NINTH EDITION

PRINCIPLES AND PRACTICE OF MARKETING

DAVID JOBBER AND
FIONA ELLIS-CHADWICK

NINTH EDITION

PRINCIPLES AND PRACTICE OF MARKETING

DAVID JOBBER AND
FIONA ELLIS-CHADWICK

Principles and Practice of Marketing, Ninth Edition

David Jobber and Fiona Ellis-Chadwick
ISBN-13 9781526847232
ISBN-10 152684723X

Published by McGraw-Hill Education
338 Euston Road,
London,
NW1 3BH
Telephone: +44 (0) 203 429 3400
Website: www.mheducation.co.uk

British Library Cataloguing in Publication Data
A catalogue record for this book is available from the British Library

Library of Congress Cataloguing in Publication Data
The Library of Congress data for this book has been applied for from the Library of Congress

Portfolio Manager: Rosie Churchill
Content Developer: Nicola Cupit
Content Product Manager: Ali Davis
Marketing Manager: Katarzyna Rutkowska

Text design by Kamae Design
Cover design by Adam Renvoize

ISBN-13 9781526847232
ISBN-10 152684723X
eISBN-13 9781526847249

Printed and bound in Great Britain by Bell & Bain Ltd, Glasgow

Dedication

To Jackson, River and Rosie.

Brief Table of Contents

Detailed Table of Contents

Vignettes

MARKETING IN ACTION

MINI CASES

Case Guide

This guide shows the key concepts covered in each of the cases in both the book and the Online Learning Centre so you can easily pick out which cases are relevant to a particular part of your course. Go to **www.mheducation.co.uk/textbooks/jobber8** to find a pdf of this guide, and search by company, industry or topic to find the ideal case to use.

Chapter	Case number	Case title and author	Key concepts covered
1	**Case 1**	Coca-Cola and Pepsi *David Jobber, Emeritus Professor of Marketing, University of Bradford.*	Marketing environment, market orientation, efficiency and effectiveness, diversification
	Case 2	Fast Fashion at H&M *David Jobber, Emeritus Professor of Marketing, University of Bradford.*	Market orientation, efficiency and effectiveness, customer value, marketing challenges and benefits
2	**Case 3**	Marketing a 'Place' in a Rapidly Changing Environment *Kim Cassidy, Professor of Services Marketing, Edgehill University; Vanessa Delhullu, team leader, Economic department, Roeselare Government; Bill Grimsey, retailer and consultant; Sheilagh Resnick, Senior Lecturer Nottingham Trent University*	Macro and micro environements, environmental influences,
	Case 4	Reaching 'Sinks, Dinks and Millennials' Worldwide *Tom McNamara and Irena Descubes, Rennes School of Business.*	SWOT, marketing challenges
3	**Case 5**	Cappuccino Wars *David Jobber, Emeritus Professor of Marketing, University of Bradford.*	Consumers, consumer behaviour, customer needs, customer satisfaction
	Case 6	The rise of influencer marketing: is it worth it for brands? *Jim Saker, senior digital manager at a leading Premier League Football Club, in conjunction with the School of Business and Economics at Loughborough University.*	Influencer marketing, influence advertising
4	**Case 7**	Naked Wines—A Community of Wine Makers and Drinkers *Brian Searle, Loughborough University*	B2B buying behaviour, B2B marketing, Buying process model, adding value, community networking, relationship marketing
	Case 8	AstraZeneca: Sweden and the UK Join Forces to Serve New Markets in the Pharmaceutical Industry *Fiona Ellis-Chadwick, Senior Lecturer, Loughborough University*	B2B buyer behaviour, nature and size of B2B markets, segmentation
5	**Case 9**	Channel 4 and Maltesers: Championing Diversity *Marie O'Dwyer, Waterford Institute of Technology*	Diversity and ethical moral duties, socially responsible advertising,Ethical advertising
	Case 10	Social Responsibility or Good Business? Coop Danmark's Anti Food Wastage Initiatives *Robert Ormrod, Associate Professor, Aarhus University*	Socially responsible business practices, environmental initiatives, ethical consumption

Chapter	Case	Title and author	Topics
6	**Case 11**	Accelerating Marketing Research How Harley-Davidson is using Artificial Intelligence to Drive Sales *Ethel Claffey, Institute of Technology.*	Big Data, Market Research, Intelligent Advertising
	Case 12	TomTom: Still Helping Us Find Our Way Around the Planet *Fiona Ellis-Chadwick, Senior Lecturer, Loughborough University*	Big Data, Market Research, New markets
7	**Case 13**	The Growing No-Alcohol and Low-Alcohol Beer Segment *Marie O'Dwyer, Waterford Institute of Technology.*	Segmentation, Emerging market segments, Millenials, positioning, differential advantage
	Case 14	Behavioural and Psychological Segmentation Criteria: The LEGO case *Robert Ormrod, Associate Professor, Aarhus University.*	Behavioural and phsychological segmentation, segmentation criteria
8	**Case 15**	Kim Kardashian: Marketing Genius? *Marie O'Dwyer, Waterford Institute of Technology.*	Brand building, personal brands, brand risks, brand extensions
	Case 16	Burberry *David Jobber, Emeritus Professor of Marketing, University of Bradford*	Augmented branding, Brand building, global branding
9	**Case 17**	Nordstrom: Using Service Excellence To Provide A Better Customer Experience *Tom McNamara and Irena Descubes, The Rennes School of Business, France*	Services, Customer Service, competitive advantage
	Case 18	Pret a Manger: Passionate About Food' *Senior Lecturer, University of Westminster.*	Market environment, competition, positioning, differential advantages, service mix
10	**Case 19**	Starbucks: Managing Customer Relationships One Cup at a Time *Tom McNamara and Irena Descubes, Rennes School of Business, Rennes-France.*	Customer relationships, customer relationship management, competitive advantage
	Case 20	Top of their Game—Technology Innovation in Manchester City Football Club (FC) *Ethel Claffey, Waterford Institute of Technology.*	Building relationships, CRM, customer relationships
11	**Case 21**	Keogh's Crisps—Home Grown Innovation *Geraldine Lavin and Christina O'Connor, Maynooth University*	Innovation, innovative products,competitive advantage
	Case 22	Innovation through Collaboration: Apple Watch Nike+ *Marie O'Dwyer, Waterford Institute of Technology.*	Innovative brands, collaboration, product replacement, New product development, product extension
12	**Case 23**	easyJet and Ryanair *David Jobber, Emeritus Professor of Marketing, University of Bradford.*	Pricing strategies, low price strategies, advantages and risks of pricing strategies
	Case 24	The Triumph of German Limited Range Discounters *Conor Carroll, Lecturer in Marketing, University of Limerick.*	Pricing strategies, Everyday low pricing, Hi-Lo pricing, Liited Range Discount format

Chapter	Case	Title and author	Topics
20	Case 39	Growth Strategies at Unilever *David Jobber, Emeritus Professor of Marketing, University of Bradford*	Brand portfolio, BCG Growth-Share Matrix, General Electric Market Attractiveness model, marginal brands, strategic divestment
	Case 40	Fever-Tree: Capitalizing on Market Trends *Brian Searle, Programme Director MSc Marketing, Loughborough University.*	Product life cycle, market development, Boston Matrix, product growth strategies, insurgent brands
21	Case 41	IKEA *David Jobber, Emeritus Professor of Marketing, University of Bradford.*	Direct investment, global brands, standardization, adaptation, international marketing strategy
	Case 42	Subway Germany: Getting Steadily Underway *Glyn Atwal*	SWOT, marketing challenges, international markets, standardization, adaptation
22	Case 43	Marimekko—a Story of Design, Determination and Leadership *Fiona Ellis-Chadwick*	Leadership, Cultural values, marketing strategy, implementation, relaunching a brand
	Case 44	Managing a Changing Musical Portfolio: HMV *Adrian Pritchard,* Adrian Pritchard, Coventry University	Implementation, internal marketing, category management, marketing metrics

Preface

Marketing is constantly adapting to meet the demands of dynamic business environments. Exploring both theoretical principles and practical business and organization practices is the key to understanding this highly dynamic and complex subject. The 9th edition brings these aspects together to engage readers in an illuminating journey through the discipline of marketing. The book explores the changing world from many different perspectives using illustrative examples of the latest applications of marketing.

The Principles and Practice of Marketing supports marketing education for students and practitioners of the subject. Students can enjoy learning from applying theoretical principles to real-world marketing problems and, in doing so, gain a richer knowledge of the value of marketing. Becoming a successful marketing practitioner also requires understanding of the principles of marketing together with the practical experience of implementing marketing ideas, processes and techniques.

This book provides a framework for understanding important marketing topics such as digital marketing, consumer behaviour, B2B marketing, segmentation, targeting and positioning, brand building, innovation, pricing, communications, marketing strategy and implementation. These core subject areas form the backbone of marketing education.

Since the last edition digital technology has had an even more profound effect on the way we do business and communicate, which has widespread implications for the way businesses and organizations operate. By understanding how to interpret the marketing environment, learning how to apply theories and concepts, students and practitioners alike can benefit from developing their knowledge of marketing.

I am joined in the writing of the 9th edition by Fiona Ellis-Chadwick, who as co-author brings to the book her expert knowledge of digital and retail marketing and detailed insight into the practical application of marketing.

Marketing is a very strong discipline, and around Europe there are specialist conferences which present the latest research: for example, the European Marketing Academy, and the Academy of Marketing in the UK. Such conferences highlight the variety and extent of marketing and ensure that there is a growing community of academics, researchers and students who are prepared to take on the challenges of modern marketing and build rewarding careers in this field.

We hope you will enjoy this book and its adds to your knowledge and understanding of the subject of marketing.

How to study

This book aims to help you to learn and understand how and why marketing works; to identify the opportunities and pitfalls of applying various marketing tools and techniques; to develop insights which enable you to become a successful marketer. The book is organised to help you build your knowledge of marketing; beginning with the fundamental principles, then how to create customer value, followed by how to communicate value through marketing and the final section, explores ways to bring all of the knowledge gained into a strategic marketing plan.

We designed the book for easy of use. Ideas, theories and concepts are explained in each chapter and there are many examples to bring these aspects to life; Marketing in Action vignettes explore some of the latest applications of marketing. There are other learning aids to help you check your understanding of new concepts: mini cases, exercises and questions at the end of each chapter. There are recommended readings, so you can stretch your knowledge further. You can also test your understanding and expand your knowledge by exploring the resources in Connect™ and LearnSmart™.

To assist you in working through this text, we have developed a number of distinctive study and design features. To familiarize yourself with these features, please turn to the Guided Tour on pages xix–xxi.

New to the 9th edition

No book on marketing can remain static, if it is to remain relevant. As always, recent events are reflected throughout this book. Here is a brief summary of the key content changes for this edition:

1. New content: in response to reviewers' feedback and changes in the practical application of digital technology within marketing practice, throughout the book there are new digital technology examples, Mini Cases, and Marketing in Action vignettes. The Marketing Research chapter has been extended to include Big data and has

been significantly updated to reflect changes in the use of data analytics. Digital coverage has been increased throughout the text with content including Digital media, display advertising SOE, mobile technologies, content marketing. There is also greater focus on co-creation of value and societal impact of marketing.

2. The structure of the ninth edition beginning with an introduction to marketing fundamentals, then focuses on how each of the elements of the marketing mix adds value and the importance of relationship marketing before exploring communication. The final part of the book brings together five chapters which focus on the strategic elements of marketing: marketing, planning and strategy.
3. Brand new vignettes, case studies and illustrations throughout the book: the principles of marketing cannot be fully grasped without solid examples of how these apply in practice. That is why in every chapter you will find a wealth of examples to support the concepts presented. These include current advertisements, Marketing in Action vignettes and Mini Cases that ask you to apply the principles learnt for yourself. Two case studies at the end of each chapter provide more in-depth examples. These features will not only help you to absorb the key principles of marketing but will also allow you to make links between the various topics and demonstrate the marketing mix at work in real-life situations. New cases look at exciting big brand e.g. Nestle, Domino's Pizzas, emerging brands e.g. Naked Wines, fever Tree, Kardashians and international brands e.g., Marrimekko, AirBnB
4. An exciting new package of supporting online resources, including new video resources and cases, as well as a rich choice of activities designed to help students develop and apply their understanding of marketing concepts. See pages xxii–xxv for further details.

Guided Tour

Real Marketing

Throughout the Principles and Practice of Marketing 9th edition product, marketing principles are illustrated with examples of real marketing practice. The following features encourage you to pause to consider the decisions taken by a rich variety of companies.

MARKETING IN ACTION 5.1
Commercial versus Social Marketing

Socially orientated marketing faces commercial challenges. Walmart and Systembolaget are examples of tensions affecting corporate organizations in different ways.

Walmart ($476 billion total revenue) annually turns over more than the following countries produce—Denmark (GDP $347 billion), Finland (GDP $276 billion)—and nearly as much Sweden (GDP $560 billion) and Norway (GDP $512 billion). Indeed, if Walmart were a country, it would rank somewhere around the 28th largest economy in the world. On a commercial level, Walmart didn't develop a sustainability strategy until 2008, when it began focusing on renewable energy, reducing waste and selling sustainable products. It now continues to focus on environmental, social and governance issues as a way of connecting with consumers and earning their trust.

However, in the USA, this positioning as a responsible retailer has been somewhat tainted as the major shareholder of Walmart's global operations has been accused of being far less generous than other wealthy philanthropists and everyday donors. The Waltons are the USA's richest family, worth in excess of $140 billion, largely due to their shares in Walmart, the world's largest retailer. The Walton Family Foundation, a non-profit organization with assets of about $2 billion, regularly invests in education reform and the environment, but recently the family have been accused of using the foundation for its tax-saving efficiencies rather than as a way to channel some of their family's great wealth into benefiting society. From a marketing perspective, the challenge is not about whether Walmart is more or less inclined towards social endeavours than other large corporations, but is about managing perceptions, and this example serves to highlight the tensions that can arise when profits meet philanthropy.

Systembolaget, the large Swedish retailer, with over 400 stores, is a state-owned monopoly with the responsibility of selling alcohol in a country where excessive drinking has been a problem. The company constantly monitors the changing world to ensure the products it sells meet current customer demand.

« **Marketing in Action** vignettes provide practical examples to highlight the application of concepts, and encourage you to critically analyse and discuss real-world issues.

» **Mini Cases** provide further examples to encourage you to consider how key concepts work in practice, and have associated questions to help you critique the principles discussed in each chapter.

MINI CASE 5.1
Not for Profit: The FA

Harry Kane is a top-rate athlete; he is a footballer, who commands a very high salary and he is not on his own. Salaries for footballers have grown on average by over 1,000 per cent in the last 20 years. Football clubs finance these high salaries through matchday revenue (approximately 13 per cent), broadcasting (approximately 60 per cent) and other commercial activities (approximately 27 per cent). Premier League club revenue is increasing in line with the massive wage bills and financial demands of the player transfer market. While football is a commercial market worth billions of pounds, the Football Association Limited (FA) (the governing body which sets the rules and regulations for the game in England and Wales) is a not-for-profit charity.

With such high stakes and volumes of money changing hands, the FA has to provide, monitor and manage standards and discipline for the game, provide safeguarding standards for young players coming through training academies, ensure opportunities for all and limit discrimination, manage anti-doping through education, testing and application of legal regulations, and protect the game, its players, supporters and many other stakeholders from betting irregularities, match fixing and insider information. The FA must ensure the viability of Club Wembley as a venue and centrepiece

EXHIBIT 7.1
The BMWi3

« **Exhibits** demonstrate how marketers have presented their products in real promotions and campaigns.

« **Interactive Case Analysis Activities** encourage students to think analytically about real-world marketing situations. Two sets of multiple choice questions prompt them to critically asses the case and then test their understanding of core concepts covered.

» **Case studies** Two are provided at the end of each chapter, based on up-to-date examples that encourage you to apply what you have learned in each chapter to a real-life marketing problem. Instructor's Teaching notes can be downloaded from the Online Learning Centre via Connect.

CASE 14

Behavioural and Psychological Segmentation Criteria: The LEGO Case

LEGO, the Danish toy manufacturer of plastic building bricks, has a large website that is translated into 19 languages across 26 different markets. Most of LEGO's 36 product lines have their own microsites with apps, games, downloads and even display sections for builders' own models—a good alignment with the needs of the digitally able generation. However, only one product line, LEGO Duplo, has external links to social media such as Facebook, Twitter and Pinterest on the product line microsite. At the other extreme, the LEGO Architecture microsite focuses on images of the current range and information about the original buildings. So, why is LEGO moving its online presence

166 CHAPTER 5 Marketing, Ethics and Society

»

Questions connect

1. **Channel 4's CSR policy claims that diversity is 'the lifeblood of the station'. Visit the Channel 4 website and access Channel 4's Diversity Charter and their latest Annual Report. Identify and discuss evidence in the report which illustrates the channel's continuing commitment to embracing diversity.**
2. **Discuss the extent to which the Maltesers' 'Look on the light side of disability' campaign can be seen as socially responsible advertising embracing diversity.**

References

Based on: Channel 4 (2017a), What does 360 degress mean?, Channel 4, https://www.channel4.com/corporate/about-4/operating-responsibly/diversity/what-does-360-mean (accessed 10 July 2018); Channel 4 (2017b), People and inclusion, *Channel 4*, https://www.channel4.com/corporate/about-4/who-we-are/people-inclusion (accessed 10 July 2018); Little Black Book (2016), Behind Maltesers' Paralympics campaign—and how it struck comedy gold, *Little Black Book*, https://lbbonline.com/news/behind-maltesers-paralympics-campaign-and-how-it-struck-comedy-gold/ (accessed 10 July 2018); Roderick, L. (2017), Channel 4 to bring back 'Superhumans wanted' competition, *Marketing Week*, https://www.marketingweek.com/2017/04/04/channel-4-relaunch-competition/ (accessed 10 July 2018); Scope (2017), Scope responds to Maltesers ad named as one of the most complained about adverts of 2016,

« **Questions** are provided at the end of each case study to allow you to test yourself on what you have read. Multiple Choice Questions are also available in Connect.

» **Videos** allow students to engage with how marketing professionals approach their day-to-day challenges through a series of interviews with marketing managers and directors from a broad range of companies.

Studying Effectively

Principles and Practice of Marketing is designed to make every study moment as efficient as possible. The following features will help you to focus your study, check your understanding and improve learning outcomes.

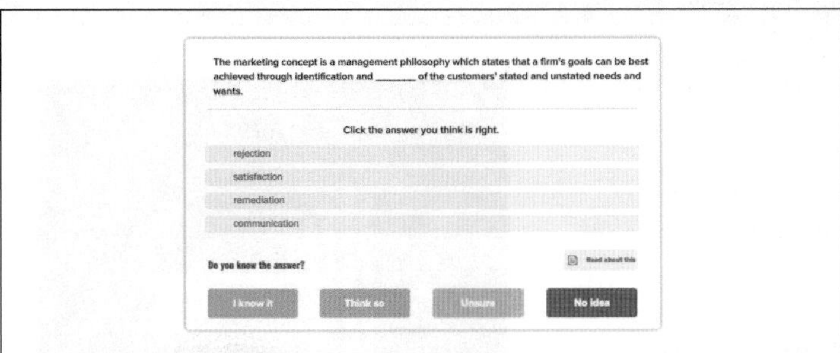

« **LearnSmart and SmartBook**
LearnSmart is the most widely used and intelligent adaptive learning resource that is proven to strengthen memory recall, improve course retention and boost grades. Fuelled by LearnSmart, SmartBook is the first and only adaptive reading experience available today.

» **Learning Objectives** are listed at the beginning of each chapter to show you the topics covered. You should aim to attain each objective when you study the chapter.

LEARNING OBJECTIVES

After reading this chapter, you should be able to:

1. define the concepts of product, brand, product line and product mix
2. distinguish between manufacturer and own-label brands
3. distinguish between a core and augmented product (the brand)
4. explain why strong brands are important
5. define brand equity, the components of customer-based and proprietary-based brand equity and brand valuation
6. explain how to build strong brands
7. distinguish between family, individual and combined brand names, and discuss the characteristics of an effective brand name

Key Terms

augmented product the core product plus extra functional and/ or emotional values combined in a unique way to form a brand

brand a distinctive product offering created by the use of a name, symbol, design, packaging, or some combination of these, intended to differentiate it from its competitors

brand assets the distinctive features of a brand

brand domain the brand's target market

brand equity a measure of the strength of a brand in the marketplace by adding tangible value to a company through the resulting sales and profits

brand extension the use of an established brand name on a new brand within the same broad market or product category

brand heritage the background to the brand and its culture

brand performance metrics how customers respond to a brand. Measures include market share, sales, sales growth, market size, share-of-wallet

brand personality the character of a brand described in terms of other entities such as people, animals and objects

brand reflection the relationship of the brand to self-identity

« **Key Terms** are provided at the end of each chapter—use the list to look up any unfamiliar words, and as a handy aid for quick revision and review.

» **Study Questions** allow you to review and apply the knowledge you have acquired from each chapter. These questions can be undertaken either individually or as a focus for group discussion in seminars or tutorials.

Study Questions

1. **Why do companies develop core products into brands?**
2. **Suppose you were the marketing director of a medium-sized bank. How would you tackle the job of building the company brand?**
3. **Think of five brand names. To what extent do they meet the criteria of good brand naming as laid out in Table 8.1?**
4. **What are the strategic options for pan-European brand building? What are the advantages and disadvantages of each option?**
5. **Why do companies rebrand product and corporate names? What is necessary for successful implementation of the rebranding process?**
6. **What are the two main forms of co-branding? What are their advantages and risks?**

Recommended Reading

Branding sets firms apart from the pack. Read the following to discover the importance of relationships in branding; how Chinese consumers are influenced by brand value and how global brands create value.

Gupta, S., Foroudi, P. and Yen, D. (2018), Investigating relationship types for creating brand value for resellers, *Industrial Marketing Management*, 72 (July), 37–47.

Luoa, J., Deyb, B.L., Yalkinc, C., Sivarajahd, U., Punjaisrie, K., Huangf, Y. and Yen, D.A., Millennial Chinese consumers' perceived destination brand value, *Journal of Business Research* https://www.sciencedirect.com/science/article/pii/S0148296318303023.

Steenkamp, J.B. (2014), How global brands create firm value: the 4V model, *International Marketing Review*, Vol. 31 Issue: 1, 5–29 https://doi.org/10.1108/IMR-10-2013-0233.

« **Further Reading** at the end of each chapter can be used to research an idea in greater depth.

McGraw Hill connect®

McGraw-Hill Connect Marketing is a learning and teaching environment that improves student performance and outcomes whilst promoting engagement and comprehension of content.

You can utilize publisher-provided materials, or add your own content to design a complete course to help your students achieve higher outcomes.

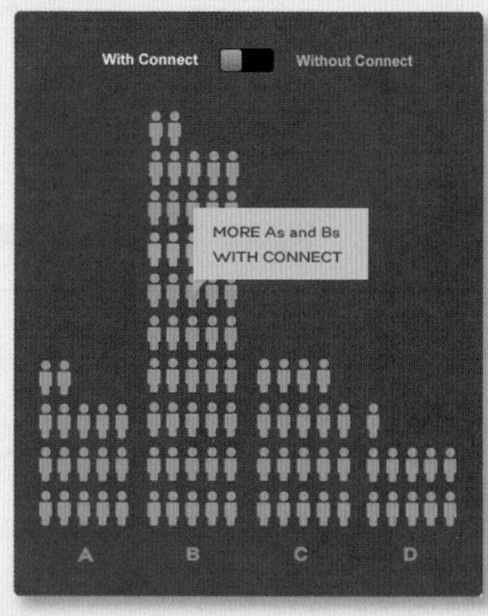

INSTRUCTORS

With McGraw-Hill Connect Marketing, instructors get:

- Simple **assignment management,** allowing you to spend more time teaching.
- **Auto-graded** assignments, quizzes and tests.
- **Detailed visual reporting** where students and section results can be viewed and analysed.
- Sophisticated **online testing** capability.
- A **filtering and reporting** function that allows you to easily assign and report on materials that are correlated to learning outcomes, topics, level of difficulty, and more. Reports can be accessed for individual students or the whole class, as well as offering the ability to drill into individual assignments, questions or categories.
- **Instructor materials** to help supplement your course.

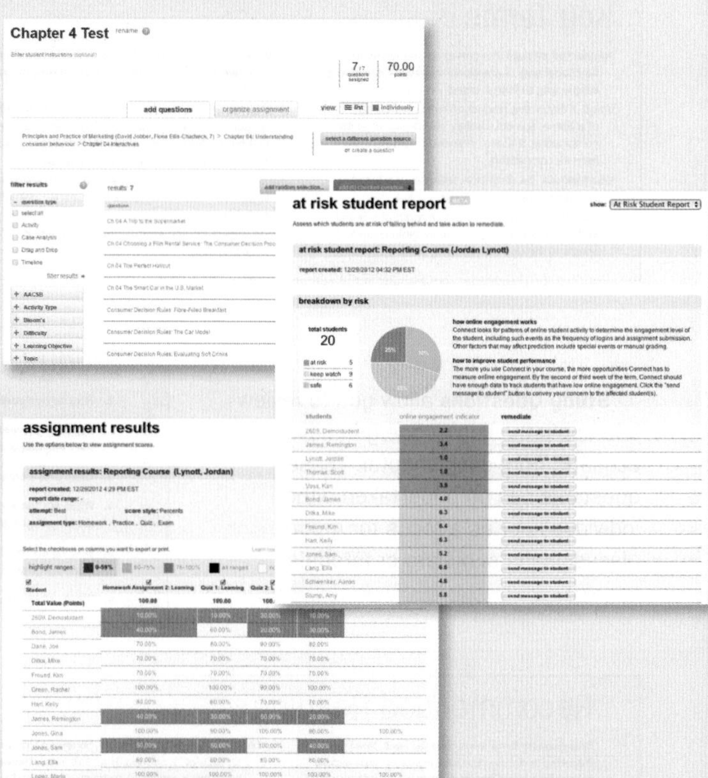

Get Connected. Get Results.

Available online via Connect is a wealth of instructor support materials, including:

- Case study teaching notes
- Fully updated PowerPoint slides to use in lectures
- A solutions manual providing answers to the Mini Cases and the end of chapter questions in the textbook.
- Image library of artwork from the textbook.
- Additional case studies.
- Tutorial activities
- Further resources including Marketing Plan, Market Research Project and Marketing Accountability and Metrics

STUDENTS

With McGraw-Hill Connect Marketing, students get:

Assigned content

- Easy **online access** to homework, tests and quizzes.
- **Immediate feedback** and 24-hour tech support.

With McGraw-Hill SmartBook, students can:

- Take control of your own learning with a personalized and adaptive reading experience.
- Understand what you know and don't know; SmartBook takes you through the stages of reading and practice, prompting you to recharge your knowledge throughout the course for maximum retention.
- Achieve the most efficient and productive study time by adapting to what you do and don't know.
- Hone in on concepts you are most likely to forget, to ensure knowledge of key concepts is learnt and retained.

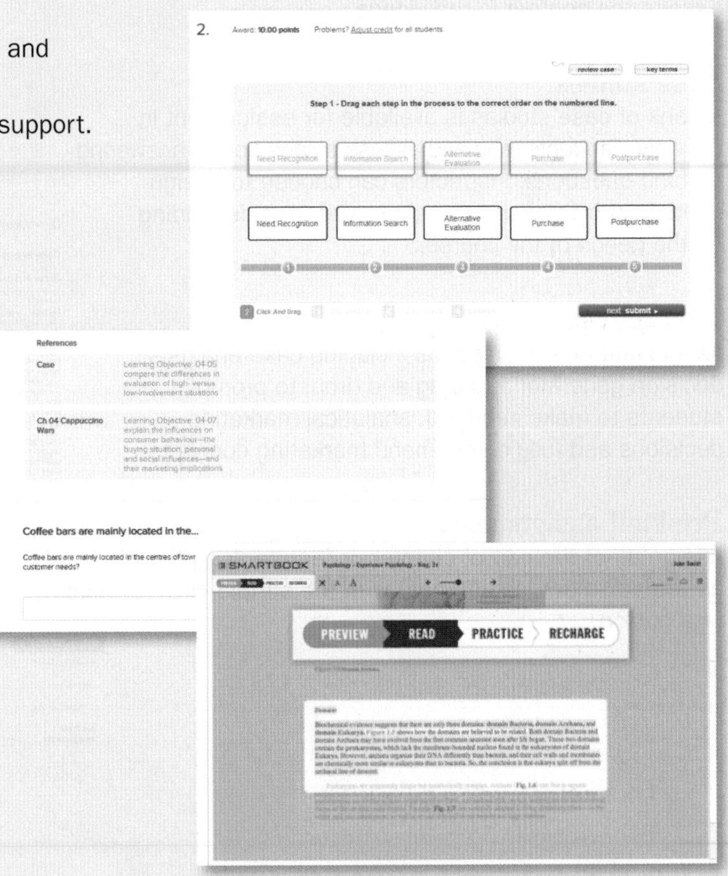

FEATURES

Is an online assignment and assessment solution that offers a number of powerful tools and features that make managing assignments easier, so faculty can spend more time teaching. With Connect marketing, students can engage with their coursework anytime and anywhere, making the learning process more accessible and efficient.

Videos

Videos featuring interviews with marketing managers and directors from a wide range of companies, along with advertising and promotional content, will engage students with the idea of marketing as a career and how the concepts they learn relate to a real world context. Autogradable questions encourage them to analyse and assess the content in the videos.

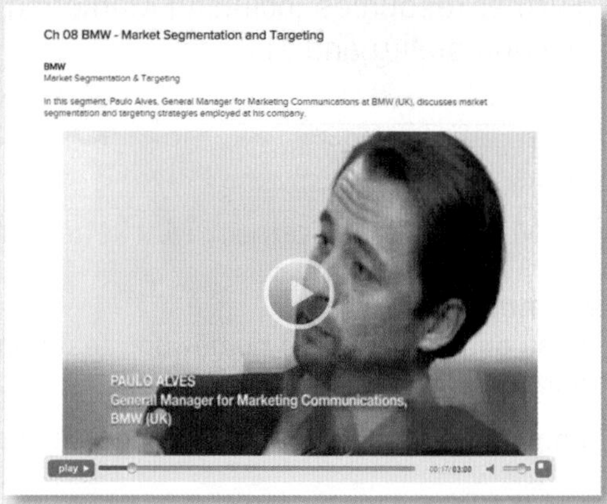

Case studies

A bank of case studies is available for assignment in Connect. Students read and assess a case before answering probing questions. Instructors can choose to assign multiple choice or short answer questions depending on the needs of the course.

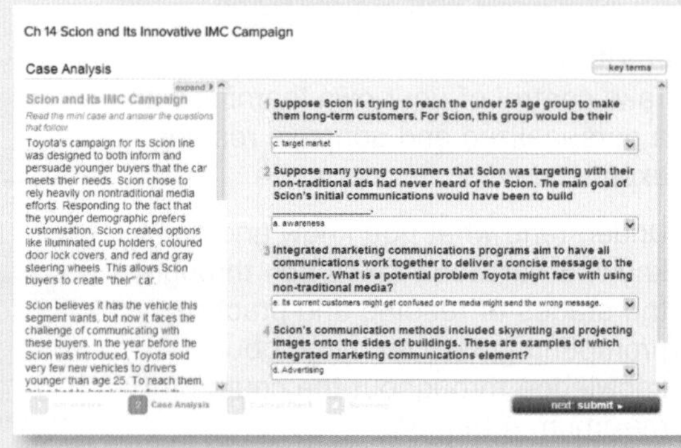

Interactives

Assign interactive questions including case analysis, decision generator and drag and drop, to prompt students to make informed, analytical marketing decisions and fully comprehend marketing concepts.

Pre-built assignments

Assign all of the end of chapter or test bank material as a ready-made assignment with the simple click of a button.

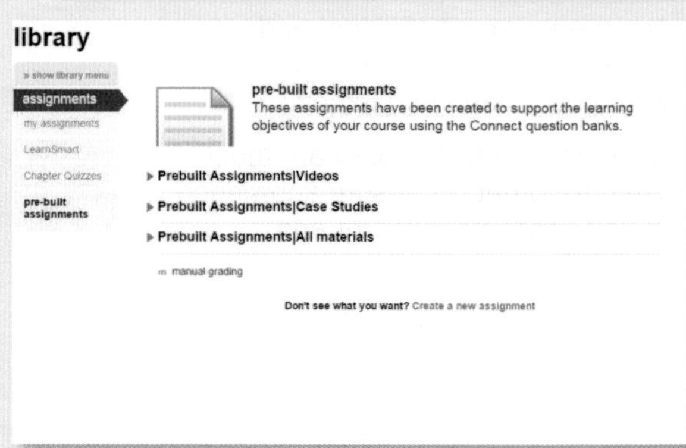

Get Connected. Get Results.

SmartBook™

Fuelled by LearnSmart—the most widely used and intelligent adaptive learning resource—SmartBook is the first and only adaptive reading experience available today. Distinguishing what a student knows from what they don't, and honing in on concepts they are most likely to forget, SmartBook personalizes content for each student in a continuously adapting reading experience. Valuable reports provide instructors insight as to how students are progressing through textbook content, and are useful for shaping in-class time or assessment.

LearnSmart™

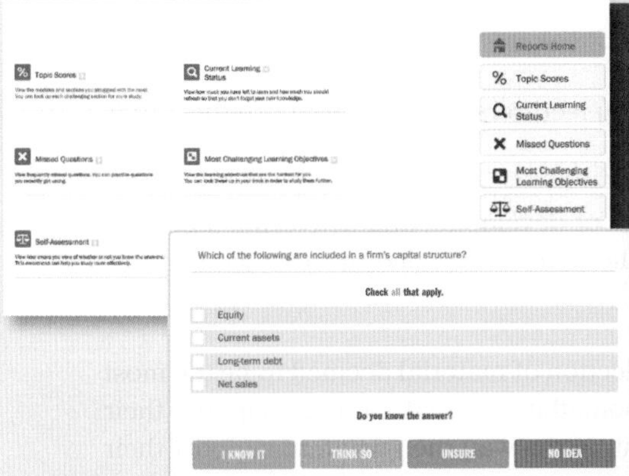

McGraw-Hill LearnSmart is an adaptive learning program that identifies what an individual student knows and doesn't know. LearnSmart's adaptive learning path helps students learn faster, study more efficiently, and retain more knowledge. Now with integrated learning resources which present topics and concepts in different and engaging formats increases student engagement and promotes additional practice of key concepts. Reports available for both students and instructors indicate where students need to study more and assess their success rate in retaining knowledge.

About the Authors

David Jobber is an internationally recognized marketing academic. He is Emeritus Professor of Marketing at the University of Bradford School of Management. He holds an honours degree in economics from the University of Manchester, a master's degree in business and management from the University of Warwick and a doctorate from the University of Bradford.

Before joining the faculty at the Bradford School of Management, David worked for the TI Group in marketing and sales, and was Senior Lecturer in Marketing at the University of Huddersfield. He has wide experience of teaching core marketing courses at undergraduate, postgraduate and post-experience levels with specialisms in business-to business marketing, sales management and marketing research. He has a proven, ratings-based record of teaching excellence at all levels. His competence in teaching is reflected in visiting appointments at the universities of Aston, Lancaster, Loughborough and Warwick in the UK, and the University of Wellington, New Zealand. He has taught marketing to executives of such international companies as BP, Allied Domecq, the BBC, Bass, Croda International, Rolls-Royce and Rio Tinto.

Supporting his teaching is a record of achievement in academic research. David has over 150 publications in the marketing area in such journals as the International Journal of Research in Marketing, MIS Quarterly, Strategic Management Journal, Journal of International Business Studies, Journal of Management, Journal of Business Research, European Journal of Marketing, Journal of Product Innovation Management, Journal of Personal Selling and Sales Management and Journal of the Operational Research Society. David has served on the editorial boards of the International Journal of Research in Marketing, Journal of Personal Selling and Sales Management, European Journal of Marketing and the Journal of Marketing Management.

He has acted as Special Adviser to the Research Assessment Exercise panel that rated research output from business and management schools throughout the UK. David has also received the Academy of Marketing's Life Achievement award for distinguished and extraordinary services to marketing.

Fiona Ellis-Chadwick has a successful professional business and academic career. She is a Senior Lecturer at Loughborough University School of Business & Economics. As part of this role, Fiona is a very active researcher and innovative educator, and frequently leads the development of innovative multi-media teaching materials, bringing together research and business. Fiona has made many films for use in higher education on a variety of different topics, including retail marketing, digital technology and economic growth from the perspective of international business leaders. As an academic consultant for the Open University and BBC productions, she has worked on highly successful and award-winning series: The Virtual Revolution, Foods That Make Billions, Evan's Business Challenges, Iceland Foods: Into the Freezer Cabinet, Business Boomers and Radio 4's The Bottom Line programme. Fiona had a successful commercial career in retailing before becoming an academic and completing her PhD. Having made a significant contribution in the area of online retailing, she continues to focus her research and academic publications on the strategic impact of the Internet and digital technologies on marketing and retailing. She is also very interested in the impact of the internet on the high street and how the increase in online shopping is reshaping our towns and cities. Her work on these topics has been widely published in the Journal of Business Research, European Journal of Marketing, Internet Research, Industrial Marketing Management, International Journal of Retail Distribution and Management plus additional textbooks and practitioner journals. Fiona is passionate about how technology and education can help business development in the future.

Acknowledgements

Authors' Acknowledgements

We would like to thank colleagues, contributors and the reviewers who have offered advice and helped develop this text. We would also like to thank our editors Alice Aldous, Nicola Cupit, Matthew Simmons for their invaluable support and assistance.

Publisher's Acknowledgements

Our thanks go to the following reviewers for their comments at various stages in the text's development:

Faisal Attazgharti, Zealand Institute of Business and Technology
Riccardo Benzo, Birkbeck, University of London
James Blackmore-Wright, University of Northampton
Laura Chamberlain, University of Warwick
Shelly Chapman, University of Leicester
Polymeros Chrysochou, Aarhus University
Jennifer Cole, University of Leicester
Christina Fona, University of Leicester
Ian Glencross, University of Sussex
Vijay Hariharan, Erasmus University
Bradley Lansdale, Oxford College of Marketing
Johan Larsson, Jönköping International Business School
Ben Marder, University of Edinburgh
Helen McGrath, University College Cork
William Mott, University of Wolverhampton
Elin Nilsson, Umeå University
Marie O'Dwyer, Waterford Institute of Technology
Eleonora Pantano, Middlesex University
Fabien Pecot, University of York
Adrian Pritchard, Coventry University
Michael Rafn, University College of Northern Jutland
Jan Sendenka, University of Skövde
Mariusz Soltanifar, Hanze University of Applied Sciences
Marcus Thompson, University of Aberdeen
Ann Torres, NUI Galway

We would like to thank the following contributors for the case study material which they have provided for this textbook and its online resources:

Glyn Atwal, Burgundy School of Business
Adele Berndt, Jönköping International Business School
Vikki Brennan, Proudly Made In Africa
Douglas Bryson, Rennes School of Business
Connor Carroll, University of Limerick
Grace Carson, Queens University Belfast
Kim Cassidy, Edgehill University
Ethel Claffey, Waterford Institute of Technology
Vanessa Delhullu, Roeselare Government
Irena Descubes, Rennes School of Business
Bill Grimsey, retailer and consultant
Clive Helm, University of Westminster
Geraldine Lavin, Maynooth University
Tom McNamara, Rennes School of Business
Christina O'Connor, Maynooth University
Marie O'Dwyer, Waterford Institute of Technology
Robert Ormrod, Aarhus University
Adrian Pritchard, Coventry University
Sheilagh Resnick, Nottingham Trent University
James Roper, Interactive Media in Retail Group
James Saker, Loughborough University
Brian Searle, Loughborough University

Picture Acknowledgements

The authors and publishers would like to extend thanks to the following for the reproduction of company advertising and/or logos:

Part and Chapter Opening Images
Part 1 Opening Image - Shutterstock / Zadorozhna Natalia 1
Part 2 Opening Image - Shutterstock / Monkey Business Images 239
Part 3 Opening Image - Shutterstock / GaudiLab 405
Part 4 Opening Image - Shutterstock / Rawpixel.com 593

Chapter 1
Chee Keong Lee / Alamy Stock Photo 11; Martin de Jong 12; Lenscap Photography 13; Zeynep Demir 13; ACnoncc / Alamy Stock Photo 18; Taa photo 18

Chapter 2
ESB Professional/Shutterstock 38; Vintage Tone/ Shutterstock 38; Evlakhov Valeriy/Shutterstock 38; McGraw-Hill Education 38; Shutterstock / samjapan 38; Glow Images 38; M4OS Photos / Alamy Stock Photo 39;

nattanai chimjanon / Alamy Stock Photo 41; zhu difeng/ Shutterstock 46; Greenpeace/KennardPhillips 48; Erica Simone Leeds 52; *Sea Shepherd Global* 52; studiomode / Alamy Stock Photo 55; gpointstudio/Shutterstock 55; stockbroker © 123RF.com 57; Shutterstock / vesna cvorovic 57

Chapter 3
WENN Ltd / Alamy Stock Photo 75; courtneyk 75; Casimiro PT 77; Shutterstock / SAPhotog 79; Gavin Rodgers / Alamy Stock Photo 84; Emilio100 85; © Jeff Morgan 15 / Alamy Stock Photo 86; Dmytro Surkov 87; chrisdorney 89; LightField Studios 92; Serhiy Kobyakov 92; javarman 92; MaraZe 92

Chapter 4
UfaBizPhoto/Shutterstock 110; robertharding / Alamy Stock Photo 111; BigTunaOnline/Shutterstock 112; Rob Wilkinson / Alamy Stock Photo 114; https://wingyip.com/#OurPhilosophy 115; © David Askham / Alamy Stock Photo 118; Juice Images/Alamy 119; Jungheinrich 120; © Bernhard Classen / Alamy Stock Photo 124; Michelin Tyre Public Limited Company 127

Chapter 5
Phil Wills / Alamy Stock Photo 141; https://www.savethechildren.org.uk/about-us/who-we-work-with/celebrity-supporters/myleene-klass 141; CosminIftode/ Shutterstock 143; Facebook 147; Adapted from Public Health England 147; Eric D ricochet69 / Alamy Stock Photo 150; European Fetal Alcohol Spectrum Disorders Alliance 156; Anna Fotyma / Alamy Stock Photo 158

Chapter 6
NicoElNino/Shutterstock 173; WAYHOME studio/ Shutterstock 190; Bloomberg / Contributor 205

Chapter 7
Fyndiq 205; Fanny Karst 214; mrfiza/Shutterstock 218; © Jeff Morgan 02 / Alamy Stock Photo 225

Chapter 8
© Alex Hinds / Alamy Stock Photo 244; Ingram Publishing/ SuperStock 245; James McDowall/Shutterstock 251; Newscast Online Limited / Alamy Stock Photo 251; Lukas Gojda/Shutterstock 255; Clynt Garnham Food & Drink / Alamy Stock Photo 260; Greenpeace 263

Chapter 9
Mim Friday / Alamy Stock Photo 282; Leggett 285; WENN Ltd / Alamy Stock Photo 286; courtesy of Sandals Resorts 291; Kathy deWitt / Alamy Stock Photo 294

Chapter 10
Michael Gordon/Shutterstock 314; Boston Conculting Group (BCG) 316; ALPA PROD/Shutterstock 320; Bloomberg / Contributor 322; Kristoffer Tripplaar / Alamy Stock Photo 326; Yuriy Vlasenko/Shutterstock 328

Chapter 11
Vuzix 344; INFOGRAPHIC CLAIRE OLIVÈS © COMITÉ COLBERT 346; Serghei Starus/Shutterstock 347; dpa picture alliance / Alamy Stock Photo 353; BSIP SA / Alamy Stock Photo 355; Jeffrey Blackler / Alamy Stock Photo 360

Chapter 12
Creative Lab 379; imageBROKER / Alamy Stock Photo 380; Martin Carlsson / Alamy Stock Photo 381; Piotr Adamowicz/Shutterstock 387

Chapter 13
Catherine Ivill / Staff 410; Mike Hewitt / Staff 410; Twitter 412; NetPhotos / Alamy Stock Photo 413; Bjoern Wylezich/Shutterstock 425; Alan Wilson / Alamy Stock Photo 426; Lifestyle pictures / Alamy Stock Photo 427

Chapter 14
Safronkin Vasilii/Shutterstock 444; Jeff Morgan 02 / Alamy Stock Photo 444; VanderWolf Images/Shutterstock 446; ©2014 Kevin Cornell, Originally appeared in A List Apart Magazine, Issue 397 449; monticello/Shutterstock 451; age fotostock / Alamy Stock Photo 452; Jeff Greenberg / Contributor 462; Nestle 466

Chapter 15
Becris/Shutterstock 483; iQoncept/Shutterstock 483; mstanley/Shutterstock 483; Creative Stall/ Shutterstock 483; elenagrevut/Shutterstock 483; lovelyday12/Shutterstock 483; Alistair Laming / Alamy Stock Photo 488; Jeffrey Blackler / Alamy Stock Photo 489; Courtesy of Butcher & Bicycle 491; Gorodenkoff/Shutterstock 494; Bakhtiar Zein/ Shutterstock 496

Chapter 16
mamanamsai/Shutterstock 525; Stanislau Palaukou/ Shutterstock 525; Vectorrex/Shutterstock 525; Shazam 527; Newscast Online Limited / Alamy Stock Photo 521; Macouno 535; ifeelstock / Alamy Stock Photo 539; Hertz Corporation 541

Chapter 17
Juan Llauro/Shutterstock 560; KPMG 562; Rentokil 563; Casimiro / Alamy Stock Photo 564; Jeffrey Blackler / Alamy Stock Photo 565; Simon Hadley / Alamy Stock Photo 566; Jim Lane / Alamy Stock Photo 568; Lucian Coman/Shutterstock 573; Bloomberg / Contributor 576; Eakvoraseth/Shutterstock 579

Chapter 18
Virgin 597; David Ryder / Stringer 601; STUART WALKER / Alamy Stock Photo 603; Glasses direct 606; Kumar Sriskandan / Alamy Stock Photo 607; Sean Gallup/ Getty 613

Chapter 19
ricochet64 /Shutterstock 630; Asia Photopress / Alamy Stock Photo 630; Ian Dagnall / Alamy Stock Photo 632; The Washington Post/Getty 645

Chapter 20
STANCA SANDA / Alamy Stock Photo 669; Images by Russell / Alamy Stock Photo 670; Rawpixel.com/Shutterstock 671; Steve Stock / Alamy Stock Photo 674; Peter Gudella/Shutterstock 675; ajt/ Shutterstock 675; Billion Photos/Shutterstock 675; Dmitri Ma/Shutterstock 675; blackliz/Shutterstock 675; imageBROKER / Alamy Stock Photo 677; M40S Photos / Alamy Stock Photo 686

Chapter 21
Ink Drop/Shutterstock 703; MSSA/Shutterstock 706; Rawpixel.com/Shutterstock 711; © McGraw-Hill Education/ Barry Barker 714; Robcartorres/Shutterstock 716; imageBROKER / Alamy Stock Photo 716

Chapter 22
Kumar Sriskandan / Alamy Stock Photo 737; Phonlamai Photo/Shutterstock 739; Jan Mika / Alamy Stock Photo 740; Konwicki Marcin/Shutterstock 742; AUTOGLASS ® and the logo are registered trademarks of Belron S.A and its affilitated companies 743; Kris Connor / Getty 746

Case 1: Nenov Brothers Images/Shutterstock 28; Case 2: Sorbis/Shutterstock 33; Case 3: Vanessa Dehullu 67; Case 3: Vanessa Dehullu 68; Case 3: Courtesy of lokaalmarkt 68; Case 4: Storms Media Group / Alamy Stock Photo 71; Case 5: © Image Source, all rights reserved. 102; Case 6: SOPA Images Limited / Alamy Stock Photo 105; Case 6: 9gifts/Shutterstock 106; Case 7: Naked Wine 133; Case 8: Steve Heap/ Shutterstock 136; Case 9: Mercante Elegance Collection / Alamy Stock Photo 164; Case 10: highwaystarz © 123RF. com 167; Case 11: Helen Sessions / Alamy Stock Photo 197; Case 12: Jan von Uxkull-Gyllenband/ Shutterstock 200; Case 13: stockbroker/123RF 234; Case 14: Seika Chujo 237; Case 15: Taylor Hill / Contributor 271; Case 16: Sorbis/Shutterstock 274; Case 17: Helen89/Shutterstock 304; Case 18: Ian Dagnall / Alamy Stock Photo 307; Case 19: Moomusician/ Shutterstock 336; Case 20: leolintang/Shutterstock 339; Case 21: Keogh's crisps Ltd 365; Case 21: Keogh's crisps Ltd 366; Case 21: Keogh's crisps Ltd 366; Case 21: Keogh's crisps Ltd 367; Case 22: Pawan Kumar / Alamy Stock Photo 368; Case 23: fazon1/ Getty 396; Case 24: monticello/Shutterstock 401; Case 25: Moomusician/Shutterstock 435; Case 26: Kyodo News / Contributor 438; Case 27: Agencja Fotograficzna Caro / Alamy Stock Photo 476; Case 28: Toyota 478; Case 29: https://twitter.com/Airbnb/ status/703128713878089729 515; Case 30: Nestle 516; Case 32: Twitter 552; Case 32: Twitter 552; Case 33: Chris Ridley - Internet Stock / Alamy Stock Photo 585; Case 34: Maurice Savage / Alamy Stock Photo 588; Case 35: Michaelpuche/Shutterstock 620; Case 36: VAA 625; Case 36: VAA 625; Case 36: VAA 626; Case 37: Goran Bogicevic 657; Case 38: Tuul and Bruno Morandi / Alamy Stock Photo 662; Case 39: joachim affeldt/Shutterstock 693; Case 40: The Grayson / Stockimo / Alamy Stock Photo 696; Case 40: Twitter 697; Case 40: dpa picture alliance / Alamy Stock Photo 697; Case 41: Tooykrub/Shutterstock 728; Case 42: https:// www.subway-franchise.de/presse/ 734; Case 44: Autumn Sky Photography 773

PART 1
FUNDAMENTALS OF MARKETING

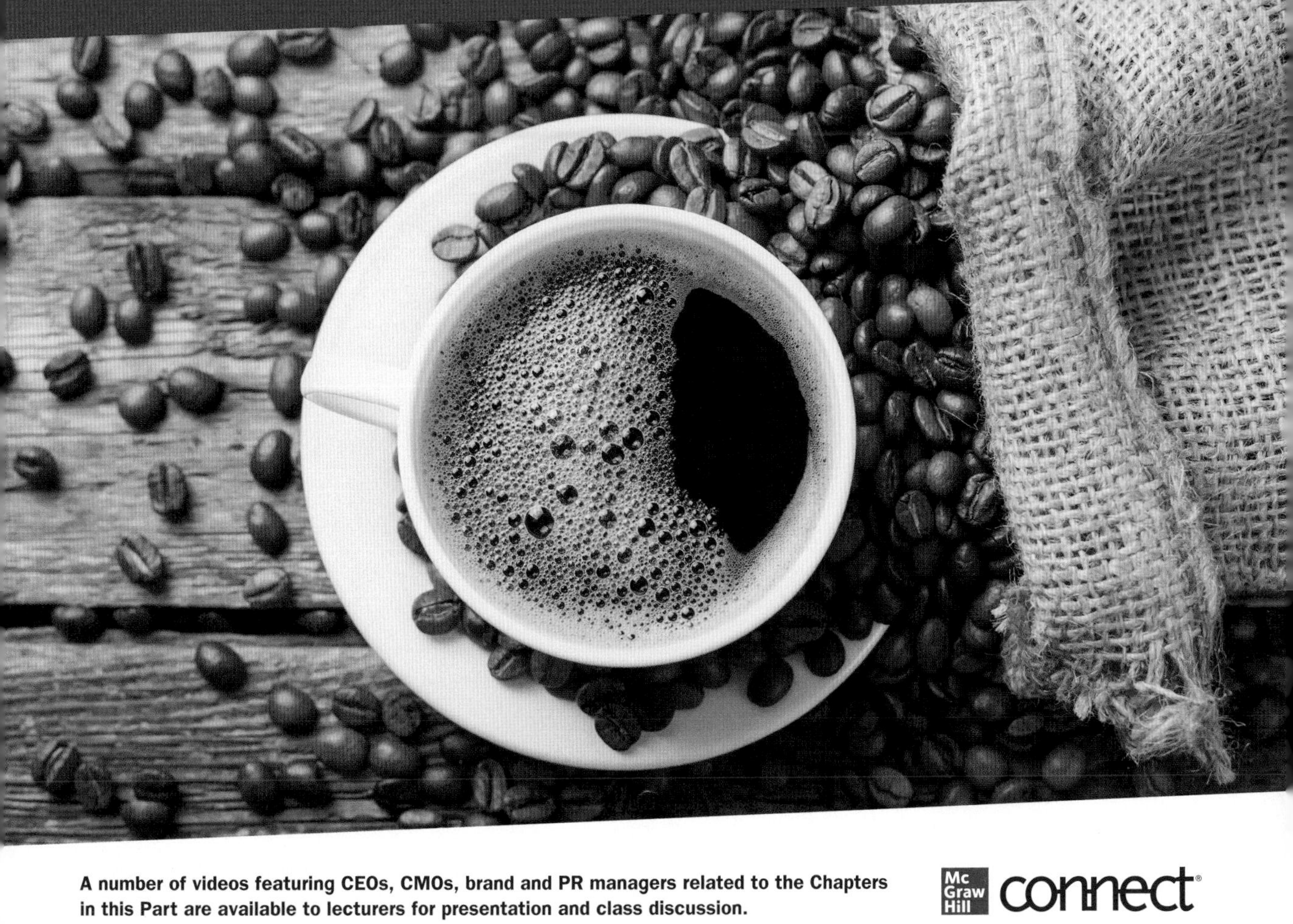

A number of videos featuring CEOs, CMOs, brand and PR managers related to the Chapters in this Part are available to lecturers for presentation and class discussion.

McGraw Hill connect®

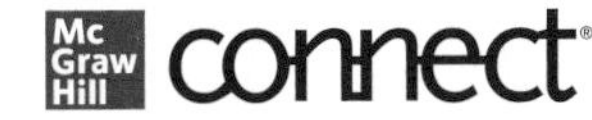

CHAPTER 1
Marketing and the Organization

> *Management must think of itself not as producing products, but as providing customer-creating value satisfactions. It must push this idea (and everything it means and requires) into every nook and cranny of the organization. It has to do this continuously and with the kind of flair that excites and stimulates the people in it.*
>
> **THEODORE LEVITT**

LEARNING OBJECTIVES

After reading this chapter, you should be able to:

1 explore the principles of marketing
2 define the marketing concept and its key components
3 explain the significance of adopting a market orientation in a changing world
4 identify the core concepts of value creation and differentiation in a market-driven economy
5 understand the differences and importance of efficiency and effectiveness
6 describe how to create customer value, satisfaction and loyalty
7 explain the relationship between marketing characteristics, market orientation and business performance
8 outline the key methods for communicating and delivering customer value
9 discuss marketing planning and strategy
10 explore the limitations of the marketing concept as a guiding principle of business
11 identify relevant business and research examples, which illustrate the application of the principles of marketing in an organization

Introduction to Principles and Practice of Marketing

The principles of marketing have been influencing business practices for centuries, but the history of marketing as a distinct discipline can be traced back to the beginning of the 1990s (Sheth and Parvatiyar, 1995). Since then, marketing has developed into a guiding philosophy for firms of every shape, size and type.

At the heart of marketing is the customer. Over time, customers' needs and wants change and, as a result, marketing practices also change to reflect and accommodate new customer demands. The authors of this book recognize the importance of reflecting such developments and the shift in marketing teaching. Accordingly, the focus has changed. Whilst the **Four-Ps** (product, price, promotion and place–see Tactical marketing below) remain a core element, the wider context of relationship marketing, value creation and other new approaches to marketing are also integrated into the book.

The text is structured around four key dimensions of marketing:

Part 1: Fundamentals of Marketing–seven chapters that explore the essential elements of marketing.
Part 2: Creating Customer Value–five chapters that focus on the main elements of delivering customer value.
Part 3: Communicating and Delivering Customer Value–five chapters concentrating on communications and distribution.
Part 4: Marketing Planning and Strategy–five chapters that adopt a more strategic focus on marketing.
See Figure 1.1.

FIGURE 1.1
Overview

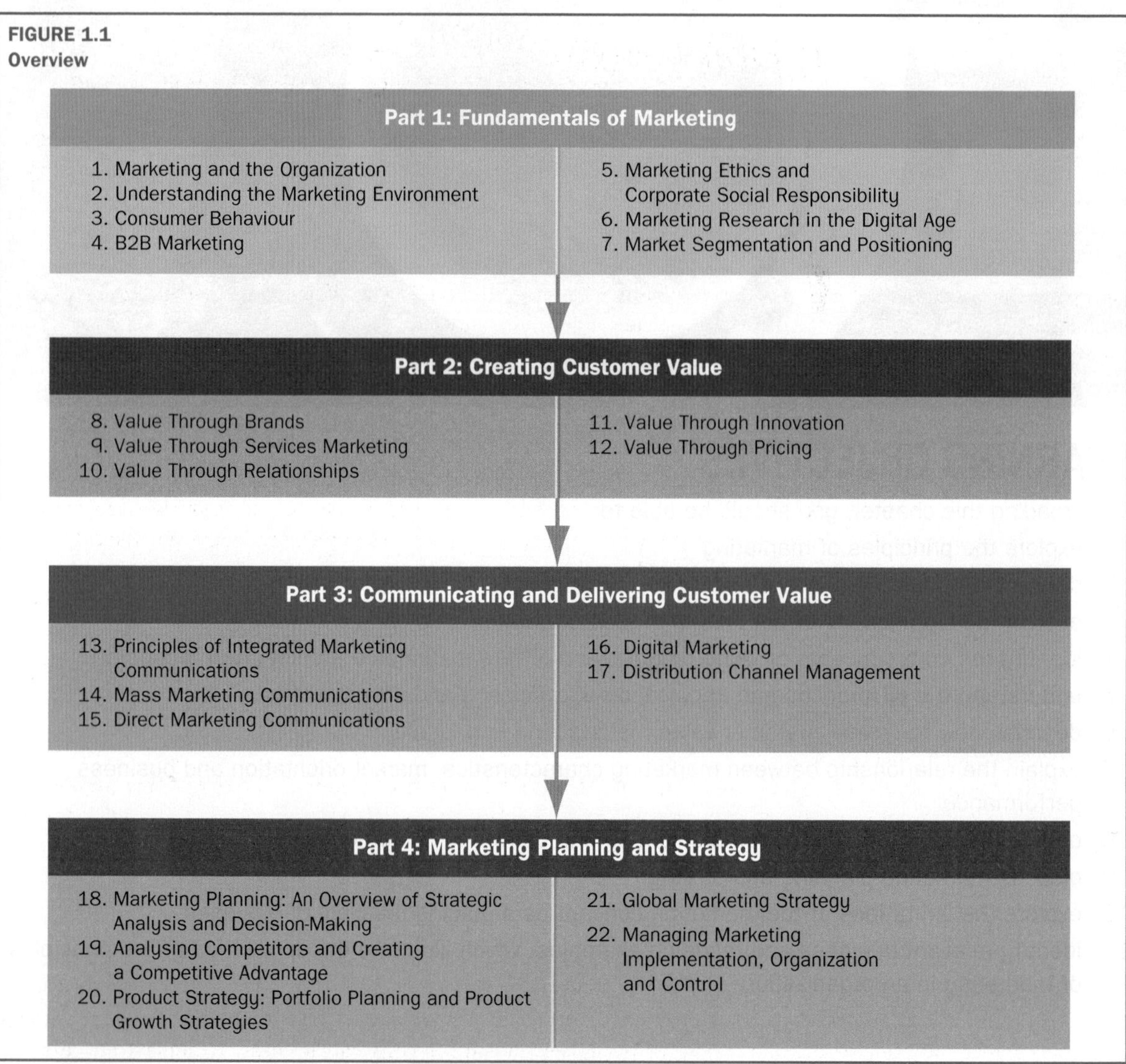

This chapter sets out the foundations for developing your understanding of the principles and practice of marketing, beginning with the fundamental question: What is marketing?

What is Marketing?

Marketing drives successful organisations, but it is often misinterpreted and sometimes gets bad press. Critics use words like marketing 'gimmicks', 'ploys' and 'tricks' to undermine the valuable effect that marketing can deliver. This is unfortunate, because the essence of marketing is value creation not trickery. Successful companies rely on customers returning to repurchase, and the goal of marketing is to facilitate this through creating long-term satisfaction not short-term deception. This theme is reinforced by the writings of top management consultant the late Peter Drucker, who stated (Drucker, 1999):

> 'Because the purpose of business is to create and keep customers, it has only two central functions—marketing and innovation. The basic function of marketing is to attract and retain customers at a profit.'

What can we learn from this statement? First, it places marketing in a central role for business success and focuses managers' attention on attracting and keeping customers.

Second, it implies that the purpose of marketing is not to chase any customer at any **price**. Drucker used profit as a criterion. Please note that profit may be used by many commercial organizations as a measure of success, whereas in the non-profit sector other measures, such as reduction of social deprivation or hunger, are equally important as profit. Consequently, the concepts, principles and techniques described in this book are as equally applicable to global corporations, e.g. Apple, Royal Dutch Shell, AXA Insurance, as charitable organizations, e.g. Barnardo's, Wellcome Trust.

Third, the investment required to attract new customers is higher than the amount needed to retain existing ones. Indeed, the costs of attracting a new customer have been found to be up to six times the costs of retaining old ones (Rosenberg and Czepeil, 1983). Companies that apply the principles of marketing recognize the importance of building relationships with customers by providing satisfaction and attracting new customers by creating added value. Grönroos (1989) stressed the importance of relationship building in his definition of marketing, in which he describes the objective of marketing as to establish, develop and commercialize long-term customer relationships so that the objectives of the parties involved are met.

Finally, most markets–e.g. consumer, industrial and not-for-profit–are characterized by strong competition. This means that organizations need not only to understand what their customers want, but also to understand what their competitors provide. If customers' needs are not met, they may switch to a rival supplier.

You should also consider that the practices of marketing are applied by organisations in dynamic and changing marketplaces. In recent years, the growth of the digital economy has significantly increased the opportunities to gather, analyse and exploit customer data and has influenced how we behave, interact, communicate and trade.

Marketing is a form of **exchange**, which is the act or process of receiving something from someone by giving something in return. The something could be a physical good, a service, an idea, information or money. Money facilitates exchanges so that people can concentrate on working at things they are good at, earn money (itself an exchange) and spend it on **products** or services that someone else has supplied. The objective is for all parties in the exchange to feel satisfied and gain something of value. This is particularly important because satisfied customers are more likely than dissatisfied ones to return for more. Hence the notion of customer satisfaction as the central pillar of marketing is fundamental to the creation of a stream of exchanges upon which organizational success depends.

These learning points are referred to throughout the book in a variety of contexts. The rest of this chapter introduces the key principles of the marketing concept, explores how marketing can create and deliver customer value and satisfaction, and considers the role of marketing planning and strategy.

The marketing concept

The traditional view of the marketing concept is based on the premise that companies achieve their profit and other objectives by satisfying (even delighting) customers (Houston, 1986). But modern marketing also needs to consider another fundamental aspect of trading exchanges: competition. In other words, the traditional marketing concept is a necessary but insufficient condition for organizational and corporate success. To achieve success,

FIGURE 1.2
Key components of the marketing concept

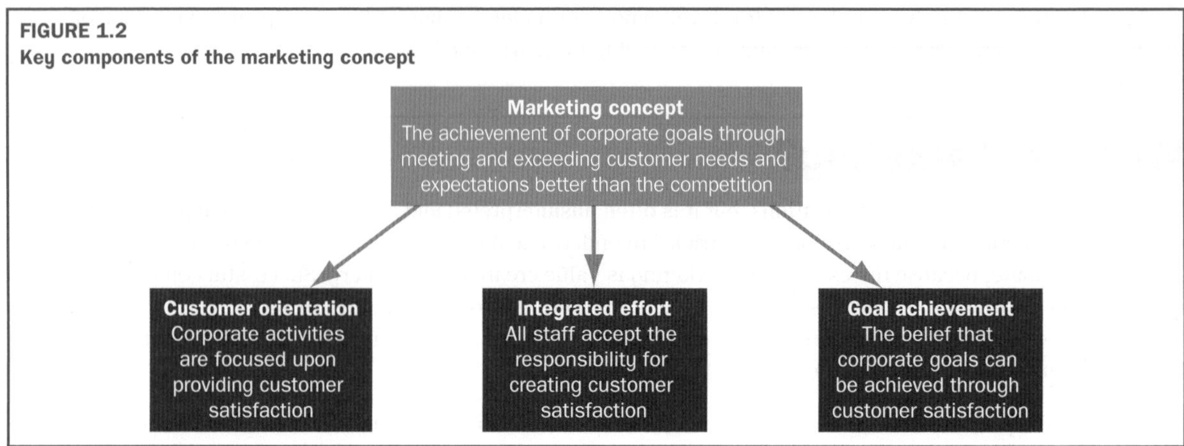

companies must go further than mere customer satisfaction; they must do better than the competition if they are to thrive and grow. International Airlines Group (IAG) is one of the world's largest airline groups, which provides national and international flights through several brands: Aer Lingus, British Airways, Iberia, Vueling. Their strategy is to provide varying levels of service through these brands. For example, British Airways (BA) has built its reputation around its brand values, which are captured by the slogan 'To Fly, To Serve' (Superbrands, 2015). BA seeks to stay ahead of the competition by providing consistently good service and quality customer experiences, whereas Vueling is a low-cost airline and IAG has invested in new systems, baggage handling and passenger queuing procedures to provide a more efficient and effective low-priced service.

The modern **marketing concept** can be expressed as the achievement of corporate goals through meeting and exceeding customer needs and expectations better than the competition.

To apply this concept, three conditions should be met. 1) Company activities should focus on providing customer satisfaction rather than making things easier and better for the producer or manufacturer. This is not an easy condition to meet, but it is a necessity to place the customer at the centre of all activity. 2) The achievement of customer satisfaction relies on integrated effort. The responsibility for the implementation of the concept lies not just within the marketing department. The belief that customer needs are central to the operation of a company should run right through production, finance, research and development, engineering and other departments. The role of the marketing department is to play *champion* for the concept and to coordinate activities. But the concept is a business philosophy, not a departmental duty. 3) For integrated effort to work successfully, management must believe that corporate goals can be achieved through satisfied customers (see Figure 1.2).

Adopting a Market Orientation in a Changing World

There is no guarantee that all companies will adopt the marketing concept. However, past research (e.g. Homburg, Vomburg, Enke and Grimm, 2015; Pulendran, Speed and Wilding, 2003; Hooley and Lynch, 1985) found evidence that the adoption of a **market orientation** could lead to significant performance benefits. Research also suggested the adoption of a market orientation approach as an evolutionary process whereby companies move from unawareness to complete acceptance of the importance of the marketing concept (Jaworski and Kohli, 1993; Hooley, Lynch and Shepherd, 1990) as a means of defining the orientation of a business. Consequently, companies focus on customer needs and change is recognized as endemic, with adaptation considered a Darwinian condition for survival. Changing needs present potential market opportunities that drive the company. Within the boundaries of their distinctive competences, market-driven companies seek to adapt their product and service offerings to the demands of current and latent markets. Figure 1.3 shows the basic elements of the market orientation.

A competing philosophy is production orientation, an inward-looking stance whereby managers become focused on the internal aspects of their business. It is particularly evident in manufacturing companies, where employees spend their working day at the point of production. In this case, firstly, management becomes cost focused and believes that its job is to attain economies of scale by producing a limited range of products

FIGURE 1.3
Basic elements of the market orientation

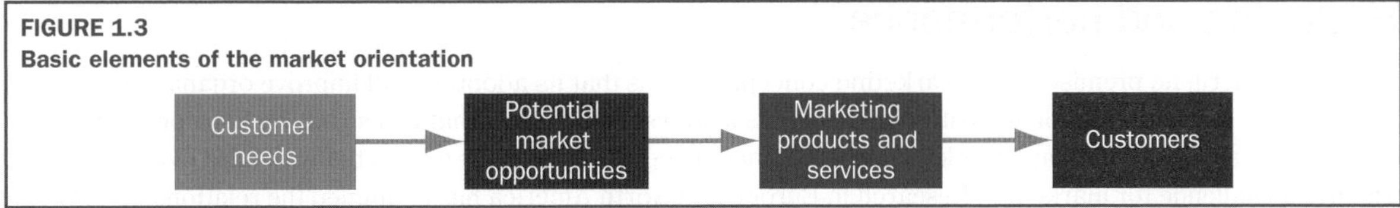

(at the extreme, just one) in a form that minimizes production costs. Henry Ford is quoted as an example of a production-orientated manager because he built just one car in one colour–the black Model T–in order to minimize costs. However, this is unfair to Mr Ford, since his objective was customer satisfaction–bringing the car to new market segments through low prices. The real production-orientated manager has no such virtues. The objective is cost reduction for its own sake, an objective at least partially fuelled by the greater comfort and convenience that comes from producing a narrow product range.

Secondly, the belief that the business should be defined in terms of its production facilities becomes ingrained in management practices. Figure 1.4 illustrates production orientation in its crudest form. If the production capabilities of an organization are allowed to define the business mission, the purpose of the organization can become organised around the manufacture of products and then aggressive selling to customers rather than focusing on delivering value and customer satisfaction.

According to Quinn, Dibb, Simkin, Canhoto and Analogbei (2016), marketing is evolving in such a way that has implications for the strategic application of the traditional market concept. Digital marketing as a discrete area of marketing activity has developed during the last 25 years from a computer-generated communication channel used by a few companies into a powerful phenomenon, which potentially affects every aspect of organizational activity across the globe. The shift toward digital marketing is changing the focus of the application of marketing, but these authors argue that its core principles are enduring:

- **Search for latent markets**: (new market opportunities) can be a challenge in well-developed economies, but digital technology has provided the capacity to delve deeply into nooks and crannies of human behaviour and, in doing so, give rise to many new market opportunities, for existing and innovative products and services. Amazon.com, Inc. developed Alexa–its range of voice activated devices–to facilitate easier access to thousands of products and services.
- **Customer focused:** sophisticated data analytics provide deeper insights into how to achieve customer satisfaction and stimulate repeat purchasing behaviour. Google LLC and Facebook, Inc. use customer data to enable the delivery of highly targeted messages and use their customer insights to sell advertising.
- **Integrated effort:** can extend to organisations outside the firm, e.g. logistics, and the delivery of the products and services are often far removed from a firm's staff members. DHL provides delivery services, dedicated warehousing and even two-man home delivery for large home appliances for many UK retailers, but in doing so focuses on giving excellent service. So, in the digital era, firms should plan how to extend their integrated efforts across multiple **touch points** that a customer might encounter.
- **Goal achievement:** perhaps an area where marketing faces its greatest challenges as performance measurement data is now gathered at every step of the way towards a corporate goal, e.g. customer acquisition, sales, delivery, return rates, customer retention, enabling more detailed and specific analysis. Homburg et al. (2015) found a tension between sales and marketing in relation to strategic decision-making, with sales challenging the dominance of the marketing function, in part due to availability and accountability of sales performance information. Technology firms like IBM are developing data science decision-making applications, which are transforming business practices. IBM Watson analytics is an analysis system that can identify business and market trends, and visualise the results on a desktop or mobile device. Marketers are increasingly being challenged to prove the benefits of marketing efforts.

FIGURE 1.4
Production orientation

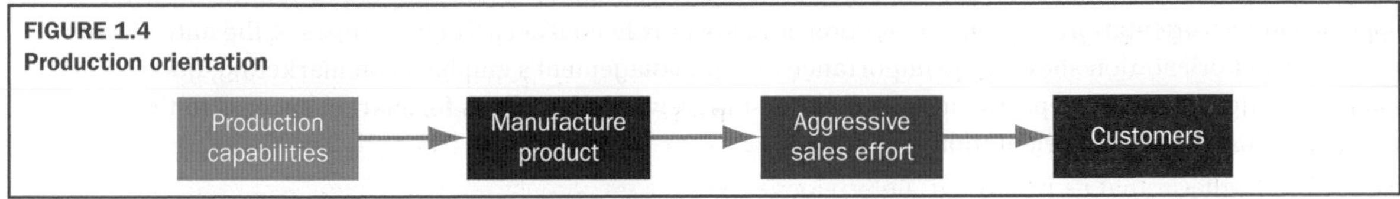

Marketing and performance

The basic underlying premise of the marketing concept remains that its adoption will improve organizational performance. Marketing is not an abstract concept: its acid test is the effect that its use has on key corporate indices, such as profitability and market share. But, increasingly, this must be supported with hard evidence, which is a challenge for marketing. Research in Europe and North America has examined the relationship between marketing and performance, and the results suggest that the relationship is positive.

In a study of 1,700 senior marketing executives, Hooley and Lynch (1985) reported the marketing characteristics of high- versus low-performing companies. The approach that they adopted was to isolate the top 10 per cent of companies (based on such measures as profit margin, return on investment and market share) and to compare their marketing practices with those of the remainder of the sample. The 'high fliers' differed from the 'also rans' in that they:

- were more committed to marketing research
- were more likely to be found in new, emerging or growth markets
- adopted a more proactive approach to marketing planning
- were more likely to use strategic planning tools
- placed more emphasis on product performance and design, rather than price, for achieving a **competitive advantage**
- worked more closely with the finance department
- placed greater emphasis on market share as a method of evaluating marketing performance.

Narver and Slater (1990) took this a step further and studied the relationship between market orientation and business performance. Market orientation was based on three measures: customer orientation, competitor orientation and degree of inter-functional coordination. They collected data from 113 strategic business units (SBUs) of a major US corporation. The businesses comprised 36 commodity businesses (forestry products) and 77 non-commodity businesses (speciality products and distribution businesses). They related each SBU's profitability, as measured by return on assets in relation to competitors' over the last year in the SBU's principal served market, to their three-component measure of market orientation.

Figure 1.5 shows the results of Narver and Slater's study. For **commodity businesses**, the relationship was U-shaped, with low and high market orientation businesses showing higher profitability than the businesses in the mid-range of market orientation. Businesses with the highest market orientation had the highest profitability, and those with the lowest market orientation had the second-highest profitability. Narver and Slater explained this result by suggesting that the businesses lowest in market orientation may achieve some profit success through a low-cost strategy, though not the profit levels of the high market orientation businesses, an explanation supported by the fact that they were the largest companies of the three groups.

For the **non-commodity businesses**, the relationship was linear, with the businesses displaying the highest level of market orientation achieving the highest levels of profitability, and those with the lowest scores on market orientation having the lowest profitability figures. As the authors state, 'The findings give marketing scholars and practitioners a basis beyond mere intuition for recommending the superiority of a market orientation.'

Kohli and Jaworski (1990) placed more emphasis on the sharing of market intelligence across an organization as a significant route towards identifying the needs of existing and new customers.

Many research studies confirm a positive relationship between market orientation and business performance on sales growth, market share and profitability (Pelham, 2000), sales growth (Narver, Jacobson and Slater, 1999), strategic orientation and overall business performance (Balodi, 2014) and international performance (Cadogan, Cui and Li, 2003). Kirca, Jayachandran and Bearden (2005) analysed the empirical findings from a wide range of studies that sought to identify the antecedents and consequences of market orientation. Their findings showed that a market orientation led to higher overall business performance (higher profits, sales and market share), better customer consequences (higher perceived quality, customer loyalty and customer satisfaction), better innovative consequences (higher innovativeness and better new product performance) and beneficial employee consequences (higher organizational commitment, team spirit, customer orientation and job satisfaction, and lower role conflict). Their analysis of the antecedents of the market orientation showed the importance of top management's emphasis on marketing, good communications between departments and systems that reward employees for market success to the implementation of market orientation.

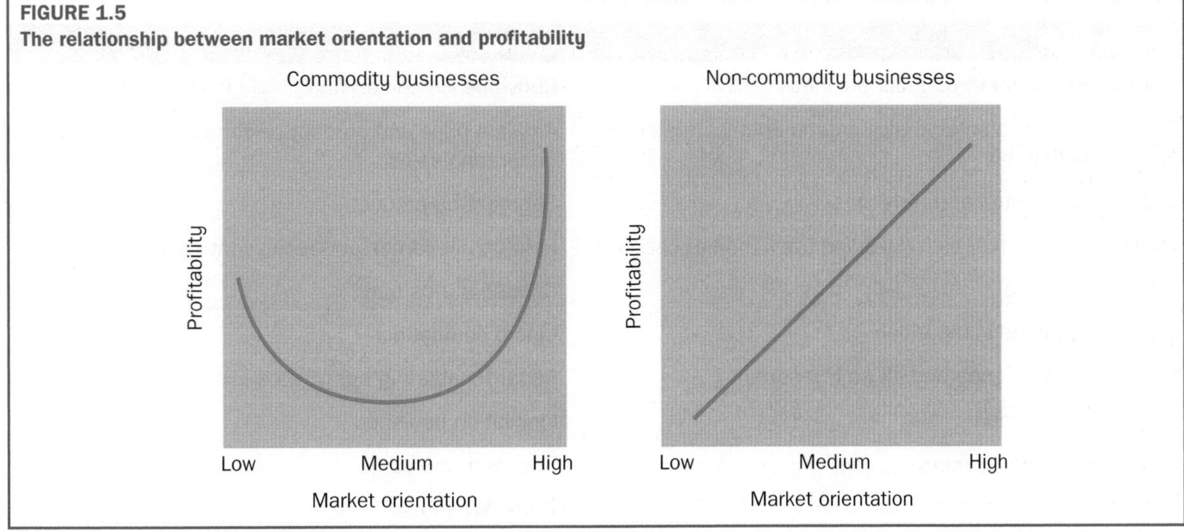

FIGURE 1.5
The relationship between market orientation and profitability

So, what overall conclusions can be drawn from these studies? In order to make a balanced judgement, limitations must be recognized. Most were cross-sectional studies based on self-reported data. With any such survey there is the question of the direction of causality. However, this clearly did not occur with the commodity sample in the Narver and Slater study (1990). What these studies have consistently and unambiguously shown is a strong association between marketing and business performance. As one condition for establishing causality, this is an encouraging result for those people concerned with promoting the marketing concept as a guiding philosophy for business.

The results of these pioneering studies have been supplemented with further empirical evidence showing a positive link between market orientation and business performance, e.g. Amazon, a company that focuses its efforts on creating customer-centric culture throughout a business.

Understanding Market-driven Businesses

In order to gain from the performance benefits of adopting the market orientation, marketers should understand the practical implications of applying this guiding philosophy. A deeper understanding of the marketing concept and orientation can be gained by contrasting a market-driven business with an internally focused business that focuses mainly on production-orientation. Table 1.1 summarizes the key differences.

Market-driven companies display customer concern throughout the business. All departments recognize the importance of the customer to the success of the business. Nestlé, for example, has placed the customer at the centre of its business philosophy by giving the company's head of marketing responsibility for the company's seven strategic business units. Marketers also control strategy, research and development, and production (Benady, 2005). For internally focused businesses, convenience comes first. If customer wants are inconvenient or expensive to produce, excuses are often used as avoidance tactics.

Market-driven businesses know how their products and services are being evaluated against those of the competition. They understand the choice criteria that customers are using and ensure that their **marketing** and **service mix** matches these criteria better than those of their competitors do. Selecting which elements of the mix to utilize can have both strategic and tactical implementations.

Businesses that are driven by the market base their segmentation analyses on customer differences that have implications for marketing strategy. Businesses that are focused internally segment by product and, consequently, are vulnerable when customers' requirements change. Rolls Royce manufactures products for

TABLE 1.1 Contrasting businesses: market versus internal focus

Market focus	Internal focus
Customer concern throughout business	Convenience comes first
Knowledge of customer choice criteria enables matching with marketing mix	Assume price and product performance is key to generating sales
Segment by customer differences	Segment by product
Invest in market research (MR) and track market changes	Rely on anecdotes and received wisdom
Welcome change	Cherish status quo
Try to understand competition	Ignore competition
Marketing spend regarded as an investment	Regard marketing spend as a luxury
Innovation rewarded	Innovation punished
Search for latent markets	Stick with the same
Are fast	Think 'Why rush?'
Strive for competitive advantage	Are happy to be 'me too'
Are efficient and effective	Are efficient

several industrial sectors: civil aviation, marine engineering and shipping, and the oil and gas industry. However, this world-leading business also recognizes the importance of its customers, who have very specific needs.

A key feature of market-driven businesses is their recognition that marketing research expenditure is an investment that can yield rich rewards through better customer understanding. Toyota is a market-led company that uses market research extensively. The Yaris was specially designed to meet the needs of the European consumer, and Toyota's Optimal Drive technology was designed to provide its customers with the benefit of enhanced performance, lower emissions and better fuel economy.

Internally driven businesses see marketing research as a non-productive intangible and prefer to rely on anecdotes and received wisdom. Market-orientated businesses welcome the organizational changes that are bound to occur as an organization moves to maintain a strategic fit between its environment and its strategies. In contrast, internally orientated businesses cherish the status quo and resist change.

Attitudes towards competition also differ. Market-driven businesses try to understand competitive objectives and strategies and anticipate competitive actions. Internally driven companies are content to ignore the competition. Marketing spend is regarded as an investment that has long-term consequences in market-driven businesses. The alternative view is that marketing expenditure is a luxury that never appears to produce benefits.

In market-orientated companies, those employees who take risks and are innovative are rewarded. Recognition of the fact that most new products fail is reflected in a reluctance to punish those people who risk their career championing a new product idea. Internally orientated businesses reward time-serving and the ability not to make mistakes. This results in risk avoidance and the continuance of the status quo. Market-driven businesses search for latent markets–markets that no other company has yet exploited. Apple, Inc., the multinational technology corporation, has exploited latent markets for many consumer electronic products: the iPhone (smart phone), iPad (tablet) and Apple watch (watch including fitness, health tracking, smart phone functionality). Read Marketing in Action 1.1 to find out how Niantic Labs, a relatively unknown US firm, with Nintendo Co. Ltd, The Pokémon Company, and Google, Inc. exploited a latent market using Artificial Intelligence and created a global phenomenon in less than 24 hours.

Internally driven businesses are happy to stick with their existing products and markets, but externally driven businesses respond to changing demands in the market. For example, the change towards ethical consumption has created opportunities for existing companies: M&S has taken actions across the supply chain to improve the ethical credentials of its products, from considering the cotton used in garment manufacture to water pollution (Moore, 2014). European fashion retailer C&A have set goals for 2020, which aim to create a culture of sustainability

MARKETING IN ACTION 1.1
Pokémon Go from Zero to Hero in 24 hours

Niantic, Inc., a US technology firm you may not instantly recognize, launched a very novel game app in the summer of 2016: Pokémon Go. The gaming app uses augmented reality technology to enable players to catch Pokémon characters using a mobile phone. Within a day, the game was at the top of every app store list and in less than 7 months generated over a billion dollars from players buying upgrades. This was not only an example of highly successful exploitation of a latent market, but also a highly profitable product. Surprisingly, there was no high-profile marketing campaign; the target markets were accessed through social media feeds. Niantic just tweeted about the app–based on Nintendo's original Pokémon game from the 1990s–saying it was available in the USA and Australasia. Nintendo (America) retweeted the announcements. However, there were pre-launch announcements and the release of a teaser video by The Pokémon Company in the autumn of the previous year, so demand had been building in anticipation of the product launch.

Within 2 years, over 20 million players lost interest in chasing Pokémon, suggesting the product had a short lifespan. But this is not the case; the app continues to be regularly downloaded by new users and has many loyal gamers who together have generated an estimated $1.8 billion. Part of this ongoing success is attributed to its wider market appeal than other gaming apps. Niantic, Inc. has led the way in the use of augmented reality in gaming apps; in the future, there are likely to be many similar products produced by competitors, like Apple, Inc., Google, Inc. and firms which are still to appear on the global stage.

Based on: Barrett (2018); Niantic, Inc. (2018); Morrison (2016)

for customers, suppliers and employees. New companies have been created using ethical principles: One Water donates 100 per cent of its profits to life-saving projects in Africa. Read Marketing in Action 1.2 to find out more about H&M's approach towards sustainability. Chapter 5 discusses ethical marketing and corporate and social responsibility in detail.

Intensive competition means market-driven companies should respond quickly to latent markets. They need to innovate, manufacture and distribute their products and services rapidly if they are to succeed before the *strategic window of opportunity* closes (Abell, 1978). In contrast, internally driven companies tend to take their time. An example of a company that was slow to respond to the opportunities in the mobile computer market is Microsoft. It introduced the tablet PC and carved a niche market in the health sector, but in 2010 Apple launched the iPad, which widened market demand, and they now dominate this sector.

A key feature of market-orientated companies is that they strive for competitive advantage. They seek to serve customers better than the competition does. Internally orientated companies are happy to produce me-too copies of offerings already on the market.

Finally, market-orientated companies are both efficient and effective; internally orientated companies achieve only efficiency. The concepts of efficiency and effectiveness are discussed in the next section.

Efficiency Versus Effectiveness

Another perspective on business philosophy can be gained by understanding the distinction between efficiency and effectiveness (Brown, 1987). **Efficiency** is concerned with inputs and outputs. An efficient firm produces goods economically–it does things right. The benefit is that the cost per unit of output is low and, therefore,

MARKETING IN ACTION 1.2
H&M: Look Good, Do Good, Feel Good

Spending on ethical products is growing each year across Europe. In the UK, the market is more than £81 billion. Demand in ethical markets for sustainable fashion, food products, transport and green energy continues to grow, and these markets appear to be more robust than other parts of the economy, even when consumers economize and spend less. Pedersen, Gwozdz and Hvass (2018) found in their study of fashion retailers in Sweden that innovative companies are more likely to actively pursue sustainable business models. Fashion brands tend to be highly flexible businesses, able to respond to changing trends. Many fashion brands in Europe have adapted their practices to improve the sustainability of their businesses and to target younger buyers of fashion, who are becoming increasingly interested in sustainability. One such company is H&M.

H&M is a retail organization that proactively searches for marketing opportunities and responds to wider market trends, such as sustainable products. The company opened its first store in 1947 in Vasteras, Sweden, selling women's clothing. The brand expanded into other parts of Scandinavia before opening its first store in London in 1976. Throughout the 1980s and 1990s, store openings continued and, by 2018, H&M was recognised as the world's second-largest fashion retailer, operating in Europe, Asia, North and South America, the Middle East and online.

H&M has put sustainability at the heart of the business. Sustainable initiatives are incorporated at every level from product design, raw materials, production and manufacturing through to logistics and sales. For example, at the product level they have launched a new brand, ARKET, which focuses on delivering sustainable designs. The company also intends this brand to lead the fashion industry as a whole toward more transparency in the supply chain. The Conscious Collection, which incorporates organic and recycled materials into its product ranges is another way in which H&M are getting across the sustainability message to customers. Last year, 17,771 tonnes of clothing were collected and reused.

The company aims to bring sustainable fashion to everyone, and to deliver this vision they are making significant and long-term changes to how the business operates.

Based on: H&M (2018); Balch (2013); Young (2018); Pedersen, Gwozdz and Hvass (2018)

the potential for offering low prices to gain market share is present, or of charging medium to high prices and achieving high profit margins. For example, car companies attempt to achieve efficiency by gaining economies of scale and building several models on the same sub-frame and with the same components. However, to be successful, a company needs to be more than just efficient–it needs to be effective as well. **Effectiveness** means doing the right things. This implies operating in attractive markets and making products that customers want to buy. Conversely, companies that operate in unattractive markets or are not producing what customers want to buy will go out of business; the only question is one of timing.

The link between performance and combinations of efficiency and effectiveness can be conceived as shown in Figure 1.6. A company that is both inefficient and ineffective will go out of business quickly, because it is a high-cost producer of products that customers do not want to buy. The Hummer SUV became a 'must have' vehicle early in the 2000s, but its high purchase cost, high running costs and high levels of carbon emissions led to its failure. High profile owners like Arnold Schwarzenegger, David Beckham and Paris Hilton abandoned their Hummers and

FIGURE 1.6
Efficiency and effectiveness

	Ineffective	Effective
Inefficient	Goes out of business quickly	Survives
Efficient	Dies slowly	Does well, thrives

the brand failed as it ceased to be a viable purchase option (Tran, 2010). In 2010, Starbucks created evening stores with product extensions, including beer and wine and table service, in thousands of outlets in the USA and a few selected stores in the UK. The aim was to increase customer traffic later in the day. But the table service for the evenings conflicted with the counter service offered in the morning and customers didn't respond well. In 2017, the programme was discontinued in many stores and Starbucks looked for other ways to tap into the night time economy (Trefis Team, 2017).

A company that is efficient and ineffective may last a little longer because its low-cost base may generate more profits from the dwindling sales volume it is achieving. Once BlackBerry devices were an innovative product and global leaders in the smart phone market, in part due to the then innovative QWERTY keyboard. But when Apple, Inc. and Android devices incorporated touch screen keyboards and larger screens in their smart phones, BlackBerry was left behind. Sales began to rapidly decline and even the new versions of the device could not compete with the sleek elegant designs of Apple and Android smart phones. The device could no longer compete or satisfy customers' needs (Worth, 2016). See Exhibit 1.1 to compare the Blackberry PDA and Samsung smart phone.

Firms that are effective but inefficient are likely to survive, however, because they are operating in attractive markets and are marketing products that customers want to buy. Department stores provide a destination for shoppers as they offer wide ranges of goods all in one **place** and are an important type of retailer for towns and cities as they attract shoppers. Debenhams and the John Lewis Partnership are examples of these types of retailers, which remain successful, but department stores are becoming an ineffective way of retailing due to the high costs of operating large expensive retail premises, managing multiple product ranges and changing shopping habits: more online and mobile shopping, and increased spending on leisure activities. There are many examples of businesses struggling to survive: House of Fraser (UK), Sears (USA), Macy's (USA).

Many small companies operating in niche markets also fall into the effective/inefficient category. One example is Morgan Motor Company, which manufactures bespoke, high-specification sports cars. Prices for the basic model start at less than £30,000 and, as a result, the company has a long waiting list of customer orders, but the factory continues to manufacture less than 30 cars a week.

A combination of efficiency and effectiveness leads to optimum business success. Such firms do well and thrive because they are operating in attractive markets, supplying products that consumers want to buy and benefiting from a low-cost base.

Toyota is an example of an efficient and effective manufacturing company. Its investment in modern production practices ensures efficiency, while effectiveness is displayed by research and development investment into new products that consumers want to buy. Inditex, owner of Zara, the Spanish fashion chain, has also thrived through a combination of efficiency and effectiveness by using its own highly efficient automated manufacturing and distribution facilities, clothing workers in 350 independently owned workshops in Spain and Portugal, and low advertising expenditures (its shops have always been its primary marketing tool). The company is highly effective, as it matches quickly changing fashion trends by means of an extremely fast and responsive supply chain. The result is that Inditex has become the world's largest clothing retailer by sales (Stothard, 2018).

The essential difference between efficiency and effectiveness is that the former is primarily cost focused, while the latter is customer focused. An effective company can attract and retain customers while remaining cost-efficient. These principles should be applied according to the market conditions and can be crucial to delivering successful performance. As markets change, the definition of efficiency and effectiveness also needs to adapt. For example, before the

EXHIBIT 1.1
Compare Blackberry PDA and Samsung smart phone

advent of online shopping, customers would be happy and satisfied if a firm delivered their ordered goods within, say, 7 days and would have very limited information about when they would arrive. But now customers expect delivery within 2 days of placing an order; ideally the next day. To achieve this new level of efficiency, firms have had to make changes and streamline their logistical operations, and to be effective they have, in many cases, had to increase the number of delivery channels and increase the predictability of when deliveries are made in order to meet customer expectations. Such changes are contributing to the evolution of marketing and also creating opportunities to meet and exceed customer expectations.

Creating Customer Value, Satisfaction and Loyalty

Customer expectations in all markets are evolving and creating value is a primary aim of market-orientated businesses. Four key benefits can be derived from adopting marketing as a guiding business philosophy:

1. customer value
2. customer satisfaction
3. customer loyalty
4. long-term customer relationships.

Customer value

Market-orientated companies attempt to create **customer value** in order to attract and retain customers. Their aim is to deliver superior value to their target customers. In doing so, they implement the marketing concept by meeting and exceeding customer needs better than the competition does. For example, the global success of McDonald's has been based on creating added value for its customers, which is based not only on the food products it sells but on the complete delivery system that goes to make up a fast-food restaurant. It sets high standards in quality, service, cleanliness and value (termed QSCV). Customers can be sure that the same high standards will be found in all McDonald's outlets around the world. This example shows that customer value can be derived from many aspects of what the company delivers to its customers, not just the basic product.

Customer value is dependent on how the customer perceives the benefits of an offering and the sacrifice that is associated with its purchase. Therefore:

$$\text{customer value} = \text{perceived benefits} - \text{perceived sacrifice}$$

Perceived benefits can be derived from the product (e.g. the taste of the hamburger), the associated service (e.g. how quickly customers are served and the cleanliness of the outlet) and the image of the company (e.g. whether the image of the company/product is favourable). If one of those factors–e.g. product benefits–changes, then the perceived benefits and customer value also change. For instance, fast food restaurants largely rely on using disposable packaging and utensils for their products, much of which is not recyclable and bad for the environment. Major brands in this industry have realised that they need to address this issue: McDonald's is to end the use of plastic straws and will switch to using paper (Vaughan, 2018), Starbucks is introducing *greener* and reusable cups and has extended its cup recycling scheme to the Netherlands (Starbucks, 2018) and KFC is focusing on using more recyclable glass, plastic and cardboard (KFC, 2018).

A further source of perceived benefits is the relationship between customer and supplier. Customers may enjoy working with suppliers with whom they have developed close personal and professional friendships, and they value the convenience of working with trusted partners.

Perceived sacrifice is the total cost associated with buying a product. This consists of not just monetary cost, but the time and energy involved in purchase. For example, with fast-food restaurants, good location can reduce the time and energy required to find a suitable eating place. But marketers need to be aware of another critical sacrifice in some buying situations. This is the potential psychological cost of not making the right decision. Uncertainty means that people perceive risk when purchasing: for example, McDonald's attempts to reduce perceived risk by standardizing its complete offer so that customers can be confident of what they will receive before entering its outlets. In organizational markets, companies offer guarantees to reduce the risk of purchase. Figure 1.7 illustrates how perceived benefits and sacrifice affect customer value. It provides a framework for considering ways of maximizing value. The objective is to find ways of raising perceived benefits and reducing perceived sacrifice.

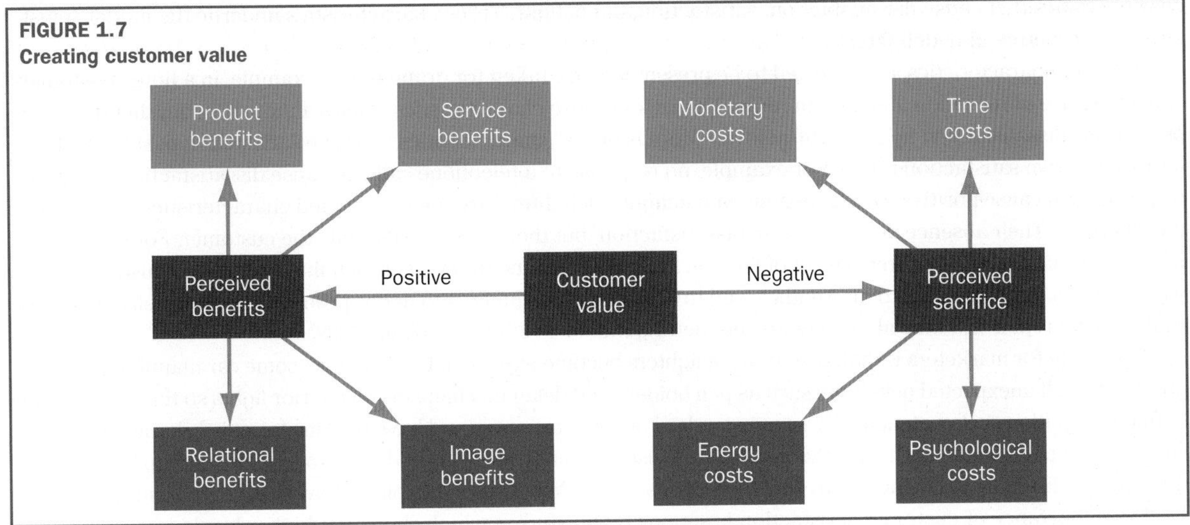

FIGURE 1.7
Creating customer value

Customer satisfaction

Exceeding the value offered by competitors is key to marketing success. Consumers decide upon purchases on the basis of judgements about the values offered by suppliers. Once a product has been bought, **customer satisfaction** depends upon the product's perceived performance compared with the buyer's expectations. Customer satisfaction occurs when perceived performance matches or exceeds expectations. Successful companies such as Canon, Toyota, Samsung, H&M, Waitrose, Apple and Virgin all place customer satisfaction at the heart of their business philosophy. Companies facing difficulties, such as General Motors, Chrysler, Gap and Kodak, have failed to do so as customers' needs and expectations have changed and so they need to find ways to refocus on the customer or potentially face business collapse. ASOS, a successful online fashion retailer, succeeding in creating customer satisfaction by looking to the digital future. The company satisfies young women's desire to replicate the look of their favourite celebrities by offering affordable versions of celebrity styles: e.g. Justin Bieber, Kayne West, Victoria Beckham. Read more about ASOS in Chapter 17 Case 33.

Customer satisfaction is taken so seriously by some companies that they link satisfaction to financial bonuses. For example, two days after taking delivery of a new car, BMW (and Mini) customers receive a telephone call to check how well they were treated in the dealership. The customer is asked various questions and their responses are measured. Dealerships have to be capable of achieving good performance scores, and existing dealerships that consistently fail to meet these standards are under threat of franchise termination. This approach makes a great deal of sense, as higher levels of customer satisfaction are associated with higher levels of customer retention, financial performance and shareholder value (see Mittal and Kamakura, 2001; Zeithaml, 2000; Anderson, Fornell and Mazvancheryl, 2004).

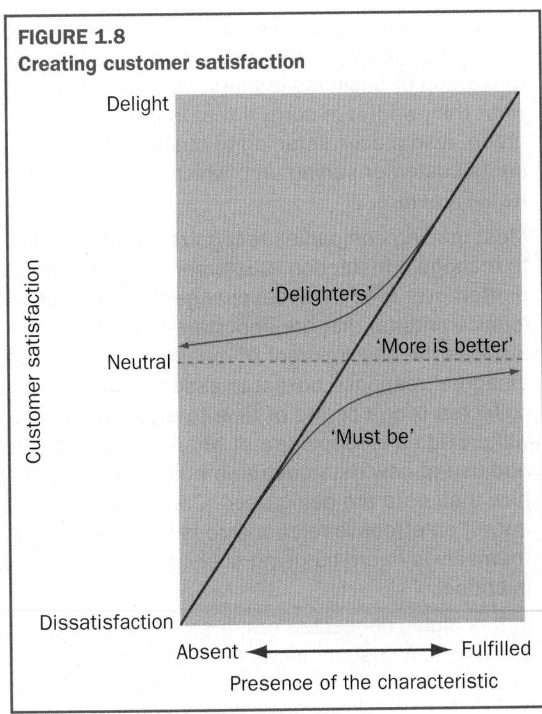

FIGURE 1.8
Creating customer satisfaction

In today's competitive climate, it is often not enough to match performance and expectations. For commercial success, expectations need to be exceeded so that customers are delighted with the outcome. In order to understand the concept of customer satisfaction, the so-called 'Kano model' (see Figure 1.8) helps to separate characteristics that cause dissatisfaction, satisfaction and delight. Three characteristics underlie the model: 'must be', 'more is better' and 'delighters'.

'Must be' characteristics are expected to be present and are taken for granted. For example, in a hotel, customers expect service at reception and a clean room. The lack of these characteristics causes annoyance, but their presence only brings dissatisfaction up to a neutral level. 'More is better' characteristics can take satisfaction past neutral into the positive satisfaction range. For example, no response to a telephone call can cause dissatisfaction, but a fast response may cause positive satisfaction or even delight. 'Delighters' are the unexpected characteristics that surprise the customer. Their absence does not cause dissatisfaction, but their presence delights the customer. For example, a UK hotel chain provides a free basket of fruit on arrival in visitors' rooms. This delights many of its customers, who were not expecting this treat. Another way to delight the customer is to under-promise and over-deliver (e.g. by saying that a repair will take about 5 hours, but getting it done in 2 hours) (White, 1999).

A problem for marketers is that, over time, delighters become expected. For example, some car manufacturers provided small unexpected delighters such as pen holders and delay mechanisms on interior lights so that there is time to find the ignition socket at night. These are standard on most cars now and have become 'must be' characteristics, as customers expect them. This means that marketers must constantly strive to find new ways of delighting. Innovative thinking and listening to customers are key ingredients in this. Mini Case 1.1 explains how to listen to customers.

The importance of customer satisfaction is supported by studies which show that higher levels of customer satisfaction lead to better performance: higher financial performance (profits and sales), greater customer loyalty (Homberg, Koschate and Hoyer, 2005) and the willingness of customers to pay higher prices (see Anderson and Sullivan, 1997; and Bolton and Drew, 1991). There is also a strong relationship between a firm's corporate social responsibility (CSR) and customer satisfaction in competitive markets, as a strong CSR strategy can reduce uncertainty and increase satisfaction (Sun and Price, 2016).

Customer satisfaction is linked to customer loyalty and profitability (Srinivasan, Anderson and Ponnavolu, 2002). It can cost up to six times more to attract a new customer than to serve an existing one (Strauss, El-Ansary and Frost, 2006).

MINI CASE 1.1
Customers

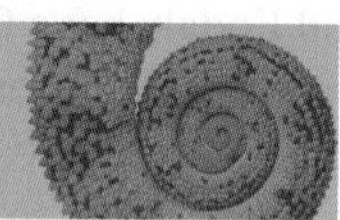

The importance of listening to customers was emphasized by Sir Terry Leahy, former chief executive of Tesco Plc, the UK's largest supermarket chain: 'Let me tell you the secret of successful retailing,' he said to a group of business leaders. 'Are you ready? It's this: never stop listening to customers and giving them what they want. I'm sorry if that is a bit of an anti-climax . . . but it is that simple.' Kwik-Fit, the car repair group, also places listening to customers high on its list of priorities. Customer satisfaction is monitored by its customer survey unit, which telephones 5,000 customers a day within 72 hours of their visit to a Kwik-Fit centre.

Most leading companies recognize the importance of listening to their customers as part of their strategy to manage satisfaction. Customer satisfaction indices are based on surveys of customers, and the results plotted over time to reveal changes in satisfaction levels. The first stage is to identify those characteristics (choice criteria) that are important to customers when evaluating competing products. The second stage involves the development of measurement scales (often statements followed by 'strongly agree'/'strongly disagree' response boxes) to assess satisfaction quantitatively. Customer satisfaction data should be collected over a period of time to measure change. Only long-term measurement of satisfaction ratings will provide a clear picture of what is going on in the marketplace. However, the marketplace is changing and use of new data-capture methods and technologies means that some customers are more aware of how their data are being used. Consequently, customers must see some benefit from the use of their data if an effective relationship is to develop, and both satisfied and dissatisfied customers are making themselves heard by using social media, for example Twitter. For marketers, understanding the digital arena is critical.

In this highly connected era, a strategy should be in place to manage customer complaints, comments and questions. A system needs to be set up that solicits feedback on product and service quality, and feeds the information to the appropriate employees, who can respond in a timely fashion. To facilitate this process, frontline employees need training to ask questions, to listen effectively, to capture the information and to communicate it so that corrective action can be taken. Walmart used to believe that no response was the best policy for handling negative tweets but has changed its strategy; now the global grocery retailer proactively manages online communication and is a top brand in content engagement. Moreover, complaint handling in some circumstances has been found to be stronger in social medial channels than traditional channels (Sugathan, Rossmann, Ranjan (2018).

TripAdvisor is one of the world's largest online travel sites, and it helps people plan their holiday and business trips by providing advice from over 60 million reviews and opinions from other travellers who have experience of services provided by hotels, restaurants and travel companies. Each service provider is ranked by a number of performance indicators, and this can make a big difference to future trade, as the opinions of other travellers can have a powerful influence.

Companies can also launch websites to solicit customers' new ideas. Dell did this after it received a flood of criticism over poor customer service, while also reaching out to online bloggers. The feedback led to a customer services overhaul and a fall in negative buzz.

Finally, Google listens to customers by releasing most products in 'beta' (which means they are not quite finished), allowing users to suggest improvements. This approach has led to the refinement of such products as Google News, Gmail and the Chrome browser.

Questions:

1. Explain why social media sites can play an important role in developing customer loyalty.
2. What strategy would you suggest to a hotelier for handling customer complaints, comments and questions?

Based on: Jones and Sasser Jr (1995); Morgan (1996); White (1999); Roythorne (2003); Ryle (2003); Mitchell (2005); Wright (2006); Jarvis (2009); Hilpern (2011); Devaney and Stein (2014); Zhang (2014); Sugathan, Rossmann and Ranjan (2018)

Customer loyalty

In most situations, returning customers are beneficial to an organization, as they can increase sales volumes through repeat purchases. Loyalty is a response that a customer shows over time. Typically, customers will repeatedly return to the same supplier if they are satisfied with the products and services they receive (Christodoulides and Michaelidou, 2011). Customer loyalty can be built on convenience, quality of service and social interaction, for example. However, loyalty can take different forms and be triggered by different marketing initiatives. For example, Tesco uses sales promotions through its loyalty card programme to trigger repeat customer purchase behaviour. Arguably, this type of loyalty is driven by price, and the promotion acts as an incentive to trigger repeat purchases. Customer loyalty can be temporarily shaken when companies change their brand identity, as Marketing in Action 1.3 explains. But customization can increase perception of service quality, satisfaction and trust, with the outcome of generating improved customer loyalty (Coelho and Henseler, 2012).

At the other end of the scale is a form of loyalty that transcends emotional boundaries: brand love. Brand love is an extension of the concept of loyalty (Batra, Ahuvia and Bagozzi, 2012). Researchers have found that the connections between individuals and the brands they choose are closely associated with the concept of interpersonal physical love. However, while brand love has been found to involve passion, positive emotional connections, long-term relationships, positive attitudes and distress at the thought of separation, it does not leave brand lovers as profoundly committed to a product as they might be to a personal partner. Nevertheless, there are consequences for marketing managers, and they should look for ways to turn *liked* brands into *loved* brands.

Looking for ways to maintain this high level of commitment to the relationship can be achieved by maximizing three key opportunities: 1) *Facilitate 'passion-driven behaviour'*, which is a strong commitment to use the brand, as in the case of luxury designer brands–e.g. Gucci, Rolex, Porsche, 2) *Build brands that engender self-brand integration.* This is the way the brand connects to an individual's values and deeper thought processes.

MARKETING IN ACTION 1.3
Brand Loyalty Wobbles when Starbucks Employs a Siren that's Just Too Perfect

Customer value is closely linked with perceptions of a brand. So, when changes are made to a brand's identity they should be meaningful to customers in such a way that they will continue to make positive brand associations and buy the products and services offered. In 2011, Starbucks launched its new global brand identity as a mark of the company's 40 years in business.

According to Steve Barrett, the Starbucks global creative vice-president, the new look tested well with loyal consumers. However, the removal of the words *Starbucks* and *coffee* from the iconic green logo initially annoyed many of its customers, and they complained in their hundreds on the brand's official Facebook page, saying the new logo 'sucks'. Part of the problem was the mermaid's face was just too perfect. So the global branding team decided the face should not be symmetrical. Take a look at the image of the Starbucks logo and see how slight changes have sought to make imperfections and in doing so humanize the image. The company aimed give the brand a less corporate and more contemporary feel.

The new identity also resonates with the introduction of new product lines, for example Tazo tea, vegan products and Starbucks Refresha–cold drinks and ice cream that are not coffee based. The initial resistance to the change of identity did not last, and customers continue to flock to Starbucks' 22,000 outlets in 66 countries around the world.

Based on: Added Value (2011); Clark (2011); Wood (2011); Leroux (2014); Berr (2014); Spary (2015); Wilson (2018)

Rewards can be used effectively to emphasize the benefits of this higher-level commitment. Samsung is an example of a brand that is attempting to connect with customers by engendering self-identity through brand values associated with the environment, and 3) *Create positive emotional connections.* Brands that succeed in being regarded as an 'old friend' and creating a strong bond with the customer benefit by finding a place in the customer's heart. Anita Roddick succeeded in making this type of connection with Body Shop customers (Batra, Ahuvia and Bagozzi (2012).

Long-term customer relationships

According to Sheth and Parvartiyar (1995), relationship marketing is a change in direction for marketing thinking and practices, and it places 'emphasis on relationships as opposed to transaction-based exchanges'. The benefit of this redefinition of marketing is that a firm's activities become focused on attracting customers and seeking ways to retain them rather than just selling the products and services that customers might need and want. Relationship marketing enhances productivity and allows the firm and its customers to develop mutual cooperation. In the digital age, technology has become increasingly important in facilitating relationship development; social media has been used to understand and engage customers. Twitter, Facebook and Instagram provide platforms for interaction and information exchange between firms, employees and customers. Social platforms maximize customer engagement and create opportunities for marketers to react instantly when a customer tweets about a bad (or good) customer experience. Rapid response in the digital arena can also deliver relational benefits, as more than 70 per cent of customers are likely to spend more if a firm has a good service history (Sklar, 2013). The concept of relationship marketing is covered in greater detail in Chapter 10.

Marketing Planning

So far in this chapter we have discussed the conceptual meaning of marketing, adopting a market orientation, the importance of efficiency and effectiveness, and ways to create customer value, satisfaction and loyalty. In this final section, we look at what is involved in developing marketing planning from three viewpoints: strategic, tactical and implementation. It is important to note that these are substantive topics, so this is merely an introduction to some of the key ideas. Each topic is covered in detail in later chapters in the book.

Marketing strategy is part of the overarching corporate strategic planning process and making marketing work requires much planning and effort across an organization. Fundamentally, marketing planning functions at two levels:

1 At a business level–here the focus is strategic in nature and involves: setting a business mission; identifying the vision driving the firm forwards; carrying out a marketing audit (an analysis of a firm's current trading situation); conducting a SWOT (strengths, weaknesses, opportunities and threats) analysis to inform strategic direction; and setting high-level marketing objectives, which define the target markets and selection of goods and services offered by a firm.
2 At a product and/or service level–here the focus is on the practical application of marketing. This level involves many decisions about how to use the product and service mix to create competitive advantage and then how these decisions are implemented.

Driving the planning process is strategic marketing, which pulls together the planning process and the tactical application of the marketing and service mix. Chapter 18 discusses marketing planning.

Strategic marketing

Strategy is defined as a firm's conscious efforts to use its resources to leverage advantage (Hamel and Prahalad, 1994) and adding a marketing perspective brings a valuable focus on how to use these resources to stand out from the competition and make it more difficult for other firms to copy (Wu, 2011). This process involves analysing competitors and creating a competitive advantage and is so important to the development of strategic marketing plans that Chapter 19 is devoted to discussing these topics.

Tactical marketing

Gupta (2009) reminds us of the importance of the customer (as well as other metrics: profits, stock valuations) when deploying marketing tactically. To gain the most benefits is it suggested that elements of the marketing and service mix should not only focus on brands, products and services, but also reach out to enhance value, customer satisfaction and loyalty in the longer term. For example, L'Oreal, a global firm, has a wide portfolio of cosmetic brands: L'Oreal Paris, Maybelline, Urban Decay, Essie. The senior management focus and invest heavily on research and development to ensure long-term customer satisfaction, that their ranges remain of interest to customers and their deployment of technology in their communications reach new and existing customers (Millington, 2015).

Tactical marketing is often viewed as the deployment of the marketing mix and consists of four major elements: *product, price, promotion* and *place.* The 'Four-Ps' highlight four key decision areas that marketers must manage to meet tactical and, ultimately, strategic goals. See Chapters 12–17 for detailed discussions of each of the elements of the marketing mix.

Furthermore, the growth of the service industries has given rise to an extended marketing mix of seven 'Ps'. The services marketing mix adds three decision areas to consider: *people, physical evidence* and *process* (Booms and Bitner, 1981). The need for the extension came about due to the high degree of direct contact between the firm and the customer, the highly visible nature of the service assembly process, and the simultaneity of production and consumption. Booms and Bitner argued for a Seven-Ps approach to services marketing, as they suggest that the Four-Ps take no account of service delivery. While it is possible to discuss people, physical evidence and process within the original Four-Ps framework (e.g. people could be considered part of the product offering), the extension allows a more thorough analysis of the marketing ingredients necessary for successful marketing planning and activities. In services, people often *are* the service itself, the process or how the service is delivered to the customer is usually a key part of the service, and the physical evidence–the décor of the restaurant or shop, for example–is so critical to success that it should be considered as a separate element in the services marketing mix. See Chapter 9 for detailed discussion of services marketing.

Marketing implementation

Marketing strategy concerns the issues of *what* should happen and *why* it should happen. Implementation focuses on actions: *who* is responsible for various activities, *how* the strategy should be carried out, *where* things will happen and *when* action will take place. So managers devise marketing strategies to meet new market opportunities, counter environmental threats and match core competences. Designing marketing strategies and positioning plans that meet today's and tomorrow's market requirements is a necessary, but insufficient, condition for corporate success. They need to be translated into action through effective implementation. While decisions regarding the extended marketing mix form a major aspect of marketing concept implementation, the emphasis and application of each of the elements of the mix will vary depending on the products and services offered: for example, BMW and Rolex are market-orientated companies that focus primarily on the Four-Ps, as they are product manufacturers, but Starbucks and Burger King focus primarily on the elements of the extended mix, as service, process and the physical evidence are at the heart of their fast-food restaurants. Marketing Implementation is the topic of Chapter 22.

Does Marketing have all the Answers?

In this chapter, we have considered how marketing as a discipline is adapting to a changing world. But academics have raised important questions regarding the value of the market concept as a guiding principle and marketing managers should guard against the following issues:

1 the marketing concept as an ideology
2 marketing and society
3 marketing as a constraint on innovation
4 marketing as a source of dullness
5 marketing as an intrusion.

The marketing concept as an ideology

Brownlie and Saren (1992) argue that the marketing concept has assumed many of the characteristics of an ideology or an article of faith that should dominate the thinking of organizations. They recognize the importance of a consumer orientation for companies but ask why, after 40 years of trying, the concept has not been fully implemented. They argue that there are other valid considerations that companies must take into account when making decisions (e.g. economies of scale), apart from giving customers exactly what they want. Marketers' attention should focus not only on propagation of the ideology but also on its integration with the demands of other core business functions in order to achieve a compromise between the satisfaction of consumers and the achievement of other company requirements.

Marketing and society

A second limitation of the marketing concept concerns its focus on individual market transactions. Since many individuals focus on personal benefits rather than the societal impact of their purchases, the adoption of the marketing concept will result in the production of goods and services that do not adequately correspond to societal welfare. Providing customer satisfaction is simply a means to achieve a company's profit objective and does not guarantee protection of the consumer's welfare. This view was supported by Wensley (1990), who regards consumerism as a challenge to the adequacy of the atomistic and individual view of market transactions. Bloom and Greyser (1981) presented an alternative view. They regard consumerism as the ultimate expression of the marketing concept, compelling marketers to consider consumer needs and wants that hitherto may have been overlooked: 'The resourceful manager will look for the positive opportunities created by consumerism rather than brood over its restraints.' But, in recent years, the role of society in marketing has become more important. Ward and Lewandowska (2008) studied marketing strategies to find out which work best for firms in Australasia, the Netherlands and China, and found societal marketing strategies to be among the most effective. They advocate that marketing managers should find ways to introduce societal marketing and match this with their trading environment and the preferences of their target markets.

Marketing as a constraint on innovation

Tauber (1974) presented a third criticism of marketing–that is, how marketing research discourages major innovation. The thrust of his argument was that relying on customers to guide the development of new products has severe limitations. This is because customers have difficulty articulating needs beyond the realm of their own experience. It is important to note that these criticisms are not actually directed at the marketing concept itself but towards its faulty implementation–an overdependence on customers as a source of new product ideas. The marketing concept does not suggest that companies must depend solely on the customer for new product ideas; rather, the concept implies that new product development should be based on sound interfacing between perceived customer needs and technological research. At Google, innovation is encouraged and innovations are tested and launched, for example, Froogle (product search engine, launched November 2004, side-lined and renamed 2007), Google Sidewiki (web annotation tool launched 2009, discontinued December 2011), Google Buzz (social networking launched in September 2010) and Google Glass (concept released 2012, suspended 2015). However, innovations only succeed if they satisfy the user and there is widespread uptake. Google is very well informed about which of its innovations are effective and which need to be discontinued.

Marketing as a source of dullness

A fourth criticism of marketing is that its focus on analysing customers and developing offerings that reflect their needs leads to dull marketing campaigns, me-too products, copycat promotion and marketplace stagnation. Instead, marketing should create demand rather than simply reflect it. On one hand, this approach can eventually lead to business failure as in the case of BlackBerry, where the products were surpassed by similar product offers from Apple and Android. But, on the other hand, 'dullness' can be a source of innovation. Charles Rolls and Tim Warrillow were at a tonic water tasting in the USA and noticed that many of these products contained preservatives and artificial sweeteners (Fever-Tree, 2018). So, they went on a journey to make a new product range that offered something different; Fever-Tree tonic was developed and very quickly became the leading brand of mixer drinks in the UK. Read more about Fever-Tree in Chapter 20 Case 40.

Marketing as an intrusion

A fifth and growing criticism of marketing has intensified as big data and digital information firms, like Facebook, Google and Instagram, gather and analyse data in such detail that they have great insight into what, when and where to send marketing messages to trigger purchases (Kotler, 2017). The capacity of marketing messages to interrupt our lives is not a new phenomenon, telephone marketing, cold calling from sales agents and direct mail are techniques that have been used to increase sales for several decades. But, as the world has become digital, the capacity and scope to send such messages has increased significantly. Google and Facebook use targeted messaging as a basis for their advertising revenue models for their platforms. This approach is highly efficient and effective; if you search for a product or service on Google, e.g. sunglasses, you are very likely to find that adverts from sunglasses brands relating to your generic search appear when you visit a different platform: Facebook, eBay, Twitter. In Europe, since May 2018, the use of data is controlled by General Data Protection Regulation (GDPR) with the intent of providing more personal data security. This legislation aims to control how organizations can use personal information. These issues are discussed further in Chapter 6.

These five emerging issues help prompt discussion about the value of the marketing concept, and together are useful for highlighting how aspects of the concept are evolving.

Review

1 **Identify the fundamental principles of marketing**
- The marketing concept sets out the core ideas that underpin the nature of marketing and provides central planks on which to build a market-orientated organization.
- Market orientation provides a guiding philosophy that enables an organization to concentrate its activities on its customers.
- Focusing on efficiency and effectiveness enables an organization to ensure that it is doing things *right* and doing the *right* things. Getting the balance correct between the two can mean the difference between success and failure.
- Customers are at the heart of marketing; consequently, understanding how to create customer value and satisfaction is very important.
- Marketing planning brings marketing into wider business strategy and developing marketing planning involves decisions at different levels: strategic, tactical and implementation.

2 **The marketing concept: an understanding of the nature of marketing, its key components and limitations**
- The marketing concept is the achievement of corporate goals through meeting and exceeding customer needs better than the competition does.
- It exists through exchanges where the objective for all parties in the exchange is to feel satisfied.
- Its key components are customer orientation, integrated effort and goal achievement (e.g. profits), and discovery and exploitation of latent markets.
- There are limitations of marketing to consider: pursuit of customer needs is only one objective companies should consider as this can lead to focusing on short-term personal satisfaction rather than longer-term societal welfare; ensuring new development leads toward innovation rather than dull marketing campaigns and me-too products; marketing can be intrusive and divisive.

3 **Adopting a market orientation**
- Focusing on customer needs identifes potential market opportunities, leading to the creation of products that create customer satisfaction.
- Production orientation focuses on production capabilities, which defines the business mission and the products that are manufactured. These are then sold aggressively to customers.

4 **The differences between market-driven and internally orientated businesses**
- Customer concern versus convenience
- Know customer choice criteria and match with marketing mix
- Segment by customer differences versus segment by product
- Marketing research versus anecdotes and received wisdom
- Welcome change versus cherish status quo
- Understand competition versus ignore competition
- Marketing spend is an investment versus marketing spend is a luxury
- Innovation rewarded and reluctance to punish failure, versus avoidance of mistakes rewarded and a failure to innovate is conspicuously punished
- Search for latent markets versus stick with the same
- Recognize the importance of being fast versus content to move slowly
- Strive for competitive advantage versus happy to be me-too
- Efficiency and effectiveness versus efficiency.

5 **The different roles of efficiency and effectiveness in achieving corporate success**
- Efficiency is concerned with inputs and outputs. Business processes are managed to a high standard so that cost per unit of output is low. Its role is to 'do things right', that is, use processes that result in low-cost production.
- Effectiveness is concerned with making the correct strategic choice regarding which products to make for which markets. Its role is to 'do the right things', that is, make the right products for attractive markets.

6 **How to create customer value and satisfaction**

- Customer value is created by maximizing perceived benefits (e.g. product or image benefits) and minimizing perceived sacrifice (e.g. monetary or time costs).
- Customer satisfaction once a product is bought is created by maximizing perceived performance compared with the customer's expectations. Customer satisfaction occurs when perceived performance matches or exceeds expectations.

7 **Marketing planning**

- Involves developing marketing planning from three viewpoints: strategic, tactical and implementation.
- Strategic marketing focuses on using a firm's resources to leverage competitive advantage.
- Tactical marketing focuses on the deployment of the marketing and service mix, but also seeks to contribute to developing longer-term customer relationships.
- The delivery of marketing is brought about through implementation. Implementation focuses on actions: *who* is responsible for various activities, *how* the strategy should be carried out, *where* things will happen and *when* action will take place.

8 **Limitations for the marketing concept**

Five limitations of marketing are discussed:

1) The marketing concept as an ideology: can lead to a narrow and mechanistic approach towards marketing.
2) Marketing and society: by pursuing individual rather than societal gains, the marketing concept can result in benefits for the individual (or firm) with little regard for the impact on the wider marketing environment and society at large.
3) Marketing as a constraint on innovation: over reliance on customers as a source of innovation can result in lacklustre innovations.
4) Marketing as a source of dullness: focus on analysing customers and developing offerings that reflect their needs leads to dull marketing campaigns, me-too products, copycat promotion and marketplace stagnation.
5) Marketing as an intrusion: in the digital age, the capacity to send frequent and high tailored messages has increased. As has the capacity of marketing messages to interrupt our lives.

9 **Identify relevant business and research examples, which illustrate the principles of marketing in a modern organization**

- This chapter has described marketing and demonstrated how the principles of marketing can be applied in the modern organization through the use of examples, marketing insights and case studies at the end of the chapter. For each of the key concepts, it is possible to identify illustrative examples.

Key Terms

commodity businesses those firms which sell goods and materials that are freely traded, e.g. agricultural products–rice, coffee, grain; raw materials, metals

competitive advantage the achievement of superior performance through differentiation to provide superior customer value or by managing to achieve lowest delivered cost

customer satisfaction the fulfilment of customers' requirements or needs

customer value perceived benefits minus perceived sacrifice

effectiveness doing the right thing, making the correct strategic choice

efficiency a way of managing business processes to a high standard, usually concerned with cost reduction; also called 'doing things right'

exchange the act or process of receiving something from someone by giving something in return

Four-Ps four key decision areas for marketing: product, price, promotion and place

latent markets markets not yet served by existing products and service offers. These markets present opportunities for market orientated companies

market orientation companies with a market orientation focus on customer needs as the primary drivers of organizational performance

marketing concept the achievement of corporate goals through meeting and exceeding customer needs better than the competition

marketing mix a framework for the tactical management of the customer relationship, including product, place, price, promotion (the Four-Ps); in the case of services, three other elements to be taken into account are process, people and physical evidence

non-commodity businesses those which are involved in facilitating processes and exchanges, but are not in themselves commodities. For example, when you buy electricity, a large proportion of the cost is attributed to the network of cables used to deliver the supply. In the UK, the National Grid owns the electricity transmission system

place the distribution channels to be used, outlet locations, methods of transportation

price (1) the amount of money paid for a product; (2) the agreed value placed on the exchange by buyer and seller

product a good or service offered or performed by an organization or individual, which is capable of satisfying customer needs

service mix an extended framework of tactical management processes specifically focusing on service delivery

touch points contact points where customers interact with a firm. Contact can occur in physical and digital situations

Study Questions

1. **What are the essential characteristics of a market-orientated company?**
2. **How has the adoption of marketing orientation evolved since the emergence of the internet?**
3. **Discuss how the desire to become efficient may conflict with being effective.**
4. **Suggest how the internet and digital technology is impacting on marketing as a guiding business philosophy.**
5. **Explain the role of marketing planning at three different levels: strategic, tactical and implementation.**

Recommended Reading

Marketing is a dynamic subject; find out more about what makes consumers satisfied in the digital economy, discover the importance of marketing as a strategy and learn about the practical application of market by reading the following:

Cheng, M. and Jin, X. (2019), What do Airbnb users care about? An analysis of online review comments, *International Journal of Hospitality Management*, 76 (A), 58–70.

Dewar, N. (2013), When marketing is strategy, *Harvard Business Review*, 91.

Dibb, S., Simoes, C. and Wensley, R. (2014), Establishing the scope of marketing practice: insights from practitioners, *European Journal of Marketing*, 48(1–2) 380–404.

References

Abell, D.F. (1978), Strategic Windows, *Journal of Marketing*, July, 21–26.

Added Value (2011), The Starbucks Debate, January http://added-value.com/the-starbucks-debate (accessed 14 February 2015).

Anderson, E.W., Fornell, C. and Lehmann, D.R. (1994), Customer Satisfaction, Market Share and Profitability: Findings From Sweden, *Journal of Marketing* 58 (July), 53–66.

Anderson, E.W., Fornell, C. and Rust, R.T. (1997), Customer Satisfaction, Productivity, and Profitability: Differences Between Goods and Services, *Marketing Science* 16 (Z), 129–45.

Anderson, E.W. and Sullivan, M.W. (1997), The Antecedents and Consequences of Customer Satisfaction for Firms, *Marketing Science* 12 (Spring), 125–43.

Anderson, E.W., Fornell, C. and Mazvancheryl, S.K. (2004), Customer Satisfaction and Shareholder Value, *Journal of Marketing* 68 (October), 172–85.

Balch, O. (2013). H&M: can fast fashion and sustainability ever really mix? *The Guardian*, 3 May http://www.theguardian.com/sustainable-business/h-and-m-fashion-sustainability-mix (accessed 30 January 2015).

Balodi, K.C. (2014) Strategic orientation and organizational forms: An integrative framework, *European Business Review*, 26 (2) (2014), pp. 188–203.

Barrett, B (2018), The Quiet, Steady Dominance of Pokémon Go, Wired, 7 July https://www.wired.com/story/pokemon-go-quiet-steady-dominance/, (accessed 7 July 2018).

Batra, R., Ahuvia, A. and Bagozzi, R.P. (2012), Brand Love, *Journal of Marketing* 76(2), 1–16.

Benady, A. (2005), Nestlé's New Flavour of Strategy, *Financial Times*, 22 February, 13.

Berr, J. (2014), Starbucks' growth plans impress Wall Street, *CBS Money Watch*, 5 December http://www.cbsnews.com/news/starbucks-ceos-growth-plans-impress-wall-street (accessed 14 January 2015).

Bloom, P.N. and Greyser, S.A. (1981), The Maturity of Consumerism, *Harvard Business Review*, Nov–Dec, 130–9.

Booms, B.H. and Bitner, M.J. (1981), Marketing Strategies and Organisation Structures for Service Firms, in Donnelly, J.H. and George, W.R. (eds.) *Marketing of Services*, Chicago: American Marketing Association, 47–51.

Bolton, R.N. and Drew, J.H. (1991), A Longitudinal Analysis of the Impact of Service Changes on Customer Attitudes, *Journal of Marketing* 55 (January), 1–9.

Booms, B.H. and Bitner, M.J. (1981), Marketing Strategies and Organisation Structures for Service Firms, in Donnelly, J.H. and George, W.R. (eds.) *Marketing of Services*, Chicago: American Marketing Association, 47–52.

Brown, R.J. (1987), Marketing: A Function and a Philosophy, *Quarterly Review of Marketing* 12(3), 25–30.

Brownlie, D. and Saren, M. (1992), The Four Ps of the Marketing Concept: Prescriptive, Polemical, Permanent and Problematical, *European Journal of Marketing* 26(4), 34–47.

BBC News (2014), Dixons Carphone unveils new stores, 7 August http://www.bbc.co.uk/news/uk-28689236 (accessed 30 January 2015).

Cadogan, J.W., Cui, C.C. and Li, E.K.Y. (2003), Export market oriented behavior and export performance: The moderating roles of competitive intensity and technological turbulence, *International Marketing Review*, 20 (5) (2003), pp. 493–513.

Cano, C.R., Carrillet, F.A. and Jaramillo, F. (2004), A Meta-Analysis of the Relationship between Market Orientation and Business Performance: Evidence from Five Continents, *International Journal of Research in Marketing* 21(2), 179–200.

Charles, J. (2007) Facebook Protest Forces Interest Rate Climbdown, Timesonline.co.uk, 31 August (retrieved from www.timesonline.co.uk/tol/money/student_finance/article2358640.ece (accessed 10 June 2018)).

Christodoulides, G. and Michaelidou, N. (2011), Shopping motives as antecedents of e-satisfaction and e-loyalty, *Journal of Marketing Management* 27(1–2), 181–97.

Clark, A. (2011), Starbucks joins Nike and Apple in the big league of no-name logos, *The Guardian*, 9 January. http://www.theguardian.com/business/2011/jan/09/starbucks-new-logo-no-name (accessed 14 February 2015).

Coelho, P.S. and Henseler, J. (2012), Creating customer loyalty through service customization, *European Journal of Marketing*, 46 (3/4), 331–56, https://doi.org/10.1108/03090561211202503.

Devaney, T. and Stein, T. (2014), Handling Haters: How To Respond To Negative Online Reviews, *Forbes*, 3 March http://www.forbes.com/sites/sage/2014/03/03/handling-haters-how-to-respond-to-negative-online-reviews (accessed 2 February 2015).

Dickinson, H. (2005), Forget Supersizing, Think Downsizing, *Marketing*, 7 December, 13.

Doherty, N.F. and Ellis Chadwick, F.E; Hart, C.A. (1999) Cyber retailing in the UK: the potential of the Internet as a retail channel, *International Journal of Retail & Distribution Management*, Vol. 27 Issue: 1, pp.22–36.

Downes, L. and Nunes, P. (2013), Big-Bang Disruption, *Harvard Business Review*, March Issue https://hbr.org/2013/03/big-bang-disruption (accessed 10 June 2018).

Drucker, P.F. (1999) *The Practice of Management*, London: Heinemann.

Euromonitor International (2011), Organics to continue to withstand downturn, http://www.just-food.com/analysis/organic-to-continueto-withstand-downturn_id117742.aspx, 20 December (accessed 10 June 2018).

Fever-tree (2018), About us, https://www.fever-tree.com/about-us#how-it-started (2008) (accessed 10 June 2018)

Fisher, J. (2013), The future of ethical retailing, *Retail Gazette*, 12 January http://www.retailgazette.co.uk/articles/04032-the-future-of-ethical-retailing (accessed 8 February 2015).

Ford, D., Håkansson, H. and Johanson. J. (1986), How Do Companies Interact? *Industrial Marketing and Purchasing* 1(1), 26–41.

Grönroos, C. (1989) Defining Marketing: A Market-Oriented Approach, *European Journal of Marketing* 23(1), 52–60.

Gupta, S. (2009) Customer-based valuation, *Journal of Interactive Marketing*, vol 23, issue 2, pp., 169–178.

H&M (2018), Sustainability, Look Good, Do Good, Feel Good http://about.hm.com/en/sustainability.html (accessed June 2018).

Hamel, G. and Prahalad, C.K. (1994), Competing for the future *Harvard Business Review*, 72 (4), 122–128.

Hilpern, K. (2011) Does your marketing serve? *The Marketer*, March, 28–31. TripAdvisor, http://www.tripadvisor.co.uk/pages/about_us.html (accessed January 2012).

Homberg, C., Koschate, N. and Hoyer, W.D. (2005), Do Satisfied Customers Really Pay More? A Study of the Relationship Between Customer Satisfaction and Willingness to Pay, *Journal of Marketing* 69 (April), 84–96.

Homburg, C., Vomberg, A. and Enke, M. (2015), *Journal of the Academy of Marketing Science* 43: 1 https://doi.org/10.1007/s11747-014-0416-3.

Hooley, G. and Lynch, J. (1985), Marketing Lessons from UK's High-Flying Companies, *Journal of Marketing Management* 1(1), 65–74.

Hooley, G., Lynch, J. and Shepherd, J. (1990), The Marketing Concept—Putting the Theory into Practice, *European Journal of Marketing* 24, 7–23.

Houston, F.S. (1986), The Marketing Concept: What It Is and What It Is Not, *Journal of Marketing* 50, 81–7.

Im, S. and Workman Jr., J.P. (2004), Market Orientation, Creativity, and New Product Performance in High Technology Firms, *Journal of Marketing* 68 (April), 114–132.

Jarvis, J. (2009), How the Google Model Could Help Detroit, *Business Week*, 9 February, 33–36.

Jaworski, B.J. and Kohli, A.K. (1993), Market Orientation: Antecedents and Consequences, *Journal of Marketing* 57(3), 53–70.

Jones, T.O. and Sasser Jr., W.E. (1995), Why Satisfied Customers Defect, *Harvard Business Review*, Nov–Dec, 88–99.

KFC (2018), Environmental sustainability At KFC Yum! Centre https://www.kfcyumcenter.com/arena-information/sustainability-efforts (accessed 10 June 2018).

Kirca, A. H., S. Jayachandran and W. O. Bearden (2005) Market Orientation: A Meta-Analytic Review and Assessment of its Antecedents and Impact on Performance, *Journal of Marketing* 69(2), 24–41.

Kohli, A.K and Jaworski, B.J. (1990), Market orientation: The construct, research propositions and managerial implications, *Journal of Marketing* 54(2), 1–18.

Kotler, P. (2017), *My Adventures in Marketing*, Idea Brite Press, USA.

Lawson, R. and Wooliscroft, B. (2004), Human Nature and the Marketing Concept, *Marketing Theory* 4(4), 311–26.

Leckart, S. (2012), The Hackathon is on: pitching programming the next killer App, Wired 18 (12) https://www.wired.com/2012/02/ff_hackathons/all/1/ (accessed 10 June 2018).

Leroux, M. (2014), Starbucks wakes up and smells... beer and wine, *The Times*, 6 December http://www.thetimes.co.uk/tto/business/industries/retailing/article4289417.ece (accessed 14 February 2015).

London, S. (2005), Rotten Cars, Not High Costs are Driving GM to Ruin, *Financial Times*, 23/24 April, 11.

Millington, A. (2015), L'Oreal's CMO on how it is evolving its marketing strategy through customer insight, *Marketing Week*, 23 April.

Mitchell, A. (2005), The Path to Success is Simple—Why Do So Few Stay the Course? *Marketing Week*, 19 May, 20–1.

Mittal, V. and Kamakura, W. (2001), Satisfaction, Repurchase Intent, and Repurchase Behaviour: Investigating the Moderating Effect of Customer Characteristics, *Journal of Marketing* 38 (February), 131–42.

Moore, B. (2014), How ethical are high street clothes? *The Guardian*, 17 June http://www.theguardian.com/sustainable-business/sustainable-fashion-blog/how-ethical-high-street-clothes (accessed 30 January 2015).

Morgan, A. (1996), Relationship Marketing, *Admap*, October, 29–33.

Morgan, O. (2006), Toyota's Spin to Pole Position is Just a Start, *Observer*, 2 April, 4.

Morgan, R.E. and Strong, C.A. (1998), Market Orientation and Dimensions of Strategic Orientation, *European Journal of Marketing* 32(11/12), 1051–73.

Morrison, M. (2016), Pokémon goes viral with no big marketing blitz, AdAge, 11 July http://adage.com/article/digital/pokemon-go-viral-marketing/304905/ (accessed 7 July 2018).

Narver, J.C. and Slater, S.F. (1990), The Effect of a Market Orientation on Business Profitability, *Journal of Marketing* 54 (October), 20–35.

Narver, J.C., Jacobson, RL. and Slater, S.F. (1999), Market Orientation and Business Performance: An Analysis of Panel Data, in R. Deshpande (ed.) *Developing a Market Orientation*, Thousand Oaks, CA: Sage Publications, 195–216.

Niantic Inc (2018), About Niantic https://www.nianticlabs.com/about/ (accessed 7 July 2018).

O'Flaherty, K. (2008), Keeping a Fresh Spin On Things, Marketing Week, 22–3.

Parkinson, S.T. (1991), World Class Marketing: From Lost Empires to the Image Man, *Journal of Marketing Management* 7(3), 299–311.

Pedersen, E.R.G., Gwozdz, W. and Hvass, K.K. (2018), Exploring the Relationship Between Business Model Innovation, Corporate Sustainability, and Organisational Values within the Fashion Industry, *Journal of Business Ethics* 149(2), 267–284.

Pelham, A.M. (2000), Market Orientation and Other Potential Influences on Performance in Small and Medium-Sized Manufacturing Firms, *Journal of Small Business Management* 38(1), 48–67.

Pelham, A.M. and Wilson, D.T. (1996), A Longitudinal Study of the Impact of Market Structure, Firm Structure, and Market Orientation Culture of Dimensions of Small Firm Performances, *Journal of the Academy of Marketing Science* 24(1), 27–43.

Pulendran, S., Speed, R. and Wilding, R.E. (2003), Marketing Planning, Market Orientation and Business Performance, *European Journal of Marketing* 37(3/4), 476–97.

Quinn, L., Dibb, S., Simkin, L., Canhoto, A. and Analogbei, M. (2016) Troubled Waters: the transformation of Marketing in a digital world. *European Journal of Marketing*, 50(12) 2103–2133.

Rafiq, M. and Ahmed, P.K. (1992), The Marketing Mix Reconsidered, *Proceedings of the Marketing Education Group Conference*, Salford, 439–451.

Reichheld, F. and Sasser Jr., E.W. (1990), Zero Defections: Quality Comes to Services, *Harvard Business Review* 68 (September/October), 105–111.

Roberson, J. (2010), Anger over Weight Watchers' endorsement of McDonald's, http://www.guardian.co.uk/business/2010/mar/03/weight-watchers-mcdonalds-obesity, 3 March (accessed 10 June 2018).

Robertson, N. (2008), Wannabe Celebs Provide the Silver on Screen, *The Guardian*, 18 April, 31.

Rosenberg, L.J. and Czepeil, J.A. (1983), A Marketing Approach to Customer Retention, *Journal of Consumer Marketing* 2, 45–51.

Roythorne, P. (2003), Under Surveillance, *Marketing Week*, 13 March, 31–2.

Ruddick, G. (2014), How Zara became the world's biggest fashion retailer, *The Telegraph*, 20 October http://www.telegraph.co.uk/finance/newsbysector/retailandconsumer/11172562/How-Inditex-became-the-worlds-biggest-fashion-retailer.html (accessed 31 January 2015).

Rust, R.T. and Zahorik, A.J. (1993), Customer Satisfaction, Customer Retention and Market Share, *Journal of Retailing* 69 (Summer), 193–215.

Ryle, S. (2003), Every Little Helps Leahy Tick, *Observer*, 13 April, 18.

Sheth, J.N. and Parvatiyar, A. (1995), The Evolution of Relationship, *International Business Review*, 4(4), 397–418.

Sklar, C. (2013), How to use social media to understand and engage your customers, *The Guardian*, 13 March http://www.theguardian.com/media-network/media-network-blog/2013/mar/13/social-media-customer-engagement (accessed 14 February 2015).

Slater, S.F. and Narver, J.C. (1994), Does Competitive Environment Moderate the Market Orientation Performance Relationship, *Journal of Marketing* 58, January, 46–55.

Smith, G. (2005), Four Wheels, *The Guardian G2*, 15 March, 26–7.

Spary, S. (2015), Starbucks to sell wine and beer in premium food push, campaign, 20 February http://www.campaignlive.co.uk/news/1334898/starbucks-sell-wine-beer-premium-food-push/?DCMP=ILC-SEARCH (accessed 10 June 2018).

Spector, M., Mattioli, D. and Stech, K. (2012) Kodak files for bankruptcy protection, *The Wall Street Journal*, 19 January http://online.wsj.com/article/SB10001424052970204555904577169920031456052.html (accessed 19 January 2012).

Srinivasan, S.S., Anderson, R. and Ponnavolu, K. (2002), Customer loyalty in e-commerce: An exploration of its antecedents and consequences, *Journal of Retailing* 78(1), 41–50.

Starbucks (2018), How Starbucks plans to make and impact by 2020 and beyond https://news.starbucks.com/news/starbucks-2016-global-social-impact-report (accessed June 2018).

Stothard, M. (2018), Zara owner Inditex logs 7% profit rise on rapid online growth, *Financial Times*, 14 March https://www.ft.com/content/f76c5804-2756-11e8-b27e-cc62a39d57a0 (accessed 10 June 2018).

Strauss, J., El-Ansary, A. and Frost, R. (2006), *E-marketing*, Upper Saddle River, NJ: Pearson Prentice Hall.

Sugathan, P., Rossmann, A. and Ranjan, K.R. (2018), Toward a conceptualization of perceived complaint handling quality in social media and traditional service channels, *European Journal of Marketing*, 52(5/6), 973–1006, https://doi.org/10.1108/EJM-04-2016-0228 (accessed June 2018).

Sun, W., Price, J.M. (2016), The impact of environmental uncertainty on increasing customer satisfaction through corporate social responsibility, *European Journal of Marketing*, 50(7/8), 1209–1238, https://doi.org/10.1108/EJM-02-2015-0077.

Superbrands (2015), British Airways http://d3iixjhp5u37hr.cloudfront.net/files/2014/02/British-Airways-for-website-aemm11.pdf (accessed 30 January 2015).

Tauber, E.M. (1974), How Marketing Research Discourages Major Innovation, *Business Horizons* 17, 22–6.

Teather, D. (2005), Kodak Cuts 10,000 More Jobs as its Film Business Weakens, *The Guardian*, 21 July, 20.

The Co-operative (2012), Ethical consumer Market Report 2012 http://www.co-operative.coop/PageFiles/416561607/Ethical-Consumer-Markets-Report-2012.pdf (accessed 30 January 2015).

The Guardian (2015), H&M searching for innovation in sustainable fashion retail, *The Guardian* http://www.theguardian.com/sustainable-business/hm-partner-zone/search-innovation-sustainable-fashion-retail (accessed 30 January 2015).

Tran, M. (2010), Hummer Brand to be wound down after sales fail, *The Guardian*, 24 February.

Trefis Team (2017), Starbucks is ending its Evening Beer and Wine program, Forbes 13 January https://www.forbes.com/sites/greatspeculations/2017/01/13/starbucks-is-ending-its-evenings-program/#58cdcde940c4 (accessed 10 June 2018).

Vaughan, A (2018), McDonald's to switch to paper straws in UK after customer campaign, *The Guardian*, 15 June https://www.theguardian.com/business/2018/jun/15/mcdonalds-to-switch-to-paper-straws-in-uk-after-customer-concern (accessed 10 June 2018).

Ward, S., Lewandowska, A. (2008), Is the marketing concept always necessary?: The effectiveness of customer, competitor and societal strategies in business environment types, *European Journal of Marketing*, 42(1/2), 222–237, https://doi.org/10.1108/03090560810840989 (accessed June 2018).

Wensley, R. (1990), The Voice of the Consumer? Speculations on the Limits to the Marketing Analogy, *European Journal of Marketing* 24(7), 49–60.

Which? (2011), Food and Drink: Brands Unwrapped, *Which*, February, 28–31.

White, D. (1999), Delighting in a Superior Service, *Financial Times*, 25 November, 17.

Wilson, M. (2018), The Starbucks logo has a secret you've never noticed. Fast company 17 January. https://www.fastcompany.com/90157014/the-starbucks-logo-has-a-secret-youve-never-noticed.

Winch, J. (2014), British Airways tops UK brand rankings, *The Telegraph*, 24 February http://www.telegraph.co.uk/finance/newsbysector/retailandconsumer/10656804/British-Airways-tops-UK-brand-rankings.html (accessed 30 January 2015).

Wood, Z. (2011), Starbucks gets a new face–and drops the mugs, *The Guardian*, 5 January http://www.theguardian.com/business/2011/jan/05/starbucks-rebranding-new-face-drops-mugs (accessed 14 February 2015).

Worth, D. (2016), 6 Reasons BlackBerry crumbled in the smartphone market., *The Insider*, 7 October.

Wright, J. (2006), *Blog Marketing*, New York: McGraw-Hill.

Wu, Chich-Wen (2011), Global marketing strategy modelling of high tech products, *Journal of Business Research*, 64(11), 1229–1233.

Young, S. (2018), H&M Launches conscious, *The Independent*, 28 April.

Zeithaml, V.A. (2000), Service Quality, Profitability, and the Economic Worth of Customers: What We Know and What We Need to Learn, *Journal of the Academy of Marketing Science* 28 (Winter), 67–8.

Zhang, M. (2014), Wal-Mart Leads Social Media Engagement for Black Friday, *Social Times*, 28 November http://www.adweek.com/socialtimes/wal-mart-leads-social-media-engagement-black-friday/208508 (accessed 8 February 2015).

CASE 1
Coca-Cola and Pepsi

Competition in a Changing Marketing Environment

For most companies, owning the number one brand name in the world (valued at over $67 billion by the Interbrand consultancy), having global brand recognition and earning $4.8 billion profits on sales of $21.9 billion a year in 2005 would spell success on a huge scale. But Coca-Cola is not 'most companies'. In the face of strong competition and a changing marketing environment, the fortunes of Coca-Cola turned for the worse during the early 2000s.

Once a Wall Street favourite, Coca-Cola created a global brand by the expert marketing of something as humble as brown carbonated water laced with caffeine and vegetable extracts. For decades the company outperformed its arch rival PepsiCo such that, in early 2000, Coca-Cola's market capitalization was $128 billion, almost three times that of PepsiCo, which was valued at $44 billion. By December 2005, all that had changed: PepsiCo had nudged ahead with a market capitalization of $98.4 billion against Coca-Cola's $97.9 billion. For the first time in the history of the two companies, PepsiCo was valued more highly than its old enemy. Suddenly, the 'real thing' was second best.

Coke's Problems

Many observers dated Coke's problems back to the death in 1997 of Roberto Goizueta, its charismatic and highly successful chief executive, who delivered double-digit annual profit growth. His success over PepsiCo led him to treat that company with contempt. He once said, 'As they become less relevant, I don't need to look at them anymore.' Shortly after his death, however, the company's shares lost a third of their value, and profit growth collapsed to the low single digits. His successors reigned during a time of bungled takeovers, disastrous product launches, contamination scares, and constant feuding between factions within the management and boardroom. A classic illustration of Coke's problems was the scandal involving the launch of Dasani, a bottled mineral water that turned out to be distilled tap water. When the harmful chemical bromate was found in a batch, the brand was withdrawn in the UK.

However, other people attributed the roots of Coke's failings to Goizueta's single-minded devotion to cola. His philosophy was that nothing could beat the low-cost, high profit-margin business of producing syrupy concentrate for bottlers, under licence, to transform into the world's favourite drink. While Coca-Cola focused on carbonated colas, PepsiCo diversified away from sugary fizzy drinks into a powerful portfolio of non-carbonated products. In 1998, it bought the fruit juice business Tropicana, which it has built to be the number one fruit juice brand in the USA. Three years later it bought Quaker Oats, thereby acquiring the energy drink Gatorade, which has also been built into a major brand. (Coca-Cola pulled out of the Quaker Oats bidding war believing its price to be too high.) PepsiCo also owns Aquafina, the leading bottled water brand in the USA. The fruit juice, energy drink and bottled water sectors all experienced double-digit growth in recent years. It continued its acquisition programme with the purchase of the South Beach Beverage Co, which manufactures the SoBe healthy drinking range, and has launched SoBe Lifewater, which it claims contains the full recommended daily amount of vitamin C together with vitamins E and B, and no preservatives or artificial flavourings.

Its bottling partner, Pepsi-Americas, also bought Ardea Beverages, which markets the Nutrisoda range containing amino acids, vitamins, CoQ10, herbs and minerals. In contrast to Coke, the culture at PepsiCo was reported to be more dynamic and customer focused and less bureaucratic.

Where Coke focused on soft drinks, Pepsi has interests in the snack food business (it bought the Frito-Lay snack food business in 1965), owning such brands as Doritos, Walkers Crisps, Quavers, Lay's Potato Crisps and Wotsits (see Table C1.1). The result is that PepsiCo generates about 23 per cent of its worldwide profits from the stagnant carbonated drinks sector, while Coca-Cola relies on fizzy drinks for 80 per cent of profits. Coca-Cola always seemed to be playing catch-up, having launched Minute Maid fruit juice to challenge Tropicana, Dasani to take on Aquafina, and Powerade, an energy drink, following the success of Red Bull and Gatorade in this sector.

PepsiCo's diversification programme and its brand-building expertise has made it the world's fourth largest food and beverage company, ranking behind Nestlé, Kraft and Unilever. Its sales were more than $67 billion compared with Coke's $47 billion in 2014; it owns 6 of the 15 top-selling food and drink brands in US supermarkets—more than any other company, including Coke, which has two. Coke, on the other hand, is market leader in carbonated drinks (43 per cent versus 32 per cent).

TABLE C1.1 Cola wars: who owns what

Coca-Cola brands	PepsiCo brands
Coca-Cola Classic	Pepsi
Diet Coke	Diet Pepsi
Coca-Cola Zero Sugar	Gatorade
Dr Pepper	Tropicana
Powerade	Aquafina
Minute Maid	Lipton Iced Tea
Dasani	Frappuccino
Fanta	Mountain Dew
Lilt	Walkers crisps
Sprite	Lay's potato crisps
Calypso	Quaker Oats
Oasis	Quavers
Just Juice	Doritos
Kia Ora	Cheetos
Five Alive	Wotsits
Malvern water	Sugar Puffs
Schweppes	7-Up

Life since Goizueta also saw Coke criticized for its fall in marketing investments, including advertising and marketing research, in an effort to maintain short-term profits, and the lack of iconic brand-building advertising. Its culture was also questioned and its high-rise headquarters building in central Atlanta was known in the industry as 'the Kremlin', because of the political intrigue and bureaucratic culture that pervaded its corridors.

A New Era?

In response to its problems, Coca-Cola brought an ex-employee, Neville Isdell, out of retirement to become chairman and chief executive in 2004. One of his first acts was to allocate an additional $400 million a year to marketing and innovation. This was in recognition of the under-investment in brands and product development. Emerging markets such as China and India were also targeted more aggressively. He also briefed advertising agencies around the world in an attempt to create new iconic campaigns to revive the core brand and reconnect with consumers. In the face of research that showed the proportion of Americans agreeing that cola is liked by everyone falling from 56 per cent in 2003 to 44 per cent in 2005, and those agreeing that the drink was 'too fattening' increasing from 48 per cent to 59 per cent, Coke increased investment in sugar-free brands such as Diet Coke and Sprite Zero. Sugar-free colas have also been launched, such as Coke Zero Sugar, which comes in black cans and bottles, and is targeted at calorie-conscious young males who have failed to connect with Diet Coke, believing that it lacks a masculine image. The brand is designed to compete with PepsiMax, which is also a diet cola targeted at men. Overall, marketing spend for the category doubled. Isdell also oversaw the acquisition of a number of small water and fruit juice companies in Europe. Isdell resisted the temptation to follow Pepsi with the acquisition of a snacks company. Instead, his strategy was to focus on building a portfolio of branded drinks. Following this strategy, Coca-Cola purchased the US firm Energy Brands, which owns Glacéau, a vitamin-enhanced water brand, and bought a stake of between 10 and 20 per cent of Innocent (increased to over 90 per cent in 2013), the market leader (68 per cent) of fruit smoothie drinks in the UK. Innocent has built a reputation for making only natural healthy products, and using only socially and environmentally aware products. At the time of the deal (2009), Innocent operated in the UK, Ireland, France, Scandinavia, Germany and Austria. Coca-Cola

»

also launched an energy drink, Relentless, aimed at 18- to 40-year-old men.

Meanwhile, PepsiCo has introduced its own labelling system in the USA to identify healthier products, using criteria set by an independent board of health experts. Now 40 per cent of sales derive from products with the green 'Smart Spot' given to healthier brands such as sugar-free colas and baked rather than fried crisps. Most of its research and development is focused on healthier products such as Tropicana-branded fruit bars, which provide the nutritional equivalent to fresh fruit. Sales of Smart Spot products are growing at twice the rate of those without the designation, and account for over half of Pepsi's product portfolio.

Continuing its focus on healthy drinks, PepsiCo launched PurVia which uses Stevia, a South American herb used to create natural sugar substitutes, as a zero-calorie sweetener. It was first used in flavours in PepsiCo's water brand SoBe Life. Coca-Cola followed this launch with its own equivalent, Truvia. PepsiCo has continued its move into healthier fare with yoghurt drinks, hummus and oatmeal bars.

Both companies have also attempted to arrest the decline in the carbonated soft drinks sector by launching a flurry of new products such as lime- and cherry-flavoured colas. Nevertheless, colas have come under attack for their contribution to obesity, with some schools banning the sale of all carbonated drinks on their premises. In the UK, the introduction of a sugar tax has caused Coca- Cola to reduce the sugar content of some of its brands, including Sprite, Fanta and Dr Pepper, although not that of Coca-Cola Classic.

Other ethical controversies have been encroaching upon Coca-Cola's global hold on the drinks market. Concern at American foreign policy and anti-American sentiment around the world has led to the launch of brands such as Mecca Cola to provide an alternative to US colas.

Under Isdell, Coca-Cola achieved steady international sales and profit growth. In 2008, he returned to retirement and was succeeded by Muhtar Kent, who has steadily built sales of Coke's brands globally. Falling sales of carbonated drinks in the USA have been offset by penetration in emerging overseas markets such as China, Brazil, Russia and India.

A new low calorie soft drink, Coca-Cola Life, was launched in 2014 to expand its range of low-calorie offerings. The brand was positioned as being based on natural ingredients (stevia extract) rather than artificial sweeteners. A new 'one name brand' advertising strategy was launched in 2015, which brought its four cola variants—Coca-Cola, Diet Coke, Coca-Cola Zero and Coca-Cola Life—together rather than advertised separately, so that consumers could clearly see the range of colas offered by Coca-Cola. 'Sugar' was added to the Coca-Cola Zero brand after research showed that half of consumers did not know that it contained no sugar. The range was reduced to three in 2017 when, in the face of declining sales, Coca-Cola Life was removed from the market.

Meanwhile, PepsiCo in 2018 launched the first ecommerce-only brand Drinkfinity, a healthy squash-like drink that comes in the form of plastic 'pods' that are added to water. Consumers are only able to buy the pods, together with a reusable bottle, on the Drinkfinity.com website.

In 2018, both companies continued their strategies of reducing their reliance on sugary fizzy drinks with Coca-Cola purchasing Costa Coffee and Pepsi buying SodaStream in multi-billion dollar deals.

Questions

1. **Compare Coca-Cola's response to the changing marketing environment before the arrival of Neville Isdell to that of PepsiCo.**
2. **Assess both companies in terms of their level of market orientation at that time.**
3. **How would you position Coca-Cola and PepsiCo on the efficiency–effectiveness matrix? Justify your answer.**
4. **What advantages, if any, does PepsiCo's greater diversification give the company over Coca-Cola?**
5. **Assess Coca-Cola's ownership of Innocent drinks from the point of view of both companies.**
6. **What future challenges is Coca-Cola likely to face?**

This case study was written by David Jobber, Emeritus Professor of Marketing, University of Bradford.

References

Based on: Devaney, P. (2006), As US Tastes Change, Coca-Cola's Supremacy Drip, Drip, Drips Away, *Marketing Week*, 6 April, 30–1; Teather, D. (2005), Bubble Bursts for the Real Thing as PepsiCo Ousts Coke from Top Spot, *The Guardian*, 27 December, 26; Ward, A. (2005), A Better Model? Diversified Pepsi Steals Some of Coke's Sparkle, *Financial Times*, 28 February, 21; Ward, A. (2005), Coke Gets Real: The World's Most Valuable Brand Wakes Up to a Waning Thirst for Cola, *Financial Times*, 22 September, 17; Sweeney, M. and Tryhorn, C. (2009), The Day Innocent Lost Its Innocence, *The Guardian*, 7 April, 3; Bokai, J. (2008), Soft Drinks Eye Herbal 'Sugar', *Marketing*, 6 August, 2;

Bokai, J. (2008), Soft Drinks Eye Premium Boost, *Marketing*, 19 March, 2; Rappeport, A. (2011), China the Real Thing for Business rather than US, *Financial Times*, 27 September, 17; Anonymous (2012), At Pepsi a Renewed Focus on Pepsi, *Bloomberg Businessweek*, 6 January–12 February, 25; Eleftheriou-Smith, L.M. (2011), Pepsi and Coke Fill War Chests, *Marketing*, 15 February, 7; Neate, R. (2013), Coca-Cola Takes Full Control of Innocent, www.theguardian.com/business, 22 February; Neate, R. (2014), Coca-Cola Enters Dairy Market with 'Milka-Cola', *The Guardian*, 26 November, 14; Smithers, R. (2014), Coca-Cola Life: Coke with Fewer Calories and Less Sugar to Tackle Obesity, www.theguardian.com/business, 11 June; Arnett, G. (2015), How Coca-Cola Is Fighting against a US Public Losing the Taste for It, www.theguardian.com/business, 13 February; Millington, A (2015), Coca-Cola Moves to 'One Brand' Strategy, Scrapping Individual Brand Campaigns, www.marketing week.com, 5 March; Rogers, C and Bacon, J. (2017), Coke Axes Coca-Cola Life Brand As Sales Tumble, www.marketing week.com, 6 April; Wood, Z. (2018), How Is Coca-Cola Preparing for Sugar Tax? Shrinking Bottles and Upping The Price, *The Guardian*, 6 January; Flaming, M. (2018), PepsiCo on The Launch of its First Ecommerce-only Brand Drinkfinity, www.marketing week.com; Reuters (2018), Pepsi's $3.2bn Soda Stream Deal Puts Fizz into Healthier Drinks, *The Guardian*, 21 August, 27; Wood, Z. and Sweney, M. (2018), Coca-Cola Snaps Up Costa in £4bn Deal to Cash in on Coffee, *The Guardian*, 1 September, 3

CASE 2
Fast Fashion at H&M

Stefan Persson, chairman of Swedish retailer Hennes & Mauritz (H&M), vividly remembers his company's first attempt at international expansion. It was 1976, the year H&M opened its London store in Oxford Circus. 'I stood outside trying to lure in customers by handing out Abba albums,' he recalls with a wry laugh. Persson, then 29, son of the company's founder, waited for the crowds. And waited. 'I still have most of those albums,' he says.

But Stefan is not crying over that unsold vinyl. In a slowing global economy, with lacklustre consumer spending and retailers across Europe struggling to make a profit, H&M's pre-tax profits were £1.8 billion in 2017 on sales of £20 billion. At current sales levels, the chain is the second largest apparel retailer in Europe after Zara. This is not just a store chain; it is a money-making machine. Table C2.1 compares H&M with Gap and Zara, its closest rivals.

Marketing at H&M

If you stop by its Fifth Avenue location in New York or check out the mothership at the corner of Regeringsgatan and Hamngatan in Stockholm, it's easy to see what's powering H&M's success. The prices are as low as the fashion is trendy, turning each location into a temple of 'cheap chic'. At the Manhattan flagship store, mirrored disco balls hang from the ceiling, and banks of televisions broadcast videos of the body-pierced, belly-baring pop princesses of the moment. On a cool afternoon in October, teenage girls in flared jeans and with two-tone hair mill around the ground floor, hoisting piles of velour hoodies, Indian-print blouses and patchwork denim skirts–each £16 (€18) or under. (The average price of an H&M item is just £10 (€12).) This is not Gap's brand of classic casuals or the more grown-up Euro-chic of Zara. It's exuberant, it's over the top and it's working. 'Everything is really nice–and cheap,' says Sabrina Farhi, 22, as she clutches a suede trenchcoat she has been eyeing for weeks.

The H&M approach also appeals to Erin Yuill, a 20-year-old part-time employee from New Jersey, USA, who explains, 'Things go out of style fast. Sometimes, I'll wear a dress or top a few times, and that's it. But I'm still in school and I don't have a lot of money. For me this is heaven.'

H&M is also shrewdly tailoring its strategy to the US market. In Europe, H&M is more like a department store–selling a range of merchandise from edgy street fashion to casual basics for the whole family. Its US stores are geared to younger, more fashion-conscious

TABLE C2.1 The clash of the clothing titans

Company	Style	Strategy	Global reach	Financials
H&M	Motto is 'fashion and quality at the best price'; translates into cutting-edge clothes.	Production outsourced to suppliers in Europe and Asia. Some lead times are just three weeks.	Has 4,300 stores in 69 countries. Largest sales are to Germany, the USA, the UK, France and China.	Pre-tax profits were £1.8 billion (€2 billion) in 2017 on sales of £20 billion (€23 billion).
Gap	Built its name on wardrobe basics such as denim, khakis and t-shirts.	Outsources all production. Slower than H&M and Zara for turnaround.	Operates 3,594 stores in 46 countries.	Pre-tax profits were £0.64 billion (€0.72 billion) in 2017 on sales of £12 billion (€13.7 billion).
Zara	Billed as 'Armani on a budget' for its Euro-style clothing for women and men.	Bulk of production is handled by company's own manufacturing facilities in Spain.	Runs 7,475 outlets in 96 countries.	Parent Inditex Group's pre-tax profits were £4.7 billion (€5.3 billion) on sales of £22 billion (€25 billion).

Source of data: company reports, about.hm.com

females. H&M's menswear line, a strong seller in Europe, hasn't proved popular with the less-fashion-conscious American male. So a number of US outlets have either cut back the selection or eliminated the line. And while the pricing is cheap, the branding isn't. H&M spends a hefty 4 per cent of revenues on marketing.

Behind this stylish image is a company so frugal that you can't imagine its executives tuning into a soft-rock station, let alone getting inside a teenager's head. Stefan Persson, whose late father founded the company, looks and talks more like a financier than a merchant prince–a penny-pinching financier, at that. 'H&M is run on a shoestring,' says Nathan Cockrell, a retail analyst at Credit Suisse First Boston in London. 'They buy as cheaply as possible and keep overheads low.' Fly business class? Only in emergencies. Taking cabs? Definitely frowned upon.

But that gimlet eye is just what a retailer needs to stay on its game–especially the kind of high-risk game H&M is playing. Not since IKEA set out to conquer the world one modular wall unit at a time has a Swedish retailer displayed such bold international ambition. H&M is pressing full-steam ahead on a programme that brought its total number of stores to 4,300 in 69 countries by the end of 2017–a 23 per cent increase in the past 3 years. In addition, its online store is open in 33 countries.

Yet H&M is pursuing a strategy that has undone a number of rivals. Benetton tried to become the world's fashion retailer but retreated after a disastrous experience in the USA in the 1980s. Gap, once the hottest chain in the USA, has lately been choking on its relatively slow reaction time to changing fashion trends and its failure to attract young shoppers, and has never taken off abroad. Body Shop and Sephora had similar misadventures.

Nevertheless, Persson and his crew are undaunted. 'When I joined in 1972, H&M was all about price,' he says. 'Then we added quality fashion to the equation, but everyone said you could never combine [them] successfully. But we were passionate that we could.' Persson is just as passionate that he can apply the H&M formula internationally.

What's that formula, exactly? Treat fashion as if it were a perishable product: keep it fresh and keep it moving. That means spotting the trends even before the trendoids do, turning the ideas into affordable clothes, and making the apparel fly off the racks. 'We hate inventory,' says H&M's head of buying, Karl Gunnar Fagerlin, whose job it is to make sure the merchandise doesn't pile up at the company's warehouses. Not an easy task, considering H&M stores sell over 600 million items per year.

Although H&M sells a range of clothing for women, men and children, its cheap-chic formula goes down particularly well with the 15-to-30 set. Lusting after that Dolce & Gabbana corduroy trench coat but unwilling to cough up £600 (€680)-plus? At £32 (€46), H&M's version is too good to pass up. It's more Lycra than luxe and won't last for ever. But if you're trying to keep *au courant*, one season is sufficient. 'At least half my wardrobe comes from H&M,' says Emma Mackie, a 19-year-old student from London. 'It's really good value for money.'

H&M's high-fashion, low-price concept distinguishes it from Gap, Inc., with its all-basics-at-all-price-points, and chains such as bebe and Club Monaco, whose fashions are of the moment but by no means inexpensive. It offers an alternative for consumers who may be bored with chinos and cargo pants, but are not able–or willing–to trade up for more fashion. H&M has seized on the fact that what's in today will not be in tomorrow. Shoppers at the flagship store agreed, particularly the younger ones that the retailer caters to.

In 2004, H&M commissioned Karl Lagerfeld, Chanel's designer, to create the limited-edition Lagerfeld range, which included a £70 (€80) sequinned jacket and cocktail dresses for under £55 (€62). The range, which was offered in the USA and 20 European countries, sold out within two hours in some stores. This was followed in 2005 by the Stella McCartney collection. McCartney, the British designer whose clothes normally retail for hundreds and sometimes thousands of pounds, designed 40 pieces for H&M, including camisoles, skinny jeans and tailored waistcoats. The average price was £40 (€45) per item, around 15 times cheaper than her own prices. The limited edition was a resounding success, with customers queuing from as early as 6.30 a.m. to get first pick of the clothes.

Since then, many other top names have lined up to work with H&M, including Kylie Minogue, Madonna and Beyoncé. In 2009, Matthew Williamson, who has designed dresses for Sienna Miller, Keira Knightley and

»

Penélope Cruz, reworked his most popular designs–kaftan dresses, beaded cardigans and print frocks–for the retailing giant. His designs sold out within hours of hitting the stores. In 2011 and 2012, H&M ran highly successful collaborations with the Versace and Marni fashion labels, in 2014 with Alexander Wang and in 2018 with Moschino.

H&M has invested heavily in social media to connect with its target audience. Fashion developments at H&M can be followed on Facebook, Twitter, Instagram, YouTube, Google + and Pinterest, as well as on mobile phone apps for iPhone and Android. Fourteen million fans follow H&M on Facebook, where they can find updates on new products and promotions. Its growing presence in global markets is supported in China by way of the Youku and Sina Weibo social network sites and in Russia through VKontakte.

The company has also made strides to improve its sustainability credentials. It has launched an ethical fashion brand called Conscious Collection as part of its drive to become a more sustainable and ethical fashion retailer. The range is made from 'green' materials such as organic cotton and recycled polyester. Its commitments include using more organic and sustainable cotton, educating farmers and developing the Sustainable Apparel Coalition, an initiative aimed at measuring the environmental impact of and labour practices for clothing and footwear manufacture.

Design at H&M

H&M's design process is as dynamic as its clothes. The 95-person design group is encouraged to draw inspiration not from fashion runways but from real life. 'We travel a lot,' says designer Ann-Sofie Johansson, whose trip to Marrakech inspired a host of creations worthy of the bazaars. 'You need to get out, look at people, new places. See colours. Smell smells.' When at home, Johansson admits to following people off the subway in Stockholm to ask where they picked up a particular top or unusual scarf. Call it stalking for style's sake.

The team includes designers from Sweden, the Netherlands, Britain, South Africa and the USA. The average age is 30. Johansson is part of the design group for 15- to 25-year-olds, and one style for the autumn they designed was Bohemian: long crinkled cotton skirts with matching blouses and sequinned sweaters for a bit of night-time glamour. Johansson and Emneryd were not pushing a whole look. They know H&M's customers ad-lib, pairing up one of its new off-the-shoulder chiffon tops with last year's khaki cargo pants for instance. The goal is to keep young shoppers coming into H&M's stores on a regular basis, even if they're spending less than £16 (€18) a pop. If they get hooked they'll stay loyal later on, when they become more affluent.

Not all designs are brand new: many are based on proven sellers such as washed denim and casual skirts, with a slight twist to freshen them up. The trick is striking the right balance between cutting-edge designs and commercially viable clothes.

To deliver 500 new designs to the stores for a typical season, designers may do twice as many finished sketches. H&M also has merchandise managers in each country, who talk with customers about the clothes and accessories on offer. When they travel, buyers and designers spend time with store managers to find out why certain items in each country have or haven't worked. In Stockholm, they stay close to the customers by working regularly in H&M's stores. Still, Johansson and her crew won't chase after every fad: 'There are some things I could never wear, no matter how trendy,' she says. Hot pants are high on that list. It's safe to say they won't be popping up at H&M anytime soon.

H&M's young designers find inspiration in everything from street trends to films to flea markets. Despite the similarity between haute couture and some of H&M's trendier pieces, copying the catwalk is not allowed, swears Margareta van den Bosch, who heads the H&M design team. 'Whether it's Donna Karan, Prada or H&M, we all work on the same time frames,' she says. 'But we can add garments during the season.'

Cutting Lead Times and Costs

Working hand in glove with suppliers, H&M's 21 local production offices have compressed lead times–the time it takes for a garment to travel from design table to store floor–to as little as three weeks. Only Zara has a faster turnaround. Zara's parent company, Inditex, owns its own production facilities in Galicia, Spain, allowing Zara to shrink lead times to a mere two weeks. Gap, Inc. operates on a much longer cycle.

H&M's speed maximizes its ability to churn out more hot items during any season, while minimizing its fashion faux pas. Every day, Fagerlin and his team tap into the company's database for itemized sales reports by country, store and type of merchandise. Stores are restocked daily. Items that do not sell are quickly marked down in price to make room for the next styles. Faster turnaround means higher sales, which helps H&M charge low prices and still log gross profit margins of 55 per cent.

All major fashion retailers aim for fast turnaround these days, but H&M is one of the few in the winners' circle. To keep costs down, the company outsources all manufacturing to a huge network of 900 garment shops located in 21 mostly low-wage countries, primarily

Bangladesh, China and Turkey. 'They are constantly shifting production to get the best deal,' says John Tisell, an analyst at Enskilda Securities in Stockholm.

Facing a New Reality

H&M is a hugely successful company, but in 2017 it was faced with a new reality: for the first time in two decades it experienced its first quarterly drop in sales. Central to the problem was that the company was being squeezed from all sides. Online-only retailers, such as Asos, Boohoo and Zalando, that offer free delivery and returns have grown partly at the expense of H&M. Zara has proven a tough competitor, taking over the number one position from H&M as the world's largest fashion retailer, and Primark has taken sales by offering cheaper clothes.

Questions

1. **To what extent is H&M market orientated? What evidence is there in the case to support your view?**
2. **Into which cell of the efficiency–effectiveness matrix does H&M fall? Justify your answer.**
3. **What is the basis of the customer value H&M provides for its customers?**
4. **What are the marketing benefits to H&M of commissioning Karl Lagerfeld, Stella McCartney and Matthew Williamson to design limited edition clothing ranges?**
5. **What challenges are likely to face H&M in the future?**
6. **Do you consider the marketing of disposable clothes contrary to societal welfare? Justify your opinion.**

This case study was written by David Jobber, Emeritus Professor of Marketing, University of Bradford.

References

Based on: Capell, K., Khermouch, G. and Sains,A. (2002), How H&M Got Hot, *Business Week*, 11 November, 37–42. Additional material from: Wilson, M. (2000), Disposable Chic at H&M, *Chain Store Age*, May, 64–66; Jones, A. and Rigby, E. (2005), A Good Fit? Designers and Mass Market Chains Try to Stitch Their Fortunes Together, *The Financial Times*, 25 October, 17; Fisher, A. (2009), Woman Who Gave Us the A-List Look, *Observer*, 22 March, 21; Venkatraman, A. (2008), Basic Instinct, *Marketing Week*, 21 August, 27; Anonymous (2011), Global Stretch, *The Economist*, 12 March, 77; Arthurs, D. (2012), Sold Out Again? H&M Strike Gold Once More with Marni Collection, *Daily Mail Online*, 12 July, www.dailymail.co.uk; Baker, R. (2011), H&M Launches Ethical Fashion Brand, www.marketingweek.com, 15 April; Neville, S. (2013),H&M Goes R&B: Beyoncé's Fashion Role, *The Guardian*, 22 March, 4; Anonymous (2018), Five Year Summary–About H&M, www.about.hm.com/en/About; Anonymous (2017), H&M, www.wikipedia.org/wiki/H&M; Milne, R. (2018), H&M faces up to a new reality, www.ft.com/content; Newbold, A. (2018), H&M teams up with GP & J Baker, www.vogue.co.uk/article.

CHAPTER 2
The Marketing Environment

> *When life gives you questions Google has the answers.*
>
> **A.J. CARPIO**

LEARNING OBJECTIVES

After reading this chapter, you should be able to:

1. describe the nature of the marketing environment
2. explain the distinction between the microenvironment and the macroenvironment
3. discuss the impact of technology, economic, political and legal factors, the physical environmental and social/cultural forces on marketing decisions
4. explain how to conduct environmental scanning
5. discuss how companies respond to environmental change

A market-orientated firm looks outwards to the environment in which it operates, adapting its practices and process to take advantage of emerging opportunities and to minimize potential threats. In this chapter, we examine the marketing environment by exploring major forces acting on companies, as shown in Figure 2.1. It has long been argued that the **marketing environment** consists of two dimensions made up of forces and actors that affect a company's capacity to operate effectively.

1 The forces shaping the first dimension—the **macroenvironment**—affect not only the company but also the actors, the people and the businesses that trade in the global business environment. These forces should be monitored, as they can affect the success of a company. But the company has limited opportunity to resist change brought on by the forces. For example, an increase in interest rates by the Bank of England will affect the economy and make the cost of borrowing higher. Companies with loans will incur higher bank charges but they have limited influence over the setting of the Bank of England base rate, which controls interest rates. Traditionally, marketers' attention has been drawn to four forces—political/legal, economic, social/cultural and technological (PEST)—when carrying out a macroenvironmental analysis. However, the growing importance of ecological/physical environmental forces on companies has led to the acronym being expanded to **PEEST analysis**. The macroenvironment shapes the character of the opportunities and threats facing a company, and these forces are largely outside the control of the company.

2 The actors shaping the second dimension—the **microenvironment**—are in the firm's immediate environment and influence how it operates in its chosen markets. The key actors are customers, competitors, distributors and suppliers, and strategic partners. The company has influence over this dimension, which can affect the nature of relationships between actors. Actors will influence the choice of target market, channel relationships, supply and distribution, and competitive marketing strategy.

Please note that the coverage of the actors in this chapter acts as a brief introduction. Actors are examined in greater detail later in the book: the influence of customers on marketing decisions in Chapters 3, 4 and 7, value through relationships in Chapter 10, the supply chain and distribution channels in Chapter 17, and marketing strategy, planning and competitive forces in Chapters 18 and 19.

The model of the marketing environment provides a framework, but, due to its changing and dynamic nature, decision-making is shrouded in uncertainty, with marketing managers sometimes unclear about what is happening and how to respond. This can delay exploitation of emerging needs and new markets, but it can also provide opportunities for the fleet of foot. For example, while large established brands may hesitate about new market opportunities, smaller *insurgent* brands take risks and respond to opportunities. For example, Justin's

FIGURE 2.1
The marketing environment

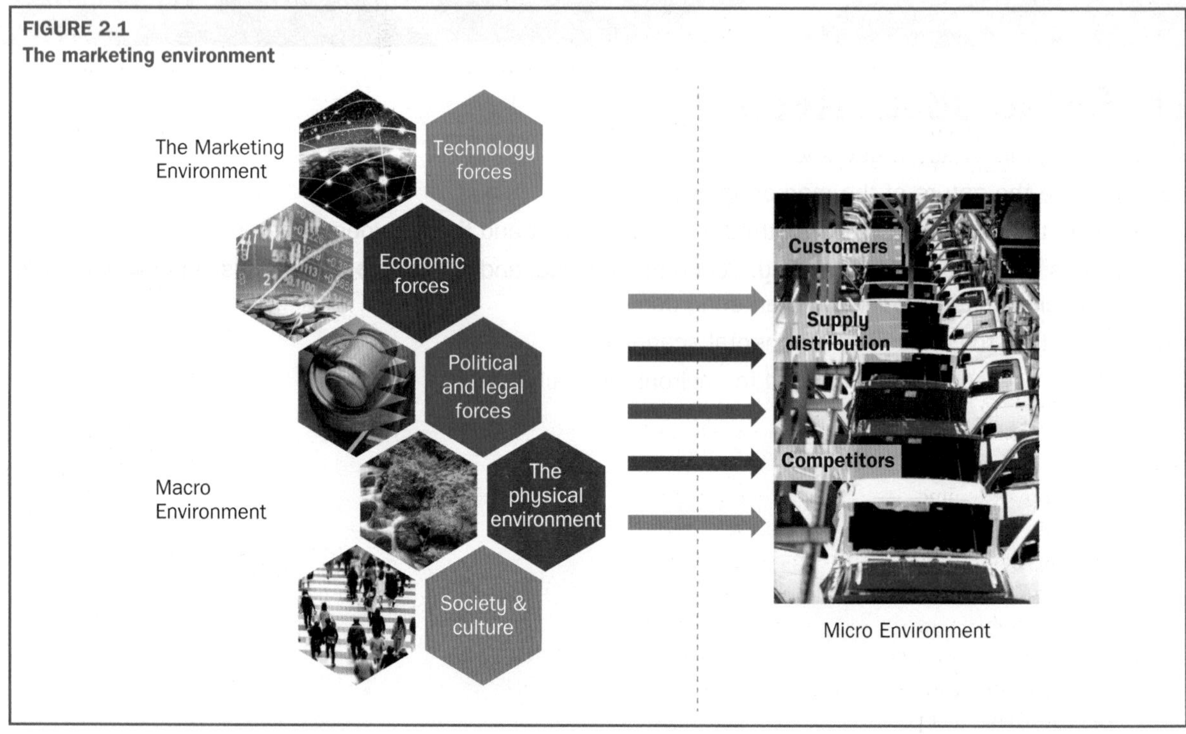

(organic peanut butter), E.L.F. (affordable beauty products) and Fever-Tree (quality tonic water and soft drinks) are companies that have grown rapidly by fulfilling unmet market demands. These smaller dynamic and flexible firms challenge established market leaders with high-quality alternatives (Bain Insights, 2018).

So, we have a framework of analysis—the market environment—which the chapter explores by looking at the elements of each dimension. Then we consider ways to map and monitor the influences and trends which have meaning for marketing, planning and strategy, since failure to respond to a changing environment can lead to poor business performance.

Technological Forces and the Digital Revolution

Each generation experiences technological change based around innovations which fundamentally change how we live. The difference with the current digital revolution is the rate of change and the speed of adoption of new products, services and ways of doing things. For example, the Internet of Things (IoT) is seamlessly linking digital devices, to facilitate the development of many new products and services. Facebook has developed into a global social networking platform since its launch in 2004, when Mark Zuckerberg and his colleagues at Harvard created a means of linking together university students. Over 25 per cent of the world's population now have an active Facebook account, three-quarters of whom use the platform at least weekly. This rapid uptake of the new digital technology is changing who people interact with. Nearly 70 per cent of the world's population own a mobile phone and so can communicate, trade and interact via the web and social media while on the move. The effects of digital technology on the marketing environment are both far-reaching and complex.

Technology can have a substantial impact on people's lives and companies' fortunes. Technological breakthroughs have given us artificial intelligence, robotics, body scanners, biotechnology, the internet, mobile phones, computers and many other products. Many technological breakthroughs have changed the rules of the competitive game: the launch of the computer and word-processing software destroyed the market for typewriters; robots are replacing humans in many manufacturing and information processes but have created markets for intelligent products. Babylon Health is a firm using artificial intelligence (AI) to provide medical expertise to people across the planet. Widespread adoption may lead to changes in the provision of medical services at local, national and global levels. Using the Babylon app, people can ask about a health condition, talk to a doctor and run a health check; see Exhibit 2.1.

Technological change can provide opportunities for new product development, create new markets, change marketing practices and communications, reshape cities and revolutionize society. Marketing-led companies seek not only to monitor technological trends but also to pioneer technological breakthroughs that can transform markets and shift competitive advantage in their favour. Innovations and technology applications are affecting every aspect of modern life, from the products and services we buy to the cities in which we live. Marketers should not only look for opportunities (and threats) surrounding their brands but also seek to use technology to improve the efficiency and effectiveness of their marketing operations. Marketers should seek to keep up to date with technological innovations, changes and trends in the following areas.

Research and development

Technology investments require sound understanding of the market. Marketing and research and development (R&D) staff should work closely together to ensure that investments are purposeful and not just for the sake of technology. A classic example of a high-technology initiative driven by technologists rather than by the market was the turbojet-powered supersonic aircraft Concorde. Although Concorde was technologically sophisticated, management knew before launch that it never stood a chance of being commercially viable. Development of the Airbus A380, the world's biggest passenger plane, has been

EXHIBIT 2.1
Babylon Health app provides instant access to healthcare information

market-based and driven by the need for greater passenger comfort on long-haul flights, pressure to reduce carbon emissions and increasing demand for these flights. But even this aircraft is struggling to be commercially viable, as there have not been enough orders (Goldstein, 2018).

R&D in new technology can pay handsome dividends and secure market share. 3M is a firm known for its R&D, and its successes include Post-it notes, fuel cells, electronic circuits, light management systems and RFID tags. R&D investment at 3M is carefully managed, with 25 per cent of the innovation budget being allocated to research and 85 per cent to product development, which has enabled the firm to continually invest in new products and manufacturing innovations (Team Trefis, 2016).

A lack of investment in high-potential technological areas can severely affect the fortunes of companies. For example, Sony—once regarded as a leader in high-tech product innovation—lost ground due to its lack of early investment in developing flat-screen TV liquid crystal displays, allowing Samsung to gain a competitive advantage in flat-screen TVs. Similarly, Nokia went through an era of complacency when it failed to monitor the competition effectively and respond accordingly; as a result, in 2013 the Finnish mobile phone company was bought out by Microsoft. Dell was a market innovator, changing the supply chain and cutting out the middleman so it could sell directly to its end customers, which created advantage over its competitors IBM and Hewllet Packard, but it then missed the shift towards mobile devices and become a market follower. However, investment in R&D in the areas of cloud computing and artificial intelligence is once again transforming Dell's fortunes (Bloomberg, 2018).

Information and data management

Technology also affects the way in which marketing is conducted. Developments in information technology have revolutionized marketing practices. Information technology describes the broad range of processes and products within the fields of computing and telecommunications. Accessibility of information has been found to be a source of competitive advantage, and data warehouses are an important new technology that offer organizations the potential to leverage such advantage from their information resources effectively. Data warehouses facilitate sharing of information and enable information to be accessible at the point of need. Indeed, research has found that accessibility of strategic information can facilitate commercial benefits (Doherty and Doig, 2011). Using better quality information, managers can make more informed decisions, save time and make a greater contribution to corporate and marketing success.

Information systems and data warehouses are used in many areas of business. Salesforce automation is improving the efficiency of salesforces; this is described and the implications examined in Chapter 15. Customer relationship management (CRM), founded on data technologies, has enabled companies to improve communications and relationships with customers; this is discussed further in Chapter 10. Multichannel retailing is underpinned by information and data technology and is discussed in Chapter 17.

Developments in data analytics and AI are enabling marketers to use intelligent personalization to predict consumer demand. Many firms are using predictive analytics to reposition their brands, improve customer satisfaction and drive loyalty. EasyJet is using data more extensively to create ongoing customer relationships. The easyJet Look&Book app is helping the airline gain more customer insights and even uses GPS to take a screen grab of the customer's location to connect them with local easyJet services (Fleming, 2018).

Communication

The internet and mobile phone technology have allowed companies to use new channels of communication and distribution (e.g. music downloads) to reach consumers. New technology speeds up communications and enables multiple interactions using various media. In the multichannel world, we communicate and gather information from multiple points: websites, apps, a multitude of TV channels, printed publications and, perhaps more importantly, each other. Digital technologies have completely altered modes of communication, but in so doing are eroding the boundaries between the message, the media, the channel and the product. The applications, issues and implications of digital communications technology are covered in detail in Chapters 13, 14, 15 and 16.

Society

Digital technologies are becoming increasingly important in most sectors of economic activity. The internet has provided the impetus for many companies to rethink the role of technology and has also had a significant effect on society. For its users, the internet has not only provided the means to find, buy and sell products, but has also created an environment for building communities where like-minded people can network, socialize and be entertained. The emergence of social networking sites such as Facebook, LinkedIn, Google and microblogging sites like Twitter have had a significant impact on global society. Social media have given a voice to masses of individuals, businesses and communities around the world, and their influence can be powerful. Social media have been used to communicate, organize protests and influence politics and governments. It has also been argued that 'Social media is reshaping human language through the unprecedented mixing of idioms, dialects, and alphabets' and this is bringing into question whether the technology will have long-term effects on the way we speak, write and listen (Schillinger, 2011). The importance of such developments for marketing is considered in detail in Chapter 16.

EXHIBIT 2.2
Songdo high tech smart apartment blocks

Smart cities

Smart cites are the cities of the future. The idea is to create an infrastructure around technology which makes use of integrated digital technologies and innovations to provide a seamlessly connected city experience. The current vision includes robots, driverless cars, cashless payment systems and items from street furniture, lamp posts, bike racks and traffic lights to home appliances and transport systems that utilise digital sensors incorporated into the fabric of a place or smart city to offer a technology-enhanced existence. The vision offers great potential for marketers and brands, and also threats, as existing services are automated and replaced by new high-tech solutions.

Some cities have made positive strides towards becoming smart. In Songdo, South Korea, pneumatic tubes take waste directly from homes, where it is then sorted, recycled and used in energy generation. A sophisticated water recycling system links to apartments which have heating and lighting that can be controlled by a mobile phone. This part of Seoul was designed to be an attractive place to live, away from the polluted, crowded streets of neighbouring districts (Poon, 2018); see Exhibit 2.2.

Economic Forces

The *economic environment* can have a critical impact on the success of companies, through its effect on supply and demand. Companies must choose those economic influences that are relevant to their business and monitor them.

Companies need to be aware of the economic forces that may affect their operations and be wary of assuming that the benign economic environment will last forever. Sudden changes in growth, interest and/or exchange rates can alter the economic climate quickly so that contingency plans are needed to cope with economy-induced downturns in demand. Firms also need to monitor the international economic environment, including the change to market-driven economies and the move into the EU by central and eastern European countries, and the opportunities and threats posed by the rise of China and India as major economic forces.

We will examine four major economic influences on the marketing environment of companies: economic growth and unemployment; interest and exchange rates; the European Union (EU), the Eurozone and Brexit; and the growth of emerging economies.

Economic growth and unemployment

The general state of national and international economies can have a profound effect on a company's prosperity. Economies tend to fluctuate according to the business cycle, although more-enlightened economic management has reduced the depth of the contraction in some countries. Most of the world's economies have gone through a period of significant growth since the mid 1990s, driven partly by productivity gains brought about by developments in computing and telecommunications technologies. This growth was followed by a period of economic slump which began in 2008 with a period referred to as the 'credit crunch'; this was followed by deepening recession and the Eurozone debt crisis (*Wall Street Journal*, 2012), which impacted on the worldwide economy. Since then the world economy has been steadily growing, especially in emerging markets, but the threat of volatility is ever-present (World Bank Group, 2018).

During periods of boom, well-managed companies experience an expansion in the demand for their products, while periods of slump may bring a decline in sales as consumers become wary of discretionary expenditures. A major marketing problem is predicting the next boom or slump. Investments made during periods of high growth can become massive cash drains when consumer spending falls suddenly. Retailers are often the first to be affected; Amazon, Carrefour, Tesco and Walmart are only too aware that they must plan to manage their national and international operations in anticipation of rising and falling consumer demand. Derived demand also affects manufacturers because, as consumer demand falls, manufacturers are affected too.

Within an economy, different sectors experience varying growth rates, leading to changing degrees of market attractiveness. For firms selling commodities, there has been low-level growth since 2015. The services sector has experienced the fastest growth and become the dominant force in most western economies. For example, in the EU, services account for over 60 per cent of gross domestic product (GDP)in some member states. GDP is a measure of the total value of goods and services produced within an economy (Eurostat, 2018).

Low growth rates tend to reflect high unemployment levels, which, in turn, affect consumer spending power. The 2008–13 recession caused unemployment rates to rise and consumer spending to fall in many European economies, for example in Greece, Portugal and Ireland. The EU set national targets for employment in 2010 as part of its long-term strategy. In emerging economies such as Brazil, China and India, economic growth is positive and employment and spending are on the increase. The UK's withdrawal from the EU will affect immigration and migrant workforces. This may have a positive effect in so far as lack of easy access to a supply of skilled immigrant workers can motivate UK workers to upskill, but there may also be shortfalls in supply of seasonal workers and workers in low-paid jobs (Tetlow and Stojanovic, 2018).

Interest and exchange rates

A key monetary tool that governments use to manage the economy is interest rates. Interest rates represent the price that borrowers have to pay lenders for the use of their money over a specified period of time. Most western economies lowered interest rates during the credit crunch to encourage borrowing and lending in an effort to avert a major slump in consumer and business demand.

An exchange rate is the price of one currency in terms of another (e.g. an exchange rate of £1 = €1.20 means that £1 buys €1.20). Fluctuations in exchange rates mean that the price a consumer in one country pays for a product and/or the money that a supplier in an overseas country receives for selling that product can change. For example, if the exchange rate between the pound sterling and the euro changes, such that a pound buys fewer euros, a German car manufacturer that receives payment in euros will receive fewer euros if the price of the car remains unchanged in the UK. In an attempt to maintain a constant euro price, the German car manufacturer may raise the UK pound sterling price to UK distributors and consumers. The following example illustrates these points.

At £1 = €1, a German car manufacturer would receive €10,000 for a £10,000 car. If the exchange rate changed to £1 = €0.5, the German car manufacturer's receipts would fall to €5,000. To maintain euro receipts at €10,000 the UK price would have to rise to £20,000.

The exchange rates between most European countries are now fixed, which avoids such problems. However, the rates at which major currencies such as the US dollar, the euro, the pound sterling and the yen are traded are still variable. As seen in the example above, this can have significant implications for sales revenues and hence the profitability of a firm's international operations. For example, during the credit crunch, the pound fell against the dollar. This meant that UK goods and services exported to Eurozone countries could be sold more cheaply or, if sold at the same price, would realize higher sterling profit margins.

The EU, the Eurozone and Brexit

The EU is a massive—largely deregulated—market, and it has far-reaching implications for marketing, as the barriers to the free flow of goods, services, capital and people among the member states are removed. A key objective of the EU is to lower the costs of operating throughout Europe and to create an enormous free market in which companies can flourish. As we have already seen, competition is encouraged through the enactment and enforcement of laws designed to remove restrictive practices and other anti-competitive activities.

TABLE 2.1 EU member states

Membership year	Member states	Total population (in millions)
Founding members	France, Netherlands, Belgium, Luxembourg, Germany, Italy	235
1970–1980	UK, Ireland, Denmark	72
1981–1990	Spain, Portugal, Greece	69
1991–2000	Austria, Sweden, Finland	23
2001–present	Poland, Estonia, Latvia, Lithuania, Czech Republic, Slovakia, Hungary, Slovenia, Romania, Bulgaria, Cyprus, Malta, Croatia	107
Candidate countries	Iceland, the former Yugoslav Republic of Macedonia, Turkey, Montenegro, Serbia	80
		586

Statistics source: http://europa.eu/about-eu/countries/member-countries

The EU currently consists of 28 member states, and it is continually expanding. Table 2.1 shows the spread of the member states, when they joined, candidate countries that are likely to become members in the future, and one country that is leaving the EU: the UK.

As the EU has expanded, new member states have contributed to the development of the community and economic growth of the union. Expansion to include eastern European countries has brought a low-cost, technically skilled workforce that has proved to be competitive with those in China and India. The strengths of the economies of member states have been boosted by EU membership and have led to considerable inward investment—for example, the Korean firm LG Electronic, which is one of the world's largest producer of TVs, committed to invest US$110 million to build a plant in Poland to produce plasma LCD TVs and car batteries for electric cars (Gottig, 2017).

The Eurozone is an economic and monetary union between 19 of the member states of the EU. Each state has adopted the euro (€) as a common currency, which is managed and controlled by the European Central Bank (ECB). A primary responsibility of the ECB is to control inflation and manage debt and economic reforms. A common currency brings advantages through facilitating the flow of free trade within the community. However, turbulence in economic markets has exposed weaknesses in areas of the Eurozone, which potentially have far-reaching implications for economies around the world.

Brexit, which refers to the vote by citizens of the UK in the referendum on 23 March 2016 to leave the EU, has caused further disruption. (The politics of this decision are discussed in the next section.) The actual economic impact on the UK and the 27 remaining member states is unclear, as the UK government has not yet negotiated the terms of the country's withdrawal. But assuming the UK's move to leave the EU continues and there is not a reversal of the decision caused by a second referendum, according to Tetlow and Stojanovic (2018) areas that will change are:

- **Trade**, which relies on overseas buyers exchanging goods and services. Prices are affected by transport costs, tariffs (imposed on import/export goods) and non-trade barriers—for example product standards, which vary from country to country. The benefit of countries being part of the EU is that, over time, agreements have been reached for all EU members.
- **Foreign direct investments** (FDI), which are important for long-term economic growth. The UK is one of the biggest beneficiaries of FDI, as over 42 per cent of FDI comes from other EU countries. Leaving the EU may mean the UK is less attractive for this form of investment, because, as a member, the UK benefits from free movement of capital, relatively frictionless trade between member states, and common regulations for the movement of goods across established complex supply chains within Europe.
- **Regulations** that determine how domestic firms can use the workforce, capital and technology resources. The argument for the UK leaving the EU is that the government may be able to adapt regulations to foster more suitable conditions. But competition and state aid regulations are already designed to promote fairness and equality among firms in Europe, and this may result in changing quality standards in relation to products, the environment and the workforce.

- **Currency valuations**. The value of sterling—which is not part of the Eurozone—floats against the Euro and other international currencies. So far, the general trend has been a lowering of the value of sterling due to uncertainty surrounding predictions of the terms under which the UK will leave the EU and negative views of the UK's economic strength. A weaker pound puts pressure on the price of imported goods, and consumers are experiencing higher prices on the high street for some goods. On a positive note, exports from the UK are cheaper, which makes it easier to sell goods overseas.

Growing and emerging economies

Dobbs et al. (2013) highlighted the growing importance of emerging regions of the global economy which are opening markets to new consumers, providing sources of skilled labour and creating opportunities for new companies to become significant global players. It is predicted that, by 2025, seven out of 10 new large companies will be based in these regions. But while there are significant opportunities in these regions, there is also increased risk—as you will discover when reading about the following emerging economies. Also see Exhibit 2.3 to see the shift of economic activity towards southeast Asia.

China and India

The economies of both China and India are growing at high and consistent rates. Moreover, both nations possess considerable strengths in low-cost labour, but increasingly also in technical and managerial skills. China possesses strengths in mass manufacturing and is currently building massive electronics and heavy industrial factories. India, on the other hand, is an emerging power in the software, design, services and precision industries. These complementary skills are persuading multinational firms to have their products built in China with software and circuitry designed in India.

China and India not only pose threats to western companies, they also provide opportunities for international firms. Chinese consumers are spending their growing incomes on all manner of consumer durables, from cars to shampoo. The Chinese buy more cars than the Americans (13.5 million compared with 11.6 million), and western

By far the most rapid shift in the world's economic center of gravity happened in 2000–10, reversing previous decades of development

Evolution of the Earth's economic center of gravity[1]
AD 1 to 2025

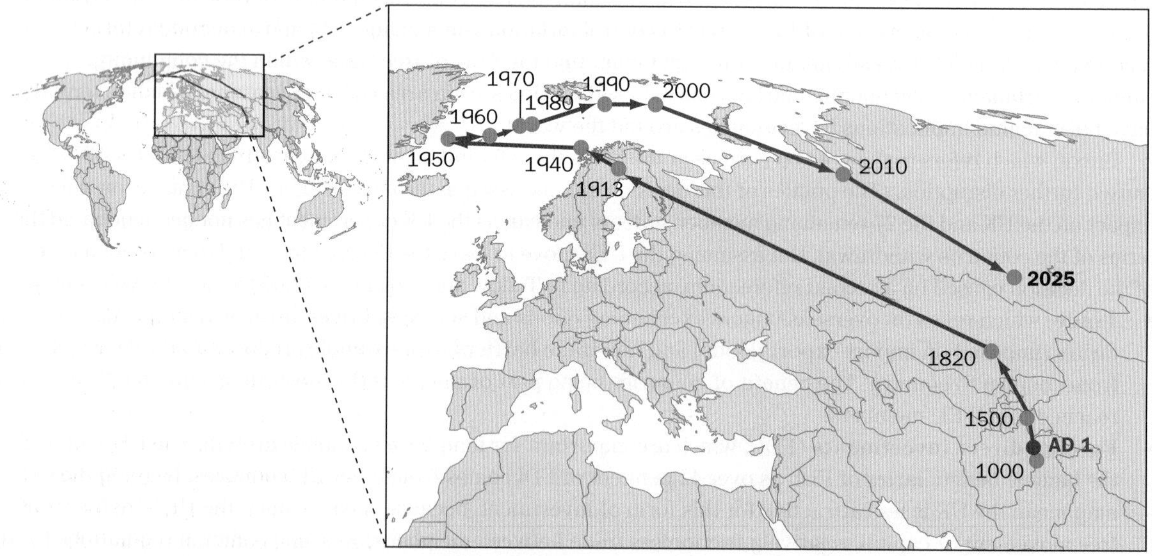

[1]Economic center of gravity is calculated by weighting locations by GDP in three dimensions and projected to the nearest point on the Earth's surface. The surface projection of the center of gravity shifts north over the course of the century, reflecting the fact that in three-dimensional space America and Asia are not only 'next' to each other, but also 'across' from each other.

SOURCE: McKinsey Global Institute analysis using data from Angus Maddison; University of Groningen

EXHIBIT 2.3
The McKinsey world economic centre of gravity

brands are becoming increasingly popular—from Burberry to Tesco, Bosch, Nestlé and Procter & Gamble—as well as healthcare and entertainment brands (Hancock, 2018).

However, companies wishing to expand in these booming markets must do adequate research, as it is important to get things right. M&S made a mistake on opening its stores in China, as it filled its rails with clothes of the wrong sizes. Chinese women are smaller and slimmer than European women and have smaller feet. In fact, many Chinese students studying in the UK buy their shoes in children's shoe shops (Muller, 2011).

In India, the economy is growing at a faster rate than China, with manufacturing and construction industries making a significant contribution (Lyengar, 2018). Consumer markets are also growing rapidly. Nestlé operates factories making many dairy products and chocolates. Hindustan Unilever is another European firm taking opportunities in India to create competitive advantage. In India, preferences for soap and shampoo vary much less than people's taste in food, so Unilever is doing even better than Nestlé, with an 18 per cent increase in profits.

China's and India's economies are not just booming in the physical world but are also rapidly expanding online and in mobile markets. Read Marketing in Action 2.1 and find out more about online shopping and social networks in China.

India's mobile phone industry is second to that of China. India produces over 11 million phones, and there are over 600 million active mobile phone subscribers—which is about one phone per two people in the population; the country also has the lowest prices anywhere in the world. Bharti Airtel was the main mobile network operator in India, and it brings phone access to everyone regardless of where they live. However, Vodafone has developed its mobile provision in India and since 2011 has been growing its market share. In 2017, the British mobile phone operator merged with Ideal Cellular to form India's largest telecoms operator. It can be challenging for international competitors trying to operate in or enter the mobile market; there are profits to be made, even though massive investment is required to improve network operations and services. Vodafone invested £1 billion into the Indian merger (Thoppil, 2018).

There are also major cultural and logistic barriers to overcome, although these apply to both online and offline markets. The retail industry in both China and India is underdeveloped. There are potentially big opportunities for western retailers (especially supermarkets) to enter Asian markets. However, in the Indian subcontinent, 'there are 20 officially recognized languages, 14 main types of cuisines and countless religious and ethnic festivals as well as a passion for cricket' (*The Economist*, 2011a), which presents exhaustive challenges when developing a national retail operation. Western companies need to understand the importance of culture in both India and China if they are to succeed. In China, *guanxi* networks are important. *Guanxi* is a set of personal relationships/connections on which a person can draw to obtain resources or an advantage when doing business. *Guanxi* is one reason why working with a Chinese partner is usually better than going it alone. When entering into business relationships, the Chinese seek stability and trust more than intimacy. They want to feel comfortable that western companies will not spring surprises that may hurt them, but they do not need to feel that they are the company's best friend. It is claimed that the failure of Rupert Murdoch's News Corp to penetrate China was largely because the company did not spend enough time and effort on building *guanxi*. See more discussion in the case study on selling in China in Chapter 15.

Russia and Brazil

Russia and Brazil are emerging economies with market development potential but also instability and uncertainty. Russia's economy has changed dramatically since the collapse of the communist state, and its centrally planned economy has moved into a globally integrated economy (The World Factbook, 2018). However, despite Russia becoming the world's largest exporter of natural gas, the second-largest of oil and third-largest of steel, the Russian economy was hit hard by the recession in 2009 caused by its reliance on such commodities. In an attempt to reduce this reliance, Russia has been investing in building up its high-tech industries, but with limited success. Fluctuations in oil prices have historically helped economic recovery and put Russia back on a growth trajectory, but oil prices have also been the cause of another downturn in 2016. Russia faces long-term challenges in the form of a shrinking workforce, a high level of corruption, difficulty in accessing capital for smaller non-energy companies, and poor infrastructure, but the government is investing in non-extraction industries as a means of diversifying the economy. Retail markets are also recovering, showing growth rates of around 13 per cent, particularly in the grocery sector, but this upturn is considerably slower than in the pre-recessionary period. Agriculture is also on the rise, as is international trade in southeast Asia (Bogod and Sukharevsky, 2017).

MARKETING IN ACTION 2.1

China: The Greatest Connected Market in the World?

Less than 10 years ago, fewer than 3 per cent of the Chinese population were online (about 33.7 million people). However, China has seen an internet boom, and the online economy is approaching $400 billion, which is more than the online spending of the USA and UK combined. It is predicted that by 2020 online retail sales will account for 24 per cent of retail spending. Around 80 per cent of adults in China's largest cities regularly shop online, and it is predicted that individual consumer spending is increasing to around the equivalent of $1,000 a year. The boom is being driven by the Chinese government, which is heavily subsidizing the roll-out of high-speed internet access, and, surprisingly, by the inefficiency of existing bricks-and-mortar retailers. Many shoppers go online because they cannot find the goods in the stores.

Alibaba is an online firm driving the growth of the online revolution. According to its founder, Jack Ma, 'In other countries, e-commerce is a way to shop, in China it is a lifestyle,' and Alibaba has become the largest e-commerce company in the world, generating most of its profits from advertising revenues.

As well as shopping, the Chinese have taken to socializing and sharing information online; shoppers are fearful of being tricked by fraudsters, so they like to share their experiences. According to research, over 40 per cent of online shoppers read and post product reviews. Social networking, like e-commerce, started slowly, but there are now three large social networks in China: QQ, Weibo and RenRen. Weibo is the Chinese equivalent of Twitter, and its top stars have more fans than their celebrity counterparts on Twitter. Also, there are over 200 million people with a social network account. Facebook, Twitter and YouTube are banned in China, which has created an opportunity for these homegrown networks to emerge. Furthermore, Chinese society is being changed extensively by the internet. Traditionally, families were reluctant to socialize with those outside their known circle of close friends and family, tending to be shy and reserved. However, now families use social networks to organize holidays and find families with similar interests from distant towns, arranging to meet, share car journeys and lots more.

Based on: Chaffey and Ellis-Chadwick (2012); The Economist (2017); Muller (2011); Stanley and Ritacca (2014)

Russia is interesting for having one of the lowest income tax rates in the world: a flat rate of 13 per cent. Also, all Russians own their own homes, having been given their own flat or house free as the Soviet era ended (most of these, however, are in a poor state of repair). Wealth tends to be centred around Moscow, where there are cash-rich consumers who enjoy spending on luxury goods.

Brazil's economy is slowly recovering from a recession in 2016, but corruption, international sanctions and political instability have hampered business growth and opportunities (The World Factbook, 2018). Brazil used to be a destination for foreign investors, but even though it is ranked eighth in the world in terms of its GDP purchasing power parity (a measure used by economists to compare the living conditions and resources of different countries), many investors are turning their backs on the country and confidence in the economy is at a low (Rapoza, 2018). Brazil's industry is linked to agribusiness and other primary products. Its main output comes from sugar, steel, oil and iron. It also has an important technological sector that ranges from submarines to aircraft, and it is involved in space research. Its economy has benefited from high levels of foreign investment by such companies as Procter & Gamble, IBM, Ford, DuPont, Peugeot Citroën, Anheuser-Busch InBev and PepsiCo. Among its largest companies are Petrobas (energy) and Vale (material), ITau Unibanco Holding (finance) and BRF—Brazil Foods (consumables). The country is also a major producer of ethanol, a sugar-based biofuel. Growth in the economy has led to rising demand for cars, mobile phones, computers and TVs among the large population of 190 million (*The Economist*, 2012).

Anti-branding and developing economies

Critics of branding say that it concentrates power and wealth in the hands of companies and economies that are already rich and powerful, whereas poor countries must compete on price. A vociferous critic of branding is Naomi Klein (Klein, 2000), who claims that branding concentrates power in the hands of the already rich and powerful, who exploit the labour force of developing countries by supporting the paying of low wages while charging high prices for their products (Klein, 2000).

Supporters of branding claim that it is not branding's fault that poor countries suffer from low wages, and that by sourcing from those countries their economies benefit. They also point out that the companies accused of being the worst offenders, such as Nike and Gap, have taken steps to introduce ethical sourcing policies that apply when dealing with the developing world.

Arguably, such anti-brand feelings are on the increase. Powerful brands are being deconstructed by vociferous online consumers who are voicing their opinions about brands and brand meaning via social networks, blogs and other online forums. The internet is liberating consumers by giving them power through debate and discourse.

Consumers are making more and more use of the internet, and instead of being passive consumers they are becoming increasingly active participants. Anti-branding websites appear high up in search listings, and such sites are surviving. Expert brand-haters (rather than just moaners and complainers) are being viewed as serious sources of information for the discerning customer who likes to review and evaluate many sources of information before making a purchase decision. Websites, blogs and social media are proving to be ideal platforms for such communications.

Research has also found an increasingly significant relationship between 'consumer-generated anti-branding activities' and 'brand value'. Furthermore, there has been a rise in the amount of anti-brand online content. Consequently, 'Consumers have total control of branding messages most of the time in such anti-branding spaces. Online anti-branding spaces, where the anti-branders deliver their messages in ways that conform to the consumers' points of view, gain more sympathy and credibility with most consumers' (Kucuk, 2008). From the brand perspective, there is value in understanding consumer/buyer concerns and issues and seeking to identify ways to address the criticism from the increasingly powerful consumer (Kucuk, 2008).

Political and Legal Forces

Political forces are complex to analyse, and the impact difficult to determine. Political issues that have implications for marketing are as diverse as threats to national security, climate change, gender equality and personal privacy. Read Mini Case 2.1 to find out how GDPR affects you.

Terrorism and unrest in the North African countries of Libya, Egypt and Tunisia has affected various industries. For example, the oil industry raised the price of a barrel of oil on the wholesale markets due to fear of loss of supply, and in the travel and tourism industry there was reducing demand for holidays in and travel to these regions. Thomas Cook is a company that has attributed some of its losses to these events.

Global warming and the politics of climate change are a source of regular action and debate. Scientists, environmental agencies, charities and activists support strong interventions to abate the effects of the changing environment. But not all world leaders and politicians hold the same views. President Trump withdrew the USA from the Paris Climate Treaty, in part due to his belief that other nations were not making equivalent financial contributions. Also, reportedly the USA is a major user of carbon-based materials, and the present administration has not been making policies which will enable it to meet its carbon-reduction commitments (Nuccitelli, 2017). For businesses, climate policies can mean adapting the manufacturing process and can require significant investment and adjustment to how products are made. But there are also opportunities to develop products which are sustainable: Allbirds is a US footwear brand that uses sugar cane and eucalyptus trees in the making of its trainers; Neste is a Finnish company producing diesel from 100 per cent renewable raw materials, which can cut carbon emissions by up to 90 per cent compared with fossil fuels. Read Marketing in Action 2.2 to find out more about the politicizing of the environment.

Equal participation is central to political decision-making in Europe, so, whatever a person's gender, they should be able to fully engage in daily life on an equal footing. But ensuring this is the case can mean making changes to overturn engrained attitudes and stereotyping. UK retailer John Lewis Partnership launched a range of gender-neutral children's clothing; it said that labels on its own-brand ranges would not say 'boys' or 'girl' and there would be no binary division in the merchandising of these garments (Pearson, 2017).

Marketing in Action 2.2 focuses on how the physical environment is being politicized.

Legal forces can influence marketing decisions by setting the rules by which business is conducted. For example, smoking bans in public places can have dramatic short- and long-term effects on the demand for cigarettes and on opportunities for introducing new products such as e-cigarettes, which are changing people's behaviour (from smoking to vaping).

But arguably the most profound change to affect legislation in Europe is the Brexit referendum. The UK joined the EU in 1973, since when companies have been affected by EU legislation. Until 23 June 2016, the UK was a committed member of the EU, but on this date a political referendum took place in which a small

MARKETING IN ACTION 2.2

Market Forces Influence Norwegian Oil Company's Investment in Arctic Oil Exploration

Norway's largest oil company, Statoil ASA, responded to opportunities to exploit untapped oil reserves in the Arctic. Statoil has invested billions of dollars exploring the remote and geographically challenging region in search of exploitable oil deposits. The outcome of the initial investment was major oil-field discoveries, for example the Johan Castberg field in the Barents Sea. The company estimates that these fields could yield more than 600 million barrels of oil. But so far no oil has been extracted, and this is largely due to market forces beyond the control of Statoil.

Oil extraction is an industry where the initial investment costs are exceedingly high; Statoil estimated that the required new infrastructure and bespoke technologies needed to exploit the Arctic field would cost over $15 billion. Statoil is no stranger to the vast wilderness of the Arctic region, yet in order to proceed with the investment the company needed to consider how market forces might affect the price of oil from these fields once it became available, in order to evaluate future investment.

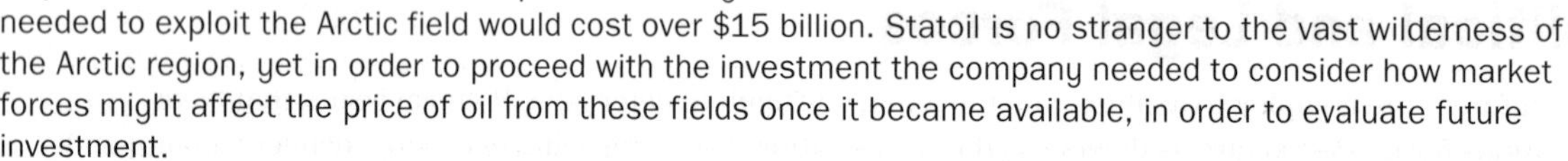

Political changes proved to have negative influences on Statoil's investment evaluation, as the Norwegian government introduced tax increases that affected the oil and gas industry. The changes mean that energy companies can only write off 22 per cent rather than 30 per cent of their capital investments against revenues from new oil fields.

Currently, economic influences are also negative. Changes in global oil prices have resulted in a fall in the price of crude oil, which has put significant pressure on the financial feasibility of huge capital investment projects like the ones proposed by Statoil. The plunge in the price of oil has been driven by a global glut in supply, shrinking demand, and a strong US dollar (global commodity prices are usually quoted in dollars). The implications for Statoil were that production from the Johan Castberg field would not break even. Statoil's breakeven point is at about $80 to $85 per barrel, but the economic changes—which are all forces beyond Statoil's control—saw the price of Brent crude fall from $116 in 2014 to below $50 in 2015.

Environmental influences are also negative, as environmental pressure groups such as Greenpeace have campaigned vigorously against drilling in the Arctic, which is seen as an extremely fragile ecosystem. The threat of oil spills has enabled Greenpeace's efforts to gather global press coverage and support.

While evaluation of the market environment suggests currently there is reduced potential for Statoil's investment in the oil fields in the Barents Sea, this situation is likely to be temporary. Statoil is not likely to be giving up on the Arctic completely, as future rises in the price of oil and ongoing innovation in cost-reducing technologies could once again make this region an attractive investment proposition. For the time being, Statoil has licences to explore the Sandino Basin off the Nicaraguan coast, which is under investigation as another potential site for future oil extraction.

Based on: Greenpeace (2014); Statoil (2015)

majority of the citizens of the UK voted to leave the EU. The impact of this vote has had a profound effect on economic and political factors (discussed in the previous sections). The UK's planned exit from the EU is likely to the affect the influence of EU-wide laws on companies operating in the UK. On 29 March 2017, Prime Minister Theresa May, on behalf of the UK government, triggered Article 50, which is the mechanism in the Lisbon Treaty that enables a member state to withdraw from the EU. The UK had until 29 March 2019 to negotiate the terms of its withdrawal. At the time of writing, it is not clear what the details of these terms will be or how they might affect companies, taxation, terms of trading, movement of people and many other aspects of the law—including intellectual property rights, which are pertinent to marketing. However, based on an assumption that the UK Government will eventually agree a withdrawal agreement, EU law will continue to affect business and trade until the beginning of 2021.

EU-wide laws

EU laws exist at two levels: 1) those that are binding on all member states, and 2) those that are enactments of a law within the member state. A major influence at the European level is EU competition, which is based on the belief that business competitiveness benefits from intense competition. The role of competition policy, therefore, is to encourage competition in the EU by removing restrictive practices, barriers to competition and other anti-competitive activities. The objectives of these legal rules are the prevention of:

- *Collusion* by price fixing, cartels and other collaborative activities. Competition is encouraged by preventing firms joining forces to act in a monopolistic way. The European Commission enforces EU rules and has had considerable success in disbanding and fining cartels. British Airways was fined £270 million for conspiring with Virgin Airways (which escaped prosecution because it alerted the regulators to the price fixing) to fix the price of passenger fuel surcharges on transatlantic flights (Milmo, 2008). Some of Europe's biggest truck makers (DAF, Daimler, Scania, Volvo) have been accused of operating a cartel for over 14 years that has potentially held up developments in emission-reducing technology; Volvo had made provision of $490 million for the likely legal action (Sharman, 2014). The European Commission has succeeded in punishing firms that collude, often with severe fines.
- *Abuse of market dominance.* Monopoly and discriminatory pricing, which could harm small buyers with little bargaining power, is discouraged. Market dominance was successfully challenged when Italian cigarette producer and distributor AAMS was found guilty of such abuse in the wholesale distribution of cigarettes. AAMS was protecting its own sales by imposing restrictive distribution contracts on foreign manufacturers, limiting the access of foreign cigarettes to the Italian market (Mercado, Welford and Prescott, 2001). Systembolaget is an interesting example of a state-run monopoly: it controls the retail sales of alcohol in Sweden. In 2007, the European Court of Justice ruled against the Swedish regulations and declared that these policies were inhibiting free movement of goods. The ruling opened opportunities for direct importing by private consumers, which in turn stimulated the growth in online alcohol retailers. However, this has led to further challenges for Systembolaget, as Swedish food retailer CityGross has teamed up with Danish wine seller Winefinder, thereby creating a legal loophole for retailers and Swedish wine drinkers (Nilsson, 2014).
- *Acquisition of excessive market power.* The objective is to control the size that firms grow to through buying or merging with other firms. Actions to prevent the build-up of excess power include blocking mergers, as in the case of the Swedish truck and coach builders Volvo, which wanted to acquire Scania. The reason for blocking the merger was that such a merger would create a near monopoly. Less severe action is to apply strict conditions to any merger, such as the requirement that Nestlé sell several Perrier brands to encourage a third force to emerge in the French mineral water market to compete with Nestlé and BSN, the second major supplier of bottled water in France.
- *Reliance on state aid.* It can be in a nation's interest for its government to give state aid to ailing firms within its boundaries; on a broader scale this can give artificial competitive advantages to recipient firms, enabling them to charge lower prices than their unsupported rivals; recipients may also be unfairly shielded from the full force of the competitive pressures affecting their markets. European Commission approval of state aid is usually given as part of a restructuring or rescue package for ailing firms. The general principle is that such payments should be one-offs to prevent uncompetitive firms being repeatedly bailed out by their governments.

MINI CASE 2.1

GDPR: A Privacy Law that Affects Everyone

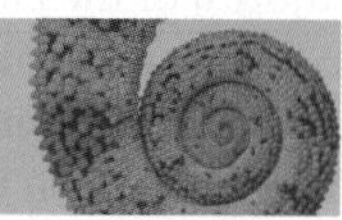

The General Data Protection Regulation (GDPR) is a Europe-wide set of legally binding principles that govern data protection. The GDPR became law on 25 May 2018. The legislation seeks to protect personal privacy, so is highly relevant to marketers wanting to gather data on their customers. Despite uncertainty over Brexit, the UK has included the principles of GDPR in its new Data Protection Act—and so the UK is in accord with the European legislation. GDPR targets the use and storage of data in the digital age and controls the processing and movement of this data; misuse of data is a criminal offence. In the past, there have been significant information breaches by Yahoo, LinkedIn and Facebook, in which unauthorized access to personal data has occurred. Post GDPR, companies must report such losses of personal data to an appropriate national data regulator.

What is GDPR?

The legislation states:

'The principles of, and rules on the protection of natural persons with regard to the processing of their personal data should, whatever their nationality or residence, respect their fundamental rights and freedoms, in particular their right to the protection of personal data. This Regulation is intended to contribute to the accomplishment of an area of freedom, security and justice and of an economic union, to economic and social progress, to the strengthening and the convergence of the economies within the internal market, and to the well-being of natural persons.'

The reasoning behind this legislation and it being Europe-wide legislation is to ensure there is a single law protecting citizens. The legislation has 99 articles which set out the rights of individuals and the obligations placed on organizations.

What does GDPR mean for me?

Individuals have eight rights:

1. The right to be informed
2. The right of access
3. The right to rectification
4. The right to erasure
5. The right to restrict processing
6. The right to data portability
7. The right to object
8. Rights in relation to automated decision making and profiling

These rights mean that an individual has greater rights—which also places more responsibility on the company holding the data—as it can ask to see the data held and can ask for data to be erased. Failure to comply can result in large fines for the companies involved.

Accountability and compliance for companies

All types of companies must comply, and there are significant implications regarding holding and using personal information for marketing and other purposes.

More specifically, companies are accountable for handling personal information and must put in place data protection policies and data protection impact assessments and must document how data is collected and managed. Companies with more than 250 employees must also be able to explain why personal information is collected and describe the type of information, where it is kept and the security measures that are in place. Systematic monitoring of people's data must be carried out, and large-scale processing of sensitive data should only be carried out by a data protection officer.

What does GDPR mean for marketers?

Markets must demonstrate that they are holding personal data lawfully and are only using data for permitted purposes. Personal data comprises name, a unique identification number, personal location data, an online identifier, and personal preferences relating to physical, physiological, economic, cultural or social identity. A marketer must have an individual's consent to gather and use such data. Many websites have been updated to comply with GDPR and require site visitors to accept terms before they can proceed to view online content.

Questions:

1. Explain the reasoning behind the changes to data protection legislation introduced by GDPR.
2. Imagine you have just been given the job of ensuring that your company is complying with GDPR. Set out the steps you might follow.
3. Read the GDPR policy for one of the following companies and then assess how the company is protecting your personal rights: Facebook (https://www.facebook.com/business/gdpr), Twitter (https://gdpr.twitter.com/en.html), eBay (https://www.ebayinc.com/our-company/privacy-center/gdpr)

Based on: Burgess (2018); Eur-Lex (2018); Gov. UK (2018); ICO (2018); Smart Insights (2018)

Legal and Regulatory Responses to Ethical Issues in Marketing

European countries are bound by several layers of laws and by regulatory bodies that restrict company actions and encourage the use of ethical practices, as described below.

- EU competition laws and regulatory bodies that seek to ban anti-competitive practices: these regulations have teeth and have resulted in fines on companies such as Microsoft (product bundling), AstraZeneca (blocking generic copies of its ulcer drug), and Hoechst, Atofina and Akzo Nobel (price fixing), imposed by the European Commission, a body set up to enforce EU competition and consumer law.
- EU laws and regulatory bodies that aim to protect the rights of consumers: consumers' rights are also protected by EU regulatory bodies and regulations. For example, consumers' interests regarding food safety are protected by the European Food Standards Authority, and the right to compensation for air travellers whose flights are overbooked, cancelled or delayed is covered by EU rules.
- National laws covering consumer rights and protection and competition regulation, supported by government-backed regulatory bodies: legislation at national level is also designed to prevent marketing and business malpractice. For example, the Financial Services Authority fined Shell £17 million under UK market abuse laws, and the Securities and Exchange Commission (SEC) fined the same company $120 million for breaches of SEC rules and US laws.
- Voluntary bodies set up by industries to create and enforce codes of practice: industries often prefer self-regulation to the imposition of laws by government. For example, most European countries are self-regulating with regard to advertising standards, through the drawing up and enforcement of codes of practice.

Marketers in Europe have great freedom with which to practise their profession. Business-imposed, societal and legal constraints on their actions not only make good sense from a long-term social and environmental perspective, but they make good long-term commercial sense, too.

The Physical Environmental Forces

The **physical environment** in a marketing context is concerned with the relationship between people and the environment. Environmentalists attempt to protect the physical environment; they are concerned with the environmental costs of consumption, not just the personal costs to the consumer. Five environmental issues are of particular concern: 1) climate change, 2) pollution control, 3) energy conservation, 4) use of environmentally friendly components, and 5) recycling and non-wasteful packaging.

Climate change

Concerns about climate change and the problems associated with global warming originate from a quadrupling of carbon dioxide emissions over the past 50 years, evidenced by more extreme weather conditions, such as hurricanes, storms and flooding. There is much discussion about whether climate change is caused by human activity and associated with carbon dioxide emissions. However, industries such as insurance, agriculture and oil have felt the impact from natural disasters like hurricane Katrina in the USA (Macalister, 2006). At the heart of the debate is the rate at which the planet is warming and the impact on global average temperature changes, which are different from the temperature changes we experience in our daily lives.

In 1992, countries joined in an international treaty to 'cooperatively consider what they could do to limit average global temperature increases and the resulting climate change and to cope with whatever impacts were, by then, inevitable' (UNFCCC, 2012). The United Nations Framework Convention on Climate Change (UNFCCC) realized that the measures in place to control climate change were insufficient. Accordingly, the UNFCC developed the Kyoto Protocol, which is an international agreement that focuses member countries on how to keep global temperature increases below 2 degrees Celsius. Thirty-seven industrialized nations and the European community, which have signed up to the Kyoto Protocol, have committed themselves to the reduction of four greenhouse gases—carbon dioxide, methane, nitrous oxide and sulphur hexafluoride—by 5 per cent (UNFCCC, 2012). The Paris Agreement, which set out further ambitious plans to control climate change came into force in December 2016. In 2018, the UK set out the Clean Growth Strategy, which aims to cut greenhouse gas emissions by nurturing low-carbon technologies and processes. The UK has had some success in reducing emissions, but at the same time the economy has been growing, indicating that it is possible to grow and simultaneously reduce or at least control the environmental impact (BEIS, 2017). See Exhibit 2.4 for an example of an energy-efficient vehicle.

EXHIBIT 2.4
Smart car was voted greenest and most energy-efficient car by the American Council for an Energy-Efficient Economy (ACEEE)

Pollution

The manufacture, use and disposal of products can have a harmful effect on the quality of the physical environment. The production of chemicals that pollute the atmosphere, the use of nitrates as a fertilizer that pollutes rivers, and the disposal of by-products into the sea have caused considerable public concern. For example, plastics, chemical sludge and debris deposited by ocean currents have accumulated in an area of the northern Pacific Ocean. This 'trash vortex', as it is called by Greenpeace (2012), is equivalent in size to the state of Texas in the USA and is a major pollution problem for the marine environment. As the waste degrades, it is ingested by marine animals, poisoning them and thereby entering the food chain. Sea Shepherd, a not-for-profit marine conservation charity, estimates that over 1 million creatures living in the oceans are killed each year because of plastic. Sea Shepherd's advert 'Plastic Ocean' depicts this scenario and is attempting to raise awareness; see Exhibit 2.5. The list of manufactured products that have found their way to the vortex is extensive and includes plastic bottles, polystyrene packaging, traffic cones, disposable lighters, vehicle tyres and even toothbrushes. Big brands are aware that this can be an emotive issue for consumers and also that they

EXHIBIT 2.5
Sea Shepherd wants to put an end to the plastic ocean

must find ways to ensure that they comply with environment legislation. Starbucks has announced it is to make a 100 per cent recyclable coffee cup and put an end to the estimated 6 billion that are discarded each year (Grant, 2018).

Also in response to pollution issues, Denmark has introduced a series of anti-pollution measures, including a charge on pesticides and a chlorofluorocarbon (CFC) tax. The Netherlands has imposed higher taxes on pesticides, fertilizers and carbon monoxide emissions. The EU has made an agreement with car manufacturers to produce colour-coded labels to make it easier for car users to understand the environmental impact of the vehicle they choose to drive. Not all initiatives mean adding costs; in Germany, for example, one of the marketing benefits of its involvement in green technology has been a thriving export business in pollution-control equipment.

Energy and scarce resource conservation

The finite nature of the world's resources is driving conservation. Energy conservation is reflected in the demand for energy-efficient housing and fuel-efficient cars. In Europe, Sweden has taken the lead in developing an energy policy based on renewable resources. The tax system penalizes the use of polluting energy sources such as coal and oil, while less polluting resources such as peat and woodchips receive favourable tax treatment. In addition, Sweden is planning to become the world's first oil-free economy by 2020, not by building nuclear power stations but by utilizing renewable resources such as wind and wave power, geothermal energy and waste heat. The plan is a response to warnings that the world may be running out of oil, together with global climate change and rising petrol prices. Companies are also making more energy-efficient products.

Another concern of environmentalists is the consumption of wood. Forest depletion by the deforestation activities of companies and the effects of acid rain damage the ecosystem. Consumers' desire for softwood and hardwood furniture and window frames is at odds with the need to preserve forests. Trees' leaves absorb carbon dioxide, and their roots help to stabilize slopes; a landslide in the Philippines that cost many lives was allegedly caused by illegal logging. A solution is the replanting of forests to maintain the long-term stock of trees. Ikea produces 100 million pieces of furniture each year and in doing so uses 1 per cent of the world's wood supply, 23 per cent of which comes from responsibly managed forests (IKEA, 2012).

Environmentally friendly ingredients and components

Environmentalists favour the use of biodegradable and natural ingredients and components when practicable. Companies have responded to the challenge by launching products such as the Estée Lauder Origins skincare and cosmetics range of vegetable-based products containing no animal ingredients. PETA (People for the Ethical Treatment of Animals) campaigns relentlessly against cruelty to animals. In response, Massimo Dutti, Topshop, Primark, H&M and Inditex (owner of Zara) have banned the use of angora wool in its garments, in an attempt to curb appalling animal-management practices in wool-producing countries (Kassam, 2015).

Recycling and non-wasteful packaging

Germany took the lead in the recycling of packaging when it introduced the Verpackvo, a law that allows shoppers to return packaging to retailers for them to pass back to suppliers. In response, suppliers promised to assume responsibility for the management of packaging waste. Over 400 companies have created a mechanism called the Dual System Deutschland (DSD). Consumers are asked to return glass bottles and waste paper to recycling bins and are also encouraged to separate other recyclable materials such as plastics, composite packaging and metals and place them in yellow bags and bins supplied by the DSD. Collections take place every month and (together with the separating of the refuse) are paid for by the DSD; the cost is eventually absorbed by the packaging manufacturers.

Recycling is also important in Sweden, where industry has established a special company to organize the collection and sorting of waste for recycling, and in Finland, where over 35 per cent of packaging is recycled. Clothing retailer H&M introduced a clothing recycle scheme in which it gathers its used products and then donates them to charitable organizations for resale. And further back along the supply chain, manufacturers are developing new fabrics for the fashion industry made from waste, for example Econyl made from abandoned fishing nets and old carpets. According to DutchAwareness (2015), these types of fabric can reduce the carbon dioxide impact by 73 per cent.

Marketing managers need to be aware of the environmental consequences of their decisions and activities and to recognize the possible impact of environmentally irresponsible actions on the reputation of their companies and brands. Managers should be alert to the opportunities created by a greater focus on the environment and should consider communicating their environmentally conscious credentials to their target markets. See Chapter 5 for further detailed discussion of marketing ethics and corporate social responsibility.

Culture and Society

Three key *social/cultural forces* that have implications for marketing are: 1) the changes in the demographic profile of the population, 2) cultural differences within and between nations, and 3) the influence of consumerism.

Demographic forces

Demographic forces concern changes in populations in terms of their size and characteristics. **Demography** is important to marketers, because it helps to predict the size and growth rates of markets and the need for facilities such as schools, one-person housing and homes for the elderly. Three major demographic forces are: 1) world population growth, 2) the changing age distribution, and 3) the changing structure of households in western countries.

World population growth

Overall, the global population is expanding at an increasing rate. However, the rate of growth is uneven across the world. In particular, the population in developed economies is expected to be stable or shrinking, whereas countries of Africa, India, 'other Asia' and Latin America are expected to account for over 90 per cent of the projected population increase during the 21st century (see Figure 2.2) (Brown, 1992). As the populations of these countries grow more youthful, the developed countries will play host to an ageing population. In 2025, half the population of Europe will be over 45 years old. For the next decade, the world population is expected to grow by an average of 97 million per year.

The changing world population distribution suggests that new markets outside the developed economies may provide attractive opportunities, although the extent to which this force progresses will depend on a rise in income levels in the less developed world. The problem is that major population growth is predicted in countries that are already poor. In Niger, the poorest place on earth, lack of food but a high fertility rate means that the average birth rate is over seven children per woman. Currently, the United Nations Population Fund is the only agency importing condoms and offering education in birth control (*The Economist*, 2014), and the economic prospects and political interest remain low.

FIGURE 2.2
World population growth

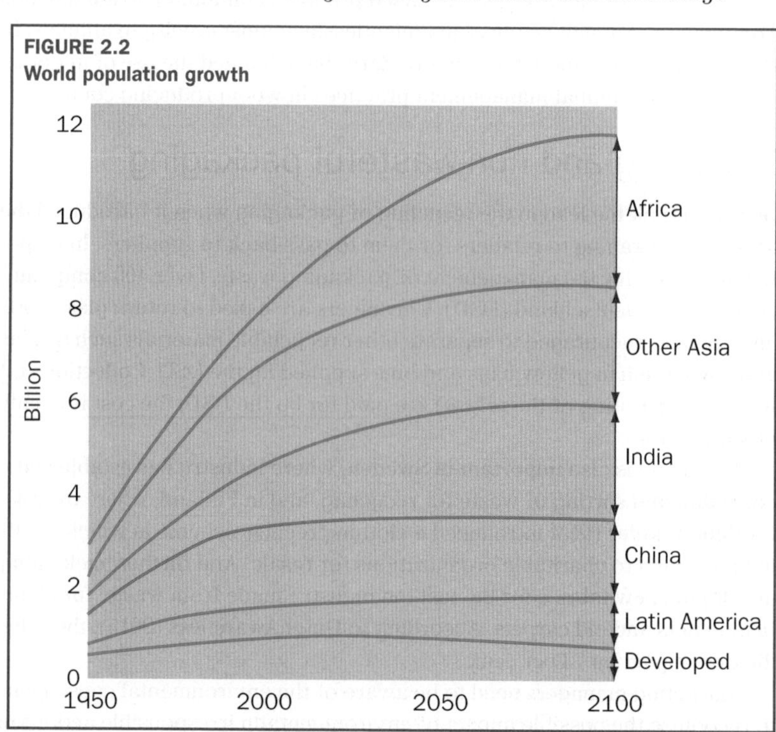

Age distribution

A major demographic change that will continue to affect the demand for products is the ageing population. In Europe, the share of the population that is over 65 is growing and life expectancy is increasing. Population pyramids, which show age distribution by sex and age group, are predicting growth of older age bands going forward to 2080. Furthermore, younger age bands are predicted to shrink relative to older groups (Eurostat, 2014).

The growth of older segments has significant implications for marketing. On the supply side, there will be an ageing workforce and a growing number of migrant workers who move according to labour demands. On the demand side, EU citizens over 45 represent substantial marketing opportunities because of their high level of per-capita income and higher disposable income and savings than younger people. With an older population who have higher disposable incomes and increased leisure time, the demand for holidays and recreational activities such as entertainment and sporting activities (e.g. golf) should increase. Older people also have different tastes and needs in terms of levels of service and style of products. As the palettes of older customers change, these people look to buy saltier and more spicy foods. See Exhibit 2.6.

EXHIBIT 2.6
Walkers extends its Sensations range of snacks to include new spicy popcorn flavours which might tempt the palettes of old snackers as well as the young

Similar ageing trends are evident in other parts of the globe, and businesses are already seeking to differentiate their offers for the lucrative ageing market. In Japan, retailers have designed a new retail concept: Funabashi. This is a shopping mall specially designed for elderly shoppers, who can access medical clinics, get discounts on pension day and enjoy leisure activities ranging from dancing to finding romantic partners (Lucas, 2014).

Household structure

Changes in household structure and behaviour that have marketing implications are the rise in one-person households and households with no children, and the growth in dual-income families.

More people are living alone by choice and through divorce or bereavement. This suggests that a key market segment is people who demand products that meet their particular needs, such as one-bedroom houses or apartments and single-portion foods. However, households are also changing their behaviour regarding employment. In many European countries, there has been a growth in dual-earner families. In the UK, for example, over half of couples with dependent children are double-income families. The rise of two-income households means this market segment possibly has higher disposable income, which can lead to reduced price sensitivity and the capacity to buy luxury furniture and clothing products and expensive services (e.g. foreign holidays, restaurant meals).

Cultural forces

Culture is the combination of traditions, taboos, values and attitudes of the society in which an individual lives. A number of distinctive subcultures in the UK provide a rich tapestry of lifestyles and create new markets. The Asian population, for example, has provided restaurants and stores supplying food from that part of the world. This influence is now seen in supermarkets, where Asian foods are readily available. The free movement of workers around the EU has also encouraged the growth of subcultures—for example, the flow of workers from central and eastern Europe to older established EU countries. To meet the needs of the Polish community in the UK, for example, Tesco sells extensive ranges of Polish foods online.

Subcultures can also span national boundaries. Youth subcultures provide cues for the development of brands, for example Levi's jeans, Coca-Cola, Pepsi and MTV. See Exhibit 2.7, which shows how Carlsberg targets young drinkers. The generation who use Facebook, Twitter, Google, and so on are different and do not gather together as hippies, punks and goths have in the past. The internet does not inspire

EXHIBIT 2.7
Carlsberg embraces the subculture of the 'everyday beer drinker' to reinvigorate the brand in the UK, Ireland, Sweden and Denmark

long-lived mass anti-fashion movements; instead it spawns brief small-scale ones that have neither longevity nor time to pervade society. But social media does encourage sharing personal information, photographs, music and videos. A *haul video* (an example of a small-scale internet trend) is made after a shopping trip and then posted on YouTube to show what has been purchased. These videos are about showing not only what you have bought but also about showing the shopping experience in a highly creative manner (Petridis, 2014).

Attitudes towards food among some sections of society in Europe are also changing. Pressures towards healthy eating have prompted moves towards food with less fat, sugar and salt, and towards health labelling. For example, the Nestlé-branded cereal range targeted at children has been reformulated with 10 per cent less sugar. New brands focusing on their healthy credentials have emerged, like Innocent smoothies, and even McDonald's has a nutrition calculator which enables savvy consumers to check what they are eating (http://www.mcdonalds.ca/ca/en/food/nutrition_calculator.html#). Market segments have appeared that are based on the concept of ethical consumption, leading to demand for vegan, fair trade and organic products, together with avoidance of companies and brands that are associated with dubious labour practices. The growth in healthy eating and ethical consumption has prompted the acquisition of small ethical brands by larger corporates, for example Rachel's Organic yoghurts by Group Lactilis, a subsidiary of BSA international, and Ben & Jerry's by Unilever.

Fair-trade marketing is the development, promotion and selling of fair-trade brands and the positioning of organizations based on a fair-trade ethos. Companies are increasingly realizing that many consumers care about how suppliers in countries of the developing world are treated and wish to support them by buying fair-trade brands, often at a price premium. For example, Cafédirect, a fair-trade company and brand, was launched to protect coffee growers from the volatility in world coffee prices. Minimum prices for coffee beans are paid, which are pegged above market fluctuations, and business support and development programmes are provided. The popularity of fair-trade brands has prompted Nestlé to launch its own fair-trade coffee, Partners' Blend, and Marks & Spencer has launched a range of fair-trade clothing which benefits Indian cotton farmers through a price that includes a premium that can be invested in their communities (Milmo, 2008).

Supermarkets are supporting fair-trade products, with Co-op stocking only own-label fair-trade tea, coffee and chocolate, and Sainsbury's selling only fair-trade bananas. Coffee bar chains such as Costa Coffee and Pret A Manger offer fair-trade varieties. Fast-moving consumer goods food manufacturers also support the spread of fair-trade products and have been acquiring ethical brands to facilitate access to these markets—for example, Unilever's acquisition of Ben & Jerry's, which is a brand that supports local farmers; all of the ingredients in its ice creams are certified as fair trade. Kraft Foods, the multinational food and beverage corporation, expanded its product portfolio with the acquisition of Green & Black's, the organic chocolate brand. From its independent origins, Green & Black's has taken a 95 per cent share of the organic chocolate market, and since 2009—with redesigned packaging—it is gaining market share in the mainstream chocolate market. Fair-trade marketing can also be based on the positioning of companies as having a fair-trade ethos. The success of fair-trade marketing is based upon consumers being willing to try and repeat-buy fair-trade brands, and organizations developing genuine fair-trade programmes. Consumers will not put up with organizations that use such schemes as an ethical veneer.

Successful marketing depends on knowing the cultural differences that exist between consumers. Cultural differences also have implications for business-to-business marketing. Within Europe, cultural variations affect the way in which business should be conducted. Humour in business life is acceptable in the UK, Italy, Greece, the Netherlands and Spain, but less commonplace in France and Germany. These facts of business life need to be recognized when interacting with European business customers. International culture is revisited in detail in Chapter 21.

Consumerism

Consumerism is organized action against business practices that are not in the interests of consumers. For decades there has been a debate about whether consumerism is driven by economic or social drivers, and what the implications are for marketing. Pinpointing the actual origins of consumerism is difficult, but, simply stated, the situation has been aggravated by 'marketing excesses, inflation, economic recession and questioning of mass-consumption society values has apparently pushed consumers to ever higher levels of dissatisfaction' (Straver, 1978). Arguably, marketing stands accused of creating opportunities for firms to sell more to the consumer, using tactical applications of the marketing mix. The response has been a growing interest in consumerism. The consumer movement has had notable successes, including improvements in car safety, the encouragement of fast-food restaurants to provide healthy-eating options, health labelling of food products, and the banning of smoking in public places in some European countries, including Ireland and the UK.

Consumers International (CI) is a worldwide federation of consumer groups that have joined together as an independent voice of the consumer. On 15 March every year, World Consumer Rights Day (WCRD) endorses the solidarity of the consumer movement and is an opportunity to promote the basic rights of the consumer. CI tackles issues from around the world. For example, in Kenya there were problems with product safety and inappropriate use of labelling which could cause serious harm to young consumers; in Asia, there is a great deal of marketing of unhealthy food to children; in Latin America, CI is working to protect consumers' right to a healthy environment. Globally, unhealthy diets are linked to four of the ten major causes of early death: obesity, and high blood pressure, glucose and cholesterol. CI is championing consumers' rights to make healthy food choices, but one key issue is the mass availability of unhealthy options. In 2018, the focus was on making digital marketplaces fairer, raising concerns about consumer safety online, equal access and transparent trading laws (Consumer International, 2018).

Marketing managers, however, should not consider the consumer movement a threat to business, but rather an opportunity to create new product offerings to meet the needs of emerging market segments. For example, in the detergent market, brands have been launched that are more environmentally friendly, while food companies have reduced the fat and salt content of some of their products and continue to introduce healthy option ranges. Pressure from the consumer movement, environmentalists, and individuals who engage in ethical consumption has resulted in most organizations adopting corporate social responsibility as a guide to their business practices. **Corporate social responsibility** (CSR) refers to the ethical principle that an organization should be accountable for how its behaviour might affect society and the environment. The importance of CSR is considered in detail in Chapter 5.

MARKETING IN ACTION 2.3
Consumerism in Sweden and Britain

British children are trapped in a cycle of compulsive consumption, according to UNICEF. But children in Sweden are different: they don't appear to crave products in the same way as UK children do and they have high levels of well-being compared with children in other European countries.

In both the UK and Sweden, the behaviour of parents is cited as a potential cause of children's behaviour. In the UK, parents are said to give their children gifts to compensate for their absence when working long hours, whereas in Sweden, where compulsive consumption is almost absent, parents spend time with their children, and families enjoy indoor and outdoor pastimes together. But research suggests there are reasons that contribute to well-being: health and safety, educational well-being, and family and peer relationships. A recent study found that when children in the UK and Sweden said they had had a good day, it was always because of people not things. A child's view of a good day is simple: time with those they love (friends, family and even pets), taking part in creative or sporting activities, and being outdoors and having fun. However, the study did reveal a desire for products: for example, phones, tablet computers, laptops and game consoles were on the wanted lists of children from both nations and from a range of different social backgrounds. Also, functional goods like footballs, creative art materials and musical instruments, which enabled the children to participate in certain activities, were also high in the list of desired items.

More firms are realizing the importance of children's rights and are seeking ways to use marketing and communications to not have an adverse impact. Through the web, companies are opening the debate to find new ways to interact with children. For example, the Swedish transport administration agency (Trafikverket) has set up workshops and invited children to share their views on traffic dangers, signage, noise and other issues.

Based on: The Swedish Wire (2011); Nairn (2011); UNICEF (2015); Lagerberg (2018)

Going forwards, changes in social and cultural aspects of the marketing environment need to be monitored and understood, so that marketing management is aware of the changing tastes and behaviour of consumers. Such changes can create demand shifts that may act as either opportunities or threats. For further discussion of consumerism, see Marketing in Action 2.3.

Societal Responses to Ethical Issues in Marketing

Societal responses to ethical issues in marketing take three forms: 1) consumerism, 2) environmentalism, and 3) ethical consumption.

Consumerism

Consumerism takes the form of organized action against business practices that are not in the interests of consumers. Organized action is taken through the **consumer movement**, which is an organized collection of groups and organizations whose objective is to protect the rights of consumers.

The consumer movement seeks to protect consumers' rights, which include the right to expect the product to be safe, for it to perform as expected and for communications for the product to be truthful and not misleading. Pressure from consumer groups in Europe has resulted in prohibitions on tobacco advertising, improvements in car safety, reductions in the levels of fat, sugar and salt in foods, restrictions on advertising alcohol to teenagers and the forcing of financial services companies to display true interest charges (the annual percentage rate, or APR) on advertisements for credit facilities. Further successes include unit pricing (stating the cost per unit of a brand), and ingredient labelling (stating the ingredients that go into a brand).

The consumer movement often takes the form of consumer associations that campaign for consumers and provide product information on a comparative basis, allowing consumers to make informed choices. These have been very successful in establishing themselves as credible and authoritative organizations and are seen as trusted providers of information to help consumer choice. Their actions help to improve consumer power when dealing with organizations.

Environmentalism

While consumerism focuses on improving the balance between consumer and organizational power and protecting the rights of consumers in consumption decisions, environmentalism is broader in scope with its focus on the physical environment. **Environmentalism** is the organized movement of groups and organizations to protect and improve the physical environment. Their concerns are: production and consumption of products that lead to global warming, pollution, the destruction of natural resources such as oil and forests, and non-biodegradable waste. Environmentalists believe that producers and consumers should take account not only of short-term profits and satisfaction but also the cost to the environment of their actions.

Environmentalists support the concept of environmental sustainability and put pressure on companies to adopt strategies that promote its objectives. Environmental sustainability means 'to maintain or prolong environmental health'. Pressure groups such as Greenpeace and Friends of the Earth have been successful in persuading organizations to produce 'greener' products such as cadmium-free batteries, ozone-safe aerosols, recycled-paper toilet tissue and packaging, catalytic converters, lead-free petrol, unbleached tea bags and cruelty-free cosmetics. Other environmental groups have successfully changed company practices. For example, UPM, Finland's largest paper and pulp company, based in over 16 countries, must replant the number of trees felled. This is the result of environmentalist action. Major electrical manufacturers like Philips and Electrolux incorporate environmental considerations systematically in new product development and have strict guidelines covering the integration of environmental considerations into product design and development.

Environmentalists have concerns about how business activity affects the environment. This means they constantly pressurize organizations to deal with issues like controlling carbon emissions, reducing global warming, eliminating harmful pollutants, and using recycled and recyclable materials in products. The overarching aim is to maintain a sustainable environment for future generations.

Ethical consumerism

Consumerism and environmentalism are organized movements designed to protect society and the environment from the harmful effects of production and consumption. However, consumers also act in an individual way to protect society and the environment through engaging in ethical consumption. **Ethical consumption** occurs when individual consumers, when making purchase decisions, consider not only personal interests but also the interests of society and the environment. Examples include boycotting products and companies that have poor records regarding social and environmental concerns, buying non-animal-tested products, choosing fair-trade or organic products, avoiding products made by sweatshop or child labour, and purchasing products that are made from recycled materials (Crane and Matten, 2004).

As discussed earlier, consumers and businesses respond differently to ethical consumption. Some are passionate about living and operating in a manner that does not impact on the environment, while others are not, and many are somewhere in between these two extremes. Marketing managers must understand their target audiences' individual values, attitudes and motivations and align these with societal values if they are to develop successful marketing strategies.

The Microenvironment

The **microenvironment** consists of the actors in the firm's immediate environment that affect its capabilities to operate effectively in its chosen markets. Those actors—customers, competitors, distributors and suppliers and strategic partners—will now be introduced and analysed in more depth.

Customers

As we saw in Chapter 1, customers are at the centre of the marketing philosophy and effort, and it is the task of marketing management to satisfy their needs and expectations better than the competition does. The starting point is an understanding of individual customers, considered in Chapter 3, and then business customers. The techniques for gathering and analysing customer and other marketing information are discussed in Chapter 6, which covers marketing research. The grouping of consumers to form market segments that can be targeted with specific marketing-mix offerings is the subject of Chapter 7.

Changing customer tastes, lifestyles, motivations and expectations need to be monitored so that companies supply the appropriate targeted marketing mix strategies that meet their needs. Changes in consumer behaviour also need to be monitored. For example, consumers are using social network sites like Twitter to communicate—a fact not lost on marketers.

Competitors

Competitors have a major bearing on the performance of companies. For example, when competitors price-cut, the attractiveness of the market can fall, and competitors' ability to innovate can ruin once highly profitable brands. Marketing history is littered with brands that were once successful but are now defunct (e.g. Nokia mobile phones, Amstrad computers and Lotus software) because rivals developed and marketed better alternatives. No longer is it sufficient to meet customer needs and expectations—success is dependent on doing it better than the competition.

Market-orientated companies not only monitor and seek to understand customers, but also research competitors and their brands to understand their strengths, weaknesses, strategies and response patterns. In this book, the importance of these issues is reflected in a section being devoted to such analysis and the strategies that can be employed to anticipate and combat competitive moves. These matters are discussed in Chapter 19.

Distributors

Some companies, such as those providing services, dispense with the use of distributors, preferring to deal directly with end-user customers. The others use the services of distributors such as wholesalers and retailers to supply end users. As we shall see in Chapter 17, which covers distribution, these channel intermediaries perform many valuable services, including breaking bulk, making products available to customers where and when they want them, and providing specialist services such as maintenance and installation.

Distributors can reduce the profitability of suppliers by putting pressure on profit margins. For example, large retailers such as Walmart and Tesco have enormous buying power and can demand low prices from their suppliers, a fact that has been criticized in the media when applied to small farmers.

Distribution trends need to be monitored. For example, the trend towards downloading music has hit traditional music outlets that sell CDs, and the growth of the internet-based sellers such as Amazon has impacted on traditional bricks-and-mortar booksellers. As the attractiveness of distribution channels changes, so suppliers must alter their strategies to keep in touch with customers.

Suppliers

The fortunes of companies are not only dependent on customers, competitors and distributors; they are also influenced by their suppliers. Increases in supply costs can push up prices, making other alternatives more attractive. For example, increases in the price of aluminium make plastic more attractive. Also, as with distributors, powerful suppliers can force up prices. The rise in the price of gas has been blamed on powerful European suppliers who, it is alleged, restricted supply to force prices higher.

Companies need to monitor supply availability, such as shortages due to labour strikes or political factors, as these can cause customer dissatisfaction and lost sales. Companies also need to be sensitive to alternative input materials that can be substituted for those of existing suppliers if the latter's prices rise or availability diminishes significantly.

The importance of suppliers is reflected in discussion of their relationship with customers in Chapter 4, which focuses on organizational buying behaviour. Many customers are increasingly forming partnerships with selected suppliers to enhance value delivery.

Strategic partners

Companies are increasing partnering with others to co-create added value, whether that be technical expertise (Google and Salesforce.com: sharing Google's marketing platform products enables Saleforce customers to gain direct access to Google's services, to enhance customer relationship management), logistical networks (DHL and Argos/Sainsbury's—DHL's two-man delivery service improves customer service quality for the retailers) or financial support (Vodaphone India and Ideal Cellular—financial investment enabled creation of a market leader). Strategic partnerships can create opportunities to expand customer bases, produce a more competitive offer and share resources and fend off the competition. Sainsbury's/Argos plans to merge with Asda/Walmart (a competitor) to create a super-sized retail operation that incorporates digital retail expertise (Argos) and logistics and global sourcing (Asda/Walmart). Further discussion of value creation through relationships is included in Chapter 10.

All elements of the microenvironment need to be monitored and assessed so that opportunities can be exploited and threats combated. This forms an essential ingredient in maintaining a strategic fit between a company and its marketing environment.

Monitoring and Responding in the Marketing Environment

The potential of external forces to affect company performance is high, but monitoring the marketing environment presents many challenges. A market-orientated firm needs to be able to respond appropriately. Guoa et al. (2018) studied the internal capabilities of firms and how these affect market performance in relation to external market forces. Guoa et al. found that the internal (micro) marketing capabilities of a firm are affected by turbulence in the external environment, especially in relation to technology forces. The authors suggest that marketing managers should carefully monitor changes in the external environment, with the help of customers—who may be more closely attuned to changes (potential opportunities and threats). By creating a dialogue, there are opportunities to co-create new products and services. LEGO, BMW and Made.com are all examples of companies that have adopted this approach and created new designs by involving their customers in the process. This research highlights the importance of gaining awareness of the nature of the environment where firms trade, to be better placed to respond adaptively to environmental changes, improve planning and decision-making, and build internal marketing capabilities. Previously, Dieffenbach (1983) found that formal environmental scanning can deliver multiple benefits such as better market awareness, improved resource allocation, greater diversification and better foreign investment.

Traditionally, the process of monitoring and analysing the marketing environment of a company is called **environmental scanning**. This process provides the essential informational input to create a strategic fit between a company's strategies, its organizational operations and the marketing environment (see Figure 2.3). Marketing strategy should reflect the environment even if this means a fundamental reorganization of operations.

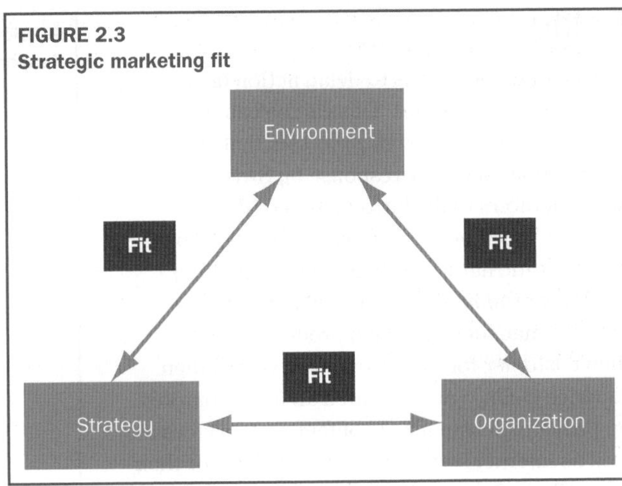

FIGURE 2.3
Strategic marketing fit

The most appropriate organizational arrangement for scanning will depend on the unique circumstances facing a firm. A judgement needs to be made regarding the costs and benefits of each alternative approach. The size and profitability of the company and the perceived degree of environmental turbulence will be factors that impinge on this decision. To establish a scanning system covering every conceivable external force would be unmanageable. Consequently, there are two key questions for managers when establishing environmental scanning: 1) what to scan, and 2) how to organize the process. To answer these questions and develop an effective scanning system, action should be taken to:

1 *Define a feasible range of forces to monitor.* These are the *potentially relevant environmental forces* that have the most likelihood of affecting future business prospects (Brownlie, 2002). Ansoff (1991) identified that environmental scanning monitors a company's environment for signals of the development of *strategic issues* that have an influence on company performance. For example, Google was slow to respond to the social media phenomenon, which could have been the result of not scanning the right forces. Not only has this allowed Facebook to develop a very powerful member base for its social network, but it is Google that has missed out on an opportunity to gather rich, detailed customer data that might enhance its core revenue stream, online advertising.

2 *Design a system that provides a fast response* to events. Some events are only partially predictable, emerge as surprises and grow very rapidly. It is essential for companies to be informed if they are to manage in increasingly turbulent marketing environments. Brownlie (2002) suggests that environmental scanning should enable a company to:
   - develop forecasts, scenarios and issues analysis as input to strategic decision-making
   - provide a focal point for the interpretation and analysis of environmental information identified by other people in the company
   - disseminate information on the business environment through newsletters, reports and lectures
   - evaluate and revise the scanning system itself by applying new tools and procedures.

The benefits of environmental scanning appear straightforward: a better understanding of the trading environment gives a company the knowledge to respond effectively to environmental changes. However, despite potential positive outcomes, companies respond differently to environmental change.

Responses to Environmental Change

Firms respond in various ways to environmental change (see Figure 2.4), and the outcomes are not always positive.

Ignorance

Because of poor environmental scanning, companies may not realize that salient forces are affecting their future prospects. They therefore continue as normal, ignorant of the environmental issues that are threatening their existence or of opportunities that could be seized. No change is made.

Delay

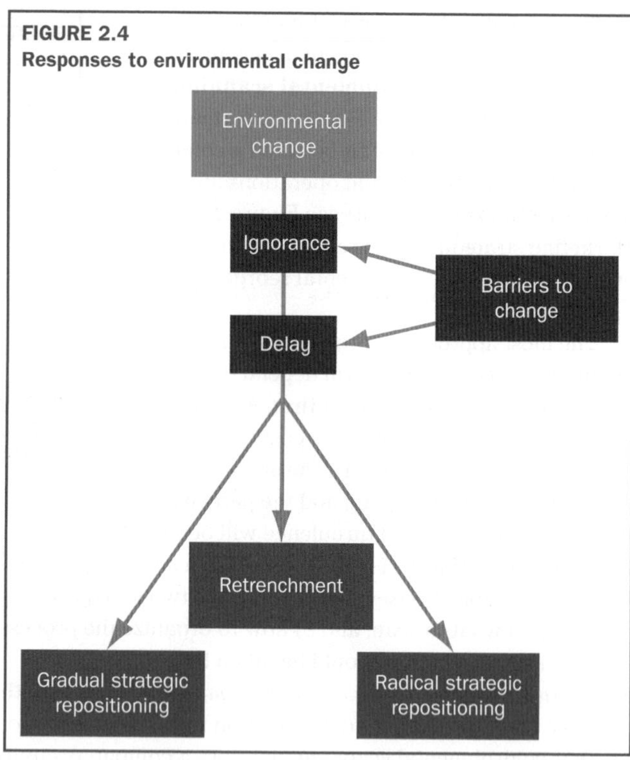

FIGURE 2.4
Responses to environmental change

The second response is to delay action once the force is understood. This can be caused by *bureaucratic decision processes* that stifle swift action. The slow response by Swiss watch manufacturers to the introduction of digital watches was thought, in part, to be caused by the bureaucratic nature of their decision-making.

Marketing myopia can slow response through management being product-rather than customer-focused. CompuServe and then America Online (AOL) created an online market by providing customized content and services as well as internet service providers (ISPs) for their subscribers. In the 1990s, when internet access was relatively new, subscribers were prepared to pay to access the internet through such custom portals. However, both companies failed to respond effectively to technological and market changes and the move to a more commoditized marketplace. In 2003, CompuServe became a division of AOL, and by 2009 it announced it would no longer operate as an ISP. AOL was rated as the worst tech product of all time by *PC World* magazine (Tynan, 2006).

A third source of delay is *technological myopia*, where a company fails to respond to technological change. An example is Kodak's slow response to the emergence of digital technology in cameras.

Finally, delay occurs because of *psychological recoil* by managers who see change as a threat and defend the status quo.

Retrenchment

This response tackles efficiency problems but ignores effectiveness issues. As sales and profits decline, management cuts costs; this leads to a period of higher profits but does nothing to stem declining sales. Costs (and capacity) are reduced once more, but the fundamental strategic problems remain. Retrenchment policies only delay the inevitable.

Gradual strategic repositioning

This involves a gradual, planned and continuous adaptation to the changing marketing environment. Tesco is a company that has continually repositioned itself in response to changing social and economic trends. Originally a supermarket based on a 'pile it high, sell it cheap' philosophy, Tesco maintained its low-price positioning while moving to higher-quality products. It has also expanded the range of products it sells (including CDs, electrical goods, financial services and clothing), to provide one-stop shopping, and has expanded into new market segments (Tesco Express convenience stores) and international markets including the Far East, the USA and central and eastern Europe.

Radical strategic repositioning

Radical strategic repositioning involves changing the direction of the entire business. Samsung has successfully repositioned itself, transferring from a copycat producer of consumer electronics into a technology company marketing mobile phones, flat-screen TVs and flash memory technology. This was followed by a move away from electronics into energy technology and solar panels (*The Economist*, 2011b). Such radical strategic repositioning is much riskier than gradual strategic repositioning and could have dramatic consequences should such a venture fail.

Review

1 The nature of the marketing environment

- The marketing environment consists of the microenvironment (customers, competitors, distributors and suppliers) and the macroenvironment (economic, social, political, legal, physical and technological forces). These shape the character of the opportunities and threats facing a company and yet are largely uncontrollable.

2 The distinction between the microenvironment and the macroenvironment

- As can be seen above, the microenvironment consists of those actors in the firm's immediate environment that affect its capabilities to operate effectively in its chosen markets.
- The macroenvironment consists of a number of broader forces that affect not only the company but also the other actors in the microenvironment.

3 The impact of political and legal, economic, ecological/physical environmental, social/cultural and technological forces on marketing decisions

- Technological forces can have an impact on marketing decisions by changing the rules of the competitive game. Technological change can provide major opportunities and pose enormous threats to companies. Marketers need to monitor technological trends and pioneer technological breakthroughs.
- Economic forces can have an impact on marketing decisions through their effect on supply and demand. Key factors are economic growth, unemployment, interest and exchange rates and changes in the global economic environment such as growth of the EU and the Eurozone and the rise of the economies of Brazil, Russia, India and China. Marketers need to have contingency plans in place to cope with economic turbulence and downturns, and to be aware of the opportunities and threats arising from changes in the global marketing environment.
- Political and legal forces influence marketing decisions by determining the rules for conducting business. In Europe, marketing decisions are affected by legislation at EU and national levels. EU laws seek to prevent collusion, prevent abuse of market dominance, control mergers and acquisitions, and restrict state aid to firms. National laws also affect marketing decisions by regulating anti-competitive practices.
- The physical environmental forces are concerned with the environmental costs of consumption. Five issues that affect marketing decisions are: combating global warming, pollution control, conservation of energy and other scarce resources, use of environmentally friendly ingredients and components, and the use of recyclable and non-wasteful packaging. Marketers need to be aware of the environmental consequences of their actions and aware of the opportunities and threats associated with ecological issues.
- Social/cultural forces can have an impact on marketing decisions by changing demand patterns (e.g. the growth of the over-50s market) and creating new opportunities and threats. Three major influences are changes in the demographic profile of the population, cultural differences within and between nations, and the impact of consumerism.

4 The microenvironment

- The microenvironment consists of the actors that shape how firms interact with and respond to macro forces. The actors are customers, competitors, suppliers and distributors, and strategic partners.

5 How to conduct environmental scanning

- Two key decisions are what to scan and how to organize the activity.
- Four approaches to the organization of environmental scanning are to use line management, the strategic planner, a separate organizational unit and joint line/general management teams.
- The system should monitor trends, develop forecasts, interpret and analyse internally produced information, establish a database, provide environmental experts, disseminate information, and evaluate and revise the system.

6 How companies respond to environmental change

- Response comes in five forms: ignorance, delay, retrenchment, gradual strategic repositioning and radical strategic repositioning.

Key Terms

consumerism organized action against business practices that are not in the interests of consumers

consumer movement an organized collection of groups with the objective of protecting consumer rights

corporate social responsibility the ethical principle that an organization should be accountable for how its behaviour might affect society and the environment

culture the combination of traditions, taboos, values and attitudes of the society in which an individual lives

demography changes in the population in terms of its size and characteristics

environmentalism the organized movement of groups and organizations to protect and improve the physical environment; their concerns are production and consumption of products that lead to global warming, pollution, the destruction of natural resources such as oil and forests, and non-biodegradable waste

environmental scanning the process of monitoring and analysing the marketing environment of a company

ethical consumption when individual consumers, when making purchase decisions, consider not only personal interests but also the interests of society and the environment

fair-trade marketing a movement that aims to help producers in developing countries to produce goods ethically and enhance the well-being and wealth of the workers in these countries; the movement also promotes sustainability

macroenvironment a number of broader forces that affect not only the company but also the other actors in the microenvironment

marketing environment the actors and forces that affect a company's capability to operate effectively in providing products and services to its customers

microenvironment the actors in the firm's marketing environment: customers, suppliers, distributors and competitors

PEEST analysis the analysis of the political/legal, economic, ecological/physical, social/cultural and technological environments

physical environment the planet and places in which we live. From a marketing perspective, it is important, as the environmental impacts of commerce are affecting how we might live our lives in the future, and this has consequences for marketing activities

Study Questions

1. **Describe the marketing environment and explain how it can inform marketing strategy and planning.**
2. **Choose an organization and identify the major forces in the environment that are likely to affect its prospects in the next three to five years.**
3. **Discuss how technology is changing the marketing landscape.**
4. **Which aspects of the technology force should a manufacturer of consumer goods consider? And why?**
5. **Discuss the importance of emerging economies to luxury car manufacturers.**
6. **Imagine you are a marketing manager of a new web based company. Discuss how you should respond to GDPR legislation.**
7. **What are the major ecological/physical environmental forces acting on marketing? What are their implications for marketing management?**
8. **Discuss the implications of a rising global population from a marketing perspective.**
9. **Explain why it is important for marketers to understand national demographic profiles and how they might use this information.**
10. **Actors in the microenvironment take on different roles. Discuss the relationships between each of the categories of actors.**

Recommended Reading

Marketing is changing and the environment is reshaping marketing practices. Read about the revolutionary changes taking place, the importance of sustainability and how disrupting marketing is creating opportunities for building global brands.

Webster, F.E. and R.F. Lusch (2012) Elevating marketing. Marketing is dead! Long live marketing! *Journal of the Academy of Marketing Science*, 41, 389–99.

Jakki J. Mohr, Linda L. Price, Aric Rindfleisch (2016) *Marketing's Quest for Environmental Sustainability: Persistent Challenges and New Perspectives*, 13, Editor: Naresh K. Malhotra ISBN: 978-1-78635-282-8 eISBN: 978-1-78635-281-1

References

Ansoff, H.I. (1991) *Implementing Strategic Management*, Englewood Cliffs, NJ: Prentice-Hall.

Bain Insights (2018) Enter the Insurgent Brands, *Forbes*, 12 July. https://www.forbes.com/sites/baininsights/2018/07/12/enter-the-insurgent-brands/#7d5bf74833f4 (accessed 8 July 2018)

BEIS (2017) The Clean Growth Strategy, Leading the way to a low carbon future, https://unfccc.int/sites/default/files/resource/clean-growth-strategy-amended-april-2018.pdf (accessed 8 July 2018)

Bloomberg, J. (2018) Dell technologies struggles to connect It infrastructure to digital transformation, *Forbes*, 6 May. https://www.forbes.com/sites/jasonbloomberg/2018/05/06/dell-technologies-struggles-to-connect-it-infrastructure-to-digital-transformation/#5d3b5d7642e3 (accessed 8 July 2018)

Bogod, D.and Sukharevsky, A. (2017) A new reality for the Russian consumer industry,McKinsey & Company. https://www.mckinsey.com/industries/consumer-packaged-goods/our-insights/a-new-reality-for-the-russian-consumer-industry (accessed 8 July 2018)

Brown, P. (1992) Rise of Women Key to Population Curb, *The Guardian*, 30 April.

Brownlie, D. (2002) Environmental Analysis, in Baker, M.J. (ed.) *The Marketing Book*, Oxford: Butterworth-Heinemann.

Burgess, M. (2018) What is GDPR? The summary guide to GDPR compliance in the UK, *Wired*, 4 October. https://www.wired.co.uk/article/what-is-gdpr-uk-eu-legislation-compliance-summary-fines-2018 (accessed 8 July 2018)

Chaffey, D. and Ellis-Chadwick, F.E. (2012) *Digital Marketing: Strategy, Implementation and Practice*, 5th edn, Harlow: Pearson.

Consumer International (2015) WCRD 2015 to focus on consumers' rights to healthy food, 1 December. https://www.consumersinternational.org/news-resources/news/releases/wcrd-2015-thunderous-support-for-healthy-diets/ (accessed 22 February 2015).

Consumer International (2018) World Rights Day https://www.consumersinternational.org/what-we-do/world-consumer-rights-day/2018-making-digital-marketplaces-fairer/ (accessed December 2018)

Crane, A. and Matten D. (2004) *Business Ethics: A European Perspective*, Oxford: Oxford University Press.

Dieffenbach, J. (1983) Corporate Environmental Analysis in Large US Corporations, *Long-Range Planning* 16 (3), 107–16.

Dobbs, R., Remes, J., Smit, S., Manyika, J., Woetzel, J. and Agyenim-Boateng, Y. (2013) Urban World: The shifting landscape of global business, McKinsey & Company. https://www.mckinsey.com/featured-insights/urbanization/urban-world-cities-and-the-rise-of-the-consuming-class (accessed 8 July 2018)

Doherty, N.F. and Doig, G. (2011) The role of enhanced information accessibility in realizing the benefits from data warehousing investments, *Journal of Organisational Transformation and Social Change* 8(2), 163–82.

DutchAwearness (2015) Dutch Awareness and Sustainability. http://dutchawearness.com (accessed 20 February 2015).

Eur-lex (2018) REGULATION (EU) 2016/679 OF THE EUROPEAN PARLIAMENT AND OF THE COUNCIL of 27 April 2016, https://eur-lex.europa.eu/legal-content/EN/TXT/?uri=uriserv:OJ.L_.2016.119.01.0001.01.ENG&toc=OJ:L:2016:119:TOC (accessed 8 July 2018)

Eurostat (2014) Population structure and ageing, Eurostat, May. http://ec.europa.eu/eurostat/statistics-explained/index.php/Population_structure_and_ageing (accessed 12 February 2015).

Eurostat (2018) Services, European Semester Thematic Factsheet, European Commission. https://ec.europa.eu/info/sites/info/files/european-semester_thematic-factsheet_services_en.pdf (accessed 8 July 2018)

Fleming, M. (2018) EasyJet's new CMO on using data to 'supercharge creative judgement', *Marketing Week*, 18 October. https://www.marketingweek.com/2018/10/18/easyjet-cmo-data-supercharge

Goldstein, M. (2018) Is there trouble in Paradise for the Airbus 380? *Forbes*, 16 October. https://www.forbes.com/sites/michaelgoldstein/2018/10/16/is-there-trouble-in-paradise-for-the-airbus-a380/#2033440872b7 (accessed 8 July 2018)

Gottig, M. (2017) LG to open Eurrope's biggest car battery factory next year, *Reuters*, 12 October. https://www.reuters.com/article/us-lgchem-factory-poland/lg-to-open-europes-biggest-car-battery-factory-next-year-idUSKBN1CH21W (accessed 8 July 2018)

Gov.UK (2018) Data Protection Act 2018, 23 May. https://www.gov.uk/government/collections/data-protection-act-2018 (accessed 8 July 2018)

Grant, K. (2018) Starbucks told to wake up and smell the coffee by environmentalists after announcing plan to create world's first 100% recyclable cup, *iNews*, 26 March. https://inews.co.uk/news/starbucks-to-create-worlds-first-totally-recyclable-compostable-takeaway-coffee-cup (accessed 8 July 2018)

Greenpeace (2012) The Trash Vortex. http://www.greenpeace.org/international/en/campaigns/oceans/pollution/trash-vortex (accessed January 2012).

Greenpeace (2014) *Save the Artic*, Greenpeace, 14 March. http://www.greenpeace.org.uk/climate/arctic (accessed May 2015).

Guoa, H., Xu, H., Tang, C., Liu-Thompkins, Y. and Guo Z Dong, B. (2018) Comparing the impact of different marketing capabilities: Empirical evidence from B2B firms in China, *Journal of Business Research* 93(12), 79–89.

Hancock, T. (2018) Increasingly wealthy Chinese go upmarket in consumer spending, *The Financial Times*, 29 May. https://www.ft.com/content/68eb6bb8-4256-11e8-97ce-ea0c2bf34a0b (accessed 8 July 2018)

ICO (2018) Individual rights. https://ico.org.uk/for-organisations/guide-to-the-general-data-protection-regulation-gdpr/individual-rights (accessed 8 July 2018)

IKEA (2012) IKEA Group Sustainability Summary FY12. http://www.ikea.com/ms/en_US/pdf/sustainability_report/sustainability_summary_2012.pdf (accessed 22 February 2015).

Kassam, A. (2015) Inditex bans angora sales worldwide after animal welfare protests, *The Guardian*, 8 January. http://www.theguardian.com/business/2015/feb/09/inditex-bans-angora-sales-animal-rights-protests (accessed 20 February 2015).

Klein, N. (2000) *No Logo*, New York: Picador.

Kucuk, S. (2008) Negative Double Jeopardy: The role of anti-brand sites on the internet, *Journal of Brand Management* 3(15), 209–22.

Lagerberg, R. (2018) Sweden—where children count. https://sweden.se/society/sweden-where-children-count (accessed 8 July 2018)

Lucas, L. (2014) Retailers target grey spending power, *The Financial Times*, 14 August. http://www.ft.com/cms/s/0/bb60a5b2-e608-11e1-a430-00144feab49a.html#axzz3SUDkZ6rd (accessed 12 February 2015).

Lyengar, R. (2018) Global slowdown? India's economy is accelerating, *CNN Business*, 31 August. https://money.cnn.com/2018/08/31/news/economy/india-economic-growth/index.html (accessed 8 July 2018)

Macalister, T. (2006) BP to Make Biggest Profit in UK History, *The Guardian*, 12 January, 26.

Mercado, S., Welford, R. and Prescott, K. (2001) *European Business: An Issue-Based Approach*, Harlow: FT Pearson.

Milmo, D. (2008) British Airways executives charged over price-fixing scandal, *The Guardian*, 7 August, 26.

Muller, R. (2011) Target: China, *The Marketer*, 32–4.

Nairn, A. (2011) Children's Well-being in UK, Sweden and Spain, Ipsos MORI Social Research Institute. https://www.unicef.org.uk/Documents/Publications/IPSOS_UNICEF_ChildWellBeingreport.pdf (accessed 20 February 2015).

Nilsson, D. (2014) *New proposal on the supervision of online retail of alcohol in Sweden*, Bird & Bird, 17 January. http://www.twobirds.com/en/news/articles/2014/global/food-law/sweden-online-retail-of-alcohol (accessed 26 February 2015).

Nuccitelli, D. (2017) Trump cemented his legacy as America's worst-ever president, *The Guardian*, 1 June.https://www.theguardian.com/environment/climate-consensus-97-per-cent/2017/jun/01/donald-trump-just-cemented-his-legacy-as-americas-worst-ever-president (accessed 8 July 2018)

Pearson, A. (2017) 'Gender neutral' children's clothing? John Lewis needs to quit getting down with the kids, *The Telegraph*, 6 September. https://www.telegraph.co.uk/women/life/gender-neutral-childrens-clothing-john-lewis-needs-quit-getting (accessed 8 July 2018)

Petridis, A. (2014) Youth subcultures: what are they now? *The Guardian*, 20 March. http://www.theguardian.com/culture/2014/mar/20/youth-subcultures-where-have-they-gone (accessed 20 February 2015).

Poon, L. (2018) Sleepy in Songdo, Korea's smartest city, *City Lab*, 22 June. https://www.citylab.com/life/2018/06/sleepy-in-songdo-koreas-smartest-city/561374 (accessed 8 July 2018)

Rapoza, K. (2018) This is where Brazil's economy is a failure, *Forbes*, 7 September. https://www.forbes.com/sites/kenrapoza/2018/09/07/this-is-where-brazils-economy-is-a-failure/#6acb9d8d17a7 (accessed 8 July 2018)

Schillinger, R. (2011) Social Media and the Arab Spring: What Have We Learned? *Huff Post: The Blog*, 20 September. http://www.huffingtonpost.com/raymond-schillinger/arab-spring-social-media_b_970165.html (accessed 8 July 2018)

Sharman, A. (2014) Top truckmakers operated cartel for 14 years, says EU, *The Financial Times*, 23 December. http://www.ft.com/cms/s/0/da53eb98-8073-11e4-872b-00144feabdc0.html#axzz3SUDkZ6rd (accessed 22 February 2015).

Smart Insights (2018) Implications of the GDPR for marketing in UK and Europe. https://www.smartinsights.com/tag/gdpr (accessed 8 July 2018)

Stanley, T. and Ritacca, R. (2014) E-commerce in China, *China 360*, January. http://www.kpmg.com/CN/en/IssuesAndInsights/ArticlesPublications/Newsletters/China-360/Documents/China-360-Issue15-201401-E-commerce-in-China.pdf (accessed 24 January 2015).

Statoil (2015) Statoil awarded licences offshore Nicaragua, Statoil.com, 29 May. http://www.statoil.com/en/newsandmedia/news/pages/default.aspx (accessed May 2015).

Straver, W. (1978) Consumerism in Europe: challenges and opportunities for marketing strategy, *European Journal of Marketing* 12(4), 316–25.

Team Trefis (2016) R&D: One of the driving factors behind 3M's Growth, *Forbes*, 20 December. https://www.forbes.com/sites/greatspeculations/2016/12/20/rd-one-of-the-driving-factors-behind-3ms-growth/#6aad6e2f6d6c (accessed 8 July 2018)

Tetlow , G. and Stojanovic, A. (2018) *Understanding the economic impact of Brexit*, London: Institute for Government, 19 October. https://www.instituteforgovernment.org.uk/publications/understanding-economic-impact-brexit (accessed 8 July 2018)

The Economist (2011a) Send for the supermarkets, 16 April, 69–70.

The Economist (2011b) The next big bet, 1 October, 73–5.

The Economist (2012) France goes soft-core, 14 January, http://www.economist.com/blogs/freeexchange/2012/01/euro-zone-crisis (accessed January 2012).

The Economist (2014) Population explosion, 16 August.

The Economist (2017) Online retail is booming in China, 26 October. https://www.economist.com/special-report/2017/10/26/online-retail-is-booming-in-china (accessed 8 July 2018)

The Swedish Wire (2011) Consumerism absent among Swedish children, 14 September. http://www.swedishwire.com/politics/11236-consumerism-absent-among-swedish-children (accessed 23 February).

The World Factbook (2018) Russia. https://www.cia.gov/library/publications/the-world-factbook/geos/rs.html (accessed January 2012).

Thoppil, D. A. (2018) Vodafone plans to infuse $1.3 billion into India operations ahead of merger with Idea, 12 June. https://asia.nikkei.com/Business/Companies/Vodafone-plans-to-infuse-1.3-billion-into-India-operations-ahead-of-merger-with-Idea2 (accessed 8 July 2018)

Tynan, D. (2006) The worst tech products of all time, *PCWorld*, 26 May.

UNFCCC (2012) Background on the UNFCCC. http://unfccc.int/essential_background/items/6031.php (accessed 8 July 2018)

UNICEF (2015) Respecting and supporting children's rights in marketing and advertising—webinar, *The Guardian*.

Wall Street Journal (2012) IMF: Without Action, Debt Crisis May Force 4% Euro-Area Contraction, 12 January. http://online.wsj. com/article/BT-CO-20120124-709079.html (accessed 8 July 2018)

World Bank Group (2018) Global Economic Prospects: The turning of the Tide?A World Bank Group Flagship Report. https://openknowledge.worldbank.org/bitstream/handle/10986/29801/9781464812576.pdf (accessed 8 July 2018)

CASE 3
Marketing a 'Place' in a Rapidly Changing Environment

Retail high streets play a crucial role in the economic and social health of towns and cities worldwide. Over the past decade, an increase in online shopping, out-of-town 'one stop' retail developments and the rise of a convenience culture has meant that many traditional retailers have closed tens of thousands of stores across the globe, with resulting high levels of shop vacancies in town centres. Town centres are part of our history and heritage and, for many, connect closely to our sense of personal identity.

Despite the gloomy outlook, there is recent evidence to suggest that some town centre managers are successfully fighting back, embracing the seismic developments in digital technology and collaborating with key stakeholders to co-create value and re-establish successful, vibrant communities. At the heart of many of these success stories lies a strong strategic plan. Such strategic plans take account of the myriad macro- and microenvironmental challenges facing the sector and strive to reinforce a distinctive positioning for the town. In this case study, we describe the plan developed by managers in one particular town in Flanders (Belgium).

Roeselare

Roeselare is a small town in the heart of West Flanders. It has a population of 62,000 and has a reputation for high-quality food production, manufacturing and retail.

Several well-known retail brands have stores in town, including Zara, H&M and Jack Jones. The town has its own brewery, producing and retailing the Rodenbach brand. A number of big-brand food manufacturers are located close to the town, including Soubry (spaghetti) and Poco loco (tortilla chips).

The population of Roeselare has been growing at a annual rate of 8.6 per cent since 2008, making it one of the fastest growing cities in West Flanders. Almost 8,500 out of 26,500 households contain single residents. The population itself is relatively young, with 18 per cent under the age of 18. The town's unemployment rate sits at around 7.6 per cent compared with 6.7 per cent in Flanders and 6 per cent in West Flanders. The economy is growing at a rate of 2.7 per cent. Roeselare has a central shopping area with more than 550 shops and bars. The Oostraat, the main shopping street, has a reputation for being the fourth best shopping street in Flanders. Around 59 per cent of the stores of the Oostraat—75 per cent of the shopping floor area—are devoted to fashion clothing and footwear outlets. Saturday is the busiest shopping day for Roeselare, followed by Tuesday, when there is a weekly market in the square. Of the citizens of Roeselare, 97 per cent buy their daily goods in the town itself. The shop vacancy rate lies at 8.3 per cent.

The Plan

In 2014, faced with the prospect of declining footfall and store closures, the head of the Department of Economic Development and the town centre manager began to look externally for ideas to revitalise the town. Inspiration came in the form of a presentation of the Grimsey Review at a meeting for civil servants in Ostend. The Mayor and his team took the recommendations in the review, tailored them to the Roeselare context, and set about developing a strategic plan to transform the town.

The team designed a plan to ensure that Roeselare would maintain and develop its position as the leading 'smart' food shopping city in Flanders. The plan consisted of seven core ambitions and 50 specific actions designed to contribute to the revenue growth of the town's traders and ensure a sustainable future for the city centre of Roeselare. The core ambitions and key actions are outlined in Table C3.1.

»

»

TABLE C3.1 The Roeselare city centre plan

Ambition	Corresponding activities
1. Create and maintain an inviting public domain	• Transforming all public libraries into ARhus, a knowledge centre in the centre of the town. It remains a meeting place for the community but is also a centre for knowledge exchange, providing resources and training for citizens and companies to enhance and develop their IT knowledge skills and capabilities. It offers access to health services for citizens, for example with training on how to do blood pressure tests and use 3D glasses. • Developing and enhancing the town squares and public spaces. The town's squares (Marketplace, Polenplein, Botermarkt and Coninckplein) have always been a key feature of Roeselare. Since 2015, they have been renewed and upgraded. The designers have focused on reducing visible parking areas, introducing more green space and providing uniform terraces and additional seating for visitors. Two streets have also been upgraded. One of these, Lemon Street, illustrates how clever design has been used to create a distinctive identity for this area of the town.  • Creating an aesthetically pleasing, clean and healthy environment. A series of measures appeared in the plan to ensure basic cleanliness of the central shopping area. These include upgrading public toilets with clear digital signage for improved access. Traders also receive fines for neglected window displays and excessive use of vacant use display notices. The local government has the authority to fine citizens up to €300 for antisocial behaviours such as dropping litter.
2. Provide active support for traders	• Introducing the B (L)OOMS programme. This is a series of tax exemptions and financial support designed to stimulate trade within the town. The aim is to encourage traders to get maximum use from town centre space. Retailers receive funding for merging commercial buildings or for opening a new retail outlet in the centre, and there is support for retailers who move their business into town or start a second business in town. A more recent initiative has been added to encourage residential development above shop space. All funds are provided by the Flemish government.
3. Smarter shopping	• Introduction of free Wi-Fi in the city centre. • Appointment of a city innovation manager. • The development of a Citie app that gives access to information about parking and shop opening hours, and a loyalty scheme with rewards linked to shopping and leisure facilities. • The introduction of digital innovations to improve the in-store shopping experience. These include a touch-and-go hands-free shopping app allowing customers to shape their shopping experience through their smartphone and interactive dressing rooms.
4. Creating a city of experience	• Building on the town's heritage, the traditional cycling museum Koers has been transformed into an interactive themed destination with a new bar and restaurant. The museum also offers an educational programme for children, teaching them how to cycle well and safely. The new museum also hosts the tourist information office.  • Every Friday the local church, under council control, hosts a covered farmer's market with a bar and children's workshop. The Lokaal brings together local producers who showcase their fresh and locally crafted products. The farmers pay a small fee to cover staffing, IT and marketing costs to sell fresh meat, fish, vegetables and fruit straight from the farm.

Ambition	Corresponding activities
	The onsite children's workshop educates the community about food health and nutrition and sustainable consumption behaviours. The Lokaal food market also organises events (e.g. BBQs, music) and offers picnic baskets for use outside the church on the new car-free square. • A coordinated series of events. Themed events capitalizing on national celebration are particularly popular, as are those that require residents to physically visit the centre to participate. • Actions to enhance the ambiance and atmosphere. A central music system has been set up in the ARhus, with eight speakers located in the central market to allow a centrally controlled and coordinated music schedule. Sustainable lights were also installed in the central shopping area.
5. Make the town accessible for all	• Streets have been widened to make the town more accessible for the less mobile, disabled or visibly impaired citizens and parents with children. • Several locations were made child- and youth-friendly with the introduction of play and sports facilities. • Parking: digital signage was introduced to show parking availability and included in the Citie app. A live roadworks scoreboard also alerts shoppers to potential delays. A more recent innovation has been shop and go, a 30-minute sensor facilitating short-term parking in the city centre. This has proved to be particularly popular with residents.
6. Ensure collaboration between stakeholders	• Providing support for networking events for traders. • Joining Bizlocator, a matchmaking business service which draws attention to new business opportunities and vacant space.
7. Coordinated promotion activity	• Publishing and communicating a city promotional plan. • Providing a central calendar that outlines all major initiatives and events a year in advance.

The plan has been implemented over a relatively short period, and success is being measured against a clear set of key performance indicators. The results to date suggest an optimistic future for the town and its citizens. There appear to have been small improvements in footfall, shop vacancy rates and patterns of use, as well as increased use of key community facilities such as ARhus and the Lokaal. As the head of economic development states 'We have been able to make many changes here in Flanders due to the power, authority and passion of our mayor. He can decide how many of one type of shop we can accommodate. We also get financial support from the government for different incentive schemes. However, we cannot be complacent; we have to be able to respond very rapidly to changes in our marketing environment. We really don't know if we have responded quickly enough. . . .'

Questions

1. **What are the key challenges in the macro- and micromarketing environment that have led to the decline of town centres around the world?**
2. **How might the influence of these factors differ for town centres in different parts of the world?**
3. **How effective do you think the town management team in Roselare have been in developing their plan in response to environmental changes?**
4. **What do you think they could do differently to future proof the town even further?**

This case study was written by: Kim Cassidy, Professor of Services Marketing, Edgehill University; Vanessa Delhullu, team leader, Economic department, Roeselare Government; Bill Grimsey, retailer and consultant; Sheilagh Resnick, Senior Lecturer, Nottingham Trent University.

References

Based on: Grimsey, B., Shellard, C., Pascoe, E., Baker, M., Vasili, S., Hopkinson, M. and Hood, N. (2013) *The Grimsey Review: An Alternative Future for the High Street*, https://cdn.britishbids.info/publications/GrimseyReview04.092_reduce-1.pdf?mtime=20180406160825; The Great British High Street (2018) Awards 2018, https://thegreatbritishhighstreet.co.uk; Rushcliffe Borough Council (2017) *West Bridgeford Commissioners' Report*, http://www.rushcliffe.gov.uk/media/1rushcliffe/media/documents/pdf/businessandlicensing/business/RBC_WB_Commissioners_Report_WEB_2.pdf; Stocchia, L., Hart, C. and Hajic, I. (2016) Understanding the town centre customer experience (TCCE), *Journal of Marketing Management* 32(17–18), 1562–87; Parker, C., Roper, S. and Meday, D. (2015) Back to basics in the marketing of place: the impact of litter upon place attitudes, *Journal of Marketing Management* 31(9–10), 1090–112.

»

CASE 4

Reaching 'Sinks, Dinks and Millennials' Worldwide

SodaStream International, a company that distributes seltzer-making units and syrups in 45 countries via 60,000 different retail locations, has a long tradition and rich history. The company's origins go back to 1903, when it was one of the first providers of a system that allowed people to make carbonated water (otherwise known as 'sparkling water') at home. Founded by W&A Gilbey, the famous London Gin distiller, its first soda-making apparatus was very popular with the British upper class. Even the royal family were equipped with a seltzer-making unit in the early 20th century. The company, constantly improving and updating its technology, now sells systems that allow people to add flavouring and produce their own soda from regular tap water, whenever they want to. SodaStream claims that its machines are cost effective, allowing people to make sparkling water for only $0.20 per litre and traditional flavoured sodas for about $0.57 per litre. A reported 1 per cent of homes in the USA have a SodaStream machine, with the proportion being an astounding one in four in Sweden. World consumption of soft drinks in 2017 was 17 billion litres, making it the fastest growing market segment, being responsible for 37 per cent of all commercial beverages sold.

SodaStream has made it clear that it plans to revamp the way it markets its products, focusing less on the making of flavoured soda and putting more emphasis on just sparkling water. The drinks brand started its transition from soft drinks to fizzy water back in 2014 in response to changing habits as consumers started to cut sugar from their diets and in expectation of restrictive legislative measures against high-sugar-content products. Events would prove the company right. In the UK, a 'sugar tax' introduced in the spring of 2018 has prompted all major manufacturers, including Coca-Cola, to reformulate their products below the tax-applicable threshold of 5 grams per 100 millilitres of beverage. From a marketing communications standpoint, SodaStream changed its slogan from 'set the bubbles free' to 'water made exciting' in 2014 to reflect the above new strategic focus, to reposition itself in the carbonated drinks market and promote its brand as the healthier option. The boxes that the machines come in now carry the slogan of 'sparkling water maker' instead of 'home soda maker'. Daniel Birnbaum, a chief executive at SodaStream, claims that users of his company's systems were only using flavouring syrups to make soda 30 per cent of the time, and the rest of the time the machines were used to just make sparkling water. These results would corroborate those of a study carried out by market research firm Canadean, which found that the sparkling water market is expected to see annual growth of 3 per cent through 2020. In mid 2017, SodaStream put at the heart of its marketing efforts the concept of 'make a difference to the world', taking on the giants of the soft drinks space with an aggressive move to cut sales of bottled water. The company has put forth the following provocative stance: 'If you're lazy, selfish and not mindful about how you contribute to the planet, keep on buying those bottles. If you want to be a leader and a change agent, you should embrace SodaStream.' In 2016, SodaStream aired a successful (and humorous) commercial in which the actress Mayim Bialik (known internationally from the US TV series *The Big Bang Theory*) plays an anthropologist in the year 2136 recalling an encounter with a near-extinct species, 'Homoschlepiens'. The Homoschlepiens—among them actor Kristian Nairn (who plays Hodor in the TV series *Game of Thrones*)—are defined by the fact that they only drink water that comes from plastic bottles. In the ad, Bialik narrates the story of Homoschlepiens to a group of school kids who have never known plastic bottles and are shocked at the 'unnatural' behaviour of Homoschlepiens. At the end of the ad, Bialik, of course, touts the benefits of SodaStream seltzer-making machines to make sparkling water at home (with no plastic bottles needed).

The goal, as announced by Laura Wilson, the brand's regional marketing officer for the Australian market, is to reach out to new demographics including the 'sinks and dinks' (single income/double income–no kids) category, as well as millennials. It's also about communicating the message of sustainability, health and wellness. 'We traditionally used to target the families market but realised through our sales data that increasingly the sinks and dinks and millennial audiences were more engaged with our brand and they were where the future is. So our social media strategy has turned to focus our content towards that audience,' she said.

Apart from marketing and strategic challenges, the company also faced political issues related to the ongoing Israeli–Palestinian conflict. The company (based in Israel) and its spokesperson at the time, Scarlett Johansson, were the targets of boycotts due to the closing of a SodaStream factory in 2015 that was situated in the Mishor Adumim industrial zone of the Ma'aleh Adumim settlement in the West Bank. In 2015, SodaStream moved its operations to Idan Hanegev in southern Israel. The company, although vocal about being a responsible and model corporate organization, could not prevent laying off about 500 Palestinians who used to work at the West Bank plant. The company's CEO, Daniel Birnbaum, claimed in 2014 that he would secure Israeli work permits for his Palestinian employees. In May 2017, his determination paid off, as 74 of SodaStream's Palestinian employees were able to join their 1,500 colleagues in the new plant in the Negev area. Birnbaum thanked the Israeli government as it 'did the moral and honorable thing to grant work permits to our employees, who can now provide for their families and also prove that coexistence is possible'. Shortly after, the brand decided to voluntarily add the Israeli flag to its packaging, along with the words 'Made in Israel', despite the risk of backlash from the Boycott, Divestment, Sanctions (BDS) movement. If you take the time to fully read the packaging, just below 'Made in Israel' it says, 'This product is produced by Arabs and Jews working side-by-side in peace and harmony.'

Despite the ever-present political challenges facing SodaStream, luckily it has one element clearly in its favour: consumer psychology. The company's home systems sell for anywhere from roughly \$80 to \$200, and for many people who buy one, this registers mentally as a type of investment rather than a simple purchase. Customers have incurred a sunk cost and as a result have a 'psychological incentive' to use the machine as many times as possible in order to recoup the purchase cost through the savings they receive by making soda more cheaply at home. Hopefully for SodaStream, people trying to save money is a trend that will never go out of style.

Questions

1. **Do a SWOT analysis for SodaStream.**
2. **What marketing challenges face SodaStream?**
3. **Apart from marketing, what other challenges is the company facing?**
4. **What strategic action is SodaStream taking in reaction to its current challenges? Do you think the company will be successful? Justify your answer.**

This case study was written by Tom McNamara and Irena Descubes, Rennes School of Business.

References

Based on: Jacobsen, J. (2015) 2015 New Product Development Outlook Survey-takers report using nearly 12 flavors in 2014, *Beverage Industry*, January 12, 2015, http://www.bevindustry.com/articles/88120-new-product-development-outlook; IBIS (2014) Global Soft Drink & Bottled Water Manufacturing Market Research Report, *IBIS World Market Research*, September 2014, http://www.ibisworld.com/industry/global/global-soft-drink-bottled-water-manufacturing.html; Cardenal, A. (2015) Is SodaStream a Top Turnaround Candidate in 2015? *The Motley Fool*, 15 January 2015, http://www.fool.com/investing/general/2015/01/15/is-sodastream-a-top-turnaround-candidate-in-2015.aspx; Rudorenoct, J. (2014) Israeli Firm, Target of Boycott, to Shut West Bank Plant, *NY Times*, 30 October, 2014, http://www.nytimes.com/2014/10/31/world/middleeast/sodastream-to-close-factory-in-west-bank.html?_r=1; IBIS (2014) Soda Production in the US: Market Research Report, Soda Production Market Research Report, NAICS 31211a, November 2014, http://www.ibisworld.com/industry/default.aspx?indid=285; AFP (2014) Sodastream Is Closing Its Controversial West Bank Plant That Caused Its Ambassador Scarlett Johansson To Quit Her Role At Oxfam, AFP, through *Business Insider*, 30 October, 2014, http://www.businessinsider.com/afp-sodastream-to-close-controversial-west-bank-plant-2014-10#ixzz3P77YIoXy; Stanford, D. D. (2012) SodaStream Takes Marketing Tactic to Coca-Cola's Hometown, *Bloomberg*, 20 June, 2012, http://www.bloomberg.com/news/2012-06-20/sodastream-takes-marketing-tactic-to-coca-cola-s-hometown.html; Esterl, M. (2014) SodaStream to Close West Bank Factory By Mid-2015, *The Wall Street Journal*, 29 October 2014, http://www.wsj.com/articles/sodastream-to-close-controversial-west-bank-factory-by-mid-2015-1414599238; Statista (2015) Soft drink sales worldwide in 2012 and 2017, by region (in million litres), *Statista*, http://www.statista.com/statistics/232794/global-soft-drink-sales-by-region; Stock, K. (2013) The Secret of SodaStream's Success, *Bloomberg Businessweek*, 31 July 2013, http://www.businessweek.com/articles/2013-07-31/the-secret-of-sodastreams-success; O'Brien,

»

»

J. (2018) SodaStream reveals why 'disruptive' influencer campaigns are vital to reaching new audiences, *CMO*, 9 February, https://www.cmo.com.au/article/633195/sodastream-reveals-why-disruptive-influencer-campaigns-vital-reaching-new-audiences; Roderick, L. (2017) SodaStream CEO on why marketing is key as it aims for 'cult' brand status, *Marketing Week*, 18 July, https://www.marketingweek.com/2017/07/18/sodastream-cult-brand; Dolsten, J. (2017) Mayim Bialik time travels in this funny new SodaStream commercial, *Jewish Telegraphic Agency*, 12 July, https://www.jta.org/2017/07/12/life-religion/mayim-bialik-time-travels-in-this-funny-new-sodastream-commercial; Sredni, Y. (2017) Made In Israel: SodaStream Now Proudly Labels Its Products With The Israeli Flag, *NoCamels*, 7 February, http://nocamels.com/2017/02/made-in-israel-sodastream-flag-bds; Schmit, F. (2018) Comments on the Sugar Tax in the UK, *Euromonitor*, 26 March, https://blog.euromonitor.com/2018/03/sugar-tax-uk.html

CHAPTER 3
Consumer Behaviour

> *No matter how insignificant it may first appear, everything in life tells a story.*
>
> **MARTIN LINDSTROM (2016)**

LEARNING OBJECTIVES

After reading this chapter, you should be able to:

1 explore the changing context of consumer behaviour
2 define the dimensions of consumer buyer behaviour
3 describe the consumer decision-making process and how people buy
4 discuss the marketing implications of need recognition, information search, evaluation of alternatives, purchase and post-purchase stages
5 compare the differences in evaluation of high- versus low-involvement situations
6 describe the nature of consumer choice criteria and their implications
7 explain the influences on consumer behaviour—the buying situation, personal and social influences—and their marketing implications

Chapter 2's discussion of the macro environment identified forces beyond the control of a firm that can influence marketing decision-making. In the next two chapters we explore customers and factors that affect their behaviour and influence decision-making. In this chapter our focus is on consumer behaviour, and in Chapter 4 on organizational buyer behaviour and business-to-business marketing. This chapter is structured around three key areas important for understanding consumer behaviour and with implications for marketing: 1) *context*, 2) *dimensions and buying processes*, and 3) *influences* on consumer behaviour.

The Changing Context of Consumer Behaviour

Consumer markets are in a state of continuous change and marketers need to understand these new and emerging contexts in which they operationalize their marketing activities if they are to succeed. For example, widespread adoption of digital technologies has connected individuals in a way not conceived as possible a decade ago. An outcome is the emergence of a global consumer culture, which overlays and affects localized lifestyles, attitudes and behaviours. While details of these contexts largely go beyond the aims of this chapter it is important to be aware of the potential influence of the following:

- *Global consumer culture* is shaping **cultural values** and the extent to which consumers conform to **cultural norms** can significantly affect how individuals respond to marketing activities (Sobol, Cleveland and Laroche, 2018). Marketers are increasingly needing to understand both *local* and the *global* nuances of a market and identify aspects of these markets that may influence consumer behaviour. This means they should consider 'how individuals acquire the knowledge, skills and behaviours' that shape the culture in which they live (Cleveland and Laroche, 2007). Global consumer culture and the connection to digital technology is occurring in response to widespread exposure to global mass media, of which coverage has expanded rapidly through satellite TV and the internet and which means that, around the world, individuals can listen to the same music, watch the same TV shows and have access to the same news. They have increased exposure to global corporations' marketing efforts; many brands have adapted product names to fit with multinational understanding, e.g. the Swedish chocolate bar Dime became Daim to be recognised in wider European markets. Similarly, Marathon chocolate bars as they were known in the UK became Snickers to align globally. Jif, a UK cleaning product, was renamed Cif to enable it to become a global brand. Greater social mobility and travel facilitates exposure to different cultures (for further discussion of globalization and marketing, see Chapter 21).
- *Co-creation of value* occurs as firms seek to differentiate their offers and make them stand out. Increasingly, firms are collaborating and getting into conversation with their customers to create experiences to complement products and services. In essence, the market becomes a forum which facilitates the value creation (Prahalad and Ramaswamy, 2004). For example, Whirlpool (home appliances) Everyday Care campaign, encouraged consumers to get involved and share their stories and thoughts via Twitter. These interactions enabled Whirlpool brand managers to discover the importance of clean clothes and that it can lead to better school attendance, so they provided washers and dryers to schools (Smiley, 2016). For co-creation to succeed, a firm should offer its customers the opportunity to co-build a service experience to suit individual needs and produce value. To do this, marketing managers need to understand how customers can contribute to the value of a brand and assess the actual value of the co-creation (Merz, Zarantonello and Grappi, 2018). Co-creation of value is a fundamental element of service dominant logic and is discussed in further detail in Chapter 10.
- *Social media and consumer behaviour*. Digital and social medial advertising spend has grown year on year and now exceeds spending on traditional media, e.g. print, TV and radio (Hobbs, 2017). Web, social media and mobile channels are connecting us to marketing messages and altering how consumers engage with firms. Digital natives are the 'anytime, anywhere' and 'always-on' consumers, from communications, to purchasing and posting reviews. Smart phones are facilitating even stronger connections to social medial and digital content, with many consumers checking their phones every few minutes of the day. Keitzmann, Hermkens, McCarthy and Silverstre (2011) developed a honeycomb framework showing the building blocks of social media: sharing content, creating a presence, having conversations, developing connected relationships, joining groups, building reputations and revealing identities; each block having different implications for marketing. Individuals are developing online identities, which enable the creation of online personas and

an extension of self (Stephen, 2016). Monikh Dale graduated in fashion design in London before becoming a full-time influential fashion blogger (see https://monikh.com/) by sharing new brands and designer wear. See Marketing in Action 3.1 to find out about how a girl from Sheffield, UK extended her identity online. These issues are discussed in further detail in Chapter 16.

As the environment around us changes so does our purchasing behaviour. Consumers are eating more convenience food; more family members are working to pay household bills and more single person households mean that convenience is a high priority for many people (Costa et al., 2007). Consumers are also getting heavier—Europe has the highest number of overweight people in the world (World Health Organization, 2010)—and this influences what they buy, that is, the likelihood of buying healthy convenience food is affected by overall liking of the meal (Olsen et al., 2012), so chicken meals are favoured over salmon. Tracking and identifying changing consumer behaviours are becoming easier as technology is enabling sophisticated analysis of every aspect of consumer decision-making, i.e. research for Carlsberg Sweden, using spectacles to track exactly what consumers are looking at, found that point-of-sale materials are more important in influencing the purchase decision than previously thought (Barda, 2011). Exhibit 3.1 illustrates how Weight Watchers are applying behavioural trends.

EXHIBIT 3.1
See how Weight Watchers has focused on behavioural trends to show how fad dieting is not for everyone and to position the brand as being 'here to help'

MARKETING IN ACTION 3.1
She Wears Fashion

Kavita Donkersley always had an interest in fashion and, at the age of 16, started taking photos and blogging about her favourite fashion items. Her passion for fashion has enabled her to become a powerful fashion blogger; she has developed photographic skills, which enable her to produce images of clothing which capture the emotions of the wearer and the imagination of her followers online. Kavita aims to tell stories through her blog. Her online identity has extended to multiple social media platforms: Facebook, Twitter, YouTube, Pinterest and Instagram; and enabled her to reach large audiences. She also has attracted attention from established brands and Kavita's blog has endorsements for a variety of brands, e.g. Wonderbra, Canestan, Sorel Footwear, Swatch, Lacoste, Mercedes and many more.

The popularity of blogs like this one is that they offer personal signals, which align with the beliefs and motivations of individuals who have similar ideals. This coming together of like minds has changed how we share information. The availability of online communities and social media is very appealing to younger age groups and many brands have benefited from engaging with these consumers through fashion bloggers' sites as many of these consumers spend upwards of 2 hours a day online.

Based: on Shewearsfashion.com (2018); Stephen (2016); Baccarella, Wagner, Keitzmann and McCarthy, (2018)

The Dimensions of Consumer Behaviour

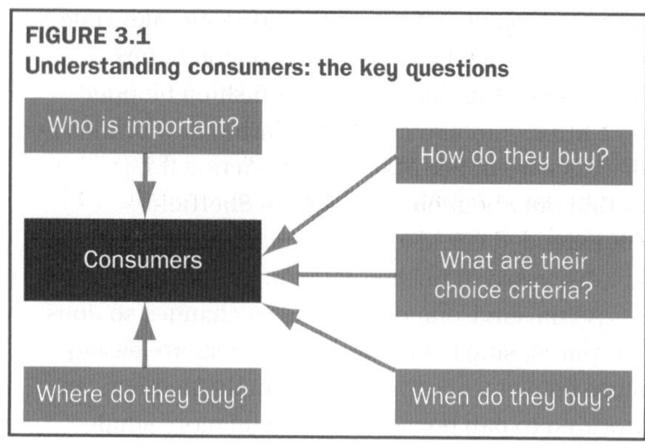

FIGURE 3.1
Understanding consumers: the key questions

In the rest of this chapter, we introduce aspects of consumer behaviour and decision-making to provide a foundation for understanding the implications for marketing. Consumer behaviour is a highly complex set of processes, and our understanding of the subject is shaped by consumer psychology and theories of human behaviour, which are extensive subject areas. At the end of the chapter, there is a selection of further recommended reading.

Consumers are individuals who buy products or services for personal consumption. Organizational buying focuses on the purchase of products and services for use in an organization's activities. The distinction is important but sometimes it is difficult to classify a product as being either a consumer or an organizational good. Cars, for example, sell to consumers for personal consumption and to organizations for use in carrying out their activities (e.g. to provide transport for a sales executive).

However, for both types of buyer, an understanding of customers can be gained by answering the following questions (see also Figure 3.1):

- *Who* is important in the buying decision?
- *How* do they buy?
- *What* are their choice criteria?
- *Where* do they buy?
- *When* do they buy?

These questions help define the key dimensions of behaviour (and are relevant to both consumer and organizational purchasers). In this chapter, we focus on the consumer perspective, and in Chapter 4 we focus on the organizational perspective. Understanding the dimensions identified by these questions is important and has implications for different levels of marketing planning. The rest of this chapter mainly focuses on the *who, how* and *what* questions as these are the more complex aspects of buyer behaviour. The more straightforward *where* and *when* questions are briefly discussed in more detail in Chapters 16 and 17.

There is an additional question to consider: *why* do they buy? For example, looking at how consumers buy through analysis of their needs recognition and problem awareness also reveals why consumers may decide on a particular purchase; discussion of choice criteria gives clues as to why one consumer may choose a Nissan Micra because of its (competitive) price, while another may choose a Mercedes S-Class for its perceived status. Exploring the influence of personality may explain why an extrovert may choose Coca-Cola, as it is a brand that seeks to please everyone, while an introvert may choose Dettol cleaning wipes, which promise 'sensitive personal care' and a more individually pleasing offer. The issue of *why* consumers buy is not treated separately as it cuts across the above questions and is integrated into the following sections.

Who buys?

Many consumer purchases are individual. When purchasing a Snickers (probably the bestselling chocolate bar in the world with sales of over $2 billion) a person may make an impulse purchase upon seeing an array of confectionery at a snack bar checkout counter. However, decision-making can also be made by a group such as a household. In such a situation, a number of individuals may interact to influence the purchase decision. Each person may assume a role in the decision-making process. Blackwell, Miniard and Engel (2005) describe five roles, as outlined below. Each may be taken by parents, children or other members of the **buying centre**.

1. *Initiator*: the person who begins the process of considering a purchase. Information may be gathered by this person to help the decision.
2. *Influencer*: the person who attempts to persuade others in the group concerning the outcome of the decision. Influencers typically gather information and attempt to impose their choice criteria on the decision.

3 *Decider*: the individual with the power and/or financial authority to make the ultimate choice regarding which product to buy.
4 *Buyer*: the person who conducts the transaction. The buyer calls the supplier, visits the store, makes the payment and effects delivery.
5 *User*: the actual consumer/user of the product.

One person may assume multiple roles in the buying group. In a smart TV purchase, for example, a teenage boy may be the *initiator* and attempt to *influence* his parents, who are the *deciders*. The boy may be *influenced* by his elder brother to buy a different brand to the one he initially preferred. The *buyer* may be one of the parents, who visits the store to purchase the smart TV and brings it back to the home. Finally, all the family maybe *users* of the TV. Although the purchase was initiated by one person, in this example, marketers have four differing viewpoints—both parents, the teenager and his older sibling—to affect the outcome of the purchase decision. The respective roles in a buying group may change during the purchasing process. The internet is also having an influence on consumer behaviour. Read Marketing in Action 3.2 to find out the influence of groups on the decision to purchase.

An implication of understanding who buys is that identification of the roles played within the buying centre is a prerequisite for targeting persuasive communications. As the previous discussion has demonstrated, the person who consumes the product may not be the most influential member of the buying centre, nor the decision-maker. Even when the user does play the predominant role, communication with other members of the buying centre can make sense when their knowledge and opinions may act as persuasive forces during the decision-making process.

A second implication is that the changing roles and influences within the family buying centre are providing new opportunities to creatively segment hitherto stable markets (e.g. cars). Read Mini Case 3.1 to understand more about influences on consumer decision-making and fine-tuning marketing directed at the previously stable age 21–35 male segment.

MARKETING IN ACTION 3.2
The Bandwagon Effect: Online Group Buying

The internet is influencing how people buy: from how they search for product alternatives, comparing purchase options, to where and when they make the purchase. Another powerful effect on the changing of consumer behaviour comes from the idea that success breeds success. Online, people look for frequently downloaded music or YouTube videos and quickly join trending news feeds which may create a Twitter storm: a spike in activity surrounding a particular news topic. Research has suggested that the actions of others have a strong influence on individual behaviour; they imply that consumers can influence and be influenced by the behaviour of others on a mass scale.

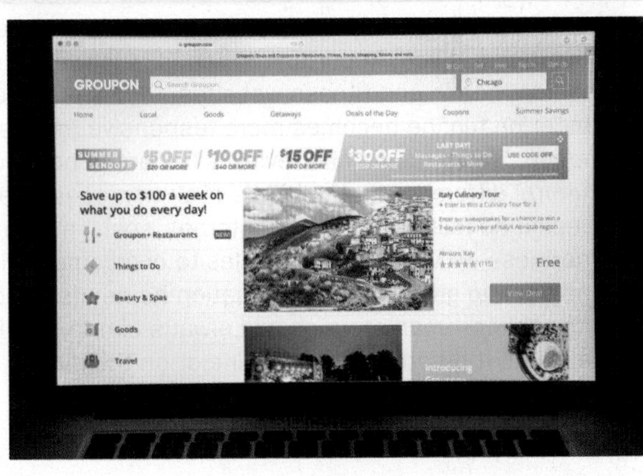

Groupon is a web portal that offers consumers promotional deals on restaurants, entertainment, sporting events and other services on a mass scale. While offers are provided on a regional basis to individuals, they are based on 'collective' buying power. The popularity of such deals has been found to have a more profound effect on positive purchase intentions and be more influential than prior shopping experiences. Another compelling finding was that the size of the discount on the service offered is more of a motivating factor than the actual price offered. To maintain its mass appeal, Groupon also uses more traditional broadcast media to grab attention and drive consumers to its website, which is positioned as a discovery platform for millions of global consumers who are looking for new experiences.

Based on: Zhang (2010); Salganik, Sheridan and Watts (2006); Groupon (2015); Luo et al. (2014); Gee (2016)

MINI CASE 3.1
Pre-family Man

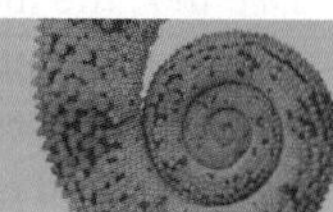

Things you ought to know about pre-family man (PFM):

- 92 per cent are online across multiple devices.
- 67 per cent don't see their friends as much as they did.
- 75 per cent see love as a top priority (Microsoft, 2012).
- 92 per cent use email at least once a day.
- 55 per cent use social networks at least once a day.
- 91 per cent watch short videos online.
- 72 per cent buy online at least once a month.

Microsoft has its eye on PFMs—young men aged 21–35—as they make up a large market. In the seven largest countries in Europe, there are over 21 million PFMs and this group is predicted to grow. Research has revealed that PFMs, who are between secondary education and having a family, should not be targeted as one group. According to Microsoft, PFM is evolving: he moves from living with parents, through living on his own or with a friend, to living with a partner. During this evolution, PFM has to achieve a balance between his desire for fun and the need to be responsible; he has to work out how to manage the things he wants to do and to set priorities, as there are always too many things he wants to do. PFM is *always switched on to digital technology* devices, and access to the internet is critical for managing his busy life.

However, depending on where PFM is on the evolutionary track, his priorities will vary according to which country he lives in. For example, between the ages of 21 and 23 in Sweden, 20 per cent of PFMs are living with parents, whereas in Spain the figure is 80 per cent. Priorities are different too: in Germany, 35 per cent are looking for more money, while in Sweden the figure is only 15 per cent. Career aspirations appear to be higher in Sweden, with 31 per cent looking for a better job, whereas in the Netherlands the figure is 7 per cent.

As technology has enabled marketers to become more informed about consumer behaviour, a complex set of rules emerge, which could give more insight into how better to serve the needs of various customers. The study by Microsoft provides guidance on targeting PFMs and suggests four golden rules that marketers should adhere to when targeting them.

1. Life stages—if targeting by age, it is key to also factor in life stages; when PFM is living with parents, his focus is on fun and he is interested in flats to rent and sports events. For the marketer, in-game advertising is very important. When PFM is living alone or with friends, marketers should target money, fashion, health and fitness websites. PFM's priorities change when living with a partner. The focus is no longer on fun: he becomes more responsive to messages about DIY, holidays, property, cooking and money. Social media and review sites are good places to advertise to capture his attention.
2. Cultural differences—the PFM's evolution goes at a different speed depending on which country he lives in; he makes use of the internet, social media and email to stay in touch through the evolution.
3. Priorities—PFM has many hurdles to overcome during his evolution. Advertisers should be aware of these and seek to give him the information he needs to achieve different priorities.
4. Information—marketers should always aim to give PFM the right type of information he needs at the point he wants it, whether that is online or on the move.

Questions:

1. Suggest how you would advise a company manufacturing tablet computers to communicate with PFM.
2. Explain how the priorities of PFM change during his evolution and suggest what the implications are for marketing managers.
3. Using the available information, suggest which country (Sweden, Germany, the Netherlands or Spain) and which accompanying PFM life stage you might target if you were responsible for developing a communication campaign for:
   a) an international property company
   b) a state-of-the-art gaming console
   c) a shopping app.

Based on: Microsoft (2012)

How they buy

How consumers buy may be regarded as a decision-making process beginning with the recognition that a problem exists. For example, a Fitbit personal activity tracker may be bought to solve a perceived problem of an unhealthy lifestyle. Problem-solving may thus be considered a thoughtful reasoned action undertaken to bring about need satisfaction. Blackwell, Miniard and Engel (2005) define a series of steps a consumer may pass through before choosing a brand. Figure 3.2 shows these stages, which form the **consumer decision-making process**. This process is shown as a set of linear steps, which lead to a purchase. It is important to understand each stage before considering how this process is influenced by the emerging contexts in which consumer behaviour takes place.

FIGURE 3.2
The consumer decision-making process

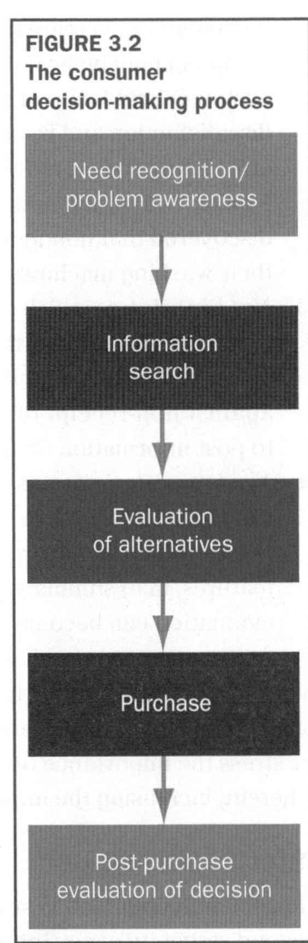

Need recognition/problem awareness

Awareness of a problem can take many forms but a *need recognition* is essentially *functional*, and realization may take place over time. So, in the case of the purchase of an activity tracker, health problems due to lack of exercise may occur due to many months of inactivity. Other problems can be the result of routine depletion (e.g. petrol, food) or unpredictability (e.g. the breakdown of a TV set or washing machine). Consumer purchasing may be initiated by more *emotional* or *psychological* needs. For example, the purchase of Davidoff Cool Water cologne (see Exhibit 3.2) is likely to be motivated by status needs rather than any marginal functional superiority over other perfumes.

The degree to which the consumer intends to resolve the problem depends on two issues: the magnitude of the discrepancy between the desired and present situation, and the relative importance of the problem (Neal, Quester and Hawkins, 2007). A problem may be perceived, but if the difference between the *current and desired situation* is small, then the consumer may not be sufficiently motivated to move to the next step in the decision-making process. For example, a person considering upgrading their mobile phone from a basic handset to a smart phone model will only make the purchase if they consider the difference in benefits to be sufficient to incur the costs involved (even though they might desire the more sophisticated product).

Conversely, a large discrepancy may be perceived but the person may not proceed to information search because the *relative importance* of the problem is small. A person may feel that a smart phone has significant advantages over a mobile phone, but that the relative importance of the advantages compared with other purchase needs (e.g. the mortgage or a holiday) might be small.

The existence of a need, however, may not activate the decision-making process in all cases. This is due to the existence of *need inhibitors* (O'Shaughnessey, 1987). For example, someone may want to buy an item on Amazon Marketplace but may be inhibited by fear of paying online and not receiving the goods. In such circumstances, the need remains passive.

EXHIBIT 3.2
The Cool Water uses emotional triggers in their adverts to communicate with target audiences

There are a number of marketing implications in the need-recognition stage:

1 *The needs* of consumers and the problems that they face. By being attuned to customers' needs,

companies can create a competitive advantage. For example, a marketing manager of a washing machine company may believe that consumers value a silent machine. But marketing research designed to assess customer problems (or needs) among people who use washing machines may identify other sources of dissatisfaction and issues they have with current models. The results of such research can have significant effects on product redesign. Samsung Electronics found there was a need to be able to add clothing missed from a load during mid-wash cycle and developed the AddWash, with an additional door; Samsung also discovered that young new home buyers have busy lives and they want speed and cleaning performance from their washing machines, so they introduced an innovative QuickDrive to meet this demand (Samsung 2018).

2 *Need inhibitors* which potentially stop a purchase. For example, eBay, Inc.—the global e-commerce platform—recognized that overcoming the need inhibitor *lack of trust* in being sent the product as important. To overcome this inhibitor, eBay introduced its PayPal payment system, which acts as financial insurance against non-receipt of goods and developed a feedback system to allow buyers (and sellers) to post information on their transactions and their experiences with particular vendors.

3 *Need stimulation* to encourage a purchase. Marketers' activities, e.g. developing advertising campaigns and training salespeople to sell product benefits, may act as cues to *needs* arousal.
For example, an advertisement displaying the features and benefits of a mobile smart phone, with new features, may stimulate potential customers to reflect on the limitations of their own current model and this evaluation can become a problem, which warrants action if they regard their phone to be lacking in some way.

Activating need/problem recognition depends on the size of the discrepancy between the current and desired situation, and the relative importance of the problem. An advertiser could therefore focus on the advantages of a smart phone over a basic mobile phone to create awareness of a larger discrepancy than originally perceived and/or stress the importance of owning a top-of-the-range model as a symbol of innovativeness and professionalism (thereby increasing the importance of the purchase relative to other products).

Information search

If problem recognition is sufficiently strong, the consumer decision-making process is likely to move to the second stage: **information search**. This involves the identification of alternative ways of problem solution. The search may be internal or external. *Internal search* involves a review of relevant information from memory. This review would include potential solutions, methods of comparing solutions, reference to personal experiences and marketing communications. If a satisfactory solution is not found, then *external search* begins. This involves *personal sources* such as, say, friends and family, and/or *commercial sources* such as advertisements, salespeople, websites and social media.

Third-party reports, such as product-testing reports, may provide unbiased information and *personal experiences* may be sought, such as asking for demonstrations and viewing, touching or tasting the product.

The objective of information search is to build up the **awareness set**—that is, the array of brands that may provide a solution to the problem. Using the smartphone example again, an advertisement may not only stimulate a search for more unbiased information regarding the advertised smartphone, but also stimulate an external search for information about rival brands.

Information search by consumers is facilitated by the growth of internet usage and companies that provide search facilities, such as Yahoo! and Google. Consumers are increasingly using the internet to gather information before buying a product and reading reviews from other customers.

Evaluation of alternatives and the purchase

The first step in *evaluation* is to reduce the awareness set to a smaller set of brands for serious consideration. The brands in the awareness set pass through a screening filter to produce an **evoked set**—those brands that the consumer seriously considers before making a purchase. In a sense, the evoked set is a shortlist of brands for careful evaluation. The screening process may use different choice criteria from those used when making the final choice, and the number of choice criteria used is often fewer (Kuusela, Spence and Kanto, 1998). One choice criterion used for screening may be price. Those smart phones priced below a certain level may form the evoked set. Final choice may then depend on such choice criteria as ease of use, speed of connection to the internet and reliability. The range of choice criteria used by consumers will be examined in more detail later in this chapter.

Although brands may be perceived as similar, this does not necessarily mean they will be equally preferred. This is because different product attributes (e.g. benefits, imagery) may be used by people when making similarity and preference judgements. For example, two brands may be perceived as similar because they provide similar functional benefits, yet one may be preferred over the other because of distinctive imagery (Creusen and Schoormans, 1997).

A key determinant of the extent to which consumers evaluate a brand is their level of *involvement.* Involvement is the degree of perceived relevance and personal importance accompanying the brand choice (Blackwell, Miniard and Engel, 2005). When a purchase is highly involving, the consumer is more likely to carry out extensive evaluation. High-involvement purchases are likely to include those incurring high expenditure or personal risk, such as buying a car or a home. In contrast, low-involvement situations are characterized by simple evaluations about purchases. Consumers use simple choice tactics to reduce time and effort rather than maximize the consequences of the purchase (Elliott and Hamilton, 1991). For example, when purchasing bread, milk or breakfast cereal, consumers are likely to make quick choices rather than agonize over the decision.

This distinction between high- and low-involvement situations implies different evaluative processes. For high-involvement purchases, the Fishbein and Ajzen theory of reasoned action (1980, 2005) provides a robust starting point for understanding purchase behaviour in situations where individuals are in complete control of the buying situation. But there are situations where buyers have limits on the control, for example limits on their mental and physical processing skills, emotions and compulsions. As a result, their intentions to buy can be moderated. So the degree to which individuals can make a reasoned decision affects their intentional behaviour (Ajzen, 1991). This issue of control has led to an extension of the theory of reasoned action model to include behavioural control (Ajzen and Madden, 1985): the theory of planned behaviour (TPB), which takes into account the degree of control individuals have over their behavioural intentions (Ajzen, 1985). Each of these models will now be examined.

Theory of reasoned action—Fishbein and Ajzen model. This suggests that an attitude towards a brand is based upon a set of **beliefs** about the brand's attributes (e.g. value for money, durability). These are the perceived consequences resulting from buying the brand. Each attribute is weighted by how good or bad the consumer believes the attribute to be. Those attributes that are weighted highly will be that person's choice criteria and have a large influence in the formation of attitude.

Attitude is the degree to which someone likes or dislikes the brand overall. The link between personal beliefs and attitudes is shown in Figure 3.3. However, evaluation of a brand is not limited to personal beliefs about the consequences of buying a brand. Outside influences also play a part. Individuals will thus evaluate the extent to which *important others* believe that they should or should not buy the brand. These beliefs may conflict with their personal beliefs. People may think that buying a sports car may have positive consequences (providing fun driving, being more attractive to other people) but refrain from buying if they believe that important others (e.g. parents, boss) would disapprove of the purchase. This collection of *normative beliefs* forms an overall evaluation of the degree to which these outside influences approve or disapprove of the purchase (*subjective norms*).

The link between normative beliefs and subjective norms is also shown in Figure 3.3. This is a *theory of reasoned action.* Consumers are highly involved in the purchase to the extent that they evaluate the consequences of the purchase *and* what others will think about it. Only after these considerations have taken place are purchase intentions formed and a purchase results. Purchase intentions are important, as they are a strong predictor of future behaviour—an intention is an indication of an individual's state of willingness to carry out an action.

Theory of planned behaviour. While the theory of reasoned action provides sound insight into how attitudes and beliefs shape intentions, it was found that an individual's behaviour is not completely controlled and rational. So the theory of planned behaviour brings in the notion of control and suggests that the *extent* to which

FIGURE 3.3
High involvement: the Fishbein and Ajzen model of reasoned action

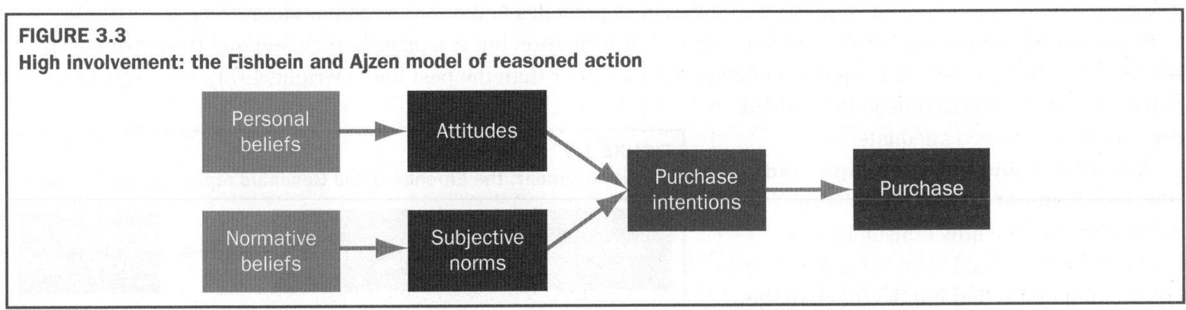

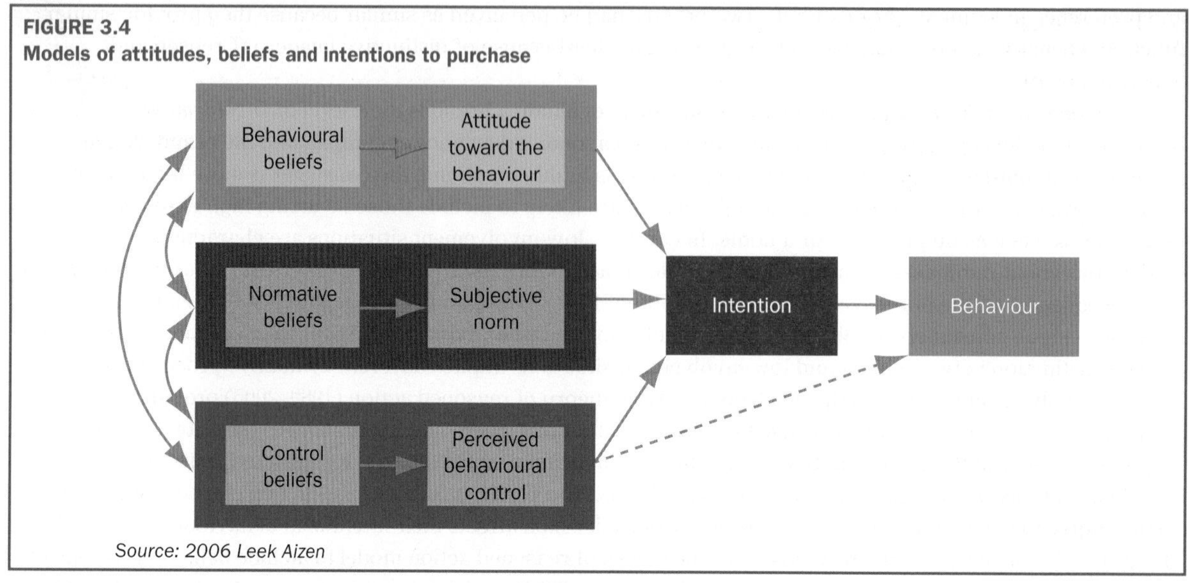

FIGURE 3.4
Models of attitudes, beliefs and intentions to purchase

Source: 2006 Leek Aizen

individuals freely make decisions will shape their intentions. In other words, our *actual shopping behaviour*, say of buying healthy foodstuffs, will be affected by *our intention to buy* healthy foodstuffs. But, also, our intentions can be changed by external influences over which we have limited control. So our healthy food purchase might be contingent on time available to make the purchase, money and our skills of being able to identify genuine healthy option foodstuffs. Ajzen (2012, 1991) suggested that measuring *perceived behavioural control*, which is an individual's belief of how easy or difficult it is to make an intended purchase, could reveal insight into a person's motivations. The *control beliefs* are the existence of factors that might facilitate or impede a person's behavioural intentions and ultimately their purchase behaviour, for example social, cultural or religious factors. See Figure 3.4. Therefore, if our healthy food buyer is a nutritionist who can readily identify healthy options, he or she is likely to be more in control and more likely to make a purchase of healthy foodstuffs based on scientific knowledge. A person who is less well informed about nutrition might be more inclined to be influenced by, say, social factors and buy skimmed milk based on presumptions about the milk, without specific knowledge of the health benefits.

Ultimately, a person's intention to perform a behaviour is a strong indicator of whether they will carry out a certain act (e.g. buy healthy foodstuffs). However, obstacles can get in the way—for example, demands from family, and work, which can limit the time available—and so a person buys a fast-food ready meal, high in fat and sugar, instead of a healthier option.

Ehrenberg and Goodhart model. In low-involvement situations (Ehrenberg and Goodhart, 1980), the amount of information processing implicit in the earlier model may not be worthwhile or sensible. A typical low-involvement situation is the *repeat purchase* of fast-moving consumer goods. The work of Ehrenberg and Goodhart suggests that a very simple process may explain purchase behaviour (see Figure 3.5). According to this model, awareness precedes trial, which, if satisfactory, leads to repeat purchase. This behavioural model indicates that consumer behaviour becomes *habitual* with little conscious thought or formation of attitudes preceding the purchase action. The notion of low involvement suggests that awareness precedes behaviour and behaviour precedes attitude. In this situation, the consumer does not actively seek information but is a passive recipient and the consumer is likely to satisfice (i.e. search for a satisfactory solution rather than the best one) (Wright, 1974). Consequently, any of several brands that lie in the evoked set may be considered adequate.

FIGURE 3.5
Low involvement: the Ehrenberg and Goodhard repeat purchase model

Awareness → Trial → Repeat purchase

Distinguishing between high- and low-involvement situations is very important because how consumers evaluate products and brands leads to contrasting marketing implications. In the high-involvement situation, marketing managers should provide a good deal of information about the positive consequences of buying as the consumer is making a significant decision. Messages with *high information content* should enhance knowledge about the brand but high levels of repetition are not needed (Rothschild, 1978). Print media and websites may be appropriate in the high-involvement case since they allow detailed and repeated scrutiny of information. Car advertisements often provide detailed information about the comfort, reliability and performance of the model, and they appeal to status considerations as all of these appeals may influence the consumer's beliefs about the consequences of buying the model. A salesforce also has an important role to play in the high-involvement situation by ensuring that the customer is aware of the important attributes of the product and correctly evaluates their consequences and provides opportunities for customers to ask questions.

For low-involvement situations, the evaluation of alternatives is much more rudimentary and attitude change is likely to follow purchase. Attempting to gain *top-of-mind awareness* through advertising and providing positive *reinforcement* (e.g. through sales promotion) to gain trial may be more important than providing masses of information about the consequences of buying the brand. Furthermore, as this is of little interest, the consumer is not actively seeking information but is a passive receiver. Consequently, advertising messages should be *short* with a small number of key points but with *high repetition* to enhance learning (Rothschild, 1978). It is important to be aware that, while these ideas are still valid, digital marketing and greater use of online channels for communicating has changed the format of communication messages and the way they are received. These issues are considered in detail in Chapters 13, 14 and 16.

Marketers must be aware of the role of emotion in consumer evaluation of alternatives. A major source of high emotion is when a product is high in symbolic meaning. Consumers believe that the product helps them to construct and maintain their self-concept and sense of identity. Furthermore, ownership of the product will help them communicate the desired image to other people. In such cases, non-rational preferences may form and information search is confined to providing objective justification for an emotionally based decision. Studies have shown the effects of emotion on judgement to be less thought, less information-seeking, less analytical reasoning and less attention to negative factors that might contradict the decision (Elliott, 1997). Instead, consumers consult their feelings for information about a decision: 'How do I feel about it?' Consequently, many marketers attempt to create a feeling of warmth about their brands. The mere exposure to a brand name over time, and the use of humour in advertisements, can create such feelings.

Impulse buying is another area that can be associated with emotions. Consumers have described a compelling feeling that is 'thrilling', 'wild', 'a tingling sensation', 'a surge of energy' and 'like turning up the volume' (see Elliott, 1998; Rook, 1987). See Marketing in Action 3.3.

Post-purchase evaluation of the decision

Effective marketing aims to create **customer satisfaction** in both high- and low-involvement situations. Marketing managers want to create positive experiences from the purchase of their products or services. Nevertheless, it is common for customers to experience some post-purchase concerns; this is called **cognitive dissonance**. Dissonance is likely to increase in four ways: with the *expense* of purchase; when the decision is *difficult* (e.g. many alternatives, many choice criteria and each alternative offering benefits not available with the others); when the decision is *irrevocable*; and when the purchaser has a tendency *to experience anxiety* (Neal, Quester and Hawkins, 2007) and is often associated with high-involvement purchases. A car buyer may attempt to reduce dissonance by looking at advertisements, websites and brochures for their model, and seeking reassurance from owners of the same model. Volkswagen buyers are more likely to look at Volkswagen advertisements and avoid Renault or Ford advertisements. Car dealers can build relationships to reduce *buyer remorse* by contacting recent purchasers to reinforce the wisdom of their decision and to confirm the quality of their after-sales service.

What are the Choice Criteria?

Choice criteria are the various attributes (and benefits) a consumer uses when evaluating products and services. They provide the grounds for deciding to purchase one brand or another. Different members of the buying centre may use different choice criteria. For example, a child may use the criterion of self-image when choosing shoes, whereas a parent may use price. Choice criteria can change over time due to changes in income through the family lifecycle. As disposable income rises, so price may no longer be the key criterion but is replaced by considerations of status or social belonging.

MARKETING IN ACTION 3.3

Chocolate Shortages and Black Friday Promotions Cause Impulsive Behaviour and Panic Buying

Impulse purchasing and panic buying are characterized by highly charged emotions, limited cognitive control and reactive rather than planned behaviour. External factors appear to increase in importance in the consumer decision-making process and encourage shoppers to engage in frenzied bouts of buying. The following examples highlight how different external influences can stimulate emotionally charged purchasing.

Panic buying

Expat British consumers living in the USA reacted aggressively towards legal action taken by the American food producer Hershey's to stop the sale of Cadbury's chocolate bars due to an infringement of its trademark. Chocolate lovers started to buy up stocks of their favourite confectionery, and warehouses emptied quickly as panic about the future lack of availability of their beloved English-made chocolate bars increased.

The source of the argument was that Cadbury entered global markets through Mondelez International, and together their chocolate accounts for nearly a third of all the chocolate consumed in the UK; but when it comes to North America, Hershey's produces Dairy Milk under license for the Cadbury brand, using a slightly different recipe. Cadbury has a long and illustrious history and chocolate with a distinctive taste to match; expat consumers were so attached to the Cadbury brand that emotions ran high and the threat of scarcity drove demand.

Impulse purchasing

Black Friday was introduced to online shoppers in the UK by Amazon in 2010. By 2014, it hit critical mass and promotions moved to the physical High Street too. ASDA/Walmart ran flash promotions in its stores, which created chaos as consumers literally fought over LED TVs, electric drills and tablet computers at heavily discounted prices. This event continues to grow in the UK, and has extended to service industries as airlines and hotels *jump on the discount bandwagon*.

Originally, Black Friday was the Philadelphia police force's answer to the chaos that ensued in the 1950s and 1960s after Thanksgiving (celebrated in the USA on the fourth Thursday in November). The name came out of the effects of the frenzied shopping on the city's retailers, as they reportedly saw profits move out of the red and into the black. Whether true or not, Black Friday represented a kick-start for Christmas shoppers, which seems set to continue, but marketers should be aware that online shoppers are savvy bargain hunters and will not be motivated to purchase if products can be found cheaper elsewhere and at other times of the year.

Based on: Euromonitor (2014); McSherry (2015); Weinberg and Gottwald (1982); Ruddick (2014); Christian (2017)

Table 3.1 lists four types of choice criteria and gives examples of each. *Technical criteria* are related to the performance of the product or service, and include reliability, durability, comfort and convenience. Convenience is often synonymous with ease of use. *Economic criteria* concern the cost aspects of purchase, and include price, running costs and residual values (e.g. the trade-in value of a car).

Social criteria concern the impact that the purchase makes on the person's perceived relationships with other people, and the influence of social norms on the person. The purchase of a BMW car may be based on status considerations as much as on any technical advantages over its rivals.

TABLE 3.1 Choice criteria used when evaluating alternatives

Type of criteria	Examples	Type of criteria	Examples
Technical	Reliability	Social	Status
	Durability		Social belonging
	Performance		Convention
	Style/looks		Fashion
	Comfort	Personal	Self-image
	Delivery		Risk reduction
	Convenience		Ethics
	Taste		Emotions
Economic	Price		
	Value for money		
	Running costs		
	Residual value		
	Lifecycle costs		

Social norms such as convention and fashion can also be important choice criteria, with some brands being rejected as too unconventional, although some advertisers do playfully use unconventional ideas to get their brands noticed. See Exhibit 3.3.

EXHIBIT 3.3
Snickers misspelt its advert to attract attention and drive social media impressions

Personal criteria are to do with how the product or service relates to the individual psychologically. Self-image is our personal view of ourselves. Some people might view themselves as 'cool' and successful, and only buy sportswear items from Under Armour, Adidas or Nike to reflect perceptions of themselves. Risk reduction can affect choice decisions, since some people are risk averse and prefer to choose 'safe' brands; an example is the purchase of designer labels, which reduces the risk of being seen wearing unfashionable clothing. Ethical criteria can be important and brands may be rejected because they are manufactured by companies that have offended a person's ethical code of behaviour.

Research has shown that consumers do consider ethical criteria and that a large majority enjoy buying products from companies that give something back to society (Confino and Muminova, 2011). The market for ethical products has grown in recent years. Some of the products currently deemed ethical include fairly traded foods and drinks that guarantee a fair deal to producers in developing countries. A company's *green credentials* can be confusing, though, and it is difficult for consumers to choose the 'best' products because, although organic may be seen as the greener and healthier food option, many scientific studies have cast doubts on such conclusions. Although ethical consumption is important in shaping and maintaining empowered ethical consumer identities and markets, there is much uncertainty about the choices to be made, and, at times, ethical trade-offs occur (e.g. products are not always organic as well as fair trade). This, in turn, generates much inconsistency about what it is possible to achieve. Although people feel empowered and responsible for environmental issues at an individual level, this is coupled with the insecurity of not knowing what the 'right choices' are and such contradictions pose huge challenges to policy-makers and marketers alike. Marketing ethics and corporate social responsibility are discussed in more detail in Chapter 5.

Emotional criteria can be important in decision-making. Many purchase decisions are experiential in that they evoke feelings such as fun, pride or pleasure. The importance of experiences to consumers has led to the growth in experiential consumption. See Exhibit 3.4 to be taken on an adventure by the Lurpak brand.

EXHIBIT 3.4
Lurpak launches new product ranges using the intangible idea of new food adventures rather than the tangible product features

Saab ran a two-page advertising campaign that combined technical and economic appeals with an emotional one. The first page was headlined '21 Logical Reasons to Buy a Saab'. The second page ran the headline 'One Emotional Reason'. The first page supported the headline with detailed body copy explaining the technical and economic rationale for purchase. The second page showed a Saab powering along a rain-drenched road. When a product scores well on a combination of choice criteria the outcome can be global success. For example, the success of the Apple smart phone derives from the convenience of being able to access emails and websites on the move (technical), and the status (social) and high self-image (personal) that is associated with owning one.

Marketing managers need to understand the choice criteria that are being used by customers to evaluate their products and services. Such knowledge has implications for priorities in product design (e.g. is style/look more important than performance?) and the types of appeals to use in marketing communications, which should be linked to the key choice criteria used by buying centre members. Concern about store design and ambience at shops such as H&M and Zara reflects the importance of creating the right experience when shopping for clothes.

Understanding consumer behaviour is important and it should be noted that people are often not just passive receivers of a firm's marketing efforts. Cultural, gender and social status differences can have a profound effect on behaviours (Jia, Zhou and Allawya, 2018). Furthermore, as discussed at the beginning of the chapter, the contexts in which buying takes place are becoming more complex and consumers are becoming participants in the creation of value (Tynan, Mckehnie and Chhuon, 2010). See Marketing in Action 3.4.

Where and when they buy

Broadly, consumers make purchases for different reasons: underlying motivations and the importance of the purchase. Traditionally, the time and place of a purchase would be at a physical point-of-sale, e.g. at a store, outdoor market, fair. This is no longer the case as the scope and opportunity of when and where to buy has been significantly extended by e-commerce systems and the growth of digital markets. More recently, mobile commerce has expanded the opportunities to purchase even further via smart phones. These issues are addressed from a digital perspective in Chapter 16 and a physical perspective in Chapter 17.

Before moving on, it is worthwhile briefly considering a darker side to consumer behaviour which relates to where and when we buy. Marketing in Action 3.3 introduced impulsive purchases and considered how certain timed promotional events can trigger excessive purchasing behaviour. Compulsive consumption is the uncontrollable desire to engage in excessive and addictive purchasing: hyperactive in-store and online purchasing (Chang, Lu, Su, Lin & Chang, 2011) is very different to impulse purchasing, which is spontaneous and unplanned buying which remains in the buyer's control. Compulsive shoppers tend to be very well informed about store prices, promotional offers and sales events; they make more purchases online and have higher credit card abuse than shoppers who do not share the same compulsion to shop. There are implications for marketers, who should be aware that compulsive buying can lead to emotional and financial difficulties and these types of shoppers should be discouraged from spending (Darrat, Darrat and Amyx, 2016).

MARKETING IN ACTION 3.4

Classic Marketing is the Surest Way to Fail in this Business

The business is luxury fashion. Since 1990, globally, the market for luxury brands has grown significantly and is now worth over $300 billion. But, during this period, manufacturer brands like Louis Vuitton, Gucci, Chanel and Hermes have been challenged by the growth of online shopping, counterfeiting, **parallel importing**, and complex social and cultural influences. The result is that marketing of luxury fashion brands is so unique that, according to Bastien and Kapferer (2009), 'classic marketing is the surest way to fail in the luxury business'. So how do these brands satisfy, delight and keep their customers? For example, for Louis Vuitton to successfully sell its clutch bags at more than £2,000, their customers need to perceive that there is sufficient value in the handbag to compensate for the high price. It should be noted that the luxury brands buyer sees high prices as a signal to ensure exclusivity and he/she rarely considers affordability when choosing goods and services.

The types of value luxury goods buyers are looking for include: utilitarian values, e.g. excellent craftsmanship, high quality materials; symbolic values, e.g. social identity, authenticity, uniqueness; experiential values, e.g. hedonic effect, aesthetics; relational values, e.g. consumer-brand relations and the cost of the purchase and perceptions of perfection, exclusivity and rarity. It is these sophisticated and complex values which brands must seek to share with their customers. Research suggests this is achieved through the process of value co-creation. This process is about defining the brand. Defining a luxury brand is not straightforward, except that generally these goods can be identifiable by the fact that demand rises because prices are higher not lower. Luxury brands take the value of their goods very seriously and, recently, Burberry, the UK fashion brand, destroyed £28 million of goods to guard against counterfeiting and their intellectual property.

Co-creation of value relies on developing relationships with active customers, brand owners and employees who are prepared to exchange knowledge and become partners in the process. This is an important and subtle difference between classic marketing, where, typically, a brand creates its products for customers who are seen as passive. Practically, luxury brands have developed (with their customers) value, creating networks and brand communities, involving high status individuals who can act as opinion leaders. These communities often form around formal planned social events that include different product categories, e.g., fashion, jewellery, yachts, luxury cars, creating experiences centred on exclusivity and opulence. Some luxury brands attract wealthy customers, who are often willing to travel the globe to acquire the goods they desire, which is also welcome news for the travel industry, but hotels, tour operators and other travel services are finding that they must also work closely with this new breed of customer in order to create the services they require.

Based on: Tynan, Mckehnie and Chhuon (2010)

Influences on Consumer Behaviour

Our discussion of *evaluation of alternatives* highlights that not all consumer decisions follow the same decision-making process, involve the same purchasers (buying centre) or use identical choice criteria. Neither do they occur at the same place or time. The consumer behaviour process, the buying centre, choice criteria, purchase situation and timing can be influenced by many factors: 1) the buying situation, 2) personal influences, and 3) social influences (see Table 3.2).

TABLE 3.2 Influences on consumer purchasing behaviour

Areas of influence	Factors affecting decision-making	Examples of marketing implications/ considerations
The buying situation	Extended problem-solving Limited problem-solving Habitual problem-solving	Level of information to provide for consumers to make informed decisions
Personal influences	Information processing Motivations Beliefs and attitudes Personality Lifestyle Lifecycle and age	Extent to which personal influences inform decision-making, e.g. an individual's perceptions can distort marketing messages; lifestyle can determine interest and opinions
Social influences	Culture Social class Geodemographics Reference groups	Extent to which social influences inform decision-making, e.g. culture can determine societal values, which might affect individual behaviour

The buying situation

Three types of buying situation can be identified: extended problem-solving, limited problem-solving and habitual problem-solving.

Extended problem-solving

Extended problem-solving involves a high degree of information searching, close examination of alternatives and the evaluation of many choice criteria (Neal, Quester and Hawkins, 2007). Information search and evaluation may focus not only on which brand/model to buy but also on where to make the purchase. The potential for cognitive dissonance is greatest in this buying situation. Extended problem-solving is usually associated with three conditions: the alternatives are differentiated and numerous; there is an adequate amount of time available for deliberation; and the purchase has a high degree of involvement (Blackwell, Miniard and Engel, 2005).

Figure 3.6 summarizes these relationships. High involvement means the purchase is personally relevant and seen as important with respect to basic motivations and needs (Bettman, 1982). Problem-solving is likely to be particularly extensive when all alternatives possess desirable features that others do not have. If alternatives are perceived as being similar, then less time is required in assessment. Extended problem-solving is inhibited by time pressure. If the decision is made quickly, the extent of problem-solving activity is curtailed. The decision-maker must also feel a high degree of involvement in the choice,

FIGURE 3.6
Determinants of the extent of problem-solving

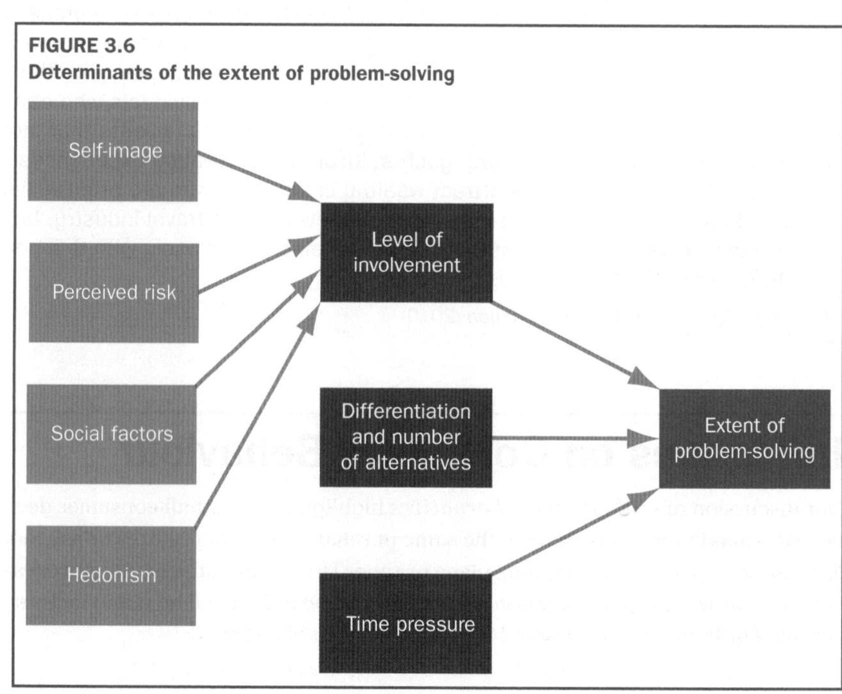

but how personally relevant and important the choice is to the decision-maker varies from person to person. Original research by Laurent and Kapferer (1985) identified four factors that affect involvement:

1 *Self-image*: involvement is likely to be high when the decision potentially affects a person's self-image. Thus, purchase of jewellery, cars and clothing invokes more involvement than choosing a brand of soap or margarine.
2 *Perceived risk*: involvement is likely to be high when the perceived risk of making a mistake is high. The risk of buying the wrong house is much higher than that of buying the wrong chewing gum, because the potential negative consequences of the wrong decision are higher. Risk usually increases with the price of the purchase.
3 *Social factors*: when social acceptance is dependent upon making a correct choice, involvement is likely to be high. Buying of the *right* golf clubs may be highly involved, as making a *wrong* decision may affect social standing among fellow golfers; the principle may apply to clothes, trainers and other products that can affect the purchaser's acceptance within a social group.
4 *Hedonistic influences*: when the purchase can provide a high degree of pleasure, involvement is usually high. The choice of restaurant when on holiday can be highly involving, since the difference between making the right or wrong choice can severely affect the amount of pleasure associated with the experience.

See Marketing in Action 3.5 for further consideration of important sources of influences.

MARKETING IN ACTION 3.5
The Active Consumer: Intuition versus Deliberation

Booking.com Review

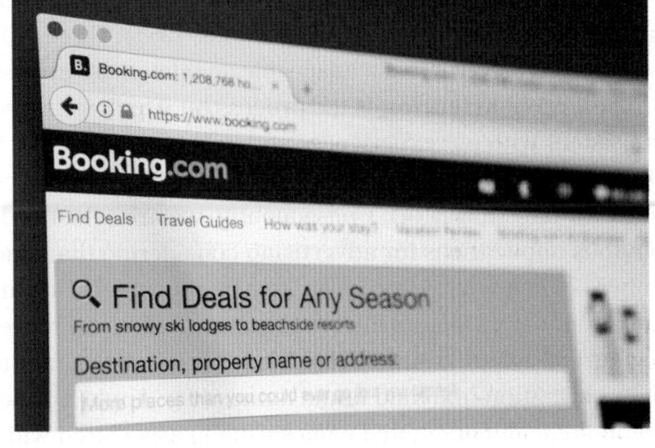

How we make buying decisions online is complex and there are two important sources of influences:

1 **Reviews**: this phenomenon has emerged as the role of personal recommendation. Person-to-person word of mouth has always been an important form of communication, but arguably the impact has been limited by the number of people reached by a person's review.
2 **Comparison**: online consumers can visit websites designed to facilitate comparison. Price is often a key criterion used to influence the decision process. Comparison websites generate referrals for retailers and service providers—for example, comparethemarket.com enables consumers to compare home, car and life insurance. Comparison websites have been found to have a significant influence on consumer behaviour, both online and offline.

Understanding how each source influences decisions is crucial for marketers, especially in the service industries as a positive online review can help to reduce uncertainties and help to increase levels of confidence. The dual theory of decision-making suggests that there are two systems operating in our brains; system one is fast and intuitive and system two is slow, deliberate and methodical. System one is said to rely on heuristics—mental short-cuts, which simplify decision processes, easing the burden of complex information processing. System two is more analytical and requires effort to be involved in the thinking processes and relies on rational judgement combined with past experiences. Research suggests that consumers who read reviews are more likely to utilize all available information to inform their decision-making. Furthermore, online reviews have become an integral part of the buying process. It is said that consumer review websites leverage the wisdom of the crowd, and photos, ratings, aggregate scores and the ease with which we can assimilate this information can help to influence the potential buyer.

There are now many review sites providing aggregated consumer reviews, e.g., Booking.com, TripAdvisor (travel and tourism industry), Feefo and Epinions (retail industry), and other websites like eBay and Amazon, which provide feedback and comments on products and services.

Based on: Dai et al (2014); Ong (2011); Nazlan, Tanford and Montgomery (2018)

Limited problem-solving

Many consumer purchases fall into the 'limited problem-solving' category. The consumer has some experience with the product in question, so an information search may be mainly internal, through memory. However, a certain amount of external search and evaluation may take place (e.g. checking prices) before purchase is made. This situation provides marketers with some opportunity to affect purchase by stimulating the need to conduct search (e.g. advertising) and reducing the risk of brand switching (e.g. warranties).

Habitual problem-solving

Habitual problem-solving occurs when a consumer repeat-buys the same product with little or no evaluation of alternatives—for example, buying the same breakfast cereal on a weekly shopping trip. The consumer may recall the satisfaction gained by purchasing a brand and automatically buy it again. Advertising may be effective in keeping the brand name in the consumer's mind and reinforcing already favourable attitudes.

Personal influences

There are six personal influences on consumer behaviour: information processing, motivation, beliefs and attitudes, personality, lifestyle and lifecycle.

Information processing

Information processing refers to the process by which a stimulus is received, interpreted, stored in memory and later retrieved (Blackwell, Miniard and Engel, 2005). It is therefore the link between external influences, including marketing activities, and the consumer's decision-making process. Two key aspects of information processing are perception and learning.

Perception is the complex process by which people select, organize and interpret sensory stimulation into a meaningful picture of the world (Williams, 1981). Three processes may be used to sort out the masses of stimuli that could be perceived into a manageable amount: these are selective attention, selective distortion and selective retention.

Selective attention is the process by which we screen out stimuli that are neither meaningful nor consistent with our experiences and beliefs. On entering a supermarket, there are thousands of potential stimuli (brands, point-of-sale displays, prices, etc) to which we could pay attention. To do so would be unrealistic in terms of time and effort. Consequently, we are selective in attending to these messages. Selective attention has obvious implications for advertising considering that studies have shown that consumers consciously attend to only 5–25 per cent of the advertisements to which they are exposed (Neal, Quester and Hawkins, 2007).

A number of factors influence attention. We pay more attention to stimuli that contrast with their background than to stimuli that blend with it. Computer and smart phone manufacturers use names of fruit to act as attention-grabbing brand names (e.g. Apple, BlackBerry, Raspberry Pi) because they contrast with the technologically orientated names usually associated with computers. The size, colour and movement of a stimulus also affect attention. Position is critical too. Objects placed near the centre of the visual range are more likely to be noticed than those on the periphery. There is intense competition to obtain eye-level positions on supermarket shelves. We are also more likely to notice those messages that relate to our needs (benefits sought) (Ratneshwar et al., 1997) and provide surprises (e.g. large price reductions).

Selective distortion occurs when consumers distort the information they receive according to their existing beliefs and attitudes. We may distort information that is not in accord with our existing views. Methods of doing this include thinking that we misheard the message and discounting the message source. Consequently, it is very important to present messages clearly without the possibility of ambiguity and to use a highly credible source, which reduces the scope for selective distortion of the message on the part of the recipient. Distortion can occur because people interpret the same information differently. Interpretation is a process whereby messages are placed into existing categories of meaning. A cheaper price, for example, may be categorized not only as providing better value for money but also as implying lower quality.

Information framing can affect interpretation. Framing refers to ways in which information is presented to people. The implications for marketing are that there is benefit in framing communication messages in a positive manner. Words, images, colours and even smell can influence interpretations. For example, blue and green are viewed as cool, and evoke feelings of security. Red and yellow are regarded as warm and cheerful. Black is seen as an indication of strength. By using the appropriate colour in pack design it is possible to affect the consumer's feelings about the product. Marketers often base complete branding concepts on colour. The Virgin group uses ‘red’ throughout its branding. Smell can influence interpretation. Singapore Airlines uses an infusion of Stefan Floridian Waters cologne into its hot towels to create a suitable aroma in its cabins. The fragrance receives consistently positive feedback from passengers and is described as exotic and feminine. Singapore Airlines was the first airline to market itself through a sensory experience appealing to the emotions, as opposed to using the approach of its competitors, which emphasized price, food and comfort (Lindstrom, 2005).

Selective retention occurs when only a selection of messages are retained in memory. We tend to remember messages that are in line with existing beliefs and attitudes. In an experiment, 12 statements were given to a group of Labour and Conservative supporters. Six of the statements were favourable to Labour and six to the Conservatives. The group members were asked to remember the statements and to return after seven days. The result was that Labour supporters remembered the statements that were favourable to Labour and Conservative supporters remembered the pro-Conservative statements. Selective retention has a role to play in reducing cognitive dissonance: when reading reviews of a recently purchased car, positive messages are more likely to be remembered than negative ones.

Learning is any change in the content or organization of long-term memory, and is the result of information processing (Neal, Quester and Hawkins, 2007). There are numerous ways in which learning can take place. These include *conditioning* and *cognitive learning.*

Classical conditioning is the process of using an established relationship between a stimulus and response to cause the learning of the same response to a different stimulus. Thus, in advertising, humour, which is known to elicit a pleasurable response, may be used in the belief that these favourable feelings will carry over to the product. Red Bull is a brand that benefits from such associations. The humour in its advertising conveys a fun image, and the promotion of Red Bull on the body of racing cars projects the feeling of excitement for the brand by association.

Operant conditioning differs from classical conditioning by way of the role and timing of the reinforcement. In this case, reinforcement results from rewards: the more rewarding the response, the stronger the likelihood of the purchase being repeated. Operant conditioning occurs as a result of product trial. The use of free samples is based on the principles of operant conditioning. For example, free samples of a new shampoo may be distributed to a large number of households. This means the shampoo can be used (desired response) without making an initial purchase. Olay introduced its body wash using this tactic. The rewards for the consumer are that they benefit by experiencing the desirable properties of the product at no cost. These experiences can then reinforce the likelihood of the consumer making a purchase. Thus, the sequence of events is different between classical and operant conditioning. In classic conditioning, liking precedes trial, whereas in operant conditioning, trial precedes liking.

For marketers, introducing a series of rewards (reinforcements) may encourage repeat buying of a product. A free sample may be accompanied by a coupon to buy the product at a discounted rate (reinforcement). Another discount coupon may be on the pack to encourage repeat buying. After this purchase, the product relies on its own intrinsic reward—product performance—to encourage purchase. This process is known as *shaping.* Repeat purchase behaviour will have been shaped by the application of repeated reinforcers so that the consumer will have learned that buying the product is associated with pleasurable experiences.

Cognitive learning involves the learning of knowledge and development of beliefs and attitudes without direct reinforcement.

Rote learning involves the learning of two or more concepts without conditioning. Having seen the headline ‘Lemsip is for flu attacks’, the consumer may remember that Lemsip is a remedy for flu attacks without the kinds of conditioning and reinforcement previously discussed.

Vicarious learning involves learning from others without direct experience or reward. It is the promise of the reward that motivates. Thus, we may learn the type of clothes that attract potential admirers by observing other people. In advertising, the ‘admiring glance’ can be used to signal approval of the type of clothing being worn. We imagine that the same may happen to us if we dress in a similar way.

Reasoning is a more complex form of cognitive learning and is usually associated with high-involvement situations. For example, some advertising messages rely on the recipient drawing their own conclusions through reasoning.

Whichever type of learning has taken place, the result of the learning process is the creation of *product positioning.* The market objective is to create a clear and favourable position in the mind of the consumer (Ries and Trout, 2001).

The ways in which consumers process information are highly complex, and while extensive research has been done in this field, the use of technology is creating opportunities for marketers to learn so much more about how consumers behave—and in a real-time basis. Online-tracking mechanisms, such as super cookies, browser fingerprinting and behavioural tracking, provide detailed information about what happens online. All a customer has to do is visit a retailer's e-commerce website, and the retailer has information about age, gender and physical location, and an estimation of income, without any input from the customer (O'Rourke, 2014). This monitoring of behaviour does not end online. Tracking through mobile phones and the use of Apple's iBeacon technology means that customers can be pinpointed within a few feet, and eye-tracking applications enable marketers to even know what we are looking at. Another technological technique that holds great potential for understanding how consumers process information is neuroscience, as Marketing in Action 3.6 discusses.

MARKETING IN ACTION 3.6

Technology Delivers Consumer Insights, and Age of Neuromarketing is Here

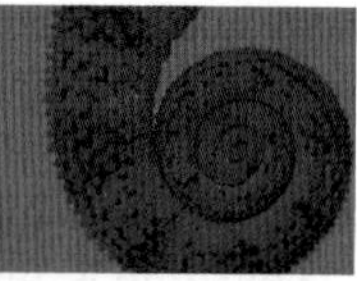

Which image would you choose to sell milk?

According to one of the world's leading neuromarketing experts, Dr A.K. Pradeep, when consumers are asked to choose 'the one that always wins out is the cow'. He suggests the underlying reasoning is that the source of a product hits a spot deep in the subconscious which is more evocative than any of the other associated images. Pradeep says that neuroscience allows marketers to find out what a brand means in the subconscious mind. One brand that he feels understands how to 'market to the buying brain' is Jo Malone. This perfume brand uses images of ingredients to trigger positive emotions, which he advocates are far more powerful than images of a man and woman in passionate embraces (McCormick, 2011).

Pradeep is not the only advocate for using technology to understand consumer behaviour. Professor O'Rourke (2014) has made a stand, and his advice to marketers looking to determine insights into consumer behaviour is to 'ditch simplistic surveys' and use instead behavioural tracking and neuroscience. Increasingly, technology is providing insights into consumer behaviour using eye tracking and electroencephalography (EEG) tests, which involve measuring brain signals. For marketers, the key question is how consumers process information, because it sheds light on how they make purchasing choices—for example, what clothes we buy or what music we like to listen to. Potentially, neuroscience and the study of the brain and nervous system by means of functional magnetic resonance imaging (FMRI) scanning and EEG tests have all the answers. The brain is made up of networks of neurons. When these cell clusters are stimulated, they use more energy. These active areas light up on FMRI scans, allowing researchers to map emotion and cognition. The scanner produces a colour-coded image of the brain that is helpful in revealing a person's unconscious feelings about a brand, an advertisement or even a media channel. For example, an understanding of the effects of different media channels (e.g. print versus the internet) on brain stimulation has been found to be useful when making media decisions. This application of the techniques of neuroscience to marketing is called neuromarketing.

Neuromarketing advocates like O'Rouke and Pradeep argue that it is an objective tool that scientifically demonstrates and quantifies human reactions and provides new insights into how people process information. However, sceptics still counter that it has not revealed huge insights into human behaviour that are not already instinctively known, and many brands still rely on surveys and focus groups. As applications of neuromarketing develop, the truth about its worth to marketers will be revealed.

Based on: McCormick (2011); Lovell (2008); O'Rourke (2014); Hannaford (2013)

Motivation

An understanding of motivation lies in the relationship between needs, drives and goals (Luthans, 2001). The basic process involves needs (deprivations) that set drives in motion (deprivations with direction) to accomplish goals (anything that alleviates a need and reduces a drive). Maslow's hierarchy of needs model has been widely used in management education, but you should be aware that it was devised in the mid-20th century and centred on American society, where individualism was very important, especially to the *middle classes* (Bennet, 2011). Arguably, this is rather one-dimensional, as the model does not accommodate the influence of others—for example family, children, work colleagues, society—on an individual's motivation. According to Pinder (1998), 'Motivation is a force that prompts action and relates to conscious or unconscious decision involving how, when, and why to allocate effort to a task or activity' (Eysenck and Eysenck, 1985). The question of why people buy is complex; the discussion of choice criteria links to motivation and can explain why one consumer may choose a Nissan car because they are price conscious while another may choose a Mercedes because they are status conscious. The influence of personality may explain the motivations that underpin why an extrovert may choose a red sports car while an introvert may prefer a grey Skoda.

It is important to note that levels of motivation vary depending on the individual, the type of purchase and the purchase occasion. For example, the motivations for buying luxury goods focus on motives such as the desire to portray a specific social class, communicate a desired self-image and provide self-concept reinforcement, a visible proof that the consumer can afford higher-priced products (Nwankwo, Hamelin and Khaled, 2014). So it is important to understand the motives that drive consumers in a wider context, particularly as motives can determine choice criteria and subsequently enable marketers get closer to their customers. For example, a consumer who is driven by the esteem and status motive may use self-image as a key choice criterion when considering the purchase of a car or clothes. Increasingly, technology is used to get inside the mind of the consumer and to develop more understanding of what drives consumer choice.

Beliefs and attitudes

A *belief* is a thought that a person holds about something. In a marketing context, it is a thought about a product or service on one or more choice criteria. Beliefs about a Volvo car might be that it is safe, reliable and high status. Marketing people are very interested in consumer beliefs because they are related to attitudes. In particular, misconceptions about products can be harmful to brand sales. Duracell batteries were believed by consumers to last three times as long as Eveready batteries, but in continuous use they lasted over six times as long. This prompted Duracell to launch an advertising campaign to correct this misconception. The promotion for Marmite crisps recognizes that the beliefs of some consumers will be favourable towards the brand and others negative. By presenting the brand in this way, the advertisement is inviting consumers to try the crisps to discover which group they are in.

An *attitude* is an overall favourable or unfavourable evaluation of a product or service. The consequence of a set of beliefs may be a positive or negative attitude towards the product or service. Beliefs and attitudes play an important part in the evaluation of alternatives in the consumer decision-making process. They may be developed as part of the information search activity and/or as a result of product use, and they play an important role in product design (matching product attributes to beliefs and attitudes), in persuasive communications (reinforcing existing positive beliefs and attitudes, correcting misconceptions and establishing new beliefs, e.g. 'Skoda is a quality car brand') and in pricing (matching price with customers' beliefs about what a 'good' product would cost).

Personality

Our everyday dealings with people tell us that they differ enormously in their personalities. **Personality** is the inner psychological characteristics of individuals that lead to consistent responses to their environment (Kassarjan, 1971). A person may tend to be warm–cold, dominant–subservient, introvert–extrovert, sociable–loner, adaptable–inflexible, competitive–cooperative, etc. If we find from marketing research that our product is being purchased by people with a certain personality profile, then advertising could show people of the same type using the product. The concept of personality is also relevant to brands. *Brand personality* is their characterization as perceived by consumers. Brands may be characterized as 'for young people' (Tommy Hilfiger), 'for winners' (Nike) or 'intelligent' (Toyota iQ). This is a dimension over and above the physical (e.g. colour) or functional (e.g. taste) attributes of a brand. By creating a brand personality, a marketer may create appeal to people who value that characterization.

Economic circumstances

During periods of economic growth, consumer spending is fuelled by rising income levels and confidence in job security. Products that are the subject of discretionary spending, such as luxury brands, expensive holidays, restaurant meals and top-of-the-range consumer durables, thrive. However, changing economic circumstances—such as recession, deflation, inflation and fears about employment prospects—drive many consumers to postpone purchases, become more price sensitive and change their shopping habits. Economic circumstances, therefore, can have a major effect on consumer behaviour.

Lifestyle

Lifestyle patterns have attracted much attention from marketing research practitioners. Lifestyle refers to the pattern of living as expressed in a person's activities, interests and opinions. Lifestyle analysis (psychographics) groups consumers according to their beliefs, activities, values and demographic characteristics, such as education and income. Lifestyle analysis has implications for marketing since lifestyles have been found to correlate with purchasing behaviour (O'Brien and Ford, 1988). A company may choose to target a particular lifestyle group (e.g. the succeeders) with a product offering and use communications that reflect the values and beliefs of this group. An example of how changing lifestyles affect consumer behaviour is the popularity of on-the-go products with people who live very busy lives. On-the-go drinks, such as bottled water and takeaway coffee, and on-the-go food, such as cereal-based breakfast snack bars, have found favour among time-pressured consumers.

Lifecycle and age

Consumer behaviour might depend on the stages reached during their lives. A person's *lifecycle stage* (shown in Figure 3.7) is relevant since disposable income and purchase requirements may vary according to stage. For example, young couples with no children may have high disposable income if both work and may be heavy purchasers of home furnishings and appliances since they may be setting up a home. When they have children, disposable income may fall, particularly if they become a single-income family and the purchase of baby- and child-related products increases. At the empty-nester stage, disposable income may rise due to the absence of dependent children, low mortgage repayments and high personal income. This type of person may be a

FIGURE 3.7
Lifecycle stages

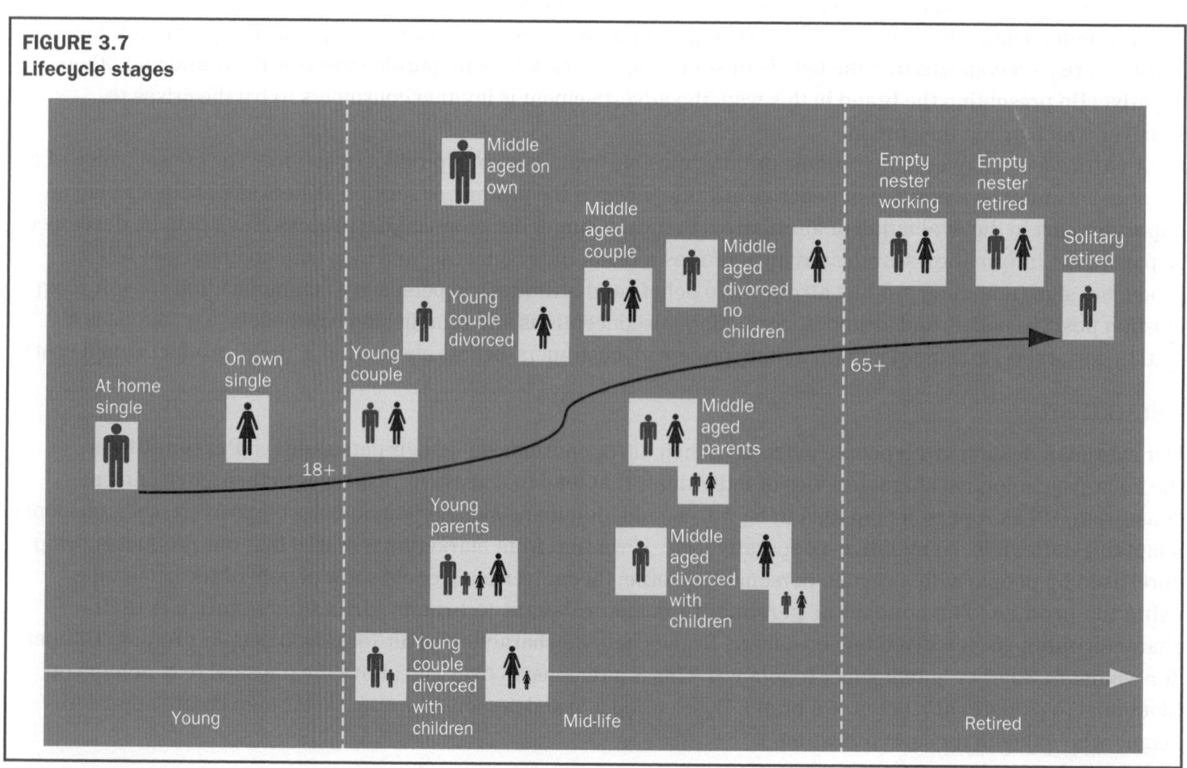

high-potential target for financial services and holidays. BMW uses lifecycle stage to segment consumers with its 4 × 4 X5 model targeted at young couples with children, and the 4 × 4 X6 model targeted at empty nesters. The X6 is designed for someone who previously owned an X5 or something similar, but now is looking for an SUV that 'doesn't scream "family"' (Smith, 2008).

However, not all people follow the classic family lifecycle stages. Figure 3.7 also shows alternative paths that may have consumer behaviour and market segmentation implications.

Age is an effective discriminator of consumer behaviour. For example, young people have very different tastes in product categories such as clothing, drinks, holidays and television viewing compared to older people. The young have always been a prime target for marketers because of their capacity to spend.

Social influences

There are four social influences on consumer behaviour: culture, social class, geodemographics and reference groups.

- **Culture** refers to the traditions, taboos, values and basic attitudes of the whole society within which an individual lives. It provides the framework within which individuals and their lifestyles develop. Cultural norms are the rules that govern behaviour and are based upon values: i.e. beliefs about what attitudes and behaviour are desirable. Conformity to norms is created by reward-giving (e.g. smiling) and sanctioning (e.g. criticism). Cultural values affect how business is conducted and also affect consumption behaviour.
- **Social class** is an important determinant of consumer behaviour. In the UK it is largely based on occupation. Advertising media (e.g. newspapers) usually give readership/viewership figures broken down by social class groupings. Every country has its own method of grouping and, in the UK, the National Statistics Socio-economic Classification system identifies eight categories based on occupation (see Table 3.3). Social class is a predictive measure of consumption although consumption patterns are likely to vary within each of the groups (e.g. some people may be more inclined to spend their money on consumer durables, while others may have more hedonistic preferences). It is important to note that the influence of social class should be tempered by lifecycle, lifestyle and age.
- **Geodemographics** Another method of classifying households is based on geographic location. This analysis—called **geodemographics**—is based on population census data. Households are grouped into geographic clusters based on information such as type of accommodation, car ownership, age, occupation, number and age

TABLE 3.3 Social class categories

Classification	Descriptors	Occupations
1	Higher managerial and professional occupations	Senior managers, directors and professionals
2	Lower managerial and professional occupations	Higher technical, administrative supervisory occupations, e.g. department managers
3	Modern professional Middle junior manager	Clerical/administrative, sales/service, technical/auxiliary and engineering occupations
4	Intermediate occupations	Non-professional and agricultural occupations, and self-employed sole traders
5	Technical craft worker	Technical craft and process operative occupations, e.g. shift manager in a factory
6	Semi-routine occupations	Service and technical operatives, agricultural, clerical and childcare occupations
7	Routine occupations	Production, technical, operative and agricultural occupations
8	Never worked	Never worked, long-term unemployed and students

Base on Source ONS (2018)

of children, and ethnicity. These clusters can be identified by postcodes, which makes targeting by mail easier. A number of systems are used in the UK, including MOSAIC and ACORN (A Classification Of Residential Neighbourhoods). The ACORN system identified 11 neighbourhood types (discussed in more detail in Chapter 7) which can be used for market segmentation and positioning. Geodemographics is an effective method of segmenting many markets.

- **Reference groups** The term **reference group** indicates a group of people that influences an individual's attitude or behaviour. Where a product is conspicuous—for example, clothing or cars—the brand or model chosen may have been strongly influenced by what buyers perceive as acceptable to their reference group. This group may consist of family members, a group of friends or work colleagues. Reference groups influence their members by the roles and norms expected of them. For example, students may have to play several roles: to lecturers, the role of learner; to other students, the role may vary from peer to social companion. Depending on the adopted role, behaviours and purchasing patterns may vary based upon group norms.

There are two main types of reference group: membership and aspirant groups. *Membership groups* are the groups to which a person already belongs. What is believed to be suitable, acceptable and/or impressive to this group may play a major role in consumption behaviour. What other people think at a party, at work or generally socializing is of great importance. *Aspirant groups* are the groups to which the individual would like to belong. Stereotypically, men supposedly want to look/feel like their favourite sport stars and women want to look/feel like famous film stars or models. This motivates the purchase of football shirts with 'Ronaldo' on the back, and the buying of clothing seen to be worn by Adele or Kate Moss. ASOS, the online fashion retailer, bases its marketing strategy on aspirant group theory. It copies the style of clothing worn by film stars and models, and sells its clothes to aspirant women who wish to dress like them. Celebrities such as David Beckham, Ronaldo, Kate Moss and Angelina Jolie also act as opinion leaders to aspirant group members, influencing their consumption behaviour.

Review

1 The context and dimensions of buyer behaviour

- Looking at the wider context, which affects the dimensions of the buying decision—how they buy, what their choice criteria are, where they buy and when they buy—helps identify what is important and has implications for the marketing mix.

2 The role of the buying centre (who buys) and its implications

- Some buying decisions are made individually, others by a group. A group decision may be in the hands of a buying centre with up to five roles: initiator, influencer, decider, buyer and user. The interaction between these roles determines whether a purchase is made.
- Marketers need to understand the formulation of buying groups as this can be helpful in targeting and segmenting markets, and for planning the core strategy.

3 The consumer decision-making process (how people buy)

- The decision to purchase a consumer product may pass through various stages: need recognition/problem awareness, information search, evaluation of alternatives, purchase and post-purchase evaluation of the decision.

4 The marketing implications of the consumer decision-making process

Each stage in the process has implications for marketing managers:

- *Need recognition*: awareness of consumer problems can create opportunities for building a competitive advantage and planning strategies to overcome any *need* inhibitors; stimulating need recognition through marketing communications might help initiate the decision-making process.

- *Information search*: knowing where consumers look for information to help solve their decision-making can aid marketing planning. Communication can direct consumers to suitable sources of information. One objective is to ensure that the company's brand appears in the consumer's awareness set.
- *Evaluation of alternatives*: when a consumer is highly involved, they require more information about the positives of making a particular buying decision than in a low-involvement buying situation. For low-involvement decisions, creating top-of-mind awareness through repetitive advertising and trial (e.g. through sales promotion) can aid the decision-making. For all consumer decisions, marketing managers must understand the choice criteria used to evaluate brands, including the importance of emotion.
- *Post-purchase evaluation*: consumers can experience cognitive dissonance after making a purchase and might need reassurance. Marketing communication initiatives can act as positive reinforcers.

5 The differences in evaluation of high- versus low-involvement situations

- *High-involvement situations*: the consumer is more likely to carry out extensive evaluation and take into account beliefs about the perceived consequences of buying the brand, the extent to which others believe they should or should not buy the brand, attitudes (which are the degree to which the consumer likes or dislikes the brand overall) and subjective norms (which form an overall evaluation of the degree to which others approve or disapprove of the purchase).
- *Low-involvement situations*: the consumer carries out a simple evaluation and uses simple choice tactics to reduce time and effort. Awareness precedes trial, which, if satisfactory, leads to repeat purchase. The behaviour may become habitual, with little conscious thought or formation of attitudes before purchase.

6 The nature of choice criteria (what are used) and their implications

- Choice criteria are the various attributes (and benefits) a consumer uses when evaluating products and services. These may be technical (e.g. reliability), economic (e.g. price), social (e.g. status) or personal (e.g. self-image).
- The implications are that knowledge of the choice criteria used by members of the buying centre aids product design (e.g. are style/looks more important than performance?) and the choice of the appeals to use in advertising and personal selling, which should be linked to the key choice criteria used by those members.

7 The influences on consumer behaviour—the buying situation, personal and social influences—and implications for marketing

- *Buying situation*: the three types are extended problem-solving, limited problem-solving and habitual problem-solving. The marketing implications for each type are: extended problem-solving—provide information-rich communications; limited problem-solving—stimulate the need to conduct a search (when their brand is not currently bought) or reduce the risk of brand switching; habitual problem-solving—repetitive advertising should be used to create awareness and reinforce already favourable attitudes.
- *Personal influences*: the six types are information processing, motivation, beliefs and attitudes, personality, lifestyle, and lifecycle and age, and they all have implications for marketing:
  1) *Information processing* involves perceptions and learning.
  2) *Motives* influence choice criteria and include physiological, safety, belongingness and love, esteem and status, and self-actualization.
  3) *Beliefs and attitudes* are linked in that the consequence of a set of beliefs may be a positive or negative attitude. Marketers attempt to match product attributes to desired beliefs and attitudes, and they use communications to influence these and establish new beliefs.
  4) *Personality* of the type of person who buys a brand may be reflected in the type of person used in its advertisements. Brand personality is used to appeal to people who identify with that characterization.
  5) *Lifestyles* have been shown to be linked to purchase behaviour. Lifestyle groups can be used for market segmentation and targeting purposes.
  6) *Lifecycle and age* stage may affect consumer behaviour as the level of disposable income and purchase requirements (needs) may depend on the stage that people have reached during their life. For similar reasons, age may affect consumer behaviour.

- There are four types of social influence: culture, social class, geodemographics and reference groups:
  1) *Culture* affects how business is conducted and consumption behaviour. Marketers have to adjust their behaviour and the marketing mix to accommodate different cultures.
  2) *Social class* can predict some consumption patterns, and so can be used for market segmentation and targeting purposes.
  3) *Geodemographics* classifies consumers according to their location and is used for market segmentation and targeting purposes.
  4) *Reference groups* influence their members by the roles and norms expected of them. Marketers attempt to make their brands acceptable to reference groups, and target opinion leaders to gain brand acceptability.

Key Terms

attitude the degree to which a customer or prospect likes or dislikes a brand

awareness set the set of brands of which the consumer is aware may provide a solution to the problem

beliefs descriptive thoughts that a person holds about something

buyers generally refers to professionals in procurement. A buyer makes business decisions on purchasing

buying centre a group that is involved in the buying decision (also known as a *decision-making unit*)

choice criteria the various attributes (and benefits) people use when evaluating products and services

classical conditioning the process of using an established relationship between a stimulus and a response to cause the learning of the same response to a different stimulus

cognitive dissonance post-purchase concerns of a consumer arising from uncertainty as to whether a decision to purchase was the correct one

cognitive learning the learning of knowledge and development of beliefs and attitudes without direct reinforcement

consumer a person who buys goods and services for personal use

consumer decision-making process the stages a consumer goes through when buying something—namely, problem awareness, information search, evaluation of alternatives, purchase and post-purchase evaluation

cultural values culture is a system of meaning, which is ingrained into society and groups. The values are shaped by individuals that are connected to the society or group

cultural norms the systems of societal (or group) beliefs and values, which are accepted by the members of the society or group

customer satisfaction a term used in both consumer and organizational purchasing situations. These are individuals and companies that have an established relationship with a seller (e.g. retailers, producers, manufacturers)

evoked set the set of brands that the consumer seriously evaluates before making a purchase

geodemographics the process of grouping households into geographic clusters based on information such as type of accommodation, occupation, number and age of children, and ethnic background

information framing the way in which information is presented to people

information processing the process by which a stimulus is received, interpreted, stored in memory and later retrieved

information search the identification of alternative ways of problem-solving

learning any change in the content or organization of long-term memory as the result of information processing

lifestyle the pattern of living as expressed in a person's activities, interests and opinions

motivation the process involving needs that set drives in motion to accomplish goals

operant conditioning the use of rewards to generate reinforcement of response

parallel importing the movement of goods from one country to another without the permission of the owner/designer. These types of imports are sometimes referred to as 'grey' imports

perception the process by which people select, organize and interpret sensory stimulation into a meaningful picture of the world

personality the inner psychological characteristics of individuals that lead to consistent responses to their environment

reasoning a more complex form of cognitive learning where conclusions are reached by connected thought

reference group a group of people that influences an individual's attitude or behaviour

rote learning the learning of two or more concepts without conditioning

selective attention the process by which people screen out those stimuli that are neither meaningful to them nor consistent with their experiences and beliefs

selective distortion the distortion of information received by people according to their existing beliefs and attitudes

selective retention the process by which people only retain a selection of messages in memory

vicarious learning learning from others without direct experience or reward

Study Questions

1. **Identify and explain the three contexts that are reshaping consumer markets.**
2. **Choose a recent purchase which involved you and other people in the decision-making. Explain what role(s) you played in the buying centre. What roles did the other people play and how did they influence your choice?**
3. **Regarding the purchase made in Question 2, what decision-making process did you go through? At each stage (need recognition, information search, etc), try to remember what you were thinking about and what activities took place.**
4. **Regarding the purchase made in Question 2, what choice criteria did you use? Did they change between drawing up a shortlist and making the final choice?**
5. **Make a list of high- and low-involvement products and suggest how marketers should plan to communicate with potential target consumers of these products.**
6. **Think of the last time you made an impulse purchase. What stimulated you to buy? Have you bought the brand again? Why or why not? Did your thoughts and actions resemble those suggested by the Ehrenberg and Goodhart model?**
7. **Discuss the difference between attitudes and beliefs and make an argument for which is the most important for markets to consider.**
8. **Find an example of how digital technology is changing the way we buy and suggest the implications for marketers.**
9. **To what kind of lifestyle do you aspire? How does this affect the types of product (particularly visible ones) you buy now and in the future?**
10. **Are you influenced by any reference groups? How do these groups influence what you buy?**

Recommended Reading

Consumers are individuals, who marketers seek to understand. Read the following articles to get inside consumers' heads to gain insights into how they think; learn about the 'moments of truth' which drive ethical consumption and gain insights into the literature that is behind consumer psychology, behaviourism, conditioning and more.

Bridger, D. (2015), *Decoding the Irrational Consumer*, London: Kogan Page.

Shewearsfashion.com (2018); (Nazlan, Tanford, & Montgomery, 2018)

Edmiston, D. (2014), The New Emerging Market Multinationals: Four Strategies for Disrupting Markets and Building Brands, *Journal of Consumer Marketing*, 31(3), 228–228, https://doi.org/10.1108/JCM-09-2013-0706.

Mohr, J.J., Price, L.L. and Rindfleisch, A. (2018), Marketing's Quest for Environmental Sustainability: Persistent Challenges and New Perspectives, *Marketing in and for a Sustainable Society*, 29–59.

References

Ajzen, I. (1985), From intentions to actions: A theory of planned behaviour, in Kuhl, J.B.J. (ed.) *Action-control: From cognition to behaviour*, Springer, 11–39.

Ajzen, I. (1991), The theory of planned behaviour, *Organizational Behaviour and Human Decision Processes* 50, 179–211.

Ajzen, I. (2012), The theory of planned behaviour, in Van Lange, P.A.M., Kruglanski, A.W. and Higgins, E.T. (eds.), *Handbook of theories of social psychology*, Vol. 1, 438–59, London, UK: Sage.

Ajzen, I. and Fishbein, M. (1980), *Understanding Attitudes and Predicting Social Behaviour*, Englewood Cliffs, NJ: Prentice-Hall.

Ajzen, I., and Fishbein, M. (2005), The influence of attitudes on behaviour, Albarracín, D., Johnson, B.T. and Zanna, M.P. (Eds.), *The handbook of attitudes*. Mahwah, NJ, US: Erlbaum.

Ajzen, I. and Madden, T. (1985), Prediction of Goal-Directed Behaviour: Attitudes, Intentions, *Journal of Experimental Social Psychology* 22, 453–74.

Anon (2011), Fragrance of flight planned to improve cabin experience http://www.independent.co.uk/travel/news-and-advice/fragrance-of-flight-planned-to-improve-cabin-experience-2344095.html (accessed May 2015).

Baccarella, C., Wagner, T., Keitzmann, J. and McCarthy, I. (2018), Social Media? It's Serious! Understanding the dark side of social media, *European Management Journal* 36(4), 431–8.

Bastien, V. and Kapferer, J-N. (2009), Luxury marketing plays by a different set of rules, *Financial Times* 15 June, vol. 2.

Barda, T. (2011), Beer Googles, *The Marketer*, April, 20–2.

Baumgartner, H. and Steenkamp, J.B. (1996), Exploratory Consumer Buying Behaviour: Conceptualisation and Measurement, *International Journal of Research in Marketing* 13, 121–37.

Bennet, B. (2011), Another criticism of Maslow's hierarchy of needs http://billbennett.co.nz/2011/07/02/criticism-maslows-hierarchy (accessed May 2018).

Bettman, J.R. (1982), A Functional Analysis of the Role of Overall Evaluation of Alternatives and Choice Processes, in Mitchell, A. (ed.) *Advances in Consumer Research 8*, Ann Arbor, MI: Association for Consumer Research, 87–93.

Blackwell, R.D., Miniard, P.W. and Engel, J. F. (2005), *Consumer Behaviour*, Orlando, FL: Dryden.

Chang, W., Lu, L., Su, H., Lin, T.A. and Chang, K. (2011), Mediating effect of buying motives between physical vanity and online compulsive buying, *African Journal of Business Management*, 5 (8), 3289–3296.

Christian, B. (2017), Black Friday in the UK makes no sense. But it isn't going anywhere, *Wired* 22 November (accessed July 2018) https://www.wired.co.uk/article/black-friday-sales-2017-future (accessed May 2018).

Cleveland, M. and Laroche, M. (2007), Acculturation to the global consumer culture: scale development and research paradigm, *Journal of Business Research*, 60 (3) 249–260.

Confino, J., and Muminova, O. (2011), What motivates consumers to make ethically conscious decisions? *The Guardian*, 11 August http://www.theguardian.com/sustainable-business/motivates-consumers-environmental-ethical-decisions (accessed 23 February 2015).

Costa, A.I.A., Schoolmeester, D., Dekker, M. and Jongen, W.M.F. (2007), To cook or not to cook: A means-end study of motives for choice of meal solutions, *Food Quality and Preference* 18, 77–88.

Creusen, M.E.H. and Schoormans, J.P.L. (1997), The Nature of Differences between Similarity and Preference Judgements: A Replication and Extension, *International Journal of Research in Marketing* 14, 81–7.

Dai, W., Lee, J., Lee, G. and Luca, M. (2014), *Optimal Aggregation of Consumer Ratings: An Application to Yelp.com*. http://www.people.hbs.edu/mluca/OptimalAggregation.pdf (accessed May 2018).

Darrat, A., Darrat, M. and Amyx, D. (2016), How impulse buying influences compulsive buying: the central role of consumer anxiety and escapism, *Journal of retailing and consumer services* 31 (July), 103–8.

Ehrenberg, A.S.C. and Goodhart, G.J. (1980), *How Advertising Works*, J. Walter Thompson/MRCA.

Elliott, R. (1997), Understanding Buyers: Implications for Selling, in Jobber, D. (ed.) *The CIM Handbook of Selling and Sales Strategy*, Oxford: Butterworth-Heinemann.

Elliott, R. (1998), A Model of Emotion-Driven Choice, *Journal of Marketing Management* 14, 95–108.

Elliott, R. and Hamilton, E. (1991), Consumer Choice Tactics and Leisure Activities, *International Journal of Advertising* 10, 325–32.

Euromonitor (2014), *Chocolate Confectionery in the United Kingdom*, Euromonitor International, September. http://www.euromonitor.com/chocolate-confectionery-in-the-united-kingdom/report (accessed 28 February 2015).

Eysenck, H.J. and Eysenck, M.W. (1985), *Personality and individual differences*, New York: Plenum.

Gee, R. (2016), Groupon returns to TV as it aims to reignite international appeal and prove its 'evolution', *Marketing Week*, 30 June (accessed July 2018) https://www.marketingweek.com/2016/06/30/groupon-returns-to-tv-as-it-aims-to-reignite-international-appeal-and-prove-its-evolution/ (accessed May 2018).

Gibson, O. (2008), Led Zep Tickets Fetch £7425 as Online 'Touts' Strike Gold in £200m Bonanza, *The Guardian*, 8 January, 13.

Global Data (2018), Growing number of female UHNWIs create new opportunities in luxury tourism, Global Data Report, https://www.globaldata.com/growing-number-female-uhnwis-create-new-opportunities-luxury-tourism/ (accessed July 2018).

Groupon (2015), About Groupon http://www.groupon.co.uk/about (accessed 23 February 2015).

Hannaford, A. (2013), 'Neuromarketing': Can science predict what we'll buy? *The Telegraph*, 13 April. http://www.telegraph.co.uk/news/science/science-news/9984498/Neuromarketing-can-science-predict-what-well-buy.html (accessed 23 February 2015).

Hobbs, T. (2017) UK ad spend hits record £21.4 bn as digital dominates again, *Marketing Week* 25 April (accessed July 2018) https://www.marketingweek.com/2017/04/25/uk-ad-spend-digital/.

Kassarjan, H.H. (1971), Personality and Consumer Behaviour Economics: A Review, *Journal of Marketing Research*, November, 409–418.

Jia, H., Zhou, S. and Allaway, A (2018), Understanding the evolution of consumer psychology research: A bibliometric and network analysis, *Journal of Consumer Behaviour*, https://onlinelibrary.wiley.com/doi/full/10.1002/cb.1734 (accessed May 2018).

Kietzmann, J., Hermkens, K., McCarthy, I. and Silvestre, B. (2011), Social media? Get serious! Understanding the functional building blocks of social media, Business Horizons, 54 (3) 241–251.

Khomami, N. (2018), Burberry destroys £28m of stock to guard against counterfeits, *The Guardian*, 19 July https://www.theguardian.com/fashion/2018/jul/19/burberry-destroys-28m-stock-guard-against-counterfeits (accessed July 2018).

Kuusela, H., Spence, M.T. and Kanto, A.J. (1998), Expertise Effects on Prechoice Decision Processes and Final Outcomes: A Protocol Analysis, *European Journal of Marketing* 32(5/6), 559–576.

Laurent, G. and Kapferer, J.N. (1985), Measuring Consumer Involvement Profiles, *Journal of Marketing Research* 12 (February), 41–53.

Levin, L.P. and Gaeth, G.J. (1988), Framing of Attribute Information Before and After Consuming the Product, *Journal of Consumer Research* 15 (December), 374–8.

Lindstrom, M. (2005) Sensing the Opportunity, *The Marketeer*, February, 4–17.

Lindstrom, M. (2016) *Small Data: The Tiny Clues that Uncover Huge Trends*, John Murray, Hodder & Stoughton, UK.

Lovell, C. (2008), Is Neuroscience Making a Difference?, *Campaign*, 3 October, 11.

Luo, X., Andrews, M., Song, Y. and Aspara, J. (2014), Group-Buying Deal Popularity, *Journal of Marketing* 78 (2), 20–33.

Luthans, F. (2001), *Organisational Behaviour*, San Francisco: McGraw-Hill.

Mairs, G. (2014), Rugby World Cup tickets: prices hit record levels amid fears touts will hold fans to ransom, *The Telegraph*, 27 October http://www.telegraph.co.uk/sport/rugbyunion/rugby-world-cup/11189239/Rugby-World-Cup-tickets-Prices-hit-record-levels-amid-fears-touts-will-hold-fans-to-ransom.html (accessed 23 February 2015).

McCormick, A. (2011), Marketing on the brain, *Marketing*, 2 November, 24–5.

McSherry, M. (2015), Hershey's lawsuit sparks British revolt for 'superior' Cadbury chocolate, *The Guardian*, 27 January. http://www.theguardian.com/business/2015/jan/27/hersheys-lawsuit-ban-imported-cadbury-from-us (accessed 26 February 2015).

Merz, M., Zarantonello, L. and Grappi, S. (2018), How valuable are your customers in the brand value co-creation process? The development of a customer Co-creation Value (CCCV) scale, *Journal of Business Research* 82 (1), 79–89.

Microsoft (2012), The Evolution of Pre-family Man, http://advertising.microsoft.com/europe/WWDocs/User/Europe/ResearchLibrary/ResearchReport/8.%20The%20Evolution%20 of%20Pre-family%20 man.pdf (accessed May 2018).

Nazlan, N.H., Tanford, S. and Montgomery, R. (2018), The Effects of availability Heuristics in online consumer reviews, *Journal of Consumer Behaviour* 17 (5) 449-460.

Neal, C., Quester, P. and Hawkins, D.I. (2007), *Consumer Behaviour: Implications for Marketing Strategy*, Boston, MA: Irwin.

Nwankwo, S., Hamelin, N. and Khaled, M. (2014), Consumer values, motivation and purchase intention for luxury goods, *Journal of Retailing and Consumer Services* 21 (5), 735–744.

O'Brien, S. and Ford, R. (1988), Can We at Last Say Goodbye to Social Class?, *Journal of the Market Research Society* 30(3), 289–332.

O'Rourke, D. (2014), Behavioural tracking and neuroscience are tools for sustainable innovation, *The Guardian*, 25 July http://www.theguardian.com/sustainable-business/behavioural-insights/behavioural-tracking-neuroscience-tools-sustainable-innovation-advertising-marketing-consumers (accessed 23 February 2015).

O'Shaughnessey, J. (1987), *Why People Buy*, New York: Oxford University Press, 161.

Olsen, N.V., Menichelli, E., Sørheim, O. and Næs, T. (2012), Likelihood of buying healthy convenience food: An at-home testing procedure for ready-to-heat meals, *Food Quality and Preference* 24(1), 171–8.

Ong, B.S. (2011), Online Shoppers' Perceptions and Use of Comparison-Shopping Sites: An Exploratory Study, *Journal of Promotion Management* 17 (2), 207–227.

ONS (2018), The National Statistics Socio-economic classification https://www.ons.gov.uk/methodology/classificationsandstandards/otherclassifications/thenationalstatisticssocioeconomicclassificationnssecrebasedonsoc2010#classes-and-collapses (accessed July 2018).

Pinder, C.C. (1998), *Work Motivation in Organizational Behaviour*, Upper Saddle River, NJ: Prentice Hall.

Prahalad, C.K. and Ramaswamy, V. (2004), Co-creation experiences: the next practice in value creation, *Journal of Interactive Marketing* 18 (3) 5–14.

Ratneshwar, S., Warlop, L., Mick, D.G. and Seegar, G. (1997), Benefit Salience and Consumers' Selective Attention to Product Features, *International Journal of Research in Marketing* 14, 245–9.

Ries, A. and Trout, J. (2001), *Positioning: The Battle for Your Mind*, New York: Warner.

Rook, D. (1987), The Buying Impulse, *Journal of Consumer Research* 14(1), 89–99.

Rothschild, M.L. (1978), Advertising Strategies for High and Low Involvement Situations, *American Marketing Association Educator's Proceedings*, American Marketing Association Chicago, 150–162.

Ruddick, G. (2014), Black Friday 2014 explained–retailers gearing up for day of deals, *The Telegraph*, 19 November. http://www.telegraph.co.uk/finance/newsbysector/retailandconsumer/11217839/Black-Friday-2014-Get-ready-for-the-biggest-online-shopping-day-in-history.HTML (accessed 26 February 2015).

Salganik, M., Sheridan, D. and Watts, D. (2006), Experimental Study of Inequality and Unpredictability, *Science* 311 (5762), 845–856.

Samsung (2018), Samsung Expands Laundry Line Up with New Premium Compact Washer (accessed July 2018) https://news.samsung.com/global/samsung-expands-laundry-line-up-with-new-premium-compact-washer (accessed May 2018).

Shewearsfashion.com (2018) travel and fashion blog, accessed October 2018

Smiley, M. (2016), Whirlpool aims to improve school attendance by providing students with access to clean clothes, *The Drum*, 1 August (accessed July 2018) https://www.thedrum.com/news/2016/08/01/whirlpool-aims-improve-school-attendance-providing-students-access-clean-clothes (accessed May 2018).

Smith, B. and Colgate M. (2007), Customer value creation: a practical framework, *Journal of Marketing Theory & Practice*, 15, 7–23.

Smith, G. (2008), On the Road, *Guardian Weekend*, 21 June, 99.

Smith, L. (2005), Ten Sales a Second: Glastonbury Tickets Go in Record Rush, *The Guardian*, 4 April, 7.

Sobol, K., Cleveland, M. and Laroche, M. (2018), Globalization, national identity, biculturalism and consumer behaviour: A longitudinal study of Dutch Consumers, *Journal of Business Research* 28 (1) 340–353.

Stephen, A. (2016), The role of digital and social media marketing in consumer behaviour, *Current Opinion in Psychology*, 10 August 17–21.

Tynan, C., Mckehnie, S. and Chhuon, C. (2010), Co-creating value for luxury brands, Journal of Business Research 63 (11) 1156–1163.

Weinberg, P. and Gottwald, W. (1982), Impulsive consumer buying as a result of emotions, *Journal of Business Research* 10 (1), 43–57.

Williams, K.C. (1981), *Behavioural Aspects of Marketing*, London: Heinemann.

World Health Organization (2010), 25–70% of adults in Europe are overweight http://www.euro.who.int/en/who-we-are/regional-director/news/news/2010/12/2570-of-adults-in-europe-are-overweight (accessed May 2018).

Wright, P.L. (1974), The Choice of a Choice Strategy: Simplifying vs Optimizing, Faculty Working Paper no. 163, Champaign, Ill: Department of Business Administration, University of Illinois.

Zhang, J. (2010), The Sound of Silence: Observational, *Marketing Science* 29 (2), 313–335.

CASE 5
Cappuccino Wars

The Battle of the Coffee Shops

The UK has come a long way from the days when a request for coffee would bring a cup of uniformly grey, unappealing liquid, sometimes served in polystyrene cups, which bore no relation to the rich, flavoursome coffee experienced on trips to continental Europe. The origin of this change was not Europe, however, but the USA, where the coffee shop culture was grounded.

Recent years have seen an explosion of coffee shops on UK high streets, with over five million lattés, cappuccinos and espressos served per week. The market is dominated by Costa Coffee (bought in 2018 by Coca-Cola from Whitbread) with over 2,300 coffee shops, US-owned Starbucks with 950, and Caffè Nero with 675 shops. In total, the UK has over 6,000 branded coffee shops, all charging over £2 (€2.30) for a small coffee. Often three or more bars will be located within 100 metres of each other.

The first US West Coast style coffee shop was opened in the UK in 1995 and was called the Seattle Coffee Company. The owners were Americans who saw an opportunity to serve the British with good-quality coffee in relaxed surroundings just like they experienced in the USA. The concept was a huge success, and by 1997 the company had 49 coffee outlets. It was joined by Coffee Republic and Caffè Nero, which also grew rapidly. In 1997, however, the coffee market in the UK was to change dramatically with the arrival of the US-based Starbucks coffee shop giant, which bought the Seattle Coffee Company.

Its strategy was to gain market share through fast rollout. For the first five years, Starbucks opened an average of five shops a month in the UK: in 1999 it had 95 shops, by 2018 this had increased to 950. Today, Starbucks is in the Fortune Top 500 US companies and has over 28,000 coffee shops in more than 70 countries. Its approach is simple: blanket an area completely, even if the shops cannibalize one another's business. A new coffee bar will often capture about 30 per cent of the sales of a nearby Starbucks, but the company considered this was more than offset by lower delivery and management costs (per shop), shorter queues at

individual shops and increased foot traffic for all the shops in an area as new shops take custom from competitors too. Over 20 million people buy coffee at Starbucks every week, with the average Starbucks customer visiting 18 times a month.

One of its traditional strengths was the quality of its coffee. Starbucks has its own roasting plant, from which the media are banned lest its secrets are revealed. In its coffee shops, coffee is mixed with a lot of milk and offered in hundreds of flavours. Its Frappuccino is positioned as a midday break in advertisements where a narrator explains 'Starbucks Frappuccino coffee drink is a delicious blend of coffee and milk to smooth out your day.' The tag-line is 'Smooth out your day, every day.'

A key problem was that Starbucks' major competitors—Costa Coffee and Caffè Nero—also followed a fast roll-out strategy, causing rental prices to spiral upwards. For example, Starbucks' Leicester Square coffee shop in London was part of a £1.5 million (€17 million) two-shop rental deal. Many coffee shops were not profitable; Starbucks, because it continued to operate them, was accused of unfairly trying to squeeze out the competition. However, the recession brought rental prices down, allowing the chains, especially Costa Coffee, to expand rapidly. All three major players are now profitable.

The typical consumers at these coffee bars are young, single and high earners. They are likely to be professionals—senior or middle managers with company cars. Students also are an important part of the market. Coffee bars are seen as a 'little bit of heaven', a refuge where consumers can lounge on sofas, read broadsheet newspapers and view New Age poetry on the walls. They provide an oasis of calm for people between their homes and offices. They are regarded as a sign of social mobility for people who may be moving out of an ordinary café or low-end department store into something more classy. Even the language is important for these consumers: terms such as latté, cappuccino and espresso allow them to demonstrate connoisseurship. Consumers are offered a wide choice of combinations, including a sprinkling of marshmallow, syrup and an extra shot of espresso.

Coffee bars also cater for the different moods of consumers. For example, Sahar Hashemi, a founding partner of Coffee Republic, explains 'If I'm in my routine, I'll have a tall, skinny latté. But if I'm feeling in a celebratory mood or like spoiling myself, it's a grand vanilla mocha with whip and marshmallows.'

Starbucks has expanded the services it provides by offering a Wi-Fi service that allows laptop users to gain high-speed internet access. This service has been copied by Costa Coffee and Caffè Nero.

Starbucks, Costa Coffee and Caffè Nero offer food alongside drinks. Starbucks targets breakfast, lunch and snack times with a limited range of both indulgent and healthy eating options. Costa Coffee has been offering hot foods and salads since 2002. Caffè Nero's food offer is integral to its Italian-style positioning, with most of the ingredients for its meals coming from Italy.

Many of the coffee shops have four zones. The first is at the front of the store, where customers can look outside and passers-by can see there are people inside. The second is an area containing perch seating, reminiscent of coffee houses in Italy. The third zone offers large community tables where groups or individuals can work on their laptops or read. Finally, softer seating creates a more intimate and relaxed zone.

The chains have also embraced the fair trade coffee idea, with Costa Coffee offering Cafédirect products since 2000 and Starbucks introducing fair trade coffee in 2002. The three chains almost entirely buy their coffee beans from sustainable sources, paying up to 12 per cent above average world prices. Low-calorie drinks are also offered.

Declining performance at Starbucks led to the reappointment in 2008 of Howard Schultz as chief executive, the man who grew the firm from just four outlets to over 28,000 today. He identified Starbucks' problems as stemming from its outlets losing their 'romance and theatre'. He pointed out that the distinctive aroma of fresh coffee was less evident because of the advent of vacuum-sealed, flavour-locked packaging. Also, the use of new automated machines meant that customers could not see their drinks being prepared—eliminating an 'intimate experience' with the barista and impairing the spectacle of coffee-making. The result he concluded was that some customers found Starbucks coffee shops sterile places that no longer reflected a passion for coffee. The situation was made worse by the smell of sandwiches, which often overpowered the aroma of coffee. Some Starbucks staff were also criticized as being unfriendly.

The problems facing Starbucks were worsened by a strong challenge from McDonald's, which opened McCafés in some of its outlets, where customers can buy similar drinks at a cheaper price. Artisan coffee shops also posed a strong threat as some consumers rejected the corporates in favour of small independent outlets. Starbucks' woes continued with a report from the consumer magazine *Which?* that showed that Starbucks coffee was inferior to that of Costa Coffee and Caffè Nero, which won. It was also the most expensive.

Schultz began to address some of these problems by introducing new, smaller expresso machines, so customers can once again see the baristas making their drinks. Coffee is once again being ground by hand, restoring the aroma, and a less potent-smelling cheese is being used in Starbucks' sandwiches. The baristas have all been retrained, not only in the art of making excellent coffee but also in connecting better with customers. The interiors of many of Starbucks' coffee shops have been renovated and redesigned.

To make the outlets more attractive during the recession, a new instant coffee brand, Via, was launched, which Starbucks claims tastes as good as ground coffee but at a much cheaper price. The company also introduced a loyalty card which allowed free extras such as a shot of whipped cream, syrup or soy in the coffee. Like Wi-Fi, this innovation was copied by its rivals. A further change was the dropping of the 'Starbucks Coffee' logo from its mugs and changing the colour of its 'siren' figure from black to green.

Starbucks has also extended its brand by an alliance with Nestlé, who has gained the global rights to sell the coffee chains' bagged coffee, drinks and Nespresso-style pods, gaining its expertise in marketing to the retail grocery sector.

Meanwhile, Costa Coffee has moved into the self-service market by buying Coffee Nation and its 900 vending machines. The offering carries the Costa Express branding and uses fresh milk and

»

»

fresh coffee beans, roasted by Costa in London. While using the machine, the customer is treated to the gentle buzz of a coffee shop and the smell of *pain au chocolat*. By 2018, the company had expanded to a total of more than 8,000 highly profitable vending machines in the UK.

Questions

1. **Why have coffee shops been so popular with consumers?**
2. **You are considering visiting a coffee shop for the first time. What would influence your choice of coffee shop to visit? Is this likely to be a high- or low-involvement decision?**
3. **Assess the coffee chains' moves to expand the offerings they provide for their customers.**
4. **Coffee shops are mainly located in the centres of towns and cities. Are there other locations where they could satisfy customer needs?**

This case study was written by David Jobber, Emeritus Professor of Marketing, University of Bradford.

References

Based on: Cree, R. (2003), Sahar Hashemi, *The Director*, January, 44–47; Daniels, C. (2003), Mr Coffee, *Fortune*, 14 April, 139–140; Hedburg, A. and Rowe, M. (2001), UK Goes Coffee House Crazy, *Marketing Week*, 4 January, 28–9; Sutter, S. (2003), Staff the Key to Marketing Success, *Marketing Magazine*, 19 May, 4; Bainbridge, J. (2005), Off the Boil, *Marketing*, 13 April, 28–9; Anonymous (2004), Starbucks to Offer 'Music to Go', *BBC News*, 12 March, http://news.bbc.co. uk.; Clark, A. (2008), Wall St Gets Palpitations Over Caffeine Fuelled Growth, *The Guardian*, 7 January, 25; Anonymous (2008), Coffee Wars, *The Economist*, 12 January, 57–8; Fernandez, J. (2009), Back To Basics, *Marketing Week*, 26 February, 18–9; Charles, E. (2011), Change Brewing at Starbucks, *Marketing*, 12 January, 14–15; Reynolds, J. (2011), Costa Targets Tesco with Express Self-Service Offer, *Marketing*, 9 March, 9; Roberts, J. (2012), Quality Quest Keeps Sector Full of Beans, *Marketing Week*, 9 February, 22–3; Bolger, M. (2013), Café Culture, *The Marketeer*, July/August, 21–3; BBC (2014), Coffee Shop Hotshots, A BBC Open University Partnership Television programme; Anonymous (2018), One In Every Two Branded Coffee Shops Is a Costa, Starbucks Or Caffee Nero, www.foodserviceequipmentjournal.com 16 January; Ritson, M. (2018), Starbucks and Nestle Must Focus On Three Key Areas To Avoid a Bitter Brew, www.marketing week.com 8 May; Guardian Staff and Agencies (2018), Nestle Swallows Starbucks Rights in $7bn Alliance, *The Guardian*, 8 May, 29; James, I. (2018), Costa Owner Blames Falling Sales On High Street Decline, www.the guardian.com/business; Wood, Z. and Sweney, M. (2018), Coca-Cola Snaps Up Costa in £4bn Deal to Cash in on Coffee, *The Guardian*, 1 September, 3.

CASE 6
The Rise of Influencer Marketing: is it Worth it for Brands?

Introduction

William Bernbach, the founder of global advertising agency DDB, once said 'good advertising does not just circulate information—it penetrates the public mind with desires and belief'.

Bernbach's thoughts still ring as true today as they did in the early 1990s. There are 3.1 billion active users on social media (https://wearesocial.com/uk/blog/2018/01/global-digital-report-2018) and the fight for brands to 'penetrate the public mind' is increasingly becoming more competitive. This has allowed for influencer marketing to take up a prominent role in the media mix across many industries. Based on the industry benchmark that peer recommendations and consumer opinion are more trustworthy than traditional advertising (http://www.nielsen.com/us/en/insights/news/2013/under-the-influence-consumer-trust-in-advertising.html), influencers have attracted brands to invest in the region of five billion dollars in 2017 (http://mediakix.com/2018/03/influencer-marketing-industry-ad-spend-chart).

Given the number of social media channels that impact onto our daily lives, brands now enjoy the ability to enlist influential people (influencers) to promote the brand. Whether this is an Instagrammer who snaps a selfie with the product or a YouTuber who produces a vlog of their experience, they come at a cost but can reach a highly engaged audience that trusts their opinion.

Example 1: Daniel Wellington (Swedish Brand) Conversion Activation—Micro Influencer Strategy

Many brands across the fashion industry led the way in this space. Daniel Wellington, the Swedish watch brand, was founded in 2011. Since its inception as a small start-up, it has bypassed traditional marketing by enlisting thousands of micro-influencers to promote their products on their social media channels. Through a combination of gifting the watch or paying the influencer, they promote the #danielwellington branded hashtag by showcasing the product in their Instagram posts. Each post features beautiful imagery of minimalistic jewellery alongside a unique discount code that their followers can use to purchase the product.

Since 2011, Daniel Wellington has eschewed traditional marketing and in doing so has gained 4.2 million Instagram followers with 1.8 million posts with the branded hashtag. The high level of social media engagement has successfully filtered down to profit, becoming the fastest growing private company in the industry, selling over a million watches a year with $228 million annual revenue (http://nordic.businessinsider.com/swedish-companies-dominate-incs-5000-fastest-growing-private-companies-in-europe—take-half-of-top-10-2017-2/; https://kingkong.com.au/how-daniel-wellington-built-a-228-million-global-fashion-empire-with-a-tiny-30k-investment-detailed-case-study/). The brand's rapid rise to the top is a great example of how a brand has reached millions across social media and successfully created a purchase journey through influencers in a very cluttered industry.

This approach has allowed the company to develop a market reach to wherever Instagram is available. Now, their target market is primarily dictated to by the social media platform being used, which, in turn, dictates the demographic of their audience.

»

»

Example 2: Adidas (German brand) Brand Awareness Activation—Macro Influencer Strategy

Across the industries that are most active in the influencer space, Instagram is the most adopted platform with 92% of retail brands having a presence on the platform (https://www.emarketer.com/Article/Brands-Worldwide-Embrace-Instagram/1013928). By comparison with the Daniel Wellington brand, who are focused on conversion to purchase by sharing discount codes, Adidas use Instagram to boost brand awareness and create user generated content (UGC).

The Adidas Neo product range is targeted towards the trendy youth market and their influencer campaign is #MyNeoShoot. The focus of the campaign was to use Instagram as a UGC tool, inviting the public to post their best 'neo inspired' modelling pictures, to be in with a chance of being one of six people selected to feature in the campaign. To kick-start the campaign, Adidas enlisted the biggest celebrity on Instagram, American singer Selena Gomez, for the launch and also recruited other high-level influencers to rapidly increase brand awareness.

The campaign was successful on several fronts for Adidas. Aside from the branded hashtag acting as a recruitment mechanic for models, by its nature it spread peer recommendations which 84% of millennials report has an influence on their purchase decision (https://www.socialmediatoday.com/marketing/masroor/2015-05-28/social-media-biggest-influencer-buying-decisions). The campaign gained 12,000 entries and amassed 71,000 mentions throughout the campaign (http://mediakix.com/2016/06/instagram-marketing-case-study-adidas-neo/).

The Adidas campaign utilised UGC to organically grow the reach of their message; the potential for people to be recruited as models provided a level of interest and engagement which also brought an enhanced focus on the 'neo' range.

Conclusion

The two campaigns had different objectives. As a start-up, Daniel Wellington aimed to directly sell products through discount codes and thus to establish itself in the industry. On the other hand, Adidas were more focused on the top-end-of-the-funnel and increasing brand awareness compared with US-based competitors such as Nike and Under Armour in a very profitable millennial demographic. In both cases, the brands leveraged the power of influencers to meet their business objective.

With the rise of over-the-top TV channels such as Amazon Prime and Netflix, traditional TV viewership has been on the decline over the past couple of years. At the same time, ad-blocking on web browsers has become more popular as the public fight to not be disturbed by a barrage of advertising. Both factors have resulted in brands being on the hunt for the most organic way of reaching their target market. Nielson Catalina Solutions state that influencer marketing provides an 11 times higher return than traditional advertising, due to its organic and often subliminal messaging (https://www.tapinfluence.com/tp_resource/nielsen-case-study/). Whether influencer marketing draws in 11 times higher return on investment for every brand across every industry is still to be determined, but brands are willing to give it a go, allowing for the marketing channel to become a multi-billion-pound industry.

Although Bernbach never lived to see the rise of influencer marketing, advertising has found a new channel based around the same principle of 'penetrating the public mind with desires and belief'.

Use the links below to explore the approach being taken by the two organisations.

Daniel Wellington – examples of campaign:

- https://www.instagram.com/p/BElot_4qtWz/
- https://www.instagram.com/p/BFA3D7-MEs1/

Adidas My Neo Shoot – examples of campaign:

- Selena Gomez video - https://www.instagram.com/p/9ZNlzCNynr/
- Selena Gomez image - https://blog.thesocialms.com/wp-content/uploads/2016/08/Bildschirmfoto-2016-08-30-um-17.01.56.png
- https://www.instagram.com/p/855VDrNT4z/
- https://www.instagram.com/p/89gwXamtw4/

Questions

1. **Using the example of Daniel Wellington, what are the advantages and disadvantages of this type of (micro) influencer strategy?**

2. **Using the Adidas example, what are the advantages and disadvantages of this type of (macro) influencer strategy?**
3. **Looking at both approaches, come up with examples of industry/product sectors that could adopt similar approaches. Are there certain characteristics of the products/ brands that lend themselves to this type of influencer activity?**
4. **Some people have called this influencer activity 'native' or 'false' advertising. What impact do you think this type of activity will have on marketing strategy generally over the next five years?**

This case study was written by James Saker, senior digital manager at a leading Premier League Football Club, in conjunction with the School of Business and Economics at Loughborough University.

References

Based on: https://wearesocial.com/uk/blog/2018/01/global-digital-report-2018; http://www.nielsen.com/us/en/insights/news/2013/under-the-influence-consumer-trust-in-advertising.html; http://mediakix.com/2018/03/influencer-marketing-industry-ad-spend-chart; http://nordic.businessinsider.com/swedish-companies-dominate-incs-5000-fastest-growing-private-companies-in-europe—take-half-of-top-10-2017-2/; https://kingkong.com.au/how-daniel-wellington-built-a-228-million-global-fashion-empire-with-a-tiny-30k-investment-detailed-case-study/; https://www.tapinfluence.com/tp_resource/nielsen-case-study/; https://www.emarketer.com/Article/Brands-Worldwide-Embrace-Instagram/1013928; https://www.socialmediatoday.com/marketing/masroor/2015-05-28/social-media-biggest-influencer-buying-decisions; http://mediakix.com/2016/06/instagram-marketing-case-study-adidas-neo/

CHAPTER 4
Business-to-Business Marketing

> *A brand for a company is like a reputation for a person. You earn a reputation by trying to do hard things well.*
>
> **JEFF BEZOS, FOUNDER OF AMAZON, INC.**

LEARNING OBJECTIVES

After reading this chapter, you should be able to:

1. understand and discuss the importance of B2B markets
2. explain the principles and practices of B2B marketing
3. discuss the people and process involved in B2B buying and marketing
4. explain the influences that shape buying behaviour
5. discuss how to segment business markets

Business-to-business (B2B) markets are a very important and vibrant part of modern marketing; networks of suppliers provide goods and services to firms of all sizes throughout global economies. This chapter examines the characteristics of B2B markets; defines B2B marketing; looks at the people and processes involved in buying and considers the implications for marketing.

Importance of Business-to-Business (B2B) Markets

Organizational markets are significant and account for nearly half of all revenues in developed countries but they are a subject area often not a key element of academic marketing courses. Before widespread adoption of the internet as a sales channel this area of marketing was called industrial marketing and mostly focused on transactions in **commodity markets**, e.g. petroleum, timber, metals. Since the growth of technology and service sector markets, the term industrial marketing has largely been replaced by B2B marketing (Lilien, 2016).

Broadly, there are three types of B2B markets:

1 *Industrial markets* consist of producers that buy products and services to help them manufacture other goods and services. Industrial goods include raw materials, components and capital goods such as machinery, as well as many leading consumers brands, which use **exclusive distribution channels** to sell their goods. See Exhibit 4.1.
2 *Reseller markets* comprise companies that buy products and services to resell. Retailers, mail order companies and online retailers are examples of resellers.
3 *Government and institutional markets* consist of government agencies and organizations that buy products and services to help them carry out their activities: for example, Local Authorities, the Police, schools, hospitals.

Trading in B2B markets tends to be complex, involving significant purchasing decisions, which can include many people in buying decisions, follow formalized procedures and operate on a global scale. B2B markets are different from Business-to-Consumer (B2C) markets as they serve demand, which is driven by firms (intermediaries) across the value chain and operate in a culture driven by manufacturing and technology as opposed to B2C markets, which serve demand at the end of the value chain and operate in a marketing culture (Grewal and Lilien, 2012). B2B marketing is shaped by many factors.

Nature and size of customers

Typically, the number of customers in B2B markets is smaller than in consumer markets. The Pareto rule often applies, with 80 per cent of output being sold to 20 per cent of customers. But it is also important to understand that there are different sizes of businesses within these markets, which operate on a local, regional, national or global scale. Read Marketing in Action 4.1 to discover more about the marketing, buying and selling of cheese. The intensity of the competition and the number of players in a market depends on how goods are manufactured and what is being sold. In the computer component manufacturing industry there are a small number of dominant global players that represent a large share of the market, e.g. Apple, Sony, Hewlett Packard, Dell, Intel and Asus. The importance of smaller numbers of large customers (compared with B2C markets, fewer suppliers serve large numbers of individual customers) is that it influences marketing behaviour. In B2B markets, suppliers (sellers) develop longer-term relationships with their buyers and invest heavily in developing collaborative relationships. Dedicated sales and marketing teams under the title of 'key account management' (KAM) are employed to service large accounts. (See Chapter 10 for detailed discussion of relationship marketing and Chapter 15 for professional selling and sales management.) Each B2B market is unique and types of products, manufacturing processes and methods of distribution affect the nature and size of customers.

EXHIBIT 4.1
Making fashion count

MARKETING IN ACTION 4.1
Quel Fromage? You can't be Serious!

France is one of the world's largest cheese producers within the dairy industry; it is important economically and has a strong export market with 36 per cent of production sold within Europe, where Europeans consume large amounts of cheese every year. The home market is strong too, individually French people–on average–consume more cheese than people in the USA, the UK, Spain, Norway and the Netherlands.

Nature and size of the market: there are many types of firms in this industry, which vary considerably in size from the typical French farm, which is small, with around 50 cows, and probably sells its milk through cooperatives to large dairy groups, e.g. Lactalis Group (largest dairy group in the world) which owns industrial manufacturing plants in 44 different countries.

In other words, there are many businesses of different sizes and functions producing many different products, which vary in price depending on whether they are industrially produced or made by craft manufacturers of artisan cheese, using milk from cows, sheep or goats. The total cheese output of all businesses in the French cheese industry is approaching two million tons per annum, with Brie, Camembert and Compte being among the favourites.

Intensity of competition is tempered by a strong sense of partnership, collaboration and cooperation. From farm to factory, relationships are key in cheese production. Dairy cooperatives have been around a very long time and have helped to transform cheese production in France, where they work in collaboration and are run in the interest of the people. France has over 60,000 farms producing milk from cows, sheep and goats, which sell their produce through 260 cooperatives (54 per cent) or private producers (46 per cent). Over 70 per cent is made into dairy products by around 650 processing units, which manufacture over 1,000 varieties of cheese. The industry is governed by partnership organizations, which manage the stewardship of the countryside, environment and heritage of the industry.

Importance of large customers: Group Lactalis is a very large customer for many businesses on the production side and a major seller of cheese in the global cheese industry. The Group owns many well-known brands of cheese: the President brand (French, sold in over 140 countries, earning €1.8 billion), Galbani (Italian, sold in 130 countries, earning €1.5 billion) and Seriously (McLelland, Scotland). Seriously is a fullyowned subsidiary of Group Lactalis; the product is manufactured in Stranraer in Scotland and the brand is positioned in the market as a heritage cheddar, with distinct character, from unspoiled rural Scotland. For Group Lactalis, all its brands need to perform well and, when Seriously Strong started to fall into decline, the Group invested in a brand refresh, so that it could compete with other popular UK cheese brands; Cathedral Cheddar and Philadelphia. The rebranding involved changing the name slightly from Seriously Strong to Seriously, new packaging and TV commercials. The £5 million investment in the brand refresh sought to reposition and help sell the cheeses to retail resellers. Following the makeover, Lactis McLelland were able to negotiate a deal with The Co-operative retail group so that the cheese would feature in its extensive network of convenience stores and, in doing so, would increase sales.

So, the next time you fancy a nibble of cheese, think about the complex global network of farmers, producers, buyers and suppliers that have been working together to bring your choice of cheese to the table.

Based on: Gee (2016); Group Lactalis (2018); Vlahović et al. (2014); FNCL (2018); Seriously (2018); Hobbs (2015); Cornall (2017)

Complexity of buying

B2B purchases involve significant investment and involve many people at different levels of the organization. Increasingly, buying has become more complex and buyers are under pressure to make cost savings, while improving the quality, flexibility and speed of delivery of the purchasing investment (Bals, Laine and Mugurusi, 2018). Due to this complexity, relationships are very important and play an important role in the buying process. Co-creation activities between buyers and sellers increasingly aim to bring added value for all parties (Chang, Wang and Arnett, 2018).

Economic and technical choice criteria

Although B2B buyers, being people, are affected by emotional factors such as liking or disliking a salesperson, B2B buying decisions are made on economic and technical criteria, as these buyers must justify their decisions to other members of their organization (Jobber and Lancaster, 2015). Also, the formalization of the buying function through the establishment of purchasing departments leads to the use of economic rather than emotional choice criteria. As purchasing becomes more sophisticated, economic criteria come to the fore, with techniques such as lifecycle cost, total cost of ownership and value-in-use analysis. Fleet buyers, for example, calculate lifecycle costs, including purchase price and running and maintenance costs, when considering which company car to buy.

Network technology and e-commerce

B2B markets led the way in using technology in purchasing with Electronic Data Interchange (EDI), that is, dedicated computer networks linking companies with suppliers to facilitate business trading via computer-to-computer exchanges. EDI has been around since the 1970s. Firms like M & S used EDI to connect with manufacturers and streamline the buying process. Buying in this way has many advantages: fast efficient processing of orders, reduction of costs as fewer people are involved, and transactions are accurate and auditable. However, dedicated EDI systems were costly to install and maintain, but widespread adoption of the internet opened up the possibilities for many firms to consider computer-enabled purchasing. EDI and e-commerce systems also facilitated online purchasing to flourish and paved the way for global purchasing via the internet. Traditional purchasing technologies had encouraged working with fewer suppliers through dedicated connections (Bakos and Brynjolfsson, 1993), whereas e-commerce via the internet opened new interactive opportunities with many suppliers (Ellis-Chadwick, 2000). These systems and networks changed the nature of buyer/supplier transactions, shortening the supply chain and bringing the end consumer closer to the manufacturer. In B2B and B2C markets, the internet revolution shifted purchasing from the physical marketplace to the virtual marketspace enabling seamless computer purchasing.

Today, value-added networks, portals (digital gateways) and virtual marketplaces give access to purchasing ecosystems, which facilitate greater communication within and across industries and to the end consumer. Alibaba.com is one of the leaders of e-commerce transactions in China selling online; see Exhibit 4.2. It provides a marketplace connecting small and medium-sized buyers and suppliers from China and around the world. Its web presence includes an international marketplace (www.alibaba.com) that focuses on global importers and exporters and a China marketplace (www.alibaba.com.cn) that focuses on suppliers and buyers trading domestically in China (Chaffey and Ellis-Chadwick, 2019). Digital technology is causing a blurring of the lines between B2B and B2C, for example Proctor and Gamble developed automated buying systems that linked retail shelves in Walmart with inventory management systems.

For manufacturing and reseller markets operating online, value-added networks bring many benefits: reduced procurement costs, fast supply, greater agility to respond to the changing marketing environment, better connectivity with suppliers, greater reach, increased opportunities to trade globally and closer working relationships between suppliers and customers. However, while e-commerce and e-procurement improve the ability of companies to source products and services globally, there are implications for logistics management.

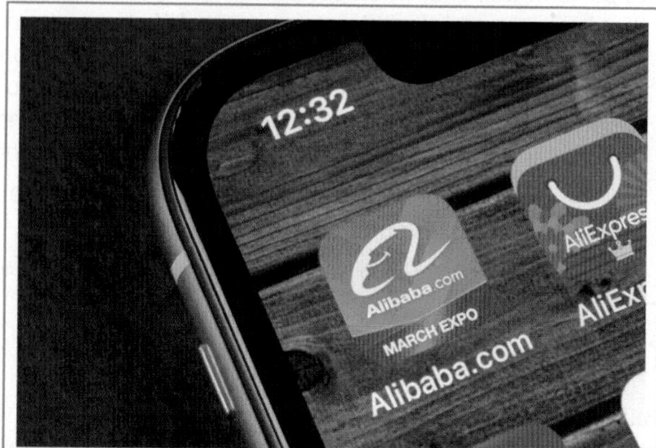

EXHIBIT 4.2
Alibaba, China's main e-commerce firm, facilitates global trading

Risks and uncertainty

Risk and uncertainty affect buying in B2B markets and influence the structure of the buying centre. The greater the uncertainty, the higher the risk, and the more people are likely to be involved in the buying decision, whereas when uncertainty is low, risks are lower, and purchases can be highly formalized and monitored by strict rules (Juha and Pentti, 2008).

B2B markets are characterized by a contract being agreed, often before the product is made due to the size of investment required. Product can be highly technical and the seller may be faced with unforeseen problems once work has started, which can mean that the buyer incurs unplanned losses. The UK's National Health Service encountered major problems when the cost of its patient record system—with an estimated budget of £6.4 billion—rose significantly, to over £10 billion. Eventually, this major IT investment project had to be abandoned, with huge losses, in this case, to the UK taxpayers. A commentator said, 'This saga is one of the most expensive contracting fiascos in the history of the public sector' (Syal, 2013).

Buying to specific requirements

Because of the large sums of money involved, B2B buyers sometimes draw up product specifications and ask suppliers to design their products to meet them. Services, too, are often conducted to specific customer requirements, marketing research and advertising services being examples. This is much less a feature of consumer marketing, where a product offering may be developed to meet a need of a market segment but, beyond that, meeting individual needs would prove uneconomic.

Derived demand

The demand for many B2B goods is derived from the demand for consumer goods. If the demand for smart phones increases, the demand for lithium-ion batteries, memory chips, cameras and other raw materials used to make phones will also increase. So component manufacturers would be wise to monitor consumer trends as well as their immediate B2B customers, like Apple, Inc., Samsung and Sony.

Negotiations

Between professional buyers and sellers, and bearing in mind the size and complexity of B2B buying, negotiation is often important. Thus, supermarkets will negotiate with manufacturers about price, since their buying power allows them to obtain discounts. Car manufacturers will negotiate attractive prices from tyre manufacturers such as Pirelli and Michelin, but the replacement brand must be an appropriate alternative. The supplier's list price may be regarded as the starting point for negotiation and the profit margin ultimately achieved will be heavily influenced by the negotiating skills of the seller. The implication is that sales and marketing personnel need to be conversant with negotiating skills and tactics and, in many situations, be aware of the complexities involved in the negotiation process, particularly when the products and services are also complicated, for example multichannel advertising deals, where both internal and media intermediaries can be involved in the negotiation. See Marketing in Action 4.2 for insight into the high stakes involved between Sky Atlantic and Volvo.

What is Business-to-Business Marketing?

B2B markets are arguably where marketing matters the most because, if manufacturers, suppliers and resellers fail in providing the *right products and services*, B2C markets cannot function effectively. The core principles of marketing apply both strategically and tactically in these markets, but differences exist, of which marketers involved in buying and selling should be aware. Broadly, the marketing capabilities to consider are those that can impact directly on customer relationships. By understanding the purchasing function, marketers can determine who to target, decide on products and services, organize sales processes and plan the communication mix. See Figure 4.1.

The purchasing dimension

Putting the customer at the core of marketing activities throughout the organization is key. Buying is one such corporate activity and, although there are similarities between consumer and B2B buying in terms of the stages of the buying process, B2B buying is different in terms of scale, risk and complexity. The implications of

MARKETING IN ACTION 4.2
Human Made Stories from Sweden Not Hollywood

Sky Atlantic HD and Volvo signed a major sponsorship deal and part of the package was a major creative media campaign, centred on the TV channel's programming, including its on-demand TV, Sky mobile TV service and SkyGo. The two organizations have come together as there is deemed to be synergy between their market positioning. Both are targeting premium markets where quality and added value are important. Volvo's core message is encapsulated in its advertising strapline, 'quality productions are made up of many parts'.

The sponsorship deal has been negotiated around opportunities for the two organizations to build long-term relationships both on and off screen. For Volvo, the benefits are extended reach for its brand messages and opportunities to build understanding of the Volvo brand among a premium viewing audience and to showcase the quality of the car. Underlining the deal for the car manufacturer is a strategic goal of selling 60,000 new cars in the UK by 2020. For Sky Atlantic, the benefits are firmly centred on the relationship opportunities.

While there are gains for both companies, this sponsorship deal was complex and was negotiated by an intermediary media agency, Mindshare. The deal involved multiple stakeholders across multiple media channels, both TV and digital, and with creative agency Grey London, which created the adverts (indents) and delivered a campaign that celebrates the art of filmmaking by playfully using a touch of Swedishness. The negotiators created a deal worth £5.3 million that involved Volvo sponsoring every programme on the Sky Atlantic Channel for two years and showing its 15-second indent adverts for 60 seconds every hour. These adverts won industry awards and led to a renewal of this partnership in 2018.

Based on: Advanced Television (2014); Sky Media (2014, 2018); Vizard (2013); Macleod (2014); Volvo Car UK (2016)

making wrong decisions in a B2B setting are potentially far-reaching, as they could eventually lead to loss of market share, job losses and even company failure. Consequently, marketing managers need to develop an understanding of buyer behaviour and the structure of the buying group within the purchasing organization to trade effectively. This type of buying requires considerable and detailed information searching and methodical evaluation of alternatives. A key challenge for B2B buyers is to be able to satisfy diverse requirements in a single offering. A product that provides engineers with the performance characteristics they demand, production managers with the delivery reliability they need, purchasing managers with the value for money they seek and shop-floor workers with the ease of installation they desire is likely to be highly successful. Understanding who is responsible for purchasing, how they buy and what is purchased is important and has implications for the sales side of business activity.

See Marketing in Action 4.3 to find out how Wing Yip developed an international trading firm by focusing on customer needs.

The sales dimension

Large B2B organizations tend to have sufficient resources for all these activities to be controlled internally under the umbrella of the marketing function. For example, personal selling strategies can be decided by the sales management team, advertising and sales promotion initiatives by the marketing communications team and a publicity event by the public relations department. Conflicts between production and marketing functions can occur and this is where the importance of an integrated effort comes to the fore. It is important to apply this mix consistently so that communications tools and techniques give out a consistent message to avoid confusing customers. For example, this can happen if the advertising department creates messages that aim to convey a brand as high quality, while at the same time the sales team are using heavy discounting and money-off sales promotions to sell their products. The result can be that customers do not know what to think about the brand. Mixed messages can seriously damage the customer perception of a brand and impede relationship development.

FIGURE 4.1
Dimensions of B2B marketing

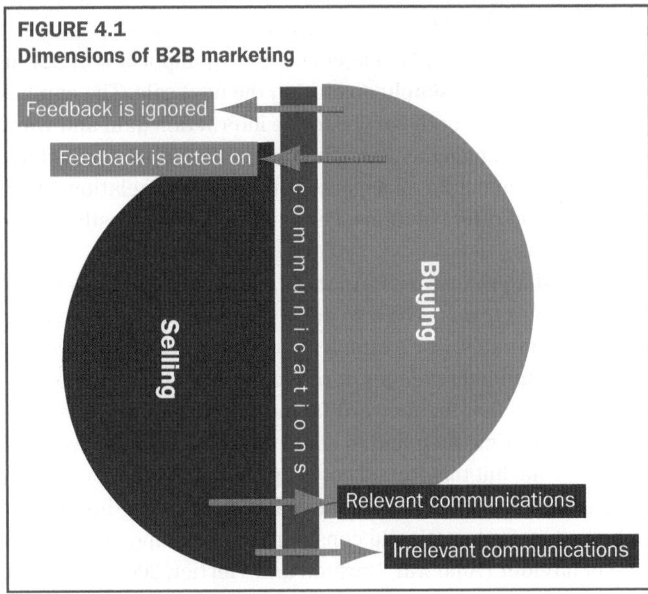

MARKETING IN ACTION 4.3
Wing Yip: All the Chinese you need to Know

When Wing Yip arrived in the UK from Hong Kong in 1959, it would have been difficult to imagine how markets for oriental food would grow to the current level of popularity. Wing worked as a waiter at a restaurant in Hull, where limited ingredients restricted the range of Chinese dishes on the menu. In the early 1960s, with partners, he opened two restaurants in Clacton-on-Sea and Ipswich, but found it increasingly difficult to obtain the quality and variety of ingredients needed to offer interesting and innovative menus to meet the growing customer demand. Eventually, he decided to sell his shares in the restaurants to fund a move into the food import business, supplying restaurants and takeaways. He used his market knowledge and said, 'after 10 years of running restaurants I knew what was required and opened a small shop in Birmingham selling Chinese ingredients to the trade'.

From humble beginnings, he worked with his brothers, Sammy and Lee, to make Wing Yip one of the UK's leading suppliers of Oriental food. Today, through their four superstores in Birmingham, Manchester, Cricklewood and Croydon, and their online store, Wing Yip supplies more than 4,500 Oriental products to the trade and has a growing consumer customer base. Having started out with an exclusively Chinese product range, they now encompass all Far Eastern cuisine. Their customers can find everything they need from live lobsters and crabs to fresh vegetables. On the sales side, Wing Yip has a personal selling sales team; direct sales and deliveries via telemarketing and sales online. Wing Yip aims to excel and to keep ahead of the competition.

Based on: Wing Yip (2018)

Personal selling

Customer relationship management is very important in B2B markets and requires the salesforce to focus on long-term goals and not simply on closing the next sale. The emphasis should be on creating win/win situations with customers so that both parties to the interaction gain and want to continue the relationship. For major customers, relationship management may involve setting up dedicated teams (key account management) to service the account and maintain all aspects of the business relationship, but for smaller customers, social media, the web and the cloud offer solutions. Personal selling is a costly form of communication, but can be ideally suited to B2B markets.

According to research (Agarwal, Harmon and Viertier, 2009), another key challenge for marketers who manage sales teams is how to achieve a balance between the cost of sales generation and the revenue such activity generates. For example, when a large telecoms company wanted to reduce the cost of its salesforce while maintaining revenues, it reduced back-office support so it could protect the frontline sales staff. But, the outcome was that the forward-facing sales representatives started doing the administrative support tasks, so reducing the time they had to concentrate on selling. Eventually, more junior sales staff were employed in the support role, but this forced costs up as they were more expensive than the original back-office staff. A good principle to use when looking at cost reductions in this area is to plan strategies that 'do no harm'; this is best achieved by systematically considering marketing systems and business practices in the light of customer needs and behaviour (Agarwal, Harmon and Viertier, 2009). See Chapter 15 for more detailed coverage of this topic.

The communications dimension

Direct marketing

The relatively low cost of direct mail and email campaigns makes them tempting alternatives to personal visits or telephone calls. Setting up a website can also be relatively inexpensive once the initial set-up costs have been met. However, wrongly targeted direct mail, a poorly designed website or a badly executed email campaign can cause customer annoyance and tarnish the image of the company and brand. B2B companies are turning to integrated marketing communications as a means of using the strengths of a variety of media to target business customers. Integrated marketing communications is a concept that sees companies coordinate their marketing communications tools to deliver a clear, consistent, credible and competitive message about the organization and its products. See Chapter 15 for more detailed coverage of this topic.

Digital marketing

According to Chaffey and Ellis-Chadwick (2019), 'Digital marketing focuses on managing different forms of online company presence, such as company websites, mobile apps and social media company pages integrated with online communications techniques' and this aspect of marketing activity has become increasingly important in B2B markets over the last two decades. For example:

- *The web:* enables firms to develop a digital destination, which can offer large resources of company information and act as a gateway to a sales portal.
- *Social media networks:* a slow initial uptake of social media platforms by B2B companies might suggest they were struggling with the technology. Research in the USA in 2012 found larger companies to be using all the major social media channels, but the same was not true for small and medium companies. In the UK, less than 30 per cent of SMEs were using social media networks to develop their brands. By 2018, its use has become much more widespread, with many companies claiming social media to be the most powerful and effective channel for deepening customer relationships, raising brand awareness and developing brand positioning. Social media marketing in B2B markets is different from consumer markets. Businesses are aiming to build significant long-term relationships with their clients.
- *Mobile marketing:* more B2B buyers are using smartphones as part of their sales and purchasing activities. Mobile buying is speeding up purchasing and research has shown this also increases customer loyalty. The new B2B seller should engage their customers through mobile marketing in the early stages of sales negotiations. According to Archacki et al (2017), 60 per cent of buyers were found to be using mobile marketing as a significant part of their purchasing behaviour.

People and Process in Purchasing

B2B buying behaviour involves the people who make the purchase decisions, the stages in the buying process and the criteria used to inform the decision-making process.

Who makes buying decisions?

Buyers are important people as they can influence many aspects of a firm's operation. They are responsible for sourcing and selecting products, which often involves complex decisions, but also for managing the buying process—decisions that can impact on company performance, suppliers and the workforce (Lewis and Arnold, 2012). However, it is important to understand in B2B buying that the buyer, or purchasing officer, is often not the only person that influences the decision or has the authority to make the ultimate decision. Rather, the decision is in the hands of a **decision-making unit** (DMU) or *buying centre* as it is sometimes called. This is not necessarily a fixed entity. Members of the DMU may change as the decision-making process continues. Thus, a managing director may be involved in the decision that new equipment should be purchased, but not in the decision as to which manufacturer to buy it from.

Six roles have been identified in the structure of the DMU, as follows (Webster and Wind, 1972).

1. *Initiators:* those who begin the purchase process, for example maintenance managers.
2. *Users:* those who actually use the product, for example welders.
3. *Deciders:* those who have authority to select the supplier/model, for example production managers.
4. *Influencers:* those who provide information and add decision criteria throughout the process, for example accountants.
5. *Buyers:* those who have authority to execute the contractual arrangements, for example purchasing officer.
6. *Gatekeepers:* those who control the flow of information, for example secretaries who may allow or prevent access to a DMU member, or a buyer whose agreement must be sought before a supplier can contact other members of the DMU.

Conceptually, a DMU resides within the buying organization. Consequently, a decision-making unit is defined as a group of people within a buying organization who are involved in the buying decision. But, external influences do come from trade promotions and advertising messages from potential trade suppliers. Increasingly, the buying function is becoming a more collaborative process as organizations seek to develop mutually beneficial long-term relationships. Read about how suppliers get involved in the purchasing process in Mini Case 4.1. Distribution and channel management is also discussed in detail in Chapter 17.

For very important decisions, the structure of the DMU will be complex, involving numerous people within the buying organization. The marketing task is to identify and reach the key members to convince them of the product's worth. Often communicating only to the purchasing officer will be insufficient, as this person may be only a minor influence on supplier choice. Relationship management is of key importance in many B2B markets (discussed in detail in Chapter 10).

When the problem to be solved is highly technical, suppliers may work with a data scientist, engineers and other experts in the buying organization to solve problems and secure the order. In fact, this is becoming increasingly important and B2B marketing is focusing more on accelerating deals through collaborations than on generating demand.

Often B2B purchases are made in committees where the salesperson will not be present. The salesperson's task is to identify a person from within the decision-making unit who is a positive advocate and champion of the supplier's product. This person (or 'coach') should be given all the information needed to win the arguments that may take place within the decision-making unit. For example, even though the advocate may be a technical person, he or she should be given the financial information that may be necessary to justify buying the most technologically superior product.

Where DMU members are inaccessible to salespeople, advertising, the internet, social media or direct marketing tools may be used as alternatives.

Stages in the buying process: how they buy

Figure 4.2 describes the basics of the **decision-making process** for a B2B product (Robinson, Faris and Wind, 1967). The exact nature of the process will depend on the buying situation. In some situations, some stages will be omitted.

MINI CASE 4.1
Iceland Frozen Foods. Made in Asia

Iceland Foods Ltd has over 300 suppliers and sources many of its products from South-East Asia, where there are highly skilled production companies that can produce the quality of foodstuff that the buying team requires at a price that enables Iceland to offer value to its customers in a highly competitive marketplace.

Iceland Foods Ltd has grown from a single retail store selling frozen foods in Oswestry, Shropshire (UK) in 1970, to a national retail chain with over 840 stores, 25,000 employees and a turnover in excess of £2.7 billion. The food retail marketplace is challenging and Iceland has faced aggressive competition from major grocery retailers such as Tesco, Sainsbury and Morrisons, from limited-range discounters Aldi and Lidl, and from a variety of retailers such as Marks & Spencer (M&S). But Iceland has managed to withstand attacks on its position by maintaining its competitive price proposition through its product ranges.

Part of Iceland's competitive armoury is its innovative food ranges; sometimes over 120 new products are introduced in one year. One of its most important ranges is its seasonal party food. Iceland was the first company to introduce large platters of Christmas party food, but its competitors have been quick to follow into this product territory. Each year, Iceland's buying team works with suppliers to produce new products to reflect changing tastes and market demand. New ranges include sushi platters, exotic mini-soufflés and new vegetarian main courses. Many of the party ranges include Chinese and Indian foods and snacks and are sourced in China.

Annually, the buying team sets objectives for the producers to enable development of new product ranges. In 2018, environmental issues came to the forefront and suppliers had to comply with Iceland's promise to its customers of a 'palm oil free Christmas'. Once the products are ready, the buying team will visit suppliers in China to sample the new product ranges and test the extent to which their objectives have been met. Iceland's buyers taste the products, evaluate the actual look of the products and determine how many items of which foodstuffs might be offered. The buyers must also ensure that they can offer sufficient value to the retail customer at a profit. Once potential ranges have been selected, they are brought back to the UK and tested by in-house teams for ease of use, cooking instructions and taste. Sometimes Iceland's buyers go back to the producer to seek modifications to products, perhaps because they don't have the right appeal, flavour or cost base. Packaging design, the amount of content and promotional offers are also considered as part of the buying decision, as it is important to be able to offer the *right value* to the consumer. The final decision about which products make it into Iceland are made by the head buyer and, following a final round of testing, by the senior management team.

The buying team at Iceland plays a very important role in ensuring that the retailer can stay ahead of the competition and retain its market share. But the buying team does not work alone; suppliers, packaging designers, taste-testers, users and the senior management team are all involved in putting together food ranges.

Questions:

1. Discuss the extent to which Iceland's buying team fits the conceptual model of a DMU.
2. Build a case report that shows the importance of the buying function at Iceland and highlight the potential impact of wrong buying decisions.

Based on: Iceland Foods Ltd (2014, 2015, 2018); Pomeroy (2013); Selwood (2018)

For example, in a routine rebuy situation the purchasing officer is unlikely to pass through the third, fourth and fifth stages (search for suppliers, and analysis and evaluation of their proposals). These stages will be bypassed, as the buyer, recognizing a need—perhaps shortage of stationery—routinely reorders from an existing supplier. In general, the more complex the decision and the more expensive the item, the more likely it is that each stage will be passed through and that the process will take more time.

The stages are:

1 *Recognition of a problem (need):* needs and problems may be recognized through either *internal or external factors* (Jobber and Lancaster, 2015). An example of an internal factor would be the realization of under-capacity leading to the decision to purchase plant or equipment. Thus, internal recognition leads to active behaviour (internal/active). Some problems that are recognized internally may not be acted upon. This condition may be termed internal/passive. A production manager may realize that there is a problem with a machine but, given more pressing problems, decides to put up with it.

Other potential problems may not be recognized internally and become problems only because of external cues. Production managers may be quite satisfied with their production process until they are made aware of another, more efficient, method. See Exhibit 4.3, Eo-n targets corporate customers.

Clearly, these different problems have important implications for marketing and sales. The internal/passive condition implies that there is an opportunity for a salesperson, having identified the condition, to highlight the problem by careful analysis of cost inefficiencies and other symptoms, so that the problem is perceived to be pressing and in need of a solution (internal/active). The internal/active situation requires the supplier to demonstrate a differential advantage of its products over those of the competition. In this situation, problem stimulation is unnecessary, but where internal recognition is absent, the marketer can provide the necessary external cues. A forklift truck sales representative might stimulate problem recognition by showing how the truck can save the customer money, due to lower maintenance costs,

FIGURE 4.2
Buy phases: the B2B decision-making process

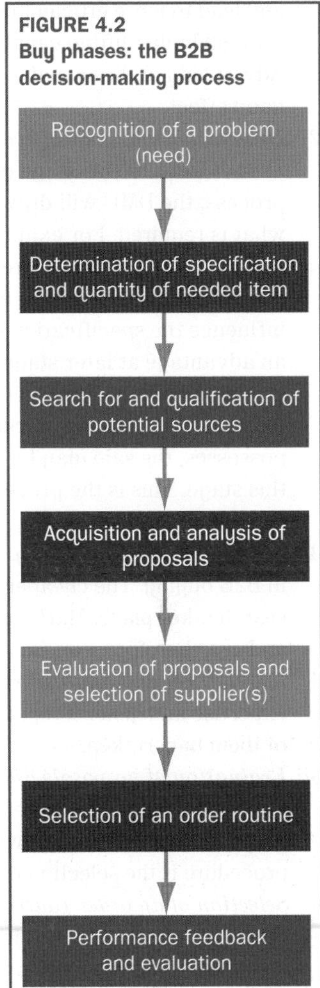

EXHIBIT 4.3
Corporate customers such as bakeries are targeted by advertisers like E.ON Energy

and lead to more efficient use of warehouse space through higher lifting capabilities. See Exhibit 4.4. Advertising or direct mail could also be used to good effect.

2 *Determination of specification and quantity of needed item:* at this stage of the decision-making process, the DMU will draw up a description of what is required. For example, it might decide that five web servers are required to meet certain specifications. The ability of marketers to influence the specification can give their company an advantage at later stages of the process. By persuading the buying company to specify features that only the marketer's own product possesses, the sale may be virtually closed at this stage. This is the process of setting up *lockout criteria*.

EXHIBIT 4.4
Jungheinrich, German Manufacturer, defines its business as providing solutions; if your problem is logistics or applications, they have a solution

3 *Search for and qualification of potential sources:* a great deal of variation in the degree of search takes place in B2B buying. The cheaper and less important the item, and the more information the buyer possesses, the less search takes place. Marketers can use advertising to ensure that their brands are in the buyer's awareness set and are, therefore, considered when evaluating alternatives.

4 *Acquisition and analysis of proposals:* having found several companies that, perhaps through their technical expertise and general reputation, are qualified to supply the product, proposals will be called for and analysis of them undertaken.

5 *Evaluation of proposals and selection of supplier(s):* each proposal will be evaluated in the light of the choice criteria deemed to be more important to each DMU member. It is important to realize that various members may use different criteria when judging proposals. Although this may cause problems, the outcome of this procedure is the selection of a supplier or suppliers.

6 *Selection of an order routine:* next, the details of payment and delivery are drawn up. Usually this is conducted by the purchasing officer. In some buying decisions—when delivery is an important consideration in selecting a supplier—this stage is merged into the acquisition and evaluation stages.

7 *Performance feedback and evaluation:* this may be formal, where a purchasing department draws up an evaluation form for user departments to complete, or informal through everyday conversations.

The implications of all this are that sales and marketing strategy can affect a sale through influencing need recognition, through the design of product specifications, and by clearly presenting the advantages of the product or service over those of the competition in terms that are relevant to DMU members. By early involvement, a company can benefit through the process of *creeping commitment*, whereby the buying organization becomes increasingly committed to one supplier through its involvement in the process and the technical assistance it provides.

Choice criteria

This aspect of B2B buyer behaviour refers to the criteria used by members of the DMU to evaluate supplier proposals. These criteria are likely to be determined by the performance criteria used to evaluate the members themselves (Draper, 1994). Thus, purchasing managers who are judged by the extent to which they reduce purchase expenditure are likely to be more cost conscious than production engineers, who are evaluated in terms of the technical efficiency of the production process they design.

In a similar manner to buying for consumers, B2B buying is characterized by *technical, economic, social* (organizational) and *personal criteria*. Economic and technical considerations are key, especially for major investment in, say, new IT systems and software, which has implications throughout an organization. While for materials and component parts, choice criteria may focus on more immediate gains: cost savings, delivery reliability, quality and technical assistance. Personal factors may also be important, particularly when suppliers' product offerings are essentially similar. In this situation, the final decision may rest upon personal relationships.

Customers' choice criteria can change in different regions of the world. For example, Xerox is generally known as a company that provides solutions for creating documents—printers and copiers—and is so well known that it is a recognized household name. Xerox aims to shift the positioning of its brand to increase recognition of the service element of its global business (Snoad, 2012), as this creates around 50 per cent of the company's business.

The motivations of key players involved in B2B purchasing and the criteria they use to compare supplier offerings are important to understand as they have implications for marketing. For example, economic considerations need to be appropriate and enable the buyers to meet their profit objectives and work within budgetary constraints. Emotional factors should not be totally ignored, as decisions are made by people who do not suddenly lose their personalities, personal likes and dislikes, and prejudices simply because they are at work. Let us examine several important technical and economic motives (quality, price and lifecycle costs, and continuity of supply) and then some organizational and personal factors (perceived risk, office politics and personal likes/dislikes).

Quality

Ensuring quality is critical for all organizations as replacing faulty components or dealing with returned goods is costly and impacts on a firm's reputation. Customers are unlikely to be satisfied if the quality is not good. There are formal procedures and standards, which apply in industrial and reseller markets, to ensure that quality requirements and procedures are met. Service quality can be assessed by reliability, responsiveness and assurance. Product quality can be assessed by performance, durability and design. Both sets of criteria are considered further in Chapters 9 and 11 respectively.

Price and lifecycle costs

For materials and components of similar specification and quality, price becomes a key consideration. For standard items, e.g. office supplies, price may be critical for a sale to be agreed as several suppliers can meet delivery and specification requirements. Much of this type of purchasing is done via e-commerce systems, but criteria are still relevant. Where personal negotiations are involved, large buying organizations can exert power to squeeze suppliers for better terms. For example, M & S, in its drive to reduce costs, demanded a 10 per cent cut in all suppliers' prices (Walsh, 2006). To remain competitive, when Tesco launched its 'Price Drop' initiative, many other supermarkets demanded reductions from their suppliers. Waitrose entered negotiations for a 5 per cent reduction from its ambient food suppliers to enable a new price-led marketing strategy, '1000s of ways to great value' (Heagarty, 2011).

Price is only one component of cost for many buying organizations. Increasingly, buyers consider **lifecycle costs**, which may include productivity savings, maintenance costs and residual values, as well as initial purchase price when evaluating products. Marketers can use lifecycle costs analysis to break into an account. By calculating lifecycle costs with a buyer, new perceptions of value may be achieved.

Continuity of supply

Another major cost to a company is disruption of a production run. Delays of this kind can mean costly machine downtime and even lost sales. Continuity of supply is, therefore, a prime consideration in many purchase situations. Companies that perform badly on this criterion lose out even if the price is competitive because a small percentage price edge does not compare with the costs of unreliable delivery. Supplier companies that can guarantee deliveries and realize their promises can achieve a significant differential advantage in the marketplace. B2B customers are demanding close relationships with *accredited suppliers* that can guarantee reliable supply, perhaps on a **just-in-time** basis.

Perceived risk

Perceived risk can come in two forms: *functional risk* such as uncertainty with respect to product or supplier performance, and *psychological risk* such as criticism from work colleagues. (For a discussion of the components of risk, see Stone and Gronhaug, 1993.) This latter risk—fear of upsetting the boss, losing status, being ridiculed by others in the department, or indeed, of losing one's job—can play a determining role in purchase decisions. Buyers often reduce uncertainty by gathering information about competing suppliers, checking the opinions of important others in the buying company, buying only from familiar and/or reputable suppliers and by spreading risk through multiple sourcing.

Office politics

Political factions within the buying company may also influence the outcome of a purchase decision. Interdepartmental conflict may manifest itself in the formation of competing camps over the purchase of a product or service.

Because department X favours supplier 1, department Y automatically favours supplier 2. The outcome not only has purchasing implications but also political implications for the departments and individuals concerned.

Personal likes/dislikes

A buyer may personally like one salesperson more than another and this may influence supplier choice, particularly when competing products are very similar. Perception is important in all B2B purchases, since how someone behaves depends upon that person's perception of the situation. One buyer may perceive a salesperson as being honest, truthful and likeable, while another may not. However, analysis and managing of spending has become more closely monitored in recent years due to the widespread adoption of procurement and information systems related to e-commerce. So many firms have actively sought to introduce purchasing policies that reduce 'maverick spending'—that is, that reduce buying from non-preferred company suppliers. See Marketing in Action 4.4.

E-procurement processes

B2B **e-procurement** accounts for significant volumes of trade and modern e-procurement systems enable companies to fulfil a range of activities and processes associated with the purchasing function: tendering, awarding contracts, establishing contractual agreements and ordering (Doherty, McConnell and Ellis-Chadwick, 2013). To action these processes, companies not only create their own websites but also develop extranets for buyers to send out requests for bids to suppliers. Online purchasing systems can take various formats.

- *Catalogue sites:* companies can order items through electronic catalogues.
- *Vertical markets:* companies buying industrial products such as steel, chemicals or plastic, or buying services such as logistics (distribution) or media, can use specialized websites (called *e-hubs*). For instance, Plastics.com permits thousands of plastics buyers to search for the lowest prices from thousands of plastics sellers.
- *Auction sites:* suppliers can place industrial products on auction sites where purchasers can bid for them.
- *Exchange* (or spot) markets: many commodities are sold on electronic exchange markets where prices can change by the minute. For example, Title Transfer Facility provides an online marketplace where gas energy can be traded instantly.
- *Buying alliances:* companies in the same market for products join together to gain bigger discounts on higher volumes.

MARKETING IN ACTION 4.4
Is Eliminating the Mavericks a Good Thing?

Maverick spending is often referred to as the deals that are done outside an organization's procurement policy. This type of spending might occur when a powerful B2B buyer has a personal preference for a particular supplier (rather than the organization itself preferring a particular supplier). In this case, the company will be referred to as 'an off-contract supplier'. Furthermore, the practice is said to be widespread, with some firms experiencing up to 80 per cent of buying being uncontrolled and sourced from off-contract suppliers.

The difference between non-preferred and preferred suppliers is that the latter are established by determining their ability to comply with a buying firm's specification, for example agreed discount targets, delivery routines and quality of goods. As a result, firms are increasingly investing in IT systems to gather data and analyse the efficiency of buying and selling with a view to reducing maverick spending, so as to bring about budget cost savings.

However, sometimes the maverick spend is not about defying purchasing policies but about finding better purchasing solutions. Also, buying is a complex function: implementing an IT system that effectively tracks all the nuances of purchasing agreements and deals can be costly and time-consuming, and may not result in the ideal purchasing outcome. So, on one hand, reducing maverick spend can ensure compliance with purchasing policy, potentially reducing the overall budget spend and maximizing purchasing power. But, on the other hand, this might lead to missed buying opportunities and increased cost through significant investment in sophisticated IT systems to manage the maverick spend.

Based on: Moretti (2013); Mitchell (2015); Batting (2014)

Industrial and reseller markets have widespread adoption of e-procurement systems but, in government markets, the adoption of e-procurement systems has been slow in comparison with the adoption in B2B and reseller markets. Indeed, recent research (Doherty, McConnell and Ellis-Chadwick, 2013) has found that, in the UK, government purchasing strategies involved less than 3 per cent of invoices being sent electronically despite the inefficiencies of the incumbent manual processing systems. The primary reasons cited for the slow rate of adoption in these markets are the complexity of the procurement processes and institutional policy restrictions.

The people and processes involved in B2B purchasing are many but it is important to be aware that, as more purchasing is done online, this does not reduce the strategic importance of choice criteria but is having an impact on the number of people and influences involved in purchasing decisions.

Influences on Buying Decisions

Figure 4.3 shows the three factors that influence how organizations buy, who buys and how they apply choice criteria: the buy class, the product type and the importance of purchase (Cardozo, 1980).

The buy class

B2B purchases can be a new task, a straight rebuy and a modified rebuy (Robinson, Faris and Wind, 1967). A **new task** occurs when the need for the product has not arisen previously, so there is little or no relevant experience in the company and a great deal of information is required. A **straight rebuy** occurs where an organization buys previously purchased items from suppliers already judged acceptable. Routine purchasing procedures are set up to facilitate straight rebuys. The **modified rebuy** lies between the two extremes. A regular requirement for the type of product exists, and the buying alternatives are known, but sufficient change (e.g. a delivery problem) has occurred to require some alteration to the normal supply procedure.

The buy classes affect B2B buying in the following ways. First, the membership of the DMU changes. For a straight rebuy, possibly only the purchasing officer is involved, whereas for a new buy senior management, engineers, production managers and purchasing officers may be involved. Modified rebuys often involve engineers, production managers and purchasing officers, but senior management, except when the purchase is critical to the company, is unlikely to be involved. Second, the decision-making process may be much longer as the buy class changes from a straight rebuy to a modified rebuy to a new task. Third, DMU members are likely to be much more receptive to new task and modified rebuy situations than to straight rebuys. In the latter case, the purchasing manager has already solved the purchasing problem and has other problems to deal with. So, why make it a problem again?

The first implication of this buy class analysis is that there are big gains to be made if a company can enter the new task at the start of the decision-making process. By providing information and helping with any technical problems that can arise, the company may be able to create goodwill and creeping commitment, which secures the order when the final decision is made. The second implication is that, since the decision process is likely to be long and many people are involved in the new task, supplier companies need to invest heavily in sales personnel for a considerable period. Some firms employ missionary sales teams comprising their best salespeople to help secure big new-task orders.

FIGURE 4.3
Influences on B2B purchasing behaviour

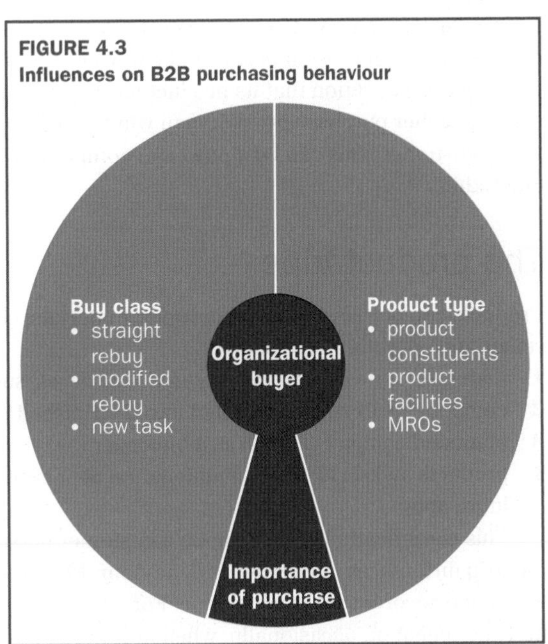

Companies in straight rebuy situations must ensure that no change occurs when they are in the position of the supplier. Regular contact to ensure that the customer has no complaints may be necessary, and the buyer may be encouraged to use automatic reordering systems. For the out-supplier (i.e. a new potential supplier), the task can be difficult unless poor service or some other factor has caused the buyer to become dissatisfied with the present supplier. The obvious objective of the out-supplier in this situation is to change the buy class from a straight rebuy to a modified rebuy. Price alone may not be enough since changing supplier represents a large personal risk to the purchasing officer. The new supplier's products might be less reliable and delivery might be unpredictable. To reduce this risk, the company may offer delivery guarantees with penalty clauses and be very willing to accept a small (perhaps uneconomic) order at first in order to gain a foothold. Supplier acquisition of a total quality management (TQM) standard such as ISP9001:2000 or ISP9004 may also have the effect of reducing perceived buyer risk. Other tactics are the use of testimonials from satisfied customers and demonstrations. Many straight rebuys are organized on a contract basis, and buyers may be more receptive to listening to non-suppliers prior to contract renewal.

Value analysis and lifecycle cost calculations enable purchases to move from a straight rebuy to a modified rebuy situation. Value analysis, which can be conducted by either supplier or buyer, is a method of cost reduction in which components are examined to see if they can be made more cheaply. The items are studied to identify unnecessary costs that do not add to the reliability or functionality of the product. By redesigning, standardizing or manufacturing by less expensive means, a supplier may be able to offer a product of comparable quality at lower cost. Lifecycle cost analysis seeks to move the cost focus from the initial purchase price to the total cost of owning and using a product. There are three types of lifecycle costs: purchase price, start-up costs and post-purchase costs (Forbis and Mehta, 1981). Start-up costs would include installation, lost production and training costs. Post-purchase costs include operating (e.g. fuel, operator wages), maintenance, repair and inventory costs. Against these costs would be placed residual values (e.g. trade-in values of cars). Lifecycle cost appeals can be powerful motivators. For example, if the out-supplier can convince the customer organization that its product has significantly lower post-purchase costs than the in-supplier's, despite a slightly higher purchase price, it may win the order. This is because it will be delivering a higher economic value to the customer. This can be a powerful competitive advantage and, at the same time, justify the premium price. See Exhibit 4.5.

EXHIBIT 4.5
SAP emphasizes the speed and efficiency of its business management network solutions

The product type

Products can be classified as four types: materials, components, plant and equipment, and MROs (maintenance, repair and operation), as follows:

1 materials to be used in the production process, such as aluminium
2 components to be incorporated into the finished product, such as headlights
3 plant and equipment, such as a bulldozer
4 products and services for maintenance, repair and operation (MRO), such as spanners, welding equipment and lubricants.

This classification is based upon a customer perspective—how the product is used—and may be employed to identify differences in B2B buyer behaviour. First, the people who take part in the decision-making process tend to change according to product type. For example, senior management tend to get involved in the purchase of plant and equipment or, occasionally, when new materials are purchased if the change is of fundamental importance to company operations: for example, if a move from aluminium to plastic is being considered. Rarely do they involve themselves in component or MRO supply. Similarly, design engineers tend to be involved in buying components and materials, but not normally MRO and plant equipment. Second, the decision-making process tends to be slower and more complex as product type moves from

MRO → components → materials → plant and equipment

For MRO items, *blanket contracts* rather than periodic purchase orders are increasingly being used. The supplier agrees to resupply the buyer on agreed price terms over a period. Stock is held by the seller and orders are automatically printed out by the buyer's computer when stock falls below a minimum level. This has the advantage to the supplying company of effectively blocking the effort of the competitors for long periods of time.

Classification of suppliers' offerings by product type gives clues as to who is likely to be influenced in the purchase decision. The marketing task is then to confirm this situation and attempt to reach those people involved. A company selling MROs is likely to be wasting effort attempting to communicate with design engineers, whereas attempts to reach operating management are likely to prove fruitful.

The importance of purchase

A purchase is likely to be perceived as being important to the buying organization when it involves large sums of money, when the cost of making the wrong decision—for example, in production downtime—is high, and when there is considerable uncertainty about the outcome of alternative offerings. In such situations, many people at different organizational levels are likely to be involved in the decision, and the process will be long, with extensive search and analysis of information. Extensive marketing effort is likely to be required, but great opportunities present themselves to those sales teams that work with buying organizations to convince them that their offering has the best payoff. This may involve acceptance trials; for example, private diesel manufacturers supply railway companies with prototypes for testing, engineering support and testimonials from other users. Additionally, guarantees of delivery dates and after-sales service may be necessary when buyer uncertainty regarding these factors is high.

An example of the time and effort that may be required to win very important purchases is the order secured by GEC to supply £250 million worth of equipment for China's largest nuclear power station. The contract was won after six years of negotiation, 33 GEC missions to China and 4,000 person-days of work.

Segmenting B2B Markets

While the B2C marketer is interested in grouping individuals into marketing-relevant segments, the B2B marketer profiles organizations and their buyers. B2B markets can be segmented on several factors that are broadly classified into two major categories: macrosegmentation and microsegmentation (see Wind and Cardozo, 1974; Plank, 1985).

Macrosegmentation focuses on the characteristics of the buying organization, such as size, industry and geographic location (see Figure 4.4). *Microsegmentation* requires a more detailed level of market knowledge, as it concerns the characteristics of decision-making within each macrosegment, based on such factors as choice criteria, decision-making unit structure, decision-making process, buy class, purchasing organization and organizational innovativeness. Often B2B markets are first grouped on a macrosegment basis and then finer sub-segments are identified through microsegmentation (Wind and Cardozo, 1974).

Figure 4.4 shows how this two-stage process works. The choice of the appropriate macrosegmentation and microsegmentation criteria is based on the marketer's evaluation of which criteria are most useful in predicting buyer behaviour differences that have implications for developing marketing strategies. Figure 4.5 shows how choice criteria can be used.

Macrosegmentation

The key macrosegmentation criteria of organizational size, industry and geographic location will now be discussed.

FIGURE 4.4
Macrosegmentation and microsegmentation of B2B markets

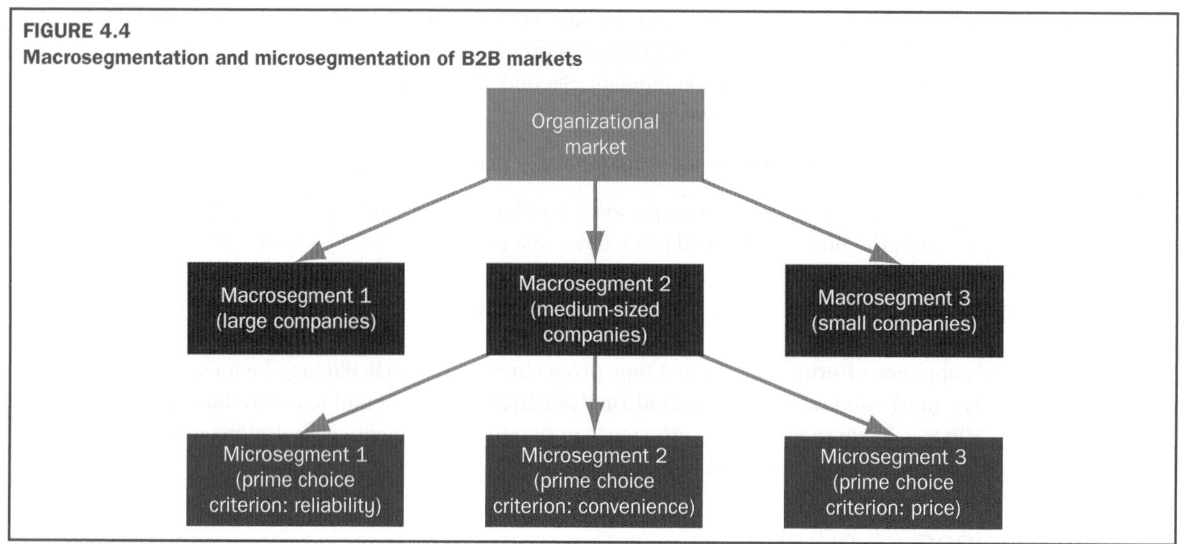

FIGURE 4.5
Segmenting B2B markets

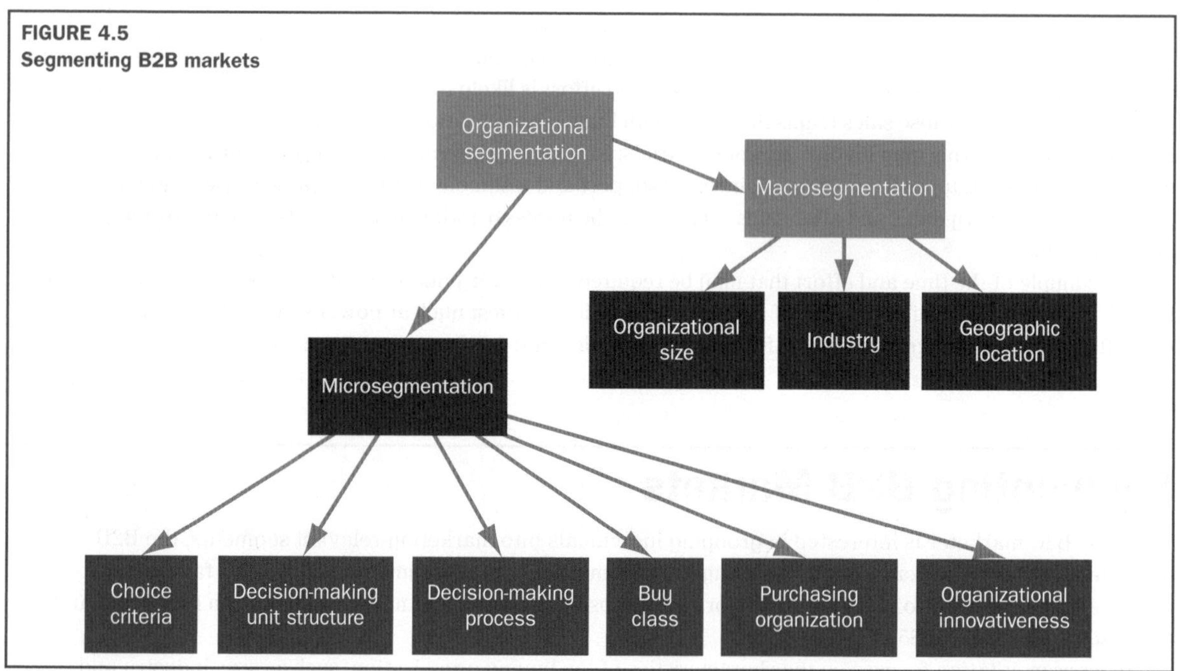

Organizational size

The size of buying organizations may be used to segment markets. Large organizations differ from medium-sized and small organizations in having greater order potential, more formalized buying and management processes, increased specialization of function and special needs (e.g. quantity discounts). The result is that they may form important target market segments and require tailored marketing mix strategies. For example, the salesforce may need to be organized on a key account basis, where a dedicated sales team is used to service important industrial accounts. List pricing of products and services may need to consider the inevitable demand for volume discounts from large purchasers, and the salesforce team need to be well versed in the art of negotiation.

Industry

Another common macrosegmentation variable is industry sector. Different industries may have unique requirements from products. For example, software application suppliers like Oracle and SAP can market their products to various sectors: banking, manufacturing, healthcare and education, each having unique needs in terms of software programs, servicing, price and purchasing practice. By understanding each industry's needs in depth, a more effective marketing mix can be designed. In some instances, further segmentation may be required. For example, the education sector may be further divided into primary, secondary and further education as their product and service requirements may differ.

Geographic location

Regional variations in purchasing practice and needs may imply the use of geographic location as a basis for differentiating marketing strategies. The purchasing practices and expectations of companies in central and eastern Europe are likely to differ markedly from those in Western Europe. Their more bureaucratic structures may imply a fundamentally different approach to doing business that needs to be recognized by companies

kets. In Chapter 2, we saw how different cultural factors affect the

Cultural differences should be reflected in marketing strategies

macrosegment into smaller microsegments based on the buyer's

re, decision-making process, buy class, purchasing organization and

on the key choice criteria used by buyers when evaluating supplier

price as the key choice criterion, another segment may favour

service orientated. These varying preferences mean that marketing and

for each segment's needs. Three different marketing mixes would be

espeople would have to stress different benefits when talking to customers

iteria can be powerful predictors of buyer behaviour. An important choice

c value to the customer, which considers not only price, but also other

es targeting business people with the aim of improving safety and year-

TS

r

e

m.

Decision-making unit structure

Another way of segmenting B2B markets is based on decision-making unit (DMU) composition: members of the DMU and its size may vary between buying organizations. As discussed earlier in the chapter, the DMU consists of all those people in a buying organization who influence supplier choice. One segment might be characterized by the influence of top management on the decision, another by the role played by engineers and a third segment might comprise organizations where the purchasing manager plays the key role. DMU size can also vary considerably: one segment might feature large, complex units, while another might comprise single members.

EXHIBIT 4.6
This advert explains how Michelin tyres offer better economic value and safety than those of its rivals

Decision-making process

The decision-making process can take a long time or be relatively short. The length of time is often correlated with DMU composition. Long processes are associated with large DMUs. Where the decision time is long, high levels of marketing expenditure may be needed, with considerable effort placed on personal selling. Much less effort is needed when the buy process is relatively short and where, perhaps, only the purchasing manager is involved.

Buy class

B2B purchases can be categorized into straight rebuy, modified rebuy and new task. The buy class affects the length of the decision-making process, the complexity of the DMU and the number of choice criteria that are used in supplier selection. It can therefore be used as a predictor of different forms of buyer behaviour, and hence is useful as a segmentation variable.

Purchasing organization

Decentralized versus centralized purchasing is another microsegmentation variable because of its influence on the purchase decision (Corey, 1978). Centralized purchasing is associated with purchasing specialists who become experts in buying a range of products. Specialization means that they become more familiar with cost factors, and the strengths and weaknesses of suppliers, than decentralized generalists. Furthermore, the opportunity for volume buying means that their power base to demand price concessions from suppliers is enhanced. They have also been found to have greater power within the DMU vis-à-vis technical people like engineers than decentralized buyers, who often lack the specialist expertise and status to challenge their preferences. For these reasons, the purchasing organization provides a good base for distinguishing between buyer behaviour and can have implications for marketing activities. For example, the centralized purchasing segment could be served by a national account salesforce, whereas the decentralized purchasing segment might be covered by territory representatives.

Organizational innovativeness

A key segmentation variable when launching new products is the degree of innovativeness of potential buyers. In Chapter 11 we discuss the characteristics of innovator firms. Marketers need to identify the specific characteristics of the innovator segment, since these companies should be targeted first when new products are launched. Follower firms may be willing to buy the product, but only after the innovators have approved it. Although categorized here as a microsegmentation variable, it should be borne in mind that organizational size (a macrosegmentation variable) may be a predictor of innovativeness too.

Table 4.1 summarizes the methods of segmenting B2B markets and provides examples of how each variable can be used to form segments.

TABLE 4.1 B2B segmentation methods

Variable	Examples
Macrosegmentation	
Organizational size	Large, medium, small
Industry	Engineering, textiles, banking
Geographic location	Local, national, European, global
Microsegmentation	
Choice criteria	Economic value, delivery, price, service
Decision-making unit structure	Complex, simple
Decision-making process	Long, short
Buy class	Straight rebuy, modified rebuy, new task
Purchasing organization	Centralized, decentralized
Organizational innovativeness	Innovator, follower, laggard

Review

1 The importance of B2B markets

- Organizational markets are significant and account for nearly half of all revenues in developed countries.
- There are three types of organizational markets: industrial, resellers and government/institutional markets.

2 The characteristics of B2B buying

- The characteristics are based on the nature and size of customers, the complexity of buying, the use of economic and technical choice criteria, network technology and e-commerce, the risky nature of buying and selling, buying to specific requirements, reciprocal buying, derived demand and negotiations.

3 What is B2B marketing

- B2B involves manufacturers, suppliers and resellers in providing the *right products and services* so that B2C markets can function effectively. All the core principles of marketing apply both strategically and tactically in these markets, but differences exist in terms of buying and selling.
- Buying is an important corporate activity and its coordination is crucial for marketing organizations.
- B2B communications primarily involve personal direct selling and digital marketing.

4 The nature and marketing implications of the people: who buys, the processes involved in how organizations buy and the choice criteria used to evaluate products

- Who buys: there are six roles in the decision-making unit—initiators, users, deciders, influencers, buyers and gatekeepers. Marketers need to identify who plays each role, target communication at them and develop products to satisfy their needs.
- How organizations buy: the decision-making process has up to seven stages–recognition of problem (need), determination of specification and quantity of needed item, search for and qualification of potential sources, acquisition and analysis of proposals, evaluation of proposals and selection of supplier(s), selection of an order routine, and performance feedback and evaluation. Marketers can influence need recognition and gain competitive advantage by entering the process early.
- Choice criteria can be technical, economic, social (organizational) and personal. Marketers need to understand the choice criteria of the different members of the decision-making unit and target communications accordingly. Other marketing mix decisions, such as product design, will also depend on an understanding of choice criteria. Choice criteria can change over time, necessitating a change in the marketing mix.

5 The influences on B2B buying behaviour—the buy class, product type and purchase importance—and their marketing implications

- The buy class consists of three types: new task, straight rebuy and modified rebuy. For a new task, there can be large gains for suppliers entering the decision process early, but heavy investment is usually needed. For straight rebuys, the in-supplier should build a defensible position to keep out new potential suppliers. For out-suppliers, a key task is to reduce the risk of change for the buyers so that a modified rebuy will result.
- Product types consist of materials, components, plant and equipment, and maintenance items. Marketers need to recognize that the people who take part in the purchase decision usually change according to product type, and channel communications accordingly.
- The importance of purchase depends on the costs involved and the uncertainty (risk) regarding the decision. For very important decisions, heavy investment is likely to be required on the part of suppliers, and risk-reduction strategies (e.g. guarantees) may be needed to reduce uncertainty.

6 Segmenting B2B marketing

- Segmenting B2B markets is a way of identifying potential customers using macro- and microsegmentation techniques.
- Macrosegmentation involves reviewing organization size, industry and geography to identify clusters of similar businesses.
- Microsegmentation involves reviewing the choice criteria, structure of the DMU, the way purchasing is organized, the buy-class and the innovativeness of the organization.

Key Terms

commodity market one where commodities—a primary good, e.g. cocoa, wheat, precious metals, oil—is traded

decision-making process the stages that organizations and people pass through when purchasing a physical product or service

decision-making unit (DMU) a group of people within an organization who are involved in the buying decision (also known as the buying centre)

e-commerce involves all electronically mediated transactions between an organization and any third party it deals with, including exchange of information

e-procurement digital systems that facilitate the management of the procurement process; often integrates with e-commerce systems

exclusive distribution channels manufacturers make agreements with specific retailers to sell the goods; the retailer is given exclusive rights, which cover a specified geographic region

just-in-time (JIT) this concept aims to minimize stocks by organizing a supply system that provides materials and components as they are required

lifecycle costs all the components of costs associated with buying, owning and using a physical product or service

modified rebuy where a regular requirement for the type of product exists and the buying alternatives are known, but sufficient change (e.g. a delivery problem) has occurred to require some alteration to the normal supply procedure

new task refers to the first-time purchase of a product or input by an organization

straight rebuy refers to a purchase by an organization from a previously approved supplier of a previously purchased item

total quality management the set of programmes designed to constantly improve the quality of physical products, services and processes

value analysis a method of cost reduction in which components are examined to see if they can be made more cheaply

Study Questions

1. **Explain the importance of B2B markets.**
2. **Discuss the activities B2B marketers might consider important.**
3. **What are the six roles that form the decision-making unit (DMU) for the purpose of a B2B purchase? What are the marketing implications of the DMU?**
4. **Why do the choice criteria used by different members of the DMU often change with the varying roles?**
5. **What are creeping commitment and lockout criteria? Why are they important factors in the choice of supplier?**
6. **Explain the difference between a straight rebuy, a modified rebuy and a new task purchasing situation. What implications do these concepts have for the marketing of B2B products?**
7. **Debate the extent to which digital technology is redefining B2B purchasing.**

Recommended Reading

B2B marketing is fundamentally important and is at the core of many brands' success. Read the following to learn about creating superior value for customers, the areas of B2B marketing that are most important to business practitioners and to gain an overview of B2B marketing from a journal editor.

Lindgreen, A., Di Benedetto, A., Geersbro, J. and Ritter, T. (2018), Past, present, and future business-to-business marketing research, Industrial marketing management 69 (February) 1–4.

O'Cass, A. and Ngo, L. (2012), Creating superior customer value for B2B firms through supplier firm capabilities, *Industrial Marketing Management* 41(1), January 2012, 125–35.

Reed, G., Story, V. and Saker, J. (2004), Business to business marketing: What is important to the practitioner?, *Marketing Intelligence & Planning*, 22(5), 501–10 https://doi.org/10.1108/02634500410551888.

References

Advanced Television (2014), Volvo Sponsors Sky Atlantic http://advanced-television.com/2014/01/02/volvo-sponsors-sky-atlantic (accessed 23 February 2015).

Agarwal, Harmon and Viertier (2009), Cutting sales costs, not revenues, Mckinsey & Company http://www.mckinsey.com/insights/marketing_sales/cutting_sales_costs_not_revenues (accessed 10 May 2015).

Archacki, R., Protextor, K., Barrios, G. and De Bellefonds, N. (2017), Mobile Marketing and the New B2B Buyer, The Boston Consulting Group https://www.bcg.com/en-gb/publications/2017/marketing-sales-digital-go-to-market-transformation-mobile-marketing-new-b2b-buyer.aspx (accessed August, 2018).

Bakos, J.Y. and Brynjolfsson, E. (1993), Information technology, incentives and the optimal number of suppliers, *Journal of Management Systems*, 10(2), pp. 37–51, Armonk.

Bals, L., Laine, J. and Mugurusi, G. (2018), Evolving Purchasing and Supply organizations: A contingency model for structural alternatives, *Journal of Purchasing and Supply Management* 24 (1) 41–58.

Batting, J. (2014), *Five things you need to know to tackle maverick spend*, Supply Management, 7 October http://www.supplymanagement.com/blog/2014/10/five-things-you-need-to-know-to-tackle-maverick-spend (accessed 26 February 2015).

Cardozo, R.N. (1980), Situational Segmentation of Industrial Markets, *European Journal of Marketing* 14(5/6), 264–76.

Chaffey, D. and Ellis-Chadwick, F. (2019), *Digital Marketing: Strategy, Implementation and Practice*, 7th Edition, Pearson, London.

Chang, Y., Wang, X. and Arnett, D. (2018), Enhancing firm performance: The role of brand orientation in business-to-business marketing, *Industrial Marketing Management* 72 (July), 17–25.

Corey, R. (1978), *The Organizational Context of Industrial Buying Behaviour*, Cambridge, MA: Marketing Science Institute, 6–12.

Cornall, J. (2017), Lactalis McLelland gets Co-op own brand cheese contract, https://www.dairyreporter.com/Article/2017/02/21/Lactalis-McLelland-gets-Co-op-own-brand-cheese-contract (accessed August 2017).

Doherty, N.F., McConnell, D. and Ellis-Chadwick, F. (2013), Institutional responses to electronic, *International Journal of Public Sector Management* 26(2), 495–515.

Draper, A. (1994), Organizational Buyers as Workers: The Key to their Behaviour, *European Journal of Marketing* 28(11), 50–62.

Ellis-Chadwick, F. (2000), An Empirical Study of Internet Adoption among Leading United Kingdom Retailers, Loughborough University Thesis.

Fleet News (2015), *Michelin Cross Climate tyres will be a 'game-changer' for UK fleets, says ATS Euromaster*, Fleet News, 16 March https://www.fleetnews.co.uk/news/2015/3/16/michelin-cross-climate-tyres-will-be-a-game-changer-for-uk-fleets-says-ats-euromaster/55157 (accessed June 2018).

Forbis, J.L. and Mehta, N.T. (1981), Value-Based Strategies for Industrial Products, *Business Horizons*, May–June, 32–42.

FNCL Fédération Nationale des Coopératives Laitières (2018), http://www.filiere-laitiere.fr/en/organizations/fncl (accessed, August 2018).

Gee, O. (2016), This is how much the French are obsessed with cheese, https://www.thelocal.fr/20160810/this-is-how-much-the-french-are-obsessed-with-cheese (accessed August 2018).

Grewal, R. and Lilien, G. (2012), Business-to-business marketing: Looking back, looking forward, Lilien and Grewal (Eds.), *Handbook of business to business marketing*, Edward Elgar Press, 1–14.

Group Lactalis (2018), Our History http://groupelactalis.co.uk/our-history.html (accessed August 2018).

Heagarty, R. (2011), Waitrose demands a 5 per cent cut from suppliers, *The Grocer*, 10 October http://www.thegrocer.co.uk/companies/waitrose-demands-a-5-cut-from-suppliers/221572.article (accessed June 2018).

Hobbs, T. (2015), Seriously Strong invests £5m as it aims to become the big cheese, *Marketing week*, 26 February (accessed August 2018).

Iceland Foods Ltd (2014) A year of major investment for sustainable future growth http://about.iceland.co.uk/_assets/files/Iceland-Foods-2014-results-FINAL.pdf (accessed 26 February 2015).

Iceland Foods Ltd (2015) Malcolm Walker's biography http://about.iceland.co.uk/the-boss/malcolm-walkers-biography (accessed 26 February 2015).

Iceland Foods Ltd (2018) Our Suppliers http://about.iceland.co.uk/our-power-for-good/our-suppliers/ (accessed July 2018).

Jobber, D. and Lancaster, G. (2015), *Selling and Sales Management*, London: Pitman, 27.

Juha, M. and Pentti, J. (2008), Managing Risks in organizational purchasing through adaptation of buying centre structure and the buying process, *Journal of Purchasing and Supply Management*, 14 (4), 253–262.

Lewis, S. and Arnold, J. (2012) Organizational career management in the UK retail buying and merchandising community, *International Journal of Retail & Distribution Management* 40(6), 451–470.

Lilien, G. (2016), The B2B Knowledge Gap, *International Journal of Research in Marketing*, 33 (3) 543–556.

Macleod, I. (2014), Volvo Cars suggests it is From Sweden Not Hollywood in Idents for Sky Atlantic, *The Drum*, 10 November http://www.thedrum.com/news/2014/11/10/volvo-cars-suggests-it-sweden-not-hollywood-idents-sky-atlantic (accessed 23 February 2015).

Mitchell, P. (2015), How to use Mavericks to solve the maverick spending problem, *Spending Matters Network*, 26 January http://spendmatters.com/cpo/use-mavericks-solve-maverick-spending-problem (accessed 26 February 2015).

Moretti, P. (2013), Spend Management: A Necessary Evil? My Purchasing Centre, 1 February. http://www.mypurchasingcenter.com/technology/technology-blogs/spend-management-a-necessary-evil (accessed 26 February 2015).

Plank R. (1985), A critical review of industrial market segmentation, *Industrial Marketing Management*, 14, 79–91.

Pomeroy, A. (producer) and Rogan, J. (director) (2013), *Iceland Frozen Foods: Life in the Freezer Cabinet* [Motion Picture], BBC Two.

Robinson, P.J., Faris, C.W. and Wind, Y. (1967), *Industrial Buying and Creative Marketing*, Boston, MA: Allyn & Bacon.

Selwood, D. (2018), Range Preview: Iceland Christmas 2018, *The grocer* 6 July, https://www.thegrocer.co.uk/stores/ranging-and-merchandising/range-preview-iceland-christmas-2018/568952.article (accessed July 2018).

Seriously (2018), http://www.seriouslystrongcheddar.co.uk/our-character/ (accessed, August, 2018).

Sky Media (2014), Volvo becomes new Sky Atlantic Sponsor, Sky Media, 1 January http://www.skymedia.co.uk/news/volvo-becomes-new-sky-atlantic-sponsor.aspx (accessed 23 February 2015).

Sky Media (2018), Sky Wins at the UK Sponsorship Awards, https://www.skymedia.co.uk/news/sky-media-wins-uk-sponsorship-awards/ March (accessed August 2018).

Snoad, L. (2012) Taking personal control of the mission redefinition, *Marketing Week*, 26 January, 16–19.

Stone, R.N. and Gronhaug, K. (1993), Perceived Risk: Further Considerations for the Marketing Discipline, *European Journal of Marketing* 27(3), 39–50.

Syal, R. (2013), Abandoned NHS IT system has cost £10bn so far, *The Guardian* http://www.theguardian.com/society/2013/sep/18/nhs-records-system-10bn (accessed 23 February 2015).

The Economist (2011), Outsourcing is sometimes more hassle than its worth, 30 July, 62.

Vlahović, B., Popović-Vranješ, A. and Mugoša, I. (2014), International Chess Marketing–Current State and Perspective, *Economic Insights–Trends and Challenges*, 1.111 (No 1/2014) http://www.upg-bulletin-se.ro/archive/2014-1/4.Vlahovic_PopovicVranjes_Mugosa.pdf (accessed June 2018).

Vizard, S. (2013), Volvo signs 2-year Sky Atlantic sponsorship deal, *Marketing Week* http://www.marketingweek.com/2013/12/19/volvo-signs-2-year-sky-atlantic-sponsorship-deal (accessed 23 February 2015).

Volvo Car UK (2016), https://www.media.volvocars.com/uk/en-gb/media/pressreleases/193871/volvo-invests-in-the-uk-motor-trade-with-the-launch-of-its-sponsored-dealer-programme (accessed August 2018).

Walsh, F. (2006), M&S Tightens Screw on Suppliers, *The Guardian*, 4 March, 27.

Webster, F.E. and Wind, Y. (1972), *Organizational Buying Behaviour*, Englewood Cliffs, NJ: Prentice-Hall, 78–80. The sixth role of initiator was added by Bonoma, T.V. (1982) Major Sales: Who Really does the Buying, *Harvard Business Review*, May–June, 111–19.

Wind, Y. and Cardozo, R.N. (1974), Industrial Market Segmentation, *Industrial Marketing Management* 3, 153–66.

Wing Yip (2018), Oriental food Report https://www.wingyip.com/ (accessed August 2018).

CASE 7

Naked Wines—A Community of Wine Makers and Drinkers

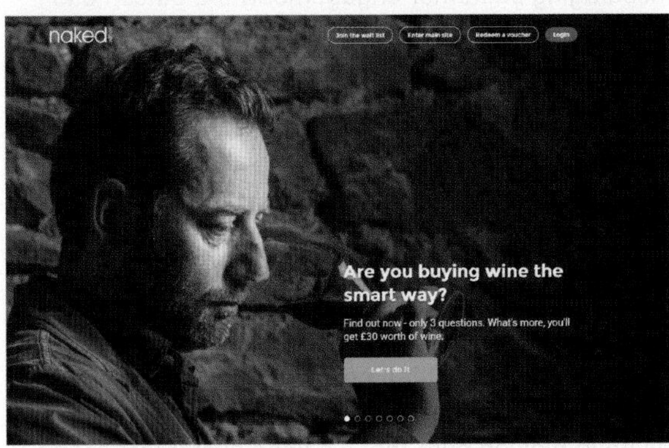

In June 2008, founder and CEO of Virgin Wines, Rowan Gormley, was attempting a management buyout from the parent group Direct Wines. The result was he got the sack. 'It was the best thing that ever happened to me,' says Rowan because, six months later, Naked Wines was born. This innovative online wine company, which does things differently, is now owned by Majestic Wine and its business model uses crowdfunding to support independent wine makers.

Community Networking Drives the Business Model

The concept was to bring crowd funding to the world of winemaking via the internet.

At its heart is 'a community of wine drinkers' who join Naked and make regular payments, starting at £20 a month, into an online account. The name given to this special group of community members is Angels, as they help those independent winemakers achieve their dreams by investing their regular contributions into the vintners' businesses. They then have no worries about selling the wine and just need to concentrate on producing quality. In return, the Angels receive a substantial discount when purchasing the wine. Paying for the product in advance is like the way we purchase airline and travel tickets. But it is an unusual approach to pricing in the retail wine industry.

Now with over 200,000 Angels, generating a cool £3.5million a month, those investments are substantial and help support a 'community of winemakers', producing new interesting wines that cannot be purchased elsewhere.

This co-creation of value approach between the winemakers and drinkers is helping Naked Wines to continue to grow. And they can attract talented, independent winemakers who want to experiment with new ideas, connecting them directly to their end consumers. This is reinforced by the reviews that people leave on the website and to which winemakers respond directly via a specially developed app. 'We knew that it would be beneficial from a customer perspective,' said Laura Riches, Marketing Director of Naked Wine. 'But what we didn't realise was that from a winemaker perspective, they'd never had that type of feedback before.'

Storytelling Saves the Day

Producers and consumers working and communicating together is delivering multiple benefits and a highly profitable value proposition. This virtuous circle, as Naked likes to call it, also includes the support for winemakers when tragedies happen. From the fires in Napa Valley to sabotage in France, the Angels are on hand to offer additional support.

Katie Jones is such a story. She followed her dream and left her 9–5 job in the UK to grow grapes in the Languedoc region of France. But, when Katie chose to leave the local wine-making co-operative, wanting to make her own wine rather than pooling her grapes with her neighbours' lower quality ones, things turned sour.

After the 2013 harvest, disgruntled co-operative members broke into her winery and opened the taps on the vats. The previous year's entire vintage of white wine was emptied down the drain and she was left with absolutely nothing.

'That's when we gave her a call,' said Laura Riches. 'We've heard about you and heard your story. We want to help.'

Naked then asked its Angels if they would be willing to buy Katie's next vintage in advance so that she could afford to continue making wine. Overnight, 30,000 bottles of her wine was bought by the Angels. She was able to carry on with her dream. 'This is no marketing

»

»

gimmick,' Riches added. 'This is someone whose life has been completely transformed.'

There are many stories just like this one, working together and supporting each other. Great wines are produced, business dreams are realised and customers are delighted with new and innovative products to suit every palate.

Marketing Secrets of Success: Call in the Archangels

Storytelling has always been an essential marketing tool and is a huge asset for Naked and aids in their delivery of lifetime value for the business from the Angels.

Marketing Director Laura suggests there are three ways she makes that happen:

1) Activation: encouraging customers to place an order and then encouraging them to place another one so they're placing more orders per year. To ensure this success, Naked needs to stay very close to its customers and understand their likes and dislikes, and they have a unique way of gathering this information and responding accordingly.

Recently. the growing community of Angels were looking online for Provence rosé and finding nothing. The reason being the available produce did not fit well with the Naked philosophy of trendy labels and so there was no such wine on the site. Laura explains how Naked resolved this marketing problem 'by involving a special group of customers in the buying process'. Naked calls them Archangels. These are committed customers, who help new Angels navigate the naked.com website as well as being a bellwether for introducing new wines. The Archangels set about their task, by sampling 40 different Provence rosés, and streaming the whole event live on Facebook, with others in this group. Unsurprisingly, their choice of wine was a small producer, Bruno Lapierre, whose wines were not available in the UK, which fits with the Naked philosophy.

Naked can now rollout the story to all its Angels and retail customers, who just buy wine online that is ready for immediate consumption. As Laura explains, 'We decided that we've got this momentum, we've got this great story, let's make it happen right now. Within four hours, they were able to pre-order the wine'. The next day, over 600 pre-orders had been placed for six-bottle packs of this wine, not bad for an expensive wine. That was in February of 2017; 4 months later, a total of 11,000 bottles had been sold and reviews from 1,000 customers had rated the wine at 92%. Laura went on to say, 'Although the story wasn't about a winemaker, it wasn't about the wine itself, bringing customers into that buying process, and making them part of the story using technology, really helped us to maximize our activation opportunity.'

Naked looks for continual improvement and is working on technology to shorten the customer sign-up process, for example, by introducing QR codes on the different wines to make them easier to find by scanning the code and then having one click through to buying and becoming an Angel. By continuously encouraging customer engagement, the outcome is helping grow customer loyalty and increase awareness of the Naked Wines brand.

2) Retention: 'if we can just retain 1 per cent more of existing UK customers, that's 2,000 customers that we don't have to go out and spend to recruit.'

Retention is the mantra of modern marketing. Solely focusing on customer acquisition is considered a short-sighted approach as many marketers' end-goal is not to just convert a consumer into a purchasing customer but to maximize the lifetime value by creating loyal customers. Laura says, 'The strength of our brand will be in making sure that we keep customers for as long as we possibly can.' And they are doing this by 'harness[ing] customers and make them part of a long-term journey with us'.

One way to achieve this is to continually surprise and involve Angels with new projects. For example, a speculative idea designed to get Angels involved was to involve then with a start-up scheme to produce method-traditional sparkling wine in England. 'We were asking Angels to take part by paying nearly £100 in advance for wines they'll receive in two years' time, and we can't even tell them how many bottles of this new wine they're going to get, because it's too early in the process.'

For this idea to work: 'We needed to get at least 1,000 people to sign up in order for this to be viable,' Laura added. She was delighted with the response. 'We got over 1,400 angels respond almost immediately saying, "Yeah, I want to be involved".'

From a marketing standpoint, this means multiple opportunities to speak to these customers, not just about buying more wine, but 'getting them involved in a conversation about this wine, and about this story'. And they'll have personal involvement in the finished product, from choosing the base blend that the sparkling wine is made from, through naming the wine and label design. 'The engagement has been extraordinary,' said Laura and reported that customers really take ownership of the wine long after they've forgotten about spending that £100. The outcome is that customers and producers have together co-created a value that goes way beyond the actual product they have made and purchased. Everyone involved in the project has had a very rich experience and taken part in the story of the development of a new English sparkling wine.

3) Profitability: encouraging customers to buy more per order and to spend a little bit more on a wine that delivers a little bit more margin. Naked takes a digital-first approach: the website is its store front and when visitors land on the site, it must capture their attention sufficiently to make them curious to find out more and eventually end up at the checkout.

Naked plays a very long game (perhaps this is due to selling a product range that increases in value with age), and has invested in making sure that when it comes to using the website it meets the ever-increasing expectations of online customers. The digital team at Naked squeeze value from every online interaction; they even find out on the landing page about the type of wines and price range customers are interested in buying. They also use its six million online reviews to increase profitably. It applies an algorithm that can match users' own taste buds and reviews to other similar customers, so they can learn from each other. 'It's a really powerful tool and something we're constantly evolving and that we hope will be even more powerful in the future.' The aim is, by analysis purchasing behaviour maps, it becomes possible to develop personally tailored marketing plans that specifically meet the needs of the individuals. Naked has more than 80 or 90 different segments, which are targeted with different products, different advertising copy and different customer experiences.

The reviews help winemakers too. One such winemaker found through the specially developed Naked Wines app that their wines received top reviews in the UK but, unfortunately, not in the USA or Australia. This knowledge allowed the producers to adapt their wines slightly to counter the criticism from customers and now they receive over 90 per cent positive ratings in both countries.

Naked Wines say in its marketing literature that 'it's not for everyone' and challenges newbies to find out if this is a smarter way to buy wine. Whether Naked is for you or not, it certainly appears to have a marketing strategy that is very smart when it comes to satisfying its customers and its producers.

Questions

1. **Explain how and why Naked Wines is doing things differently.**
2. **Describe the ways in which Naked puts its customers at the core of its B2B marketing activities.**
3. **Discuss which type of B2B market Naked Wines is operating in and identify who are its customers.**
4. **Apply the buying process model to this case and evaluate the role of the end consumer.**
5. **Suggest how producers and manufacturers are involved in creating added value.**

This case study is by Brian Searle, Loughborough University

References

Based on: Carruthers, B. (2017), How Naked Wines' storytelling helps crowdfund wine making, WARC June www.warc.com; Clarke, L. (2018), How Naked Wines is bringing a digital-first approach to a vintage industry, ComputerworldUK 20 July https://www.computerworlduk.com/data/how-naked-wines-is-bringing-digital-first-approach-vintage-industry-3681049/; Naked Wines (2018), https://www.nakedwines.com; Wikipedia (2018), Naked Wines https://en.wikipedia.org/wiki/Naked_Wines

CASE 8
AstraZeneca: Sweden and the UK Join Forces to Serve New Markets in the Pharmaceutical Industry

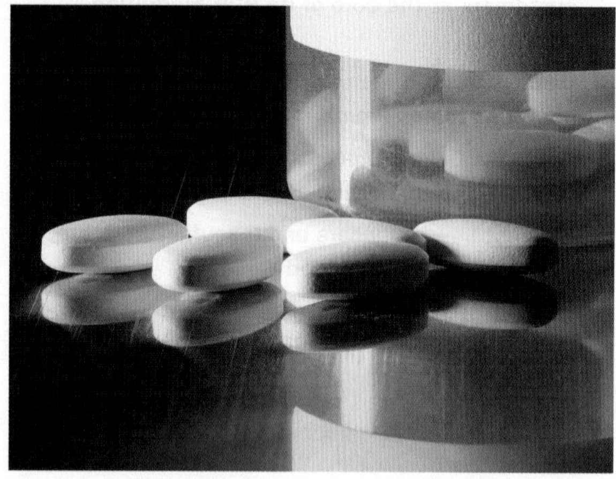

Healthcare is the largest business sector in the world, around three times the size of the banking industry, but the return on research and development into new products is not as high as might be expected as often traditional business practices stifle innovation. But this is not the case at AstraZeneca, which was developed following a merger between Astra AB of Sweden and Zeneca PLC of the UK. These two companies had similar organizational cultures and views of the pharmaceutical industry. The purpose of the merger was to take advantage of market growth opportunities, extend the reach of the business to global markets to create a more powerful innovation-led research and development platform, and to improve financial flexibility. AstraZeneca became the fourth-largest pharmaceutical company in the world when the Swedish and UK companies merged. This created a challenge for the supply side of the business. This case explores the complexity of the buying process and associated issues in procurement in the pharmaceutical industry.

AstraZeneca is a manufacturer of drug treatments and specializes in cardiovascular, oncology and respiratory healthcare, which are the major areas of metabolic disease. The organization is involved in all stages of production and distribution, from the initial research and development required to find new drugs and treatments, through manufacture, to delivery to its business customers.

Pharmaceuticals is a complex industry, especially when it comes to procurement. So companies in this industry need to be very clear about their buying objectives and product requirements, and have strategies in place that can guide their purchasing. Over the last few decades, there has been a seismic shift in the pharmaceuticals industry in terms of the way value is defined, and in the markets that products are created for. To understand this market sector, we need to briefly delve into its evolution and development.

Evolution of Pharmaceutical Industry

Over the years, this industry has evolved and new business models have emerged. Until 1870, there was just one business model and that was the apothecary shop; this was a robust approach to buying and selling drugs and is how Astra AB came into being, with over 400 of these shops. This low-tech approach to medicine supply served the market demands well for over 600 years. But, as the marketing environment changed through the period of the industrial revolution, social attitudes altered, populations grew, urbanization of living spaces was extended to a larger population, increased knowledge of technology opened up product-development opportunities, and the result was demand for different types of drug to treat a range of new and existing conditions. The pharmaceutical industry evolved to meet this new demand. There were then two types of approach to buying and selling drugs—prescription drugs and over-the-counter drugs—and this became the module used for many decades.

Moving rapidly forward to the 1990s, the marketing environment again experienced major changes from social and technology perspectives, and there were major advances in medicines—for example, antibiotics and beta blockers—which led to further and more sophisticated business models of buying and selling emerging. The evolution of the pharmaceutical industry, driven by technological and social change, has continued to intensify over the last 25 years. Now we have an even more complex set of business models guiding the way pharmaceutical products are bought and sold.

Figure C8.1 illustrates how there are different types of market emerging that are being shaped by: 1) the demand for fitness, 2) who defines the value and 3) how the value is created. The habitats shown are potential markets for particular types of product. For example, the 'Lazarus and Narcissus' habitat is where there is demand for very innovative and expensive treatments that are highly personalized, for example gene therapy. Buyers of these types of product will be serving a target market of 'wealthy well' individuals who are seeking to maintain their health. In the centre of Figure C8.1 is the core state provision habitat. This is where government procurement processes define the value—which currently is to seek maximum efficiency from drugs at the lowest possible cost to serve a large state healthcare market. At the other end of the spectrum is the 'limited choice' habitat, which is like state provision but tends to occur more in emerging, poorly served healthcare markets (Smith, 2011).

In 2010, greater diversification occurred as the changing demand created opportunities for new types of firms to enter the market. Fujifilm has moved from photography to pharmaceuticals and is developing a wide range of new drugs for treatment of cancer and infectious diseases, and is using innovative technology and biologics (genetically engineered proteins). The outsourcing of Research and Development (R&D) by more traditional pharma firms has enabled new entrants to benefit from lower entry barriers as they too can use similar resources.

So, in summary, forces in the marketing environment are increasingly shaping demand, and the buying practices within the pharmaceutical industry and the emerging habitats (markets) are driving the market-based approach to purchasing.

Market-based Approach to Purchasing

Drugs are specialized products made from chemical substances that interact with the human body to produce a biological response. These products are manufactured to a high specification by companies

FIGURE C8.1
Different types of healthcare market

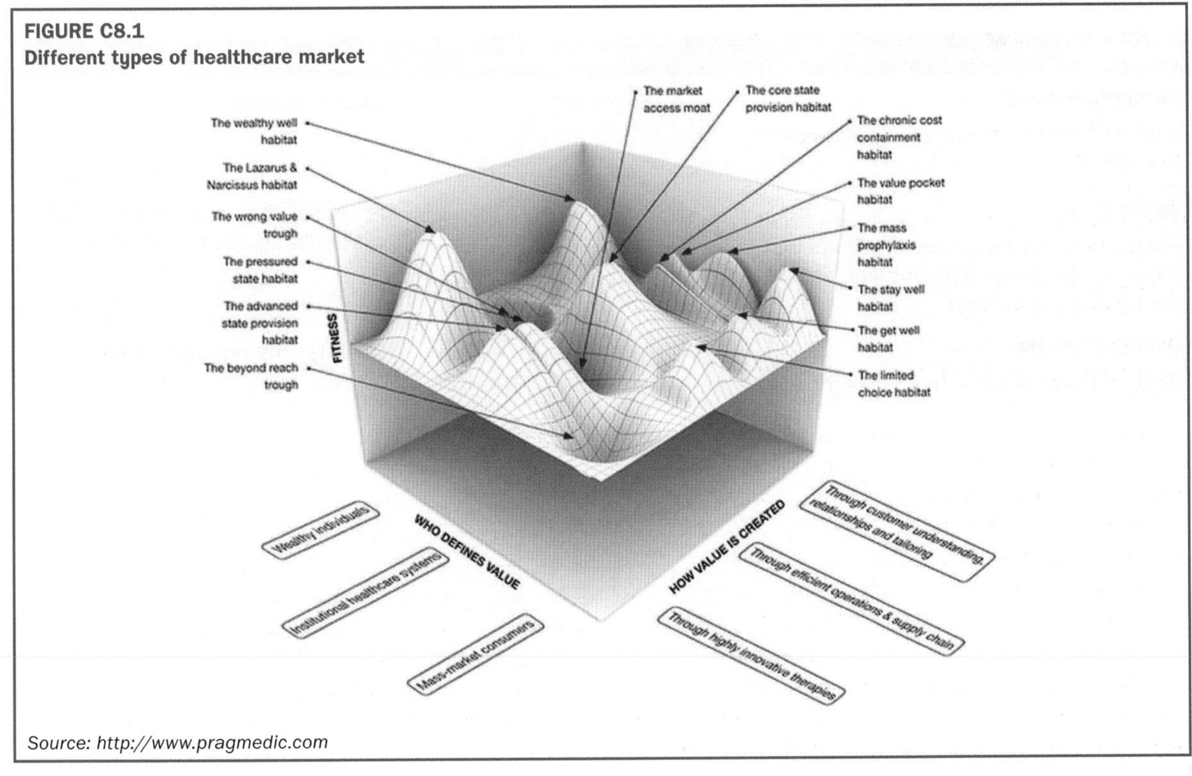

Source: http://www.pragmedic.com

»

like AstraZeneca. Developing and clinical testing of new drugs can take many years before they are made available for sale, to ensure they are safe and effective. Finally, drugs must have regulatory approval and continuous monitoring. Once AstraZeneca has developed a new drug, it holds a patent, which gives the company protection to produce the product for, say, 20 years. Once the patent runs out, then cheaper copies can be manufactured by other companies; these are called generics.

Buyers that are looking to purchase drugs from AstraZeneca must navigate through a complex set of choice criteria. See Table C8.1 for definition of the broad types of product bought and sold in the pharmaceutical industry.

Increasingly, buyers in this industry are under pressure to meet many different purchasing criteria, and determination of product specification and quality is very important. Berk et al (2013) suggest it is important to consider all three of the broad types of product shown in Table C8.1 if a buying group is to meet its order requirements and the different routes to the emerging market segments, for example direct to consumer, direct to pharmacy. Berk et al. also suggest that manufacturers and buyers throughout the supply chain select a procurement model to guide their buying practices. The procurement models are based on the service requirement and demands for cost-effectiveness and value.

Questions:

1. **Discuss the extent to which buyers in the pharmaceutical industry need to consider the marketing environment when making purchasing decisions.**
2. **Imagine you are a buyer of cardiovascular drugs and treatments for a large state healthcare provider. Identify a set of choice criteria you might use.**
3. **Explore the nature and size of manufacturers in the pharmaceutical industry and discuss the extent to which the Pareto rule applies.**

This case study was written by Fiona Ellis-Chadwick, Senior Lecturer, Loughborough University.

References

Based on: Berk, P., Gilbert, M., Herlant, M. and Walter, G. (2013), Rethinking the Pharma Supply Chain: New Models for a New Era, BCG Perspectives by the Boston Consulting group https://www.bcgperspectives.com/content/articles/biopharma_supply_chain_management_rethinking_ pharma_supply_chain_new_models_new_era/#chapter1 (accessed July 2015); AstraZenec (2015), About Us—History http://www.astrazeneca.com/About-Us/History (accessed July 2015); Smith, B. (2011), *The Future of Pharma: evolutionary threats and opportunities*, Aldershot: Gower Publishing Ltd

TABLE C8.1 Drug types and example products

Drug type	Product examples	Description
Perception drugs Sold by the drug manufacturer who holds the patent	Pulmicort	Asthma treatment
Generics Made under licence, these are drugs that are no longer under a patent, and as a result the price is much lower	Nexium	Decreases the acid in the stomach and treats symptoms of reflux
Over the counter Sold by pharmacists without prescription	Ibuprofen	Anti-inflammatory, pain relief

CHAPTER 5
Marketing, Ethics and Society

> *The premise of this Foundation is one life on this planet is no more valuable than the next.*
>
> **MELINDA FRENCH GATES**

LEARNING OBJECTIVES

After reading this chapter, you should be able to:

1 explain the dimensions of sustainable marketing
2 explain the meaning of ethics, and business and marketing ethics
3 describe ethical issues in marketing
4 explain the stakeholder theory of the firm
5 discuss corporate social responsibility (CSR)
6 discuss societal marketing, describe the dimensions of CSR
7 discuss non-profit organizations

This chapter builds on and explores marketing in order to discover the role of ethics and how this is impacting on society and how organizations, large and small, should and are responding. First, we look at the dimensions of **sustainable marketing**, then we review the principles and applications of marketing ethics, and finally we examine marketing approaches towards implementing sustainable marketing.

Dimensions of Sustainable Marketing

Over the decades, marketing and branding have enabled firms to grow into global corporations, turning over billions if not trillions of dollars a year. Strong brands develop relationships with their customers, which enable the creation of mutual benefits and increased value. All is good so far? Not without consideration of the wider societal impact. Many companies are adopting environmental and social policies that fit with their organizational structure and stakeholder expectations. Concern for the physical environment and sustainability—a company's survival into the future over say 10, 50 or 100 years—has become highly significant and generally forms part of most companies' corporate and strategic marketing planning. Nestlé is a global corporation that touches people's lives from end-to-end of the supply chain: that is, from producer to consumer. They have made 41 public commitments which seek to ensure that all their operations are contributing to *enhancing the quality of lives and contributing to a healthier future* for the planet. Water and its future supply are key concerns, and the corporation has been investing in raising water stewardship standards across their operations, which means reducing consumption in manufacturing processes, facilitating use of recycled water and increasing access to safe drinking water and sanitation (Nestlé, 2018).

But how do businesses, large and small, local and global—from a marketing viewpoint—determine which are the *right* and *ethical* paths to follow to ensure future sustainability? Tension exists between the environmental, social and economic contexts, and the extent to which a company leans towards high or low sustainability policies and environmental credentials will determine where the emphasis is placed (see Figure 5.1). For example, high-sustainability companies pay attention to stakeholder relationships—for example, relationships with employees, customers and non-governmental organizations (NGOs) in the environment—engaging with them in a proactive way. Low-sustainability companies will concentrate on the traditional corporate model of profit maximization (Eccles, Ioannou and Serafeim, 2011). In other words, each of the context: environmental, social and economic bring different priorities to the fore.

Environmental context highlights sustainability. Arguably, companies should create marketing strategies to address issues facing the physical world. And some do: Nestlé is investing heavily to ensure substantiality of resources and low impact of its activities on the planet in its long-term strategic planning. To give focus to guide (and enforce) environmental policies, governments are tackling environmental issues through the use of legislation and target setting, e.g. the Climate Change Act (2008) commits the UK to an 80 per cent reduction in greenhouse gas emissions by 2050, and the Paris Agreement (2015), which is seeking to control global temperature. For companies, this means identifying sources of greenhouse gas emissions, e.g. transportation activities, waste disposal, production. The Stobart Group operates transportation and services to the energy, aviation and rail industries, which means managing emissions effectively. The Eddie Stobart's rail freight division, working with Tesco Distribution and Direct Rail Services, significantly improved the efficiency of the movement of goods and helped Tesco move closer to becoming a zero-carbon business by 2050 (Stobart Group, 2018) and won environmental awards. See Exhibit 5.1 for how Tesco is marketing this achievement. In some industries, the options for adopting greener alternatives is very limited, for example, while aircraft are becoming more fuel efficient, electric or solar aeroplanes are not likely to be available for several decades. So, airlines are more likely to stick to traditional corporate models and to maximizing profits rather than deterring passengers from flying by raising awareness of the extent of aviation emissions (Tyers, 2017).

FIGURE 5.1
Dimensions of sustainable marketing

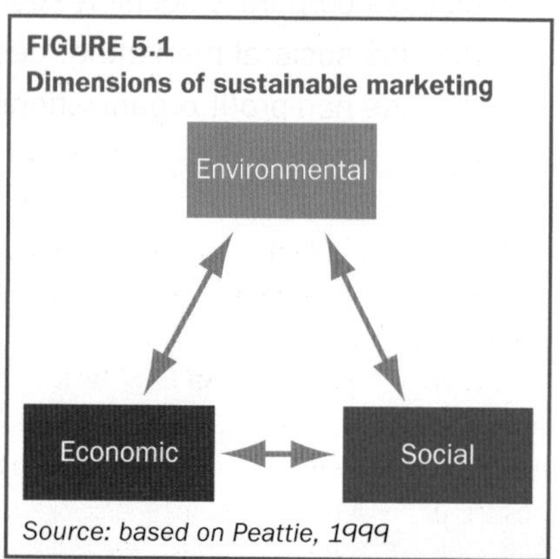

Source: based on Peattie, 1999

Additionally, there are global movements that are seeking to make fundamental changes in production methods and environmental impact. The Fairtrade movement has focused on the impact of sustainability on the environment and society. To become certified as a fair-trade producer, farmers must ensure that they are providing 'decent working conditions, local sustainability, and fair terms for farmers and workers in the developing world' (Fairtrade Foundation, 2018). This movement has invested in raising public awareness through education and promotional campaigns, and has seen significant changes in public attitude towards fair procurement.

EXHIBIT 5.1
Tesco promotes its achievements with an adaptation of its logo

Social context highlights the need for change in society, inequality and deprivation. For example, according to the World Bank, in 2011 over 2.2 billion people lived on less than $2 a day, but progress is very slow in moving them out of poverty (World Bank, 2015). But the world poverty clock shows that achievements are being made in helping people escape from poverty in real time (see https://worldpoverty.io/) and targets are being met by expanding social protection programmes, which foster sustainable developments so that when natural disasters occur there are better survival rates, and many other initiatives (United Nations, 2017). Save the Children is a **not-for-profit organization** which seeks to give children a healthy start in life and an education to give them prospects of a better life. The charity uses advertising campaigns to maintain awareness of such issues, using thought-provoking subjects, e.g. war in Syria, and often high-profile celebrity brand ambassadors to promote the need for action and change (see Exhibit 5.2). Starbucks Foundation has also focused on self-improvement and partnered with the Malala Fund to create educational opportunities in India and Latin America for girls and young women, aiming to help to end poverty (Starbucks, 2018).

Likewise, but at the other end of the age spectrum, Help Age International are committed to protecting the rights of older people. Due to wider benefits of achieving social good, many corporate organizations are also finding ways to get involved, e.g. through philanthropy, community engagement and many other social initiatives. But each firm must balance societal and environmental issues with its economic demands. Read Marketing in Action 5.1 to find out more about these tensions.

Economic context focuses on strong economic performance as being the bedrock of business activity, and on economic growth as being vital to future business sustainability. However, environmental issues have begun to impact on economic performance. For example, accessible reserves of oil and natural gas have dwindled, causing prices to rise across many raw materials and manufactured goods, but many sectors of the industrial economy rely on performing activities that are economically rewarding but potentially environmentally damaging. For some industries, social and environmental challenges are difficult to address. For example, aviation contributes around 2.5 per cent to the world's total carbon emissions and there is no slow-down in demand for short- and long-haul flights. In fact, the airline industry is booming; driving down the cost of travel has increased passenger numbers and the industry is set to see revenues reach the level of 1 per cent of global GDP. There are predictions that, by 2035, there will be double the number of passenger aircraft compared with 2019. Additionally, governments are benefiting in the form of tax revenues (around $133 billion) and employment (70 million jobs across the supply chain) from this high level of performance across the industry (Tyers, 2017).

Companies have responded in various ways to the dimensions of sustainable marketing. Corporate social responsibility (CSR) and operating in an ethical way are becoming increasingly important in the modern world. Globally, companies are taking CSR seriously and responding positively: for example, TNT (Netherlands logistics firm) has 50 people on standby to respond within 48 hours to world emergencies and IBM's (USA computer corporation) philanthropic spending involves deploying staff to work on worthy projects in the developing world.

EXHIBIT 5.2
Musician Myleene Klass supports Save the Children's work to keep children alive in their early years

Positive responses can benefit an organization's market position but, equally, unethical behaviour can lead to bad publicity and have a negative effect on customers' willingness to buy. Examples that have had a negative influence include: BA (price fixing),

MARKETING IN ACTION 5.1

Commercial versus Social Marketing

Socially orientated marketing faces commercial challenges. Walmart and Systembolaget are examples of tensions affecting corporate organizations in different ways.

Walmart ($476 billion total revenue) annually turns over more than the following countries produce—Denmark (GDP $347 billion), Finland (GDP $276 billion)—and nearly as much Sweden (GDP $560 billion) and Norway (GDP $512 billion). Indeed, if Walmart were a country, it would rank somewhere around the 28th largest economy in the world. On a commercial level, Walmart didn't develop a sustainability strategy until 2008, when it began focusing on renewable energy, reducing waste and selling sustainable products. It now continues to focus on environmental, social and governance issues as a way of connecting with consumers and earning their trust.

However, in the USA, this positioning as a responsible retailer has been somewhat tainted as the major shareholder of Walmart's global operations has been accused of being far less generous than other wealthy philanthropists and everyday donors. The Waltons are the USA's richest family, worth in excess of $140 billion, largely due to their shares in Walmart, the world's largest retailer. The Walton Family Foundation, a non-profit organization with assets of about $2 billion, regularly invests in education reform and the environment, but recently the family have been accused of using the foundation for its tax-saving efficiencies rather than as a way to channel some of their family's great wealth into benefiting society. From a marketing perspective, the challenge is not about whether Walmart is more or less inclined towards social endeavours than other large corporations, but is about managing perceptions, and this example serves to highlight the tensions that can arise when profits meet philanthropy.

Systembolaget, the large Swedish retailer, with over 400 stores, is a state-owned monopoly with the responsibility of selling alcohol in a country where excessive drinking has been a problem. The company constantly monitors the changing world to ensure the products it sells meet current customer demand. In the Nordic economies, social initiatives rank highly. Whilst Sweden is relatively small in terms of population, it tops the league tables in many things, from economic competitiveness to social health and happiness. Indeed, along with the other Nordic nations (Denmark, Norway, Iceland and Finland), Sweden is seen as offering a blueprint for reform of the public sector and delivering societal well-being. This is a nation where social welfare is considered a priority. It is said that 'A Swede pays tax more willingly than a Californian because he gets decent schools and free healthcare.'

Soft factors such as equality and social cohesion are at the foundation of the Swedish economic model and the response has been to invest in initiatives at all levels to change behaviour. Upstream, the government has set clear goals for behaviour change: alcohol-free childhood, postpone the age of first drink experiences, provide more alcohol-free environments, prevent drink-driving. Mid-stream, Systembolaget trains its employees to be expert advisers on alcohol consumption, and downstream individual consumption of alcohol has reduced, as many 15- to 16-year-olds change their behaviour and attitudes towards alcohol (Hallgren, Leifman and Andréasson, 2012).

Systembolaget is positioned in the minds of its consumers as a brand that takes social responsibility very seriously and its sustainability strategy continues to focus on the harmful effects of alcohol on customers and their friends and families. The tensions occur because they are in a monopoly position when it comes to the sale of alcohol and have been criticized for reaping profits from industrially produced wines rather than producing more specialized selections and pursuing a single goal to sell as much wine as possible. So, they too walk a challenging path between delivering high levels of customer satisfaction and trust and making a good profit.

Based on: Dibb and Carrigan (2013); Milne (2014); Cheng, Kotler and Lee (2011); Walmart (2014, 2018); Knoema (2015); O'Connor (2014); Systembolaget (2018); Hagstrom (2018)

BAE Systems (bribery), BP and Shell (oil spills in the USA and Nigeria), Walmart (allegations of poor employee relations), McDonald's (health concerns), Coca-Cola (marketing positioning of Dasani in the UK) and Procter & Gamble (Sunny D, the drink found to turn children yellow). These examples bear witness to the importance of business and marketing ethics, not only in their own right but also for the well-being of the organizations themselves.

Consequently, organizations are now reflecting on and defining their standards of behaviour by focusing on social marketing principles. Read Mini Case 5.1 to discover the extent to which football is regulated by social principles.

MINI CASE 5.1

Not for Profit: The FA

Harry Kane is a top-rate athlete; he is a footballer, who commands a very high salary and he is not on his own. Salaries for footballers have grown on average by over 1,000 per cent in the last 20 years. Football clubs finance these high salaries through matchday revenue (approximately 13 per cent), broadcasting (approximately 60 per cent) and other commercial activities (approximately 27 per cent). Premier League club revenue is increasing in line with the massive wage bills and financial demands of the player transfer market. While football is a commercial market worth billions of pounds, the Football Association Limited (FA) (the governing body which sets the rules and regulations for the game in England and Wales) is a not-for-profit charity.

With such high stakes and volumes of money changing hands, the FA has to provide, monitor and manage standards and discipline for the game, provide safeguarding standards for young players coming through training academies, ensure opportunities for all and limit discrimination, manage anti-doping through education, testing and application of legal regulations, and protect the game, its players, supporters and many other stakeholders from betting irregularities, match fixing and insider information. The FA must ensure the viability of Club Wembley as a venue and centrepiece of the game of football. This is an almost impossible task.

So how does the FA fund its operations and prioritise what it does?

Funding: The FA reinvests over £120 million a year into the game, which it generates through its partnerships both commercial (e.g. Nike, Buildbase, Mars, EE, McDonald's, BT Sport) and with other charities (e.g. Cancer Research); Other sources are grant income (e.g. Sport England), broadcasting, sponsorship and licencing, and Club Wembley revenues. Investment is made into the following strategic priorities.

Priorities: The FA's mission is to widen participation in the game, promote diversity and regulate the sport to ensure enjoyment for all. The strategic priorities are: producing England winning teams in men's and women's football; world-leading education from the grassroots upward through coaching programmes; expanding the women's game, and widening participation and engagement across society; improving the trust and efficiency of the game.

While the FA can generate enough income to reinvest in its good works, the charity constantly faces criticism that it is not capable of meeting its priorities. The FA has been accused of being ineffective, especially regarding match fixing. 'Fixing goes on but the FA are oblivious to it': high profile legal cases have found coaches guilty of abuse against children and its management has been criticised for being slow, ineffectual, too conservative and male dominated.

In support of the FA's achievements against its priorities, there are now more women's and girls' teams than ever before, attendance at Women's Super League games has been rising year-on-year, mini soccer teams have seen increasing participation by young players and there are now over 186 disability teams.

Arguably, the FA is doing (some) good, but this is clearly not enough; they must be perceived as doing good by all stakeholders.

Questions:

Imagine you are the Strategy and Communications Director for the FA and you are responsible for providing the strategic focus for the charity's next sustainable marketing strategy.

1 Review the extent to which the FA is achieving a balance in its application of sustainable marketing contexts.

2 Using the output of your review, suggest changes for their next sustainable marketing strategy that can help the charity to deliver on its priorities.

Based on: Deloitte (2018); Northcroft (2017); Rumsby (2013); The FA (2017); BBC (a), (2018); Burt, (2016)

Marketing and Ethics

Underpinning sustainable marketing and shaping its implementation is the concept of ethics. **Ethics** are the moral principles and values that govern the actions and decisions of an individual or group (Berkowitz et al., 2004). They involve *values* about right and wrong conduct. **Business ethics** are the moral principles and values that guide a firm's behaviour. Until recently, for many companies, business ethics consisted mainly of compliance-based, legally driven codes and training that provided details of what employees could or could not do regarding such areas as conflicts of interest or improper use of company assets. Now, an increasing number of companies are designing value-based ethical programmes that are consistent across global operations. The aim is to provide employees with an in-depth understanding of ethical issues to help them make correct decisions when faced with new ethical situations and challenges.

Marketing ethics are the moral principles and values that guide behaviour within the field of marketing, and cover issues such as product safety, truthfulness in marketing communications, honesty in relationships with customers and distributors, pricing issues, and the impact of marketing decisions on the environment and society. There can be a distinction between the legality and ethicality of marketing decisions. Ethics concern personal moral principles and values, while laws reflect society's principles and standards that are enforceable in the courts.

Not all unethical practices are illegal. For example, it is not illegal to include genetically modified (GM) ingredients in products sold in supermarkets. However, some organizations, such as Greenpeace, believe it is unethical to sell GM products when their effect on health has not been scientifically proven. Such concerns have led some supermarket chains to withdraw GM ingredients from their own-brand products.

Ethical principles reflect the cultural values and norms of society. Norms guide what ought to be done in a particular situation. For example, being truthful is regarded as good. This societal norm may influence marketing behaviour. Hence—since it is good to be truthful—deceptive, untruthful advertising should be avoided. Often, unethical behaviour may be clear-cut but, in other cases, deciding what is ethical is highly debatable. Ethical dilemmas arise when two principles or values conflict. For example, Ben & Jerry's, the US ice cream firm, was a leading member of the Social Venture Network in San Francisco, a group that promotes ethical standards in business. A consortium, Meadowbrook Lane Capital, was part of this group and was formed to raise enough capital to make Ben & Jerry's a private company again. However, its bid was lower than that of Anglo–Dutch food multinational Unilever NV. Arguably, on the one hand, for Ben & Jerry's to stick to its ethical beliefs it should have accepted the Meadowbrook bid. On the other hand, the company also had to perform financially in the interests of its shareholders. Ben & Jerry's faced an ethical dilemma: one of its values and preferences inhibited the achievement of financial considerations. Ultimately, it accepted the Unilever bid (Reed, 2000).

Many ethical dilemmas derive from the conflict between the desire to increase profits and the wish to make decisions that are ethically justified. For example, the decision by Google to launch a self-censored search engine in China was driven by the need to be competitive in a huge market where it was lagging behind competitors. In order to secure a deal in China, Microsoft accepted censorship by the government in its agreement with Baidu (China's largest search engine) (Arthur, 2011). Companies do seek to address such conflicts: for example, Nike and Reebok monitor their overseas production of sports goods to ensure that no child labour is used, while still producing cost-efficient ranges.

Ethical issues in marketing

Ethical concerns impinge on all aspects of the marketing mix and, in many instances, are regulated by law. Marketing practices have been criticized by consumers, consumer groups and environmentalists, who accuse marketing managers of harming the interests of consumers, society and the environment. In this section, these ethical concerns are examined in relation to the marketing mix; this is followed by consideration of general societal, environmental and political issues (see Figure 5.2).

Product: product safety

Consumers expect products to be safe to use. They are legally protected by the Consumer Rights Act 2015, which means manufacturers and resellers must ensure that all products, physical and digital, are of satisfactory quality, fit for purpose and as described. The duty of care falls onto the supplier of the goods and services as they are responsible and experts. However, there have been many instances where it has been argued that these guiding principles have not been adhered to.

The tobacco, food and drinks industries have attracted criticism in recent years regarding the potential harm their products may cause to consumers. Tobacco companies have been criticized for marketing cigarettes, which cause lung cancer. The food industry has been criticized for marketing products that have high levels of fat, which can lead to obesity, and in the drinks industry concern has been expressed over the marketing to children of sugar-rich fizzy drinks, which cause tooth decay and can also lead to obesity.

In response, these industries have argued that they are taking steps to reduce the harmful effects of products, with bans on tobacco promotion and the creation of bodies such as the Food Standards Agency (the independent food safety body set up to protect public health and consumer interests in relation to food in the UK) and the Portman Group (the industry-sponsored organization that oversees the UK's alcoholic drinks industry). Most European countries have similar organizations which also provide advice to industry and seek to guide manufacturers and retailers towards the production and distribution of safe produce.

FIGURE 5.2
Ethical issues in marketing

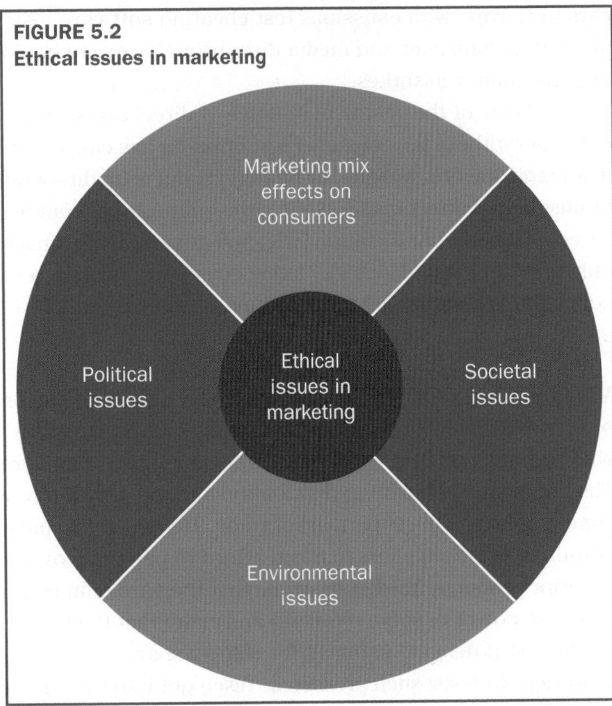

Pricing: price fixing and anti-trust laws

An anti-competitive practice associated with marketing is price fixing, where two or more companies collude to force up the price of products. Price fixing is considered unethical because it interferes with the consumer's freedom of choice and raises prices artificially. European Union (EU) competition policy provides a legal framework that is designed to prevent companies from carrying out this practice. The EU anti-trust policy rules out two firms making agreements that can restrict competition and prohibits firms with a dominant market position from charging unfair prices (European Commission (a), 2018).

For example, the European Commission has fined technology companies ASUS, Denon & Marantz, Phillips and Pioneer over €111 million for price fixing online and breaching EU competition and anti-trust laws. These companies were attempting to control the price of their electronic products (kitchen appliances, hair dryers, notebook computers, headphones) being sold online and were found to be threatening retailers selling at discounted prices with blocking supplies. The manufacturers were also found to be using digital monitoring tools to track their goods to help control pricing (European Commission (b), 2018). Similarly, Google has been fined €4.3 billion for imposing restrictions on manufacturers that were deemed anti-competitive. Google required manufacturers to pre-install the Google search app, made large payments to manufacturers and mobile network operators to ensure that only the Google app was preloaded, and prevented the use of unauthorised versions of Android (European Commission (c), 2018).

Promotion: misleading advertising

Marketers argue that in most European countries advertising is tightly regulated, minimizing opportunities for advertisers to mislead. Misleading advertising can take the form of exaggerated claims or concealed facts. A claim that a diet product was capable of 1 kilogram of weight loss per week, when in reality much less was the case, is an example of an exaggerated claim. When Coca-Cola launched its bottled water brand Dasani in the UK, it concealed the fact that it was made from local Sidcup tap water. Consumers were enraged and felt they had been cheated. A damaging media frenzy followed; traces of bromate (a possible carcinogen) were found in the water. Volkswagen was sued for making false claims in TV commercials promoting its vehicles as being environmentally friendly and using 'clean diesel'. US regulators found 40 times the allowed levels of air pollutants coming from these vehicles when tested in real-world driving conditions and the fines added up to over $30 billion. Volkswagen has also been fined €1 billion by German prosecutors for selling over 10 million cars in Europe with emissions test-cheating software installed (BBC (b), 2018). These high-profile scandals that meet with consumer and media disapproval are (or should be) a major deterrent to companies contemplating making similar mistakes.

The issue of the unethical practice of direct marketing companies entering names and addresses onto a database without the consumer's permission has caused concern. Some consumers fear that the act of subscribing to a magazine or a website, or buying products by direct mail, will result in the inconvenience of receiving streams of unsolicited direct mail or *spam* (the online equivalent to junk mail). Regulation in Europe by bodies such as the Direct Marketing Association (UK) and governments aims to ensure that consumers are protected and their data is only used and stored legally. Online consumers are given various options to opt in or opt out of non-essential data collection and subsequent promotional mailings.

Place: slotting allowances

Manufacturers promote their products and aim to outperform the competition. Consequently, they sometimes offer inducements to retailers to place special emphasis on particular products. A slotting allowance is a fee paid by a manufacturer to a retailer in exchange for an agreement to place a product on the retailer's shelves. The importance of gaining distribution and the growing power of retailers means that slotting allowances are commonplace in the supermarket trade. They may be considered unethical since they distort competition, favouring large suppliers that can afford to pay them over small suppliers who may, in reality, be producing superior products. Marketers argue that they are only responding to the realities of the marketplace (i.e. the immense power of some retailers) and claim that the blame should rest with the purchasing practices of those retailers that demand payment for display space, rather than with the marketing profession who are often powerless to resist such pressures. Tesco got into trouble over slotting allowances and marketing/distribution fees, which had a widespread effect on the value of the brand. The grocery chain demanded high fees from suppliers to position their goods in prominent locations in stores and to favour their brands over the supermarket's own label goods. But these fees raised the prices paid by customers and allowed competition from discount supermarkets such as Aldi and Lidl—which mainly sell own label goods—to offer consumers a better deal on a basket of shopping. Following substantial financial issues relating to over-inflated profits from these types of rebates, Tesco is aiming to reduce the fees it charges suppliers, although payments for prominent shelf positions will remain (Economist, 2015).

Ethics and societal, environmental and political issues

Critics of marketing practices suggest that there is too much promotion of materialism; emphasis on the short-term and limited concern for long-term environmental consequences. Arguably, marketers should consider the interests of consumers and society, and how this is influenced by political issues.

Societal issues: materialism and short-termism

Materialism is an ethical concern associated with an overemphasis on material possessions. Critics argue that people judge themselves and are judged by others, not by who they are, but by what they own. Marketers use this trait to drive consumption. For example, status symbols such as expensive houses, cars, second homes, yachts, high-tech gadgets and designer clothing are marketed as representations of success and social worth. Such conspicuous consumption is fuelled by the advertising industry, which equates materialism and success with happiness, desirability and social worth. Materialism is not considered natural by the critics, but a phenomenon created by business, to drive sales and deliver high profit margins. Such companies devote large marketing expenditures to these types of brands.

Supporters of marketing argue that sociological studies show how remote communities in Africa—never exposed to marketing's pervasive and persuasive powers—also display signs of materialism. For example, in some tribes, people use the number of cows owned as a symbol of status and power. Some marketers argue that desire for status is a natural state of mind, with marketing simply promoting the kinds of possessions that may be regarded as indicators of status and success.

Accruing symbols of power is not limited to the physical world. Online, the Facebook 'Like' button drives people to show their commitment to individuals, brands and communities. At a personal level, self-esteem can be boosted by getting 'Likes' thumbs-up affirming a post as something good (see Exhibit 5.3). The underlying reasoning is that receiving positive feedback makes us feel good and raises our perceptions of our relational value. Billions of 'Likes' are generated every day and those who receive them feel good and those who don't can feel lonely and rejected (Burrow and Rainone, 2017).

Short-termism Marketing is often accused of short-termism; putting the immediate interests of consumers before society's long-term interests. As we have seen when discussing product safety, marketers supply and promote products that can have long-term adverse health repercussions for consumers. Cigarettes may aid short-term relaxation, but they have harmful long-term health effects for both smokers and those people forced to breathe in their smoke. Fatty food may be tasty, but it may also lead to obesity and heart problems. Too much salt and sugar in food and drinks may enhance the taste, but also lead to long-term health problems. See Exhibit 5.4 to see how recommended sugar intakes correspond to the amount of sugar in soft drinks. Alcohol may remove inhibitions and help to create a convivial atmosphere, but may also lead to dependency and liver problems. The UK has introduced a sugar tax, so manufacturers must pay a levy for high sugar content drinks. Many brands which target children with soft drinks have already reduced the sugar content: Fanta, Ribena, Lucozade (BBC (c), 2018).

EXHIBIT 5.3
Facebook uses the thumbs up symbol as a mechanism for displaying loyalty

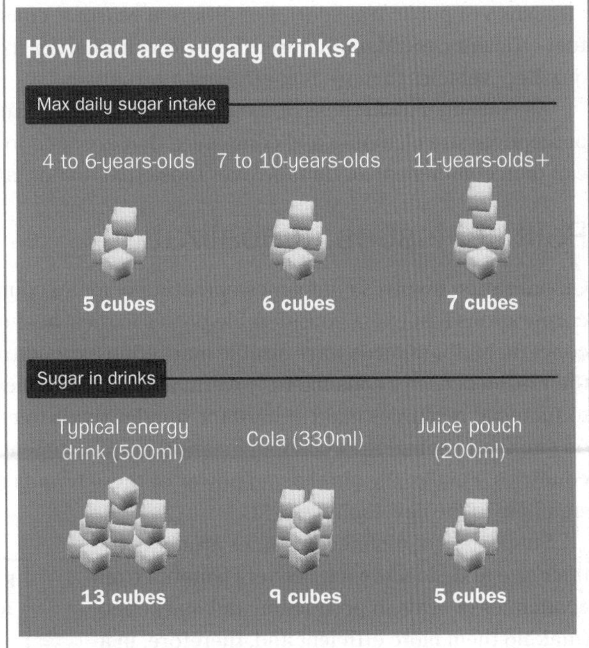

EXHIBIT 5.4
Public Health England demonstrates the sugar content of popular soft drinks

Environmental issues: production and consumption

Production should enable efficient manufacture of goods and services. Businesses may also want the cheapest ingredients and components in their products and look for countries where low cost manufacturing is highly profitable using local work forces. Environmentalists favour using sustainable resources, which may be more costly due to being biodegradable or recyclable, and cost could also be raised as they involve providing staff with safe working conditions and good levels of pay, rather than being exploitive. Doing good and making the *right* choices when producing goods can be fraught with challenges. Globally, events, like the building collapse in Rana Plaza, Bangladesh, which killed 1,135 garment workers, highlights problems with unethical low-cost production methods. This tragic event put pressure on manufacturers in the area to improve working conditions for workers, who are typically paid less than a quarter of those in mainland China. However, the region has duty-free access to Western markets and the low-paid workers have helped to make this trade a major part of Bangladesh's economy and export trade ($28 billion a year) (Reuters, 2016).

Consumption is arguably driven by marketers' desire to satisfy consumers' wants, but again there are conflicts of interest when it comes to the environment. Consumers are given a confusing range of choices; marketers do not always help: a brand may favour large packaging that gains the attention of consumers in stores, whereas environmentalists favour smaller pack sizes and refill packs. Eco-friendly labelling does not always help to alleviate confusion. Lots of brands use the word *organic* on their packaging, especially on health and beauty products, and in the UK this market has grown by 20 per cent, to over £60 million. The Soil Association has accused manufacturers of investing in marketing products which claim to be *green*, rather than into research and development to produce toxin-free products. In the EU, beauty products are not subject to the same stringent regulations as organic foods and so almost any product can be labelled natural or organic, leaving the consumer confused (Smithers, 2017).

Governments have tried to take positive actions in an attempt to reconcile business and environmental interests—for example, with car scrappage schemes that aim to cut pollution and stimulate demand for new cars. The politically and economically desirable option would be to create incentive structures for the advancement of innovation in the area of energy-efficient cars, which could reduce emissions and maintain a healthy automotive industry. The French government introduced a car scrappage scheme of €1,000 for consumers who exchange their old cars for fuel-efficient models; the result was improved sales. Prompted by European regulations, manufacturers in the automotive industry are continually fostering innovations that aim to meet carbon-reduction targets (Everitt, 2009). However, environmentalists have questioned the benefits of such schemes, saying that new cars might be operationally greener but efficiency gains tend to be offset by the carbon footprint involved in the manufacture of a new car. They would prefer governments to invest in increasing access to and improving the efficiency of public transport. For different reasons, consumers are also yet to be convinced *en masse* to adopt fuel-efficient cars. Manufacturers have to work harder to counter consumer resistance to switch from their 'gas guzzling' vehicles to more fuel-efficient alternatives.

As consumer awareness of the impact of climate change and the use of non-renewable resources grows, perceptions are changing and companies that are seen to be taking a serious approach towards sustainability can gain commercial advantage over those that do not take positive action (Barnett, 2011).

Political issues: globalization

Globalization involves companies operating in many countries and is a term usually applied to multinational corporations that exert considerable power in their host countries. It is the abuse of such power that is of ethical concern. Multinationals have sizable marketing expenditures and global mega brands; concern is expressed over their influence over consumers, governments and suppliers. Critics argue that the organizations' size and access to financial resources make it hard for smaller rivals to compete, and thus reduces consumer choice. The impact on employment and the economy means that governments vie with each other to attract multinationals to their countries. Finally, the purchasing power of these brands means that they can negotiate very low prices from suppliers in the developing world.

Supporters of global companies argue that their size and global reach delivers benefits from economies of scale in production and marketing (making them more efficient and, therefore, in a better position to charge low prices to consumers) and in Research and Development (R&D), enabling them to develop better-quality products and make technological breakthroughs—for example, in the area of healthcare. They further claim that their attraction to governments is evidence of the value they provide to host nations. Regarding their ability to negotiate down prices from developing-world suppliers, global organizations need to recognize their responsibilities to their supplier stakeholders. This is happening as more of them adopt corporate responsibility programmes and global corporations recognize the marketing potential of fair-trade products (for example, Nestlé markets Partners' Blend, a fair-trade coffee).

Having discussed the examples of ethical issues relating to marketing, in the next section we will explore specific marketing approaches to responding to ethical concerns.

FIGURE 5.3
Typical key stakeholders for a company

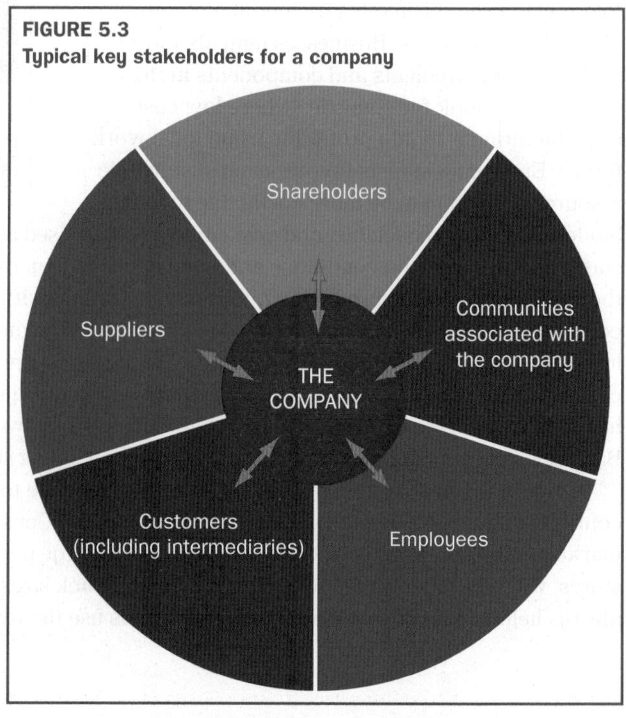

Marketing Approaches and Society

So far in this chapter we have discussed the tensions, challenges and difficult choices a firm must make if they are to adopt sustainable marketing into their marketing strategy. In this final part of the chapter, we explore, corporate and social responsibility and societal and not-for-profit marketing, which can help to give a firm structure to what they need to do, when striving to satisfy customer needs from a sustainable perspective. For marketing managers, sustainability is possibly the biggest challenge of the 21st century. Not only are there issues of what to reduce, but there is also the problem of understanding the real impact of any action. Research by Trucost (2012) found environmental sustainability is at the top of most companies' agendas.

Corporate social responsibility (CSR)

Business has taken action to address ethical concerns in marketing and other functional areas by adopting the philosophy of CSR. CSR has become increasingly important and commands the attention of executives around the world. It would be difficult to find a recent annual report of any large multinational company that does not talk proudly of its efforts to improve society and safeguard the environment (Crook, 2005). We shall now examine the idea in depth by exploring the nature and dimensions of CSR and assessing the arguments for and against its adoption.

Corporate social irresponsibility can have painful consequences for organizations. The case of Siemens illustrates the negative fallout that can follow. Accused of paying bribes to win lucrative overseas telecoms and power contracts, Siemens was fined US$800 million (£523 million) by the US Department of Justice. A further €395 million was paid to settle a case in Munich over the failure of its former board to fulfil its supervisory duties. The total cost to Siemens, a symbol of German engineering excellence, was more than €1.3 billion, including lawyers' and accountants' fees, plus the loss of its reputation and that of former senior executives (Gow, 2008).

The fallout from this and other cases raises the issue of how harmful corporate social irresponsibility can be to companies and wider society. As a result, companies are increasingly examining how their actions affect not only their profits but society and the environment. CSR refers to the ethical principle that an organization should be accountable for how its behaviour might affect society and the environment.

CSR is not new. For many years, companies have been aware of the obligations of being an employer and a consumer of natural resources. For example, the town of Bourneville was created by the founder of Cadbury to house the workers of that company (Moon, 2002). Nevertheless, there is little doubt that CSR is now higher on the agenda of many companies than it was in the past. Most multinational corporations now have a senior executive, often with staff at his/her disposal, specifically charged with developing and coordinating the CSR function (Crook, 2005). Furthermore, most large companies engage in corporate social reporting within their annual financial statements, as separate printed reports and/or on websites. The importance of CSR is also reflected in membership organizations, which offer services to members, such as providing information, lobbying and promoting the CSR cause. For example, the UK-based Business in the Community (www.bitc.org.uk) has a membership of over 700 companies and includes in its activities cause-related marketing and the promotion of CSR internationally. Other notable organizations in Europe include Business and Society Belgium, Finnish Business and Society, Business in the Community Ireland, Samenleving and Bedrijf (Netherlands), CSR Europe (www.csreurope.org) and the European Business Ethics Network (www.eben-net.org). However, it is not straightforward to determine the best course of action for future sustainability. Read Marketing in Action 5.2 to find out more about Ikea's approach to CSR.

CSR is based on the **stakeholder theory** of the firm, which contends that companies are not managed purely in the interests of their shareholders alone. Rather, there is a range of groups (stakeholders) that have a legitimate interest in the company as well (Donaldson and Preston, 1995). Following this theory, a **stakeholder** of a company is an individual or group that either:

- is harmed by or benefits from the company, *or*
- whose rights can be violated, or have to be respected, by the company (Crane and Matten, 2004).

Other stakeholder groups—besides shareholders, who typically would be considered stakeholders—are communities associated with the company, employees, customers of the company's products and suppliers (see Figure 5.3). The key point is that stakeholder theory holds that the company has obligations not only to shareholders but to other parties that are affected by its activities.

MARKETING IN ACTION 5.2
IKEA People and the Planet

IKEA operates 380 stores in 48 countries and is the world's largest furniture retailer, which seeks to deliver better prices and quality to its customers who buy $38 billion worth of goods each year. To ensure the success of its CSR policies, IKEA is constantly reviewing its practices across the supply chain to ensure that it provides sustainability on a large scale. On the production side, their strategy involves shortening the need for transportation, so in the USA, for example, almost a quarter of the products sold are manufactured in the USA.

According to Steve Howard, IKEA's Chief Sustainability Officer, the company is 'using IWay, a code of conduct that specifies environmental and social requirements for sourcing and distributing products, which is bringing sustainable and affordable cotton and timber products to millions of consumers around the world'. He also said that IKEA is 'committed to future proofing' the company in advance of the many challenges it is likely to face in the future. IKEA owns wind turbines and has introduced nearly half a million solar panels. In the USA, IKEA is the second largest private commercial solar power owner. The company is aiming to isolate itself from the volatilities of the energy markets and has reported significant savings on energy consumption across the business.

Based on: Jeffries (2011); King (2012); Kelly-Detwiler (2014); Gillies (2017)

The nature of CSR

A useful way of examining the nature of CSR is Carroll's four-part model of CSR (see Carroll and Buchholtz, 2000; Carroll, 1991). Carroll views CSR as a multi-layered concept that can be divided into four interrelated responsibilities: economic, legal, ethical and philanthropic. The presentation of these responsibilities is in the form of layers within a pyramid, and the full achievement of CSR occurs only when all four layers are met consecutively (see Figure 5.4).

FIGURE 5.4
The pyramid of social responsibility

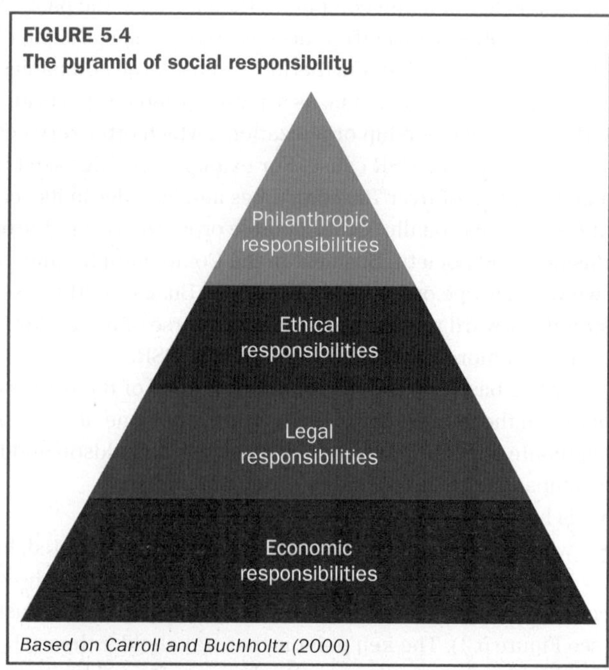

Based on Carroll and Buchholtz (2000)

Economic responsibilities

Carroll recognized that the principal role of a firm was to produce goods and services that people wanted and to be as profitable as possible in so doing. Economic responsibilities include: maintaining a strong, competitive position; operating at high levels of efficiency and effectiveness; and aiming for consistently high levels of profitability. Without the achievement of economic responsibilities, the other three are redundant, since the firm would go out of business. Economic success is the *sine qua non* (literally translated 'without which not', which in other words means 'without economic success, the other responsibilities cannot succeed') of CSR.

Legal responsibilities

Companies must pursue their economic responsibilities within the framework of the law. Laws reflect society's principles and standards that are enforceable in the courts. Occasionally, the drive to maximize profits can conflict with the law—as with Microsoft, which has faced heavy financial penalties both in Europe and the USA for anti-competitive behaviour (e.g. bundling Media Player into the Windows operating system, thereby squeezing out competitors' software). Like economic responsibilities, the meeting of legal responsibilities is a requirement of CSR.

Ethical responsibilities

Although the establishment of laws may be founded on ethical considerations, as we have seen there can be important distinctions, as with the selling of genetically modified (GM) products, which may raise ethical questions and yet be lawful. The same could be said of the meat production industry, where 90 per cent of pork is produced by raising female pigs in metal cages that are so small that the pregnant sow can hardly move. This practice is not currently illegal, but is thought by many to be inhumane (Gunther, 2012).

Ethical responsibilities mean that companies should perform in a manner consistent with the principles and values of society and prevent ethical norms being compromised in order to achieve corporate objectives. Companies such as BP draw up codes of ethical conduct and employ teams to govern legal compliance and business ethics (252 BP employees were dismissed in one year for unethical behaviour in a drive to weed out bribery and corruption) (Boxell and Harvey, 2005). Ethical responsibilities therefore comprise what is expected by society over and above economic and legal requirements.

Philanthropic responsibilities

At the top of the pyramid are the philanthropic responsibilities of companies—these are corporate actions that meet society's expectation that businesses should be good corporate citizens. This includes promoting human welfare, or goodwill, such as making charitable donations, the building of leisure facilities or even homes for employees and their families, arts and sports sponsorship, and support for local schools (Crane and Matten, 2004). The key difference between philanthropy and complying with ethical responsibilities is that the former is not expected in an ethical sense. Communities may desire companies to contribute to their well-being, but do not consider them unethical if they do not. Philanthropic responsibilities are presented at the top of the pyramid, as they represent the 'icing on the cake'—actions that are desired by society, but not expected or required. Warren Buffet, one of the world's richest men, made a record-breaking $37-billion donation to the Gates Foundation. The foundation, set up by former head of Microsoft, Bill Gates, and his wife, aims to give every life across the planet equal value, through philanthropic donations that support global, development and health programmes (Gates Foundation, 2012).

The dimensions of CSR

A strength of the four-part model of CSR is its realism in recognizing that, without the fulfilment of economic responsibilities, a company would not have the capability to engage in ethical and/or philanthropic activities. However, to gain a deeper understanding of the scope of CSR activities, it is necessary to explore its dimensions as well as its responsibilities.

CSR has four layers of responsibility: economic, legal, ethical and philanthropic. By examining the dimensions of CSR, an insight into where those responsibilities may be discharged can be gained. CSR dimensions are based on four key stakeholders—the individuals or groups affected by a company's activities—plus the physical environment, which, equally, can be affected by a company's activities, such as pollution or usage of scarce natural resources (see Maignan and Ferrell, 2004; Fukukawa and Moon, 2004).

Table 5.1 outlines the CSR dimensions, lists associated key issues and describes marketing responses for each dimension. Please note that the key issues relating to each CSR dimension are not all exclusively marketing related. For example, pollution control at a chemical plant is a production-related issue, whereas standard setting for supplies is a procurement-related topic and the setting of fair pay is a human resources issue. Nevertheless, for most of the issues listed in Table 5.1, marketing practices can affect outcomes. For example, car design can affect pollution levels and the rate at which oil reserves are depleted, and the creation of healthy-eating brands can improve consumers' diets through the reduction in fat, sugar and salt levels.

TABLE 5.1 Dimensions of CSR

Dimension	Key issues	Marketing response
Physical environment	Combating global warming Pollution control Conservation of energy and scarce resources Use of environmentally friendly ingredients and components Recycling and non-wasteful packaging	Sustainable marketing
Social (community involvement)	Support for the local community Support for the wider community	Societal marketing Cause-related marketing
Consumer	Product safety (including the avoidance of harmful long-term effects) Avoidance of price fixing Honesty in communications Respecting privacy	Societal marketing
Supply chain	Fair trading standard-setting for supplies (e.g. human rights, labour standards and environmental responsibility)	Fair-trade marketing
Employee relations	Fair pay Equal opportunities Training and motivation Information provision (e.g. on career paths, recruitment policies and training opportunities)	Internal marketing

Physical environment

Key issues in the physical environment, such as the use of environmentally friendly ingredients and components, recycling and non-wasteful packaging and pollution control, were introduced in Chapter 2. Marketers' response to these issues can be summarized under the term 'sustainable marketing'. Environmental sustainability means to maintain or prolong the physical environment. It involves action towards the use of renewable rather than finite raw materials, and the minimization and eventual elimination of polluting effluents and toxic or hazardous wastes.

Since marketing operates at the interface between the organization and its environment, it is uniquely positioned to lead the move towards more sustainable products and strategies. Typically, companies move through several stages (see Figure 5.5). To facilitate the process, marketing as a function needs to address a range of questions from the strategic to the tactical. Key questions are as follows (Charter et al., 2002).

- Have the effects of sustainability issues on company activities been analysed as part of the marketing planning process?
- Has the company conducted marketing research into the probable impacts on the organization of sustainability issues?
- Can the company modify existing products, services or processes to take account of sustainability considerations, or will innovations be required?
- Is the firm developing positive links with environmental groups?
- Do communications strategies accurately emphasize environmental considerations?

Responding positively to environmental issues is important in order to protect and sustain brands. Market-leading brands are always susceptible to attack by media and/or pressure groups following any environmental incident. It is, therefore, sensible to build into brand strategies sustainability issues to nurture and maintain brand trust.

Environmental issues can be a source of threats to organizations, but they can also provide opportunities. Toyota responded to environmental trends by successfully launching the Toyota Prius hybrid car, which supplements normal fuel with an electric-powered engine. The electric engine starts the car and operates at low speeds using a battery. At higher speeds, the Prius automatically switches to a normal engine and fuel. This saves on fuel and is less polluting. The success of the Prius has led many of its rivals to enter the hybrid and electric vehicle markets, e.g. Nissan Leaf, Renault Zoe and Kangoo Z.E. van. These models seek to put an end to all the myths about driving electric cars and give the motorist energy-efficient driving.

The production of biofuel has risen dramatically as companies have seized the opportunity to replace petrol. For example, BP has invested £284 million in biofuels. However, opposition from environmentalists may hamper further development. They fear that carbon-absorbing rainforests in countries such as Brazil are being depleted to make way for fuel crops such as soya and palm, and that such crops are displacing land use for food, forcing up prices (Macalister, 2008). Detergent companies like Unilever have also embraced sustainable marketing by producing concentrated soap powder that both helps the environment and improves profitability. Environmental damage is reduced because the product requires less plastic, less water, less space for transportation, fewer chemicals and less packaging (Skapinker, 2008). Procter & Gamble has also promoted the benefit of low-temperature washing with its award-winning Ariel 'Turn to 30' campaign, which raised awareness of the impact of washing temperatures on emissions (Murphy, 2008).

FIGURE 5.5
The stages in the move towards excellence in environmental performance

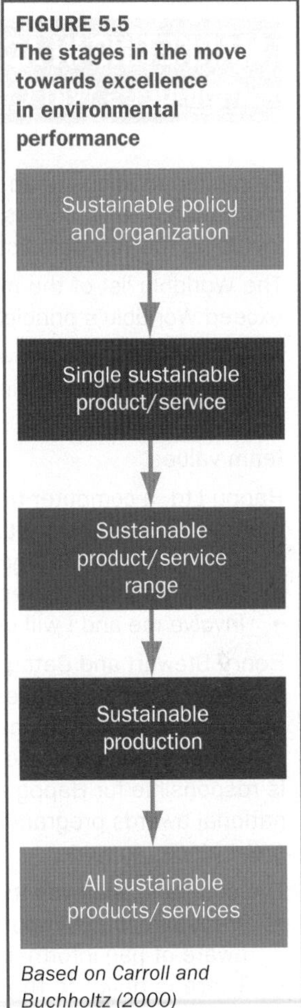

Based on Carroll and Buchholtz (2000)

Social and consumer dimensions

A social concern that businesses have sought to address is the need to support local and wider communities. Consumer concerns include the effect of business activities on product safety, including the avoidance of harmful long-term effects, the avoidance of price fixing, honesty in communications and respecting privacy. Although social and consumer dimensions of CSR are distinct because their key issues differ, the two dimensions are analysed together as marketing's major response—societal marketing—embraces both. Whereas sustainable marketing focuses on the physical environment, societal marketing relates to marketing's direct effect on people, both in the form of consumers and society in general.

Supply chain

Unfair trading arises when large buyers exert their power on small commodity producers to force prices to very low levels. This can bring severe economic hardship to the producers, who may be situated in countries of the developing world. Many of the growers of such products as coffee, tea and cocoa live in poverty and face hardship in the form of poor working conditions, health problems and prices that fail to provide a living wage. Fairtrade seeks to improve the prospects of suppliers through ethical trading, including the guaranteeing of minimum prices.

Employee relations

Poor employee relations can have harmful marketing consequences. For example, Walmart has suffered from years of allegations regarding low pay and sexually discriminatory hiring and employment practices, a situation it is seeking to address (Hines, 2012). Bad publicity can deter ethically aware consumers from buying from companies that suffer such criticism.

While most employee relations issues are the province of the human resources function, marketing can play a role through internal marketing programmes. **Internal marketing** is the development, training and motivation of employees designed to enhance their performance in providing customer satisfaction. The idea began in service organizations such as hotels and restaurants, where staff are in daily communication with customers, but has spread to all sectors in reflection of the need for all employees who come into contact with customers to be trained in how to deal with such issues as giving help, dealing with complaints and treating customers respectfully. Such training avoids, as far as possible, employee–customer arguments and conflict, which not only improves customer satisfaction but is good for staff morale, reduces stress levels and aids staff retention. Marketing in Action 5.3 describes the importance of democracy and supportive working environments.

MARKETING IN ACTION 5.3
Employees Win Company Awards

Employee relations is an important dimension of CSR. Happy Computers is a company that has an enviable reputation when it comes to staff training and has won many industry and service excellence awards, including the Worldblu list Top Practice award in 2013.

The Worldblu list of the most democratic places to work gives annual awards to companies that meet and exceed Worldblu's principles of organizational democracy.

AISEC International, the world's largest youth-run organization, based in Rotterdam, the Netherlands, has regularly been featured in the list since 2007. This organization aims to unlock the potential of young people.

Dreamhost, a leading web hosting firm in Los Angeles, USA, enables its workforce to make choices based on team values.

Happy Ltd, a computer training company, believes that learning should be fun. The training programmes bring together technical expertise and excellent training skills. The training is based on the following ideas:

- Tell me and I will forget.
- Show me and I will remember.
- Involve me and I will understand.

Henry Stewart and Cathy Busani founded Happy Ltd in 1990 in response to their clients asking for help to create *great* workplaces. At Happy, there is a relatively small workforce of 45 employees, and a unique approach to CSR training. The company has won numerous awards for innovative approaches to training, customer service and the quality of the working environment. Cathy is Managing Director of Happy Ltd and is responsible for Happy employees. She has been rated one of the best bosses in the UK in two separate national awards programmes. She is passionate about valuing people and the role they play in creating truly great places to work.

The company achieves its success by applying some straightforward principles:

- Transparency is important throughout (e.g. employees at both the top and bottom of the scale are all aware of pay information).
- There is belief in the ability of the individual—members of the Happy team hold a fundamental belief that all people (with no exceptions) are born with enormous intelligence and tremendous eagerness to learn.
- Celebrate mistakes as part of the culture to engender learning and development—Happy believes that if you do not make mistakes you are not actively learning; it believes that you should enable an employee's natural learning abilities and delight in new possibilities to allow them to come to the fore.
- Create a feel-good environment, as individuals work to their best ability when they feel good about themselves. Happy has created a workplace where people are trusted to make the key decisions about their work.
- Share information—as Francis Bacon said, 'knowledge is power'. Happy's management team takes the view that information is required to make informed decisions and to enable individuals to take responsibility and full ownership of their jobs. As more companies turn to e-learning, Happy Computers has been finding additional ways to help. Learnfizz is one of Happy's products designed to 'find, organize and share the best free learning on the web'.

Applying these principles has enabled Happy to do more than win awards, and it has zero recruitment costs. This is due to its employee-focused working environment, high staff morale and demand from potential employees desiring to work for this unique organization.

Based on: www.happy.co.uk; Worldblu (2013)

CSR leads to enhanced brand/corporate image and reputation

One argument *for* CSR is that a strong reputation in environmental and social responsibility can help a company build trust and enhance the image of its brands. For example, BP has taken steps to reduce harmful emissions. Orange has enhanced its image through sponsorship of the arts.

This approach can help when a company is faced with media criticism or regulatory scrutiny. Also, if a company is moving to a new area or new market, or opening a new site such as a distribution centre, store or factory, it helps to be seen as trustworthy and a 'good neighbour' (Sclater, 2005).

CSR provides marketing opportunities

Environmental and social responsibility has created new markets for business-to-business and business-to-consumer goods and services. For example, GE is expanding its marketing of 'clean' technological goods to companies, and Cafédirect, Green & Black's, Innocent drinks and the Body Shop have built their businesses on CSR ideals.

Market segments have emerged based on 'green' credentials that provide targeting opportunities. One segment—known as ethical hard cores or dark greens—researches companies and their practices thoroughly before buying their products. These consumers view ethical consumerism as a way of life, whatever the sacrifice.

A second segment—known as ethical lites or light greens—do their bit but do not have the time to research products or companies thoroughly (Parkinson, 2005). They are happy to recycle newspapers, plastics and other material from their homes and buy ethical brands, provided there is not too much of a price premium.

CSR increases organizations' ability to attract and retain employees

Many employees are attracted to employers that are active in social issues. For example, membership of netimpact.org, a network of socially conscious MBA graduates, rose from 4,000 in 2002 to over 10,000 in 2009. Some companies, such as salesforce.com (an internet-based services company), have a policy of good corporate citizenship (staff are encouraged to devote time, at the company's expense, to charitable works) that they believe helps to attract, retain and motivate employees (see Grow, Hamm and Lee, 2005; *The Economist*, 2005).

CSR is a form of risk management

There are real penalties for companies that are not environmentally or socially responsible. The media criticisms of such companies as Nike (child labour in the developed world), BNFL (toxic discharges in the Irish Sea), Enron and Royal Bank of Scotland (financial scandals), and News of the World (phone hacking) have shown the harm that can arise from being perceived as irresponsible. CSR, then, can be employed as a form of risk management that reduces the chances of being the subject of the next corporate scandal to hit the headlines.

Societal Marketing

Societal marketing considers consumers' and society's wider interests rather than short-term consumption. It aims to rectify potential conflicts between consumers' short-term needs—for example, for fast food, which may contain high levels of fat, sugar and salt—and their long-term needs—in this case, health. In the face of intense media pressure, including the hit movie *Super Size Me*, which records a film-maker's descent into serious illness while living on a McDonald's-only diet, McDonald's introduced healthy-eating options including salads and mineral water (instead of the ubiquitous cola). While cynics may view this as a public relations exercise, the response of McDonald's may be regarded as a move towards implementing societal marketing principles. Kraft is another company responding to consumers' demands for healthier foods, by cutting fat in its Philadelphia Lite soft cheese and cutting salt in its Dairylea product line by over 30 per cent (Clarke, 2008). One is also a company that produces various products—from bottled water, eggs and toilet tissue, to condoms—and uses the profits to fund social projects in Africa that are improving health and welfare for communities there (Costa, 2011).

Critics of societal marketing suggest it is a short-term public relations exercise that cynically manipulates a company's stakeholders. Supporters argue that the stakeholder principle suggests that it is in a company's long-term interests to support the long-running concerns of consumers and society, resulting in a win–win situation.

However, by combining sustainable principles and societal marketing initiatives, organizations become better prepared to meet the requirements of triple bottom-line reporting, which considers not only financial matters but also environmental and social issues.

But societal marketing is nothing new; it was referred to as the applications of marketing to the solution of social and health problems early in the 1970s by Kotler and Zaltman (1971). But this marked a departure point, whereby marketing began to evolve into more than just customer-focused strategies, tools and techniques to encourage people to buy more. Today, societal marketing is a framework that involves changing behaviour in complex economic, social and political environments (Lefebvre D. and G.H., 1997). The development of this sub-discipline within marketing has passed through four key stages of development (Dibb and Carrigan, 2013):

Stage 1: Focusing on behaviour—this involves clarifying the objectives that social marketers should pursue. Such objectives focus on the actual behaviour and not the attitudes towards the behaviour, for instance, the intention to eat a healthier diet is not the same as switching to healthy alternatives, as in the UK government's 'Change4Life eat well, move more, live longer' campaign.

Stage 2: Modelling the planning process—taking the classic steps in the marketing planning process, but redefining them in the context of the social marketing framework.

Stage 3: Three levels of social marketing—downstream, mid-stream and upstream. This introduced the idea that just targeting behaviour change in an individual was only partially effective (downstream level). So, the idea of also targeting peers of the individuals in the target market—friends, family acquaintances—was introduced in order to broaden the scope of the social marketing initiatives (mid-stream level); for example, mid-stream advocates can be targeted to encourage healthy eating behaviour. The final level (upstream) was to target organizations that could play a supporting role in the desired behaviour change (also see Marketing in Action 5.1). This extension of social marketing brings extra challenges—especially at the upstream level, which often involves bringing on side manufacturers that, say, produce sugary soft drinks and high fat content products.

Stage 4: Incorporating social media into social marketing—digital marketing and social media platforms have enabled the widespread distribution of social marketing messages. Also, it is possible for individuals to find information on how to change a particular behaviour, for example by adopting a healthier lifestyle.

Societal marketing seeks to change behaviour for the benefit of the individual and society, and its applications come in many different guises. For example, cars are built with mechanisms to remind the driver to wear a seat belt; there are social movements for wider change, for example green and climate change organizations, the consumerism movement, the international campaign to raise awareness of the risks of drinking in pregnancy (see Exhibit 5.5) and social engineering (e.g. in Sweden, the government introduced into schools a 'say no to drugs initiative' (Dibb and Carrigan, 2013)).

Inevitably, laudable social issues have to be funded, and so there is an inevitable link between social and more traditional commercial marketing. Where the lines are drawn is not entirely clear, as some new commercial products clearly exhibit social marketing ideals—for example, hybrid and electric cars designed to reduce fuel emissions and the consumption of carbon-based fuels, and fair-trade products aimed at helping the producers earn a reasonable living. Marketing in Action 5.4 explores these ideas further.

EXHIBIT 5.5
International campaign to raise awareness of the risks of drinking in pregnancy uses shock tactics

MARKETING IN ACTION 5.4
Using Social Marketing to Combat the Obesity Crisis

Overeating has become a pressing health issue in many developed countries. In the UK, there are 9,000 premature deaths per year linked to obesity. Government data suggests that obesity-related illnesses will cost the taxpayer £50 billion by 2050, and up to 90 per cent of today's children will be obese or overweight by the same year if current trends continue.

To raise public awareness of the link between obesity and life-threatening diseases such as coronary heart disease and diabetes, the UK government financed a £75 million social marketing campaign, which drew an additional £200 million-worth of services and marketing support from a variety of companies and organizations, including supermarkets, large food producers, health clubs, the London Marathon, voluntary groups and a wide-ranging media coalition. Rather than shocking people into healthier lifestyles, the Change4Life TV campaign used light-hearted animation to inform consumers of the threats posed by sedentary lifestyles and drew particular attention to the need for children to eat more healthily and become more active.

The campaign was a social marketing effort aimed at employing the power of marketing tools and concepts to achieve specific behavioural goals for increased societal welfare.

Although the initiative was welcomed by most stakeholders, some have criticized the government's choice to engage in corporate partnerships, as food corporations and supermarkets are seen as part of the issue by selling junk food and pushing foods high in salt, fat and sugar as cheap and credit-crunch-friendly options for hard-pressed consumers. Critics have suggested that the use of legislation to protect children from junk food marketing, and effective nutritional labelling enforcement, would be far better investments than the Change4Life campaign.

However, when the UK government reported on the Change4Life campaign, it found that, in its first year, the movement had become more widespread than expected and had many more supporters and partners, in business and government. The focus of the campaign widened and now includes Sugar Swap, Change4Life cooking guide, Change4Life healthy eating, Smart ReStart for the new school year, and Start4Life targeting pregnant women and families with very young children. The report stated that 'Over one million mums are already claiming to have made changes to their children's diets or activity levels as a result of Change4Life.' Change4Life has continued to have an impact, and its branding has become synonymous with improvement.

Based on: HM Government (2010); Boseley (2009); Sweeney (2009); Watts (2009); National Social Marketing Centre (2009); Public Health England (2015)

Non-profit marketing

Non-profit organizations attempt to achieve objectives other than profit. This does not mean they are uninterested in income, as they have to generate cash to survive, but their primary goal is societal—for example, to provide cultural enrichment (an orchestra), to protect birds and animals (Royal Society for the Protection of Birds, Royal Society for the Prevention of Cruelty to Animals), to alleviate hunger (Oxfam), to provide education (schools and universities), to foster community activities (community association), or to supply healthcare (hospitals) and public services (local authorities). Their worth and standing are not dependent on the profits they generate. The not-for-profit sector is gaining importance and even organizations that rely on government-sponsored grants need to show how their work is of benefit to society. Many non-profit organizations rely on membership fees or donations, which means marketing the organizations and its aims effectively.

Non-profit characteristics

Despite the growing use of marketing in the non-profit sector, it is important to be aware of the characteristics that distinguish this form of marketing from that of profit-orientated marketing organizations.

Education versus meeting current needs

Some non-profit organizations see their role as not only meeting the current needs of their customers but also educating them in terms of new ideas and issues, research, cultural development and social awareness. Cancer Research UK has big ambitions 'to see 3 in 4 people surviving cancer by 2034' and to do this it generates significant revenues to spend on research (£423 million in 2017). But it also invests resources in education, both in learning resources about various form of cancer and through advertising to reach a wider audience. The 'Right Now' advertising campaign used personal stories to show the advances being made in research into the fight against the disease (Roderick, 2017).

Multiple publics

Most non-profit organizations serve several groups, or publics (discussed further in Chapter 14 under the topic of public relations), who form three markets: clients and customers; volunteers; and donors and/or funders.

Measurement of success and conflicting objectives

Profit-orientated organizations' success is ultimately measured in financial terms. For non-profit organizations, measuring success is not so easy, and decision-making is therefore complex in non-profit-orientated organizations.

Public scrutiny

While all organizations are subject to public scrutiny, public-sector non-profit organizations are closely monitored. The reason is that they are publicly funded from taxes.

Marketing procedures for not-for-profit organizations

Despite non-profit organizations needing to take into account these characteristics, marketing procedures relevant to profit-orientated companies can largely be applied to non-profit organizations. Target marketing, differentiation and marketing-mix decisions need to be made. Each target market is quite distinct and not-for-profit organizations should identify benefits and clearly communicate with their different publics. The **customers** are relatively straightforward as they benefit from the products and services offered by the charity. For example, Mary's Living and Giving shops, which are part of Save the Children, offer customers a unique proposition: boutique charity shops, which sell second-hand designer and top quality goods. The **volunteers** are a more challenging market and few charities are well-equipped to run recruitment campaigns or have the internal management skills needed to retain good volunteers. The main benefit for this target group is making a difference; so, whether it is a fund-raising event, working in a charity shop or helping to deliver good work, it is important for volunteers to have fun, be given meaningful roles and be appreciated (Findlay, 2013). Sport England is a not-for-profit organisation that relies heavily on volunteers, which can involve marshalling a fun run, managing finances or getting involved in sporting events (Sport England, 2018). The **donors** need to understand why they might provide monies to charitable organizations. They need to understand the benefits, and have trust in the charity's ability to deliver on its promises. Organizations seeking funding and donations need to target individuals and organizations with an interest in the work of the charity. See Exhibit 5.6 for an emotional appeal from The RSPCA animal welfare charity.

EXHIBIT 5.6
Cute dogs and kittens are widely used in advertising appeals. The RSPCA is focusing on emotions to encourage donations

Developing a marketing mix

Non-profit organizations often use *event marketing*. Events including dinners, dances, coffee mornings, book sales, sponsored walks and theatrical shows, which are organized to raise funds. Not all events are designed to raise funds for the sponsoring organization. For example, the BBC hosts the Comic Relief and Children in Need telethons to raise money for worthy causes.

Like most services, distribution systems for many non-profit organizations are short, with production and consumption taking place almost simultaneously. Such organizations have to think carefully about how to deliver their services to accommodate the convenience that customers require. For example, the Hallé orchestra is based in Manchester, but over half of its performances are in other towns or cities. Some non-profit organizations have their own retail outlets. For example, Oxfam, an organization that seeks to reduce poverty and suffering around the world through fundraising and issue-awareness campaigns, has 750 shops around the UK that sell donated second-hand clothing, books, music and household items.

Many non-profit organizations can use all aspects of the promotional mix to further their objectives. Print media and direct mail have been widely used to elicit donations for major disasters, for example for famine relief in Africa and for victims of the tsunami in Japan. Advertising is widely used by charities such as Oxfam and Barnardo's to create awareness of issues and raise funds, so that they can continue to provide services. Public relations has an important role to play in generating positive word-of-mouth communications and to confirm the non-profit identity of the charity.

Review

1 Explain the dimensions of sustainable marketing

- Environmental context highlights sustainability.
- Social context highlights the need for change in society, inequality and deprivation.
- Economic context focuses on strong economic performance.

2 The meaning of ethics, and business and marketing ethics

- Ethics are the moral principles and values that govern the actions and decisions of an individual or group.
- Business ethics are the moral principles and values that guide a firm's behaviour.
- Marketing ethics are the moral principles and values that guide behaviour within the field of marketing.

3 Ethical issues in marketing

- Ethical issues in marketing relate to concerns about how the marketing mix is applied to consumers, and more general societal, environmental and political issues. Specific examples include: product safety, price fixing, misleading advertising, deceptive selling, invasion of privacy through direct and internet marketing activities, and the use of promotional and slotting allowances.
- Societal concerns focus on materialism and short-termism; environmental concerns focus on the impact of marketing decisions on the environment; and political concerns focus on the power that global companies can exert on consumers, governments and suppliers.

4 Corporate Social Responsibility

- The main response from businesses has been the adoption of CSR as a philosophy guiding decisions and actions.
- Societal responses take the form of consumerism, environmentalism and ethical consumption.
- Legal and regulatory responses are the enactment of laws at European and national levels to protect the consumer and to outlaw anti-competitive business practices, and the establishment of regulatory bodies to enforce those laws. Many industries have also established organizations to apply self-regulation through the drawing up and enforcement of codes of practice.

5 The stakeholder theory of the company

- CSR is based on the stakeholder theory of the company, which contends that companies have multiple stakeholders, not just shareholders, to whom they hold a responsibility. These include communities associated with the company, employees, customers (including intermediaries) and suppliers.

6 **The nature of CSR**

- CSR refers to the ethical principle that an organization should be accountable for how its behaviour might affect society and the environment.
- Organizations have responsibilities to ensure that economic performance meets stakeholder requirements, operational practices do not break the law and ethical principles are consistent with the values of society. Additionally, an organization has a responsibility to be a good corporate citizen: e.g. supporting good causes and making philanthropic donations.

7 **The dimensions of CSR**

- CSR involves five dimensions of organizational activity: the physical environment, social, consumer, supply chain and employee relations.
- Marketing's response to each dimension involves responding to relevant issues, for example:
  - *physical environment issues*—combating global warming by applying business practices which create, produce and deliver sustainable solutions to environmental problems, while continuing to satisfy customers and other stakeholders.
  - *societal and consumer issues*—community support and attention to product safety. This is an example of societal marketing, as it takes account of consumers' and society's wider interests rather than just their short-term consumption. Societal welfare is also enhanced by cause-related marketing, which is the commercial activity by which businesses and charities form a partnership to market an image or product for mutual benefit.
  - *supply chain issues*—low prices to producers in the developing world, applying fair-trade marketing, which is the development, promotion and selling of brands and the positioning of organizations on the basis of a fair-trade ethos.
  - *employee relations issues*—training and motivation. This is referred to as internal marketing, which is the development, training and motivation of employees, designed to enhance their performance in providing customer satisfaction.

8 **The focus of social marketing and not-for-profit marketing**

- The four stages of the development of social marketing, focusing on behaviour, modelling the planning process, the three levels of social marketing and incorporating social media into social marketing.
- Marketing procedures for non-profit organizations: target marketing, differentiation, developing a marketing mix.

Key Terms

business ethics the moral principles and values that guide a firm's behaviour

ethics the moral principles and values that govern the actions and decisions of an individual or group

fair-trade marketing the development, promotion and selling of fair-trade brands and the positioning of organizations on the basis of a fair-trade ethos

internal marketing training, motivating and communicating with staff to cause them to work effectively in providing customer satisfaction; more recently the term has been expanded to include marketing to all staff, with the aim of achieving the acceptance of marketing ideas and plans

marketing ethics the moral principles and values that guide behaviour within the field of marketing

not-for-profit organization this type of organization often employs a volunteer workforce and relies on donations and external funding

social marketing seeks to change behaviour for the benefit of the individual and society, and its applications come in many different guises

societal marketing focuses on consumers' needs and long-term welfare as keys to satisfying organizational objectives and responsibilities by taking into account consumers' and societies' wider interests rather than just their short-term consumption

stakeholder an individual or group that either (i) is harmed by or benefits from the company, or (ii) whose rights can be violated or have to be respected by the company

stakeholder theory this contends that companies are not managed purely in the interests of their shareholders alone, but for those of a broader group including communities associated with the company, employees, customers and suppliers

sustainable marketing focuses on reducing environmental damage by creating, producing and delivering sustainable solutions while continuing to satisfy customers and other stakeholders

Study Questions

1. **Explain the three contexts which frame sustainable marketing activities.**
2. **Discuss the extent to which you believe the marketing practices of global corporations are unethical.**
3. **What are the key responsibilities of CSR and to what extent do you believe businesses should accept them?**
4. **Describe the five dimensions of CSR. Evaluate marketing's response to the issues underlying each dimension.**
5. **Evaluate the contention that if ethical consumption was the norm there would be no need to legislate to protect consumers.**
6. **Discuss the differences in meaning of sustainability and CSR.**
7. **Suggest why societal marketing is becoming more important in commercial markets.**
8. **Discuss how non-profit companies might identify and communicate with their three main target markets.**
9. **Make an argument for and against the adoption of a sustainable marketing approach.**

Recommended Reading

Ethics and sustainability are important topics in marketing. Read about modern marketing ethics and society; discover ideas on how sustainable marketing can bring human consumption and nature together to greater benefit for all; and explore the 'wicked' problems faced by marketing and find some solutions.

Eagle, L. and Dahl, S. (2015), *Marketing Ethics & Society*, London: Sage Publications Ltd.

Fodness, D. (2015), Managing the wickedness of socially responsible marketing, *Journal of Business Strategy*, 36(5), 10–17, https://doi.org/10.1108/JBS-07-2014-0077.

Löbler, H. (2017), Humans' relationship to nature—framing sustainable marketing", *Journal of Services Marketing*, 31(1), 73–82, https://doi.org/10.1108/JSM-01-2016-0037.

References

Arthur, C. (2011), Microsoft accepts censorship in Chinese search engine deal, *The Guardian*, 5 July, 16.

Barnett, M. (2011), Driving home the benefits of green wheels, *Marketing Week*, 7 April, 24–6.

BBC (a) (2018), After Barry Bennell convictions, where now for football's sexual abuse scandal? https://www.bbc.co.uk/sport/football/42993689 (accessed August 2018).

BBC (b) (2018), Diesel emissions scandal: VW fined €1 billion by German prosecutors, https://www.bbc.co.uk/news/business-44474781 (accessed August 2018).

BBC (c) (2018), Soft drink sugar tax start, but will it work? 6 April https://www.bbc.co.uk/news/health-43659124 (accessed August 2018).

Berkowitz, E.N., Kerin, R.A., Hartley, S.W. and Rudelius, W. (2004), *Marketing*, Boston, MA: McGraw-Hill.

Boseley, S. (2009), Matter of Life and Death: Wallace and Gromit Makers get Animated over UK Obesity Crisis, Guardian.co.uk, 2 January www.guardian.co.uk/politics/2009/jan/02/wallace-gromitobesity-ad-health (retrieved 6 April 2009).

Boxell, J. and Harvey, F. (2005), BP Sacked 252 in Corruption Drive, *The Financial Times*, 12 April, 22.

Burrow, A. and Rainone, N. (2017), How many likes did I Get?: Purpose moderates links between positive social media feedback and self-esteem, *Journal of Experimental Social Psychology*, 69 (March) 232–6.

Burt, J. (2016), The FA is too old, too white, too male—radical change is needed for this outdated organization, *The Telegraph* 12 December https://www.telegraph.co.uk/football/2016/12/12/fa-old-white-male-radical-change-needed-outdated-organization/ (accessed August 2018).

Carroll, A.B. (1991), The Pyramid of Corporate Social Responsibility: Toward the Moral Management of Organizational Stakeholders, *Business Horizons*, July/August, 39–48.

Carroll, A.B. and Buchholtz, A.K. (2000), *Business and Society: Ethics and Stakeholder Management*, Cincinnati: South-Western College.

Charter M., Peattie, K., Ottman, J. and Polonsky, M. (2002), *Marketing and sustainability*, Centre for Business Relationships, Accountability, Sustainability April http://www.cfsd.org.uk/smart-know-net/smart-know-net.pdf (accessed June 2018).

Cheng, H., Kotler, P. and Lee, N. (2011), *Social Marketing for Public Health: Global Trends and Success Stories*, London, UK: Jones & Bartlett LLC.

Clarke, B. (2008), Good Marketing Beats Regulation, *The Marketer*, March, 15.

Costa, M.L. (2011), One man's vision, *Marketing Week*, 5 May, 18–21.

Crane, A. and Matten, D. (2004), *Business Ethics: A European Perspective*, Oxford: Oxford University Press.

Crook, C. (2005), The Good Company, *The Economist*, 22 January, 3–4.

Deloitte LLP (2018), Roar Power Annual Review of Football Finance since 2018 https://www2.deloitte.com/uk/en/pages/sports-business-group/articles/annual-review-of-football-finance.html# (accessed August 2018).

Dibb, S. and Carrigan, M. (2013), Social Marketing Transformed, *European Journal of Marketing* 47(9), 1376–1398.

Donaldson, T. and Preston, L.E. (1995), The Stakeholder Theory of the Corporation: Concepts, Evidence, and Implications, *Academy of Management Review* 20(1), 15–91.

Eccles, R., Ioannou, I. and Serafeim, G. (2011), The Impact of a Corporate Culture of Sustainability on Corporate Behaviour and Performance, *Harvard Business Review: Working Papers*, 14 November.

Economist (2000), Slipping Slopes, 15 April, 85.

Economist (2005), A Union of Concerned Executives, 22 January, 7–12.

Economist (2015), Buying Up Shelves, *The Economist*, 18 June https://www.economist.com/business/2015/06/18/buying-up-the-shelves (accessed July 2018).

European Commission (a) (2018), Competition http://ec.europa.eu/competition/antitrust/overview_en.html (accessed July 2018).

European Commission (b) (2018), Antitrust: Commission Fines four consumer electronics manufacturers for fixing online resale prices, 24 July http://europa.eu/rapid/press-release_IP-18-4601_en.htm (accessed July 2018).

European Commission (c) (2018), Antitrust: Commission fines Google €4.34 billion for illegal practices regarding Android mobile devices to strengthen dominance of Google's search engine, 18 July http://europa.eu/rapid/press-release_IP-18-4581_en.htm (accessed July 2018).

Everitt, P. (2009), Car Scrappage Schemes are Not a Motor Industry Green Scam, Guardian.co.uk, 19 March 2009, www.guardian.co.uk/commentisfree/2009/mar/19/paul-everitt-response (retrieved 3 April 2009).

Fairtrade Foundation (2018), What is fair trade https://www.fairtrade.org.uk/en/what-is-fairtrade (accessed November 2018).

Findlay, R. (2013), What can charities do to improve the volunteering experience?, *The Guardian*, 15 November https://www.theguardian.com/voluntary-sector-network/2013/nov/15/charities-improve-volunteering-experience (accessed August 2018).

Fukukawa, K. and Moon, J. (2004), A Japanese Model of Corporate Social Responsibility: A Study of Online Reporting, *Journal of Corporate Citizenship* 16, Winter, 45–59.

Gates Foundation (2012), Programs and Partnerships, http://www.gates foundation.org/programs/Pages/overview.aspx (accessed August 2018).

Gillies, T. (2017), IKEA's strategy: Stick to the basics and expand in the US, CNBC, https://www.cnbc.com/2017/01/15/ikeas-strategy-stick-to-the-retail-basics-and-expand-in-the-us.html (accessed August 2018).

Gow, D. (2008), Record US Fine Ends Siemens Bribery Scandal, *The Guardian*, 16 December, 24.

Grow, Hamm & Lee 2005, The rebates over doing good, *The Economist*, 5 December 70–80.

Gunther, M. (2012), A big push to move meat production terrible to just bad, 23 February http://www.greenbiz.com/topic/food–agriculture?page 2 (accessed June 2012).

Hagstrom, B. (2018), Opinion: Systembolaget's image is based on bluff, https://www.thelocal.se/20170404/opinion-systembolagets-image-is-based-on-a-bluff (accessed August 2018).

Hallgren, M., Leifman, H. and Andréasson, S. (2012), Drinking Less But Greater Harm: Could Polarized Drinking Habits Explain the Divergence Between Alcohol Consumption and Harms among Youth? *Alcohol and Alcoholism*, 4 July, 47(5), 581–90 doi:http://dx.doi.org/10.1093/alcalc/ags071.

www.happy.co.uk, about, accessed October 2018

Hines, A. (2010), Walmart Sex discrimination claims filed by 2000 women, *Huffington Post*, 6 June https://www.huffingtonpost.co.uk/entry/walmart-sex-discrimination-women-_n_1575859HM Government (2010), Change4life, 17 February http://www.dh.gov.uk/prod_consum_dh/groups/dh_digitalassets/@dh/@en/documents/digitalasset/dh_115511.pdf (accessed June 2018).

Jeffries, E. (2011), A clearer footprint, *Marketing*, 19 October, 26–7.

Kelly-Detwiler, P. (2014), IKEA's Aggressive Approach To Sustainability Creates Enormous Business Opportunities, *Forbes*, 7 February http://www.forbes.com/sites/peterdetwiler/2014/02/07/ikeas-aggressive-approach-to-sustainability-creates-enormous-business-opportunities (accessed 3 March 2015).

King, H. (2012), Ikea's Steve Howard on bringing sustainability to the masses, Greenbiz.com, http://www.greenbiz.com/blog/2012/02/23/ikeas-cso-steve-howard-bringing-sustainability-masses (accessed June 2012).

Knoema (2015), World GDP Ranking 2014 | Data and Charts, Knoema http://knoema.com/nwnfkne/world-gdp-ranking-2014-data-and-charts (accesed August 2018).

Kotler, P. and Zaltman, G. (1971), Social marketing: an approach to planned social change, *Journal of Marketing* 35, 3–12.

Lefebvre, D. and G.H. (1997), De-marketing: Putting Kotler and Levy's ideas into practice, *Journal of Marketing Management* 13(4), 315–25.

Macalister, T. (2008), Undercut and Under Fire: UK Biofuel Feels Heat From All Sides, *The Guardian*, 1 April, 28.

Maignan, I. and Ferrell, O.C. (2004), Corporate Social Responsibility and Marketing: An Integrated Framework, *Journal of the Academy of Marketing Science* 32(1), 3–19.

Milne, R. (2014), Scottish nationalists look to Nordic model for independence, *The Financial Times*, 2 February http://www.ft.com/cms/s/0/57664dc2-8bf8-11e3-bcf2-00144feab7de.html#axzz3ToDmmcSK (accessed 2 March 2015).

Moon, J. (2002), Corporate Social Responsibility: An Overview, in *The International Directory of Corporate Philanthropy*, London: Europa Books.

Murphy, C. (2008), Green Gold, *The Marketer*, September, 30–3.

National Social Marketing Centre (2009), www.nsms.org.uk/public/default.aspx (accessed 6 April 2009).

Nestlé Corporation (2018), Caring for Water https://www.nestle.com/csv/impact/water (accessed July 2018).

Northcroft, J. (2017), Joey Barton: Fixing goes on but the FA are oblivious, *The Sunday Times* 18 June https://www.thetimes.co.uk/article/fixing-goes-on-but-the-fa-are-oblivious-to-it-fdvpqbggg (accessed August 2018).

O'Connor, C. (2014), Report: Walmart's Billionaire Waltons Give Almost None Of Own Cash To Foundation, Forbes, 3 June http://www.forbes.com/sites/clareoconnor/2014/06/03/report-walmarts-billionaire-waltons-give-almost-none-of-own-cash-to-family-foundation (accessed 8 March 2015).

Parkinson, C. (2005), Make the Most of Your Ethics, *Marketing Week*, 9 June, 30–1.

Peattie, K. (1999), Trappings versus substance in the greening of marketing, *Journal of Strategic Marketing* 7(2), 131–48.

Public Health England (2015), Campaign Resource Centre, Public Health England http://campaigns.dh.gov.uk/category/change-4-life (accessed 8 March 2015).

Reed, C. (2000), Ethics Frozen Out in the Ben & Jerry Ice Cream War, *The Observer*, 13 February, 3.

Reuters (2016), Rana Plaza collapse: 38 charged with murder over garment factory disaster, *The Guardian* 18 July https://www.theguardian.com/world/2016/jul/18/rana-plaza-collapse-murder-charges-garment-factory (accessed August 2018).

Roderick, L. (2017), Cancer research UK merges emotional and practical messages to drive donations, *Marketing Week* https://www.marketingweek.com/2017/12/18/cancer-research-uk-emotional-practical/ (accessed August 2018).

Rumsby, B. (2013), Premier Leagues game almost certainly rigged claims betting expert, *The Telegraph*, 29 November https://www.telegraph.co.uk/sport/football/news/10485329/Premier-League-game-almost-certainly-rigged-claims-betting-expert.html (accessed August 2018).

Sclater, I. (2005), Thank Goodness for Success, *The Marketer*, January, 11–13.

Skapinker, M. (2008), Taking a Hard Line On Soft Soap, *The Financial Times*, 7 July, 16.

Smithers, R (2017), Consumers being misled by labelling on ' organic' beauty products, report shows, *The Guardian* 24 April. https://www.theguardian.com/environment/2017/apr/24/consumers-being-misled-by-labelling-on-organic-beauty-products-report-shows (accessed August 2018).

Sport England (2018), about us https://www.sportengland.org/ (accessed August 2018).

Starbucks (2018), Starbucks partner with Malala Fund in a global commitment to invest in 250,000 Women by 2025 https://news.starbucks.com/press-releases/starbucks-partners-with-malala-fund-to-invest-in-women (accessed August 2018).

Stobart Group (2018), http://www.stobartgroup.co.uk/stobart-group/community-and-environment (accessed August 2018).

Sweeney, M. (2009), Government in £275m Anti-obesity Drive, Guardian.co.uk, 2 January 2009 www.guardian.co.uk/media/2009/jan/02/change4life-obesity (retrieved 6 April 2009).

Systembolaget (2018), Launch Plan 2018 https://www.systembolaget.se/imagelibrary/publishedmedia/rayb9y5gctbnprjg3pkg/Launch_plan_2018.pdf (accessed August 2018).

The FA (2017), Report and Financial Statements, The Football Association Limited http://www.thefa.com/ (accessed August 2018).

Trucost (2012), State of Green Business 2012 http://www.trucost.com/published-research/75/state-of-green-business-2012 (accessed August 2018).

Tyers, C. (2017), It's Time to wake up to the devastating impact flying has on the environment. *The Conversation* 11 January http://theconversation.com/its-time-to-wake-up-to-the-devastating-impact-flying-has-on-the-environment-70953 (accessed August 2018).

United Nations Sustainable Development Goal 1 (2017), https://sustainabledevelopment.un.org/sdg1 (accessed August 2018).

Vandermerwe, S. and Oliff, M. (1990), Customers drive corporations green, *Long Range Planning*, 23(6), 10–16.

Walmart (2014), Walmart 2014 Annual Report http://cdn.corporate.walmart.com/66/e5/9ff9a87445949173fde56316ac5f/2014-annual-report.pdf (accessed 24 February 2015).

Walmart (2018), Global responsibility report https://corporate.walmart.com/global-responsibility/global-responsibility-report (accessed August 2018).

Watts, R. (2009), Taking a Wrong Turn in Tackling Obesity, Guardian.co.uk, 2 January 2009 www.guardian.co.uk/society/joepublic/2008/dec/31/change4lifecampaign-obesity (retrieved 6 April 2009).

World Bank (2015), Poverty, The World Bank http://www.worldbank.org/en/topic/poverty/overview (accessed August 2018).

Worldblu (2013), The Worldblu List 2013 http://www.worldblu.com/awardee-profiles/2013.php (accessed August 2018).

CASE 9
Channel 4 and Maltesers Championing Diversity

Introduction

Channel 4 is a publicly-owned and commercially-funded UK public service broadcaster, with a statutory remit to deliver high-quality, innovative and alternative content that challenges the status quo. Channel 4 has for many years promoted inclusion and, in January 2015, launched a Diversity Charter in an effort to place diversity at the heart of everything they do. The Charter reflects Channel 4's commitment to diversity at every level of their organization, on screen, off screen and including Channel 4's leadership. Their goal is to ensure that the TV station is inclusive of diversity that encompasses all under-represented groups: Black, Asian and minority ethnic (BAME); lesbian, gay, bisexual and transgender (LGBT); disability; gender; social mobility; those who live outside London; and more (Channel 4, 2017a). In 2016, Channel 4's 'Year of Disability', they placed an increased emphasis on providing opportunities for candidates with disability; they awarded 50% of Channel 4's apprenticeships and 35% of work experience placements to disabled people and they also increased the number of staff declaring a disability from 3% to 11% (Channel 4, 2017b).

Challenging the Advertising Industry

During the channel's 'Year of Disability', their Chief Marketing and Communications Officer chastized the advertising industry for its unrealistic and unrepresentative approach to disability, announcing 'It's almost as if disabled people don't exist in adland'. Not content to simply raise the issue, Channel 4 launched their inaugural Channel 4 Diversity in Advertising Award. The award would see advertisers compete to win £1 million of free advertising space from Channel 4. In 2016, the competition entitled 'Superhumans Wanted' offered £1 million of free advertising space during the Paralympic Games 2016 opening ceremony to a brand or agency that submitted the strongest campaign idea focused on changing consumer attitudes towards disability. The aim was to get

UK advertisers to think differently about how they represent disability (Little Black Book, 2016).

Channel 4 expected between 20 and 30 applicants, but saw nearly 100 brands and agencies enter the competition. One of the brands to take up the challenge was Maltesers. The British confectionery brand, manufactured by Mars, has been around for almost 80 years. It positions itself as 'a lighter way to enjoy chocolate' and its advertisements often encourage people to look on the light side of life. (Little Black Book, 2016) Maltesers, along with its agency Abbott Vickers Mead BBDO, won the Channel 4 competition and as a result had three months to bring their ideas to life and create an advertising campaign that had diversity and disability at its heart (Roderick, 2017).

'Look on the Light Side of Disability' Campaign

Maltesers wanted to ensure that any ads created for this campaign were human and real and stayed true to the light-hearted tone of Maltesers' previous advertising campaigns. In order to create an effective advertising campaign that was inclusive, Maltesers consulted with the disability charity Scope and also conducted workshops with people of different disabilities during the campaign's development (Scope, 2017). What this research showed them was that people with disabilities have lives and experiences just like everyone else; they don't want to be treated more gently because of their disability and that just because they have a disability doesn't mean that they've lost their sense of humour! (Little Black Book, 2016).

Armed with these insights, Abbot Vickers Mead BBDO released their campaign entitled 'Look on the light side of disability' during Channel 4's Paralympic Games coverage. The campaign consisted of three Maltesers' ads featuring disabled people in everyday situations discussing awkward encounters and experiences. One ad 'New Boyfriend' focuses on the story of a woman in a wheelchair who experiences spasms, a result of her cerebral palsy, during an intimate moment with her new boyfriend (Oakes, 2017). A second ad 'Theo's Dog' tells the story of a deaf woman whose hearing aid is swallowed by a dog. This ad was aired for the first time using British Sign Language and without the use of subtitles (Marketing Society, 2017). The final ad in the series called 'Wedding' features a disabled woman making a joke about running over the bride's foot at a wedding with her wheelchair, but 'getting the best man's number' (Tweedy, 2016).

Using the free airtime that was won as part of Channel 4's 'Superhumans Wanted' competition, Maltesers invested in TV advertising for this campaign. However, they also used online video to ensure that they were effectively reaching their younger audiences who are increasingly consuming content online. In addition, they supported their TV ads on Facebook and Twitter through the creation of gifs of the TV ads' most engaging moments. The use of social media was critical to the campaign as it allowed its reach to extend beyond TV and ensured continued conversation about the brand online (Marketing Society, 2017).

Response to the Campaign

Maltesers knew that this campaign was different from what the public had seen before and knew that it would challenge the public's perceptions of disabled people. As such, they knew this campaign was risky and could be viewed as somewhat controversial. Mars knew that the ads could provoke mixed reactions, including criticism from those who might see the ads' storylines as treating disability insensitively. However, they strongly believed that it was a risk worth taking for the brand and didn't want to play it safe (Kiefer, 2016). In general, the public welcomed these ads and praised Maltesers for championing diversity and disability in this campaign. Through these ads, Maltesers helped change how people viewed disability and showed that diversity initiatives don't have to be tear-jerking, inspirational or maudlin efforts and that disability can be part of the joke in an ad, without being the butt of the joke (Griner, 2018). However, not all commentary about the campaign has been positive. For example, the 'New Boyfriend' ad was in fact one of the Advertising Standards Authority's (ASA) most complained about ads in the UK in 2016. Most of these complaints centred around claims that the ads were offensive to disabled people or were overly sexual in nature. However, the ASA did not uphold any of the 151 complaints it received regarding the campaign (Rath, 2017).

Despite the criticism, this campaign has proved to be Maltesers' most successful campaign in over a decade. At the launch of the campaign, the brand set itself a number of targets including a 4% growth in sales and a 10% uplift in brand affinity. Maltesers' expectations were more than exceeded as sales grew by 8.1% and brand affinity grew by 20%. YouTube views for the launch ad 'New Boyfriend' broke the two million barrier within the first 24 hours, more than double Maltesers' one million target and the effectiveness of the campaign encouraged the confectionery brand to consider using its diversity and inclusion themes in Maltesers ads in other markets such as the USA and Australia (Mortimer, 2017).

Building on Success

What Maltesers has done is to build differentiation into their brand by putting inclusivity at the heart of its positioning. Maltesers has managed to challenge the advertising industry's views on disability and sparked a conversation about the under-representation of minority groups in advertising. According to 2016 research by Lloyds Banking Group, minority groups such as disabled people, the LGBT community and single parents continue to be let down by brands who are failing to create diverse and inclusive advertising. Just 19% of people featured in advertising are from minority groups, and of that only 0.06% of people portrayed are disabled or from the LGBT community and just 0.29% are single parents. These figures are drastically out of kilter with the proportion these minority groups represent in the wider population. Failing to engage with the issue of diversity could ultimately prove damaging to brands. According to the Lloyds report, 65% of respondents say they feel more favourable towards a brand that reflects diversity in advertising, while 67% surveyed expect advertisers to represent the diverse aspects of society. It appears that the time has come for marketers to promote diversity and inclusivity in their advertising by depicting a variety of people in a realistic and authentic way. Some argue that advertisers have a voice and a responsibility to use the power of their brands for good. The Maltesers' campaign has gone some way towards promoting the conversation about inclusivity in advertising, but some would argue that there is still a long way to go (Rogers, 2017).

»

»

Questions

1. **Channel 4's CSR policy claims that diversity is 'the lifeblood of the station'. Visit the Channel 4 website and access Channel 4's Diversity Charter and their latest Annual Report. Identify and discuss evidence in the report which illustrates the channel's continuing commitment to embracing diversity.**
2. **Discuss the extent to which the Maltesers' 'Look on the light side of disability' campaign can be seen as socially responsible advertising embracing diversity.**
3. **Responding to public complaints about the Maltesers' 'New Boyfriend' ad, the Advertising Standards Authority (ASA) ruled that it was not unethical in its approach or tone. View the advertisement at https://www.youtube.com/watch?v=YgUqmKQ9Lrg and the ASA ruling at https://www.asa.org.uk/news/2016-s-most-complained-about-ads.html. Discuss the extent to which you agree with the ASA ruling. Fully justify your answer.**
4. **Discuss the extent to which you think advertisers have a moral duty to embrace diversity and represent society at large in its output. Outline the benefits and risks.**

This case study is by Marie O' Dwyer, Waterford Institute of Technology.

References

Based on: Channel 4 (2017a), What does 360 degress mean?, Channel 4, https://www.channel4.com/corporate/about-4/operating-responsibly/diversity/what-does-360-mean (accessed 10 July 2018); Channel 4 (2017b), People and inclusion, *Channel 4*, https://www.channel4.com/corporate/about-4/who-we-are/people-inclusion (accessed 10 July 2018); Little Black Book (2016), Behind Maltesers' Paralympics campaign—and how it struck comedy gold, *Little Black Book*, https://lbbonline.com/news/behind-maltesers-paralympics-campaign-and-how-it-struck-comedy-gold/ (accessed 10 July 2018); Roderick, L. (2017), Channel 4 to bring back 'Superhumans wanted' competition, *Marketing Week*, https://www.marketingweek.com/2017/04/04/channel-4-relaunch-competition/ (accessed 10 July 2018); Scope (2017), Scope responds to Maltesers ad named as one of the most complained about adverts of 2016, *Scope*, https://www.scope.org.uk/press-releases/maltesers-ad-most-complained-about-ad-2016 (accessed 10 July 2018); Oakes, O. (2017), Maltesers' disability campaign 'most successful' in decade, *Campaign Live*, https://www.campaignlive.co.uk/article/maltesers-disability-campaign-most-successful-decade/1433980 (accessed 10 July 2018); Marketing Society (2017), Maltesers: Looking on the light side of disability, *Marketing Society*, https://www.marketingsociety.com/sites/default/files/thelibrary/MSOC_CauseRelated_Maltesers.pdf (accessed 10th July 2018); Tweedy, J. (2016), 'One person said I put them off eating chocolate: Disabled star of the Maltesers advert reveals how she was targeted by trolls, *Daily Mail*, http://www.dailymail.co.uk/femail/article-3937578/That-midget-freak-advert-putting-eating-chocolate-Disabled-star-Malteasers-advert-reveals-targetted-online-trolls-making-TV-debut.html (accessed 10 July 2018); Marketing Society UK (2017) Maltesers: Looking on the light side of disability, WARC, https://www.warc.com/content/article/Maltesers_Looking_on_the_Light_Side_of_Disability/111624 (accessed 10 July 2018); Kiefer, B. (2016) Sex, Chocolate and disability: What marketers can learn from Maltesers campaign, *Campaign Live*, https://www.campaignlive.co.uk/article/sex-chocolate-disability-marketers-learn-maltesers-campaign/1407980 (accessed 10 July 2018); Griner, D. (2018), Maltesers' wonderfully awkward diversity ads are back, featuring hot flashes and lesbian dating, *Adweek*, https://www.adweek.com/creativity/maltesers-wonderfully-awkward-diversity-ads-are-back-featuring-hot-flashes-and-lesbian-dating/ (accessed 10 July 2018); Rath, J. (2017), These were the most complained about UK ads of 2016, *Business Insider*, http://uk.businessinsider.com/uk-advertising-standards-authority-ten-most-complained-ads-of-2016-2017-1?r=US&IR=T (accessed 10 July 2018); Mortimer, N. (2017), Maltesers' ad featuring disabled actors prove to be the 'most successful' advert for the brand in 10 years, *The Drum*, http://www.thedrum.com/news/2017/04/05/maltesers-ads-featuring-disabled-actors-prove-be-most-successful-advert-the-brand-10 (accessed 10 July 2018); Rogers, C. (2017), Just 19% of people in ads are from minority groups, new research finds, *Marketing Week*, https://www.marketingweek.com/2016/12/06/lloyds-diversity-report/ (accessed 10 July 2018).

CASE 10
Social Responsibility or Good Business? Coop Danmark's Anti Food Wastage Initiatives

Food wastage, and the efforts of supermarkets to combat this problem, is not a new phenomenon; in the UK. WRAP (Waste and Resources Action Programme) has estimated that there has been a 12 per cent reduction in food and drink waste by grocery retailers and manufacturers between 2007 and 2015. The public has also been playing their part: as compared with 2007, consumers spend £3.4 billion a year less on food products. However, there is room for improvement; in 2015, 7.3 million tonnes of food was still simply thrown away. In Denmark, the figures are slightly better, but, according to the Danish Environmental Agency (Miljóstyrelsen), Danish households still throw away 260,000 tonnes of food annually, while retailers throw away around 163,000 tonnes, together amounting to more than 60 per cent of the total food wastage in Denmark. This case looks at the way in which the Danish supermarket retail cooperative Coop Danmark A/S (www.coop.dk) is addressing this issue by reducing the amount of food that its supermarkets throw away and raising awareness among consumers about the problem of food wastage.

Coop's 'Stop Food Wastage' Magazine and In-store Initiatives

Coop Danmark A/S (COOP) is the largest supermarket retailer in Denmark, employing more than 36,000 people in over 1,200 retail outlets of varying sizes. Coop defines wasted food as 'food that could have been eaten by humans but for one reason or another ends up being thrown away'. Giving away unsold food to food banks is not possible, as, unlike in France, Danish law prohibits the donation of food that has passed its sell-by date. So how does Coop do its part to reduce the amount of food that is wasted? Coop acknowledges that the Danish food retail

industry has a large influence over the food that is wasted by both producers and consumers, and so Coop has produced a 'stop food wastage' magazine in conjunction with the Danish consumer movement Stop Wasting Food (www.stopspildafmad.dk). The magazine contains articles that inform consumers of Coop's aims for reducing food waste in its supermarkets, by consumers and by producers. Coop has also begun to donate food close to its sell-by date to charities such as the Food Bank, and to participate in the app-based 'too good to go' scheme that enables restaurants and retailers to sell prepared food that would otherwise be thrown away at reduced prices.

Coop states in its food wastage magazine that the aims can be achieved through concrete in-store initiatives, such as reducing the price on food products as they get closer to their sell-by date, developing a visual concept that can help draw consumer attention to the need to reduce food waste, and through providing knowledge about food waste—and how to prevent it—to consumers. Coop has also pledged to hold an annual campaign in all its stores that aims to increase awareness of the problem of food wastage, together with becoming an active participant

»

»

in the public debate surrounding food wastage. So, rather than simply passing the responsibility for reducing food wastage on to consumers, Coop has taken an active role.

Coop has long considered social responsibility to be part of the company's mission. Coop was the first company in Denmark to introduce a programme for improving consumer awareness and health, together with the production of educational materials for schools to encourage healthy eating. Today, Coop's corporate social responsibility initiatives focus on the avoidance of food wastage, and thus continues to support the company's social mission of changing consumer attitudes to consumption. These educational initiatives are supported by changes in pricing strategy and by highlighting the issue of food wastage: for example, Coop's discount format Fakta has stopped the 'buy one get one free' offers, instead offering lower prices on purchases of single products. When it was discovered that around 40,000 bananas were thrown away annually for the simple reason that the fruit was single rather than in a bunch of two or more. Coop then held an event in Copenhagen's Central Square where 40,000 single bananas were handed out to passers-by. Whilst the results of the event have yet to be measured in terms of bananas, there was wide coverage in the national media, which thus fulfilled Coop's pledge to participate in the public debate.

In a survey, Danish consumers were asked what would encourage them to purchase products close to the sell-by date. Given the high cost of food products in Denmark relative to other European countries, respondents answered that a lower price would make them more likely to purchase food products close to the sell-by date. In response to this, Coop has changed its pricing strategy by systematically reducing the price of food products that are approaching their sell-by date. For Coop, reduced prices leads to a lower profit margin on each item; however, unsold food that is just thrown away does not contribute anything to the costs associated with the production and warehousing of the products prior to them being put on the shelves of the supermarket, and the safe disposal of food items leads to other costs.

In order to address consumer concerns about the quality of food that is near its sell-by date, several of Coop's supermarket formats have introduced special counters where food items that are close to their sell-by date are placed, with slogans such as 'Save the Food' and 'Enjoy Soon, Save More'. While the intention of this labelling strategy is positive, one result may be that food that the supermarket would have been forced to dispose of is actually thrown away at home. Coop has also addressed this issue in several ways: by developing a cookbook with the title 'Rich on Leftovers' (the recipes are also available for free online), and by experimenting with labels on shrink-wrapped broccoli that remind consumers that all of the stalk can be used.

Impact on the Supply Chain

In addition to the direct wastage that supermarkets are responsible for due to unsold food, supermarket retailers' power in the supply chain means that the impact of short-term demand fluctuations is passed back to farmers. Farmers are therefore forced to produce more than is necessary to ensure that they can supply the supermarkets. At the same time, the requirement for aesthetically pleasing produce to support a supermarket brand image focusing on quality leads to misshaped vegetables being thrown away by farmers before they even reach the supermarket shelves. By selling 'unorthodox'-shaped vegetables and fruit, Coop eases pressure on the supply chain, as farmers throw away less produce when demand is high.

Impact of the Initiatives

So, have Coop's initiatives had any impact on the attitudes and purchasing behaviour of Danish consumers? The numbers speak for themselves: in 2017, an investigation by the Danish Statistical Office found that 45% of consumers had a greater focus on food wastage compared with the year before. However, one problem that Coop and all supermarkets face is that customers expect full shelves at all times of the day; if the products are not available, consumers will shop elsewhere—maybe for good (Ritzau, 2014). So, while consumers have become better at buying products that are closer to their sell-by date, consumers' purchasing behaviour appears to be driven by lower prices rather than a change in social attitudes towards food wastage and an acceptance of the logistical challenges that lead to empty supermarket shelves. So, the question remains: have social attitudes towards food wastage really changed, or is it just the impact of a change in price?

Questions

1. **Coop Danmark A/S prides itself on its socially responsible business practices. Can Coop's pricing strategy be seen as a socially responsible business practice or just a way to pass on to consumers the responsibility of reducing food wastage?**

2. **What do you think is the main reason for Coop Danmark's anti-food wastage initiatives: reducing Coop's costs, increasing Coop's income by selling food that would otherwise be wasted, or reinforcing Coop's socially responsible brand?**
3. **Do you think that it is possible for Coop to reduce costs, increase income *and* reinforce their brand, all at the same time?**
4. **Do you think that Coop's initiatives will have an impact on purchase and consumption behaviour?**

This case study was written by Robert Ormrod, Associate Professor, Aarhus University.

Further reading

COOP Danmark A/S (www.coop.dk); Stop Spild af Mad (http://www.stopspildafmad.dk).

References

Based on: landbrugsavisen.dk (2015), COOP reducerer madspil, http://landbrugsavisen.dk/coop-reducerer-madspild (accessed 7 July 2015); Ritzau (2014), COOP om madspil: Kunder kræver fyldte hylder: http://www.msn.com/da-dk/finans/other/coop-om-madspild-kunder-kr%c3%a6ver-fyldte-hylder/ar-BB8isaf.

CHAPTER 6
Marketing Analytics and Research

"I firmly believe that if you can't measure it, you cannot manage it."

BOB NAPIER, EXECUTIVE VICE PRESIDENT, HEWLETT-PACKARD

LEARNING OBJECTIVES

After reading this chapter, you should be able to:

1. contextualize the use of big data for marketing decision-making
2. discuss marketing analytics, goal setting and performance measurement
3. identify and discuss different types of data sources
4. discuss the scope of market and marketing research
5. describe the stages in the market research process
6. distinguish between qualitative and quantitative research
7. explain how to prepare a research brief and proposal
8. discuss the role of exploratory research
9. discuss approaches to research design decisions: sampling, survey method and questionnaire design issues
10. explain the processes involved with interpreting and presenting data and writing reports
11. discuss the ethical issues that arise in market research

In this chapter, we explore, marketing analytics and how the changing **information** landscape is influencing the practice of market research.

In recent years, the marketing landscape has changed beyond recognition as the internet, smart phones, social media networks and other digital innovations have profoundly altered the way we communicate. Digital technologies are disrupting traditional methods of gathering, processing and utilizing marketing information: **data** can be collected and analysed instantaneously, enabling measurement of real-time behaviour (Poynter, Williams and York, 2014). Understanding marketing analytics is increasingly producing efficiency gains and creating opportunities for marketing activities to be more effective. Marketers use big data to inform decision-making, aid organizational goals setting and ensure control. Moreover, the capacity to interpret meaning from big data becomes more important as the sources of data increase. In the last few years, the flow of big data has grown dramatically as use of the internet has extended throughout the supply chain and into the hands of consumers as they shop online and via mobile devices. Big data is generated in quantities that are difficult to comprehend, for example petabytes, zettabytes and yottabytes. These volumes of data are generated from many sources, from scanners to smartphones and cars, and come in different forms, including videos, documents, spreadsheets, online purchases, blogs and tweets. The list is becoming ever longer as the Internet of Things (IoT) connects more and more elements of human interaction to a plethora of digital devices (Kerschberg, 2014). It is estimated that there are 2.5 quintillion bytes of data created every day (Marr, 2018).

There are significant implications for marketing as customers (B2B and B2C) interact with firms, products and services differently via digital platforms. Also, these interactions—whether Google searches, Facebook posts or tweets—are being monitored and the data analysed. Supercookies, tiny pieces of data stored in web browsers, are used to record website visits and the dwell time on each site and page (Pagliery, 2015). Browser fingerprinting is used to provide behavioural advertisers (BA) with information they need to develop highly targeted and personalized promotional offers. From watching browsing behaviour and analysing the data, BAs can infer age, gender and personal interests without ever asking your permission (Truste, 2015). But data collection does not stop with web browsing; Samsung's Smart TV enabled the company to gather viewing behaviour directly from the television (BBC, 2015) and voice activated speakers like Amazon's Echo range are constantly gathering data.

However, it is important to understand that big data is only of value once it is analysed and turned into **business intelligence** (Kerschberg, 2014). Read Marketing in Action 6.1 to find out how GlaxoSmithKline (GSK) is using big data in this way.

Then let's explore the links between data, marketing goals, performance and measurement.

Marketing Analytics: Goals, Performance and Measurement

Marketing analytics play an increasingly significant role in demonstrating how marketing activities translate into revenue. As discussed in Chapter 1, marketers are increasingly being challenged to prove the benefits of their marketing efforts, especially in relation to goal achievement and performance. Marketing analytics are the tools, technologies, systems and processes that are used to reveal insights, measure performance, drive growth and lead to more informed decision-making.

In the past, marketing information systems were designed to provide quality information that had an impact on the effectiveness of decision-making (Daniels, Wilson and McDonald, 2003). As use of these systems became widespread, previous piecemeal systems were replaced by integrated customer relationship management systems to provide a unified view of the customer and actionable market intelligence.

A **marketing information system** has been defined as a system in which marketing information is formally gathered, stored, analysed and distributed to managers in accord with their informational needs on a regular planned basis (Jobber and Rainbow, 1977). These systems were built on an understanding of the information needs of marketing management, and supply information when, where and how to suit management needs.

MARKETING IN ACTION 6.1
What is Big Data? GSK Shares its Big Data

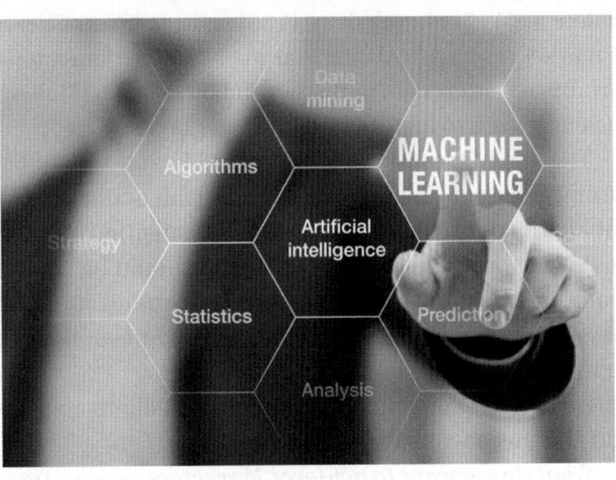

Big data is not a new idea; since the linking of low-cost computing and scanners at the point of sale in shops, large quantities of data have been generated. This early form of big data improved understanding of shopper behaviour and enabled retailers to manage their stock more effectively. Retailers also had access to the information from their scanners almost immediately instead of waiting for weeks for the traditional accounting reports. Another major benefit of this new stream of information was more targeted sales promotions and advertising campaigns, and improved profitability.

GlaxoSmithKline (GSK) is a company attempting to make use of big data from end-to-end of the supply chain by sharing its data with the world. This multinational pharmaceutical firm has a portfolio of brands stretching from prescription medicines like Amoxil and Betnovate cream to consumer healthcare brands including Aquafresh, Beechams and Sensodyne. Marketing research comes in many forms because of the nature of the business—carrying out clinical trials and research associated with bringing healthcare products to the market. However, when it comes to the analysis of consumer data, GSK has invested in its marketing research operation to ensure that collection and dissemination of findings happen at a company-wide level. The company has experts in every area of the business who concentrate on specific marketing research problems. They have taken the very bold step of sharing their data with outsiders and have posted over 450 studies online. This transparency and openness are strategic moves aiming to benefit the industry and humankind by enabling faster innovations through collaboration.

In the organization, it is felt that the most useful information is generated when experts work together on common goals, gathering data from large, complex data sources, including internal data and online sources, and from weblogs, social media, web and smartphone analytics, through which consumers provide signals about what they are thinking at a given point in time. GSK works with companies that provide data management services to help its clients reach a better understanding of their own customers. Ultimately, GSK aims to build relationships with over a million of its customers through social media and to use these relationships as a base for market research and for multichannel marketing. Data collection takes place when customers are directed to targeted offers and promotions for brand websites, where external data are integrated with existing internal data. The process involves tracking a brand and analysing what customers are saying and thinking specifically about the brand. The process also involves looking at everything else the customers are talking about (in areas of public access) to build a consumer profile. GSK then employs internal data management and processing analysts to make sense of the data and uses the information to inform its marketing strategy and planning at both strategic and tactical levels.

Capacity to analyse and use data is constantly developing and GSK is using artificial intelligence (AI) systems to deliver transformational changes to the way it does things and bring new products to market much faster.

Based on: GlaxoSmithKline (2012); Hemsley (2011); Leonard (2018); Weintraub (2014); Fulgoni (2013)

Data from the marketing environment is translated into information. The difference between data and information is as follows.

- **Data** are the most basic form of knowledge, for example the brand of butter sold to a customer in a certain town; this statistic is of little worth but may become meaningful when combined with other data.
- **Information** is a combination of data that provides decision-relevant knowledge, for example the brand preferences of customers in a certain age category in a geographic region could enable butter producer Lurpak to plan a targeted marketing campaign.

Digital technology is transforming the opportunities to collect data from multiple sources in real time. As a result, the volume of data being generated has increased significantly and is now referred to as 'big data' (very large data sets). Big data analytics can identify hidden patterns in behaviour, which can be translated into market advantage (Erevelles, Fukawa, Swayne, 2016). For marketers to benefit from this glut of data, it must be managed and analysed correctly. But the problem with big data is that it 'just happens', is unstructured and (unlike market research data) is not collected to answer a specific question (see later in the chapter for discussion of market research). Also, it is argued that the data-intensive digital era is fundamentally changing approaches towards research, data gathering and processing (Muller, Junglas, vom Brocke, Debotoli, 2017), moving information systems closer to performance measurement.

The need for marketing-orientated businesses to have structured approaches for obtaining big data and turning it into marketing intelligence (the actionable knowledge produced by the analysis of big data with implications for decision-making) is intensified. According to Chaffey and Ellis-Chadwick (2019), marketing goals, performance and measurement should be considered on an organization-wide basis, reflect information requirements in relation to the level of organizational decision-making and relate to varying levels of marketing control. Figure 6.1 shows key questions for planning performance measurement and marketing control systems.

Answering these broad questions can help to achieve a structured approach to creating a marketing performance measurement system:

1 *What do we want to achieve?* Marketers need to frame the questions they want big data and marketing analytics systems to solve and relate their questions to organizational goals (at both strategic and tactical levels). For example, a firm may incorporate Google Analytics into their website, which will produce reports, e.g. website traffic, visitor behaviour, site performance, but this data needs to be linked to specific marketing objectives to effectively inform decision-making. The website traffic might increase at a point in time due to a one-off promotional event, but customer retention may be in decline as customers are utilizing the offer but not returning or creating a long-term relationship. If the goal is to build a sustainable online customer base, monitoring the pull of one-off promotions is not providing the information needed. So, careful planning is required to ensure that the *right* data is collected to answer appropriate questions, and ensure the effectiveness of strategic and or tactical goals.

2 *What is happening?* Performance measurement is central to understanding efficiency. According to Chaffey (2000), organizations create management frameworks around specific groupings of metrics, which assess marketing performance. He suggested that macro-level metrics can assess the efficiency of strategic goals and micro-level metrics assess the efficiency of tactical goals. There are many software systems that create performance measurement dashboards, e.g. IBM Cognos Analytics; see Exhibit 6.1.

3 *Why (is it happening)?* Performance diagnostics systems can then identify details of why certain outcomes are succeeding or failing against planned marketing goals. To achieve a good level of understanding of what is happening, marketers should review *when* marketing campaigns and plans are being implemented and *who* is involved. Roche (global healthcare) utilizes a diagnostic system to ensure that supplies and end consumers receive the best healthcare products when they are needed, which has helped to develop new levels of customer engagement and deeper understanding of customer requirements (Roche—Diagnostic, 2018).

FIGURE 6.1
Adapted from Chaffey and Ellis-Chadwick (2019): The Marketing Performance Measurement Framework

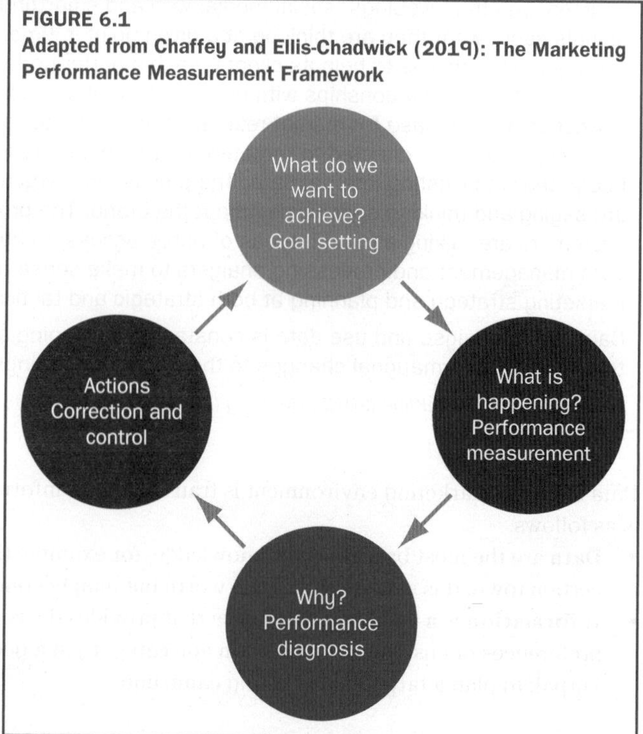

EXHIBIT 6.1
Marketing analytic performance dashboard

4 *What should we do?* Once the actual performance has been reviewed against the set goals, the next stage in the process is to take corrective action; to improve performance.

While much data is gathered through digital channels, there are also three other aspects and sources of data to consider: internal continuous data; internal ad-hoc data and data from environmental scanning; and market research.

Internal continuous data

Companies possess an enormous amount of marketing and financial data that can be used for marketing decision-making and should be incorporated into the performance management system as this can enable the conversion of financial data and a range of other data into a form usable by marketing management.

A marketing information system (MkIS) provides managers with analysis and marketing information, which can be used to support decision-making and strategic planning. An Mk-IS may stimulate the provision of information that marketing managers can use, for example about the profitability of a particular product, customer or distribution channel, or even the profitability of a particular product to an individual customer. Widespread integration of information systems across businesses provides great insight into customers and provides more informed decision-making. An MkIS can incorporate big data and then provide opportunities to delve deeply into consumer behaviour, by monitoring consumers' profiles, attitudes, preferences and purchasing behaviour (Salvador and Ikeda, 2014). Internal data become more complex as information and data-collection points start to include websites, mobile apps and social media.

Read Marketing in Action 6.2 to find out how stationery distributor Viking was targeting the *wrong* customers.

Another application of the MkIS concept to internal continuous data is within the area of salesforce management. As part of the sales management function, many salesforces are monitored by means of recording sales achieved, number of calls made, size of orders, number of new accounts opened, and so on. This can be recorded in total or broken down by product or customer/customer type. The establishment of an MkIS where these data are stored and analysed over time can provide information on salesforce effectiveness. For example, a fall-off in performance of a salesperson can quickly be identified and remedial action taken.

MARKETING IN ACTION 6.2
Viking Targets the Wrong Customers

One of the fundamental principles of marketing is understanding and satisfying customer needs, so for Viking Direct (part of Office Depot), a global company and one of the world's largest suppliers of office stationery for B2B customers, targeting the wrong customer had serious implications for its promotion strategy.

Viking operates in the UK in Leicester, London and Manchester, and claims to sell more office products than any other company. Through the website, Viking sells writing materials, office equipment, warehouse and cleaning supplies. Viking competes with retail brands, e.g. Tesco and Amazon, as well as B2B competitors.

When the company streamlined its information systems to improve customer insight, it discovered that the stereotypical '35-year-old female secretary' was not the primary buyer as previously thought. New survey data revealed that middle-aged men were more likely to be the primary stationery buyers. This shift occurred in part because the economic recession led to many men leaving the corporate world to start their own businesses. The data analysis also revealed that, not only were men buying the stationery, but they were older than previously thought and were working in smaller companies. As a result of this new customer insight, Viking Direct re-branded; changing its marketing materials and sales initiatives, digital platforms and developing a mobile application. Tony Dobbs (Head of Customer Relationship Management) developed a loyalty ladder for driving sales using motivational triggers such as relevance of product, ease of ordering, delivery, price and fulfilment. They also began using TV advertising on subscription services like Sky to reach their newly discovered target market.

Based on: Viking Direct (2018); Costa (2011)

Internal ad-hoc data

Company data can also be used for a specific (ad-hoc) purpose. For example, management may look at how sales have reacted to a price increase or a change in advertising copy. Although this could be part of a continuous monitoring programme, specific one-off analyses are inevitably required from time to time. Capturing the data on the MkIS allows specific analyses to be conducted when needed.

Environmental scanning

The environmental scanning procedures discussed in Chapter 2 also form part of the MkIS, and this includes environmental analysis—whereby the economic, social, political, legal, technological and ecological/physical forces are monitored. These forces can be difficult to monitor, due to their amorphous nature, but are important as they can shape the context within which the company, suppliers, distributors and the competition do business, as in the case of Viking Direct. Environmental scanning provides an early warning system for the forces that may impact on a company's products and markets in the future (Jain and Haley, 2009). In this way, scanning enables an organization to act on, rather than react to, opportunities and threats. The focus is on the longer-term perspective, allowing a company to be in the position to plan ahead, and information from data analysis provides a major input into strategic decisions such as which future products to develop and markets to enter, and the formulation of a competitive strategy (e.g. to attack or defend against competition).

Market research

While environmental scanning focuses on the longer term, **market research** considers the more immediate situation and is primarily concerned with providing information about markets and customer reactions to various product, price, distribution and promotion decisions (Moutinho and Evans, 1992). As such, market research is a key part of the MkIS because it makes a major contribution to marketing mix planning.

There are two main types of external market research:

1 *External continuous data sources* include TV audience monitoring and **consumer panels** where household purchases are recorded over time. Loyalty cards are also a source of continuous data, providing information on customer purchasing patterns and responses to promotions. The growth of digital technology and the uptake of e-commerce has led to new forms of continuous data collection, as has the development of mobile apps. See Marketing in Action 6.3 to find out more about the power of apps as a source of data collection.

MARKETING IN ACTION 6.3
Proximity Apps and Customer Information

Proximity marketing is creating endless possibilities for marketing to link consumers to events to generate revenue. Beacons send messages to mobile devices and then, through a system of servers, location-based marketing messages are delivered to the consumer's device. Nodes is a specialist agency, based in London and Copenhagen, which develops proximity marketing mobile apps for big brands such as Carlsberg, GSK, BMW, Unilever and Samsung and aims to make strong connections with users. Its apps can be designed to meet various objectives, for example for social engagement, product demonstrations, tracking user experiences and proximity marketing campaigns. For example, Crowdit developed a social bar finder app as a proximity marketing tool. The aim for Crowdit was to enable customers to generate a voucher on their mobile phones that could be used in a nearby bar. The app also included other features so that its users could order a cab, find a particular type of bar, and be informed of events and promotions. The app was designed for Carlsberg, but there was none of the beer's branding on the app, so any bar was able to sign up to use the app. Bar owners in Denmark responded as quickly as their customers, with over 100,000 downloads soon after its launch.

Customers were offered a voucher that they could also share with their friends. iBeacons were used to send out notifications when a customer was within close proximity of a Crowdit bar. An iBeacon is a small Bluetooth device that transmits signals from a chosen location to smart phones that come within its range. Once the customer had the voucher, the bar redeemed the voucher in exchange for a drink.

The bar owners benefited, as they received all of the information about each particular user of the voucher and could view the analytics, which enabled them to update events based on customer adoption rates and engagement. Additional data gathering from vouchers being shared with friends meant the iBeacons also acted as a bridge between the digital and the physical world and kept track of how long a particular user was within range. This then enabled bar owners to send highly targeted offers, for example a second drink notification. The second voucher is sent at the critical point at which the consumer decides whether to stay or move to a new location. The information provided by the app and the iBeacons can be used to develop customer loyalty and customer retention.

Proximity apps are not just for B2C markets. DFDS developed an app with Nodes for its ferry service between Copenhagen and Oslo. The aim was to strengthen loyalty and retention, and to encourage customers to opt for sea rather than air travel. The app provided information about travel times and sailing, but also shopping offers. The success of the consumer-facing app sparked the development of an app for freight clients. The app enables heavy goods vehicle freight drivers to also have access to all the information they need, when and where they need it, to ensure the smoothest movement of goods. DFDS envisages being able to streamline its whole freight division due to the efficient communication system provided by the proximity app.

Based on: Nodes (2018); Mobile Marketing (2014); Beaconstat, (2018); DFDS (2018)

2 *External ad-hoc data* are often gathered by means of surveys into specific marketing issues, including usage and attitude studies, advertising and product testing, and corporate image research. More traditional forms of market research—telephone and face-to-face interviews—are being replaced by digital survey techniques. Digital platforms (web and mobile) are being used, not only for gathering quantitative survey data, but also for gathering qualitative data through real-time audio and online video discussions. Social media is also providing access to an innovative form of digital discussion group, and companies are analysing online conversations to find out what their consumers really think about their products (Manning, 2011).

The rest of this chapter will examine the process of marketing research and the factors that affect the use of research information.

Marketing research has been used by an increasing range of types of organization, from political parties to community groups. Some marketing research agencies specialize in particular types of market research. For example, Ipsos MORI specializes in brand loyalty, advertising, and political and social research; Sherbert Research focuses on qualitative research with children and teenagers.

Furthermore, not only are organizations making more use of technology, but the technology itself is also enabling more insightful analysis. The market research industry is penetrating deeper into the psyche of individual consumers.

Marketing and Research

Market research and marketing research are two terms often used interchangeably; distinctions can be drawn but be aware that there is significant overlap. Marketing research refers to work that explores broader fundamental issues and/or highly specific areas, e.g. advertising research, services marketing, changing marketing environment, consumer behaviour; whereas market research refers to research that looks at markets, trends and how actors (customers) behave. It has a relatively narrow focus and represents the process of gathering, analysing and interpreting data. Market research also tends to be done on a commercial basis unlike marketing research, which is more academic. This chapter focuses on the application of market research. The Market Research Society (MRS) is the UK's professional body for research insights and analytics. Its role is to ensure that high standards are maintained by its members, who carry out market research for many thousands of organizations. The market research sector has grown by 60% in the last five years, is worth nearly £5 billion annually in the UK and employs 78,000 people. Recently, the MRS have observed changing requirements in the industry, with increasing demand for data analytics, storytelling and data visualization. The focus has shifted towards use of big data, data analytics, social media analysis, data mining and predictive analytics, qualitative research, and online and mobile surveys, and away from using survey data (MRS, 2018).

This is an emerging field of data science that combines statistics, computer science and behavioural science with the aim of extracting meaningful insights and predicting future outcomes. To achieve this the data used for the analysis must be good. Poor data quality leads to potentially damaging and inaccurate outputs. To be sufficiently accurate, data must be free of errors, up-to-date and complete (Hazen, Boone, Ezell, Janes-Farmer, 2016).

Qualitative and quantitative

An important distinction in market research is that between qualitative and quantitative research. Qualitative research usually precedes quantitative research and forms the basis for an understanding of consumers that can aid planning questionnaires, which can then be designed to focus on what is important to the consumer and worded in language that consumers use and understand. However, when the objectives of the research are to gain rich, in-depth insights into consumer motivations, attitudes and behaviour, the study may be based on qualitative research alone without the quantitative follow-up.

Whichever approach is taken, there are several essential differences between these two key primary data-gathering methods which mean that the skills required vary. Indeed, many market research practitioners specialize in one or the other approach. These differences relate to the research purpose and whether it is to gather verbal or numerical data. Qualitative research can provide deep insights into consumer behaviour, whereas the purpose of quantitative research is to provide information that can be generalized across the study population.

Also, the methods used for data collection tend to be different. Qualitative data are often gathered through focus groups and in-depth interviews, whereas quantitative data is gathered using a structured questionnaire. Qualitative methods offer more flexibility than quantitative studies, as questions can be varied to some degree depending on the answers given by a respondent. Although a structured questionnaire can provide the means for varying questions through the use of filter questions (e.g. 'If the answer to question 6 is yes, go to question 7, if no go to question 10'), there is much less flexibility to vary the questions at the discretion of the interviewer.

It is also important to note that sample sizes differ. Qualitative methods such as in-depth interviews and focus groups have a higher cost per respondent and so tend to focus on insight rather than statistical precision, which means that qualitative studies are associated with smaller samples than quantitative research. Quantitative studies can involve thousands of people. For example, OnePoll conducts surveys on a local, national or international scale, using tailor-made surveys, teams of researchers and selected relevant participants. A typical qualitative study, however, may involve fewer than 30 people.

Analysis and presentation of results can also vary. Qualitative data is analysed using content analysis, which can result in a report that provides summary statements and uses quotes from research respondents. Quantitative survey data is approached by statistical analysis, and reporting back is by means of graphs, tables and other methods of statistical presentation. In both cases, careful interpretation is required.

The Market Research Process

Many firms wanting to conduct market research outsource the work to a specialist company. But it is important for marketers to be aware of how to identify an appropriate company to be able to commission good research, which can be used to inform corporate and marketing decision-making (MRS, 2018). Both large and small firms commission market research studies as the insights and evidence produced can help with development of new products, increase customer retention, developing more effective advertising campaigns.

This section presents a framework for understanding the main steps in the marketing research process, shown in Figure 6.2. This 'map' highlights what is involved in a major marketing research study covering both qualitative and quantitative research.

FIGURE 6.2
Overview of market research process

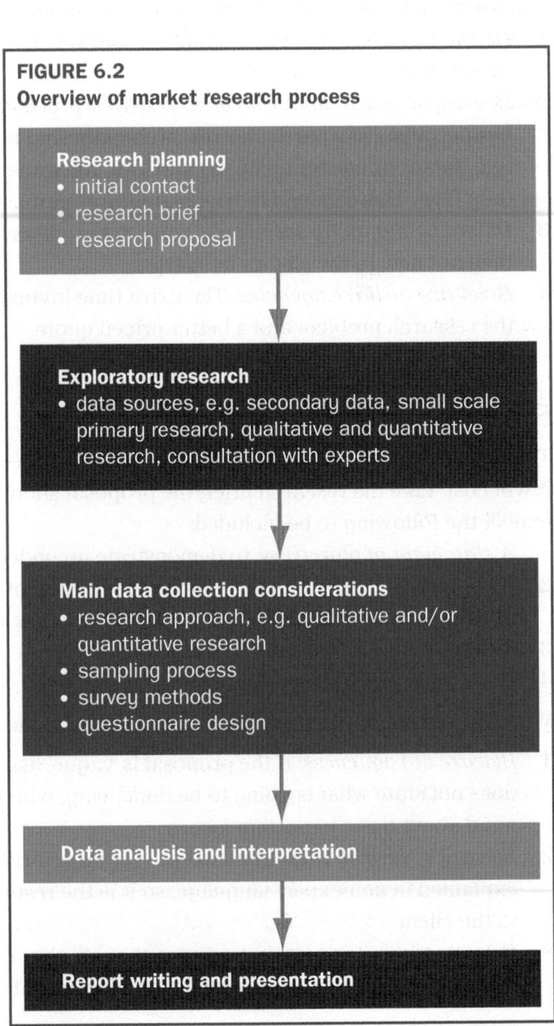

Research planning

Decisions made at the research planning stage will fundamentally affect what is done later, so planning is required prior to any data collection. A commercial marketing research project is likely to involve marketing management at the client company, internal marketing research staff and, usually, research staff at an outside marketing research agency. The following discussion provides a generic view of the commercial marketing research process.

Initial contact

The start of the process is usually the realization that a marketing problem (e.g. a new product or advertising decision) requires information to help find a solution. Marketing management may contact internal marketing research staff or an outside agency. Let us assume that the research requires the assistance of a marketing research agency. A meeting will be arranged to discuss the nature of the problem and the client's research needs.

Research brief

At the meeting with the marketing research agency, the client will explain the marketing problem and outline the research objectives. The marketing problem might be to attract new customers to a product line, and the research objectives could be to identify groups of customers (market segments) that might have a use for the product, and the characteristics of the product that appeal to them most (Crouch and Housden, 2003). The key point is that clients should not only tell research agencies what they want to understand but what the research will be used for (Dye, 2008).

Other information that should be provided for the research agency includes the following (Crouch and Housden, 2003):

1 *Background information*: the product's history and the competitive situation.
2 *Sources of information*: the client may have a list of industries that might be potential users of the product. This helps the researchers to define the scope of the research.
3 *The scale of the project*: is the client looking for a 'cheap and cheerful' job or a major study? This has implications for the research design and survey costs.
4 *The timetable*: when is the information required?

The client should produce a specific written **research brief**. This may be given to the research agency prior to the meeting and perhaps modified as a result of it but, without fail, should be in the hands of the agency before it produces its **research proposal**. The research brief should state the client's requirements and should be in written form to minimize misunderstandings. In the event of a dispute later in the process, the research brief (and proposal) form the benchmark against which any grievances can be settled.

Commissioning good research is similar to buying any other product or service. If marketing managers can agree on why the research is needed, what it will be used for, when it is needed and how much they are willing to pay for it, they are likely to make a good buy. Four suggestions for buying good research are as follows.

1 *Define terms clearly*. For example, if market share information is required, the term 'market' should clearly be defined.
2 *Beware of researchers who bend research problems* so that they can use their favourite technique. They may be specialists in a particular research-gathering method (e.g. group discussion) or statistical technique (e.g. factor or cluster analysis) and look for ways of using these methods no matter what research problem they face. This can lead to irrelevant information and unnecessary expense.
3 *Do not be put off by seemingly naïve researchers* who ask what appear to be simple questions, particularly if they are new to the client's industry.
4 *Brief two or three agencies*. The extra time involved should be rewarded by better feedback on how to tackle the research problem and a better priced quote.

Research proposal

The research proposal defines what the marketing research agency promises to do for its client, and how much it will cost. Like the research brief, the proposal should be written to avoid misunderstandings. A client should expect the following to be included:

1 *A statement of objectives*: to demonstrate an understanding of the client's marketing and research problems.
2 *What will be done*: an unambiguous description of the research design, including the survey method, the type of sample, the sample size and how the fieldwork will be controlled.
3 *Timetable*: if and when a report will be produced.
4 *Costs*: how much the research will cost and what, specifically, is/is not being included in those costs.

When assessing proposals, a client might usefully check the following points:

1 *Beware of vagueness*: if the proposal is vague, assume that the report is also likely to be vague. If the agency does not state what is going to be done, why, who is doing it and when, assume that it is not clear in its own mind about these important issues.
2 *Beware of jargon*: there is no excuse for jargon-ridden proposals. Marketing research terminology can be explained in non-expert language, so it is the responsibility of the agency to make the proposal understandable to the client.
3 *Beware of what is missing*: assume that anything not specified will not be provided. For example, if no mention of a presentation is made in the proposal, assume it will not take place. Any doubts, ask the agency.

Exploratory research

Exploratory research involves the preliminary exploration of a research area prior to the main data-collection stage. The discussion that follows assumes that the initial proposal has been accepted and that exploratory research is to be carried out as the basis for survey design.

A major purpose of exploratory research is to guard against the sins of omission and admission (Wright and Crimp, 2003).

- *Sin of omission*: not researching a topic in enough detail, or failing to provide sufficient respondents in a group to allow meaningful analysis.
- *Sin of admission*: collecting data that are irrelevant to the marketing problem or using too many groups for analysis purposes and thereby unnecessarily increasing the sample size.

Exploratory research techniques allow the researcher to understand the people who are to be interviewed in the main data-collection stage, and the market that is being researched. The main survey stage can thus be designed with this knowledge in mind rather than being based on the researcher's ill-informed prejudices and guesswork.

Figure 6.3 displays the four exploratory research activities. An individual research project may involve all or some of them.

Please note that qualitative and quantitative research methods may be used at both the exploratory and main data-collection stage and it will be the market research project manager's responsibility to determine which methods will be the best methods to meet the research objectives.

Secondary research

Secondary research is so called because the data come to the researcher 'second-hand' (other people have compiled the data). When the researcher actively collects new data—for example, by interviewing respondents—this is called primary research (discussed in the next section).

Secondary data come from sources such as internal company records, reports and previous research carried out for the company. External sources of secondary data include: government and European Union (EU) statistics; publishers of reports and directories on markets, countries and industries; trade associations; banks; and newspapers, magazines and journals.

The internet provides access to rich sources of secondary information. Websites like Trendwatching (www.trendwatching.com) specialize in identifying emerging global consumer and marketing trends. Some online sources are free to access, others are paid-for services; for example, IDC, Gartner and Experian have an internet presence and provide both free and paid-for resources. Companies that specialize in providing secondary information also provide electronic content either by subscription or by selling individual reports. For example, a visit to Mintel—the world's leading market intelligence agency (www.mintel.com)—can provide hundreds of industry reports from the very specific, such as on innovations in German barbeques, to broader subjects such as personal health and beauty care. A word of caution when using online resources (especially free information): remember to verify the authenticity of the data; be critical of the findings and establish the origin of the data.

FIGURE 6.3
Forms of exploratory research

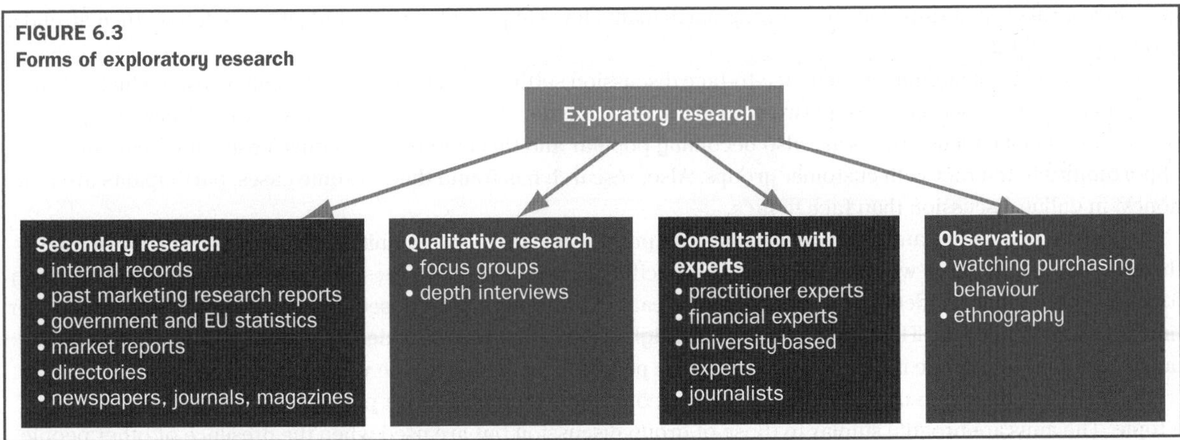

In the EU, there are many secondary sources of data, e.g. Euromonitor—industry reports (http://www.euromonitor.com); Kompass—competitor information (http://gb.kompass.com); and European statistics (http://ec.europa.eu/eurostat). These and other resources can supply information for specific industries, details of market competitors and economic trend statistics.

Secondary research should be carried out before primary research. Without the former, an expensive primary research survey might be commissioned to provide information that is already available from secondary sources.

Primary research methods

Each ad-hoc marketing research project may be different. This is in order to fit the particular requirements and resources of various clients. For example, one study may focus on **qualitative research** using small numbers of respondents, while another may be largely **quantitative research**, involving interviewing hundreds or thousands of consumers. Therefore, it is important to take care to ensure that the data-collection method is suitable and best able to meet the objectives of the market research activity.

Qualitative research

Qualitative research has been defined as 'the analysis and understanding of patterned conduct and social process of society' (Denzin and Lincoln, 2000). The main forms of qualitative research used in market research which help us to understand the complex patterns of human behaviour are group discussions and **in-depth interviews** and **ethnography**, which involve bringing together personal encounters, life events and understandings into a more meaningful context (Tedlock, 2000). Qualitative research aims to establish customers' attitudes, values, behaviour and beliefs, and aims to understand consumers in a way that traditional methods of interviewing people using questionnaires cannot. Qualitative research seeks to understand the 'why' and 'how' of consumer behaviour (Clegg, 2001). The key differences between qualitative and quantitative research are explored later in this chapter.

Focus groups involve unstructured or semi-structured discussions between a *moderator*, or group leader, who is often a psychologist, and a group of consumers. The moderator has a list of areas to cover within the topic, but allows the group considerable freedom to discuss the issues that are important to them. The topics might be organic foods, men's cosmetics, motor sports or activity holiday pursuits. By arranging groups of 6–12 people to discuss their beliefs, attitudes, motivation, behaviour and preferences, a good deal of knowledge may be gained about the consumer. This can be helpful when planning questionnaires, which can then be designed to focus on what is important to the respondent (as opposed to the researcher) and worded in language that the respondent uses and understands.

A further advantage of the focus group is that the findings may provide rich insights into consumer motivations and behaviour because of the group dynamics where group members 'feed off' each other and reveal ideas that would not have arisen on a one-to-one basis. Such findings may be used as food for thought for marketers, without the need for quantitative follow-up.

The weaknesses of the focus group are that interpretation of the results is highly subjective, the quality of the results depends heavily on the skills of the moderator, sample size is usually small, making generalization to wider populations difficult, and there exists the danger that the results might be biased by the presence of 'research groupies', who enjoy taking part in focus groups and return again and again. Such people sometimes even take on different identities, skewing survey results, and have led the Association of Qualitative Research Practitioners to introduce a rule which says that focus group participants have to provide proof of identity each time they attend a group (Flack, 2002).

Technology is impacting on such face-to-face discussion settings and high-tech labs can be used which allow participants to be observed through two-way glass, enabling the client organization to view the focus group session live. Online focus groups are also becoming popular and this method can reduce costs and create more opportunities to interact with customer groups. Also, research has found that, in some cases, participants are more honest in online discussion than face to face.

Internet communities and social media sites can provide access to 'communities of interests', which can take the form of chat rooms or websites dedicated to specific interests or issues. These are useful forums for conducting focus groups, or at least identifying suitable participants. Questions can be posed to participants who are not under time pressure to respond. This can lead to richer insights since they can think deeply about questions put to them online. Another advantage is that they can comprise people located all over the world at minimal cost.

In-depth interviews involve the interviewing of consumers individually for perhaps one or two hours about a topic. The aims are broadly similar to those of group discussion but are used when the presence of other people could inhibit honest answers and viewpoints, when the topic requires individual treatment, as when discussing an individual's decision-making process, and where the organization of a group is not feasible (e.g. it might prove impossible to arrange for six busy purchasing managers to come together for a group discussion).

Care has to be taken when interpreting the results of qualitative research in that the findings are usually based on small sample sizes, and the more interesting or surprising viewpoints may be disproportionately reported. This is particularly significant when qualitative research is not followed by a quantitative study.

Consultation with experts

Qualitative research is based on discussions and interviews with actual and potential buyers of a brand or service. However, consultation with experts involves interviewing people who may not form part of the target market, but who, nevertheless, can provide important marketing-related insights. Many industries have their experts in universities, financial institutions and the press, who may be willing to share their knowledge. They can provide invaluable background information and can be useful for predicting future trends and developments.

Observation

Observation can also help in exploratory research when the product field is unfamiliar. For example, watching people buy wine in a supermarket or paint in a DIY store may provide useful background knowledge when planning a survey in these markets. Another form of observational research that focuses on employee performance is *mystery shopping*. The 'shopper' acts like any other customer in visiting a store, but is trained to ask particular questions and to assess performance on such criteria as service time, friendliness and product knowledge. The objective is to identify service weaknesses and strengths, and to provide input into staff training.

Ethnography Ethnography is a form of observation that involves detailed and prolonged observation of (in the context of this book) consumers. Its origins are in social anthropology, where researchers live in a studied society for months or years. Consumer researchers usually make their observations more quickly and use a range of methods, including direct observations, interviews and video and audio recordings (Peter, Olson and Grunert, 1999).

This method of data collection has become popular as it connects important personal experiences to specific contexts (Tedlock, 2000) and enables researchers to get closer to consumers in order to understand their behaviour in new and more detailed ways. Such research investigates how people behave in their own environment and interact with the world around them. Unlike focus groups, where consumers are brought to the researcher, ethnography takes the researcher to the consumer. Advocates of this form of research argue that focus groups only provide part of the story and do not yield the kinds of 'consumer insights' that ethnography can.

One company that has embraced ethnographic research is Procter & Gamble. 20 families in the UK and a further 20 in Italy were chosen to take part in a study that involved recording their daily household behaviour by video camera. The idea was that, by studying people who buy Procter & Gamble products—such as Max Factor cosmetics, Ariel washing powder and Pampers nappies—the company could gain valuable insights into people's consumer habits. The findings have had implications for its approach to product design, packaging and promotion. For example, it was ethnographic research that revealed that the nappy was not as important as Procter & Gamble had previously thought. New mothers were more interested in information and knowledge than nappies. Using these consumer insights, Procter & Gamble launched Pampers.com, an online community for mothers that attracts over 650,000 users across Europe. Procter & Gamble has also used ethnographic research in China. It observed low-income consumers doing their washing and found that they were prepared to do the extra hand washing needed to compensate for water hardness. Procter & Gamble's response was to launch a cut-price version of its China Tide detergent without water softener (ESOMAR, 2005). A Procter & Gamble spokesman pointed out that ethnography will not replace other forms of research and that ethical issues concerning privacy are dealt with by getting full permission beforehand and giving the families complete editorial control over what is eventually shown to the marketing team.

The objective of ethnographic research is to bridge the gap between what people say they do and what they actually do. Its usefulness is reflected in the fact that companies such as Toyota, Land Rover, Intel, Adidas and Nike have used this genre of research.

The objective of the exploratory research stage in the marketing research process is not to form conclusions but to get better acquainted with the market and its customers. This allows the researcher to base the next stage, which involves wider data collection, on *informed assumptions* rather than guesswork.

FIGURE 6.4
Types of quantitative data-collection

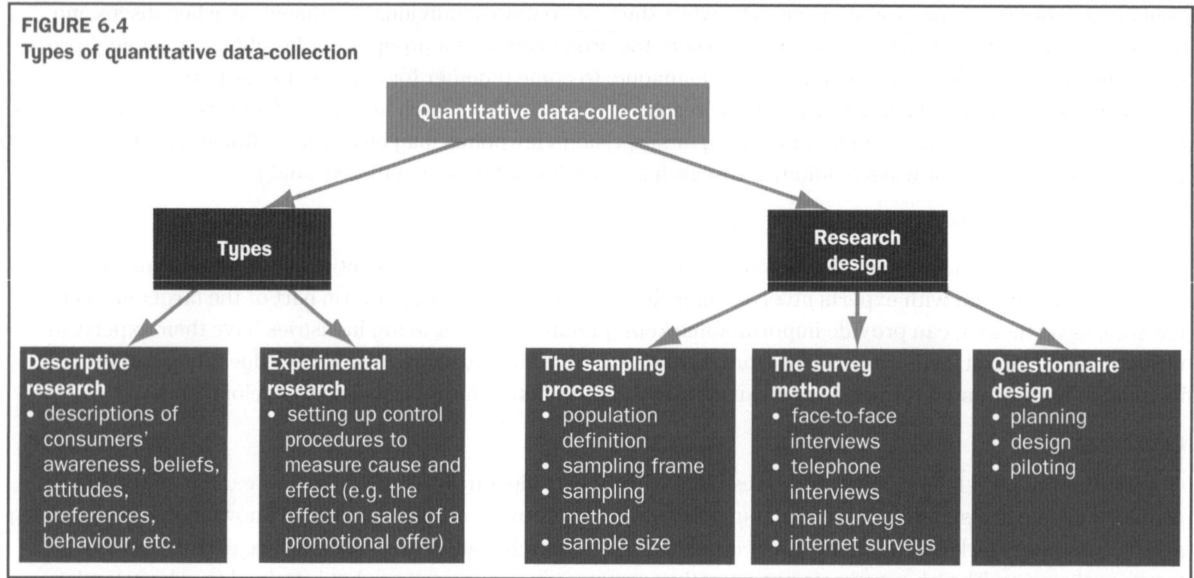

The main data-collection stage

Following careful exploratory research, the design of the main data-collection procedures will be made. In Figure 6.4, the assumption is that quantitative research methods are the most appropriate. However, in some situations, it may be better to extend the use of qualitative research methods used at the exploratory stage of a project. In either case it is important for the project manager to select the data-collection methods that are most likely to achieve the research objectives.

At the main data-collection stage, two alternative approaches are descriptive and experimental research.

Assuming the main data-collection stage requires interviewing, the research design will be based on the following factors:

- who and how many people to interview (the sampling process)
- how to interview them (the survey method)
- what questions to ask (questionnaire design).

Figure 6.4 displays the two types of approach and the three research design methods associated with the main quantitative data-collection stage. These research approaches and methods will now be examined.

Descriptive research

Descriptive research may be undertaken to describe consumers' beliefs, attitudes, preferences, behaviour, etc. For example, a survey into advertising effectiveness might measure awareness of the brand, recall of the advertisement and knowledge about its content.

Experimental research

The aim of **experimental research** is to establish cause and effect. Experimental research involves setting up control procedures to isolate the impact of a factor (e.g. a money-off sales promotion) on a dependent variable (e.g. sales).

The key to successful experimental design is the elimination of other explanations of changes in the dependent variable. One way of doing this is to use random sampling. For example, the sales promotion might be applied in a random selection of stores, with the remaining stores selling the brand without the money-off offer. Statistical significance testing can be used to test whether differences in sales are likely to be caused by the sales promotion or are simply random variations. The effects of other influences on sales are assumed to impact randomly on both the sales promotion and the no-promotion alternatives.

The sampling process

Figure 6.5 outlines the **sampling process**. It begins by *defining the population*—that is, the group that forms the subject of study in a particular survey. The survey objective will be to provide results that are representative of this group. Sampling planners, for example, must ask questions like: 'Do we interview all people over the age of 18 or restrict it to those of the population aged 18–60?' and 'Do we interview purchasing managers in all textile companies or only those that employ more than 200 people?'

Once the population has been defined, the next step is to search for a *sampling frame*—that is, a list or other records of the chosen population from which a sample can be selected. Examples include a register of electors or the *Kompass* directory of companies. The result determines whether a random or non-random sample can be chosen. A random sample requires an accurate sampling frame; without one, the researcher is restricted to non-random methods.

FIGURE 6.5
The sampling process

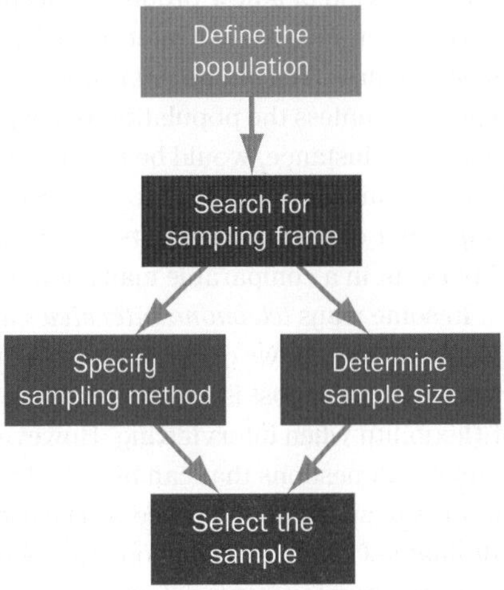

Define the population → Search for sampling frame → Specify sampling method / Determine sample size → Select the sample

Three major *sampling methods* are simple random sampling, stratified random sampling and quota sampling. It is also important to determine *sample size*.

- With simple random sampling, each individual (or company) in the sampling frame is given a number, and numbers are drawn at random (by chance) until the sample is complete. The sample is random because everyone on the list has an equal chance of selection.
- With stratified random sampling, the population is broken down into groups (e.g. by company size or industry) and a random sample is drawn (as above) for each group. This ensures that each group is represented in the sample.
- With quota sampling, a sampling frame does not exist but the percentage of the population that falls in various groupings (e.g. gender, social class, age) is known. The sample is constructed by asking interviewers to select individuals on the basis of these percentages, for example roughly 50 : 50 females to males. This is a non-random method since not everyone has an equal chance of selection, but it is much less expensive than random methods when the population is widely dispersed.
- Sample size is a further key consideration when attempting to generate a representative sample. Clearly, the larger the sample size the more likely it will represent the population. Statistical theory allows the calculation of sampling error (i.e. the error caused by not interviewing everyone in the population) for various sample sizes. In practice, the number of people interviewed is based on a balance between sampling error and cost considerations. Fortunately, sample sizes of around 1,000 (or fewer) can provide measurements that have tolerable error levels when representing populations counted in their millions.

Data-collection methods: interviews and surveys

There are two basic *methods of gathering data*: personal interviews and non-personal surveys. Personal interviews, where there is direct contact between interviewer and interviewee, may be face to face, by telephone or through video. In contrast, with non-personal surveys contact is through impersonal media—that is, the internet, mail or mobile phone. Each method has a number of different techniques which can be applied, and each has its own strengths and limitations.

Face-to-face, and video interviews

A major advantage of *face-to-face interviews* is that response rates are generally higher than for telephone interviews (Yu and Cooper, 1983). Seemingly, the personal element in the contact makes refusal less likely. This is an important factor when considering how representative of the population the sample is and when using experimental designs. Testing the effectiveness of a stimulus would normally be conducted by face-to-face interview rather than a mail survey, where high non-response rates and the lack of control over who completes the questionnaire would invalidate the results. Face-to-face interviews are more versatile than telephone.

The use of many open-ended questions can be used effectively when interviewing, although time restrictions for a telephone interview can limit their use. Probing is easier with face-to-face interviews. Two types of probes are *clarifying probes* (e.g. 'Can you explain what you mean by . . . ?'), which help the interviewer understand exactly what the interviewee is saying, and *exploratory probes*, which stimulate the interviewee to give a full answer (e.g. 'Are there any other reasons why . . . ?'). A certain degree of probing can be achieved with a telephone interview, but time pressure and the less personalized situation will inevitably limit its use. Visual aids (e.g. a drawing of a new product concept) can be used where clearly they cannot with a telephone interview.

However, face-to-face interviews have their drawbacks. They are more expensive than telephone and mail questionnaires. Telephone interviews are cheaper because the cost of contacting respondents is much less expensive, unless the population is very concentrated (face-to-face interviewing of students on a Business Studies course, for instance, would be relatively inexpensive). The presence of an interviewer can cause bias (e.g. socially desirable answers) and lead to the misreporting of sensitive information. For example, O'Dell (1962) found that only 17 per cent of respondents admitted borrowing money from a bank in a face-to-face interview compared with 42 per cent in a comparable mail survey, which gave the respondent more privacy when answering questions.

In some ways *telephone interviews* are a halfway house between face-to-face and mail surveys. Telephone interviews generally have a higher response rate than mail questionnaires, but lower than face-to-face interviews; their cost is usually less than face-to-face, but higher than for mail surveys; and they allow a degree of flexibility when interviewing. However, the use of visual aids is not possible and there are limits to the number of questions that can be asked before respondents either terminate the interview or give quick (invalid) answers to speed up the process. The use of computer-aided telephone interviewing (CATI) is common as is Automated Computer Telephone Interviewing (ACTI). Centrally located interviewers read questions from a computer monitor and input answers via the keyboard. *Routing* through the questionnaire is computer-controlled, helping the process of interviewing.

Video interviews via the web and mobile phones offer a solution to get over some of the issues of face-to-face and telephone interviews and focus groups (Mindswarms, 2015). Clients are able to set research objectives and then view the results, which can gather detailed behavioural data. Companies like Virgin America, Dell and Microsoft have used this form of interviewing to gain deep insight into their customers' needs when developing new products.

Online and mobile surveys

Digital forms of data gathering are increasingly popular and here are some compelling reasons why. Surveys represent a lower cost option than interviewing, they can be used to reach a widely dispersed population and can be delivered in a variety of ways, for example via the web and by mail and mobile phone. However, the major problem is the potential of low response rates and the accompanying danger of an unrepresentative sample.

In recent years there has been a significant shift away from mail surveys to using internet-based approaches. Digital platforms (web and mobile) are increasingly used to conduct survey research. With **digital surveys**, the questionnaire is administered by email, on a website, by registering key words, or it appears in banner advertising on search engines such as Yahoo! or Google, which drive people to the questionnaire. Mobile devices can also be used. Digital surveys have grown in popularity to such an extent that they now account for a significant proportion of all the quantitative data collected in Europe and the USA. There are now many bespoke online survey and poll companies, for example Survey monkey (http://www.surveymonkey.com), eSurveysPro (http://www.esurveyspro.com) and EZpolls (http://www.ezpolls.com), which provide survey tools and methods of analysis.

Major advantages of digital marketing research platforms are:

- flexibility of content—visual aids such as video and graphics can be used, as well as audio input
- reach—there are no geographical limitations
- speed of delivery (Gigliotti, 2011)
- automated digital data collection—data sets are readily available in digital format for analysis
- potential cost saving.

However, the more complex the survey—for example, when it includes video and interactive experiments—the higher the cost of production. So, while these digital techniques can be highly flexible, the size of the survey should be taken into consideration when evaluating the relative cost. Sampling problems are a potential disadvantage, as they can arise because of the skewed nature of internet users (if the online target populations are from younger and more affluent groups in society), although this issue is becoming less important as the global internet user population increases.

In summary, it is suggested that digital surveys are faster, easier, cheaper and better. However, research has found that the benefits do not come in equal quantities when compared with other survey tools. For example:

- Digital surveys are *faster* to distribute than mail surveys, but telephone surveys can provide the most instantaneous response.

- Digital surveys may be *easier* to compile and use, but this will be subjective as it depends on the technological literacy of those involved.
- Digital surveys may be *cheaper* in terms of sample size, as the larger the sample the greater the cost of the other methods of data collection, but there can be significant up-front costs involved in setting up a digital survey and accessing the desired target respondents.
- To be *better* than other survey tools, digital surveys need to ensure the validity of response.

An absence of accurate contact lists remains a problem when using email to survey populations. Even when lists can be found, researchers need to tread very carefully, as 'spamming'—sending junk mail—is seen as very offensive by most email users and messages may be blocked by firewalls and therefore never get to the recipient's mail box.

MARKETING IN ACTION 6.4
Mobile Ethnography Reveals Motherhood is not a Job

Mobile technology has brought innovation to ethnographic research and enables research teams to get even closer to people's lives by observing their actions in real time. For example, Mumsnet and Saatchi & Saatchi teamed up to study mothers to find out more about the roles they play in the family, the relationships they have with their children and the implications for marketing. The mobile ethnographic study was conducted over a week with a representative sample of 1,022 mothers in the UK. The aim was to gain in-depth understanding about the mother's role, and her home and personal environment.

The study revealed eight emotional roles that mothers assume when caring for their families. These roles were created from 35 emotions that were identified in the ethnographic study.

TABLE 6.1 Emotional roles adopted by mothers in their daily lives

Roles	Examples of raw emotions	Implications for the role of brands
Carer	Comforting, helpful, needed, loving, trusted	Help the mother feel great that she can be there for her children
Safe house	Safe, reliable, control, stability, strong, trusted	Help the mother be there when she's needed
Coach	Knowledgeable, experienced, impactful, important	Give support for mentoring
Fan	Proud, inspired, amazed	Help the mother have more time to enjoy her children's achievements
Partner in crime	Playful, creative, entertained	Focus on opportunities to create fun
Rule breaker	Rebellious, fun, silly	Give the mother permission to break her rules
Friend	Understanding, accepted, admired, cool	Focus on the balance between parent and friend
Hero	Encouraging, successful, impactful, confident	Help the role the mother wants for herself and her family

The marketing implications for the research are that, if brands find ways to enable mothers to spend more time with their families, this is seen as an important potential benefit. Another finding from the study is that mothers would like to spend more time having fun with their children rather than just being providers of entertainment. While mothers are primary carers in the family unit, with 58 per cent saying they take on the majority of the parenting role, they would like more time to 'break the rules' and have the freedom to let go and have fun. Further research has revealed that price cutting can increase engagement with brands. But mums are more likely to return if there is an element of gamification of their brand experiences, which works by capturing the shoppers' attention.

Based on: Vince (2015); Saatchi & Saatchi (2015); Burrows (2014)

A possible way to reap the benefits and counter the problems associated with digital surveys is to use a mixed-method approach that allows for different modes of data collection to be used to address validity issues. The use of two methods will, however, slow the survey process and increase the costs, but it should ensure greater validity in the findings, which is one of the fundamentals when using survey data to make strategic and tactical marketing decisions (Gigliotti, 2011). Read Marketing in Action 6.4 to discover how digital mobile ethnography has been used to find out the emotional roles that mothers play in family lives.

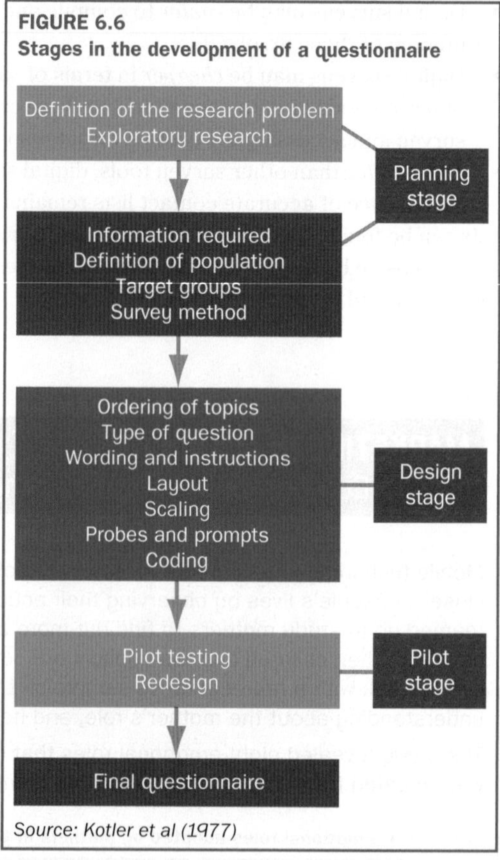

FIGURE 6.6
Stages in the development of a questionnaire

Source: Kotler et al (1977)

Questionnaire design

Three conditions are necessary to get a true response to a question.

1 Respondents must *understand* the question.
2 Respondents must be *able to provide* the information.
3 Respondents must be *willing to answer.*

Researchers must remember these conditions when designing questionnaires. Questions need to be phrased in language the respondent understands and is able to interpret. Equally, researchers must not ask about issues that respondents cannot remember or that are outside their experience. For example, it would be invalid to ask about attitudes towards a brand of which the respondent is unaware. Finally, researchers need to consider the best way to elicit sensitive or personal information. As we have already seen, willingness to provide such information depends on the survey method employed.

Figure 6.6 shows the three stages in the development of the questionnaire: planning, design and pilot.

The *planning stage* involves the types of decision discussed so far in this chapter. It provides a firm foundation for designing a questionnaire that provides relevant information for the marketing problem that is being addressed.

The *design stage* involves a number of interrelated issues:

1 *Ordering of topics*: an effective questionnaire has a logical flow. It is sensible to start with easy-to-answer questions. This helps to build the confidence of respondents and allows them to relax. Respondents are often anxious at the beginning of an interview, concerned that they might show their ignorance. Other rules of thumb are simply common sense: for example, it would be logical to ask awareness questions before attitude measurement questions, and not vice versa. Unaided awareness questions must be asked before aided ones. Classificatory questions that ask for personal information such as age and occupation are usually asked last.
2 *Types of question*: closed questions specify the range of answers that will be recorded. If there are only two possible answers (e.g. 'Did you visit a cinema within the last seven days?' YES/NO) the question is *dichotomous* (either/or). If there are more than two possible answers, then the question is *multiple choice* (e.g. 'Which, if any, of the following cinemas have you visited within the last seven days?' Odeon, Vue, Cineworld, None). *Open-ended questions* allow respondents to answer the question in their own words (e.g. 'What did you like about the cinema you visited?'). The interviewer then writes the answer in a space on the questionnaire.
3 *Wording and instructions*: great care needs to be taken in the wording of questions. Questionnaire designers need to guard against ambiguity, leading questions, asking two questions in one and using unfamiliar words. Table 6.2 gives some examples of poorly worded questions and suggests remedies. Instructions should be printed in capital letters or underlined so that they are easily distinguishable from questions.
4 *Layout*: the questionnaire should not appear cluttered. In mail questionnaires, it is a mistake to squeeze too many questions onto one page so that the questionnaire length (in pages) is shortened. Response is more likely to be lower if the questionnaire appears heavy than if its page length is extended (Jobber, 1985).

TABLE 6.2 Poorly worded questions and how to avoid them

Question	Problem and solution
What type of wine do you prefer?	'Type' is ambiguous; respondents could say 'French', 'red', 'claret', depending on their interpretation. Showing the respondent a list and asking 'from this list . . .' would avoid the problem.
Do you think that prices are cheaper at Asda than at Aldi?	Leading question favouring Asda; a better question would be 'Do you think that prices at Asda are higher, lower or about the same as at Aldi?' Names should be reversed for half of the sample.
Which is more powerful and kind to your hands: Ariel or Bold?	Two questions in one: Ariel may be more powerful, but Bold may be kinder to the hands. Ask the two questions separately.
Do you find it paradoxical that X lasts longer and yet is cheaper than Y?	Unfamiliar word: a study has shown that less than a quarter of the population understand such words as 'paradoxical', 'chronological' or 'facility'. Test understanding before use.

5 *Scaling*: careful exploratory research may allow attitudes and beliefs to be measured by means of scales. Respondents are given lists of statements (e.g. 'My company's marketing information system allows me to make better decisions') followed by a choice of five positions on a scale ranging from 'strongly agree' to 'strongly disagree'. Furthermore, computer advances are enabling the measurement of emotions using avatars (pictorial representations of people).

6 *Probes and prompts*: probes seek to explore or clarify what a respondent has said. Following a question about awareness of brand names, the *exploratory probe* 'Any others?' would seek to identify further names. Sometimes respondents use vague words or phrases like, 'I like going on holiday because it is nice.' A *clarifying probe* such as, 'In what way is it nice?' would seek a more meaningful response. *Prompts*, on the other hand, aid responses to a question. For example, in an aided-recall question, a list of brand names would be provided for the respondent.

7 *Coding*: by using closed questions the interviewer merely has to ring the code number next to the respondent's choice of answer. In computer-assisted telephone interviewing, and with the increasing use of laptop computers for face-to-face interviewing, the appropriate code number can be keyed directly into the computer's memory. Such questionnaires are *pre-coded*, making the process of interviewing and data analysis much simpler. Open-ended questions, however, require the interviewer to write down the answer verbatim. This necessitates *post-coding*, whereby answers are categorized after the interview. This can be a time-consuming and laborious task.

Once the preliminary questionnaire has been designed, it should be piloted with a representative sub-sample to test for faults. The *pilot stage* is not the same as exploratory research. Exploratory research helps to decide upon the research design, whereas piloting tests the questionnaire design and helps to estimate costs. Face-to-face piloting, where respondents are asked to answer questions and comment on any problems concerning a questionnaire read out by an interviewer, is preferable to impersonal piloting, where the questionnaire is given to respondents for self-completion and they are asked to write down any problems found (Reynolds and Diamantopoulos, 1998). If desired, several kinds of question on the same topic can be asked in order to assess the effects of the wording on respondents (Sigman, 2001). Once the pilot work proves satisfactory, the final questionnaire can be administered to the chosen sample.

Digital technology is now widely used in the research process but, as discussed at the beginning of the chapter, the difference is that big data is largely collected automatically and used to provide companies with business intelligence that is informing marketing decision-making online. A widely used term is 'web analytics', and this refers to measurement and analysis of how a website is performing in terms of visitor numbers, unique visitors, keyword search terms used to find a site, areas of the site most frequently visited, time spent on the site, responses to promotions and, for online retailers, the proportion of visitors proceeding to the checkout (Fahy and Jobber, 2015). Further discussion of website analysis is provided in Chapter 16. On the web, Google has led the way in providing such data and information about how the web is used. Google Analytics is a suite of marketing research solutions that help companies track customer engagement and improve site visits. Read Mini Case 6.1 to find out more about how analytics can help and how data capture is changing.

MINI CASE 6.1
Does Google Track our Every Move?

Website analysis enables the assessment of site performance and helps to identify key areas for improvement, such as web pages on a site that are rarely visited or features on the home page that are rarely clicked on. In other words, marketing managers can summarize the actions of visitors to their websites by statistically analysing users' data. Google Analytics provides a range of statistics such as bounce rates, unique visitors, page views and average time a user spends on a particular site.

Understanding website performance can be important for customer relationship management strategies by helping to identify areas for improvement that might increase customer acquisition, conversion, retention and enjoyment during website visits. For example, a website might include personalized recommendations for loyal customers or introduce interactive tools to help with product selection.

Sophisticated analytical tools and software applications mean that all eyes are on the consumer, but marketing managers should be aware that consumers are becoming increasingly unwilling to hand over their personal data, especially online. In the past, retailers and consumer-facing brand websites have been able to entice consumers into signing up to newsletters, surveys and other data capture devices by offering a small incentive such as discount vouchers for handing over their personal details. However, some consumers are increasingly reluctant to knowingly hand over personal information. In fact, research has found that consumers now expect more free information from brand websites than ever before. Sectors yet to experience this trend are insurance, charities and some alcoholic drink brands, where consumers are signing up and handing over personal details in record numbers.

Paradoxically, it is perhaps the increase in our ability to analyse data and make more meaningful interpretations that is making collecting data from some consumers harder. Part of the problem is that consumers are concerned about online security and identity fraud. Google is doing little to alleviate these fears as it integrates more data-collection methods into its search engine and links together with social media, encouraging consumers to unwittingly divulge more and more personal details. This means that consumer profiles can become very transparent and this information can be used for marketing initiatives. For instance, before you receive your next email marketing message, the time of day you are most likely to open and respond to the message will have been analysed, the contents of the mailing may have been personalized to suit your preferences, and sophisticated software will be ready to monitor your next move. If you access the web using a smart phone, someone somewhere may have read your electronic diary and know when you are free next week and already be planning which marketing initiatives you are going to receive. As one of the internet giants, Google provides a very efficient information search engine for 90 per cent of users in Europe. Google has also been rebuked by the European Commissioner for Justice over what are seen as weak protection policies for personal data. EU member states were concerned because Google has made changes that mean it could pool data about registered users and how they use the web, make video searches, find map directions and browse the web, and which adverts they click. This pooling of data means that no stone is left unturned and Google can capture data on every aspect of an individual's life and build personalized profiles, which it can then use for its lucrative Adwords pay-for-search advertising. The EU has responded with its General Data Protection (GDPR) legislation, designed to protect privacy and make firms like Amazon, Google, Facebook, or indeed any firms that gather personal data, conform to new and more restrictive methods of storing and using personal data. GDPR replaces older data protection legislation which has become outdated and it restricts how personal data is collected, stored and used.

The Market Research Society's (MRS's) code of conduct advocates maintaining anonymity for any opinions deduced from analysing online content, and has guidance on applying GDPR (https://www.mrs.org.uk/standards/gdpr-faq).

Questions:

1 Give an example of an online marketing campaign that targets consumers.
2 Suggest the broad types of consumer data that a digital marketer might need to carry out the campaign.
3 Carry out desk research to find out which of the data suggested in your answer to Q2 can be legally stored under GDPR legislation.

Based on: Chaffey and Ellis-Chadwick (2019); Cowlett (2011); Arthur (2012); Costa (2011); EUGDPR (2018); MRS (2018)

Report writing, presentation and visualization

The key elements in a research report are:

1 title page
2 list of contents
3 preface (outline of agreed brief, statement of objectives, scope and methods of research)
4 summary of conclusions and recommendations
5 previous related research (how previous research has had a bearing on this research)
6 research method
7 research findings
8 conclusions
9 appendices.

Sections 1–4 provide a concise description of the nature and outcomes of the research for busy managers. Sections 5–9 provide the level of detail necessary if any particular issue (e.g. the basis of a finding or the analytical technique used) needs checking. The report should be written in language the reader will understand; jargon should be avoided.

Visualisation Software packages such as PowerPoint considerably ease the production of pie charts, histograms, graphs, and so on, for use in the report or for presentational purposes (such as the production of acetates for overhead projection). Clients are increasingly asking for live discussions in which ideas are thought about and the implications for marketing decisions discussed. Some agencies recommend the use of workshops, following the presentation of results, to encourage this kind of discussion (Dye, 2008). See Exhibit 6.2.

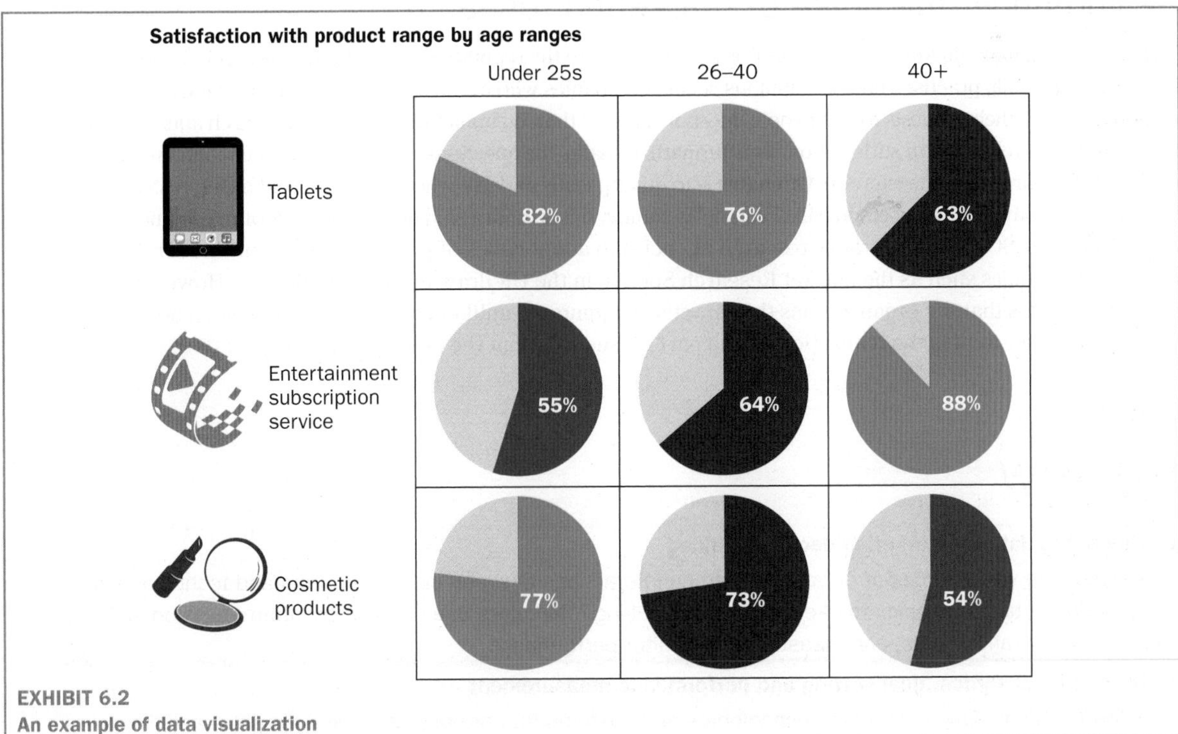

EXHIBIT 6.2
An example of data visualization

Ethical Issues in Marketing Analytics

Despite these good intentions of benefiting customers and sellers, there are three ethical concerns about marketing research, which are discussed below.

Intrusion of privacy

Many consumers recognize the positive role that marketing research plays in the provision of goods and services, but some resent the intrusive nature of marketing research surveys. Most consumer surveys ask for classificatory data such as age, occupation and income. While most surveys ask respondents to indicate an age and income band rather than requesting specific figures, some people feel that this is an intrusion of privacy. Other people object to receiving unsolicited telephone calls or mail surveys, dislike being stopped in the street to be asked to complete a face-to-face survey, and resent unsolicited online surveys and email questionnaires.

The right of individuals to privacy is incorporated in the guidelines of many research associations. For example, a code of conduct of the European Society for Opinion and Marketing Research (ESOMAR, 2018) states that 'No information which could be used to identify informants, either directly or indirectly, shall be revealed other than to research personnel within the researchers' own organization who require this knowledge for the administration and checking of interviews and data processing' (Schlegelmilch, 1998). Under no circumstances should the information from a survey combined with the address/telephone number of the respondent be supplied to a salesperson.

Misuse of market research findings

When market research findings are to be used in an advertising campaign or as part of a sales pitch, the results could be manipulated to show a bias in favour of the desired outcome. Respondents could be chosen who are more likely to give a favourable response. For example, a study comparing a domestic versus foreign brand of car could be biased by only choosing people that own domestic-made cars.

Another potential source of bias in the use of marketing research findings is where the client explicitly or implicitly communicates to the researcher the preferred research result. Most market researchers, however, accept the need for objective studies where there is room for more than one interpretation of study findings.

In the long term, it is in everyone's interest to produce *accurate* findings, as these are likely to be used for marketing planning decision-making. Using misinformation can prove to be very risky.

Selling under the guise of marketing research

This practice, commonly known as 'sugging', is a real danger to the reputation of marketing research. Despite the fact that it is usually practised by unscrupulous selling companies who use marketing research as a means of gaining compliance with their requests to ask people questions, rather than by bona fide marketing research agencies, the marketing research industry suffers from its aftermath. Usually, the questions begin innocently enough but quickly move on to the real purpose of the exercise. Often this is to qualify leads and ask whether they would be interested in buying the product or having a salesperson call. 'Fruging' is similar, but is fundraising under the *cover* of marketing research.

In Europe, ESOMAR encourages research agencies to adopt codes of practice to prevent this sort of behaviour, and national bodies such as the Market Research Society in the UK draw up strict guidelines. However, the problem remains that the organizations that practise sugging are unlikely to be members of such bodies. The ultimate deterrent is the realization on the part of 'suggers' that the method is no longer effective.

Review

1 Use of big data for marketing decision-making

- Access to vast sources of data generated by interactions between individual, firms and technology is fundamentally reshaping marketing decision-making. Marketers use big data to inform decision-making, set organization goals, and measure and monitor performance.

2 Marketing analytics, goal setting and performance measurement

- Marketing analytics are tools, technologies and systems that are used to reveal insights, and they play a significant role in measuring performance and demonstrating how marketing activities translate into revenue.

- Previously, marketing information systems were a means of gathering, storing, analysing and distributing information across organizations. Use of such systems is now widespread and more sophisticated than in the past.
  - Planning analytics and performance measurement requires marketeers to consider four key questions:
  - What do we want to achieve?
  - What is happening?
  - Why (is it happening)?
  - What actions should we take to ensure correction (if required) and control?

3 Identify and discuss different types of data sources

- Data is the most basic form of knowledge, which become meaningful when translated into information. Information is a combination of data that provides decision-relevant knowledge. Data can be found in different forms within a firm and beyond: internal and continuous data; internal ad-hoc data; data generated from environmental scanning; market research data.

4 Scope of market and marketing research

- Market research and marketing research are two terms used interchangeably. The former leans towards looking at trends in marketing activities of consumers, firms and society, which have implications for practical and commercial marketing activities. Marketing research has a wider and more academic scope.

5 The distinguishing features between qualitative and quantitative research

- Qualitative research usually precedes quantitative research. Qualitative research can provide rich, in-depth insights into consumer behaviour, whereas the purpose of quantitative research tends to be to provide information that can be generalized across the study population.

6 Stages in the marketing research process

- The stages in the marketing research process are research planning (research brief and proposal), exploratory research (secondary research, qualitative research, consultation with experts and observation), the main (quantitative) data-collection stage (descriptive and experimental research, sampling, survey method, questionnaire design), data analysis and interpretation, and report writing and presentation.

7 The nature and role of exploratory research

- Exploratory research involves the preliminary exploration of a research area prior to the quantitative data-collection stage. Its major purpose is to avoid the sins of omission and admission. By providing an understanding of the people who are to be interviewed later, the quantitative survey is more likely to collect valid and reliable information.
- Exploratory research comprises secondary research, qualitative research, consultation with experts and observation.

8 How to prepare a research brief and proposal

- A research brief should explain the marketing problem and outline the research objectives. Other useful information is background information, possible sources of information, the proposed scale of the project and a timetable.
- A research proposal should provide a statement of objectives, what will be done (research design), a timetable and costs.

9 Quantitative research design decisions: sampling, survey method and questionnaire design issues

- Sampling decisions cover who and how many people to interview. The stages are population definition, sampling frame search, sampling method specification, sample size determination and sample selection.
- Survey method decisions relate to how to interview people. The options are face-to-face, by telephone or mail, and over the internet.
- Questionnaire design decisions cover what questions to ask. Questionnaires should be planned, designed and piloted before being administered to the main sample.

10 Analysis and interpretation of data

- Qualitative and quantitative analysis can be facilitated by using specialist software packages.
- Care should be taken when interpreting marketing research results. One common failing is inferring cause and effect when only association has been established.

11 Report writing and presentation

- The contents of a marketing research report should be title page, list of contents, preface, summary, previous related research, research method, research findings, conclusions and appendices.
- Software packages such as PowerPoint can be used to make professional presentations.
- *Research means*: focus groups or depth interviews versus structured questionnaires.
- *Operation*: high flexibility in data collection versus low flexibility in data collection.
- *Data capture*: audio recording requiring post-coding versus pre-coded response categories on a structured questionnaire.
- *Sampling*: small samples versus large samples.
- *Analysis*: content analysis of respondent statements from audio recording versus statistical analysis of pre-coded responses from a structured questionnaire.
- *Reporting*: underlying themes illustrated by quotes from respondents and summary statements versus statistical.

12 Ethical issues in marketing research

- These are potential problems relating to intrusions on privacy, misuse of marketing research findings and selling under the guise of marketing research.

Key Terms

ad-hoc research a research project that focuses on a specific problem, collecting data at one point in time with one sample of respondents

business intelligence the actionable knowledge produced by the analysis of 'big data' (very large data sets)

consumer panel household consumers who provide information on their purchases over time

continuous research repeated interviewing of the same sample of people

data the most basic form of knowledge, the result of observations

descriptive research research undertaken to describe customers' beliefs, attitudes, preferences and behaviour

digital surveys various methods of gathering qualitative (and in some cases quantitative) data using email or web-based surveys

ethnography a form of qualitative research which involves detailed and prolonged observation of consumers in the situations that inform their buying behaviour

experimental research research undertaken in order to establish cause and effect

exploratory research the preliminary exploration of a research area prior to the main data-collection stage

focus group a group normally of 6–12 consumers brought together for a discussion focusing on an aspect of a company's marketing

in-depth interviews the interviewing of consumers individually for perhaps one or two hours, with the aim of understanding their attitudes, values, behaviour and/or beliefs

information combinations of data that provide decision-relevant knowledge

marketing information system a system in which marketing information is formally gathered, stored, analysed and distributed to managers in accordance with their informational needs on a regular, planned basis

marketing research the gathering of data and information on the market and consumer reactions to product, pricing, promotional and distribution decisions

omnibus survey a regular survey, usually operated by a marketing research specialist company, which asks questions of respondents for several clients on the same questionnaire

qualitative research exploratory research that aims to understand consumers' attitudes, values, behaviour and beliefs

quantitative research a structured study of small or large samples using a predetermined list of questions or criteria

research brief a written document stating the client's requirements

research proposal a document defining what the marketing research agency promises to do for its client and how much it will cost

retail audit a type of continuous research tracking the sales of products through retail outlets

sampling process a term used in research to denote the selection of a sub-set of the total population in order to interview them

secondary research data that have already been collected by another researcher for another purpose

Study Questions

1. **Explain how market research practices are being re-shaped by digital technology.**
2. **What is big data and how is it used to help companies make marketing decisions?**
3. **Discuss how marketing analytics can help to inform goal setting and performance measurement.**
4. **Discuss the difference between market research and marketing research.**
5. **Discuss when you would use qualitative research and when you would use quantitative research.**
6. **What are secondary and primary data? Why should secondary data be collected before primary data?**
7. **What is the difference between a research brief and a proposal? What advice would you give a marketing research agency when making a research proposal?**
8. **'Digital survey techniques offer the best solution for gathering data.' Discuss this statement.**
9. **Discuss the problems facing market research as a method of generating information about consumer behaviour.**
10. **Why are marketing research reports more likely to be used if they conform to the prior beliefs of the client? Does this raise any ethical questions regarding the interpretation and presentation of findings?**

Recommended Reading

Marketing decision-making increasingly relies on big data. Read the following to discover how to manage big data, what consumer behaviour insights can be gained from big data and how UK firms are creating competitive advantage using marketing analytics.

Cao, G., Duan, Y. and El Banna, A. (2018), A dynamic capability view of marketing analytics: Evidence from UK firms, Industrial marketing management https://www.sciencedirect.com/science/article/pii/S0019850117306892 (accessed September 2018).

Hofacker, C.F., Malthouse, E.C. and Sultan, F. (2016), Big Data and consumer behavior: imminent opportunities, *Journal of Consumer Marketing*, 33(2), 89–97, https://doi.org/10.1108/JCM-04-2015-1399.

McFee, A. and Brynjolfsson, E. (2012), Big data: The management revolution, *Harvard Business Review* 90(10), 60–8.

References

Arthur, C. (2012), Search giant 'sneaking' citizens' privacy away warns EU justice chief, *The Guardian*, 2 March, 18–19.

BBC (2015), News Technology, 9 February http://www.bbc.co.uk/news/technology-31296188 (accessed September 2018).

Beaconstat (2018), What is proximity marketing and how does it work? https://www.beaconstac.com/proximity-marketing (accessed September 2018).

Burrows, D. (2014), How to use ethnography for in-depth consumer insight, *Marketing Week*, 9 May https://www.marketingweek.com/2014/05/09/how-to-use-ethnography-for-in-depth-consumer-insight (accessed 9 June 2015).

Chaffey, D. and Ellis-Chadwick, F.E. (2019), *Digital Marketing: Strategy, Implementation and Practice*, 7th edn., Harlow: Pearson.

Chaffey (2000), Achieving Internet Marketing Success, *The Marketing Review*, 1 (1), 35–60.
Clegg, A. (2001), Policy and Opinion, *Marketing Week*, 27 September, 63–5.
Costa, M. (2011), All roads to improvement start at insight, *Marketing Week*, 19 May, 31.
Cowlett, M. (2011), A Social Insight, Marketing, 31–3.
Crouch, S. and Housden, M. (2003), *Marketing Research for Managers*, Oxford: Butterworth-Heinemann, 253.
Daniels, E., Wilson, H. and McDonald, M. (2003), Towards a map of marketing information systems: an inductive study, *European Journal of Marketing* 37(5/6), 821–47.
DFDS (2018), Freight Ferry Alerts App https://www.dfds.com/en-gb/about/media/news/dfds-releases-freight-ferry-alerts-app (accessed August 2018).
Denzin, N.K. and Lincoln, Y.S. (eds) (2000), *The Handbook of Qualitative Research*, 2nd edn., Thousand Oaks CA: Sage Publications, 11.
Dye, P. (2008), Share The Knowledge, *Marketing*, 19 March, 33–34.
Erevelles, S., Fukawa, N. and Swayne, L. (2016), Big Data consumer analytics and the transformation of marketing, *Journal of Business Research*, 69(2) 897–904.
ESOMAR (2005), Industry Study on 2004, ESOMAR World Research Report.
ESOMAR (2018), Market Research Explained, ESOMAR, 8 March. http://www.esomar.org/knowledge-and-standards/market-research-explained.php (accessed August 2018).
EUGDPR (2018), https://www.eugdpr.org/.
Fahy, J. and Jobber, D. (2015), *Foundations of Marketing*, Maidenhead: McGraw-Hill Education.
Flack, J. (2002), Not So Honest Joe, *Marketing Week*, 26 September, 43.
Fulgoni, G. (2013), Big Data: Friend or Foe of Digital Advertising? *Journal of Advertising Research*, 1 December.
Gigliotti, L.M. (2011), Comparison of an Internet Versus Mail Survey: A Case Study, *Human Dimensions of Wildlife* 16(1), 55–62.
GlaxoSmithKline plc (2012), http://www.gsk.com (accessed September 2018).
Hazen, B., Boone, C., Ezell, J., Skipper, J. (2016), Big Data and predicative analytics for supply chain sustainability, *Computers and Industrial Engineering*, 101 (C) 592–8.
Hemsley, S. (2011), Embracing the elephant in the room, *Marketing Week*, October, 39–43.
Jain, S.C. and Haley, G.T. (2009), *Marketing: Planning and Strategy*, USA: South Western Publishing.
Jobber, D. (1985), Questionnaire Design and Mail Survey Response Rates, *European Research* 13(3), 124–9.
Jobber, D. and Rainbow, C. (1977), A Study of the Development and Implementation of Marketing Information Systems in British Industry, *Journal of the Marketing Research Society* 19(3), 104–11.
Kerschberg, B. (2014), How Big Data, Business Intelligence and Analytics Are Fuelling Mobile Application Development, *Forbes*, 17 December http://www.forbes.com/sites/benkerschberg/2014/12/17/how-big-data-business-intelligence-and-analytics-are-fueling-mobile-application-development (retrieved 9 June 2015).
Kotler, P., Gregor, W. and Rodgers, W. (1977), The Marketing Audit Comes of Age, *Sloan Management Review*, Winter, 25–42.
Leonard, J (2018) GSK's chief data officer reveals how machine learning has been used to speed up drug discovery, Computing 2nd March 2018 https://www.computing.co.uk/ctg/interview/3027675/interview-gsks-chief-data-officer-on-machine-learning-to-speed-up-drug-discovery-and-changes-in-the-cdo-role (accessed August 2018).
Manning, J. (2011), Online Research insights, *The Marketer*, June, 42–3.
Market Research Society (MRS, 2018), https://www.mrs.org.uk/standards/gdpr-faq (accessed September 2018).
Marr, B. (2018), How much data do we create every day? The mind-blowing stats everyone should read, *Forbes*, 21 May https://www.forbes.com/sites/bernardmarr/2018/05/21/how-much-data-do-we-create-every-day-the-mind-blowing-stats-everyone-should-read.
Mindswarms (2015), How our mobile video Survey works, Mindswarms, 20 May https://www.mindswarms.com/for-researchers/how-mobile-video-surveys-work (accessed September 2018).
Mobile Marketing (2014), Making Sense: watch Nodes Making sense of Proximity Marketing, *Mobile Marketing Magazine*, 23 July http://mobilemarketingmagazine.com/tag/making-sense.
Moutinho, L. and Evans, M. (1992), *Applied Marketing Research*, Wokingham: Addison-Wesley, 5.
Muller, O., Junglas, I., vom Brocke, J. and Debotoli, S. (2017), Utilising big data analytics for information systems research: challenges, promises and guidelines, *European Journal of Information Systems*, 25(4) 289–302.
Nodes (2015), Voucher and proximity marketing http://www.nodesagency.com/cases (accessed June 2015).
O'Dell, W.F. (1962), Personal Interviews or Mail Panels, *Journal of Marketing* 26, 34–9.
Pagliery, J. (2015), 'Super cookies' track you, even in privacy mode, CNN Money, 9 January http://money.cnn.com/2015/01/09/technology/security/super-cookies (accessed September 2018).
Peter, J.P., Olson, J.C. and Grunert, K.G. (1999), *Consumer Behaviour and Marketing Strategy*, Maidenhead: McGraw-Hill.
Poynter, R., Williams, N. and York, S. (2014), *Handbook of Mobile Market Research*, ESOMAR. doi:978-1-118-93562-0 (accessed September 2018).
Reynolds, N. and Diamantopoulos, A. (1998), The Effect of Pretest Method on Error Detection Rates: Experimental Evidence, *European Journal of Marketing* 32(5/6), 480–98.
Roche Diagnostic (2018), About Roche Diagnostics https://www.roche.com/about/business/diagnostics/about-diagnostics.htm (accessed September 2018).
Saatchi & Saatchi (2015), Less of a housekeeper, more of a rule breaker http://saatchi.co.uk/en-gb/news/less-of-a-house-keeper-more-of-a-rule-breaker (accessed June 2015).
Salvador, A. and Ikeda, A. (2014), Big Data Usage in the Marketing Information System, *Journal of Data Analysis and Information Processing* 2, 77–85 doi:http://dx.doi.org/10.4236/jdaip.2014.23010.
Schlegelmilch, B. (1998), *Marketing Ethics: An International Perspective*, London: International Thomson Business Press.
Sigman, A. (2001), The Lie Detectors, *Campaign*, 15 June, 29.
Tedlock, B. (2000), Ethnography and ethnographic representation, in *The Handbook of Qualitative Research*, Denzin, N.K. and Lincoln, Y.S. (eds), 2nd edn., Thousand Oaks CA: Sage Publications, 455–86.
Truste (2015), Understanding Online Behavioral Advertising (OBA), Truste, 6 March http://www.truste.com/consumer-privacy/about-oba Viking Direct, http://www.viking-direct.co.uk/specialLinks.do;jsessionid=0000iLL4HvfFivp2SWXHkkxKk2P:130mjq8ku? ID=rb_company_info (accessed August 2018).
Viking Direct (2018), About Viking direct www.viking-direct.co.uk.
Vince, L. (2015), Motherhood is not a job, London: Saatchi & Saatchi London http://saatchi.co.uk/uploads/142676674036405/original.pdf (accessed 6 June 2015).
Weintraub, A. (2014), Big Pharma Opens Up Its Big Data, MIT Technology Review, 21 July http://www.technologyreview.com/news/529046/big-pharma-opens-up-its-big-data (accessed September 2018).
Wright, L.T. and Crimp, M. (2003), *The Marketing Research Process*, London: Prentice-Hall.
Yu, J. and Cooper, H. (1983), A Quantitative Review of Research Design Effects on Response Rates to Questionnaires, *Journal of Marketing Research* 20, February, 156–64.

CASE 11

Accelerating Marketing Research

How Harley-Davidson is using Artificial Intelligence to Drive Sales

Introduction

Harley-Davidson motor company was founded in 1903 by William Harley and Arthur Davidson with its headquarters in Milwaukee, Wisconsin. The company quickly expanded to become a global success in the heavy-weight motorcycles segment. The distinct and innovative design helped the company make Harley motorcycles popular across the world. Today it has manufacturing facilities in Wisconsin, Pennsylvania and Missouri, and subsidiaries in Germany, the UK, Benelux, France and Japan. Harley-Davidson has been singled out as one of the strongest brand names—in an exclusive circle of cult brands, including Apple and Mini. In 2018, the company boasted a top-80 global brand valued at $5.6 billion (Forbes, 2017). Although the last decade has been turbulent, a key driver of the company's recent success is their usage of data analytics and artificial intelligence (AI) to refocus their marketing strategy.

Challenges for Harley-Davidson

Dwindling market share: despite a promising start, the road to success wasn't always straight for Harley as they faced significant challenges in the global market. US motorcycle sales peaked at over 1.1 million in 2005, then plummeted during the global recession, leaving Harley-Davidson facing extinction. The brand value dropped 43 per cent in 2009, with a 66 per cent drop in company profits in 2008 (Penhollow, 2014). In 2010, Harley-Davidson shed hundreds of jobs in the USA and saw a decline in shipments worldwide (Forbes, 2017).

Loss of market positioning: whilst Harley bikes were hugely popular with the Baby Boomer generation, this segment was now aging and Harley was struggling to replenish its core customer base. The brand had also become associated with biker gangs, notably the Hells Angels, and was perceived as old-fashioned and outdated. Younger generations were reluctant to embrace the brand, as 'millennials' were typically more price-conscious, risk averse and tended to hold off on making discretionary expenditures (Hanbury, 2017). Finally, Harley-Davidson was characterised as having a more 'male' identity, with the brand selling to a predominately male, white middle-class market (Khulbe, 2016).

Intense competition: in Europe, despite having a typical market share of 6–12 per cent in the past few years, Harley continued to trail behind its main competitors (BMW, Triumph, Yamaha, Suzuki, Honda and Kawasaki) (The Statistics Portal, 2017). These competitors focus their efforts on producing quality motorcycles that are affordable to attract a wider customer base. Honda, Suzuki, Yamaha and Kawasaki are sportier bikes with relatively lower prices compared with Harleys (Khulbe, 2016).

So, the challenges for Harley-Davidson were many, not least to fend off competition and grow their share of a slowing market. The company was forced to take a hard look at every facet of its marketing strategy. A radical plan for recovery and growth was introduced. Central to this plan was Harley's AI-driven market analytics and intelligence. Harley needed to gain insights into the factors responsible for attracting consumers to buy motorcycles as well as influences on consumer satisfaction and dissatisfaction. The company wanted to know about the attitudes of young adults (aged 18 to 34), especially women.

»

»

It aimed to discover the features consumers find most useful when buying a motorcycle and whether these features vary depending on their age, gender and global location. The company needed to learn how the Harley-Davidson brand was positioned in the minds of its customers compared with its competitors.

AI-driven Market Intelligence

Harley-Davidson knew that, to increase their market share, they had to reach as many people as possible. In 2016, Harley-Davidson deployed an artificial intelligence system, 'Albert', that could discover trending behaviour at a pace that only a machine can handle. Albert has several distinct beneficial features. First, Albert can identify and automatically target new audiences based on online social behaviours. Using existing customer data, Albert can detect the characteristics of existing customers and build an online profile for 'lookalike customers' who have similar demographic and behavioural profiles. After the AI system identifies the lookalikes and their behavioural patterns, it learns what these individuals do and don't respond to, enabling the company to tailor interactions. Albert also identifies customers who spend one to two minutes on the Harley website, and begins targeting them and customising responses, knowing that they're engaged prospects. It can also disregard visitors who leave the site within 15 seconds because that indicates a lack of interest in the product.

In addition, Albert provides feedback about when and where Harley should display content on their website or banner ads and how that content is performing (Jacobi, 2016). For example, Albert identified that, by changing wording used in advertising content, sales leads would increase—telling potential customers to 'call now' rather than 'buy now' created a substantial sales increase. This was achieved by running test campaigns and analysing the outcomes. In addition to analysing the performance of word combinations, Albert identified the most compelling colour combinations to be used for particular market segments. This allows Harley to identify the highest impact combinations of creative design and marketing messages. It also enables them to automatically identify high performance advertisements and discontinue poor performers. Critically, Albert enables Harley to dynamically update its pricing and budget allocation across all digital channels, enabling 'on the fly' marketing mix modelling (Albert.ai, 2017).

Harley leverages its virtual community 'HOG' (Harley Owners Group) to gather substantial data to feed its AI system. Although HOG was born in 1983 as a way for the brand's highly passionate consumers to connect as a group, Harley harnesses the power of Web 2.0 technology to expand the global reach of the community. The virtual community provides the firm with access to invaluable information about members' behaviours and lifestyles. It also provides opportunities for Harley-Davidson to tailor offerings to the specific needs of their customers.

The Results

To date, Harley's AI-assisted marketing research uncovered several critical results. Findings showed that under 35s, particularly in Europe, liked less-chromed, lighter, faster and smaller bikes. As a result, the company added a product line 'Dark Custom', including the 1200CX Roadster (Harley-Davidson, 2016). Company officials said at its launch in 2016 that the new model's design was optimal for more challenging European driving conditions. Additionally, in 2020, based on an identified market-desire for cleaner, more efficient vehicles which emulate the sound and feel of riding a Harley, Harley-Davidson will launch its first electric motorcycle (Bright, 2018). The company also hopes to take advantage of the customization craze, which it has largely ceded to third-party vendors.

Findings of the work with Albert revealed that, in order to appeal to the female market, the brand had to diversify its offerings. Although the brand was already positioned as a 'lifestyle brand', research showed that Harley must emphasize its brand extensions such as clothing, accessories and perfumes (for example, L'Oréal licensed the name Harley-Davidson for a line of perfumes and colognes). The company also added Harley-Davidson branded gear and apparel to its product line specifically designed for women (Thompson, 2017).

Additionally, research showed a requirement from the HOG community for the provision of specialized services and products. These include official Harley-Davidson insurance, financial services, Harley-Davidson apparel, touring guides and member recognition rewards (Harley-Davidson, 2016).

Three months after introducing Albert, daily website visits increased by 566 per cent and sales leads increased by 2,930 per cent (50 per cent were lookalikes) (Brown, 2016). Today, the company credits 40 per cent of motorcycle sales to Albert. Based on the success of this AI deployment, multiple Harley outlets are rolling out AI solutions to drive business (Vankar, 2017).

Continuing the Journey

In the future, Harley will continue to listen to the market and embrace change through the implementation of new techniques to capture consumer data. In another AI-driven insightful move, during the summer of 2018, the company ran its first 12-week #FindYourFreedom internship, which allowed students to ride Harleys across the USA and get paid to explore and discover 'motorcycle culture' (Harley-Davidson, 2016). Trainees learned how to ride a motorcycle and, in collaboration with Harley-Davidson's marketing team, they helped create content for the company's social media accounts.

Recently, the company launched a new social media platform, 'All for Freedom, Freedom for All,' as part of their 10-year strategy to create the next generation of riders (American Iron, 2017). Harley recruited its network of riders, dealers and employees on social media to post their images and stories. This empowered their consumers to share their experience online. It also enabled the firm to harness customer innovation and insights. These highly engaged customers, in terms of their levels of participation and commitment, are an important source of new product ideas for the brand.

Questions

1. **Discuss the benefits of deploying AI technology for marketing research purposes.**
2. **Can a chatbot always replace humans in marketing research? Discuss the downside of using computer-aided methods in market research.**
3. **Suggest alternative methods that Harley-Davison might use to research its market.**
4. **Critically evaluate the ethical issues that may be associated with the use of AI technology.**

This case study is written by Dr Ethel Claffey, Waterford Institute of Technology.

References

Based on: Forbes (2017), Company overview Harley Davidson. Available at: https://www.forbes.com/companies/harley-davidson (accessed 10 August 2018); Penhollow, S. (2014), Harley-Davidson and the Quest for Female Customers. Available at: http://www.brittonmdg.com/the-britton-blog/Harley-Davidson-targeting-women-and-young-customers-in-marketing (accessed 11 August 2018); Forbes (2017), Harley-Davidson Works To Reverse The Declining Sales Trend In The Home Market. Available at: https://www.forbes.com/sites/greatspeculations/2017/02/07/harley-davidson-works-to-reverse-the-declining-sales-trend-in-the-home-market/#2ca8f38b6a89 (accessed 10 August 2018); Hanbury, M. (2017), Millenials could be a problem for America's most iconic motorcycle brand. Available at: http://uk.businessinsider.com/millennials-are-hurting-harley-davidson-sales-2017-7 (accessed 12 August 2018); Khulbe, Y. (2016), The Startling Decline of Harley Davidson. Available at: https://www.huffingtonpost.com/yatin-khulbe/the-startling-decline-of-_b_12796210.html (accessed 10 August 2018); The Statistics Portal (2017), Harley-Davidson's worldwide motorcycle retail sales in FY 2016 and FY 2017, by country or region (in units). Available at: https://www.statista.com/statistics/252220/worldwide-motorcycle-retail-sales-of-harley-davidson (accessed 12 August 2018); Jacobi, A. (2016), Harley-Davidson Says Artificial Intelligence Drives 40% of New York Sales. Available at: https://www.emarketer.com/Article/Harley-Davidson-Says-Artificial-Intelligence-Drives-40-of-New-York-Sales/1014642 (accessed 12 August 2018); Albert.ai (2017), Harley Davidson NYC hits all time high with Albert. Available at: https://albert.ai/harley-davidson-nyc (accessed 10 August 2018); Harley-Davidson (2016), Dark Custom. Available at: https://www.harley-davidson.com/ap/en/motorcycles/dark-custom.html (accessed 10 August 2018); Bright, J. (2018), Harley Davidson's EV debut could electrify the motorcycle industry. Available at: https://techcrunch.com/2018/02/22/harley-davidsons-ev-debut-could-electrify-the-motorcycle-industry/?guccounter=1 (accessed 20 August 2018); Thompson, A. (2017), Harley-Davidson's Vision Statement & Mission Statement. Available at: http://panmore.com/harley-davidson-vision-statement-mission-statement (accessed 20 August 2018); Harley-Davidson (2016), Store. Available at: https://www.harley-davidson.com/store/ (accessed 20 August 2018); Brown, A. (2016), Harley-Davidson Boosts Digital Marketing With AI. Available at: http://www.baselinemag.com/innovation/harley-davidson-boosts-digital-marketing-with-ai.html (accessed 10 August 2018); Vankar, P. (2017), Artificial Intelligence: Providing new muscle to marketing. Available at: https://www.hcltech.com/blogs/artificial-intelligence-new-marketing-frontier (accessed 12 August 2018); Harley-Davidson (2016), Student and Rotational Programs. Available at: https://www.harley-davidson.com/us/en/about-us/careers/students-rotational-programs.html (accessed 10 August 2018); American Iron (2017), Harley-Davidson Launches "All For Freedom, Freedom for All" Campaign. Available at: https://www.aimag.com/harley-davidson-launches-all-for-freedom-freedom-for-all-campaign (accessed 10 August 2018).

CASE 12

TomTom: Still Helping Us Find Our Way Around the Planet

TomTom was founded in 1991 by a group of Dutch entrepreneurs. Harold Goddijn is a tenacious Dutchman, Peter-Frans Pauwles wanted to be his own boss, Corinne Vigreux knew about international selling and the importance of building business relationships, and Alexander Ribbink had an eye for technology innovations. All four went to university, three to the University of Amsterdam and the fourth to ESSEC Business School in France. Harold studied economics, Peter-Frans studied business and computer science, Corinne studied international affairs and Alexander studied law. Together, their skills and expertise gave them what they needed to bring an innovation to market: satellite navigation system TomTom. This case study explores how TomTom uses different types of data to ensure its satellite navigation system retains traction in the marketplace.

From Cars to Watches to Telematics

In the early days, TomTom's team realized that, in order to make sure their product would sell, they needed to look at the target market carefully and sell directly to the users of the product. They initially developed a mobile-phone-based mapping system, with Ericsson as the mobile handset producer and digital navigation software supplied by TomTom. However, they soon realized that, to make this into a product they could market effectively, they needed to build the hardware too.

Together, they researched the market and discovered that, at the time, car navigation devices cost around £3,000 and were too costly for most consumers. The aim for TomTom was to develop a good, simple and robust design that would be easy to use and an affordable price to consumers. The team realized that, at the time, this would be a small market, but they felt there was vast potential. Arguably, growth in the market came sooner than expected when Bill Clinton liberalized the global positioning system (GPS) for public use during his term as president of the USA and opened the way for the development of satellite navigation (satnav) that was more affordable for everyone.

The company grew rapidly and became the most popular navigation device in 2007. But, TomTom was not the only satellite navigation system available in the market; Garmin, a US manufacturer, had a competing brand and, in 2009, TomTom's revenues slumped, as the effects of the global economic crisis, smartphones and Google maps (offered via Android-powered phones) took their toll on market share. However, by 2015, global markets had revived and TomTom had begun to develop new devices, which were not all about cars. Their GPS navigation for watches and other wearable sports, e.g. TomTom Runner, a fitness watch, enabled the brand to expand its reach into new markets and, for a while, this looked promising. However, stiff competition from Fitbit, Xiaomi, Apple and Garmin in the wearables market made it hard for TomTom to maintain and grow its market share. In 2017, TomTom's share in the wearables market was declining by 20 per cent year on year, so they decided to shift direction again and focus on automotive licencing and telematics. For example, TomTom agreed a multi-year deal with Uber, the peer-to-peer ridesharing taxi company, to provide maps for drivers in more than 300 cities globally. TomTom also works with Apple on its in-house mapping.

So, TomTom continues to be widely used in consumer markets as a means of navigation and the company is expanding its telematic services in business-to-business and government markets. Its WebFleet is a software service, used in commercial vehicle management and vehicle tracking. The TomTom Telematic service uses big data on a secure platform and is used by leasing firms, car rental companies, for insurance applications and by car dealers and importers Volkswagen, Daimler, Fiat, Chrysler and Hyundai.

The brand's competitive advantage is based on providing up-to-date maps and accurate real-time information.

More than just Traffic Updates

TomTom uses vast amounts of data to give accurate and up-to-the-minute maps of global road networks. It produces high-quality digital maps that provide a rich range of data, which can be used and analysed to guide us around the planet. TomTom can analyse addresses and find places. To do this, it uses various sources of private and government data, which enable the geo-navigation systems to pinpoint individual buildings.

Historical traffic data is used to factor in known hazards and difficulties that can be encountered. Satnavs can use this data to determine the effects of the school run and bank holidays and can even anticipate the effect of changing weather conditions on our road journeys. Actual speed data from millions of users make calculations on actual journeys, rather than using permitted speed limits. Traffic flow data reveals what is happening in real time for every part of the road network. By combining these sources of data, TomTom can supply real-time navigation information.

TABLE C12.1 Sources of data used by TomTom

Professional mapmaking			Community input		
Mobile mapping vans	Field survey	Authoritative sources	Probe data	Community input	Sensor data

Source: TomTom

The Technology

TomTom has built up years of innovation and geospatial expertise, which is available to the government and the public sector, and through continuous investment and a vast workforce it is able to provide the most accurate maps and navigation using satellite imagery, field surveys, mobile mapping vans and fleets with rigorously controlled community input. TomTom has many live (community) input sources, which provide greater accuracy and increased consumer confidence, and gives it the ability to publish data on any road.

TomTom's key data assets, available to government and public sector customers, are:

- millions of connected GPS devices, 80 million GSM probes, millions of government road sensors and thousands of journalists collecting incident information
- OpenLR technology (for dynamic location referencing); TomTom can describe incidents or congestion on any road, including secondary roads, on any map
- mature and proven fusion engine
- class-leading traffic information.

Frequency of data:

- every second, new road data is received
- every 30 seconds, the traffic status is updated
- every minute (or less), all data is made available to customers.

Driverless Cars are the Future and TomTom is Ready

TomTom may not have always led the way in consumer products, but it has built core competencies in mapping data management and processing power, and these capabilities are creating opportunities in the emerging market associated with automated driving and automated vehicles. TomTom's mapping accuracy has enabled it to take a powerful position and it is designing next generation maps, which will fine tune the software to such a level that it is able to provide the standards required for automated vehicles.

Questions

1. **Discuss how TomTom has used data to identify new markets.**
2. **Identify and explain the different types of data TomTom uses to supply navigational information for drivers.**
3. **Imagine you are the marketing director for TomTom and you are responsible for new market development. Discuss how you would go about finding growth opportunities.**

This case study was written by Fiona Ellis-Chadwick, Senior Lecturer, Loughborough University.

»

References

Based on: Garside, J. (2011), Harold Godijin: TomTom's founder needs his business to turn the corner, *The Guardian*, http://www.theguardian.com/business/2011/nov/24/harold-goddijn-tomtom; Bickerton, I. (2007), TomTom's Road Less Travelled, *The Financial Times*, http://www.ft.com/cms/s/1/99581e48-c1b3-11db-ae23-000b5df10621.html#axzz3fnURO1tf; TomTom (2015), http://www.tomtom.com/lib/doc/licensing/S-GOV.EN.pdf; Arthur, C. (2015), Navigation decline: What happened to TomTom? *The Guardian*, 21 July https://www.theguardian.com/business/2015/jul/21/navigating-decline-what-happened-to-tomtom-satnav; Kokalitcheva, K. (2015), Uber signs a mapping deal with TomTom, *Fortune*, 12 Nov http://fortune.com/2015/11/12/uber-tomtom-partnership/ (accessed Nov 2018); Lamkin, P. (2017), TomTom struggles in wearables tech market, admits focus is elsewhere, *Forbes*, 26 July https://www.forbes.com/sites/paullamkin/2017/07/26/tomtom-struggles-in-wearable-tech-market-admits-focus-is-elsewhere/#48b1a3d82f7c (accessed Nov 2018); TomTom (2018), From Business and Government https://www.tomtom.com/en_gb/business-and-government/ (accessed Nov 2018).

CHAPTER 7
Market Segmentation and Positioning

Finding the most revealing way to segment a market is more an art than a science. . . Any useful segmentation scheme will be based around the needs of customers and should be effective in revealing new business opportunities.

PETER DOYLE (2008)

LEARNING OBJECTIVES

After reading this chapter, you should be able to:

1. define the concepts of market segmentation and target marketing, and discuss their use in developing marketing strategy
2. discuss the methods of segmenting consumer markets
3. consider the rise of tribal marketing and trends in target market development
4. identify the factors that can be used to evaluate market segments
5. distinguish between the four target marketing strategies—undifferentiated, differentiated, focused and customized marketing
6. define the concept of positioning and discuss the keys to successful positioning
7. discuss positioning and repositioning strategies
8. discuss the characteristics of developing an effective marketing mix

Few products or services satisfy all customers even Google with its two billion users, only has approaching 50% of all internet users across the globe (Internet World Stats, 2018). Nevertheless, what makes Google so widely used is its utility. Whether you can spell or not, its search facility will help you find what you are looking for (arguably) and this is a free service (so long as you don't mind being digitally tracked). Google uses what it knows about us to serve up organic results to our questions and sponsored advertising links, which are generated based on search behaviour and location. If you sign in to your Google account and look at ad settings, you can see the profile Google has built based on your search history and your profile: age, gender, interests, shopping behaviour, location (Burgess, 2018).

This type of knowledge is important and forms the basis for **market segmentation**, targeting and **positioning**, and aids the implementation of the marketing concept by satisfying customer needs, as product and service offerings can be tailored to meet the diverse requirements of different customer groups. Marketers use personal profile information to get to grips with the diverse nature of markets and this technique is called market segmentation. Market segmentation may be defined as 'the identification of individuals or organizations with similar characteristics that have significant implications for the determination of marketing strategy'. Market segmentation involves dividing a diverse market into several smaller, more similar, sub-markets. The objective is to identify groups of customers with similar requirements so that they can be served effectively while being of a sufficient size for the product or service to be supplied efficiently. Usually, in consumer markets, it is not possible to create a marketing mix that satisfies every individual's requirements exactly but, as the Google example has shown online, high levels of personalisation are increasingly possible (see Chapters 6 and 16 for further discussion of new trends and techniques for using digital analytics). Grouping together customers with similar needs provides a commercially viable method of serving customers in the chosen target market and gives focus to how to position the market offer. This is at the heart of strategic marketing and these three techniques are the subject of this chapter.

Why Bother to Segment Markets?

Why go to the trouble of segmenting markets? What are the gains to be made? Figure 7.1 identifies four benefits.

Target market selection

Market segmentation provides the basis for the *selection of target markets*. A *target market* is a chosen segment of market that a company has decided to serve. As customers in the target market segment have similar characteristics, a single marketing mix strategy can be developed to match those requirements. Creative approaches towards segmentation may result in the identification of new segments that have not been served adequately and may form attractive target markets. For example, Google regularly introduces new product offers to serve the functional needs of different target markets, such as Google Wallet for shoppers who want to buy while on the move, Google+—a social network, providing an alternative to Facebook—and Google Maps for smartphone users.

Tailored marketing mix

Market segmentation allows the grouping of customers based upon similarities (e.g. benefits sought) that are important when designing marketing strategies. Consequently, this allows marketers to understand in-depth the requirements of a segment and *tailor a marketing mix package* that meets its needs. This is a fundamental step in the implementation of the marketing concept; segmentation promotes the notion of customer satisfaction by viewing markets as diverse sets of needs that suppliers must understand and meet.

FIGURE 7.1
The advantages of market segmentation

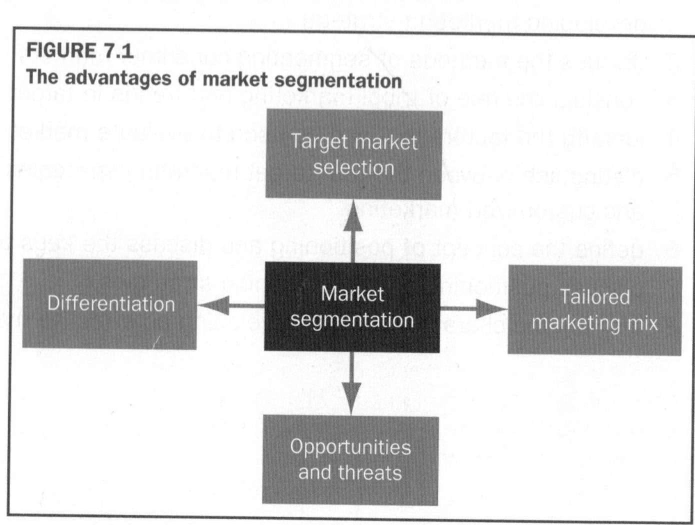

For example, BMW has introduced the BMWi3, a high-performance but low-emission saloon car, to serve a target market that wants a more sustainable mode of transport than a conventional carbon-fuel car. See Exhibit 7.1 to discover how BMW uses psychographic segmentation focusing on lifestyle variables to target customers for the BMWi3.

EXHIBIT 7.1
The BMWi3

Differentiation

Market segmentation allows the development of **differential marketing strategies**. By breaking a market into its constituent sub-segments, a company may differentiate its offerings between segments (if it chooses to target more than one segment) and, within each segment, it can differentiate its offering from the competition. By creating a differential advantage over the competition, a company is giving the customer a reason to buy from it rather than the competition. For example, Apple created the smartphone market with the launch of its first iPhone in 2007. Bundling a new set of applications and functionality into its mobile handset gave the iPhone the difference needed to attract a new generation of mobile users. For a while, Apple led the way, but now competition in this market is intense. Nearest rival, Samsung, sells smartphones that are technically similar and so both firms are seeking ways to differentiate their offer (Davis, 2014). Read Marketing in Action 7.1 to find out how Fyndiq is differentiating its business from internet giants Amazon and eBay.

Opportunities and threats

Market segmentation is useful when attempting to spot opportunities and threats. Markets are rarely static. As customers become more affluent, seek new experiences and develop new values, new segments emerge. The company that first spots a new and underserved market segment and meets its needs better than the competition

MARKETING IN ACTION 7.1
Start-up Business Fyndiq Creates a Marketplace with a Difference

Fyndiq is a Swedish start-up business launched in 2010, which has created an e-commerce platform for online retailers and shoppers. The marketplace is differentiated from its competitors by focusing on bargain products. It targets bargain hunters and positions the business online as The Bargain Superstore. The items on sale are end-of-lines and slow-selling products that are heavily discounted. Sellers are currently allowed to list their products free of charge and then pay a fee of just 5 per cent once the items are sold. Currently, there are over 1,700 merchants selling to millions of customers and the company is expanding to serve markets across Europe. CEO Dinesh Nayar and co-founder Fredrik Norberg aim for Fyndiq to become 'Amazon for bargain products'.

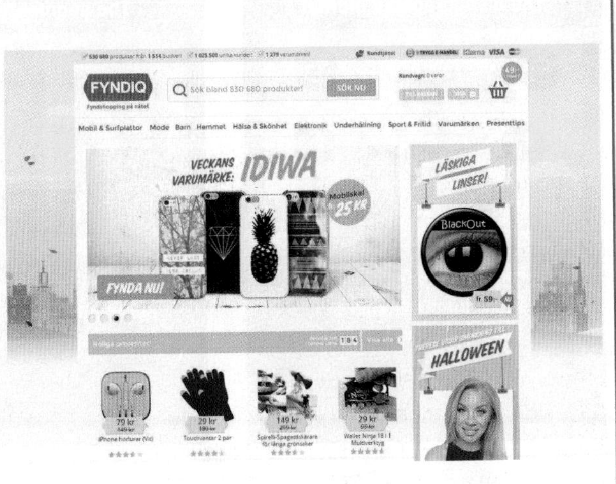

Based on: Lunden (2014); Fyndiq (2014); Dawson (2017)

can benefit from increasing sales and profit growth. Zara is a fashion brand built on a market opportunity—to supply fashionable clothing to the market quickly. Zara pioneered the concept of fast fashion, which means that new designs are available in weeks rather than the fashion industry standard of six months. Spotting this opportunity has enabled Zara to develop into one of the world's largest fashion brands.

Similarly, the neglect of a market segment can pose a threat if the competition uses it as a gateway to market entry. Gap, US fashion brand and rival to Zara, failed to spot the changing trends among fashion-conscious shoppers, so, as Gap's core target market aged, the brand failed to attract younger fashion-hungry consumers and so lost its market lead to Zara; this remains a position that Gap has not been able to recapture (Keely and Clark, 2008; Bearne, 2015).

The point is that market segments need to be protected from competitors. Otherwise there is a threat that new entrants might establish a foothold and grow market share in the poorly served segment of a market.

The Process of Market Segmentation and Target Marketing

The selection of a target market or markets is a three-step process (see Figure 7.2).

1. *Understand the requirements and characteristics of the individuals and/or organizations* that comprise the market. Marketing research can be used here.
2. *Divide the market, according to these requirements and characteristics, into segments* that have implications for developing marketing strategies. Note: a market can be segmented in various ways depending on the choice of criteria. For example, the market for cars could be segmented by type of buyer (individual or organizational), major benefit sought in a car (e.g. functionality or status) and family size (empty nester versus family with children). There are no rules about how a market should be segmented. Using a new criterion or using a combination of well-known criteria in a novel way may give fresh insights into a market. For example, TomTom changed the way drivers navigate with the launch of its satellite navigation device TomTom Go.
3. *Choose market segment(s) to target.* A marketing mix can then be developed, based on a deep understanding of target-market customers' needs and values. The aim is to design a mix that is distinctive from competitors' offerings. This theme of creating a *differential advantage* will be discussed in more detail when we examine how to position a product in the marketplace.

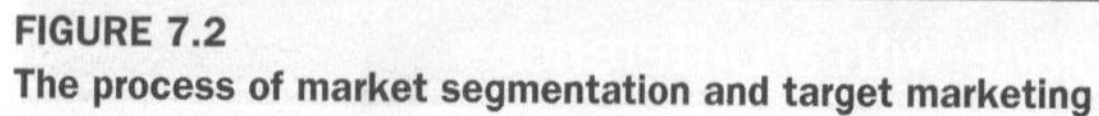

FIGURE 7.2
The process of market segmentation and target marketing

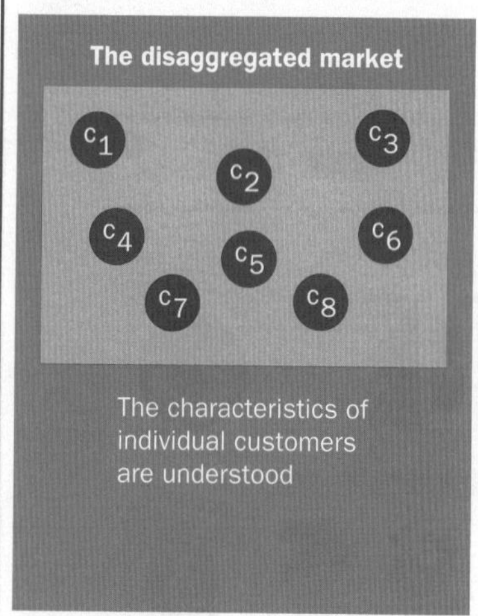

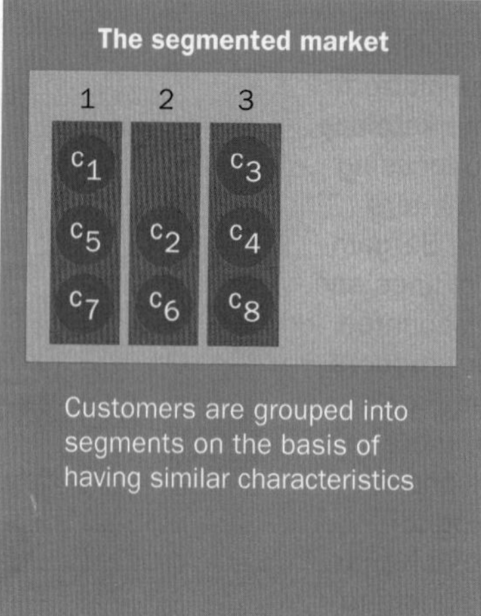

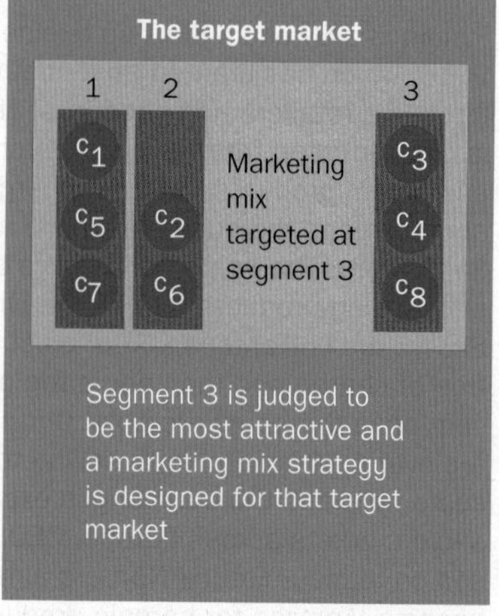

Segmenting Consumer Markets

Markets can be segmented in many ways. Segmentation variables are the criteria that are used for dividing a market into segments. When examining criteria, the marketer is trying to identify good predictors of differences in buyer behaviour. There is an array of options and no single prescribed way of segmenting a market (Wind, 1978). Now we look at possible ways of segmenting consumer markets.

There are three broad groups of consumer segmentation criteria: 1) *behavioural*, 2) *psychographic* and 3) *profile* variables. Since the purpose of segmentation is to identify differences in behaviour that have implications for marketing decisions, *behavioural variables* such as benefits sought from the product and buying patterns may be considered the basis for segmentation. Psychographic variables are used when researchers believe that purchasing behaviour is correlated with the personality or lifestyle of consumers; consumers with different personalities or lifestyles have varying product or service preferences and may respond differently to marketing mix offerings. Having found these differences, the marketer needs to describe the people who exhibit them and this is where profile variables such as socio-economic group or geographic location are valuable (Van Raaij and Verhallen, 1994). For example, a marketer may see whether there are groups of people who value low calories in soft drinks and then attempt to profile them in terms of their age, socio-economic groupings and so on.

FIGURE 7.3
Segmenting consumer markets

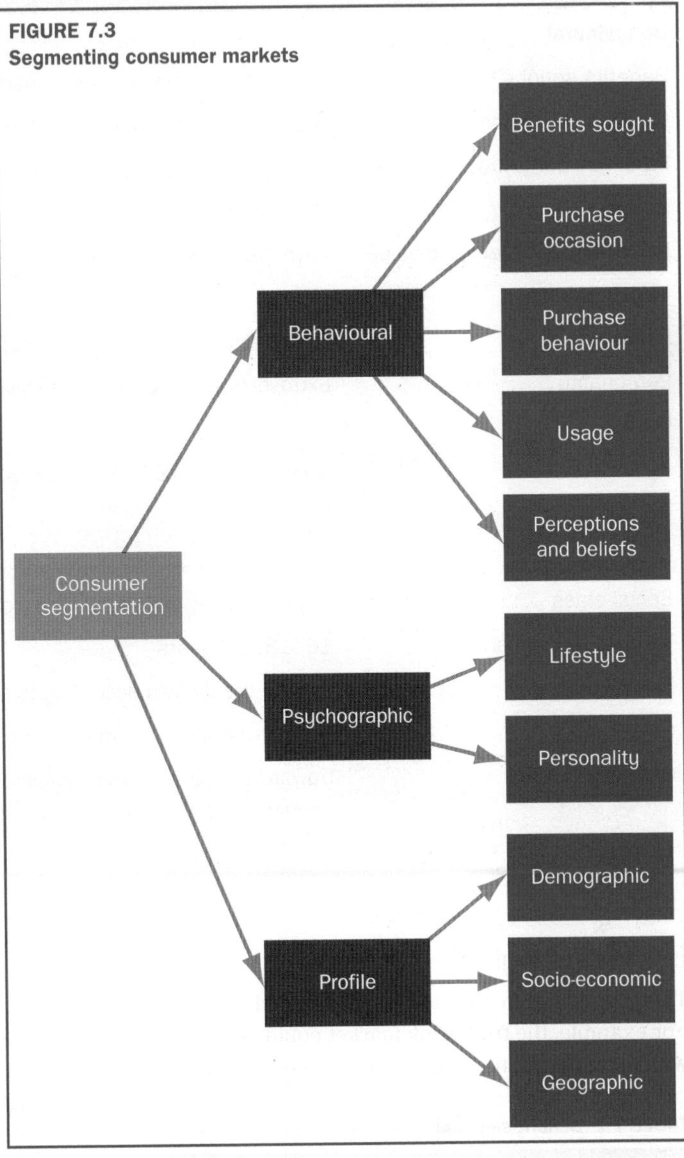

In practice, however, segmentation may not follow this logical sequence. Often, profile variables will be identified first and then the segments so described will be examined to see if they show different behavioural responses. Age or income groups are frequently used as a basis for identifying market segments, and marketing managers examine groups of individuals to see if they show different attitudes and requirements towards particular products and initiatives. For example, Abercrombie & Fitch have found their market to be 25-year-olds with attitude (Ritson, 2011). Figure 7.3 shows the major segmentation variables used in consumer markets and Table 7.1 describes each of these variables in greater detail.

Behavioural segmentation

The key behavioural bases for segmenting consumer markets are: benefits sought; purchase occasion; purchase behaviour; usage; and perceptions, attitudes beliefs and values. Each will now be discussed.

TABLE 7.1 Consumer segmentation methods

Variable	Examples
Behavioural	
Benefits sought	Convenience, status, performance, price
Purchase occasion	Self-buy, gift, special occasions, eating occasions
Purchase behaviour	Solus buying, brand switching, innovators
Usage	Heavy, light
Perceptions, beliefs and values	Favourable, unfavourable
Psychographic	
Lifestyle	Trendsetters, conservatives, sophisticates
Personality	Extroverts, introverts, aggressive, submissive
Profile	
Age	Under 12, 12–18, 19–25, 26–35, 36–49, 50–64, 65+
Gender	Female, male
Lifecycle	Young single, young couples, young parents, middle-aged empty nesters, retired
Social class	Upper middle, middle, skilled working, unwaged
Terminal education age	16, 18, 21 years
Income	Income breakdown according to study objectives and income levels per country
Geographic	North versus south, urban versus rural, country
Geodemographic	Upwardly mobile young families living in larger owner-occupied houses; older people living in small houses; European regions based on language, income, age profile and location

Benefits sought

This segmentation criterion can be applied when the people in a market seek different benefits from a product. For example, the fruit drink market could be segmented by benefits sought. Table 7.2 shows such a breakdown with examples of the brands targeting each segment.

TABLE 7.2 Benefit segmentation in the fruit drink market

Benefits sought	Products favoured
Extra energy	Lucozade Energy Orange
Vitamins	Ribena Blackcurrant juice drink
Natural	Innocent apple and mango
Low calorie	PLJ Lemon juice cordial
Convenience	Capri-Sun Orange sachets

Benefit segmentation provides an understanding of why people buy in a market and can aid the identification of opportunities. For example, previously the Lego Group focused predominantly on toys for boys, with its packs of building bricks designed to assemble helicopters, trains, rockets and 'warrior-themed' product ranges. However, after four years of research into how girls play, the company introduced a range called Lego Friends aimed at 6- to 12-year-old girls. Now, both boys and girls playing with Lego bricks can enjoy the product's educational benefits—for example, developing spatial awareness, mathematical and fine motor skills through play (Wieners, 2011; Wachman, 2012).

Many markets are segmented on the basis of price sensitivity. Often a market will be characterized by a segment of customers who value the benefit of low price and another that values high quality or service and is prepared to pay more for that benefit. In the grocery market, the UK market leader, Tesco, has developed several product ranges, for example Tesco Everyday Value and Tesco Finest, to cater for different market segments, while Sainsbury's has over 1,000 products in its Taste the Difference range of premium quality products, which have enabled the supermarket chain to capture market share and drive sales growth

(Cattermole, 2012). In the travel industry, established national airlines missed an opportunity to cater for the price-sensitive market segment, which created an opportunity for the so-called 'no-frills' airlines EasyJet and Ryanair to grow rapidly.

Benefit segmentation is a fundamental method of segmentation, because the objective of marketing is to provide customers with benefits they value. Knowing the various benefits people value is therefore a basic prerequisite of understanding markets. Benefit segmentation provides the framework for classifying individuals based upon this knowledge. Profile analyses can then be performed to identify the type of people (e.g. by age, gender, socio-economic grouping) in each benefit segment so that targeting can take place.

Purchase occasion

Customers can be distinguished according to the occasions when they purchase a product. For example, a product (e.g. tyres) or service (e.g. plumbing) may be purchased as a result of an emergency or as a routine unpressurized buy. Price sensitivity, for example, is likely to be much lower in an emergency buying situation. Some products (e.g. mobile phones) may be bought as gifts or as self-purchases. These different occasions can have implications for marketing mix and targeting decisions. If it is found that the gift market is concentrated at Christmas, advertising budgets will be concentrated in the pre-Christmas period. Package design may differ for the gift versus personal-buy segment also. Many brands of chocolate are targeted at the gift segment of the confectionery market, for example, Thorntons (UK), Bonnat (France) and Ritter Sport (Germany).

Segmentation by purchase occasion is also relevant in the grocery market. Tesco, the UK's leading supermarket, has different store formats according to the occasions when consumers purchase groceries. For the weekly shop, there are Tesco superstores offering a wide range of food and non-food items; for convenience purchases, a more restricted range of food products are offered by Tesco Metro shops in central urban locations and Tesco Express shops next to petrol stations.

Often, special occasions such as Easter and Christmas are associated with higher prices. However, prices fall rapidly after the occasion: for example, chocolate eggs are discounted after Easter Sunday.

Purchase behaviour

Differences in purchase behaviour can be based on the time of purchase relative to the launch of the product or on patterns of purchase. When a new product is launched, a key task is to identify the innovator segment of the market. These people (or organizations) may have distinct characteristics that allow communication to be targeted specifically at them (e.g. young, middle class). Innovators are more likely to be willing to buy the product soon after launch. Other segments of the market may need more time to assess the benefits and delay purchase until after the innovators have taken the early risks of purchase. Only when the credentials have been established among these 'innovators' is the brand moved to a wider target audience. For example, the number of electric cars is still relatively low and prices are typically high, and as yet this type of car still has to appeal to a wide audience.

The degree of *brand loyalty* in a market may also be a useful basis for segmenting customers. Solus buyers are totally brand loyal, buying only one brand in the product group, such as a person who buys only Ariel washing powder. Most customers brand-switch; some may have a tendency to buy Ariel but also buy two or three other brands (e.g. Persil, Fairy); others might show no loyalty to any individual brand but switch brands on the basis of special offers (e.g. money off) or because they are variety-seekers who look to buy a different brand each time. By profiling the characteristics of each group, a company can target each segment accordingly. By knowing the type of person (e.g. by age, socio-economic group, media habits) who is brand-loyal, a company can channel persuasive communications to defend this segment. By knowing the characteristics and shopping habits of the offer-seekers, sales promotions can be targeted correctly.

In the consumer durables market, brand loyalty can be used as a segment variable to good purpose. For example, Volkswagen has divided its customers into first-time buyers, replacement buyers (model-loyal replacers and company-loyal replacers) and switch replacers. These segments are used to measure performance and market trends, and for forecasting purposes (Hooley et al, 2012).

A recent trend in consumer services sectors has been towards biographics. This is the linking of actual purchase behaviour to individuals. The growth in retailer loyalty schemes has provided a mechanism for gathering behavioural data. Customers are given cards that are swiped through an electronic machine at the checkout so that points can be accumulated towards discounts and vouchers. The more loyal the shopper, the higher the number of points gained. The retailer benefits by knowing the purchasing behaviour of named individuals. Online behavioural targeting and browser fingerprinting are discussed in Chapter 16.

Usage

Customers can also be segmented on the basis of heavy users, light users and non-users of a product category. The profiling of heavy users allows this group to receive most marketing attention (particularly promotion efforts) on the assumption that creating brand loyalty among these people will pay heavy dividends. Sometimes the 80% : 20% rule applies, where about 80 per cent of a product's sales come from 20 per cent of its customers.

However, information technology has increased access to and knowledge of niche markets, and the 'long tail' is a term used to reflect the increase in interest in niche products by marketers (Brynjolfsson et al, 2011). Brands are increasingly developed to target niche market segments. For example, as populations are ageing, there is more demand for specialist healthcare products, and car manufacturers like Ford and BMW are adding healthcare technology to their cars so they can access niche segments—for example, the electrocardiogram (ECG) seat measures the heart rate of the driver automatically (Barnett, 2011).

Marketing managers need to be aware that selecting heavy-user segments can deliver benefits in terms of volume of potential sales, but analysing the light-user segments can provide insights that can deliver advantages over the competition. Target Group Index Europa is a good source of consumer product usage information and provides actionable marketing information on adults (Kantar Media, 2012). An important point to note is that while *use* may prove helpful for identifying buyers of particular products, it may not necessarily give insight into an individual's 'shopping basket' of items. For example, luxury foods and drinks may be purchased for a special event like a birthday, but value groceries may be selected for everyday use.

The key issue to remember is that market segmentation concerns the grouping of individuals or organizations with similar characteristics that have implications for the determination of marketing strategy.

Perceptions, attitudes, beliefs and values

The final behavioural base for segmenting consumer markets is by studying perceptions, attitudes, beliefs and values. This is classified as a behaviour variable because perceptions, attitudes, beliefs and values are often strongly linked to behaviour. Consumers are grouped by identifying those people who view the products in a market in a similar way (perceptual segmentation) and have similar beliefs (belief segmentation). These kinds of segmentation analyses provide an understanding of how groups of customers view the marketplace. To the extent that the groups' perceptions and beliefs are different, opportunities to target specific groups more effectively may arise.

Attitudes towards products and services can prove fruitful as a basis for segmenting a market. Research in the UK found that 71 per cent of the population said they were middle class, but this very large section of the population represented a wide spectrum of incomes, wealth and attitudes. Six distinct *tribes* were identified, showing different attitudes towards brand preferences. For example: 'squeezed strugglers' liked Gillette and ITV but disliked the National Trust and Sainsbury's; 'bargain hunters' liked eBay and Muller but disliked John Lewis; 'Daily Mail disciplinarians' liked British Airways but disliked L'Oréal and Channel 4; 'comfortable greens' liked Fairtrade and Green & Black's but disliked Asda and Coca-Cola (Chorley and Rentoul, 2011). But there is more to being part of a tribe than liking or disliking a particular brand. See Exhibit 7.2 for further discussion of tribal marketing.

Car manufacturers use belief segmentation to divide the market and target specific groups. For example, Toyota aimed to attract a new generation of car buyers in Europe with its Yaris model. In targeting 20- to 30-year-olds, Toyota used direct marketing to persuade this group that these cars are fun, entertaining and enjoyable to own. The new models have added attributes such as touch-screen multimedia systems and other gadgets to attract the attention of the target group (Brownsell, 2011).

Values and lifestyles (VALS)

Values-based segmentation is based on the principles and standards that people use to judge what is important in life. Values are relatively consistent and underpin behaviour. Values form the basis of attitudes and lifestyles, which, in turn, manifest as behaviour. Marketers have recognized the importance of identifying the values that trigger purchase for many years, but now it is possible to link value groups to profiling systems that make targeting feasible. A values and lifestyles (VALS) framework profiles consumer attitudes, needs, beliefs and values and links with their demographic profile. This system of customer analysis extends the reach of segmentation.

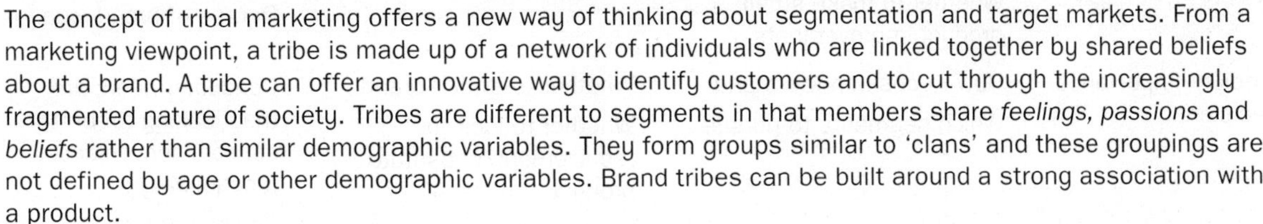

MARKETING IN ACTION 7.2
Tribal Marketing

The concept of tribal marketing offers a new way of thinking about segmentation and target markets. From a marketing viewpoint, a tribe is made up of a network of individuals who are linked together by shared beliefs about a brand. A tribe can offer an innovative way to identify customers and to cut through the increasingly fragmented nature of society. Tribes are different to segments in that members share *feelings, passions* and *beliefs* rather than similar demographic variables. They form groups similar to 'clans' and these groupings are not defined by age or other demographic variables. Brand tribes can be built around a strong association with a product.

Unilever used the concept of tribalism and the medium of social media to create a tribe called the Marmarati—a group of consumers who were so passionate about Marmite XO (especially strong) that they were prepared to publicly demonstrate their love of the product through Facebook and Twitter. Their approach created excitement around the product both online and offline.

Games Workshop has built its global business by connecting Warhammer gaming fanatics, who recreate battles and conflicts with its fantasy figures. Warhammer gamers are a passionate tribe, committed to their war game hobby. At Warhammer World in Lenton, Nottingham—where the brand originated—is an event centre, which attracts tribe members from across the world. Gamers devote time and money, and have a lot to say about what they expect from the brand by working together. Games Workshop now produces regular releases of new products and play tables in-stores, where staff give lessons in game strategy and practical advice on painting the models, all of which create value for the tribe of customers.

To create a successful tribe, marketers need to identify what it is that brings these individuals together. Tribes are not homogenous like segments; they are linked by passion for a brand and are capable of collective action. Tribes are fuzzy, more like societal sparkle than socio-economic certainty, and so can be difficult to identify, but technology is helping expand online communities.

Online brand communities

Online social networks have facilitated the growth of brand communities, which are becoming an increasingly important marketing phenomenon. These digital forums provide a perfect place for like-minded consumers to congregate and co-produce shared value. Interestingly, such communities have gained power in their relationship with brands and are somewhat empowered almost to the extent that they manage the brands by producing their own interpretations of a brand, its value and market position. At the technological extremes, online communities are creating their own brands and products, e.g. Linux (open source operating system), Geocaching (a global treasure hunt, followed and created by its treasure-hunting users). There is also a darker side, which marketers should be aware of: if strong online communities become dissatisfied with a brand—they even feel exploited by pricing policies and value offers—they may rebel by boycotting the brand, openly criticizing and supporting competing brands.

Based on: Cova and Cova (2002); Cova and White (2010); Dixon (2005); Veloutsou and Moutinho (2009); Uncles (2008); Wood (2018)

Focusing on different segments, the types of decisions they are making and the issues they want to address enables marketers to understand consumers' deeply held beliefs. This has implications for marketing planning and campaigns (Yankelovich and Meer, 2006); see Table 7.3.

The VALs is a global segmentation system (Strategic Business Insights, 2018) that can provide consumer insights that have implications for marketing strategy and planning.

The VALS framework was developed by SBI International as an innovative market research tool for determining the motivations which underpin consumer purchasing decision-making. Further research found that psychological traits are more stable than societal trends and consumer values (SBI International, 2018), and are a useful way to identify segments.

VALS Types

There are eight types in the framework and each type have a set of typical characteristics which can be used to identify them as a target group: innovators (e.g. sophisticates, with high self-esteem), thinkers (e.g. mature, satisfied

TABLE 7.3 Framework for aligning marketing, consumer and segmentation issues, adapted from Yankelovich and Meer, 2006

	Marketing issues	Consumer concerns	Segmentation insights
Low importance decisions	Whether to make small price increases Whether to make small product improvements	How relevant is the product and the value it offers	Buyer usage behaviour Price sensitivity Degree of brand loyalty
Medium importance decisions	How to position the brand Which segments to pursue	Whether to switch brands Whether to look for replacement/substitute product	Consumer need: are they looking for better service, convenience, functionality Social statues, self-image and lifestyle
High importance decisions	Whether to completely revise the business in response to changing market trends, e.g. IBM moved out of computer hardware into software solutions	Making sustainable purchasing choices Changing diet regime, e.g. becoming vegan	Core values and beliefs which inform buying decisions, e.g. environmental concerns

reflective), believers (e.g. traditional, moral, deep-rooted), achievers (e.g. goal-orientated), strivers (e.g. fun-loving, financially stretched), experiencers (e.g. enthusiastic, impulsive), makers (e.g. practical, constructive) and survivors (e.g. cautious, resource-poor).

Motivation

The framework focuses on three consumer motivations: 1) ideals, 2) achievement, and 3) self-expression. By identifying the dominant motivating factors, methods for developing deeper understanding of their customers' needs and how to use this knowledge in their marketing campaigns should be addressed. For example, there is a growing trend for consumers to become more health conscious and, as a result, the markets for health, fitness and well-being products and services are growing rapidly. Individuals who are motivated by ideals are likely to be interested in detailed information about the origins and sourcing of products, e.g. where food ingredients come from and how the produce is transported to its destination market. Targeting a young consumer who is motivated by demonstrating to their peers how well they are doing is ideal for wearable fitness products, which measure achievements (e.g. FitBit, Apple Watch). Consumers motivated by self-expression desire social or physical activity and variety. Leon is a restaurant chain which offers *naturally fast food* and is suited to this type of customer.

Resources

This refers to how individual consumer goods and services go beyond basic demographic variables into psychographic variables and intimate personal lifestyle characteristics, e.g. energy levels, self-confidence, intellect and innovativeness. Looking at both types of variables in conjunction with motivation can deliver detailed insights. The next section adds to this discussion.

Psychographic segmentation

Psychographic segmentation involves grouping people according to their lifestyle and personality characteristics.

Lifestyle

This form of segmentation attempts to group people according to their way of living, as reflected in their activities, interests and opinions. As discussed, the VALS framework makes use of these values. The question with lifestyle segmentation is the extent to which general lifestyle patterns are predictive of purchasing behaviour in specific markets (Sampson, 1992). Nevertheless, **lifestyle segmentation** has proved popular among advertising agencies, which have attempted to relate brands (e.g. Hugo Boss) to a particular lifestyle (e.g. aspirational). In television, Sky has used lifestyle segmentation to target special interest groups, including sports enthusiasts (Sky Sports), film lovers (Sky Movies) and news followers (Sky News).

Personality

The idea that brand choice may be related to personality is intuitively appealing. However, the usefulness of personality as a segmentation variable is likely to depend on the product category. Buyer and brand personalities are likely to match where brand choice is a direct manifestation of personal values, but, for most fast-moving consumer goods (e.g. detergents, tea, cereals), the reality is that people buy a repertoire of brands (Lannon, 1991). Personality (and lifestyle) segmentation is more likely to work when brand choice is a reflection of self-expression; the brand becomes a *badge* that makes public an aspect of personality—'I choose this brand to say this about me and this is how I would like you to see me.' For example, Mercedes' brand personality is all about the brand's *assertiveness*, and is reflected in its strapline, 'the best or nothing', whereas BMW uses the phrase 'the ultimate driving machine' to reflect the desirable aspects of its more *sensuous* personality (Millward Brown, 2015).

Profile segmentation

Profile segmentation variables allow consumer groups to be classified in such a way that they can be reached by the communications media (e.g. advertising, internet communications). Even if behaviour and/or psychographic segmentation have successfully distinguished between buyer preferences, there is often a need to analyse the resulting segments in terms of profile variables such as age and socio-economic group to communicate to them. The reason is that readership and viewership profiles of newspapers, magazines and television programmes tend to be expressed in that way.

We shall now examine a number of demographic, socio-economic and geographic segmentation variables.

Demographic variables

The demographic variables we shall look at are age, gender and lifecycle.

Age has been used to segment many consumer markets (Tynan and Drayton, 1987). For example, children receive their own TV programmes; cereals, computer games and confectionery are other examples of markets where products are formulated with children in mind. The sweeter tooth of children is reflected in sugared cereal brands targeted at children (e.g. Kellogg's Rice Krispies, Coco Pops). It should be noted that recent pressure to reduce sugar consumption has led to manufacturers lowering the amount of sugar in their brands. L'Oréal targets the over-50s with its Age Perfect and Revitalift brands, while Vodafone targets 35- to 55-year-olds with an easy-to-use, no-frills mobile phone that offers the uncomplicated functionality that many in this segment group value (Simms, 2005). See Exhibit 7.2 for how Fanny Karst views fashion and age.

Age is not only widely used for segmenting product markets, it is also used as a segmentation variable in services. The holiday market is heavily age segmented, with offerings targeted at the under-30s and the over-60s segments, for example. This reflects the different requirements of these age groups when on holiday. Mini Case 7.1 explores some of the issues associated with using age as a segmentation variable.

Despite the latest challenges raised by using age as a segmentation variable, many companies covet the youth segment, which comprises the major purchasers of items such as clothing, consumer electronics, drinks, personal care products and magazines. One popular way to communicate with these segments is through digital media communications. Marketing in Action 7.3 explores some of the issues related to understanding this key market segment.

Gender also offers much for a marketing manager planning a segmentation strategy. The different tastes and customs of men and women are reflected in specialist products aimed at these market segments. Magazines, clothing, hairdressing and cosmetics are product categories that have used segmentation based on gender.

The classic family *lifecycle* stages offer opportunities to segment by a range of related variables such as: disposable income; family responsibilities; and consumption patterns based on family circumstances, for example single, married, divorced, living with or without children. Lifecycle stages are discussed in detail in Chapter 3.

Based upon population census data, 'People UK' is arranged in eight life stages: starting out, young with toddlers, young families, singles/couples/no kids, middle-aged families, empty nesters, retired couples and older singles. Produced by CACI, the system is particularly useful for targeted mailing, because it can be applied to everyone on the UK electoral roll. People are classified according to the neighbourhood in which they live (Chisnall, 2005). The methodology is described a little later in this section, when we discuss the ACORN geodemographic system.

EXHIBIT 7.2
Old Ladies' Rebellion range, created by Fanny Karst for women over 60

Socio-economic variables

Socio-economic variables include social class, terminal education age and income. Here we shall look at social class as a predictor of buyer behaviour.

Social class is measured in varying ways across Europe. In the UK, occupation is used, whereas in other European centres a combination of variables is used. Like the demographic variables discussed earlier, social class is relatively easy to measure, and is used for creating media readership and viewership profiles. However, as shown in Table 7.1, social class can be multi-layered and consequently may be more difficult to identify. Furthermore, many people who hold similar occupations have very dissimilar lifestyles, values and purchasing patterns. Nevertheless, social class has proved useful in discriminating on the basis of owning a dishwasher, having central heating and privatization share ownership, for example, and therefore should not be discounted as a segmentation variable (O'Brien and Ford, 1988).

Geographic variables

The final set of segmentation variables is based on geographic differences. A marketer can use pure geographic segmentation or a hybrid of geographic and demographic variables called *geodemographics*.

The *geographic* segmentation method is useful where there are geographic locational differences in consumption patterns and preferences. For example, variations in food preferences may form the basis of geographic segments; differences in national advertising expectations may also form geographic segments for communicational purposes. Germans expect a great deal more factual information in their advertisements than French or British audiences do. France, with its more relaxed attitude to nudity, broadcasts commercials that would be banned in the UK. In the highly competitive Asian car market, both Honda and Toyota have launched their first 'Asia-specific' cars, designed and marketed solely for Asian consumers, but they face emerging competitors—for example, Tata Motors in India, a company manufacturing cars specifically for the home market (e.g. Nano, a small, affordable, reliable car for Indian families (Tata Motors, 2009).

Geodemographic: in countries that produce population census data, the potential for classifying consumers on the combined basis of location and certain demographic (and socio-economic) information exists. Households are classified into groups according to a wide range of factors, depending on what is asked for on census returns.

MINI CASE 7.1
Age

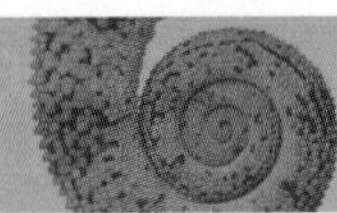

Personality-based profiles and ageist stereotyping are becoming less effective as a segmentation strategy as boundaries between segments blur and attitudes morph. For example, a rebellious person who is a keen media consumer and interested in the latest innovations could be a teenager, but these days this description more aptly fits the 'baby boomer'. Interestingly, baby boomers (born between 1946 and 1964) are the *original* teenagers and are equally as likely to use Skype as their 15- to 24-year-old counterparts; they feel more up to date than today's youngsters and very eager to use new communication technology. However, the boomers are often missed by marketers who prefer to use age to discriminate and so target the 18–34 market segment.

Perhaps it is not surprising that marketers are getting it wrong when using age as a segmentation variable. In Europe, young people seem to be different ages up to a point where they become 'old people', but even this distinction lacks precision. In the UK, you are an old person at 59; youth ends at 35 and middle age spans the 24 years in between. In Greece, youth does not end until you are 52, and old age does not start until you reach 67, leaving just 15 years to be middle-aged. Moreover, stereotyped groupings of old and young have often been defined using measures of competence, with the 'old' regularly being placed in the low competence group.

However, wherever the lines are drawn between young and old, marketers need to take care not to alienate the 'old people', as they account for a rapidly growing and increasingly wealthy market segment. Furthermore, analysis suggests that the median age in Europe will increase from 37 to 52 by 2050. In Britain, the government is increasing the minimum retirement age (by 2046 it could be 68), so the trend is set to continue and grow in the future.

Marketers need to be aware that attitudes and preferences change as we age: for example, the desire for sweet tastes dwindles and is replaced by a preference for dryer, sharper and more sophisticated flavours, while responsibilities tend to increase with age as marriage, children and property ownership come along. Some new and existing brands are taking advantage of the potential opportunities afforded by targeting 'old people'. Old Ladies' Rebellion is a fashion label created by Fanny Karst for over-60 women. She developed the brand based on her knowledge of traditional tailoring skills and respect for 'the older generation' when she was a young designer in London. Her designs reflect the age of the customers but also incorporate a sense of fun. Her 'old is the new black' slogan epitomizes her sense of fun and underlying determination to make a statement about the importance of older women in fashion. More-established brands from Marks & Spencer to Aviva motor insurance specifically aim to develop their customer base among the 50-somethings.

How to communicate with 'old people' is another consideration. New media are proving to be effective in communicating with this market segment: for example, women over 55 are the fastest-growing user segment on Facebook and they are the most unlikely to reply to direct mailing. More consumers (of all ages) are turning to the web to find pre-purchase information and compare what is on offer online before deciding where and from whom to buy.

The reality is that the world is changing rapidly and using stereotypes and easily accessible demographic variables such as age is likely to prove ineffective as consumers grow older. A possible solution is to take a more rounded view by seeking to identify how customers interact with brands and examining the different channels through which they connect with a brand.

Questions:

1. Think of a segmentation classification for 'old people' that would enable you to access this target group more precisely.
2. Discuss the implications for the lifecycle stage model discussed in Chapter 3.
3. Make a list of the brands that might profitably target 'old people'.

Based on Edwards (2011); Handley (2011); Hilpern (2011); Rochon (2014); Fanny Karst (2018)

In the UK, variables such as age, social status, family size, ethnic background, joint income, type of housing and car ownership are used to group small geographic areas (known as *enumeration districts*) into segments that share similar characteristics. The two best-known geodemographic systems in the UK are ACORN and Mosaic. Both use census data and postcodes to produce categorizations of the population in the UK. See Table 7.4 for details of ACORN's system of classification.

MARKETING IN ACTION 7.3
The A–Z of Digital Generations

During the last two decades, a generation of digitally informed new consumers has been born to shop online. But they are not the only generations who have learned how to function in the technology-enhanced world: others, too, are learning how to become digital natives. So, marketers need to understand and be able to identify these consumers in order to engage with the generations. Here are just a few of the digitally able generations:

B is for baby boomers—46 years old and over, who have no intention of retiring or opting for a quiet life. People in this group tend to be both mentally and physically active, and as a segment are likely to drive future growth in retail spending; they are high online spenders, but spend a smaller percentage of their income online than the millennials. They are tech-savvy consumers and have taken to mobile commerce too.

C is for content—generation C are the group of customers who, rather than being consumers of content, are in fact the creators of content, or *prosumers* as they have been called. Highly sophisticated digital devices enable consumers to produce content such as images, videos and audio tracks. There are individuals of all ages and backgrounds, so age is not a useful segmentation variable. For marketers, the commercial advantage of consumer-generated content is that it reveals hidden preferences. For example, the rise in popularity of 'unboxing', where a person films the unwrapping and the initial operation of a new purchase (invariably a newly released piece of technology), and the film that demonstrates things about the product that the buyer finds difficult and what he or she enjoys about a particular product. Increasingly, marketers are engaging consumers in the product development process, working together to produce finely tuned market offerings.

D is for digital natives—a broad term coined in 2001 to capture the group of people who were 'born digital'. This term has come to mean people born after 1980, who have always been exposed to computer technology and digital communications.

M is for millennials—a key target group of online consumers because they spend more money online than any other group. Millennials are 18- to 34-year-olds. Their attitudes vary and millennials have been labelled the 'me, me, generation', but also the 'nice generation'. Arguably, those in this generation have grown up with more structure in their lives, and family values are important. During their early years, there was a downturn in violence against children and an increase in child-friendly gadgets to promote their safe upbringing. Millennials are risk averse, aspire to stable careers and are less likely to have a credit card than Generation Xers.

S is for silent generation—born between 1925 and 1945. This generation started out life in turbulent economic times; the great depression and World War II both had an influence in making a generation who took no chances and kept quiet about things.

X is for generation Xers—born between 1965 and 1980. This is a generation of extremes: during childhood, they tended to experience indulgent parenting styles from their baby boomer parents, but, as they got older, divorce, poor schooling and other social factors led to this group being called the 'baby bust generation'. The Xers were hit hard by the 2008 recession and tended to downsize and live a DIY lifestyle.

Y is for generation Y—young boomers that followed the baby boomers. They tend to be 32 or younger and have unique product preferences and different attitudes to brands; multi-channel shopping particularly appeals to this group. They are accused of being selfish and love spending time online.

Z is for generation Z—this group has a relatively low income, but spends the largest percentage of time online. Born since the millennium and in their mid-teens, they have grown up in a world of political and financial turmoil. They care about the world they live in and see education as a thing to be treasured. They are more likely to volunteer than their generation X parents and the millennials.

Based on: Kimmel (2010); Smith (2014); KPMG (2013); Prensky (2001); Howe (2014); Wallop (2014); Trendwatching.com (2004)

ACORN is a powerful consumer classification that segments the UK population. By analysing demographic data, social factors, population and consumer behaviour, it provides precise information and an understanding of different types of people.

Mosaic is a classification system that provides insight into demographics and lifestyles in the world's major economies. In the UK, the system classifies individuals, household and/or postcodes into homogenous consumer segments. There are 141 Mosaic person types, which can be aggregated into 67 household types and 15 groups. For example, groups include: alpha territory; career and kids; claimant culture. The classification system can then be overlaid onto a map of an area to show the areas in relation to the person types, household types and groups (Experian, 2015).

TABLE 7.4 ACORN categories, groups and types (ACORN CACI, 2014)

Category	Traits	Group	Type—examples
1 Affluent achievers	Financially successful, middle-aged plus, mainly empty nesters; confident with new technology	Lavish lifestyles Executive wealth Mature money	Exclusive enclaves Asset-rich families Upmarket downsizers
2 Rising prosperity	Highly educated younger singles and couples, living in modern flats, with good incomes; earlier adopters of the internet	City sophisticates Career climbers	Socializing young renters Career-driven young families
3 Comfortable communities	Tend to live in suburbs or smaller towns, own their homes (average value for region), have average income and average education; professional, managerial and clerical jobs	Countryside communities Successful suburbs Steady neighbourhoods Comfortable seniors Starting out	Farms and cottages Large family homes, multi-ethnic Suburban semis, conventional attitudes Older people; neat and tidy neighbourhoods Smaller houses and starter homes
4 Financially stretched	Tend to live in terraced houses or semi-detached; more single, separated and divorced than average; less likely to have a credit card, but use the internet socially	Student life Modest means Striving families Poorer pensioners	Term-time terraces Fading owner-occupied terraces Families in right-to-buy estates Elderly people in social rented flats
5 Urban adversity	Deprived areas of large and small towns; low household incomes, refused credit; low levels of qualifications; higher levels of health problems than other areas	Young hardship Struggling estates Difficult circumstances	Young families in low cost private flats Low-income terraces Deprived areas and high-rise flats
6 Not private households	Communal establishments, e.g. military bases, hotels, other holiday accommodation	Not private households	Active communal Inactive communal

A major strength of these geodemographics systems for marketers is the capacity to link buyer behaviour to customer groups and locations. There are a wide range of variables that can be used to segment consumer markets. Often a combination of variables will be used to identify groups of consumers that respond in the same way to marketing mix strategies.

Research companies are also combining lifestyle- and values-based segmentation schemes with geodemographic data. For example, CACI's Census Lifestyle system classifies segments using lifestyle and geodemographic data.

Influences of digital technology on segmentation variables

According to research (Doherty and Ellis-Chadwick, 2010a and b), online consumer markets can be identified by considering demographic variables and behavioural and psychographic variables, which have implications for segmentation. While there is a similarity between categories of variables online and offline, each group of variables has different characteristics in the virtual world. For example, research suggests that in terms of their personal profiles—age, gender, education, salary, and so on—internet shoppers are likely to be similar to their offline counterparts (Jayawardhena, Wright and Dennis, 2007). However, it is still possible to distinguish the most enthusiastic and profitable internet shoppers on the basis of their perceptions, beliefs and behaviours. For example, it has recently been found that the internet is a favourite channel for the compulsive shopper, as consumers are able to 'buy unobserved', 'without contact with other shoppers', and, in so doing, 'experience strong positive feelings during the purchase episode'.

Furthermore, the demographic variables which have significant implication for online targeting are those found to remain static throughout an individual's lifetime, or to evolve slowly over time—such as education, race, age (Hoffman, Novak and Schlosser, 2003), gender (Slyke, Comunale and Belanger, 2002) and lifestyle (Shui and Dawson, 2004).

Important psychographic and behavioural variables are those that shape the perceptions, beliefs and attitudes that might influence consumers' online behaviour and their intention to shop or engage with an online offer. Online behavioural characteristics—such as knowledge, attitude, innovativeness and risk aversion—have been found to have significant implications when segmenting online markets and when considering a consumer's likelihood to shop online. For example, it has been found that consumers who are primarily motivated by convenience were more likely to make purchases online, while those who value physical social interactions were found to be less interested (Swaminathan, Lepkowska-White and Rao, 1999; Kukar-Kinney, Ridgway and Monroe, 2009). Moreover, a study of internet shoppers from six countries (developing and developed) found a surprisingly high degree of homogeneity in their characteristics and habits (Brashear et al., 2009). It concluded that internet shoppers share 'their desire for convenience, are more impulsive, have more favourable attitudes towards direct marketing and advertising, are wealthier, and are heavier users of both email and the internet'. Further discussion of digital technology and social media can be found in Chapter 16.

Target Marketing

Market segmentation is a means to an end: **target marketing**. This is the choice of specific segments to serve and is a key element in marketing strategy. A company needs to evaluate the segments and decide which ones to serve. For example, CNN targets its news programmes at what are known as 'influentials'. This is why CNN has, globally, focused so much of its distribution effort into gaining access to hotel rooms. Business people know that, wherever they are in the world, they can see international news on CNN in their hotel. Eurosport uses a similar targeting approach and provides plenty of coverage of upmarket sports such as golf and tennis for viewers in Europe. In high-tech markets, Apple's introduction of the iPad enabled the company to gain a stronghold in corporate markets for its multi-touch devices. When Coca-Cola targeted consumer markets in China, it gave its soft drinks brand a makeover, including a new name (see Exhibit 7.3) and a strapline which, when translated from Mandarin, becomes 'delicious happiness' (Muller, 2011).

Entering markets can be costly, especially when products need to be altered, so it is important to take care in selecting those target markets that will meet marketing objectives. Accordingly, first we examine how to evaluate potential market segments and then we consider how to make a balanced choice about which markets to serve.

EXHIBIT 7.3
Coca-Cola targeted consumer markets in China with a new image and strapline

Evaluating market segments

When evaluating market segments, a company should examine two broad issues: market attractiveness and the company's capability to compete in the segment. Market attractiveness can be assessed by looking at market factors, competitive factors, and political, social and environmental factors (Abell and Hammond, 1979; Day, 1986; Hooley et al, 2012). Figures 7.4 and 7.5 illustrate the factors that need to be examined when evaluating market segments.

Market factors

Segment size: generally, large-sized segments are more attractive than small ones, since sales potential is greater, and the chance of achieving economies of scale is improved. However, large segments are often highly competitive

FIGURE 7.4
Factors used to assess market attractiveness

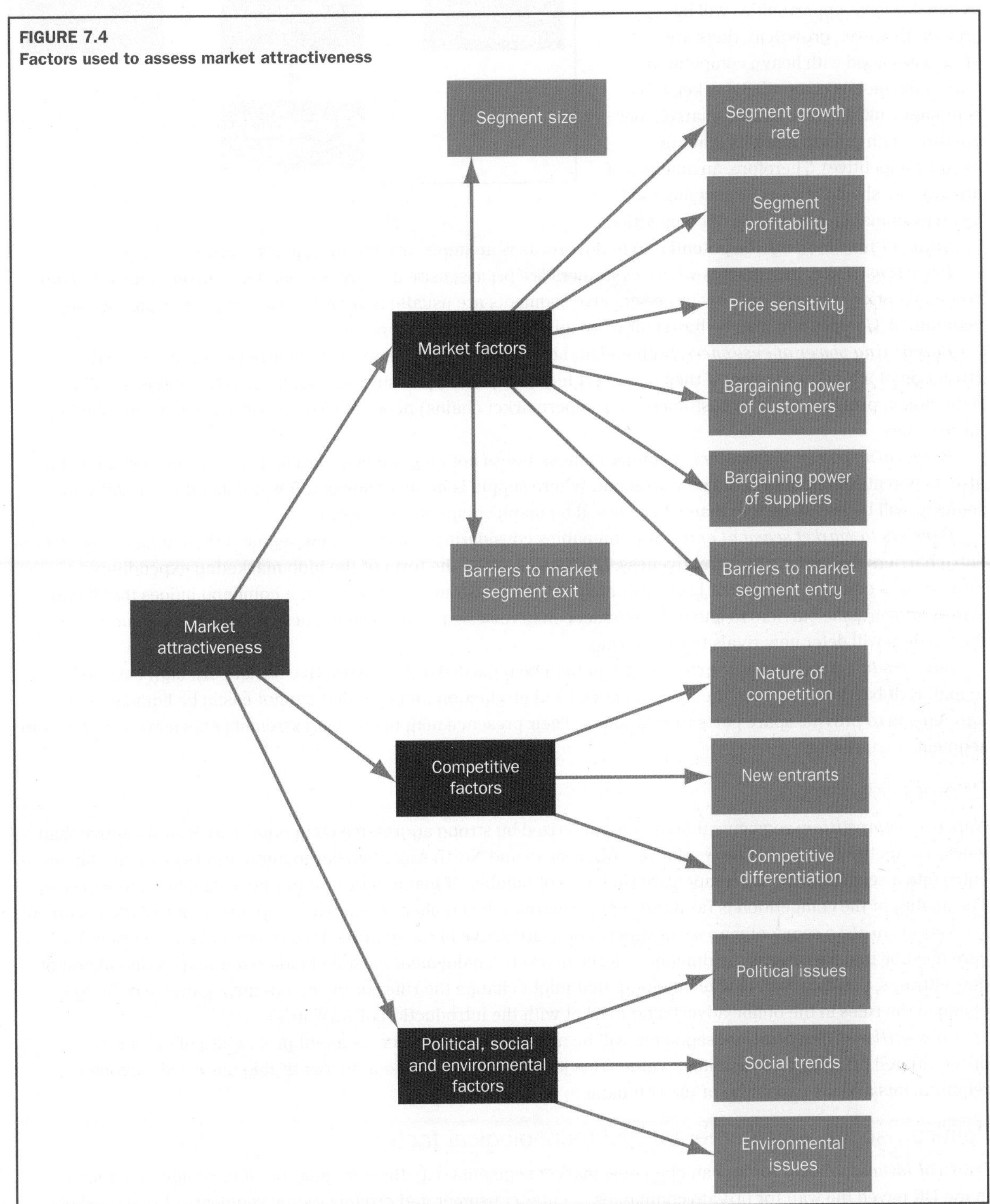

since other companies are realizing their attraction, too. Furthermore, smaller companies may not have the resources to compete in large segments and so may find smaller segments more attractive.

Segment growth rate: growing segments are usually regarded as more attractive than stagnant or declining segments, as new business opportunities will be greater. However, growth markets are often associated with heavy competition (e.g. in the mobile computing market, tablet computers, ultra netbooks and smartphones are three high-growth markets that are highly competitive). Therefore, an analysis of growth rate should always be accompanied by an examination of the state of competition.

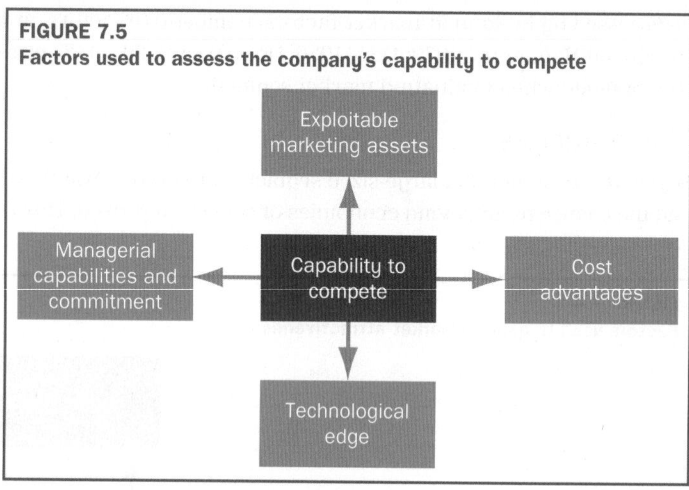

FIGURE 7.5
Factors used to assess the company's capability to compete

Segment profitability: the potential to make profits is an important factor in market attractiveness.

Price sensitivity: in segments where customers are price sensitive, there is a danger of profit margins being eroded by price competition. Low price-sensitive segments are usually more attractive, since margins can be maintained. Competition may be based more on quality and other non-price factors.

Bargaining power of customers: both end and intermediate customers (e.g. distributors) can reduce the attraction of a market segment if they can exert high bargaining pressure on suppliers. The result is usually a reduction in profit margins as customers (e.g. supermarket chains) negotiate lower prices in return for placing large orders.

Bargaining power of suppliers: a company must assess not only the negotiating muscle of its customers but also its potential suppliers in the new segment. Where supply is in the hands of a few dominant companies, the segment will be less attractive than when served by many competing suppliers.

Barriers to market segment entry: for companies considering entering a new segment there may be substantial entry barriers that reduce its attractiveness. Barriers can take the form of the high marketing expenditures necessary to compete, patents or high switching costs for customers. However, if a company judges that it can afford or overcome barriers to entry, its existence may raise segment attractiveness if the company judges that the barriers will deter new rivals from entering.

Barriers to market segment exit: a segment may be regarded as less attractive if there are high barriers to exit. Exit barriers may take the form of specialized production facilities that cannot easily be liquidated or agreements to provide spare parts to customers. Their presence may make exit extremely expensive and therefore segment entry riskier.

Competitive factors

Nature of competition: segments that are characterized by strong aggressive competition are less attractive than where competition is weak. The weakness of European and North American car manufacturers made the Japanese entry into a seemingly highly competitive (in terms of number of manufacturers) market segment relatively easy. The quality of the competition is far more significant than the number of companies operating in a market segment.

New entrants: a segment may seem superficially attractive because of the lack of current competition, but care must be taken to assess the dynamics of the market. A judgement must be made regarding the likelihood of new entrants, possibly with new technology, that might change the rules of the competitive game (e.g. Google changed the rules in the online advertising market with the introduction of AdWords).

Competitive differentiation: segments will be more attractive if there is a real probability of creating a differentiated offering that customers value. This judgement is dependent on identifying unserved customer requirements and the capability of the company to meet them.

Political, social, environmental and technological factors

Political issues: political forces can open new market segments (e.g. the deregulation of telecommunications in the UK paved the way for private companies to enter consumer and organizational segments of that market).

Alternatively, the attraction of entering new geographic segments may be reduced if political instability exists or is forecast: for example, unrest in Turkey, Egypt and Tunisia caused a reduction in the number of tourists travelling to such regions; hurricanes caused damage in the Caribbean and such events cause downturn in sales for travel firms like Thomas Cook and Tui Group (Davies, 2017).

Social trends: changes in society need to be assessed to measure their likely impact on the market segment. Changes can give rise to latent market segments, under-served by current products and services. For example, changing perceptions of gender roles means reviewing who is the main income earner in a household (traditionally male) and who is responsible for childcare (traditionally women). These changing patterns of family life mean that women are working more, and men are more likely to be involved actively in parenting. Fathers are often overlooked as a target market, but they are increasingly influencing brand choices. New dads are taking responsibility for decisions in the home and tend to look for healthier and more environmentally friendly products. Behavioural science research suggests it is important for marketers to strike a balance between dad as a *parent* and as a *man* (Fleck, 2018), but also to be aware that gender stereotyping should be avoided (Friedmann, 2018).

Environmental issues: the trend towards more environmentally friendly products has affected market attractiveness both positively and negatively. The Body Shop took the opportunity afforded by the movement against animal testing of cosmetics and toiletries; conversely, the market for CFCs has declined in the face of scientific evidence linking their emission with depletion of the ozone layer.

Technology issues: digital technology is now ubiquitous and a part of almost every aspect of modern life. These technologies are affecting how we consume, what we consume, and when and where we consume goods and services, and should not be overlooked as new market segments are constantly emerging and big gains can be made by first entrants (e.g. Apple's entry into the mobile music market with iTunes, and Amazon's early entry into virtual assistance and voice activated speakers with Amazon Eco, gained advantage and established a dominant market position).

Capability

Against the market attractiveness factors must be placed the company's *capability to serve the market segment*. The market segment may be attractive, but outside the resources of the company. Capability may be assessed by analysing exploitable marketing assets, cost advantages, technological edge, and managerial capabilities and commitment.

Exploitable marketing assets: does the market segment allow the firm to exploit its current marketing strengths? For example, is segment entry consonant with the image of its brands or does it provide distribution synergies? However, where new segment entry is inconsistent with image, a new brand name may be created. For example, Toyota developed the Lexus model name when entering the upper-middle class executive car segment.

Cost advantages: companies that can exploit cheaper material, labour or technological cost advantages to achieve a low-cost position compared with the competition may be in a strong position, particularly if the segment is price sensitive.

Technological edge: strength may also be derived by superior technology, which is the source of differential advantage in the market segment. Patent protection (e.g. in pharmaceuticals) can form the basis of a strong defensible position, leading to high profitability. For some companies, segment entry may be deferred if they do not possess the resources to invest in technological leadership.

Managerial capabilities and commitment: a segment may look attractive, but a realistic assessment of managerial capabilities and skills may lead to rejection of entry. The technical and judgemental skills of management may be insufficient to compete against strong competitors. Furthermore, the segment needs to be assessed from the viewpoint of managerial objectives. Successful marketing depends on implementation. Without the commitment of management, segment entry will fail on the altar of neglect.

Target marketing strategies

The purpose of evaluating market segments is to choose one or more segments to enter. Target market selection is the choice of which and how many market segments compete in. There are four generic target marketing strategies from which to choose: **undifferentiated marketing**, **differentiated marketing**, **focused marketing** and **customized marketing** (see Figure 7.6). Each option will now be examined.

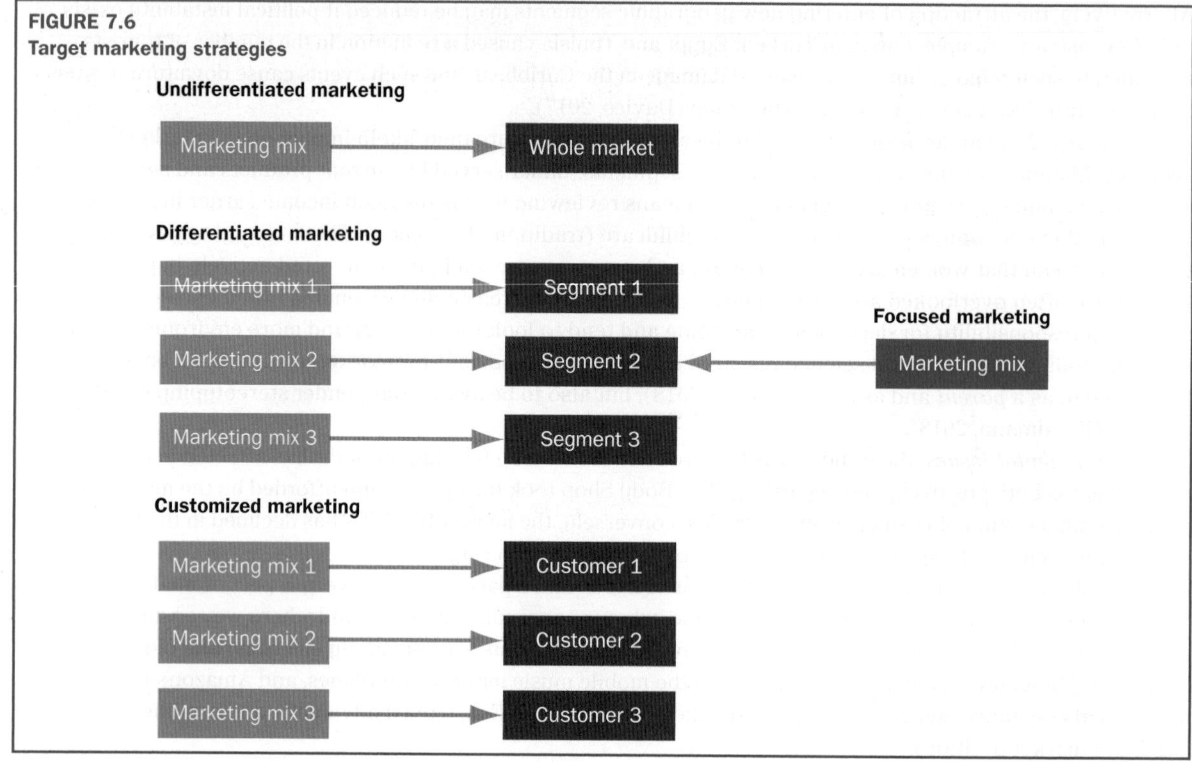

FIGURE 7.6
Target marketing strategies

Undifferentiated marketing

Occasionally, a market analysis will show no strong differences in customer characteristics that have implications for marketing strategy. Alternatively, the cost of developing a separate market mix for separate segments may outweigh the potential gains of meeting customer needs more exactly. Under these circumstances, a company may decide to develop a single marketing mix for the whole market. This absence of segmentation is called undifferentiated marketing.

Unfortunately, this strategy can occur by default. For example, companies that lack a market orientation may practise undifferentiated marketing through lack of customer knowledge. Furthermore, undifferentiated marketing is more convenient for managers, since they have to develop only a single product. Finding out that customers have diverse needs that can be met only by products with different characteristics means that managers have to go to the trouble and expense of developing new products, designing new promotional campaigns, training the salesforce to sell the new products and developing new distribution channels. Moving into new segments also means that salespeople have to start prospecting for new customers. This is not such a pleasant activity as calling on existing customers who are well known and liked.

The process of market segmentation is normally the motivator to move such companies from practising undifferentiated marketing to one of the next three target marketing strategies.

Differentiated marketing

When market segmentation reveals several potential targets, specific marketing mixes can be developed to appeal to all or some of the segments. This is called differentiated marketing. For example, airlines design different marketing mixes for first-class and economy passengers, including varying prices, service levels, quality of food, in-cabin comfort and waiting areas at airports. A differentiated target marketing strategy exploits the differences between marketing segments by designing a specific marketing mix for each segment. Marketing in Action 7.4 describes how Tesco and Sky have designed different products to cater for the segments that exist in their markets.

One potential disadvantage of a differentiated compared with an undifferentiated marketing strategy is the loss of cost economies. However, the use of flexible manufacturing systems can minimize such problems.

MARKETING IN ACTION 7.4

Companies Use Different Brands to Meet the Needs of their Various Target Markets

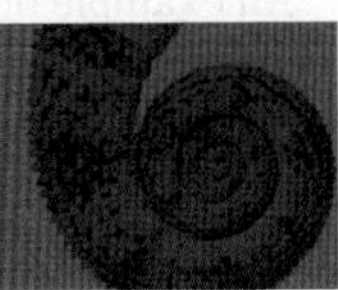

Market segmentation is a creative act that relies upon a clear understanding of the groups of customers that make up a target market. The actual basis of segmentation will vary by market sector. However, large corporations frequently aim to ensure that their product portfolios offer a mix of product ranges and brands that meet the needs of different market segments. For example, Tesco differentiates its various offers by channel choice and store format. The weekly shopper tends to look for a store where they can purchase all of their needs in one location, while the convenience shopper is looking for a limited range of products and is prepared to pay a slightly higher price and select from a limited range of products as the store is very conveniently located, often within walking distance of the consumer's home. The online shopper often wants a mix of both convenience and range, but is prepared to wait for their shopping to be delivered. Each of these shoppers is looking for a different type of convenience.

By utilizing three distinct brands, Tesco is able to target different segments, extend its reach and protect its market share from competitors:

Tesco Stores → targets weekly shoppers
Tesco Express → targets convenience shoppers
Tesco.com → targets online shoppers

Sky has also differentiated some of its product offerings to target specific segments:

Sky Sports → targets sports enthusiasts
Sky Movies → targets film lovers
Sky News → targets news followers
Sky Atlantic → targets drama lovers
Sky Witness → targets prime-time TV lovers

Airlines apply similar principles. For example, United Airlines is based in North America and is one of the world's largest airlines, operating a fleet of over 700 aircraft. The airline serves many target markets, catering for domestic and commercial customers, and operates internal, transcontinental and transatlantic routes. On all United Airlines flights, passengers are offered a choice of classes:

First class → targets top business executives
Business class → targets senior managers
Economy class → targets other business travellers and domestic travellers

All of these companies—whether they be retail or broadcast orientated, or travel related—have recognized that market segmentation can lead to higher rates of satisfaction of consumer needs than producing a single offering and hoping it will meet all the diverse expectations of a given market.

Based on: United Airlines (2012); Rose (2008); Smith (2008); Jack (2009)

Focused marketing

The identification of several segments in a market does not imply that a company should serve all of them. Some may be unattractive or out of line with business strengths. Perhaps the most sensible route is to serve just one of the market segments. When a company develops a single marketing mix aimed at one target market (*niche*) it is practising **focused marketing**.

This strategy is particularly appropriate for companies with limited resources. Small companies may stretch their resources too far by competing in more than one segment. Focused marketing allows research and development expenditure to be concentrated on meeting the needs of one set of customers, and managerial activities can be devoted to understanding and catering for their needs. Large organizations may not be interested in serving the needs of this one segment, or their energies may be so dissipated across the whole market that they pay insufficient attention to their requirements.

An example of focused marketing in the consumer market is given by Bang & Olufsen (B&O), the Danish audio electronics firm. It targets upmarket consumers who value self-development, pleasure and open-mindedness, with its stylish TV and music systems. B&O describes its positioning as 'high quality but we are not Rolls-Royce—more BMW'. The company places emphasis on distinctive design, good quality and simplicity of use. Focused targeting means that B&O defies the conventional wisdom that a small manufacturer could not make profits marketing consumer electronics in Denmark (Bang & Olufsen, 2018).

One form of focused marketing is to concentrate efforts on the relatively small percentage of customers that account for a disproportionately large share of sales of a product (the heavy buyers). For example, in some markets, 20 per cent of customers account for 80 per cent of sales. Some companies aim at such a segment because it is so superficially attractive. Unfortunately, they may be committing the *majority fallacy* (Zikmund and D'Amico, 1999). The majority fallacy is the name given to the blind pursuit of the largest, most easily identified, market segment. It is a fallacy because that segment is the one that everyone in the past has recognized as the best segment and, therefore, it attracts the most intense competition. The result is likely to be high marketing expenditures, price cutting and low profitability. A more sensible strategy may be to target a small, seemingly less attractive, segment rather than choose the same customers that everyone else is after.

Customized marketing

Customised marketing is included in this chapter to complete the discussion of the model, but refers more specifically to organizational target market. In some markets, the requirements of individual customers are unique and their purchasing power sufficient to make designing a separate marketing mix for each customer viable. Segmentation at this disaggregated level leads to the use of customized marketing. Many service providers, such as advertising and marketing research agencies, architects and solicitors, vary their offerings on a customer-to-customer basis. They will discuss face-to-face with each customer their requirements and tailor their services accordingly. Customized marketing is also found within organizational markets, because of the high value of orders and the special needs of customers. Locomotive manufacturer Siemens design and build products to specifications given by rail transport providers, e.g. the Electric Freight Locomotive has been customised for Australian customers and the Electric Locomotive for Russian customers. Customized marketing is often associated with close relationships between supplier and customer, in these circumstances because the value of the order justifies large marketing and sales efforts being focused on each buyer.

Positioning

So far, we have discussed market segmentation and target market selection. The next step in developing an effective marketing strategy is to clearly position a product or service offering in the marketplace. Figure 7.7 summarizes the key tasks involved and shows where positioning fits into the process. Positioning is the choice of:

- *target market—where* we want to compete
- *differential advantage—how* we wish to compete.

Both of these elements of positioning should be considered in conjunction with customer needs. The objective is to create and maintain a distinctive place in the market for a company and/or its products.

Target market selection has accomplished part of the positioning job already. But to compete successfully in a target market involves providing the customer with a differential advantage. See Exhibit 7.4 to see how Glacéau Water is positioned as a problem solver. This requires giving the target customer something better than the competition is offering. Creating a differential advantage is discussed in detail in Chapter 19. Briefly, it involves using the marketing mix to create something special for the customer. Product differentiation may result from added features that give customers benefits that rivals cannot match. Promotional differentiation may stem from unique, valued images created by advertising, or superior service provided by salespeople.

FIGURE 7.7
Key tasks in positioning

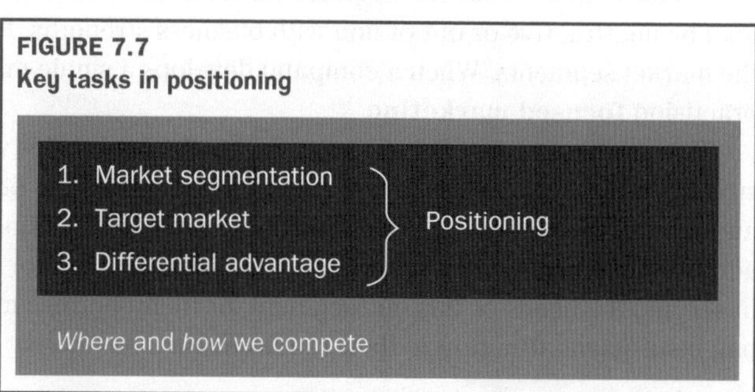

Distribution differentiation may arise through making the buy situation more convenient for customers. Finally, price differentiation may involve giving superior value for money through lower prices.

A landmark book by Ries and Trout (2001) suggested that marketers are involved in a battle for the minds of target customers. Successful positioning is often associated with products possessing favourable connotations in the minds of customers. For example, Samsung is associated with high-technology, reliable and fashionable mobile phones. These add up to a differential advantage in the minds of its target customers, whether they be in London, Amsterdam or Moscow. Similarly, the success of Cillit Bang has been based on its positioning of Cillit as the most powerful and versatile household cleaner on the market. Such positioning is hard won and relies on four factors, as shown in Figure 7.8 and listed below.

EXHIBIT 7.4
Glacéau appeals to members of its target audience by identifying their problems and providing solutions that match their preferences

1. *Clarity*: the positioning idea must be clear in terms of both target market and differential advantage. Complicated positioning statements are unlikely to be remembered. Simple messages such as Walmart's 'always low prices' and Stella Artois' 'reassuringly expensive' are clear and memorable.
2. *Consistency*: people are bombarded with messages daily. To break through this noise, a consistent message is required. Confusion will arise if this year marketers position on 'quality of service', then next year they change it to 'superior product performance'. Two examples of brands that have benefited from a consistent message being communicated to their target customers are Gillette ('the best a man can get') and L'Oréal ('because you're worth it'). Both receive high recall when consumers are researched because of the consistent use of a simple message over many years.
3. *Credibility*: the differential advantage that is chosen must be credible in the minds of the target customer. Nokia introduced the world to the smartphone and led the market with its Symbian series phones until 2007. But, when Apple launched its iPhone with touch screen and app-based operating system, Nokia did not respond and so the Symbian technology got older while the iPhone developed. The significant growth in demand for smartphones fuelled market growth, but Nokia lost credibility and market share due to its outdated technology platform (Chang, 2012).
4. *Competitiveness*: the differential advantage should have a competitive edge. It should offer something of value to the customer that the competition is failing to supply. For example, Fever Tree's range of mixer drinks has become a market leading and award-winning brand, which filled a gap in the market for premium quality tonic to accompany the growing number of premium brands of gin.

Perceptual mapping

A useful tool for determining the position of a brand in the marketplace is the *perceptual map*—a visual representation of consumer perceptions of the brand and its competitors using attributes (dimensions) that are important to consumers. The key steps in developing a perceptual map are as follows.

1. Identify a set of competing brands.
2. Identify important attributes that consumers use when choosing between brands, using qualitative research (e.g. group discussions).

FIGURE 7.8
Keys to successful positioning: the Four-Cs framework

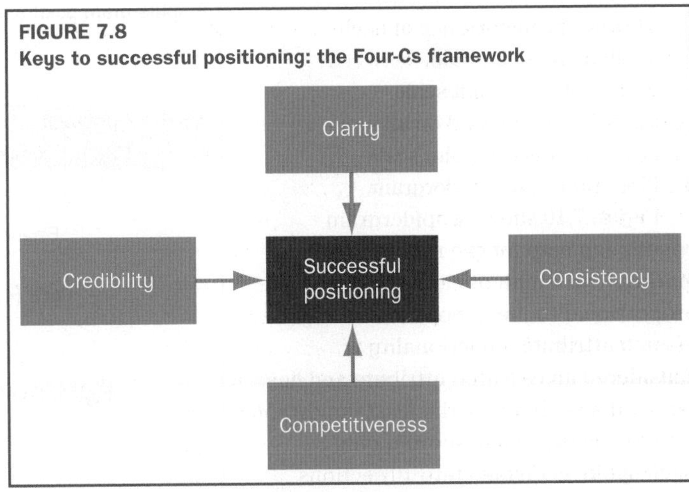

3 Conduct quantitative marketing research where consumers score each brand on all key attributes.
4 Plot brands on a two-dimensional map(s).

Figure 7.9 shows a perceptual map for seven supermarket chains. Qualitative marketing research has shown that consumers evaluate supermarkets on two key dimensions: price and width of product range. Quantitative marketing research is then carried out using scales that measure consumers' perception of each supermarket on these dimensions. Average scores are then plotted on a perceptual map.

The results show that the supermarkets are grouped into two clusters: the high quality, wide product range group, and the low quality, narrow price range group. These are indicative of two market segments and show that supermarkets C and D are close rivals, as measured by consumers' perceptions, and have very distinct perceptual positions in the marketplace compared with E, F and G.

FIGURE 7.9
A perceptual map of supermarket chains

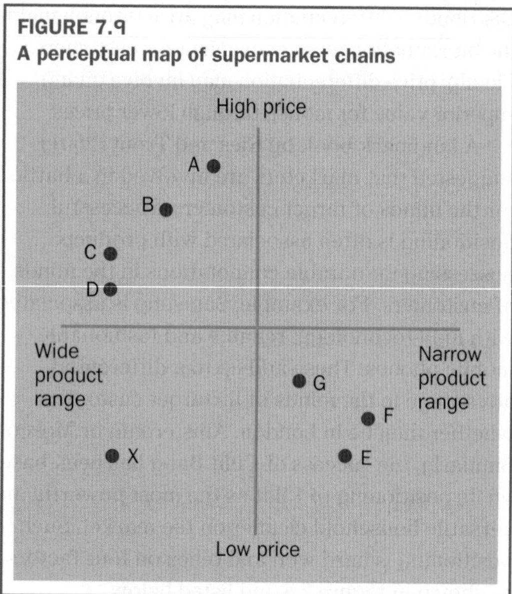

Perceptual maps are useful in considering strategic moves. For example, an opportunity may exist to create a differential advantage based on a combination of wide product range and low prices (as shown by the theoretical position at X).

Perceptual maps can also be valuable in identifying the strengths and weaknesses of brands as perceived by consumers. Such findings can be very revealing to managers, whose own perceptions may be very different from those of consumers. Consumers can also be asked to score their ideal position on each of the attributes so that actual and ideal positions can be compared.

Spidergram analysis

An alternative approach to perceptual mapping for understanding the position of a brand in the marketplace is spidergram analysis. Like perceptual mapping, spidergram analysis provides a visual representation of consumer perceptions of the brand and its competitors using attributes (dimensions) that are important to consumers when evaluating those brands. However, this analysis also asks consumers to rate the importance of the attributes, and their relative importance is represented visually by the length of the spoke on the spidergram.

The key steps are as follows.

1 Identify a set of competing brands.
2 Identify important attributes that consumers use when choosing between brands, using qualitative research (e.g. group discussions).
3 Conduct quantitative marketing research in which consumers:
a) rate the importance of each attribute in their choice between brands on a 10-point scale
b) score each brand on all key attributes on a 10-point scale.
4 Plot brands on a spidergram.

Figure 7.10 shows a spidergram positioning map for the robotic systems market. The length of each spoke is proportional to the importance ratings of each attribute. Functionality is considered an essential attribute and has received a score of 10; the least important attribute is financing, scoring only 3. Each spoke is divided into 10 sections

FIGURE 7.10
A spidergram positioning map for the robotic systems market

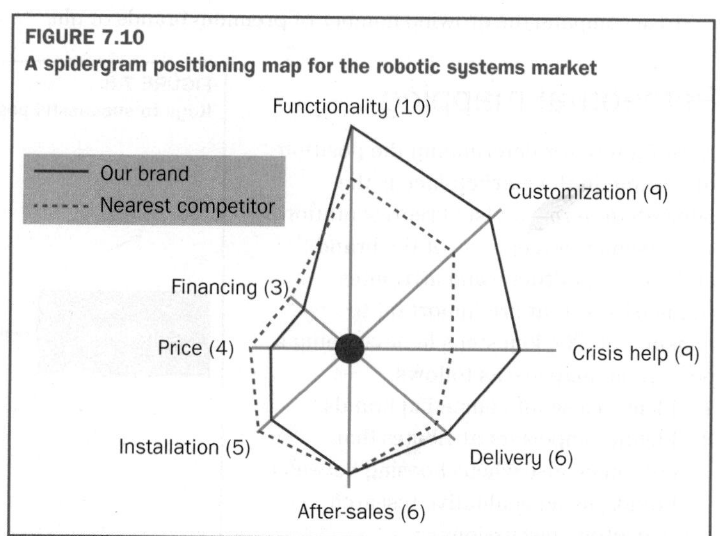

and each brand's score is plotted on each attribute. Our brand has received higher perceptual scores than its nearest competitor for functionality, customization, crisis help and delivery. Our brand and its nearest competitor are similarly rated for after-sales service, but for installation, price and financing, our nearest competitor is rated more highly. Since our company is rated more highly on those attributes that are more important to consumers, it is likely that our brand has a larger market share than its
nearest competitor.

Like a perceptual map, spidergram analysis is valuable in identifying how consumers (as opposed to managers) perceive the strengths and weaknesses of competing brands. It provides a visual portrayal of the positions of brands along multiple dimensions. Spidergram software is available from the Aliah Corporation, USA, which permits the simultaneous analysis of up to six brands.

FIGURE 7.11
Repositioning strategies

Target market	Product: Same	Product: Different
Same	Image repositioning	Product repositioning
Different	Intangible repositioning	Tangible repositioning

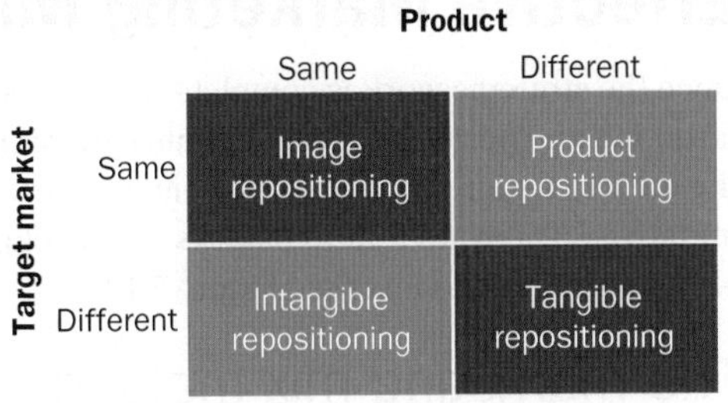

Repositioning

Occasionally a product or service will need to be repositioned because of changing customer tastes or poor sales performance. **Repositioning** involves changing the target markets, the differential advantage, or both.

A useful framework for analysing repositioning options is given in Figure 7.11. Using product differentiation and target market as the key variables, four generic repositioning strategies are shown.

Image repositioning

The first option is to keep product and target market the same, but to change the image of the product. In markets where products act as a form of self-expression, the product may be acceptable in functional terms but fail because it lacks the required image. Many organizations—from McDonald's to low-cost airlines like Ryanair (Eletheriou-Smith, 2011) to giant industrial corporations like BASF, the German chemical company—have changed their image by altering business practices to be perceived as sustainable, environmentally friendly and better able to meet the needs of the target audience.

Product repositioning

With this strategy, the product is changed while the target market remains the same. For example, IBM has used product repositioning very successfully by moving away from the manufacture of computers (IBM sold its PC division to Lenovo) to the provision of software and services to essentially the same type of business customers.

Intangible repositioning

This strategy involves targeting a different market segment with the same product. Beecham Foods initially targeted Lucozade, a carbonated drink, at sick children. But, in the 1980s, it was realized that the drink could become an everyday drink. So, the strapline for its adverts changed from 'Lucozade aids recovery' to 'Lucozade replaces lost energy'. This shift allowed the product to be sold to new target markets. Since then, Lucozade has successfully targeted the health drink and sports markets (Ward, 2009).

Tangible repositioning

When both product and target market are changed, a company is practising tangible repositioning. For example, a company may decide to move upmarket or downmarket by introducing a new range of products to meet the needs of the new target customers.

Highly successful tangible repositioning was undertaken by Samsung Electronics, which was once an unfocused manufacturer of cheap undifferentiated TVs and microwaves, selling to all age groups, but is now a premium-priced flat-screen television and mobile handset brand focused on, as we have seen, the 'high-life seeker' segment of the market—consumers who are willing to adopt technology early and pay a high price for it (Pesola, 2005).

Mercedes-Benz found it necessary to use tangible and product repositioning in the face of Japanese competition. Tangible repositioning took the form of developing new products (e.g. a city car) to appeal to new target customers. Product repositioning was also required in its current market segments to bring down the cost of development and manufacture in the face of lower-priced rivals such as Toyota's Lexus.

Key Characteristics of an Effective Marketing Mix

Once the strategic work is complete on segmentation, targeting and positioning, the outputs can inform the tactical actions needed to implement marketing initiatives. There are four hallmarks for developing an effective marketing mix (see Figure 7.12).

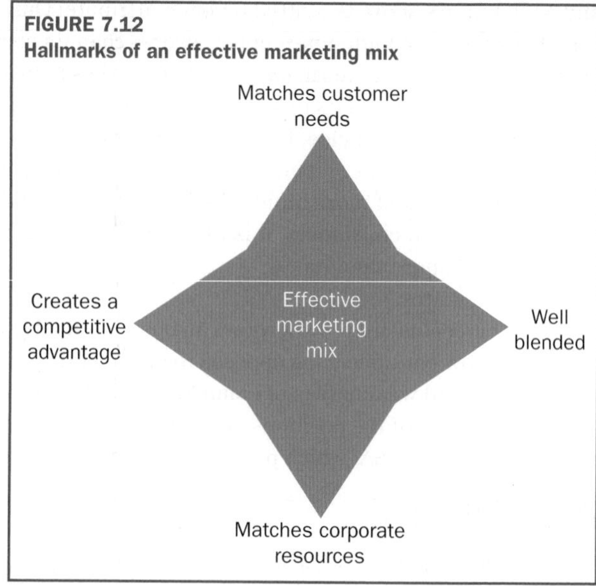

FIGURE 7.12
Hallmarks of an effective marketing mix

The marketing mix matches customer needs

Sensible marketing mix decisions can be made only when the target customer is identified and understood. Once the target market(s) is identified, marketing management needs to understand how customers choose between rival offerings so they can develop a market position. Managers should consider the product or service through customers' eyes and consider segmentation variables and choice criteria (discussed in Chapter 3), which inform how individuals in the market might behave.

Figure 7.13 illustrates the link between customer choice criteria and the marketing mix. The starting point is the realization that customers evaluate products on economic and psychological criteria. Economic criteria include factors such as performance, availability, reliability, durability and productivity gains to be made by using the product. Examples of psychological criteria are self-image, a desire for a quiet life, pleasure, convenience and risk reduction (see Chapter 3). The important point at this stage is to note that an analysis of customer choice criteria reveals a set of key customer requirements that must be met in order to succeed in the marketplace. Meeting or exceeding these requirements better than the competition leads to the creation of a competitive advantage.

The marketing mix creates a competitive advantage

A competitive advantage is the achievement of superior performance through differentiation to provide superior customer value or by managing to achieve lowest delivered cost. Competitive advantage can be derived from decisions about the Four-Ps.

Lidl and Aldi, the German supermarket chains, achieve a competitive advantage by severely controlling costs, allowing them to make profits even though their prices are low, a strategy that is attractive to price-sensitive shoppers.

The strategy of using advertising as a tool for competitive advantage is often employed when product benefits are particularly subjective and amorphous in nature. Thus, the advertising for perfumes such as those produced by Chanel, Givenchy and Yves St Laurent is critical in preserving the exclusive image established by such brands.

Finally, distribution decisions need to be made with the customer in mind, not only in terms of availability but also with respect to service levels, image and customer convenience. The Radisson SAS hotel at Manchester

FIGURE 7.13
Matching the marketing mix to customer needs

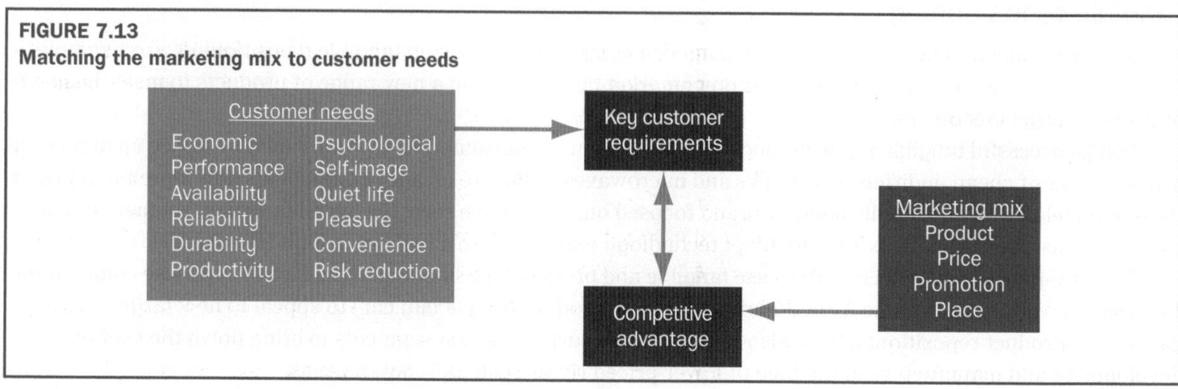

airport is an example of creating a competitive advantage through customer convenience. It is situated 5 minutes' walk from the airport terminals, which are reached by covered walkways, while guests at rival hotels must rely on taxis or transit buses to reach the airport.

The marketing mix should be well blended

The third characteristic of an effective marketing mix is that the four elements—product, price, promotion and place—should be well blended to form a consistent theme. If a product gives superior benefits to customers, price, which may send cues to customers regarding quality, should reflect those extra benefits. All the promotional mix should be designed with the objective of communicating a consistent message to the target audience about these benefits, and distribution decisions should be consistent with the overall strategic position of the product in the marketplace. The use of exclusive outlets for upmarket fashion and cosmetics brands—Armani, Christian Dior and Calvin Klein, for example—is consistent with their strategic position.

The marketing mix should match corporate resources

The choice of marketing mix strategy may ultimately be down to the available financial resources of the company. For example, Amazon was only able to establish its global presence by massive financial investment in online advertising. Certain media—for example, TV advertising—require a minimum threshold investment before they are regarded as feasible. In the UK, a rule of thumb is that at least £5 million per year is required to achieve impact in a national advertising campaign. Clearly, those brands that cannot afford such a promotional budget must use other less expensive media—for example, digital marketing, posters or sales promotion—to attract and hold customers.

A second internal resource constraint may be the internal competences of the company. A marketing mix strategy may be too ambitious for the limited marketing skills of personnel to implement effectively. While an objective may be to reduce or eliminate this problem in the medium- to long-term, in the short-term marketing management may have to heed the fact that strategy must take account of competences.

Each of the elements of the marketing mix are covered in detail in later chapters.

Review

1 The concepts of market segmentation and target marketing and their use in developing marketing strategy

- Market segmentation is the identification of individuals or organizations with similar characteristics that have significant implications for the determination of marketing strategy.
- Its use aids target market selection, the ability to design a tailored marketing mix, the development of differential marketing strategies, and the identification of opportunities and threats.
- Target marketing is the choice of specific segment(s) to serve. It concerns the decision of where to compete.
- Its use is focusing company resources on those segments that it is best able to serve in terms of company resources and segment attractiveness. Once chosen, a tailored marketing mix that creates a differential advantage can be designed based on an in-depth understanding of target customers.

2 Discuss the methods of segmenting consumers

- Segmentation involves looking at the characteristics of the disaggregated market and then dividing this market into meaningful segments. Consumer segmentation can use many different variables as the basis for identifying a market. There are three broad categories of variables that a marketer might use: behavioural, psychographic and profile variables.

3 Consider the rise of tribal marketing and the implications for marketing

- Tribal marketing offers a new way of thinking about identifying target markets. Tribal clans are self-selecting and are formed by mutual interest in a brand, product or service.
- Online communities formed through social media networks can be very powerful and may have the capacity to influence the development of a brand and its value.
- Tribal markets tend to be more about co-creation of value than traditional marketing segmentation.

4 The factors that can be used to evaluate market segments

- Two broad issues should be used: market attractiveness and the company's capability to compete.
- Market attractiveness can be assessed by examining market factors (segment size, segment growth rate, price sensitivity, bargaining power of customers, bargaining power of suppliers, barriers to market segment entry and barriers to market segment exit), competitive factors (nature of competition, the likelihood of new entrants and competitive differentiation) and political, social and environmental factors (political issues, social trends and environmental issues).
- Capability to compete can be assessed by analysing exploitable marketing assets, cost advantages, technological edge, and managerial capabilities and commitments.

5 Four target market strategies: undifferentiated, differentiated, focused and customized marketing

- Undifferentiated marketing occurs when a company does not segment but applies a single marketing mix to the whole market.
- Differentiated marketing occurs when a company segments the market and applies separate marketing mixes to appeal to all or some of the segments (target markets).
- Focused marketing occurs when a company segments the market and develops one specific marketing mix to one segment (target market).
- Customized marketing occurs when a company designs a separate marketing mix for each customer.

6 The concept of positioning and the keys to successful positioning

- There are two aspects of positioning: the choice of target market (where to compete) and the creation of a differential advantage (how to compete).
- The objective is to create and maintain a distinctive place in the market for a company and/or its products.
- The four keys to successful positioning are: clarity, consistency, credibility and competitiveness.

7 Positioning and repositioning strategies

- A useful tool for determining the position of a brand in the marketplace is the perceptual map.
- Positioning strategy should be formulated on a clear choice of target market, based on market segment attractiveness and company capability, and the creation of a differential advantage (based on an understanding of the attributes—choice criteria—that consumers use when choosing between brands).
- Repositioning strategies can be based on changes to the product and/or target market. Four strategies are: image repositioning, product repositioning, intangible repositioning and tangible repositioning.

8 Discuss the characteristics of developing an effective marketing mix

Once the strategic work is complete on segmentation, targeting and positioning, the outputs can inform the tactical actions needed to implement marketing initiatives. An effective mix:

- matches the customer's needs
- creates competitive advantage
- is well-blended
- matches corporate resources.

Key Terms

benefit segmentation the grouping of people based on the different benefits they seek from a product

customized marketing the market coverage strategy where a company decides to target individual customers and develops separate marketing mixes for each

differential marketing strategies market coverage strategies where a company decides to target several market segments and develops separate marketing mixes for each

focused marketing a market coverage strategy where a company decides to target one market segment with a single marketing mix

lifestyle segmentation the grouping of people according to their pattern of living as expressed in their activities, interests and opinions

market segmentation the process of identifying individuals or organizations with similar characteristics that have significant implications for the determination of marketing strategy

positioning the choice of target market (where the company wishes to compete) and differential advantage (how the company wishes to compete)

profile segmentation the grouping of people in terms of profile variables, such as age and socio-economic group, so that marketers can communicate to them

psychographic segmentation the grouping of people according to their lifestyle and personality characteristics

repositioning changing the target market or differential advantage, or both

target marketing the choice of which market segment(s) to serve with a tailored marketing mix

undifferentiated marketing a market coverage strategy where a company decides to ignore market segment differences and develops a single marketing mix for the whole market

Study Questions

1. **What are the advantages of market segmentation? Can you see any advantages of mass marketing, that is of treating a market as homogeneous and marketing to the whole market with one marketing mix?**
2. **Choose a market you are familiar with and use benefit segmentation to identify market segments. What are the likely profiles of the resulting segments?**
3. **In what kind of markets is psychographic segmentation likely to prove useful? Why?**
4. **How might age affect online market segmentation?**
5. **Explain how you might select segmentation variables when aiming to access online markets.**
6. **Define the VALs framework and discuss how this can be used as a method for identifying a target market.**
7. **Explain the difference between a tribe and a segment.**
8. **What is the majority fallacy? Why should it be considered when evaluating market segments?**
9. **What is the difference between positioning and repositioning? Choose three products and services and describe how they are positioned in the marketplace—that is, what is their target market and what is their differential advantage?**

Recommended Reading

Customers can be clumped together in many different ways. Read the following to discover more about the importance of tribes to marketing; get first hand practical experience on how leading consumer analytics firm Experian segments populations, take a deep dive into how to serve a particular segment: the millenials.

Cova, B. and V. (2002), Tribal marketing: The tribalisation of society and its impact on the conduct of marketing, *European Journal of Marketing* 36(5/6), 595–620.

Experian Mosaic (2018), https://www.experian.co.uk/marketing-services/products/mosaic/mosaic-resources.html (accessed August 2018).

Anon. (2011), Special issue on marketing challenges in serving millenials, *Journal of Consumer Marketing*, 28(1), https://doi.org/10.1108/jcm.2011.07728aaa.003 (accessed August 2018).

References

The author is indebted to Professor David Shipley, Trinity College, University of Dublin, for material used in the description of spidergram analysis.

Abell, D.F. and Hammond, J.S. (1979), *Strategic Market Planning: Problems and Analytical Approaches*, Hemel Hempstead: Prentice-Hall.

ACORN CACI (2014), *The User Guide: The Consumer Classification*. London http://acorn.caci.co.uk/downloads/Acorn-User-guide.pdf (accessed 17 March 2015).

Bang & Olufsen (2018), Bang & Oulfsen report double digit growth and improved profitability, Press release file:///C:/Users/Fiona/Downloads/annual-report-17-18-bangolufsen-press-release-uk.pdf (accessed August 2018).

Barnett, M. (2011), Hi-tech healthcare, *Marketing Week*, 30 June, 14–17.

Bearne, S. (2015), How Gap Failed to fill a gap in the fashion market, *Retail week*, 30 January http://www.retail-week.com/sectors/fashion/analysis-how-gap-failed-to-fill-a-gap-in-the-fashion-market/5071599.article?blocktitle=Zara:-Latest-news-and-insight&contentID=9719 (accessed 28 February 2015).

Brashear, T.G., Kashyap, V., Musante, M.D. and Donthu, N. (2009), A profile of the internet shopper: evidence from six countries, *Journal of Marketing Theory and Practice* 17(3), 267–81.

Brownsell, A. (2011), Toyota targets young drivers in £7.5m push, *Marketing Magazine*, 10 August, 3.

Brynjolfsson, E., Hu, Y.J. and Simester, D. (2011), Goodbye Pareto Principle, Hello Long Tail: the effect of search costs on the concentration of product sales, *Management Science* 57(8), 1373–86.

Burgess, M. (2018), You and your personal data , *Wired*, 16 March https://www.wired.co.uk/article/google-history-search-tracking-data-how-to-delete (accessed August 2018).

Cattermole, G. (2012), Sainsbury's boosted by Christmas food sales growth, *The Guardian*, http://www.guardian.co.uk/business/2012/jan/11/sainsburys-christmas-food-sales (accessed February 2015).

Chang, A. (2012), 5 Reasons why Nokia Lost its Handset Sales Lead and Got Downgraded to 'Junk', *Wired*, 27 April http://www.wired.com/2012/04/5-reasons-why-nokia-lost-its-handset-sales-lead-and-got-downgraded-to-junk (accessed 6 March 2015).

Chisnall, P. (2005), *Marketing Research*, Maidenhead: McGraw-Hill.

Chorley, M. and Rentoul, J. (2011), Seven in 10 of us belong to middle class Britain, *The Independent on Sunday*, 20 March, 13–17.

Cova, B. and V. (2002), Tribal marketing: The tribalisation of society and its impact on the conduct of marketing. *European Journal of Marketing* 36(5), 595–620.

Cova, B. and White, T. (2010), Counter-brand and alter-brand communities: the impact of Web 2.0 on tribal marketing approaches, *Journal of Marketing Management* 26 (3–4) 256–70.

Davis, A. (2014), Cut-throat competition grips smartphone market, *The Telegraph*, 28 July http://www.telegraph.co.uk/sponsored/finance/macroeconomics-investment/10995602/cutthroat-competition-grips-smartphone-market.html (accessed 10 March 2015).

Dawson, C. (2017), Meet the market place: Fyndiq, 25 September https://tamebay.com/2017/09/meet-marketplace-fyndiq.html (accessed August, 2018).

Day, G.S. (1986), *Analysis for Strategic Market Decisions*, New York: West.

Davies, R. (2017), Thomas Cook profits fall after political turmoil and food poisoning claims, *The Guardian*, 22 November https://www.theguardian.com/business/2017/nov/22/thomas-cook-shares-fall-political-turmoil-tourist-spots-profits (accessed August 2018).

Dixon, P. (2005), Wake up to stronger tribes and longer life, *Financial Times*, 31 October http://www.globalchange.com/financialtimesdixonfeature31oct2005.pdf (accessed 7 April 2012).

Doherty, N.F. and Ellis-Chadwick, F. (2010a), Evaluating the role of electronic commerce in transforming the retail sector, *The International Review of Retail, Distribution and Consumer Research* 20(4), 375–8.

Doherty, N.F. and Ellis-Chadwick, F. (2010b) Internet retailing: the past, the present and the future, *International Journal of Retail & Distribution Management* 38, 11/12, 943–65.

Doyle, P. (2008), *Value-Based Marketing*, John Wiley & Sons.

Edwards, H. (2011), Sixty is the new old, *Marketing Magazine*, 9 November, 19.

Eletheriou-Smith, L.M. (2011), Ryanair signal brand U-turn with eco-claims, *Marketing*, 27 July, 1.

Experian (2015), *Mosaic United Kingdom* http://cld.bz/RUfDTGu (accessed July 2018).

Fanny Karst (2018), http://www.fannykarst.com/ (accessed August 2018).

Fleck, A. (2018), What advertisers should know about marketing to fathers, *AdWeek*, 13 June https://www.adweek.com/creativity/infographic-fathers-present-unique-targets-for-advertisers/ (accessed August 2018).

Friedmann, E. (2018), The context of choice as boundary conditions for gender differences in brand choice considerations, *European Journal of Marketing* 52 (5/6) 1280–1304.

Fyndiq (2014), *'Amazon for bargain products' Fyndiq reaches break-even, over 200 000 products sold in December*, Mynewsdesk, 30 January http://www.mynewsdesk.com/se/fyndiq/pressreleases/amazon-for-bargain-products-fyndiq-reaches-break-even-over-200-000-products-sold-in-december-955282 (accessed July 2018).

Handley, L. (2011), Original teenagers kick segmentation into touch, *Marketing Week*, 1 December, 18–19.

Hilpern, K. (2011), An ageless strategy, *The Marketer*, November/December, 28–31.

Hoffman, D.L., Novak, T.P. and Schlosser, A. (2003), The evolution of the digital divide: how gaps in internet access may impact electronic commerce, in Steinfield, C. (ed.) *New Directions in Research on E-Commerce*, West Lafayette, IN: Purdue University Press, 245–92.

Hooley, G.J., Saunders, J., Piercy, N. and Nicoulaud, B. (2012), *Marketing Strategy and Competitive Positioning: The Key to Market Success*, Hemel Hempstead: Prentice-Hall, 148.

Howe, N. (2014), Generation X: Once Xtreme, Now Exhausted, *Forbes*, 27 August http://www.forbes.com/sites/neilhowe/2014/08/27/generation-x-once-xtreme-now-exhausted-part-5-of-7 (accessed 12 March 2015).

Internet World Stats (2018), The Big Picture https://www.internetworldstats.com/stats.htm (accessed August 2018).

Jack, L. (2009), Cleaning Up Its Act, *Marketing Week*, 12 February, 21.

Jayawardhena, C., Wright, L.T. and Dennis, C. (2007), Consumers online: intentions, orientations and segmentation, *International Journal of Retail & Distribution Management* 35(6), 512–26.

Kantar Media (2012) TGI Europa, http://kantarmedia-tgigb.com/tgi-surveys/tgi-europa/ (accessed February 2015).

Keely, G. and Clark, A. (2008), Zara overtakes Gap to become world's largest clothing retailer, *The Guardian*, 11 August http://www.theguardian.com/business/2008/aug/11/zara.gap.fashion (accessed 10 March 2015).

Kimmel, A.J. (2010), *Connecting with consumers: marketing for new marketplace realties*, Oxford University Press, 15–19.

KPMG (2013), *How will demographic trends affect the retail sector?* http://www.kpmg.com/uk/en/issuesandinsights/articlespublications/newsreleases/pages/how-will-demographic-trends-in-the-uk-affect-the-retail-sector.aspx (accessed 23 February 2015).

Kukar-Kinney, M., Ridgway, N.M. and Monroe, K.B. (2009), The relationship between consumers' tendencies to buy compulsively and their motivations to shop and buy on the internet, *Journal of Retailing* 85(3), 298.

Lannon, J. (1991), Developing Brand Strategies across Borders, *Marketing and Research Today*, August, 160–8.

Lunden, I. (2014), *Fyndiq Raises $20M To Take Its Bargain Marketplace Beyond Sweden*, Techcrunch, 7 November http://techcrunch.com/2014/11/07/fyndiq-raises-20m-to-take-its-bargain-marketplace-beyond-sweden (accessed 15 March 2015).

Millward Brown (2015), *Brand Personality*, MillwardBrown, 20 March http://www.millwardbrown.com/mb-global/brand-strategy/brand-equity/brandz/top-global-brands/previous-years-results/2012-brandz-top-100/brand-personality (accessed August 2018).

Muller, R. (2011), Target China, *The Marketer*, July/August, 32–5.

O'Brien, S. and Ford, R. (1988), Can We at Last Say Goodbye to Social Class?, *Journal of the Market Research Society* 30(3), 289–332.

Pesola, M. (2005), Samsung plays to the young generation, *Financial Times*, 29 March.

Prensky, M. (2001), Digital Natives, Digital Immigrants, *On the Horizon* 9(5), 1–6.

Ries, A. and Trout, J. (2001), *Positioning: The Battle for your Mind*, New York: Warner.

Ritson, M. (2011), Know when to shut the door on your customer, *Marketing Week*, 25 August, 50.

Rochon, M.E. (2014), Conversation with Fanny Karst, young designer but old lady at heart, La Passerelle, 6 May http://lapasserellemontreal.com/2014/05/06/conversation-with-fanny-karst-young-designer-but-old-lady-at-heart/#sthash.6FrqL5ui.dpuf (accessed 12 March 2015).

Rose, S. (2008), There Are Plenty of Reasons Why Britain Still Loves M&S, *The Guardian*, 25 January, 41.

Sampson, P. (1992), People are People the World Over: The Case for Psychological Market Segmentation, *Marketing and Research Today*, November, 236–44.

SBI International (2018), https://www.sri.com (accessed August 2018).

Shui, E. and Dawson, J. (2004), Comparing the Impacts of Technology and National Culture on Online Usage and Purchase from a Four-Country Perspective, *Journal of Retailing and Consumer Services* 11(6), 385–94.

Simms, J. (2005), Strategising Simplicity, *Marketing*, 25 May, 15.

Slyke, C.V., Comunale, C.L. and Belanger, F. (2002), Gender differences in perceptions of Web-based shopping, *Communications of the ACM* 45(7), 82–6.

Smith, C. (2014), 7 Statistics About E-Commerce Shoppers That Reveal Why Many Consumer Stereotypes Don't Apply Online, *Business Insider*, 13 August http://www.businessinsider.com/the-demographics-of-who-shops-online-and-on-mobile-2014-8?IR=T (accessed February 2015).

Smith, G. (2008), On The Road, *Guardian Weekend*, 21 June, 99.

Swaminathan, V., Lepkowska-White, E. and Rao, B.P. (1999), Browsers or buyers in cyberspace? An investigation of factors influencing electronic exchange, *Journal of Computer-Mediated Communication* 5(2), 1–19.

Strategic Business Insights (2018), http://www.strategicbusinessinsights.com/vals/ustypes.shtml (accessed August 2018).

Tata Motors (2009), The story of the Nano http://www.tatanano.com (accessed August 2018).

Tynan, A.C. and Drayton, J. (1987), Market Segmentation, *Journal of Marketing Management* 2(3), 301–35.

United Airlines (2012), www.united.com.

Uncles, M.D. (2008), Know thy changing consumer, *Journal of Brand Management*, 15(4), 227–31.

Van Raaij, W.F. and Verhallen, T.M.M. (1994), Domain-specific Market Segmentation, *European Journal of Marketing* 28(10), 49–66.

Veloutsou, C. and Moutinho, L. (2009), Brand relationships through brand reputation and brand tribalism, *Journal of Business Research* 62(3), 314–322.

Wachman, R. (2012), Lego's profits rise as it thinks pink, *The Guardian*, 1 March http://www.theguardian.com/business/2012/mar/01/lego-profits-rise-pink (accessed February 2015).

Wallop, H. (2014), Gen Z, Gen Y, baby boomers—a guide to the generations, *The Telegraph*. http://www.telegraph.co.uk/news/features/11002767/Gen-Z-Gen-Y-baby-boomers-a-guide-to-the-generations.html (accessed 12 March 2015).

Ward, L. (2009), The history of Lucozade, The Fact Site http://www.thefactsite.com/2009/03/history-of-lucozade.html (accessed August 2018).

Wieners, B. (2011), Lego is for girls, *Bloomberg Business Week*, 19 December, 68–73.

Wind, Y. (1978), Issues accessed February 2015 and Advances in Segmentation Research, *Journal of Marketing Research*, August, 317–37.

Wood, Z. (2018), Fantasy miniatures bring roaring success to UK's Games Workshop, *The Guardian*, 3 March https://www.theguardian.com/business/2018/mar/03/fantasy-miniatures-bring-roaring-success-to-uks-games-workshop (accessed August 2018)

Yankelovich, D. and Meer, D. (2006), Rediscovering Market Segmentation, *Harvard Business Review* http://www.viewpointlearning.com/wp-content/uploads/2011/04/segmentation_0206.pdf (accessed August 2018).

Zikmund, W.G. and D'Amico, M. (1999), *Marketing*, St Paul, MN: West, 249.

CASE 13
The Growing No-Alcohol and Low-Alcohol Beer Segment

Introduction

Growth in conventional beer sales is stalling around the world, as an increasing number of people become more focused on health and well-being (EUCAM, 2018). A growing push among consumers to live healthier lives has completely refocused the food and drinks industry over the last few years. Consumers shop differently, cook differently, eat differently and drink differently. The shift towards health and wellness has shaken up the alcohol sector and resulted in rising demand for no-alcohol beers and low-alcohol beers (NABLABs) (Kowitt, 2017). No-alcohol beers are generally considered as those under 0.5% ABV, while low-alcohol beers are considered as those between 0.5% and 3% ABV. ABV refers to alcohol by volume and is a standard measure of how much alcohol (ethanol) is contained in a given volume of an alcoholic beverage (expressed as a volume per cent) (Arthur, 2016).

A Growing Segment

According to insights from Global Data, the compound annual growth rate for beer overall was less than 1 per cent between 2010 and 2016, but low and no alcohol beers provided a glimmer of hope at 5.2 per cent growth. Euromonitor (2017) found non-alcoholic beer still represents the fastest growing area of the beer market in Europe. This rate of growth has made the category a major priority for big brewers. The industry had limited choice but to act, as increasing demand for these products is pushing the brewers into action. Currently, alcohol-free beer accounts for about 2% of overall beer consumption, but despite such a low base, it is expected that the move towards health will make NABLABs one of the fastest growing categories of beers (Kowitt, 2017). Zero and low alcohol beers may be a niche market for leading global brands like Budweiser brewer Anheuser-Busch InBev, Heineken and Carlsberg, but these big brewers are now introducing zero and low alcohol beer brands to appeal to wider markets. Anheuser-Busch InBev, the biggest of the brewers, aims to make a fifth of its sales from low and no alcohol beers by 2025, investing in new products such as Budweiser Prohibition, the alcohol-free version of their famous brand. Meanwhile, Carlsberg has also set targets to double sales of its alcohol-free variants by 2022 (EUCAM, 2018).

According to Global Market Insights, the global non-alcoholic beer market is projected to surpass US$25 billion by 2024 (Global Market Insights, 2018). Spain is the leader in Europe, with roughly 13 per cent of the total beer market consisting of low or no alcohol products. This is well ahead of the UK (0.5 per cent), France (1 per cent), the Netherlands (3 per cent) and Austria (4 per cent).1 However, even though the market share of NABLABs is low in the UK, sales of no and low alcohol drinks have soared by more than a fifth between 2017 and 2018. These figures, revealed by the Department of Health in the UK, show that, in just 12 months, sales of NABLABs rose by 20.5 per cent, while sales of high strength beers fell by 12 per cent in the same time period. (Donnelly, 2018).

Drivers of Growth

Designated drivers, pregnant women, nursing women and those who abstain from alcohol for religious reasons are all target groups for the category. These beers are ideal for occasions when people want a great tasting beer, but either cannot or do not wish to consume more or any alcohol. However, experts believe that health-conscious millennials are increasingly driving demand for NABLABs. Millennials are becoming increasingly health-conscious and are aware of long-term effects of alcohol. Gym membership is up among millennials and they don't want alcohol to undo all their efforts. More and more millennials are embracing sobriety and may be reacting against the 'laissez faire' attitude shown by the boozier older generation. Data from the Office for National Statistics (2018) showed the proportion of adults saying they drank alcohol was at the lowest level on record. In total, 56.9 per cent of those aged over 16 had a drink in the week before they were interviewed, a fall from 64.2 per cent in 2005. The figures also showed that those aged 16 to 24 were the least likely to drink of any other age group, with 27 per cent teetotal, a rise from 19 per cent a decade before (Donnelly, 2018).

The drinks industry is responding to trends and to the growing success of movements like 'Dry January' (the month-long abstinence campaign launched by Alcohol Concern 2013). The growing success of 'Dry January' has also resulted in other networks springing up, such as 'One Year No Beer', 'Go Sober for October' and 'Club Soda' (a group which encourages 'mindful drinking') to champion the mindful drinking movement. It has also led to spin-off events (Spitalfields' biannual Mindful Drinking Festival) and a rash of recently published books (e.g. *Mindful Drinking*, the *Sober Diaries* and the *28 Day Alcohol-Free Challenge*). Mindful drinking, a modern-day temperance movement, is becoming increasingly fashionable among millennials who are looking to moderate their alcohol intake, embrace periods of sobriety or even become fully teetotal (Hurst, 2017).

As millennials spend more time interacting with friends online rather than in person, they are increasingly shaping their personal identity around the feedback and the popularity of the content they share on their social media channels. Young users of social media are extremely image aware, carefully curating content and sharing purchases that in some way enhance their personal brands on their channels (Wood and Brennan, 2017). Interestingly, some millennials are also choosing to drink NABLABs because of concern about pictures of them drinking haunting them on social media. They are very attuned to social media and are very conscious that being drunk on social media does not look good (Hurst, 2017).

Challenges

As zero and low alcohol beers are relatively new, stimulating market growth has meant overcoming a number of challenges for leading brewers: overcoming negative consumer perception of the beers and their taste; defining a competitive market position for the beers; working out how to differentiate NABLABs from existing products and from other competing low and no alcohol products. Additionally, many smaller craft brewers are introducing new low-alcohol and alcohol-free beers. There is also the threat of substitution from other non-alcoholic soft drinks, which continue to be popular and pose a major challenge for NABLABs looking to gain a share in the drinks market. Persuading consumers to try the new beers and choose them on a regular basis has been challenging as this segment has traditionally suffered from taste and image problems. For example, the category has been associated with weaker flavours and poor quality. NABLABs face the challenge of trying to make their beers appealing to both men and women and moving away from outdated views. Traditionally, beer companies have mainly focused on males, but a real opportunity exists to target both genders (Roderick, 2017). Yet another challenge facing brewers of these NABLABs is that there is a perception that these products are a 'distress purchase'. Consumers have often felt forced to choose products from this category because they were the designated driver or were watching their weight, therefore creating an association with sacrifice or a negative (Kowitt, 2017). Finally, the future of the NABLAB segment is still uncertain. While this segment is experiencing more growth compared to the overall beer sector, it is coming from a small base. The big question remains—does this category have real growth potential, or will it never be more than a niche add-on to standard beer?

Questions

1. **Suggest what to consider when marketing NABLABs to millennials.**
2. **Discuss the main challenges facing brewers in the NABLAB segment. What can companies and brands do to overcome these challenges?**
3. **Choose any one no-alcohol beer or low-alcohol beer that you are familiar with. Identify the positioning of this beer, i.e. its target market and differential advantage. How is the beer's positioning communicated?**
4. **NABLABs often suffer from negative public perceptions regarding their image and taste. Suggest how these beers can be repositioned to make them more appealing to consumers?**

This case study was written by Marie O' Dwyer, Waterford Institute of Technology.

References

Based on: EUCAM (2018), Growth in the alcohol-free beer market: A threat to soft drinks or to ordinary beer?, EUCAM. Available at: https://eucam.info/2018/02/19/growth-in-the-alcohol-free-

»

beer-market-a-threat-to-soft-drinks-or-to-ordinary-beer/ (accessed 15 July 2018); Kowitt, B. (2017), Big beer's plan for growth? Dropping the alcohol, *Fortune*. Available at: http://fortune.com/2017/08/04/health-wellness-zero-low-no-alcohol-beers/ (accessed 15 July 2018); Arthur, R. (2016), Non-alcoholic and low alcohol beers: opportunities and challenges, *Beverage Daily*. Available at: https://www.beveragedaily.com/Article/2016/02/26/Non-alcoholic-and-low-alcohol-beers-Opportunities-and-challenges (accessed 15 July 2018); Global Market Insights (2018), Worldwide non-alcoholic beer market worth over $25 billion by 2014, *Global Market Insights*. Available at: https://globenewswire.com/news-release/2018/03/20/1442488/0/en/Worldwide-Non-alcoholic-Beer-Market-worth-over-25-billion-by-2024-Global-Market-Insights-Inc.html (accessed 15 July 2018); Donnelly, L. (2018), Sales of 'nanny state' low-alcohol beers are soaring, *Telegraph*. Available at: https://www.telegraph.co.uk/news/2018/04/29/sales-nanny-state-low-alcohol-beers-soaring-figures-show/ (accessed 15 July 2018); Hurst, G. (2017), Mindful drinking is new trend among millennials, *The Times*. Available at: https://www.thetimes.co.uk/article/mindful-drinking-is-new-trend-among-millennials-one-year-no-beer-club-soda-big-drop-brewing-co-rzb03g6rr (accessed 15 July 2018); Wood, S. and Brennan, P. (2017), The art of drinks marketing is changing as demand for NOLO (no and low) alcohol reaches its peak, *The Drum*. Available at: https://www.thedrum.com/opinion/2017/04/20/the-art-drinks-marketing-changing-the-demand-nolo-no-and-low-alcohol-reaches-its (accessed 15 July 2018); Roderick, L. (2017), Four challenges Heineken needs to overcome to make its non-alcoholic beer a success, *Marketing Week*. Available at: https://www.marketingweek.com/2017/05/19/heineken-non-alcoholic-beer/ (accessed 15 July 2018).

CASE 14

Behavioural and Psychological Segmentation Criteria: The LEGO Case

LEGO, the Danish toy manufacturer of plastic building bricks, has a large website that is translated into 19 languages across 26 different markets. Most of LEGO's 36 product lines have their own microsites with apps, games, downloads and even display sections for builders' own models—a good alignment with the needs of the digitally able generation. However, only one product line, LEGO Duplo, has external links to social media such as Facebook, Twitter and Pinterest on the product line microsite. At the other extreme, the LEGO Architecture microsite focuses on images of the current range and information about the original buildings. So, why is LEGO moving its online presence away from an exclusive focus on Web 2.0 on most of the product line microsites to include social media for one customer segment, and back to more traditional 'Web 1.0' marketing for another? This case looks at why demographic segmentation criteria are not enough; behavioural and psychological segmentation also have a role to play in reaching out to target consumers.

The LEGO Duplo and LEGO Architecture Product Lines

LEGO Duplo bricks are designed to be used by young children, in the age range two to five years. The LEGO Duplo bricks are only found in the range of sets that make up the LEGO Duplo product line and focus on themes that toddlers and pre-school children can relate to, such as animals, food and trains. LEGO Duplo bricks are also much larger than the standard LEGO bricks, making it easier for the youngest children to build creatively without the need for the fine motor skills that older children have.

The LEGO Architecture product line, on the other hand, is primarily targeted towards the adult segment. Standard LEGO bricks are used to build scale models of famous buildings such as the Eiffel Tower, the Great Wall of China and the Statue of Liberty. Only one LEGO Architecture product encourages independent creativity, containing white bricks and a booklet

explaining the principles of modernist architecture, developed in conjunction with architectural design bureaus from around the world.

Target Segments

The majority of LEGO's main website focuses on reaching out to school children up to the age of about 14, and emphasizes interaction and the co-creation of content through the ability to upload the builder's own models to forums.

The LEGO Duplo and LEGO Architecture microsites are fundamentally different, as both of these microsites focus on adults. The British LEGO Duplo microsite (http://www.lego.com/en-gb/duplo) focuses on mothers and children and links to five social media platforms.

The image on the Duplo site and the links to social media are unique to the LEGO Duplo microsite; for comparison, the microsite of LEGO Junior, a product line that targets the four- to seven-year-old segment, has an image of two children building a LEGO product together and no offsite links to social media, despite being aimed mostly at parents. It makes sense to reach out to adults through social media using mobile devices, as the majority of adults are constantly online and have a high consumption of social media, especially Facebook and Pinterest, using a variety of

»

»

devices. Whilst pre-schoolers do not understand the internet in the same way as their parents do and do not have the fine motor skills to use a mouse, they can use tablets and smartphones due to the intuitive user interface of these mobile devices, which, coupled with the high level of consumption by parents, makes the mobile platform ideal.

In contrast, a key aim of the LEGO Architecture product line is to entice adults back to building with LEGO bricks, as LEGO tends to 'lose' builders after the age of about 14. Rather than focusing on themes that may be seen as childish by some, its aim is building a scale model of a famous structure. The target segment for LEGO Architecture understands the web in the same way as the LEGO Duplo target segment does; however, the value that needs to be provided by the LEGO Architecture microsite is different.

Behavioural and Psychological Segmentation Criteria, and the LEGO Duplo and LEGO Architecture Microsites

From a market segmentation perspective, a key difference between the LEGO Duplo and LEGO Architecture product lines on the one hand, and LEGO's other product lines on the other, are the segmentation criteria that are used. Instead of targeting children, LEGO targets adults, with the core demographic characteristics being individuals who are middle class, middle income and between the ages of 25 and 40. Behavioural and psychological segmentation criteria are used to understand the needs of adults. The key value proposition that is provided by both the LEGO Duplo and LEGO Architecture microsites is information. The information on the LEGO Duplo microsite details how the building bricks can be used to support child development, with text boxes providing information to parents about general child development in the first five years of their child's life, and shows how LEGO Duplo can contribute to this development using colours, shapes and language. LEGO also underlines on the Duplo microsite how building with the bricks can improve fine motor skills and provide a way for children to express themselves and use their imagination; to support this, most LEGO Duplo products do not contain an instruction booklet. The value provided on the LEGO Architecture microsite for customers consists of information about the buildings themselves—the architect, the building and its history—together with details of the process through which a LEGO Architecture model is developed and realized.

Conclusion: Segmentation and Online Marketing

The LEGO Duplo and LEGO Architecture microsites have a different target segment to the other LEGO microsites: adults rather than children. This provides LEGO with a challenge: how can the product line microsites address the needs of adults rather than children? The answer lies in enabling those in the target segment to receive the most important content in the format from which they gain the most value. In the case of LEGO Duplo, this means optimizing content to focus on social media through mobile devices; in the case of LEGO Architecture, information about the real-world building that inspired the model. So even though both microsites target the same demographic segment—adults—behavioural and psychological segmentation criteria enable LEGO to identify and add extra value on the product line microsites.

Questions

1. **Do you think that LEGO targets the right segment with its LEGO Duplo microsite? Can you think of any other segments that the focus on social media might miss? What about the LEGO Architecture microsite?**
2. **How can LEGO ensure a smooth transition from how parents and children interact with the Duplo range to the LEGO ranges targeted to older children?**
3. **Apply the behavioural and psychological segmentation criteria presented in this chapter to the LEGO Duplo and LEGO Architecture product lines. Which criteria are the same for both product lines, and which are different?**
4. **Who buys LEGO Duplo and LEGO Architecture products? When and why do they buy LEGO Duplo and LEGO Architecture products? Using your answer to question 3, discuss whether LEGO is using the right segmentation criteria to target customers.**

This case study was written by Robert Ormrod, Associate Professor, Aarhus University.

References

The material in the case has been drawn from a variety of published sources.

PART 2 CREATING CUSTOMER VALUE

A number of videos featuring CEOs, CMOs, brand and PR managers related to the Chapters in this Part are available to lecturers for presentation and class discussion.

CHAPTER 8
Value Through Brands

> *The first lesson of branding is memorability. It is very difficult to buy something you can't remember.*
>
> **JOHN HEGARTY (2011)**

LEARNING OBJECTIVES

After reading this chapter, you should be able to:

1 define the concepts of product, brand, product line and product mix
2 distinguish between manufacturer and own-label brands
3 distinguish between a core and augmented product (the brand)
4 explain why strong brands are important
5 define brand equity, the components of customer-based and proprietary-based brand equity and brand valuation
6 explain how to build strong brands
7 distinguish between family, individual and combined brand names, and discuss the characteristics of an effective brand name
8 discuss why companies rebrand and explain how to manage the process
9 discuss the concepts of brand extension and stretching, and their uses and limitations
10 describe the two major forms of co-branding, and their advantages and risks
11 discuss the arguments for and against global and pan-European branding, and the strategic options for building such brands

Marketing success goes beyond merely satisfying customer needs. Brand manufacturers must consider ways to focus market opportunities, using their customers' values. In this chapter we focus on value creation from the perspective of brands.

The core element in the marketing mix is the company's product because this provides the functional requirements sought by customers. Marketing managers develop their products into brands that help to create a unique position (see Chapter 7) in the minds of customers. Brand superiority leads to high sales, the ability to charge price premiums and the power to resist distributor power. Firms attempt to retain their current customers through brand loyalty. Loyal customers are typically less price sensitive, and the presence of a loyal customer base provides the firm with valuable time to respond to competitive actions (DeKimpe et al., 1997). The management of products and brands is therefore a key factor in marketing success.

This chapter will explore the nature and importance of branding, how successful brands are built and how brand equity is created. Then we explore a series of key branding decisions: brand name strategies and choices, rebranding, brand extension and stretching, and co-branding. Finally, we explore global and pan-European branding.

Products, Services and Brands

A product is anything that is capable of satisfying customer needs. For example, a Belvita breakfast biscuit, a pair of Nike trainers, a Ford Focus car or a haircut by Toni & Guy are all capable of satisfying different needs from hunger, through clothing, transportation and self-image. However, we often distinguish between products and services, with products being tangible (e.g. a can of Heinz soup) and services being mainly intangible (e.g. a haircut). Consequently, it is logical to include services within the definition of the product but to be aware that there are differences. Hence, there are *physical products* (goods) such as a watch, a car or a wind turbine, or *service products* such as insurance or banking.

Products satisfy customer needs: for example, a hamburger satisfies hunger, a wind turbine provides sustainable power and insurance products reduce financial risk. The principles discussed in this chapter apply equally to physical and service products. However, because there are special considerations associated with service products (e.g. intangibility), and as service industries (e.g. restaurants, tourism, banking, and the public sector) are an important and growing sector in most developed countries, Chapter 9 is dedicated to examining service products and services marketing in detail.

Branding is the process by which companies distinguish their product offerings from the competition. By developing a distinctive name, packaging and design, a **brand** is created. Most brands are supported by logos—for example, the Nike 'swoosh' and the prancing horse of Ferrari. By developing an individual identity, branding permits customers to develop associations with the brand (e.g. prestige, style, low cost) and eases the purchase decision (De Chernatony, 1991). The marketing task is to ensure positive associations between the chosen positioning objectives (see Chapter 7), the product and the brand.

Branding affects perceptions. In blind product testing, consumers often fail to distinguish between brands in each product category and often cannot correctly identify what they perceive to be their favourite brand. For example, the Pepsi Challenge used a series of taste tests and blind tests (i.e. the brand identities were concealed) to determine preferred brand. The results showed that, while more people bought Coca-Cola, they preferred the taste of Pepsi when blindfolded. Advances in neuroscience may go some way to explaining the results. A recreation of the test produced identical results, but when the tasters were wired to a brain scanner, there was a flurry of activity in the part of the brain that is stimulated by taste in the blind test. However, when the consumers were told which brand they were drinking, the part of the brain associated with higher thinking was activated during tasting (Valantine, 2009).

The word 'brand' is derived from the Old Norse word 'brandr', which means 'to burn', as brands were and still are the means by which livestock owners mark their animals to identify ownership (Keller, 2008). This definition is still pertinent today, as modern branding aims to permanently capture a part of the buyer's mind (Hegarty, 2011), with the aim that buyers always choose a particular brand.

The Product Line and Product Mix

Brands are not often developed in isolation. They normally fall within a company's **product line** and mix. A product line is a group of brands that are closely related in terms of their functions and the benefits they provide (e.g. Apple, Inc. smart watches, Royal Philips of the Netherlands, Ambilight TVs; Driscoll's berries). The *depth* of the product line depends upon the pattern of customer requirements (e.g. the number of segments to be found in the market), the product depth being offered by competitors and company resources. For example, although customers may require wide product variations, a small company may decide to focus on a narrow product line serving only sub-segments of the market.

A **product mix** is the total set of brands marketed in a company: the sum of the product lines offered. Thus, the *width* of the product mix can be gauged by the number of product lines an organization offers. Royal Philips of the Netherlands has a diversified product mix offer, from healthcare ranges for business markets to consumer electronics and lighting. But the company has a consistent brand message for this diverse range of products, which is 'improving people's lives through meaningful innovation' (Phillip, 2015). Other companies have a much narrower product mix comprising just one product line—such as Aston Martin, which produces high-performance cars.

The management of brands and product lines is a key element of product strategy. First, we shall examine the major decisions involved in managing brands: the type of brand to market (manufacturer versus own-label), how to build brands, brand name strategies, brand extension and stretching, and the brand acquisition decision. Then, we shall explore how to manage brands: the product life-cycle. Finally, we discuss managing brand and product line portfolios.

Brand Types

The two alternatives regarding brand type are manufacturer and own-label brands. **Manufacturer brands** are created by producers and bear their own chosen brand name. The responsibility for marketing the brand lies in the hands of the producer. Examples include Kellogg's Cornflakes, Gillette Sensor razors and Norton Securities anti-virus software. The value of the brand lies with the producer and, by building major brands, producers can gain distribution and customer loyalty.

A fundamental distinction needs to be made between category, brands and variants (see Figure 8.1). A category (or product field) is divided into brands, which in turn may be divided into variants based on flavour, formulation or another feature (East, 1997). For example, Heinz tomato soup is the tomato variant of the Heinz brand of the

FIGURE 8.1
Categories, brands and variants

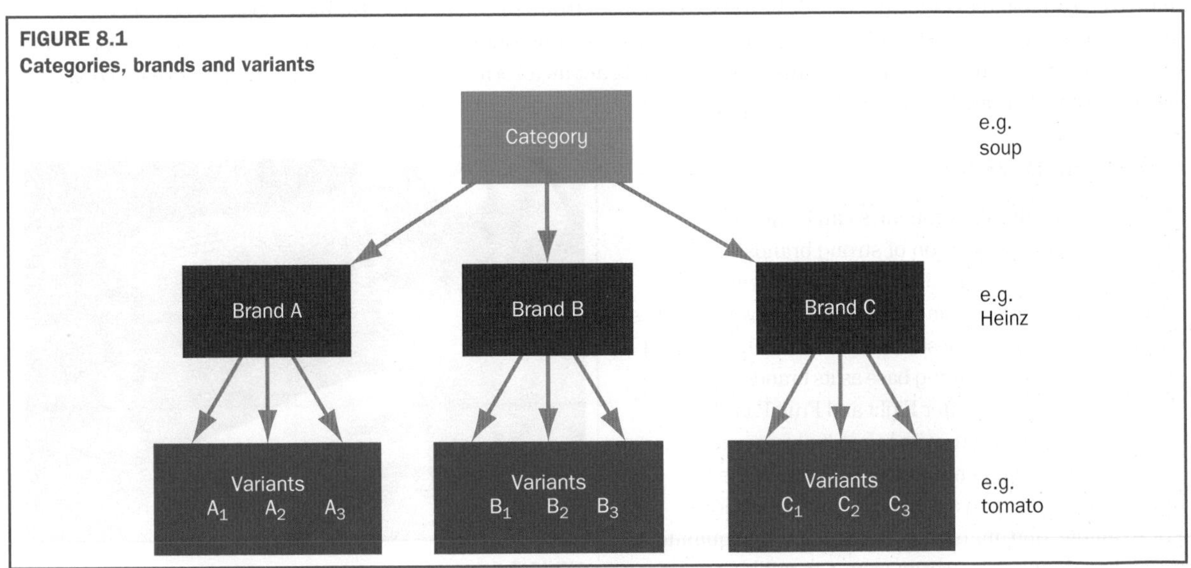

category 'soup'. In recent years, several products have emerged which have become category-creating products: for example, the iPod, Yakult probiotic drinks, Spanx body-shaping underwear and Twitter (Carter, 2011).

Own-label brands (sometimes called *private label* or *distributor brands*) are created and owned by distributors. Own-label branding, if associated with tight quality control of suppliers, can provide consistent high value for customers and be a source of retail power as suppliers vie to fill excess productive capacity with manufacturing products for own-label branding. The power of low-price supermarket own-label brands has focused many producers of manufacturer brands to introduce so-called **fighter brands** (i.e. their own low-price alternative). Own-label food lines is certainly where supermarkets do battle. Discounters Aldi and Lidl have jointly grown their market share in the UK to 13 per cent with their low-priced own-label product, taking market share from larger rivals Sainsbury's and Tesco. Both larger chains offer a suite of own-label propositions from 'value' ranges to premium-priced e.g. Tesco's Finest, Sainsbury's Taste the Difference. But Sainsbury's is experiencing declining market share; even large price cuts to its Taste the Differences range made limited impact, suggesting that consumers are looking for good quality lower priced goods and are moving away from top-end own-labels in supermarkets (Vincent, 2018).

Fighter brands are not just low-price alternatives, but are generally developed as part of a competitive strategy to protect market share from predatory competitors. Examples include Qantas launching Jetstar to fight the entry of Virgin Australia Airlines into Australian airspace. Intel introduced the Intel Celeron both to protect its premium market produce, the Pentium, and to fight off its cheaper competitors.

A major decision for producers is whether to agree to supply own-label products for distributors. The danger is, should customers find out, they may believe that there is no difference between the manufacturer's brand and its own-label equivalent. Some companies, such as Kellogg's, refuse to supply own-label products; indeed, this global food manufacturer has developed secret recipes for its Special K brand to fight against the rise of supermarket own brands (Reynolds, 2015). For other producers, supplying own-label goods is a means of generating income from the high sales volumes contracted with distributors. Bokomo Foods is a leading cereal maker and produces branded own-label foods for the UK and Scandinavia. For example, it produces cereals for Sainsbury's, Tesco and Morrisons in the UK, and makes Belso exclusively for Danish stores Netto, Fotex and Bilka (Bokomo Foods Ltd, 2015).

Why Strong Brands are Important

Apple, Google, IBM, China Mobile and General Electric are world-leading brands valued at over $50 billion (Costa, 2011) and customers are prepared to pay for the assurances they offer. Strong brands, typically product category leaders, are important to both companies and consumers. Companies benefit because strong brands add value to companies, positively affect consumer perceptions of brands, act as a barrier to competition, improve profits and provide a base for brand extensions. Strong brand names also have positive effects on consumer perceptions and preferences. See Mini Case 8.1 to find out how Douwe Egberts is more than just coffee to its consumer. Consumers gain because strong brands act as a form of quality certification and create trust. We now look at these factors.

Company value

The financial value of companies can be greatly enhanced by the possession of strong brands. For example, Nestlé paid £2.5 billion for Rowntree, a UK confectionery manufacturer, a sum that was six times its balance sheet value. Nestlé was not so much interested in Rowntree's manufacturing base as its brands—such as Kit Kat, Quality Street, After Eight and Fruit Pastilles—which were major brands with brand-building potential.

Strong branding enhances company value and brand makeovers can seriously affect valuations. For example, ghd, manufacturer of haircare equipment, more than doubled its profits from £16 million to £32 million when its CEO, Paul Stoneham, gave the brand a makeover (White, 2014); see Exhibit 8.1.

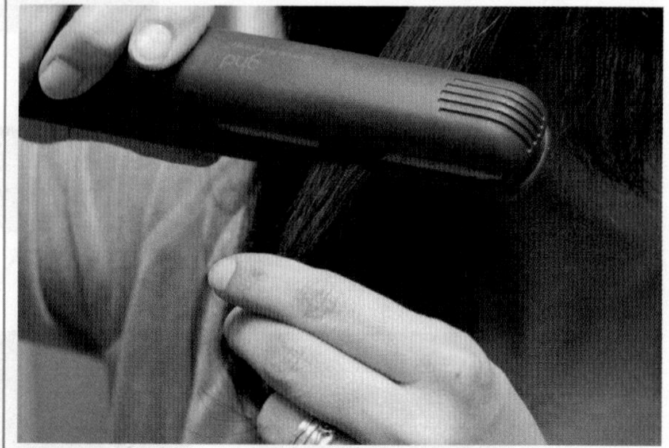

EXHIBIT 8.1
ghd developed their brand to become synonymous with hair straighteners

MINI CASE 8.1
Douwe Egberts is No Ordinary Coffee

Egbert Douwes opened his first coffee shop in Joure, Netherlands, in 1753 with his wife Akke. Together they laid the foundations for what was to become a powerful global mega brand. Their mission was simple: to sell products that could deliver 'the pleasure of daily living'. As a result, the coffee they produced was very popular and the business continued to grow. The brand strength was built around the taste and functionality of the coffee.

The company was always keen to adapt to the changing needs of its coffee-drinking customers. For example, in 1954, Douwe Egberts instant coffee was introduced and, later, instant cappuccino. Then Douwe Egberts started to notice changes in coffee drinking habits; it found that brewed coffee needed to provide customers with a more personalized, individual and luxury feel. So, they worked with Dutch technology company Philips to produce a coffee machine that could be used with their coffee to make an expresso-like foamy coffee in an instant. In 2001, the launch of the Senseo was a revolution in coffee drinking and provided a way for individual customers to have freshly brewed coffee. The Senseo got a positive reaction and was bought by millions of customers around the world.

Despite being a major player in the global coffee market, in 2010 Douwe Egberts was in danger of falling behind its competitors. As a result, it set about refreshing its identity, drawing on the heritage of the brand and using its 250 years of history and craftsmanship to reinforce the brand's position and be perceived positively by its customers. This action significantly boosted the brand's popularity and sales, enabling further growth. Recently, the company joined forces with Modelèz International in a mega merger, bringing it together with the US group's Carte Noire, Kenco and Tassimo brands. This move meant the newly named Jacobs Douwe Egberts held a market-leading position in many countries.

Despite the size of this powerful global brand, it constantly aims to be in touch with its customers and respond to the ever-changing market environment. In 2014, it partnered with Prostate Cancer; the company encouraged its customers to drink a cup of its coffee and post a selfie on Facebook showing foamy moustaches to raise the profile of the global Movember fundraising campaign. In 2015, Douwe Egberts joined forces with Actimel yoghurt, Bonne Maman preserves, HP sauce, Nestlé cereal and other leading brands in the 'A Better Breakfast' campaign designed to encourage the population of the UK not to skip breakfast, because it is a very important meal.

Since opening a single store in the Netherlands, Douwe Egberts has built its reputation and its business around being first in the minds of its customers when they think about drinking coffee. Consider the following questions.

Questions:

1. Explain how Douwe Egberts has extended the brand and how this has enabled the brand to reach more customers.
2. Discuss the extent to which this company has built customer-based brand equity for its brand.
3. From a branding perspective, suggest why Douwe Egberts has become involved with Prostate Cancer and the 'A Better Breakfast' campaign.

Based on: Douwe Egberts Coffee Company (2018); Hilpern (2010); Armstrong (2014); Kimberly (2014); Cassidy (2012)

eBay increased its brand value by 15 per cent ($10.7 billion) by undergoing a transformation driven by launching its online outlet dedicated to fashion. Amazon is another very successful brand, valued at over $64 billion (three times more than eBay). In emerging markets, China Mobile (valued at $50 billion) and Baidu search engine (valued at $30 billion) (Brandz, 2015) are growing rapidly. Brands can also lose market share for various reasons;

for example, Angry Birds, produced by Finnish firm Rovio Entertainment, experienced a significant drop in sales due to declining interest in its merchandise (Dregde, 2015). German power group E.ON reported difficulties in its fossil fuel businesses as wholesale electricity prices plummeted (Macalister, 2015).

Barrier to competition

The impact of the strong, positive perceptions held by consumers about top brands means it is difficult for new brands to compete (even if the new brand performs well on blind taste testing). As we have seen, this may be insufficient to knock the market leader off the top spot. This is one of the reasons Virgin Coke failed to dent Coca-Cola's domination of the cola market. The reputation of strong brands may be a powerful barrier to competition. However, in technology markets the top spot is not so assured. Digital brands can grow quickly, as they spread like infectious diseases across the internet, but they can fall out of favour in the same manner: for example, MySpace (Cannarella and Spechler, 2014), Friends Reunited and Second Life. Even Facebook, the world's largest social network, is losing its core customers; millions of teenagers in the UK and USA have stopped regularly using the platform because 'as soon as parents got in they killed it'. Founder Mark Zuckerberg has faced further challenges for the brand as the algorithm, which links families and friends and other mechanisms on the platform, has been found to be exploiting behavioural traits for profit and their proliferation of fake news has eroded the credibility of the brand (Sweeny and De Liz, 2018).

High profits

Strong, market-leading brands are rarely the cheapest. Brands such as Heinz, Kellogg's, Mercedes, Rolls Royce, Apple, Michelin, L'Oréal and Microsoft are all associated with premium prices. This is because their superior brand equity means that consumers receive added value over their less powerful rivals. Strong brands also achieve distribution more readily, gain economies of scale and are in a better position to resist retailer demands for price discounts. These forces feed through to profitability. Digital brands are disrupting this model. Google, Facebook and Twitter are massive global brands which give away their core product for free. But there is a price to pay: lack of privacy. Google uses the personal data it collects from our search behaviour and voice interactions to create its products. Google generates billions of dollars of revenue through targeted advertising and has plans to use visual information from your camera to tell you everything about the objects you can see in your personal spaces (Tiku, 2018).

Base for brand extensions

A strong brand provides the foundation for leveraging positive perceptions and goodwill from the core brand to brand extensions. Examples include Diet Coke, Dove Visible Care body wash, Baileys Chocolat Luxe and H&M's Modern Essentials. The new brand benefits from the added value that the brand equity of the core brand bestows on the extension. There is a full discussion of brand extensions later in this chapter.

Quality certification

Strong brands also benefit consumers in that they provide quality certification, which can aid decision-making. The following example illustrates the lengths consumers will go to when using strong brands as a form of quality certification.

Hyundai cars were not noted for their quality. Chung Ju-Yung, founder of the car company in South Korea, used to count clapped-out deserted cars as a measure of his brand's performance. So long as there were more Hyundais abandoned on the roadside than his competitors' cars, he was convinced the company was doing well. Things are very different today, and the launch of the Prada Genesis cars from the Hyundai stable shows how the brand has changed. Hyundai joined with the Italian designer fashion house Prada to produce an exclusive, high-quality version of its Genesis range. Buyers in the Gulf and China are the main target audience. While this model will not significantly increase annual revenues, it is a clear indication and informal certification of the quality of the brand. For online brands, consumer trust is paramount (Oliver, 2011). VeriSign produces formal certification for online brands to indicate security of an e-commerce website. In the case of Hyundai, Prada is acting as an intangible form of quality certification, whereas VeriSign certificates are highly tangible.

Trust

Consumers tend to trust strong brands and, ultimately, the belief that a brand will deliver on its promises is a deal breaker when everything else is equal. For example, Aviva and the AA both offer motor insurance in this highly competitive consumer market. Price is still a strong discriminating factor in this market, but motorists are looking for something extra. Market research found that if all motor insurance companies were offering the same rate and terms, consumers' favourite brand would be the AA as it is most trusted to deliver on its brand promises (Barnett, 2012). Arguably, the AA has risen to this position in the minds of its target audiences by increasing its media spend and subsequently improving brand awareness.

Examples of trusted European brands are C&A (clothing), Samsung (mobile phones), Miele (domestic appliances) and Nivea (cosmetics).

When consumers stop trusting a brand, the fallout can be catastrophic. For example, Gerald Ratner destroyed his chain of high street jewellery stores when he repeatedly spoke about the poor quality of the merchandise at public speaking engagements; Sunny Delight, Procter & Gamble's highly successful children's fruit drink, fell from grace instantly once it was revealed that drinking too much could turn children yellow; when Coca-Cola launched its Dasani bottled water in the UK, all went well until consumers were made aware that it was actually bottled tap water. In each of these examples, consumers lost trust in the brands because they felt they had been cheated and, while the brands made every attempt to recover, consumers were not willing to forget.

Brand Equity

Strong brands are rich in a property called **brand equity**. Brand equity is a measure of the strength of a brand in the marketplace by adding tangible value to a company through the resulting sales and profits. There are two types of brand equity: customer-based and proprietary-based brand equity. **Customer-based brand equity** resides in the minds of consumers and consists of brand awareness and brand image. Proprietary-based brand equity is based on assets that are attributable to the company and consists of patents and channel relationships.

Customer-based brand equity

The type of brand equity that resides in the minds of consumers who hold more favourable perceptions and associations towards the brand than towards its rivals is called *customer-based brand equity*, which is defined as the differential effect that brand knowledge has on consumer response to the marketing of a brand (Keller, 2008), e.g. when consumers react more favourably to a branded product over one of its rivals. Positive, customer-based brand equity is likely to result in high customer loyalty, low price sensitivity, a high willingness for customers to visit more than one outlet to purchase the brand and a strong base for brand extensions.

There are two sources of customer-based brand equity: brand awareness and brand image (see Figure 8.2).

Brand awareness

Brand awareness is related to brand equity in two ways. First, by raising brand awareness, the likelihood of the brand entering a consumer's evoked set (those brands that a consumer seriously considers before making a purchase) is increased since awareness is a pre-condition of evaluation of a brand. Second, in low-involvement situations (discussed in Chapter 3), a purchase may follow awareness of a brand with little information processing

FIGURE 8.2
Sources of brand equity

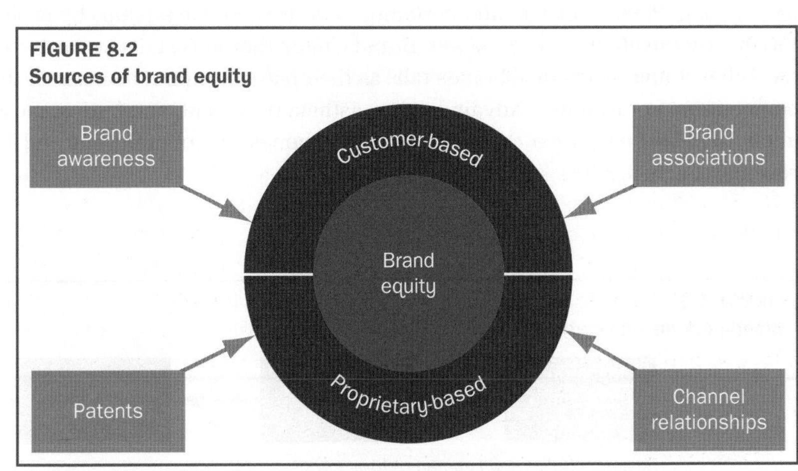

since the purchase is of low importance or low price. In both these cases, increasing brand awareness can lead to higher sales and profits, and hence increased brand equity. The global brand awareness of brands like Coca-Cola, Philips, Google, Facebook, Apple, Samsung and IKEA is a major contributor to their brand equity.

Brand image

Brand equity can also be increased by creating a strong brand image. A positive brand image is formed by generating strong, favourable and unique associations to the brand in the memory (Keller, 2008). A brand image is created using all elements of the marketing mix.

The brand image of a car may be influenced by product quality (associating it with perceptions of comfort, reliability, durability and so on), promotion (marketing communications campaign may infuse the car with high-status connotations), price (a competitive price may confer associations with value for money) and place (a smart, modern dealership may associate the car with efficient after-sales service). Advertising is often employed to create a brand image. A positive brand image increases the likelihood of purchase and hence brand equity. Brands like Johnson & Johnson, Dulux and Colgate gain equity through their image of being trustworthy.

The long-term future of a brand relies on understanding (and measuring) the mindset of its customers. Many academics suggest that brand equity is built in the minds of the consumer, and is then converted into market performance and revenue, but measuring performance is a problem and tends to look at short-term outcomes (Aneslmsson and Bondesson, 2015). **Brand performance metrics** focus on the basics of brand equity and lean towards tangible economic values shown in the brand value chain, see Figure 8.3. But, research suggests that there are gains in linking economic metrics with market performance and customer mindset measurement.

Marketing programme actions typically involve the actions taken by brands to raise awareness and get into the minds of potential customers.

Customer mindset includes any association that links the brand to the customer's memory. For example, emotions, feelings, experiences, images, perceptions, beliefs and attitudes (Keller & Lehmann, 2003).

Market/brand performance refers to how customers respond to a brand. Measures include market share, sales, sales growth, market size, share-of-wallet. Aneslmsson and Bondesson (2015) suggest that the best predictors of long-term sustainable performance are measures of purchase intention and attitudinal loyalty because they reflect choice and intended future behaviour.

Financial impact refers to shareholder value and can be measured by stock price and market capitalization.

Proprietary-based brand equity

Proprietary-based brand equity is derived from company attributes that deliver value to the brand. These can be found in many aspects of corporate activity, but the two main sources are patents and channel relationships.

Patents

A common method to calculate the value of a brand is by considering future profits and discounting them to the present day. Patents give greater certainty to future revenue streams by protecting a brand from competitive threat over the lifetime of the patent. Brand equity, therefore, falls towards the end of this period. For example, the value of pharmaceutical brands falls as their patents expire, because of the likely launch of low-priced generic competitors. For example, Advair, leading asthma treatment, and Lyrica, muscle pain relief drug, are among those about to fall off the *patent cliff* and parent companies GlaxoSmithKline and Pfizer could lose billions of dollars of revenue (Parrish, 2018).

FIGURE 8.3
Brand performance metrics

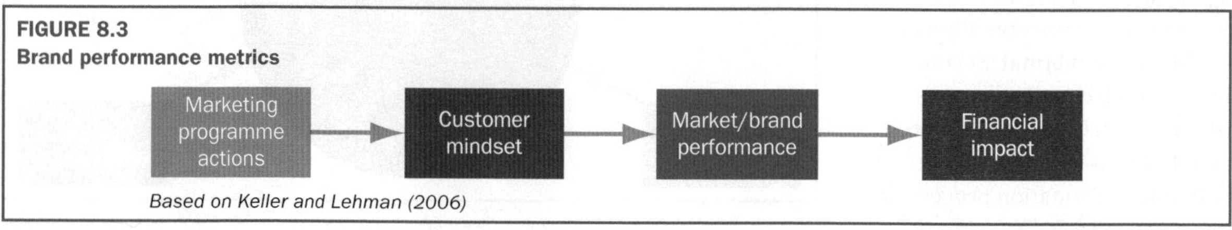

Based on Keller and Lehman (2006)

Channel relationships

Experience, knowledge and close relationships with distributors and suppliers can enhance the value of company brands. For example, Procter & Gamble has a global distribution network across 180 countries facilitating the movement of fast moving consumer brands, e.g. Gillette Oral-B and Pampers, which enhances the value of these brands.

Brand valuation is a difficult task. It is the process of estimating the financial value of an individual or corporate brand. A widely cited list of the top 100 global brands by financial value is produced by Interbrand. It bases its calculations on a brand's financial performance (profits on products and services, earnings attributable to the brand), its influence on customer choice and the strength of the brand relative to the competition (Interbrand, 2018).

Although Interbrand's approach does not give estimates of the value of brands in the future (something that would be useful to investors), it does provide a picture of the value of brands in any one year. Calculating the value of brand equity is an important task since it indicates the rewards that can be reaped from marketing investments. Apple and Google are valued at almost $200 billion and are at the top of the list of 100 global brands; Amazon ranks fifth, Disney 14th, Nike 18th, IKEA 25th, Huawei 70th (the Chinese telecoms corporation) and one of the fastest growing brands, and a new entrant, Netflix is 78th (Interbrand, 2018).

Brand Building

The importance of strong brands means that brand building is an essential marketing activity. Successful brand building can reap benefits in terms of premium prices, achieving distribution more readily, and sustaining high and stable sales and profits through brand loyalty (Ehrenberg, Goodhardt and Barwise, 1990). Strong brands are also better able to withstand external market forces such as economic recessions and financial downturns (Millward Brown, 2014).

A brand is created by augmenting a **core product** with distinctive values that distinguish it from the competition. To understand the notion of brand values, we first need to understand the difference between features and benefits. A feature is an aspect of a brand that may or may not confer a customer benefit. For example, adding fluoride (*feature*) to a toothpaste confers the customer *benefits* of added protection against tooth decay and decreased dental charges. Not all features necessarily confer benefits to all users. For example, Microsoft Office is a bundle of software programs. However, for a user who only wishes to use the word processor, the spreadsheet and PowerPoint software confer no benefits.

Core benefits derive from the core product (see Figure 8.4). Toothpaste, for example, cleans teeth and therefore protects against tooth decay. But all toothpastes achieve that. Branding allows marketers to create added values that distinguish one brand from another. Successful brands are those that create a set of brand values that are superior to other rival brands. So, brand building involves a deep understanding of both the functional (e.g. ease of use) and emotional (e.g. confidence) values that customers use when choosing between brands, and the ability to combine them in a unique way to create an augmented *product* that

FIGURE 8.4
Creating a brand

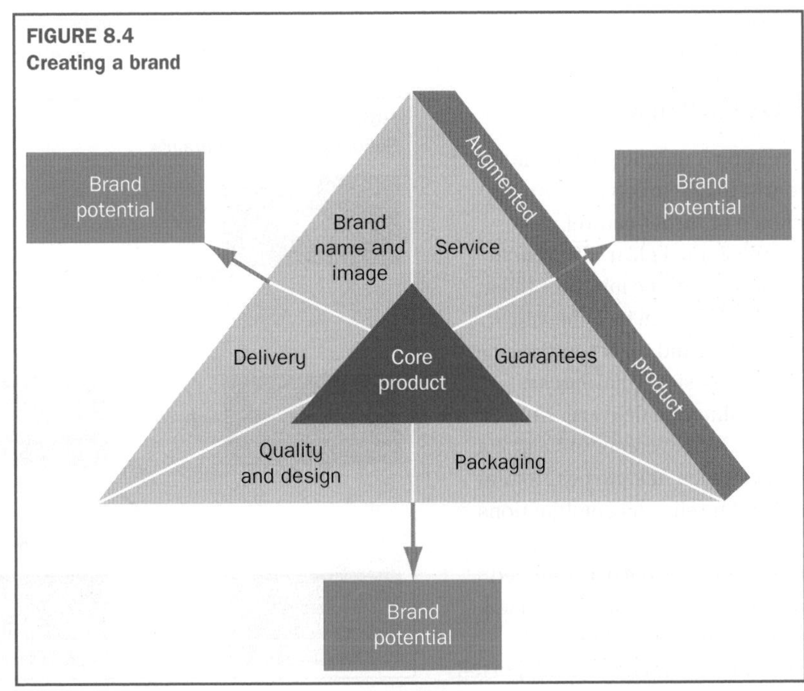

customers prefer. This unique, **augmented product** is what marketers call the *brand*. The success of the Swatch brand was founded on the recognition that watches could be marketed as fashion items to younger age groups. By using colour and design, Swatch successfully augmented a basic product—a watch—to create appeal for its target market. Swatch combined functional and emotional values to create a successful brand. Focusing on functional values is rarely sufficient. Once Blackberry set itself apart from other mobile devices by offering email on the go, but when the iPhone entered the marketplace with touchscreen phones, the benefits of Blackberry's phone with a keyboard were eroded; it was no longer seen as the phone for business professionals.

Figure 8.4 shows how products can be augmented. Singapore Airlines has augmented its brand by providing superior *service*. Kia has differentiated its cars by offering seven-year *guarantees* (warranties) when most of its competitors offer only three years (see Exhibit 8.2 and how Kia conveys the extent to which it offers benefits to its customers). Nivea was the first to differentiate its sunblock brand using innovative *packaging* that allowed it to be sprayed onto the body. Netflix created a differential advantage through its innovative internet distributed TV services and offering a wide variety of online content, which satisfy global audiences' viewing tastes (Lotz, 2017). Apple expanded its offer by creating its app store for its iPhone, which allows anyone to create and sell an application, providing efficient *delivery* of extra *services* to customers. Finally, BMW has augmented its brand by its *image*, embodied in its 'the ultimate driving machine' strapline, which differentiates it from the competition.

Managing brands involves a constant search for ways of achieving the full brand potential. To do so means the creation of major global brands: e.g. Apple, Google, Coca-Cola, Microsoft, IBM, General Electric, AT&T, China Mobile. But how are successful brands built? A combination of some or all of seven factors can be important (see King, 1991; Doyle, 1989). These are shown in Figure 8.5 and described below.

Quality

It is vital to build quality into the core product; a major reason for brand failure is the inability to get the basics right. Marketing a tablet computer that overheats, a vacuum cleaner that does not pick up dirt effectively or a garden fork that breaks is courting disaster. The core product must achieve the basic functional requirements expected of it. A major study of factors that affect success has shown statistically that higher quality brands achieve greater market share and higher profitability than their inferior rivals (Buzzell and Gale, 1987). Product quality improvements have been shown to be driven mainly by market pull (changing customer tastes and expectations), organizational push (changes in the technical potential and resources of a company) and competitor actions (Lemmink and Kaspar, 1994).

Top companies such as Canon, BBC, Apple, Guinness, FedEx, Siemens, Intel, Toyota and Google understand the importance of quality in the brand-building process. Their success has been based on high-quality foundations. Once a brand is associated with quality, it forms a formidable barrier for competitors to overcome.

Positioning

FIGURE 8.5
Building successful brands

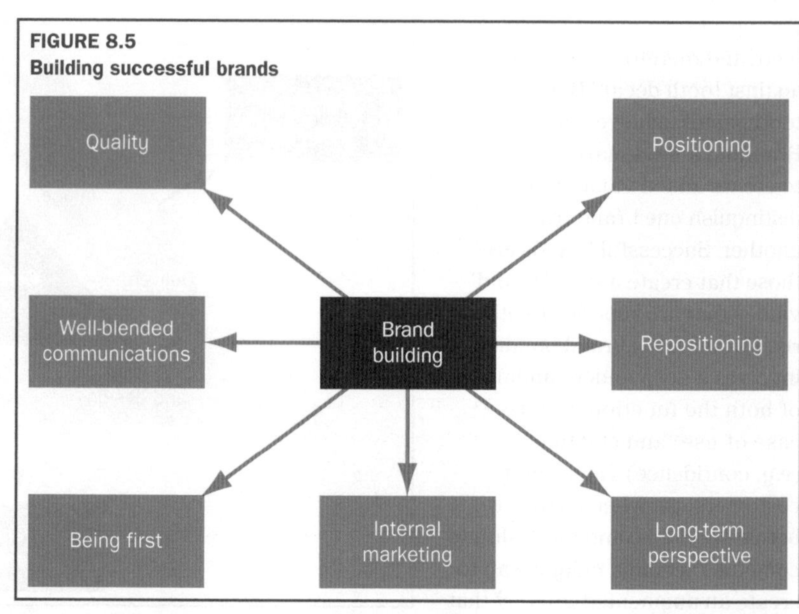

Creating a unique position in the marketplace involves a careful choice of target market and establishing a clear differential advantage in the minds of those people. This can be achieved through brand names and image, service, design, guarantees, packaging and delivery. In today's highly competitive global marketplace, unique positioning normally relies on combinations of these factors. For example, the success of BMW is founded on a high-quality, well-designed product, targeted at distinct customer segments and supported by a carefully nurtured exclusive brand name and image. The Four-Cs framework (clarity, consistency, credibility and competitiveness) discussed in Chapter 7 acts as a guide to the factors to consider when positioning a brand. Often the essence of the Four-Cs is used in a brand's positioning statement. For example, Mercedes' 'precision engineered luxury' or DHL's 'Excellence. Simply Delivered.'

An analytical framework that can be used to dissect the current position of a brand in the marketplace and form the basis of a new brand positioning strategy is given in Figure 8.6. The strength of a brand's position in the marketplace is built on six elements: **brand domain**, **brand heritage**, **brand values**, **brand assets**, **brand personality** and **brand reflection**. The first element, brand domain, corresponds to the choice of target market (where the brand competes); the other five elements provide avenues for creating a clear differential advantage with these target consumers.

FIGURE 8.6
The anatomy of brand positioning

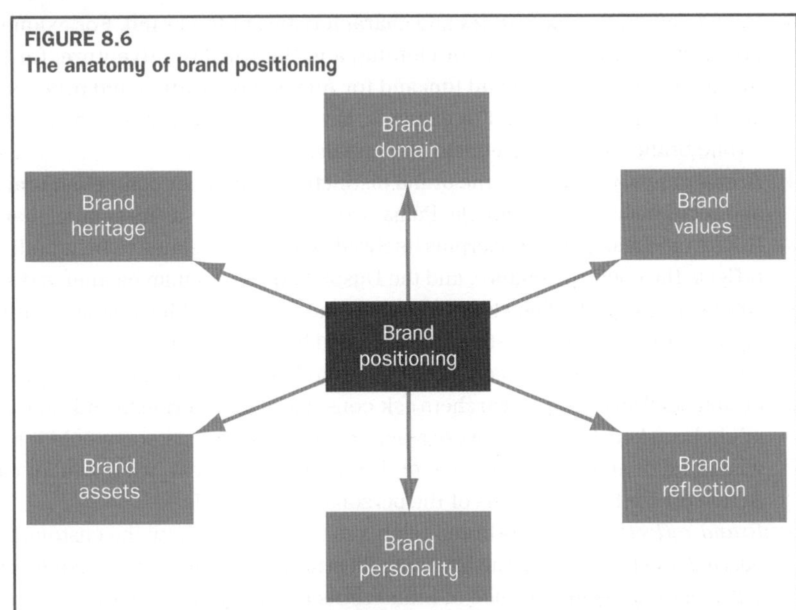

1 *Brand domain*: the brand's target market: that is, where it competes in the marketplace. For example, the brand domain for Innocent drinks is the general consumer, whereas they also produce Innocent Smoothie for Kids designed especially for children. See Exhibit 8.2.
2 *Brand heritage*: the background to the brand and its culture, i.e. how it has achieved success (and failure) over its life. Brand heritage can form an extremely useful platform to build on, and some brands have long histories to help them stand out. For example, the foundations of Wolsey (knitwear, hosiery and underwear for men) stretch back to 1755 and the company has built its reputation on a longstanding history of quality design and fabrics, and its Britishness. Burberry is another fashion brand that has gained from its history: founded in 1856, its reputation has been built on producing hard-wearing coats and outerwear, even for polar explorers and pilots. The Burberry trench coat designed in the 1940s remains a popular choice for men and women. Exhibit 8.3 shows how Kerrygold butter uses its heritage to convey the richness and pureness of the brand—an approach that it uses around the world.

EXHIBIT 8.2
Innocent Smoothies designed for children with colourful packs, easy to grip packaging and suitable quantities

EXHIBIT 8.3
Heritage can be used in advertisements to position brands, in the marketplace. Irish Brand Kerrygold uses its heritage to position the brand in the minds of consumers

3 *Brand values*: the core *values* and characteristics of the brand. For example, the brand values of Berghaus are high-performance outdoor clothing and the spirit of adventure; for Lycra they are comfort and fit; for Absolut Vodka purity and fun; and for Audi sophistication and progression. Ethical values for brands and companies are important. For example, Ecover, Green & Black's chocolate and Café Direct coffee all combine strong brand values with ethical credentials.

4 *Brand assets*: what makes the brand distinctive from other competing brands, such as symbols, features, images and relationships. For example, Puma uses its namesake as its symbol that distinguishes it from other brands, IKEA's blue and yellow underpins its Swedishness and relates to being full of light and yet restrained, which reflects the country's culture, and the Dyson bagless vacuum cleaner is distinguished from traditional vacuum cleaners. Nivea's 'feeling closer' strapline and distinctive blue colour captures the image of the brand, and the close relationship with customers developed by IBM over many years is a major brand asset for the company.

5 *Brand personality*: the character of the brand described in terms of other entities, such as people, animals or objects. Marketing researchers ask consumers to describe brands in these terms. For example, consumers might be asked, 'If brand X were a person, what kind of person would it be?', 'If brand X were an animal, what kind of animal would it be?' or 'If brand X were a car, what kind of car would it be?' See Marketing in Action 8.1 for further details of the personality of brands.

6 *Brand reflection*: how the brand relates to self-identity; how the customer perceives him/herself because of buying/using the brand. The branding illustration visualizes how people use brands to reflect and project their self-identity. The importance of brand reflection is apparent in the demand for aspirational brands such as Gucci handbags, Cartier or Rolex watches, and Mercedes cars.

By analysing each element, brand managers can form an accurate portrait of how brands are positioned in the marketplace. From there, thought can be given to whether and how the brand can be repositioned to improve performance.

Repositioning

As markets change and opportunities arise, repositioning may be needed to build brands from their initial base. Skoda was repositioned from a downmarket car brand of dubious quality to a mid-market brand whose quality has led to several awards, significant sales and profit growth. Samsung successfully repositioned from being perceived as a producer of cheap TVs and microwave ovens to being regarded as a 'cool' youth brand producing mobile phones and flat-screen TVs for the 'techno savvy'. Marks & Spencer (M&S) relies on own-label products

MARKETING IN ACTION 8.1
The Personality of a Brand

A brand's personality is an intangible but important part of the market position of goods and services. Like individuals, brands aspire to convey their uniqueness and the characteristics of their personalities as this can help it, both in terms of a customer's understanding of the brand, and also from the company's perspective when selecting appropriate messages and media to use to communicate a brand's position.

According to Millward Brown (2012), to understand a brand personality it is important to consider the personality characteristics and archetypes. For example, generous and caring characteristics could be combined with the archetype 'mother' in a similar way as adventurous and brave could be combined with a 'hero' archetype. The next step is to consider what the archetype represents: for example, a 'mother' archetype could relate to stability and well-being. To be successful, a brand personality should link to archetypes that interest a brand's target audience. For example, the 'wise' archetype, with its characteristics of trustworthiness, has been attributed to Google, China Mobile and Visa. L'Oreal has been classified as fitting the 'seductress' archetype (with characteristics of being sexy and desirable); its Age Perfect campaign featuring Dame Helen Mirren added to the list of characteristics, using the words 'outrageous' and 'bold' in its advertising message. Some archetypes are less likely to deliver success; having a *friendly* personality (like Airtel, Home Depot and KFC) might be straightforward and easy to understand, but is less likely to stand out from the crowd.

Based on: Millward Brown (2012)

for most of its sales and is positioned as a good quality retailer, but recently has suffered declining sales and market share. In response, M&S is planning a 'radical transformation' to stem losses and revive the business (Wood and Butler, 2018). This involves repositioning the brand as an agile digital retailer by operational changes: getting rid of 25 per cent of its high street store floor space in clothing and homewares, investing in technology and moving more sales online. Historically, M&S has been slow and lacking in innovation in the online retailing space and so is now looking to 'radically' reshape the brand by redefining its brand values and culture to become a vibrant and agile 'digital-first' brand (Hammett, 2018).

Integrated marketing communications

Brand positioning is based on customer perception. To create a clear position in the minds of a target audience requires considerable thought and effort regarding the tools (e.g. advertising, sales promotions) and media (e.g. broadcast, internet) used to communicate brand messages. Integrated marketing communications, combining the strengths of traditional and digital media, are often used to promote such successful brands as Coca-Cola, Virgin Atlantic, Hertz car hire, Marmite and Birds Eye.

Marketers can make their brands more noticeable through attractive display or package design, and through generating customer familiarity with brand names, brand logos and a brand's visual appearance. All the considerations for developing well-blended and integrated communication campaigns are discussed in detail in Chapter 13.

Being first

Research has shown that pioneer brands are more likely to be successful than follower brands. For example, Urban et al. (1986) showed that, for frequently purchased consumer goods, the second firm in the market could expect only 71 per cent of the market share of the pioneer and the third only 58 per cent of the pioneer's share. Lambkin (1992) found that those pioneers that invest heavily from the start in building large production scale, in securing wide distribution and in promoting their products achieve the strongest competitive position and earn the highest long-term returns. (For a useful summary and further evidence, see Denstadli, Lines and Grønhaug (2005).) Being first gives a brand the opportunity to create a clear position in the minds of target customers before the competition enters the market. It also gives the pioneer the opportunity to build customer and distributor loyalty (Bainbridge, 2013). Nevertheless, being first into a market with a unique marketing proposition does not guarantee success; it requires sustained marketing effort and the strength to withstand competitor attacks. For example, Blackberry failed to retain its position once Apple entered the market with its iPhone.

Being first does not necessarily mean pioneering the technology. Bigger returns may come to those who are first to enter the mass market: for example, the Apple iPad. Microsoft had introduced the tablet PC in 2000, but did not successfully launch the product in the mass market, whereas Apple seized the opportunity in 2010 to capture and develop the market. Indeed, some of the world's most successful brands have benefited from following rather than leading, as they have gained important insights from first movers. For example, Google followed Alta Vista in the search engine marketplace as it realized the importance of a clean, clear user interface not cluttered with adverts (McWillians, 2009). Gillette is often considered to have invented the safety razor, but it was not the first brand to sell this product. Gillette made an important change by adding the disposable blade to the earlier design, and this enabled it to dominate the market.

Long-term perspective

Brand building is a long-term activity and can take many years to achieve. There are many demands on people's attention, so generating awareness, communicating brand values and building customer loyalty requires significant commitment. Management should constantly evaluate brand investment to ensure that they establish and maintain the desired position of a brand in the marketplace. Unfortunately, it can be tempting to cut back on expenditure in the short term. Cutting the marketing communication spend by half a million euros may immediately cut costs and increase profits. Conversely, for a well-established brand, sales are unlikely to fall substantially in the short term because of the effects of past advertising. The result is higher short-term profits. This may be an attractive proposition for managers in charge of a brand for less than two years. One way of overcoming this danger is to monitor brand manager (and brand) performance by measuring brand equity in terms of awareness levels, brand associations and intentions to buy, and being vigilant in resisting short-term actions which may cause harm.

MARKETING IN ACTION 8.2
Why Do Some Brands Fall from Grace?

Brands live in an unforgiving, harsh environment. Their survival depends on many factors, and their demise can be swift when they are not met.

Here are some suggestions as to why brands fall out of favour and lose their place in the market.

1 Leading brands are more likely to fail than to persist as leaders over time. Hoover used to dominate the vacuum cleaner market, but was knocked off the top spot when Dyson's bagless cleaner gained popularity. The Co-op was the UK's leading grocery retailer, but over the years its dominance has been eroded by Tesco, Sainsbury's and, more recently, by discounters Lidl and Aldi. Toyota, Mercedes and BMW have been top-performing brands in the car market for some years, but Volkswagen, Audi and Nissan are rising stars that could challenge the market leaders, especially as demands for fuel efficiency and non-carbon fuel substitutes become more important to car buyers.

2 Once brand leadership is lost, it is likely to be gone forever. In 2000, Gap was 29th in the 100 global brands list, but by 2018 had fallen out of the top 100. It was a leader in the youth fashion market, but has been overtaken by new fashion brands like Zara and H&M. The newcomers battle it out in the fast-fashion market. H&M offers its customers a larger range and tends to achieve a lower average price over all its merchandise than Zara. H&M frequently offers discounts, but this is rarely the case for Zara. But Zara has an extremely efficient supply side, which supports the 'catwalk-inspired' fashion ranges. The demand for fast fashion helped the rapid growth of these brands, but both will need to monitor external market trends for fundamental shifts in buying behaviour that might affect their brands' prominence in the future.

3 Difficult economic circumstances are good for leading brands. While consumers might be inclined to turn to private labels and own brands during difficult economic trading conditions, leading brands tend to be robust and maintain market share. Nestlé, Kraft and Kellogg's performed well in the recent economic crises as more consumers turned to eating at home the brands they knew.

4 Brand leadership can be dependent on category. Some product categories offer better long-term brand leadership than others; fashion apparel and consumer electronics are the most difficult to stay ahead in, as fashion tastes change and technological advances can springboard new entrants such as Google and Amazon to the top of the list. Foods and household supplies tend to be more durable, as consumers can seek familiarity and avoid risk—for example, Heinz, Colgate and Danone. Such brands tend to constantly remind their customers about the benefits the brands offer in their communication messages; for example, see how Colgate reminds us about how its toothpaste can aid oral health.

Based on: Golder, Irwin and Mitra (2013); Interbrand (2018); Anon (2009)

Companies also need to be prepared to suffer losses when marketing brands in entirely new markets. Tesla, Inc. moved into the sustainable transport market with an innovative electric vehicle, but recently reported record losses on its Model 3 mass market electric cars. However, the company expects to return to profits as it becomes established in this market (Tesla, Inc., 2018). Read Marketing in Action 8.2 to find out why brands fail.

Key Branding Decisions

Besides the branding decisions so far discussed, marketers face four further key branding decisions: brand name strategies and choices, rebranding, brand extension and stretching, and co-branding.

Brand name strategies and choices

Another key decision area is the choice of brand name. Three brand name strategies can be identified: family, individual and combination.

Family brand names

A **family brand name** is used for all products (e.g. Philips, Microsoft, Heinz, Procter & Gamble, Samsung and Apple—see Exhibit 8.4). The goodwill attached to the family brand name benefits all brands, and the use of the name in advertising helps the promotion of all the brands carrying the family name. The risk is that, if one of the brands receives unfavourable publicity or is unsuccessful, the reputation of the whole range of brands can be tarnished. This is also called *umbrella branding*. Some companies create umbrella brands for part of their brand portfolios to give coherence to their range of products. For example, Lego created the umbrella brand of Duplo for its range of bricks and toys targeting small children.

EXHIBIT 8.4
Apple uses family brand symbols for all its products, including its latest watches

Individual brand names

An **individual brand name** does not identify a brand with a particular company (e.g. Procter & Gamble does not use the company name on brands such as Ariel, Fairy Liquid, Daz and Pampers). This may be necessary when it is believed that each brand requires a separate, unrelated identity. Toyota also abandoned its family brand name when it launched its upmarket executive car, which was simply called the Lexus. In some instances, the use of a family brand name when moving into a new market segment may harm the image of the new product line. The same can be true when brands make acquisitions. For example, when Coca-Cola acquired Innocent, the reputation of the latter was damaged as it was viewed as selling out to a large corporation (Barda, 2010) and setting aside its ethical brand principles. BMW also chose not to attach its family brand name to the Mini, since it would have detracted from the car's sense of 'Britishness'.

Combination brand names

A **combination brand name** combines family and individual brand names to capitalize on the reputation of the company, while allowing the individual brands to be distinguished and identified. For example, in the Apple family, there are the iPad, iPhone, iPod Touch, MacBook, iTunes and, the latest, Apple Watch.

Criteria for choosing brand names

The choice of brand name should be carefully thought out, since names convey images. For example, the brand name Pepsi Max was chosen for Pepsi's diet cola targeted at men, as it conveyed a masculine image in a product category that was associated with women. So, one criterion for deciding on a good brand name is that it evokes *positive associations*.

A second criterion is that the brand name should be easy to *pronounce and remember*. Short names such as Esso, Shell, Daz, Ariel, Orange and Mini fall into this category. There are exceptions to this general rule, as in the case of Häagen-Dazs, which was designed to sound European in the USA where it was first launched. A brand name may suggest *product benefits*, such as with Right Guard (deodorant), Head & Shoulders (anti-dandruff shampoo) and MacBook Air (lightweight computer). Technological products may benefit from *numerical* brand naming (e.g. Airbus 380, Aston Martin DB9) or *alpha-numeric* brand names (e.g. Audi A4, Samsung Galaxy S6). This also overcomes the need to change brand names when marketing in different countries.

The question of brand *transferability* is another brand name consideration. With the growth of global brands, names increasingly need to be able to cross geographical boundaries. Companies that do not check the meaning of a brand name in other languages can be caught out, as when General Motors launched its Nova car in Spain only to discover later that the word meant 'it does not go' in Spanish. The lesson is that brand names must be researched for cultural meaning before being introduced into a new geographic market. One advantage of non-meaningful names such as Diageo and Exxon is that they transfer well across national boundaries.

Specialist companies have established themselves as brand name consultants. Market research is used to test associations, memorability, pronunciation and preferences. Legal advice is important so that a brand name *does not infringe an existing brand name*. Table 8.1 summarizes the issues that are important when choosing a brand name.

Brand names can also be categorized, as shown in Table 8.2.

TABLE 8.1 **Brand name considerations**

A good brand name should:
1. evoke positive associations
2. be easy to pronounce and remember
3. suggest product benefits
4. be distinctive
5. use numerals or alpha-numerics when emphasizing technology
6. be transferable
7. not infringe an existing registered brand name

TABLE 8.2 **Brand name categories**

People	Adidas, McDonald's, Chanel, Heinz, Marriott, Louis Vuitton
Places	Singapore Airlines, Deutsche Bank, Air France
Descriptive	China Mobile, Body Shop, Federal Express, Airbus, Weetabix
Abstract	KitKat, Kodak, Prozac, IKEA
Evocative	Orange, Apple, Häagen-Dazs, Dove
Brand extensions	Diet Coke, Pepsi Max, Lucozade Sport
Foreign meanings	Lego (from 'play well' in Danish)

Rebranding

The act of changing a brand name is called **rebranding**. It can occur at the product level (e.g. confectionery Dime bar to Daim, Opal Fruits to Starburst, Marathon to Snickers) and at the corporate level (e.g. Orange and T-Mobile merged and were rebranded as Everything Everywhere (EE); Norwich Union, insurer, became Aviva, and TNT Post has rebranded as Whistl and announced that its postmen will deliver mail on electric unicycles (Mortimer, 2014)).

Rebranding is risky and the decision should not be taken lightly, as potentially a rebranding exercise can cause a loss of sales of between 5 and 20 per cent (Klara, 2015). Abandoning a well-known and, for some, favourite brand runs the risk of customer confusion, resentment and loss of market share. When Coca-Cola was rebranded (and reformulated) as New Coke, negative customer reaction forced the company to withdraw the new brand and reinstate the original one (Muzellec and Lambkin, 2006). When Italo Suisse chocolates decided to rebrand, it came up with a new name: ISIS. But this name change ended up getting the chocolates removed from retailers' shelves in 2014 when the Islamic State of Iraq and Syria (ISIS) began releasing its terror videos. The chocolate-maker quickly rebranded again using the name of the founder, Libeert (Klara, 2015).

Why rebrand?

Despite such well-publicized problems, rebranding is a common activity. The reasons are as follows (see Keller, 2008; Riezebos, 2003).

Merger or acquisition

When a merger or acquisition takes place, a new name may be chosen to identify the new company. Sometimes a combination of the original corporate names may be chosen (e.g. when Glaxo Wellcome and SmithKline Beecham formed GlaxoSmithKline), a completely new name may be preferred (e.g. when Grand Metropolitan and Guinness became Diageo) or the stronger corporate brand name may be chosen (e.g. when Nestlé acquired Rowntree Mackintosh).

Desire to create a new image/position in the marketplace

Some brand names are associated with negative or old-fashioned images. The move by BT Wireless to drop its corporate brand name was because it had acquired an old-fashioned, bureaucratic image. The new brand name, O_2, was chosen because it sounded scientific and modern, and because focus groups saw their mobile phones as an essential part of their lives (like oxygen). O_2 was bought out by Spanish telecom Telefonica in 2006 but retained the brand name. The negative image of the cable television company ntl, caused by poor service, was part of the reason for buying Virgin Mobile, which allows it to use the Virgin brand under licence across its consumer businesses (Wray, 2006). Similar motivations were behind the rebranding of Andersen Consulting to Accenture. Image considerations were also prominent when the negative association of the word 'fried' in Kentucky Fried Chicken stimulated the move to change the name to KFC.

The sale or acquisition of parts of a business

Brands acquire other brands for various reasons. In luxury fashion markets, Michael Kors acquired Jimmy Choo and Coach acquired Kate Spade to bolster their product portfolios and enable greater marketing capacity to compete with Moet Hennessy Louis Vuitton, Kering and Richemont (Danziger, 2017). GlaxoSmithKline sold multiple brands in a strategic initiative to reduce costs and re-focus parts of the business. Brands to be divested included Horlicks, Schwartz spices and other food brands, to focus on consumer healthcare, respiratory and HIV medicines (BBC, 2018).

Corporate strategy changes

When a company diversifies out of its original product category, the original corporate brand name may be considered too limiting. Esso (Standard Oil) changed its name to Exxon as its product portfolio extended beyond oil. Also, Dixons Retail has become Dixons Carphone because the company has widened its product range strategically to place more emphasis on mobile technology.

Brand familiarity

Sometimes the name of a major product brand owned by a company becomes so familiar to customers that it supersedes the corporate brand. In these circumstances, the company may decide to discard the unfamiliar name in favour of the familiar. That is why Consolidated Foods became Sara Lee and Boussois-Souchon-Neuvesel (BSN) became Danone.

International marketing considerations

A major driver for rebranding is the desire to harmonize a brand name across national boundaries to create a global brand. Companies may also change brand names to discourage parallel importing. When sales of a premium-priced brand in some countries are threatened by reimports of the same brand from countries where the brand is sold at lower prices, rebranding may be used to differentiate the product. This is why the Italian cleaning agent Viakal was rebranded in some European countries as Antikal.

Legal problems

A brand name may contravene an existing legal restriction on its use. For example, the Yves St Laurent perfume brand Champagne required a name change because the brand name was protected for use only with the sparkling wine from the Champagne region of France.

Managing the rebranding process

Rebranding is usually an expensive, time-consuming and risky activity, and should only be undertaken when there is a clear marketing and financial case in its favour and a strong marketing plan in place to support its implementation (Keller, 2008). Management should recognize that a rebranding exercise cannot by itself rectify more deep-seated marketing problems.

Once the decision to rebrand has been made, two key decisions remain: choosing the new name and implementing the name change.

Choosing the new brand name

The issues discussed earlier in this chapter regarding choosing brand names are relevant when changing an existing name. These are that the new brand name should evoke positive associations, be easy to pronounce and remember, suggest positive benefits, be distinctive, be transferable, not infringe an existing registered brand name and consideration should be given to the use of numerals when emphasizing technology. These issues should form the basis of the first step, setting the rebranding objectives (see Figure 8.7). For example, a key objective of the new name might be that it should be easily remembered, evoke positive associations and be transferable across national boundaries.

The second step is to generate as many brand names as possible. Potential sources of names include consumers, employees, distributors, specialist brand name consultants and advertising agencies.

The third step is to screen the names to remove any with obvious flaws, such as those that are difficult to pronounce, too close to an existing name, have adverse double meanings and do not fit with the rebranding objectives. The objective is to reduce the names to a shortlist of around 6—12. For the fourth step, an information search is carried out to check that each name does not infringe on an existing registered brand name in each country where the brand is, or may be, marketed.

The fifth step is to test the remaining names through consumer research. The key criteria, such as memorability, associations and distinctiveness, chosen in step one (rebranding objectives), will be used to assess the performance of the new names.

Finally, management will assess the virtues of each of the shortlisted brand names and conclude which one should be chosen and registered.

FIGURE 8.7
The rebranding process

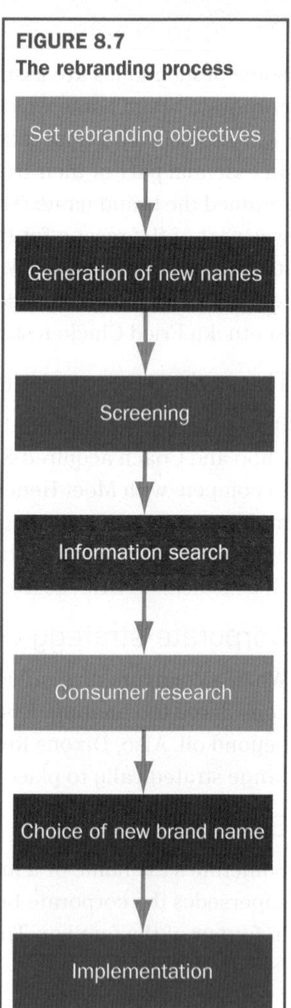

Implementing the name change

Name changes can meet considerable resistance from consumers, employees and distributors. All three groups can feel that their loyalty to a brand has been betrayed. Attention also has to be paid to the media and financial institutions, particularly for corporate name changes. Careful consideration is required to change a name and all interested parties should be involved in the process and understand the logic underlying the change. Implementing a brand name change requires attention to five key issues (Kapferer, 2008).

1 *Coordination*: name change requires harmonious working between the company departments and those groups most involved—marketing, production, the salesforce, logistics and general management. All must work together to avoid problems and solve any that may arise.
2 *Communication*: all stakeholders—for example, customers, employees and investors—need to be targeted with communications that notify them early and with a full explanation. When the chocolate bar known as Raider in continental Europe changed its name to Twix, which was the name used everywhere else, consumers in Europe were informed by a massive advertising campaign (two years' advertising budget was spent in three weeks). Retailers were told of the name change well in advance by a salesforce whose top priority was the Twix brand. Trial was encouraged by promotional activities at retail outlets. The result was a highly successful name change and the creation of a global brand.
3 *Understanding what the consumer identifies with the brand*: consumer research is required to understand what consumers identify as the key characteristics of the brand. Shell made the mistake of failing to include the new colour (yellow) of the rebranded Shell Helix Standard (from Puissance 7) in its advertising, which stressed only the name change from Puissance 7 in France. Unfortunately, customers, when looking for their favourite brand of oil, paid most attention to the colour of the can, so they could not find their usual brown can of Puissance 7 and did not realize it was now in a yellow can and had a new and unfamiliar name. The lesson is that rebranding means making sure that target audiences are informed of all of the brand changes.
4 *Providing assistance to distributors/retailers*: to avoid confusion at distributors/retailers, manufacturers should avoid double-stocking of the old and new brand, and ensure barcodes and product management systems are updated. Mars management took great care to ensure that, on the day of the transfer from Raider to Twix, no stocks of Raider would be found in the shops, even if this meant buying back stock.
5 *Speed of change*: consideration should be given to whether the change should be immediate (as with Twix) or subject to a transitional phase where, for example, the old name is retained (perhaps in small letters)

on the packaging after the rebrand. Old names are retained during a transitional period when the old name has high awareness and positive associations among consumers. Retaining an old brand name following a takeover may be wise for political reasons, as when Nestlé retained the Rowntree name on its brands for a few years after its takeover of the UK confectionery company.

Brand Extension and Stretching

A **brand extension** is the use of an established brand name on a new brand within the same broad market or product category. For example, the Anadin brand name has been extended to related brands Anadin Extra, Maximum Strength, Soluble, Paracetamol and Ibuprofen. The Lucozade brand has undergone a very successful brand extension with the introduction of Lucozade Sport, with isotonic properties that help to rehydrate people more quickly than other drinks and replace the minerals lost through perspiration. Coca-Cola has extended its Coke brand into Diet Coke, and its variant form, Diet Coke with cherry. Google extended its core search brand with many variants including Google Chrome, Google Home, Google Maps, Google Street View. These are examples of *line* extensions.

An extreme form of brand extension is known as brand stretching. **Brand stretching** is when an established brand name is used for brands in unrelated markets or product categories, such as the use of the Yamaha pianos brand name on hi-fi equipment, skis and motorcycles. Menswear designer fashion brands like Paul Smith, Ted Baker and Tommy Hilfiger have also been extended from clothing to fragrances, footwear and home furnishings. Google has moved into smartphones with Pixel2 and voice-activated speakers with Google Home. Table 8.3 gives some examples of brand extensions and stretching.

Some companies have used brand extensions and stretching very successfully. Richard Branson's Virgin company is a classic example. Beginning in 1970 as Virgin Records, the company grew through Virgin Music (music publishing), Megastores (music retailing), Radio, Vodka, Cola, Atlantic Airways (long-haul routes), Express (short-haul routes), Rail, Money (insurance, credit cards, mortgages, etc.), One (one-stop online banking), Media (digital TV, broadband, phone and mobile), Healthcare and many more. The Virgin Group has over 400 subsidiaries.

Brand extension is an important marketing tactic. Two key advantages of brand extension in releasing new products are that it reduces risk and is less costly than alternative launch strategies (Sharp, 1990). Both distributors and consumers may perceive less risk if the new brand comes with an established brand name. Distributors may be reassured about the 'saleability' of the new brand and therefore be more willing to stock it. Consumers appear to attribute the quality associations they have of the original brand to the new one (Aaker and Keller, 1990). An established name enhances consumer interest and willingness to try the new brand (Aaker, 1990). Consumer attitudes towards brand extensions are more favourable when the perceived quality of the parent brand is high (Bottomley and Doyle, 1996). For example, Yakult Light is an extension of the Yakult brand.

Launch costs can also be reduced by using brand extension. Since the established brand name is already well known, the task of building awareness of the new brand is eased. Consequently, advertising, selling

TABLE 8.3 Brand extensions and stretching

Brand (line) extensions	Brand stretching
Anadin brand name used for Anadin Extra, Maximum Strength, Soluble, Paracetamol and Ibuprofen	Dyson, from vacuum cleaners to hand dryers and bladeless room fans
McDonald's launched McCafé, a coffee-house style food chain	Yamaha (pianos) brand name used on motor cycles, hi-fi, skis, pianos and summerhouses
Lucozade extended to Lucozade Sport, Energy, Hydroactive and Carbo Gel	Jimmy Choo, the luxury shoemaker, has moved into bags, men's fragrances, jewellery and clothing
McCain Chips extended its range with Home Chips (Authentic), Oven Chips (Healthier), French Fries, ready baked jacket potatoes, micro chips	Mont Blanc (pen specialist) has moved into watches, jewellery and glasses

and promotional costs are reduced. Furthermore, there is the likelihood of achieving advertising economies of scale since advertisements for the original brand and its extensions reinforce each other (Roberts and McDonald, 1989).

Brand extensions can also benefit the core brand due to the increase in marketing expenditure. Core brand sales can increase this enhancement of consumers' perception of brand values and image through increased communication (Grime, Diamantopoulos and Smith, 2002). But, consumers shop around and brand extensions that fail to meet expectations will be rejected. *Cannibalization*, which refers to a situation where the new brand gains sales at the expense of the established brand, can also occur. For example, additional flavour extensions of the Absolut Vodka brand were found to cannibalize sales of existing ones, leading to a refocus on the original brand (Bokaie, 2008). Further, brand extension has been criticized as leading to a managerial focus on minor modifications, packaging changes and advertising, rather than the development of real innovations (Bennett and Cooper, 1981).

MARKETING IN ACTION 8.3
Developing the Lotus Bakeries Brand of Caramelized Biscuit

Caramelized biscuits are an original Belgian specialty. Lotus Bakeries, family-owned since 1932, has acquired international exposure thanks to this flagship product. This Belgian company is very small compared with Mondelèz International or United Biscuits, but it has succeeded in cornering a growing share of a niche market. The market in question is the speculoos market, which consists of suppliers of a type of spiced shortcrust biscuit. In Belgium, Lotus's version of speculoos is a top product across the biscuit market. The biscuits are also proving increasingly popular internationally, so that today more than 75 per cent of sales are realized outside Belgium. Lotus Bakeries annually manufactures six billion of the lightly spiced, thin and crunchy biscuits for export to 40 countries. With its modern rectangular shape, the Lotus biscuit has been widely adopted by bars and quality restaurants around the world.

Speculoos is the name used to market Lotus original caramelized biscuits in Belgium and France. However, Biscoff (a fusion of 'biscuits for coffee', a shorter, snappier name) was chosen as a product brand name for the USA, quickly replacing the original caramelized biscuit brand in other international markets, including the UK, where the Biscoff brand name was introduced in March 2014. Speculoos is Lotus Bakeries' largest and most important product group, and has driven the group's growth in recent years, especially outside Belgium. Given its strategic importance, major sales and marketing efforts have been made to stimulate the product's further development and growth.

Brand line extensions

Alongside family packs and pocket-size formats of the Original Speculoos, developed in most countries, as well as a chocolate version, Lotus Bakeries is testing, in its traditional markets of Belgium and France, other line extensions, among which are Original Speculoos Crumbs, Rolls and Minis.

Brand stretching

After launching a Lotus Speculoos ice cream, Lotus Bakeries innovated in 2008 and conquered a new market with its spreadable version of the Original Lotus Speculoos. Introduced year-by-year to many countries, including the UK where the brand has become a firm favourite, it is creatively used in a range of recipes shared by customers. Retail giants Sainsbury's and Waitrose saw sales of Biscoff Spread (smooth and crunchy versions) rocket. Following its successful debut, the product was launched in 20g packs for catering and food services. A chocolate version of the spread can also be found in Quebec, Canada.

Lotus Bakeries continues to expand by focusing on the quality of its core products: caramelized biscuits, gingerbread, waffles, specialty cakes and Dinosaurs biscuits.

Based on: Flambard-Ruaud and Daly (2012); Lotus Bakeries (2018)

Brands should be aware of the risks. A major test of any brand extension opportunity is to ask whether the new brand concept is compatible with the values inherent in the core brand: it will not be viable when a new brand is being developed for a target group that holds different values and aspirations from those in the original market segment. When this occurs, the use of the brand extension tactic would detract from the new brand. The answer is to develop a separate brand name, as with Toyota's Lexus, and Seiko with its Pulsar brand developed for the lower-priced mass market for watches.

Finally, management needs to guard against the loss of credibility if a brand name is extended too far. This is particularly relevant when brand stretching. The use of the Pierre Cardin name for such disparate products as clothing, toiletries and cosmetics has diluted the brand name's credibility (Aaker, 1990).

Brand extensions are likely to be successful if they make sense to the consumer. If the values and aspirations of the new target segment(s) match those of the original segment, and if the qualities of the brand name are likewise highly prized, then success is likely. The prime example is Marks & Spencer, which extended from clothing to food based on its core values of quality and reliability.

Co-branding

There are two major forms of co-branding: **product-based co-branding** and **communications-based co-branding** (see Figure 8.8).

FIGURE 8.8
Forms of co-branding

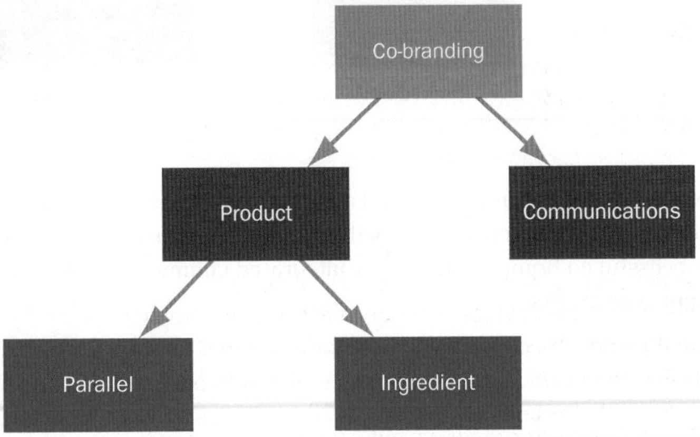

Product-based co-branding

Product-based co-branding involves the linking of two or more existing brands from different companies or business units to form a product in which the brand names are visible to consumers. There are two variants: parallel and ingredient co-branding. **Parallel co-branding** occurs when two or more independent brands join forces to produce a combined brand. An example is Häagen-Dazs ice cream and Baileys liqueur combining to form Häagen-Dazs with Baileys flavour ice cream. Other examples are, BlackBerry (RIM), which partnered with Sky in the Sky Atlantic channel, and both brand names appear together on the channel communications, and Siemens and Porsche Design, which produce a range of kettles, toasters and coffee machines under the Siemens Porsche co-brand (Tomkins, 2005).

Ingredient co-branding is found when one supplier explicitly chooses to position its brand as an ingredient of a product. Intel is an ingredient brand. It markets itself as a key component (ingredient) of computers. The ingredient co-brand is formed by the combination of the ingredient brand and the manufacturer brand—for example, Hewlett-Packard or Sony. Usually the names and logos of both brands appear on the computer. Although Baileys liqueur may at first sight seem to be an ingredient brand, it is not since its main market positioning is as an independent brand (a liqueur), not as an ingredient of ice cream (Riezebos, 2003). Figure 8.9 shows the distinction between parallel and ingredient co-branding.

Advantages

The advantages of product-based co-branding are as follows.

Added value and differentiation The co-branding alliance of two or more brands can capture multiple sources of brand equity, and therefore add value and provide a point of differentiation. For example, Disney has launched a service called Disney Movies Anywhere; it has expanded its alliance with Apple to include Google's Android to allow the unlimited streaming of Disney movies (Nieva, 2014). Target (mass-market USA retailer) has joined with Italian designer Missoni to introduce a range of 400 fashion garments (Ritson, 2011).

If co-branding is going to work, there needs to be certain contrasts between the brands so that joining together brings synergistic benefits. In the case of Target (the US retail department store brand), the Missoni design flare adds value and enables the retailer to associate more closely with premium brands. For Missoni, the

FIGURE 8.9
Parallel and ingredient co-branding

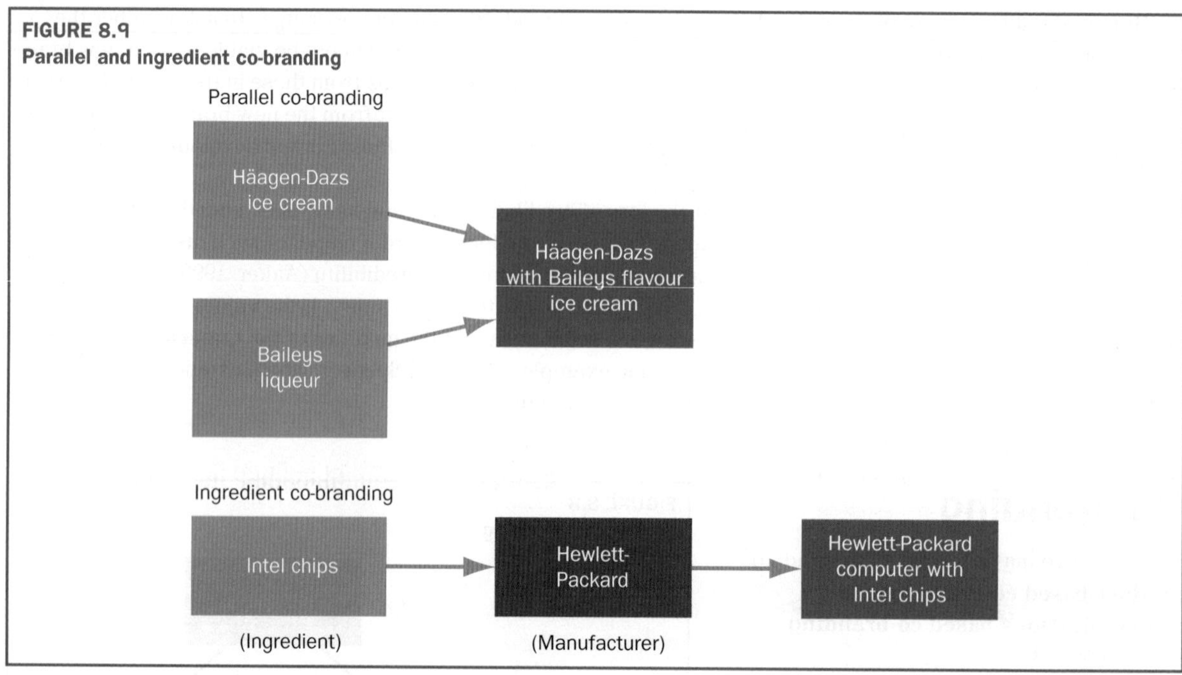

biggest benefit is creating brand awareness in North America. Both companies cater for different audiences, so strong co-branding can again deliver added benefits by giving access to new customers. The potential benefits of successful co-branding are better integrated communication, organizational learning, increased brand equity and improved profits.

Positioning A co-brand can position a product for a target market. Best Western International hotel group and Harley Davidson Motor Company entered into partnership to promote Rider Friendly hotels. The deal brought advantages for both companies and the customers: Best Western gained access to motorcycling enthusiasts who like to travel; Harley Davidson demonstrated its commitment to getting the best for its customers, who on arrival at the hotel could enjoy selected benefits (PRNewswire, 2013). Apple and Volkswagen joined forces, bringing together the Beetle and iPhone to produce a new car called the iBeetle.

Reduction of cost of product introduction Co-branding can reduce the cost of product introduction since two well-known brands are combined, accelerating awareness, acceptance and adoption (Keller, 2008). Consumer technology manufacturer LG and Google joined forces and agreed to share their patent portfolios in a deal that aimed to reduce costs and create opportunities for the development of future innovative products and services (Boxall, 2014).

Risks

There are also risks involved in product-based co-branding, as with other co-branding exercises.

Loss of control Given that the co-brand is managed by two different companies (or at the very least different strategic business units of the same company), each company loses a degree of control over decision-making. There is potential for disagreement, misunderstanding and conflict. For example, American Express decided to end its co-branding relationship with Costco Wholesale because the two corporations could not agree on acceptable terms. The credit card company has seen its stock price fall significantly over the break-up of this unusual partnership, in which Costco exclusively accepted AMEX cards (Sidel, 2015). Lego ended its partnership with Royal Dutch Shell Plc after getting embroiled in an environmental debate over drilling in the Artic. Events came to a head when Greenpeace launched a video which attracted over six million views online. This is a longstanding partnership between the toy maker and the oil producer, extending back over 40 years. Lego had distribution agreements with Shell to sell its toys in petrol stations in 25 countries and made branded Shell petrol station toys (Vaughan, 2014). See Exhibit 8.5 to see how Lego's actions were portrayed.

Loss of brand equity Poor performance of the co-brand could have negative effects on the original brands. In particular, each or either of the original brands' images could be tarnished.

Communications-based co-branding

Communications-based co-branding involves the linking of two or more existing brands from different companies or business units for the purposes of joint communication. This type of co-branding can take the form of recommendation. For example, Ariel and Whirlpool launched a co-branded advertising campaign where Ariel was endorsed by Whirlpool (Kapferer, 2008). In a separate co-branding campaign, Whirlpool endorsed Finish Powerball dishwasher tablets. A second variant is when an alliance is formed to stimulate awareness and interest, and to provide promotional opportunities. An example is Shell's sponsorship of the Ferrari Formula One motor racing team. As part of the deal, the Shell brand name appears on Ferrari cars.

EXHIBIT 8.5
Greenpeace, Lego and Shell Oil

Advantages

The advantages of communications-based co-branding are as follows.

Endorsement opportunities e.g. Whirlpool and Ariel engaged in mutual endorsement in their advertising campaign. Endorsement may also be one-way: Shell gains by being associated with the highly successful international motor racing brand, Ferrari.

Cost benefits One of the parties in the co-brand may provide resources to the other. Shell's deal with Ferrari demands that Shell pays huge sums of money, which helps Ferrari support the costs of motor racing. Also, joint advertising alliances mean that costs can be shared.

Awareness and interest gains The McDonald's/Disney alliance means that new Disney movies are promoted in McDonald's outlets, enhancing awareness and interest, and Happy Meals contain figures from the Disney brands.

Promotional opportunities As we have discussed, McDonald's gained by the in-store promotional opportunities afforded by its co-branding alliance with Disney.

Risks

The risks involved in communications-based co-branding are like those of product-based co-branding.

Loss of control Each party to the co-branding activity loses some of its control to the partner. For example, in joint advertising there could be conflicts arising from differences of opinion regarding creative content and the emphasis given to each brand in the advertising. For example, Lego ended its partnership with Shell Oil because Greenpeace campaigned against the oil company's plans to start drilling for oil in the Arctic. Lego felt that it should not be drawn into this dispute, and so to protect the brand it withdrew (Trangbaek, 2014).

Brand equity loss No one wants to be associated with failure. Poor performance of one brand could tarnish the image of the other. For example, an unsuccessful Disney movie prominently promoted in McDonald's outlets could rebound on the latter. Conversely, bad publicity for McDonald's might harm the Disney brand by association.

Global and Pan-European Branding

Global branding is the achievement of brand penetration worldwide. Levitt, a champion of global branding, argues that intensified competition and technological developments will force companies to operate globally, ignoring superficial national differences. Globally, consumers seek reliable, quality products at a low price, and the marketing task is to offer the same products and services in the same way, thereby achieving enormous global economies of scale. Levitt's position is that the new commercial reality is the emergence of global markets for standardized products and services on a previously unimagined scale. The drivers behind this trend are the twin forces of customer convergence of tastes and needs, and the prospect of global efficiencies in production, procurement, marketing, and research and development. Asian economies are being successful in achieving these kinds of economies to produce high-quality, competitively priced global brands (e.g. Japan: Toyota, Honda, Sony and Canon). Exhibit 8.6 depicts the world's largest brands by industry and turnover. The dominance of technology brands in the top 100 brands is clear. Facebook, Amazon, Apple and Google lead the way in brand valuations. Automotive brands are the next highest in terms of collective brand value. Consumer goods brand Coca-Cola maintains its position in the top ten, while retail brands have lower valuations.

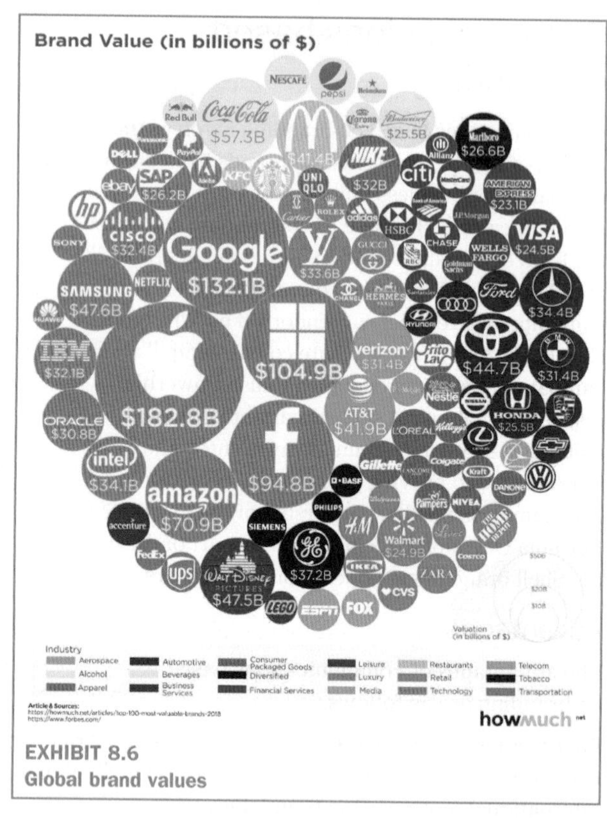

EXHIBIT 8.6
Global brand values

The creation of global brands also speeds up a brand's time to market by reducing time-consuming local modifications. The perception that a brand is global has also been found to affect positively consumers' belief that the brand is prestigious and of high quality (Steenkamp, Batra and Alden, 2003).

In Europe, the promise of pan-European branding has caused leading manufacturers to seek to extend their market coverage and to build their portfolio of brands. Nestlé has widened its brand portfolio by the acquisition of such companies as Rowntree (confectionery) and Buitoni-Perugina (pasta and chocolate), and has formed a joint venture (Cereal Partners) with US giant General Mills to challenge Kellogg's in the European breakfast cereal market. Mars has replaced its Treets and Bonitos brands with M&Ms and changed the name of its third-largest UK brand, Marathon, to the Snickers name used in the rest of Europe.

Some global successes, such as Coca-Cola, BMW, Gucci and McDonald's, can be noted, but national varieties in taste and consumption patterns will ensure that such achievements in the future will be limited. For example, the fact that the French eat four times yoghurt than the British, and the British buy eight times as much chocolate than the Italians, reflects the kinds of national differences that will affect the marketing strategies of manufacturers (Barwise and Robertson, 1992). Indeed, many so-called global brands are not standardized, claim the 'local' marketers. For example, Coca-Cola in Scandinavia tastes different from that in Greece, and Nescafé has many different varieties of its classic instant coffee blend, the aim being to suit local tastes.

When entering international markets, brands should consider which parts of the brand can be standardized and which must be varied across countries. A useful way of looking at this decision is to separate out the elements that comprise the brand, as shown in Figure 8.10.

FIGURE 8.10
Global branding decisions

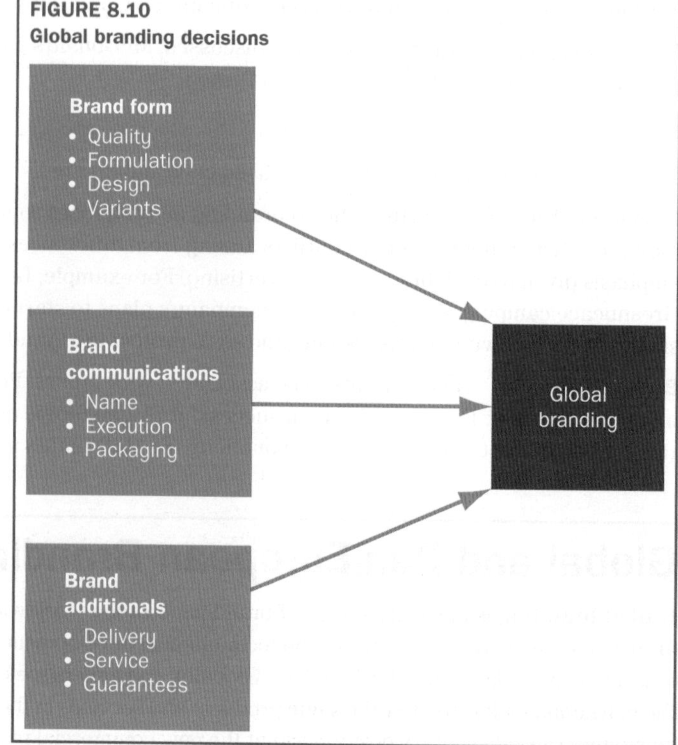

Can brand name and image, advertising, service, guarantees, packaging, quality and design, and delivery be standardized?

Gillette's global success with its Sensor, Fusion and Mach 3 razors was based on a highly standardized approach: the product, brand name, the message 'the best a man can get', advertising visuals and packaging were standardized; only the voice-overs in the advertisement were changed to cater for 26 languages across Europe, the USA and Japan.

Lever Brothers found that, for detergent products, brand image and packaging could be standardized, but the brand name, communications execution and brand formulation needed to vary across countries (Halliburton and Hünerberg, 1993). Brand image and packaging were the same, but the name and formulation (fragrance, phosphate levels and additives) differed between countries.

In other circumstances, the brand form may remain the same across countries, but the brand communications may need to be modified. Consequently, differing advertising appeals would be needed to communicate the concept of exclusiveness in these countries.

Much activity has taken place over recent years to achieve global and pan-European brand positions. There are three major ways of doing this, as outlined below (Barwise and Robertson, 1992).

1 *Geographic extension*: taking present brands into the geographic markets
2 *Brand acquisition*: purchasing brands
3 *Brand alliance*: joint venture or partnerships to market brands in national or cross-national markets.

Brand managers should evaluate the strengths and weaknesses of each option, and Figure 8.11 summarizes these using as criteria speed of market penetration, control of operations and the level of investment required.

Brand acquisition gives the fastest method of developing global brands. For example, Unilever's acquisition of Fabergé, Elizabeth Arden and Calvin Klein immediately made it a major player in fragrances, cosmetics and skincare.

Brand alliance usually gives moderate speed. For example, the use of the Nestlé name for the Cereal Partners (General Mills and Nestlé) alliance's breakfast cereals (e.g. Cheerios, Shreddies and Shredded Wheat) in Europe helped retailer and consumer acceptance.

Geographic extension may be the slowest, unless the company is a major global player with massive resources, as brand building from scratch is a costly process. Many brands are attempting to enter the rapidly expanding markets in China, with varying success. For example, B&Q and Best Buy have opened and then closed stores, but Tesco and Bosch are succeeding. Bosch attributes its success to understanding the needs of the market. The company has been trading in China for over a century using the name Bo Shi and develops specific products for the local markets, such as power tools (Costa, 2011).

However, geographic extension provides a high degree of control since companies can choose which brands to globalize and can plan their global extensions. Brand acquisition gives a moderate degree of control, although many may prove hard to integrate with in-house brands. Brand alliance fosters the lowest degree of control, as strategy and resource allocation will need to be negotiated with the partner. Figure 8.11 provides a framework for assessing the strategic alternatives when developing global and pan-European brands.

Review

1 The concept of a product, brand, product line and product mix

- A product is anything that is capable of satisfying customer needs.
- A brand is a distinctive product offering created using a name, symbol, design, packaging, or some combination of these, intended to differentiate it from its competitors.
- A product line is a group of brands that are closely related in terms of the functions and benefits they provide.
- A product mix is the total set of products marketed by a company.

2 The difference between manufacturer and own-label brands

- Manufacturer brands are created by producers and bear their chosen brand name, whereas own-label brands are created and owned by distributors (e.g. supermarkets).

3 The difference between a core and an augmented product (the brand)

- A core product is anything that provides the central benefits required by customers. The augmented product is produced by adding extra functional and/or emotional values to the core product, and combining them in a unique way to form a brand.

4 Why strong brands are important

- Strong brands are important because they enhance company value, act as a barrier to competition because of their impact on consumer perceptions and preferences, produce high profits and market share, act as a form of quality certification, aid consumers' decision-making, and build trust among consumers.

5 Brand equity, its components and the concept of brand valuation

- Brand equity is a measure of the strength of a brand in the marketplace by adding tangible value to a company through the resulting sales and profits.
- Sources of customer-based brand equity are brand awareness and brand image.
- Sources of proprietary-based brand equity are patents and channel relationships.
- Brand valuation is the process of estimating the financial value of an individual or corporate brand.

6 How to build strong brands

Strong brands can be built by:

- building quality into the core product, creating a unique position in the marketplace
- repositioning to take advantage of new opportunities
- using well-blended communications to create a clear position in the minds of the target audience
- being first into the market with a unique marketing proposition.

7 The differences between family, individual and combined brand names

- A family brand name is one that is used for all products in a range; an individual brand name does not identify a brand with a company; a *combination brand name* combines family and individual brand names.
- The characteristics of an effective brand name are that it should evoke positive associations, be easy to pronounce and remember, suggest product benefits, be distinctive, use numerics or alpha-numerics when emphasizing technology, be transferable and not infringe on existing registered brand names.

8 Why companies rebrand, and how to manage the process

- Companies rebrand: to create a new identity after merger or acquisition; to create a new image/position in the marketplace; to reflect that a major product brand is more familiar to consumers than the old corporate brand; for international marketing reasons (e.g. name harmonization across national borders); for consolidation of brands within a national boundary; in response to legal problems (e.g. restrictions on its use).
- Managing the rebranding process involves choosing the new brand name and implementing the name change.

9 The concepts of brand extension and stretching, their uses and limitations

- A brand extension is the use of an established brand name on a new brand within the same broad market or product category; brand stretching occurs when an established brand is used for brands in unrelated markets or product categories.
- The advantages are: reduced perceived risk of purchase on the part of distributors and consumers; the use of the established brand name raises consumers' willingness to try the new brand; the positive associations of the core brand should rub off onto the brand extension; the awareness of the core brand lowers advertising and other marketing costs; and the introduction of the extension can raise sales of the core brand due to the enhancement of consumers' perception of brand values and image through increased communication.
- The limitations are that poor performance of the brand extension could rebound on the core brand, the brand may lose credibility if stretched too far, sales of the extension may cannibalize sales of the core brand and the use of a brand extension strategy may encourage a focus on minor brand modifications rather than true innovation.

10 The two major forms of co-branding, and their advantages and risks

- The two major forms are product-based (parallel and ingredient) co-branding and communications-based co-branding.
- The advantages of product-based co-branding are added value and differentiation, the enhanced ability to position a brand for a particular target market, and the reduction of the cost of product introduction.
- The risks of product-based co-branding are loss of control and potential brand equity loss if poor performance of the co-brand rebounds on the original brands.
- The advantages of communications-based co-branding are endorsement opportunities, cost benefits, awareness and interest gains, and promotional opportunities.
- The risks of communications-based co-branding are loss of control, and potential brand equity loss.

11 The arguments for and against global and pan-European branding, and the strategic options for building such brands

- The arguments 'for' are that intensified global competition and technological developments, customer convergence of tastes and needs, and the prospect of global efficiencies of scale will encourage companies to create global brands.
- The arguments 'against' are that national varieties in taste and consumption patterns will limit the development of global brands.
- The strategic options are geographic extension, brand acquisition and brand alliances.

Key Terms

augmented product the core product plus extra functional and/or emotional values combined in a unique way to form a brand

brand a distinctive product offering created by the use of a name, symbol, design, packaging, or some combination of these, intended to differentiate it from its competitors

brand assets the distinctive features of a brand

brand domain the brand's target market

brand equity a measure of the strength of a brand in the marketplace by adding tangible value to a company through the resulting sales and profits

brand extension the use of an established brand name on a new brand within the same broad market or product category

brand heritage the background to the brand and its culture

brand performance metrics how customers respond to a brand. Measures include market share, sales, sales growth, market size, share-of-wallet

brand personality the character of a brand described in terms of other entities such as people, animals and objects

brand reflection the relationship of the brand to self-identity

brand stretching the use of an established brand name for brands in unrelated markets or product categories

brand valuation the process of estimating the financial value of an individual or corporate brand

brand values the core values and characteristics of a brand

combination brand name a combination of family and individual brand names

communications-based co-branding the linking of two or more existing brands from different companies or business units for the purposes of joint communication

core product anything that provides the central benefits required by customers

customer-based brand equity the differential effect that brand knowledge has on consumer response to the marketing of that brand

family brand name a brand name used for all products in a range

fighter brands low-cost manufacturers' brands introduced to combat own-label brands

global branding achievement of brand penetration worldwide

individual brand name a brand name that does not identify a brand with a particular company

ingredient co-branding the explicit positioning of a supplier's brand as an ingredient of a product

manufacturer brands brands that are created by producers and bear their chosen brand name

own-label brands brands created and owned by distributors or retailers

parallel co-branding the joining of two or more independent brands to produce a combined brand

product-based co-branding the linking of two or more existing brands from different companies or business units to form a product in which the brand names are visible to consumers

product line a group of brands that are closely related in terms of the functions and benefits they provide

product mix the total set of products marketed by a company

proprietary-based brand equity is derived from company attributes that deliver value to the brand

rebranding the changing of a brand or corporate name

Study Questions

1. **Why do companies develop core products into brands?**
2. **Suppose you were the marketing director of a medium-sized bank. How would you tackle the job of building the company brand?**
3. **Think of five brand names. To what extent do they meet the criteria of good brand naming as laid out in Table 8.1?**
4. **What are the strategic options for pan-European brand building? What are the advantages and disadvantages of each option?**
5. **Why do companies rebrand product and corporate names? What is necessary for successful implementation of the rebranding process?**
6. **What are the two main forms of co-branding? What are their advantages and risks?**

Recommended Reading

Branding sets firms apart from the pack. Read the following to discover the importance of relationships in branding, how Chinese consumers are influenced by brand value and how global brands create value.

Gupta, S., Foroudi, P. and Yen, D. (2018), Investigating relationship types for creating brand value for resellers, *Industrial Marketing Management*, 72 (July), 37–47.

Luoa, J., Deyb, B.L., Yalkinc, C., Sivarajahd, U., Punjaisrie, K., Huangf, Y. and Yen, D.A., Millennial Chinese consumers' perceived destination brand value, *Journal of Business Research* https://www.sciencedirect.com/science/article/pii/S0148296318303023 (accessed July 2018).

Steenkamp, J.B. (2014), How global brands create firm value: the 4V model, *International Marketing Review*, 31(1), 5–29 https://doi.org/10.1108/IMR-10-2013-0233.

References

Aaker, D.A. (1990), Brand extensions: The Good, the bad and the ugly, *Sloan Management Review*, Summer 47–56.

Aaker, D.A. and Keller, K.L. (1990), Consumer evaluation of brand, *Journal of Marketing* 54 (January), 27–41.

Aneslmsson, J. and Bondesson, N. (2015), Customer-based brand equity and human resource management image: Do retail customers really care about HRM and the employer brand?, *European Journal of Marketing*, 50(7/8), 1185–1208.

Bainbridge, J. (2013), Last-mover advantage: when brands should avoid taking the lead, Campaign 24 January https://www.campaignlive.co.uk/article/last-mover-advantage-when-brands-avoid-taking-lead/1167648 (accessed Nov 2018).

Barda, T. (2010), Reforming reputation, *The Marketer*, 23 Nov.

Barnett, M. (2012), Brands build trust through media spend, *Marketing Week*, 23 February, 14–16.

Barwise, F. and Robertson, T. (1992), Brand Portfolios, *European Management Journal*, 10 (3) 277–85.

BBC News (2018), GSK may sell Horlicks to fund Novartis deal https://www.bbc.co.uk/news/business-43552765 (accessed Nov 2018).

Bennett, R.C. and Cooper, R.G. (1981), The Misuse of the Marketing Concept: An American Tragedy, *Business Horizons*, Nov.–Dec., 51–61.

Bokaie, J. (2008), Absolut Scales Back Flavoured Roll-Outs, *Marketing*, 13 August, 8.

Bokomo Foods Ltd. (2015), *WE LOVE OUR CUSTOMERS*, Bokoma http://www.bokomo.co.uk/about/our-customers (accessed Nov 2015).

Bottomley, P.A. and Doyle, J.R. (1996), The Formation of Attitudes towards Brand Extensions: Testing and Generalising Aaker and Keller's Model, *International Journal of Research in Marketing* 13, 365–77.

Boxall, A. (2014), LG and Google hope more innovative products will come from new patent sharing deal, *Digital Trends*, 6 November http://www.digitaltrends.com/mobile/lg-google-sign-patent-sharing-dealBrandz (accessed June 2015).

Brandz (2015), Top 100 Global, Brandz http://www.brandz100.com/#/tabbed/global-100/149?tab_id=150&tab_url=%2Ftop-table%2Ftop-100-48673d91-a201-4477-aefd-86db2db2b656%2F150 (accessed 20 March 2015).

Buzzell, R. and Gale, B. (1987), *The PIMS Principles*, London: Collier Macmillan.

Cannarella, J. and Spechler, J. (2014), Epidemiological modelling of online social network dynamics http://arxiv.org/abs/1401.4208 (accessed 22 March 2015).

Carter, M. (2011), 21st century alchemy, *The Marketer*, April, 28–32.

Cassidy, A. (2012), Ad agencies vie for £4m Douwe Egberts brief, *Campaign*, 30 August.

Costa, M. (2011), Brand value is jewel in the crown for marketers, *Marketing Week*, 12 May, 12–14.

Danziger, P. (2017), Luxury Brand Mergers and Acquisitions set to Explode. *Forbes*, 16 April https://www.forbes.com/sites/pamdanziger/2017/08/16/luxury-brand-mergers-and-acquisitions-set-to-explode/ (accessed July 2018).

De Chernatony, L. (1991), Formulating Brand Strategy, *European Management Journal* 9(2), 194–200.

DeKimpe, M.C., Steenkamp, J.B.E.M., Mellens, M. and Vanden Abeele, P. (1997), Decline and Variability in Brand Loyalty, *International Journal of Research in Marketing* 14, 405–20.

Denstadli, J.M., Lines, R. and Grønhaug, K. (2005), First Mover Advantage in the Discount Grocery Industry, *European Journal of Marketing* 39(7/8), 872–84.

Douwe Egberts Coffee Company (2018), DE Coffee Company, History of Douwe Egberts http://www.decoffeecompany.com/History_of_Douwe_Egberts_s/31.htm (accessed March 2015).

Doyle, P. (1989), Building Successful Brands: The Strategic Options, *Journal of Marketing Management* 5(1), 77–95.

Dregde, S. (2015), Angry Birds revenues fell in 2014 due to sharp decline in merchandise sales, *The Guardian*, 19 March http://www.theguardian.com/technology/2015/mar/19/angry-birds-revenues-2014-rovio (accessed July 2018).

East, R. (1997), *Consumer Behaviour*, Hemel Hempstead: Prentice-Hall Europe.

Ehrenberg, A.S.C., Goodhardt, G.J. and Barwise, T.P. (1990), Double Jeopardy Revisited, *Journal of Marketing* 54 (July), 82–91.

Flambard-Ruaud, S. and Daly, P. (2012), Which Growth Strategy for Lotus Original Speculoos on the French market: Focusing on the core market or diversifying into new ones?, Case study M1783(GB), Paris: CCMP.

Gale Encyclopedia of E-commerce (2002), http://www.encyclopedia.com/topic/Jeffrey_Bezos.aspx (accessed June 2018).

Golder, P., Irwin, J. and Mitra, D. (2013), Four Insights On How Great Brands Fail, *Forbes*, 12 July http://www.forbes.com/sites/onmarketing/2013/07/12/four-insights-on-how-great-brands-fail (accessed 30 March 2015).

Grime, I., Diamantopoulos, A. and Smith, G. (2002), Consumer evaluation of extensions and their effects on the core brand: key issues and research propositions, *European Journal of Marketing* 36(11/12) 1415–38.

Gupta, S., Foroudi, P. and Yen, D. (2018), Investigating relationship types for creating brand value for resellers, *Industrial Marketing Management*, 72 (July) 37–47.

Halliburton, C. and Hünerberg, R. (1993), Pan-European Marketing—Myth or Reality, *Proceedings of the European Marketing Academy Conference*, Barcelona, May, 490–518.

Hammett, E. (2018), M&S looks to unify brand and culture after profits decline, *Marketing Week*, 23 May https://www.marketingweek.com/2018/05/23/ms-unify-brand-culture/ (accessed August 2018).

Hegarty, J. (2011), *Hegarty on advertising: turning intelligence into magic*, London: Thames & Hudson, 21–39.

Hickman, M. (2006), Disney Drops McDonald's Amid Health Fears, *Independent*, 10 May, 24.

Hilpern, K. (2010), Douwe Egberts bagged a bigger share of the luxury coffee market with its master blend, *The Marketer* http://www.themarketer.co.uk/archives/case-studies/brand-blend (accessed 22 March 2015).

Interbrand (2018), Interbrand's 18th annual Best Global Brands Report, Interbrand, October https://www.interbrand.com/best-brands/best-global-brands/2017/ranking/Interbrand (2014) Methodology, Interbrand; http://www.bestglobalbrands.com/2014/methodology (accessed June 2015).

Kapferer, J.N. (2008), *The New Strategic Brand Management*, London: Kogan Page.

Keller, K.L. (2008), *Strategic Brand Management*, New Jersey: Pearson.

Keller, K. and Lehmann, D. (2003), How do brands create value? *Marketing Management*, 12(3), 26–31.

Keller, K. and Lehmann, D. (2006), Brands, Branding: Research Findings and Future Priorities, *Marketing Science* 25(6), 740–59.

Kimberly, S. (2014), Douwe Egberts launches selfie campaign for Prostate Cancer, *Campaign*, 27 October http://www.campaignlive.co.uk/news/1319010/douwe-egberts-launches-selfie-campaign-prostate-cancer (accessed 24 March 2015).

King (1991), Brand /building in the 1990s, *Journal of Marketing Management*, 7(1), 3-14.

Klara, R. (2015), 11 Brand Names That Simply Couldn't Survive the Times Ayds diet candy and Isis Chocolates were doomed, *Adweek*, 18 March http://www.adweek.com/news-gallery/advertising-branding/11-brand-names-simply-couldnt-survive-times-163440 (accessed 30 March 2015).

Lambkin, M. (1992), Pioneering New Markets: A Comparison of Market Share Winners and Losers, *International Journal of Research in Marketing* 9(1), 5–22.

Lemmink, J. and Kaspar, H. (1994), Competitive Reactions to Product Quality Improvements in Industrial Markets, *European Journal of Marketing* 28(12), 50–68.

Lotus Bakeries (2018), Annual Review https://www.lotusbakeries.com/corporate/investor-relations/doclist/half-yearly-annual-reports (accessed Sept 2018).

Lotz, A. (2017), The Unique strategy Netflix deployed to reach 90 million worldwide subscribers, *The Conversation* 5 April https://theconversation.com/the-unique-strategy-netflix-deployed-to-reach-90-million-worldwide-subscribers-74885 (accessed July 2018).

Luoa, J., Dey, B.L., Yalkinc, C., Sivarajahd, U., Punjaisrie, K., Huangf, Y., Yen, D.A. (2018), Millennial Chinese consumers' perceived destination brand value, *Journal of Business Research* In Press July https://www.sciencedirect.com/science/article/pii/S0148296318303023 (accessed July 2018).

Macalister, T. (2015), E.On reports group losses as prepares to hive off fossil fuel business, *The Guardian*, 11 March http://www.theguardian.com/business/2015/mar/11/eon-reports-record-group-losses-hive-off-fossil-fuel-business-german (accessed 27 March 2015).

McWillians, J. (2009), How Facebook beats MySpace, *The Guardian*, 23 June http://www.theguardian.com/commentisfree/cifamerica/2009/jun/23/facebook-myspace-social-networks (accessed 10 February 2015).

Millward Brown (2012), *Brand Personality*, Millward Brown http://www.millwardbrown.com/mb-global/brand-strategy/brand-equity/brandz/top-global-brands/2012/brand-personality (accessed 31 July 2015).

Millward Brown (2014), *Most Valuable Brands 2014*, MillwardBrown.com https://www.millwardbrown.com/brandz/2014/Top100/Docs/2014_BrandZ_Top100_Chart.pdf (accessed 31 July 2015).

Mortimer, N. (2014), Royal Mail challenger TNT Post rebrands as Whistl and trials electric unicycle deliveries, *The Drum*, 15 September http://www.thedrum.com/news/2014/09/15/royal-mail-challenger-tnt-post-rebrands-whistl-and-trials-electric-unicycle (accessed 20 March 2015).

Muzellec, L., Lambkin, M.C. (2006), Corporate rebranding: destroying, transferring or creating brand equity?, *European Journal of Marketing* 40(7/8), 803–24.

Nieva, R. (2014), Google partnership with Disney streams its catalog to Android, 4 November http://www.cnet.com/uk/news/google-partnership-with-disney-streams-its-catalog-to-android (accessed March 2015).

Oliver, C. (2011), Hyundai shifts gear with move to quality, *Financial Times*, 19 May, 22.

Parrish, M. (2018), 10 Major Drugs Losing Patent Protection in 2018, Pharmaceutical Manufacturing, 16 May https://www.pharmamanufacturing.com/articles/2018/10-major-drugs-losing-patent-protections-in-2018/ (accessed August 2018).

Philips (2015), Company Profile, Philips, 20 March http://www.philips.co.uk/about/company/companyprofile.page (accessed March 2015).

PRNewswire (2013), Best Western And Harley-Davidson Partnership Goes Global, PRNewswire, 20 February http://www.prnewswire.com/news-releases/best-western-and-harley-davidson-partnership-goes-global-192015471.html (accessed July 2018).

Reynolds, J. (2015), Kellogg's hits back at own-label with top secret Special K recipe, *Marketing*, 17 May http://www.marketingmagazine.co.uk/article/1182787/kelloggs-hits-back-own-label-top-secret-special-k-recipe (accessed 20 March 2015).

Riezebos, R. (2003), *Brand Management*, Harlow: Pearson Education.

Ritson, M. (2011), Opposites attract higher brand equity, *Marketing Week*, 22 September, 62.

Roberts, C.J. and McDonald, G.M. (1989), Alternative Naming Strategies: Family versus Individual Brand Names, *Management Decision* 27(6), 31–7.

Sharp, B.M. (1990), The Marketing Value of Brand Extension, *Marketing Intelligence and Planning* 9(7), 9–13.

Sidel, R. (2015), AmEx-Costco Divorce Shakes Up Card Industry, *The Wall Street Journal*, 12 February http://www.wsj.com/articles/american-express-to-lose-costco-exclusivity-1423746408 (accessed 16 March 2015).

Steenkamp, J.B.E.M., Batra, R. and Alden, D.L. (2003), How Perceived Brand Globalness Creates Brand Value, *Journal of International Business Studies* 34(1), 53–65.

Steenkamp, J.B.E.M. (2014) How global brands create firm value: the 4V model, *International Marketing Review*, 31(1), 5–29 https://doi.org/10.1108/IMR-10-2013-0233 (accessed Oct 2018).

Sweeny, M. and De Liz, A. (2018), Parents killed it: why Facebook is losing its teenage users, *The Guardian*, 16 February https://www.theguardian.com/technology/2018/feb/16/parents-killed-it-facebook-losing-teenage-users (accessed August 2018).

Tesla, Inc. (2018), Tesla First Quarter http://ir.tesla.com/static-files/1b240f1e-b519-4b40-b14b-fea44698c3af (accessed August 2018).

Tiku, N. (2018), The price of Google's new data conveniences? Your data. *Wired*, 5 August, https://www.wired.com/story/the-price-of-googles-new-conveniences-your-data/ (accessed August 2018).

Tomkins, R. (2005), A Desire for Pairings Leads Brands on a Wild Goose Chase, *Financial Times*, 29 November, 13.

Trangbaek, R. (2014), About Us, Lego, 8 October http://www.lego.com/en-GB/aboutus/news-room/2014/october/comment-on-the-greenpeace-campaign-and-the-lego-brand (accessed 30 March 2015).

Urban, G.L., Carter, T., Gaskin, S. and Mucha, Z. (1986), Market Share Rewards to Pioneering Brands: An Empirical Analysis and Strategic Implications, *Management Science* 32 (June), 645–59.

Valantine, M. (2009), It's All in the Mind, *Marketing Week*, 2 April, 29.

Vaughnan, A. (2014), Lego ends Shell partnership following Greenpeace campaign, *The Guardian*, 9 Oct, https://www.theguardian.com/environment/2014/oct/09/lego-ends-shell-partnership-following-greenpeace-campaign (accessed Nov 2018).

Vincent, M. (2018), Sainsbury's taste for discounts shows its hunger for Asda deal, *Financial Times*, 4 July https://www.ft.com/content/c41b36d8-7f98-11e8-8e67-1e1a0846c475 (accessed August 2018).

White, A. (2014), How ghd is getting ahead, *The Telegraph*, 4 January http://www.telegraph.co.uk/finance/newsbysector/retailandconsumer/10549768/How-ghd-is-getting-ahead.html (accessed 18 March 2015).

Wood, Z. and Butler, S. (2018), Marks & Spencer to close 100-plus stores by 2022, *The Guardian*, 22 May https://www.theguardian.com/business/2018/may/22/marks-spencer-close-stores (accessed August 2018).

Wray, R. (2006), NTL Buys Virgin Mobile and Prepares to Battle with BSkyB, *The Guardian*, 5 April, 23.

CASE 15
Kim Kardashian: Marketing Genius?

Introduction

If you are looking for a conversation starter, just mention the Kardashians. You are likely to get a deeply impassioned response to this famous family and their widely publicised lives. Whether you love them or hate them, most people know who they are (Mirza, 2017). The Kardashian family, consisting of momager Kris, her son Rob and daughters Kim, Kourtney, Khloe, Kylie and Kendall, is one of the most well-known reality TV families. In 2007, 'Keeping up with the Kardashians', an L.A. family's unvarnished docuseries launched on E! and catapulted the family to instant fame. Since then, they have built themselves a global brand empire and have managed to create a colossal money-spinning franchise (Leslie, 2017).

The Rise of Brand Kim Kardashian

Of all the Kardashian/Jenner family members, Kim is one of the most successful, with an enviable social media following of over 200 million (Bengani, 2018). The history of Kim Kardashian (also known as Kim K) is a very public one. She was a personal stylist to Paris Hilton and Lindsay Lohan back in the early 2000s. However, she received even greater notoriety in 2007 when a sex tape made by Kim and her partner back in 2003 was leaked to the press, allegedly by her own mother! Since then, she has married rapper Kanye West, has had three children and has transformed herself into a multimillionaire business woman and the most successful reality TV star in history (Morgan, 2016).

While some might refer to her as a 'television personality' or 'socialite', Kim Kardashian has become a marketable product and has brilliantly practiced personal branding. Personal branding is the practice of marketing yourself and your career as a brand. By creating strong personal brands, celebrities such as Kim can become famous for more than just their talent, but also for the values, attributes and ideas they represent. Like any successful business, Kim has embraced branding, marketing and sales to carefully craft a personal brand strategy and message. She has managed to successfully move away from the idea that she is *only* a socialite and is now seen as an influential business woman and couture fashion icon. Like all brands, personality and positioning is sculptured through clear messaging and, when crafted effectively, can change the way a brand is perceived by the audience. Kim and her army of publicists have worked hard to create and implement her personality and social media has played a significant part in shaping this. With an Instagram occupied with images of luxury garments and a Twitter full of fashion conscious posts, Kim tailors her brand strategy message around the interests of her desired audience—designers and fashionistas. We can now find Kim in the front row of Fashion Week or donning the cover of *Vogue*. Kim also understands and uses her influence. She increases brand awareness through the use of engaging content and is often involved in publicity stunts to ensure that she stays relevant in the media. For example, she attempted to break the internet by posing nude (for free) for *Paper* magazine. This wasn't a financially driven deal, but rather a very successful attempt to further fuel awareness of her brand. She knows how to present herself, and how to leverage media attention and her brand to increase her success. This has allowed her to turn her personal brand into a money-making machine (Robinson, 2015).

Kim's estimated worth in 2018 was $175 million and, according to Forbes, Kim earned a whopping $45.5 million in 2017 alone. This makes her the wealthiest of the Kardashian/Jenner clan (Calfas, 2017).

»

»

She has earned a substantial amount of money as a result of her role as executive producer on her family's reality show, her involvement with her family's DASH clothing stores and her many brand deals and celebrity appearances (e.g. endorsing waist trainers, hair vitamins, laser hair removal, etc.). She has also accumulated substantial wealth through her Kim Kardashian West (KKW) Beauty and Fragrance businesses, her app empire, her acting career, her recent clothing collaboration with her husband Kanye West—'Kids Supply' and her new lingerie and shapewear line (Bobb, 2017). A substantial proportion of Kim's wealth comes from her app development. She has developed a number of apps, including 'Kim Kardashian: Hollywood', 'Kimojis' and 'Kim Kardashian West'. These apps provide an exclusive look into her daily life through the use of exclusive livestreams, beauty tutorials, behind-the-scenes photos and videos, personal journals, fashion content and more (Apple, 2018).

Lessons in Personal Branding

Many have described Kim as a shrewd businesswoman and a successful entrepreneur, and there has been much speculation about the possible reasons for this success. Some have argued that it is not just her association with the Kardashian business or her marriage to one of the world's most brilliant and controversial recording artists, or her selfies, nakedness or the conversations she generates in real life and online on a daily basis that has made her famous. Some laud her as a savvy marketing genius who can teach others a valuable lesson about the power of personal branding (Pattie, 2017). *Time* magazine included Kim on their list of 2015's 100 most influential people, while in 2016 *Vogue* described her as a 'pop culture phenomenon'. She received a further accolade in 2018 when she was awarded an inaugural Influencer Award from the Council of Fashion Designers of America (CFDA) to recognise her influence in the beauty and fashion world (Irish Examiner, 2018).

Some argue that Kim's personal branding success may be down to the fact that she understands her audience and does everything she can to appeal to them. She has a diverse portfolio of products, but each is centred on her core themes of beauty, glam and luxury, and these are themes her audience associates with (Patel, 2017). Every time she steps out of the door or puts a photo of herself on social media, she is instantly recognizable as Kim and it's this brand consistency that has kept people coming back for more. Diversifying her product offering has also allowed her to continue to grow her brand and make a name for herself in other markets (Mattice, 2018). More importantly, Kim is a social media mogul who recognizes the power of branding on social media. She uses a number of different social media platforms to engage with her audience, giving them an insight into her world. Her public documenting of her life on social media makes people feel they have some kind of a connection to her. With millions of Instagram followers, she is the fifth most followed person on Instagram worldwide (Patel, 2017).

Conclusion

There is no doubt that Kim Kardashian is hugely successful and has built herself a substantial empire over the years. As a celebrity, she also has significant cultural influence, shaping a broader conversation around what's attractive in terms of a woman's appearance, how women do their makeup, how they take selfies, etc. Her body is her money-maker and she has set a new standard for what society considers a desirable female body (Romanoff, 2017). Kim may be worshipped by fans across the world, but she is at the same time reviled as someone who is self-absorbed, materialistic, fame-hungry and vain. She has been accused of being spoiled, privileged and a symbol of 'empty celebrity', someone who came to prominence not because of any particular talent but who is 'famous for being famous'. Critics argue that Kim promotes a toxic form of femininity, heaping pressure on young women and girls to maintain a picture-perfect, Instagram worthy image around the clock (McGrath, 2016). For those people who are so repelled by her and who will do anything to stay out of the Kim Kardashian bubble, it is now possible to download a 'K-Blocker' app that purges all Kardashian references and allows you to enjoy Kardashian-free browsing online! (Stachowiak, 2015). Whatever people think of Kim, she has launched a successful personal brand that most would envy. Her brand has managed to stay relevant and profitable over the years, in what is a volatile industry. The Kim Kardashian brand may not be around forever, but she has definitely capitalized on it while she is still the talk of the town (Palihakkara, 2017).

Questions

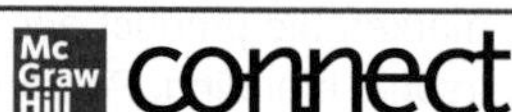

1. **What are the key factors that have contributed to the success of the Kim Kardashian brand? In particular, comment on the role and importance of social media in growing this brand.**
2. **What are the difficulties and risks associated with building a personal brand, as opposed to building a brand for a product or service?**

3. **How has the Kim Kardashian brand been leveraged through brand extension? Conduct online desk research to find examples of Kim's endorsement of other companies' products and services. What are the risks associated with using a celebrity such as Kim to endorse your brand?**
4. **Justify whether you think Kim Kardashian can be described as a marketing genius? Do you think she is a positive role model for women and young girls?**

This case study was written by Marie O' Dwyer, Waterford Institute of Technology.

References

Based on: Mirza, H. (2017), Six brand lessons from the Kardashian clan, LinkedIn https://www.linkedin.com/pulse/six-brand-lessons-from-kardashian-clan-hannah-mirza/ (accessed July 2018); Leslie, B. (2017), The Kardashian decade: how a sex tape led to a billion-dollar brand, *Hollywood Reporter* https://www.hollywoodreporter.com/features/kardashian-decade-how-a-sex-tape-led-a-billion-dollar-brand-1029592 (accessed July 2018); Bengani, S. (2018), Decoding the Kardashian business model: what makes them so successful?, *NewsBytes* https://www.newsbytesapp.com/timeline/Entertainment/16604/82524/keeping-up-with-the-kardashians (accessed July 2018); Morgan, E. (2016), Why is Kim Kardashian so famous? You asked Google—here's the answer, *The Guardian* https://www.theguardian.com/commentisfree/2016/apr/20/why-is-kim-kardashian-famous (accessed July 2018); Robinson, P. (2015), Kim Kardashian has three things to teach us about brand strategy, *Meltwater* https://www.meltwater.com/blog/kim-kardashian-brand-strategy-tips/ (accessed July 2018); Calfas, J. (2017), Kim Kardashian's new makeup line sold out in under 3 hours, *Money* http://time.com/money/4825195/kim-kardashian-kkw-beauty-make-up-line/ (accessed July 2018); Bobb, B. (2017), Here's a first look at Kim Kardashian West and Kanye West's Kids Supply clothing line, dropping today, *Vogue* https://www.vogue.com/article/kim-kardashian-kanye-west-the-kids-supply-childrens-line (accessed July 2018); Apple (2018), Kim Kardashian West app, Apple App Store https://itunes.apple.com/us/app/kim-kardashian-west-app/id1000716588?mt=8 (accessed July 2018); Pattie, L. (2017), Kim Kardashian: Marketing genius, *Digiground* https://digiground.com.au/kim-kardashian/ (accessed July 2018); Irish Examiner (2018), Kim Kardashian is receiving a prestigious award: Here's why she's such a huge fashion influence, *Irish Examiner* https://www.irishexaminer.com/breakingnews/lifestyle/kim-kardashian-is-receiving-a-prestigious-award-heres-why-shes-such-a-huge-fashion-influence-846864.html (accessed July 2018); Patel, S. (2017), Four marketing lessons you can learn from the ubiquitous reality TV star, *Entrepreneur* https://www.entrepreneur.com/article/298532 (accessed July 2018); Mattice, B. (2018), Is Kim Kardashian really a marketing genius?, *Shoemoney* https://www.shoemoney.com/2018/03/15/kim-kardashian-really-marketing-genius/ (accessed July 2018); Romanoff, Z. (2017), The Kardashians' greatest trick, *Racked* https://www.racked.com/2017/9/26/16363484/kardashian-makeup-kylie-cosmetics-kim-kkw-beauty (accessed July 2018); McGrath, M. (2016), Selfie society: Are the Kardashians ruining womanhood?, *Independent* https://www.independent.ie/style/voices/selfie-society-are-the-kardashians-ruining-womanhood-35201655.html (accessed July 2018); Stachowiak, S. (2015), Tired of the Kardashians? Get K Blocker and eliminate them, AppAdvice https://appadvice.com/appnn/2015/11/tired-of-the-kardashians-get-k-blocker-and-eliminate-them (accessed July 2018); Palihakkara, E. (2017), Why the Kardashian marketing strategy is one for the books, *Huffpost* https://www.huffingtonpost.com/erandi-palihakkara/why-the-kardashian-market_b_9136006.html (accessed July 2018).

CASE 16
Burberry

Reinventing the Brand

It is called 'doing a Gucci' after Domenico De Sole and Tom Ford's stunning success at turning nearly bankrupt Gucci Group into a £7 billion (€10 billion) (market capitalization) fashion powerhouse. Since 1997, when she took over, Rose Marie Bravo's makeover of the 143-year-old Burberry brand followed the same path.

The Burberry story began in 1856 when Thomas Burberry opened his first gentlemen's outfitters. By the First World War, business was booming as Burberry won the contract to supply trench coats to the British army. Its reputation grew when it proved its contribution to the national cause. The Burberry check was introduced in the 1920s and became fashionable among the British middle to upper classes. Later, when it was worn by Humphrey Bogart in *Casablanca* and Audrey Hepburn in *Breakfast at Tiffany's*, the Burberry trench coat gained widespread appeal.

Bought by Great Universal Stores in 1955, the brand's huge popularity from the 1940s to the 1970s had waned by the 1980s. A less deferential society no longer yearned to dress like the upper classes, and the Burberry brand's cachet fell in the UK. This was partially offset by a surge in sales to the newly rich Japanese after they discovered its famous (and trademarked) tan, black/red and white check pattern. This trend spread across other areas in South-East Asia and, by the mid-1990s, this region accounted for an unbalanced 75 per cent of Burberry sales. British and American consumers began to regard it as an Asian brand and rather staid. Furthermore, distribution was focused on small shops with few big fashion chains and upmarket stores like Harrods stocking the brand. In the USA, stores like Barney's, Neiman Marcus and Saks only sold Burberry raincoats, not the higher-profit-margin accessories (e.g. handbags, belts, scarves and wraps).

Change of Strategy

These problems resulted in profit falls in the 1990s culminating in a £37 million (€42 million) drop in profits to £25 million (€28 million) in 1997. This prompted some serious managerial rethinking and

the recruitment of American Rose Marie Bravo as a new chief executive. Responsible for the turnaround of the US store chain Saks Fifth Avenue, she had the necessary experience to make the radical changes required at Burberry.

One of her first moves was to appoint young designer Roberto Menichetti to overhaul the clothing range. His challenge was to redesign Burberry's raincoats and other traditional products to keep them fresh and attractive to new generations of younger consumers. Furthermore, he sought to extend the Burberry image to a new range of products. The Burberry brand name began to appear on such products as children's clothes, personal products, watches, blue jeans, bikinis, homewares and shoes in order to attract new customers and broaden the company's sales base. Commenting on Menichetti, Bravo said, 'Coming in, I had studied Hermes and Gucci and other great brands, and it struck me that even during the periods when they had dipped a bit, they never lost the essence of whatever made those brands sing. And I thought, "This man will retain what's good and move us forward".'

Design was further strengthened in 2001 with the appointment of Christopher Bailey (from Gucci) as Burberry's creative director. He created Burberry 'classics with a twist' (for example, recasting the classic trench coat in hot pink). Bailey's job was to design clothes that met Bravo's vision of heritage and classic, but young, modern, hip and fashionable.

A second element of her strategy was to bring in advertising agency Baron & Baron and celebrity photographer Mario Testino to shoot ads featuring models Kate Moss and Stella Tennant. Other celebrities, such as the Beckhams, Callum Best, Elizabeth Jagger, Nicole Appleton and Jarvis Cocker, also featured in Burberry advertising. The focus was to emphasize the new credentials of the Burberry brand without casting off its classic roots. Getting key celebrities to don the Burberry check in its advertising was highly important in achieving this. Bravo once remarked that the famous picture of Kate Moss in a Burberry check bra cut the average age of its customers by 30 years.

A third strand in Bravo's strategy was to sort out distribution. Unprofitable shops were closed and an emphasis placed on flagship stores in cosmopolitan cities. Prestige UK retailers including Harvey Nichols were selected to stock exclusive ranges. Bravo commented, 'We were selling in 20 small shops in Knightsbridge alone, but we weren't in Harrods.' Also, stores that were selling only raincoats were persuaded to stock high-margin accessories as well. Burberry accessories increased from 20 per cent to 25 per cent of turnover. This was part of a wider focus on gifts—the more affordable side of luxury that can drive heavy footfall through the stores. As Bravo said, 'Burberry has to be thought of as a gift store. Customers have to feel they can go into Burberry and buy gifts at various price points.'

International expansion was also high on Bravo's priority list. A succession of new stores were opened, including flagship stores in London, New York and Barcelona. The New York store on 57th Street was the realization of a personal dream for Bravo, whose vision was to replace the store the company had been running in Manhattan for almost 25 years with one that was bigger, better and far more profitable. It is the biggest Burberry store worldwide and has a number of Burberry 'firsts': a lavish gift department, a large area for accessories, private shopping and an in-store Mad Hatters tea room. It also offers a service called Art of the Trench where customers can get made-to-measure trench coats customized by allowing them to pick their own lining, collar, checks and tartan. The Barcelona store was regarded as vital in helping to reposition the Burberry brand in Spain. Prior to its opening, the brand was slightly less fashionable and sold at slightly lower prices than in the UK. The opening of the Barcelona store saw the London product being displayed for the first time as Burberry moved towards one global offering. Besides the USA and Spain, Burberry's third priority country was Japan, since it was an enormous market for the company already.

The results of this activity were astonishing. Profits soared to £162 million (€183 million) by 2005, a six-fold increase since Bravo took over, and in 2002 Great Universal Stores floated one-third of Burberry, its subsidiary, on the stock market, raising £275 million (€310 million). Then, in December 2005, it demerged Burberry completely, allocating Burberry stores to GUS shareholders in proportion to their holdings in a deal worth £1.4 billion (€1.6 billion).

Burberry did face problems, however. One was the weeding-out of grey-market goods, which were offered cheaply in Asia only to be diverted back to Western markets at discounts. Not only were sales affected but brand image was tarnished. Like Dior before it, Burberry was willing to spend the necessary money to try to eliminate this activity. Another problem was that of copycats that infringed its trademark. Burberry claim to spend about £2 million (€2.3 million) a year fighting counterfeits, running advertisements in trade publications and sending letters to trade groups, textile manufacturers and retailers reminding them about its trademark rights. It uses an internet-monitoring service to help pick up online discussion about counterfeits. It also works with Customs officials and local police forces to seize fakes and sue infringers.

The fondness with which so-called 'chavs' regarded the Burberry check was a third problem. One observer defined a chav as a young, white, under-educated underclass obsessed with brands and unsuitable jewellery. One product with which chavs became particularly associated was the Burberry baseball cap. They were also associated with violence, particularly at football matches. The sight of football hooligans appearing in the media adorned in beige and black check was not one appreciated at Burberry HQ. In response, the company stopped producing the infamous cap and shifted emphasis to other non-check lines, including its Prorsum line of luxury clothing designed by creative director, Christopher Bailey.

A fourth problem arose in 2005 with the announcement that Bravo had decided to step down as chief executive. The woman who had built Burberry into an ultra-fashionable major global brand would need to be replaced. Her successor was Angela Ahrendts, who was recruited from US clothing company Liz Claiborne. After a period of working together, Ahrendts took the helm in July 2006 with Bravo taking the newly created role of vice-chairperson, a part-time executive position.

A New Era

Ahrendts made changes to the Burberry product line by making the check more subtle and using it mainly in linings and discreet areas of garments. She also placed greater emphasis on higher margin accessories such as handbags and perfumes, and top-of-the-range fashion. She continued to use British celebrities such as Agnes Deyne and Emma Watson to represent the brand. Burberry also opened stores in emerging markets such as China, India, Russia,

»

»

the Middle East and eastern Europe. In 2008, Burberry's first standalone children's-wear store in Hong Kong was opened, and in 2011 the company bought out its Chinese franchise partner in order to tighten its rein on its global image. It also built up its presence in the USA with the opening of its new headquarters in New York and further store openings.

Ahrendts also improved efficiency by installing new IT systems and replacing 21 scattered distribution centres with three regional hubs in the USA. Her attention was also placed on better sourcing in an effort to improve margins.

Another major focus was to revive Burberry's heritage to the digital generation. Where once luxury brands were reluctant to use the internet, believing it would cheapen their image, Burberry embraced digital, for example being the first luxury brand to embrace Snapchat to connect to the next generation of consumers. Now digital represents over 60 per cent of the marketing budget. Burberry live-streams seasonal shows online and in stores, allowing customers to order products for early delivery with a personalized touch, such as an engraved nameplate in a coat or bag. Pictures of the latest designs are posted on Twitter before they are released to traditional media. Burberry has over eight million Facebook fans, who can watch most of its catwalk shows live and purchase Burberry products direct from its virtual store.

Burberry's digital presence extends to China, where sales have soared. The brand features on Chinese sites such as Sina Weibo (China's equivalent to Twitter) and Youku (similar to YouTube), helping the brand to outperform its rivals in the country. Asia now accounts for over 40 per cent of Burberry's revenues.

As well as global and digital expansion, Ahrendts saw menswear and male accessories such as bags and scarves as key to Burberry's continuing success. In 2012, its first standalone menswear store, next to its branch in Knightsbridge, London, was opened. By 2014, menswear accounted for a quarter of Burberry's sales.

The expansion of fragrance and beauty products has also driven sales growth. In 2014, its first dedicated makeup and perfume shop was opened in Covent Garden, London.

Changes at the Top

By 2014, Burberry sales had soared to £2.33 billion (€2.7 billion) with profits of £461 million (€520 million). However, in the same year, Ahrendts was tempted by an offer to join Apple and was succeeded by creative director Christopher Bailey, who had received much of the credit for the success of Burberry's digital marketing operations, including streaming its fashion shows live, and had been named British designer of the year in 2009. His promotion saw him take over the dual roles as chief executive and creative director. His aims were to continue global expansion, particularly in Japan, where Burberry has underperformed, expansion of its beauty business, including entering the £26 billion (€29 billion) skincare market in 2015, and to continue to penetrate the menswear market.

However, in the face of less than impressive financial results and criticism of his ability to manage two roles, he was replaced as chief executive by Marco Gobbetti in 2017, while taking on the positions of president and creative director. Gobbetti was hired from Celine, where he transformed the ailing brand by making it more exclusive and expensive. The intention was for them work together but, after nine months, Bailey decided to leave the company.

Gobbetti's strategy is to move Burberry further upmarket to take on super-luxury exclusive brands such as Gucci, Dior and Hermes. He gave the example of Burberry polo shirts priced at £145–275 (€165–310), which he believed should be priced 50% higher to match other luxury brands. He announced that he would close some outlets in department stores, beginning in the USA before doing so in Europe. He admitted that the plan would require considerable investment and patience from shareholders. His new creative director is Riccardo Tisci, recruited from Givenchy.

Questions

1. **How were the clothes bearing the Burberry name augmented to create a brand before the 1980s?**
2. **What elements of the brand-building factors discussed in this chapter have been used by Burberry to rebuild its brand?**
3. **What problems might arise in trying to build Burberry into a global brand?**
4. **What are the dangers inherent in Burberry's strategies since 1997?**

This case was written by David Jobber, Emeritus Professor of Marketing, University of Bradford.

References

Based on: Heller, R. (2000), A British Gucci, *Forbes*, 3 April, 84–86; White, E. (2003), Protecting the Real Plaid from a Lineup of Fakes, *Wall Street Journal*, 7 May; Barns, E. (2005), Are Advertisers Wise to Chase the Chav Pound?, *Campaign*, 24 March, 18; Walsh, F. (2006),

Burberry Chief Turns on Charm with 19 per cent Growth in Retail Sales, *The Guardian*, 13 July, 28; Kollewe, J. and Wearden, G. (2008), Burberry Sees Profits Rise While Laura Ashley Suffers, *The Guardian*, 29 May, 26; Gumbel, P. (2008), The Luxury Market Loses Its Lustre, *Fortune*, 22 August, 27; Wardell, J. (2009), Burberry Makes Loss For Year, *Business Week*, 19 May, 64; Wood, Z. (2010), Burberry Buys Out Chinese Partner to Unify the Brand, *The Guardian*, 17 July, 33; Ritson, M. (2011), Burberry Offers a Lesson in Consistency, *Marketing Week*, 2 June, 54; Barrett, C. and Bradshaw, T. (2011), Burberry in Step with Digital Age, *Financial Times*, 1 September, 16; Leroux, M. and Thompson, S. (2012), Burberry Banks on the Ascent of (Fashionable) Man, *The Times*, 24 May, 43; Butler, S. (2013), Chilly Spring Warms Hearts at Burberry, *The Guardian*, 11 July, 26; Butler, S. and Rankin, J. (2014), Doubt Over Leaving Date for Outgoing Boss at Burberry, *The Guardian*, 17 April,31; Rankin, J. (2014), Bailey Outlines His Design for Burberry Seamless Move, *The Guardian*, 22 May, 29; Vizard, S. (2015), 'Commitment to Customer Experience' Helps Burberry to Festive Sales Boost, marketingweek.com, 14 January; Cartner-Morley, J. (2017), Checking Out of Burberry: Fashion Star Who Sparked Rebirth of the Trenchcoat, *The Guardian*, 1 January, 3; Wood, Z. (2017), Burberry Value Drops £850m as Plan is Unveiled to Move More Upmarket, *The Guardian*, 10 November, 40; Kollewe, J. (2018), Sales Slide at Burberry As Sterling's Rise Puts Chinese Shoppers Off, *The Guardian*, 12 July, 36.

CHAPTER 9
Value Through Service

> *It is not so much the products you sell that guarantee success but the service you provide to customers.*
>
> **LUKE JOHNSON, ENTREPRENEUR**

LEARNING OBJECTIVES

After reading this chapter, you should be able to:

1. describe the nature and special characteristics of services
2. describe the activity sectors in the services industry
3. explain how customer relationships should be managed
4. explain how to manage service quality, productivity and staff
5. explain how to position a service organization and brand
6. discuss the services marketing mix
7. describe the nature and special characteristics of non-profit marketing

This chapter discusses the marketing of **services** and how they deliver value. Throughout this text we adopt the stance that physical products and service products are equally important in terms of the marketing requirements. It is also essential to be aware of how principles of marketing apply to services. In addition to the Four-Ps, the marketing of services requires understanding of the services marketing mix. Furthermore, it is important to be aware of how superior value is created in the service industries by bringing together a company and its customers in the value creation process. This approach has been called service *dominant logic* and it focuses marketers' attention on the creation of value and the importance of relationships in contrast to the traditional model of marketing, which has the exchange of manufactured goods as its dominant logic. From this point of view, marketers should think about how best to manage and co-create value with customers. This means developing long-term relationships that are mutually beneficial (Karpen, Bove and Lukas, 2012). The management of customer relationships is discussed in detail in Chapter 10.

Services become increasingly valuable to industrialized economies as advances in technology lead to the development of sophisticated products that require more design, production and maintenance services. Another reason for the rising contribution of services to the global economy is growth in per capita income. This gives citizens a greater percentage of their income to spend on non-essentials such as restaurant meals and national and international travel, which are all service-intensive products. Greater discretionary income increases demand for financial services such as investment trusts and personal pensions. It is not just in the consumer sector where there is an increase in demand for services. In industrial sectors, the trend towards outsourcing means that manufacturers are buying in services. Often it is more efficient for a company to use external expertise to manage distribution, warehousing and catering, leaving time to focus on its core competencies. Deregulation has also increased the level of competition in certain service industries (e.g. telecommunications, television, airlines) and this has also been a driver of expansion of services.

To give you an idea of the growing significance of the services industry in significant economies around the world, Table 9.1 shows the percentage that each sector (industrial, agricultural and service) contribute to the GDP of each country listed. In the UK and the USA, services contribute over 80 per cent and the dominance of services can be seen around the world. In addition, public administration and other services industries, which include work carried out in private households, and employed persons contribute to the service economy.

TABLE 9.1 Contribution of industrial, agricultural and service industry sectors to GDP can be divided into sectors

Country	GDP (purchasing power parity)	Industrial sector (%)	Agricultural sector (%)	Services sector (%)
USA	$19.39 trillion	18.8	0.9	80.2
China	$23.7 trillion	39.5	8.3	52.2
India	$9.46 trillion	23.00	15.4	61.5
Japan	$5.43trillion	29.7	1.00	69.3
Russia	$4.01 trillion	32.4	4.7	62.3
Germany	$4.17 trillion	30.1	0.6	69.3
United Kingdom	$2.91 trillion	19.00	0.6	80.4
France	$2.83 trillion	20.1	2.00	77.9

Source: CIA World Facts Book (2018) Figures based on 2017 estimates https://www.cia.gov/library/publications/the-world-factbook/geos/xx.html

The Service Industries

The sectors that make up the service industries vary considerably and are constantly evolving as new service concepts are developed, for example web developers and social media engagement analysts. Various forces are driving the changes, such as technological innovations and changing patterns of ownership. For example, privatization of parts of the UK National Health Service opened up opportunities for private service providers to perform medical scans and carry out diagnostic tests and X-rays on patients (Campbell, 2015). Servitization of products is also encouraging firms to rethink their business strategies. This approach has created many

TABLE 9.2 The UK service industry sectors

Sector	Areas of activity	Examples of leading companies
Creative industries	Advertising, IT technology, software design, web services, film industry, theatres, TV and radio, publishing, music	Abbott Mead Vickers BBDO, McCann Erickson, Bloomsbury Publishing, Google, Microsoft, IBM, BBC, Tiger Aspect Productions, Sky, Channel 4
Government services	Education, health and social work	NHS Direct, UK Universities, schools and colleges, British council
Financial and business services	Banking, accountancy, financial management, legal services	HSBC, Barclays Bank, Admiral insurance, Aviva, PWC, Deloitte
Hospitality and tourism	Tourism, fast food, pubs, leisure clubs, accommodation	Intercontinental Hotels, Thomas Cook, TUI Travel Plc Whitbread, Greene King, Centre Parcs
Property management	Real estate, renting, computer related	Savills, Knight Frank, Strutt & Parker
Transport, storage and communications	Land, air transport, business services, post and telecoms	Vodafone, Virgin, EE, British Airways
Retailing	Motor, wholesale, supermarkets	Amazon, Aldi, Boots, Marks & Spencer, Next Plc, Costco
Non-profit	Alleviation of hunger, protection of children, vulnerable individuals, animals	Oxfam, RSPCA, Worldwide Fund for Nature, Save the Children, English Heritage

opportunities for firms to extend their 'product' sales by selling wraparound services that complement the original sale. For example, industrial equipment manufacturers regularly provide add-on support services, which can extend relationships. Bains and Lightfoot (2013) found that some pioneering companies, e.g. Rolls Royce, Xerox, London Underground, were undergoing a transformation in their business strategy and pushing performance helped these and other firms create competitive advantage by developing customer intimacy (detailed knowledge of customer requirements) so that they could produce the best solutions, operational excellence (controlling processes) through delivering the *best* solutions and product leadership (selling the best products on the market). As a result, these authors classified services as Basic (providing products), Intermediate (repair, maintenance and customer help) and Advanced (flexible payment solutions, fleet management, collaborative integrated solutions) and suggested that they provide a pathway for firms to develop their own servitization strategies.

In this section, we briefly consider each of the areas of activity highlighted in Table 9.2. The basic premise in each of the sectors is that businesses engage in economic activity, which involves using particular knowledge, skills and expertise in the production of specialist services, as opposed to manufacturing products (e.g. car production), growing produce (e.g. farming) or extracting minerals (e.g. mining). We will explore this idea in more detail in the next section when discussing the physical goods–service continuum model.

Creative industries

Sometimes referred to as the new economy, creative industries and creative clusters, defining this sector is not straightforward. However, creative industries has become the widely accepted name (Lazzeretti and Vecco, 2018) and these areas of activity are enjoying a period of growth across Europe. In the UK, around 3.1 million people work in this sector. Exhibit 9.1 shows an infographic of the UK creative economy in terms of employment opportunities and regional differences. The rise of creative industries has become an important area of research and an important economic driver. This sector relies on developing services based on creative skills; for example, creative (advertising), writers, fashion designers, artists, musicians and TV producers. Software development and electronic publishing are the most active parts of the sector—in economic terms—followed by publishing, advertising, architecture, music and the visual arts, film, TV and radio, and design. Creative industries generate distinctive and authentic 'products' which are difficult to replicate, for example Electronic Arts' (video game publisher) *Need for Speed* and *Battlefield* games. So, creative labour 'is geared to the production of original or distinctive commodities that are primarily aesthetic and/or symbolic–expressive rather than utilitarian and

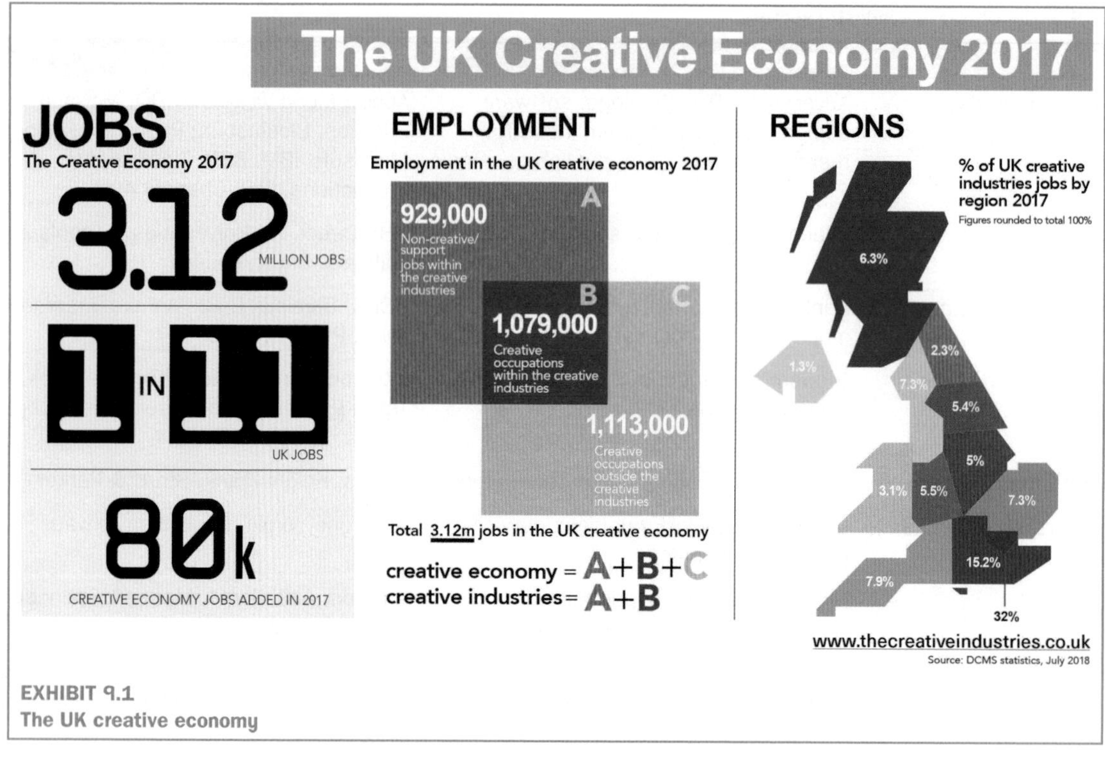

EXHIBIT 9.1
The UK creative economy

functional' (Hirsch, 1972). Nick Park (creator, animator and director, perhaps best known for Wallace and Gromit and Shaun the Sheep), J.K. Rowling (writer, best known for Harry Potter) and First Aid Kit (international singer/songwriters best known for 'My Silver Lining') are all examples of successful individuals who began and developed their careers in the creative industries. Increasingly, creative people understand the importance of leveraging market advantage from their skills and talents. In the past, commercial values and artistic autonomy were seen as being in opposition. But now 'the very best artists are also some of the most effective entrepreneurs' (Arts Council, 2004).

See Marketing in Action 9.1 to learn more about how Nordic film makers and production companies have influenced the global creative industry.

MARKETING IN ACTION 9.1
Nordic Noir Changes the Mood in the Creative Industry

Moody, brooding epic productions like *Fortitude*, produced by UK production company Fifty Fathoms/Tiger Aspect, demonstrated the extent to which 'Nordic noir' has percolated through the creative industries' psyche. Filmed in Reyðarfjörður on the eastern Fjords of Iceland, *Fortitude* used the appeal of the Nordic landscape and the fresh, clean environment, entwined with complex, dark undertones of social deviation to create a blockbuster drama series shown on Sky Atlantic (pan-European satellite broadcaster). But this is literally the tip of the iceberg of the Nordic creative industry, as there are hundreds of writers, film producers and drama series that have emerged from Sweden, Denmark, Finland, Iceland and associated territories such as the Hebrides.

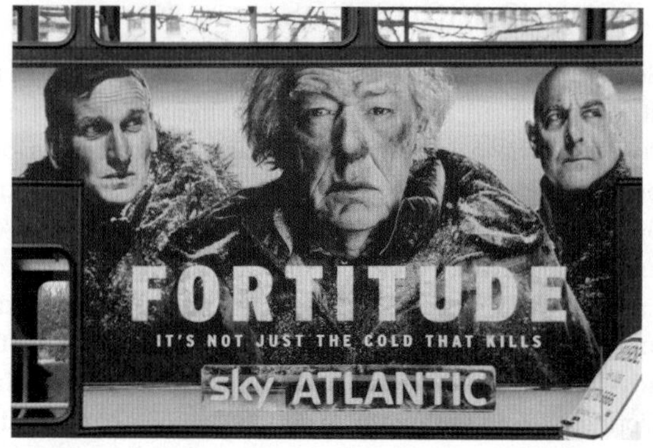

Furthermore, this powerhouse of creative development has become an important source of economic growth. The distinctive and authentic nature of these creative products has captured the hearts and minds of readers, TV viewers and film goers globally.

For example, *Wallander* (adapted from Henning Mankell's novels) was a series of crime drama novels (published in Swedish in 1991) that arguably began the popularization of Nordic noir in the UK and unwittingly helped to nudge this emerging genre into the mainstream. Initially, European crime dramas were in the bargain basement for broadcasters looking for cheap, watchable alternatives to high-cost US productions. As well as price, demand has driven growth: due to the proliferation of TV channels, there was the need to find new drama to attract viewers. The Swedish version of *Wallander* was aired in the UK with English subtitles on BBC 4 (new satellite channel). But the UK's BBC 1 also produced its own version of the series, with leading actor Sir Kenneth Branagh; this version was aired on BBC 1 at prime viewing times. Although critically acclaimed, the English version is said to have been outpaced by the Swedish language version, which proved very popular with viewers and created demand for similar foreign language drama productions, paving the way to success for other series such as *Borgen, The Killing* and *The Bridge*. In a similar vein, the work of author Stieg Larsson, writer and creator of the best-selling *Millennium* trilogy, which included *The Girl with the Dragon Tattoo*, has become internationally acclaimed. The books, which were published after Larsson's death, topped best-seller lists around the world and inspired film makers in Scandinavia and the USA.

Nordic noir has become so popular that producers and broadcasters are seeking every opportunity to partner with individuals and businesses in the Nordic creative industry to secure an opportunity to find the next best-selling blockbuster and, in response, authors and publishers have increased their outputs.

Based on: Booth (2014); Gallagher (2009); Jodelka (2015); Stougaard-Neilsen (2016)

Furthermore, it is important to remember that creative skills are also at the centre of product innovation, and a company's innovation in the design area can contribute significantly to its overall level of performance (Rubera and Kirca, 2012).

Government services

The public sector in many countries around the world involves the provision and delivery of services by the government for the country's citizens. The sector typically includes education, health, social care, police, defence and transport. This is a highly complex part of the service industry, and processes are central to much of the activity that takes place. For example, maintaining relationships with suppliers is important to ongoing success of procurement processes. For example, Computacenter works closely with the UK central government, providing IT solutions which meet exacting efficiency standards, but also add value through tailored long-term solutions and ongoing support packages.

E-procurement has been widely adopted as a means of reducing operational cost while maintaining organizational standards. However, while it is arguably easy to measure the performance of the process of procurement (especially since the advent of e-procurement systems), it is more difficult to monitor the process of, say, a patient being taken into hospital, as the individual circumstances can vary considerably—as can the outcome, depending on the patient's health at presentation at the hospital (or point of care).

This sector also tends to have less clear goals, which makes setting objectives complex. Another complexity that is arguably unique to this sector is the involvement of politics. In the UK, the National Health Service is often subject to public scrutiny through the media (Collinson, 2012).

Nevertheless, marketing has an important role to play, and organizations from councils to hospitals can use the marketing mix in their strategy and planning. For example, Gov.uk is a digital service provided to help UK citizens find helpful information and access services. It is important to note that much of the marketing activity in this sector is concerned with customer satisfaction, despite the lack of direct competition.

Financial services

In this sector of the industry, banking and insurance are the key areas of activity. The focus of the industry is financial management, which includes investment, the lending of money, insurance issues and pensions. This industry sector serves both large corporations and individuals. Investment banking typically provides services to corporate clients. We have mentioned mergers, acquisitions and takeovers earlier, and these activities are likely to be handled by investment banks that provide the required skill sets to handle the moves. Commercial banks handle deposits and loans for companies and individuals. In the UK, the financial services sector employs one million people and contributes around 12 per cent to GDP, it is the world's second largest financial centre, just behind the USA, but ahead of China and Japan (Allen, 2018). But the UK's decision to leave the EU is throwing doubt as to how long its dominance will continue. The City of London is a centre of excellence for financial expertise and has attracted many leading financial organizations to locate part of their businesses there. However, because of the Brexit referendum vote for the UK to leave the EU, banks and asset management firms are looking to relocate on mainland Europe and Paris, and Dublin and Frankfurt are vying for their business (Edmund, 2018). Nevertheless, this sector of the services industry plays a significant part in the economic well-being of local and global economies and remains very important to the UK.

Hospitality, travel and tourism

This part of the sector is very diverse. Under this heading we are primarily thinking about the providers of travel and hospitality services rather than the transportation element, which is covered separately. Hospitality is made up of many facets, from pubs, restaurants and hotels, to theme parks and special-interest activities like wine-tasting events. The hospitality industry caters for the needs of businesses and individuals alike. Exhibit 9.2 shows the economic impact of the UK tourism industry.

From a marketing perspective, an important point to be aware of is that many of the services offered in this part of the sector are highly perishable. In other words, the vacancy rate in a hotel is an important determinant of its likely success. If the rate is high and there are many empty rooms, the business is performing poorly. The same is true of the travel industry. Service suppliers such as travel agents and operators, both online and offline, are constantly aiming to fill their holidays and tours. Sales promotions are widely used to sell available places. Travelling for pleasure has been on the increase for many years. While travel used to be an activity associated with the rich, package holidays and, more recently, low-cost air travel have made foreign travel accessible to more consumers. This sector also includes business travel.

Property management

As with other parts of the sectors, a range of activities are involved and, although provided primarily for business-to-business markets, there is a part of the sector that provides services for the individual. Property management includes handling day-to-day management of clients, maintenance and repairs, and this can mean handling residential or commercial properties. In the past, this industry collected rent and maintained buildings, but

EXHIBIT 9.2
Visit England estimates the potential for growth in the tourism industry in the UK
Source: https://www.visitbritain.org/visitor-economy-facts

today property investors want engagement between individual customers, commercial occupiers and the management team. Knight Frank is investing in technology platforms that provide property management systems to facilitate such engagement, concierge services and help desks. By automating part of the facilities, managers are then able to spend more time on improving services to property users. Read Marketing in action 9.2 to find out more about how French property agent Leggett Immobillier reinvented its services to become the best estate agent in France.

Transport, storage and communications

This part of the sector covers rail, road, water and air transportation, and communication services for both individuals and businesses. Communication services include postal and telecommunication services. There are many billions of service encounters in this sector and opportunities to engage customers. Many firms are finding

MARKETING IN ACTION 9.2
Leggett Immobillier Voted the Best Estate Agency in France for the Fifth Year

Property sales in France are buoyant and President Macron is keen for this market to continue to grow and attract both domestic and international buyers. In recent years, there has been approaching a million properties sold every year; good rates for long-term loans, tax incentives and low interest rates for mortgages all help to support this vibrant and valuable market. Research suggests that international buyers of French properties, of whom 32 per cent are British, 15.5 per cent Belgian and 7.2 per cent Swiss, need help in finding the right property and understanding how to buy property in France. Leggett Immobilier is an estate agency which not only helps domestic and international buyers find the right property, but has also developed a unique approach.

Trevor Leggett moved to France and began a house renovation business, but soon realized there was a market opportunity for a quality estate agent service for property buyers. At the time, French agencies tended to focus on the domestic market, leaving international buyers without good property services and there was almost no online support. Trevor started Leggett Immobilier at the end of the 1990s and the business has grown into France's leading international estate agency, which regularly wins awards for customer care and is also one of the ten fastest growing property consultancies in Europe. The company has a large support centre, with people on hand to answer questions (in many languages) and an online portal, providing access to properties for sale, information and links to company agents who have specialist knowledge of local areas.

Based on: Notaires.fr (2018); Leggett Immobilier (2018); Financial Times Survey (2017)

ways to improve their services, delight customers and develop relationships with customers. London Underground transports over one billion passengers each year, it has recently invested £billions in rail infrastructure, new trains and upgrading existing carriages, and is committed to making life in the city better, with a safe and reliable underground rail network (TFL, 2018).

Retailing

Retailing is an important element of the service industry: it is the activity involved in the sale of products to the ultimate consumer. Retailing is a major employer of the European Union's workforce. Again, this is a very diverse industry, and retailers make use of every aspect of the product and services marketing mix. In order to deliver the service expectations of their customers, retailers have to ensure that they have the right products in the right place and at the right time, which has implications for purchasing and logistics (discussed in detail in Chapter 17). One of the key functions of retailing is to 'break-bulk so that consumers can buy goods in small quantities to satisfy their needs' (Ellis-Chadwick, 2011).

Consumer decision-making involves not only the choice of product and brand, but also of retail outlet. Most retailing is conducted in stores such as supermarkets, catalogue shops and departmental stores, but non-store retailing such as mail order and automatic vending also accounts for a large amount of sales. Retailing provides an important service to customers, making products available when and where customers want to buy them.

Many large retailers exert enormous power in the distribution chain because of the vast quantities of goods they buy from manufacturers. The purchasing power of retailers has meant that manufacturers have to maintain high service levels and good buyer–supplier relationships.

Non-profit organizations

Non-profit organizations contribute to service sector activity, but are not driven by the profit motive to satisfy their stakeholders. These types of organizations can focus their activities on social change and encouraging communities to think and act in new ways. Firms with this focus are sometimes referred to as engaging in social entrepreneurship (Kelly & Lewis, 2009). This is not new thinking, as Ansoff (1979) argued that not-for-profit organizations would need to become more socially relevant to survive. What is new is the need for greater efficiency and effectiveness throughout the organizations, so, even though the profit motive is different, the need to provide great service is not diluted. Read Marketing in Action 9.3 to find out how a different approach to selling in the charity shop sector has revitalised business for Save the Children

This sector is also discussed in some detail in Chapter 5.

MARKETING IN ACTION 9.3
Mary's Living and Giving Shops

Since 2009, a new style of retailing has emerged in the third sector (non-governmental and not-for-profit organizations). Charity shops have become more sophisticated and have begun looking at how to create a brand image, which is attractive to their customers. One such example is Mary's Living and Giving Shop for Save the Children. This is a charity shop that is positioned in a premium and luxury goods market; rather unusual for a store concept, which relies on donations of clothing and accessories from members of the public and other organizations to provide its products. The concept for the store was devised by Mary Portas (retail consultant and broadcaster), who saw an opportunity to embed the charity shop more positively in the local environment as well as improving the returns for Save the Children.

»

The connection with a larger charity was important, as there was a parenting advantage for Mary's fledgling concept as the larger charity provided structure, leadership, focus and networks of volunteers and, in return, the Living and Giving stores provided enhanced value for Save the Children. The store concept has led to 21 stores and even a pop-up store in the world-renowned Liberty of London department store.

Save the Children is not the only charity to open niche stores. Oxfam has developed specialized book and music stores, The British Red Cross, Traid and Amnesty International also operate niche stores, selling 'upcycled' clothes, wedding outfits and more.

Based on: Charles et al. (2018); McColl et al. (2018); Wood (2017); Liberty London (2018)

The Nature of Services

In the previous section, we briefly introduced different areas of activity in the services industry. Next, we shall examine the nature of services, as these principles guide much of the management activity in all of the above.

Cowell (1995) states that 'what is significant about services is the relative dominance of *intangible attributes* in the make-up of the 'service product'. Services are a special kind of product. They may require special understanding and special marketing efforts. Services often involve the use of something without ever gaining ownership, for example renting an apartment, a car or a hotel room. However, while pure services do not result in ownership, they may be linked to a physical good. For example, a machine (physical good) may be sold with a one-year maintenance contract (service).

Many offerings, however, contain a combination of the tangible and intangible. For example, a marketing research study would provide a report (physical good) that represents the outcome of a number of service activities (discussions with client, designing the research strategy, interviewing respondents and analysing the results). In the creative industries, the service is the generation of the ideas and concepts, which are then delivered in a tangible form: for example, an author writes a manuscript, and the publisher then produces a book or a production company a film.

This distinction between physical and service offerings can, therefore, best be understood as a matter of degree rather than in absolute terms. Figure 9.1 shows a physical goods–service continuum, with the position of each offering dependent upon its ratio of tangible/intangible elements. At the pure goods end of the scale is clothing, as the purchase of a skirt or socks is not normally accompanied by a service. Carpet purchases may involve an element of service if they require professional laying. Machinery purchase may involve more service elements in the form of installation and maintenance. Software design is positioned on the service side of the continuum since the value of the product is dependent on design expertise rather than the cost of the physical product (disk). Marketing research is similarly services based, as discussed earlier. Finally, internet banking

FIGURE 9.1
The physical goods–service continuum

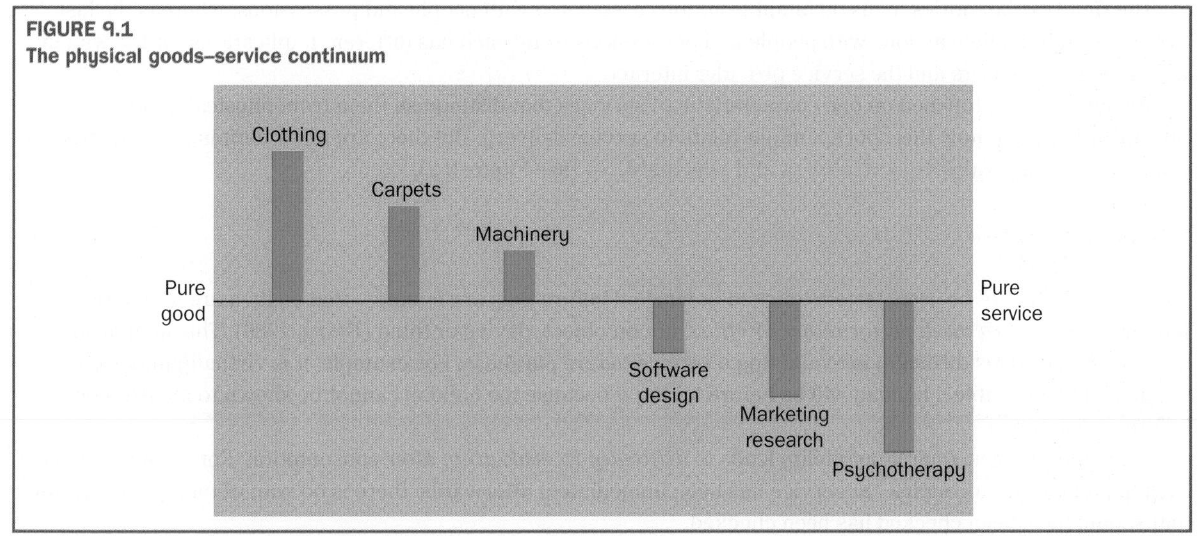

(management of digital assets) or psychotherapy (treatment of a mental health issue) may be regarded as a pure service since the client receives nothing tangible from the transaction.

Drawing a line between goods and services is difficult. Indeed, it has been argued that any such attempt to do so misses the point. Vargo and Lusch (2006) suggest that the marketers' 'love affair' with products is over and has been superseded by a new 'service-aligned ethos'. This means that managers should make services central to their activities rather than the product. Ultimately, in this model the product becomes a 'keepsake' of the service experience and the customer is a 'co-creator of value'. The paper by Vargo and Lusch has been influential in marketing literature, but the terminology has been hotly debated by academics (Brown and Patterson, 2009; O'Shaughnessy and O'Shaughnessy, 2009). Nevertheless, there is a growing body of work that supports the notion that marketing now extends well beyond the Four-Ps framework. Indeed, services have been defined in marketing literature as 'the application of specialized competences (knowledge and skills) through deeds, processes, and performances for the benefit of another entity or the entity itself' (Lusch and Vargo, 2011; Vargo and Lusch, 2004).

Furthermore, services are everyday occurrences or acts (in a commercial setting) that provide assistance or help to a customer. This action entails activities, tasks and processes to be performed, and they can be carried out directly or indirectly; for example, 'I have received excellent service from my hairdresser' (directly) or 'I received excellent service through my bank account' (indirectly) (Lusch and Vargo, 2011).

Ultimately, service-dominant logic sets out a model that suggests that marketing can serve as a framework for integrating marketing and supply chain management (SCM) practices in a manner that enables the 'target user/consumer' to take part in the creation process (Lusch, Vargo and Tanniru, 2010). According to Wirtz and Chew (2003) and Wirtz, Chew and Lovelock (2012), there are different categories of services which can be defined by looking at service users and their possessions, and the extent to which the services provided are tangible or intangible.

- People processing: the services are directed at the individual, as in the case of a manicurist, a barber and an optician. In this situation, the service user visits the service provider in order to receive the services on offer.
- Possession processing: the services are directed at physical possessions, for example dry cleaners, a shoe repairer and a cleaner. Here, the service user is less involved in the actual process, and to a certain extent the production of the services (repairing the shoes) can be separated from the consumption of the service (enjoyment of wearing the shoes with a newly replaced heel).
- Mental stimulus processing: the services are aimed at the mind of the individual, for example education. In this case, the service is information-based.
- Information processing: services are associated with an intangible asset, for example accounting, banking and insurance. This is the most intangible type of service production, whereby intangible assets are processed to produce intangible outputs for the user, for example insurance cover for a car driver. Until the point at which the driver needs the insurance cover, there is limited physical evidence of its existence.
  Should the driver be involved in an accident, then tangible features of the product might increase, for example a courtesy car and medical healthcare. If the driver never needs to use his or her insurance cover, then the only tangible evidence of its existence is the payment for the service and a policy number.

The first two categories focus on tangible actions associated with people and possessions, whereas the last two focus on intangible actions with people and possessions—and each has different implications for the way in which the service users and the service provider interact.

We have already touched on one characteristic of services that distinguish them from physical goods—**intangibility**—and how this concept might relate to service delivery. But there are other defining characteristics to consider: **inseparability**, **variability** and **perishability** (see Figure 9.2).

Intangibility

Pure services cannot be seen, tasted, touched or smelled before they are bought—that is, they are intangible. Rather, a service is *a deed, performance or effort*, not an object, device or thing (Berry, 1980). This may mean that a customer finds difficulty in evaluating a service before purchase. For example, it is virtually impossible to judge how enjoyable a holiday will be before taking it because the holiday cannot be shown to a customer before consumption.

For some services, their intangibility leads to *difficulty in evaluation* after consumption. For example, it is not easy to judge how thorough a car service has been immediately afterwards: there is no way of telling if everything that should have been checked has been checked.

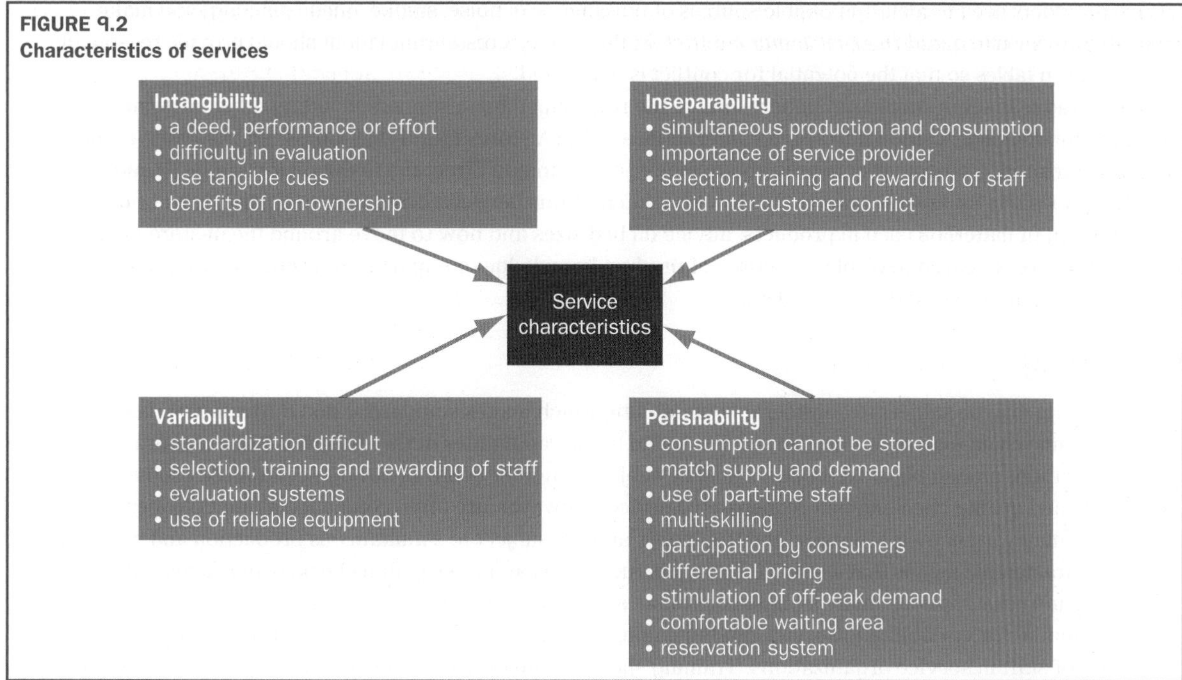

FIGURE 9.2
Characteristics of services

The challenge for the service provider is to *use tangible cues* to service quality. For example, a holiday firm may show pictures of the holiday destination, display testimonials from satisfied holidaymakers and provide details in a brochure of the kinds of entertainment available. A garage may provide a checklist of items that are required to be carried out in a service, and an indication that they have been completed.

The task is to provide evidence of service quality. McDonald's does this by controlling the physical settings of its restaurants and by using its 'golden arches' as a branding cue. By having a consistent offering, the company has effectively dealt with the difficulties that consumers have in evaluating the quality of a service. Standard menus and ordering procedures have also ensured uniform and easy access for customers, while allowing quality control (Edgett and Parkinson, 1993).

Intangibility also means that the customer cannot own a service. Payment is for use or performance. For example, a car may be hired or a medical operation performed. Service organizations sometimes stress the *benefits of non-ownership* such as lower capital costs and the spreading of payment charges.

Inseparability

Unlike physical goods, services have inseparability—that is, they have *simultaneous production and consumption*. For example, a haircut, a holiday and a rock concert are produced and consumed at the same time. This contrasts with a physical good, which is produced, stored and distributed through intermediaries before being bought and consumed. This illustrates the *importance of the service provider*, which is an integral part of the satisfaction gained by the consumer. How service providers conduct themselves may have a crucial bearing on repeat business over and above the technical efficiency of the service task. For example, how courteous and friendly the service provider is may play a large part in the customer's perception of the service experience. The service must be provided, not only at the right time and in the right place, but also in the right way (Berry, 1980).

Often, in the customer's eyes, the airline cabin crew member *is* the company. Consequently, the *selection, training and rewarding of staff* who are the frontline service people are of fundamental importance in the achievement of high standards of service quality. This notion of the inseparability of production and consumption gave rise to the idea of relationship marketing in services. In such circumstances, managing buyer–seller interaction is central to effective marketing and can only be fulfilled in a relationship with the customer (Aijo, 1996).

Furthermore, the consumption of the service may take place in the presence of other consumers. This is apparent with restaurant meals, air, rail or coach travel, and many forms of entertainment, for example. Consequently, enjoyment of the service is dependent not only on the service provided, but also on other consumers. Therefore, service providers need to identify possible sources of nuisance (e.g. noise, smoke, queue jumping) and make adequate provision to *avoid inter-customer conflict*. For example, a restaurant layout should provide reasonable space between tables so that the potential for conflict is minimized.

Marketing managers should not underestimate the role played by customers in aiding other customers in their decision-making. A study into service interactions in IKEA stores found that almost all customer–employee exchanges related to customer concerns about 'place' (e.g. 'Can you direct me to the pick-up point?') and 'function' (e.g. 'How does this folding chair work?'). However, interactions between customers took the form of opinions on the quality of materials used in products, advice on bed sizes and how to move around the in-store restaurant. Many customers appeared to display a degree of product knowledge or expertise bordering on that of contact personnel (Baron, Harris and Davies, 1996).

Variability

Service quality may be subject to considerable variability, which makes standardization difficult. Two restaurants within the same chain may have variable service owing to the capabilities of their respective managers and staff. Quality variations among physical products may be subject to tighter controls through centralized production, automation and quality checking before dispatch. Services, however, are often conducted at multiple locations, by people who may vary in their attitudes (and tiredness), and are subject to simultaneous production and consumption. The last characteristic means that a service fault (e.g. rudeness) cannot be quality checked and corrected between production and consumption, unlike a physical product such as misaligned car windscreen wipers.

The potential for variability in service quality emphasizes the need for rigorous selection, training and rewarding of staff in service organizations. Training should emphasize the standards expected of personnel when dealing with customers. *Evaluation systems* should be developed that allow customers to report on their experiences with staff.

Service standardization is a related method of tackling the variability problem. The *use of reliable equipment* rather than *people* can also help in standardization—for example, the supply of drinks via vending machines or cash through bank machines. However, great care needs to be taken regarding equipment reliability and efficiency. For example, bank cash machines have been heavily criticized for being unreliable and running out of money at weekends.

Perishability

The fourth characteristic of services is their perishability in the sense that *consumption cannot be stored* for the future. A hotel room or an airline seat that is not occupied today represents lost income that cannot be gained tomorrow. If a physical good is not sold, it can be stored for sale later. Therefore, it is important to *match supply and demand* for services. For example, if a hotel has high weekday occupancy but is virtually empty at weekends, a key marketing task is to provide incentives for weekend use. This might involve offering weekend discounts, or linking hotel use with leisure activities such as golf, fishing or hiking.

Service providers also have the problem of catering for peak demand when supply may be insufficient. A physical goods provider may build up inventory in slack periods for sale during peak demand. Service providers do not have this option. Consequently, alternative methods need to be considered. For example, supply flexibility can be varied through the *use of part-time staff* during peak periods. *Multi-skilling* means that employees may be trained in many tasks. Supermarket staff can be trained to fill shelves and work at the checkout at peak periods. *Participation by consumers* may be encouraged in production (e.g. self-service breakfasts in hotels) and in avoiding queues (e.g. self-service checkouts in supermarkets). Demand may be smoothed through *differential pricing* to encourage customers to visit during off-peak periods (e.g. lower-priced cinema and theatre seats for afternoon performances). *Stimulation of off-peak demand* can be achieved by special events (e.g. spa breaks or gourmet weekends for hotels). If delay is unavoidable, then another option is to make it more acceptable—for example, by providing a comfortable waiting area with seating and free refreshments. Finally, a *reservation system*, as commonly used in restaurants, hair salons and theatres, can be used to control peak demand and assist time substitution.

While these characteristics of services have been widely criticized due to the changing focus of services marketing in today's world and the advancement of digital technology, Moeller (2010) argues that this framework remains valid and provides a very useful lens through which to begin studying services marketing and build a foundation of understanding. It is then important to consider the extent to which service encounters and servicescapes form a service ecosystem where co-creation by multiple stakeholders can occur (Akaka and Vargo, 2015).

Service ecosystems discussed by Lusch and Vargo (2011) and Vargo and Lusch (2016) are defined as 'relatively self-contained, self-adjusting system(s) of resource-integrating actors connected by shared institutional arrangement and mutual value creation through service exchange'. This means that value co-creation can take place in a socially constructed setting amidst a network of actors and organizations. The reason for considering service ecosystems is that they extend beyond the characteristics of services, service encounters and servicescapes, and draw attention to the setting (both past and present) in which the service encounter occurs. This also allows for the consideration of service from a more dynamic perspective (Akaka and Vargo, 2015).

Managing Services

In order to manage services effectively, the service provider should understand the whole of the customer journey, which involves five key aspects: managing customer relationships, managing service quality, managing service productivity, managing service staff and positioning services. Customer relationship management is covered in Chapter 10. Read Mini Case 9.1 to consider how Sandals Resorts manages its service offering.

MINI CASE 9.1

Sandals Resorts: Knowing your Customers is the Key to their Hearts and a Way to Stand out in a Crowded Marketplace

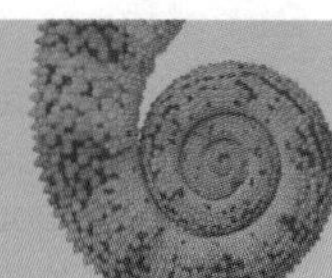

The hospitality and tourism industry offers many opportunities for service providers to devise highly targeted offers. This is an industry where competition is intense and opportunities to create a differentiated offer are hard to find. But, at Sandals Resorts International (SRI) success has been built on providing very specialized services.

The first Sandals resort was established in Montego Bay, Jamaica. Largely due to the reputation built on excellent personalized service, the business has grown and now employs over 10,000 people and operates 13 couples-only and 6 family-oriented resorts under the brand names Sandals and Beaches. These all-inclusive resorts are located close to some of the best beaches in the Caribbean. The business has been built around the idea of 'giving customers more than they expect or think they need'. Sandals are classified in the industry as all-inclusive resorts, but they have successfully differentiated themselves in this sector too by offering 'Ultra All-inclusive' offers, which include special packages for weddings and honeymoons, with features such as access to private offshore islands and themed gourmet restaurants, and some holiday packages even include personal butler services.

At the heart of the company's operation is a business intelligence system, which enables the marketing team at SRI to have the right tools to carry out the analysis needed to ensure that customers are completely satisfied, and also to ensure that the company operates profitably. The system gathers data on a daily basis, and close attention is paid to key performance indicators such as occupancy rates, staffing levels, food costs and spend per room. Daily management updates enable the team to monitor performance and take immediate action if any issues are detected.

In addition to the emphasis on exceeding guests' expectations, SRI invests substantially in its employees, who they call 'team members', through the Sandals Corporate University (SCU). Each team member is specially selected and trained to carry out his/her role, and continually encouraged to develop personally. The SCU ensures that team members understand that they are as important as their guests, which is fundamental to a successful service organization, because happy team members give excellent service, resulting in happy, loyal guests.

»

SRI does not stop with its customers; it also has a commitment to society. The Sandals Foundation makes investments to support the development of local communities. There are three core elements to the foundation: the community, education and the environment. By working with the community, the foundation tackles social issues relating to violence, poverty, unemployment and healthcare, and community programmes have succeeded in 'giving people a chance to change their lives'. Education initiatives have provided scholarship and learning for thousands of students in the Caribbean of all ages and across all aspects of life. For example, in Montego Bay, parenting workshops raise awareness of the importance of education and lifelong learning. Preserving the environment is very important, and the foundation increasingly is taking a leadership role in environmental programmes in both the public and private sector. At the Boscobel marine sanctuary, ecologists are working to protect coral and fish stocks, and also engage local community fishermen to raise awareness of behaviour that is damaging the fragile underwater environment.

Over the past 30 years, SRI has been consistently rewarded for its emphasis on people. It receives high satisfaction levels from guests, and more than half return; SRI's employees are happy and remain loyal, and SRI holds numerous awards from the hospitality sector. Furthermore, Gordon 'Butch' Stewart, the founder of the Sandals vision, has shown how a successful hospitality brand can foster wide economic and social development that has made a significant contribution to helping communities in the Caribbean have a more sustainable way of living.

Questions:

1. Customer retention is at the centre of relationship management. Suggest why SRI has been successful in encouraging over half of its customers to return.
2. Imagine you are the customer service manager for one of the Sandals resorts and there has been a serious incident of food poisoning that has resulted in several guests becoming ill. Suggest how you are going to manage this situation.

Based on: Brown, Hassan and Teare (2011); Pike (2011); Sandals Resorts International Websites–sandals.com and beaches.com; Aptech Computer Systems (2014); http://www.aptech-inc.com/index.php/2014/11/sandals-upgrades-bi-to-latest-aptech-execuvue-with-dashboards-for-21-resorts, Sandals (2018).

Managing service quality

Intuitively, it makes sense to suggest that improving service quality will increase customer satisfaction, leading to higher sales and profits. Indeed, it has been shown that companies that are rated higher on service quality perform better in terms of market share growth and profitability (Buzzell and Gale, 1987). Yet, for many companies, high standards of service quality remain elusive. There are four causes of poor perceived quality (see Figure 9.3). These are the barriers that separate the perception of service quality from what customers expect (Parasuraman, Zeithaml and Berry, 1985).

FIGURE 9.3 Barriers to the matching of expected and perceived service levels

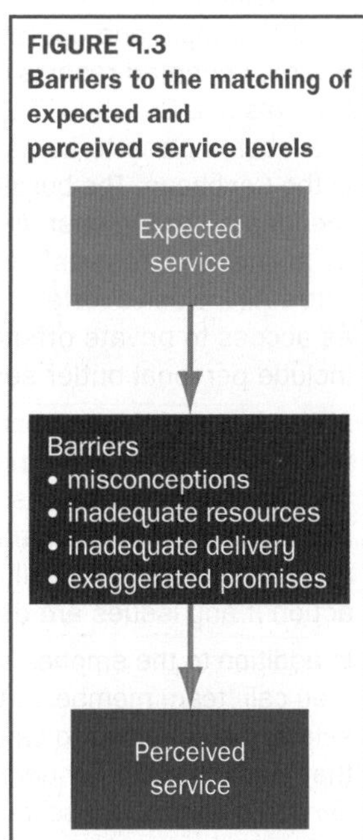

Misconception barrier: this arises from management's misunderstanding of what the customer expects. Lack of marketing research may lead managers to misconceive the important service attributes that customers use when evaluating a service, and the way in which customers use attributes in evaluation. For example, a restaurant manager may believe that shortening the gap between courses may improve customer satisfaction, when the customer actually values a pause between eating.

Inadequate resources barrier: managers may understand customer expectations but are unwilling to provide the resources necessary to meet them. This may arise because of a cost reduction or productivity focus, or simply because of the inconvenience it may cause.

Inadequate delivery barrier: managers may understand customer expectations and supply adequate resources, but fail to select, train and reward staff adequately, resulting in poor or inconsistent service. This may manifest itself in poor communication skills, inappropriate dress or unwillingness to solve customer problems.

Exaggerated promises barrier: even when customer understanding, resources and staff management are in place, a gap between customer expectations and perceptions can still arise through exaggerated promises. Advertising and selling messages that build expectations to a pitch that cannot be fulfilled may leave customers disappointed even when receiving good service. For example, a tourist brochure that claims that a hotel is 'just a few minutes from the sea' may lead to disappointment if the walk takes 10 minutes.

Meeting customer expectations

A key to providing service quality is the understanding and meeting of *customer expectations*. To do so requires a clear picture of the criteria used to form these expectations, recognizing that consumers of services value not only the *outcome* of the service encounter but also the *experience* of taking part in it. For example, an evaluation of a haircut depends, not only on the quality of the cut, but also the experience of having a haircut. Clearly, a hairdresser needs, not only technical skills, but also the ability to communicate in an interesting and polite manner. Meeting and exceeding customers' expectations is even more important as good and bad experiences can easily be shared via social media such as Twitter and Instagram.

Ten criteria may be used when evaluating the outcome and experience of a service encounter, and these form a checklist for service providers to monitor performance (Parasuraman, Zeithaml and Berry, 1985).

1. *Access*: is the service provided at convenient locations and times, with little waiting?
2. *Reliability*: is the service consistent and dependable?
3. *Credibility*: can customers trust the service company and its staff?
4. *Security*: can the service be used without risk?
5. *Understanding the customer*: does it appear that the service provider understands customer expectations?
6. *Responsiveness*: how quickly do service staff respond to customer problems, requests and questions?
7. *Courtesy*: do service staff act in a friendly and polite manner?
8. *Competence*: do service staff have the required skills and knowledge?
9. *Communication*: is the service described clearly and accurately?
10. *Tangibles*: how well managed is the tangible evidence of the service (e.g. staff appearance, décor, layout)?

Where service quality is dependent on a succession of service encounters (e.g., a hotel stay may encompass the check-in, the room itself, the restaurant, breakfast and check-out), each should be measured in terms of its impact on total satisfaction so that corrective actions can be taken (Danaher and Mattson, 1994). Customer service questionnaires are widely used in the service industry to gather feedback on customer experiences. Social media are also widely used in the same context.

Managing service productivity

Productivity is a measure of the relationship between an input and an output. For example, if more people can be served (output) using the same number of staff (input), productivity per employee has risen. Clearly, there can be conflict between improving service productivity (efficiency) and raising service quality (effectiveness). For example, a beauty therapist who reduces time spent with a client may increase the number of clients per day, but the reduction in time spent on service delivery is likely to affect the quality of service and customer retention.

Clearly, a balance must be struck between productivity and service quality. At some point, quality gains become so expensive that they are not worthwhile. However, there are ways of improving productivity without compromising quality. Technology, obtaining customer involvement in production of the service, and balancing supply and demand are three methods of achieving this.

Technology

Technology can be used to improve productivity and service quality. For example, airport X-ray surveillance equipment raises the throughput of passengers (productivity) and speeds the process of checking-in (service quality). Automatic cash dispensers in banks increase the number of transactions per period (productivity), while reducing customer waiting time (service quality). Automatic vending machines increase the number of drinks sold per establishment (productivity), while improving accessibility for customers (service quality).

Retailers have benefited from barcodes and electronic fund transfer at point of sale (EFTPOS). Timely and detailed sales information can aid buying decisions and provide retail buyers with a negotiating advantage over suppliers. Other benefits from this technology include better labour scheduling, stock management and distribution systems. Read Marketing in action 9.4 to discover how the humble hashtag has been transformed into a marketing tool.

MARKETING IN ACTION 9.4
Social Media Transformed the Hashtag into a Marketing Tool

Social media have provided popular platforms on which to engage with customers, and the hashtag has enabled messages to be found and shared. Coca-Cola's #shareacoke originally involved bottles of coke with names on and the campaign drove sales and created extensive social media coverage. The approach was so successful that 'share-a-coke' has become a regular summer campaign in North America.

The hashtag # was just a simple symbol used in the IT industry to highlight a special meaning for computer coders, but now it has been transformed into a powerful marketing tool. Twitter started using hashtags in 2007, and a bush fire in the same year proved the usefulness of the hashtag, as messages tagged #sandiegofire were shared across California. Twitter then began linking anything preceded by # so that its users could share their experiences and find other tweets with similar things to say. Instagram and Flickr followed suit, and then leading brands began making use of the hashtag in their marketing campaigns.

Marketers realized that tweets containing hashtags were more likely to be shared and retweeted, and could be used to build different types of powerful communications campaigns, e.g. the #IceBucketChallenge used by the Motor Neurone Disease charity. The challenge encouraged people to throw a bucket of icy water over their heads, and exceeded expectations by raising in excess of $100 million. British Airways wanted to remind its customers about the 'magic of flying', so the company used #Lookup as part of its campaign. It used interactive digital advertising boards that tracked aircraft using sophisticated surveillance technology and interrupted other advertisers' displays with a child pointing to the sky every time a plane flew overhead.

The beer industry in the UK wanted to change behaviour and to urge consumers to drink differently (cutting down on alcohol consumption) during the month of January rather than completely abstain from visiting bars and pubs. Its campaign was #DryJanuary.

The hashtag symbol is widely used by marketers to build interest in a brand and to create successful campaign-specific hashtags to generate genuine user content. Hashtags can also be used to follow trends and create campaigns to manage customer expectations and to address social issues. The #MeToo campaign against sexual violence against women initially raised awareness of the treatment of women in the Hollywood film industry but became so powerful that it attracted attention globally. Within 24 hours of the first tweet, more than 4.7 million people and 12 million posts appeared online.

Based on: Offerpop (2013); Milington (2015); Tesseras (2014); Coca-Cola (2018); CNN (2017); Lawton (2017)

Customer involvement in production

The inseparability between production and consumption provides an opportunity to raise both productivity and service quality. For example, self-service breakfast bars and petrol stations improve productivity per employee and reduce customer waiting time (service quality). The effectiveness of this tactic relies heavily on customer expectations, and on managing transition periods. It should be used when there is a clear advantage to customers in their involvement in production. In other instances, reducing customer service may reduce satisfaction. For example, a hotel that expected its customers to service their own rooms would need a persuasive communications programme to convince customers that the lack of service was reflected in cheaper rates.

Balancing supply and demand

Because services cannot be stored, balancing supply and demand is a key determinant of productivity. Hotels or aircraft that are less than half full incur low productivity. If, in the next period, the hotel or airline is faced with excess demand, the unused space in the previous period cannot be used to meet it. The combined result is low productivity and customer dissatisfaction (low service quality). By smoothing demand or increasing the flexibility of supply, both productivity and service quality can be achieved.

Smoothing demand can be achieved through differential pricing and stimulating off-peak demand (e.g. weekend breaks). Increasing supply flexibility may be increased by using part-time employees, multi-skilling and encouraging customers to service themselves.

Managing service staff

Many services involve a high degree of contact between service staff and customers. This is true for such service industries as healthcare, banking, catering and education. The quality of the service experience is therefore heavily dependent on staff–customer interpersonal relationships. John Carlzon, the head of Scandinavian Airlines System (SAS), called these meetings *moments of truth*. He explained that SAS faced 65,000 moments of truth per day, and that the outcomes determined the success of the company.

Research on customer loyalty in the service industry showed that only 14 per cent of customers who stopped patronizing service businesses did so because they were dissatisfied with the quality of what they had bought. More than two-thirds stopped buying because they found service staff indifferent or unhelpful (Schlesinger and Heskett, 1991). Clearly, the way in which service personnel treat their customers is fundamental to success in the service industry.

Also, frontline staff are important sources of customer and competitor information and, if properly motivated, can provide crucial inputs in the development of new service products (Lievens and Moenaert, 2000). For example, discussions with customers may generate ideas for new services that customers would value if available on the market.

In order for service employees to be in the frame of mind to treat customers well, they need to feel that their company is treating them well. In companies where staff have a high regard for the human resources policy, customers also have a positive opinion of the service they receive.

The *selection of suitable people* is the starting point of the process. Personality differences mean that it is not everyone who can fill a service role. The nature of the job needs to be defined and the appropriate personality characteristics needed to perform effectively outlined. Once selected, training is required to familiarize recruits with the job requirements and the culture of the organization. *Socialization* allows the recruit to experience the culture and tasks of the organization. Usually, the aim is creative individualism, whereby the recruit accepts all of the key behavioural norms, but is encouraged to display initiative and innovation in dealing with problems. Thus, standards of behaviour are internalized, but the creative abilities of the individual are not subjugated to the need to conform.

Service quality may also be affected by the degree to which staff are *empowered*, or given the authority to satisfy customers and deal with their problems. Google is a business that empowers its staff to be creative. Google cafés are an initiative designed to encourage interaction and innovation among employees. However, empowerment programmes need to recognize the increased responsibility thrust on employees. Not everyone will welcome this, and reward systems (e.g. higher pay or status) need to be thought through. At the luxury hotel chain Ritz-Carlton, customer service is of paramount importance and, as a result, the frontline staff are given the *right* be involved with the work they are doing and make decisions on how to best serve the hotel guests. The company empowers its employees through training and trusting in them to make accurate decisions that will wow their customers (Solomon, 2014).

Maintaining a motivated workforce in the face of irate customers, faulty support systems and the boredom that accompanies some service jobs is a demanding task. The motivational factors include recognition of achievement, role clarity, opportunities for advancement, the interest value of the job, monetary rewards and setting challenging but achievable targets. A key factor in avoiding demotivation is to monitor support systems so that staff work with efficient equipment and facilities to help them carry out their job.

Service evaluation is also important in managing staff. Customer feedback is essential to maintaining high standards of service quality. McDonald's continually monitors quality, service, cleanliness and value, and if a franchisee fails to meet these standards they are dropped. The results of customer research should be fed back to employees so that they can relate their performance standards to customer satisfaction. Enlightened companies tie financial incentives to the results of such surveys.

Positioning services

Positioning is the process of establishing and keeping a distinctive place in the market for a company and its products. Most successful service companies differentiate themselves from the competition on attributes that their target customers value highly. They develop service concepts that are highly valued and communicate to target customers so that they accurately perceive the position of the service.

FIGURE 9.4
Positioning for services

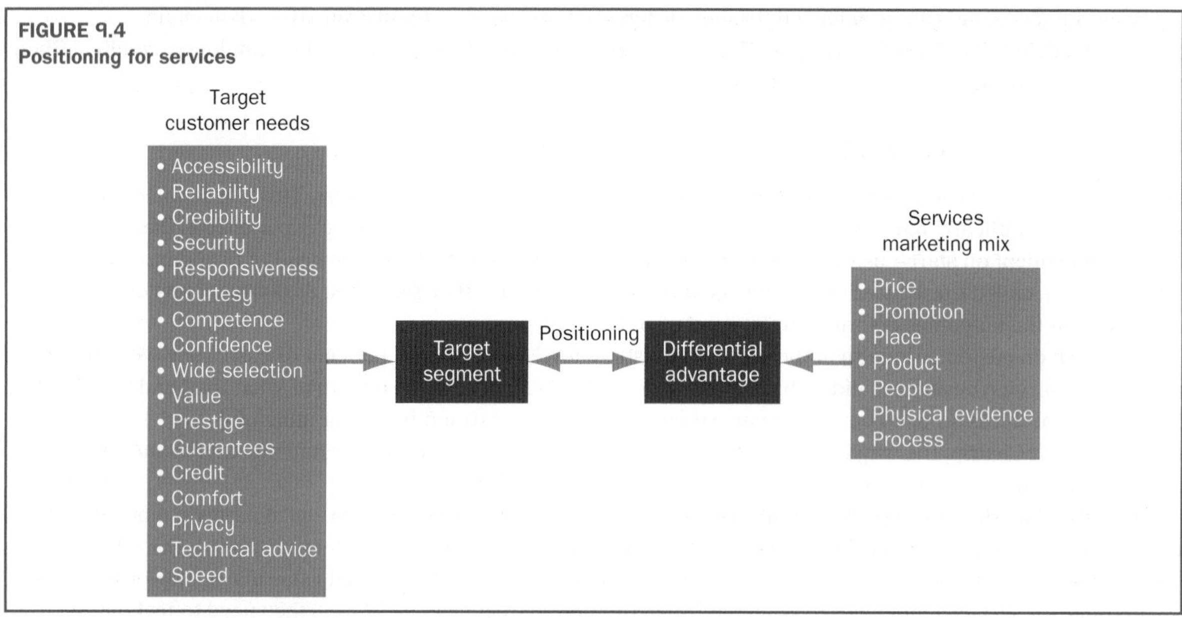

The positioning task entails two decisions:

1 choice of target market (where to compete)
2 creation of a differential advantage (how to compete).

These decisions are common to both physical products and services. Creating a differential advantage is based on understanding the target customers' requirements better than the competition. Figure 9.4 shows the relationship between *target customer needs* and the *services marketing mix*. On the left of the figure is an array of factors (choice criteria) that customers may use to judge a service. How well a service company satisfies those criteria depends on its marketing mix (on the right of the figure). Marketing research can be useful in identifying important choice criteria, but care needs to be taken in such studies. Asking customers which are the most important factors when buying a service may give misleading results. For example, the most important factor when travelling by air may be safety. However, this does not mean that customers use safety as a choice criterion when deciding which airline to use. If all major airlines are perceived as being similar in terms of safety, other less important factors like the quality of in-flight meals and service may be the crucial attributes used in decision-making.

Target marketing

The basis of target marketing is market segmentation. A market is analysed to identify groups of potential customers with similar needs and price sensitivities. The potential of each of these segments is assessed on such factors as size, growth rate, degree of competition, price sensitivity, and the fit between its requirements and the company's capabilities.

The most attractive markets are often not the biggest (as discussed in Mini Case 9.1 on Sandals Resorts International), as saturated markets often confer high levels of competition. So, a service organization should apply segmentation and target marketing analysis to determine a suitable marketing mix for the specific groups of customers, thereby creating an opportunity to differentiate its offer. For example, Southwest Airlines uses this strapline to differentiate itself in the crowded airline industry: 'We like to think of ourselves as a Customer Service company that happens to fly airplanes' (Southwest Airlines, 2015).

FIGURE 9.5
Target and halo customers

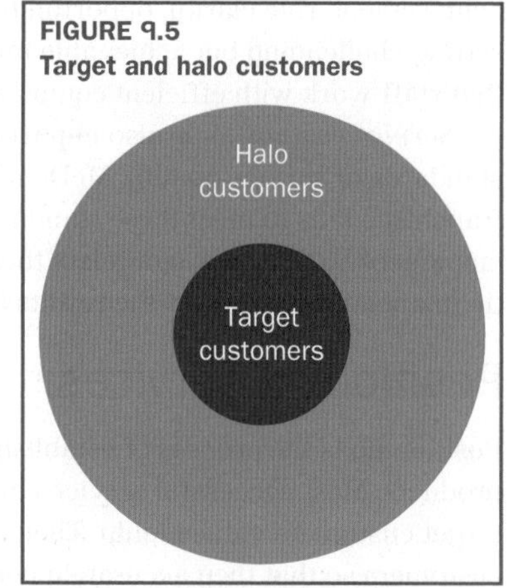

Marketing managers also need to consider those potential customers who are not directly targeted, but may find the service mix attractive. Those customers that are at the periphery of the target market are called **halo customers** and can make a substantial difference between success and failure (see Figure 9.5). Launching into a new target market may require trials to test the innovation and refine the concept. For example, when KFC was considering moving into the breakfast segment of the fast-food market it ran trials in selected outlets before the full launch (Charles, 2008). Sometimes the changing marketing environment can also expand the reach of a service. In the case of KFC, they have realised that changing consumer tastes and more emphasis on healthy living means a change of menu. By 2020, the fast food company plans to have menu options that are under 600 calories.

Differential advantage

Understanding customer needs will be the basis of the design of a new service concept that is different from competitive offerings, is highly valued by target customers, and therefore creates a differential advantage. It will be based on the creative use of marketing-mix elements, resulting in such benefits as more reliable or faster delivery, greater convenience, more comfort, higher-quality work, higher prestige or other issues (listed on the left of Figure 9.4). Mini Case 9.1 describes how Sandals Resorts International has differentiated itself from larger chains through the use of service excellence.

Research can indicate which choice criteria are more or less valued by customers, and how customers rate the service provider's performance on each (Christopher and Yallop, 1990). For marketers, it is important to achieve a balance between what is valued by the customer as important and how the customer perceives the service provider's performance. For both the service provider and its customers, there is no point in going too far to provide quality service. FedEx, the international shipping company, has guidelines on how to avoid customer *overkill*. It suggests avoiding too much contact (hotel guests constantly contacted by front desk), asking too many questions, providing excessive perks (e.g. lavish baskets of fruit in a hotel room and private boxes at sporting events). Furthermore, it suggests that listening to what the customer wants and making appropriate decisions about when to say no is the key to providing a balanced and highly regarded service (FedEx, 2015).

The services marketing mix

The **services marketing mix** is an extension of the Four-Ps framework introduced in Chapter 1. The essential elements of *product, promotion, price* and *place* remain, but three additional variables—*people, physical evidence* and *process*—are included to produce a Seven-Ps mix (Booms and Bitner, 1981). The need for the extension is due to the high degree of direct contact between the company and the customer, the highly visible nature of the service assembly process, and the simultaneity of production and consumption. While it is possible to discuss people, physical evidence and process within the original Four-Ps framework (e.g. people could be considered part of the product offering), the extension allows a more thorough analysis of the marketing ingredients necessary for successful services marketing. Each element of the marketing mix will now be examined.

Product Physical products can be inspected and tried before buying, but pure services are intangible; you cannot go to a showroom to see a marketing research report or medical operation that you are considering. This means that service customers suffer higher perceived risk in their decision-making and that the three elements of the extended marketing mix—people, physical evidence and process—are crucial in influencing the customer's perception of service quality. These will be discussed later.

The *brand name* of a service can also influence the perception of a service. Four characteristics of successful brand names are as follows (Berry, Lefkowith and Clark, 1980).

1 *Distinctiveness*: it immediately identifies the services provider and differentiates it from the competition.
2 *Relevance*: it communicates the nature of the service and the service benefit.
3 *Memorability*: it is easily understood and remembered.
4 *Flexibility*: it not only expresses the service organization's current business, but is also broad enough to cover foreseeable new ventures.

Examples of effective brand names are: Visa, which suggests internationality; Travelodge, which implies travel accommodation; and Virgin Atlantic, which associates the airline with flights to and from North America.

Service providers such as hotels are constantly seeking ways of differentiating themselves from their competitors. For example, Marriott has invested heavily in new super-comfortable beds and bedding to gain an advantage over its competitors.

The quality of the physical product is also used as a differentiator by airlines—for example, stainless steel rather than plastic cutlery, more leg room, personal television screens showing up-to-date movies and, for first-class long-haul passengers, more comfortable beds. Service companies need to reassess their product offerings to keep up with changing consumer tastes. For example, to appeal to a generation of young people who spend a lot of time playing computer games, Disneyland has designed attractions that offer theme park guests the chance to 'get interactive', and is experimenting with mobile phones and other handheld electronic devices to add interactive appeal (Garrahan, 2005).

Promotion The intangible element of a service may be difficult to communicate. For example, it may be difficult to represent courtesy, hard work and customer care in an advertisement. Once again, the answer is to use *tangible cues* that will help customers understand and judge the service. A hotel can show its buildings, swimming pool, friendly staff and happy customers. An investment company can provide tangible evidence of past performance. Testimonials from satisfied customers can also be used to communicate services benefits. Netto, the Danish-based supermarket chain, used testimonials from six customers in its UK advertising to explain the advantages of shopping there.

Advertising can be used to communicate and reinforce the image of a service. For example, store image can enhance customer satisfaction and build store loyalty (Bloemer and de Ruyter, 1998). Advertising can also be used to create awareness of the benefits that consumers can expect from the service provider, as the advertisement for HSBC shows.

Digital marketing is widely used to encourage engagement with service brands. Marks & Spencer spent 25 per cent of its marketing budget on digital communications. Personal selling can also be effective in services marketing because of the high perceived risk inherent in many service purchases. For example, a salesperson can explain the details of a personal pension plan or investment opportunity, answer questions and provide reassurance.

Because of the high perceived risk inherent in buying services, salespeople should develop lists of satisfied customers to use in reference selling. Also, salespeople need to be trained to ask for referrals. Customers should be asked if they know of other people or organizations that might benefit from the service. The customer can then be used as an entrée and point of reference when approaching and selling to the new prospect.

Word of mouth is critical to success for services because of their experiential nature. For example, talking to people that have visited a resort or hotel is more convincing than reading holiday brochures. Social media are playing an increasingly important part in this form of communication: for example, the Four Seasons hotel group used Facebook and Twitter to share both guest and staff messages about what the hotels had on offer, things to do at particular destinations, and local tips and deals.

Communication should also be targeted at employees because of their importance in creating and maintaining service quality. Internal communications can define management expectations of staff, reinforce the need to delight the customer and explain the rewards that follow from giving excellent service. External communications that depict service quality can also influence internal staff if they include employees and show how they take exceptional care of their customers.

Care should be taken not to exaggerate promises in promotional material since this may build up unachievable expectations. For example, Delta Airlines used the advertising slogan 'Delta is ready when you are'. This caused problems because it built up customers' expectations that the airline would always be ready—an impossible task. This led Delta to change its slogan to the more realistic 'We love to fly and it shows' (Sellers, 1988).

Price Price is a key marketing tool, for three reasons. First, as it is often difficult to evaluate a service before purchase, price may act as an indicator of perceived quality. For example, in a travel brochure the price charged by hotels may be used to indicate their quality. Some companies expect a management consultant to charge high fees, otherwise they cannot be particularly good. Second, price is an important tool in controlling demand: matching demand and supply is critical in services because they cannot be stored. Creative use of pricing can help to smooth demand. Third, a key segmentation variable with services is price sensitivity. Some customers may be willing to pay a much higher price than others.

Time is often used to segment price-sensitive and price-insensitive customers. For example, the price of international air travel is often dependent on length of stay. Travellers from Europe to the USA will pay a lot less if they stay a minimum of six nights (including Saturday). Airlines know that customers who stay for less than that are likely to be business people who are willing and able to pay a higher price. An exception is the budget hotel chain Travelodge. The company has adopted a demand-led online pricing system similar to that pioneered by easyJet and Ryanair. Rooms are often priced cheaply to begin with, but the price rises as the hotel becomes fully booked (Fernandez, 2009).

Some services, such as accounting and management consultancy, charge their customers fees. A strategy needs to be thought out concerning fees. How far can fees be flexible to secure or retain particular customers? How will the fee level compare to that of the competition? Will there be an incentive built into the fee structure for continuity, forward commitment or the use of the full range of services on offer? Five pricing techniques may be used when setting fee levels:

1. *Offset*: low fee for core service but recouping with add-ons.
2. *Inducement*: low fee to attract new customers or to help retain existing customers.
3. *Diversionary*: low basic fees on selected services to develop the image of value for money across the whole range of services.
4. *Guarantee*: full fee payable on achievement of agreed results.
5. *Predatory*: competition's fees undercut to remove them from the market; high fees charged later.

The internet is making price transparency a reality. This has caused problems for premium-price service companies such as Avis. In the face of online holiday companies offering cheap holidays and car rental deals, and the ease with which consumers can compare prices, Avis has had to reduce prices, thereby depressing profitability (Davoudi, 2005). But, price transparency online extends further. Honest By is an online company which claims to be totally transparent and provides full details of the component parts of the garments it sells.

Place Distribution channels for services are usually more direct than for many physical goods. Because services are intangible, the services marketer is less concerned with storage, the production and consumption is often simultaneous, and the personal nature of services means that direct contact with the service provider (or at best its agent) is desirable. Agents are used when the individual service provider cannot offer a sufficiently wide selection for customers. Consequently, agents are often used for the marketing of travel, insurance and entertainment. However, the advent of the internet means that direct dealings with the service provider are becoming more frequent.

Growth for many service companies means opening new facilities in new locations. Whereas producers of physical goods can expand production at one site to serve the needs of a geographically spread market, the simultaneous production and consumption of hotel, banking, catering, retailing and accounting services, for example, means that expansion often means following a multi-site strategy. The evaluation of store locations is therefore a critical skill for services marketers. Much of the success of top European supermarket chains has been due to their ability to choose profitable new sites for their retailing operations.

People Because of the simultaneity of production and consumption in services, the company's personnel occupy a key position in influencing customer perceptions of product quality (Rafiq and Ahmed, 1992). In fact, service quality is inseparable from the quality of the service provider. Without courteous, efficient and motivated staff, service organizations will lose customers. A survey has shown that one in six consumers have been put off making a purchase because of the way they were treated by staff (Wilkinson, 2002). An important marketing task, then, is to set standards to improve the quality of service provided by employees and monitor their performance. Without training and control, employees tend to be variable in their performance, leading to variable service quality.

Service providers need to adopt a customer-first attitude rather than putting their own convenience and enjoyment before that of their customers.

Marketing should also examine the role played by customers in the service environment and seek to eliminate harmful interactions. For example, the enjoyment of a restaurant meal or air travel will very much depend on the actions of other customers. At seasonal festival times and special events, restaurants are often in demand by groups of work colleagues for staff parties. These can be rowdy affairs that can detract from the pleasure of regular patrons. This situation needs to be managed, perhaps by segregating the two types of customer in some way.

Physical evidence Physical evidence is the environment in which the service is delivered, and any tangible goods that facilitate the performance and communication of the service. Customers look for clues to the likely quality of a service by inspecting the tangible evidence. For example, prospective customers may gaze through a restaurant window to check the appearance of the waiters, the décor and furnishings. The ambience of a retail store is highly dependent on décor, and colour can play an important role in establishing mood because colour has meaning. For example, black signifies strength and power, whereas green suggests mildness. The interior of jet aircraft is pastel-coloured to promote a feeling of calmness, whereas many nightclubs are brightly coloured, with flashing lights to give a sense of excitement.

The layout of a service operation can be a compromise between operations' need for efficiency, and marketing's desire to serve the customer effectively. For example, the temptation to squeeze in an extra table at a restaurant or extra seating in an aircraft may be at the expense of customer comfort.

Process This describes the procedures, mechanisms and flow of activities by which a service is acquired. Process decisions radically affect how a service is delivered to customers. For example, a self-service cafeteria is very different from a restaurant. Marketing managers need to know whether self-service is acceptable (or indeed desirable). Queuing may provide an opportunity to create a differential advantage by reduction/elimination, or making the time spent waiting more enjoyable. Certainly, waiting for service is a common experience for customers and is a strong determinant of overall satisfaction with the service and customer loyalty. Research has shown that an attractive waiting environment can prevent customers becoming irritated or bored very quickly, even though they may have to wait a long time. Both appraisal of the wait and satisfaction with the service improved when the attractiveness of the waiting environment (measured by atmosphere, cleanliness, spaciousness and climate) was rated higher (Pruyn and Smidts, 1998). Providing a more effective service (shorter queues) may be at odds with operations, as the remedy may be to employ more staff.

Reducing delivery time—for example, the time between ordering a meal and receiving it—can also improve service quality. As discussed earlier, this need not necessarily cost more if customers can be persuaded to become involved in the production process, as successfully reflected in the growth of self-service breakfast bars in hotels.

Review

1 The nature and special characteristics of services

- Services are a special kind of product that may require special understanding and special marketing efforts because of their special characteristics.
- The key characteristics of pure services are intangibility (they cannot be touched, tasted or smelled); inseparability (production and consumption takes place at the same time, e.g. a haircut); variability (service quality may vary, making standardization difficult); and perishability (consumption cannot be stored, e.g. a hotel room).

2 Managing service quality, productivity and staff

- Two key service quality concepts are customer expectations and perceptions. Customers may be disappointed with service quality if their service perceptions fail to meet their expectations. This may result from four barriers: the misconception barrier (management's misunderstanding of what the customer expects); the inadequate resources barrier (management provides inadequate resources); the inadequate delivery barrier (management fails to select, train and adequately reward staff); and the exaggerated promises barrier (management causes expectations to be too high because of exaggerated promises).
- Service productivity can be improved without reducing service quality by using technology (e.g. automatic cash dispensers); customer involvement in production (e.g. self-service petrol stations); and balancing supply and demand (e.g. differential pricing to smooth demand).
- Staff are critical in service operations because they are often in contact with customers. The starting point is the selection of suitable people; socialization allows the recruit to experience the culture and tasks of the organization; empowerment gives them the authority to solve customer problems; they need to be trained and motivated; and evaluation is required so that staff understand how their performance standards relate to customer satisfaction.

3 **How to position a service organization or brand**

- Positioning involves the choice of target market (where to compete) and the creation of a differential advantage (how to compete). These decisions are common to both physical products and services. However, because of the special characteristics of services, it is useful for the services marketer to consider not only the classical Four-Ps marketing mix but also an additional three-Ps—people, physical evidence and process—when deciding how to meet customer needs and create a differential advantage.

4 **The services marketing mix**

- The services marketing mix consists of Seven-Ps: product, price, place, promotion, people (important because of the high customer contact characteristic of services), physical evidence (important because customers look for cues to the likely quality of a service by inspecting the physical evidence, e.g. décor) and process (because the process of supplying a service affects perceived service quality).

Key Terms

exaggerated promises barrier a barrier to the matching of expected and perceived service levels caused by the unwarranted building up of expectations by exaggerated promises

halo customers customers that are not directly targeted but may find the product attractive

inadequate delivery barrier a barrier to the matching of expected and perceived service levels caused by the failure of the service provider to select, train and reward staff adequately, resulting in poor or inconsistent delivery of service

inadequate resources barrier a barrier to the matching of expected and perceived service levels caused by the unwillingness of service providers to provide the necessary resources

inseparability a characteristic of services, namely, that their production cannot be separated from their consumption

intangibility a characteristic of services, namely, that they cannot be touched, seen, tasted or smelled

misconception barrier a failure by marketers to understand what customers really value about their service

perishability a characteristic of services, namely, that the capacity of a service business, such as a hotel room, cannot be stored—if it is not occupied, this is lost income that cannot be recovered

service any deed, performance or effort carried out for the customer

services marketing mix product, place, price, promotion, people, process and physical evidence (the 'Seven-Ps')

variability a characteristic of services, namely, that, being delivered by people, the standard of their performance is open to variation

Study Questions

1. **Choose one service industry sector, identify three businesses operating in your chosen sector, and then evaluate the differences and similarities of each firm from a service perspective.**
2. **To what extent is the marketing of services the same as the marketing of physical goods? Discuss.**
3. **What are the barriers that can separate expected from perceived service? What must service providers do to eliminate these barriers?**
4. **Discuss the role of service staff in the creation of a quality service. Can you give examples from your own experience of good and bad service encounters?**
5. **Explain service-dominated logic and how this helps to define services.**
6. **Choose a company you are familiar with and have had reason to complain about. Discuss the barriers of service quality that the company might need to overcome for you to become a regular customer.**

7. **Identify and evaluate how hotels can differentiate themselves from their competitors. Choose three hotel groups and evaluate their success at differentiation.**
8. **Discuss the problems of providing high-quality service in retailing in central and eastern Europe.**
9. **Discuss the benefits to organizations and customers of developing and maintaining strong customer relationships.**
10. **Suggest how the internet and associated technologies are changing the nature of services.**

Recommended Reading

Services are delivered when customers and firms come together. Read the following seminal papers to deepen your understanding of services marketing.

Anker, T., Sparks, L., Moutinho, L., Gronroos, C. and L. (2015), Consumer dominant value creation: A theoretical response to the recent call for a consumer dominant logic for marketing, *European Journal of Marketing* 49(3/4), 532–60.

Gummesson, E. and Grönroos, C. (2012), The emergence of the new service marketing: Nordic School perspectives, *Journal of Service Management* 23(4), 479–97.

Vargo, S.L. and Lusch, R.F. (2004), The Four Service Marketing Myths, *Journal of Service Research* 6(4), 324–35.

References

Aijo, T.S. (1996), The Theoretical and Philosophical Underpinnings of Relationship Marketing, *European Journal of Marketing* 30(2), 8–18.

Akaka, M.A. and Vargo, S.L. (2015), Extending the context of service: from encounters to ecosystems, *Journal of Services Marketing*, 29(6/7), 453–62 https://doi.org/10.1108/JSM-03-2015-0126.

Akaka, M.A., Vargo, S.L. and Schau, H.J. (2015), The context of experience, *Journal of Service Management*, 26(2), 206–223.

Allen, K. (2018), UK Finance industry dominates European Scene *Financial Times*, 5 September https://www.ft.com/content/88cdec40-b03c-11e8-8d14-6f049d06439c (accessed July 2018).

Ansoff (1979), *Strategic Management*, Macmillan, London.

Aptech Computer Systems (2014), Sandals Upgrades BI to Latest Aptech Execuvue with Dashboards for 21 Resorts, Aptech http://www.aptech-inc.com/index.php/2014/11/sandals-upgrades-bi-to-latest-aptech-execuvue-with-dashboards-for-21-resorts (accessed 11 November 2014).

Arts Council (2004), Market matters: the dynamics of the contemporary art market, London: Arts Council.

Baines, T. and Lightfoot, H. (2013), Servitization of the manufacturing firm: Exploring the operations practices and technologies that deliver advanced services, *International Journal of Operations & Production Management*, 34(1), 2–35.

Baron, S., Harris, K. and Davies, B.J. (1996), Oral Participation in Retail Service Delivery: A Comparison of the Roles of Contact Personnel and Customers, *European Journal of Marketing* 30 (9), 75–90.

Berry, L.L. (1980), Services Marketing is Different, *Business Horizons*, May–June, 24–9.

Berry, L.L., Lefkowith, E.E. and Clark, T. (1980), In Services: What's in a Name?, *Harvard Business Review*, Sept.–Oct., 28–30.

Bloemer, J. and de Ruyter, K. (1998), On the Relationship Between Store Image, Store Satisfaction and Store Loyalty, *European Journal of Marketing* 32(5/6), 499–513.

Booms, B.H. and Bitner, M.J. (1981), Marketing Strategies and Organization Structures for Service Firms, in Donnelly, J.H. and George, W.R. (eds.) *Marketing of Services*, Chicago: American Marketing Association, 47–51.

Booth, M. (2014), Dark lands: the grim truth behind the 'Scandinavian miracle', *The Guardian*, 27 January http://www.theguardian.com/world/2014/jan/27/scandinavian-miracle-brutal-truth-denmark-norway-sweden (accessed 22 March 2015).

Brown, P., Hassan, S. and Teare, R. (2011), The Sandals philosophy: exceeding guest expectations–now and in the future, *Worldwide Hospitality and Tourism Themes* 3(1), 8–13.

Brown, S. and Patterson, A. (2009), Harry Potter and the Service-Dominant Logic of marketing: a cautionary tale, *Journal of Marketing Management* 25(5–6), 519–33.

Buzzell, R.D. and Gale, B.T. (1987), *The PIMS Principles: Linking Strategy to Performance*, New York: Free Press, 103–34.

Campbell, D. (2015), NHS agrees largest ever deal to tackle backlog, *The Guardian*, 12 March http://www.guardian.com/society/2015/mar/nhs-agrees-largest-ever-provatisation-deal-to-tackle-backlog (accessed 18 March 2015).

Charles, E., Marciniak, R. and McColl, J. (2018), The nature of parenting advantage in Third Sector retailing: case of Mary's living and giving Shop for Save the Children, *EIRASS 25th Recent Advances in Retailing and Services Studies* 25th Vol. 25th Proceedings (p. 16), Funchal Madeira: Technishe Universiteit Eindhoven.

Charles, G. (2008), KFC Launches Breakfast Menu, *Marketing*, 7 May, 1.

Christopher, M. and Yallop, R. (1990), Audit your Customer Service Quality, *Focus*, June–July, 1–6.

CNN (2017), *CNN, Cassandra Santiago and Doug Criss*. An activist, a little girl and the heartbreaking origin of 'Me too CNN, archived from the original on 17 October 2017. Retrieved 18 October 2017.

Coca-Cola (2018), https://www.coca-colacompany.com/stories/share-a-coke-and-share-the-summer-2018-campaign-focuses-on-special-moments (accessed July 2018).

Collinson, S. (2012), Why is the public sector so complex? http://flipchartfairytales.wordpress.com/2012/03/19/why-is-thepublic-sector-so-complex (accessed June 2012).

Cowell, D. (1995), *The Marketing of Services*, London: Heinemann, 35.

Danaher, P.J. and Mattson, J. (1994), Customer Satisfaction during the Service Delivery Process, *European Journal of Marketing* 28(5), 5–16.

Davoudi, S. (2005), From Brand Leader to Struggler in Eight Years, *Financial Times*, 17 June, 24.

Edgett, S. and Parkinson, S. (1993), Marketing for Services Industries: A Review, *Service Industries Journal* 13(3), 19–39.

Edmund, T. (2018), Financial services European aspects, *House of commons briefing paper*, http://researchbriefings.files.parliament.uk/documents/CBP-7435/CBP-7435.pdf (accessed July 2018).

Ellis-Chadwick, F. (2011), *B22 An introduction to retail management and marketing: Book 1 What is retailing?* The Open University, 7.

FedEx (2015), Customer Service Overkill, Fedex, 30 March https://getahead.fedex.ca/customer-service-overkill (accessed July 2018).

Fernandez, J. (2009), Sparking a Hotel Price War, *Marketing Week*, 12 March, 22–3.

Financial Times Survey (2017), https://ig.ft.com/ft-1000/ 24 April.

Gallagher, P. (2009), Henning Mankell creates a 'female Wallander' following star's suicide, *The Observer*, 27 December http://www.theguardian.com/uk/2009/dec/27/wallandar-hemming-mankell-tv-books-detective (accessed 21 March 2015).

Garrahan, M. (2005), The Ride of a Lifetime, *Financial Times*, 18 August, 19.

Grönroos, C. (1990), *Services Management and Marketing: Managing the Moments of Truth in Service Competition*, Lexington, MA: Lexington Books.

Hirsch, P. (1972), Processing fads and fashions: an organization set analysis of culture industry systems, *American Journal of Sociology*, 77, 639–59. In Banksa, M. and Hesmondhalgh, D. (2009), Looking for work in creative industries policy, *International Journal of Cultural Policy* 15(4), 415–30.

Jodelka, F. (2015), Fortitude: 'not another chunk of Nordic noir', *The Guardian*, 29 January http://www.theguardian.com/tv-and-radio/2015/jan/29/fortitude-sky-atlantic (accessed 21 March 2015).

Karpen, I., Bove, L. and Lukas, B. (2012), Linking service-dominant logic and strategic business practice: A conceptual model of a service-dominant orientation, *Journal of Service Research* 15(1), 21–38; DOI: 10.1177/1094670511425697.

Kelly, D. and Lewis, A. (2009), Human service sector nonprofit organization's social impact, Business Strategy Series, 10(6) 374–82 https://doi.org/10.1108/17515630911005664 (accessed August 2018).

Lawton, G. (2017), #MeToo is here to stay. We must challenge all men about sexual harassment *The Guardian* 28 October https://www.theguardian.com/lifeandstyle/2017/oct/28/metoo-hashtag-sexual-harassment-violence-challenge-campaign-women-men (accessed August 2018).

Lazzeretti, L. and Vecco, M. (2018), *Creative industries and Entrepreneurship: Paradigms in transition from a global perspective*, Edward Elgar, Cheltenham, UK.

Leggett Immobilier (2018), http://blog.frenchestateagents.com/uncategorized/brits-are-still-the-biggest-buyers-in-france-2374 (accessed July 2018).

Liberty London (2018), https://www.libertylondon.com/uk/marys-living-and-giving-shop.html.

Lievens, A. and Moenaert, R.K. (2000), Communication Flows During Financial Service Innovation, *European Journal of Marketing* 34(9/10), 1078–110.

Lusch, R.F. and Vargo, S.L. (2011), Service-dominant logic: a necessary step, *European Journal of Marketing* 45(7/8), 1298–1309.

Lusch, R.F., Vargo, S.L. and Tanniru, M. (2010), Service, value networks and learning, *Journal of the Academy of Marketing Science* 38, 19–31.

McColl, J., Marciniak, R. and Charles, E. (2018), Brand separation Strategy in Charity retailing: the case of luxury product offerings. In EIRASS 25th Recent Advances in Retailing and Services Studies 25th Vol. 25th Proceedings (pp. 65). Funchal Madeira: Technishe Universiteit Eindhoven.

Milington, A. (2015), Pubs and bars hit back at New Year health campaigns with 'Try January' push, *Marketing Week*, 6 January http://www.marketingweek.com/2015/01/06/pubs-and-bars-hit-back-at-new-year-health-campaigns-with-try-january-push (accessed 22 March 2015).

Moeller, S. (2010), Characteristics of services–a new approach uncovers their value, *Journal of Services Marketing*, 24(5), 359–68 https://doi.org/10.1108/08876041011060468 (accessed June 2010).

Notaires.fr (2018), French property analysis https://www.notaires.fr/en/housing-tax-system/french-property-market/french-property-market-analysis (accessed July 2018).

O'Shaughnessy, J. and N. (2009), The service-dominant perspective: a backward step? *European Journal of Marketing* 43(5/6), 784–93.

Offerpop (2013), *History of the Hashtag*, Offerpop, 6 November http://www.offerpop.com/resources/blog/history-hashtags (accessed June 2013).

Parasuraman, A., Zeithaml, V.A. and Berry, L.L. (1985), A Conceptual Model of Service Quality and its Implications for Future Research, *Journal of Marketing*, Fall, 41–50.

Pike, J. (2011), Sandals' Success Story, Travel Agent, Questex Media Group, 25 July, 19–21.

Pruyn, A. and Smidts, A. (1998), Effects of Waiting on the Satisfaction with the Service: Beyond Objective Times Measures, *International Journal of Research in Marketing* 15, 321–34.

Rafiq, M. and Ahmed, P.K. (1992), The Marketing Mix Reconsidered, *Proceedings of the Annual Conference of the Marketing Education Group*, Salford, 439–51.

Rubera, G. and Kirca, A. (2012), Firm Innovativeness and Its Performance Outcomes: A Meta-Analytic Review and Theoretical Integration, *Journal of Marketing* 76(May), 130–47.

Sandals (2018), About Sandals https://www.sandals.co.uk/about/ (accessed July 2018).

Schlesinger, L.A. and Heskett, J.L. (1991), The Service-Driven Service Company, *Harvard Business Review*, Sept.–Oct., 71–81.

Sellers, P. (1988), How to Handle Customers' Gripes, *Fortune* 118 (October), 100.

Solomon, M. (2014), Self-Leadership The Best Leadership? Ritz-Carlton's Employee Empowerment, *Forbes*, 13 May http://www.forbes.com/sites/micahsolomon/2014/05/13/ritz-carltons-corporate-culture (accessed 20 March 2015).

Southwest Airlines (2015), Customer Service, Southwest Airlines. https://www.southwest.com/html/customer-service DOI: 10.3402/jac.v8.32704 (accessed June 2015).

Stougaard-Neilsen, J. (2016), Nordic Noir in the UK: the allure of accessible difference, *Journal of Aesthetics & Culture* 8(1).

TFL (2018), Our customer commitments, https://tfl.gov.uk/corporate/about-tfl/how-we-work/our-customer-commitments (accessed July 2018).

Tesseras, L. (2014), The Marketing Year: The top campaigns of 2014, *Marketing Week*, 8 December http://www.marketingweek.com/2014/12/08/the-marketing-year-the-top-campaigns-of-2014 (accessed 12 December 2014).

Vargo, S.L. and Lusch, R.F. (2004), Evolving to a new dominant logic for marketing, *Journal of Marketing*, 68(January), 1–17.

Vargo, S.L. and Lusch, R.F. (2006), Service-Dominant Logic: What It Is, What It Is Not, What It Might Be, in Lusch, R.F. and Vargo, S.L. (eds), *The Service-Dominant Logic of Marketing: Dialog, Debate, and Directions*, Armonk: M.E. Sharpe, 43–56.

Vargo, S.L. and Lusch, R.F. (2016), Institutions and axioms: an extension and update of service-dominant logic, *Journal of the Academy of Marketing Science.*

Wilkinson, A. (2002), Employees can get the Message Across, *Marketing Week*, 3 October, 20.

Wirtz, J. and Chew, P.L. (2003), *Essentials of Services Marketing*, Pearson Education, London.

Wirtz, J., Chew, P.L. and Lovelock, C. (2012), *Essentials of Services Marketing*, 2nd edn, Pearson Education, London.

Wood, R. (2017), Interview: Mary Portas on the Save the Children Charity Shops, *The Times* 6 August https://www.thetimes.co.uk/article/interview-mary-portas-on-her-save-the-children-charity-shops (accessed September 2018).

CASE 17
Nordstrom: Using Service Excellence To Provide A Better Customer Experience

'Use your best judgement in all situations. There will be no additional rules.' That is all the guidance that Nordstrom, the famous Seattle-based upscale fashion retailer, gives its employees regarding how to handle all customer service interactions. The company, famous for its 'no-questions-asked' returns policy, is also well known for providing some of the highest levels of customer service in the retail industry. Nordstrom's reputation for service is so great that a book was actually written about it, *The Nordstrom Way to Customer Service Excellence*. It offers a guideline for managers who are looking to emulate best practices and improve the levels of service at their companies.

Nordstrom, founded in 1901, has always had a strong presence in the Pacific Northwest of the USA. Currently, it has 122 full-service stores in the USA, Puerto Rico and Canada. From the very beginning, providing the best customer service as well as the best service experience was at the heart of everything that Nordstrom did. The company says that it has a 'relentless drive to exceed expectations'.

Analysts believe that Nordstrom's exemplary levels of customer service are based on two key factors: 1) the increased level of attention to detail regarding the customer's experience when shopping (regardless of the channel) and 2) the high degree to which employees are empowered to take decisions and solve problems autonomously.

Examples of Nordstrom's commitment to service are legendary. A former employee, Ambra Benjamin, explained in an interview some of the policies and expectations regarding behaviour that workers were required to adhere to. The most important was the company's returns policy. It doesn't matter how long ago an item was bought, what condition it is in or whether the customer does not have the receipt. As an employee, you are expected to accept the item without question.

Nordstrom also provides its customers with a better experience by not consolidating checkout counters into endless rows near the exit, like other retailers do. Every department has its own cashier dedicated to helping customers who are looking to buy a certain category of item. The company also offers personal shoppers and concierges to give an even higher level of personalized service and a customized shopping experience. Other in-store amenities are comfortable and clean toilets as well as nursing and changing rooms for mothers with infants.

Realizing that its employees are the 'face' of the company, Nordstrom tends to provide good pay and benefits, with commission running as high as 10 per cent and salaries going into six figures for high performers. The company even has something called the 'million-dollar club'. This is a select group of salespeople who bring in more than $1 million in sales per year. This 'elite of the elite' go out of their way to cultivate personal relationships with Nordstrom's customers, contacting them directly about certain events and promotions that might be of interest, as well as sending hand-written thank-you cards.

As you would expect from a company demanding service excellence, courtesy and politeness are paramount. That is why Nordstrom employees do not point you in the right direction when you ask where something is. Instead, they walk you there themselves. They do not hand you your purchased items over the counter. They walk around and place the items into your hands. Also, customers are never rushed, even when it is closing time.

Nordstrom is also obsessed with using the latest technology, starting in the late 1990s with trying to find new ways to improve customer service and the overall shopping experience by incorporating the latest IT developments into its operations. Its goal is to become the world's best 'omni-channel' retailer—that is to say, provide as many different ways for customers to shop as possible (both online and offline) and making all the channels perform seamlessly from a service experience point of view. Analysts say that Nordstrom is 'at the forefront of e-commerce and omni-channel retail', having reportedly spent at least $1 billion developing its technological capabilities. For Nordstrom's part, they insist that they are 'leading the charge to redefine the role that technology and digital tools play in the retail environment'.

An example of Nordstrom's commitment to IT is the introduction of an inventory system as far back as 2002 that provided customers with a 'consistent multi-channel experience'. Nordstrom was one of the first retailers to have a point-of-sale system that allowed salespeople to track an individual customer's order and service needs through the internet. Nordstrom was also an early innovator and adopter of apps and social media, as well as mobile checkout systems that allow people to purchase an item in a store without having to wait in a checkout line and see a cashier. The company recently made it possible to buy items posted on Instagram immediately through a link. Nordstrom also analyses marketing and fashion trends, using information it receives from its Pinterest page to help it to identify items that it should display more prominently in its stores. This results in higher service by more effectively providing customers with the items that they themselves believe are popular. The company also acquired the 'flash-sale' site Hautelook in an effort to provide high fashion at lower prices. All these innovations have helped Nordstrom to provide a personalized and superior customer experience to shoppers in the USA and 96 countries worldwide through its website.

In March of 2018, the company signalled an even bigger commitment to use technology to provide customers with a world class shopping experience. Nordstrom announced that it was buying (for an undisclosed sum) two cutting edge retail technology companies, BevyUp and MessageYes, in an effort to 'serve customers on their terms'. BevyUp is a designer of digital selling tools, while MessageYes is an e-commerce platform. The goal is to ultimately provide a shopping experience that is seamless. One way the company plans to do this is by integrating BevyUp's platform into a mobile app used by Nordstrom's employees, allowing them to have better information and capabilities to more efficiently serve customers' needs. MessageYes will bring its expertise in artificial intelligence, machine learning and data science to Nordstrom's already impressive IT team.

While technology is important, Nordstrom realizes that people (for now) still spend most of their time in the real world. And in order to fulfill their personal, as well as retail, needs the company recently launched the innovative concept known as 'Nordstrom Local'. These are roughly 3,000 square foot (almost 279 square meter) shopping spaces that will provide 'experiential' services like manicures and personalized styling, as well as a bar. Experts believe that, in addition to providing customers with a better service experience, the new format will allow Nordstrom to experiment with different experiential offerings, as well as give the company the opportunity to reach ever more refined consumer segments.

In 2014, Nordstrom decided to spread its excellence north, expanding into Canada. The company opened its first store in Calgary, a second store opened in Ottawa in March 2015, and a third store opened in Vancouver around September 2015. Since 2018, the company has been present in British Columbia and Toronto as well. In an attempt to get closer to its Canadian customers, the company announced the launch of its 'True Nord' (in French, 'Nord' means 'North') marketing campaign in August of 2018. This is Nordstrom's first effort at a national Canadian marketing effort and is designed to better identify its brand with the 'inclusive and welcoming spirit of Canadians'.

In a further sign of its commitment to service excellence, Nordstrom said that it plans 'to stay focused on serving customers one at a time and getting to know and understand our customers in each city in which we are opening'. As an example of perhaps learning from the mistakes of others, Nordstrom's market entry plan appears to be on a much smaller and cautious scale than that of another US retailer, Target. At the end of 2014, Target announced that it would be leaving Canada due to poor performance (the company reportedly lost $2 billion on its venture in the 'great white north'). Unfortunately, in business, sometimes when a weak competitor leaves a market a stronger one enters. Saks Fifth Avenue, another US luxury retailer known for high levels of customer service, announced plans to open two stores in Toronto in 2016. Analysts believe that many Canadians are familiar with, and have shopped, at both Nordstrom and Saks Fifth Avenue. This is good news for the competing companies and their respective expansion plans. The challenge is that Canadian customers will most likely have extremely high expectations regarding customer service and their overall shopping experience. If disappointed, it will probably be a long time before they return again, if they ever do.

»

Questions

1. **What kind of services does Nordstrom offer its customers?**
2. **What role do employees play in providing excellent customer service?**
3. **How does Nordstrom use technology to improve its customer service?**
4. **What steps can Nordstrom take to be successful in its expansion abroad, maintain its excellent customer service and keep its competitive advantage?**

This case study was written by Tom McNamara and Irena Descubes, The Rennes School of Business, France

References

Based on: Lutz, A. (2014), How Nordstrom Became The Most Successful Retailer, *Business Insider*, December 30, 2014 http://www.businessinsider.com/nordstroms-business-strategy-is-working-2014-12#ixzz3PAx3pRKo; Khan, H. (2014), How Nordstrom Made Its Brand Synonymous With Customer Service (and How You Can Too), *Shopify*, 2 October http://www.shopify.com/blog/15517012 how-nordstrom-made-its-brand-synonymous-with-customer-service-and-how-you-can-too; Janus, A. (2015), Nordstrom take note, here's what Target's Canadian failure can teach you, CTV News, 15 January http://www.ctvnews.ca/business/nordstrom-take-note-here-s-what-target-s-canadian-failure-can-teach-you-1.2190662#ixzz3P7eeR6lT; Solomon, M. (2014), Take These Two Steps To Rival Nordstrom's Customer Service Experience, *Forbes*, 15 March http://www.forbes.com/sites/micahsolomon/2014/03/15/the-nordstrom-two-part-customer-experience-formula-lessons-for-your-business; Martinez, A. (2011), Tale of lost diamond adds glitter to Nordstrom's customer service, *Seattle Times*, May 11 http://seattletimes .com/html/businesstechnology/2015028167_nordstrom12.html; Udland, M. (2015), Target Is Leaving Canada, *Business Insider*, 15 January http://www.businessinsider.com/target-shuts-down-canada-operations-2015-1#ixzz3PBURMzRa; Quora (2014), Why is Nordstrom known for their good customer service? *Quora*, 19 February http://www.quora.com/Why-is-Nordstrom-known-for-their-good-customer-service; Ross, J.W., Beath, C.M. and Sebastian, I. (2015), Why Nordstrom's Digital Strategy Works (and Yours Probably Doesn't), *Harvard Business Review*, 14 January https://hbr.org/2015/01/why-nordstroms-digital-strategy-works-and-yours-probably-doesnt; Nordstrom Press Release (2018), Canada Plays Starring Role In First-Ever National Canadian Brand Campaign For Nordstrom, August 27. Accessed at: http://press.nordstrom.com/phoenix.zhtml?c=211996&p=irol-newsArticle_print&ID=2364914; Nordstrom Press Release (2018), Nordstrom Names Edmond Mesrobian Chief Technology Officer, August 6. Accessed: http://press.nordstrom.com/phoenix.zhtml?c=211996&p=irol-newsArticle&ID=2362208; Nordstrom Press Release (2018), Nordstrom Announces Investments In Digital Technology, March 8. Accessed at: http://press.nordstrom.com/phoenix.zhtml?c=211996&p=irol-newsArticle_Print&ID=2337118; Thompson, S. (2008), Nordstrom buys BevyUp and MessageYes, Retail Technology Innovation Hub, March 12. Accessed at: https://retailtechinnovationhub.com/home/2018/3/12/nordstrom-buys-bevyup-and-messageyes; Schulties, J. (2017), To Reimagine the Store Experience, Nordstrom Experiments with 'Local' Concept, pmx agency, September 12. Accessed at: https://www.pmxagency.com/blog/2017/09/reimagine-store-experience-nordstrom-experiments-local-concept/.

CASE 18
Pret A Manger: 'Passionate About Food'

Introduction

Pret a Manger (French for 'ready to eat') is a chain of shops that sell a range of high-quality sandwiches, salads, sushi, desserts and coffee to an increasingly discerning set of lunchtime customers. Started in London, England, in 1986 by two university graduates, Pret now has more than 500 stores across the UK and in many high profile international locations: New York and Boston, Paris, Hong Kong, Shanghai, Singapore. Being positioned as a quality food outlet rather than a coffee shop which sells food (like other popular brands such as Starbucks, Costa and Caffé Nero), which in the past has reportedly made regular lunch time deliveries of sandwiches to royalty, celebrities and politicians for working lunches, has enabled the chain to develop competitive advantage and be differentiated from its competitors. This value-added market positioning did not go unnoticed and, in 2018, German conglomerate JAB paid £1.5 billion to acquire Pret. This case explores the growth and development of Pret as a leading consumer-facing service business.

Background and Company History

Pret was founded with a single shop in central London by two property law graduates, Julian Metcalf and Sinclair Beecham, who had been students together in the early 1980s. At that time, the choice of lunchtime eating in London and other British cities was much more limited than it is today. Some chose restaurants or those well-known British institutions, pubs. However, lunchtime habits were changing. There was a growing awareness of the benefits of healthier eating, and also a trend among office workers towards taking shorter lunch breaks and eating at their desks. The choice in carry-out food was dominated by fast-food chains such as McDonald's, Burger King and KFC. Sandwiches also played an important part in lunchtime eating. Prior to Pret's arrival, sandwiches had been sold mainly pre-packed in supermarkets and high street chain stores or made to order in the many small, owner-run sandwich bars found in city centres and business districts.

Dissatisfied with both the food and service from traditional sandwich bars—Metcalf described the food

as 'soggy sandwiches and mush'—Metcalf and Beecham were determined that Pret should offer something different and much better. They wanted Pret's food to be, not only high quality, but also preservative- and additive-free, using natural ingredients. According to Metcalf, this proved to be a lot harder than it looked. In the beginning, with only one store, they shopped for the food themselves at local markets and then returned to the shop, where they made the sandwiches each morning. Metcalf would go in on Sunday evenings to cook 25 chickens ready to make sandwiches for the following day. As he recalls: 'Half the battle was getting preservative-free, chemical-free food. And it was an immense logistical challenge to get the ingredients delivered each morning.'

Pret's offer was based around premium quality sandwiches, other food and coffee, all priced higher than existing sandwich bars, sold in attractive packaging ready to carry out or eat in a comfortable store environment, with a focus on best quality natural ingredients and high-quality service.

The Pret Vision—'Passionate About What We Do'

From the very outset, Pret strongly focused on the quality of its food and ingredients in line with its own distinctive set of values. On its website, Pret claims to be: 'Passionate about food. The company's mission is to create, handmade, natural food, avoiding

»

»

the obscure chemicals, additives and preservatives common to so much of the 'prepared' and 'fast' food on the market today. Using natural ingredients is sacred to Pret.' And this approach has been enduring, as it continues to be 'The simple recipe for success' according to Clive Schlee, the current Chief Executive.

Great importance is placed on freshness. Uniquely, unlike those sold in other coffee chains, shops or supermarkets, Pret's sandwiches are all made and pre-packed for sale by hand in the kitchens of most Pret shops, starting at 6.30 each morning, rather than being prepared by a supplier or at a central location. No sandwiches or salads are kept overnight—any that aren't sold by the end of the day are offered free to local charities or disposed of. This means that store managers have the difficult logistical balancing act of keeping the shelves sufficiently full while at the same time not ordering or making too much food, which has to be disposed of at the end of the day. If a store runs out of a particular sandwich during the day, customers can ask to have one made especially for them.

Pret puts its customers central to the brand and does this by being aware of current trends in food consumption. For example, there are several Veggie Pret stores, where over half the food is vegetarian or vegan. Turmeric is the most popular new ingredient in salads and sandwiches. Great products, which are market relevant, are just part of the story. Pret also carries out random acts of kindness. In 2016, Pret launched their 'make someone smile campaign' which involved barista selecting 120,000 random customer and giving them a free coffee. Customers are encouraged to share their *free* experiences of drinking coffee via social media.

Careful sourcing of supplies has also always been critical, and Pret has taken time to build relationships with a number of suppliers it can trust to provide food of the quality and standard it requires. The organic coffee, for example, is supplied by small growers that operate as co-operatives and follow sustainable growing policies under the Fairtrade banner. (Fairtrade is a scheme that tries to ensure that sellers of agricultural products in developing countries receive a fair price for their products.) The milk, which is also organic, is from British farms where cows are allowed to graze and eat naturally. Genetically modified ingredients are banned, and the tuna used in Pret sandwiches has to be 'dolphin friendly'. The eggs in the egg mayonnaise are free range, and the ham comes from pigs fed on a strictly vegetarian diet on Farm Assured farms.

At the same time, Pret is also continually searching for new supplies of ingredients of the quality and standard it requires. There is also a drive for constant product improvement and innovation—Pret claims that its chocolate brownie has been improved more than 30 times over the years. New product ideas meetings are held in the company head office every Wednesday, and on average a new product is tried out every four days. There is also a sustainability strategy in place to reduce energy usage and waste, and build long-term partnerships with other suppliers in developing countries. Pret also has a charitable foundation, set up in 1995, which contributes to charities that help homeless people in the UK.

Pret is aware that some of its customers are increasingly health conscious. Its website menu carefully lists all the ingredients and nutritional values of every menu item in terms of energy, protein, fat and dietary fibre. But even this attention to detail has led to a food related fatality and. In 2018, the inclusion of sesame seeds in an artichoke, olive and tapenade baguette caused an extreme allergic reaction and eventually death of the customer. There was no allergen advice on the wrapper -this was legally allowable due to the baguette being mode on the premises- which caused a tragic outcome. Pret responded by introducing full ingredient labelling on it packaging,

Although the stores are mainly self-service, the quality of service provided by staff in the few moments that a customer spends buying coffee and paying at the counter is also critical in providing an experience that can differentiate Pret and build loyalty with customers who are usually in a hurry and buying on impulse. The service in Pret is friendly and efficient, in contrast to that in many restaurants and retailers in Britain, where historically service quality has not always been high. Customer-facing store staff are young, enthusiastic and motivated, and they are often given discretion to offer customers a free replacement for any item that is out of stock. There is a strong emphasis on staff recruitment and training to achieve this service quality—Pret claims it takes 12 weeks to fully train a coffee barista to the standard it needs—pay is above the industry average, and there are opportunities for career development into management. While staff turnover at 98 per cent a year may seem high, it is low against the fast-food industry average of around 150 per cent. As many Pret stores open early for breakfast, depending on customer demand, staff may be required to work on rotas that begin early in the morning. Advertised jobs are many times oversubscribed by applicants, and the company has been voted by *Fortune Magazine* as one of the top 10 companies to work for in Europe.

Monitoring the quality of the service in the stores is important, and quality is checked regularly by using mystery shoppers. If a shop receives a good report, then all the staff there receive an hourly bonus for the week of the visit. Managers also regularly visit and work as buddies for a week in stores every few months to help them keep in touch with how things are working on the shop floor. Store staff work in teams and are briefed daily, often on the basis of customer feedback, which Pret actively encourages through its website, in-store reply cards or by phone. Pret takes this very seriously and places great importance on this customer feedback, both positive and negative, which is discussed at weekly management meetings.

The design of the store environment is also distinctive. Shops are fitted out in a light and airy style featuring walls in bare and white-painted brick, Pret's trademark dark red, and furniture and fittings with natural wood finishes. Some stores play music, which helps to create a lively, fast-moving environment. Pret does not advertise, but attractive point-of-sale promotional material and graphics are on the walls of most shops, explaining Pret's values and philosophy, and announcing new products. The paper napkins are made from unbleached paper, while packaging, cutlery and paper cups are simply and attractively designed and recyclable. Pret also offers an online delivery service for businesses.

Competition

As Pret's chain expanded throughout the 1990s and 2000s into city centres, business and shopping areas, as well as airports and railway stations throughout the UK, so did the competition. Rivals such as Caffè Nero, Costa Coffee and USA-based Starbucks all entered the market, as well as a number of smaller independent chains. All offered a choice of coffees but with varying offerings in terms of sandwiches and food. In a London shopping street, it is not uncommon to see three or four rival coffee shops next door to or within a few metres of each other. Prices in each chain are roughly comparable. Pret, however, currently sees its main competitor as Eat, a chain of around 120 outlets throughout the UK, founded in 1996, with a similar offering of coffee, sandwiches and other hot and cold food. Eat describes its food as, 'made from scratch and served fresh', but does not claim that it is made in the store, nor that its ingredients are natural or organic.

The Future

As work and lifestyles get busier, the demand for convenience and fast food continues to grow. But, while the growth in sales of some types of fast food like burgers are showing signs of slowing down, sandwiches continue to increase in popularity. Customers are also generally getting more health-conscious and choosy about what they eat, particularly about the levels of fat, sugar and additives in food. They are also getting increasingly concerned about finding nutritional information from food labelling.

After a long run of success, Pret has plans for further growth. It hopes to open more new stores in the UK, but as Pret owns and manages all its stores and does not franchise their format, its plan is, as always, to expand carefully and cautiously. It also aims to open more stores internationally, particularly in New York and Hong Kong, where the brand has already been successful.

Questions

Go to Pret's website at http://www.pret.com and use it in conjunction with the case study to answer the following questions:

1. **Define the market environment and product category that Pret a Manger operates in?**
2. **Which companies do you think are Pret a Manger's competitors?**
3. **How does Pret a Manger differentiate its brand from its competitors in this market? In a few key words or phrases, define what you think is the defining positioning or 'essence' of the Pret a Manger brand.**
4. **Discuss how Pret a Manger manages each of the elements of its services marketing mix, to deliver a distinctive customer experience and build its brand equity.**

This case study was written by Clive Helm, Senior Lecturer, University of Westminster.

References

Based on: Pret A manger (2018), Financial statement 2017 https://www.pret.co.uk/en-gb/pret-a-manger-announces-financial-results-for-2017 (accessed Nov 2018); Pret (2018), Our menu https://www.pret.co.uk/en-gb/2565-salads-sweet-potato-falafel-&-smashed-beets-veggie-box.aspx, Pret empowers over 100,000 customers to 'make someone smile' new initiative enables customers to give the gift of free coffee https://www.pret.co.uk/en-gb/make-someone-smile Jan 18; Doward, J. (2018), Pret allergy death: parents describe final moments with their daughter, *The Guardian*, 29 September https://www.theguardian.com/society/2018/sep/29/pret-allergy-death-parents-demand-label-laws (accessed Dec 2018); BBC (2018), Pret a Manger to label products after allergy death https://www.bbc.co.uk/news/business-45731201 3 Oct (accessed Dec 2018).

CHAPTER 10
Value Through Relationships

Expectation is the root of all heartache.

ANONYMOUS

LEARNING OBJECTIVES

After reading this chapter, you should be able to:

1 define the concept of relationship marketing
2 discuss the nature of relationship marketing and how to build customer relationships
3 explain how customer relationships should be managed
4 suggest ways of developing customer relationship strategies
5 explain the significance and benefits of customer retention
6 discuss approaches towards customer loyalty programmes
7 explain and discuss the function of customer relationship management (CRM) systems

Marketers are increasingly considering societal as well as economic factors when developing their strategies, so that they can deliver value not only for customers but also for employees, their families and many other stakeholders. The benefits that can be derived from a value-driven approach are many. In this chapter, we examine how value can be created through relationship marketing.

Relationship marketing is a philosophy that involves 'marketing initiatives being based on relationships, networks and interaction and recognizing that marketing is embedded in the total management of the networks of the selling organization, the market and society' (Gummesson, 2002; Berry, 2008) and is common practice in business-to-consumer and business-to-business markets (Jones, et al 2015). Hence, developing successful relationships between buyer and supplier becomes a firm's ultimate goal, which arguably can deliver value for all involved.

The principles of relationship marketing are nothing new (McGarry, 1953), but do represent a fundamental change in marketing practice. Since the 1990s, the shift in marketing research and practice (Grönroos, 1994) away from the Four-Ps, which had dominated marketing thinking since 1960, occurred in response to growing customer demands and an ever more complex business environment (Singh, Agrariya and Deepali, 2011). The significance of relationship marketing has continued to gather momentum as companies have moved away from developing short-term transactional relationships towards building long-term relationships (Kotler, 1991). At the heart of relationship building theory is the idea of value creation by managing customer expectations and experiences within societal networks.

In this chapter, we build on earlier discussions of customer value (Chapter 1) to explore relationship marketing and associated management practices. Throughout the chapter, illustrative examples are provided from both business-to-business and business-to-consumer contexts. More specifically, this chapter examines the concepts of value creation, relationship marketing and relational networks, before considering building and managing relationships, the benefits of developing organizational and consumer relationships, developing customer retention strategies, customer loyalty programmes and **customer relationship management** (CRM) systems.

Value Creation

Value creation occurs when companies enter into exchanges with their customers. In Chapter 9, we discussed Vargo and Lusch's (2004) work on the value of co-creation and how value should be created at every point where a customer touches a firm. Moreover, to achieve this, every area of a firm throughout the value chain must be dedicated to value creation Merz et al. (2018). They give the example of two fast food restaurants in the USA: Wendy's and McDonald's. Value is co-created at Wendy's when the company provides the dining facilities, cooks the food and drink and delivers it to the customer to enjoy. If their customers value this experience, they may choose to return to Wendy's rather than going to McDonald's. Customers may also share their positive experiences on social media and reply to an opinion survey. Customers are likely to review their experiences at Wendy's and compare them in relation to the positioning shown in advertising. This series of interactions is an example of how customers can help contribute to co-creation of value for the brand. Two further aspects to consider are customer-owed resources and customer motivation (Merz et al., 2018).

- Customer-owned resources:
  a. Brand knowledge a customer has acquired. This experience makes them a valuable resource to the brand (Harmeling et al., 2017), especially if this knowledge is used to write reviews and blog about their experiences.
  b. Brand skills refer to the customer's influence over potential customers. The more informed the customer, the greater the authority with which they can speak about the brand.
  c. Brand connectedness is the customer's personal links and networks (Harmeling et al., 2017). Customers who are part of a social media network can connect, communicate and interact, not only with their own friends and family, but also with the brand and its employees, which might be able to extend reach and diversity of the target audience.
- Customer motivation:
  a. Brand passion is *love*, and strong feeling, towards a brand (Albert et al., 2013) and is central to the development of strong brand relationships. Brands can use the customer's enthusiasm by encouraging word-of-mouth (online and offline) to extend reach.

b. Brand trust refers to a customer confidence that the brand will deliver on its promises. It is also an important aspect of maintaining customer relationships.
c. Brand commitment is defined as the extent to which customers will work with the brand. A committed customer will help to co-create brand value, through brand communities, positive reviews and even product development. Booking.com relies on the quality of services provided by the hotels and accommodation advertised on its platform. Customers using the accommodation booking platform are actively encouraged to review places after their trip. The co-creation of value through customer reviews enables booking.com, accommodation suppliers and the end customer to develop strong customer motivation. They also reward returning customers with offers, discounts and elevated booking status (Genius loyalty programme for frequent travellers).

Co-creation of value through exchange relationships in B2B markets are important and happen when an arrangement is established between trading partners. Value is created using the resources and management structures that the exchange partners control (Hammervoll, 2012). Various types of value creation initiative can be established depending on the extent of the interaction between the trading partners and the aims for the value creation interaction (Grönroos and Voima, 2012). For example:

- **Information sharing to aid supplier learning**: a buyer might supply market intelligence about market demand and competitors in a new market to its supplier, to aid learning that might deliver future improvements in the seller's offer. In this situation, the success of the interaction is dependent on the quality of the information provided by the buyer and the supplier's ability to use the intelligence effectively (Ciborra, 1991).
- **Supplier development**: a supplier improves the quality of its products through insights derived from discussion and consultation with buyers. In this case, there is a shared initiative that focuses on improvements that can contribute to creating a competitive advantage, which will ultimately benefit both companies. Such initiatives might result in better quality service achieved through improved training, reduced costs, and more innovative product design (Hammervoll, 2012).
- **Strategic knowledge sharing**: a supplier improves its production processes by engaging in joint projects with a buyer. Both companies (buyer and supplier) participate in such ventures by contributing ideas, suggestions and feedback to gain mutual benefit (Hammervoll, 2009). For this level of interaction to be successful, both parties need to be willing to share sensitive strategic information, utilise their company's capabilities and fully engage in the co-creation of value.

As a result, relationship management plays an essential role in value creation, because both buyer and supplier need to work together in the pursuit of mutual gains. Managers in all markets can consider the idea of value creation, as it may be a way to identify new opportunities to differentiate a company's offer. To benefit, managers should allocate time and resources to learning about their customers' requirements, and then considering how to improve their products and services. In consumer markets, service providers need to demonstrate their commitment, not only towards their customers, but also towards employees, suppliers and other stakeholders, to create trusting relationships and excellent customer experiences. For example, the coffee shop sector has focused on how to create customer experiences that matter. See Marketing in Action 10.1 for discussion of how Starbucks created the third place concept and in doing so revolutionised the coffee shop industry.

MARKETING IN ACTION 10.1
The Third Place: Creating and Managing Customer Value in the Coffee Shop Industry

Howard Schultz joined Starbucks when it had just four coffee shops. Then he went on a trip to Italy and came back with an idea that would change coffee drinking behaviour and stimulate the development of a multi-billion-dollar industry. Schultz wanted to give Americans the Italian coffee experience, but realised that he needed to adapt the product and the service offer to suit the needs of his customers, as they would not want the strong, bitter espresso coffee drunk by Italians. So, he invented a version of coffee to entice young adults away from sugary drinks like Coke and sought to change their beverage-drinking behaviour. He added milk and sugary syrups to strong black coffee, so that his customers could get their caffeine 'kick' in a different way. Schultz encouraged people to drink frothy cappuccinos and milky lattés, and their response was overwhelming: they queued in their hundreds outside the company's coffee shops in Seattle.

»

Adapting the product was only part of Schultz's strategy; he also realised the importance to the customers of creating a unique environment in which to experience their coffee drinking. Schultz conceived the third place—a place between work and home, a place to meet friends. The coffee shops were designed to provide a warm and convivial atmosphere to appeal to customers, a principle that has remained important to the company throughout its development into a global mega-brand. The third place idea was so successful that it is a model that has been used by all the world's successful coffee shop brands, such as Costa Coffee and Caffé Nero.

Each Starbucks store is designed to be as unique as possible, even though the company operates over 22,000 stores globally. But, as well as the look and feel, distinct zones within many stores aim to provide different customer experiences. For example: seating by windows allows customers to watch passers-by are for customers while they sip their macchiatos; stylish bars while they drink to stand at drink frothy espressos which aims to create an experience reminiscent of traditional coffee houses in Italy; communal tables, for groups of customers or individuals, have space to drink, eat, socialise, read or work on a laptop; softer seating areas offer more 'intimate' coffee drinking experiences.

Also, the heart of Starbucks' success is a set of core principles that focus on value creation, the development of relational capital and the capture of customer value. Relationships with customers, employees, suppliers and alliance partners are considered so valuable that they form a central part of the company's activities.

For customers, it is important to understand the service operation from the perspective of the person the service exists for, so Starbucks works with its customers to get ideas on how to improve its service. For example, the My Starbucks Idea website invites customers to submit ideas and suggestions. Many new product ideas and service improvements have been introduced from customer ideas, for example 'buy 10 get one free', reduced fat cinnamon swirl coffee cake, Evolution Fresh (fruit and veg) smoothies, and Teavana, premium loose-leaf tea.

For employees, learning is an important part of the value creation process at Starbucks. For example, Starbucks and the Schultz Family Foundation work with disengaged young adults to help them find employment; they also provide job training programmes as well as life skills coaching to support young people throughout their lives, not only at work. Mutual benefits are generated: for the company, happier and more satisfied employees mean genuine good service experiences for Starbucks customers, and for the individual, there is a sense of purpose and belonging.

For suppliers and alliance partners, supplier development and knowledge sharing for strategic development is vital to the company's ongoing success. Starbucks works with its suppliers and farmers to ensure that its coffee beans are grown in a sustainable manner, for example through the Coffee and Farmer Equity Practices; this not only provides high quality beans but also ensures the livelihoods of the farmers and their families.

Based on: Hammervoll (2012); Centrum för Tjänsteforskning (2015); Starbucks (2015a and b); Wilson (2014); Liozu (2017)

Value and Relational Networks

Value and relational networks involve people and the roles they play within the networks. 'Network' is a term used to describe a set of connections among people, which from a marketing perspective might be used as a resource to solve problems, share knowledge and extend the network by adding new connections (Wenger, Trayner and de Latt, 2011). Networks are highly complex and intangible entities, but are formed to co-produce service offerings, exchange service offerings and facilitate the co-creation of value (Lusch, Vargo and Tanniru, 2010). LinkedIn is an example of an online network that connects professional workers together. However, it is important to note that the roles people assume within a network can be highly complex and an individual may assume different identities in social situations (Edvardsson, Tronvall and Gruber, 2011). For example, a software company may be made up of several individuals who play various roles, for example leader, problem-solver, designer or service provider. A role within a value network is different from a job title. So, at the software company, the leader may have the job title senior developer but may also act as a problem-solver.

Networks are important, especially as all markets are now electronically connected through the internet. A network relationship should facilitate the sharing of competencies and aid the development of relationships to enable companies to perform better (Lusch, Vargo and Tanniru, 2010). For example, eBay is an electronic marketplace made up of buyers and sellers that has created new opportunities for different types of seller (hobbyists and collectors) who previously did not have access to a commercial platform. As eBay has grown, so have the connections and number of buyers and sellers that use the marketplace. Working together, eBay and its participants have created a highly successful value network that is clearly differentiated from its competitors.

Having briefly explored value and relational networks, the next section considers the core concepts of relationship marketing, followed by discussion of managerial issues and practical implications of adopting a relationship marketing approach.

As discussed earlier, service quality, trust and commitment feature strongly in the creation of satisfaction between parties in the relationship. Read Mini case 10.1 to find out more about how to engage millennials in a meaningful relationtionship.

MINI CASE 10.1
New Rules of Engagement: Marketing to Millennials

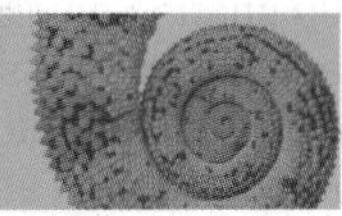

Millennials are a maturing generation born in the period around 1980 and 2000. They are a different breed of consumers; they have grown up with digital media and are experts in the use of the web, social media and mobile technology to facilitate every aspect of their lives. They have been portrayed in mainstream media as 'lazy, debt-laden, social-media obsessed fame seekers' and yet they are a generation most wanted by brands (Barton et al., 2012). There is little doubt that marketers must think and act differently to build relationships with this generation, who are adept at using technology as part of their daily lives. According to Sinomson and Rosen (2014): 'In the past, buyers typically made relative comparisons ("Is Brand A better than Brand B?") or went by the maxim "You get what you pay for.'" Buyers largely had to rely on information provided by suppliers, media reports and word of mouth from personal friends and acquaintances who had personal experience of a brand. Before 2004, there was limited scope for gathering independent information on product performance, quality and customer experiences, which could then inform purchase decisions. But the launch of Facebook helped consolidate the social media revolution started by Friends Reunited and Myspace and paved the way for online reviews. Millennials tend to be the most active at consulting social media for information about physical products, brand experiences and service quality to inform their purchasing decisions. Social media provides an increasingly rich tapestry of reviews of customer experiences. Millennials are also very keen to use and provide peer-to-peer reviews on products and services, giving potential buyers the opportunity to get a sense of what it's like to own or use the goods they're considering.

So, what are the new rules of engagement, when it comes to building relationships with millennials?

»

Hip-ennial
"I can make the world a better place."
29%
- Cautious consumer, globally aware, charitable, and information hungry
- Greatest user of social media but does not push/contribute content
- Female dominated, below-average employment (many are students and homemakers)

Gadget Guru
13%
"It's a great day to be me."
- Successful, wired, free spirited, confident, and at ease
- Feels this is his best decade
- Greatest device ownership, pushes/contributes to content
- Male dominated, above-average income, single

Millennial Mom
"I love to work out, travel, and pamper my baby."
22%
- Wealthy, family oriented, works out, confident, and digitally savvy
- High online intensity
- Highly social and information hungry
- Can feel isolated from others by her daily routine
- Older, highest income

Clean and Green Millennial
10%
"I take care of myself and the world around me."
- Impressionable, cause driven, healthy, green, and positive
- Greatest contributor of content, usually cause related
- Male dominated, youngest, more likely to be Hispanic, full-time student

Anti-Millennial
"I'm too busy taking care of my business and my family to worry about much else."
16%
- Locally minded, conservative
- Does not spend more for green products and services
- Seeks comfort and familiarity over excitement/change/interruption
- Slightly more female, more likely to be Hispanic and from the western U.S.

Old-School Millennial
10%
"Connecting on Facebook is too impersonal, let's meet up for coffee instead!"
- Not wired, cautious consumer, and charitable
- Confident, independent, and self-directed
- Spends least amount of time online, reads
- Older, more likely to be Hispanic

Source https://www.bcg.com/documents/file103894.pdf

The differences:

Desires—this generation wants more from the brands they choose to engage with, they are keen to co-create by sharing opinions, reviews, feedback through social media and the web. They will endorse the things they approve of, but shout about things they despise. They are also happy to engage in such activites around the clock and tend to react instantaneously. The implications for marketers are that brands do not have to wait to poll opinion about a new product launch; they can accurately gauge consumer reactions almost instantly online. But brands must ensure authenticity and transparency if they wish to avoid the wrath of a millennial backlash to a product offer perceived to be 'phoney' or unfair.

Demands—experiences are important, as are new and innovative products and services. While rational functionality is key, as a millennial is likely to be the 'chief technology officer' in many households, they also like emotional rewards and instant gratification, which must be delivered appropriately and quickly. Pleasure, fun and adventure are also cravings of this generation, who are prepared to do things differently, from ordering an instant taxi (Uber), staying in someone else's home instead of using a recognized accommodation provider (AirBNB), to having a personal shopper manage your luxury clothing online orders (net-a-porter).

Influencers—millennials' lives are directly interconnected with others and so are heavily affected by the view of their peers. Their purchasing behaviour is strongly influenced by their large network of online 'friends' and, unlike previous generations, they turn more readily to online peer-networks for advice and ideas, which they openly share online. So, what are the new rules for marketers, wishing to develop relational networks with millennials.

The new rules of millennial network building

1. Do not stereotype: millennials have been referred to as lazy, entitled, spoiled, but this does not fit well with their own ideals.
2. Understand the target customer profile: broadly, this generation are tech savvy, digital natives, relaxed, in love with convenience, want things easy, and have a strong sense of self. But their birthdays span 20 years so there are sub-segments to consider.

3 Engage through digital media; millennials are prepared to become brand advocates and co-create, but an engagement strategy needs to be interesting and throught-provoking if it is not to be dismissed by this generation.
4 Plan to reward your customers—be able to provide instant and appropriate rewards.
5 Do not try to hide mistakes; seek millennials' 'expert advice' when things are going right, but also when they go wrong.
6 Make it fun; this is a constantly on-the-go generation and they want new experiences to enjoy.
7 Use, don't abuse, information. Adapt marketing strategies to take account of the increased influence of customer opinions.

Questions:

1 How can brands use digital media to support brand development?
2 How might social media affect the value of a brand name when targeting millennials? Discuss positive and negative influences.
3 For a brand of your choice, decide which distinct millennial segment is the most likely target group. Then suggest which digital media they are most likely to use and where the brand is mostly likely to be able to begin to develop a connected relationship.

Based on: Maheshwari (2013); Barton, Fromm and Egan (2012); Simonson and Rosen (2014); Ellis-Chadwick (2013)

Key Concepts of Relationship Marketing

The term 'relationship marketing' was coined by Berry, Shostak and Upah (1983), who defined it in terms of the marketing strategies that companies need to apply to retain customers over a longer time. This new paradigm redefined marketing, moving it away from being a transactional exchange process to a relational perspective. This also led to greater understanding of the lifetime value of a customer and the potential value of strategic partnering (Sheth, 2017). Much of the logic that underpins the core elements of relationship marketing comes from the marketing of services rather than physical products. But, there is debate about the meaning of relationship marketing: for some it means customer relationship management (CRM) and to others it is the marketing activities a firm engages in after an exchange has occurred, e.g. loyalty programmes, and is considered more as customer support (Sheth, 2017). This issue is returned to later when discussing relationship management. Nevertheless, there are two important elements of relationship marketing to consider:

1) **Core service** A core service can be developed around a company's offer that meets customers' needs in a distinctive manner. Retail banks have developed tailored financial products that enable customers to choose the level of service that is wrapped around their personal bank account: for example, HSBC plc offers a Basic account, an Advanced account and a Premier account.
2) **Relationship quality** Customers develop relationships with companies by engaging in the exchange process and are motivated to do so by the potential value that might be gained. But, from a relationship marketing perspective, the ongoing interaction between parties is of primary importance. In other words, companies seek to build relationships that develop customer **loyalty** and, in doing so, encourage customers to engage in repeated purchasing. Ultimately, the quality of a relationship is likely to affect customer loyalty and determine whether a company can retain its customers (Vize et al., 2013).

   Relationship quality is a complex subject, but there are several key factors to consider (Vize, 2012) which potentially affect the outcome of a relationship:

   - **Service quality**—this involves the experience a customer has of a company's offer. Services vary in complexity and in the investment and risk a customer makes in the purchase—for example, having a haircut or buying a cup of coffee. Service quality is discussed in detail in Chapter 9, but it is important to note that service quality plays an important part in the development of relationships, especially in service industries (Chenet, Dagger and O'Sullivan, 2010).

- **Trust**—this refers to a customer's level of confidence in a company's ability to supply the required goods, and its reliability and integrity (Hunt, Morgan and Shelby, 1994). Trust is developed over time as customers base their perceptions and expectations on past purchase experiences. Trust plays a very important role in relationships, especially in an online setting. Building trust is a very effective way to increase satisfaction and subsequently develop commitment to long-term relationships (Geyskens, Steenkamp and Kumar, 1998; Selnes, 1998; Vlaga and Eggert, 2006; Hunt et al., 1994). It can also help weaker partners in a business relationship to gain power over time in their dealings with more powerful companies (Narayandas and Rangan, 2004). As a relationship develops, a customer may develop positive feelings about a company as he or she comes to rely on the credibility of a brand and the competency with which the goods and services are provided. When customers trust a brand, they are more likely to recommend it to others and also to continue to use the brand themselves (Adams, 2014).
- **Commitment**—this involves the extent to which customers seek to develop an enduring relationship with a company (Moorman, Zaltman and Deshpande, 1992), and is likely to affect their loyalty to a company. Commitment is a driver of loyalty, as some of the benefits of a committed relationship are reduced uncertainty, greater satisfaction and enhanced performance, through the synergies of an effective relationship. There are different types of commitment. Some customers can form emotional attachments to a brand, and this forms the basis of their commitment to a brand. For example, when food manufacturer Heinz used the slogan 'Beanz, Meanz, Heinz' to promote its baked beans in 1967, little did it realise that this would become one of the most enduring and long-lasting advertising slogans of all time (Gerges, 2012), and, arguably, it still acts as a mantra for committed loyal customers of the brand. Other customers base their commitment on more rational calculations: for example, some mobile phone companies offer contracts that bundle together benefits, including handsets and internet and telephone services, which provide an overall discount.
- **Satisfaction**—customers are likely to reflect on their experiences and evaluate the extent to which their choice has generated the results they wanted. There are many influences which might determine a customer's level of satisfaction, for example level of knowledge, prior experience, economic requirements and social influences (Geyskens, Steenkamp and Kumar, 1999).

From a buyer's (business and consumer) point of view, the proliferation of *choice* and the development of the online marketplace has made moving between competitors easier than ever before. When customers are faced with many alternatives while making purchasing decisions, they can switch between suppliers (Singh, Agrariya and Deepali, 2011), so the greater the number of suppliers and product choice the easier it becomes to change. Mobile phone operators use this knowledge and often develop *relational price incentives* (Berry, 2008) to encourage customers to move to a new network operator. European phone carrier EE, for example, includes unlimited calls, inclusive cloud storage, free music, data rollover, and a bundle of other services to retain and attract new customers. In this dynamic marketing environment, it becomes increasingly important for companies to seek ways to develop lasting relationships with their customers. In response to these changes, companies have begun to focus on how to develop long-term relationships.

Relationship Management and Managing Customer Relationships

Relationships can take different forms and achieve different levels of success for all parties concerned. At a very basic level, buyers and suppliers can engage in simple transactional relationships that centre on a single purchase, and neither party makes contact again after a sale is completed. For example, a business passenger at an international airport who needs road transportation will probably never meet the taxi driver again, and the choice of taxi supplier depends on the passenger's position in the queue rather than free choice. In this case, the exchange—cash for the journey—is a pure transaction; the driver knows that it is unlikely that there will ever be a repeat purchase (Egan, 1997; see also Coviello et al., 2002). Nowadays, this limited level of involvement is relatively rare, as most companies look for opportunities to begin to build a relationship. In the most light-touch relationships, there is usually a means of seeking redress in the case where the buyer wishes to complain about their purchase experience. Building on this approach, a company may actually contact the buyer to find out about the purchase experience in order to determine whether the customer expectation has been met. Online sellers like Amazon and Ebuyer send post-purchase surveys to poll customers' views and seek customers' reviews of the product and service. The more a seller commits to the notion of a *relationship* with its customers (in both business and consumer markets), the more inclined it is towards being proactive about the development of the relationship.

Ultimately, at the most engaged level of relationship building, buyer and supplier develop a partnership approach, and this results in working together for mutual benefit (McDaniel, 1998). Therefore, the nature of the relationship can increase the complexity of the task of managing relationships. No longer is it enough to just focus on the transactional element of a sale. New approaches are needed that move on from market-mix-based solutions towards those that are built on relationship development and the specific types of relationship (Harker and Egan, 2010).

Managing relationships is a key ingredient in successful organizational marketing. In practical terms, **relationship marketing** concerns the shifting from activities focusing on attracting customers to activities concerned with current customers and how to retain them. Customer retention is critical, since small changes in retention rates have significant effects on future revenues (Andreassen, 1995). At its core is the maintenance of relations between a company and its suppliers, channel intermediaries, the public and its customers.

Ultimately, the key idea is for companies to act to create customer loyalty so that a stable, mutually profitable and long-term relationship is developed (Ravald and Grönroos, 1996). Furthermore, loyal customers are likely to spend more than non-loyal customers and recommend a company to others. So, for relationship marketing to be successful, two essential conditions should be met:

1 A relationship should be a mutually rewarding connection between two or more parties.
2 The parties involved in the relationship should commit to the relationship over time and be willing to make adaptations to their own behaviour to maintain its continuity (Takala and Uusitalo, 1996).

Relationship marketing in services has attracted much attention in recent years as organizations focus their efforts on retaining existing customers rather than just attracting new ones. It is not a new concept, however, since the idea of a company earning customer loyalty was well known to the earliest merchants, who had the following saying: 'As a merchant, you'd better have a friend in every town' (Grönroos, 1994). From a marketing viewpoint, it is important to recognize that relationship marketing involves shifting away from activities concerned with attracting customers to activities that focus on current customers and how to retain them and convert them into loyal advocates of the brand (and/or company). Although the idea of relationship marketing can be applied to many industries, it is particularly important in services, where there is often direct contact between service provider and customer—for example, the client–agency relationship in the advertising industry, the relationship between a web service provider and its clients, and that between hotel staff and guests. See Marketing in Action 10.2 for further discussion of building communities in the web service industry.

The quality of the relationship is likely to determine the length of a relationship, levels of satisfaction and loyalty. Companies therefore need to decide when the practice of relationship marketing is most applicable. The following conditions suggest potential areas for the use of relationship marketing activities (Berry, 1995):

- where there is an ongoing or periodic desire for the service by the customer, e.g. insurance, banking, telephone, internet services
- where the customer controls the selection of a service provider, e.g. selecting a hotel, a restaurant, an entertainment provider or an airline.

There are situations where the supplier may have few competitors, and in these circumstances may feel it is less important to develop strong customer relationships—for example, utility providers such as gas, water and electricity companies, and health services. While there is some competition in these markets, the suppliers tend to hold the power and it is not always easy, affordable or viable for customers to switch suppliers.

We will now explore how to build a relationship and then the benefits of relationship marketing to organizations and customers, and the customer retention strategies used to build relationships and tie customers closer to companies.

How to Build Relationships

Once marketers have made the decision that it is appropriate to invest resources into building a relationship, they should also consider the degree of effort to put into relationship building. In most exchange relationships, there is some potential benefit to be gained from relationship development, and Sheth (2017) argues that emphasis should be placed on managing 'share of the heart' rather than 'share of the wallet' and also that relationship marketing practices such as loyalty programs, Key Account Management and Customer Relationship Management schemes have become universal and therefore commoditized. His solution is to focus on winning 'share of the heart', which involves close bonding with the customers in much the same way as you would develop a relationship with a friend.

The section on value creation highlighted some of the important features of close partnership relationships and highlighted how parties engaged in relationship development adapt their processes and products to achieve a better match with each other, and how they share information and experience, which reduces insecurity and uncertainty.

Sharing information is a good starting point for the development of a close connected relationship and for building a better atmosphere for future business (Zineldin, 1998). Many companies are using the internet to encourage their customers to share information. For example, John Deere, business-to-business supplier of agricultural machinery, uses social media sites (e.g. Facebook and Twitter) to communicate with farmers with similar interests around the world.

Effective relationship building can create opportunities to develop competitive advantage and is especially powerful if embedded within the culture of the organization. This makes it more difficult for competitors to copy (see O'Driscoll, 2006; Winklhofer, Pressey and Tzokas, 2006). Exchanging information is potentially a low-level approach to relationship building, so to create a more involved relationship-orientated culture a company needs to identify aspects of its business that could be considered part of a relationship-building strategy. There are several potential sources a company might consider.

Technical support

Technical support can take the form of research and development cooperation, before-sales or after-sales service, and providing training to the customer's staff. The supplier is thus enhancing the customer's know-how and productivity.

For example, leading European retailer of consumer electronics Dixons Carphone has developed strong relationships with its suppliers, and, consequently, suppliers trust Dixons Carphone to carry out repairs on high-tech equipment. Much learning, training and sharing of information has taken place, so that the retailer and manufacturers can ensure better service for the end consumer. So, retail customers with faulty goods can have repairs carried out through the retailer, and in doing so enjoy better service and faster turnaround times on repairs. This is an example of how strong relationships can benefit many companies in the supply chain.

Expertise

Suppliers can look for opportunities to provide expertise for their customers, which enables them to improve their service quality. The customer can benefit through acquiring extra skills at a minimal cost, the benefits of which they can pass on to their own customers.

For example, French cosmetics and beauty company L'Oreal Professionnel (Paris) develops specialist haircare products for salons and beauty specialist businesses. This business-to-business division provides specialist training for stylists and salon owners and shares the expertise it has built up over years of researching and developing new haircare products. L'Oreal has an extensive range of educational programmes which it offers to its customers, from learning about how to apply new hair care products to how to build and run a successful business in the beauty industry (see Exhibit 10.1).

EXHIBIT 10.1
L'Oreal provides training for stylists and salon owners

MARKETING IN ACTION 10.2
Most Valued People Award Helps Drive Umbraco's Success

Umbraco is an open source content management system (CMS) that offers solutions to the web industry. CMSs are important in the increasingly complex online world, where a website has become an essential part of a company's marketing presence. Additionally, most companies now have a website with links to social media platforms like Twitter, Instagram and Facebook. The result is that there are now more and more complex websites that need effective management of all the content, transactional elements and social media to achieve market goals.

Umbraco offers a solution that was created by Niels Hartvig, who developed a simple CMS framework at his first job at Snabel & Co in Denmark. From here, Niels developed a prototype, which was released in 2003. This proved to be very popular and has become widely adopted by leading retail brands, telecommunications companies, financial institutions, government and other public sector organizations, and others. Indeed, Umbraco currently ensures the smooth running of more than 400,000 major websites worldwide.

One contribution to Umbraco's success is that it was launched as an open source project—a method widely used in the software development industry to enable open access to products via a free licence, which enables and promotes collaboration.

Another contributing factor was Umbraco's Most Valued People (MVP) award, which has enabled Umbraco, not only to reward excellence in the software development community, but also to build a strong collaborative community of like-minded individuals. What makes Umbraco's MVP award unique is that nominations from amateurs and professionals alike are welcomed. The value of this approach is that the community can be expanded but, at the same time, Umbraco ensures that the project remains grounded and relevant to everyone's needs. The Umbraco community is quoted as being 'the friendliest CMS community on the planet' and is a great example of collaborative working on a global scale.

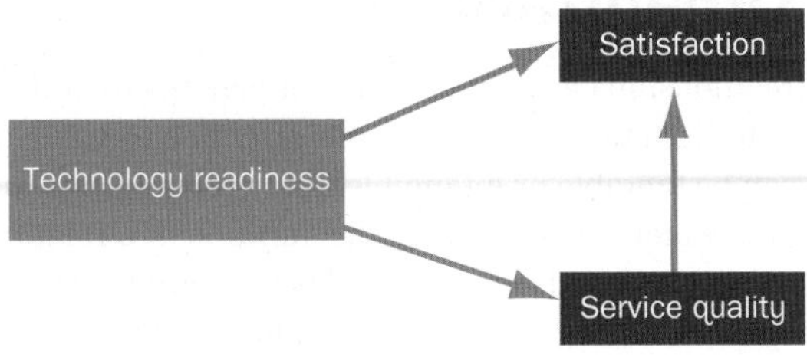

Based on: Vize et al (2013); Umbraco (2018)

Resource support

Suppliers can support the resource base of customers, for example by extending credit facilities, giving low-interest loans, agreeing to cooperative promotion and accepting reciprocal buying practices, where the supplier agrees to buy goods from the customer. The overall effect of these activities is a reduced financial burden for the customer.

Service levels

Suppliers can improve their relationships with customers by improving the level of service offered to them. This can involve providing more reliable delivery, fast or just-in-time delivery, setting up computerized reorder systems, offering fast, accurate quotes and reducing defect levels. In so doing, the customer gains by lower inventory costs, smoother production runs and lower warranty costs. By creating systems that link the customer to the supplier—for example, through recorder systems or just-in-time delivery—*switching costs* may be built in, making it more expensive to change supplier (Jackson, 1985). Advances in technology are providing opportunities to improve service levels. For example, BMW is using IBM's big data analytics technology to improve its repair and maintenance services as well as its products. IBM's predictive analytics can detect and fix potentially faulty elements of new cars, and BMW and IBM are working on ways to personalise in-car computing and driver support systems using Watson cognitive computing (Guerrini, 2016); see Exhibit 10.2.

EXHIBIT 10.2
BMW and IBM bring a whole new meaning to smart cars

Risk reduction

If a company is looking to acquire new customers, it may encounter resistance as target customers are familiar with their existing suppliers. So, to use risk reduction as part of a relationship-building strategy, a company should identify initiatives that enable it to show that there are low levels of risk in switching suppliers. This may involve free demonstrations, the offer of products for trial at zero or low cost to the customer, product and delivery guarantees, preventative maintenance contracts, swift complaint handling and proactive follow-ups. These activities are designed to provide customers with reassurance. Birds Eye, a European manufacturer of frozen foods, launched a new range of pasta and rice dishes called Stir Your Senses. To launch the product range, it ran a 'try me for free' campaign, giving away 1.6 million packs through leading UK supermarkets (IPM, 2015). Additionally, this product range has been developed by working with consumers to understand how the frozen food manufacturer can best cater for the changing needs of its customers. These products were developed to provide a hassle-free meal solution for busy consumers.

Benefits for the Organization

Ultimately, building a successful relationship can bring a range of benefits to both the supplier and the buyer. Social exchange theory (attributed to Homans, 1958) draws our attention to value and processes involved in an exchange relationship, which can be tangible or intangible. But, crucially, it is an evaluation of the balance between perceived costs and benefits which will determine the duration of a relationship. As relationships develop, a history of knowledge of past experiences builds up and, if all is favourable, trust and commitment will grow between parties in the exchange process (Dwyer et al., 1981) and, in this context, reciprocal value exists. The nature of the value is likely to be dependent on the context of the exchange and the benefits sought. Let's examine possible benefits for organizations and then consumers.

There are six major benefits to service companies in developing and maintaining strong customer relationships (Zeithaml, Bitner and Gremier, 2005).

1 *Increased purchases*: which help to develop trust between the company and the customer as they become more and more satisfied with the quality of services provided by the supplier.
2 *Lower cost*: the start-up costs associated with attracting new customers are likely to be far higher than the cost of retaining existing customers. Start-up costs include the time for making repeat calls in an effort to persuade a prospect to open an account, the advertising and promotional costs associated with making prospects aware of the company and its service offering, the operating costs of setting up accounts and systems, and the time costs of establishing bonds between the supplier and customer in the early stages of the relationship. Furthermore, costs associated with solving early teething problems and queries are likely to fall as the customer becomes accustomed to using the service.
3 *Lifetime value of a customer*: the lifetime value of a customer is the profit made on a customer's purchases over the lifetime of that customer. If a customer spends £80 in a supermarket per week, resulting in £8 profit, and uses the supermarket 45 times a year over 30 years, the lifetime value of that customer is £10,800. Thus, a bad service experience early on in this relationship which results in the customer defecting to the competition would be very expensive to the supermarket, especially when the costs of bad word of mouth are added, as this may deter other customers from using the store.
4 *Sustainable competitive advantage*: the intangible aspects of a relationship are not easily copied by the competition. For example, the friendships and high levels of trust that can develop as the relationship matures can be extremely difficult for competitors to replicate. This means that the extra value to customers that

derives from the relationship can be a source of sustainable competitive advantage for suppliers (Roberts, Varki and Brodie, 2003).

5 *Word of mouth*: word of mouth is very important in services due to their intangible nature which makes them difficult to evaluate prior to purchase. In these circumstances, potential purchasers often look to others who have experienced the service (e.g. a hotel, financial service) for personal recommendation. See Mini Case 10.1 for further discussion of the growing importance of online reviews. A company that has a large number of loyal customers is more likely to benefit from word of mouth than another without such a resource.

6 *Employee satisfaction and retention*: satisfied, loyal customers benefit employees in providing a set of mutually beneficial relationships and less hassle. This raises employees' job satisfaction and lowers job turnover. Employees can spend time improving existing relationships rather than desperately seeking new customers. This sets up a virtuous circle of satisfied customers leading to happy employees, which raises customer satisfaction even higher.

The net result of these six benefits of developing customer relationships is high profits. A study has shown across a variety of service industries that profits climb steeply when a company lowers its customer defection rate (Reichheld and Sasser Jr, 1990). Companies could improve profits significantly (depending on the industry) by reducing customer defections by as little as 5 per cent. The reasons are that loyal customers generate more revenue for more years, and the costs of maintaining existing customers are lower than the costs of acquiring new ones. An analysis of a credit card company revealed that improving the defection rate from 10 to 20 years increased the lifetime value of a customer from $135 to $300.

Benefits for the Customer

Entering a long-term relationship can also reap the following four benefits for the customer.

1 *Risk and stress reduction*: since the intangible nature of services makes them difficult to evaluate before purchase, relationship marketing can benefit the customer as well as the company. This is particularly so for services, which are personally important, variable in quality, complex and/or subject to high-involvement buying (Berry, 1995). Such purchases are potentially high risk in that making the wrong choice has severe negative consequences for the buyer. Banking, insurance, motor servicing and hairstyling are examples of services that exhibit some or all of the characteristics—importance, variability, complexity and high involvement—that would cause many customers to seek an ongoing relationship with a trusted service provider. Such a relationship reduces consumer stress, as the relationship becomes predictable, initial problems are solved, special needs are accommodated and the consumer learns what to expect. After a period, the consumer begins to trust the service provider, can count on a consistent level of quality service and feels comfortable in the relationship (Bitner, 1995).

2 *Higher-quality service*: experiencing a long-term relationship with a service provider can also result in higher levels of service. This is because the service provider becomes knowledgeable about the customer's requirements. For example, beauticians and hairstylists learn about the preferences of their clients. Knowledge of the customer built up over a series of service encounters facilitates the tailoring or customizing of the service to each customer's special needs.

3 *Avoidance of switching costs*: maintaining a relationship with a service supplier avoids the costs associated with switching to a new provider. Once a service provider knows a customer's preferences and special needs, and has tailored services to suit them, to change would mean educating a new provider and accepting the possibility of mistakes being made until the new provider has learnt to accommodate them. This results in both time and psychological costs to the customer. Bitner (1995) suggests that a major cost of relocating to a new geographic location is the need to establish relationships with unfamiliar service providers such as banks, schools, doctors and hairdressers.

4 *Social and status benefits*: customers can also reap social and status benefits from a continuing relationship with a supplier. Since many service encounters are also social encounters, repeated contact can assume personal as well as professional dimensions. In such circumstances, service customers may develop relationships resembling personal friendships. For example, hairdressers often serve as personal confidantes and restaurant managers may get to know some of their customers personally. Such personal relationships can feed a person's ego (status): for example, a hotel customer commented, 'When employees remember and recognize you as a regular customer, you feel really good' (Parasuraman, Berry and Zeithaml, 1991).

Developing Customer Retention Strategies

The potential benefits of developing long-term relationships with customers mean that it is worthwhile for organizations to consider designing customer retention strategies. This involves targeting customers for retention, bonding, internal marketing, promise fulfilment, building of trust and service recovery (see Figure 10.1).

While these retention strategies are important in both business-to-business and consumer markets, the following discussion gives examples from the consumer perspective.

Targeting customers for retention

Not all customers deliver benefits from relationship building—for example, habitual brand switchers who respond to the lowest priced deal available regardless of the brand, low spenders who may not generate sufficient revenue to justify the expense of acquiring them and maintaining the relationship and disruptive customers who may be so troublesome, and whose attitudes and behaviour may cause so much disruption to the service provider, that the costs of servicing them outweigh the benefits. Consequently, companies need to analyse their customers and identify those customers that they wish to engage in a long-term relationship, those for whom a transactional marketing approach is better suited and those with whom they would prefer not to do business. This is the classical market segmentation and targeting approach discussed in Chapter 7. The characteristics of those customers that are candidates for a relationship marketing approach are high-value, frequent-use, loyalty-prone customers for whom the actual and potential service offerings that can be supplied by the company have high utility.

Targeting customers for retention involves the analysis of loyalty- and defection-prone customers. Service suppliers need to understand why customers stay or leave, what creates value for them and their profile. Decisions can then be made regarding which types of customer defector they wish to try to save (e.g. price or service defectors) and the nature of the value-adding strategy that meets their needs, while at the same time maintaining bonds with loyalty-prone customers (Berry, 1995).

Bonding

Retention strategies vary in the degree to which they bond the parties together. One framework that illustrates this idea distinguishes between three levels of retention strategy based on the types of bond used to cement the relationship (Berry and Parasuraman, 1991).

- *Level 1*: at this level the bond is primarily through financial incentives, for example higher discounts on prices for larger-volume purchases, or loyalty points and associated tailored promotions which can result in lower future prices. The problem is that the potential for a sustainable competitive advantage is low, because price incentives are easy for competitors to copy even if they take the guise of frequent-flyer or loyalty points. Most airlines and retailers compete in this way, and consumers have learnt to join more than one scheme, which thus negates the desired effect.
- *Level 2*: this higher level of bonding relies on more than just price incentives, and, consequently, raises the potential for a sustainable competitive advantage. Level 2 retention strategies build long-term relationships through social as well as financial bonds, capitalizing on the fact that many service encounters are also social encounters. Customers become clients, the relationship becomes personalized and the service customized. Characteristics of this

FIGURE 10.1
Developing customer retention strategies

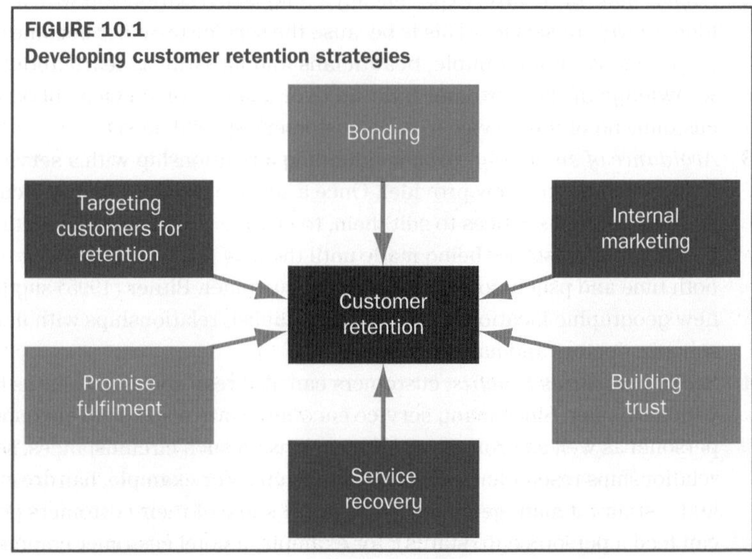

type of relationship include frequent communication with customers, providing continuity of service through the same person or people employed by the service provider, providing personal treatment like sending cards, and enhancing the core service with educational or entertainment activities such as seminars or visits to sporting events. Often hotels keep records of their guests' personal preferences, such as food allergies and requirements for non-smoking rooms. This builds a special bond between the hotel and its customers, who feel they are being treated as individuals. Increasingly, social media and other forms of digital communication are used to develop such relationships.
- *Level 3*: this top level of bonding is formed by financial, social and structural bonds. Structural bonds tie service providers to their customers through providing solutions to customers' problems that are designed into the service delivery system. For example, logistics companies often supply their clients with equipment that ties them into their systems. When combined with financial and social bonds, structural bonds can create a formidable barrier against competitor inroads and provide the basis for a sustainable competitive advantage.

Internal marketing

A fundamental basis for customer retention is high-quality service delivery. This depends on high-quality performance from employees, since the service product is a performance and the performers are employees (Berry, 1995). Internal marketing concerns training, communicating with and motivating internal staff. Staff need to be trained to be technically competent at their jobs as well as to handle service encounters with customers. To do this well, they must be motivated and understand what is expected of them. Service staff act as 'part-time marketers', since their actions can directly affect customer satisfaction and retention (Gummesson, 1987). Staff are critical in the 'moments of truth' when they and customers come into contact in a service situation.

A key focus of an internal marketing programme should be employee selection and retention. Service companies that suffer high rates of job turnover are continually employing new, inexperienced staff to handle customer service encounters. Employees that have worked for the company for years know more about the business and have had the opportunity to build relationships with customers. By selecting the right people and managing them in such a way that they stay loyal to the service organization, higher levels of customer retention can be achieved through the build-up of trust and personal knowledge gained through long-term contact with customers.

Promise fulfilment

The fulfilment of promises is a cornerstone for maintaining service relationships. This implies three key activities: *making* realistic promises initially and *keeping* those promises during service delivery by *enabling* staff and service systems to deliver on promises made (Bitner, 1995).

Making promises is done through marketing communications channels, for example the web, and more traditional advertising, selling and promotion, as well as the specific service cues that set expectations, such as the dress of the service staff and the design and décor of the establishment. It is important not to over-promise with marketing communications or the result will be disappointment and, consequently, customer dissatisfaction and defection. The promise should be credible and realistic. Some companies adhere to the adage 'under-promise and over-deliver'. For example, UK retailer John Lewis has made an enduring commitment to its customers that they can shop with confidence as the retailer operates a 'never knowingly undersold' policy. If a customer buys a product from John Lewis and finds that he or she could have bought it cheaper elsewhere, the retailer will refund the difference.

Keeping of promises occurs when the customer and the service provider interact—the 'moment of truth' mentioned earlier. Research has shown that customers judge employees on their ability to deliver the service right the first time, their ability to recover if things go wrong, how well they deal with special requests, and on their spontaneous actions and attitudes (see Bitner, Booms and Tetreault, 1990; Bitner, Booms and Mohr, 1994). These are clearly key dimensions that must play a part in a training programme and should be borne in mind when selecting and rewarding service staff. Not all service encounters are equal in importance, however. Research conducted on behalf of Marriott hotels has shown that events occurring early in a service encounter affect customer loyalty the most. Based on these findings, Marriott developed its 'first 10 minutes' strategy. It is hardly surprising that first impressions are so important, since before that the customer has had no direct contact with the service provider and is uncertain of the outcome. Marriott hotels has become an international market leader, with over 422 luxury destinations worldwide and plans for 40 more (Gollan, 2017) and customers' experiences are key to their future marketing strategy. See Exhibit 10.3 for Marriott's plans for Solaz, one of their latest luxury openings.

Enabling staff is a necessary condition for promises to be kept. This means that staff must have the skills, competences, tools, systems and enthusiasm to deliver. Some of these issues have been looked at in the earlier discussion of internal marketing, and are dependent on the correct recruitment, training and rewarding of staff, and on providing them with the right equipment and systems to do their jobs. Finally, we need to recognize that the keeping of promises does not depend solely on service staff and technology. Because service delivery is often in a group setting (e.g. a meal with friends or family in a restaurant, watching a film or travelling by air), the quality of the experience can be as dependent on the behaviour of other customers as on that of the service provider. Lovelock, Vandermerwe and Lewis (1999) label the problem customers 'jaycustomers'. These are people who act in a thoughtless or abusive way, causing problems for the organization, its employees and other customers. One kind of jaycustomer is the belligerent person who shouts abuse and threats at service staff because of some service malfunction. Staff need to be trained to develop the self-confidence and assertiveness required to deal with such situations, and to know what to do if the situation escalates beyond their control and more senior staff are required to be involved. Ultimately, the jaycustomer should be moved away from contact with other customers to minimize the discomfort of the latter.

EXHIBIT 10.3
Marriott's plans for Solaz, one of their latest luxury openings
Source: https://www.forbes.com/sites/douggollan/2017/12/10/marriott-international-will-open-40-luxury-hotels-in-2018/#c2a165469957

Building trust

Customer relationships *per se* depend on building trust. But trust is also a very important aspect of customer retention, particularly where the intangible nature of a service means that the customer can find it difficult to evaluate prior to purchase. Buying a service for the first time can leave the customer with a feeling of uncertainty and vulnerability, particularly when the service is personally important (see Chapter 9 for more detailed discussion of the impact of the characteristics of services). Consequently, when customers have developed trust in a supplier, they are often reluctant to switch to a new supplier and experience the uncomfortable feelings of uncertainty and vulnerability all over again.

Companies that wish to build up their trustworthiness should keep in touch with their customers by regular two-way communication to develop feelings of closeness and openness, provide guarantees to symbolize the confidence they feel in their service delivery, reduce their customers' perceived risk of purchase, and operate a policy of fairness and high standards of conduct with their customers (Berry, 1995).

Service recovery

Service recovery strategies should aim to solve problems and restore customers' trust in the company, and also improve the service system so that the problem does not recur (Kasper, van Helsdingen and Gabbott, 2006). Recovery is crucial, because if carried out effectively it can encourage customers to become advocates for a company and will reduce the likelihood of dissatisfied customers telling others of their negative experiences.

There are three important considerations when establishing a service recovery strategy:

1 *Set up a tracking system to identify system failures.* Customers should be encouraged to report service problems, since those customers that do not complain are the least likely to purchase again. Systems should be established to monitor complaints, follow up on service experiences (e.g. through the web, using feedback surveys, by phone) and provide opportunities for both service staff and customers to feed back on their experiences.
2 *Train and empower staff* to respond to service complaints. This is important, because research has shown that the successful resolution of a complaint can cause customers to feel more positive about the company than before the service failure.

The first response from a service provider to a genuine complaint is to apologize. Often this will take the heat out of the situation and lead to a spirit of cooperation rather than recrimination.

The next step is to attempt to solve the problem quickly. Marriott hotels facilitate this process by empowering frontline employees to solve customers' problems quickly, even though this may mean expense to the hotel, and without recourse to seeking approval from higher authority.

Other key elements in service recovery are to appear pleasant, helpful and attentive, show concern for the customer and to be flexible. Regarding problem resolution, service staff should provide information about the problem, take action and appear to put themselves out to solve the problem (Johnson, 1995).

It is important to note that while careful and appropriate handling of a complaint can result in a customer developing a positive attitude, if a second problem occurs, this effect (called the 'recovery paradox') disappears (Maxham and Netemeyer, 2002).

3 *Encourage learning among staff* so that service recovery problems are identified and corrected. Service staff should be motivated to report problems and solutions so that recurrent failures are identified and fixed. In this way, an effective service recovery system can lead to improved customer service, satisfaction and higher customer retention levels.

Customer retention is fundamental to the success of a modern company, and technology is now widely used to gather customer feedback and manage the whole of the customer experience. The remaining part of this chapter examines customer relationship management, focusing on relationship development in both consumer and business markets.

Technology-enhanced Customer Relationship Management

Customer relationships are increasingly managed using technology in consumer and business-to-business markets and, while Sheth (2017) considers such systems to be responsible for the commoditization of customer relationship, these systems are still very important to marketing efforts. Effective customer relationship management (CRM) begins by understanding the value, attitudes and behaviour of various customers and prospects, which might form part of a relationship marketing strategy. Rapid development of digital, mobile and remote computer technologies has enabled the development of highly sophisticated CRM systems that can manage relationships, interactions and customer journeys. These journeys include all the touchpoints where a customer interacts with a business and then creates a data collection point. CRM is seen by many marketers as the practical implementation of relationship marketing (Harker and Egan, 2010). 'CRM' is a term for the methodologies, technologies and e-commerce capabilities used by companies to manage customer relationships. CRM software packages aid the interaction between the customer and the company, enabling the company to coordinate all of the communication effort so that the customer is presented with a unified message and image.

CRM companies offer a range of IT-based services such as call centres, data analysis and website management. The basic principle behind CRM is that company staff have a single-customer point of view of each client. As customers are now using multiple channels more frequently, they may buy one product from a salesperson and another from a website. A website may provide product information, which is used to buy the product from a distributor. Interactions between a customer and a company may take place through the salesforce, call centres, websites, email and social media. However, it is important to ensure that data is gathered and shared effectively.

For example, Volvo Construction Equipment (Volvo CE) has built its reputation on producing high quality market-leading equipment and excellent customer support (Volvo Construction Equipment, 2015). In this business, relationships are very important and sales are primarily through local dealers. The company has been proactive about using the web as a way for customers to interact with the brand and submit enquiries through online forms on the website. But there was an issue because Volvo was only receiving limited feedback and a limited number of leads collected from the website; also, customers completing the online form merely received a simple 'thank you' message. It was decided that the company should try to make better use of internet technology to interact with customers, provide more dynamic information, automate the customer communication process and gather more data about customer interactions. Volvo CE had to devise a cost-efficient system to achieve its goals. The team's response was to create a process that evaluated the customer lifecycles and their online interactions using the newly implemented CRM system. Using customer data, the system was able to send relevant information to customers and up-to-date reports to dealers and internal staff.

Although the term 'CRM' is seen as referring to a recent management technology, the ideas and principles behind CRM are not new. Businesses have long practised some form of CRM. What sets present-day CRM apart is that companies now have an increased opportunity to use technology and manage one-to-one relationships with huge numbers of consumers. This is facilitated by companies such as Salesforce.com, IBM, SAP and Oracle.

Therefore, it is crucial that no matter how a customer contacts a company, all staff have instant access to the same data about the customer, such as his/her details and past purchases. This usually means the consolidation of the many databases held by individual departments in a company into one centralized database that can be accessed by all relevant staff on a computer screen. CRM is much more than simply the technology, as demonstrated by the E.ON CRM update in Marketing in Action 10.3.

Success factors in CRM

CRM projects have met with mixed success. As the customer journeys and experiences become a more important feature in marketing initiatives, so does the successful deployment of CRM systems and associated technologies.

MARKETING IN ACTION 10.3
E.ON, European Energy Supplier, Updates its CRM Systems

E.ON is a brand that supplies energy to residential and corporate clients in Europe. The brand was created with the merger of VEBA and VIAG—two large German corporations—in 2000 and it quickly entered US, UK and Swedish markets. Through a number of large acquisitions of Powergen (UK), Enel (Italy) and Endesa (Spain), E.ON was able to expand its operation significantly.

However, whilst E.ON was committed to providing 'cleaner and better energy' to its corporate and domestic clients, the technology it was using to facilitate the relationships was not delivering. Whilst CRM systems can deliver technology-enhanced relationships by managing the relationship at every touchpoint across a company, there are many aspects involved in effective customer management. E.ON faced difficulties, particularly in Scandinavia, as its CRM systems were out of date and difficult for employees to use. When selling energy in business-to-business markets, the stakes are high, the volumes are large and the agreements placed between supplier and buyer are highly complex. The problems facing E.ON salespeople in Sweden was that they could not develop a clear picture of customers' needs, due to the antiquated CRM system.

As a result, E.ON started to look for solution providers who could deliver a CRM technology solution. Stratiteq, an IT solution provider in Sweden, provided a CRM solution based on the Microsoft platform, which required a change in working practices at E.ON. Employees had to adapt to new ways of working and, in doing so, also realised the benefits offered from the new system. At the heart of the success of the implementation was the commitment and support provided by Stratiteq. The collaborative nature of the relationship enabled a successful roll-out of the technology and, as a result, E.ON was able to link together all aspects of its engagement with customers. The sales process is now streamlined and sales managers are able to review all the customer data in one place, which has significantly improved levels of service and customer relationships.

Based on: E.ON (2015); Stratiteq (2015)

It has been found that nearly half of CRM projects fail due to insufficient attention being paid to the *processes* involved and the function the system was designed to achieve. *People* can also create issues in the adoption of new CRM systems by resisting the use of the new technology or having a lack of adequate training. Many CRM systems have been found to fail due to lack of planning and clear objectives. Finally, about a third of CRM systems fail due to lack of suitable technology (Band, 2013).

Research has revealed that the following factors are associated with successful CRM implementations:

- having a customer orientation and organizing the CRM system around customers
- taking a single view of customers across departments, and designing an integrated system so that all customer-facing staff can draw information from a common database
- having the ability to manage cultural change issues that arise as a result of system development and implementation
- involving users in the CRM design process
- designing the system in such a way that it can readily be changed to meet future requirements
- having a board-level champion of the CRM project, commitment within each of the affected departments to the benefits of taking a single view of the customer, and an understanding of the need for common strategies—for example, prioritizing resources on profitable customers
- creating 'quick wins' to provide positive feedback on the project programmes
- ensuring face-to-face contact (rather than by paper or email) between marketing and IT staff
- piloting the new system before full launch.

Much of the development of CRM systems and solutions is being driven through digital marketing and customer experience initiatives, as customers expect to have instantaneous access to information. Consequently, it has become more of an imperative to ensure that CRM systems perform effectively, especially as they are being used in all business sectors. For example: in the not-for-profit sector, donations are increasingly being given by mobile phone and through social media platforms; retailers are selling more online; and airlines and other transport companies use mobile phones to supply travel updates (Frost and Sullivan, 2011). Social media is also taking a more important role as individuals share their experiences on everything from grocery shopping and eating out to engagement in large-scale fundraising campaigns such as #icebucketchallenge.

CRM systems are becoming progressively more complex as the number of potential **touchpoints** where a customer can interact with a company increases (see Figure 10.2). Touchpoints are where customers interact with

FIGURE 10.2
Touchpoints where customers might interact with a company

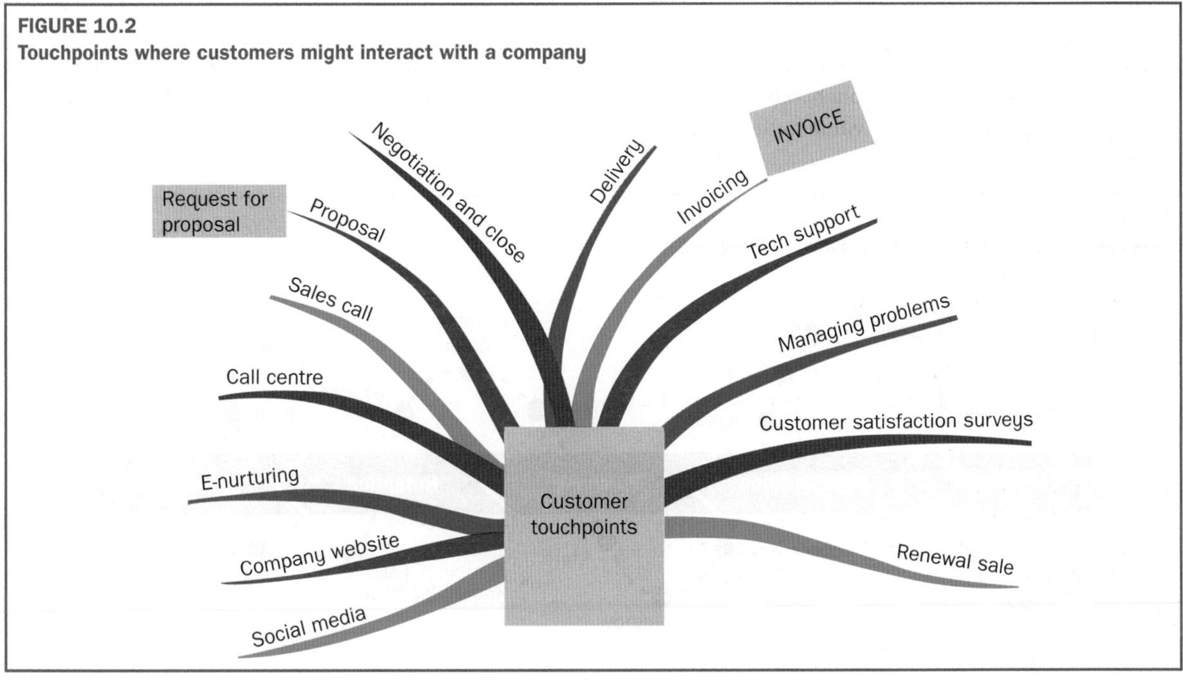

a company and data about their interactions can be gathered. Interactions with customers can be through physical human interactions, for example with customer service staff or sales representatives, or where customers interact virtually, for example through loyalty schemes, online reviews and search enquiries. Interactions can also occur at any stage in a customer journey and give rise to opportunities for companies to use the touchpoint productively. For example, a retailer might offer existing customers a future discount if they refer a friend through the company website, or on receipt of a delivery a customer might be encouraged to comment on the quality of the product and the delivery service.

As customers engage with companies through a variety of touchpoints, it becomes increasingly challenging to ensure the quality of the customer experience. Figure 10.3 shows a potential cross-channel touchpoint customer experience (Gill, 2014). Initially, customers may become aware of a new product or service through traditional channels, for example broadcast media, TV and radio. As they begin to consider, evaluate and move toward selecting a particular product, they may move over to digital channels, for example online reviews and blogs. Once customers are ready to make a purchase, they may choose from various channels, for example online, in store or through a direct mail catalogue. After the sale is complete, customers may seek advice about how to use their product, for example through an online FAQs database, or comment on their experience in a forum. Finally, they might become an advocate for their chosen product and make future purchases, read newsletters, and even write a blog post about their experiences.

Cross-channel touchpoints test companies who wish to manage their customers' journeys to ensure a uniform experience. Many brands struggle to provide a seamless customer experience. For example, Gap offers its customers a flexible click-and-collect service to pick up their online orders through any of the group's stores, such as Gap, Old Navy and Banana Republic. But, when it comes to returning goods, customers must take the returns back to the specific store selling the brand they have purchased. The problem for retailers is reverse logistics—in other words, getting the goods back where the stock was originally held, especially if a retailer manages online and offline stock through different locations (Gill, 2014), and customers are left struggling to work out where to return their goods.

Air Canada is another example where there are breaks in the cross-channel customer experience: its customers can book flights via mobile devices, but cannot amend the details or change flights via any digital touchpoints. Customers wishing to make changes must use the telephone. As a result, the cross-channel experience can be frustrating rather than rewarding.

So, how can companies manage multiple cross-channel touchpoints and use their CRM systems effectively? According to research (Gill, 2014), companies should consider the overall customer experience and aim to 'identify, design, implement and optimise end-to-end customer journeys'. In order to do this, they should aim to follow three rules (Gill, 2014).

1 **Do not try to please everyone**. Marketing managers should aim to concentrate on creating high-value experiences which involve touchpoints that create meaningful journeys for target customers. They should also identify tasks that add value to the experience.

FIGURE 10.3
Touchpoints in a cross-channel customer journey

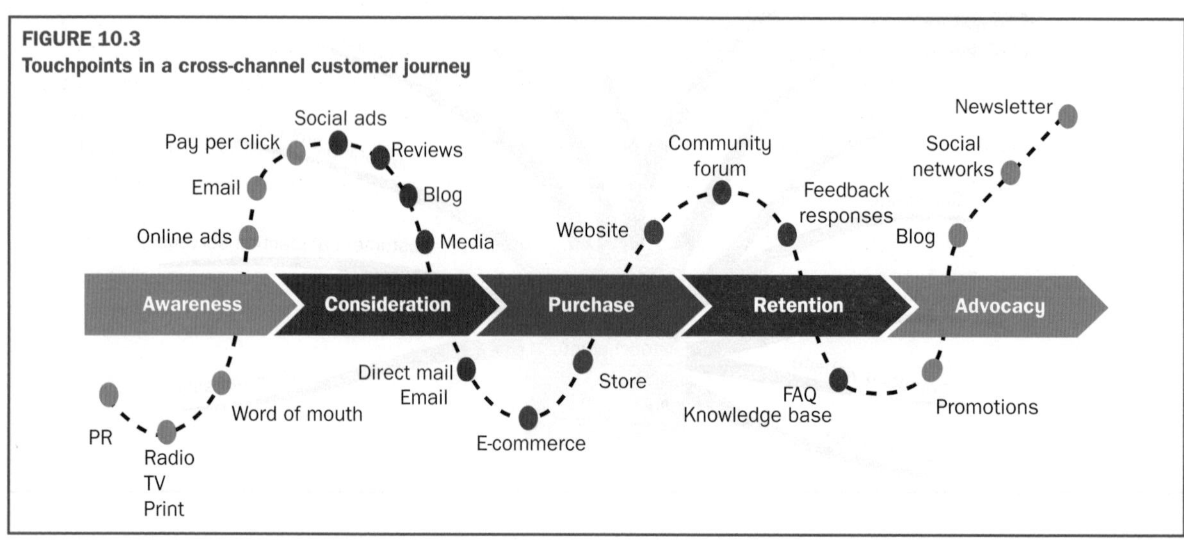

For example, Starbucks has developed a cross-touchpoint experience for its tech-savvy customers. It uses sophisticated software and GPS positioning to push time-specific offers to its customers in particular locations. The aim is to increase footfall in Starbucks coffee shops. The My Starbucks app enables pre-payment and acts as a point-of-sale using QR codes and also links to an individual's loyalty data to be used for future promotions.

Finally, the focus should also be on a frequently occurring task, as it is not viable to try to streamline every customer journey. For example, Debenhams has integrated its mobile app with its e-commerce site so that it can ensure a seamless mobile-to-store-to-web customer shopping journey.

2 **Optimise the journey, not the touchpoint**. Marketing managers responsible for mapping customer journeys have to decide which channels and technologies will provide the best customer journey. They should also ensure that each touchpoint is deemed important.

Prisma, one of Finland's most advanced online retailers, designed its customer journey by mapping out a series of common touchpoints that shoppers wanted to use. The journey maps showed how customers used mobile phones, the web and physical stores; when the maps were combined with historical customer data, the retailer was able to improve the customer experience.

Ultimately, the marketer should aim to understand how an individual touchpoint contributes to the total customer journey.

3 **Manage the transitions**. Marketing managers should look for innovative ways to move customers from one touchpoint to another and across channels. One way to achieve this is to make sure that the customer is in control. So, if customers need to move from the digital to physical space, for example in getting their eyes tested and buying a pair of glasses, the online appointment system should ensure that there is sufficient choice of appointment times. The earlier Starbucks example demonstrates how to link the digital and physical space using a mobile device.

As customers become more connected and more familiar with using multiple touchpoints, it will become increasingly important for all companies to manage their customer journeys effectively in order to deliver a seamless customer experience.

Relationship Marketing—Summary

In summary, relationship marketing has grown in importance in the last two decades, largely because of increased competition and wider application of technology-based CRM systems and growing user acceptance of digital technologies. The emerging generation of digitally savvy customers has raised customer expectations of what it means to engage with a brand and they have also widened opportunities to get involved in co-creation activites. The implication of change is that companies seek to build closer long-term relationships with their customers, unlike in the past when short-term transactional relationships sufficed.

For a company to become successful in its application of relationship marketing, it must be able to manage customer expectations and experiences in such a way that there are opportunities to deliver added value. There are various types of relationship management which a company should be aware of if it is to successfully shift attention away from physical products towards customers. Furthermore, customer retention is important in creating a long-term relationship. From a practical point of view, relationships can be built through the use of technical support, expertise and high levels of service, and can result in long-term benefits for a company, for example a sustainable competitive advantage and lower operating costs.

Technology is central to CRM, and CRM systems are often seen as the practical application of relationship marketing. CRM systems are used in both consumer- and business-facing industries.

Review

1 **Value creation**
- Companies engage in value creation when they enter exchanges with their customers and this is central to building relationships. Co-creation of value involves information sharing to aid supplier learning, supplier development and strategic knowledge sharing.

2 **The key concepts of relationship marketing**
- The concepts are: relationship quality, service quality, trust, satisfaction, commitment and loyalty.

3 **The nature of relationship marketing and how to build customer relationships**
- Relationship marketing concerns the shift from activities associated with attracting customers to activities concerned with current customers and how to retain them. A key element is the building of trust between buyers and sellers.
- Relationship building can be enhanced by the provision of customer services, including giving technical support, expertise, resource support, improving service levels and using risk-reduction strategies.

4 **Value and relational networks**
- People and the roles they play within the network.
- A network is a term used to describe a set of connections among people, which, from a marketing perspective, might be used as a resource to solve problems, share knowledge and extend the network.

5 **Types of relationship management**
- Relationships can take different forms. There are four key types of relationship:
  1) Classic market relationships: supplier–customer, supplier–customer–competitor and the physical distribution network.
  2) Special market relationships, such as between the customer as a member of a loyalty programme and the interaction in the service encounter.
  3) Relationships with the economy and society in general.

6 **The management of customer relationships**
- This concerns focusing a company's activities on building long-term relationships and identifying opportunities for relationship development, for example where there is a desire from the customer for delivery of an ongoing service, where the customer makes a choice of service provider or where the customer has many alternative suppliers to choose from.

7 **Building customer relationships**
- Effective relationships can be a source of competitive advantage and are developed through a number of different operational aspects of a business: technical support, expertise, resource support, service levels and risk reduction.

8 **Benefits to the organization**
- Engaging in relationship management can deliver a number of benefits to the organization: increased purchases, lower costs, lifetime value of a customer, sustainable competitive advantage, employee satisfaction and retention.

9 **Benefits to the customer**
- For relationships to work, there should be mutual benefits for all parties involved in the relationship.
- For the customer, potential benefits are: stress reduction, higher quality service, avoidance of switching costs, social and status benefits.

10 Customer retention strategies are central to the marketing effort of relationship marketing

- Customer retention involves the targeting of customers for retention, bonding, internal marketing, promise fulfilment, building of trust and service recovery.

11 Technology-enhanced customer relationship management (CRM)

- Technology is key to the development of successful relationships.
- CRM systems are technology-based solutions that facilitate interactions between the customer and the company, enabling the company to coordinate all of the communication effort so that the customer is presented with a unified message and image.
- Cross-channel customer journeys occur when customers interact with different channels during the purchasing process.

Key Terms

commitment a process whereby individuals (and companies) establish a bond to reduce negative aspects of a relationship

customer relationship management (CRM) a term for the methodologies, technologies and e-commerce capabilities used by companies to manage customer relationships

loyalty a term used to explain repeated purchasing behaviour

relationship marketing the process of creating, maintaining and enhancing strong relationships with customers and other stakeholders

satisfaction an indicator of the extent to which customer expectations have been met. As a concept, it is important to long-term relationship building

service quality involves the experience a customer has of a company's offer. Services vary in complexity and the investment and risk a customer makes in the purchase

touchpoints points at which a customer interacts with a company across a customer journey and where data can be collected

trust a customer's level of confidence in a company's ability to supply the required goods; its reliability and integrity

Study Questions

1. **Explain the concept of value from a relationship marketing perspective.**
2. **Why is relationship management important in many supplier–customer interactions?**
3. **How can suppliers build close relationships with organizational customers?**
4. **How are millennials different from other target segments and in what ways should marketers adapt their strategies to build relationships with this generation?**
5. **What are the benefits derived from engaging in a relationship for a) the organization, b) the customer?**
6. **To what extent is technology involved in the development of successful relationships?**
7. **Is social media a tool which can be harnessed to facilitate relationships? Discuss the pros and cons.**
8. **Why is customer retention important in relationship marketing?**
9. **Suggest how CRM can be used to develop customer relationships.**
10. **Discuss the importance of touchpoints in a cross-channel customer journey.**

Recommended Reading

Relationships are everything. Read more:

Vargo, S. and Lusch, R. (2010), It's all B2B . . . and beyond: toward a system perspective of markets, *Industrial Marketing Management* 40(11), 181–7.

References

Adams, M. (2014), Three ways to build customer trust, *Forbes*, 22 April.

Albert, N., Merunka, D. and Valette-Florence, P. (2013), Brand passion: Antecedents and consequences, *Journal of Business Research* 63, 904–9.

Andreassen, T.W. (1995), Small, High Cost Countries' Strategy for Attracting MNC's Global Investments, *International Journal of Public Sector Management* 8(3), 110–18.

Band, W. (2013), How to succeed with CRM: The Critical Success Factors http://blogs.forrester.com/william_band/13-07-31-how_to_succeed_with_crm_the_critical_success_factors (accessed 20 April 2015).

Barton, C., Fromm, J. and Egan, C. (2012), *The Millennial Consumer: Debunking Stereotypes*, The Boston Consulting group https://www.bcg.com/documents/file103894.pdf.

Berry, L.L. (1995), Relationship Marketing of Services—Growing Interest, Emerging Perspectives, *Journal of the Academy of Marketing Science* 23(4), 236–45.

Berry, L.L. (1995), Relationship Marketing, in Payne, A., Christopher, M., Clark, M. and Peck, H. (eds), *Relationship Marketing for Competitive Advantage*, Oxford: Butterworth-Heinemann, 65–74.

Berry, L.L. (2008), Relationship Marketing Perspectives 1983 and 2000, *Journal of Relationship Marketing* 1(1), 59–77.

Berry, L.L. and Parasuraman, A. (1991), Marketing Services, New York: Free Press, 136–42.

Berry, L.L., Shostak, G.L. and Upah, G.D. (eds.) (1983), *Emerging Perspectives on Services Marketing*, Chicago, IL: American Marketing Association.

Bitner, M.J. (1995), Building Service Relationships: It's All About Promises, *Journal of the Academy of Marketing Science* 23(4), 246–51.

Bitner, M.J., Booms, B.H. and Mohr, L.A. (1994), Critical Service Encounters: The Employee's View, *Journal of Marketing* 58, October, 95–106.

Bitner, M.J., Booms, B.H. and Tetreault, M.S. (1990), The Service Encounter: Diagnosing Favourable and Unfavourable Incidents, *Journal of Marketing* 43, January, 71–84.

Centrum för Tjänsteforskning (2015), *Value Creation Through Service*, Sweden: Karlstad University.

Chenet, P., Dagger, T. and O'Sullivan, D. (2010), Service quality, trust, commitment and service differentiation, *Journal of Services Marketing* 24, 336–46.

Ciborra, C. (1991), Alliances as learning experiments: cooperation, competition and change in high-tech industries, in Mytelka, L.K. (ed.), *Strategic partnerships and the world economy*, 51–77.

Coviello, N.E., Brodie, R.J., Danaker, P.J. and Johnson, W.J. (2002), How Firms Relate to Their Markets: An Empirical Examination of Contemporary Marketing Practices, *Journal of Marketing* 66, July, 33–46.

Dwyer, F.R. and Walker, O.C. (1981), Bargaining in an asymmetrical power structure, Journal of Marketing, 45 (Winter): 104–15.

Edvardsson, B., Tronvall, B. and Gruber, T. (2011), Expanding understanding of service exchange and value co-creation: a social construction approach, *Journal of the Academy of Marketing Science* 39(2), 327–39.

Egan, C. (1997), Relationship Management, in Jobber, D. (ed.) *The CIM Handbook of Selling and Sales Strategy*, Oxford: Butterworth-Heinemann, 55–88.

Ellis-Chadwick, F. (2013), *History of Online Retail*, Open University.

E-ON (2015), E-On History 2000–2014 http://www.eon.com/en/about-us/profile/history/2000-2015.html (accessed June 2015).

Frost & Sullivan (2011), A smarter approach to CRM, IBM https://www-935.ibm.com/services/uk/gbs/pdf/SMW03042WWEN.PDF.

Gerges, D. (2012), Beanz Meanz Heinz beats out Nike's Just Do It to be named top advertising slogan of all time, *The Daily Mail*, 26 January.

Geyskens, I., Steenkamp, J.B.E.M. and Kumar, N. (1998), Generalizations About Trust in Marketing Channel Relationships Using Meta-Analysis, *International Journal of Research in Marketing* 15, 223–48.

Geyskens, I., Steenkamp, J.B.E.M. and Kumar, K. (1999), A meta-analysis of Satisfaction in Marketing Channel Relationships, *Journal of Marketing Research* 36, 223–38.

Gill, M. (2014), Manage The Cross-Touchpoint Customer Journey http://www.genesys.com/resources/Manage_The_Cross_Touchpoint_Customer_Journey.pdf (accessed 20 April 2015).

Gollan, D. (2017), Marriott International will open 40 luxury hotels in 2018, *Forbes* 10 December https://www.forbes.com/sites/douggollan/2017/12/10/marriott-international-will-open-40-luxury-hotels-in-2018/#c2a165469957 (accessed December 2016).

Grönroos, C. (1994), From Marketing Mix to Relationship Marketing: Towards a Paradigm Shift in Marketing, *Management Decision* 32(2), 4–20.

Grönroos, C. and Voima, P. (2012), Critical service logic: making sense of value creation and co-creation, *Journal of Academy of Marketing Science* 41(1), 133–50.

Guerrini, F. (2016), BMW partners with IBM to add Watson computing capabilities to its cars, *Forbes* 15 December https://www.forbes.com/sites/federicoguerrini/2016/12/15/bmw-partners-with-ibm-to-add-watsons-cognitive-computing-capabilities-to-its-cars/#7b748cbd1a90 (accessed December 2016).

Gummesson, E. (1987), The New Marketing–Developing Long-term Interactive Relationships, *Long Range Planning* 20, 10–20.

Gummesson, E. (2002), Relationship Marketing in the New Economy, *Journal of Relationship Marketing* 1(1), 37–57.

Hammervoll, T. (2009), Value-creation logic in supply chain relationships, *Journal of Business to Business Marketing* 16(3), 220–41.

Hammervoll, T. (2012), Managing interaction for learning and value creation in exchange relationships, *Journal of Business Research* 65(2), 128–36.

Harker, M. and Egan, J. (2010), The past, present and future of relationship marketing, *Journal of Marketing Management* 2(1), 215–42.

Harmeling, C.M., Moffett, J.W., Arnold, M.J. and Carlson, B.D. (2017), Toward a theory of customer engagement marketing, *Journal of the Academy of Marketing Science*, 1–24.

Homans, G.C. (1958), Social behavior as exchange, *American Journal of Sociology* 63: 597–606.

Hunt, R., Morgan, M. and Shelby, D. (1994), The Commitment-Trust Theory of Relationship Marketing, *Journal of Marketing*, July, 58(3), 20–39.

IPM (2015), Birds Eye runs 'Try Me Free' on 1.6m 'Stir Your Senses' packs http://www.theipm.org.uk/news/2015/02/birds-eye-runs-try-me-free-on-16m-stir-your-senses-packs (accessed 14 April 2015).

Jackson, B.B. (1985), Build Customer Relationships that Last, *Harvard Business Review*, Nov–Dec, 120–25.

Johnson, R. (1995), Service Failure and Recovery: Impact, Attributes and Process, in Swartz, T.A., Bowen, D.E. and Brown, S.W. (eds.) *Advances in Services Marketing and Management* 4, 52–65.

Jones, M., Reynolds, K., Arnold, M., Gabler, C., Gillison, S. and Landers, V. (2015), Exploring consumers' attitude towards relationship marketing, *Journal of Services Marketing*, 29(3), 188–99 https://doi.org/10.1108/JSM-04-2014-0134.

Kasper, H., van Helsdingen, P. and Gabbott, M. (2006), *Services Marketing Management*, Chichester: Wiley, 528.

Kotler, P. (1991), Philip Kotler Explores the New Marketing Paradigm, *Marketing Science Institute Review*, Spring, 1, 4–5.

Liozu, S. (2017), Customer Value is not just created, its formally managed, *Journal of Creating Value* 3(2) https://doi.org/10.1177%2F2394964317728136.

Lovelock, C.H., Vandermerwe, S. and Lewis, B. (1999), *Services Marketing—A European Perspective*, New York: Prentice-Hall, 176.

Lusch, R., Vargo, S. and Tanniru, M. (2010), Service, value networks and learning, *Journal of the Academy of Marketing Science*, 38, 19–31.

Maheshwari, S. (2013), How millennials are described by public companies to wall street, available at: www.buzzfeed.com/sapna/what-public-companies-are-telling-wall-street-about-millenni (accessed 13 March 2014).

Maxham III, J.G. and Netemeyer, R.G. (2002), A Longitudinal Study of Complaining Customers' Evaluations of Multiple Service Failures and Recovery Efforts, *Journal of Marketing* 66, October, 57–71.

McDaniel, S.W. (1998), The Seven Habits of highly effective marketers, *Federal Highway Administration*, Nov/Dec, 62 (3).

McGarry, E. (1953), Some viewpoints in marketing, *Journal of Marketing* 17(3), 36–43.

Merz, Michael A., Zarantonello, L. and Grappi, S. (2018), How valuable are your customers in the brand value co-creation process? The development of a Customer Co-Creation Value (CCCV) scale, *Journal of Business Research*, 82, issue C, 79–89 https://EconPapers.repec.org/RePEc:eee:jbrese:v:82:y:2018:i:c:p:79–89.

Moorman, C., Zaltman, G. and Deshpande, R. (1992), Relationships between providers and users of market research: The dynamics of trust within and between organizations, *Journal of Marketing Research*, 29, 314–29.

Narayandas, D. and Rangan, V.K. (2004), Building and Sustaining Buyer–Seller Relationships in Mature Industrial Markets, *Journal of Marketing*, 68 (July), 63–77.

O'Driscoll, A. (2006), Reflection on Contemporary Issues in Relationship Marketing: Evidence from a Longitudinal Case Study in the Building Materials Industry, *Journal of Marketing Management* 22(1/2), 111–34.

Parasuraman, A., Berry, L.L. and Zeithaml, V.A. (1991), Understanding Customer Expectations of Service, *Sloan Management Review*, Spring, 39–48.

Ravald, A. and Grönroos, C. (1996), The Value Concept and Relationship Marketing, *European Journal of Marketing* 30(2), 19–30.

Reichheld, F.F. and Sasser Jr, W.E. (1990), Zero Defections: Quality Comes to Services, Sept.–Oct., 105–11.

Roberts, K., Varki, S. and Brodie, R. (2003), Measuring the Quality of Relationships in Consumer Services: An Empirical Study, *European Journal of Marketing* 37(1/2), 169–96.

Selnes, F. (1998), Antecedents and Consequences of Trust and Satisfaction in Buyer–Seller Relationships, *European Journal of Marketing* 32(3/4), 305–22.

Sheth, J. (2017), Revitalizing relationship marketing, *Journal of Services Marketing*, 31(1), 6-10 https://doi.org/10.1108/JSM-11-2016-0397.

Singh, A., Agrariya, K. and Singh, D. (2011), What Really Defines Relationship Marketing? A Review of Definitions and General and Sector-Specific Defining Constructs, *Journal of Relationship Marketing* 10(4), 203–37.

Simonson, I. and Rosen, E. (2014), What Marketers Must Understand about Online Reviews, *Harvard Business Review*.

Starbucks (2015a), C.A.F.E Practices http://gr.starbucks.com/en-US/_Social+Responsibility/_Social+Responsibilities/C.A.F.E+Practices.htm (accessed 18 April 2015).

Starbucks (2015b), Starbucks and the Schultz Family Foundation Give Young Job Seekers a Roadmap to Opportunity. https://news.starbucks.com/news/starbucks-and-schultz-family-foundation-give-young-job-seekers-a-roadmap (accessed 18 April 2015).

Stratiteq (2015), Corporate home page http://www.stratiteq.com (accessed September 2018).

Takala, T. and Uusitalo, O. (1996), An Alternative View of Relationship Marketing: A Framework for Ethical Analysis, *European Journal of Marketing* 30(2), 45–60.

Umbraco (2018), http://umbraco.com/about-us/history accessed November 2018.

Vargo, S.L. and Lusch, R.F. (2004), The Four Service Marketing Myths, *Journal of Service Research* 6(4), 324–35.

Vize, R. (2012), *Exploring Relationship Quality (RQ) in an online B2B retail context: A Structural Equation Modelling Approach*, Dublin: Dublin Institute of Technology.

Vize, R., Coughlan, J., Kennedy, A. and Ellis-Chadwick, F. (2013), Technology readiness in a b2B online retail context: an examination of antecedents and outcomes, *Industrial Marketing Management* 42(6), 909–18.

Vlaga, W. and Eggert, A. (2006), Relationship Value and Relationship Quality, *European Journal of Marketing* 40(3/4), 311–27.

Volvo Construction Equipment (2015), Volvo CE shortlisted for prestigious innovation award http://www.volvoce.com/constructionequipment/corporate/en-gb/press_room/articles/company_stories/pages/innovation_award.aspx (accessed March 2015).

Wenger, E., Trayner, B. and de Latt, M. (2011), *Promoting and assessing, value creation in communities and networks: a conceptual framework*, Dutch Ministry of Education.

Wilson, M. (2014), Can Starbucks Make 23,000 Coffee Shops Feel Unique? http://www.fastcodesign.com/3034441/starbucks-secrets-to-make-every-store-feel-unique (accessed 18 April 2015).

Winklhofer, H., Pressey, A. and Tzokas, N. (2006), A Cultural Perspective of Relationship Orientation: Using Organizational Culture to Support a Supply Relationship Orientation, *Journal of Marketing Management* 22(1/2), 169–94.

Zeithaml, V.A., Bitner, M.J. and Gremier, D.D. (2005), *Services Marketing*, New York: McGraw-Hill, 174–78.

Zineldin, M. (1998), Towards an Ecological Collaborative Relationship Management: A 'Co-operative Perspective', *European Journal of Marketing* 32(11/12), 1138–64.

CASE 19

Starbucks: Managing Customer Relationships One Cup At a Time

Starbucks is on a roll. The company, which has over 21,000 stores in 65 different countries, reported record net revenue of US$22.39 billion for the fiscal year 2017 (an increase of 5 per cent from the previous year). The company that provides you with delicious (if pricey) coffee as well as free Wi-Fi is trying to provide you with something else—a personal relationship. So far, it seems to be succeeding.

Starbucks famously described its vision of reaching its customers as 'one neighbourhood, one person and one cup at a time'. And thanks to its effective use of digital marketing, social media, customer relationships and technology management, the company is doing just that.

Starbucks appears to be one of the few companies that truly understands the intricate triangulation between consumers, a product and social media, and how the three, when successfully managed, can increase a brand's profile and develop a relationship between that brand and a customer (while, at the same time, generating higher sales). As proof of Starbucks getting its customer relationship management right, a reported nine out of ten people who use Facebook are either fans of Starbucks or know somebody who is.

Starbucks, for quite some time now, has been at the cutting edge of incorporating the latest technological developments into its operations, allowing it to almost seamlessly merge its brick and mortar stores with the numerous digital marketing channels available. The company has also been adept at developing relationships with its customers, using the latest online innovations and social media platforms. Starbucks is adamant when it says that the purpose of new technology is not just to improve its website or to process payments more quickly for people who are queueing up. It is really about getting in touch with its customers and trying to better understand them, so as to improve service levels and their experience with the brand. As a sign of its commitment, the company has reportedly taken all the money that it used to spend on traditional media outlets and shifted it into digital and social media marketing in an effort to deepen and consolidate its relationship with its customers.

Experts believe that, when trying to build or protect customer relationships, there are certain rules of etiquette that should be respected. One important principle is to engage with customers on their own terms and to the degree that they want to be engaged with. 'Pushing' an ad in this always-connected age really does not work, especially with the generation known as millennials, who were basically born into a world of social media. Today, the expectation for many is that they will 'invite' a brand or product into their lives, while at the same time actively resisting something that was 'forced' upon them. As with any relationship, 'desperation' is the world's worst cologne.

In the spring of 2018, Starbucks tweaked its relationship marketing strategy again, saying that it was moving away from 'a short-term "one and done" focus to a sustained platform, ongoing relationship focus with [its] customers.' One part of this renewed emphasis on relationship building was the company's decision to allow all customers to place orders using its mobile apps. Previously, this feature was the exclusive domain of people who were registered in the Starbucks rewards programme and had personal customer accounts that were preloaded with money. There are 15 million registered users in the rewards programme, and it is a vital source of revenue. In fact, most of the same-store year-on-year sales growth has come from the rewards programme's mobile app. According to Chief Financial Officer (CFO) Scott Maw, by encouraging more people to download the pay and order app, the company will gain access to critical email addresses and smart phone information. This will allow for more customized ads targeted at a whole new group of consumers, allowing for better promotion of the Starbucks brand, in addition to a more personalized customer relationship.

Another key element in Starbucks' successful relationship development is the quality of recruitment of new employees and the emphasis that it puts on training and excellence. If you were to ask top management at Starbucks, 'What is your main product?', the answer would not be fine coffee. Rather, Starbucks sees itself as a purveyor of a unique 'experience' (much like McDonald's, which sees itself as, not just providing hamburgers, but rather a service experience). And that experience (and by extension, the relationship with the customer) is built on employees 'creating meaningful moments of connection more than 70 million times every week' with the people who visit Starbucks. The company says that it is committed to developing 'new choices and experiences that surprise and delight our customers at every interaction' in an effort to better serve them as well as develop a relationship with them.

One cup of coffee at a time.

Questions

1. **What are some of the ways in which Starbucks 'engages' its consumers in customer relationships?**
2. **How can an understanding of digital marketing and social media help companies gain a competitive advantage when it comes to customer relationship management?**
3. **Analyse the methods used by Starbucks and explain how the company has been successful in increasing its brand recognition, while at the same time improving its customer relationship management.**

This case study was written by Tom McNamara and Irena Descubes, Rennes School of Business, Rennes-France.

References

Based on: Wharton (2014), Brand Challenge: Is There a 'Recipe' for Going Viral?, Knowledge@Wharton, Opinion North America, 19 September http://knowledge.wharton.upenn.edu/article/is-there-a-recipe-for-going-viral; Divol, R., Edelman, D. and Sarrazin, H. (2012), Demystifying social media, *McKinsey Quarterly*, April, https://www.mckinsey.com/business-functions/marketing-and-sales/our-insights/demystifying-social-media; Moth, D. (2014), Eight awesome social campaigns from Starbucks, Econsultancy, 13 February https://econsultancy.com/blog/64328-eight-awesome-social-campaigns-from-starbucks; Digital Strategy Consulting (2014), Facebook investigated for secret experiment, Digital Strategy Consulting, July 3 http://www.digitalstrategyconsulting.com/intelligence/2014/07/facebook_investigated_for_secret_experiment.php; Fitgerald, M. (2013), How Starbucks Has Gone Digital, *MIT Sloan Management Review*, 4 April http://sloanreview.mit.edu/article/how-starbucks-has-gone-digital; Sivitz, L. and Holup, M. (2012), Inside Starbucks Digital Marketing—Going 'Beyond The Big, Seattle 24x7, 23 November https://www.seattle24x7.com/community/shoptalk/2012/11/23/starbucks-digital-marketing-going-beyond-the-big-idea/; Bold, B. (2014), Starbucks admits opening brand to social media is 'doubled-edged sword', *Marketing Magazine* UK, 7 February http://www.marketingmagazine.co.uk/article/1301515/starbucks-admits-opening-brand-social-media-doubled-edged-sword; Allison, M. (2013), Starbucks presses social media onward, *The Seattle Times*, 27 April http://seattletimes.com/html/businesstechnology/2020862483_starbuckssocialxml.html; Statista (2018), Revenue of Starbucks worldwide from 2003 to 2017 (in billion US dollars), https://www.statista.com/statistics/266466/net-revenue-of-the-starbucks-corporation-worldwide/; PYMNTS (2018), Starbucks Plans To Step Up Digital Marketing Efforts, 27 April https://www.pymnts.com/news/retail/2018/starbucks-earnings-coffee-ordering/; Taylor, K. (2018), Starbucks just quietly made a change that reveals the future of the company—here's how it works, *Business Insider*, March 27 http://www.businessinsider.fr/us/starbucks-mobile-order-and-pay-for-all-customers-2018-3; Fleming, M. (2018), Starbucks moves away from the 'drumbeat of promotions' to build longer term relationships with customers, *Marketing Week*, April 27 https://www.marketingweek.com/2018/04/27/starbucks-drumbeat-promotions/?message=4&action=adresponse&status=error&ct_5b585ab6131a2=5b585ab61324e.

CASE 20
Top of their Game—Technology Innovation in Manchester City Football Club (FC)

Introduction

Manchester City FC was founded in 1880, under the name of St. Mark's—changing their name to Manchester City in 1894. In 2008, the club received a significant financial boost when taken over by billionaire Sheikh Mansour. Today, Manchester City has risen to become one of the most successful clubs in the Premier League. In 2018, Forbes ranked it as the world's fifth-most valuable football club, worth US$2.47 billion. On the surface, Manchester City is a typical football club, with a primary focus on player acquisition and Premier League performance. However, what sets the club apart are its dedicated early technology pushes, which focus on building a strong bond with fans. According to Diego Gigliani, SVP of Media and Innovation, when asked about the drive for technology innovation, he noted that: 'We want to grow the sport, league and club . . . strengthening our connection with people will help us achieve that. You can't fit more than 55,000 people in a stadium, but online you can have 10 million people engaged with the club. It's really powerful' (Wollaston, 2017).

This case examines Manchester City FC's newly designed co-creation platform, where building relationships with their fans is central to all marketing activities. In addition, the club's 'Cityzens' loyalty programme for fans, its virtual reality platform, its use of Facebook bots, Hackathons and eSports, which all help build the trustworthiness of the club, will be discussed. Manchester City FC are pioneers of these innovations in Premier League football and are adept at developing relationships with their fans.

Website Co-creation

Through the development of its new website in 2016, Manchester City FC have firmly adopted the fans-first ethos. The website was completely overhauled and designed in conjunction with the team's fans. The club engaged in value co-creation with its fans by involving them in every aspect of the design—from colour schemes, usability, content provision, to device compatibility (desktop, mobile and app). Furthermore, the team crest was co-created with fans through focus groups, prototype designs and user testing. By engaging with the fan base, listening to their needs and observing their behaviour, the club has empowered their fans and facilitated the development of direct and deeper relationships.

Cityzens

In parallel to the website revamp, the club launched its 'Cityzens' initiative (Connelly, 2017). Through a dedicated mobile app and/or social media, fans were enabled to gather as a community of support for the club. The app allows fans to locate each other on maps and to initiate chat sessions. The mapping functionality is leveraged to provide fans with experiences, such as trips to matches and meetings with players. Rewards are also offered (e.g. invitations to match screenings, special events and free merchandise) based on the fan's level of participation in the community. Additionally, as fans register with the app, they are sent personalized video messages from the club's management and players. Fans also gain rewards when they reach certain milestones, such as attending every match in a season. Community-based features include match day add-ons—such as games in which fans try to predict the score, guessing line-ups and voting for the best players. Providing direct incentives to the fans increases their positivity toward the club and encourages fans to engage more with the 'Cityzens' community. Fans have also remarked at the sense of pride they feel when interacting with others via the community, which, in turn, influences their level of engagement and loyalty towards Manchester City FC.

Virtual Reality (VR)

In 2017, in conjunction with Sky Sports, Manchester City FC launched a VR experience for fans in London, New York and Melbourne, in which a selection of

fans could watch a match via VR headsets while it was played live in the Etihad Stadium in Manchester. Fans were able to immerse themselves in different elements of the match day—from watching players train via wearable cameras, to viewing the changing room preparations and walks down the blue carpet. The latest VR addition places the fans in a virtual private VIP suite in which they can watch matches and other related content. This is enabled on multiple VR headsets ranging from Google Cardboard, Samsung Gear VR to the Oculus Rift, so that fans from all walks of life can engage in the experience. While watching a match in VR, viewers can switch between multiple pitch cameras at will by simply looking at various virtual icons.

Facebook Bots

In another innovate move, the club launched a Facebook messenger bot through which fans can choose to receive multiple news items and tailored content. This includes interesting updates on the club, such as the latest interviews with the club manager, news about player transfers, match replays and behind-the-scenes videos. Messaging apps have become an important way of delivering content directly to the fans, enabling the club to increase their global, digital and mobile fan base (Begum, 2016).

Beyond the Pitch—Hackathons and eSports

In 2017, encroaching into the domain of tech giants such as Google and Facebook, Manchester City FC organized a hackathon. A hackathon is an event where computer programmers, graphic designers, interface designers and subject matter experts get together for a defined period (typically a day) to collaborate and create new innovations (Wikipedia, 2018). The event helped the club uncover new insights on player performance, while also enhancing their innovative image. Multiple hackathon teams came together and were provided with access to player datasets and analytics (such as club/player performance). The teams were also provided with the technology to provide real-time data visualizations, which are typically used for news and sports reporting, so that they could develop their own designs. The winning team created a machine learning system that focused on in-match decision-making, and which has the potential to improve decisions made by management in terms of set-pieces, player substitutions and so on (Leyden, 2016).

Manchester City FC also entered the eSports arena, which is an exponentially growing industry with a massive fan base, by sponsoring a celebrity gamer 'Kez' (a renowned expert in the world's leading football simulation video game, FIFA 16). Kez now represents the club in eSports tournaments globally. This has created further brand awareness for the club, bringing the fans into the eSports arena, and enabling the brand to engage with a new audience—typically younger generation eSports fanatics (Elder, 2018).

The Future

The club continues to innovate by using technology such as Snapchat spectacles (sunglasses with inbuilt cameras) to provide fans with a first-person perspective of player life through the eyes of star players. For example, Yara Touré spent an afternoon in 2017 wearing them while walking through the Etihad stadium, talking to teammates and participating in training sessions (Spectacles, 2018). The club also uses a dedicated app on Amazon Fire TV to allow fans to stream content from mobile devices to their TV (Andrews, 2016). Essentially, this means that fans can access all their personal CityTV content via their mobile device and cast it to their TV at home. This initiative has encouraged fans to engage with the Manchester City app rather than accessing content on their TV via YouTube.

Manchester City's innovations have increased global awareness of the club, while significantly improving levels of service and customer (fan) relationships. It is the fastest-growing club on Facebook for the last number of seasons. For example, since the start of the 2013/14 season, Manchester City's Facebook page grew by 287 per cent, compared with Chelsea (168 per cent), Arsenal (159 per cent), Real Madrid (135 per cent) and Manchester United (107 per cent). Manchester City also almost doubled its YouTube video views during the 2015/16 season compared with the same time in the previous year

»

»

(44 million views versus 82 million views). In 2018, the club was the most subscribed-to Premier League club channel on YouTube, with just short of 1.4 million subscribers. Their long-term goal is to become the premium team, both on and off the pitch, while always maintaining and building relationships with their fans.

Questions

1. **Discuss the benefits for Manchester City FC of building relationships with their fans.**
2. **Discuss the importance of using technology to engage and develop relationships with fans.**
3. **Suggest how CRM can be used to develop customer relationships. In your answer, discuss the types of fan-related data that should be captured for Manchester City FC. Explain why you need to capture this data.**

This case study was written by Dr Ethel Claffey, Waterford Institute of Technology.

References

Wollaston, V. (2017), Innovating the beautiful game: how Man City is taking football from the terraces to the web https://www.wired.co.uk/article/football-tech-innovation-manchester-city (accessed August 2018); Connelly, T. (2017), Manchester City get smart with data to create a personalised fan experience platform https://www.thedrum.com/news/2017/08/07/manchester-city-get-smart-with-data-create-personalised-fan-experience-platform (accessed August 2018); MCFC Editorial (2016), Watch City in Virtual Reality with New App https://www.mancity.com/news/club-news/club-news/2016/september/city-vr-launch (accessed August 2018); Begum, S. (2016), Manchester City FC connect with fans with Facebook Messenger; https://www.manchestereveningnews.co.uk/business/media/manchester-city-fc-connect-fans-11546286 (accessed August 2018); Wikipedia (2018), Hackathon; https://en.wikipedia.org/wiki/Hackathon (accessed August 2018); Leyden, J. (2016), Fancy hacking Man City? Happy days: Footy club to host hackathon https://www.theregister.co.uk/2016/06/29/football_hackathon_manchester_city_fc/ (accessed August 2018); Elder, R. (2018), The eSports competitive video game market continues to grow revenues and attract investors; http://uk.businessinsider.com/esports-market-growth-ready-for-mainstream-2018-3-21 (accessed August 2018); Spectacles (2018), A new way to look; https://www.spectacles.com/ie/ (accessed August 2018); Andrews, K. (2016), Manchester City launches first EPL Amazon Fire TV app https://www.si.com/tech-media/2016/11/02/manchester-city-epl-amazon-fire-tv-app (accessed August 2018).

CHAPTER 11
Value Through Innovation

> *You learn more from failure . . . but the key is to fail early, fail cheaply, and not to make the same mistake twice.*
>
> **A.G. LAFLEY, CEO, PROCTER & GAMBLE**

LEARNING OBJECTIVES

After reading this chapter, you should be able to:

1. discriminate between innovation and a new product
2. describe the different types of new products that can be launched
3. describe how to create and nurture an innovative culture
4. discuss the organizational options that apply to innovations and new product development
5. explain the concepts of idea realization and new product development
6. describe the stages in the new product development process
7. discuss the key ingredients in commercializing technology quickly and effectively
8. explain the martech landscape

Arguably, innovation is the lifeblood of corporate success. From a marketing perspective, it is important to consider how innovations and new products can add value. Changing customer tastes, technological advances and competitive pressures mean that companies cannot afford to rely on past product success. Companies must look closely at the needs of customers and other stakeholders and the impact on the wider environment if they are to develop innovative products and services that add value.

Innovations require testing and development, and new product development is a risky activity as most new products fail. But judgement in terms of the percentage of failures should be avoided, as this could stifle the spirit of innovation. The acid test is the number of successes. Failure must be tolerated.

To fully understand innovation and new product development, we need to distinguish between invention and innovation. **Invention** is the discovery of new ideas and methods. Not all countries have the same capacity for invention. The UK has a history of being inventive, from the steam engine and bicycle to the television, computer and jet engine. In Scandinavia, many businesses were built on a local invention. For example, Tetra Pak was founded by a person who conceived of 'pouring milk into a paper bag'. Lego bricks revolutionized toys, and IKEA's invention of a new way to deliver furniture was central to its phenomenal growth. In these cases, the key was not just the invention but the capability to innovate by bringing the product successfully to market (Richard, 1996).

Innovation is a concept which has no clear definition and yet is widely used in many different disciplines. Baregheh et al. (2009) identified 60 definitions of innovation from widespread areas of research—marketing and management to economic research and entrepreneurship. They also concluded that a general (and multi-disciplinary) definition of innovation should consider the nature and type of innovation as well as the stages of the innovation process and new product development, the social context and the aim of the innovation.

All countries are not equal when it comes to realizing new innovations, and the USA is a major source of innovation, particularly in the technology industry. Table 11.1 shows some of the world's most innovative companies' activity sectors, country of origin and products. The selection of firms in this list is based on the extent to which industries invest in innovation (Dyer and Gregersen, 2018), the capitalization of each firm and the previous trading performance.

A key point to remember is that the focus of innovation should be on providing new solutions that better meet customer needs. Innovative solutions often do not always require breakthroughs in technology.

TABLE 11.1 The world's most innovative companies

Company	Industrial sector	Innovative products
ServiceNow	IT service sector (USA)	Intelligent applications; security, IT, HR solutions
Workday	IT sector (USA)	Cloud applications, innovative and adaptable applications
Salesforces.com	IT sector (USA)	Customer relationship management solutions, Internet of Things (IoT) integration and collaboration
Tesla	Automotive sector (USA)	Electric vehicles, cars and trains
Amazon	Internet and catalogue retail (USA)	Online shopping services, delivery solutions, artificial intelligence (AI) devices
Netflix	Media, film and television (USA)	Video streaming services
Incyte	Biotech (USA)	Medical health products
Hindustan Unilever Ltd	Household and personal products (India)	Soaps detergents, personal healthcare, foodstuffs
Naver	IT services (South Korea)	Community services, blogs, cafes knowledge shopping maps
Facebook	IT services (USA)	Social media network and apps

Based on: Forbes List https://www.forbes.com/innovative-companies/#75f6b13a1d65

For example, the growth of Starbucks was fuelled by redefining what city-centre coffee drinking meant, and Ryanair built its success by creating a different consumer appeal from that of traditional airlines, based on low prices and strict cost control (Doyle, 1997).

In this chapter, we consider the definition of innovation to be the process that occurs when an invention is commercialized by bringing it to market and we focus on new product development. We begin by asking the question 'What is an innovation and what is new product?' and examine three key issues in new product development: 1) organization, 2) developing an innovation culture, and 3) the new product development process. Then we examine the strategies involved in product replacement, the most common form of new product development. Finally, we look at the consumer adoption process, which is how people learn about innovations and new products, try them, and adopt or reject them.

What is an Innovation and What is a New Product?

Not all new products are innovations. Innovation is the process of translating an idea into a product or service. Some new products are so fundamentally different from existing products that they reshape markets and competition; for example, in the past, satellite navigation systems have created a new market for digital navigation devices and reduced the sale of printed road maps significantly. Publisher HarperCollins said sales of maps and atlases declined from £13.5 million in 2006 to £9.7 million in 2010 (Geoghegan, 2011). Table 11.2 shows some of the latest innovations that are reconfiguring the world in which we live and work (Forbes Technology Council, 2018).

TABLE 11.2 Innovations that are reshaping our world

The idea	The products	The company
Practical augmented reality digital displays that deliver information to various devices	Vuzix Blade AR glasses (see Exhibit 11.1) Brand building visual identity for Chelsea Market (New York)	Vuzix https://www.vuzix.com/products/blade-smart-glasses Square360 https://www.square360.com
Real-time language translation Voice recognition technology with inbuilt artificial intelligent enables speakers to have conversations	Pixel Buds (instant language translation earphone for 40 different languages) Alexa smart speakers	Google https://store.google.com/sg/product/google_pixel_buds Amazon https://blog.aboutamazon.co.uk/supporting-small-businesses/small-british-businesses-use-alexa-to-innovate
Chatbots Computer programs that facilitate dialogue (audio or text) and collect and analyse information	LivePerson conversational commerce IBM Watson chatbots	LivePerson Inc https://www.liveperson.com IBM https://www.ibm.com/watson/how-to-build-a-chatbot/
Artificial intelligence and machine learning Data modelling, analyzing speech, driving a car, operating a robot; enable machines to become smart	Deep learning platforms Network security solutions	AMAX Total computing solutions https://www.amax.com/solutions/deep-learning-solutions/deep-learning-platform Cisco Systems https://www.cisco.com/
The cloud Flexible computing solutions, data streaming to web browsers, mobile apps, IoT devices	Serverless connectivity Microsoft Azure cloud platform	Kaazing.IO https://kaazing.com/kaazingio/ Microsoft https://azure.microsoft.com/en-gb/

Based on Forbes Technology Council (2018)

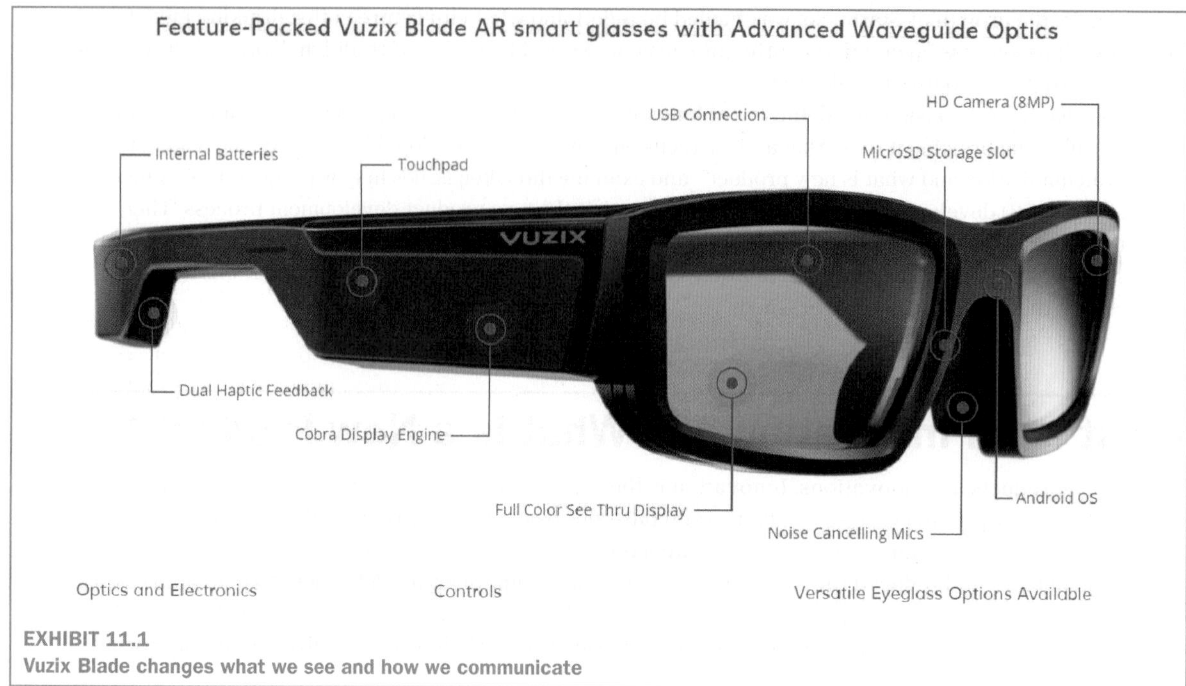

EXHIBIT 11.1
Vuzix Blade changes what we see and how we communicate

World-shaping innovations are at one end of the scale; at the other extreme are products and services that are incremental improvements on existing ones, for example a shampoo that is different from existing products only by means of its brand name, fragrance, packaging and colour but will still be referred to as a new product. There are four broad categories of new product to consider (Booz, Allen and Hamilton, 1982):

1 *Product replacements*: which account for about 45 per cent of all new product launches and include revisions and improvements to existing products; for example, Lucozade Sport has been reimagined and positioned as a 'body fuel' and 'fitwater' to access new market segments. Some product replacements are lower cost versions of existing products reformulated or redesigned to cost less to produce. The Toyota Corolla hatchback is a reimagined version of the car manufacturer's lower cost vehicle. Dyson releases new products based on improvements to an existing product. Its new vacuum cleaner has an innovative ball to improve manoeuvrability and is smaller and more flexible than previous models.
2 *Additions to existing lines*: these account for about 25 per cent of new product launches and take the form of new products that add to a company's existing product lines. This produces greater product depth. Chocolate Weetabix is an extension that enables the well-known cereal brand to compete with chocolate cereals. Another example is the addition to the Crest toothpaste brand of Crest Pro-Health whitening toothpaste.
3 *New product lines*: these total around 20 per cent of new product launches and represent a move into a new market. For example, in Europe, Volvic introduced the 'Touch of Fruit' range of bottled waters, and Evian brought out a facial spray—both targeted at different audiences. This strategy widens a company's product mix.
4 *Innovations of new-to-the-world products*: these total around 10 per cent of new product launches and create entirely new markets. For example, smartphones and voice-activated speakers have created new markets because of the highly valued customer benefits they provide.

Clearly, the degree of risk and reward varies according to the new product category. New-to-the-world products normally carry the highest risk, since it is often very difficult to predict consumer reaction. Effective new product development is based on creating and nurturing an innovative culture, organizing effectively for new product development and managing the new product development process. We shall now examine these three issues.

Creating and Nurturing an Innovative Culture

The foundation for successful new product development is the creation of a corporate culture that promotes and rewards innovation. Unfortunately, many marketing managers regard their company's corporate culture as a key constraint to innovation (Matthews, 2002). Managers, therefore, need to pay more attention to creating a culture that encourages innovation. Figure 11.1 shows the kinds of attitudes and actions that can foster an innovative culture. People in organizations observe those actions that are likely to lead to success or punishment. The surest way to kill innovative spirit is to conspicuously punish people who are prepared to create and champion new product ideas and to reward those people who are content to manage the status quo. Such actions breed the attitude 'Why should I take the risk of failing when by carrying on as before I will probably be rewarded?' Research has shown that those companies that have supportive attitudes to rewards and risk and a tolerant attitude towards failure are more likely to innovate successfully (see Shrivastava and Souder, 1987; Gupta and Wileman, 1990; Koshler, 1991). Read Marketing in Action 11.1 to find out more about innovative luxury industries in Europe.

FIGURE 11.1
Creating and nurturing an innovative culture

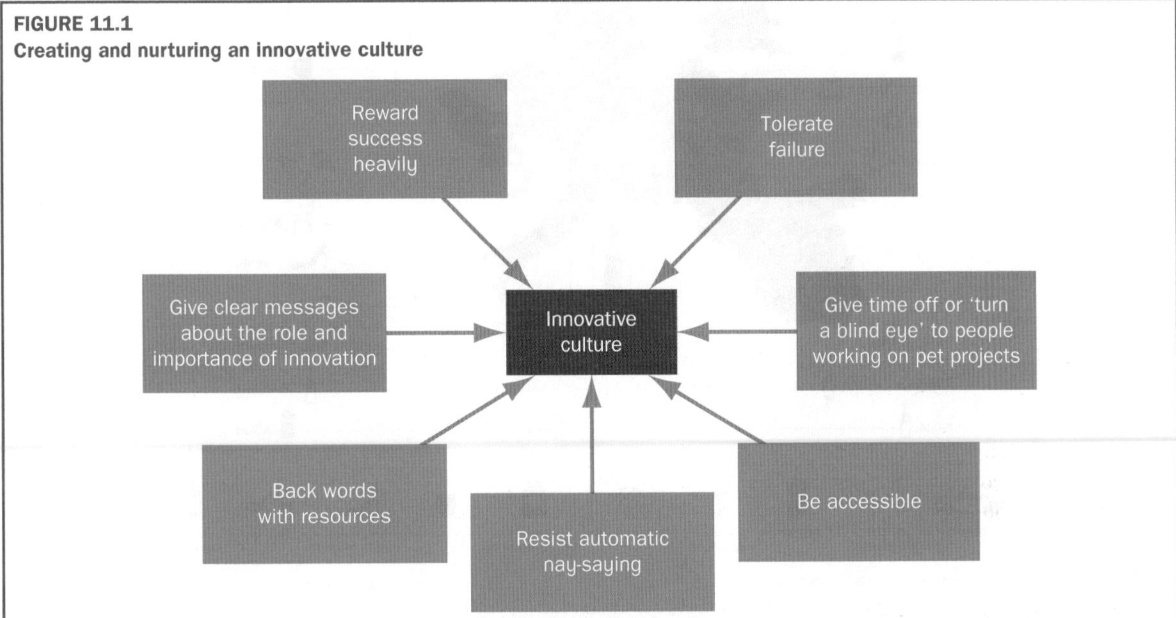

MARKETING IN ACTION 11.1
Innovation in Luxury Industries in Europe

Luxury industries drive forward excellent new product development. Firms constantly innovate, but in Europe it is recognised that there are areas that offer the opportunity to bring firms together and foster even greater creative output. Many regional industries across Europe form clusters of excellence based on specific skills and product expertise. By investing in skills and innovation, European governments can support and encourage further development of artistic cultures and inherited craftmanship.

Luxury manufacturers invest in long-term strategies and look for sources of inspiration in creative style and design innovations and in innovations emerging from scientific research. To foster the development of innovations, these firms invest in training facilities and business development so that they can bridge gaps between skills and the needs of their industry.

Europe has a strong artistic culture that has supported craftsmanship and which has been handed down through generations, but this does not mean luxury businesses are stuck in the past; they have grown from solid foundations and have a high capacity for innovation and creativity.

»

»

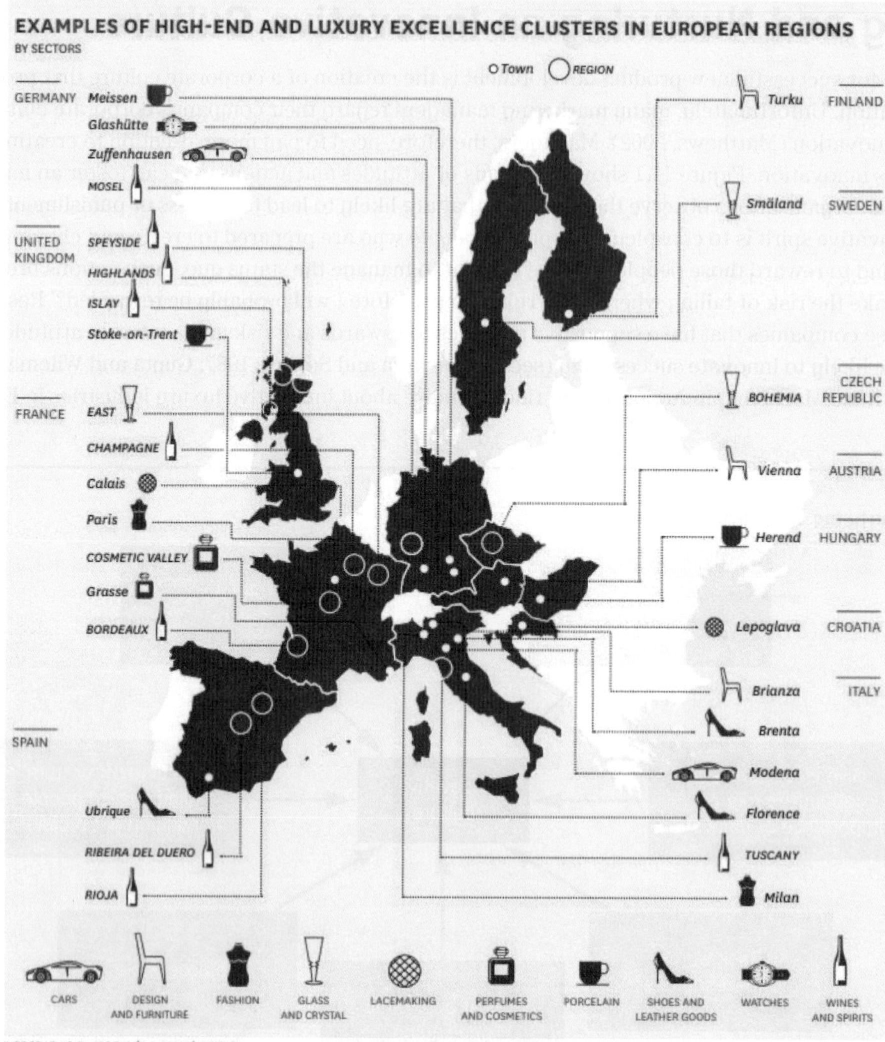

INFOGRAPHIC CLAIRE OLIVÈS © COMITÉ COLBERT

In an interview, the CEO of Moser (a crystal and glass manufacturer in the Czech Republic) said: ‘Clusters of excellence [with] craftsmanship based on traditional know-how have become a significant aspect of European regions’ history and cultural heritage, and high-end and luxury industries play an important role in the vitality of these clusters. Czech glass was always regarded as an excellent article of trade, and as an artefact it has become synonymous with business skills, inventiveness and high quality to become the product of its country—Czech Republic.’ Moser, founded 160 years ago, produces unique luxury crystal objects and is one of the country’s leading glass producers.

In an interview, Andrea Illy, Chairman of Illycafe (Italy), said: ‘Our industries are creative and innovative par excellence, from products to processes, from manufacturing to distribution, from communication to business model. And they are cultural industries because they redefine the tastes and the lifestyles of the world’s most sophisticated consumers—more than 400 million people, trendsetters who create an imitation process for an even larger share of the population. Our companies shape the world’s contemporary material culture, modelling the future. For these reasons, our products are very close to contemporary art. We’ve been mostly referring to the civilization that was born and evolved in the Mediterranean area and in Europe.’

The luxury sector is highly competitive and has many firms with a small market share; as a result, brands are constantly looking to innovate and renew their products and market position. The nature of this sector gives it a vibrancy which attracts new market entrants, promotes fair competition and generates sustainable employment opportunities.

Based on: European Cultural and Creative Industries Alliance (2017)

An innovation culture can also be nurtured by senior management visibly supporting new product development in general and high-profile projects (see Booz, Allen and Hamilton, 1982; Maidique and Zirger, 1984). Besides sending clear messages about the role and importance of new product development, senior management should reinforce their words by allowing time off from their usual duties to people who wish to develop their own ideas, making available funds and resources for projects, and making themselves accessible when difficult decisions need to be taken (see Bergen, Miyajima and McLaughlin, 1988; Hegarty and Hoffman, 1990).

Finally, management at all levels should resist the temptation of automatic 'nay saying'—that is, whenever a new idea is suggested, there is a tendency for doubters in a firm to make negative comments and question the feasibility of the new idea. This does not mean that all ideas should immediately be developed, as each will be scrutinized and has to pass through many stages of development before becoming a reality. The point is that stifling new ideas at conception only serves as a constraint on innovation. Managers need to seek ways to create an innovative culture.

Creative leadership is required to release the passions, imagination and energy needed for outstanding innovation. Such leadership encourages staff to reject the status quo and operate in a productive discomfort zone, has a clear vision of the future, and provides support for exploration (e.g. Apple Inc, Google, Haier, 3M, Hyundai).

Arguably, there is an underlying assumption that all innovation by commercial profit-based businesses is for affluent markets where customers will eventually pay for the research, development and marketing of new products and deliver surplus profits by paying high prices for such goods and services. On the one hand, perhaps this is a reasonable assumption, as over half the world's population survive on less than $2.50 dollars a day and therefore are deemed to be uninterested in or unable to purchase innovative products (Shah, 2012). On the other hand, is it a classic example of marketing myopia as suggested by Theodore Levitt in the 1960s (Levitt, 1960), whereby companies are short-sighted about growth opportunities in the market? Read Mini Case 11.1 to find out more about how a shift towards frugal innovation is creating innovative products for billions of underserved consumers.

MINI CASE 11.1
Frugal Innovations: From Clay Fridges to Cardboard Splints

Historically, over half the world's population have been ignored by global corporations as a segment capable of being interested in innovation. However, Eric von Hippel, a professor of technological innovation, has argued for many years that the key to innovation comes from customers, not corporate thinking, and that everyone has *needs* that can be satisfied by new products and services.

Sustained global recession has affected many areas of business, and governments around the world have taken to using austerity as a watchword for managing national and regional affairs. This shift in emphasis has profound implications for marketers. For example, the engineers in India won the day with the Tata Nano when Renault–Nissan asked its engineers in France, India and Japan to come up with some cost-saving ideas. The Haier Group, a Chinese consumer electronics manufacturer, has undercut western competitors by producing goods ranging from air conditioners and washing machines to wine coolers often at half the usual cost. The result has been that Haier has taken significant percentages of US and European markets. However, the shift towards frugal innovation is more far-reaching than just producing goods for western markets more cheaply. According to Prahalad and Mashelkar (2010), a form of new product development called *frugal innovation* or *reverse innovation* specifically engineers products to meet the needs of developing countries—for example, a rough-terrain wheelchair or a $20 prosthetic knee that can be assembled in an hour.

»

In the developing world, the various champions of frugal innovations include Anil Gupta, who is an academic at one of India's top business schools, the Indian Institute of Management. Anil is a champion of individuals who are deemed to be 'knowledge-rich yet economically poor'. Anil believes that there is a solution to world poverty but it requires a different approach: a bottom-up one. He established the Honey Bee Network in the 1980s with the aim of nurturing innovation, knowledge and creativity at a grassroots level. This initiative led to the development of a village-to-government approach towards innovation. Innovation scouts go to rural villages in India looking for potential products to develop.

Mansukhbhai Prajapati is an example of a successful entrepreneur who has emerged from this initiative. He developed the Mitticool brand, which includes clay pans, pressure cookers and non-electric refrigerators and which is making a difference to local communities' health through better-kept and better-cooked food.

Mohammad Mehtar designed a windmill that cost less than $120 dollars but could irrigate a paddy field to a sufficient level to grow rice that is more nutritious than that using the conventional production method, making this not only low cost but also more sustainable and environmentally friendly.

Jugaad is an example of a company that began creating products from recycled material in 1997 through a Delhi-based children's home that organized work for disadvantaged children. *Jugaad* is a unique Hindi word that refers to the practice of getting required results by using whatever limited resources are available. People Tree (a retailer) provided outlets and supported Jugaad until it became an independent brand in 2004. This creative manufacturer now provides employment and training and helps members of its workforce to become independent entrepreneurs.

The Tata Nano may not have changed the world, but frugal innovation will!

Questions:

1 What are 'frugal' innovations and how might they change the world?
2 If you worked for a large multinational, suggest how you would incorporate frugal innovations into your marketing strategy.

Based on: Day (2012); The Economist (2012); Jugaad (2012); Kadri (2010); Duggan (2012); Honey Bee (n.d.); Prahalad and Mashelkar (2010); Priya (2017)

Organizing Effectively for Innovation and New Product Development

The second building block of successful new product development and innovation is an appropriate organization structure. Most companies use one or a combination of the following methods: project teams, product and brand managers, new product departments and new product committees.

Project teams

Project teams involve the bringing together of staff from such areas as research and development (R&D), engineering, manufacturing, finance and marketing to work on a new product development project. Research has shown that assigning the responsibility of new product development to such cross-functional teams has a positive effect on new product performance (Joshi and Sharma, 2004). Specialized skills are combined to form an effective team to develop the new product concept. Furthermore, if the members of the team remain stable for the duration of a project, there is greater potential to foster better decision-making, engender shared responsibility and leverage advantage from the collective expertise. Ultimately, this approach helps develop better new product advantage. Working together in stable teams can also help to avoid 'tunnel vision' and inflexibility in problem solving, up to a point.

Slotegraaf and Atuahene-Gima (2011) discuss how stable teams benefit from better decision-making. However, a key challenge associated with developing a new product is that innovation requires the conversion of knowledge into something tangible, and the stability of a product team can help the process. There is a certain point where the benefits begin to diminish. So, long-term stability beyond a project may be less successful. Google supported new product development by allowing employees 20 per cent of their work time to spend on innovative projects. Gmail and AdSense and artificial intelligence driven Smart Compose and Google Assistant have all been developed in this manner.

Product and brand managers

Product and brand management entails the assignment of product managers to product lines (or groups of brands within a product line) and/or of brand managers to individual brands. These managers are then responsible for the products'/brands' success and have the task of coordinating functional areas (e.g. production, sales, advertising and marketing research). They are also often responsible for new product development, including the creation of new product ideas, improving existing products and designing brand extensions. Product managers may be supported by a team of assistant brand managers and a dedicated marketing researcher. In some companies, a new product development manager may help product and brand managers in the task of generating and testing new product concepts. This form of organization is common for high-volume, relatively low-value products such as groceries and toiletries, and in the drinks industries.

New product departments and committees

The review of new product projects is normally in the hands of high-ranking functional managers, who listen to progress reports and decide whether further funds should be assigned to a project. The functional managers may also be charged with deciding new product strategies and priorities. It doesn't matter whether the underlying structure is a venture team, product and brand management, or a new product department, a new products committee often oversees the process and services to give projects a high corporate profile through the stature of its membership.

The importance of teamwork

Whichever method (or combination of methods) is used, effective cross-functional teamwork is crucial for success (see Hise et al., 1990; Johne and Snelson, 1988; Walsh, 1990) and there must be effective communication and teamwork between R&D and marketing. Although all functional relationships are important during new product development, the cultural differences between R&D and marketing are potentially the most harmful and difficult to resolve. The challenge is to prevent technical people developing only things that interest them professionally, and to get them to understand the realities of the marketplace.

Innovation leadership

Businesses must encourage innovation, but if they are to achieve sustainable performance they should also provide management leadership to drive innovation. Lukoschek et al. (2018) studied the behaviours of 194 firms of various sizes and from different industries, for example manufacturing, retail, engineering, IT and construction, and found different approaches towards fostering idea generation and idea realization. They argue that innovation leaders need to foster two types of management behaviour:

1 *Idea generation*, which is encouraging the creation and development of new ideas. A leader should seek to create a supportive working environment in which individuals and teams can be inspired, open to new ideas and eager to explore to find new opportunities. But from a business perspective, this can be a costly way of working and may impact on units (organizational success). Nevertheless, leaders should focus on how to develop the creative knowledge and skills of individuals and teams.

2 *Idea realization*, which is the implementation of new ideas into marketable products and services. Leaders need to find ways to ensure that the realization delivers increased value, innovativeness and efficiency.
So, a successful innovation leader should not only encourage creativity and innovative thinking, but also do this within the financial and structural constraints of the organization. Building prototypes that can be tested, applying ideas in real-world settings and evaluating the process are important elements of idea realization which need to be managed.

The Lukoschek et al. (2018) study of innovation leadership concluded that these two behaviours require different skills, and yet innovation leaders must be able to foster both creativity and efficiency if they are to succeed.

Managing Idea Realization (New Product Development)

There are three inescapable facts about idea realization (new product development): it is expensive, risky and time-consuming. For example, Gillette spent in excess of £100 million over more than 10 years developing its Sensor razor brand. The new product concept was to develop a non-disposable shaver and use new technology to produce a shaver that would follow the contours of a man's face, giving an excellent shave (through two spring-mounted platinum-hardened chromium blades) with fewer cuts. This made commercial sense, since shaving systems are more profitable than disposable razors and allow more opportunity for creating a differential advantage. Had the brand failed, Gillette's position in the shaving market could have been damaged irreparably. Nike is another company that invests heavily in new product development to maintain its lead in the specialist sports shoe market. Read Marketing in Action 11.2 to discover how innovation drives the Decathlon service brand.

Managing the processes involved efficiently is an important factor in reducing cost, time and risk. Studies have shown that having a formal process with review points, clear new product goals and a strong marketing orientation underlying the process leads to greater success, whether the product is a physical good or a service (de Brentani, 1991; Johne and Storey, 1998).

An eight-step new product development process to provide these characteristics is shown in Figure 11.2 and consists of setting new product strategy, idea generation, screening, concept testing, business analysis, product development, market testing and commercialization. Although the reality of new product development may resemble organizational chaos, the discipline imposed by the activities carried out at each stage leads to a greater likelihood of developing a product that not only works but also confers customer benefits. We should note, however, that new products pass through each stage at varying speeds; some may dwell at a stage for a long period, while others may pass through very quickly (Cooper and Kleinschmidt, 1986).

FIGURE 11.2
The eight-step new product development process

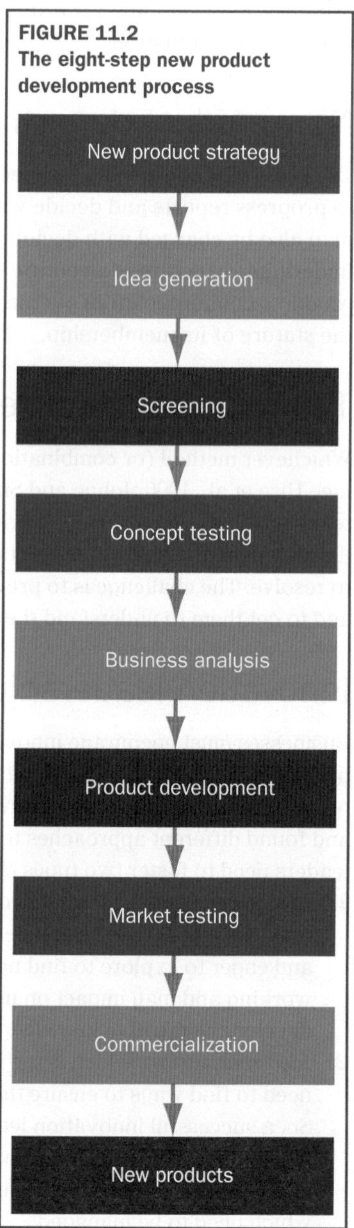

New product strategy

As we have already seen, innovation leaders value strategic guidance from senior management about their vision and priorities for new product development. By providing clear guidelines about which products/markets the company is interested in serving, senior management staff can provide a focus for the areas in which idea generation should take place. Also, by outlining their objectives (e.g. market share gain, profitability, technological leadership) for new products they can provide indicators for the screening criteria that should be used to evaluate those ideas. A key issue in new product strategy is where to allocate resources. A company may have several divisions and a multitude of product lines, so the company has to decide where funds should be invested.

Idea generation

One of the benefits of developing an innovative corporate culture is that it sparks the imagination (see Marketing in Action 11.2). The objective is to motivate the search for ideas, so that salespeople, engineers, top management, marketers and other employees are all alert to new opportunities. Interestingly, questioning Nobel Prize winners about the time and

MARKETING IN ACTION 11.2
Innovation Drives Passion Brands and Builds Sporting Universes at Decathlon

'*Create the need and make the pleasure and the benefits of sport accessible to as many people as possible*', is the promise that Decathlon has offered its clients since 1976. The idea of 'sport for all' enabled this French company to differentiate from other major brands focusing on competition and performance. This led it to the innovative concept of bringing together all sports (from cycling to fishing) under one roof and offering a large range of self-service sport products at the best price. Decathlon continued to develop the business and in 1999 opened its first store in the UK and its first Oxylane Village in France—an innovative sports environment based around a Decathlon store. By 2018, Decathlon had 285 shops and 11 Oxylane Villages in France and over 1,414 stores in more than 45 different countries. Worldwide sales are important to the company as they account for 58 per cent of sales. Central to the Decathlon offer are the Passion brands. Each Passion brand represents a sporting universe, and collectively they accounted for more than 60 per cent of Decathlon's turnover of €11 billion. See Table 11.3 for examples.

TABLE 11.3 Examples of Passion brands, sporting universes and innovative products

Passion Brand	Sporting universe	Examples of products
Geologic	Darts, archery and boules	Soft archery kit, totally safe to use anywhere T-light, a safe dartboard
Newfeel	Walking	Propulse Walk 400, shoes that aid fitness Fullwalk 540 design shoes, with lightness in mind
Oxelo	Urban skate sport	Town 7 Easyfold scooter—easy to assemble anywhere Sneak-in inline skates to be worn with own shoes
Tribord	Nautical water sports	Easybreathe full-face snorkel; see and breathe underwater Izeber 50 floating system lifejacket to aid buoyancy

Each Passion brand conceives the products, which are exclusively distributed by Decathlon stores. The own-brand offer is due to Decathlon placing innovation at the heart of its activities. With a very advanced internal R&D department composed of researchers, engineers and designers, Decathlon's international design network is prolific, producing about 40 patents and nearly 3,000 products each year. Decathlon rewards excellence in innovation at an annual award-giving event, the Oxylane Awards.

Domyos is another Passion brand (dedicated to fitness) and is the best example of the firm's willingness to immerse the employees among its customers. Who better than sportspeople know what they need to improve their game? Decathlon provides them with a website, Openoxylane (http://www.openoxylane.com), dedicated to the co-creation of new products. Anyone can put forward ideas and participate in projects submitted by members of the community. At each stage of the creative process—from defining functions to selecting materials or colours and choosing a name and even the price—users can submit proposals, interact and give their opinion. Prototype workshops are also available for teams to observe the behaviour and test the components of finished products; they help speed up the design process. Organizing this innovation culture allows the group to compete with major brands such as Nike and Adidas, who traditionally highlight their innovation and design.

Based on: http://www.decathlon-united.com

circumstances when they had the important germ of an idea that led them to great scientific discovery revealed that it can occur at the most unexpected time: just before going to sleep, on waking up in the morning, or at a place of worship. The common factor seems to be a period of quiet contemplation, uninterrupted by the bustle of everyday life and work.

Successful new product ideas are not necessarily based on technological innovation. Often, they are based on novel applications of existing technology (e.g. Velcro poppers on disposable nappies). The iPhone created a need for a place to buy 'portable music', which led to the development of the iTunes store.

The sources of new product ideas can be internal to the company: scientists, engineers, marketers, salespeople and designers (as at 3M). Some companies timetable sessions to think about new ways of doing things, often asking the question 'how might we . . . ?' as a technique to stimulate the creation of ideas, and use financial incentives to persuade people to put forward the ideas they have had. At Royal Dutch Shell, virtual teams meet via the internet to share ideas. These sessions have generated many ideas, from ways to reduce paperwork to using sophisticated laser sensors to find oil (Viklund, 2015).

The prediction by Hamel and Prahalad (1991) that global competitive battles will be won by those companies that have the corporate imagination to build and dominate fundamentally new markets has been proved right, especially in high-tech markets. Often, fundamentally new products/markets are created by small businesses that are willing to invent new business models or radically redesign existing models. Sources of new product ideas can also be external to the company. Examining competitors' products may provide clues to product improvements. Competitors' new product plans can be gleaned by training the salesforce to ask distributors about new activities. Distributors can also be a source of new product ideas directly, since they deal with customers and have an interest in selling improved products. Another source of externally generated new product ideas is the millions of scientists, engineers and other companies globally. By collaborating with them, a firm can gain access to innovative solutions. Procter & Gamble leads the way by using online networks to get in touch with thousands of experts.

Anyone anywhere can connect with Procter & Gamble (P&G) through the web and share ideas. P&G taps in to a vast well of expertise through its Connect + Develop programme. It practises open innovation, which is a means of accessing externally developed intellectual property while allowing internally developed assets and know-how to be used by others. This two-way process has led to innovation in such areas as technology, engineering, marketing, packaging, design and business services. For example, Bounce, the world's first dryer-aided softener, was created by an independent Canadian inventor. By P&G and the inventor working together, this innovative product was patented and licensed and sold throughout the world. The internet has enabled the creation of Connect + Develop hubs, joining together innovators as far and wide as in China, Japan, Europe and North and South America. Febreze, which has become a billion-dollar brand for P&G, is another example of an innovation developed through the Connect + Develop programme (Proctor & Gamble, 2018).

Major sources of good ideas are consumers themselves. Their needs may not be satisfied by existing products and they may be genuinely interested in providing ideas that lead to product improvement. Sometimes, traditional marketing research techniques such as focus groups can be useful. Other companies require a less traditional approach. Procter & Gamble, for example, has used ethnographic research, by observing consumers using its products, to develop new and improved products. Philips has employed anthropologists and cognitive psychologists to gather insights into the needs and expectations of consumers around the world. Online, researching blogs and social community sites can reveal ideas for new products and give insights into the strengths and weaknesses of existing products, which can lead to improved product replacements.

In organizational markets, keeping in close contact with customers who are innovators and market leaders in their own marketplace is likely to be a fruitful source of new product ideas (Parkinson, 1982). These '*lead customers*' are likely to recognize required improvements ahead of other customers, as they have advanced needs and are likely to face problems before other product users do. For example, GE's healthcare division researches 'luminaries', who tend to be well-published doctors and research scientists from leading medical institutions. Up to 25 luminaries are brought together at regular medical advisory board sessions to discuss developments in GE's technology. GE then shares some of its advanced technology with a subset of these people. The result is a stream of new products that emerge from collaboration with these groups. Marketing research can play a role in providing feedback when the product line is familiar to customers. However, for radically new products, customers may be unable to articulate their requirements, and so conventional marketing research may be ineffective as a source of ideas. In this situation, as can be seen in Marketing in Action 11.3, companies need to be proactive in their search for new markets rather than rely on customer suggestions (Johne, 1992).

MARKETING IN ACTION 11.3
Creating Radical Innovation

Many new products are incremental, such as Diet Coke from Coca-Cola, or Persil Bio Action laundry capsules from Unilever; others fundamentally change the nature of a market and may be based on technological breakthroughs, such as wearable technologies like the iWatch from Apple, the invention of new business models, such as that of Google, which freely gives away its core search product for free, or Starbucks' reinvention of city-centre coffee drinking. Radical innovation is risky but can bring huge rewards, creating new markets and destroying old ones. The focus is on making the competition irrelevant by creating a leap in value for customers and entering new and uncontested market space.

Avoiding an incremental approach to new product development involves a sharpening of the corporate imagination to become more alive to new market opportunities. Five factors can aid this development.

1 *Escaping the tyranny of served markets*: looking outside markets that are currently served can be assisted by defining core competences and looking at products/markets that lie between existing business units. For example, Motorola's core competences in wireless technology led it to look beyond current products/markets (e.g. mobile phones) and towards global positioning satellite receivers.
2 *Searching for innovative product concepts*: this can be aided by viewing markets as a set of customer needs and product functionalities. This has led to adding an important function to an existing product (e.g. Yamaha's electronic piano), creating a new way to deliver an existing function (e.g. electronic notepads) or creating a new functionality (e.g. web browsers, search engines).
3 *Weakening traditional price-performance assumptions*: traditional price–performance assumptions should be questioned. For example, the price of drone technology, or unmanned aerial vehicles (UAVs), used to provide satellite signals to inaccessible parts, has fallen dramatically. Originally, this highly sophisticated technology cost thousands of dollars, but firms like Google and Facebook have been developing low-flying solar-powered drones to widen internet access in remote locations, and in doing so have significantly reduced the cost. 3D Robotics is selling UAVs at less than $700.
4 *Leading customers*: a problem with developing truly innovative products is that customers rarely ask for them. Successful innovating companies lead customers by imagining unarticulated needs rather than simply following them. They gain insights into incipient needs by talking in depth to and observing closely a market's most sophisticated and demanding customers. For example, Gillette held focus groups with female customers to find out how often they used its razors. In the focus groups, the women said they changed their razor blades regularly. However, Gillette carried out an ethnographic study by going to the homes of the women in the survey. The researchers found that the women regularly forgot to keep a supply of spare blades close to their shower. The outcome was the launch of the Venus razor with an in-shower blade dispenser making it more convenient for consumers. This also sold many more razor blades to women.
5 *Building a radical innovation hub*: a hub is a group of people who encourage and oversee innovation. It includes idea hunters, idea gatherers, internal venture capitalists, members of project evaluation committees, members of overseeing boards and experienced entrepreneurs. The hub's prime function is to nurture hunters and gatherers from all over the company to foster a stream of innovative ideas. Innovation hubs foster innovation and enterprise have developed across the globe, from Silicon Valley to Zurich and Helsinki.

The attitudes and practices within innovative firms are also important and help to create a culture that assists in driving radical innovation. Attitudes include a tolerance for risk-taking and a future market focus that encourages managers to seek to identify customer needs through strategic futures research. Key practices are the empowerment of product champions, which encourages them (supported by resources) to explore research and build on promising but uncertain future technologies, and the use of generous financial and non-financial (e.g. recognition and autonomy) rewards for innovative employees.

Based on: Belton (2015); Nadworny (2014); Moules (2013); Moosmayer and Koehn (2011); Tellis, Prabhu and Chandy (2009)

Screening

Having developed new product ideas, these need to be screened to evaluate their commercial worth. Some companies use formal checklists to help them judge whether the product idea should be rejected or accepted for further evaluation. This ensures that no important criterion is overlooked. Criteria may be used that measure the attractiveness of the market for the proposed product, the fit between the product and company objectives, and the capability of the company to produce and market the product.

Concept testing

Once the new idea has been accepted as worthy of idea realization it can be developed into a concept/ prototype for initial market testing. Different versions of the product concepts may be tested with different target customers. Products, services and even marketing messages are evaluated in this way to gain understanding of customer needs. Each variant should be carefully documented and benchmarked where appropriate. **Concept testing** thus allows the views of customers to enter the new product development process at an early stage.

Focus group discussion can also be used to develop and test product concepts. The concept may be described verbally or pictorially so that the major features are understood. Potential customers can then state whether they perceive any benefits accruing from the features.

Online marketing research is being used increasingly to test concepts, partly because of its relatively low cost. Companies such as Lego, BA, Philips and P&G have set up their own digital communities where they can test consumers' reactions to new product concepts. Considerable ingenuity is needed to research new product concepts. Some companies, such as Diageo, have developed their own highly innovative centres for concept testing. Shop Direct's user experience lab (UX lab) has been designed to help develop better understanding of online shoppers at its websites, for example very.co.uk, isme.co.uk and littlewoods.co.uk. Many innovations have emerged and contributed to Shop Direct's online success.

Often a consideration of buying intentions is a key factor in judging whether any of the concepts are worth pursuing further. In the grocery and toiletries industries, for example, companies (and their marketing research agencies) often use '*action standards*' (e.g. more than 70 per cent of respondents must say they intend to buy) based on experience to judge new product concepts. Concept testing allows a relatively inexpensive judgement to be made by customers before embarking on a costly product development programme. Although concept testing is not foolproof, obvious non-starters can be eliminated early in the process.

Business analysis

Based on the results of the concept test and considerable managerial judgement, estimates of sales, costs and profits will be made. This is the **business analysis** stage. To produce sensible figures, a marketing analysis will need to be undertaken. This will identify the target market, its size and projected product acceptance over several years. Consideration will be given to various prices, and the implications for sales revenue (and profits) discussed. By setting a tentative price, this analysis will provide sales revenue estimates.

Costs will also need to be estimated. If the new product is like existing products (e.g. a brand extension) it should be fairly easy to produce accurate cost estimates. For radical product concepts, costings may be nothing more than informal 'guesstimates'.

Break-even analysis, where the quantity needed to be sold to cover costs is calculated, may be used to establish whether the project is financially feasible. *Sensitivity analysis*, in which variations from given assumptions about price, cost and customer acceptance, for example, are checked to see how they impact on sales revenue and profits, can also prove useful at this stage. Optimistic, most likely and pessimistic scenarios can be drawn up to estimate the degree of risk attached to the project.

If the product concept appears commercially feasible, this process will result in marketing and product development budgets being established based on what appears to be necessary to gain customer awareness and trial and the work required to turn the concept into a marketable product.

Read Marketing in Action 11.4 to find out how 3D printers can turn ideas into reality.

MARKETING IN ACTION 11.4
3D Printers

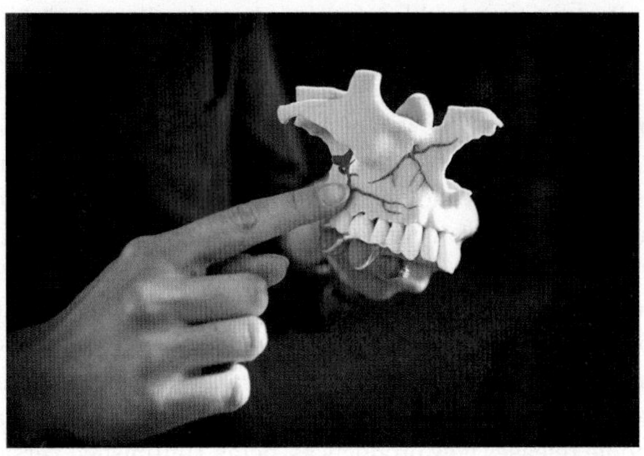

3D technology is now widely available commercially. 3D printing brings manufacturing to your desktop. 3D printers create physical replicas of images from computer screens. A 3D form can be created layer by layer.

Globally, it is estimated that by 2018 the market for 3D printers will be approaching $20 billion. But this is just the beginning as more and more practical applications for this new technology emerge. According to Lisa Harouni (2011), we are witnessing 'an industrial revolution in the digital age'. This type of technology is not new; it has been around for about 20 years, but it is only now that the bespoke products built on demand are beginning to find a niche (but growing) market. There are advantages to this form of bespoke manufacturing: it is very localized and significantly reduces carbon footprints, and there is less waste too.

Currently, this technology is being increasingly used to produce body parts and medical devices. 3D printing is improving efficiency and significantly lowering the cost of production in the area of medical health. Additionally, the printers produce high quality products and have even been used to form face replicas and soft tissue used in bone grafts.

The car industry is also using 3D printer technology. Fiat Chrysler has developed models that can be used in engine testing. So, in the future, we may be able to download physical goods like car parts, jewellery, phone covers and even chocolates in a similar way to which we download music, software and movies today.

Based on: Rowan (2011); Wheeler (2015)

Product development

At this stage, the new product concept is developed into a physical product. As we have seen, the trend is to move from a situation where this is the sole responsibility of the R&D and/or engineering department. Multi-disciplinary project teams are established with the task of bringing the product to the marketplace.

The aim is to integrate the skills of designers, engineers and production, finance and marketing specialists so that product development is quicker, less costly and results in a high-quality product that delights customers. For example, the practice of **simultaneous engineering** means that designers and production engineers work together rather than passing the project from one stage of development to another once the first department's work is finished. Costs are controlled by a method called *target costing*. Target costs are worked out on the basis of target prices in the marketplace and given as engineering/design and production targets.

Cutting time to market by reducing the length of the product development stage is a key marketing factor in many industries. This process, known as *virtual engineering*, has been used by Fiat, which, when designing its Bravo and 500, chose to rely solely on computer simulations rather than take the traditional route of making prototypes. This cut design-to-production time from 26 to 18 months (*The Economist*, 2008).

Marketing has an important role to play in the product development stage. R&D and engineering may focus on the functional aspects of the product, whereas seemingly trivial factors may have an important bearing on customer choice. For example, the foam that appears when washing-up liquid is added to water has no functional value—a washing-up liquid could be produced that cleans just as effectively but does not produce bubbles. However, the customer sees the foam as a visual cue that indicates the power of the washing-up liquid. Marketing needs to keep the project team aware of such psychological factors when developing the new product. Marketing staff need to make sure that project team members understand and communicate the important attributes that customers are looking for in the product.

In the grocery market, marketing will usually brief R&D staff on the product concept, and the latter will be charged with the job of turning the concept into reality. For example, Yoplait, the French dairy cooperative and market leader in fruit yoghurts, found through marketing research that a yoghurt concept based on the following attributes could be a winner.

- Top-of-the-range dessert
- Position on a health–leisure scale at the far end of the pleasure range—the ultimate taste sensation
- A fruit yoghurt that is extremely thick and creamy.

This was the brief given to the Yoplait R&D team that had the task of coming up with recipes for the new yoghurt and the best way of manufacturing it. Its job was to experiment with different cream/fruit combinations to produce the right product—one that matched the product concept—and to do it quickly. Time to market was crucial in this fast-moving industry. To help, Yoplait employed a panel of expert tasters to try out the new recipes and evaluate them in terms of texture, sweetness, acidity, colour, smell, consistency and size of the fruit.

Product testing focuses on the functional aspects of the product and on consumer acceptance. Functional tests are carried out in the laboratory and out in the field to check such aspects as safety, performance and shelf life. For example, a car's braking system must be efficient, a jet engine must be capable of generating a certain level of thrust, and a food package must be capable of keeping its contents fresh. Product testing of software products by users is crucially important in removing any 'bugs' that have not been picked up by internal testers. For example, Google releases new products as 'betas' (unfinished versions) so that users can check for problems and suggest improvements (Jarvis, 2009).

Market testing

So far in the development process, potential customers have been asked if they intend to buy the product, but have never been placed in the position of having to pay for it. **Market testing** takes measurement of customer acceptance one crucial step further than product testing by forcing consumers to 'put their money where their mouth is'. The basic idea is to launch the new product in a limited way so that consumer response in the marketplace can be assessed. Two major methods are used: the simulated market test and test marketing.

The *simulated market test* can take several forms, but the principle is to set up a realistic market situation in which a sample of consumers choose to buy goods from a range provided by the organizing company, usually a marketing research company. For example, a sample of consumers may be recruited to buy their groceries from a mobile supermarket that visits them once a week. They are provided with a magazine in which advertisements and sales promotions for the new product can appear. This method allows measurement of key success indicators such as *penetration* (the proportion of consumers that buy the new product at least once) and *repeat purchase* (the rate at which purchasers buy again) to be made. If penetration is high but repeat purchase low, buyers can be asked after trial why they rejected the product. Simulated market tests are therefore useful as a preliminary to test marketing by spotting problems, such as in packaging and product formulation, that can be rectified before test market launch. They can also be useful in eliminating new products that perform so badly compared with competition in the marketplace that test marketing is not justified. Indeed, as techniques associated with simulated market tests become more sophisticated and distributors increasingly refuse to cooperate in test marketing, simulated market tests have become an attractive alternative to a full test market (Chisnall, 2005).

Test marketing involves the launch of the new product in one or a few geographical areas chosen to be representative of the intended market. Towns or television areas are chosen in which the new product is sold into distribution outlets so that performance can be gauged face to face with rival products. Test marketing is the acid test of new product development since the product is being promoted as it would during a national launch and consumers are being asked to choose it against competitor products as they would if the new product went national. It is a more realistic test than the simulated market test and therefore gives more accurate sales penetration and repeat purchasing estimates. By projecting test marketing results to the full market, an assessment of the new product's likely success can be made. But be aware that sample locations may not be representative of the national market, and thus sales projections may be inaccurate. Competitors may invalidate the test market by giving distributors incentives to stock their product, thereby denying the new product shelf space. Also, test marketing needs to run over a long enough period to measure the repeat purchase rate for the product, since this is a crucial indicator of success for many products (e.g. groceries and toiletries). This can mean a delay in national launch stretching to many months or even years. In the meantime, more aggressive competitors can launch a rival product nationally and therefore gain market pioneer advantages. The advantages of test marketing are that the information it provides facilitates the 'go/no go' national launch decision, and the effectiveness of the marketing mix elements—price, product formulation/packaging, promotion and distribution—can be checked for effectiveness. On a global scale, many international companies roll out products (e.g. cars and consumer electronics) from one country to another. In so doing, they are gaining some of the benefits of test marketing in that lessons learned early on can be applied to later launches.

Commercialization

Commercialisation involves considering three issues.

Developing a commercialization strategy for a new product

An effective commercialization strategy relies upon marketing management making clear choices regarding the target market (where it wishes to compete), and the development of a marketing strategy that provides a differential advantage (how it wishes to compete). These two factors define the new product positioning strategy, as discussed in Chapter 20.

A useful starting point for choosing a target market is an understanding of the **diffusion of innovation process** (Rogers, 2003). This explains how a new product spreads throughout a market over time. Particularly important is the notion that not all people or organizations who make up the market will be in the same state of readiness to buy the new product when it is launched. In other words, different actors in the market will have varying degrees of innovativeness—that is, their willingness to try something new. Figure 11.3 shows the *diffusion of innovation* curve, which categorizes people or organizations according to how soon they are willing to adopt the innovation.

The curve shows that those actors (*innovators* and *early adopters*) who were willing to buy the new product soon after launch are likely to form a minor part of the total number of actors who will eventually be willing to buy it. As the new product is accepted and approved by these customers, and the decision to buy the new product therefore becomes less risky, so the people that make up the bulk of the market, comprising the *early and late majority*, begin to try the product themselves. Finally, after the product has gained full market acceptance, a group suitably described as the *laggards* adopt the product.

By the time the laggards have begun buying the product, the innovators and early adopters have probably moved on to something new.

This diffusion of innovation categories has a crucial role to play in the choice of target market. The key is to understand the characteristics of the innovator and early adopter categories and target them at launch. Simply thinking about the kinds of people or organizations that are more likely to buy a new product early after launch may suffice. If not, marketing research can help. To stimulate the thinking process, Rogers suggests the following broad characteristics for each category (Rogers, 2003). It is important to note this is an introduction to this theory; you should read about the impact of technology and the 'big bang effect' in Chapter 20.

- *Innovators*: these are often venturesome and like to be different; they are willing to take a chance with an untried product. In consumer markets they tend to be younger, better educated, more confident and more financially affluent, and, consequently, can afford to take a chance on buying something new. In organizational markets, they tend to be larger and more profitable companies if the innovation is costly, and have more progressive, better-educated management. They may themselves have a good track record in bringing out new products and may have been the first to adopt innovations in the past. As such, they may be easy to identify.
- *Early adopters*: these are not quite so venturesome; they need the comfort of knowing someone else has taken the early risk. But they soon follow their lead. They still tend to have similar characteristics

FIGURE 11.3
The diffusion of innovation process

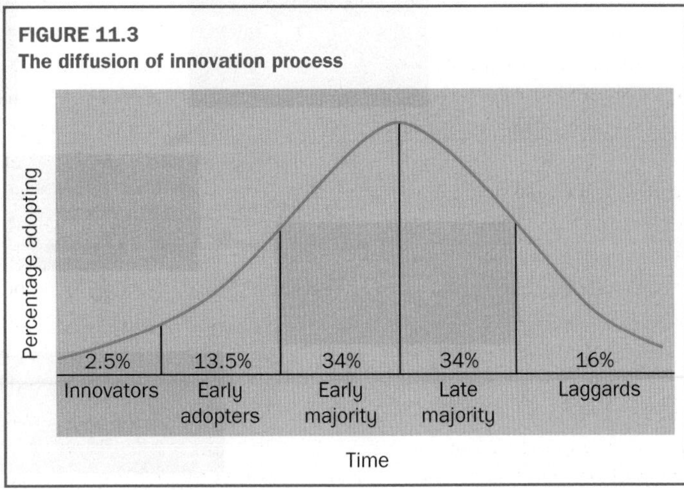

to the innovator group, since they need affluence and self-confidence to buy a product that has not yet gained market acceptance. They, together with the innovators, can be seen as opinion leaders who strongly influence other people's views on the product. As such, they have a major bearing on the success of the product. One way of looking at the early adopters is that they filter the products accepted by the innovator group and popularize them, leading to acceptance by most buyers in the market (Zikmund and D'Amico, 1999).

- *Early and late majorities*: these form the bulk of the customers in the market. The early majority are usually deliberate and cautious in their approach to buying products. They like to see products prove themselves on the market before they are willing to part with cash for them. The late majority are even more cautious and possibly sceptical of new products. They are willing to adopt only after most people or organizations have tried the products. Social pressure may be the driving force moving them to purchase.
- *Laggards*: these are tradition-bound people. The innovation needs to be perceived almost as a traditional product before they will consider buying it. In consumer markets, they are often the older and less well-educated members of the population.

By understanding the characteristics of at each stage of adoption it becomes possible to extract meaningful insights for marketing planning. At introduction, innovators buy the product, followed by early adopters as the product enters the growth phase. Growth is fuelled by the early and late majority, and stable sales during the maturity phase may be due to repurchasing by these groups. Laggards may enter the market during late maturity or even decline. Thus promotion designed to stimulate trial may need to be modified as the nature of new buyers changes over time.

The second key decision for commercialization is the choice of marketing strategy to establish a differential advantage. The approach will be dependent on the characteristics of the target market and the type of new product or service. As we have seen, the characteristics of customers affect the rate of adoption of an innovation, and marketing's job is to identify and target those with a high willingness to adopt upon launch. The characteristics of the product being launched also affect the diffusion rate and have marketing strategy implications (see Figure 11.4).

1 What is the *differential advantage* of the new product compared with existing products, as this will affect the speed of adoption. The more added customer benefits a product gives to a customer, the more customers will be willing to buy.

2 What is the innovation's *compatibility* with consumers' values, experiences, lifestyles and behaviours? The congruence between mobile phones and the lifestyles of many young people helped their diffusion. The iPhone's rapid diffusion was also aided by such compatibility. The new product also needs to be compatible with consumers' behaviour. Although the telephone is now part of our everyday lives, diffusion was slow because its adoption required significant behaviour change (Gourville, 2006). The diffusion of e-books

FIGURE 11.4
How the characteristics of a product affects its rate of diffusion

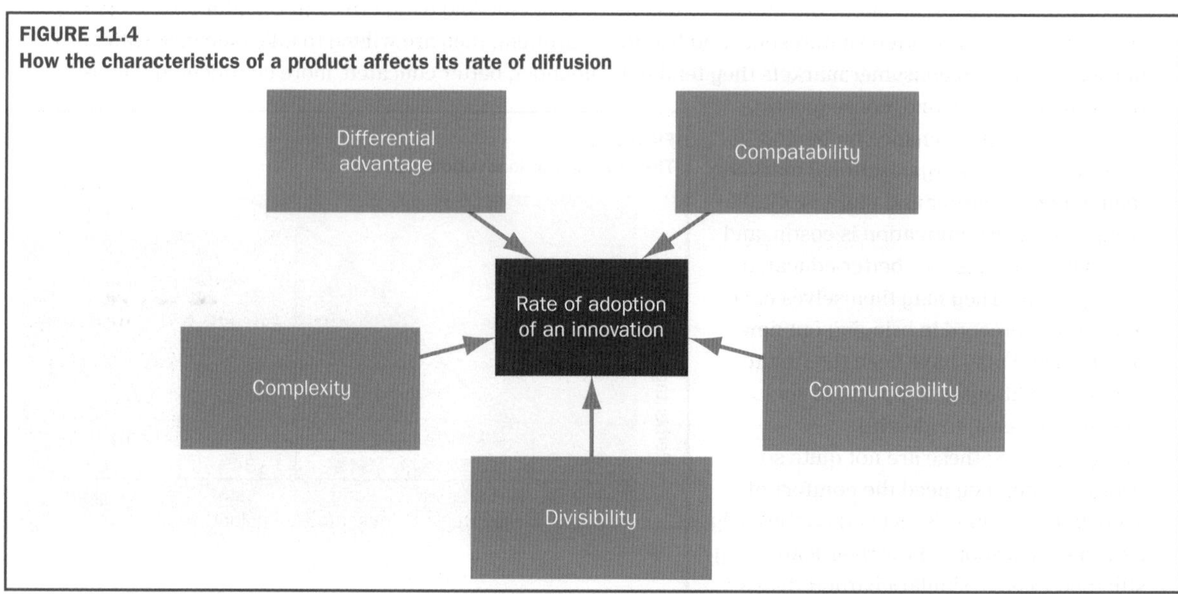

has also been slow, partly because people value the tactility and aesthetics of books rather than reading from an electronic screen.

3 What is the innovation's *complexity?* Products that are difficult to understand or use may take longer to be adopted. For example, Apple launched its Macintosh computer backed by the proposition that existing computers were too complex to gain widespread adoption. By making its model more user friendly, Apple gained fast adoption among the large segment of the population that was repelled by the complexity of using computers.

4 To what extent can the product or service be tried/experimented with? This also affects its speed of diffusion. This is called *divisibility* and refers to the degree to which the product can be tried on a limited basis. Inexpensive products can be tried without risk of heavy financial loss. The rapid diffusion of Google was aided by the fact that its functionality could be accessed free of charge. This mode of diffusion has been adopted by many high-tech products, for example Facebook, Twitter and Gmail.

5 What is the innovations *communicability?* Adoption is likely to be faster if the benefits and applications of the innovation can be readily observed or described to target customers. If product benefits are long term or difficult to quantify, then diffusion may take longer. For example, Skoda's attempt to produce more reliable cars took time to communicate, as buyers' acceptance of this claim depended on their long-term experience of driving the cars. In service industries, marketing innovations like providing more staff to improve the quality of service are hard to quantify in financial terms (i.e. extra revenue generated) and therefore have a low adoption rate by the management of some companies. The marketing implications are that marketing management must not assume that what is obvious to them will be clear to customers. They need to devise a communications strategy that allows potential customers to become aware of the innovation and understand and be convinced of its benefits.

Product replacement strategies

Product replacement is the most common form of new product introduction. A study of the marketing strategies used to position product replacements in the marketplace found eight approaches based on a combination of product change and other marketing modifications (i.e. marketing mix and target market changes) (Saunders and Jobber, 1994a). Figure 11.5 shows the eight replacement strategies used by companies.

1 *Facelift*: minor product change with little or no change to the rest of the marketing mix or target market. Cars are often given facelifts midway through their lifecycle by undergoing minor styling alterations; for example, Chinese and Japanese companies constantly use facelifts for current electronic products such as cameras, LCD screen and smart televisions, tablet and laptop computers and smartphones by changing product features, a process known as **product churning**.

2 *Inconspicuous technological substitution*: a major technological change with little or no alteration of the other elements of the marketing mix. The technological change is not brought to the consumer's attention, a strategy often used by washing powder manufacturers, where the improved performance rather than the technological change is brought to the consumers' attention (e.g. Skip intelligent liquid detergent, which has Fibre Protect technology).

3 *Remerchandising*: a modification of name, promotion, price, packaging and/or distribution, while maintaining the basic product. For example, Danone's Bio yoghurt changed to Activia; Jif cleaning products were rebranded as Cif; Orange mobile became Everything Everywhere (EE) in the UK when it merged with T-Mobile (Exhibit 11.2).

4 *Relaunch*: both the product and other marketing mix elements are changed. Relaunches are common in the car industry, where, every four to five years,

FIGURE 11.5
Product replacement strategies

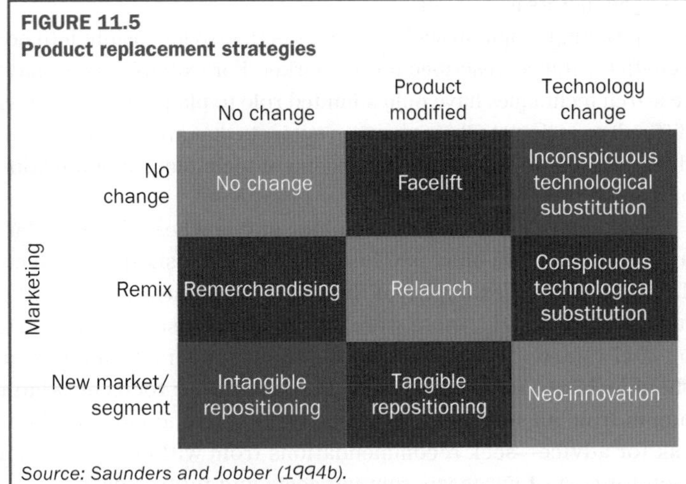

Source: Saunders and Jobber (1994b).

a model is replaced with an upgraded version. Sky has relaunched Sky 1, 2 and 3 channels as Sky Atlantic, Sky Living and Sky HD. Sky Living has subsequently been rebranded to Sky Witness to better reflect the programming of the channel and the introduction of more crime dramas.

5 *Conspicuous technological substitution*: a major technological change is accompanied by heavy promotional and other mix changes to stimulate awareness and trial. An example is the replacement of the Rover Mini with the BMW Mini, which, despite remaining faithful to the character of the original, is technologically a fundamentally different car.

EXHIBIT 11.2
Orange mobile became Everything Everywhere (EE) in the UK when Orange merged with T-Mobile

6 *Intangible repositioning*: the basic product is retained, but other mix elements and target customers change. Diageo has retained the product Le Piat d'Or wine, but is targeting a new audience of 45- to 50-year-old female wine drinkers. New packaging is designed to give clearer branding and shelf appeal (Fox, 2010).

7 *Tangible repositioning*: both the product and target market change. Skoda is an example of the product being significantly improved to appeal to a more upmarket, wealthier target market.

8 *Neo-innovation*: a fundamental technology change accompanied by target market and mix changes. For example, Samsung's move into the sustainable energy market has seen the development of new technology for new target customers.

Companies, therefore, face an array of replacement options with varying degrees of risk. Figure 11.5 categorizes these options and provides an aid to strategic thinking when considering how to replace products in the marketplace.

Commercializing technology

Superior commercialization of technology has been, and will continue to be, a key success factor in many industries. Some companies make a significant commitment to developing the capability to bring sophisticated high-tech products to market faster than other companies that treat the commercialization process in a less disciplined manner. For example, Volkswagen is to invest over €34 billion in electric and self-driving cars (Storbeck, 2017). Samsung spent over €13 billion on R&D into smart televisions and other advanced projection devices. Intel spends over $13 billion on R&D to keep pace with the demands for ever-increasing computing power and outspends its major competitors Qualcomm Broadcom and Samsung, where the annual spend on semiconductors in $3.4 billion.

Marketing's input in such situations is to provide insight into how the technology may provide customer benefits within a prescribed target market. For example, as we have already discussed, traditional marketing research techniques have only a limited role to play when using technology to create new markets; people find it difficult to articulate their views on subjects that are unfamiliar, and acceptance may come only over time (the diffusion of innovation). The marketing of technological innovations, therefore, calls for a blend of technology and marketing.

Martech is a growing marketplace and is where the boundaries between marketing and technology firms are becoming very blurred. There are currently six distinct sectors with numerous specific activity areas. Table 11.4 shows examples of the areas of business activity where marketing and technology are inseparable. In 2011, there were just 150 firms listed in the martech sector; this had grown to close to 5,000 by 2017 (Martech, 2018). For marketing managers wishing to navigate this highly complex landscape, they should stick to some basic marketing principles: focus on what is needed, not the latest cool gizmo; get buy-in from all stakeholders who are likely to engage with the latest technology application(s) needed; ask for advice—seek recommendations from within the relevant industry; evaluate the recommendations; monitor cost of purchase, running costs and future costs.

TABLE 11.4 The Martech industry by sector and activity

	Sector					
	Advertising and promotion	**Content and experiences**	**Social and relationships**	**Commerce and sales**	**Data**	**Management**
ACTIVITIES	Mobile marketing	Mobile apps	Call analytics and management	Retail and proximity marketing	Audience/ market data and data enhancement	Talent management
	Display and programmatic advertising	Video marketing	Events, meetings and webinars	Channel, partner and local marketing	Marketing analytics, performance and attribution	Product management
	Search and social Advertising	Interactive content	Social media marketing and mentoring	Sales automation, enablement and intelligence	Mob and web analytics	Budgeting and finance
	Native/content advertising	Email marketing	Advocacy, loyalty and referrals	Affiliate marketing and management	Dashboards and data visualization	Collaboration
	Video advertising	Content marketing	Influencers	E-commerce marketing	Business/ customer intelligence and management	Project and workflow
	Print	Optimization, personalization and testing	Feedback	E-commerce platforms and carts	Predictive analytics	Agile and lean management
	Public relations	DAM and MRM	Community and reviews		Customer data platforms	Vendor analysis

DAM – Digital asset management

MRM Market resource management

Review

1 What is an innovation and what is a new product?

- Innovation is the process of translating an idea into a product or service; innovative products are those that can reshape markets and reconfigure marketing environments.
- New products are much less revolutionary and tend to be incremental improvements. They fall into four broad types: product replacements, additions to existing lines, new product lines and new-to-the-world products.

2. How to create and nurture an innovative culture

- Creating and nurturing an innovative culture can be achieved by rewarding success heavily, tolerating a certain degree of failure, and senior management sending clear messages about the role and importance of innovation. Their words should be supported by allowing staff time off to develop their own ideas, making resources available, being accessible when difficult decisions need to be taken, and resisting automatic nay-saying.

3 The organizational options applying to innovations and new product development

- The options are project teams, product and brand managers, and new product departments and committees. Whichever method is used, effective cross-functional teamwork is essential for successful innovation leadership.

4 **Managing idea realization (new product development)**

- Idea realization and new product development is expensive, risky and time-consuming. Managing the process effectively is important, as is controlling budgets, production time and lowering risk. There is an eight-step new product development process, which consists of setting new product strategy, idea generation, screening, concept testing, business analysis, product development, market testing and commercialization.

5 **The new product development process**

- A formal process with review points, clear new product goals and a strong marketing orientation underlying the process leads to greater success.
- The stages are new product strategy (senior management should set objectives and priorities), idea generation (sources include customers, competitors, distributors, salespeople, engineers and marketers), screening (to evaluate the ideas' commercial worth), concept testing (to allow the views of target customers to enter the process early), product development (where the concept is developed into a physical product for testing), market testing (where the new product is tested in the marketplace) and commercialization (where the new product is launched).

6 **Commercialization**

- Commercialization involves three issues:
  1) Developing a commercialization strategy, which involves selecting target markets and understanding the diffusion of innovation categories and their marketing implications. The categories are innovators, early adopters, early and late majorities, and laggards. The marketing implications are that the categories can be used as a basis for segmentation and targeting (initially the innovators/early adopters should be targeted). As the product is bought by different categories, so the marketing mix may need to change. The speed of adoption can be affected by marketing activities—for example, advertising to create awareness, sales promotion to stimulate trial, and educating users in product benefits and applications. The nature of the innovation itself can also affect adoption—that is, the strength of its differential advantage, its compatibility with people's values, experiences, lifestyles and behaviours, its complexity, its divisibility and its communicability.
  2) Product replacement strategies—deciding when it is appropriate to introduce a new form of an existing product.
  3) Commercializing technology, innovative technology firms are constantly developing new products and they tend to have significant R&D budgets. The marketing of technology products calls for a blend of technology and marketing. This blend has given rise to a whole new industry sector called martech. This sector is growing in complexity, the type of activities and the number of firms.

Key Terms

business analysis a review of the projected sales, costs and profits for a new product to establish whether these factors satisfy company objectives

concept testing testing new product ideas with potential customers

diffusion of innovation process the process by which a new product spreads throughout a market over time

innovation the realization of an invention by bringing it to market

invention the discovery of new methods and ideas

market testing the limited launch of a new product to test sales potential

martech the growing technology and marketing landscape of companies, who are involved in relevant activities

product churning a continuous and rapid spiral of new product introductions

project teams the bringing together of staff from such areas as R&D, engineering, manufacturing, finance and marketing to work on a project such as new product development

test marketing the launch of a new product in one or a few geographic areas chosen to be representative of the intended market

Study Questions

1. **Explain the difference between an invention, innovation and new product development.**
2. **Discuss how creative clusters in the high-end luxury markets in Europe foster innovation and new product development.**
3. **Suggest how marketing leaders can nurture, support and manage innovation.**
4. **Explain the different skills needed to be an innovation leader.**
5. **Think of an unsatisfied need that you feel could be solved by the introduction of a new product. How would you set about testing your idea to examine its commercial potential?**
6. **What are the advantages and disadvantages of test marketing? In what circumstances should you be reluctant to use test marketing?**
7. **Your company has developed a new range of Thai curry sauce, intended to compete with the market leader. How would you conduct product tests for your new line?**
8. **What are the issues associated with the commercialization phase of new product development?**
9. **Debate the importance of innovation as a driver of economic growth.**
10. **Choose a successful innovation and then find out the history of its development. Identify the barriers and hurdles that were overcome between initial design stage and market success.**

Recommended Reading

Innovations drives future growth. Read more about the diffusion of innovations, the importance of collaboration and innovation culture in small and medium-sized firms.

Aksoym, H. (2017) How do innovation culture, marketing innovation and product innovation affect the market performance of small and medium-sized enterprises (SMEs)? *Technology in Society*, 51: 133–41. Available at: https://www.sciencedirect.com/science/article/pii/S0160791X1730088X (accessed August 2018)

Fossas-Olalla, M., Minguela-Rata, B., López-Sánchez, J. and Fernández-Menénde, J. (2015) Product innovation: when should suppliers begin to collaborate? *Journal of Business Research*, 68(7): 1404–6.

Rogers, E.M. (2010) *Diffusion of Innovations*, Simon and Schuster. New York.

Tellis, G. (2013) *Unrelenting Innovation*, John Wiley & Sons Inc. San Francisco.

References

Baregheh, A., Rowley, J. and Sambrook, S. (2009) Towards a multidisciplinary definition of innovation, *Management Decision*, 47(8): 323–1339. Available at: https://doi.org/10.1108/00251740910984578 (accessed August 2018).

Belton, P. (2015). Game of drones: As prices plummet drones are taking off, BBC.co.uk, 16 January. Available at: http://www.bbc.co.uk/news/business-30820399 (accessed August 2018).

Bergen, S.A., Miyajima, R. and McLaughlin, C.P. (1988) The R&D/production interface in four developed countries, *R&D Management*, 18(3): 201–16.

Booz, Allen and Hamilton (1982) *New Products Management for the 1980s*. New York: Booz, Allen and Hamilton, Inc.

de Brentani, U. (1991) Success factors in developing new business services, *European Journal of Marketing*, 15(2): 33–59.

Chisnall, P. (2005) *Marketing Research*. Maidenhead: McGraw-Hill.

Cooper, R.G. and Kleinschmidt, E.J. (1986) An investigation into the new product process: steps, deficiencies and impact, *Journal of Product Innovation Management*, June, 71–85.

Day, P. (2012), Frugal Feast, http://www.bbc.co.uk/programmes/b01gvtjj (accessed August 2018).

Doyle, P. (1997) From the top, *Guardian*, 2 August.

Duggan, M. (2012) Frugal innovation, http://knowinnovation.com/frugal-innovation (accessed August 2018)

Dyer, J. and Gregersen, H. (2018) How we rank the most innovative companies 2018, *Forbes*, 29 May, https://www.forbes.com/sites/innovatorsdna/2018/05/29/how-we-rank-the-most-innovative-companies-2018/#b3663201e3cb (accessed August 2018).

European Cultural and Creative Industries Alliance (2017) *Securing the Leadership of the European High-end and Luxury Industries in the Digital Era*, https://www.eccia.eu/assets/activities/files/ECCIA_Manifesto_HD.pdf (accessed August 2018).

Forbes Technology Council (2018) The best tech innovation of the last three years, *Forbes*, 25 May, https://www.forbes.com/sites/forbestechcouncil/2018/05/25/the-best-tech-innovations-of-the-last-three-years/#70f7afec25a4 (accessed August 2018).

Fox, P. (2010) Piat d'Or launches first Sauvignon Blanc, http://www.talkingretail.com/products/drinks-news/piat-dor-launches-first-sauvignon-blanc, 1 July (accessed August 2018).

Geoghegan, J. (2011) Satnavs and smartphones put traditional maps on the road to nowhere as sales drop massively, The Mail Online, 3 September, http://www.dailymail.co.uk/sciencetech/article-2033227/Satnavs-smart-phones-traditional-maps-road-sales-drop-massively.html#ixzz1rwFKziSX (accessed August 2018).

Gourville, J. (2006) *The Curse of Innovation: Why Innovative Products Fail*, MSI Report No. 05-117.

Gupta, A. K. and Wileman, D. (1990) Improving R&D/marketing relations: R&D perspective, *R&D Management*, 20(4): 277–90.

Hamel, G. and Prahalad, C.K. (1991) Corporate imagination and expeditionary marketing, *Harvard Business Review*, July–August, 81–92.

Harouni, L. (2011) A Primer on 3d Printing, https://www.ted.com/talks/lisa_harouni_a_primer_on_3d_printing?language=en (accessed August 2015).

Hegarty, W.H. and Hoffman, R.C. (1990) Product/market innovations: a study of top management involvement among four cultures, *Journal of Product Innovation Management*, 7: 186–99.

Hise, R.T., O'Neal, L., Parasuraman, A. and McNeal, J.U. (1990) Marketing/R&D interaction in new product development: implications for new product success rates, *Journal of Product Innovation Management*, 7: 142–55.

Honey Bee (n.d.) http://www.sristi.org/hbnew

Huston, L. and N. Sakkab (2006) Connect and Develop: Inside Procter & Gamble's New Model for Innovation, *Harvard Business Review* 84(3), 58–72.

Jarvis, J. (2009) The foresight of Google, *Media Guardian*, 9 February.

Jobber, D., J. Saunders, G. Hooley, B. Gilding and J. Hatton-Smooker (1989) Assessing the Value of a Quality Assurance Certificate for Software: An Exploratory Investigation, *MIS Quarterly*, March, 19–31.

Johne, A. (1992) Don't let your customers lead you astray in developing new products, *European Management Journal*, 10(1): 80–4.

Johne, A. and Storey, C. (1998) New source development: a review of the literature and annotated bibliography, *European Journal of Marketing*, 32(3/4): 184–251.

Johne, A. and Snelson, P. (1988) Auditing product innovation activities in manufacturing firms, *R&D Management*, 18(3), 227–33.

Joshi, A.W. and Sharma, S. (2004) Customer knowledge development: antecedents and impact on new product performance, *Journal of Marketing*, 68 (October): 47–9.

Jugaad (2012) http://www.jugaad.org/?page_id=2 (accessed August 2018)

Kadri, M. (2010) Finding innovation in every corner, 2 August, http://changeobserver.designobserver.com/feature/findinginnovation-in-every-corner/12691 (accessed August 2018).

Koshler, R. (1991), in Mueller-Boehling, D. *et al.* (eds) *Innovations—und Technologiemanagement*. Stuttgart: C.E. Poeschel Verlagi.

Levitt, T. (1960) Marketing myopia, *Harvard Business Review*, July–August.

Lukoschek, C., Gerlach, G., Stock, R. and Xin, K. (2018) Leading to sustainable organizational unit performance: antecedents and outcomes of executives' dual innovation leadership, *Journal of Business Research*, 91: 266–76.

Maidique, M.A. and Zirger, B.J. (1984) A study of success and failure in product innovation: the case of the US electronics industry, *IEEE Transactions in Engineering Management*, EM-31 (November): 192–203.

Martech (2018), what is martech? The marketing and technology landscape, April, https://martechtoday.com/library/what-is-martech (accessed August 2018)

Matthews, V. (2002) Caution versus creativity, *Financial Times*, 17 June.

Moosmayer, D.C. and Koehn, A. (2011) The moderating role of managers' uncertainty avoidance values on the performance impact of radical and incremental innovation, *International Journal of Business Research*, 11(6): 32–9.

Moules, J. (2013) Tech start-ups: innovation hubs all over world seek to follow Silicon Valley lead, *The Financial Times*, 11 June. Available at: http://www.ft.com/cms/s/2/e357a258-b3d2-11e2-b5a5-00144feabdc0.html#axzz3YdUGITLb (accessed 20 April 2015).

Nadworny, R. (2014) Observe your customers to unlock innovation, Burlington Free Press, 18 December, http://www.burlingtonfreepress.com/story/money/industries/2014/12/18/nadworny-observe-customers-unlock-innovation/20554685 (accessed August 2018).

Parkinson, S.T. (1982) The Role of the User in Successful New Product Development, *R&D Management*, 12, 123–31.

Prahalad, C.K. and Mashelkar, R.A. (2010) Innovation's Holy Grail, *Harvard Business Review*, July–August.

Priya, K.V. (2017) Interview with Professor Anil Kumar Gupta, Indian Institute of Management, Ahmedabad, February, https://mediaindia.eu/interview/interview-with-professor-anil-kumar-gupta-indian-institute-of-management-ahmedabad/ (accessed August 2018).

Procter & Gamble (2018) Connect + develop, https://www.pgconnectdevelop.com/ (accessed August 2018)

Richard, H. (1996) Why Competitiveness is a Dirty Word in Scandinavia, *European*, 6–12 June, 24.

Rogers, E.M. (2003) *Diffusion of Innovations*. New York: Free Press.

Rowan, D. (2011) 3D printing—an industrial revolution in the digital age? *IWired*, 9 May, http://www.wired.com/epicenter/2011/05/3d-printing-an-industrial-revolution-in-the-digital-age (accessed August 2018).

Saunders, J. and Jobber, D. (1994a) Product replacement strategies: occurrence and concurrence, *Journal of Product Innovation Management* (November).

Saunders, J. and Jobber, D. (1994b) Strategies for product launch and deletion, in Saunders, J. (ed.) *The Marketing Initiative*. Hemel Hempstead: Prentice-Hall, 227.

Shah, A. (2012) Causes of poverty, http://www.globalissues.org/issue/2/causes-of-poverty, 8 April.

Shrivastava, P. and Souder, W.E. (1987) The strategic management of technological innovation: a review and a model, *Journal of Management Studies*, 24(1): 24–41.

Slotegraaf, R.J. and Atuahene-Gima, K. (2011) Product development team stability and new product advantage: the role of decision-making processes, *Journal of Marketing*, 75(1), 96–108.

Storbeck, O. (2017) VW to invest more than €34 billion in electric and self-driving vehicles, *Financial Times*, 17 November, https://www.ft.com/content/6ed3b1d2-cbbb-11e7-aa33-c63fdc9b8c6c (accessed August 2018).

Tellis, G., Prabhu, J.C. and Chandy, R.K. (2009) Radical innovation across nations: the preeminence of corporate culture, *Journal of Marketing*, 73(1): 3–23.

The Economist (2008) Rebirth of a Carmaker, 26 April, 91–3.

The Economist (2012) Asian Innovation, http://www.economist.com/node/21551028, 24 March (accessed August 2018).

Viklund, A. (2015) Brainstorming, http://teamvirtute.wordpress.com/promotingcreativity/brainstorming/ (accessed August 2018)

Walsh, W.J. (1990) Get the whole organisation behind new product development, *Research in Technological Management*, Nov–Dec, 32–6.

Wheeler, A. (2015) 3D Printing Industry, *3D Printing Industry*, 23 April. http://3dprintingindustry.com/3dp-applications (accessed August 2018).

Zikmund, W.G. and D'Amico, M. (1999) *Marketing*. St Paul, MN: West.

CASE 21

Keogh's Crisps—Home Grown Innovation

Introduction

Innovation is in the roots of Keogh's Crisps, with a business dating back 200 years. The family business, now known for its tasty crisp and potato offerings, was originally a traditional potato farm supplying Dublin city wholesale markets. However, change was imminent with the Keogh family observing a 50 per cent decline in potato consumption in the early 2000s. The Irish, a nation of potato eaters, had developed a taste for convenience and a broader palate for global food. As a result, the business needed to adapt and innovate to reconnect with the Irish consumer.

Facilitating Consumer Convenience through Innovation

In 2006, the team developed easy-cook potatoes as a solution for the time-poor, money-rich consumer. This product—the first such product in the world at the time—was cooked in a bag in the microwave and tasted as good as a boiled potato but in a more convenient and efficient way. Initially this product went under a private label for a supermarket retailer and didn't really take off. It was only after insight from focus groups that it emerged that consumers did not fully trust a supermarket to brand this product and would prefer the Peter Keogh and Son's farm brand. This insight ultimately led to the decision to rebrand into the family-farm brand 'Keogh's' in 2007. At this time, the use of farm brands for fresh produce was emerging, with Keogh's being one of the first to highlight its name on both products. The easy-cook potatoes were then rebranded with the Keogh's name and relaunched in the original retailer, with an immediate increase in sales, just as the focus groups had predicted.

Diversification to New Product Offering—Crisps

While potato sales remained a core product offering, Keogh's knew it had to diversity to maintain growth in a market increasingly interested in pasta and rice as alternatives to potatoes. Crisps emerged as the new and ultimately successful arm of the business and its product offerings. While on a visit to the USA, the Managing Director, Tom Keogh, met consumers who were interested in buying Keogh's potato products, but after samples been sent to the USA they were returned by the Food and Drug Administration (FDA) before they could be tested. An FDA official explained that fresh potatoes would be blocked from entering the USA, but they could get through customs if they were cooked! As a result, Keogh's started to look at the options. New product suggestions such as frozen chips arose; however, it was the popularity of premium crisps in the UK in 2007 that captured Keogh's attention. As a result, Keogh's looked to multiple markets to carry out research. This research immediately told Keogh's that its offering had to be 'uber' premium, and it took four years to get the know-how and resources in place to action this new product range.

The new product development started in the kitchen of the Keogh family farmhouse, which at the time was a cookery school. Experimentation began with frying, seasoning and using different oils to create a product. The first business plan was to be at a farmers' markets for three years, but this product resonated with the

»

Irish market much sooner than this and performed way beyond the expectations of the business. Keogh's artisan potato crisps was launched in the depth of a recession in 2011, and focus groups with Bord Bia, the Irish government organisation responsible for supporting food businesses, showed that the product was well received, with a new Irish brand being seen as a good news story. The brand started to gain traction as the whole potato, including the skin, was being used with high quality oil and seasonings. All authentic local Irish brands were sourced for flavourings, and Keogh's Crisps started working with companies that were equally as passionate about their products. Examples include salt from the Barra peninsula, cider vinegar from David Llewellyn's orchard and chorizo from Gubbeen Smokehouse.
Not only have the flavourings been sourced locally, but the imagery used on each individual flavour is unique and personal to the family business and where the flavours have been sourced from.

This image of cheese and onion is placed on the red van that Peter Keogh used when bringing his products to wholesale in the early days of the potato business.

This image of sea salt derives from Ballinskelligs, County Kerry, and the view of the Skelligs in the background known also for the filming of *Star Wars*.

A Growing Innovative Culture

As the business develops, idea generation has become an important team role and not just the role of the Managing Director. Recognising the consolidation of ideas, Keogh's Crisps developed a five-year strategic plan to deliver a progressive and shared vision for the business. The growing staff consist of four senior managers—Tom as managing director alongside a head of operations, financial controller and head of sales—supported by management in human resources, export sales, marketing and quality management. In total, 48 people are employed within Keogh's Crisps and 45 are employed for potatoes.
To assist in the more efficient and consistent delivery of new product developments, a specialist consultancy company was brought into the business in 2016 to assist Keogh's Crisps in the new product development process from idea generation, to understanding the market, to understanding the consumer. Traditionally, new product development was delivered by Keogh's Crisps, but with no great depth of research undertaken. However, with a bigger team, it now practises a stage-gate process with continual review of new product development decisions by management at distinct stages, taking into consideration market information available alongside risk analysis and availability of resources. As a result, a new product development pipeline is available for the next three years. Idea generation and sharing are encouraged in Keogh's Crisps, as management value and include inputs from all team members. These ideas are listened to and fed into the idea generation process. With ideas coming back even while employees are travelling, both on holiday and for business, innovation within Keogh's Crisps is active and varied.

The Authentic Taste of Ireland

In 2012, Keogh's Crisps wowed the world with the sensational shamrock-seasoned potato crisp.
The concept came from the popularity of seasonal products, so Keogh's wanted to launch a crisp product around the seasonal calendar. The plan was launched in November 2011 with the team sourcing shamrocks from a list of Bord Bia approved shamrock growers. With the upcoming St Patrick's Day in March, Keogh's was set on developing a flavoured crisp from shamrocks. With quick turnaround needed in the development of the product, Keogh's received welcome confirmation that shamrocks were recognised as a food product, and oil infusion was used to extract

the shamrock flavouring. From concept to launch of the shamrock-flavoured crisps took a total of 14 weeks, and within one day global PR was achieved. This product launched the business into mainstream media attention and into the mouths of consumers. Despite delisting the product after the St Patrick's festival period, the product received continued demand and today it is Keogh's third biggest seller after mature Irish cheese and onion, and Irish sea salt and cider vinegar.

The Crisp Consumer and Crisp Market

Due to the growing success of Keogh's core range, crinkle-cuts and multipack potato crisp ranges, Keogh's feel the pressure from the crisp consumer to keep innovating. As well as combining travel abroad for research purposes, Keogh's Crisps continually utilizes focus groups to assist with new product developments, which maintains its understanding of the consumer at all times. In more recent years, Keogh's Crisps has been faced with challenges from similar ('me-too') products by bigger players while trying to retain its current 8 per cent of the crisp market in Ireland. The team work hard to maintain their distinct offering through their high quality and the exceptional taste of their products, with consumer trust underpinning the business and who they are. This is particularly important in a market where 'fake farm' brands are emerging. One example of this authentic connection between the consumer and Keogh's Crisps is evident through the creative 'Spud Nav', in which consumers can trace the origins of their crisps by field and flavour at www.keoghs.ie/spud-nav.

Exciting New Products are 'Flying' in . . .

In January 2016 as a result of Keogh's Crisps development, the business was in a position to expand the factory. In this expansion, Tom used the opportunity to introduce new technological innovation in the sizing of crisps, separating small and larger crisps, with the small crisps suitable for a 20 g bag versus the usual 50 g offering. As a result of this new packaging solution, Emirates Airline was attracted to 20 g smaller bags of crisps for its first class passengers. But it was only after the product went to blind taste testing with 15 different products that it was taken on board by Emirates Airline. This was a particularly welcome outcome for Keogh's Crisps, as the company had tried twice before to get its products accepted by Emirates Airline. As a result of the flying success, Keogh's now services Cityjet and Lufthansa and is exploring other options.

New development and perceived areas of growth will accompany the continual development of new crisp flavours and exports, but there are exciting developments as a new product for the healthy snack market is receiving attention by Keogh's . . . so the future looks extremely tasty and certainly looks innovative for the deeply rooted family farm business.

Questions

1. **How has Keogh's Crisps used innovation in marketing to build its brand?**
2. **What approach does Keogh's take to developing innovative products?**
3. **How has Keogh's Crisps achieved competitive advantage?**
4. **What is Keogh's Crisps doing to ensure it will continue to innovate in the future?**

This case study was written by Geraldine Lavin and Christina O'Connor, Maynooth University.

Special acknowledgement to Tom Keogh, MD of Keogh's for providing access to his business and for his time in interview.

CASE 22

Innovation through Collaboration: Apple Watch Nike+

Introduction

Apple is widely considered as the number one innovative company in the world. Founded by Steve Jobs and Steve Wozniak in 1976, the company revolutionized personal technology with the introduction of the Mackintosh in 1984. Apple grew throughout the 80s and 90s, despite both Wozniak and Jobs moving on to newer and bigger things. The company peaked in 1990, but by 1996 experts believed Apple to be doomed and on the verge of bankruptcy. It was not until 1997, when Steve Jobs returned to Apple and became the interim CEO, that the company's fortunes began to turn around. Jobs revamped Apple computers and introduced the iBook (a personal laptop). He also started branching out into mp3 players (iPod) and media player software (iTunes). While Steve Jobs died on 5 October, 2011, Apple continues with his legacy (Richardson and Terrell, 2008). In 2018, Apple made history by becoming the first private sector company to surpass US$1 trillion market value, to make it the most valuable company on Earth (Gurman, 2018). The tech giant has staged an unparalleled turnaround since its near bankruptcy in the 1990s, and experts credit the company's ongoing commitment to innovation as key to its continued success. Apple now leads the world in innovation, with the iPhone, iPad, Mac, Apple TV and the Apple Watch. Apple's four software platforms—iOS, macOS, watchOS and tvOS—provide seamless experiences across all Apple devices and empower people with breakthrough services such as the App Store, Apple Music, Apple Pay and iCloud (Apple, 2018).

A Perfect Partnership

Making your brand stand out from the crowd in a hugely competitive marketplace has been one of the biggest challenges facing Apple. The company has long seen the value of teaming up and collaborating with other brands for commercial projects, to increase its brand exposure and to reap dividends for the business. Over the years, Apple has teamed up with numerous manufacturers and retailers, but its partnership with Nike is like no other. Nike and Apple have long had a good relationship when it comes to the convergence of technology and athletics. One of the first products that came from the relationship was the Nike+ running initiative launched in 2006, which started with a small chip placed inside a Nike running shoe paired with a connected Apple iPod (Westlake, 2015). Having Tim Cook, then Apple's CEO, on Nike's board allowed an effortless partnership with Apple by leveraging Apple's hardware as the chip's receiver to track users' distances and speed (Anonymous, 2016). Since this initial collaboration in 2006, there have been an abundance of collaborative product launches from the two powerhouses.

One of their most successful collaborations resulted in Apple unveiling a new product in collaboration with its long-standing partner Nike in 2016: the Series 2 Apple Watch Nike+. With a price tag of $399, the device was geared towards runners and was promoted as the ultimate companion for those with a passion for running, whether they were emerging runners or marathon veterans. To get the most out of the watch, users needed to wirelessly tether to an iPhone, allowing users to receive notifications and other updates. However, the Apple Watch Nike+ could also be autonomously used for exercise and using apps. Apple unveiled its co-branded watch with Nike to appeal to customers who wanted more specialized exercise tracking compared with the standard Apple Watch model (Apple, 2016). The watch was intended to compete against the likes of Fitbit, Jawbone and Samsung, all of which offered fitness trackers that doubled as smartwatches (Reisinger, 2016).

For both Apple and Nike, it was important that the watch had a differential advantage over rival brands in the competitive wearable technology market. The watch featured GPS, water resistance to 50 metres, a powerful dual-core processor and watch OS3. The Apple Watch Nike+ also included exclusive Siri commands and iconic Nike watch faces, along with deep integration with Nike's new Nike+ Run Club app for motivation to go for a run, coaching plans that adapt to the user's unique schedule and progress, and guidance from the world's best coaches and athletes. According to Trevor Edwards, the President of the Nike brand, the collaborative effort between Nike and Apple resulted in a device that had an immediate differential advantage: 'The market is full of hard-to-read devices that focus on your data. This focuses on your life. It's a powerful device with a simple solution—your perfect running partner.' Ultimately, the Apple Watch Nike+ leveraged Apple's incredible tech know-how with Nike's deep understanding of athletes (Tillman and Grabham, 2018).

Since its initial launch in 2016, Apple and Nike have continued to work closely to improve the quality of the Apple Watch Nike+, adding features and improving the watch's design. For example, in 2018 Apple again teamed up with Nike to introduce a version of the Apple Watch designed for runners. The Series 4 Apple Watch Nike+ watch uniquely featured a different strap design and specialized software to make it easier for runners to put it on quickly and make use of the device's built-in GPS. Like the standard Apple Watch, users could change the straps. It featured new watch-band colours and included a pure platinum/black sport band (with a perforated design that was designed to be more durable and breathable) and a summit white sport loop with reflective yarn. As for software, Nike+ had additional perks over the standard version of the Apple Watch: it came with exclusive Nike-themed watch faces and allowed the user to directly launch the Nike+ Run Club app, which came pre-installed, allowing users to track their runs, view running history, and more (Ismael and Picks, 2018).

Since its original release in 2016, the Apple Watch has been one of the most popular smartwatches to date. While the device is appreciated by everyone from tech geeks to trend chasers, it is especially loved by athletes, and Nike's collaborative efforts with Apple have always been their versions of choice (Kunert, 2017). According to Jason Low, Canalys analyst, 'What sets the Apple Watch apart is a renewed focus on fitness, its co-branding with Nike helping to support this move. In addition, the availability of a wide range of accessories means the Apple Watch appeals to tech savvy consumers with an eye for fashion' (Riley, 2018).

Conclusion

Apple has long nurtured collaborations with heritage luxury brands, starting with Hermès in 2015. Since then, designers including Coach, Kate Spade and Nike have all designed trendy bands at high price points for the Apple watch. However, Apple's relationship with Nike has proved to be one of its most successful collaborations. Apple recognized the potential of working with Nike, and vice versa. They had similar audiences. They both had brand loyalists, and the union encouraged Apple die-hards to try Nike+, and Nike+ lovers to buy the Apple Watch (Young, 2018).

Recent research suggests that consumers' love affair with fitness bands looks to have run its course, with smartwatches shaping up to be the preferred choice. Channel analyst Canalys has indicated that sales of fitness bands fell 7 per cent year-on-year to just over 9 million units in the first quarter of 2017. At the same time, smartwatch sales jumped 26 per cent to more than 6 million—some 40 per cent of the total wearable band market. Apple Watch accounted for 3.8 million of these sales (up 77 per cent from the year before) according to Canalys (Kunert, 2017). In addition, Apple became the biggest shipper of wearables in 2017, owning 21 per cent of market share, according to the International Data Corporation (IDC). With Allied Market Research projecting that the smartwatch market will reach $32.9 billion globally by 2020, Apple appears well positioned for the future (Riley, 2018).

Questions

1. **In 2018, Fast Company identified Apple as the number one most innovative company in the world. Why do you think Apple has been given this accolade?**
2. **Comment on how the collaboration between Nike and Apple has been advantageous to both brands. Identify other high profile examples of successful brand collaborations.**
3. **How has the collaboration between Nike and Apple given the Apple Watch Nike+ a competitive edge over rival wearable technology brands?**
4. **Conduct additional secondary research and comment on the different types of new products that have resulted from the collaboration between Apple and Nike, i.e. product replacements,**

additions to existing lines, new product lines and new-to-the-world products.

This case study was written by Marie O' Dwyer, Waterford Institute of Technology.

References

Based on: Anonymous (2016) Is Nike the next big tech giant?, Harvard Business School, https://rctom.hbs.org/submission/is-nike-the-next-big-tech-giant/ (accessed 12 September 2018); Apple (2016) Apple and Nike launch the perfect running partner, Apple Watch Nike+, Apple Inc, https://www.apple.com/newsroom/2016/09/apple-nike-launch-apple-watch-nike/ (accessed 12 September 2018); Apple (2018) Apple's worldwide developers conference kicks off June 4 in San Jose, Apple Inc, https://www.apple.com/ie/newsroom/2018/03/apples-worldwide-developers-conference-kicks-off-june-4-in-san-jose/ (accessed 12 September 2018); Gurman, M. (2018) Apple becomes the first U.S. company to hit $1 trillion value, Bloomberg, https://www.bloomberg.com/news/articles/2018-08-02/apple-becomes-first-u-s-company-to-hit-1-trillion-market-value (accessed 12 September 2018); Ismael, A. and Picks, I. (2018) Nike has quietly put its exclusive Apple Watch Series 3 on sale—here's how to save 20% before it sells out, *Business Insider*, http://uk.businessinsider.com/apple-watch-nike-plus-series-3-sale-2018-8?r=US&IR=T (accessed 12 September 2018); Kunert, P. (2017) Sweaty fitness bands fall behind as Apple Watch outpaces sales, *The Register*, https://www.theregister.co.uk/2017/05/12/apple_watch/ (accessed 12 September 2018); Reisinger, D. (2016) Here's when you can get the Apple Watch Nike+, *Fortune*, http://fortune.com/2016/10/14/apple-watch-nike/ (accessed 12 September 2018); Richardson, A. and Terrell, E. (2008) Apple Computers Inc., Business Reference Services, http://www.loc.gov/rr/business/businesshistory/April/apple.html (accessed 12 September 2018); Riley, T. (2018) The Apple Watch has a secret weapon that helps it dominate the market, CNBC, https://www.cnbc.com/2018/05/03/apple-watch-has-a-secret-weapon-that-helps-it-dominate-the-market.html (accessed 12 September 2018); Tillman, M. and Grabham, D. (2018) What is Apple Watch Nike+? And how is it different to the standard Apple Watch?, Pocket-lint, https://www.pocket-lint.com/smartwatches/news/apple/139179-what-is-apple-watch-nike-plus-and-when-can-you-buy-it (accessed 12 September 2018); Westlake, A. (2015) Nike CEO 'excited' about possible Apple collaboration in future, Slashgear, https://www.slashgear.com/nike-ceo-excited-about-possible-apple-collaboration-in-future-09382794/ (accessed 12 September 2018); Young, T. (2018) How to choose a co-selling partner, *Business Journal*, https://www.bizjournals.com/bizjournals/how-to/marketing/2018/05/how-to-choose-a-co-selling-partner.html (accessed 12 September 2018)

CHAPTER 12
Value Through Pricing

There are two fools in every market. One charges too little; the other charges too much.

RUSSIAN PROVERB

LEARNING OBJECTIVES

After reading this chapter, you should be able to:

1. explain the economist's approach to price determination
2. distinguish between full-cost and direct-cost pricing
3. discuss your understanding of going-rate pricing and competitive bidding
4. explain the advantages of market-orientated pricing over cost and competitor-orientated pricing
5. discuss the factors that affect price setting when using a market-orientated approach
6. identify when and how to initiate price increases and cuts
7. identify when and when not to follow competitor-initiated price increases and cuts, when to follow quickly and when to follow slowly
8. discuss ethical issues in pricing

Price is the odd one out of the marketing mix, because it is the revenue earner. The price of a product is what the company gets back in return for all the effort that is put into producing and marketing the product. The other three elements of the marketing mix—product, promotion and place—are costs. Therefore, no matter how good the product, how creative the promotion or how efficient the distribution, unless price covers costs the company will make a loss. Managers need to understand how to set prices, because both undercharging (lost margin) and overcharging (lost sales) can have dramatic effects on profitability.

The obvious way of adding value to an offering is to cut price. However, this can be a dangerous tactic since it can lead to price wars and can damage perceptions of the brand. In this chapter, we will consider how pricing can be used as a strategic weapon to achieve corporate and brand objectives without necessarily cutting price.

One of the key factors that marketing managers need to remember is that price is just one element of the marketing mix. Price should not be set in isolation; it should be blended with product, promotion and place to form a coherent mix that provides superior customer value. The sales of many products, particularly those that are a form of self-expression—such as drinks, cars, perfume and clothing—could suffer from prices that are too low. As we shall see, price is an important part of positioning strategy, since it often sends quality cues to customers.

Understanding how to set prices is an important aspect of marketing decision-making, not least because of changes in the competitive arena that many believe will act to drive down prices in many countries. One major force is technological change, as Marketing in Action 12.1 explains. Since price is a major determinant of profitability, developing a coherent pricing strategy assumes major significance.

Many people's introduction to the issue of pricing is a course in economics. We will now consider, very briefly, some of the ideas discussed by economists when considering price.

Economists' Approach to Pricing

Although a full discussion of the approach taken by economists to pricing is beyond the scope of this chapter, the following gives a flavour of some of the important concepts relating to price. The discussion will focus on demand, since this is of fundamental importance in pricing. Economists talk of the *demand curve* to conceptualize the relationship between the quantity demanded and different price levels. Figure 12.1 shows a typical demand curve.

MARKETING IN ACTION 12.1
Technology Drivers of Price

Technology is having a major impact on prices. First, the internet has spawned price-comparison sites such as Kelkoo and PriceRunner that allow consumers, at the click of a button, to check prices to find bargains. Before the internet, consumers often needed to spend time and money searching retail outlets for the best offers. Auction houses, the most successful of which is eBay, have allowed the creation of virtual marketplaces where sellers and buyers can trade products and arrive at prices by competitive bidding.

The internet has also facilitated the growth of yield management systems that allow price to change according to supply and demand. American Airlines was the pioneer in developing yield management, and the system has been adopted by other airlines such as easyJet, hotel chains such as Premier Inn, and intercity bus companies such as Megabus in the UK and Onnibus in Finland. Using hotels as an example, when a room is first offered on the market, the price is typically set low to attract customers. As the hotel moves closer to full capacity, the price rises by an amount that is dependent on demand. If demand is low, the price rise will be small or the price could even fall, but if demand is high, meaning that there are very few rooms available, the price will rise sharply. Customers are never told how soon or by how much the price will be changed. The objective is to maximize occupancy and thereby revenue (yield), because when selling airline or bus seats or hotel rooms, vacancies cannot be stored; if seats or rooms are not occupied, the revenue from them is lost. The system is based on sophisticated statistical modelling with the key variable being the number of seats/rooms unsold, but other factors, such as the number of clicks on the website, also influence price, as a high number of clicks is often indicative of forthcoming sales.

Technological forces are also driving down the cost of manufacture, with consequent price reductions. For example, the prices of desktop computers, laptops and tablets have fallen over 76 per cent since 2005, with advances in technology, changing consumer tastes and economies of scale driving down costs.

Based on: Office for National Statistics (2017)

At a price of P_1, demand is Q_1. As price drops, so demand rises. Thus at P_2, demand increases to Q_2. For some products, a given fall in price leads to a large increase in demand. The demand for such products is said to be *price elastic*. For other products, a given fall in price leads to only a small increase in demand. The demand for these products is described as *price inelastic*. Clearly it is useful to know the price elasticity of demand. When faced with elastic demand, marketers know that a price drop may stimulate much greater demand for their products. Conversely, when faced with inelastic demand, marketers know that a price drop will not increase demand appreciably.

FIGURE 12.1
The demand curve

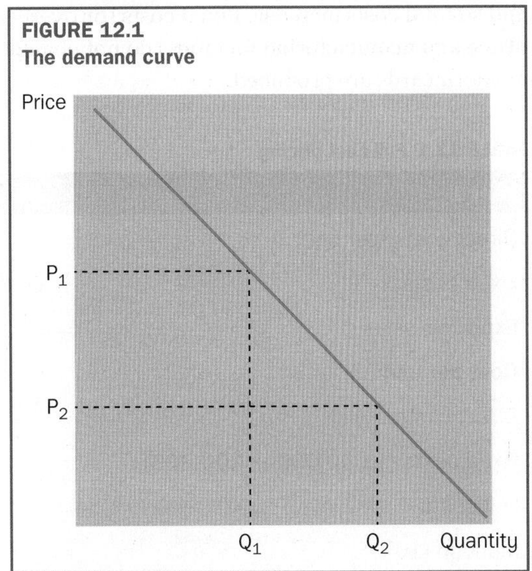

FIGURE 12.2
Pricing methods

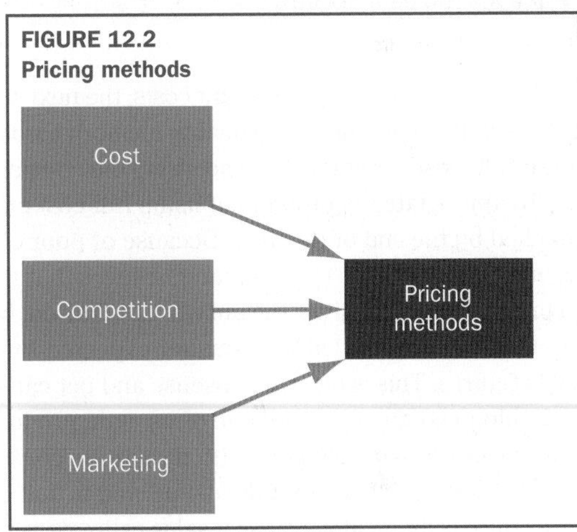

An obvious practical problem facing marketers who wish to use demand curve analysis is plotting demand curves accurately. There is no one demand curve that relates price to demand in real life. Each demand curve is based on a set of assumptions regarding other factors such as advertising expenditure, salesforce effectiveness, distribution intensity and the price of competing products, which also affect demand. For the purposes of Figure 12.1, these have been held constant at a level so that one unique curve can be plotted. A second problem regarding the demand curve relates to the estimation of the position of the curve even when other influences are held constant. Some companies conduct experiments to estimate likely demand at various price levels. However, it is not always feasible to conduct experiments, since companies may rely on the cooperation of retailers, who may refuse or may demand unrealistically high fees. Second, it is very difficult to implement a fully controlled field experiment. Where different regions of the country are involved, differences in income levels, variations in local tastes and preferences, and differences in the level of competitor activities may confound the results. The reality is that while the demand curve is a useful conceptual tool for thinking about pricing issues, in practice, its application is limited. In truth, traditional economic theory was not developed as a management tool but as an explanation of market behaviour. Managers therefore turn to other methods of setting prices, and it is these methods that we shall discuss in this chapter.

Shapiro and Jackson (1978) identified three methods used by managers to set prices (see Figure 12.2). The first reflects a strong internal orientation and is based on costs. The second is to use competitor-orientated pricing, where the major emphasis is on competitor activities. The final approach is called market-orientated pricing, as it focuses on the value that customers place on a product in the marketplace and on the product's marketing strategy. In this chapter, we shall examine each of these approaches and draw out their strengths and limitations. We shall also discuss how to initiate and respond to price changes.

Cost-orientated Pricing

Companies often use cost-orientated methods when setting prices (see Shipley, 1981; Jobber and Hooley, 1987). Two methods are normally used: full-cost pricing and direct- (or marginal-) cost pricing.

Full-cost pricing

Full-cost pricing can best be explained by using a simple example (see Table 12.1). Imagine that you are given the task of pricing a new product (a memory card) and the cost figures given in Table 12.1 apply. Direct costs such as labour and materials work out at £10 per unit. As output increases, more people and materials will be needed, and so total costs increase. Fixed costs (or overheads) per year are calculated at £1,000,000. These costs (such as office and manufacturing facilities) do not change as output increases. They must be paid whether 10 or 1 million memory cards are produced.

TABLE 12.1 Full-cost pricing

Year 1		Year 2	
Direct costs (per unit)	= £10	Expected sales	= 50,000
Fixed costs	= £1,000,000		
Expected sales	= 100,000		
Cost per unit		**Cost per unit**	
Direct costs	= £10	Direct costs	= £10
Fixed costs (1,000,000 ÷ 100,000)	= £10	Fixed costs (1,000,000 ÷ 50,000)	= £20
Full costs	= £20	Full costs	= £30
Mark-up (10%)	= £2	Mark-up (10%)	= £3
Price (cost plus mark-up)	= £22	**Price** (cost plus mark-up)	= £33

Having calculated the relevant costs, the next step is to estimate how many memory cards we are likely to sell. We believe that we produce good-quality memory cards and therefore sales should be 100,000 in the first year. Therefore, total (full) cost per unit is £20 and, using the company's traditional 10 per cent mark-up, a price of £22 is set.

To appreciate the problem of using full-cost pricing, let us assume that the sales estimate of 100,000 is not reached by the end of the year. Because of poor economic conditions or because of setting the price too high, only 50,000 units are sold. The company believes that this level of sales is likely to be achieved next year. What happens to price? Table 12.1 gives the answer: it is raised, because cost per unit goes up. This is because fixed costs (£1,000,000) are divided by a smaller expected sales volume (50,000). The result is a price rise in response to poor sales figures. This is clearly nonsense and yet can happen if full-cost pricing is followed blindly. A major European technology company priced one of its main product lines in this way and suffered a downward spiral of sales as prices were raised each year with disastrous consequences.

The first problem with full-cost pricing is that it leads to an increase in price as sales fall. Second, the procedure is illogical, because a sales estimate is made *before* a price is set. Third, it focuses on internal costs rather than customers' willingness to pay. Finally, there may be a technical problem in allocating overheads in multi-product firms (Christopher, 1982).

However, since the method forces managers to calculate costs, it does give an indication of the minimum price necessary to make a profit. Once direct and fixed costs have been measured, *break-even analysis* can be used to estimate the sales volume needed to balance revenue and costs at different price levels. Therefore, the procedure of calculating full costs is useful when other pricing methods are used, since full costs may act as a constraint. If full costs cannot be covered, then it may not be worthwhile launching the product.

Direct-cost pricing

In certain circumstances, companies may use **direct-cost pricing** (sometimes called *marginal cost pricing*). This involves the calculation of only those costs that are likely to rise as output increases. In the example shown in Table 12.1, direct cost per unit is £10. As output increases, so total costs will increase by £10 per unit. Like full-cost pricing, direct-cost pricing includes a mark-up (in this case 10 per cent) giving a price of £11.,

The obvious problem is that this price does not cover full costs, and so the company would be making a loss selling a product at this low price. However, there are situations where selling at a price above direct costs but below full cost makes sense. Suppose a company is operating below capacity and the sales director receives a call from a buyer who is willing to place an order for 50,000 memory cards but will pay only £11 per unit. If, in management's judgement, to refuse the order would mean machinery lying idle, a strong case for accepting the order can be made since the £1 per unit (£50,000) over direct costs is contributing to fixed costs and would not be made if the order were turned down. The decision is not without risk, however. The danger is that customers who are paying a higher price become aware of the £11 price and demand a similar deal.

Direct-cost pricing is useful for services marketing—for example, where seats in aircraft or rooms in hotels cannot be stored; if they are unused at any time, the revenue is lost. In such situations, pricing to cover direct costs plus a contribution to overheads can make sense. As with the previous example, the risk is that customers who have paid the higher price find out and complain.

Direct costs indicate the lowest price at which it is sensible to take business if the alternative is to let machinery (or seats or rooms) lie idle. Also, direct-cost pricing does not suffer from the 'price up as demand down' problem that was found with full-cost pricing, as it does not take account of fixed costs in the price calculation. Finally, it avoids the problem of allocating overhead charges that is found with full-cost pricing, for the same reason. However, when business is buoyant, it gives no indication of the correct price, because it does not take into account customers' willingness to pay. Nor can it be used in the long term as, at some point, fixed costs must be covered to make a profit. Nevertheless, as a short-term expedient or tactical device, direct-cost pricing does have a role to play in reducing the impact of excess capacity.

Competitor-orientated Pricing

A second approach to pricing is to focus on competitors rather than costs when setting prices. This can take two forms: **going-rate pricing** and **competitive bidding**.

Going-rate pricing

In situations where there is no product differentiation—for example, when selling a certain grade of coffee bean—a producer may have to take the going rate for the product. This accords most directly to the economist's notion of perfect competition. To the marketing manager it is anathema.

A fundamental marketing principle is the creation of a differential advantage which enables companies to build monopoly positions around their products. This allows a degree of price discretion dependent upon how much customers value the differential advantage. Even for what appear to be commodity markets, creative thinking can lead to the formation of a differential advantage on which a premium price can be built. A case in point was Austin Trumans, a steel stockholder, which stocked the same kind of basic steels held by many other stockholders. Faced with a commodity product, Austin Trumans attempted to differentiate on delivery. It guaranteed that it would deliver on time or pay back 10 per cent of the price to the buyer. So important was delivery to buyers (and so unreliable were many of Austin Trumans' rivals) that buyers were willing to pay a 5 per cent price premium for this guarantee. The result was that Austin Trumans was consistently the most profitable company in its sector for a number of years. This example shows how companies can use the creation of a differential advantage to move away from going-rate pricing.

Competitive bidding

Many contracts are won or lost based on competitive bidding. The most usual process is the drawing up of detailed specifications for a product and putting the contract out to tender. Potential suppliers quote a price that is confidential to each supplier and to the buyer (sealed bids). All other things being equal, the buyer will select the supplier that quotes the lowest price. A major focus for suppliers, therefore, is the likely bid prices of competitors.

Statistical models have been developed by management scientists to add a little science to the art of competitive bidding (Edelman, 1965). Most use the concept of *expected profit*, where:

$$\text{expected profit} = \text{profit} \times \text{probability of winning}$$

Expected profit is clearly a notional figure based on actual profit (bid price—costs) and the probability of the bid price being successful.

Table 12.2 gives a simple example of how such a competitive bidding model might be used. Based on past experience, the bidder believes that the successful bid will fall in the range of £2,000–£2,500. As price is increased, so profits will rise (full costs = £2,000) and the probability of winning will fall. The bidder uses past experience

TABLE 12.2 Competitive bidding using the expected profit criterion

Bid price (£)	Profit	Probability	Expected profit
2,000	0	0.99	0
2,100	100	0.90	90
2,200	200	0.80	160*
2,300	300	0.40	120
2,400	400	0.20	80
2,500	500	0.10	50

**Based on the expected profit criterion, recommended bid price is £2,200.*

to estimate the probability of each price level being successful. In this example, the probability ranges from 0.10 to 0.99. By multiplying profit and probability, an expected profit figure can be calculated for each bid price. Expected profit peaks at £160, which corresponds to a bid price of £2,200. Consequently, this is the price at which the bid will be made.

Unfortunately, this simple model suffers from a number of limitations. First, it may be difficult, if not impossible, for managers to express in precise statistical probability terms their views on the likelihood of a price being successful. Note that if the probability of the £2,200 bid were recorded as 0.70 rather than 0.80, and likewise the £2,300 bid were recorded as 0.50 rather than 0.40, the recommended bid price would move from £2,200 (expected profit £140) to £2,300 (expected profit £150). Clearly the outcome of the analysis can be dependent on small changes in the probability figures. Second, use of the expected profit criterion is limited to situations where the bidder can play the percentage game over the medium to long term. In circumstances where companies are desperate to win an order, they may decide to trade off profit for an improved chance of winning. In the extreme case of a company fighting for survival, a more sensible bid strategy might be to price at below full cost (£2,000) and simply contribute to fixed costs, as we discussed above under direct-cost pricing.

Clearly, the use of competitive bidding models is restricted in practice. However, successful bidding depends on having an efficient competitor information system. One Scandinavian ball-bearing manufacturer which relied heavily on effective bid pricing installed a system that was dependent on salespeople feeding into its computer-based information system details of past successful and unsuccessful bids. The salespeople were trained to elicit successful bid prices from buyers and then to enter them into a customer database that recorded order specifications, quantities and the successful bid price. Because not all buyers were reliable when giving their salespeople information (sometimes it was in their interest to quote a lower successful bid price than actually occurred), competitors' successful bid prices were graded as category A (totally reliable—the salesperson had seen documentation supporting the bid price or it came from a totally trustworthy source), category B (probably reliable—no documentary evidence but the source was normally reliable) or category C (slightly dubious—the source may be reporting a lower than actual price to persuade us to bid very low next time). Although not as scientific as the competitive bidding model, this system, built up over time, provided a very effective database that salespeople could use as a starting point when they were next asked to bid by a customer.

Market-orientated Pricing

Market-orientated pricing is more difficult than cost-orientated or competitor-orientated pricing, because it takes a much wider range of factors into account. In all, ten factors need to be considered when adopting a market-orientated approach; these are shown in Figure 12.3.

Marketing strategy

The price of a product should be set in line with *marketing strategy*. The danger is that price is viewed in isolation (as with full-cost pricing), with no reference to other marketing decisions such as positioning, strategic objectives, promotion, distribution and product benefits. The result is an inconsistent mess that makes no sense in the marketplace and causes customer confusion.

The way around this problem is to recognize that the pricing decision is dependent on other earlier decisions in the marketing planning process (see Chapter 18). For new products, price will depend on positioning strategy; for existing products, price will be affected by strategic objectives. First, we will examine the setting of prices for new products. Second, we will consider the pricing of existing products.

FIGURE 12.3
Market-orientated pricing

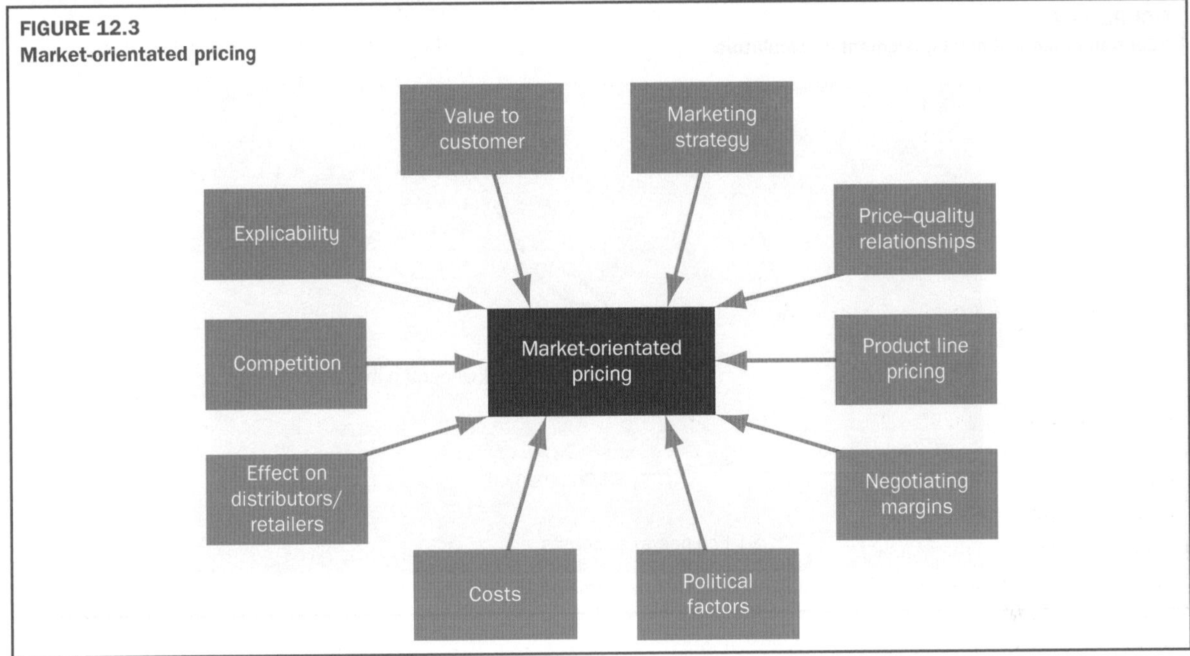

Pricing new products

The usual pricing objective for new products is to gain profitable market penetration. However, occasionally organizations will sacrifice short-term profits to achieve long-term goals. For example, Sky UK priced its next-generation Sky Q boxes below cost to encourage consumers to subscribe to its multichannel television service.

In this section, we explore the way in which positioning strategy affects price, launch strategies based upon skimming and penetration pricing, and the factors that affect the decision to charge a high or low price.

Positioning strategy: a key decision that marketing management faces when launching new products is **positioning strategy**. This in turn will have a major influence on price. As discussed in Chapter 7, product positioning involves the choice of target market and the creation of a differential advantage. Each of these factors can have an enormous impact on price.

When strategy is being set for a new product, marketing management is often faced with an array of potential target markets. In each, the product's differential advantage (value) may differ. For example, when calculators were developed commercially for the first time, three distinct segments existed: S1 (engineers and scientists who placed a high value on calculators because their jobs involved a lot of complex calculations), S2 (accountants and bankers who also placed a high value on a calculator because of the nature of their jobs, although not as high as S1) and S3 (the general public, who made up the largest segment but placed a much lower value on the benefits of calculators) (Brown, 1991).

Clearly, the choice of target market had a massive impact on the price that could be charged. If engineers/scientists were targeted, a high price could be set, reflecting the large differential advantage of the calculator to them. For accountants/bankers the price would have to be slightly lower, and for the general public a much lower price would be needed. In the event, the S1 segment was chosen and the price set high (around £250/€360). Over time, the price was reduced to draw into the market segments S2 and S3 (and a further segment, S4, when exam regulations were changed to allow schoolchildren to use calculators). Much later, when Casio entered the market, it targeted the general public with calculators priced at less than £10. The development of the market for calculators, based upon targeting increasingly price-sensitive market segments, is shown in Figure 12.4.

Two implications follow from this discussion. First, for new products, marketing management must decide on a target market and on the value that people in that segment place on the product (the extent of its differential advantage); only then can a market-based price be set which reflects that value. Second, where multiple segments appear attractive, modified versions of the product should be designed and priced differently, not according to differences in costs but in line with the respective values that each target market places on the product.

FIGURE 12.4
Adoption of innovations by segments: calculators

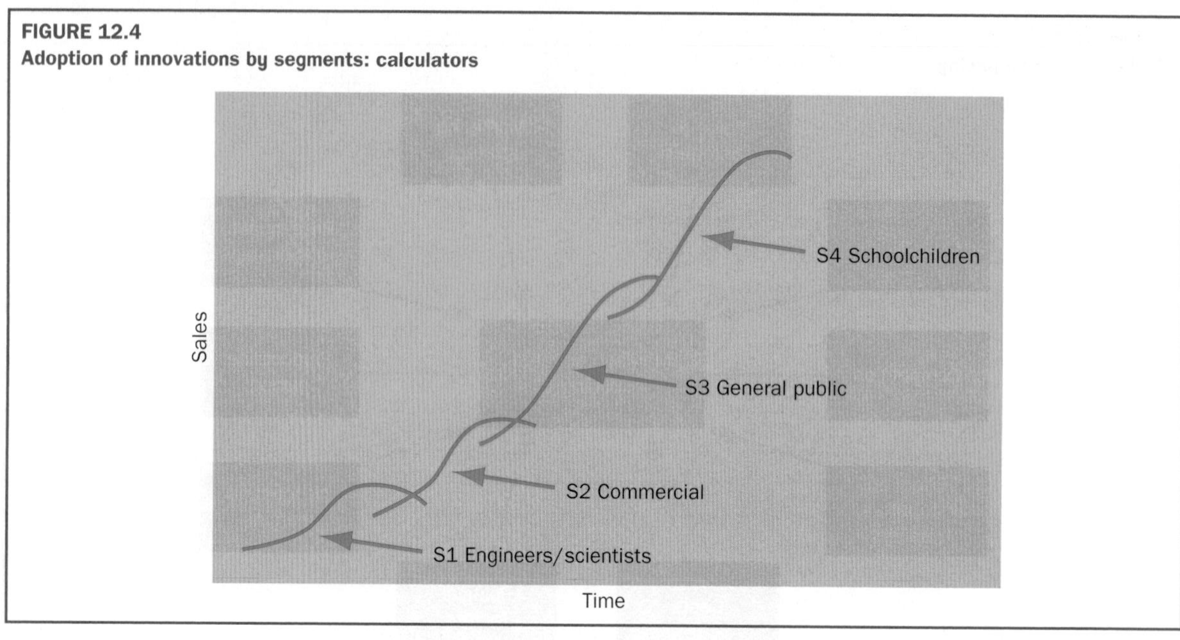

Launch strategies: price should also be blended with other elements of the marketing mix. Figure 12.5 shows four marketing strategies based on combinations of price and promotion. Similar matrices could also be developed for product and distribution, but for illustrative purposes promotion will be used here.

A combination of high price and high promotion expenditure is called a *rapid skimming strategy*. The high price provides high margin returns on investment, and the heavy promotion creates high levels of product awareness and knowledge. Nike usually employs a rapid skimming strategy when it launches new ranges of trainers. Coca-Cola also employs rapid skimming strategies. A *slow skimming strategy* combines high price with low levels of promotional expenditure. High prices mean big profit margins, but high levels of promotion are believed to be unnecessary, perhaps because word of mouth is more important and the product is already well known (e.g. Rolls-Royce) or because heavy promotion is thought to be incompatible with product image.

Companies that combine low prices with heavy promotional expenditure are practising a *rapid penetration strategy*. The aim is to gain market share rapidly, perhaps at the expense of a rapid skimmer. For example, no-frills airlines such as easyJet and Ryanair have successfully attacked British Airways by adopting a rapid penetration strategy. Direct Line is an example of a company that challenged traditional UK insurance companies with great success by using heavy promotion and a low charge for its insurance policies. Supermarkets also use a rapid penetration strategy with low prices being heavily promoted. For example, Tesco uses the strapline 'Every little helps'; Asda uses 'Permanently low prices forever', 'Price guarantee 10 per cent lower than other supermarkets'; Lidl uses 'Big on quality Lidl on prices'.

Finally, a *slow penetration strategy* combines a low price with low promotional expenditure. Own-label brands use this strategy: promotion is not necessary to gain distribution, and low promotional expenditure helps to maintain high profit margins for these brands. The supermarket chains Netto and Lidl adopted a slow penetration strategy in their early years in the UK. The low promotional expenditures help to promote the low cost base necessary to support their low prices. This price/promotion framework is useful in thinking about marketing strategies at launch. A major question remains, however: when is it sensible to use a *high price (skimming) strategy* and when should a *low price (penetration) strategy* be used (Jobber and Shipley, 1998)?

FIGURE 12.5
New product launch strategies

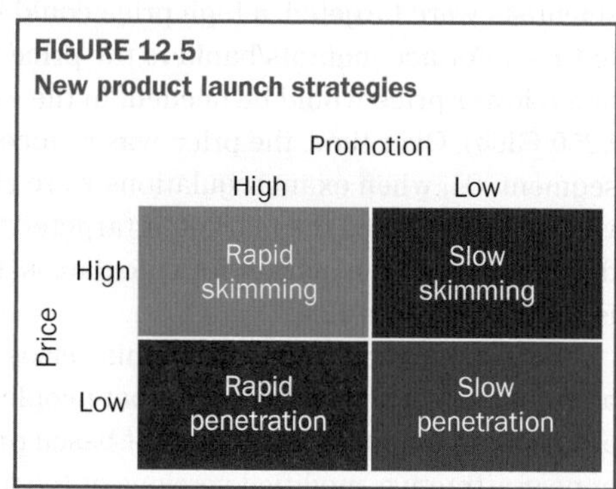

EXHIBIT 12.1
Designer handbags demand high prices as they have the potential to deliver high psychological value to some consumers

To answer this question, we need to understand the characteristics of market segments that can bear a high price. These characteristics are shown in Table 12.3. The more that each of these characteristics is present, the more likely that a high price can be charged (Jobber and Shipley, 2012).

The first characteristic is that the market segment should place a *high value on the product*, based on the customer benefits it provides. Calculators provided high functional value to engineers and scientists; other products (e.g. perfumes and clothing) may rely more on psychological value, where brand image is crucial (e.g. Chanel perfume or Gucci shoes)—see Exhibit 12.1.

Second, high prices are more likely to be viable where *customers have a high ability to pay. Cash-rich segments* in organizational markets often correlate with profitability. For example, the financial services sector and the textile industry in Europe may place a similar value on marketing consultancy skills, but in general the former has more ability to pay.

TABLE 12.3 Characteristics of high-price market segments

1 Product provides high value
2 Customers have high ability to pay
3 Consumer and bill payer are different
4 Lack of competition
5 Excess demand
6 High pressure to buy
7 Switching costs

In certain markets, the *consumer of the product is different from the bill payer*. This distinction may form the basis of a high-price market segment. Rail travel is often segmented by price sensitivity. Early-morning long-distance trips are more expensive than midday journeys, since the former are usually made by business people and often the company they are working for will pay for their travel.

The fourth characteristic of high-price segments is *lack of competition* among supplying companies. The extreme case is a monopoly where customers have only one supplier from which to buy. When customers have no, or very little, choice of supply, the power to determine price is largely in the hands of suppliers. This means that high prices can be charged if suppliers so wish.

The fifth characteristic of high price segments is *excess demand*. When demand exceeds supply, there is the potential to charge high prices. For example, when the demand for gold/petrol/cocoa exceeds supply, the price of gold/petrol/cocoa usually rises. Conversely when there is excess supply, prices usually fall. The power of supply and demand in affecting prices is discussed in Marketing in Action 12.2.

The next situation where customers are likely to be less price sensitive is where there is *high pressure to buy*. For example, in an emergency where a vital part is required to repair a machine that is needed to fulfil a major order, the customer may be willing to pay a high price if a supplier can guarantee quick delivery.

The final situation where high prices can be charged is where there are high *switching costs*. Buyers may have made investments in dealing with a supplier that they would have to make again if they switched suppliers. Production, logistical or marketing operations may be geared to using the equipment of a supplier (e.g. computer systems). Customers may have invested heavily in product-specific training that would have to be repeated if they chose to switch. These factors are likely to make customers less sensitive to the price charged by existing suppliers in such circumstances.

The task of the marketing manager is to evaluate the chosen target market for a new product using the checklist provided in Table 12.3. It is unlikely that all seven conditions will apply, and so judgement is still required. But the more these characteristics are found in the target market, the greater the chances that a high price can be charged.

MARKETING IN ACTION 12.2
Oil Price Collapse: A Classic Case of Supply and Demand

During the latter part of 2014, the price of oil more than halved from $116 a barrel in June to around $50 in December. Such an immense price drop could only be caused by powerful forces. These were the classic economists' drivers of supply and demand.

Supplies boomed as the USA increased oil production by investing in fracking projects. Between 2008 and 2014, US oil companies increased production by 70 per cent, or 3.5 million barrels per day. While US output soared, the Organization of the Petroleum Exporting Countries (OPEC), led by Saudi Arabia, refused to cut production, leading to a glut of oil on the international market.

The supply effect could have been offset by growing demand, but this did not happen. Consumption in Europe and Japan fell in 2014 as economies struggled to cope with stagnation. In the USA, tighter fuel economy standards for vehicles and the closure of petrochemical plants reduced demand. These demand issues were compounded by a marked slowdown in the Chinese economy.

The combined effects of a glut in supply, not compensated for by a rise in demand, were the underlying causes of the dramatic oil price fall. This example provides evidence of how powerful the forces of supply and demand can be on prices.

Based on: Associated Press (2014); Rankin (2015)

Table 12.4 lists the conditions when a *low price (penetration) strategy* should be used. The first situation is when an analysis of the market segment using the previous checklist reveals that a low price is the *only feasible alternative*. For example, for a product that has no differential advantage launched onto a market where customers are not cash rich, pay for themselves, have little pressure to buy and have many suppliers to choose from, there is no basis for charging a price premium. At best it could take the going-rate price but, more likely, would be launched using a penetration (low-price) strategy, otherwise there would be no incentive for consumers to switch from their usual brand. The power of consumers to force down prices is nowhere greater than on the internet, as it improves price transparency.

TABLE 12.4 Conditions for charging a low price

1 Only feasible alternative
2 Market penetration or domination
3 Experience curve effect/low costs
4 Make money later
5 Make money elsewhere
6 Barrier to entry
7 Predation

There are, however, more positive reasons for using a low-price strategy. A company may wish to gain *market penetration* or *domination* by pricing its products aggressively. This requires a market containing at least one segment of price-sensitive consumers. See Exhibit 12.2. Direct Line priced its insurance policies aggressively to challenge traditional insurance companies and is now market leader for home and motor insurance in the UK. Tesco, the UK supermarket chain, became the market leader through charging low prices for good-quality products, although its position is being eroded by Aldi and Lidl, who offer even lower prices.

EXHIBIT 12.2
Intel is a supplier of computer components and is positioned as a low-cost supplier

Penetration pricing for market presence is sometimes followed by price increases once market share has reached a satisfactory level. Tata cars has followed this approach with the Nano, partly as a strategic move and partly in response to increased production costs.

Low prices may also be charged to increase output and so bring down costs through the *experience curve effect*. Research has shown that, for many products, costs decline by around 20 per cent when production doubles (Abell and Hammond, 1979). Cost economies are achieved by learning how to produce the product more effectively through better production processes and improvements in skill levels. Economies of scale through, for example, the use of more cost-effective machines at higher output levels also act to lower costs as production rises. Marketing costs per unit of output may also fall as production rises. For example, an advertising expenditure of £1 million represents 1 per cent of revenue when sales are £100 million, but rises to 10 per cent of revenue when sales are only £10 million. Therefore, a company may choose to price aggressively to become the largest producer and, if the experience curve holds, the lowest-cost supplier.

Intel has taken full advantage of the cost economies that come with being the dominant market leader in the microprocessor market, with over 80 per cent share and the investment of billions of dollars in hyper-productive plants that can produce more processors in a day than some of its rivals can produce in a year (Edwards, 2006). This has given it the option of achieving higher profit margins than its competitors or charging low prices, as it did with its top-performing Pentium processor; prices dropped by 57 per cent in a six-week period in a move designed to hurt its major rival, AMD (Popovich, 2002).

Indeed, *low costs* through ruthless cost-cutting may be necessary to achieve profits using low-price strategies. For example, Costco, the US membership warehouse club, keeps costs low by displaying products on racks and in the packaging in which they are delivered. With its no-frills service and focus 'on marketing not advertising', Costco has become number one in its sector (Frazier, 2005).

A low-price strategy can also make sense when the objective is to *make money later*. Two circumstances can provoke this action. First, the sale of the basic product may be followed by profitable after-sales service and/or spare parts. For example, the sale of an aero-engine at cost may be worthwhile if substantial profits can be made on the later sale of spare parts. Canon Pixma is a budget all-in-one colour printer that sells for less than £50. Replacement ink cartridges, however, sell at around £15, so the lifetime cost of the printer can be quite high. Technology firms have exploited this strategy. Dropbox, which offers cloud-based file storage, gives away its basic product but places storage limits; once limits are exceeded, users of the service must buy more capacity by signing up to a payment subscription. See Exhibit 12.3 to find out more about how Cannon promotes its budget printers.

Second, the price sensitivity of customers may change over time as circumstances change. For example, digital cameras were highly priced initially then prices began to fall as more competitors entered the market. Prices then fell further as mobile phones and smartphones incorporated highly sophisticated cameras as part of a bundle of features.

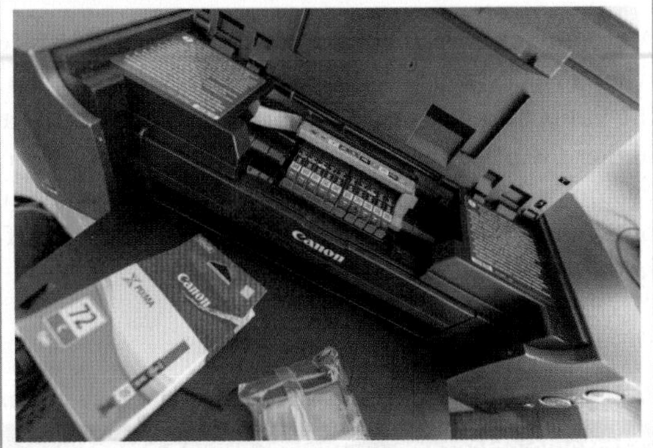

EXHIBIT 12.3
Canon focuses on the benefits of Pixma printer; most profits are made on its high-priced printer inks

Marketers also charge low prices to *make money elsewhere*. For example, retailers often use loss leaders, which are advertised to attract customers into their stores and to create a low-cost image. Supermarkets compete with traditional petrol retailers using petrol as a loss leader to attract motorists to their stores. Manufacturers selling a range of products to organizations may accept low prices on some goods to be perceived by customers as a full-range supplier. In both cases, sales of other higher-priced and more profitable products benefit.

Low prices can also act as a *barrier to entry*. A company may decide that the longer-term benefits of deterring competition by accepting low margins are greater than the short-term advantages of a high-price, high-margin strategy, which may attract rivals into its market.

Finally, low prices may be charged to put other companies out of business; this is known as *predation*. However, this approach is rarely used, because it can cause harmful price wars and in many countries is considered an anti-competitive practice.

Pricing existing products

For new products, the pricing objective is usually straightforward: to build profitable sales and market share. However, for existing products, the choice is not so clear-cut. The pricing of existing products should be set within the context of strategy. Specifically, the *strategic objective* for each product has a major bearing on pricing objectives and actions. As with new products, existing products should not be priced in isolation, but pricing should be consistent with strategic objectives. Three strategic objectives are relevant to pricing: build, hold and harvest. These will impact on pricing objectives and actions (see Table 12.5).

- *Build objective*: relevant pricing objectives would be *market penetration* and *market share leadership*. Achieving these goals should result in long-term profit maximization. For price-sensitive markets, an appropriate pricing action would be to *price lower than the competition* or use *value leadership*, where the customer benefit-to-price ratio is kept higher than that of the competition. If the competition raises its prices, the response is to be *slow to match* it, whereas for price falls it is to be *fast to match*. For price-insensitive markets, the best pricing strategy becomes less clear-cut. Price in these circumstances is dependent on the overall *positioning strategy* that is deemed appropriate for the product.
- *Hold objective*: the corresponding pricing objective is to maintain sales and/or market share. Appropriate pricing actions are to *maintain or match price relative to the competition* or to use *value parity*, where the customer benefit-to-price ratio is maintained vis-à-vis the competition. The response to competitors' price changes is to match them quickly.
- *Harvest objective*: appropriate pricing objectives are to *maintain or raise profit margins* for the purposes of *short-term profit maximization*, even if the result is long-term falling sales and/or market share. Pricing actions are to *set or maintain premium prices*. For products that are being harvested, there would be much greater reluctance to match price cuts than for products that are being built or held. On the other hand, price increases would swiftly be matched, consistent with raising profit margins. Examples of brands that are being harvested (high price/low promotion) are Bovril, Horlicks, Ovaltine and Vaseline.

The above examples show how developing clear strategic objectives helps the setting of price and clarifies the appropriate reaction to competitive price changes. Price setting, then, is much more sophisticated than simply asking 'How much can I get for this product?' The process starts by asking more fundamental questions like 'How is this product going to be positioned in the marketplace?' and 'What is the appropriate strategic objective for this product?' Only after these questions have been answered can price sensibly be determined.

Value to the customer

A second marketing consideration when setting prices is estimating a product's value to the customer. Already when discussing marketing strategy its importance has been outlined: price should be accurately keyed to the value to the customer. In brief, the more value a product gives compared with that of the competition, the higher the price that can be charged. In this section, we explore a number of ways of estimating value to the customer. Estimating value is critical because of the close relationship between value and price. Three methods of estimating value will now be discussed: trade-off analysis, experimentation, and analysis of economic value to the customer.

TABLE 12.5 Strategic objectives, pricing objectives and pricing actions

Strategic objectives	Typical pricing objectives	Pricing actions
Build	Market penetration	Low price relative to rivals
	Market share leadership	Value leadership
	Long-term profit maximization	Slow/fast to match rivals' price increases/decreases
		Positioning strategy
Hold	Maintain sales/market share	Maintain or match price relative to competition
		Value parity
		Fast to match rivals' price falls and rises
Harvest	Maintain or raise profit margins	Premium prices
	Short-term profit maximization	Reluctance to match price cuts
		Fast matching of price rises

Trade-off analysis

Trade-off analysis (otherwise known as *conjoint analysis*) measures the trade-off between price and other product features so that their effects on product preference can be established (Kucher and Simon, 1987). Respondents are not asked direct questions about price; instead product profiles consisting of product features and price are described and respondents are asked to name their preferred profile. From their answers, the effect of price and other product features can be measured using a computer model. The following is a brief description of the procedure.

The first step is to identify the most important product features (attributes) and the benefits that are expected to be gained as a result of buying the product. Product profiles are then built using these attributes (including price) and respondents are asked to choose which product they would buy from pairs of product profiles. Statistical analysis allows the computation of *preference contributions* that permit the preference for attributes to be compared. For example, if the analysis was for a business-to-business product, trade-off analysis might show that improving delivery time from one week to one day is worth a price increase of 5 per cent. In addition, the relative importance of each of the product attributes, including price, can be calculated. By translating these results into market share and profit figures for the proposed new product the optimal price can be found.

This technique has been used to price a wide range of industrial and consumer products and services and can be used to answer such questions as the following (Cattin and Wittink, 1989).

- What is the value of a product feature, including improving service levels, in price terms?
- What happens to market share if price changes?
- What is the value of a brand name in terms of price?

Experimentation

A limitation of trade-off analysis is that respondents are not asked to back up their preferences with cash expenditure. Consequently, what they say they prefer may not be reflected in actual purchase when they are asked to part with their money. *Experimental pricing research* attempts to overcome this drawback by placing a product on sale at different locations with varying prices.

The major alternatives are to use a controlled store experiment or test marketing. In a *controlled store experiment*, a number of stores are paid to vary the price levels of the product under test. Suppose 100 supermarkets are being used to test two price levels of a brand of coffee; 50 stores would be chosen at random (perhaps after controlling for region and size) and allocated the lower price; the rest would use the higher price. By comparing sales levels and profit contributions between the two groups of stores, the most profitable price would be established. A variant of this procedure is to test price differences between the test brand and major rival brands. For example, in half the stores a price differential of 2p may be compared with one of 4p. In practice, considerable sums need to be paid to supermarkets to obtain approval to run such tests, and the implementation of the price levels needs to be monitored carefully to ensure that the stores do sell at the specified prices.

Test marketing can be used to compare the effectiveness of varying prices as long as more than one area is chosen. For example, the same product could be sold in two areas using an identical promotional campaign but with different prices between areas. A more sophisticated design could measure the four combinations of high/low price and high/low promotional expenditure if four areas were chosen. Obviously, the areas would need to be matched (or differences allowed for) in terms of target customer profile so that the result would be comparable. The test needs to be long enough so that trial and repeat purchase at each price can be measured. This is likely to be between 6 and 12 months for products whose purchase cycle lasts more than a few weeks.

A potential problem of using test marketing to measure price effects is competitor activity designed to invalidate the test results. For example, competitors could run special promotions in the test areas to make sales levels atypical if they discovered the purpose and location of the test marketing activities. Alternatively, they might decide not to react at all. If they know that a pricing experiment is taking place and that syndicated consumer panel data are being used to measure the results, they may simply monitor the results since competitors will be receiving the same data as the testing company (Moutinho and Evans, 1992). By estimating how successful each price has been, they are in a good position to know how to react when a price is set nationally.

Analysis of economic value to the customer

Experimentation is more usual when pricing consumer products. However, industrial markets have a powerful tool at their disposal when setting the price of their products: **economic value to the customer (EVC)** analysis. Many organizational purchases are motivated by economic value considerations, since reducing costs and increasing revenue are prime objectives of many companies. If a company can produce an offering that has a high EVC, it can set a high price and yet still offer superior value compared with the competition. A high EVC may be because the product generates more revenue for the buyer than the competition does or because its operating costs (such as maintenance, operation or start-up costs) are lower over its lifetime.

The Lexus was marketed on low lifetime operating costs, with the tag line 'Lowest cost of ownership' based on its decent fuel economy, durability and resale value. Lexus salespeople were trained to provide the financial evidence to justify the claim (Helm, 2008). Microsoft also used EVC analysis to defend its Windows platform against the threat from the lower-cost Linux operating system. Microsoft commissioned independent tests that showed how the total lifetime cost of open-source operating systems could exceed the costs of Windows, despite their lower purchase price (Nagle and Hogan, 2006).

EVC analysis is usually particularly revealing when applied to products whose purchase price represents a small proportion of the lifetime costs to the customer (Forbis and Mehta, 1979). Figure 12.6 illustrates the calculation of EVC and how it can be used in price setting.

A reference product is chosen (often the market leader) with which to compare costs. In the example, the market leader is selling a machine tool for £50,000. However, this is only part of a customer's lifecycle costs. In addition, £30,000 start-up costs (installation, lost production and operator training) and £120,000 post-purchase costs (operator, power and maintenance) are incurred. The total lifecycle costs are, therefore, £200,000.

A new machine tool (product X) has a different customer cost profile. Technological advances have reduced start-up costs to £20,000 and post-purchase costs to £100,000. Therefore, total costs are reduced by £30,000 and the EVC our new product offers is £80,000 (£200,000 – £120,000). Thus, the EVC figure is the amount a customer would have to pay to make the total lifecycle costs of the new and reference products the same. If the new machine tool were priced at £80,000, this would be the case. Below this price there would be an economic incentive for customers to buy the new machine tool.

EVC analysis is clearly a powerful tool for price setting, since it establishes the upper economic limit for price. Management must then use judgement regarding how much incentive to give the customer to buy the new product and how much of a price premium to charge. A price of £60,000 would give customers a £20,000 lifetime cost saving incentive while establishing a £10,000 price premium over the reference product. In general, the more entrenched the market leader, the more loyal its customer base, and the less well known the newcomer, the higher the cost-saving incentive needs to be. In the second example shown in Figure 12.6,

FIGURE 12.6
Pricing using economic value to the customer (EVC) analysis

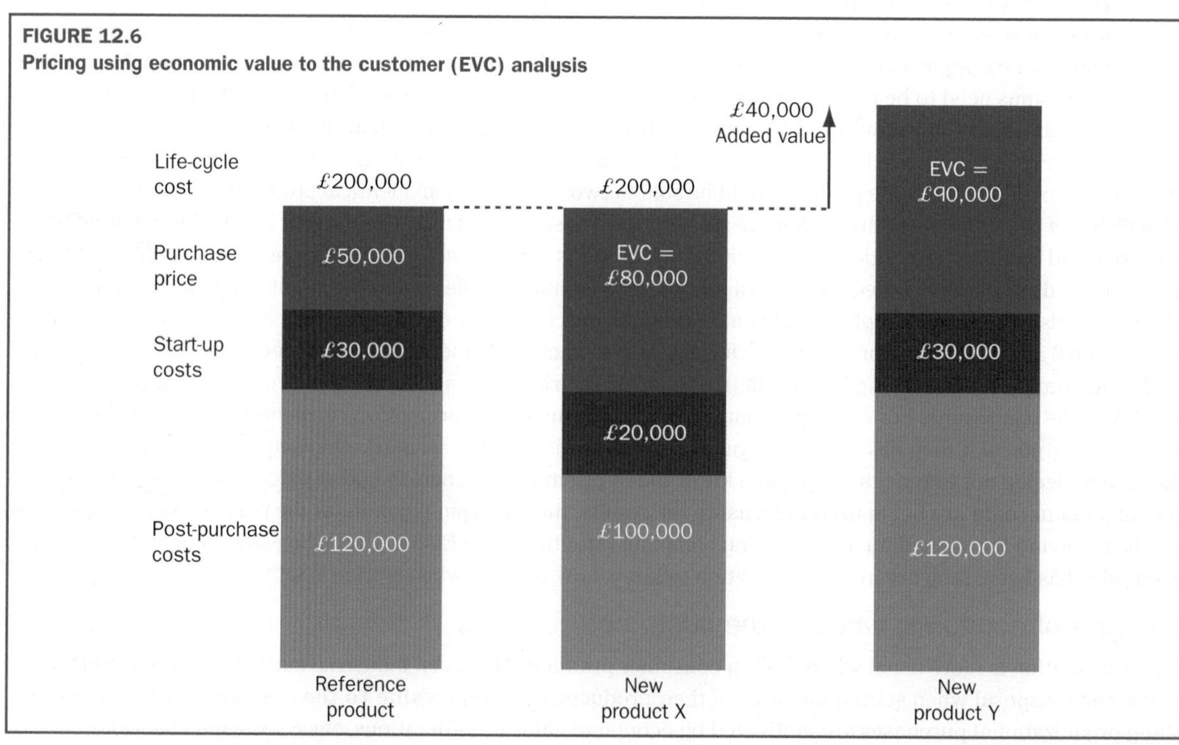

the new machine tool (product Y) does not affect costs but raises the customer's revenues. For example, faster operation may result in more output, or greater precision may enhance product quality leading to higher prices. This product is estimated to give £40,000 extra profit contribution over the reference product, because of higher revenues. Its EVC is, therefore, £90,000, indicating the highest price the customer should be willing to pay. Again, marketing management must decide how much incentive to give to customers and how much of a price premium to charge.

EVC analysis can be useful in target market selection, since different customers may have varying EVC levels. A decision may be made to target the market segment that has the highest EVC figure, since for these customers the product has the greatest differential advantage. The implementation of an EVC-based pricing strategy relies on a well-trained sales force that is capable of explaining sophisticated economic value calculations to customers, and field-based evidence that the estimates of cost savings and revenue increases will occur in practice.

Price–quality relationships

A third consideration when adopting a market-orientated approach to pricing is the relationship between price and perceived quality. Many people use price as an indicator of quality. This is particularly the case for products where objective measurement of quality is not possible, such as drinks and perfume. But the effect is also to be found with consumer durables and industrial products.

A study of price and quality perceptions of cars, for example, found that higher-priced cars were perceived to possess (unjustified) high quality (Erickson and Johansson, 1985). For example, the Seat Leon is built using many of the same components as the Audi A3, but the two cars are perceived differently, with the latter often being perceived to be of higher quality. Also, sales of a branded agricultural fertilizer rose after the price was raised above that of its generic competitors, despite the fact that it was the same compound. Interviews with farmers revealed that they believed the fertilizer to improve crop yield compared with rival products. Clearly, price had influenced quality perceptions.

Mini Case 12.1 discusses some interesting results of experiments conducted to investigate the influence of price on quality perceptions. A potential problem, therefore, is that by charging a low price, brand image may be tarnished.

MINI CASE 12.1
Does Price Really Influence Perceptions of Quality?

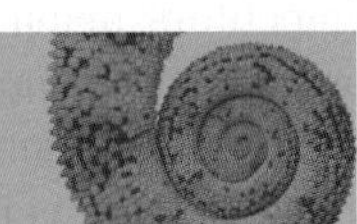

The question of the influence of price on quality perceptions has interested marketing managers for decades. Two experiments have investigated this issue. The first was a study into the effect of the price of placebos (dummy pills) on the killing of pain. Both pills were identical (a sugar compound), but patients who took the $2.50 placebo judged it better at killing pain than those that took one costing only 10 cents.

In the second experiment, 20 occasional red-wine drinkers were asked to taste a Cabernet Sauvignon marked with a $5 price tag and one with a $45 price label. However, both came from the same $5 bottle. The higher-priced wine was selected as tasting superior by most of the drinkers. To explain the results, neuroscience was called upon. In a second experiment, the drinkers were asked to drink again while wired up to a brain scanner. When they drank the 'more expensive' wine, the part of the brain associated with pleasure became more active than when the 'less expensive' wine was drunk. Clearly, the higher price caused the drinkers to experience more pleasure, even if the product itself was no different.

Question:

1 As a marketer, how could you use this information to promote lower-priced goods against competitors selling higher-priced goods? Use further examples to justify your argument.

Based on: The Guardian (2008); Rangel, O'Doherty and Shiv (2008); Ritson (2008a)

Product line pricing

Market-orientated companies also need to take account of where the price of a new product fits into their existing product line. For example, when Apple developed the iPod nano, it had to carefully price-position the device against the original iPod mobile music player. Given that some potential buyers of the original iPod might now buy the nano, pricing it too cheaply could have resulted in lower overall profits.

Some companies prefer to extend their product lines rather than reduce the price of existing brands in the face of price competition. They launch cut-price fighter brands to compete with the low-price rivals. This has the advantage of maintaining the image and profit margins of existing brands. For example, Apple found itself being attacked by low-priced competitors in the mobile music player market. The company chose a fighter brand strategy to compete. The iPod shuffle, originally retailing at £49 compared with £219 for the iPod, was launched to compete with low-price mp3 players. By producing a range of brands at different price points, companies can cover the varying price sensitivities of customers and encourage them to trade up to the more expensive, higher-margin brands.

Explicability

The capability of salespeople to explain a high price to customers may constrain price flexibility. In markets where customers demand economic justification of prices, the inability to produce cost and/or revenue arguments may mean that high prices cannot be set. In other circumstances, the customer may reject a price that does not seem to reflect the cost of producing the product. For example, sales of an industrial chemical compound that repaired grooves in drive-shafts suffered because many customers believed that the price of £500 did not reflect the cost of producing the compound. Only when the sales force explained that the premium price was needed to cover high research and development expenditure did customers accept that the price was not exploitative.

Competition

Competition factors are important determinants of price. At the very least, competitive prices should be considered; yet it is a fact of commercial life that many companies do not know what the competition is charging for its products.

Care has to be taken when defining competition. When asked to name competitors, many marketing managers list companies that supply technically similar products. For example, a paint manufacturer will name other paint manufacturers. However, as Figure 12.7 illustrates, this is only one layer of competition. A second layer consists of dissimilar products solving the same problem in a similar way. Polyurethane varnish manufacturers would fall into this category. A third level of competition would come from products solving the problem (or eliminating it) in a dissimilar way. Since window frames are often painted, PVC double glazing manufacturers would form competition at this level.

This analysis is not simply academic, as the effects of price changes can be misleading if these three layers of competition are not taken into consideration. For example, if all paint manufacturers raised their prices simultaneously, they might believe that overall sales would not be dramatically

FIGURE 12.7
Layers of competition

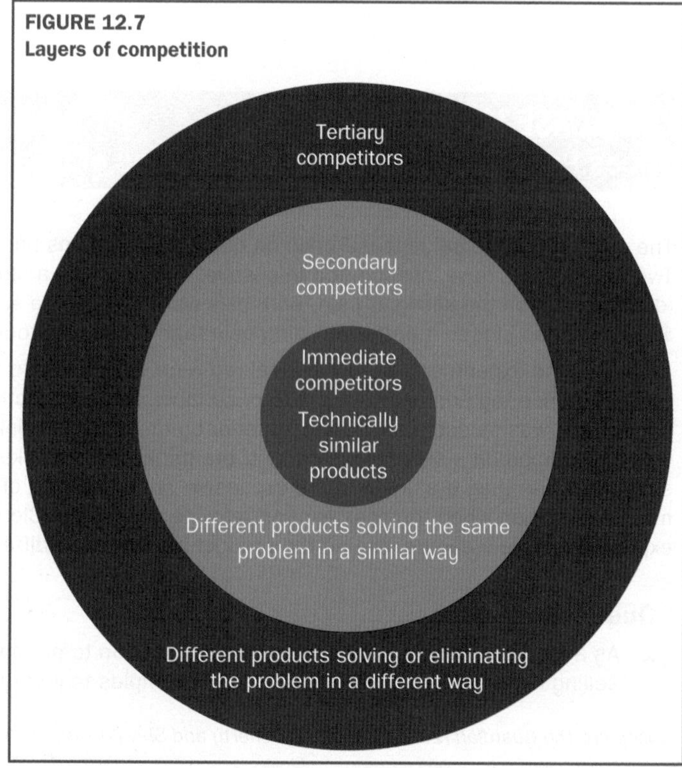

MARKETING IN ACTION 12.3
The price of the Free

For Google, Facebook, Twitter, You Tube and many more digital brands, there is only one price for their core product: it is free. But each digital brand comes with a price to pay, although not in the monetary sense to enjoy the free services.

YouTube—you can view multiple channels of video and subscribe to your favourites, but you must often watch related adverts before watching your chosen videos.

Spotify—music for everyone; Spotify has millions of audio tracks from recording artists. You can use this service on your computer, phone and other peripherals. The free service requires you to listen to audio adverts, which are interspersed with your chosen music selections.

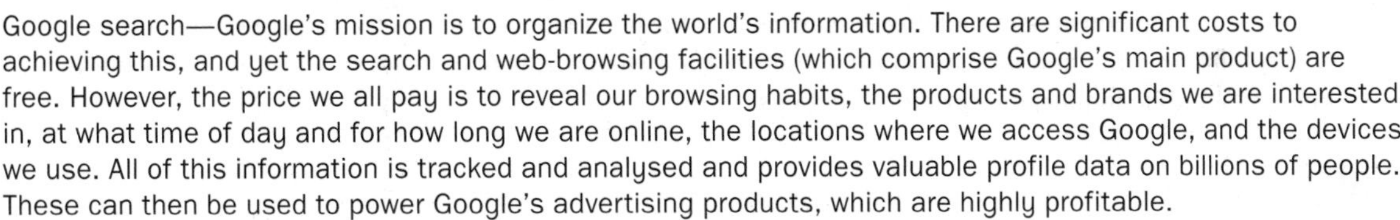

Google search—Google's mission is to organize the world's information. There are significant costs to achieving this, and yet the search and web-browsing facilities (which comprise Google's main product) are free. However, the price we all pay is to reveal our browsing habits, the products and brands we are interested in, at what time of day and for how long we are online, the locations where we access Google, and the devices we use. All of this information is tracked and analysed and provides valuable profile data on billions of people. These can then be used to power Google's advertising products, which are highly profitable.

Facebook—a social networking site, where many of us share our lives, loves, hates, photos and personal details with our friends. Another 'free' service? The price is once again the information, which enables Facebook, like Google, to sell highly targeted advertising. Facebook has also been involved in a political scandal and accused of enabling targeted content to be used for political gains.

These are just four examples of how digital brands are making us 'pay' for their services with personal behavioural information. This has significant implications for the pricing of products and services in the digital space and how services are costed.

Based on: Cadwalladr and Graham-Harrison (2018)

affected if they mistakenly defined competition as technically similar products. The reality is, however, that such price collusion would make polyurethane varnish and, over a longer period, PVC double glazing more attractive to customers. Online competitive pricing can take a different form see Marketing in Action 12.3. The implication is that companies must consider all three levels of competition when setting and changing prices.

Negotiating margins

In some markets, customers expect a price reduction. The price paid is therefore very different from the list price. In the car market, for example, customers expect to pay less than the asking price. For organizational customers, Marn and Rosiello describe the difference between list price and realized or transaction price as the **price waterfall** (Marn and Rosiello, 1992). The difference can be accounted for by order-size discounts, competitive discounts (a discretionary discount negotiated before the order is taken), a fast payment discount, an annual volume bonus and promotional allowances.

Managing this price waterfall is a key element in achieving a satisfactory transaction price. Market-orientated companies recognize that such discounting may be a fact of commercial life and build in *negotiating margins* that allow prices to fall from list price levels but still permit profitable transaction prices to be achieved.

Effect on distributors/retailers

When products are sold through intermediaries such as distributors or retailers, the list price to the customer must reflect the margins required by intermediaries. When Müller yoghurt was first launched in the UK, a major factor in gaining distribution in a mature market was the fact that its high price allowed attractive profit margins for the supermarket chains. Conversely, the implementation of a penetration pricing strategy may be hampered if distributors refuse to stock the product because the profit per unit sold is less than that for competitive products.

The implication is that pricing strategy is dependent on understanding not only the ultimate customer but also the needs of the distributors and retailers that form the link between the customer and the manufacturer. If distributors' and retailers' needs cannot be accommodated, product launch may not be viable or a different distribution system (e.g. direct selling) may be required.

Political factors

High prices can be a contentious public issue and may invoke government intervention. Where price is out of line with manufacturing costs, political pressure may act to force down prices. The European Commission and national bodies such as the Competition Commission have been active in discouraging anti-competitive practices such as price-fixing. Indeed, the establishment of the single European market was a result of the desire to raise competitive pressures and thereby reduce prices throughout the European Union.

Companies need to take great care that their pricing strategies are not seen to be against the public interest. For example, in the UK, sharp increases in energy prices have brought much adverse publicity and threats from politicians to curb further increases. Ofcom, the independent regulator for the UK communications industries, provides advice to help consumers and businesses make informed choices when selecting communication products. Exploitation of a monopoly position or collusion between firms may bring short-term profits but incur the backlash of a public inquiry into pricing practices.

Costs

The final consideration that should be borne in mind when setting prices is costs. This may seem in contradiction to the outward-looking market-orientated approach, but costs do enter the pricing equation. The secret is to consider costs alongside all the other considerations discussed under market-orientated price setting rather than in isolation. In this way, costs act as a constraint: if the market will not bear the full cost of producing and marketing the product, it should not be launched.

What should be avoided is the blind reference to costs when setting prices. Simply because one product costs less to make than another does not imply that its price should be less.

Initiating Price Changes

Our discussion of pricing strategy so far has looked at the factors that affect pricing. By considering the ten market-orientated factors, managers can judge the correct level at which to set prices. But in a highly competitive world, pricing is dynamic: managers need to know when and how to raise or lower prices, and whether to react to competitors' price moves. First, we shall discuss initiating price changes, before analysing how to react to competitors' price changes.

Three key issues associated with initiating price changes are the *circumstances* that may lead a company to raise or lower prices, the *tactics* that can be used, and *estimating competitor reaction*. Table 12.6 illustrates the major points relevant to each of these considerations.

Circumstances

A price increase may be justified as a result of marketing research (e.g. trade-off analysis or experimentation) which reveals that customers place a higher *value* on the product than is reflected in its price. *Rising costs*, and hence reduced profit margins, may also stimulate price rises. Another factor that leads to price increases is *excess demand*. A company that cannot supply the demand created by its customers may choose to raise prices in an effort to balance demand and supply. This can be an attractive option, as profit margins are automatically widened. The final circumstance when companies may decide to raise prices is when embarking on a *harvest objective*. Prices are raised to increase margins, even though sales may fall.

TABLE 12.6 Initiating price changes

	Increases	Cuts
Circumstances	Value greater than price Rising costs Excess demand Harvest objective	Value less than price Excess supply Build objective Price war unlikely
Tactics	Price jump Staged price increases Escalator clauses Price unbundling Lower discounts	Price fall Staged price reductions Fighter brands Price bundling Higher discounts
Estimating competitor reaction	Strategic objectives Self-interest Competitive situation Past experience Statements of intent	

Correspondingly, price cuts may be provoked by the discovery that price is high compared with the *value* that customers place on the product, *falling costs* (and the desire to bring down costs further through the experience curve effect), and where there is *excess supply* leading to excess capacity. As we have seen, excess supply in the oil industry led to a dramatic fall in the price of oil. A further circumstance that may lead to price falls is the adoption of a *build objective*. When customers are thought to be price-sensitive, price cutting may be used to build sales and market share. The final circumstance that might lead to price cuts is the desire to *preempt competitive entry* into a market. Proactive price cuts—before the new competitor enters—are painful to implement, because they incur short-term profit sacrifices but immediately reduce the attractiveness of the market to the potential entrant and reduce the risk of customer annoyance if prices are reduced only after competitive entry.

Tactics

Price increases and cuts can be implemented in many ways. The most direct is the *price jump* or *fall*, which increases or decreases the price by the full amount in one go. A price jump avoids prolonging the pain of a price increase over a long period but may raise the visibility of the price increase to customers. Using *staged price increases* might make the price rise more palatable but runs the risk of a company being charged with always raising its prices. A *one-stage price fall* can have a high-impact dramatic effect that can be heavily promoted, but also has an immediate impact on profit margins. *Staged price reductions* have a less dramatic effect but may be used when a price cut is believed to be necessary but the amount necessary to stimulate sales is unclear. Small cuts may be initiated as a learning process that proceeds until the desired effect on sales has been achieved.

Price can also be raised by using *escalator clauses*. The contracts for some organizational purchases are drawn up before the product has been made. Constructing the product—for example, a new defence system or motorway—may take several years. An escalator clause in the contract allows the supplier to stipulate price increases in line with a specified index—for example, increases in industry wage rates or the cost of living.

Price unbundling is another tactic that effectively raises prices. Many product offerings actually consist of a set of products for which an overall price is set (e.g. computer hardware and software). Price unbundling allows each element in the offering to be priced separately in such a way that the total price is raised. A variant on this process is charging for services that were previously included in the product's price. For example, manufacturers of mainframe computers have the option of unbundling installation and training services and charging for them separately.

A final tactic is to maintain the list price but *lower discounts* to customers. In periods of heavy demand for new cars, dealers lower the cash discount given to customers, for example. Quantity discounts can also be manipulated to raise the transaction price to customers. The percentage discount per quantity can be lowered, or the quantity that qualifies for a particular percentage discount can be raised.

Companies that are contemplating a price cut have three options besides a direct price fall. A company defending a premium-priced brand that is under attack from a cut-price competitor may choose to maintain its price while introducing a *fighter brand*. The established brand keeps its premium-price position while the fighter brand competes with the rival for price-sensitive customers. Where several products and services that tend to be bought together are priced separately, *price bundling* can be used to effectively lower price. For example, televisions can be offered with free three-year repair warranties or cars offered with free labour at first service. Finally, *discount terms* can be made more attractive by increasing the percentage or lowering the qualifying levels. However, giving higher discounts over too long a period can be risky, as General Motors found to disastrous effect. By pursuing a four-year price discounting strategy in the USA in the face of poor sales, it provoked a price war with Ford and Chrysler, caused consumers to focus on price rather than value offered by the product, and reduced profits (Simon, 2005).

Estimating competitor reaction

A key factor in the price change decision is the extent of competitor reaction. A price rise that no competitor follows may turn customers away, while a price cut that is met by the competition may reduce industry profitability. Four factors affect the extent of competitor reaction: competitors' strategic objectives, what is in their self-interest, the competitive situation at the time of the price change, and past experience.

Companies should try to gauge their *competitors' strategic objectives* for their products. By observing pricing and promotional behaviour, talking to distributors and even hiring their personnel, estimates of whether competitor products are being built, held or harvested can be made. This is crucial information: the competitors' response to a price increase or cut will depend upon it. They are more likely to follow a price increase if their strategic objective is to hold or harvest. If they are intent on building market share, they are more likely to resist following a price increase. Conversely, they are more likely to follow price cuts if they are building or holding, and more likely to ignore price cuts if they are harvesting.

Self-interest is also important when estimating competitor reactions. Managers initiating price changes should try to place themselves in the position of their competitors. What reaction is in their best interests? This may depend on the circumstances of the price change. For example, if price is raised in response to a general rise in cost inflation, the competition is more likely to follow than if price is raised because of the implementation of a harvest objective. Price may also depend upon the *competitive situation*. For example, if the competition has excess capacity, a price cut is more likely to be matched than if this is not the case. Similarly, a price rise is more likely to be followed if the competition is faced with excess demand.

Competitors' reaction can also be judged by looking at their reactions to previous price changes. While *past experience* is not always a reliable guide, it may provide insights into the way in which competitors view price changes and the likely responses they might make. Experience may be supplemented by *statements of intent*.

Reacting to Competitors' Price Changes

When competitors initiate price changes, companies need to analyse their appropriate reactions. Three issues are relevant here: when to follow, when to ignore, and the tactics required if the price change is to be followed. Table 12.7 summarizes the main considerations.

When to follow

Competitive price increases are more likely to be followed when they are due to general *rising cost* levels or industry-wide *excess demand*. In these circumstances, the initial pressure to raise prices is the same on all parties. Following a price rise, when customers are relatively *price insensitive* the follower (competitor) will not gain much advantage by resisting the price increase. Where *brand image is consistent* with high prices, a company is more likely to follow a competitor's price rise, as to do so would be consistent with the brand's positioning strategy. Finally, a price rise is more likely to be followed when a company is pursuing a *harvest or hold objective*, because, in both cases, the emphasis is more on profit margin than sales/market share gain.

TABLE 12.7 Reacting to competitors' price changes

	Increases	Cuts
When to follow	Rising costs Excess demand Price-insensitive customers Price rise compatible with brand image Harvest or hold objective	Falling costs Excess supply Price-sensitive customers Price fall compatible with brand image Build or hold objective
When to ignore	Stable or falling costs Excess supply Price-sensitive customers Price rise incompatible with brand image Build objective	Rising costs Excess demand Price-insensitive customers Price fall incompatible with brand image Harvest objective
Tactics: – quick response – slow response	Margin improvement urgent Gains to be made by being customer's friend	Offset competitive threat High customer loyalty

Price cuts are likely to be followed when they are stimulated by general *falling costs* or *excess supply*. Falling costs allow all companies to cut prices while maintaining margins, and excess supply means that a company is unlikely to allow a rival to make sales gains at its expense. Price cuts will also be followed in *price-sensitive markets*, since allowing one company to cut price without retaliation would mean large sales gains for the price cutter. The image of the company can also affect reaction to price cuts. Some companies position themselves as low-price manufacturers or retail outlets. In such circumstances, they would be less likely to allow a price reduction by a competitor to go unchallenged, for to do so would be *incompatible with their brand image*. Finally, price cuts are likely to be followed when the company has a *build* or *hold strategic objective*. In such circumstances, an aggressive price move by a competitor would be followed to prevent sales/market share loss. In the case of a build objective, response may be more dramatic, with a price fall exceeding the initial competitive move.

When to ignore

The circumstances associated with companies not reacting to a competitive price move are, in most cases, simply the opposite of the above. Price increases are likely to be ignored when *costs are stable or falling*, which means that there are no cost pressures forcing a general price rise. In the situation of *excess supply*, companies may view a price rise as making the initiator less competitive, and therefore allow the price rise to take place unchallenged, particularly when customers are *price sensitive*. Companies occupying low-price positions may regard a price rise in response to a price increase from a rival to be *incompatible with their brand image*. Finally, companies pursuing a *build objective* may allow a competitor's price rise to go unmatched to gain sales and market share.

Price cuts are likely to be ignored in conditions of *rising costs, excess demand* and when servicing *price-insensitive customers*. Premium-price positioners may be reluctant to follow competitors' price cuts, for to do so would be *incompatible with brand image*. Lastly, price cuts may be resisted by companies using a *harvest objective*.

Tactics

When a company decides to follow a price change, it can do so quickly or slowly. A *quick price reaction* is likely when there is an urgent need to *improve profit margins*. Here the competitor's price increase will be welcomed as an opportunity to achieve this objective.

Conversely, a *slow reaction* may be desirable when an *image of being the customer's friend* is sought. The first company to announce a price increase is often seen as the high-price supplier. Some companies have mastered the art of playing the low-cost supplier by never initiating price increases and following competitors' increases slowly (Ross, 1984). The key to this tactic is timing the response: too quick, and customers do not notice; too slow, and profit is foregone. The optimum period can be found only by experience but, during it, salespeople should be told to stress to customers that the company is doing everything it can to hold prices for as long as possible.

A *quick response* to a competitor's price fall will happen to ward off a *competitive threat*. In the face of undesirable sales/market share erosion, fast action is needed to nullify potential competitor gains. However, reaction will be slow when a company has a *loyal customer base* willing to accept higher prices for a period as long as they can rely on price parity over the longer term.

Ethical Issues in Pricing

Key issues regarding ethical issues in pricing are price fixing, predatory pricing, deceptive pricing, penetration pricing and obesity, price discrimination and product dumping.

Price fixing

One of the driving forces towards lower prices is competition. Therefore, it can be in the interests of producers to agree among themselves not to compete on price. Groups of companies that collude are said to be acting as a cartel. If discovered, there can be heavy fines. For example, some of the world's largest consumer products companies, including Unilever, Proctor & Gamble, Gillette and Reckitt Benckiser, were fined a combined €951 million by the French competition authorities for price fixing in supermarkets (Kollewe, 2014).

Opponents of price fixing claim that it is unethical because it restrains the consumer's freedom of choice and interferes with each firm's interest in offering high-quality products at the best price. Proponents argue that under harsh economic conditions, price fixing is necessary to ensure a fair profit for the industry and to avoid price wars that might lead to bankruptcies and unemployment.

Predatory pricing

This refers to the situation where a firm cuts its prices with the aim of driving out the competition. The firm is content to incur losses with the intent that high profits will be generated through higher prices once the competition is eliminated.

Deceptive pricing

This occurs when consumers are misled by the price deals offered by companies. One example is misleading price comparisons. Misleading price comparisons occur when a store sets artificially high prices for a short time so that much lower 'sale' prices can be claimed later. The purpose is to deceive customers into believing they are being offered bargains. Some countries, such as the UK and Germany, have laws that state the minimum period over which the regular price should be charged before it can be used as a reference price in a sale.

Penetration pricing and obesity

A controversial issue is the question of the ethics of charging low prices for fatty food targeting young people. Critics claim that, by doing so, fast-food companies encourage obesity. Others claim that such companies cannot be blamed when consumers are made aware by the media of the consequences of eating fatty foods.

Price discrimination

This occurs when a supplier offers a better price for the same product to one buyer and not to another, resulting in an unfair competitive advantage. Price discrimination can be justified when the cost of supplying different customers varies, where the price differences reflect differences in the level of competition, and where different volumes are purchased.

Product dumping

This involves the export of products at much lower prices than charged in the domestic market, sometimes below the cost of production. Products are 'dumped' for a variety of reasons. First, unsold stocks may be exported at a low price rather than risk lowering prices in the home market. Second, products may be manufactured for sale overseas at low prices to fill otherwise unused production capacity. Finally, products that are regarded as unsafe at home may be dumped in countries that do not have such stringent safety rules. For example, the US Consumer Product Safety Commission ruled that three-wheel cycles are dangerous. Many companies responded by selling their inventories at low prices in other countries (Schlegelmilch, 1998).

Review

1 The economist's approach to price determination

- The economist's approach to pricing was developed as an explanation of market behaviour and focuses on demand and supply. There are limitations in applying this approach in practice, which means that marketers turn to other methods in business.

2 The differences between full-cost and direct-cost pricing

- Full-cost pricing takes into account both fixed and direct costs. Direct-cost pricing takes into account only direct costs such as labour and materials.
- Both full-cost and direct-cost pricing suffer from the problem that they are internally orientated methods. Direct-cost pricing can be useful when the corporate objective is survival and there is a desperate need to fill capacity.

3 An understanding of going-rate pricing and competitive bidding

- Going-rate pricing is setting price levels at the rate generally applicable in the market, focusing on competitors' offerings and prices rather than on company costs. Marketers try to avoid going-rate pricing by creating a differential advantage.
- Competitive bidding involves the drawing up of detailed specifications for a product and putting the contract out to tender. Potential suppliers bid for the order, with price an important choice criterion. Competitive bidding models have been developed to help the bidding process, but they have severe limitations.

4 The advantages of market-orientated pricing over cost-orientated and competitor-orientated pricing methods

- Market-orientated pricing takes into account a much wider range of factors that are relevant to the setting of prices. Although costs and competition are still taken into account, marketers will take a much more customer-orientated view of pricing, including customers' willingness to pay as reflected in the perceived value of the product. Marketers will also evaluate the target market of the product to establish the price sensitivity of customers. This will be affected by such factors as the degree of competition, the degree of excess demand, and the ability of target customers to pay a high price. A full list of factors that marketers take into account is given in point 5 below.

5 The factors that affect price setting when using a market-orientated approach

- A market-orientated approach involves the analysis of marketing strategy, value to the customer, price–quality relationships, explicability, product line pricing, competition, negotiating margins, effect on distributors/retailers, political factors and costs.

6 When and how to initiate price increases and cuts

- Initiating price increases is likely to be carried out when value is greater than price, in the face of rising costs, when there is excess demand and where a harvest objective is being followed.
- Tactics are a price jump, staged price increases, escalator clauses, price unbundling and lower discounts.
- Initiating price cuts is likely to be carried out when value is less than price, when there is excess supply, where a build objective is being followed, where a price war is unlikely and when there is a desire to preempt competitive entry.
- Tactics are a price fall, staged price reductions, the use of fighter brands, price bundling and higher discounts.

7 When and when not to follow competitor-initiated price increases and cuts; when to follow quickly and when to follow slowly

- Competitor-initiated price increases should be followed when there are rising costs, excess demand, price-insensitive customers, where the price rise is compatible with brand image, and where a harvest or hold objective is being followed.
- Competitor-initiated price increases should not be followed when costs are stable or falling, with excess supply, with price-sensitive customers, where the price rise is incompatible with brand image, and where a build objective is being followed.

- The price increase should be followed quickly when the need for margin improvement is urgent, and slowly when there are gains to be made by being seen to be the customer's friend.
- Competitor-initiated price cuts should be followed when there are falling costs, excess supply, price-sensitive customers, where the price cut is compatible with brand image, and where a build or hold objective is being followed.
- Competitor-initiated price cuts should not be followed when there are rising costs, excess demand, price-insensitive customers, where the price fall is incompatible with brand image, and where a harvest objective is being followed.
- The price cut should be followed quickly when there is a need to offset a competitive threat, and slowly where there is high customer loyalty.

8 **Ethical issues in pricing**
- There are potential problems relating to price fixing, predatory pricing, deceptive pricing, price discrimination and product dumping.

Key Terms

competitive bidding drawing up detailed specifications for a product and putting the contract out to tender

direct-cost pricing the calculation of only those costs that are likely to rise as output increases

economic value to the customer (EVC) the amount a customer would have to pay to make the total lifecycle costs of a new and a reference product the same

full-cost pricing pricing so as to include all costs based on certain sales volume assumptions

going-rate pricing pricing at the rate generally applicable in the market, focusing on competitors' offerings rather than on company costs

market-orientated pricing an approach to pricing that takes a range of marketing factors into account when setting prices

positioning strategy the choice of target market (*where* the company wishes to compete) and differential advantage (*how* the company wishes to compete)

price unbundling pricing each element in the offering so that the price of the total product package is raised

price waterfall the difference between list price and realized or transaction price

trade-off analysis a measure of the trade-off customers make between price and other product features so that their effects on product preference can be established

Study Questions

1. **Accountants are always interested in profit margins, sales managers want low prices to help promote sales, and marketing managers are interested in high prices to establish premium positions in the marketplace. To what extent do you agree with this statement in relation to the setting of prices?**
2. **You are the marketing manager of a company that is about to launch an electric car. What factors should you take into consideration when pricing this product?**
3. **Why is value to the customer a more logical consideration when setting prices than cost of production? What role can costs play in the setting of prices?**
4. **Discuss the advantages and disadvantages of experimentation in assessing customers' willingness to pay.**
5. **What is analysis of economic value to the customer? Under what conditions can it play an important role in price setting?**
6. **Under intense cost-inflationary pressure, you are considering a price increase. What other considerations would you take into account before initiating the price rise?**

7. **You are the marketing manager of a range of premium-priced all-weather tyres. A competitor has launched a cut-price alternative that possesses 90 per cent of the effectiveness of your product. If you do not react, you estimate that you will lose 30 per cent of sales. What are your strategic pricing options? What would you do?**

8. **The only reason that companies set low prices is that their products are undifferentiated. Discuss.**

Recommended Reading

Deciding on a pricing strategy requires much insight into market demand. Find out more by reading about marketing-oriented pricing, using pricing to create shared value and having to consider pricing strategies in the long term.

Baker, W.L., Marn, M.V. and Zawada, C.C. (2010) Do you have a long-term pricing strategy? *McKinsey Quarterly*, October, 1–7.

Bertini, M. and Gourville, J. (2012) Pricing to create shared value, *Harvard Business Review*, 90(6): 96–104.

Jobber, D. and Shipley, D. (2012) Marketing-orientated pricing: understanding and applying factors that discriminate between successful high and low pricing strategies, *European Journal of Marketing*, 46(11/12): 1647–70.

References

Abell, D.F. and Hammond, J.S. (1979) *Strategic Marketing Planning*. Englewood Cliffs, NJ: Prentice-Hall.

Associated Press (2014) Collapse in Oil Prices: Producers Howl, Consumers Cheer, Economists Fret, *The Guardian*, 16 December. www.the guardian.com/business (accessed October 2018)

Brown, R. (1991) The S-curves of innovation, *Journal of Marketing Management*, 7(2): 189–202.

Cadwalladr, C. and Graham-Harrison, E. (2018) Revealed: 50 million Facebook profiles harvested for Cambridge Analytica in major data breach, *The Guardian*, 17 March. https://www.theguardian.com/news/2018/mar/17/cambridge-analytica-facebook-influence-us-election (accessed October 2018)

Cattin, P. and Wittink, D.R. (1989) Commercial use of conjoint analysis: an update, *Journal of Marketing*, July, 91–6.

Christopher, M. (1982) Value-in-use pricing, *European Journal of Marketing*, 16(5): 35–46.

Edelman, F. (1965) Art and science of competitive bidding, *Harvard Business Review*, July–August, 53–66.

Edwards, C. (2006) Inside Intel, *Business Week*, 9 January, 43–8.

Erickson, G.M. and Johansson, J.K. (1985) The role of price in multi-attribute product evaluations, *Journal of Consumer Research*, September, 195–9.

Forbis, J.L. and Mehta, N.T. (1979) *Economic Value to the Customer*, McKinsey Staff Paper. Chicago: McKinsey & Co., Inc., February,1–10.

Frazier, M. (2005) Costco, *Ad Age*, 7 November, https://adage.com/article/special-report-marketing-50/costco/105099 (accessed October 2018)

Helm, B. (2008) How to sell luxury to penny-pinchers, *Business Week*, 10 November, 60.

Jobber, D. and Hooley, G.J. (1987) Pricing behaviour in the UK manufacturing and service industries, *Managerial and Decision Economics*, 8: 167–71.

Jobber, D. and Shipley, D. (1998) Marketing-orientated pricing strategies, *Journal of General Management*, 23(4): 19–34.

Jobber, D. and Shipley, D. (2012) Marketing-orientated pricing: understanding and applying factors that discriminate between successful high and low pricing strategies, *European Journal of Marketing*, 46(11/12): 1647–70.

Kollewe, J. (2014) France Fines Thirteen Consumer Goods Firms Euro951m for Price Fixing, *The Guardian*, 18 December. Available at: www.theguardian.com/business (accessed October 2018)

Kucher, E. and Simon, H. (1987) Durchbruch bei der Preisentscheidung: conjoint-measurement, eine neue Technik zur Gewinnoptimierung, *Harvard Manager* 3, 36–60.

Marn, M.V. and Rosiello, R.L. (1992) Managing price, gaining profit, *Harvard Business Review*, Sept–Oct, 84–94.

Moutinho, L. and Evans, M. (1992) *Applied Marketing Research*. Wokingham: Addison-Wesley, 161.

Nagle, T.T. and Hogan, J.E. (2006) *The Strategy and Tactics of Pricing*. New Jersey: Pearson Education.

Office for National Statistics (2017) The changing price of everyday goods and services. https://www.ons.gov.uk/economy/inflationandpriceindices/articles/thechangingpriceofeveryday goodsandservices/2017-07-11 (accessed October 2018)

Popovich, K. (2002) Intel to Cut Chip Pricing by 57 per cent, *eWeek*, 4 January, 16.

Rangel, A., O'Doherty, J. and Shiv, B. (2008) *Marketing Actions Can Modulate Neural Representations of Experienced Pleasantness*, Stanford University Working Paper.

Rankin, J. (2015) Oil Prices: Why Are They Falling And Who Are the Winners and Losers, *The Guardian*, 6 January. http://www.theguardian.com/business/2015/jan/06/why-are-oil-prices-falling (accessed October 2018)

Ritson, M. (2008a) Why brands are at a premium, *Marketing*, 30 April, 19.

Ross, E.B. (1984) Making money with proactive pricing, *Harvard Business Review*, Nov–Dec, 145–55.

Schlegelmilch, B. (1998) *Marketing Ethics: An International Perspective*. London: International Thomson Business Press.

Shapiro, B.P. and Jackson, B.B. (1978) Industrial pricing to meet customer needs, *Harvard Business Review*, Nov–Dec, 119–27.

Shipley, D. (1981) Pricing objectives in British manufacturing industry, *Journal of Industrial Economics* 29 (June): 429–43.

Simon, B. (2005) Detroit Giants Count Cost of Four Year Price War, *Financial Times*, 19 March. *The Guardian* (2008) In Praise of Placebos, 5 March.

CASE 23
easyJet and Ryanair

Flying High with Low Prices

The story behind the success of Europe's no-frills airlines began in the USA. Southwest Airlines, a Texas-based carrier, was the first to benefit from the deregulation of American skies in 1978. The airline began the operation of a no-frills, low-fare business model, involving no free meals or coffee, only peanuts. The attraction was fares set at about one-fifth of those of the mainstream airlines. The Southwest Airlines fleet was made up entirely of one type of aircraft, the Boeing 737, to keep costs down by reducing pilot training and maintenance costs. The airline flew between secondary airports, which were sometimes over an hour's drive from city centres.

An essential component in the Southwest Airlines approach was fast turnaround times from uncongested airports, which could be as short as 20 minutes. This meant that aircraft could be used for 15 hours per day. In comparison, conventional airlines that ran a 'hub and spoke' network, flew aircraft for only half that length of time, as aircraft must wait to connect with incoming flights. Southwest Airlines embraced internet transactions to cut paperwork and administrative costs, and rejected corporate acquisitions in favour of organic growth. The result has been a continual stream of profits (unlike for other American airlines) and a business that attracts around 65 million passengers a year.

Southwest Airlines' approach and success has been mirrored by easyJet and Ryanair, who have pioneered low-fare, no-frills flying in Europe. Growth has been spectacular, with both airlines consistently recording annual increases in passenger numbers of 15–20 per cent, although this has slowed in recent years.

The growth in the low-cost sector has been fuelled by the burgeoning market for short-haul city breaks, the desire of more adventurous holidaymakers to arrange their own vacation packages, and people's wish to own holiday homes in warm, sunny climates. These factors, together with the drive by business to trim back on travel costs, have fuelled growth in passenger numbers.

Marketing Strategy at easyJet

A key element in the success of easyJet has been its approach to pricing. The conventional method of selling airline seats was to start selling at a certain price and then lower it if sales were too low. What Stelios Haji-Ioannou, owner of easyJet, pioneered was the opposite: the start was a low headline price that grabbed attention, then it was raised according to demand. Customers are never told how soon or by how much the price will be changed. This system, called *yield management*, is designed to allow airline seats to be priced according to supply and demand and achieve high seat occupancy. This reflects the fact that a particular seat on a specific flight cannot be stored for resale; if it is empty, the revenue is lost.

For the customer, the result has been fares much lower than those offered by conventional airlines such as BA and Lufthansa. To be profitable, easyJet has needed to control costs strictly. Following the example of Southwest Airlines, easyJet has achieved this through simplicity (using one aircraft type), productivity (fast turnaround times to achieve high aircraft use) and direct distribution (using the internet for upfront payment and low administrative charges). Also, onboard costs are reduced by not providing free drinks or meals to passengers.

Although easyJet operates out of secondary airports such as Luton in the UK, it is increasingly using mainstream airports such as Gatwick in a direct attempt to take passengers from more conventional rivals such as BA. Its approach is to fly to relatively few destinations but with a higher frequency on each route. This provides a barrier to entry, and the higher frequency attracts high-volume business travellers who prize schedule over price and are, therefore, willing to pay a little more for the service (the average easyJet seat price is reported to be higher than that of Ryanair). EasyJet also offers flexible fares that are attractive to business travellers, as they allow free date changes. One in five of easyJet's passengers are business customers. The airline also derives revenue from the sale of onboard food and drinks, check-in charges, priority boarding fees, car hire and hotel bookings.

In 2002, easyJet bought the rival Go airline for £374 million (€ 423 million), a price lower than expected by many analysts. For easyJet, the deal was about creating a route network that stretched across Europe. With the exception of domestic routes, the two airlines had few destinations in common. EasyJet's top routes included Amsterdam, Geneva and Paris, while Go took holidaymakers to Faro, Bologna and Bilbao. There was overlap on only a handful of destinations, both flying to Barcelona, Nice, Majorca and Malaga. Furthermore, the UK bases of the two airlines were complementary, with easyJet operating from Luton, Gatwick and Liverpool, while Go operated from Stansted, Bristol and East Midlands airports. At the time, the combined companies were about the same size as Ryanair in terms of passenger numbers. The takeover alone gave easyJet scale and increased buying power, a factor that was important when it decided to abandon its policy of using only Boeing 737s, by buying a fleet of aircraft from Airbus in 2002 at a knockdown price.

In 2007, easyJet bought GB Airways in a £103 million (€116 million) deal that allowed easyJet to expand operations at London Gatwick airport and also establish a base at Manchester airport.

Under its entrepreneurial leader, Stelios Haji-Ioannou, the easyJet group moved into other areas such as car hire, internet cafés and cruises, using the same low-price model. Another venture was the setting up of easyCinema to challenge the established cinema chains. The motivation was the half-empty cinema auditoria Haji-Ioannou saw when visiting conventional cinemas. He could not understand why price was not varied according to demand (by day and by film). Although some cinemas did reduce prices midweek, their pricing policies were not considered flexible enough compared with pricing using yield management. Also, he argued, why pay the same to see a blockbuster as a flop? And why is the price of the blockbuster the same on the opening night as it is six weeks later? What he proposed was an infinite number of prices depending on supply and demand, following his success in the airline business.

The easyCinema formula worked as follows. The pricing structure began at 20 pence (less than €0.25). People logged on to easyCinema.com, where they found three options. First, they could select the movie they most wanted to see, the dates when they could see it and at what prices; second, they could select the day on which they wanted to visit the cinema, what films were showing and at what prices; and third, they could come to the site with a budget of, say, £1 (€1.13) and find all the movies that could be seen for £1 or less. Bookings could be made up to two weeks in advance. As with aircraft seats, the likelihood was that, the earlier the booking was made, the cheaper the seat would be. Also, after examining costs, Haji-Ioannou decided not to install food and drink stands, saying, 'If ya want popcorn, go to a popcorn vendor. For movies come to easyCinema.' Staff costs were also reduced, since there were no tickets. Booking was done through the website, and a membership card was printed out that admitted visitors to the cinema via a turnstile. Finally, no advertising for unrelated products (e.g. the local curry house) prior to the movie showing was allowed. The first easyCinema was opened in Milton Keynes with a view to expanding the business across the UK. In 2006, however, three years after its opening, it closed, and the plan to transform the movie business was abandoned in the face of meagre audiences.

While Haji-Ioannou remains the largest shareholder, he became embroiled in a dispute with the board, believing that its plans for expansion were too ambitious in the light of a looming recession, so in 2010 he stood down as chairman to take on the role of non-executive director. Nevertheless, in 2013 easyJet ordered 135 Airbus A320s for delivery between 2015 and 2022, and in 2014 added a further 27 aircraft to its order. The A320s were more fuel efficient and were 15 per cent larger than easyJet's previous aircraft, the A319. In 2018, the company unveiled the first of a fleet of A321neo planes which carried 49 more passengers, were 15 per cent more fuel efficient and were 50 per cent quieter on take-off and landing than the A320s. The airline converted an order for 30 A320s to the new larger model.

In the same year, 2018, easyJet announced it would provide feeder flights to some long-haul carriers. Passengers taking connecting flights through Gatwick, such as those travelling from Aberdeen to New York, would be able to book the entire flight on easyJet's website.

»

»

Marketing Strategy at Ryanair

Ryanair is run by Michael O'Leary, who is famous for his outspoken views and controversial advertising campaigns. Like easyJet, Ryanair has followed the Southwest Airlines business model but, if anything, has been more ruthless on cost-cutting. It provides cheap point-to-point flying from secondary airports, rather than shadowing and undercutting the major carriers as easyJet increasingly does. Sometimes the airports can be 60 miles from the real destination: for Frankfurt read Hahn, for Hamburg read Lübeck, for Stockholm read Vesteraas or Skavsta, and for Brussels read Charleroi. Ryanair has kept to its single-aircraft policy, using Boeing 737s which it bought second-hand and cheaply, reducing maintenance, spares and crew training. Its fleet of 737–800s were purchased at record low prices at the bottom of the market. They offer 45 per cent more seats at lower operating costs and the same number of crew. Ryanair continued this policy with the purchase of a further 70 Boeings in 2005 at an even lower price. In 2009, it entered negotiations with Boeing and Airbus over the purchase of up to 300 short-haul jets and announced plans to become a transatlantic carrier. In the event, Ryanair continued its policy of buying only one type of aircraft. By 2011, it operated over 300 Boeing 737s, and in 2013 ordered 200 Boeing 737 Max 200s, which provided more passenger legroom than its existing fleet while increasing capacity by nine seats.

Turnaround times at airports are fast, to keep more aircraft in the air, and online booking has slashed sale and distribution costs. Ryanair.com has become the largest travel website in Europe, selling more than 2 million seats per month. Ryanair's focus on cost reduction has resulted in profit margins about double those of easyJet, despite the latter's higher prices. Some of the cost savings are passed on to the customers in the form of lower fares (the plan is an average fall in fare levels of 5 per cent per year) to make Ryanair even more attractive to its target market: the leisure customer. By contrast, easyJet has increasingly targeted business passengers. Ryanair is the only European airline to record profits for each of the last 20 years. Even during the recession, it continued to make a small operating profit despite soaring fuel prices. An important part of its revenue comes from the sale of onboard food and drinks and scratch cards, charges for passengers checking in rather than doing so online, priority boarding and for putting luggage in the hold, and income from car hire and hotel bookings.

Ryanair has also been on the acquisition trail by buying Buzz, the budget division of KLM Royal Dutch Airlines, for £15.8 million (€18 million). Loss-making Buzz was immediately given the Ryanair cost-cutting treatment, including the loss of 440 jobs and the introduction of new contracts for pilots that raised pay but meant longer flying hours. Half of Buzz's routes were axed, but Ryanair still intended to increase passenger load from 2 million to 3 million through lower prices—£31.50 (€36) versus £56 (€ 64) previously—and more frequent flying along the retained routes.

Competitive Response

The stellar growth in low-cost flying has attracted new entrants such as Flybe and Jet2 in the UK, and TUI fly, Goodjet and Transavia elsewhere in western Europe. There are now over 50 no-frills airlines operating in Europe. Traditional airlines have also responded. For example, Air France, Lufthansa and BA have cut prices on many of their European flights in an attempt to stem the flow to the low-price carriers.

BA has embarked on an aggressive strategy of slashing prices from Heathrow and Gatwick to almost all its European short-haul destinations. Fares to places such as Berlin, Paris and Barcelona have been cut by up to 50 per cent. In response to the low-cost carriers, BA stopped offering free food and drink on economy-class short-haul flights in 2016. Unlike at Ryanair, there are no charges for checking in luggage. The strategy of competitive fares and the convenience and flight transfers offered by Heathrow and Gatwick is designed to win large numbers of passengers from no-frills operators. In support of the strategy, BA's former chief executive Willie Walsh, whose nickname—The Slasher—was earned during his time at Aer Lingus, cut 600 managerial jobs and announced a further 1,000 job losses at the airline's call centres and travel shops in 2006.

Ryanair's reaction was to claim that BA's prices were still higher than its own after the cuts. It also claimed better punctuality—90 per cent of flights arriving on time compared with BA's 74 per cent—and a significantly lower missing bags ratio: 0.5 per 1,000 passengers against 17.7 for BA.

Customer Service

The need to trim costs to the bone has meant that some customers have been dissatisfied with the service provided by both no-frills airlines. For example, the need for fast turnaround times at airports has meant that customers who check in late are usually refused entry. Where lateness is the fault of another travel provider, such as a rail company, customers have been known to complain bitterly about entry refusal. Fast turnaround times also mean that there is little slack should a flight be delayed, with a knock-on effect on other flights.

Another problem is the reluctance of the no-frills airlines to pay compensation. For example, when easyJet cancelled a flight after it admitted it had no crew to fly the aircraft, it offered a refund of the ticket price but no compensation for the other costs such as the lost hotel deposit and car parking fees incurred by one of its customers. Ryanair, similarly, was reported to have said, 'We never offer compensation, food or hotel vouchers.' Ryanair also experienced teething problems with lost and delayed luggage after switching baggage contractors, and in the past has appeared reluctant to pay compensation with respect to lost luggage.

Of particular concern to customers was the lack of pre-booking of seats, leading to a rush to board a plane. EasyJet was the first to respond to customer complaints and introduced an allocated seating policy in 2012. No longer would families need to worry about being split up, and passengers were spared the mad rush across the tarmac. EasyJet also invested in its website, making booking easier than when using the Ryanair website, which was criticized for its poor user-friendliness. A fare-finder app was launched that allowed budget-conscious travellers to find the lowest fares across a month. These innovations saw easyJet's performance outstrip that of Ryanair.

In the face of falling sales and profits and a survey by the consumer magazine *Which?* that placed Ryanair in the worst of 100 biggest brands serving the UK market, Ryanair changed tack and sought to improve customer service. In 2014, the company introduced allocated seating along with a series of measures that were designed to quell the flow of complaints from customers. These included a more flexible baggage allowance, lighter penalties for reissuing boarding cards (a passenger had complained that she had been charged several hundred euros, resulting in half a million people on Facebook backing her complaint), reduced baggage fees and the curbing of in-flight sales announcements. It also invested in upgrading its website to make booking quicker and easier, and followed easyJet by introducing a fare-finder tool. A new staff training programme was designed to improve the customer experience.

Ryanair also began to improve its marketing to business customers. It introduced a flexible business fare that allowed passengers to change their flights, and business-plus fares that provided premium seats at the front of the plane for quick boarding or exit and rows with extra legroom. Flight schedules to locations like Madrid, Milan and Barcelona, which are popular with business people, were improved to three daily returns so that passengers could travel there and back in a day. Ryanair also began targeting more primary airports around Europe rather than out-of-the-way secondary airports.

In 2017, after facing problems caused by disgruntled pilots and cabin crew and also after errors with the pilot holiday rotas that led to the cancellation of around 20,000 flights, Ryanair agreed to recognize trade unions. A series of strikes in 2018 over pay and conditions such as annual leave and more transparency when deciding on promotions led the company to threaten that jobs could be lost jobs in Dublin, where most of the strikes originated.

Questions

1. **How do easyJet and Ryanair achieve success using low-price strategies?**
2. **What are the advantages and risks associated with low-price strategies?**
3. **To what extent do the conditions for charging low prices discussed in this chapter hold for easyJet and Ryanair?**
4. **Why did the low-price, no-frills business model fail with easyCinema?**

This case was prepared by David Jobber, Emeritus Professor of Marketing, University of Bradford.

References

Press Association (2017) Easy Jet to Connect with Other Airlines' Long-Haul Flights for First Time, HYPERLINK "http://www.theguardian.com/business" www.theguardian.com/business, 13 September. Anonymous (2018) Ryanair Has Grown to a SizeThat Belies Its Image as an Upstart, The Observer, 8 July.

Press Association (2018) Ryanair to Shrink Dublin Fleet After Pilot Strikes,The Guardian, 26 July.

CASE 24
The Triumph of German Limited Range Discounters

Shifts in the Retail Landscape

Discount retailers have been surging ahead. Grocery retailers like Aldi and Lidl are proving formidable competitors. Non-grocery retailers like fixed-price stores (e.g. Poundland, Poundstretcher) are reaping rich dividends through their focus on frugality. Value fashion brands like Primark are booming, while online retailers (e.g. Boohoo) are garnering larger customer bases. There is a huge appetite among customers for value for money. Discounters are powering ahead with their expansion plans throughout Europe and beyond. Their formula of low prices and offering a limited assortment of products on their shelves appears to be a winning pan-European formula for retailing. The retailing concept was pioneered by German hard discounter Aldi, and has now been successfully duplicated by other discounters such as the German Lidl, Italian Eurospin and Danish Netto chains. In Germany, over 90 per cent of the German population lives within 15 minutes of an Aldi store. The discounter has control of 40 per cent of the German market.

These limited-range discounters (LRDs) believe that success can be achieved through offering good-quality products at low prices and stocking minimal assortments that match consumers' basic needs, such as staple items that consumers buy regularly. Success is achieved through the generation of high volumes and the LRDs' ability to communicate to consumers, their price gaps with traditional retailers, and them placing costs at the forefront of all their business activities. Their continued success has led to dramatic changes within the retail sector, leaving manufacturers with difficult decisions as to how to supply these LRDs effectively while not damaging their brands and relations with other retailers.

German discounters are growing rapidly; Aldi and Lidl account for £1 pound in every £8 spent in supermarkets across the UK. LIDL became the fasted growing supermarket in 2017, with sales increases of 19.2 per cent in three months, which gave it 5.3% market share. Aldi also performed well and its market share rose to 6.9%. Both discounters challenge other supermarket brands; Waitrose was overtaken by Lidl in 2017, putting it into 7thplace, and Aldi in 5thplace behind the big four: Tesco, Sainsbury, Asda and Morrisons. Both discounters have ambitions to grow and Aldi aims to build over 400 news stores and have 1200 stores in the UK by 2025.

So, how do these LRDs operate? LRDs have four central planks in their operating philosophies. First, they stock a very limited product assortment (around 1,000 stock-keeping units), whereas a traditional store may have 25,000 different product variants. These are typically fast-moving, high stock rotation items. Usually, a shopper is offered only one type of brand from a category. Second, these stores are very simple in layout, design and operation. They require lean management and very few employees to operate. A hard discounter will typically have longer queues, which people bear for greater savings. Third, the retailers have a low-cost and highly efficient supply chain infrastructure, utilizing large regional distribution centres to service their retail outlets. Last and most importantly, these stores operate on the principle of 'everyday low prices'.

Competition between discounters is rife. Price wars are common between these retailers. However, if they stock similar products, they typically stock different size variants and at different prices to avoid direct confrontation, where possible. Their success has led traditional supermarkets to introduce cheaper brand ranges, such as Tesco Value, in an attempt to deter customers from switching. Some consumers view these discounters as too frugal and downmarket to give them their custom. LRDs' decision to locate in socially deprived areas has contributed to this image even further, although this is changing. Open pallets, lack of assortment and lack of extra value-added services alienate some shoppers. However, in Germany, where many of these discounters initially emerged, wealthy Mercedes drivers typically frequent these retailers. In Germany, the LRDs' appeal spans across different socio-economic groups.

Aldi is completely privately owned by the secretive Albrecht family. Its owners are now one of Europe's wealthiest families. The name originated from Albrecht Discount. Aldi pioneered the hard discounter market. The Aldi Group from its German base has two main divisions: Aldi Nord and Aldi Sud. Both operate

independently and have clearly defined operating markets and different own-label brands, but both co-operate in terms of pricing and assortment decisions. Aldi Sud is responsible for Southern Germany, Austria and English-speaking countries, while Aldi Nord is responsible for all other non-German-speaking European countries. Aldi has saturation coverage within the German market and possesses limited growth opportunities. Every German is within a 15- to 20-minute drive of an Aldi outlet. Indeed, the actual number of Aldi and Lidl stores is reducing in Germany. As a result, the chain has grown aggressively abroad. It aims to open up to 1,000 Aldi stores in the UK by 2022.

The emphasis within Aldi is on efficiency and productivity. Each store is responsible for its own revenues and cost base. Costs are kept to an absolute minimum. By having a basic store layout and design, low staff numbers, non-expensive in-store storage displays, and a limited number of products on shelves, it keeps costs to an absolute minimum, which other retailers find hard to compete against. It has built up a reputation among its loyal consumers based on the strength of the quality of its product offering. Products are strenuously tested for quality and are only allocated to stores once they are proved to be fast movers. The company has also moved into selling an organic range of produce. Aldi sources products from leading food manufacturers and sells them under the Aldi own-label brand. Indeed, the discounters now have two-tier private label strategies offering both standard and premium variants of their own-label brands. Its sheer size enables Aldi to save through bulk buys, and through strong price negotiation with suppliers. The company now sells products that are specific to a particular country in a bid to attract local customers. Through its scale, it can then source country-specific products suitable for market needs. If it still does not have the necessary scale, it will import brands into that country. Aldi utilizes huge regional distribution centres to service up to 50 outlets at a time. Goods are brought into the store on pallets and are gradually emptied by consumers before being replenished with another new pallet. The company is famous for its frugality and thriftiness at all levels of its operations, utilizing a strong, decentralized operation, with the focus on simplicity.

The first Lidl discount outlet opened in 1973. Lidl originated as a clone of the successful Aldi format, but has since evolved into having its own strong brand identity. Like Aldi, Lidl has grown rapidly by expanding its international operations. It is privately owned by the Schwarz Group, which is notoriously secretive about its operations. The group owns a suite of different retailing divisions such as hypermarkets, traditional supermarkets and discounters. The company is still number two in its domestic German market, but it has been pursuing a rapid internationalization strategy, hoping to achieve over 70 per cent of its revenues from overseas markets. Its scope of operations is limited to Europe, unlike Aldi which also owns stores in the USA and Australia. The company uses a rapid property-acquisition programme and establishes large regional distribution centres to service these new markets. The majority of its stores in international markets are non-unionized; however, in some markets it has appeased local interests by allowing trade union activity.

One of the biggest weapons in the armoury of discounters is their 'one-off' specials. These promotions typically entail the sale at substantial discount of a non-food item (e.g. ski, gardening or DIY equipment). These specials are promoted on a weekly basis through local press advertising and leaflet drops. They act as a major inducement and increase footfall to these stores. These heavily discounted items are allocated to stores, where there are only a handful of units per store. This creates a weekly sale frenzy at these stores. The biggest problem with 'one-off specials' is that it is very hard to estimate demand and, if a special proves unpopular, the stores are left with unsold stock, which can create logistical difficulties and contributes to costs.

One of the main reasons behind the LRDs' success and apparent unstoppable growth is their store location strategy. Each of these discounter stores is substantially smaller in size than a typical traditional supermarket. In addition, they require smaller property sites and ancillary works such as car parking and special entry and exit points. This has allowed the LRDs to obtain planning permission at a much faster rate than typical retailers and with enhanced likelihood of success. In France, Lidl achieved rapid growth rates through store adaptation of its business formula which overcame strict planning laws through having higher shelves, smaller aisles and lower product assortments.

The LRDs are continually evolving, with some offering in-store bakeries, fresh produce and premium regional products to bolster their brand. In addition, Aldi has signed up several celebrity chefs as endorsers for its

»

TABLE C26.1 LRDs: A profile—a comparison of Lidl and Aldi

Lidl	Aldi
Owned by Schwarz Group, privately owned	Owned by Albrecht family, privately owned
Stores in the UK 694 Stores in Spain 545 Stores in the Netherlands 412 Stores in Germany 3,182 Stores in France 1,520 Stores in Ireland 150 Total no. of stores 10,496	Stores in the UK 762 Stores in Spain 278 Stores in the Netherlands 490 Stores in Germany 4,159 Stores in USA 1,600 Stores in Ireland 129 Total no. of stores 10,719
Estimated sales by 2017 of over €79 billion	Estimated sales by 2017 of over €77 billion
Stocks up to 1,600 products	Stocks around 1,000 products
A third of products are branded items	Over 90 per cent are private label
Typical store size 1,000 sq metres	Typical store size 900 sq metres

brands. In essence, the LRDs are moving away from the imagery of a pure hard discounter. The middle tier of supermarkets are under pressure from the discounters, as their operating philosophy of offering large assortments places them at a cost disadvantage. The discounters themselves are facing a number of new challenges with the likes of Tesco testing discount outlets in eastern Europe, and Asda testing discount store concepts. This is a similar strategy to that carried out by continental retailers in response to the threat of discounters.

In the wake of the discounters' onslaught, leading UK supermarket chain Sainsbury's formed a joint venture with Danish discounter chain Netto. They each invested £12.5 million in a joint venture to relaunch Netto in the UK. Netto had originally sold its UK stores to Asda in 2010, but then planned to roll out 18 new discount stores. This strategy had inherent risks for Sainsbury's. The chain is primarily seen as middle market, with a focus on the south of England. Its thinking was to launch the Netto concept in northern areas, thereby mitigating against possible cannibalisation. Surprisingly, however, some of these new stores were located right beside those of their co-owner. These stores typically stock 2,000 products, combining own-label and some popular branded best-selling goods. Two-thirds own-label goods, 20 per cent were less well-known brands, with the remaining 10 per cent popular brand staples. The stores also promoted regular one-off weekly specials to act as inducements. However, in 2016, Sainsbury's abandoned the endeavour, with all of Netto's 16 stores closing, signalling a full-scale retreat. Now Sainsbury's is trying to consolidate through a mega merger with Asda—an acknowledgment of both stores struggling to compete against the rising German discounters, despite massive cost-cutting programmes. This merger will turn the retailer into the UK's largest retailer ahead of Tesco.

In some overseas markets, market share has plateaued after the initial success of the discounters. Shoppers are still drawn to their traditional supermarket retailers because of the attraction of wide choice, one-stop shopping and the availability of low-price product ranges. However, LRDs are here to stay and leave both retailers and suppliers with difficult decisions to face: how do they compete, and how do they supply these retailers?

Questions

1. **Discuss the strengths and weaknesses associated with the limited-range discounter format.**
2. **What are the advantages associated with the 'everyday low prices' concept versus Hi-Low pricing for retailers?**
3. **How should branded manufacturers respond with their pricing strategies if they want to supply an LRD while simultaneously supplying traditional retailers?**

This case was written by Dr Conor Carroll, Lecturer in Marketing, University of Limerick. Copyright © Conor Carroll (2018).

References

Butler. S. (2017) Lidl overtakes Waitrose as UK shoppers turn to discounters, The Guardian, 22ndAugust, HYPERLINK "https://nam05.

safelinks.protection.outlook.com/?url=https%3A%2F%2Fwww.theguardian.com%2Fbusiness%2F2017%2Faug%2F22%2Flidl-overtakes-waitrose-uk-grocer-chain-discounters&data=01%7C01%7CAli.Davis%40mheducation.com%7Ccb5673a0658f492424fd08d6b373709d%7Cf919b1efc0c347358fca0928ec39d8d5%7C0&sdata=Pi%2ByYK6C8re7%2FJ8xNTK6ZW48K7FQbUKnH6xaP44Cpgl%3D&reserved=0" https://www.theguardian.com/business/2017/aug/22/lidl-overtakes-waitrose-uk-grocer-chain-discounters (accessed March 2019).

Butler. S. (2017) Aldi and Lidi increase share of British shoppers as inflation hits spending, The Guardian, 19thSeptember HYPERLINK "https://nam05.safelinks.protection.outlook.com/?url=https%3A%2F%2Fwww.theguardian.com%2Fbusiness%2F2017%2Fsep%2F19%2Faldi-and-lidl-increase-share-of-british-shoppers-as-inflation-hits-spending&data=01%7C01%7CAli.Davis%40mheducation.com%7Ccb5673a0658f492424fd08d6b373709d%7Cf919b1efc0c347358fca0928ec39d8d5%7C0&sdata=7qoaRYgqjSO4lY4gv24%2FvnlnH0lTtuGUQzmihsYTG8Q%3D&reserved=0" https://www.theguardian.com/business/2017/sep/19/aldi-and-lidl-increase-share-of-british-shoppers-as-inflation-hits-spending (accessed March 2019).

Davey, J. (2018) Not let up for rivals as Aldi UK raises store target to 1200. Reuters, 1st October HYPERLINK "https://nam05.safelinks.protection.outlook.com/?url=https%3A%2F%2Fuk.reuters.com%2Farticle%2Fuk-aldi-uk-results%2Faldi-uk-plans-130-new-stores-in-next-two-years-as-profits-rise-idUKKCN1MB1MX&data=01%7C01%7CAli.Davis%40mheducation.com%7Ccb5673a0658f492424fd08d6b373709d%7Cf919b1efc0c347358fca0928ec39d8d5%7C0&sdata=Nb1s75mdgfATF20QojCz44jLzlAJB5WJBp0n7vL88oo%3D&reserved=0" https://uk.reuters.com/article/uk-aldi-uk-results/aldi-uk-plans-130-new-stores-in-next-two-years-as-profits-rise-idUKKCN1MB1MX (accessed March 2019)

PART 3 COMMUNICATING AND DELIVERING CUSTOMER VALUE

A number of videos featuring CEOs, CMOs, brand and PR managers related to the Chapters in this Part are available to lecturers for presentation and class discussion.

McGraw Hill connect®

CHAPTER 13
Integrated Marketing Communications

> *Probably the most powerful form of communication we have at our disposal is storytelling. It has been incorporated by virtually every civilization into their culture. It is the simplest, most memorable device we have for engaging, learning, entertaining and persuading.*
>
> **JOHN HEGARTY (2011), WORLDWIDE CREATIVE DIRECTOR AND FOUNDER OF BARTLE BOGLE HEGARTY**

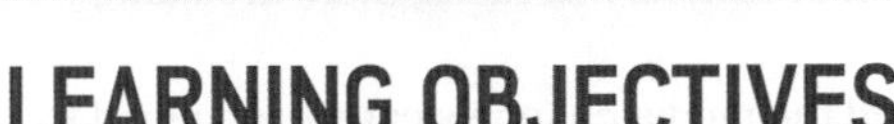

LEARNING OBJECTIVES

After reading this chapter, you should be able to:

1. explain how to develop an integrated marketing communications strategy and set relevant communication objectives
2. describe the elements of integrated marketing communications
3. explain the distinction between mass and direct communications
4. discuss the promotional communication mix
5. explain the key characteristics of each of the main media channels
6. consider the implications for planning communications for different audiences and contexts

Good communications are the lifeblood of successful market-orientated companies and their brands, but creating good communications presents many challenges. As discussed in Chapter 8, all companies need to communicate what they stand for and the benefits they have on offer if they are to earn their customers' trust. Trust is at the core of a brand's very existence (Hegarty, 2011). However, the way in which businesses communicate with their audiences is constantly evolving. Currently, digital technology is reshaping both the tools and the media through which we communicate. The martech landscape discussed in Chapter 11 is reshaping how marketing and technology firms are joining together and revolutionizing the communications industry. There are also more channels and opportunities for a customer to engage with a brand. In the UK alone, over 500 television channels compete to catch the attention of consumers; around the world tens of millions of company websites provide product and marketing information to stimulate buyer behaviour. Social media tools are used by individuals and companies as a means of extending their communication networks.

This increase in the number of opportunities to engage and interact with customers has created a need for better coordination of all an organization's communications activities. Additionally, to manage these challenges of the changing communication environment and the proliferation of channels, organizations wishing to promote themselves must understand which communications tools to use in which situations. They must also consider operational issues associated with the management of promotional campaigns and assess whether to place responsibility for campaigns with an internal department or to employ external specialist communication agencies. For example, for large manufacturing organizations producing fast-moving consumer goods (e.g. Kraft Foods, Unilever, Procter & Gamble), promotional activity might involve various types of communication tools, such as digital marketing, advertising, sales promotion and public relations. These large manufacturing firms may have the resources for all these activities to be controlled internally under the umbrella of the marketing function. For example, personal selling strategies can be decided by the sales management team, advertising and sales promotion initiatives by the marketing communications team, and a publicity event by the public relations department. But they are equally likely to employ external specialists, as they can bring talent and fresh creativity and the organizational skills needed to deliver highly effective and coordinated communication campaigns. For example, Bartle Bogle Hegarty (BBH) devised the 'Keep walking' campaign for drinks manufacturer Diageo. Not only did BBH revive the brand, but it also delivered a 7 per cent increase in sales (McMains, 2014). Procter & Gamble is another large manufacturer that employs external specialists to handle its marketing communications campaigns. Its approach is to appoint a brand agency leader that acts as a single point of contact for all the agencies working on brands in its portfolio.

Finding communication solutions to these challenges has been a driver of change in the communication environment and has led to the **integrated marketing communications (IMC)** school of thought. This approach delivers many benefits through integration, but as the use of digital communications increases, there are many challenges for marketing managers to consider.

This chapter will focus on IMC and how brand messages, the tools and the media channels can be managed to develop coordinated communication strategies that maximize the efficiency and effectiveness of the promotional element of the marketing mix.

The chapter begins with a consideration of the drivers of IMC then looks at the planning process and how to develop a communication strategy. Next, we explore the elements of IMC, including the principles of communication and the importance of the message, the communication tools and their characteristics, and then we briefly introduce the media channels, touch on the people involved in communications and finally consider communication contexts: business to business (B2B) and business to consumer (B2C). Chapter 14 focuses in detail on mass communications tools by examining advertising, the media, sales promotions and public relations (PR). Chapter 15 discusses direct communications tools—personal selling and sales management, direct marketing and customer relationship management—while Chapter 16 explores the digital marketing and social media landscape.

Integrated Marketing Communications Approach

The IMC school of thought aims to move the emphasis of communications away from a step-by-step, linear, transactional process to an ongoing relational dialogue. Another fundamental shift is to move away from transactional communications to make communications customer-centred by capturing and using the reality of how individuals and businesses engage and come into contact with communications.

The transactional approach means promotional campaigns are designed to meet specific communication objectives such as creating awareness or stimulating action, using separate communications tools. Rarely are there any linkages between the messages carried by each tool. For example, in the past, Heinz had a long-running television advertising campaign for its baked beans that aimed to position the product as a quality brand. However, at times, it also used sales promotions techniques (e.g. multipack of four cans for the price of three) to combat supermarket value brands being sold at a few pence per can, although there were no explicit links between the television advertising campaign and the sales promotion initiatives. Now Heinz takes a very different approach. Its highly successful 'Grow your own' campaign, currently implemented for the third year running, seeks to remind sauce lovers across Europe about the quality of the brand and encourage engagement. Shoppers are encouraged to grow their own tasty tomatoes. This IMC campaign was activated via a mobile app, had its own Facebook page and is supported by a £1 million television campaign. Additionally, there was also in-store activation of the campaign, with on-pack labelling featuring the 'Grow your own' message, and at selected stores shoppers could also pick up a free pack of seeds. The campaign encouraged the whole family to take part. School children got involved and teachers were asked to sign up to take part in an educational part of the campaign (Glenday, 2017).

IMC campaigns seek to rationalize the approach to communications. By focusing on developing relational and coordinated communication strategies, it becomes possible to bring together communication tools, techniques, messages and media channels favoured by a target audience (Fill, 2011). It is difficult to pinpoint exactly when this change in communication planning took place. However, IMC began to be accepted as a valid approach for communications in the early 1990s. Duncan and Everett (1993) commented that the new customer-focused, technology-driven communications were an *orchestration, whole egg, seamless communication* approach, and Schultz referred to it as 'the process of developing and implementing various forms of persuasive communication programs with customers and prospects over time' (Schultz, 1993). From the mid 1990s, IMC adoption has become increasingly widespread, and now IMC means integrating all useable promotional tools and appropriate media to deliver synergistic communication campaigns. In other words, promotional campaigns select the most appropriate tools and channels which can be used in harmony with one another to maximize communication effectiveness so that the sum is greater than the individual parts.

The principles of IMC are that organizations coordinate their use of marketing communications tools, branding, images, logos and CRM strategies to deliver a clear, consistent, credible and competitive message about the organization and its products. The objective is to position products and organizations clearly and distinctively in the marketplace by providing target audiences with multiple opportunities to see, hear, read and/or interact with consistent marketing messages. As we discussed in Chapter 7, successful positioning is associated with products and services being favourably positioned in the minds of target audiences. 'A brand is the most valuable piece of real estate in the world: a corner of someone's mind' (Hegarty, 2011). IMC facilitates the positioning process by sending out consistent messages through all the components of the promotional mix, and in doing so reinforces the core message. LinkedIn's IMC campaign sought to raise awareness of the value the network can bring. The 'In it together' campaign deployed digital display ads, paid social media, online video, outdoor marketing, radio, podcasts, search engine marketing and partnership relationships to reach target markets in the USA. The message of the campaign was about working together to succeed and thinking outside the box about what is possible, and that LinkedIn is there to help, support and inspire (Cohen, 2018).

Drivers of IMC

Currently, advances in communication technology account for many changes taking place in the marketing industry, but there are other key drivers that help to explain why more organizations are adopting the IMC approach.

- *Organizational drivers* focus on the benefits IMC can bring from an operational perspective—for example, streamlining communications activities, creating opportunities for increased profits through efficiency gains. Many organizations are faced with having to show greater accountability in the communication budget and more measurable outcomes. IMC creates opportunities to create competitive advantage through coordinated brand development, and across an organization can deliver improved productivity and greater focus.

EXHIBIT 13.1
The Premier League changed its positioning with the help of a new visual image

- *Target-market-based drivers* focus on changes that are affecting the delivery of communication messages. For example, the cost and availability of media channels is changing. Audiences are becoming more fragmented, and organizations are using different media and different timings to grab the attention of their audiences. Technology-enabled communications are used more frequently as target audiences' skills and communication literacy are increasing.
- *Communication drivers* focus on the potential benefits associated with the delivery of the message—for example, increased effectiveness of the message—through constant reinforcement of the core ideas, consistent product and brand communication across a range of touchpoints, less confusion over the meaning of the message, and opportunities to build brand reputation and position clearly a product, brand or firm (based on Fill, 2011).

For marketing managers, achieving high levels of consistency across a range of communications is challenging. On the one hand, well-planned IMC campaigns can contribute to the development of competitive advantage, building stronger relationships between a brand and its stakeholders, improved consistency and clearer positioning of brands in the minds of customers. This approach can also be a source of further advantages insofar as there are opportunities to:

- *reduce costs* by standardizing communication messages across a selected promotional mix
- *create synergies* between the use of communication tools: for example, television advertising can be linked to in-store sales promotions and social media, so that members of a target audience receive a consistent message wherever they 'touch' an IMC campaign
- *reinforce competitive advantage* by creating a more consistent communication experience for customers. IMC campaigns potentially garner greater advantage than isolated campaigns. The Premier League reinvented its image to attract more sponsors. The new image heralded the new market positioning for the brand and sought to shed the brand's corporate image and focus more on the personality and story of the brand (Roderick, 2016).

See Exhibit 13.1 for the Premier League's new visual image.

On the other hand, however, organizations might have to change management structures and organizational culture to accommodate IMC, and creativity can be stifled if campaigns go wrong—which they can do on a grander scale and with greater potential to damage a brand's reputation. Increased use of digital channels and social media is intensifying the demands on both creating and controlling campaigns. There are now many more opportunities to 'touch' a brand. Marketers must consider the multiple touchpoints in a customer journey if they are to bridge the gap between the physical and digital world (Bylykbashi, 2015). Furthermore, according to Fill (2011), other potential disadvantages of adopting an IMC approach are that it:

- *requires greater management commitment* throughout the development and implementation of the IMC campaign
- *requires increased agency commitment* with the integration of all the stages across several platforms, media and promotional tools, leading to a need for more involvement from all agencies involved
- *encourages uniformity*, since increased commitment from management and agencies can lead to demand for uniformity and might stifle creativity.

Managers should consider the advantages and disadvantages when planning and developing an IMC approach to campaigns.

Planning for Integrated Marketing Communications

So far, we have discovered that many drivers are now encouraging wider uptake of IMC as a framework for planning and managing communication campaigns and initiatives. We have, however, also identified several management considerations and challenges to be addressed if a brand is to maximize the potential advantages and avoid the disadvantages of adopting an IMC approach. A framework for applying an IMC approach is given in Figure 13.1.

FIGURE 13.1
A framework for implementing integrated marketing communications

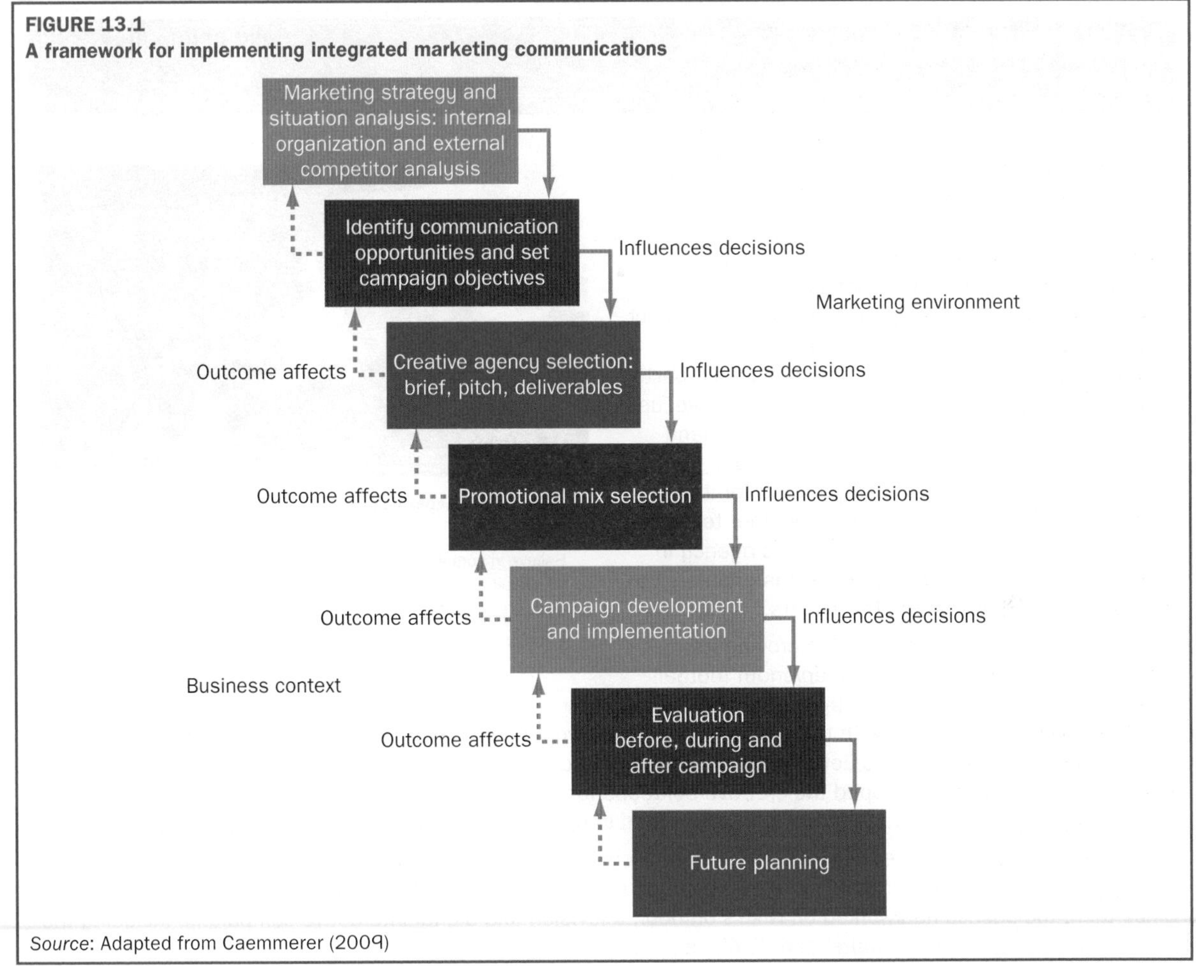

Source: Adapted from Caemmerer (2009)

Marketing strategy and situation analysis

IMC is a framework for planning the use of the promotional mix. Therefore, it is important to remember that the objectives, the brand positioning statement and more come from the marketing strategy (see Chapter 18 for more details). Opportunities identified from the marketing situation analysis and the target market analysis should be captured to enable use of promotions to contribute to the creation of differential advantage. This initial stage in the planning framework serves to ensure integration between the marketing strategy and promotional mix selection. The analysis should also clarify the overarching objectives that guide the campaign. The promotional mix decisions depend on the marketing strategy, competitive positioning and target market. For example, target market definition will lead to an understanding of the needs of the target audiences and how the audiences can be reached by different promotional tools and media channels. Furthermore, differential advantage will affect message decisions.

IMC campaign objectives

Once issues from the marketing strategy and situation analysis have been decided, communication objectives will be set and promotional options selected (e.g. advertising, direct marketing and personal selling) to form a brand-led approach. However, it should be noted that among practitioners there is debate over which comes first—the marketing and brand strategy or the objectives for the communication campaign. (Further discussion of these issues and specific communication objectives appears in Chapters 14, 15 and 16; also see Marketing in Action 13.1.)

So, how do companies decide communication objectives for integrated campaigns?

MARKETING IN ACTION 13.1
Nike Scores By Getting Controversial

Nike is a brand that creative agencies want to work for, and it is seen as an innovative and thought-provoking brand. Nike's clothing and digital sport divisions are constantly conducting research and development so the brand can lead the way in wearable sport technologies. An example of a product is the FuelBand, which measures the wearer's movements throughout the day and produces reports on calorie intake, distance covered and total NikeFuel points accumulated. R/GA picked up the FuelBand business from Nike due to its prowess as a digital agency. The agency won industry awards for its cross-platform campaigns, bringing together television and digital channels. The success of this agency in meeting Nike's communication goals has enabled it to be retained for European football events.

Nike is constantly developing and improving its product offerings such as the Hypervenom football boot, and this means plenty of opportunities for creative agencies to engage with the brand. Agencies are very keen to work with innovative companies, as it gives them an opportunity to develop highly differentiated communication campaigns. ManvsMachine, an award-winning agency, developed the creative solutions for Nike's Hypervenom II campaign. The creative theme was used at every stage of the campaign: film, in print, in stores and online.

Wieden + Kennedy is another highly creative global communications agency, which has worked with Nike since creating the brand's first-ever national television advert, aired in 1982 during the New York City Marathon. Since then, the agency has worked on Nike's outdoor, television and digital interactive campaigns, including the iconic 'Just do it', 'Write the future' and 'Endless possibilities' campaigns.

When the 'Just do it' campaign reached the age of 30, Wieden + Kennedy built on previous themes and developed a controversial campaign, Dream Crazy, featuring former US National Football League (NFL) player Kaepernick. Kaepernick encourages consumers to dream in the creative campaign, which showcases a wrestler with no legs, a football player with a missing hand, as well as known sporting celebrities like tennis player Serena Williams. The integrated campaign used digital, print and broadcast channels and was highly successful both in terms of engagement and commercially, with revenues up 10 per cent and increased profits. Kaepernick's inclusion in the campaign hit the headlines, as he was linked to the NFL players who protested about police brutality by kneeling during the national anthem played at the beginning of a game. Nike's customers were divided, with many protesting that the leading sportwear brand was being unpatriotic; some even burnt trainers as a sign of their disgust, and social media threads #justburnit and #boycottNike kept the debate alive. Kaepernick reaffirmed his passion for following a dream, by tweeting: 'Believe in something. Even if it means sacrificing everything else."

Even though Nike is an attractive brand from a creative agency's perspective, both client and agency must build foundations to ensure that a good working relationship is established, especially when embarking on a controversial campaign. Setting clear and measurable goals, working collaboratively and choosing an agency with exploitable skills are some of the key areas that need to be right for a successful working partnership to develop.

Based on: Carr (2013); Anon (2015a); Beltrone (2014); Swift (2015); Manvsmachine (2015); Vizard (2018), Schultz and Pasquarelli (2018); Kelner, M. (2018)

There are benefits to following the top-down, market-strategy-driven, brand-led approach, as it means the marketing team are aware of what is required to position the brand and can tailor communications accordingly. This approach means that campaigns are coordinated and efficient. See Exhibit 13.2 for how Virgin Media used its film *Birds Behind Bars* to promote a new season of the Netflix hit *Orange is the New Black*. This multi-platform campaign used social media, retail channels and video on demand. However, sometimes marketing managers use their large IMC budgets to determine the shape of the campaign (Ritson, 2011). In other words, they select promotional tools that are affordable, desirable or in vogue, with only a limited consideration of the IMC campaign objectives. This approach means that campaigns can become disjointed and inefficient, and the outcome can be that they perform poorly and achieve little for the brand when driven by the promotional tools rather than the marketing and branding strategy.

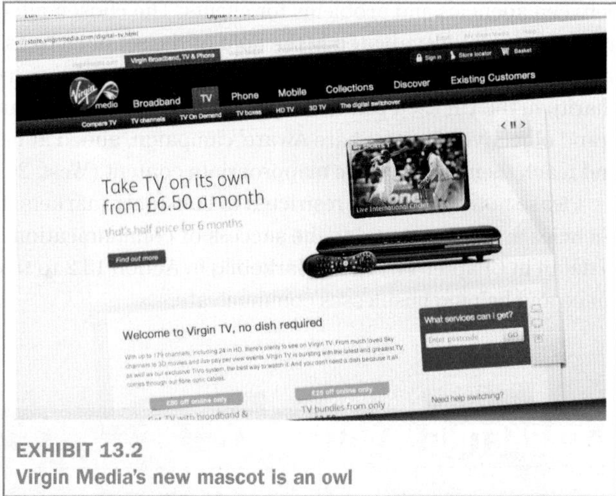

EXHIBIT 13.2
Virgin Media's new mascot is an owl

The key point to be aware of is this: clear objectives are imperative for IMC if it is to be considered as a valid and achievable framework for planning communications. (Specific communication objectives for each of the tools are discussed in Chapters 14, 15 and 16.)

Creative agency selection

Once the objectives are set, the next step is to select creative **agencies** (which includes using internal teams and departments) to develop a communication brief and determine the deliverables. Once the creative brief has been developed, creative agencies will be selected to pitch for the campaign. It should be noted that often communications are developed by the internal marketing team, but there should still be a briefing document, as this sets down on a single page the core requirement of the campaign, which acts as a guide for everyone in terms of the message, target audiences, tone, budget and deliverables. Agencies and/or internal departments will prepare a pitch for the client that shows how their ideas and use of the communication budget will meet the client's requirements. Marketing managers must decide how to determine whether an agency can deliver on its promises. This has always been an issue, but it is a problem that has become increasingly difficult to solve in the digital age. Agencies are not opposed to claiming that they offer a full range of services when, in fact, they are not able to deliver seamless integration across all the communication tools (Bendaby, 2011). (The issue of agency selection is revisited in Chapters 14 and 16.) See Marketing in Action 13.1 to find out how Nike gets record engagement with a controversial IMC campaign. A full-service agency should offer the capacity to provide all the promotional tools. Some agencies (e.g. BBH advertising agency) offer a complete service across all the communication tools. However, there are specialist agencies with particular expertize (e.g. Fever PR, an agency specializing in public relations online and offline) or an internal company team.

Once the agency selection is complete, the creative teams, account managers and other service providers will work together to produce each of the elements of the campaign. Media schedulers will be involved in making sure that any media requirements are available and fulfilled. A Gantt chart or similar project management timetable will be set out as a guide to make sure that each of the elements of the campaign is ready at the prescribed time. Timing is very important to IMC campaigns, especially as different tools might be required to fulfil different functions, and digital technology is enabling brands to communicate with their supporters in real time.

The Lawn Tennis Association (LTA) has always been positioned as quintessentially English, and its approaches to communication have fitted this stance. However, the LTA teamed up with a new sponsor Nature Valley in an IMC campaign aimed at encouraging the British public to go out and play tennis in order to demonstrate the association's commitment to encouraging greater participation in the sport (LTA, 2018).

The advantage of using one agency is better communication and specialist expertise, but using several agencies gives clients more flexibility regarding the choice of the best agencies to handle each media type (Weissberg, 2008). However, using several agencies can lead to conflict regarding who is paid for what and who takes charge. Suppose an integrated campaign is mainly direct marketing but includes an online game created by a digital specialist who also thinks of the main campaign strapline. Which agency has contributed more to the campaign, and which deserves the greater financial reward (Bidlake, 2008)? Such questions can create conflict between agencies and problems for clients. The chosen integrated communication strategy will be executed and subsequently evaluated in the light of the set objectives. At the NSPCC, communication messages are often informative and aim to change behaviour. In a thought-provoking campaign, 'Alex's willy', this leading children's charity in the UK used prime-time television, social media and digital spaces to deliver messages to achieve its new brand objectives for its 'Share Aware' campaign, aimed at helping parents keep their children safe on social media and teach them not to share inappropriate content (West, 2015).

Please note, IMC is not restricted to consumer markets. Furthermore, relationships between clients and agencies are fundamental to the success of communication initiatives. (Client—agency relationships are covered in detail in Chapter 14.) Read Marketing in Action 13.2 to find out how the IMC concept is developing in the digital space and helping businesses communicate.

MARKETING IN ACTION 13.2

Digital Platforms, Managed Content and Customer Journeys Move IMC to a New Level

Some commentators argue that manufacturers have to go beyond just integrating their brand communications across a number of different media. In the digital space, it is suggested that communications are synchronized to ensure that a company's campaigns allow everyone who touches a product from *cradle to grave* to get the communication messages. This approach requires collaborative cross-stakeholder involvement to produce a seamless brand experience.

Arguably, an IMC campaign uses communication tools sequentially, and the core communication message is translated into a format that is appropriate for the media channel. For example, Tesco spends over £110 million a year on its brand communications, which are key to it retaining is market leadership position; its 'Every little helps' campaign, along with the introduction of its Tesco Value range and the Tesco Clubcard, helped the brand move into number one spot in the UK grocery market by 1995, overtaking its rival Sainsbury's. The 'Every little helps' campaign message was used first in the 1990s and was launched on television, followed by sales promotions in print media, in-store and through the Tesco Clubcard. The initial campaign attracted 1.3 million new customers to Tesco. Since then, the message has been consistently applied through various communication tools as a fully integrated series of campaigns. But as Tesco moves forward, its new communications agency BBH will have to consider how to engage customers simultaneously across multiple platforms.

Arguably, synchronized campaigns change the emphasis by focusing on the strengths of each communication technique and identifying each step of the customer journey and the touchpoints where customers will engage with a brand. This allows creatives to plan how to manage the execution of the campaign in real time and respond to engagement from the target audience. The reason for the shift in emphasis is that, previously, choosing the message and then controlling how it was received by the target audience was more straightforward. Today, a customer's first encounter with a brand could be a Twitter feed, a shared Facebook message or a mobile app.

Content is also developed in conjunction with communication campaigns. Brands are increasingly aiming to tell an enduring story that will foster engagement and customer loyalty. Content management also needs to be planned around campaign objectives, the target audience and the targeting opportunities. Content marketing enables a brand to focus on its core values and reflect customers' needs. But it is important that the content does not become a rambling dialogue that dilutes the meaning of a brand. According to Hertz Europe, 'The secret is to ensure the content focuses on what a product enables someone to do or the experiences it opens up for them.' Taking this approach enables Hertz to ensure that the content is constantly refreshed and on-message.

Consequently, companies have new challenges if they wish to take IMC campaigns to a new level. They must consider their customers' journeys and where, when and how customers encounter various communication tools and digital platforms, before developing specific communication messages. Companies also must devise a strategy for managing content that might support the campaign to ensure that the brand positioning is not diluted by an off-topic digital conversation.

Based on: Magee (2015); Anon (n.d.); DeSantis Breindel (2015); Hill (2015); Hemsley (2015); Clark and Chan (2014)

The promotional mix

The communication objectives can help to determine which communication tools to include in a campaign (Caemmerer, 2009). Furthermore, the creative pitch enables an agency to make suggestions about which tools are the most likely to achieve the campaign objectives set by the client. Ultimately, the client (the company commissioning the campaign) decides which tools to use, which creative message and combination of agencies represent the best value, and which are likely to achieve their communication aims.

Campaign development and implementation

At this stage, the promotional mix decision is finalized and the message and creative execution confirmed. Other major decisions taken at this stage are the media channel selection, planning and scheduling. The media decision will affect the budget. For example, television advertising reaches a large television audience but can be expensive, whereas print media advertising using regional newspapers can be a relatively low-cost option but will not have the same reach, and digital platforms offer scope for interactive campaigns which can foster high levels of engagement. The relative merits of media channels are discussed later in the chapter and in Chapter 14.

Evaluation

Following the implementation, each of the elements of the campaign will be evaluated to assess overall effectiveness. Evaluation should take place at all stages of the campaign, including during pre-testing, tracking studies and post testing. This approach can help to assess the effectiveness and efficiency of the IMC campaign (Sherwood, Stevens and Warren, 1989). Measurements are taken to determine the extent to which a campaign has achieved communication objectives and whether it is moving target audiences in the planned direction. Evaluation also feeds into future planning.

Future planning

After the implementation of an IMC campaign, each of the elements should be reviewed. Findings from the review should be fed back and recorded to inform the development of future campaigns. Throughout the campaign, information should be fed back. While the planning framework shows a linear process which moves from one stage to another, in reality the process is rather more iterative with information and learning influencing and informing developments at every stage of the process.

This section has examined the IMC planning process. The next section looks at the elements that underpin the IMC planning process and are fundamental to its successful application: the message, the tools, the media channels and the contexts.

Elements of Integrated Marketing Communications

To survive, organizations need to communicate with their customers; marketing messages tell buyers about the meaning of a brand and the benefits it can deliver. Arguably, 50 years ago delivering a message to a target audience was relatively straightforward: there were a small number of commercial television and radio channels and a few well-known printed publications, which a marketer might use to get the messages across. Now the communications environment has changed: it is more complex, integrated and universal. There are more interconnections between the core elements of communications to consider when planning an IMC campaign. The core elements are: the message, which is used to position a product, brand and/or an organization in the minds of the customer; the tools—the six key methods that provide the means of achieving communication objectives; the media, which are the channels that carry the message to the audience; the people who collectively are responsible for creating, planning, managing and implementing the communication campaign; and the context—the setting in which communication takes place (see Table 13.1).

TABLE 13.1 Core elements of IMC

Elements	Examples
The message	Rational, emotional
The tools	Advertising, personal selling, sales promotions, digital marketing, direct marketing, public relations
The media channels	Broadcast, print, internet, mobile, social networks, outdoor
The people	Account managers, clients, agencies, schedulers, planners, web service providers, martech specialist agencies
The context	Industrial, consumer, public sector, social

The message

In this section, we explore the function of the **message** and how it might be communicated to target audiences using both simple and complex processes.

At the heart of communications is the message. Messages are very important as they not only transfer information from a message sender to its recipient, but can also determine the nature of a relationship, establish credibility (Fill, 2011), set the tone for a *conversation* and cross tangible and intangible boundaries. Effective messages can become so powerful that they can be heard around the globe when used with suitable media channels. For example, when Bob Geldof, the Irish rock star, wanted to communicate the message that millions of people in Africa were dying of starvation, he decided to use a rock concert to get the message across to young audiences around the world. His core message was famine relief for Africa. The rock concert was Live Aid. This concert was transmitted from the UK and the USA on live television. Bob Geldof's message brought together a global audience, united music and youth, and spread the message of famine relief to a 400 million television viewers in over 50 countries (Hegarty, 2011).

In marketing, messages take on a special meaning—they are not mercurial asides between individuals, or unplanned, off-the-cuff remarks, but are carefully planned and crafted. Messages play an important role in positioning. To create effective messages, marketers need to consider the credibility of the message and its source (Kelman, 1961). For a target audience to engage with a marketing message, it has to be attractive and interesting, and the source (the sender of the message) has to be perceived as credible and believable to have the power to deliver the message promise. The next step is to establish suitable brand messages to communicate with target audiences.

As discussed earlier, product (Chapter 8) and service (Chapter 9) brands are distinctive market offerings that can be easily identified by target audiences for whom they deliver a parcel of benefits. During the development of a brand, its quality, value, features, name, design and packaging are determined. These features of the brand can then be used in crafting marketing messages.

Marketing messages take many forms, for example emotional and rational appeals that are designed to stimulate different responses such as fear, humour and action. In Chapters 4 and 5 we discovered how consumers react to both emotional and factual stimuli, whereas business buyers respond to more rational, information-based messages.

Information-based messages

Sometimes companies want to provide their customers with information that will enable them to make an informed decision about the brands they choose.

Increasingly, brands are using digital platforms to provide their customers with the information they need to make their choices, as well as more traditional print and broadcast channels.

Information-based messages use different formats: for example, Weetabix's 'incredible inside', a £10-million campaign, reached out to all its customers with a television advert that aimed to remind them how important their bodies are, and in doing so delivered hard facts. This style of message delivery is sometimes referred to as a *slice of life*.

Emotional messages

Sometimes messages are designed to stimulate a response and possibly connect with the target audience through an emotion. For example, Procter & Gamble's 'Like a girl' campaign focused on a girl's life to promote its Always brand and used male/female perceptions, relationships and music to create a highly emotional appeal. The brand extended the reach of its campaign by raising awareness of period poverty and donating to Kind Direct, a not-for-profit charity that works to end hygiene poverty. Thousands of young girls regularly miss school because they do not have access to sanitary protection; this affects their confidence, and they miss out on learning and experiences (Always, 2018).

Messages that shock are often used to attract not only the attention of the target audiences but also that of the wider media. To accompany the poster campaign, the United Nations ran a YouTube animation that sought to demonstrate the level of sexism within society, using a global Google autofill study. While not necessarily accurate in the inference of its finding of the levels of discrimination against women (as autofill searches make many bizarre suggestions), this campaign raised awareness of the injustices against women on a global scale (Mahdawi, 2013).

In Chapter 14 we explore messages in more detail and look at how to create different types of message appeal—informative, interactive or actionable. Now we are going to consider how the message is delivered through the communication process.

The communication process: simple and complex

While messages are at the heart of the process, the actual way in which we communicate is also very important. In this section, we examine the elements of the simple communication model which shows how a message is transferred from one person to another. Then we consider how messages are spread within and across communities.

A simple model of the *communication process* is shown in Figure 13.2. The *source* (or communicator) *encodes* a message by translating the idea to be communicated into a symbol consisting of words, pictures and numbers. Some advertisements attempt to encode a message using the minimum of words, while others provide extensive detail. We explore message content later in this section.

Noise—distractions and distortions during the communication process—may prevent transmission to some of the target audience. A television advertisement may not reach a member of the household because of conversation or the telephone ringing. Similarly, a press advertisement may not be noticed because of editorial competing for attention.

When a *receiver* sees or hears the message, it is *decoded*. This is the process by which the receiver interprets the symbols transmitted by the source. The aim is for the receiver's decoding to coincide with the source's encoding process. The receiver thus interprets the message in the way intended by the source. Messages that rely on words more than pictures can also be decoded differently. For example, a message such as 'the most advanced washing machine in the world' may be accepted by some receivers but rejected by others.

Communicators need to understand their targets before encoding messages, so that they are credible. Otherwise the response may be disbelief and rejection. In a personal selling situation, *feedback* from buyer to salesperson may be immediate, as when objections are raised or a sale is concluded. For other types of marketing such as advertising and sales promotion, feedback may rely on marketing research to estimate reactions to commercials and increases in sales due to incentives.

FIGURE 13.2
Simple model of communication

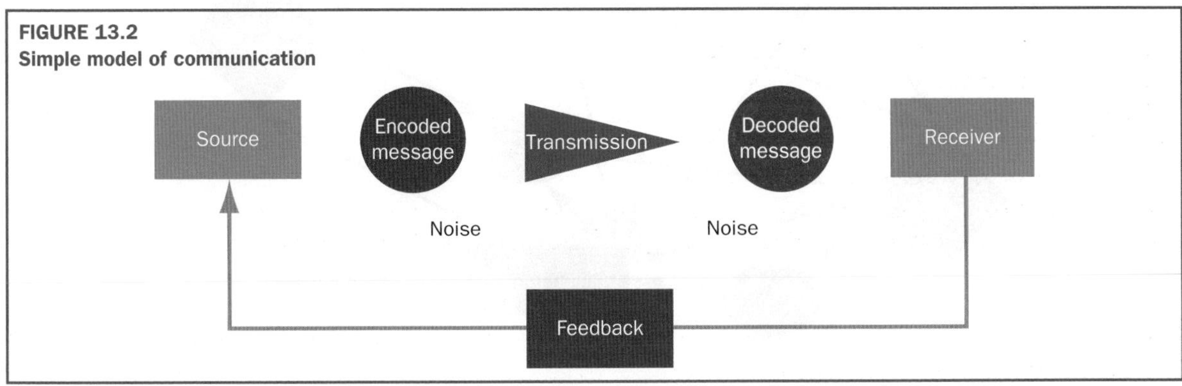

An important point to recognize in the communication process is the sophistication of receivers and how they can play different roles in the wider dissemination of the message. The simple model of communication explains the basic concepts and transmission of a message from sender to receiver, but the communication of a message rarely takes place in such isolation. Message receivers interact with one another, and consequently they can act as conduits to spread messages further afield.

The message is *transmitted* through media such as television or posters, which are selected for their ability to reach the desired target audience in the desired way. Communication requirements may affect the choice of media. For example, if the encoded message requires the product to be demonstrated, the internet, television and cinema may be preferred to posters and printed publications.

There are also other levels of complexity to consider: different message recipients play different roles in the wider diffusion of messages. Katz and Lazarfield (1955) found that some individuals were able to exert greater influence than others. These opinion leaders (Rogers, 1983)—as they have become known—enjoy higher status within social groups, and their views are considered more highly by other members of the social/peer group. Opinion leaders play an important role in the communication process, as 'they are receptive to new ideas' and are happy to try and buy new products and services (Fill, 2011); they are prepared to lead opinion. Opinion formers are individuals who can exert personal influence because of authority, education or status associated with the objects of the communication process (Fill, 2011); they shape opinion. The influence of opinion formers is also important in the communication process. A theatre critic writing reviews in a local or national newspaper or blogging online has also become an important type of opinion former. For example, Elin Kling is a Swedish fashion blogger who collaborated with H&M and then became a fashion designer; Pete Cashmore, the Scottish founder of the famous blog site Mashable, is a highly influential voice in technology, business, social media and entertainment.

The simple model of communication suggests that communications are unidirectional, passing from sender to receiver. In the past, this model has been used to explain the spread of many mass-marketing campaigns. But the world of communications has become highly complicated. There are many ways for individuals and companies to communicate and interact. Indeed, the boundaries between the pillars of the marketing mix are becoming eroded as products and communications come closer together.

In a multichannel world where message receivers gather information from multiple points such as websites, apps, a multitude of television channels, printed publications and, perhaps more importantly, each other, a more complex model is needed to understand how communication messages are disseminated. Figure 13.3 shows the complexity of communication networks.

FIGURE 13.3
Complex model of communication

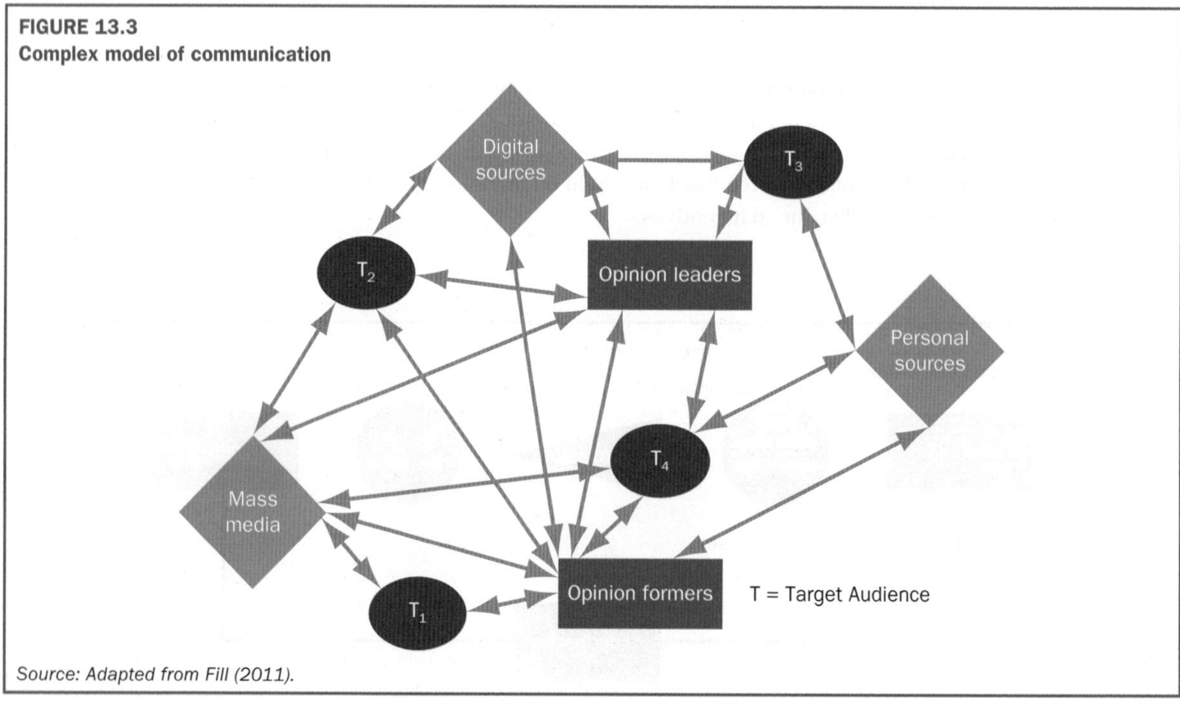

Source: Adapted from Fill (2011).

Figure 13.3 shows how complex two-way linkages can form between target audiences, opinion formers and leaders, the media (television, radio, internet), digital sources of influence (e.g. websites, social media) and personal sources of information (experiences). The implications for developing IMC campaigns are that multiple two-way integrated communications become formal and informal. This means that message senders need to use multiple methods and channels to ensure that messages are being received by the intended target audience. For instance, a website selling innovative products (digital source) may provide information that may then be picked up by a journalist (opinion former) who does a review for a special-interest magazine (mass media) that is read by the local computer expert (opinion leader), who informs her friends (target audience). The communication message potentially is the central core of a conversation between multiple participants. Read more about how conversations and storytelling can help to spread a message in Mini Case 13.1.

MINI CASE 13.1
Conversations, Storytelling and Happy Endings

Conversations

When Owen Baxter and Geoffrey Lewis (executives of the then-failing Hush Puppy brand of shoes) had a conversation with a New York stylist, they were told that Hush Puppies had suddenly become hip in the clubs and downtown bars of Manhattan, and that there were resale shops in the Village in Soho where the Hush Puppies were being sold (Gladwell, 2000). Reportedly, what followed was that the shoes were chosen by fashion buyers to feature in their new ranges, and the basset hound (symbol for the brand) was used by a Los Angeles designer on his store in Hollywood. The sales of Hush Puppies quadrupled year on year, and so the brand that was on its way out was not only saved but became a staple item in every young trendy American's wardrobe. In this tale, the informal communication network enabled the message to be filtered back from the target audience (young people in East Village Manhattan) to the opinion leaders (fashion designers and stylists) and eventually to more formal traditional mass media communication channels.

Storytelling

Storytelling is part of our daily lives and helps us make sense of the complex world around us. Often we become part of the story, and brands utilize storytelling as a platform for developing meaning. John Hegarty, Creative Director of Bartle Bogle Hegarty (BBH), is one of the world's advertising aficionados. Hegarty advocates that storytelling is probably the most powerful form of communication, as it can be used very effectively to make brands memorable (see quote at opening of chapter). However, he suggests that messages and stories need to be created for the screen-based culture (television, computers, mobile phones) that is now so prevalent in modern society. To be successful in the screen-based world of communications, it is important to get the balance right between visuals and words. In many of the highly successful Levi's 501 jeans commercials, the story is a visual narrative. For example, in the 1985 classic advert, set in a 1950s launderette, Nick Kamen (the lead character) walks into the launderette wearing sunglasses, which he proceeds to remove. He then fills the washing machine with soap powder, removes his top and Levi's and then, wearing just his boxer shorts, sits down to read a magazine while he waits for his jeans to be washed. The slogan shown on screen at the end of the commercial, 'Levi's 501 the original shrink-to-fit jeans', neatly brings the tale to an end.

Another tip—from William Goldman, award-winning novelist and screenwriter—is 'Come in late, leave early.' What this means is that the scriptwriter should leave space for the target audience to fill in some of the gaps and should not over-explain. Scripts for commercials do tend to be brief and give the creative director space to tell the story visually. According to John Hegarty, 'Great writing and storytelling also has to understand the principle of input and out-take. For example, if I want to make you think I'm funny, I don't tell you that I'm really funny, I tell you a joke. You laugh and think, "Wow, that guy is really funny."' He also explains that communicators should inspire people to do something, rather than merely giving them instructions, and should never forget that 'a brand is an agglomeration of stories linked together by a vision'.

Happy endings

Creating successful communication messages is a challenge for marketing managers, and identifying opportunities to stimulate meaningful conversations or create a story that *captures the hearts and minds* of the target audience is difficult. Furthermore, the attitude of the recipient will be influenced by whether they are favourably disposed towards advertising in general, as this will affect the effectiveness of the

»

communication message. Despite these challenges, manufactures of generic products like butter, milk, tea and toilet rolls have frequently been successful in ticking all the boxes and creating messages with the best happy endings in the communication industry, by developing stories involving animals and children.

In 1972, the likeable Labrador puppy first appeared in Andrex toilet-roll commercials and proved so successful that it has since appeared in over 130 campaigns. The puppies feature on the products and the website, and over the years the slogans have evolved from 'soft, strong and very long' through 'tuggable, huggable softness' to 'be kind to your behind'. The loveable puppies continue to make the brand memorable and deliver happy endings all round for Andrex and its customers. More recently, Budweiser is another brand to use 'puppy love' to produce highly emotional adverts with happy endings.

There are many other examples of products that have successfully used animals in their campaign stories: Kerrygold butter with its cows; PG Tips tea and its chimpanzees; Cesar dog food with a white West Highland terrier; and the Felix cat food brand, which uses the iconic black and white cartoon cat. From shoes to car commercials, animals score highly on the likeability scale and are usually a safe bet for delivering a happy ending that captures the imagination of the target audience and delivers a good return on investment for the brand.

But not all happy endings are born out of cuteness and likeability. Social media and video on demand have opened new routes to follow Hegarty's principles. In a viral campaign, #epicstrut, Moneysupermarket.com arguably applied the general principles of the Levi's classic advert to capture attention and drive engagement. In the advert, which features the Pussycat Dolls' hit 'Don't cha', Dave expresses his satisfaction at the saving on his car insurance by strutting in a combination of suit, hot pants and black patent high heels, much to the surprise of passers-by. Within the first few days, this campaign went viral.

Questions:

1. How does the interactional model of communication work for Hush Puppies?
2. Explain more fully why coming in late might be a valid approach for developing communication messages. Give examples of commercials that take this approach.
3. Why do certain brands use animals in their campaigns?

Based on: Anon (2015b); Gladwell (2000); Hegarty (2011); Mehta (2000); Fill (2011); Cordiner (2009)

The increasing complexity of communications channels, the shift towards informal away from formal lines of communications, and the growing importance of digital and mobile channels and media are blurring the divisions between communication tools, sales channels and the media. Research (Doherty, Ellis-Chadwick and Hart, 1999) into the use of digital technology in the retail sector has highlighted that, for this industry, the internet is a channel that facilitates communications, interactions and sales. For example, Dixons Carphone uses SMS to send text messages to its customers, informing them of the latest offers, but also uses this channel to provide product delivery information. Additionally, the firm's brand websites are used for sales, communications and aftersales care. For the customer, the message, the media and the channel work seamlessly together, while for the firm the main point is that the basic premise of its messages has not changed, but the opportunities to leverage advantage through greater functionality and extended touchpoints of the message have increased significantly.

The tools

In this section, we explore the promotional communication tools that deliver the message to the target audiences. We also examine the tools' key characteristics and the impact on selection of tools to use for IMC campaigns. In addition to this brief section introducing the tools, all the elements of the promotional communication mix and how they can be used in campaigns is covered in more detail in the following chapters. Three chapters cover specific tools: Chapter 14 covers mass communications, which are those tools that reach wide audiences using non-personal communication techniques, such as advertising, public relations and sales promotions; Chapter 15 covers direct communications, the tools that communicate with specific members of the target audience, such as direct marketing and personal selling; and Chapter 16 covers digital promotions and social media, tools that connect with target audiences through digital and mobile channels and foster engagement through digital channels.

Before looking at the specific tools, we briefly consider the division of tools into the following groups: mass, direct and digital.

Mass, direct and digital communications

As explored earlier, messages can take many forms and be communicated to various audiences. Because of the volume of marketing messages that are currently aimed at consumers and businesses, there is a likelihood that many of these messages will not reach the target recipients in the way that might be intended. This fact makes the study of marketing communications a fascinating aspect of marketing. Currently, there are three major groups of tools available to the marketer.

1 *Mass marketing communications* include advertising, sales promotions and public relations. These are methods of communication that can be styled to meet IMC campaign objectives. Mass communications methods are those that primarily involve sending non-personal messages to wide target audiences. The main media for mass communications are broadcast, print and digital. Mass communications are sometimes criticized because their impact is difficult to measure—particularly that of advertising and public relations—therefore it can be difficult to value the return on investment.
2 *Direct marketing communications* include personal selling, exhibitions and direct marketing. These are also methods of communication that can be styled to meet IMC campaign objectives, but the main difference is that direct communications can be personalized, highly specific and tend to be used to target narrow or niche audiences. These tools rarely use broadcast or print media to deliver the message. Direct communications are also easier to measure than mass communications. The measurement aspect has been a key driver in the increase in the use of these tools in recent years.
3 *Digital promotions and social media communications* include websites, email marketing, buzz marketing and social media. Digital communications can also be styled to meet IMC campaign objectives, but are more difficult to categorize because of their flexibility. For example, a company website can accommodate many aspects and elements of IMC (Chaffey and Ellis-Chadwick, 2012). The BBC uses its websites as a communication channel, an information resource, a media player and a sales channel. Digital communications can reach wide, narrow and individual target audiences. These forms of communication are the most measurable; sophisticated analytics and metric programs provide a wealth of data ranging from what a website user downloads to the time of day that person opens and reads their email messages. Digital marketing and social media are explored in detail in Chapter 16.

The rest of this section introduces the individual tools that make up the promotional mix and considers their impact for IMC campaigns.

The challenge for marketing managers responsible for communications is selecting the *right* mix of tools and then the media channels to deliver the message. The promotional communication mix is a key element in any IMC campaign. The reason is that the mix provides the means by which the message achieves campaign objectives and determines the style used to craft the message. There are six major components of the mix: advertising, personal selling, direct marketing, digital promotions, sales promotion and public relations.

1 **Advertising**: any paid form of non-personal communication of ideas or products in the prime media, i.e. television, the press, outdoor, cinema, radio and the internet.
2 **Personal selling**: oral communication with prospective purchasers with the intention of making a sale.
3 **Direct marketing**: the distribution of products, information and promotional benefits to target consumers through interactive communication in a way that allows response to be measured.
4 **Digital promotions**: the promotion of products to consumers and businesses through digital media channels.
5 **Sales promotion**: incentives to consumers or the trade that are designed to stimulate purchases.
6 **Public relations**: educating and informing an organization's public through the media without paying for the time or space directly.

In addition, product placement, sponsorship, exhibitions and branding are also used to communicate with target audiences. These tools are covered in Chapters 14 and 15.

To develop an IMC campaign, the marketing manager must make a choice of the promotional blend needed to communicate to the target audience. Each of the six major promotional tools has its own strengths and limitations, and these are summarized in Table 13.2. Marketers will carefully weigh these factors against communication objectives to decide the amount of resources to channel into each tool. Usually, five considerations will have a major impact on the choice of the promotional mix.

1 *Resource availability and the cost of promotional tools*: to conduct a national advertising campaign may require several million pounds. If resources are not available, cheaper tools such as sales promotion or public relations may have to be used.
2 *Market size and concentration*: if a market is small and concentrated, then personal selling may be feasible, but for mass markets that are geographically dispersed, selling to the ultimate customer would

not be cost-effective. In such circumstances, advertising, digital promotion or direct marketing may be the correct choice.

3 *Customer information needs*: if a complex technical argument is required, personal selling may be preferred. If all that is required is the appropriate brand image, then advertising may be more sensible.

4 *Product characteristics*: because of the above arguments, business-to-business companies tend to spend more on personal selling than on advertising, whereas consumer goods companies tend to do the reverse.

5 *Push versus pull strategies*: a push strategy involves an attempt to sell into channel intermediaries (e.g. retailers) and is dependent on personal selling and trade promotions. A pull strategy bypasses intermediaries to communicate to consumers directly. The resultant consumer demand persuades intermediaries to stock the product. Advertising and consumer promotions are more likely to be used.

TABLE 13.2 Key characteristics of the core tools of the promotional mix

Advertising
• Good for awareness-building, because it can reach a wide audience quickly • Repetition means that a brand-positioning concept can be communicated effectively; television is particularly strong, but the level of use is changing due to the internet • Can be used to aid the sales effort, to legitimize a firm and its products • Impersonal, lacks flexibility and questions cannot be answered • Limited capability to close the sale
Personal selling
• Interactive: questions can be answered and objectives overcome • Adaptable: presentations can be changed depending on customer needs • Complex arguments can be developed • Relationships can be built, because of its personal nature • Provides the opportunity to close the sale • Sales calls are costly
Direct marketing
• Individually targets those consumers most likely to respond to an appeal • Communication can be personalized • Short-term effectiveness can easily be measured • A continuous relationship can be built through periodic contact • Activities are less visible to competitors • Response rates are often low • Poorly targeted direct marketing activities cause consumer annoyance
Digital promotions
• Global reach to consumers and businesses at a comparatively low cost • Highly measurable • Interactive digital promotions enable a dialogue between companies and their customers and suppliers • Highly adaptable, as messages, prices, products and content can be changed rapidly • Highly flexible; can be used to create sales and communication channels • Highly targeted and can be personalized • Convenient form of access to product and firm information and purchasing • Avoids the necessity of negotiating and arguing with salespeople • High cost of development of websites and mobile content • Poses security issues and risk of intrusion
Sales promotion
• Incentives provide a quick boost to sales • Effects may be only short-term • Excessive use of some incentives (e.g. money off) may damage brand image
Public relations
• Highly credible, as message comes from a third party • Higher readership than advertisements in trade and technical publications • Loss of control: a press release may or may not be used, and its content may be distorted

Two points need to be stressed. First, marketing communications are not the exclusive province of the promotional mix. All the marketing mix communicate to target customers. The product itself communicates quality; price may be used by consumers as an indicator of quality, and the choice of distribution channel will affect customer exposure to the product. Secondly, effective communication is not a one-way producer-to-consumer flow. Producers need to understand the needs and motivation of their target audience before they can talk to them in a meaningful way. For example, marketing research may be used to understand large consumer segments before designing an IMC campaign, and salespeople may ask questions of buyers to reveal their circumstances, problems and needs before making a sales presentation. Furthermore, using the internet and the web, members of the target audience can freely express their views and opinions through customer feedback, reviews, blogs and social media.

Developing a successful IMC campaign involves careful planning and implementation, topics which are discussed in more detail later in the chapter. However, at the start of a campaign, companies should ensure that they have completed a situation analysis and have identified communication opportunities before selecting the communication mix. Furthermore, communication mix decisions should not be taken in isolation. Marketers need to consider the complete communication package by selecting tools that create a suitable blend with other components of the promotional campaign mix. The aim is to ensure that a clear and consistent message is received by target audiences. The media channel that carries the message is a further consideration. In the past, media decisions were mainly associated with advertising, but now other tools can be involved in media selection. For example, sales promotions can appear on broadcast media, outdoor media, in store or be delivered via email. Direct marketing uses the internet, mail services and mobile, and even personal selling is now possible via the web. Public relations messages can also involve similar media selection, as they can be sent via the internet and through mobile messaging.

The Renault IMC campaign highlights how combining tools and media to deliver a consistent message can be effective in generating the interest of a wide audience and eventually changing the attitudes of target consumers.

Media channels

This section introduces the channels that carry the message, using the selected communication tool, to the target audience. There used to be a joke among media people that the client's attitude to its part in advertising was, '10 minutes to go before lunch. Just enough time to discuss media' (Syedain, 1992). However, as media costs have risen and brands become more targeted, and as the choice of media channels has increased, this attitude has disappeared. Table 13.3 shows the different media channels available to marketing communication managers.

TABLE 13.3 Media channels

Media channel	Type
Broadcast	Television, radio
Print	Newspapers, magazines, fanzines
Digital	Websites, intranets, portals, email, interactive TV, mobile, social networks
Social	Online communities, blogs
Outdoor	Billboards, street furniture, transport, guerrilla
Indoor	Point of sale, in-store posters, window and shelf displays, ambient
Cinema	Multiplex, Imax, outdoor

Arguably, before the internet was available commercially (pre 1989), media decisions were clear-cut. They involved deciding which **media class** (e.g. broadcast or print) and which media vehicle (e.g. which specific newspaper) would carry the message. Print was the most widely used, followed by television. However, since the commercialization of the internet, the whole media world has changed. The internet now accounts for more of the communication budget spend than any other media (e.g. television, newspapers, radio, outdoor). The reason for its increasing popularity is bound up in its flexibility. The internet (the web and associated technology) can act not only as a multimedia channel, offering marketing communication managers the opportunity to send video, audio and text-based messages, but also creates an environment for advertising, sales promotions, direct marketing, personal selling and public relations. Consequently, digital technologies now accommodate almost every aspect of the communication and media mix. The technology also adds innovative ways to communicate messages to a target audience, for example animation, interaction, social communities and crowd-sourcing (discussed further in Chapter 16).

Currently, organizations use various media channels to carry their message. Probably the key media decision is which forms of **media channel** to use (e.g. broadcast, print, digital).

Media channel choice

When considering which media channel, the media planner faces the choice of using television, press, cinema, outdoor, radio, digital platforms and digital channels or some combination of media classes. Various aspects will be considered, and *creative factors* may have a major bearing on the decision, for example the type of message and the audio/visual elements that make up the appeal. Turkish Airlines used animation, humour and characters from *The Lego Movie* to make an in-flight video to communicate all the safety features of their airlines. The film is shown on all the airline's flights and, additionally, has been viewed nearly 20 million times on YouTube (Gibson, 2018). The key question that needs to be addressed is 'Does the medium allow the communication objectives to be realized?' For example, if the objective is to position the brand as having a high-status aspirational personality, television is better than posters. However, if the communication objective is to remind the target audience of a brand's existence, a poster campaign may suffice. Each medium possesses its own set of creative qualities and limitations, as described below.

The creative opportunities afforded by the media channel can add to the richness of the message. Other considerations when selecting media are the **media type** (newspaper, website, poster, mobile), the **media vehicle decision** (e.g. a particular newspaper, *The Times, Le Monde*) and **media planning** (the media buying, scheduling, timing, frequency). These issues are covered in detail in Chapter 14.

Broadcast television: advertisers can demonstrate the product in action. For example, a lawnmower can be shown to cut grass efficiently, or the ease of application of a paint can be demonstrated. The capability of television (unlike the press, posters and radio) to combine colour, movement and sound means that it is often used when building brand image and introducing new products. It is easier to create an atmosphere using television than using other media that lack its versatility. Traditionally, viewers could not refer to the advertisement once it had been broadcast (unlike the press); however, with the advent of YouTube and other online video platforms, adverts can be viewed repeatedly. Indeed, adverts are often launched through YouTube and social media. John Lewis's highly successful Christmas adverts were shown first online to great success, and now leading supermarkets vie for position, measured by digital engagement analytics.

Despite the increase in popularity of television commercials online, a potential threat to mainstream television advertising is digital recording devices (e.g. digi-boxes like Sky, FreeSat), which can store over 100 hours of programmes, allowing viewers to record their choice of programmes, watch them when convenient and skip through the adverts, potentially reducing television advertising effectiveness. Also, the rise of media service providers like Netflix and Amazon prime is disrupting the industry, as these media service providers use a subscription model rather than advertising revenue to fund their operation.

Some advertisers have been producing their adverts as mini movies and creating a buzz online. Sainsbury's used the 100-year anniversary of the World War I football match between English and German soldiers to deliver its 'Christmas is for sharing' message. The advert was a highly emotional appeal, and at an unprecedented 3.18 minutes in length, it took up the whole of the commercial break when it was launched. Television companies have also been taking actions to encourage more viewer engagement. See Marketing in Action 13.3 to find out how Sky is providing advertisers with precision targeting opportunities.

Digital television technology means that signals can be compressed, allowing more to be sent to the viewer. The result is the escalation of the number of channels that can be received. The extra 'bandwidth' created by digital technology is likely to reduce costs, enabling small players to broadcast to small target audiences such as small geographical areas and special-interest groups (e.g. shoppers). Also, digital technology allows the development of additional interactive services, promoting the potential for home shopping (Ellis-Chadwick, Doherty and Anastasakis, 2007).

Television programmes can now be watched via a computer and mobile phone, with the development of such online services as the BBC's iPlayer and ITV Hub. Following the success of YouTube, companies have found that setting up their own-brand television channel is proving very successful for fostering consumer engagement.

Many companies have taken advantage of this opportunity to communicate with their target audiences, for example Apple, Coca-Cola, and fashion retailers H&M and New Look. Audi has found that potential car buyers return 12 times during the decision-making process, and the channel features several streams of video-on-demand content: sport, lifestyle, behind the scenes, on the road, adventure, people, culture, places. (Press and media vehicles are discussed in more detail in Chapter 14, in the section on advertising.)

MARKETING IN ACTION 13.3
Sky Adsmart: Clas Ohlson uses Precision Advertising to Penetrate the UK High Street

Sky Adsmart gives advertisers the opportunity to use highly sophisticated targeting techniques to deliver specific adverts at specific times to individual homes. Advertisers can set highly specific variables for the viewing audience they want to communicate to, for example by age, region and demographic profile. This means that companies can develop specific adverts for target audiences; for example, young families with children may receive one version of an advert, whereas older households without children another.

Clas Ohlson is a large Swedish retailer that used precision television advertising to promote its hardware brand in the UK. Its Adsmart campaigns aimed to raise awareness and drive traffic to specific metropolitan regions where its stores are situated. Adsmart not only allowed Clas Ohlson to distribute its adverts geographically, but it also made sure it was targeting 'young and mature home sharers and families of mid to very high affluence'. It had a relatively low budget of £57,000, but the precision approach reached 219,000 Sky households and delivered millions of impressions. The results were that brand awareness of Clas Ohlson was increased and the brand was also put into the purchase-consideration set of a new set of customers.

Based on: SkyAdsmart (2015); Stevens, B (2018)

Broadcast radio: this is creatively limited to sound, and thus may be better suited to communicating factual information (e.g. a special price reduction) than attempting to create a brand image. The nature of the audience changes during the day (e.g. motorists during rush hours), and so a measure of targeting is possible. Production costs are relatively low. The arrival of digital radio has increased the number of radio stations available and marginally improved sound quality. Digital radios have screen displays, which allows websites and telephone numbers to be run at the same time as an advertisement is being played (Hicks, 2005). Radio listening has also increased through voice-activated devices such as the Amazon Echo and Google Home.

Press: factual information can be presented in a press advertisement (e.g. specific features of a washing machine, car or computer), and the readers are in control of how long they take to absorb the information. Allied to this advantage is the possibility of re-examination of the advertisement at a later date. But print media lacks movement and sound, and advertisements in newspapers and magazines compete with editorial for the reader's attention. However, the boundaries are blurring, and the introduction of the iPad and other tablet computers is enabling print publications to be delivered digitally; when delivered digitally, they are able to carry multimedia content. (Press and media vehicles are discussed in more detail in Chapter 14, in the section on advertising.)

Digital: this medium allows global reach at relatively low cost. The number of website visits, clicks on advertisements and products purchased can be measured. Interactivity between supplier and consumer is possible, either by website-based communication or email. Direct sales are possible, which is driving the growth of e-business in such areas as hotels, travel and information technology. Advertising content can be changed quickly and easily. Catalogues and price lists can be amended rapidly, and a dialogue between companies and their customers and suppliers can be established. Placing sponsored links to websites on search engines can give firms almost instant advertising; Google is the market leader for 'paid search' or 'pay-per-click' advertising. The basic idea is that advertisers bid in an online auction for the right to have their link displayed next to the results for specific search terms, such as 'used cars' or 'digital cameras', and then pay only when a visitor to the site actually clicks on that link (hence 'pay-per-click'). An advantage to the advertiser is that the consumer has already expressed interest and intent—first by typing in the search term and then by clicking on the advertiser's link—and, therefore, is more likely to make a purchase than someone passively watching an advertisement on television or looking at one in a newspaper (*The Economist*, 2005). Digital advertising is on the increase and now accounts for more of the media spend than any other form of media-based advertising. (Digital marketing, social media and the internet are discussed in greater detail in Chapter 16.)

Social media: messages can be straightforward and direct, but the way in which messages are transmitted through social media communities can be highly complex and multi-layered. To make creative use of social media, it is important to understand the concept of social capital and how power is attached to particular members of the online community (Coleman, 1988). Such communities provide an area for digital conversations, where members of the community can feel a sense of belonging (Tuten and Solomon, 2013). For example, Facebook enables its billions of users to start conversations with their friends and share thoughts, pictures and conversations with like-minded people around most parts of the globe.

This type of medium can act as a conduit to access homogeneous groups of individuals, but commercial organizations that use this type of space to carry their messages should be aware that social media can be many things to many people—from a community, to a publishing space, to entertainment and a social commerce arena—and, consequently, great care needs to be taken to ensure that the content and tone of the message are in keeping with the expectations of the chosen target community (Tuten and Solomon, 2013). For example, Mumsnet.com is an online community for parents seeking help and advice on bringing up children. Many issues have been debated within this community, from the sexualization of children to the growth in occurrence of childhood diabetes. (Social media are discussed in greater detail in Chapter 16.)

Outdoor: simplicity is required in the creative work associated with outdoor advertising, because many people (e.g. car drivers) will have the opportunity only to glance at a poster. Like the press, outdoor advertising is largely visual and is often used as a support medium alongside television, internet or press campaigns, because of its creative limitations. For example, in conjunction with poster campaigns, Thames Reach's communication director also used print media. Outdoor advertising, is, however, an effective medium for carrying messages that remind target audiences of issues and products. Poster campaigns can be created with a limited promotions budget but can be used to good effect.

Possibly the most effective use of outdoor advertising was by Benetton's creative director, Oliviero Toscani. With a series of highly controversial poster campaigns, Toscani led the brand from being a medium-sized European brand to being a global one. In 2011, to gain attention for its 'Unhate campaign'—which aims to break down cultural barriers—a series of thought-provoking images carrying the Benetton logo appeared on billboards around the world.

Often, outdoor advertising sites are sold as a package targeting specific audiences. For example, supermarket shoppers can be targeted by advertisers buying space close to supermarket stores; if business people are the target, it is possible to buy a package of sites at major airports (Tomkins, 1999). This form of advertising can also be low-key. Exhibit 13.3 shows how Costa coffee uses an A-frame board to promote the quality of its coffee.

Technology is helping outdoor advertising to gain a bigger share of advertising in the prime media. Backlit and scrolling sites are gradually replacing more traditional glued posters. Digital technology is allowing animated posters, the content of which alters during the day, and high-definition quality moving images. For outdoor advertising, the keyword is simplicity. An ad has, on average, just six seconds to get a message across, which has led to the golden rule 'no more than seven words on a poster' (Fitzsimmonds, 2008). Piccadilly Circus in London is an ideal place for outdoor messages, as millions of pedestrians and drivers pass by every week. The Piccadilly Lights complex carries static and animated adverts, and messages can be changed according to the time of day.

EXHIBIT 13.3
Costa uses a board to attract customers away from the competition

Guerrilla is potentially a controversial way to use outdoor media. The aim is often to deliver communication messages through unexpected means and in ways that almost 'ambush' the consumer to gain attention (Fahy and Jobber, 2015). One of the most effective guerrilla marketing campaigns was that used by Carlsberg in the UK, which also employed its well-known positioning slogan, 'Carlsberg don't do [. . .] but if they did it would probably be the best [. . .] in the world'. The company dropped £50,000 worth of £5 and £10 notes all over London on which were stickers containing the slogan 'Carlsberg don't do litter, but if they did, it would probably be the best litter in the world.' For a small investment, the brand received enormous publicity. Another example is when DSL55 launched its first London store aimed at young skateboarders. It employed people to place stickers showing the firm's winged angel at locations where the target audience might be, for example close to skateboard parks, on street furniture and lamp posts. To use this form of medium, communicators must be prepared to connect with their target audience in a very unusual, unconventional, surprising and often illegal manner. This is not a mainstream medium, and is often used when the communication budget is small.

Indoor media: these include in-store point-of-purchase materials, packaging, window display signs and the on-shelf display. These forms of media are used predominantly by retailers and consumer-facing service providers, but may also be used at transit stations, within shopping malls, and at entertainment and sports arenas. These types of media are increasingly using digital technology to deliver highly creative messages. For example, East Midlands Airport has a cut-out figure of a member of the airport service staff; a moving image is projected onto the face of the model, informing passengers how to streamline their journey through the airport.

In addition, both outdoor and indoor media can apply techniques called *ambient media*. These non-traditional forms of media are often used to take the target audience by surprise. Ambient advertising generally refers to the established outdoor categories such as billboards (Fahy and Jobber, 2012), bus signs or point-of-sale or in-store posters found at checkouts. Advertising that appears on shopping bags, petrol pump nozzles, balloons or banners towed by aeroplanes, on street pavements, overhead lockers on aircraft, and so on, are also classed as ambient. Ambient media are only limited by the advertiser's imagination.

Cinema: advertisements can benefit from colour, movement and sound, and exposure is high, due to the captive nature of the audience. Repetition may be difficult to achieve, given the fact that people visit cinemas intermittently. In the past, cinema-goers tended to be between 15 and 25 years of age. Brands like BMW Mini, Volkswagen, Toyota, Citroën and Ford have used the cinema to target young audiences (Donnelly, 2008). However, the demographic of cinema-goers has changed as cinema has become more family orientated. Family films such as the *Lego Movie, Muppets Most Wanted* and *Paddington* (Exhibit 13.4) continue to attract the younger audience, and this has led companies to invest in longer adverts for delivery through cinemas; for example, Disney purchased 60-second slots before family feature films. Older audiences are attracted by comedy dramas; for example, *The Best Exotic Marigold Hotel* series and Marks & Spencer have been attracted by this target market. Marks & Spencer offered its first movie-related promotion, offering a 'buy one, get one free' film ticket deal on Mother's Day (Durrani, 2015).

The people

Managing communications involves complex decision-making. There are also many challenges involved in bringing together teams and departments in an integrated manner to satisfy the marketing objectives of the advertising agency while engaging the attention of target audiences. Research proposes a two-stage approach: the first stage is the client/agency level; the second stage is target audience level (Mishra and Muralie, 2010). Consequently, there are three types of people to consider: the customer, the client and the agency.

Customers vary from single individuals, to families and groups, to business customers and global corporations. Consequently, their motivations, interests, spending power and needs

EXHIBIT 13.4
Movies for under-12s attract more families to the cinema

vary considerably. Nevertheless, it is becoming increasingly important to ensure that any firm (the client) wishing to communicate does so by understanding its customers' needs and how they engage with communications.

Clients come in many different shapes and sizes from large corporate clients with multimillion-dollar communication budgets to spend in promoting a wide portfolio of products and building brands (e.g. Unilever, Kraft Foods, GE, Mercedes) to small independent companies planning their first website.

Agencies that develop communications also vary considerably in terms of what they have to offer. Agencies generally provide account management and liaison with the client, the creative teams and production of the communication campaigns. They also plan the media and can be responsible for research. Types of agencies include: full service, creative boutiques, specialized agencies, digital agencies and web service providers.

The client is generally the originator of communication initiatives and is also likely to make key decisions and ultimately be responsible for the planning approach: target market selection (the customer), financial resources and agency selection. Corporate marketing is where decisions are made about a firm's image and corporate identity. Again, the client (the firm) will strongly influence communication decisions. Selection of the marketing communication mix and media coordination is where the agency can become much more influential in the decision-making process; the agency is likely to be responsible for the management of these elements of IMC. Ensuring consistency of the message is the responsibility of both the client and the agency, and they need to ensure that, whatever form the IMC campaign takes, it delivers a consistent message throughout to the target audiences (the customer).

Office politics can occur, especially in the form of clashes between advertising creatives who, say, have radical ideas to take a brand forward with the latest of a series of television commercials, and brand executives with very conservative values who want to protect a brand's traditional target markets. Difficult situations can arise when IMC strategies call for a shift in expenditure from advertising to direct or digital promotion. Other problems surround the specialist nature of different communication disciplines that can narrow people's minds to such an extent that they fail to understand how some marketing objectives can be better achieved by using a different communications technique (Murgatroyd, 2004).

However, for a campaign to be successful, issues and problems must be overcome, and this is often achieved by appointing a senior level communications officer to oversee all of the firm's communications activities. A director of marketing communications is likely to be responsible for deciding the extent to which each of the components of the promotional mix is used to achieve business and marketing objectives. The person needs to be a visionary and someone with passion who can persuade everyone of the benefits of an integrated approach to marketing communications (Eagle and Kitchen, 2000).

Client and agency relationships are discussed in more detail in Chapter 14, and types of digital agencies and web service providers in Chapter 16. Figure 13.4 shows the core tasks that people must manage to create an integrated campaign.

FIGURE 13.4
The core tasks the people must manage to create an integrated campaign

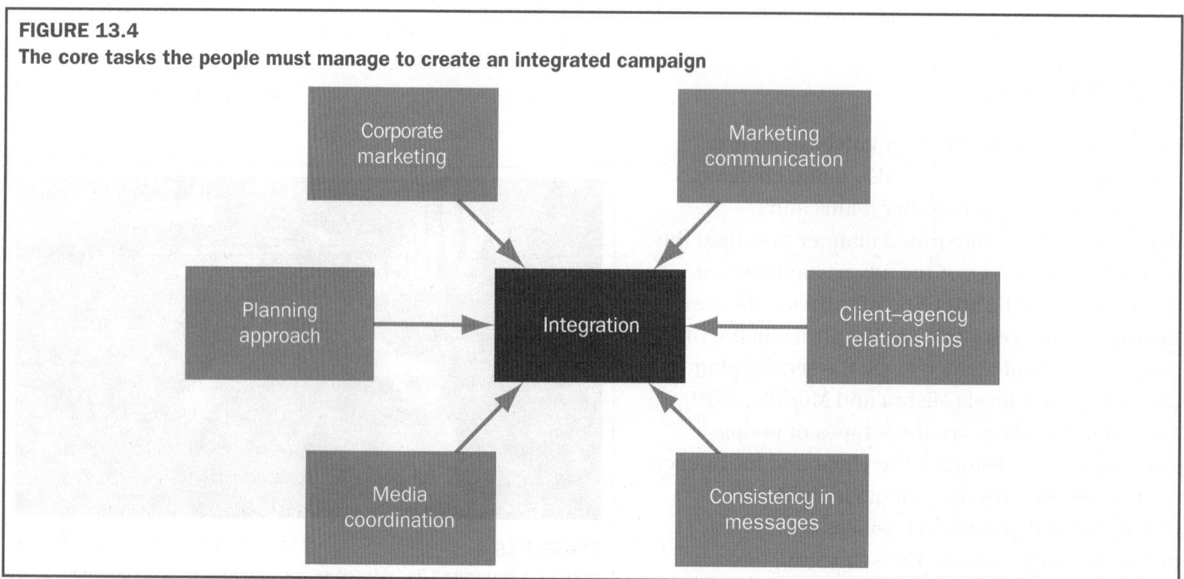

The contexts

In this chapter, we have explored the changing nature of the communication environment, looked at the drivers for the adoption of an IMC approach, considered the processes associated with developing a campaign, and examined important elements that form the core constituents of an IMC campaign. In this final section, we look at the different contexts for IMC campaigns, namely, business-to-consumer and business-to-business settings and corporate profiles.

There are three main contexts that define the target audience and nature of IMC campaigns. These contexts determine the focus, strategy and the actions that a campaign aims to achieve.

FIGURE 13.5
Direction of communication flow in pull-positioning strategies

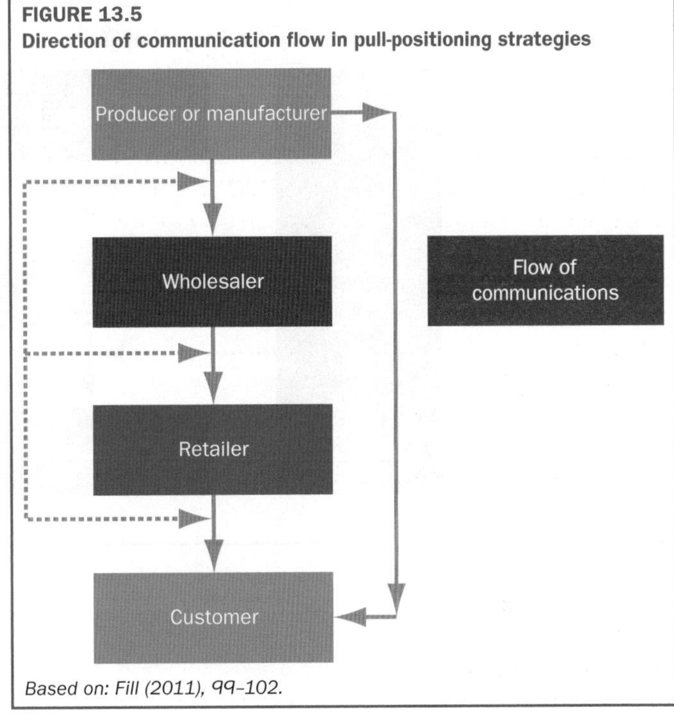

Based on: Fill (2011), 99–102.

1 Pull-positioning strategies aim to encourage consumers and end-user business customers to make a purchase, thereby pulling goods through the supply chain from the manufacturer to the retailer (or final purchase point in the supply chain) (see Figure 13.5).

In a pull-positioning strategy, messages tend to be designed to create awareness and *stimulate action among members of the* **target audience**. The underlying idea is that target audiences expect the product to be available when they wish to make a purchase. Many consumer brands use pre-announcement and give launch dates to stimulate interest and excitement. For example, Apple gives launch dates for its new products and latest versions of existing products. This raises anticipation, causes excitement and creates pre-sale demand. High-tech shoppers and Apple aficionados form queues at Apple stores and stockists on the launch date hoping to be able to purchase the latest iPhone or iPad. The pull strategy also enables Apple to encourage its stockists (e.g. PC World, EGiganten, Ledfal, Electro World) to have stock available in store to meet consumer demand.

2 Push-positioning strategies aim to *move goods through the supply chain*. The target audiences for this type of communications initiatives are channel intermediaries. Often, communication objectives aim to build relationships between channel intermediaries and influence trade partners to take stock and allocate shelf space and help to develop trade partners' awareness of product features and benefits (Fill, 2011). Push communications also tend to take place in a channel network moving goods from one point to another (see Figure 13.6).

This strategy is widely used between businesses, and the most prevalent communication tools are personal selling and trade promotions (see Chapter 14 for further details). For example, Costco is a large intermediary in the retail supply chain. It supplies both trade and retail customers with top fast-moving consumer goods brands (e.g. Heinz, Coca-Cola, Gillette, Colgate), white goods (e.g. Beko, Bosch), small electricals (e.g. Breville), electric kettles and fresh foods from various producers. Each of the suppliers engages in push communications designed to ensure that Costco continues to stock its ranges. Manufacturers also work together with Costco to increase purchases, using a range of techniques from tastings to bonus packs.

3 Profile-positioning strategies aim to *develop the image and identity of an organization*. In addition to consumer and business target audiences, there are many other stakeholders that might be interested in an organization, for example investors, the local community, the media, trade unions, pressure groups and employees. Perceptions and views of such stakeholders are increasingly important, and this has given rise to greater use of IMC campaigns to raise corporate reputations. Public relations, sponsorship, lobbying, **media relations** and internal communications are examples of the methods used in this instance to develop a corporate profile (further discussion of these methods is in Chapters 15 and 22).

FIGURE 13.6
Direction of communication flow in push-positioning strategies

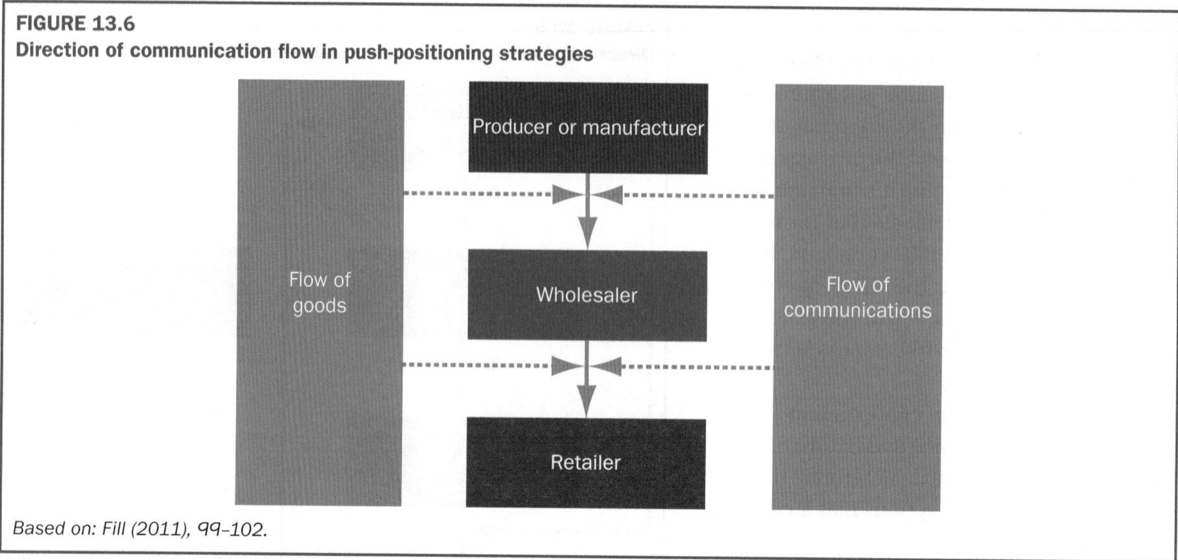

Based on: Fill (2011), 99–102.

Review

1 The elements of integrated marketing communication (IMC) campaigns

- The elements include the message, the tools, the media channel and the context applied in a coordinated campaign designed to create multiple opportunities to engage with the target audience.

2 The value of IMC campaigns

- IMC is the concept by which companies coordinate their marketing communications tools to deliver a clear, consistent, credible and competitive message about the organization and its products.
- The achievement of an IMC campaign can be hampered by office politics. A high-ranking communications officer may be needed to see through its successful implementation.
- The IMC philosophy has led to the rise in media-neutral planning, which is the process of solving communications problems through an unbiased evaluation of all media.

3 How IMC campaigns are organized

- Planning campaigns develop from a situation analysis, which should aid a firm in identifying communication opportunities. Following on from this is agency selection, the briefing process and setting out the deliverables that an agency will produce. The next stage in the process is the development of the campaign and its implementation. The penultimate stage is evaluation of the effectiveness of all the elements of the campaign. The final stage is future planning.

4 Elements of IMC

- The core elements are: the messages which are used to position a product, brand and/or an organization in the minds of the customer; the tools, the six key methods of achieving communication objectives; the media, which are the channels that carry the message to the audience; the people who collectively are responsible for creating, planning, managing and implementing the communication campaign; and the context, the setting in which communication takes place.

5 The message

- At the heart of communications is the message. Messages are very important as they not only transfer information from a message sender to its recipient, but can also determine the nature of a relationship, establish credibility (Fill, 2011), set the tone for a *conversation* and cross tangible and intangible boundaries. Effective messages can become so powerful that they can be heard around the globe, when used with suitable media channels.

6 **The communication process**

- The communication process begins with the source encoding a message that is transmitted through media to the receiver who decodes. Noise (e.g. distractions) may prevent the message reaching the receiver. Feedback may be direct when talking to a salesperson or through marketing research. The simple model explains the basic elements of the communication process, whereas the complex model explains how communication messages pass by formal and informal messages between message senders and different types of message recipient.

7 **The factors that affect the choice of the promotional mix for IMC campaigns**

- The factors are resource availability and the cost of promotional tools, market size and concentration, customer information needs, product characteristics and push versus pull strategies.

8 **The key characteristics of the major promotional tools**

- Advertising: strong for awareness building, brand positioning, firm and brand legitimization, but it is impersonal and inflexible and has only a limited ability to close a sale.
- Personal selling: strong for interactivity, adaptability, the delivery of complex arguments, relationship building and the closing of the sale, but is costly.
- Direct marketing: strong for individual targeting, personalization, measurement, relationship building through periodic contact, low visibility to competitors, but response rates are often low and direct marketing can cause annoyance.
- Digital marketing: strong for global reach, measurement, establishing a dialogue, quick changes to catalogues and prices, convenience and avoiding arguments with salespeople, but impersonal and requires consumers to visit website.
- Sales promotion: strong on providing immediate incentive to buy, but effects may be short-term and can damage brand image.
- Public relations: strong on credibility and high readership, but loss of control.

9 **The media channels**

- When considering which media channel to use, the media planner faces the choice of using television, the press, cinema, outdoor, radio, the internet or some combination of media classes. Various considerations will be taken into account; *creative factors* may have a major bearing on the decision. The key question that needs to be addressed is 'Does the medium allow the communication objectives to be realized?'

10 **The people**

- Managing communications involves complex decision-making. There are also many challenges involved in bringing together teams and departments in an integrated manner to satisfy the marketing objectives while engaging the attention of target audiences.
- Research proposes a two-stage approach: the first stage is the client/agency level; the second stage is target audience level (Mishra and Muralie, 2010). Consequently, there are three types of people to consider: the customer, the client and the agency.

11 **The contexts**

- There are three main contexts that define the target audience and nature of IMC campaigns. These contexts determine the focus, strategy and the actions that a campaign aims to achieve.

Key Terms

advertising any paid form of non-personal communication of ideas or products in the prime media: i.e. television, the press, posters, cinema and radio, the internet and direct marketing

agency an organization that specializes in providing services such as media selection, creative work, production and campaign planning to clients

digital promotion the promotion of products to consumers and businesses through electronic media

direct marketing (1) acquiring and retaining customers without the use of an intermediary; (2) the distribution of products, information and promotional benefits to target consumers through interactive communication in a way that allows response to be measured

integrated marketing communications (IMC) the concept that companies coordinate their marketing communications tools to deliver a clear, consistent, credible and competitive message about the organization and its products

media channel the means used to transmit a message, including spoken words, print, radio, television or the internet. Also called the *medium*

media class the press, cinema, television, posters, radio, or some combination of these

media planning an advertising strategy most commonly employed to target consumers using a variety of informational outlets. Media planning is generally conducted by a professional media planning or advertising agency and typically finds the most appropriate media outlets to reach the target market

media relations the communication of a product or business by placing information about it in the media without paying for time or space directly

media type (also referred to as a *content type*) is a general category of data content, such as application (executable program), audio content, an image, a text message or a video stream

media vehicle decision the choice of the particular newspaper, magazine, television spot, poster site, etc.

message the use of words, symbols and illustrations to communicate to a target audience using prime media

personal selling oral communication with prospective purchasers with the intention of making a sale

public relations the management of communications and relationships to establish goodwill and mutual understanding between an organization and its public

sales promotion incentives to customers or the trade that are designed to stimulate purchase

Study Questions

1. **Compare the possible use of advertising and personal selling in an IMC campaign.**
2. **Discuss how communication messages can be used to build a brand.**
3. **Explain how digital media and platforms are changing the focus of IMC campaigns.**
4. **Explain when a company might use different elements of the promotional mix.**
5. **Suggest why media channel choice is increasingly important in the digital age.**
6. **Outline the stages in the IMC planning framework.**
7. **Discuss the drivers of an IMC and suggest possible limitations when developing a pan-European campaign.**
8. **Discuss the advantages and disadvantages of adopting an IMC approach towards communication planning.**

Recommended Reading

Good communications are the lifeblood of successful marketing firms. Read the following to learn more about new thinking around communications online, offline and in social media networks.

Finne, A. and Gronroos, C. (2009) Rethinking marketing communication: From integrated marketing communication to relationship communication, *Journal of Marketing Communications*, 15 (2–3): 179–95.

Henninger, C.E., Alevizou, P.J. and Oates, C.J. (2017) IMC, social media and UK fashion micro-organisations, *European Journal of Marketing*, 51(3): 668–91, https://doi.org/10.1108/EJM-08-2015-0599

Zook, Z. and Smith, P.R. (2016) *Marketing Communications Offline and Online Integration, Engagement and Analytics*. London: Kogan Page.

References

Anon (2015a) Nike to crown its football 'Ice Kings', The 12ethman, 27 January, http://12elfthman.com/2015/01/27/nike-to-crown-its-football-ice-kings (accessed October 2018).

Anon (2015b) Why Moneysupermarket's #EpicStrut is a viral hit, *Marketing*, 23 January, http://www.marketingmagazine.co.uk/article/1330549/why-moneysupermarkets-epicstrut-viral-hit (accessed 10 June 2015).

Anon (n.d.) Tesco—how 'Every little helps' was a big help to Tesco, Thinkbox, http://www.thinkbox.tv/server/show/ConCaseStudy.1642 (accessed 10 June 2015).

Always (2018) Always & Tampax-Free Puberty Kits for schools "about you" puberty education programme. https://www.always.co.uk/en-gb/puberty-education-programme-always-tampax (accessed October 2018).

Beltrone, G. (2014) How R/GA dominated digital by finding its TV groove, *AdWeek*, 15 December, http://www.adweek.com/news/advertising-branding/agency-year-how-rga-dominated-digital-finding-its-tv-groove-161925 (accessed 8 June 2015).

Bendaby, D. (2011) Marketers divided on the merits of integration, *Pitch Agency Reputation Survey*, 40.

Bidlake, S. (2008) Goodwill to all agencies, *Campaign*, 5 December, 3.

Bylykbashi, K. (2015) Brands are struggling to join up multichannel customer journeys, *Marketing Week*, 14 April. Available at: https://www.marketingweek.com/2015/04/14/brands-are-struggling-to-join-up-multichannel-customer-journeys (accessed October 2018).

Caemmerer, B. (2009) The planning and implementation of integrated marketing communications, *Marketing Intelligence & Planning* 27(9): 524–38.

Carr, A. (2013) *NIKE: THE NO. 1 MOST INNOVATIVE COMPANY OF 2013*, Fastcompany, 11 February, http://www.fastcompany.com/most-innovative-companies/2013/nike (accessed October 2018).

Chaffey, D. and Ellis-Chadwick, F.E. (2012) *Digital Marketing: Strategy, Implementation and Practice*, 5th edn. Harlow: Pearson.

Clark, T. and Chan, S.P. (2014) A history of Tesco: The rise of Britain's biggest supermarket, *The Telegraph*, 14 October.

Coleman, S. (1988) Social capital in the creation of human capital, *The American Journal of Sociology*, 94: 95–120.

Cohen, D. (2018) LinkeIn's New integrated marketing campaign seeks to smash its white collar stereotypes, *AdWeek*, 8 January, https://www.adweek.com/digital/linkedins-new-integrated-marketing-campaign-seeks-to-smash-its-white-collar-stereotype (accessed October 2018).

Cordiner, R. (2009) Set free your core native: the brand as a storyteller, *Admap*, October.

Croft, M. (1999) Listeners keep radio on air, *Marketing Week*, 8 July, 30–1.

DeSantis Breindel (2015) Integrated Marketing is No Longer Enough: Why B2B Brands Need to be Synchronized, DeSantis Breindel.com, 10 June, http://www.desantisbreindel.com/integrated-marketing-is-no-longer-enough (accessed October 2018).

Doherty, N.F., Ellis-Chadwick, F.E. and Hart, C.A. (1999) Cyber retailing: the potential in the UK: the potential of the internet as a retail channel, *International Journal of Retail & Distribution Management*, 27(1).

Donnelly, A. (2008) Big screen draw, *Marketing*, 9 July, 19.

Duncan, T. and Everett, S. (1993) Client perceptions of integrated communications, *Journal of Advertising Research*, 3(3): 30–9.

Durrani, A. (2015) M&S makes debut film promotion for The Second Best Exotic Marigold Hotel, *Media Week*, 5 March, http://www.mediaweek.co.uk/article/1336864/m-s-makes-debut-film-promotion-second-best-exotic-marigold-hotel (accessed October 2018).

Eagle, L. and Kitchen, P.J. (2000) Brand communications and corporate cultures, *European Journal of Marketing*, 35(5/6): 667–86.

Ellis-Chadwick, F., Doherty, N.F. and Anastasakis, L. (2007) E-strategy in the UK retail grocery sector: a resource-based analysis, *Managing Service Quality*, 17(6): 702–27.

Fahy, J. and Jobber, D. (2015) *Foundations of Marketing*. London: McGraw-Hill Education, 242–3.

Fill, C. (2011) *Essentials of Marketing Communications*. London: Prentice Hall, 7–8.

Fitzsimmonds, C. (2008) Outdoor's digital future, *Campaign*, 18 July, 24–5.

Gladwell, M. (2000) *The Tipping Point*. London: Abacus, 3–5.

Glenday, J. (2017) Kraft Heinz seeds 'grow your own' schools campaign, *The Drum*, 17 February, https://www.thedrum.com/news/2017/02/17/kraft-heinz-seeds-grow-your-own-schools-campaign (accessed October 2018).

Gibson, D. (2018) The five most impactful ad campaigns of 2018 so far, *The Drum* 4th September https://www.thedrum.com/news/2018/09/04/the-five-most-impactful-ad-campaigns-2018-so-far (accessed October 2018)

Hegarty, J. (2011) *Hegarty on advertising: turning intelligence into magic*, London: Thames & Hudson, 95.

Hemsley, S. (2015) How to create content relevant to your business, *Marketing Week*, 12 June. Available at: http://www.marketingweek.com/2015/06/12/how-to-create-content-relevant-to-your-business (accessed October 2018).

Hicks, R. (2005) Special Report: Radio, *Campaign*, 4 November, 26.

Hill, C. (2015) 10 steps to an effective content strategy, *The Guardian*, 10 June. http://www.theguardian.com/media-network-outbrain-partner-zone/content-strategy-marketing-customer-engagement (accessed October 2018).

Katz, E. and Lazarfield, P.F. (1955) *Personal Influence*. Glencoe, Il: Free Press.

Kelner, M. (2018) Nike's controversial Colin Kaepernick ad campaign its most diverse yet, *The Guardian*, 4 September, https://www.theguardian.com/sport/2018/sep/04/nike-controversial-colin-kaepernick-campaign-divisive (accessed October 2018).

Lawn Tennis Association (LTA) (2018) Nature Valley becomes new sponsor title for LTA major events, 13 April, https://www.lta.org.uk/about-us/tennis-news/news-and-opinion/general-news/2018/april/nature-valley-announced-as-title-sponsor-nottingham-birmingham-eastbourne (accessed October 2018).

Kelman, H. (1961) Process of opinion change, *Public Opinion Quarterly*, 25(spring): 57–78.

Magee, K. (2015) Tesco shifts trade and tactical ad work to BBH, *Brand Republic*, 12 June, http://www.brandrepublic.com/article/1351209/tesco-shifts-trade-tactical-ad-work-bbh (accessed October 2018).

Mahdawi, A. (2013) Google's autocomplete spells out our darkest thoughts, *The Guardian*, 22 October, http://www.theguardian.com/commentisfree/2013/oct/22/google-autocomplete-un-women-ad-discrimination-algorithms (accessed 10 June 2015).

Manvsmachine (2015) Hypervenom case study, http://manvsmachine.co.uk/project/hypervenom-2 (accessed October 2018).

McCarthy, J. (2017) Nature Valley's 'perfectly times' tennis tie up delivered a 20% uplift in sales, *The Drum*, 30 November, https://www.thedrum.com/news/2017/11/29/nature-valleys-foray-british-tennis-was-perfect-timing-says-marketing-lead-0 (accessed October 2018).

McMains, A. (2014) Even BBH's rivals wonder why Johnnie Walker is in review—after all, the shop's 'Keep walking' campaign has delivered results, *Adweek*, 10 November, http://www.adweek.com/news/advertising-branding/even-bbhs-rivals-wonder-why-johnnie-walker-review-161311 (accessed 10 May 2015).

Mehta, A. (2000) Advertising attitudes and advertising effectiveness, *Journal of Advertising Research*, May/June, 67–72.

Mishra, S. and Muralie, S. (2010) Managing dynamism of IMC anarchy to order, *Journal of Marketing & Communications*, 6(2): 29–37.

Murgatroyd, L. (2004) All together now, *Marketing Business*, March, 39.

Ritson, M. (2011) What if your customers are silent? *Marketing Week*, 14 April, 70.

Roderick, L. (2016) Premier League looks to shed 'corporate' image as it unveils new brand identity, *Marketing Week*, 9 February, https://www.marketingweek.com/2016/02/09/premier-league-looks-to-shed-corporate-image-as-it-unveils-new-brand-identity (accessed October 2018).

Rogers, E. (1983) *Diffusion of Innovations*, 3rd edn. New York: Free Press.

Schultz, D. (1993) Integrated marketing communications: maybe definition is in the point of view, *Marketing News*, 18 January, 17.

Schultz, E.J. and Pasquarelli, A. (2018) Nike Unveils Lengthy Kaepernick spot, *AdAge*, 5 September, https://adage.com/article/cmo-strategy/nike-unveils-lengthy-kaepernick-spot/314830 (accessed October 2018).

Sherwood, P. K., Stevens, R.E. and Warren, W.E. (1989) Periodic and continuous tracking studies: matching methodology with objectives, *Marketing Intelligence and Planning*, 7(1/2): 11–14.

SkyAdsmart (2015) *Clas Ohlson & Sky AdSmart*, Skymedia, 10 June, http://www.skymedia.co.uk/sky-adsmart/Case-Studies/clas-ohlson-&-sky-adsmart.aspx (accessed October 2018).

Stevens, B (2018). Clas Ohlson to close all but one UK stores *Retail Gazette* 6th December https://www.retailgazette.co.uk/blog/2018/12/clas-ohlson-close-uk-stores/ (accessed October 2018).

Swift, J. (2015) R/GA and Dare win Nike football brief, *Campaign*, 28 May. http://www.campaignlive.co.uk/news/1348941 (accessed October 2018).

Syedain, H. (1992) Taking the Expert Approach to Media, *Marketing*, 4 June, 20–1.

The Economist (2005) Pay Per Sale, 1 October, 73.

Tomkins, R. (1999) Reaching new heights of success, *Financial Times*, 28 May, 16.

Tuten, T.L. and Solomon, M.R. (2013) *Social Media Marketing*. Harlow: Pearson, 86.

Vizard, S. (2018) Nike proud of Colin Kaepernick ad as campaign drives record engagement, *Marketing Week*, 26 September, https://www.marketingweek.com/2018/09/26/nike-proud-of-colin-kaepernick-ad-campaign (accessed October 2018).

Weissberg, T. (2008) One Message, Many Media, *Marketing Week*, 18 September, 31–4.

http://www.thedrum.com/news/2015/01/12/ad-day-nspcc-share-aware (accessed 10 June 2015).

CASE 25
Domino's Journey to Number One

Introduction

Domino's Pizza, Inc., now branded simply as Domino's, is an American pizza restaurant chain founded in 1960. In the mid-2000s, Domino's was a faltering competitor in a global chain pizza landscape dominated by Pizza Hut. Customers complained about Domino's product quality, sales were falling and the chain's stock price hovered at an all-time-low of $3. When Patrick Doyle came on board as CEO of Domino's Pizza in 2010, he vowed to transform the struggling pizza company into a 'technology-enabled, nimble, category-disrupting machine'. The radical action Domino's then took included publicly admitting that its pizzas were bad, in the unusually frank 'Oh yes we did' campaign, with executives reading brutal customer comments on camera (Campaign, 2017). By 2018, Domino's turnaround had achieved spectacularly successful results, with the company being declared the 'largest pizza company in the world', having generated $12.3 billion in global revenue and the share price reaching a high of over $300 (Rogers, 2018).

Domino's transformation from failing disappointment to market leader directly stems from its vigorous and consistent efforts to perfect digital marketing practices. It built an impressive, and immersive, digital experience that rivals many traditional e-commerce brands. David Wild, Chief Executive Officer of Domino's Pizza Group plc (DPG, the franchise that operates the UK and six other European operations), explains: 'In 1999, UK online sales were £100K per annum, in 2003 online sales of £100K were achieved in a week, in 2018 sales worth £100K are being taken in four minutes' (Wild, 2018).

Early adoption of mobile apps and channels provided by far the largest lift to Domino's direct product sales. The iOS app became popular on iPhones and iPads for its customization features, which included graphical abilities to design a unique pizza and save individual orders.

By 2018, 80 per cent of Domino's sales were via digital ordering channels, and over half of all sales were placed on mobile devices, whether from the apps developed for iPhone and Android, from Slack or Twitter, or even from the 'one tap' feature that allows mobile customers to repeat an order without entering any information.

The Domino's 'Pizza Legend' campaign was developed for the UK market in 2015

Digital Transformation

Domino's adoption of digital marketing began with its use of social media to find fresh ideas for improving its business. In 2012, Domino's launched its 'Think Oven', a Facebook page where participants were encouraged to submit ideas in two categories: the 'Idea Box' (for general ideas, e.g. new menu items and tips for going green.) and 'Current Project' (for specific things Domino's needs help with, e.g. new Domino's uniforms). The ideas that attracted most attention were rewarded with a monetary prize and actually implemented with executive approval.

Following the success of social media initiatives, Domino's began a radical overhaul of the company's entire ethos, with a focus on creating an 'e-commerce company that happens to sell pizza'. To accomplish this, Domino's entire corporate structure was revised—beginning from the top down—to focus on digital sales and advertising.

Digital Focus

In an interview (Wong, 2018), Domino's SVP of eCommerce Development and Emerging Technologies, Kelly Garcia, explained the steps of modernizing the company. After focusing on talent acquisition, the biggest drive was to create new opportunities for

>>

online customers. Domino's was keen to insist that ordering be possible on every popular internet platform, on any of its customers' favourite devices, in any way they want, anywhere, which is an ongoing effort facilitated by its AnyWare platform (Barrett, 2016).

Currently, pizza can be ordered using, for example:

- a mobile in in-app voice assistant
- SMS and GIF's
- Slack
- Facebook Messenger
- Twitter with the use of emojis
- Google Home and Amazon Echo
- Samsung and Apple Smart TVs
- Ford Synch
- Apple Watch.

The platform diversity of its solution also enabled Domino's to attract top talent to work on product development and the phrase 'Surprise and delight' was used to position a loyalty programme designed to reward Domino's best customers and keep them away from the competition.

Forward Thinking, Creativity and Innovation

While digital marketing remained the heart of Domino's transformation, other areas of development focused squarely on innovation, raising the brand image, building public trust and pushing investors to take the plunge. The company gained wide media recognition for experiments with autonomous vehicles, drones, artificial intelligence and mobile marketing stunts. A seamless delivery experience is core to the business's success, so it has been investing heavily in improving the service, installing GPS in half of its stores and creating an online tracker that maps the driver's route.

TV Sponsorship

Despite the fact that digital makes up 80 per cent of Domino's sales, Tony Holdway, DPG's Sales and Marketing Director, firmly believes that the company does not need to divert all its spend online. High-profile TV sponsorships and above-the-line advertising remain at the core of Domino's marketing strategy, which is built around the key occasions when consumers might want to order a pizza. Holdway argues that rather than focusing on big events like Father's Day, it is far more exciting to tap in to the little truisms in customers' lives that put them in the mood for pizza, and then expand on those over time (Rogers, 2018).

Holdway explains: 'The key passion points for customers are things like sport—football in particular—and the big events when the family sit down. Then you say, how could we associate ourselves better with football? And that's how we ended up with the Sky Sports News sponsorship.'

Domino's also sponsors ITV Hub and Channel 4 series *Hollyoaks*. 'With the ITV Hub, clearly if you are going to watch something on catch up you really want to watch it. You're hunting it down and it becomes a proper TV moment so that could be a moment to order a pizza. Then *Hollyoaks*' audience is a strong demographic for us and it's that perfect timing [6.30pm on weeknights]. Even if you don't order pizza that night, it's reminding you that we're there.'

If This, Then Domino's

A 2018 initiative called 'If This, Then Domino's' enables customers to use a microsite that links apps and devices together to select personal and cultural events to trigger a pizza order. Users can choose a variety of scenarios like 'if it's raining, then Domino's', or 'if my favourite football team is playing, then Domino's' or 'if I need to work past 9:00 pm, then Domino's'. When these events occur, the user receives a text asking, 'Do you want your Domino's Easy Order?', which they can confirm with a 'yes' or 'no' reply. This manifestation of Domino's partnership with 'If This, Then That' continues easing the customer path to purchase while helping position Domino's as a digital-first pioneer (Contagious, 2018).

Three Key Ingredients of Domino's Digital Transformation

Kelly Garcia, Domino's SVP of eCommerce Development and Emerging Technologies, sets out the three key ingredients of Domino's digital transformation (Wong, 2018).

1 Organizational buy-in from the top down

Because it would require a massive technology investment to deliver a world-class e-commerce experience, it was crucial that everyone at the top, from the board of directors to the CEO and on down, needed to be on board. In 2012, Garcia and Dennis Maloney, the Chief Digital Officer, went to the board and outlined the threats to the business. They introduced the idea that, to survive, they had to start thinking themselves as an 'e-commerce company that happens to sell pizza.' The CEO already believed in, and fully supported, this vision, and once the board was behind it as well, the technology plan was funded.

Along with gaining support from the top down, it was critical to develop a strong culture at the company. Early on they were selling the vision as a means of recruiting talent. As they began to see success, the culture became one of passion and excitement, with very little staff turnover.

2 Relentless dedication to measuring results

With the help of an outstanding analytics team, Domino's was able to employ A/B testing (the testing of different versions of advertising tools and messages to determine the most effective for a given target group) against every new tool and process it implemented. Digital products, especially those based on ordering, by nature provide massive amounts of data. By understanding what was driving bottom-line results and sales, both across the board and by franchise, Domino's was able to offset costs and prove value. This, in turn, enabled the company to attract more of the marketing budget to scale the areas that were working.

3 Marketing around telling customers about technology investment

With brand image being a crucial area in need of improving, Domino's new unified, tech-forward vision was shared broadly across owned, earned and paid channels. It was important for the brand to be transparent about both its need to change as well as the huge investment it was making in its digital transformation. In addition to investing heavily in telling consumers about its new digital products, it built platforms like 'Think Oven' to maintain a two-way dialogue with them. According to Garcia, it was important from the start to promote a culture where the marketing and IT teams were collaborative and strategically aligned.

What's Next?

There is no sign of the transition to digital slowing, and new third-party delivery 'disruptors' that are flush with venture capital or subject to less stringent expectations when it comes to profits, like Just Eat, Deliveroo and Uber Eats, are fuelling the trend.

To compete, Domino's is pushing to make even better use of its data in order to personalize its communications as well as analyse and predict consumer behaviour.

An example of this is Domino's Hotspots, which enable pizza ordering for delivery to parks, beaches and other destinations that do not have traditional addresses. Delivery is all about convenience, and Domino's Hotspots establish set drop-off points that customers can find with the location services on their smartphones. Some 150,000 new US delivery hotspots were introduced in April 2018 (Baertlein, 2018).

Asked what he's most excited about from a technology perspective in 2018, Garcia highlighted voice interface, chat and conversational commerce as key areas for continued growth. Viewing this as the next wave of mobile evolution, he believes that conversational commerce is where the industry is moving in the next three to five years.

Questions

1. **Discuss how Domino's has reinvented the brand using integrated marketing communications.**
2. **Suggest how digital communications have enriched the communication process during the transformation.**
3. **Debate the extent to which the success of the digital focus of Domino's marketing efforts has surpassed the actual product.**
4. **Explain the characteristics of all the promotional tools used by Domino's and then suggest which are the most significant in driving the brand forward.**
5. **Imagine you own a regional chain of Chinese/ Indian takeaway restaurants; explain what you have learnt from Dominos transformation that could help you grow this business.**

This case study was written by James R.J. Roper, FRSA James Roper is founder of IMRG (Interactive Media in Retail Group), the UK industry association for e-retailing and e-commerce, and was formerly vice president of EMOTA, the European e-commerce industry association. He has worked exclusively on interactive e-retail projects since the mid-1980s, and in 1990 directed the original IMR (Interactive Media in Retail) survey that led to the formation of IMRG.

References

Based on: Baertlein, L. (2018) Domino's unveils pizza delivery 'hotspots' as competition rages, *Reuters*, 16 April, https://www.reuters.com/article/us-dominos-pizza-delivery/dominos-unveils-pizza-delivery-hotspots-as-competition-rages-idUSKBN1HN18R; Barrett, B. (2016) HOW DOMINO'S PUT AUTOMAGIC PIZZA ON EVERY DEVICE. LIKE, EVERY DEVICE, *Wired*, 29 April, https://www.wired.com/2016/04/dominos-anyware-pizza/; Campaign (2017) Case study: How Domino's and Crispin Porter & Bogusky transformed the pizza chain into a tech company, 15 February 2017, https://www.campaignlive.co.uk/article/case-study-dominos-crispin-porter-bogusky-transformed-pizza-chain-tech-company/1422647; Contagious (2018) Campaign of the Week: Domino's, If This, Then Domino's, https://www.contagious.com/news-and-views/campaign-on-the-week; Wild, D. (2018) Presentation by David Wild, Chief Executive Officer of Domino's Pizza Group plc at IMRG's conference ECOOMERCE EXPO, 27 September, London; Rogers, C. (2018) Domino's: It's not as simple as 'we're digital so let's spend all our money on digital', *Marketing Week*, 6 July, https://www.marketingweek.com/2018/07/06/dominos-marketing-strategy/; Wong, K. (2018) How Domino's Transformed into an E-commerce Powerhouse Whose Product is Pizza, *Forbes*, 26 January, https://www.forbes.com/sites/kylewong/2018/01/26/how-dominos-transformed-into-an-ecommerce-powerhouse-whose-product-is-pizza/#69e32f067f76

CASE 26
eSports Sponsorship: Game On

The atmosphere in the indoor stadium was frenzied. The tension was building up. The team players were using all their experience and expertise to attempt to outfox the opposition. Who would get the upper hand? A reflex delay of a millisecond could make the difference between victory and defeat. There can be only one winner, and it was 'Flash Wolves' who were crowned 2017 League of Legends Intel Extreme Masters World Champions. It was a sporting event that didn't involve kicking or striking a ball, but rather the clicking of a super-sensitive laser mouse and keys of a LED-decorated gaming keyboard.

The annual eSports championship attracted more than 173,000 attendees during a two-weekend event at the Polish city of Katowice. However, if fans couldn't make it to Poland for the big event, it didn't really matter: the tournament was broadcast in 19 languages by numerous internet-based platforms. Viewers could even take advantage of a viewing experience that included an immersive 360° virtual reality broadcast. The reach was truly global. The championship, besides *League of Legends*, included other leading games such as *Counter-Strike: Global Offensive* and *StarCraft II*, and attracted 46 million unique viewers. The eSports championship, with a prize pool of $650,000, had captured the attention and enthusiasm of a growing community of fans. It was a truly exceptional eSports event, which showcased an emerging channel for brand communications: eSports sponsorship.

Marketers have only very recently taken eSports sponsorship seriously. ESports had been generally regarded as a niche leisure-time activity and a natural fit for brands that have an affinity towards the gaming community. For example, HyperX, a manufacturer of gaming gadgets such as headsets, is one of the technology sponsors of the Intel Extreme Masters. Other brands such as energy drinks Red Bull and Monster have also invested heavily in eSports sponsorship, which targets a predominantly young, male profile.

However, the eSports landscape is changing rapidly as it enters the mainstream, and this is impacting on how brands play the sponsorship game. According to Newzoo's 2018 Global eSports Market Report, by 2018 the global eSports audience will reach 380 million, made up of 165 million eSports 'enthusiasts' and 215 million 'occasional viewers'. It is expected that the size of the eSports audience will increase to nearly 600 million people by 2020. eSports is still lagging behind major sports leagues such as the NFL, NBA and Football Premiership, but the growth of the eSports audience is gaining with unprecedented momentum.

This is challenging common misconceptions about the profile of the eSports fan. First, eSports is an activity for teenagers. Some marketing executives may have personal experience of their children playing eSports instead of doing their homework. Yet, according to a recent report, the median age for eSports viewers in the USA is, in fact, 28 years, and nearly half of them hold a university degree. What is even more interesting is that according to Nielsen's 2017 ESports Playbook, which draws on survey data from the USA, UK, Germany and France, 61 per cent of eSports fans live in households with three or more people. This implies that eSports fans are part of household purchase decisions, which makes them a vital target for marketers, as they can influence purchase decisions, from savoury snacks to cars. A second misconception is that eSports is run on male adrenaline. Although some games such as *Counter Strike: Global Offensive* are male dominated, other games such as *FIFA* enjoy a strong female following. For example, 32 per cent of *FIFA* and 21 per cent of *Overwatch* fans are female.

eSports is maturing, and the increasingly mainstream appeal has attracted the attention of brands that may not have initially considered eSports as being part of a sponsorship strategy. Newzoo reports that, in 2018, the global eSports economy will grow to $905.6 million, a year-on-year growth of 38 per cent, in which $174 million and $359 can be attributed to advertising and sponsorship respectively. Brands have started to explore how to maximize the return on the eSports sponsorship dollar, which has focused on being not on the sidelines, but at the top of the game.

Event Sponsorship

Gaming tournaments are the lifeblood of the eSports industry which brings together fans from over the world. Mercedes-Benz partners with ESL, one of the world's largest eSports companies. This sponsorship of tournaments by BMW goes beyond building brand awareness for the car brand. For example, throughout the ESL One Hamburg 2017 Dota 2 tournament, fans were able to vote online for the most valuable player (MVP) to win a Mercedes-Benz car. The Vice-President Marketing of Mercedes-Benz Passenger Cars noted that the new involvement in eSports will accommodate the interests of the brand's diverse target groups, 'As a brand, we maintain close contact with our customers, are able to build up empathy and to become an accepted part of their world.' Its global 'Grow Up' brand campaign has even integrated an eSports storyline. Mercedes-Benz is willing to break the rules in order to connect with a new generation of car owners. (The 'Grow Up' campaign can be viewed at https://www.youtube.com/watch?v=X5Z4doe1x2g.)

Team Sponsorship

Fnatic has over 2.6 million followers on Facebook and gives behind-the-scenes exclusives from professional teams competing in major tournaments. Although on a different scale, eSports fans are similar to those fans that follow a favourite football team. Ironically, leading football clubs such as Paris Saint-Germain, Manchester City, and AS Rom have formed eSports teams. Team sponsorship enables brands to leverage their association in terms of brand exposure and engagement. For example, Audi is the sponsor of the Danish Counter-Strike: Global Offensive team, Astralis. Media exposure of the four-ring logo is clearly visible on the team's jersey. The team enjoys a strong social media presence thanks to its competitive standing: Astralis won the ELEAGUE 2017, a professional eSports league. However, the sponsorship deal has also enabled Audi to deliver exclusive content which connects with a wider and younger audience. A TV commercial was developed for the Audi Q2, which featured members of the Astralis team with the tagline of #Untaggable. (The #Untaggable campaign can be viewed at https://www.youtube.com/watch?v=QbN4zHKfDD8.)

Brand Ambassador

Gillette has signed up a number of sporting stars, including footballers Neymar Jr (Paris Saint-Germain), Thomas Müller (Bayern Munich) and Antoine Griezmann (Atlético Madrid) as brand ambassadors. It has also enlisted professional League of Legends eSports player xPeke as a brand ambassador. This may be a surprising addition, but it is, in fact, consistent in reaching out to a male-grooming audience and showcasing cutting-edge performance at the highest level. The pro eSports athlete is seen as an ideal fit who has also been featured as part of the long-running 'the best a man can get' communications campaign.

eSports sponsorship can create synergies with other communication activities such as branded content and spin-off promotional activities. For example, Coca-Cola hosted 200 simultaneous viewing parties at cinemas in North America and Europe for the League of Legends World Championship. And it seems that eSports fans are receptive of brands getting involved. Nielsen (2017) reported that 50–60 per cent of respondents have favourable responses towards brand involvement in tournaments, streams or eSports events. Remarkably, less than 10 per cent gave a negative response to this kind of brand activity.

eSports sponsorship is set to become the next communications battleground. And there is a new dimension to the sport that will elevate the sport to a higher level: Epic Games will be offering $100 million in prize money for the inaugural season of Fortnite eSports. Undeniably, the hype surrounding eSports is breaking new records. Over 127 million people watched the 2018 League of Legends Midseason Invitational Finals, making it the most watched eSports match in history. To put this in perspective, the 2018 Super Bowl was watched by 103.4 million viewers. The dynamism of the sport is even changing how people actually define sports. eSports might be included as a demonstration sport at the 2024 Olympic Games in Paris. It is likely to feature as a medal event at the 2022 Asian Games. Sports sponsorship will need to move in conjunction with these developments. Brands will ultimately need to ask themselves if they are ready to be a winner or a loser in the fast-moving track of eSports. It may be time for brands to put on their new game faces.

Questions

1. **Discuss the different factors that influence a brand to invest in eSports sponsorship.**
2. **Discuss how eSports sponsorship differs from traditional sports sponsorship.**
3. **Suggest how would you measure the effectiveness of eSports sponsorship.**

This case was written by Glyn Atwal, Burgundy School of Business, France, and Douglas Bryson, Rennes School of Business, France, from various published sources as a basis for classroom discussion rather than to show effective or ineffective management.

References

Based on: Armstrong, P. (2017) +46 Million Watched Live Esports Event (+10 Million More Than Trump Inauguration Broadcast), *Forbes*, 16 March, https://www.forbes.com/sites/paularmstrongtech/2017/03/16/46-million-watched-live-esports-event-10-million-more-than-trump-inauguration-broadcast/#419a17e191f4; Asarch, S. (2018) 'Fortnite' Esports Offers $100 Million Prize Pool, Can It Break The Battle Royale Curse?, *Newsweek*, 21 May, https://www.newsweek.com/fortnite-esports-100-million-prize-pool-largest-competitive-play-937615; Business Wire (2017) Who Watches eSports? Interpret Releases Report that Busts Myths about eSports Viewers, 23 February, https://www.businesswire.com/news/home/20170223005219/en/; Daimler (2018) Mercedes-Benz in eSports: International eSports competition ESL One in the hotbed Katowice, https://media.daimler.com/marsMediaSite/en/instance/ko/Mercedes-Benz-in-eSports-International-eSports-competition-ESL-One-in-the-hotbed-Katowice.xhtml?oid=33548228; ESL (2017) Mercedes-Benz enters esports in partnership with ESL, https://www.eslgaming.com/press/mercedes-benz-enters-esports-partnership-esl; Nielsen (2017) The Esports Playbook, https://www.nielsen.com/content/dam/nielsenglobal/ru/docs/nielsen-esports-playbook.pdf; Pannekeet, J. (2018) Newzoo: Global Esports Economy Will Reach $905.6 Million in 2018 as Brand Investment Grows by 48%, 21 February, https://newzoo.com/insights/articles/newzoo-global-esports-economy-will-reach-905-6-million-2018-brand-investment-grows-48/; Rogers, C. (2018) Taking control: Why brands are seizing the eSports opportunity, *Marketing Week*, 2 May, https://www.marketingweek.com/2018/05/02/esports-opportunity/; Newzoo (2018) Global 2018 Global Esports Market Report, https://newzoo.com/insights/trend-reports/global-esports-market-report-2018-light/

CHAPTER 14
Mass Marketing Communications

> *Nobody counts the number of ads you run; they just remember the impression you make.*
>
> **BILL BERNBACH**

LEARNING OBJECTIVES

After reading this chapter, you should be able to:

1. explain the role of each of the tools in the mass communication promotional mix
2. discuss the role of advertising, how it works and when to use advertising
3. discuss the reasons for the growth of product placement
4. define public relations, key objectives, targets and characteristics
5. discuss the objectives and methods of sponsorship
6. explain how to select and evaluate a potential sponsored event
7. identify the major sales promotion types, including objectives
8. explain how to evaluate sales promotion
9. describe trade promotions
10. discuss ethical issues in mass marketing communications

Integrated communications campaigns use different communication methods. Mass marketing communications primarily involve sending non-personal messages to wide target audiences. These key tools are the focus of this chapter and are discussed in the following order: advertising and product placement, public relations (PR) and sponsorship, and sales promotions. The chapter also explores the main media channels, building on coverage in the previous chapter and looking specifically at media vehicle selection.

Introduction

Mass communications can facilitate wide dispersion of brand and company messages. The simple and complex models of the communication processes explain how messages spread (see Chapter 13). Mass communication tools, advertising, product placement, PR, sponsorship and sales promotions are used to provide the focus, style and tone of the message. This is then delivered to the **target audience** by a variety of media channels. Each aspect shapes the communication message and impacts on how it might be received. For example, highly emotional messages can trigger certain behaviours. Cadbury's used a drumming gorilla to reinvigorate the brand. Sitting in a rehearsal studio, the gorilla plays the drums to the 1980s hit song 'In the air tonight' by Phil Collins. Juan Cabral (ad director) wanted 'to go to the heart and not the brain' with this iconic campaign, which is credited with driving sales of the Dairy Milk chocolate bar by an increase of nearly 10 per cent, and the ad continued to influence sales throughout the year (Wood, 2010; Caird, 2016).

Television adverts can touch our emotions in various ways and sometimes they are even designed to irritate the target audience. Gocompare.com, webuyanycar.com and Cillit Bang have been cited as being among the most irritating television commercials (Burn-Callander, 2015). Textual adverts in printed newspapers and magazines and online can present rational and logical arguments to encourage target audiences to make a buying decision. Text can also be accompanied by powerful imagery to both stimulate emotionally and provide detailed arguments to persuade the message receiver to act. Hellmann's award-winning 'Food pioneers—on the side of food' campaign used print adverts, television, radio and social media for this global campaign visually showcasing foods and the people who eat them, and simultaneously highlighting the brand's commitment to responsible food production (Ogilvy, 2017).

Innovative digital advertising formats are creating opportunities to appeal to target audiences dynamically and can instantly be tailored to the consumers viewing an **advertising message**. Ocean Outdoor is pioneering the use of large-screen digital advertising screens to deliver targeted messages to passing shoppers (Ocean Outdoor, 2017).

Advertising in its many forms is not the only type of mass communication tool to reach our emotions and foster engagement. PR, stories in the media and organized events provide a source of public information and experience, which can raise awareness and educate various publics (target audiences) about a brand and its corporate image. Carefully designed PR campaigns can enhance corporate reputations and increase competitive advantage.

Sales promotions, another form of mass communication, are often used to elicit action, and this technique is used widely in situations from selling fast-moving consumer goods (FMCGs) to car finance. For example, PC World regularly offers promotional discounts to encourage purchases of consumer electronics. Typical promotions offer customers the opportunity to make financial savings, receive bonus items, and enjoy free delivery. HSBC Bank Plc in partnership with Visa offers its customers the opportunity to receive cashback when they shop with certain brands. This is just one type of sales promotion; more types are discussed later in the chapter.

Digital marketing offers scope to engage target audiences and create communities using the web and social media platforms. For example, Nike used a fully integrated digital marketing campaign to launch its Epic React running shoes. The campaign used video, web and social media. Nike China took the campaign to a different level, sending customers into a virtual world as digital avatars that then appeared on a treadmill, running past World Heritage landmarks in Reactland. Using the web in this way is transcending the divide between television and print media and developing highly dynamic and creative campaigns. Digital marketing is covered in detail in Chapter 16. These are examples of the variety of ways in which mass communications are used to communicated with target audiences.

Broadly speaking, advertising and PR raise awareness, while sales promotion is used to stimulate action. But each tool has much more to offer a marketing manager who is planning an integrated marketing communications campaign. These tools are now explored in more detail.

Advertising

What is the role of **advertising**? How does it work? When should it be used and how can we evaluate its effectiveness? These questions, asked about advertising, have tormented academics and practitioners alike and filled thousands of pages of hundreds of publications. Jones (1991) explained how advertising can persuade, while Barnard and Ehrenberg suggested it is more about 'nudging' the buyer towards a decision and reinforcing their perceptions of a brand (Barnard and Ehrenberg, 1997). Industry experts have their own views: John Hegarty, co-founder of Bartle Bogle Hegarty, says success in advertising comes from the big idea, and he places high importance on creativity to differentiate a brand. For Sir Martin Sorrell—founder of WWP, one of the world's largest advertising agencies—it is all about the capacity to deliver return on investment (Tylee, 2018). And just when you think you might have some answers, throw into the debate *disruptive* technology like the internet. Here, newcomers to the world of business, like college students Page and Brin (Google) and Zuckerberg (Facebook), have created new environments that are part of the networks that encase the planet and operate at the speed of light.

Furthermore, digital channels and social media networks are changing the way we communicate through advertising and the nature of the content of the messages we use to influence others. Digital advertising is measurable, and so it is easier to see how customers respond to messages delivered through digital channels. For example, Weetabix used Skyview as a research tool to evaluate the effectiveness of its intensive television advertising campaigns. Skyview is a panel of over 30,000 viewers who have Sky boxes to record their watching behaviour, and this data is linked to TNS's Worldpanel, which gathers data on purchasing habits. Weetabix was able to confirm the effectiveness of its television campaign and saw an over 10 per cent increase in sales. Weetabix was also able to determine the frequency needed to get the best results: one exposure to the advert prompted awareness and intention to purchase, but two to four exposures were needed to achieve action and actual sales; any more was a waste, which was a very important finding for Weetabix (SkyMedia, 2015).

So where do we start? First, we look at the role of advertising and the theories that seek to explain how it works, and then we look at when advertising should be used. Finally we discuss how its effectiveness can be measured.

The Role of Advertising

Advertising helps brands to establish a dialogue with their target audiences, to communicate with them and engage their interest through appeals, stories and messages. More specifically, advertising is generally used to persuade and encourage message receivers to respond, so as to meet various communication objectives: for example, it may be used to stimulate sales and ultimately increase profits. To deliver operational value from advertising, it is important to set clear communication *objectives*. Advertising can create awareness, stimulate trial, differentiate and position products in customers' minds, correct misconceptions, remind and reinforce, and provide support for the salesforce.

Create awareness

Advertising can create awareness of a company, a brand, a website, an event, or something of interest to target audiences. It can even alert buyers to a solution to a problem. For example, Colgate toothpaste can stop plaque, bad breath, and tooth and gum decay. Discount supermarket Lidl aims to help its customers deal with the problem of the cost of shopping with its 'shop a Lidl smarter' campaign. It is widely agreed (in principle) that advertising can help to legitimize a company, its products, brands and sales teams in the minds of the target audience. In doing so, it can also improve acceptance of what a company has on offer. Brand awareness is considered as a precondition of purchase and can be achieved through advertising. Advertising is a means of informing target audiences and encouraging recall and recognition; awareness is necessary for successful communication (Jakeli and Tchumburidze, 2012). Level of awareness is important to advertisers, as customers need to instantly recall a brand or product if they are to make a purchase.

EXHIBIT 14.1
Jackfruit, the all-vegan superfood

Stimulate trial

Advertising can create interest and stimulate trial. The sale of some products can suffer because of lack of trial. Marketing research has shown that, for some products, once consumers try the product, acceptance is high but for some reason only a small proportion of the target group go on to buy the product. In such circumstances, advertising focuses on stimulating trial.

For example, jackfruit grows easily without pesticides and artificial irrigation and is a good, versatile food source that is 100 per cent vegan. The jackfruit company makes products that range from smoked, pulled jackfruit (texture and taste like pulled pork) to low-calorie ice cream, to target the growing market of people identifying themselves as vegan. The Gourmet Burger Kitchen gave away 900 jackfruit burgers on World Vegan Day, to stimulate trial (Chiorando, 2018). See Exhibit 14.1.

Differentiate and position products in customers' minds

Advertising copy and visuals have a major role to play in positioning brands in the minds of the target audience (Ries and Trout, 2001). Creative positioning involves the development or reinforcement of an image or set of associations for a brand; see Exhibit 14.2. Brands often use advertising campaigns to differentiate them from competitors: McDonald's makes claims of longer opening hours than Burger King; BMW claims it produces better quality vehicles than Audi (Bambauer-Sachse and Heinzle, 2018). Aaker, Batra and Myers (1996) identified seven ways to position a product.

1 *Product characteristics and customer benefits*: for example, Ryanair launched an advertising campaign to let its customers know about changes to its previously restrictive baggage rules, the introduction of seating allocation, and improvements to its online booking website. Headphone manufacturer Dre positioned its products as offering top-quality sound and reliability. Ford Focus uses its high-tech features and characteristics—for example, Wi-Fi hotspot, driver assist, voice-control navigation and entertainment system, active parking assistance, EcoBoost, low-speed safety system, traffic sign recognition—to portray its car's benefits to the user, and this is summed up in the statement 'Ford Focus—together we go further'.

   Another tactic used for positioning is being first: for example, Sky News claims the number one position with respect to its claim to be 'first for breaking news'. Occasionally, two or more attributes are used, as with Ecover laundry liquid (cleans clothes with its non-biological ingredients and is good for the environment as it uses less packaging and fewer transport miles). L'Oreal Men Expert Pure Power claims to help to improve skin by making it cleaner.

2 *Price*: this positioning approach focuses on price as a weapon to deliver higher value to

EXHIBIT 14.2
L'Oreal appeals to its target audience by identifying their problems and providing solutions that match consumer preferences

consumers. Many airlines use price as a differentiator, for example low-cost airlines like Air Asia, easyJet, Ryanair and Wizz Air. Sainsbury's promotes low-price lines branded under its 'basics' range, and Morrisons has its M Saver range. Price positioning is not always focused on low prices, however. Occasionally a brand is positioned based on its high price, as is the case with Stella Artois ('reassuringly expensive').

3 *Product use*: another positioning method is to associate the product with a use. Examples are: Cillit Bang, with its 'power to wow' cleaning products, which are easy to use and shift dirt and grime easily; L'Oreal Elnett Satin, hairspray, 'Nothing holds you like Elnett'; the Co-operative Bank, 'Good with money'.
4 *Product user*: another way of positioning is to associate a brand with a user or user type. Polo by Ralph Lauren portrays its users to be bohemian romantics who live on the edge of the city, with an interest in antiques, art and music (Stubbs, 2014). Celebrity endorsements are often used, such as by David Beckham (Adidas, H&M, Breitling), Michael Jordan (Nike), Helen Mirren (L'Oreal) and Nicole Kidman (Chanel No 5). Fashion models Kendall Jenner, Karlie Kloss, and Bella and Gigi Hadid, with large social media followings, have become powerful influencers for brands like Versace, Fendi, Maybelline and Pepsi (Fleming, 2018).
5 *Product class*: some products can benefit by positioning themselves within a product class. For example, Red Mountain coffee positioned itself within the ground coffee class with the tagline 'Ground coffee taste without the grind', and a margarine called 'I Can't Believe It's Not Butter' was positioned within the butter class by virtue of its name and advertising; and, of course, there is the enduring classic 'Beanz Meanz Heinz'.
6 *Symbols*: the use of symbols to position brands in the marketplace has been achieved by Michelin (Michelin Man), McDonald's (golden arches) and Apple (white apple logo). The use of symbols is particularly effective when the symbol reflects a quality desired in the brand, as with the Andrex puppy (softness).
7 *Competition*: positioning against well-entrenched competitors can be effective, since their image in the marketplace can be used as a reference point. For example, Subaru positioned against Volvo by claiming that 'Volvo has built a reputation for surviving accidents. Subaru has built a reputation for avoiding them,' based on ABS for better braking and four-wheel drive for better traction. Dyson positions itself against the competition by claiming that, unlike those of its rivals, its vacuum cleaners do not lose suction, thanks to Dyson's patented technology. Adidas positions its products against other brands of trainers (e.g. Nike). In the Steadicam campaign, a runner in the desert is wearing Nike trainers, but the cameraman, carrying a heavy camera and filming the event, is wearing Adidas. The message is that Adidas trainers offer better performance and enable users to remain fresh and lively even after an extreme run. Positioning against competitors can be effective when consumers base their purchase decision on facts. Hence, a well-adjusted statement claiming a factual advantage against a key competitor can be highly successful. However, research has shown that, if used inappropriately, such positioning can tarnish the image of the brand that is using the technique. There is also the risk of legal action. Aldi upset Tesco with its 'Swap & Save' campaign. Aldi claimed that 84 out of 98 people had saved money by switching to shopping with the discount supermarket. Tesco disagreed, and the Advertising Standards Authority (ASA) banned Aldi's advert, claiming it was misleading to customers. (In the UK, the ASA is an independent regulator that controls advertising standards across all media.)

Correct misconceptions

Correcting misconceptions that consumers hold against brands can be achieved with carefully designed advertising campaigns. Brands can spend millions on repositioning a brand in the minds of consumers. Unilever's £12.5 million 'Powered by plants' campaign was designed to celebrate the plant-based ingredients of its Flora spreads and position them as all-vegetable alternatives to butter. This approach has delivered positive results, and the FMCG manufacturer's sustainable living brands are driving growth (Willan, 2017). Another example is McCain's, the market leader in the UK for oven chips, which ran a successful advertising campaign claiming that oven chips contained 40 per cent less fat than home-cooked chips. However, marketing research showed that consumers still believed that McCain's oven chips contained 30 per cent fat. A new campaign was designed to correct this misconception by stating that the oven chips contained only 5 per cent fat. Advertising cosmetic surgery has become increasingly commonplace. Service providers are keen to dispel fears and often use advertising as a way of conveying the message that cosmetic procedures and treatments are safe. However, in the UK, the ASA has often ruled against such advertising on the grounds of it being misleading, exaggerated or breaching social responsibility.

Remind and reinforce

Once a clear position in the minds of the target audience has been established, the objective of advertising may be to remind consumers of the brand's existence and to reinforce its image. For many leading brands in mature markets, such as Coca-Cola, Heinz Beans or Nestlé's Kit Kat, the objective of their advertising is to maintain top-of-mind awareness and favourable associations. Given leading brands' strong market positions, a major advertising task is to defend against competitive inroads, and thus maintain high sales, market share and profits. Guinness has managed to maintain its brand for over 250 years, making it one of the world's most successful alcoholic drink brands; see Exhibit 14.3.

EXHIBIT 14.3
Guinness uses a thought-provoking campaign to maintain top-of-mind awareness among its target audiences

Provide support for the salesforce

Advertising can provide invaluable support for the salesforce by identifying 'warm' prospects and communicating with otherwise unreachable members of a decision-making unit. Some business-to-business advertising contains return coupons that potential customers can send to the advertiser to indicate a degree of interest in the product.

Read Marketing in Action 14.1 to find out about the advice that the Saatchi & Saatchi global creative agency gives its clients when setting advertising objectives.

MARKETING IN ACTION 14.1
Saatchi & Saatchi Advocates Love and Respect When Planning Communication Objectives

Advertising is a way that brands set themselves apart from their competitors. Today, most goods work in the way they are expected to, as the ramifications of a customer revolt through social media can destroy a brand's reputation very quickly. So how do marketers make their cars, chocolates, wine or clothing stand out from the crowd? Saatchi & Saatchi suggests that is it a matter of love and respect. '*Lovemarks*' are brands that are '*owned by the people (customers) who love them, and they (brand owners) use their respect equity to build new mysterious, sensual and intimate relationships*'—see http://www.lovemarks.com.

Source of image: http://www.saatchi.be/lovemarks

Creators of the love—respect axis at Saatchi & Saatchi suggest that if a brand has high respect and high love, it is considered a '*Lovemark*'. However, if it has high respect and low love, then it is merely a *brand*. High love and low respect is the domain of fads, and low love and low respect is where commodities (products) reside on the matrix. The purpose of the matrix is to inspire companies to shift the positioning of their market offers until they achieve the high status of a Lovemark. And to help, Saatchi & Saatchi has a '*Lovemarker*', which is an index that allows it to score companies on levels of *respect*, which is made up of the three constructs—performance, trust and reputation—and *love*, which is similarly made up of mystery, sensuality and intimacy. In total, 14 respect and 13 love variables are used to determine a score. The Lovemarker allows companies to determine whether they are hot (2 points), warm (1 point) or cold (0 points) against each variable, and they must score over 41 points to be a Lovemark. Examples of Lovemarks are McDonald's and Harley Davidson.

Achieving Lovemark status is done by not only getting the storytelling right and connecting it in a logical and coherent way from the past to the future, but also by tapping in to customer emotions to inspire and excite. However, some goods have a head start. For example, we might know that green beans are better for us than sweets and are something we need to eat, but the sugar boost makes confectionary more likely to be a heart-pumping *want* than is a plate of healthy vegetables, which means that it is easier for us to love a bag of M&Ms than a packet of Florette salad mix.

According to Dina Howell, Worldwide CEO at Saatchi & Saatchi, a *want* is more powerful than a *need*. Howell advocates three ways for companies to unlock positive emotions.

1 ***Know the market, understanding the culture and triggers that might prompt emotion and excitement***. When Cadbury's Dairy Milk sought to enter Arabian markets by targeting young single adults, the company had to find a way to make its products more exciting than market leader Galaxy. Its solution was to invite young shoppers to sample the 'Joy Elevator'. Saatchi & Saatchi devised the campaign, which was delivered through store experiences, online and using traditional media channels.

2 ***Know the channel and what it has to offer***. When Swiffer mops set out to revive its sales, the Saatchi & Saatchi team identified a *lovegap* between the manufacturer (Procter & Gamble) and potential new customers. The problem was that while customers were aware of the brand, when they got to the store to buy the product, they often could not find it, touch it or see how it worked, as the Swiffer mop was sealed in a box. The solution was to supply the mop ready assembled, so customers could see in store how easy it would be to use. Adapting the product to the channel and promoting the brand through media channels raised its profile and moved it into Lovemark territory.

3 ***Know the shopper***. In the USA, 86 per cent of purchases are made in the store by women. So, when Quaker Oats asked Saatchi & Saatchi for help, together they devised the 'power their potential' campaign. The challenge was how to get children to concentrate more at school (by eating breakfast and heathy snacks) and at the same time how to give parents an easy solution for providing children with the 'fuel' they needed to get them through to lunch time. The solution was a combination of brands of hot cereals and ready-to-eat healthy snacks and cookies that were highly visible when parents went shopping. Using in-store displays and online media, this campaign enabled Quaker to increase its market share.

Based on: Saatchi & Saatchi (2015); Roberts (2015a and b); Howells (2015)

Advertising Expenditure

Fulfilling the various roles often requires significant resources, and vast sums of money are spent on developing advertising campaigns every year. Digital media have changed how we consume advertising and shifted how the advertising budget is allocated to the various media. For many years, print media were where most of this money was spent. Figure 14.1 shows how companies in the UK spend their advertising budgets.

In 2017, advertising expenditure in the UK exceeded £20 billion. Since 2009, we can see year-on-year growth in total spend—a trend that is forecast to continue beyond 2021. The UK market has grown beyond expectations (Bourn et al., 2018). Search advertising—keyword advertising through search engines—attracts the largest amount of spend, followed by, television, mobile display, desktop display, and online classified. Cinema, Radio and Outdoor advertising.

Setting the advertising budget requires consideration of many variables. The achievement of any of the roles outlined above will depend upon the size of the budget and how effectively it is spent. There are various methods of setting budgets.

How Advertising Works

For many years, there has been considerable debate about how advertising works. The consensus is that there can be no single all-embracing theory that explains how all advertising works, because advertising has varied tasks (Wright and Crimp, 2003). For example, advertising that attempts to make an instant sale by incorporating a return coupon that can be used to order a product is very different from corporate image advertising that is designed to reinforce attitudes and shape beliefs.

FIGURE 14.1
UK advertising spend by type of media

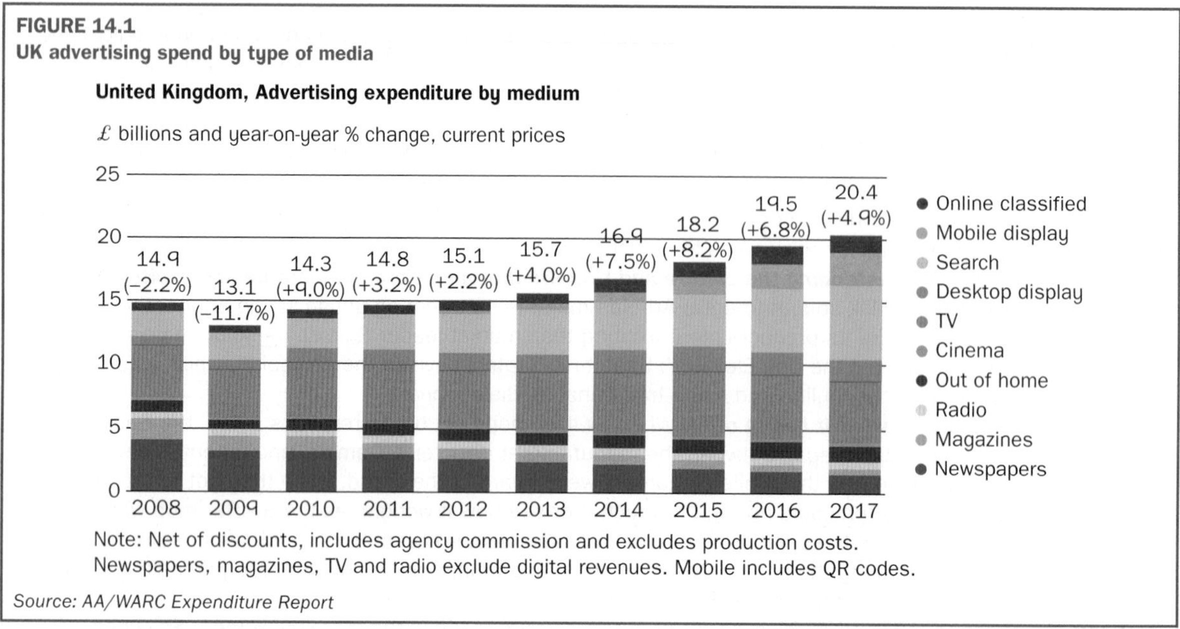

Source: AA/WARC Expenditure Report

Two competing views on how advertising works are the **strong theory of advertising** and the **weak theory of advertising** (Jones, 1991). The strong theory has its base in the USA and is shown on the left-hand side of Figure 14.2. A person passes through the stages of awareness, interest, desire and action (AIDA). According to this theory, advertising is strong enough to increase people's knowledge and change people's attitudes, and therefore is capable of persuading people who had not previously bought a brand to buy it. It is therefore a conversion theory of advertising: non-buyers are converted to buyers. Advertising is assumed to be a powerful influence on consumers.

FIGURE 14.2
Strong and weak theories of how advertising works

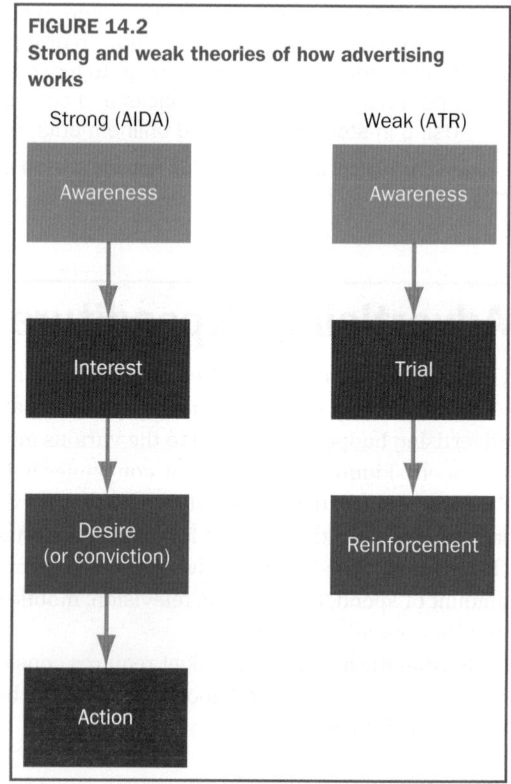

This model has been criticized on two grounds (Ehrenberg, 1992). First, for many types of product there is little evidence that consumers experience a strong desire before action (buying the brand). For example, in the case of an inexpensive product, a brand might be bought on a trial basis without any strong conviction that it is superior to competing brands. Second, the model is criticized because it is limited to the conversion of a non-buyer to a buyer. It ignores what happens after action (i.e. first purchase). Yet in most mature markets, advertising is designed to affect people who have already bought the brand at least once.

The major alternative to the strong advertising theory is shown on the right-hand side of Figure 14.2. The steps in this model are awareness, trial and reinforcement (ATR). The ATR model, which has received support in Europe, suggests that advertising is a much less powerful influence than the strong theory would suggest. As Ehrenberg explains, 'Advertising can first arouse awareness and interest, nudge some customers towards a doubting first trial purchase (with the emphasis on trial, as in maybe I'll try it) and then provide some reassurance and reinforcement after that first purchase. I see no need for any strong AIDA-like Desire or Conviction before the first purchase is made' (Ehrenberg, 1992). Ehrenberg's work in fast-moving consumer goods (FMCG) markets has shown that loyalty to one brand is rare. Most consumers purchase a selection of brands. The proportions of total purchases represented by the different brands show little variation over time, and new brands join the selection only in exceptional circumstances. A major objective of advertising in such circumstances is to defend brands: it does not work to increase sales by bringing new buyers to the brand advertised; its main function is to retain existing buyers and sometimes to increase the frequency with which they buy the brand (Jones, 1991). Therefore, the target is existing buyers who are well disposed to the brand (otherwise they would not buy it), and advertising is designed to reinforce these favourable perceptions, so consumers continue to buy the brand (Dall'Olmo Riley et al., 1997). Level of involvement also has an important role in determining how people make purchasing decisions. Jones (1991) suggested that involvement may also explain when the strong and weak theories apply.

For high-involvement decisions such as the purchase of expensive consumer durables, cars, complex financial services products the decision-making process is thorough, with many alternatives considered and an extensive information search undertaken. Advertising, therefore, is more likely to follow the strong theory either by creating a strong desire to purchase (as with mail order) or by convincing people that they should find out more about the brand (e.g. by visiting a showroom). Since the purchase is expensive, it is likely that a strong desire (or conviction) is required before purchase takes place.

However, for low-involvement purchase decisions (such as low-cost packaged goods), people are less likely to consider a wide range of brands thoroughly before purchase, and it is here that the weak theory of advertising almost certainly applies. Advertising is mainly intended to keep consumers doing what they already do by providing reassurance and reinforcement. Advertising repetition will be important in maintaining awareness and keeping the brand among the consumer's selection of brands from which individual purchases will be chosen.

Moving beyond strong and weak theories of advertising, Kitchen et al. (2014) argue that the Elaboration Likelihood Model (ELM) introduced by Petty and Cacioppo (1981) gives us a model of advertising that encapsulates attitudinal change. It is important to understand attitudinal changes if we are to get to the bottom of why certain behaviours occur in response to the stimulus of a piece of advertising. The ELM aims to explain how humans process stimuli (Geddes, 2016). Exhibit 14.4 shows a cartoon image which captures the essence of the ELM. The cartoon mouse has different options (stimulus to interact with) to reach the cheese. Whichever choice the mouse makes, the next mouse may make a different decision based on its past experiences and willingness to become involved.

The ELM presents the idea that there are different routes a person may follow when responding to advertising messages (see Figure 14.3).

1 The central route—high processing of the advertiser's message equals high elaboration.
2 The peripheral route—low processing of the advertiser's message equals low elaboration.

The route people take will be influenced by their levels of motivation and cognitive ability when processing advertising messages. Petty and Cacioppo (1981a,b) tested the theory by exposing different groups of people to adverts for a disposable razor. One group were encouraged to be highly involved with the product, while the other group were not provided with the same stimulus and therefore were assumed to have low involvement.

The ELM is still widely used in advertising research and is respected by academics for being well constructed, able to accommodate many different outcomes (in response to advertising) and widely cited. Marketers, however, need to be aware of the context and the media environment in which they seek to apply the principles of the ELM; it has certain limitations, as actual behaviour is not necessarily as clear cut as the model suggests and people may engage in dual processing and follow both the central and the peripheral route simultaneously (Kitchen et al., 2014). Shi et al. (2018) applied the ELM in a social media context and found the central and peripheral route behaviours to be evident among Twitter users. The researchers chose to use the ELM to find out why some tweets go viral, as understanding this could help marketers promote brands online. Oreo biscuits is one such example: the brand created a Twitter storm by tweeting 'you can still dunk in the dark' when the power failed during a Super Bowl tournament. There were strong connections and relevance, and individuals readily retweeted the message to friends and family. Shi et al.'s study found that there is a

EXHIBIT 14.4
How will the mouse react to different stimuli?
©2014 Kevin Cornell, Originally appeared in A List Apart Magazine, Issue 397

FIGURE 14.3
ELM model

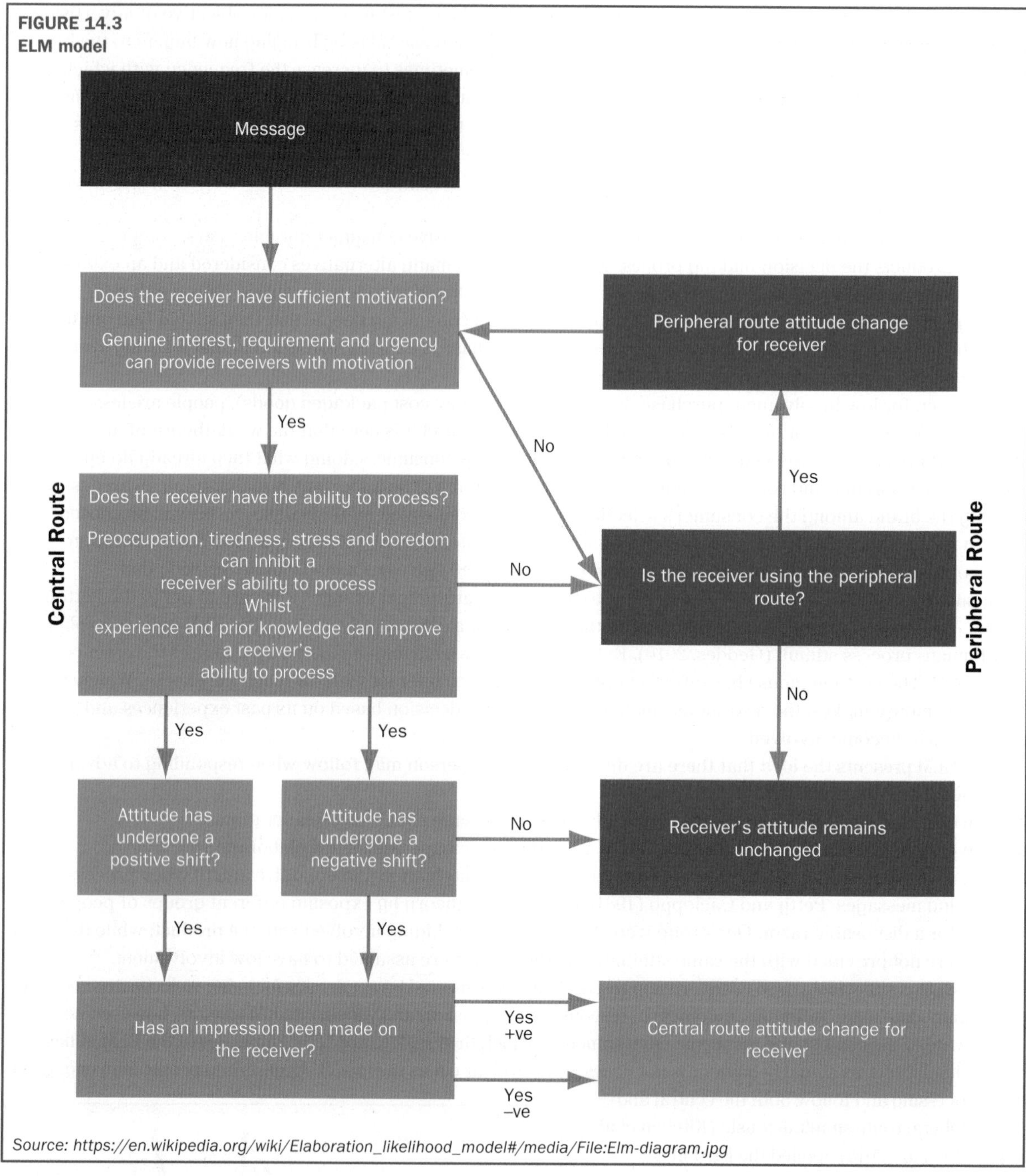

Source: https://en.wikipedia.org/wiki/Elaboration_likelihood_model#/media/File:Elm-diagram.jpg

wealth of information in social media networks but a 'scarcity of attention', so the context is important. Members of social media platforms are much less receptive to unsolicited messages than to those that are from a trusted source.

Shi et al. also found that the ELM is suitable for planning campaigns designed to encourage re-tweeting behaviour. To influence a person using the central route, the content of a tweet should match the individual's topical preferences: for example, if a cosmetics brand is linked to a celebrity favoured by the individual, that person is more likely to pay attention to the tweet. Marketers can provide rich information content to stimulate higher elaboration. To engage individuals who follow the peripheral route is more challenging in social media networks but if clusters of similar minded individuals (with similar needs) are identified, they can then be targeted successfully. Read Marketing in Action 14.2 to find out about how giving target audiences a choice of media might help them to engage with brand advertising.

MARKETING IN ACTION 14.2

Nordic Brands Invite Audiences to Experience the Benefits of a Brutal Landscape

Arguably, Volvo cars, Arla yoghurt and Finlandia vodka share a common message theme in their adverts: they want their customers to know how the harsh Nordic environment and the strength needed to survive builds better brands. But why might the brooding, melancholy film produced by Volvo attract more car buyers? And how does Arla's journey of a young boy across Iceland's desolate landscapes help sell yoghurt? Why might spending over two minutes viewing snippets of Nordic wisdom encourage us to drink more vodka?

Gratification researchers offer some insight into why such approaches might work. User gratification theory (UGT) suggests that audiences voluntarily engage with media, motivated by their own needs and goals. And their reward for actively participating in the communication process (e.g. viewing adverts on television, downloading video on demand, sharing via social media) is the gratification that results. UGT hangs on the premise that it is different to mass communication theories, because it endows the consumer of the media with the power to determine which media they engage with rather than being passively captivated by powerful brand messages. Researchers in this field suggest various ways in which audiences achieve gratification and satisfy their needs. For example, utility is seen as using the media to achieve certain tasks; selectivity is seen as audiences using the media to support their own interests and beliefs; and personal interest is seen as serving psychological needs through reassurance and self-understanding.

So when Volvo decided to adopt a global approach to communications, it produced its Nordic noir film as a centrepiece for the campaign. In the advert (a four-minute film), a Volvo car was shown traversing the tough Nordic landscape accompanied by emotive music and lyrics to match. Viewers were invited to experience and gain insights into how these extremes ensure that Volvo cars are able to deal with all eventualities. Engaging with this advert arguably reassures car buyers that a car *made by Sweden* offers performance and safety for the precious things in life.

For Arla Icelandic yogurt, there are also gains for those who engage with this advert. The personal benefits are said to be the offer of a healthy alternative and giving health-conscious consumers *'a great treat after exercise, since protein contributes to maintaining and growing muscle mass'*. In the advert, the journey of a boy named Orri, seen delivering an important message, seeks to convey that nothing is too difficult once you've eaten Arla, a product with 1,000 years' worth of heritage.

With Finlandia, audiences are offered insight and wisdom from quirky individuals. If they engage with this *knowledge collective*, amassed from 1,000 years (combined age of the knowledge providers in the advert) of insight, it offers a guide to vodka drinkers on how they might live a 'life less ordinary'.

Possibly these and other brands do look for ways to engage their audiences and give something back. As media channels become more fragmented and digital platforms more widely used, there are more opportunities to deliver benefits that go beyond the simple message of 'buy more product'.

Based on: Levy and Windahl (1985); Oster (2015); Gilbert (2015); Magee (2015); Elihu, Blumer and Gurevitch (1974); West and Turner (2010)

When to use Advertising

Planning campaigns and the FCB matrix

Adverts that provide factual information can aid consumers who are uncertain about making a purchasing decision. But how much information is required? Which media channels should be used and how frequently should the message be repeated? These questions are often asked by marketers planning to use advertising. Richard Vaughn, Director of Advertising Research at Foote, Cone & Belding, a global advertising agency, developed the FCB matrix as an aid to help write advertising copy—an aid that could potentially take account of consumer behaviour. See Figure 14.4 for an adapted version of the FCB matrix.

FIGURE 14.4
FCB matrix

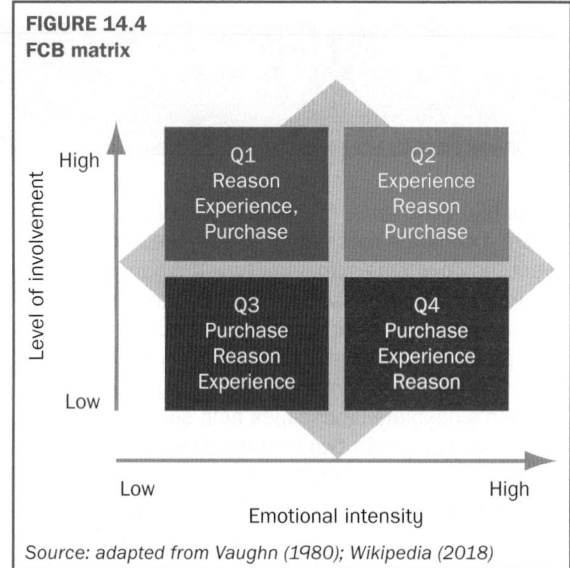

Source: adapted from Vaughn (1980); Wikipedia (2018)

In its simplest form, the FCB matrix enables advertising planners to consider whether a product (or service) is high or low involvement and where it might be positioned on a scale of the emotional connection a consumer might attach to the purchase. Depending on whether the consumer is making a rational low-involvement purchase or a high-involvement highly emotional purchase, the matrix can aid decision-making about when to use particular types of advertising message.

Quadrant 1 (Q1) decisions are high involvement and require information to enable consumers to think through their decision-making. For example, when buying a car, a computer, financial investment products or high-value jewellery. Products which fall into this area need advertising formats that can help the consumer learn about the product and develop positive feelings before they are likely to make a purchase. On the Rolex website, for example, powerful imagery showcases the features of Rolex watches; there is also detailed product information and information about the history of the brand and where and how to buy the products from an exclusive network of retailers around the world.

Quadrant 2 (Q2) decisions are also high involvement, and strong emotional considerations like ego and self-esteem also feature in the decision-making process. Fragrances and luxury fashion tend to fall into this quadrant. These types of products require consumers to feel emotionally connected to the product before they want to learn more and then make a purchase. Glossy magazines, television and web advertising can be effective for creating powerful visual and experiential campaigns. Chanel's Gabrielle perfume advert featured Kristen Stewart dancing to Beyoncé's 'Runnin'. The consumer is invited to feel freedom and independence before considering whether to make this all-important personal purchase (Niven-Phillips, 2017).

Quadrant 3 (Q3) focuses on low-involvement decisions, which involve routinely purchased items like laundry liquids—items that have practical use in our daily lives. The tendency is for the consumer to buy first then experience the product and develop feeling and attitudes after the purchase. With this type of habitual purchasing, advertising should seek to remind and reinforce. FMCG brands regularly use catchy tunes, jingles and lyrics to achieve this: for example, the Cadbury's classic 'Finger of Fudge is just enough to give the kids a treat', Proctor and Gamble's Fairy Liquid 'Hands that do dishes can feel as fell soft as your face' and Nike's 'Just do it' capture the essence of this quadrant.

Quadrant 4 (Q4) decisions are also low involvement but are about pleasure seeking and the potential to be quickly satisfied. Outdoor advertising can be effective, as it arouses immediate interest and stimulates action, and it enables consumers to develop feelings and finally to learn about their product decisions. Benetton's controversial billboard campaigns worked in this way and were initially very successful for building the brand globally. See Exhibit 14.5.

EXHIBIT 14.5
Benetton courts controversy to stimulate action, develop feelings and eventually learn about what the brands stand for

The FCB matrix has been criticized for being overly simplistic and because informational motivations cannot be so easily classified, as there are multiple layers of motives which are dependent on the metal state of the consumer (Rossiter and Percy, 1987). Claeys et al. (1995) tested the basic principles of the model and concluded they were valid, but added that, when thinking about products, consumers also use their emotions, so this should be taken into consideration when planning the use of advertising. The greater the 'emotional involvement' the stronger the emotional message. For example, luxury fragrances use highly emotional messages, as this is a very personal product choice.

Target audience

Deciding when to use advertising and which type of advertising format to use will be dependent on the **target audience** at which the advertisement is aimed. In consumer markets, the target audience may be defined in terms of socio-economic group, age, gender, location, buying frequency (e.g. heavy versus light buyers) and/or lifestyle. In organizational markets, target audience may be defined in terms of role (e.g. purchasing manager, managing director) and industry type.

Message decisions

Once the target audience has been identified, it needs to be understood. Buyer motives and choice criteria need to be analysed. Choice criteria are those factors buyers use to evaluate competing products. Understanding criteria in line with the needs of the target audience is vital: doing so has fundamental implications for message and media decisions.

Advertising messages should clearly communicate with the target audience, be important to them, communicate benefits and aim to secure competitive advantage. This is why an understanding of the motives and choice criteria of the target audience is essential for effective advertising. Without this knowledge, a campaign could be built upon an advertising platform that is irrelevant to its audience. See Marketing in Action 14.3 for further insights.

MARKETING IN ACTION 14.3
Keep Calm and Carry On

Successful advertising slogans (sometimes referred to as straplines) are short, memorable phrases. They can focus on a particular aspect of a product or service and can be long lasting. Or they may be created for a single campaign. They are not a new phenomenon. The iconic Keep Calm and Carry On poster was originally designed for the British government to be used in the advent of an invasion, and the message aimed to encourage the nation to be positive and to boost morale. However, the poster was never used officially. The 2.5 million copies were held in reserve and remained largely unseen by the British public until 2000.

Stuart Manley, owner of Barter Books (www.barterbooks.co.uk), a second-hand bookshop in Alnwick, Northumberland, found a copy of the poster and had it framed for his wife, who liked it so much she displayed it by the side of the shop checkout. The bookshop is unusual insofar as it allows its customers to barter for goods as well as making cash purchases. But, more notably, the shop has become famous for finding the poster. Since the discovery of the 'Keep Calm and Carry On' poster, millions of copies have been sold worldwide. The posters can be seen in places far and wide, from Buckingham Palace and the US Embassy in Belgium, to David Beckham's chest (on a T-shirt). The slogan appears on mugs, jewellery, baby clothes, T-shirts, travel bags and screen savers.

Simple, timeless and succinct, this slogan has longevity. Although not used for its intended purpose, the slogan eschews common values and brings people together in a common goal and, according to Alain Samson (social psychologist at the London School of Economics), 'The words are also particularly positive, reassuring, in a period of uncertainty, anxiety, even perhaps of cynicism.' The number of uses of the slogan has been expanded, and the slogan has appeared on products around the world. The Keep Calm and Carry On website has a product creator that enables shoppers to make their own products using this iconic logo.

Based on: Wikipedia (2012); Barter Books (2012); Henley (2009); Keep Calm and Carry On (n.d.)

Media decisions

Media planning is an important part of deciding when to use advertising. It has changed significantly in recent years, as digital platforms, mobile, the web, and so on account for a much larger part of a communication budget.

Building on the discussion in Chapter 13, we discuss media channels and the implications of channel choice. Each of the media can be used to carry different types of message: for example, television advertising is often used to convey the desired emotional response, and print media to supply objective information. In low-involvement situations, such as with the choice of drinks and convenience foods, humour is sometimes used to create a feeling of warmth about a brand; even regular exposure to a brand name over time can generate the desired feeling of warmth (Elliott, 1997). Finnair used a subtle form of humour in its 'Just like the movies' campaign, which used outdoor, print, web, cinema and television to promote flights to America; Interestingly, different media are perceived to have different levels of 'trustworthiness': for example, television, print and cinema advertising is generally seen as more trusted than outdoor, online and direct mail (Barnett, 2011). Consequently, selecting media can be complex.

The five aspects to be considered when selecting media are:

1 *Creative factors*. The key question that needs to be addressed is 'Does the medium allow the communication objectives to be realized?' For example, if the objective is to position the brand as having a high-status aspirational personality, then television or a carefully planned PR or digital media campaign may be best. If the communication objective is to remind the target audience of a brand, then a poster campaign or outdoor media may be better. Outdoor media are becoming more dynamic thanks to technological advancements that mean many of the benefits of television can be conveyed to outdoor adverts. JCDecaux is an example of a company making use of new technology to bring outdoor advertising to life (see https://www.jcdecaux.co.uk/specifications/westfield-london-landscape-digital-screens).

2 *Size of the advertising budget*. Some media are naturally more expensive than others. For example, £500,000 may be enough for a national poster campaign, but woefully inadequate for national television and a multi-channel integrated marketing communications campaign. However, widespread uptake of digital media has created opportunities for smaller companies that cannot afford to advertise on national television.

3 *Relative cost per opportunity to see*. The target audience may be reached much more cheaply using one medium rather than another. However, the calculation of opportunity to see differs according to media class, making comparisons difficult. For example, in the UK an opportunity to see for the press is defined as 'read or looked at any issue of the publication for at least two minutes', whereas for posters it is 'traffic past site', and online it is the number of unique visits or downloads. See table 14.1.

4 *Competitive activity*. The key decision is whether to compete in the same medium or to seek to dominate an alternative medium. Deciding to compete in the same medium may be appropriate if it is seen as the most effective one by the competition, so that to ignore it would be to hand the competition a massive communication advantage.

5 *Opinions of the retail trade* (e.g. supermarket buyers). These may influence the choice of media class. Advertising expenditure is often used by salespeople to convince the retail trade to increase shelf space for existing brands and to stock new brands. Since distribution is a key success factor in these markets, the views of retailers will be important. For example, if it is known that supermarkets favour television advertising in a certain product market, the selling impact on the trade of £3 million spent on television may be viewed as greater than the equivalent spend of 50:50 between television and the press.

Media vehicles

Media vehicle refers to the choice of a specific newspaper, magazine, television slot, location of a poster site, and so on. Although creative considerations still play a part, calculation of *cost per thousand exposures* is more important. This requires readership and viewership figures. In the UK, readership figures are produced by the National Readership Survey, based on over 36,000 interviews per year. Viewership is measured by the Broadcasters' Audience Research Board (BARB), which produces weekly reports based on a panel of 5,300 households equipped with metered television sets. Poster research is conducted by an organization called Route. It provides information on not only the number of people who pass each poster, but also on the number of people who are likely to see a particular site.

TABLE 14.1 Definition of an opportunity to see

Television	Presence in room with set switched on, at turn of clock minute, to relevant channel, provided that presence in room with set on is for at least 15 consecutive seconds
Press	Read or looked at any issue (for at least two minutes) within the publication period (e.g. for weeklies, within the last seven days)
Posters	Traffic past site (including pedestrians)
Cinema	Actual cinema admissions
Mobile	Ad impressions

Sometimes a combination of media classes is used in an advertising campaign to take advantage of the media classes' relative strengths and weaknesses. For example, a new car launch might use television to gain awareness and project the desired image, the internet to foster engagement, the press to supply more technical information, and, later in the campaign, outdoor media posters may be used as a support medium to remind and reinforce earlier messages.

Execute campaign

Once the advertisements have been produced and the media selected, the advertisements are sent to the relevant media for publication, transmission or launch online. A key organizational issue is to ensure that the right advertisements reach the right media at the right time. Each media vehicle has its own deadlines after which publication or transmission may not be possible.

Evaluate advertising effectiveness

All marketing communications, not just advertising, should be evaluated to determine a) whether the message and the tools that are to be used to deliver the campaign are likely to be effective, and b) the impact and effectiveness of the campaign once it has been released (Fill, 2009). This means pre-testing (before the campaign) and post-testing (during and after the campaign).

What should be measured depends on whatever the advertising is trying to achieve. As we have already seen, advertising objectives include gaining awareness, trial, positioning, correcting misconceptions, reminding and providing support for the salesforce (e.g. by identifying 'warm' prospects). By setting targets for each objective, advertising research can assess whether objectives have been achieved. For example, a campaign might have the objective of increasing awareness from 10 to 20 per cent, or of raising beliefs that the product is the 'best value brand on the market' from 15 to 25 per cent of the target consumers. If advertising objectives are couched in sales or market-share terms, campaign evaluation methods should monitor the sales or market share effects of the advertising. If trade objectives are important, distribution and stock levels of wholesalers and/or retailers, and perhaps their awareness and attitudes, could be measured. Each tool has different methods of evaluation. In the rest of this section, we focus on advertising research methods by looking at pre- and post-testing.

Pre-testing before the campaign is part of the creative process. Adverts can be tested at various stages of development, from testing the concept to finished adverts (before they are released). For example:

- *Concept testing* is part of the development of the advertising campaign and helps the creative team to identify the ideas that are most likely to be effective. This method works by showing the target audience a rough outline of the ideas, for example storyboards or photographs. The advantages are that a variety of ideas can be tested prior to further development. A limitation of this approach is that it takes place in an artificial setting, which must be considered when evaluating the results.
- *Focus groups*—a small number of target audience members are brought together to discuss ideas and relevant topics. There will be a moderator who is experienced in interviewing and who uses the gathering to probe thoughts and emotions. The advantage is that this is a relatively low-cost approach that can reveal in-depth information about target audience preferences, but the results can lack objectivity and be potentially biased.
- *Readability tests* are used for testing finished print-based adverts. The comprehensibility of the words used in the copy is tested.

Post-testing is carried out after the release of the advert and can be used to assess the advert's effectiveness throughout and when the campaign is over. Checking how well an advertising campaign has performed provides information for future campaigns. A key advantage of post-testing is that it is carried out in the 'live' environment. Methods of post-testing include:

- *Inquiry tests* that measure the number of direct inquiries and responses resulting from the advertising, which may include completed coupons or requests for more information. This method has become more widely used with the rise in the use of direct marketing.
- *Recall tests* are designed to measure the impact of adverts on the target audience. Recall tests usually rely on responses from many members of the target audience who are interviewed within a short time after seeing the advert. This form of measurement is reasonably accurate (e.g. each time an advert is tested, the results are the same). However, the ability of recall tests to predict sales is generally considered to be low (bringing the validity of this method into question). Despite these issues, recall testing is widely used, especially to evaluate television advertising, and can also be used for press advertisements.
- *Recognition tests* are based on memory and the ability of members of the target audience to reprocess information in an advert. This is one of the main methods used for measuring magazine readership. The reliability of the recognition test is high and much better than that of recall tests (Fill, 2009: 453–9).
- *Likeability* has been found to be a very powerful predictor of sales (Gordon, 1992). The problem with likeability is that it is difficult to measure. For example, if one person says 'I like the advert a lot,' how does this compare with a person who says 'I like the advert a little'? For each person the evaluation will have a different meaning and relevance and will stimulate different levels of interest.
- *Financial analysis* requires the cost of the resources to be evaluated, which includes the media spend. This is usually carried out continuously and acts as an early warning system if costs are spiralling out of control. Financial control and accountability of the advertising spend have become increasingly important in recent years.

In Chapter 16, we discuss digital analytics and other forms of digital testing that are responding to the changing ways that audiences receive communication methods.

Organizing for Campaign Development

There are various options when developing an advertising campaign and the choice will be largely dependent on the resources, skills and capabilities of the company wishing to develop the campaign. In principle, campaigns may be developed:

- *in cooperation* with people from the media; for example, advertising copy may be written by company staff, but the artwork and layout of the advertisement may be done by the newspaper or magazine
- *in-house* by the advertising department staffed with copy-writers, media buyers and production personnel
- *in cooperation with an* **advertising agency**. Larger agencies offer a full service, comprising creative, media planning and buying, planning and strategy development, market research and production.

In reality, given the growing complexity of communication campaigns and wider use of digital media platforms, companies wishing to advertise use a combination of approaches. Central to the success of any campaign is the relationship between clients and agencies. Key roles in the development of a campaign are account directors and executives, who liaise with client companies and coordinate the work of the other departments on behalf of their clients. Because agencies work for many clients, they have a wide range of experience and can provide an objective outsider's view of what is required and how problems can be solved.

When an advertiser uses an agency, managing the relationship is of critical importance. Therefore, a company should aim to find the type of agency that best suits its needs. Types of agency include: *full service agencies*, which offer strategic planning, research, creative development, brand building, media buying and scheduling and a full range of expertise across all of the communication tools; *boutiques or creative shops*, which provide specialist services, for example copywriting and creative content development expertise; smaller agencies, often chosen for their ability to develop specialist creative ideas; and digital agencies (and/or web service providers), which can offer an extensive range of web-based and mobile services, such as content development, blogging, online PR, buzz marketing, social media, and search engine optimization (SEO). The internet and mobile and digital marketing have extended the choice of agencies, and these issues are discussed in more detail in Chapter 16.

The formal part of an agency selection is the pitching process, where the client produces a creative brief and the agency prepares a pitch to demonstrate how it will meet that brief. However, the communication industry is a 'people' business, and therefore it is critically important to get the relationships right in order to develop trust and commitment that will see the campaign through to a successful conclusion.

Managing the client–agency relationship

Strong relationships between clients (advertisers) and their agencies can provide the platform for effective advertising. A survey of clients and agencies focused on those issues that were causing problems in achieving this desired state (Rauyruen and Miller, 2007; Morgan and Hunt, 1994).

Many clients demanded that agencies become more involved in their business, with comments like 'they need to spend more time understanding our challenges and goals' and 'they need to take more notice of the client's view with regard to creative work'. Clearly, clients were looking for agencies to spend more time and attention on understanding their business objectives before beginning the creative process (Curtis, 2002a and b).

The importance of the early stages of the advertising development process was also emphasized by agencies. Some complained about having to deal with junior people at the briefing stage who had not been trained to write a clear brief. This was critical, because unless clients get the briefing stage right, things will inevitably go wrong further down the line. This problem was connected to the lack of accessibility of senior marketing staff because they have too much other work to do. This means that briefing is left in the hands of junior staff, who have the power to say 'no' but not 'yes'. This can be very frustrating for agencies. One agency complained about not enough 'ear time' with a senior member of his client's marketing team: 'he is too busy and there is too big an experience gap between him and his team'. Two further consequences of this were insufficient access to business objectives and strategy and an inability to provide constructive feedback on their proposals.

One issue that can spoil client–agency relationships is client conflict. This occurs when an advertising agency wins a new account from a rival to an existing client, or when an agency is taken over by an agency that holds the account of a rival. Both of these scenarios have happened to Procter & Gamble. Media planning agency Zenith Optimedia won the L'Oreal account, causing potential client conflict with its existing Procter & Gamble account. Procter & Gamble was also concerned when its advertising agency Grey Global was acquired by the WPP Group, which counts arch-rival Unilever among its client base. Such situations can end relationships or, as was the case with WPP, the client's fears may be assuaged if it is satisfied that separate agency networks will be working for the two clients (Singh, 2005).

Research into relationships with web and internet agencies indicates that firms will be more successful if they build long-term, mutually supportive relationships with their customers. However, to work together, both parties rely on making agreements that are dependent on high levels of trust and commitment. Furthermore, the need for understanding how to build successful relationships in highly complex and challenging online trading environments is not only important but critical for the success of digital campaigns (Vize et al., 2011).

Three key factors are critical in managing client relationships. First, the agency should be client-centric. This means understanding the client's market and business, and how both are changing. There can be a tendency for such an understanding to dwindle over time. To combat this, agencies should invite clients to talk about their business. Second, agencies should not neglect personal contact. With digital communication the easy option, it can be tempting to communicate remotely. However, face-to-face contact is critical as it is difficult to build and maintain a business relationship purely through email. Finally, the strength of the relationship needs to be checked regularly. Assuming that everything is fine because nobody has complained is a dangerous path to follow.

Agency selection

As with buying any product, agency selection begins by defining requirements, which can vary considerably depending on whether the advertising is for a discount grocery store, a new car or a luxury designer fashion brand, for example. While grocery retailer Lidl might communicate clear messages about pricing, BMW and Gucci are brands that give priority to the creative talents of prospective agencies.

Consequently, agency selection involves: defining advertising objectives and creative message requirements to brief potential agencies; creating a list of possible agencies; arranging for agencies to pitch their creative ideas; analysing each agency's offer; and selecting and contracting the preferred agency.

Once an agency has been selected and the contract agreed, it is important to brief the agency carefully, giving as much relevant information about the company that is developing the campaign as possible: for example, product history in terms of past sales, market share and previous campaigns; product features and benefits;

target audiences—who they are, their motives and choice criteria. In addition, communication objectives and the timetable for delivery and launch of the campaign should be clearly stated and agreed, and the budget set, as this might affect choice of media.

Product Placement

Product placement is the deliberate placing of products and/or their logos in films, television programmes, songs and video games, usually in return for money, and is sometimes referred to as 'embedded marketing'. This form of marketing is lucrative, and placement opportunities often command high prices from brand owners. For example, Heineken struck a 15-year multi-picture deal for product placement in the James Bond films. It paid a reported $45 million for its products to appear in *Skyfall*, which included a 30-second commercial and an online game featuring Daniel Craig in the Bond role (Nathanson, 2013). According to research, placements can be particularly effective if the respective brand is also advertised during the television show or film.

Product placement has been used in the USA for some time. However, in Europe there have been restrictions preventing product placement until now, when the rules are being gradually relaxed. Since 2011, paid-for product placement has been allowed in UK television programmes. The new rules for product placement are more stringent than in the USA. Product placement of tobacco, alcohol, gambling, medicines, baby milk and any foods that are high in fat, salt or sugar is not permitted. Furthermore, the product is not allowed to distort the editorial content or affect its independence. On the plus side, broadcasters are now able to access the revenue generated by product placement. In the future, many interesting relationships/issues may develop between advertisers and programme makers (Williams, 2011).

Product placement has grown significantly in recent years, for the following reasons: media fragmentation means it is increasingly hard to reach mass markets; the brand can benefit from the positive associations it gains from being in a film or television show; many consumers do not realize that the brand has been product-placed; repetition of the film or television show means that the brand is seen again and again; careful choice of film or television show means that certain segments can be targeted; and promotional and merchandising opportunities can be generated on the show's website. For example, the popular television series *Coronation Street* now has its own Costa Coffee Shop and Co-op in its fictional town, Weatherfield. This is the first peak-time viewing serial to include such extensive brand placement. When aired, the shows must display a 'P' logo to indicate the placements (Khomami, 2018).

Technological developments in the online gaming sector allow for different products to be placed in games at different times of the day or in different geographic locations, expanding the marketing possibilities available to companies. For example, Blizzard Entertainment, a video game developer, looked to recruit a specialist who can work with consumer brands, so that real products can be licensed and then appear in Blizzard's next generation of games (Dumitrescu, 2012).

While product placement is becoming very popular, it is important to remember that there are risks involved. If the film or television show fails to take off, it can tarnish the image of the brand and reduce its potential exposure. Even when a film is highly successful, there may still be issues that prevent brands from wanting to be involved. For example, Danny Boyle, when making his film *Slumdog Millionaire*, was not allowed to use Mercedes-Benz products in a slum setting (Wikipedia, 2012), and all images of the brand had to be removed from the film.

Furthermore, audiences can become annoyed by blatant product placement, damaging the brand image, and brand owners may not have complete control over how their brand is portrayed. Also, the popularity of product placement is fast giving rise to claims that it constitutes deceptive advertising. Lobby groups in the USA claim that one of the difficulties with product placement is that it cannot be controlled by the consumer in the way that traditional advertising breaks can, through 'zapping' (switching to another channel), and they want it restricted.

However, Coker and Altobello (2018) found that the social setting in which product placements are viewed can have a significant influence on effectiveness and recall. For instance, if product placement is viewed when a person is accompanied by friend(s) rather than viewing alone, the shared experience strengthens recall. As more viewing is being carried out through subscription services like Amazon Prime and Netflix, where there is limited opportunity for traditional adverts to be viewed, the importance of product placement is likely to increase and it may even become the 'primary way consumers see, hear, and learn about brands' (Coker and Altobello, 2018). This trend also affects television viewership in a slightly different way, as people skip through advertisements using live pause and recording features on the latest television sets.

Product placement is subject to the same kinds of analysis as all the other promotional techniques described in this chapter. For example, in the James Bond film *Die Another Day*, the Ford Motor Company had three of its car brands 'starring' in the film: an Aston Martin Vanquish, a Thunderbird and a Jaguar XKR. Movie-goers were interviewed both before and after seeing the film to see if their opinions of the brands had changed. In addition, the product placement was part of an integrated campaign including PR and advertising, which ensured that even people who had not seen the film were aware of Ford's association with it. During the film's peak viewing periods in the USA and UK, Ford's research found that the number of times its name appeared in the media increased by 34 per cent and that Ford corporate messages appeared in 29 per cent of the Bond-related coverage (*Campaign*, 2002; Dowdy, 2003; Tomkins, 2003; Armstrong, 2005; Silverman, 2005).

Public Relations and Sponsorship

In a 365-day, 24/7 interconnected global society, every move a company makes can be shared. Intended and unintended messages about a product, a brand or a company can appear online. This means corporate reputation is constantly in the spotlight, and this change in emphasis has meant a rise in the importance of PR (Roper and Fill, 2012). The role of digital media in PR is discussed in Chapter 16.

A company is dependent on many groups if it is to be successful. The marketing concept focuses on customers and distributors, but the needs and interests of other groups such as employees, shareholders, the local community, the media, government and pressure groups are also important. **Public relations (PR)** is concerned with all of these groups and may be defined as:

> '. . . the management of communications and relationships to establish goodwill and mutual understanding between an organization and its public'.

PR is therefore wider ranging than marketing, which focuses on markets, distribution channels and customers. By communicating to other groups ('publics'), PR creates an environment in which it is easier to conduct marketing (White, 1991). These publics are shown in Figure 14.5.

FIGURE 14.5
An organization and its publics

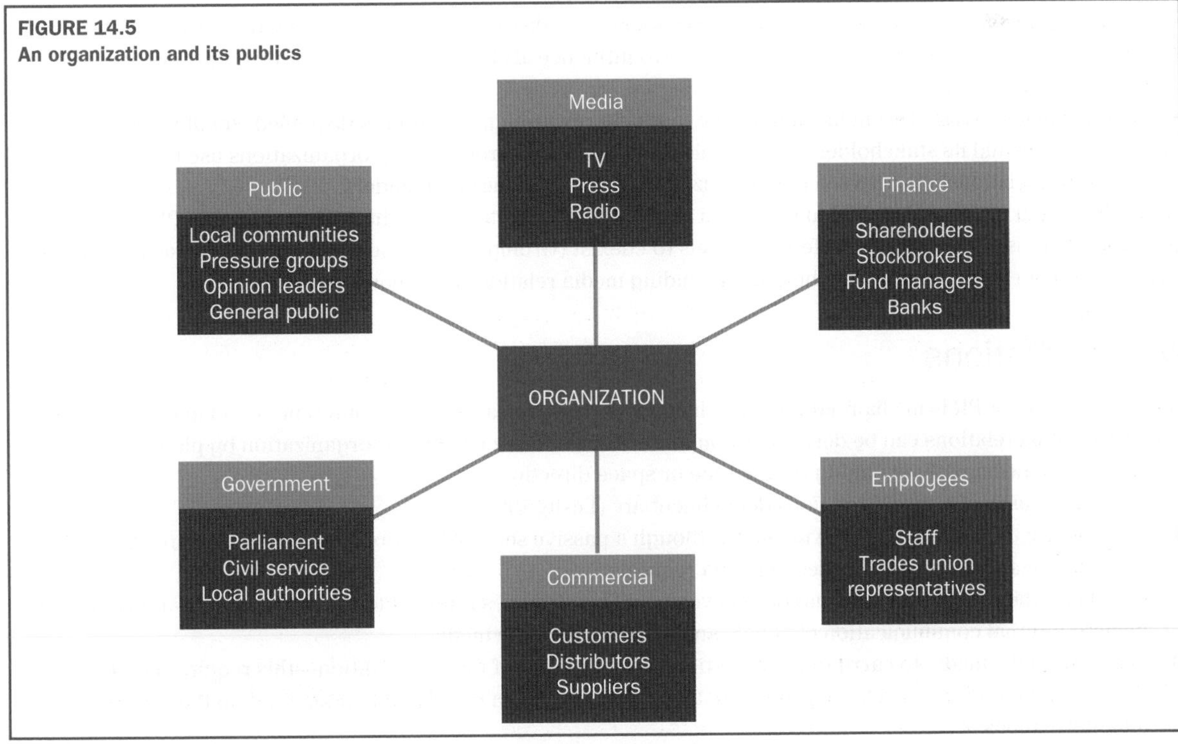

PR activities include media relations, lobbying, corporate advertising and sponsorship (Fill, 2009: 256–72). PR can accomplish many objectives, as outlined below (Lesly, 1998).

- *Prestige and reputation*: it can foster prestige and reputation, which can help companies to sell products, attract and keep good employees, and promote favourable community and government relations.
- *Promotion of products*: the desire to buy a product can be helped by the unobtrusive things that people read and see online, in the press, and on radio and television. Awareness of and interest in products and companies can be generated.
- *Dealing with issues and opportunities*: the ability to handle social and environmental issues to the mutual benefit of all parties involved.
- *Goodwill of customers*: ensuring that customers are presented with useful information, are treated well and have their complaints dealt with fairly and speedily.
- *Goodwill of employees*: promoting the sense of identification and satisfaction of employees with their company. Activities such as internal newsletters, recreation activities and awards for service and achievement can be used.
- *Overcoming misconceptions*: managing misconceptions about a company so that unfounded opinions do not damage its operations.
- *Goodwill of suppliers and distributors*: building a reputation as a good customer (for suppliers) and a reliable supplier (for distributors).
- *Goodwill of government*: influencing the opinions of public officials and politicians so that they think the company operates in the public interest.
- *Dealing with unfavourable press coverage*: responding quickly, accurately and effectively to negative publicity such as an oil spill or an air disaster.
- *Attracting and keeping good employees*: creating and maintaining respectability in the eyes of the public so that the best personnel are attracted to work for the company.

PR can take two basic models. In the first model, communication messages flow one way—for example, a company's press agent produces favourable information in the form of press releases and media events. A variation of this approach is to disseminate information that presents a more balanced view (including positive and negative information). This is sometimes referred to as a *public information model* (Fill, 2009: 55).

The second model focuses on two-way communications, so feedback from target audiences is paramount. There are a further two derivatives of this model:

- *Two-way asymmetric*. In this model, power is not equally distributed between the stakeholders and the organization. The purpose of this form of PR is to influence attitudes and behaviour through persuasion (Fill, 2009: 256).
- *Two-way symmetric*. This model aims to be mutually rewarding, as power is dispersed equally between the organization and its stakeholders. Communication flow is reciprocal. Some organizations use PR as a means of mediating relationships between the organization and its various stakeholders.

In the highly connected multichannel media world it is difficult to isolate the various forms of PR, and therefore there is a tendency for different models to coexist (Grunig, 1997). The remainder of this section on PR examines different methods and techniques, including media relations and sponsorship.

Media relations

A major element of PR is media relations, which includes press releases, press conferences and interviews, and publicity. Media relations can be defined as communication about a product or organization by placing news about it in the media without paying for the time or space directly.

Three key tasks of a media relations department are (Lesly, 1998):

1. Responding to requests from the media—although a passive service function, it requires well-organized information and prompt responses to media requests
2. Supplying the media with information on events and occurrences relevant to the organization—this requires general internal communication channels and knowledge of the media
3. Stimulating the media to carry the information and viewpoint of the organization—this requires creative development of ideas, developing close relationships with media people and understanding their needs and motivations.

Characteristics of media relations

Information dissemination may be through the web, news releases, news conferences, interviews, feature articles, photo calls and public speaking (at conferences and seminars, for example). No matter which method is used to carry the information, media relations has five important characteristics.

1 *The message has high credibility*: the message has higher credibility than advertising, because it appears to the reader to have been written independently (by a media person) rather than by an advertiser.
2 *No direct media costs*: since space or time in the media is not bought, there is no direct media cost. However, this is not to say that it is cost-free. Someone must write the news release, take part in the interview or organize the news conference. This may be organized internally, by a press officer or media relations department, or externally, by a PR agency.
3 *Loss of control of publication*: unlike advertising, there is no guarantee that the news item will be published. This decision is taken out of the control of the organization and into the hands of an editor. A key factor in this decision is whether the item is judged to be newsworthy. Table 14.2 lists several potentially newsworthy topics.
4 *Loss of control of content*: there is no way of ensuring that the viewpoint expressed by the news supplier is reflected in the published article. For example, a news release might point to an increase in capital expenditure to deal with pollution, but this might be used negatively (e.g. saying the increase is inadequate).
5 *Loss of control of timing*: an advertising campaign can be coordinated to achieve maximum impact. The timing of the publication of news items, however, cannot be controlled. For example, a news item publicizing a forthcoming conference to encourage attendance could appear in a publication after the event has taken place or too late to have any practical effect on attendance.

TABLE 14.2 Potentially newsworthy topics

Being or doing something first
Marketing issues
New products
Innovative research
Large orders/export contracts
Changes to the marketing mix, e.g. price
Rebranding
Production issues
Productivity achievements
Employment changes
Capital investments
Financial issues
Financial statements
Acquisitions
Sales/profit achievements
Personal issues
Training awards
Winners of company contests
Promotions/new appointments
Success stories
Visits by famous people
General issues
Conferences/seminars/exhibitions
Anniversaries of significant events

Sponsorship

Sponsorship has been defined by Sleight as (Sleight, 1989):

> '. . . a business relationship between a provider of funds, resources or services and an individual, event or organization which offers in return some rights and association that may be used for commercial advantage'.

Potential sponsors have a wide range of entities and activities from which to choose, including sports, arts, community activities, teams, tournaments, individual personalities or events, competitions, fairs and shows. Sports sponsorship is by far the most popular sponsorship medium, as it can offer high visibility through extensive television press coverage, the ability to attract a broad cross-section of the community and to service specific niches, and the capacity to break down cultural barriers (Bennett, 1999).

Sponsorship can achieve several communicational objectives, but there are also risks (Barrand, 2005). For example, the highly publicized arrests of senior officials and allegations of financial corruption at FIFA have caused its major partners and sponsors—for example, Visa, Coca-Cola, Kia and Adidas—to consider withdrawing (Wilson, 2015). Companies should be clear about their reasons for spending money on sponsorship. The four principal objectives of sponsorship are to gain publicity, create entertainment opportunities, improve community relations and create promotional opportunities.

Gaining publicity

Sponsorship provides ample opportunities to create publicity in the news media. Worldwide events such as major golf, football and tennis tournaments supply the platform for global media coverage. Sponsorship of such events can provide brand exposure to millions of people. Some events, such as athletics championships, have mass audience appeal, while others, such as golf, have a more upmarket profile. Rolex supports more than 150 sporting events around the world, exposing the brand name to its more upmarket customer segment. Budweiser's sponsorship of the FA Cup has given it exposure to the young male demographic (Reynolds and Charles, 2011). Many companies sponsor large events like the Olympic Games: for example, Tokyo 2020 sponsors include Shimizu Corporation (official sponsor), Coca Cola, AOKI Holdings Inc, and Proctor & Gamble.

The publicity opportunities of sponsorship can produce major *awareness* shifts. For example, Etihad Airways, LavAzza, Maybelline and Toni&Guy were among the sponsors of London Fashion Week in 2018. Together with the Department for International Trade, the aim is to promote the prominent role of the London fashion industry globally. Brands carefully select organizations to sponsor that align with their values, such as WWF (environment), European Red Cross (social responsibility) and the Canon Foundation (education).

Sponsorship can also be used to position brands in the marketplace. See Mini Case 14.1

MINI CASE 14.1
What do Sharp Electronics, Vodafone and Chevrolet have in Common?

Manchester United Football Club (MUFC) has a long history of Premiership football and is reported to be among the top-earning clubs in the world, with an income of £590 million. During the last decade, it has become a brand that has global recognition. This means that MUFC is potentially an attractive sponsorship proposition for companies that are prepared to offer financial investment, for example in the club's ground at Old Trafford in Manchester or the team's football kit. Sharp Electronics was the first company to invest around £0.5 million in the kit in 1982, a partnership which lasted 17 years. Vodafone replaced Sharp Electronics in 1999, making an investment of £36 million. In 2012, Chevrolet then put together a seven-year deal worth more than £362 million. The size of the investment has increased significantly, but why are companies prepared to invest such significant sums in MUFC?

First, MUFC eschews several values that could be transferred to sponsors, for example sporting achievements, winners, energetic, masculinity. These are values shared by current shirt sponsor Chevrolet—an American car brand looking for opportunities to build its global presence. MUFC is an interesting sponsorship partner: it is not a point of entry into the UK domestic market only, as the club also has strong international connections. The global fan base for MUFC is over 700 million, over half of whom live in emerging markets in China and other parts of Asia, making it one of the world's most popular football clubs.

When the partnership with shirt sponsors Chevrolet was announced in 2012, over 1 billion page impressions were downloaded from the car manufacturer's website within two weeks. This news and subsequent online activity exceeded previous (similar scale) marketing campaigns by Chevrolet in the USA Super Bowl, making this a valuable communication and brand awareness campaign. The MUFC management team realize the importance to the club's global presence of collaborative communications with its supporting partner and engage in many entertainment activities to ensure that the club remains at the forefront of the minds of its fans: for example, during the summer pre-season when there are no domestic league matches, the team goes on extensive tours to help develop the brand globally. MUFC toured China in 2016, despite the many challenges surrounding the physical demands players faced due to the climate and availability of training facilities. In 2018, the team toured the USA.

Other partners with MUFC have included: Aon (principal partner), DHL (logistics partner), Aeroflot (carrier), Bulova (timekeeping partner) and Adidas (official supplier of the team's football kit).

Questions:

1. Explain what should be considered when selecting an event to sponsor.
2. Identify and discuss the potential challenges for Chevrolet and other partners when sponsoring Manchester United Football Club.
3. Select a leading European football team, identify its main sponsors and then suggest the benefits of the partnership for both sponsor and team.

Source: Based on: manutd.com, about (2018); Flanagan (2015); Gibson (2015); O'Leary (2014); Telegraph Sport (2012); Ogden (2015)

Creating entertainment opportunities

A major objective of much sponsorship is to create entertainment opportunities for customers and the trade. Sponsorship of music, the performing arts and sports events can be particularly effective. For example, Rolex supports classical concerts and the arts (e.g. the Vienna Philharmonic Orchestra's New Year's Concert; the Royal Opera House in London). Waitrose sponsored the England Cricket team. Often sports personalities are invited to join the sponsor's guests. Attendance at sponsored events can also be used to reward successful employees.

Figure 14.6 shows some broad values conferred on the sponsor from five sponsorship categories. These are composite views. Values may depend on a specific activity or event—for example, football versus tennis.

Improving community relations

Sponsorship of schools—for example, by providing low-cost personal computers—and supporting community programmes can foster a socially responsible, caring reputation for a company. For example, Lloyds Bank's Social Entrepreneurs programme sponsors young adults in community and environmental projects.

For example, Levi's became an official sponsor of Liverpool FC. Both brands are focusing on developing a long-term partnership which can give added value for football fans through music and art. The Levi's music project provides local young adults with the opportunity to develop creative talents in the arts and aims to enhance the community and people's lifestyles (Liverpool FC, 2018).

Creating promotional opportunities

Sponsored events provide an ideal opportunity to promote company brands. Sweatshirts, bags, pens, etc. carrying the company logo and the name of the event can be sold to a captive audience. Where the brand can be consumed during the event (e.g. Nestlé at the Cannes Film Festival), this provides an opportunity for customers to sample the brand.

Sponsorship can also improve the effectiveness of other promotional vehicles. For example, responses to direct marketing materials issued by the Visa credit card organization and featuring its sponsorship of the Olympic Games were 17 per cent higher than responses from a control group to which the sponsorship images were not transmitted (Crowley, 1991).

Expenditure on sponsorship

Six factors account for the growth of sponsorship.

1 Restrictive government policies on tobacco and alcohol advertising
2 Escalating costs of media advertising
3 Increased leisure activities and sporting events
4 The proven record of sponsorship
5 Greater media coverage of sponsored events
6 The reduced efficiencies of traditional media advertising, for example as a result of people being exposed to 'clutter' (huge volumes of advertising messages) and as a result of people 'zapping' between television programmes during advertising breaks.

Although most money is spent on **event sponsorship**, such as sports or arts events, of increasing importance is **broadcast sponsorship**, where a television or radio programme is the focus. An example of event sponsorship is the sponsorship of music designed to target the youth market, as Figure 14.6 illustrates.

FIGURE 14.6
Values transferred from sponsorship categories

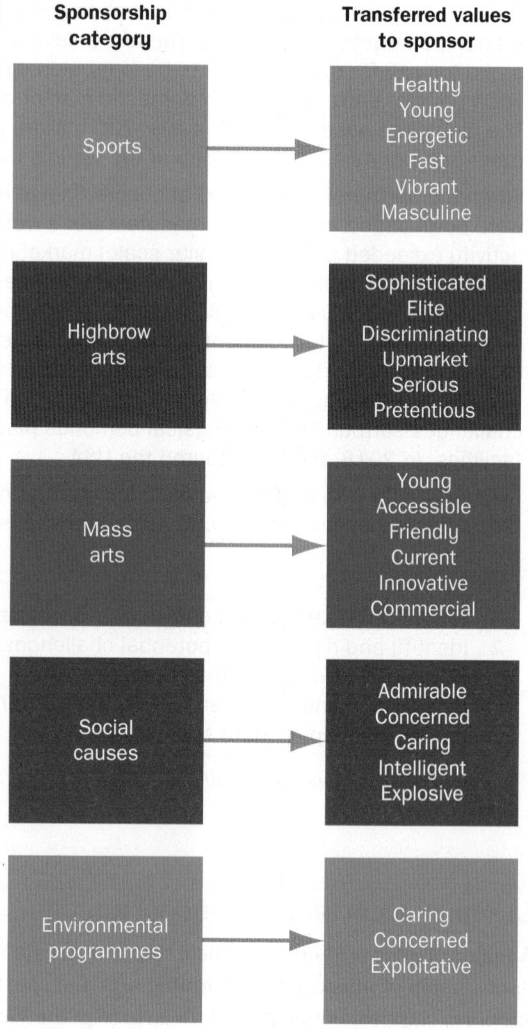

Sponsorship category	Transferred values to sponsor
Sports	Healthy Young Energetic Fast Vibrant Masculine
Highbrow arts	Sophisticated Elite Discriminating Upmarket Serious Pretentious
Mass arts	Young Accessible Friendly Current Innovative Commercial
Social causes	Admirable Concerned Caring Intelligent Explosive
Environmental programmes	Caring Concerned Exploitative

Source: based on Meenaghan and Shipley (1999).

Broadcast sponsorship of programmes can extend into the sharing of production costs. This is attractive to broadcasters, who otherwise face increasing costs of programming, and sponsors, who gain more influence in negotiations with broadcasters. Volvo signed up for a two-year deal as sponsor for a whole channel: Sky Atlantic. In this exclusive deal, no other brand can sponsor content on the channel. Casillero del Diablo, a wine producer, entered a major sponsorship deal with Sky movies. There were key benefits for both companies: the wine producer had the opportunity to reach an estimated 44 million individuals during the 12-month campaign and, in return, promoted Sky on over 4 million bottles of wine using promotional offers of free Sky subscriptions and competitions (The UK Sponsorship Database, 2015). Another growth area is that of **team sponsorship**, such as the sponsorship of a football, cricket or motor racing team. For example, Emirates, Europcar and Citroen are among the sponsors of Arsenal Football Club.

Selection and evaluation of an event or programme to sponsor

Selection of an event or programme to sponsor should be undertaken by answering a series of questions.

- *Communications objectives*: What are we trying to achieve? Are we looking for awareness or image, improvement in community relations or entertainment opportunities? Does the personality of the event match the desired brand image?
- *Target market*: Who are we trying to reach? Is it the trade or final customers? How does the profile of our customer base match the likely audience of the sponsored event or programme?
- *Risk*: What are the associated risks? What are the chances that the event or programme might attract adverse publicity (e.g. football hooliganism tainting the image of the sport and, by implication, the sponsor)? To what extent would termination of the sponsorship contract attract bad publicity (e.g. mean the closing of a theatre)?
- *Promotional opportunities*: What are the potential sales promotion and publicity opportunities?

- *Past record*: If the event or programme h
previous sponsor withdraw?
- *Cost*: Does the sponsorship opportunit

The evaluation process should lead t
Understanding *sponsorship objectives* i
deals, evaluation is likely to be more f
sightings using a specialist monitorin

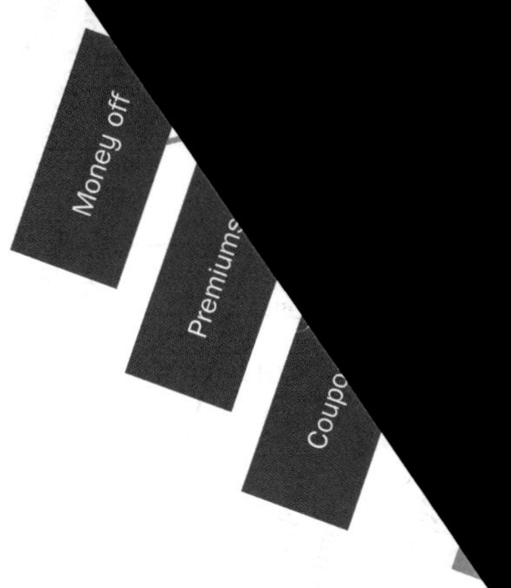

Sales Promotion

Sales promotions are incentiv
Examples include money off a
(trade promotions).

Sales promotions have b
market erosion caused by n
their promotional budgets

The effects of

Sales promotions are used as a short
influence consumers' (and firms') purchasing
in competitive markets and act as an incentive to mou

The sales promotion boosts sales during the promotion per
important tool for matching supply and demand (Demirag, Keskinocak
in a fall in sales after the campaign, as customers stock up on the product at the
sales effect of the promotion could be positive, neutral or negative. Buil, De Chernatony
that the effect of sales promotions on brand equity varies depending on the type of promotion. Mo
(price discounts) can negatively affect perception of quality, whereas gifts can have a positive effect and
brand associations. Marketing managers should carefully consider when to give price incentives, as extended use is likely to damage the perceived quality of a brand in the longer term. See Figure 14.7 for different types of sales promotion.

Major sales promotion types

Sales promotions can be directed at the consumer or the trade. Major consumer sales promotion types are money off, bonus packs, premiums, free samples, coupons, prize promotions and loyalty cards. A sizeable proportion of sales promotions are directed at the trade, including price incentives and discounts, free goods, competitions, allowances, promotional price support, and in-store display and promotional support.

Consumer promotions

The following sections examine the main types of *consumer promotions*.

Money off **Money-off promotions** provide direct value to the customer, and are therefore an unambiguous incentive to purchase. They have a proven track record of stimulating short-term sales increases and encouraging trial (Wilson, 2005). However, price reductions can easily be matched by the competition and if used frequently can devalue brand image. Consumer response may be 'If the brand is that good, why do they need to keep reducing the price?' A variant on the normal money-off promotion is the *value pack*. With value packs, the consumer pays a higher price for the larger pack, but the per-unit price (e.g. per gram or per tablet) is less.

Bonus packs These give *added value* by giving consumers extra quantity at no additional cost. **Bonus packs** are often used in the drinks, confectionery and detergent markets. For example, cans of lager may be sold based on '12.5 per cent extra free'. Because the price is not lowered, this form of promotion runs less risk of devaluing brand image. Extra value is given by raising quantity rather than cutting price. With some product groups, this encourages buyers to consume more. For example, a chocolate bar will be eaten or a can of lager drunk whether there is extra quantity or not.

FIGURE 14.7
Consumer and trade promotions

Money off
Premiums
Coupo

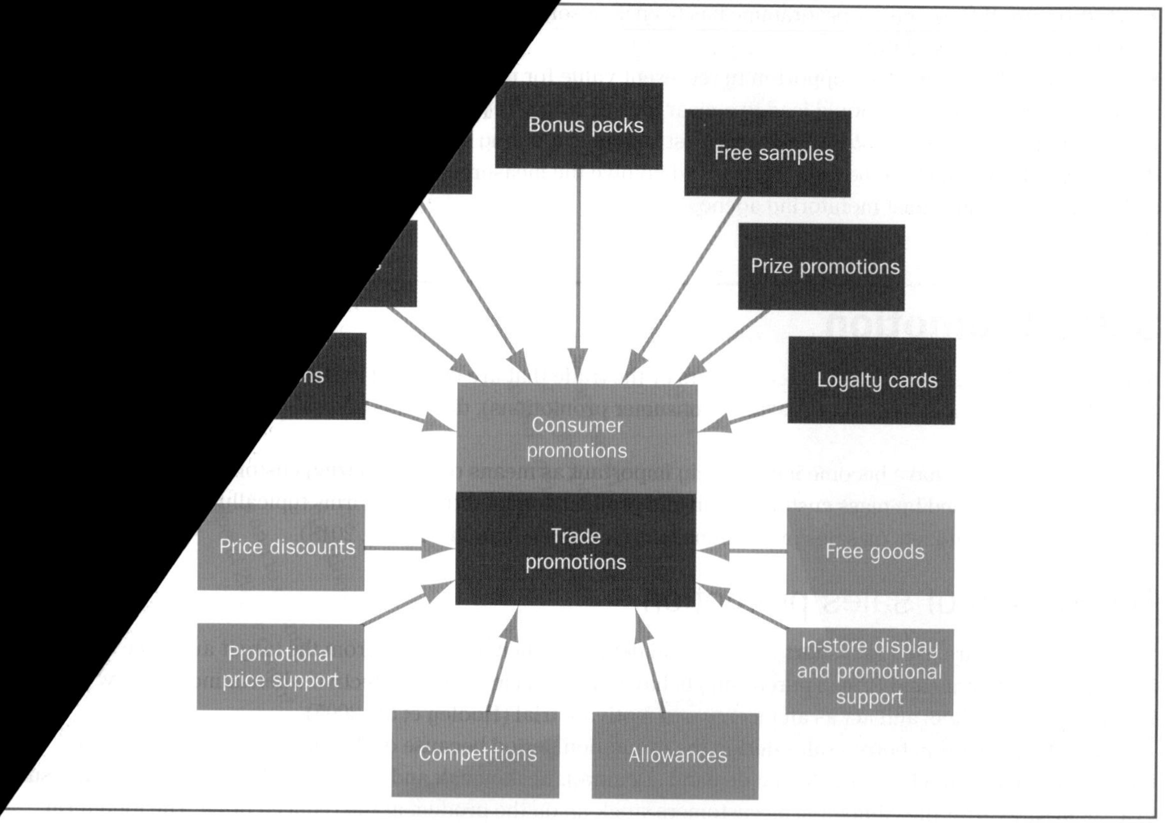

Bonus packs
Free samples
Prize promotions
Loyalty cards
Consumer promotions
Trade promotions
Price discounts
Free goods
Promotional price support
In-store display and promotional support
Competitions
Allowances

Premiums **Premiums** are any merchandise offered free or at low cost as an incentive to purchase a brand. There are four major forms: free in- or on-pack gifts, free in-the-mail offers, self-liquidating offers, and buy-one-get-one-free offers. For example, as a *free in- or on-pack gift*, Heinz offered free tomato seeds linked to its 'grow your own' campaign.

FMCG manufacturer brands use premiums to promote sales. This technique is widely used in the cosmetics industry as an incentive to purchase more high-priced items. Clinique, Estee Lauder and L'Occitane frequently have offers that provide free gifts when the customer spends over a certain amount of money.

Occasionally, the gift is a free sample of one brand that is banded to another brand (*branded pack offer*). The free sample may be a new variety or flavour that benefits by getting trial. In other cases, the brands are linked, as when Nestlé promoted its children's confectionary brands (Smarties, Fruit Pastilles and Milky Bar) with a 'Kids go Free' promotion for hundreds of family days out at local attractions. See Exhibit 14.6.

When two or more items are banded together, the promotion is called a *multibuy* and can involve a number of items of the same brand being offered together. Multibuys are a popular form of promotion. They are frequently used to protect market share by encouraging consumers to stock up on a particular brand when two or more items of the same brand are packaged together. However, unlike price reductions, they do not encourage trial, because consumers do not bulk-buy a brand they have not tried before. When multibuys take the form of two different brands,

EXHIBIT 14.6
'Kids go Free' promotion for family days out, by Nestlé and local entertainment and event venues

range trial can be generated. For example, a manufacturer of a branded coffee launching a new brand of tea could band the two brands together, and thus leverage the strength of the coffee brand to gain trial of the new tea brand (Killigran and Cook, 1999).

Free in-the-mail offers: this sort of promotion involves the collection of packet tops or labels, which are sent in the mail as proof of purchase to claim a free gift or money-off voucher: Kellogg's Fruit 'n Fibre has been promoted by such an offer.

Gifts can be quite valuable, because redemption rates can be low (less than 10 per cent redemption is not unusual). This is because of *slippage*: consumers collect labels with a view to mailing them but never collect the requisite number.

Self-liquidating offers: these are similar to free in-the-mail offers except that consumers are asked to pay to cover the costs of the merchandise plus administration and postage charges. The consumer benefits by getting the goods at below normal cost, because the manufacturer passes on the advantage of bulk buying and prices at cost. The manufacturer benefits by the self-funding nature of the promotion, although there is a danger of being left with surplus stocks of the merchandise.

Buy-one-get-one-free offers: sometimes known as a BOGOF: with this type of promotion, the consumer is, in effect, getting two items for the price of one. Wine is sometimes offered as a BOGOF promotion so that the consumer can buy two bottles of a particular brand for the price of one. The danger of running BOGOF promotions for heavily advertised brands is that they lose their premium positioning and are seen as just another brand available in bulk at discount prices (Ritson, 2005).

Free samples *Free samples* of a brand may be delivered to the home or given out in a store. The idea is that having tried the sample, a proportion of consumers will begin to buy it. For new brands or brand extensions (e.g. a new shampoo or fabric conditioner), this form of promotion is an effective if expensive way of gaining consumer trial. However, sampling may be ineffective if the brand has nothing extra to offer the consumer, but there may be other incentives a brand may add for free. For existing brands that have a low trial but high purchasing rate, sampling may be effective. As many of those who try the brand like it and buy it again, raising the trial rate through free samples could have a beneficial long-term effect.

Coupons Coupons can be delivered online or to the home, appear in magazines or newspapers, or appear on packs. *Home couponing*, after home sampling, is the best way to achieve trial for new brands (Davidson, 2003). *Magazine or newspaper couponing* is much cheaper than home delivery and can be used to stimulate trial, but redemption rates are much lower at around 5 per cent on average. The purpose of *on-pack couponing* is to encourage initial and repeat purchasing of the same brand or trial of a different brand. Redemption rate is high, averaging around 40 per cent (Cummins and Mullin, 2008). The coupon can offer a higher face value than the equivalent cost of a money-off pack, since the effect of the coupon is on both initial and repeat sales. However, a coupon is usually less effective in raising initial sales than money off is, because there is no immediate saving and its appeal is almost exclusively to existing consumers (Davidson, 2003).

Prize promotions There are three main types of *prize promotion*: competitions, draws and games. Unlike other promotions, the cost can be established in advance and does not depend on the number of participants.

Competitions require participants to exercise a certain degree of skill and judgement. For example, a competition to win free cinema seats might require entrants to name five films based upon stills from each. Entry is usually dependent on at least one purchase. Compared with premiums and money off, competitions offer a less immediate incentive to buy, and one that requires time and effort on the part of entrants. However, competitions can attract attention and interest in a brand.

Draws make no demands on skill or judgement: the result depends on chance. For example, a supermarket may run an out-of-the-hat draw in which customers fill in their name and address on an entry card and on a certain day a draw is made. Another example of a draw is when direct mail recipients are asked to return a card on which there is a set of numbers. This is then compared against a set of winning numbers.

An example of a *game promotion* is where a newspaper encloses a series of bingo cards and customers are told that, over a period of time, sets of bingo numbers will be published. If these numbers form a line or full house on a bingo card, a prize is won. Such a game encourages repeat purchases of the newspaper.

The national laws governing sales promotions in Europe vary tremendously, and local legal advice should be taken before implementing a sales promotion. The UK, Ireland, Spain, Portugal, Greece, Russia and the Czech Republic have relaxed laws about what can be done. Germany, Luxembourg, Austria, Norway, Switzerland and Sweden are much more restrictive. For example, in Sweden, free mail-ins, free draws and money-off-next-purchase promotions are not allowed, and in Norway self-liquidating offers, free draws, money-off vouchers and money-off-next-purchase, are not allowed (PromoWatch, 2012).

Trade promotions

We will now look at *trade promotions*.

Price discounts The trade may be offered (or may demand) *discounts* in return for purchase. The concentration of buying into fewer trade outlets has placed increasing power with these organizations. This power is often translated into discounts from manufacturers. The discount may be part of a joint promotion, whereby the retailer agrees to devote extra shelf space, buy larger quantities, engage in a joint competition and/or allow in-store demonstrations. Volume discounts are given to retailers that hit sales targets (Quilter, 2005).

Free goods An alternative to a price discount is to offer more merchandise at the same price. For example, the *baker's dozen* technique involves offering 13 items (or cases) for the price of 12.

Competitions A competition may involve a manufacturer offering financial inducements or prizes to distributors' salesforces in return for them achieving sales targets for the manufacturer's products. Alternatively, a prize may be given to the salesforce with the best sales figures.

Allowances A manufacturer may offer an *allowance* (a sum of money) in return for retailers providing promotional facilities in store (*display allowance*). For example, an allowance would be needed to persuade a supermarket to display cards on its shelves indicating that a brand was being sold at a special low price. An *advertising allowance* would be paid by a manufacturer to a retailer for featuring its brands in the retailer's advertising. *Listing allowances* are paid by the manufacturer to have a brand stocked.

Promotional price support Promotional price support occurs when the manufacturer/supplier of particular goods or services works with the retailer to give money-off deals. For example, HSBC Bank had an introductory offer for its customers, offering a £50 wine voucher to spend with Laithwaites Wine. This technique is often used by manufacturers and retailers.

In-store display and promotional support Another form of trade promotion is when the manufacturer pays for in-store displays and promotions. For example, a supplier could pay for a gondola-end display or a 10-second advertisement on the retailer's in-store television network (Quilter, 2005).

Sales promotion objectives

The most basic objective of any sales promotion is to provide extra value that encourages purchase. When targeted at consumers, the intention is to stimulate **consumer pull**; when the trade is targeted, **distribution push** is the objective. We will now look at specific sales promotion objectives.

Fast sales boost

Sales promotions deliver short-term sales increases, which may be required for a number of reasons: needing to reduce inventories or meet budgets prior to the end of the financial year, moving old stocks, or increasing stockholding by distributors in advance of the launch of a competitor's product (Cummins and Mullin, 2008). Promotions that give large immediate benefits, such as money off or bonus packs, have bigger effects on sales volume than more distant promotions such as competitions or self-liquidators. However, whatever the objective for the sales promotion, it should not be used as a means of patching up more fundamental inadequacies such as inferior product performance or poor positioning.

A classic sales promotion that went seriously wrong was Hoover's attempt to boost sales of its washing machines, vacuum cleaners, refrigerators and tumble driers by offering two free USA flight tickets for every Hoover product purchased over £100. The company was the target of much bad publicity as buyers discovered that the offer was wreathed in difficult conditions (found in the promotion's small print) and complained bitterly to Hoover and the media. In an attempt to limit the damage done to its reputation, the company announced that it would honour its offer to its customers, at an estimated cost of £20 million.

Encourage trial

Sales promotions can be highly successful by encouraging trial. If new buyers like the brand, the long-term effect of the promotion may be positive. Home sampling and home couponing are particularly effective methods of inducing trial. Promotions that simply give more product (e.g. bonus packs) are likely to be less successful, since consumers will not place much value on the extra quantity until they have decided that they like the product.

Encourage repeat purchase

Certain promotions, by their nature, encourage repeat purchase of a brand over a period of time. Any offer that requires the collection of packet tops or labels (e.g. free mail-ins and promotions such as bingo games) is attempting to raise repeat purchases during the promotional period. Loyalty cards are designed to offer consumers an incentive to repeat purchase at a store.

Stimulate purchase of larger or more expensive packs

Promotions that are specifically linked to larger pack sizes may persuade consumers to switch from the less economical smaller packs. However, there has been a trend within the FMCG market for more concentrated products that come in smaller packages and are more expensive, but last longer and give better value for money (e.g. Ecover, 40 washes; Fairy liquid concentrated lasts 50 per cent longer). Even own-label value brands offer concentrated versions of their products (Tesco Value Bio Concentrated Liquid Wash).

Gain distribution and shelf space

Trade promotions are designed to gain distribution and shelf space. These are major promotional objectives, since there is a strong relationship between sales and these two factors. Discounts, free gifts and joint promotions are methods used to encourage distributors to stock brands. Also, consumer promotions that provide sizeable extra value may persuade distributors to stock products or give extra shelf space to them.

Traditionally, sales promotions have been associated with achieving objectives for supermarket brands. However, their presence has spread to other sectors such as financial services, cars, IT and telecoms. There is a trend towards integrated media campaigns. For example, the Royal Mail postal service in the UK launched a major direct mail campaign called 'Mail Men' in a bid to tempt advertisers away from digital channels (Ghosh, 2015).

Evaluating sales promotion

There are two types of research that can be used to evaluate sales promotions: *pre-testing research* is used to select, from a number of alternative promotional concepts, the most effective in achieving objectives; *post-testing research* is carried out to assess whether promotional objectives have been achieved.

Ethical Issues in Advertising

Advertising has an influence on society and subsequent behaviours. There are many controversial issues.

Advertising to children

Critics argue that children are especially susceptible to persuasion and therefore need special protection from advertising. Others claim that children are remarkably streetwise and can look after themselves. However, many European countries have regulations that control advertising to children. For example, in Germany, advertising specific types of toys is banned, and, in the UK, alcohol advertising is controlled (Schlegelmilch, 1998). In Sweden, advertising to under-12s on terrestrial television stations is banned, and, in Belgium and Australia, advertising within children's programmes is limited.

The UK has a code of practice to control advertisements aimed at children, which is designed to make sure that advertisers avoid the misleading presentation of product information. For example, when advertising toys, accurate information about their size, price and operation should be included (Oates, Blades and Gunter, 2003). Pepsi and McDonald's have also introduced voluntary restrictions on their advertising to children in response to rising levels of obesity in the USA and western Europe (Ward and Grant, 2005).

Misleading advertising

This takes the form of exaggerated claims and concealed facts. For example, it would be unethical to claim that a car achieved 50 miles to the gallon when it was only 30 miles. Nevertheless, most countries accept a certain amount of *puffery*, recognizing that consumers are intelligent and interpret the claims in such a way that they are not deceptive. In the UK, the advertising slogan 'Carlsberg: probably the best lager in the world' is acceptable because of this. However, in Europe, advertisers should be aware that a European directive on misleading advertising states that the burden of proof lies with the advertiser should the claims be challenged.

Many industrialized countries have their own codes of practice that protect the consumer from deceptive advertising. For example, in the UK, the Advertising Standards Authority (ASA) administers the British Code of Advertising Practice. It insists that advertising should be 'legal, decent, honest and truthful'. This means that advertisers need to be very careful about the claims they make.

For example, supermarket retailer Waitrose claimed in a television and cinema advert that 'Everyone who works for Waitrose owns Waitrose.' However, cleaning services are outsourced, so this precluded certain workers. The supermarket and the ASA agreed that the case could be closed if Waitrose amended the advert.

VIP Electronic cigarettes was accused of glamourizing e-cigarettes in its television adverts. This complaint was upheld, and as a result the adverts were banned (ASA, 2015). However, the industry has grown to be worth over £1 billion in the UK, and e-cigarette manufactures have been accused of developing products that might encourage children into nicotine addiction. Names like Tango Tipple, Lime Zest and Juicy Pineapple Chunks are likely to suggest a fruity drink to a child. E-cigarettes are now the most commonly consumed form of nicotine among children, and research has suggested that young adults who try e-cigarettes are four times more likely to start smoking regularly than those who try conventional cigarettes (Ungoed-Thomas and Neal, 2018).

Advertising's influence on society's values

Critics argue that advertising images have a profound effect on society. They claim that advertising promotes materialism and takes advantage of human frailties. Advertising is accused of stressing the importance of material possessions, such as the ownership of an expensive car or the latest consumer electronics. Critics argue that this promotes the wrong values in society.

The ASA takes very seriously any campaigns that might bring advertising into disrepute. For example, Paddy Power, an Irish bookmaker, launched a series of adverts offering incentives to bet on the outcome of the Oscar Pistorius murder trial. The ASA received 5,525 complaints, which were upheld, as it ruled that '*The ad caused serious offence by trivializing the issues surrounding a murder trial, the death of a woman and disability.*' The ASA also concluded that these adverts brought advertising into disrepute.

Review

1 The role of advertising in the promotional mix

- Advertising is any paid form of non-personal communication of ideas or products in the prime media, i.e. digital, television, the press, posters, cinema and radio.
- It possesses strengths and limitations and should be combined with other promotional tools to form an integrated marketing communications campaign.

2 How advertising works, strong and weak theories of advertising, the Elaboration Likelihood Model (ELM)

- The strong theory of advertising considers advertising to be a powerful influence on consumers, increasing knowledge, changing attitudes, and creating desire and conviction, and therefore persuading people to buy brands.
- The weak theory of advertising considers advertising to be a much less powerful influence on consumers. It suggests that advertising may arouse awareness and interest, nudge some consumers towards trial, and then provide some reassurance and reinforcement after the trial.
- The ELM explains how some consumers are highly engaged with a product purchase and then carefully consider information and linkages to their personal circumstances. Such highly engaged consumers are said to take the central route of elaboration, whereas consumers with fewer connections and less commitment are said to take the peripheral route. The route taken can provide insights for designing advertising campaigns.

3 **When to use adverting and advertising evaluation**

- The FCB matrix sets out options for when to use different types of advertising. Planning is based on the type of product, whether it elicits high or low involvement and the propensity of the consumer to think/or feel.
- Advertising decisions should not be taken in isolation but should be based on a clear understanding of campaign objective, message execution and media decisions.
- Execution: care should be taken to meet publication deadlines.
- Evaluation of advertising: three key questions are what, when and how to evaluate.

4 **How campaigns are organized, including advertising agency selection**

- An advertiser has four organizational options:
  1 Advertising can be developed directly in cooperation with the media.
  2 An in-house advertising department can be created.
  3 A full-service advertising agency can be used.
  4 A combination of in-house staff (or the full-service agency) can be used for some functions and a specialist agency (media or creative) for others.
- Agency selection should begin with a clear definition of requirements. A shortlist of agencies should be drawn up and each agency briefed on the product and campaign. Selection will take place after each has made a presentation to the client.

5 **The reasons for the growth in product placement and its risks**

- Product placement activity is growing because of its mass-market reach, ability to confer positive associations to brands, high credibility, message repetition, ability to avoid advertising bans, targeting capabilities, the opportunities it provides for new linked brands and promotions, and the ability to measure its impact on audiences.
- Its risks are that the film or television programme may fail, tarnishing brand image; there is the possibility that the placement may not get noticed or may cause annoyance; and there is also the reduction in control, compared with advertisements, over the way in which the brand will be portrayed in the film or television programme.

6 **The objectives and targets of public relations**

- The objectives of public relations (PR) are to foster prestige and reputation, promote products, deal with issues and opportunities, enhance the goodwill of customers and employees, correct misconceptions, improve the goodwill of suppliers, distributors and government, deal with unfavourable publicity, and attract and keep good employees.
- The targets of PR are the public, the media, the financial community, government, commerce (including customers) and employees.

7 **The key tasks and characteristics of media relations**

- Three key tasks are: responding to requests from the media; supplying the media with information on events relevant to the organization; stimulating the media to carry the information and the viewpoint of the organization.
- The characteristics of publicity are that the message has higher credibility than advertising, there are no direct media costs, and there is no control over what is published (content), whether the item will be published or when it will be published.

8 **The objectives and methods of sponsorship**

- The objectives of sponsorship are to gain publicity, create entertainment opportunities, foster favourable brand and company associations, improve community relations and create promotional opportunities.
- The two key methods of sponsorship are event sponsorship (such as a sports or arts event) and broadcast sponsorship (where a television or radio programme is sponsored).

9 **How to select and evaluate a potential sponsored event or programme**

- Selection should be based on asking what are we trying to achieve (communication objectives), who are we trying to reach (target market), what are the associated risks (e.g. adverse publicity), what are the potential promotional opportunities, what is the past record of sponsorship of the event or programme, and what are the costs.

- Evaluation should be based on measuring results in terms of sponsorship objectives (e.g. changes in awareness and attitudes). Formal evaluation involves measurement of media coverage and name mentions/sightings, using a specialist monitoring agency.

10 The growth in sales promotion

- The reasons for growth are increased impulse purchasing, the growing respectability of sales promotions, the rising costs of advertising and amount of advertising clutter, shortening time horizons for goal achievement, competitor activities and the fact that their sales impact is easier to measure than that of advertising.

11 The major sales promotion types

- Major consumer promotions are money off, bonus packs, premiums (free in- or on-pack gifts, free in-the-mail offers, self-liquidating offers and buy-one-get-one-free offers), free samples, coupons, prize promotions (competitions, draws and games) and loyalty cards; major trade promotions are price discounts, free goods, competitions, allowances, promotional price support, and in-store display and promotional support.

12 The objectives of sales promotion

- The objectives of sales promotion are to provide a fast sales boost, encourage trial, encourage repeat purchases, stimulate purchase of larger packs, and gain distribution and shelf space.

13 Ethical issues in mass marketing communication

- There are potential problems relating to misleading advertising, advertising's influence on society's values and advertising to children.
- There are potential problems relating to the use of trade inducements and the promotion of anti-social behaviour.

Key Terms

advertising any paid form of non-personal communication of ideas or products in the prime media, i.e. television, the press, posters, cinema and radio, the internet and direct marketing

advertising agency an organization that specializes in providing services such as media selection, creative work, production and campaign planning to clients

advertising message the use of words, symbols and illustrations to communicate to a target audience using prime media

bonus pack giving a customer extra quantity at no additional cost

broadcast sponsorship a form of sponsorship where a television or radio programme is the focus

consumer pull the targeting of consumers with communications (e.g. promotions) designed to create demand that will pull the product into the distribution chain

distribution push the targeting of channel intermediaries with communications (e.g. promotions) to push the product into the distribution chain

event sponsorship sponsorship of a sporting or other event

media vehicle the choice of the particular newspaper, magazine, television spot, poster site, etc.

money-off promotions sales promotions that discount the normal price

premiums any merchandise offered free or at low cost as an incentive to purchase

product placement the deliberate placing of products and/or their logos in movies and television, usually in return for money

public relations (PR) the management of communications and relationships to establish goodwill and mutual understanding between an organization and its public

sales promotions incentives to customers or the trade that are designed to stimulate purchase

sponsorship a business relationship between a provider of funds, resources or services and an individual, event or organization that offers, in return, some rights and association that may be used for commercial advantage

strong theory of advertising the notion that advertising can change people's attitudes sufficiently to persuade those who have not previously bought a brand to buy it; desire and conviction precede purchase

target audience the group of people at which an advertisement or message is aimed

team sponsorship sponsorship of a team—for example, a football, cricket or motor racing team

weak theory of advertising the notion that advertising can first arouse awareness and interest, nudge some consumers towards a doubting first trial purchase and then provide some reassurance and reinforcement; desire and conviction do not precede purchase

Study Questions

1. **Discuss the role of advertising and how this might affect the choice of media used to carry an advertiser's messages.**
2. **Describe the strong and weak theories of how advertising works. Consider the extent to which each theory is more likely to apply to the purchase of a branded fragrance and a bar of soap.**
3. **Using the FCB matrix as a guide, suggest the different types of advertising you might use for the following products: shampoo, a designer handbag, a digital media subscription service (e.g. Netflix), a sports car.**
4. **Describe the structure of a large advertising agency. Why should an advertiser prefer to use an agency rather than set up a full-service internal advertising department?**
5. **Create an argument to support the use of product placement rather than more traditional forms of advertising.**
6. **When you next visit a supermarket, examine three sales promotions. What types of promotion are they? What are their likely objectives?**
7. **Why would it be wrong to measure the sales effect of a promotion only during the promotional period? What are the likely long-term effects of a promotion?**
8. **Explain the difference between public relations (PR) and media relations.**
9. **Discuss the extent to which PR provides free advertising.**
10. **Discuss the main reasons for an organization becoming involved in event sponsorship.**

Recommended Reading

Reaching a large global audience with a single message has become increasingly popular. Read about the power and complexity of advertising, the rise in the influence of mobile advertising and the importance of money in sales promotions.

Eui-Bang Lee, Sang-Gun Lee, Chang-Gyu Yang (2017) The influences of advertisement attitude and brand attitude on purchase intention of smartphone advertising, *Industrial Management & Data Systems* 117(6), 1011–36.

Oliver, B., Büttner, A., Florack, A. and Göritz, S. (2015) How shopping orientation influences the effectiveness of monetary and nonmonetary promotions, European Journal of Marketing 49(1/2), 170–89.

Pieters, R., Wedel, M. and Batra, R. (2010) The stopping power of advertising: measures and effects of visual complexity, *Journal of Marketing* 74(5), 48–60.

References

Aaker, D.A., Batra, R. and Myers, J.G. (1996) *Advertising Management*, New York: Prentice-Hall.

Armstrong, S. (2005) How to Put Some Bling into Your Brand, *Irish Times, Weekend*, 30 July, 7.

ASA (2015) *2014 most complained about adverts*, ASA, 20 February. https://www.asa.org.uk/News-resources/Media-Centre/2015/2014 -most-complained-about-ads.aspx#.VX3tEPlVhBc (accessed October 2018)

Barnett, M. (2011) In advertising we've a broad level of trust, *Marketing Week*, 2 May, 28–30.

Barrand, D. (2005) When Disaster Strikes, *Marketing*, 9 March, 35–6.

Barter Books (2012) http://www.keepcalmhome.com/about.htm (accessed October 2018)

Bennett, R. (1999) Sports Sponsorship, Spectator Recall and False Consensus, *European Journal of Marketing* 33(3/4), 291–313.

Burn-Callander, R. (2015) The most annoying adverts from the past 15 years, *The Telegraph*, 22 January. http://www.telegraph.co.uk/finance/newsbysector/retailandconsumer/11359924/The-most-annoying-adverts-from-the-past-15-years.html (accessed October 2018)

Barnard, N. and Ehrenberg, A. (1997) Advertising: Strongly Persuasive or Nudging? *Journal of Advertising Research* 37, 21–28.

Caird, J. (2016) 'I was basically told: you are never showing this'—how we made Cadbury's gorilla ad, *The Guardian*, 7 Jan, https://www.theguardian.com/media-network/2016/jan/07/how-we-made-cadburys-gorilla-ad (accessed October 2018)

Claeys, C., Swinnen, A. and Vanden Abeele, P. (1995) Consumers' means-end chains for 'think' and 'feel' products, *International Journal of Research in Marketing* 12(3), 193–208.

Chiorando, M. (2018) GBK to give away 900 free vegan burgers for World Vegan Day, Plant Based News, 30 October. https://www.plantbasednews.org/post/gbk-to-give-away-900-free-vegan-burgers-for-world-vegan-day (accessed October 2018)

Coker, K.K. and Altobello, S.A. (2018) Product placements in social settings: The impact of coviewing on the recall of placed brands, *Journal of Business Research* 87(6), 128–36.

Bambauer-Sachse, S. and Heinzle, P. (2018) Comparative advertising: Effects of concreteness and claim substantiation through reactance and activation on purchase intentions, *Journal of Business Research* 84(3), 233–42. https://www.sciencedirect.com/science/article/pii/S014829631730471X (accessed October 2018)

Buil, I., De Chernatony, L. and Martínez, E. (2013) Examining E the role of advertising and sales promotions in brand equity creation, *Journal of Business Research* 66(1), 115–22.

Bourn, M., Evans, M. and Mason, E. (2018) UK advertising spend achieves record for Q1 2018, WARC, http://expenditurereport.warc.com/FreeContent/AA-WARC%20Q1%202018.pdf (accessed October 2018)

Campaign (2002) The Top Ten Product Placements in Features, 17 December, 36.

Chaudhuri, M., Calatone, R, Voorhees, C. and Cockerell, S. (2018) Disentangling the effects of promotion mix on new product sales: An examination of disaggregated drivers and the moderating effect of product class, *Journal of Business Research* 90(9) 286–94.

Crosier, K. (1983) Towards a Praxiology of Advertising, *International Journal of Advertising* 2, 215–32.

Crowley, M. G. (1991) Prioritising the Sponsorship Audience, *European Journal of Marketing* 25(11), 11–21.

Cummins, J. and Mullin, R. (2008) *Sales Promotion*, London: Kogan Page, 79.

Curtis, J. (2002a) Clients Speak Out on Agencies, *Marketing*, 28 March, 22–3.

Curtis, J. (2002b) Agencies Speak Out on Clients, *Marketing*, 4 April, 20–1.

Dall'Olmo Riley, F., Ehrenberg, A.S.C., Castleberry, S.B., Barwise, T.P. and Barnard, N.R. (1997) The Variability of Attitudinal Repeat-Rates, *International Journal of Research in Marketing* 14, 437–50.

Davidson, J.H. (2003) *Offensive Marketing*, Harmondsworth: Penguin, 249–71.

Demirag, O.C., Keskinocak, P. and Swann, J. (2011) Customer rebates and retailer incentives in the presence of competition and price discrimination, *European Journal of Operational Research* 215(1), 268–80.

Dowdy, C. (2003) Thunderbirds Are Go, *Financial Times*, Creative Business, 24 June, 10.

Dumitrescu, A. (2012) Blizzard's Project Titan Will Have Product Placement, 25 January, *Softpedia*, http://news.softpedia.com/news/Blizzard-s-Project-Titan-Will-Have-Product-Placement-248355.shtml (accessed October 2018).

Ehrenberg, A.S.C. (1992) Comments on How Advertising Works, *Marketing and Research Today*, August, 167–9.

Elihu, K., Blumer, G. and Gurevitch, M. (1974) Uses and Gratifications Research, *The Public Opinion Quarterly* 37(4), 509–23.

Elliott, R. (1997) Understanding Buyer Behaviour: Implications for Selling, in D. Jobber (ed.) *The CIM Handbook of Selling and Sales Strategy*, Oxford: Butterworth-Heinemann.

Fleming, M. (2018) Models-turned-influencers are the biggest celebrity endorsers in 2017, *Marketing Week*, 10th Jan, https://www.marketingweek.com/2018/01/10/model-influencers-e/ https://www.marketingweek.com/2018/01/10/model-influencers-e (accessed October 2018)

Fill, C. (2009) *Marketing Communications: Interactivity, communication and content*, Prentice Hall, 153.

Flanagan, E. (2015) Ron Atkinson, Bryan Robson and the Sharp vertical record player: How Manchester United did kit launches in 1982, *Manchester Evening News*, 7 Jan, http://www.manchestereveningnews.co.uk/sport/football/pictured-manchester-united-kit-launch-7388441 (accessed October 2018)

Geddes, J. (2016) Elaboration Likelihood Model Theory—Using ELM to Get inside the User's Mind, https://www.interaction-design.org/literature/article/elaboration-likelihood-model-theory-using-elm-to-get-inside-the-user-s-mind (accessed October 2018)

Gibson (2015) Manchester United fall behind Barcelona on Deloitte rich list, *The Guardian*, 2 March 2015 http://www.theguardian.com/football/2010/mar/02/manchester-united-barcelona-deloitte-rich-list (accessed October 2018)

Ghosh, S. (2015) Royal Mail launches 'Mail Men' campaign to boost direct mail, *Campaign*, 28 January. http://www.campaignlive.co.uk/news/1331384/royal-mail-launches-mail-men-campaign-boost -direct-mail/?HAYILC=RELATED (accessed 10 June 2015).

Gilbert, H. (2015) Arla makes new play for UK yogurt market with high protien quark products, *The Grocer*, 19 January. http://www.thegrocer.co.uk/buying-and-supplying/new-product-development/arla-makes-new-play-for-uk-yoghurt-market-with-high-protein-quark-product/512227.article (accessed October 2018)

Gordon, W. (1992) Ad pre-testing—hidden maps, *Admap* (June) 23–7.

Grunig, J.E. (1997) A situational theory of publics: conceptual history, recent challenges and new research, in D. Moss, T. MacManus and D. Vercic (eds), *Public Relations Research: An International Perspective*, London: International Thomson Business, 3–48.

Henley, J. (2009) What crisis? *The Guardian*, 18 March, http://www.guardian.co.uk/lifeandstyle/2009/mar/18/keep-calmcarry-on-poster (accessed October 2018).

Howells, D. (2015) Love and Respect, key note, Academy of Marketing Science Annual Conference, Denver, Colorado (accessed October 2018).

Jones, J.P. (1991) Over-Promise and Under-Delivery, *Marketing and Research Today*, November, 195–203.

Jakeli, K. and Tchumburidze, T. (2012) Brand awareness matrix in political marketing area

Journal of Business, 1 (1), pp. 25-28

Hooley, G.J., Greenley, G.E., Cadogan, J.W. and Fahy, J. (2005) The performance impact of marketing resources, *Journal of Business Research* 58(1), 18–27.

Keep Calm and Carry On (n.d.) http://www.keepcalmandcarryon.com (accessed October 2018)

Kitchen, P.J., Kerr, G., Schultz, D.E., McColl, R. and Pals, H. (2014) The elaboration likelihood model: review, critique and research agenda, *European Journal of Marketing* 48(11/12), 2033–50.

Killigran, L. and Cook, R. (1999) Multibuy Push May Backfire, *Marketing Week*, 16 September, 44–5.

Khomani, N. (2018) Coronation street signs product placement deal with Co-op and Costa, *The Guardian*, 18 Jan, https://www.theguardian.com/media/2018/jan/30/coronation-street-product-placement-deal-co-op-costa-coffee (accessed October 2018)

Lesly, P. (1998) *The Handbook of Public Relations and Communications*, Maidenhead: McGraw-Hill, 13–19.

Levy, M.W. and Windahl, S. (1985) The concept of audience activity, *Media Gratification Research*, 109–22.

Liverpool FC (2018) Reds welcome Levi's as official partner, 22 August, https://www.liverpoolfc.com/news/announcements/312990-liverpool-fc-levis-official-partnership (accessed October 2018)

Magee, K. (2015) Volvo shifts global creative account out of Grey London, *Campaign*, 11 June. http://www.campaignlive.co.uk/news/1351070/ (accessed October 2018)

Manutd.com (2018) Manchester United, (accessed December 2018).

Meenaghan, T. and Shipley, D. (1999) Media Effect in Commercial Sponsorship, *European Journal of Marketing* 33(3/4), 432.

Morgan, M.R. and Hunt, S.D. (1994) The Commitment-Trust Theory of Relationship Marketing, *Journal of Marketing* 58(July), 20–38.

Nathanson, J. (2013) *The Economics of Product Placements*, Priceonomics, 4 December. http://priceonomics.com/the-economics-of-product-placements/ (accessed October 2018)

Oates, C., Blades, M. and Gunter, B. (2003) Marketing to Children, *Journal of Marketing Management* 19(4), 401–10.

Ogden, M. (2015) Manchester United face pre-season tour to China in 2016, *The Telegraph*, 29 July. http://www.telegraph.co.uk/sport/football/teams/manchester-united/11771517/Manchester-United-face-pre-season-tour-to-China-in-2016.html (accessed October 2018)

O'Leary, N. (2014) Chevy Paid $560 Million to sponsor Manchester United, *Adweek*, 2 Feb. http://www.adweek.com/news/advertising-branding/chevy-paid-560-million-sponsor-manchester-united-and-now-its-pulling-out-europe-155399 (accessed October 2018)

Oster, E. (2015) W+K London Shares '1,000 Years of Less Ordinary Wisdom' for Finlandia, *Adweek*, 12 June. http://www.adweek.com/agencyspy/wk-london-shares-1000-years-of-less-ordinary-wisdom-for-finlandia/88040 (accessed October 2018)

Niven-Phillips, L. (2017) Kristen Stewart dances to beyonce For Chanel, and it's brilliant, *Vogue*, 29 August, https://www.vogue.co.uk/article/kristen-stewart-dances-to-beyonce-for-chanel-advert (accessed October 2018)

Ocean Outdoor (2017) Ocean Outdoor and intu partnership to engage shoppers with Nottingham's first large format digital screen, 21 June, https://oceanoutdoor.com/ocean-news/news/ocean-outdoor-and-intu-partnership-to-engage-shoppers-with-nottinghams-first-large-format-digital-screen (accessed October 2018)

Ogilvy (2017) Hellmann's Food Pioneer's, https://ogilvy.co.uk/work-article/hellmanns-1 (accessed October 2018)

Petty, R.E. (1986) *Communication and Persuasion: Central and Peripheral Routes to Attitude Change*, New York: Springer-Verlag.

Petty, R.E. and Cacioppo, J.T. (1981a) *Attitudes and Persuasion: Classic and Contemporary Approaches*, Wm. C. Brown Company Publishers, Dubuque, IA.

Petty, R.E. and Cacioppo, J.T. (1981b) Issue involvement as a moderator of the effects on attitude of advertising content and context, *Advances in Consumer Research* 8, 20–24.

Petty, R.E. and Cacioppo, J.T. (1983) Central and peripheral routes to persuasion: application to advertising, in Percy, L. and Woodside, A.G. (eds), *Advertising and Consumer Psychology*, D.C. Lexington, MA: Heath and Company, 3–23.

PromoWatch (2012) Shreddies Win 1 of 75 summer holidays with Eurocamp, 5 April. http://www.mosaicmarketing.co.uk/promowatch/2012/april/shreddies-win-1-of-75-summer-holidays-with-eurocamp.aspx (accessed October 2018)

Quilter, J. (2005) Aisles of Plenty, *Marketing*, 10 August, 15.

Rauyruen, P. and Miller, K.E. (2007) Relationship Quality as a Predictor of B2B Customer Loyalty, *Journal of Business Research* 60(1), 21–31.

Reynolds, J. and Charles, G. (2011) A game of four brands, *Marketing*, 29 June, 14–15.

Ries, A. and Trout, J. (2001) *Positioning: The Battle for your Mind*, New York: McGraw-Hill.

Ritson, M. (2005) Cadbury's Decision to BOGOF is a Strategic Error, *Marketing*, 25 May, 24.

Roberts, K. (2015a) *Love/Respect Axis*, Saatchi & Saatchi, 10 June. http://www.saatchikevin.com/lovemarks/loverespect-axis (accessed October 2018)

Roberts, K. (2015b) *Brand Loyalty Reloaded*, red paper, Saatchi & Saatchi. http://www.saatchikevin.com/wp-content/uploads/2014/09/Loyalty-Beyond-Reason-Red-Paper-Jan-2015.pdf (accessed October 2018)

Roper, S. and Fill, C. (2012) *Corporate Reputation: Brand and communication*, London: Pearson, 5.

Rossiter, J.R. and Percy, L. (1987) *Advertising and Promotion Management*, McGraw-Hill.

Saatchi & Saatchi (2015) Lovemarks. http://www.saatchi.be/lovemarks (accessed 10 May 2015).

Schlegelmilch, B. (1998) *Marketing Ethics: An International Perspective*, London: International Thomson Business Press.

Shi, J., Hu, P., Lai, K. and Chen, G. (2018) Determinants of users' information dissemination behavior on social networking sites: An elaboration likelihood model perspective, *Internet Research* 28(2), 393–418. https://www.emeraldinsight.com/doi/abs/10.1108/IntR-01-2017-0038 (accessed October 2018)

Silverman, G. (2005) After the Break: The 'Wild West' Quest to Bring the Consumers to the Advertising, *Financial Times*, 18 May, 17.

Singh, S. (2005) P&G Reads the Riot Act Over Client Conflict, *Marketing Week*, 4 August, 9.

SkyMedia (2015) Weetabix—SkyView TV Effectiveness, Skymedia, 10 June. http://www.skymedia.co.uk/Insight/Case-Studies/ weetabix.aspx (accessed October 2018)

Sleight, S. (1989) *Sponsorship: What It Is and How to Use It*, Maidenhead: McGraw-Hill, 4.

Stubbs, D. (2014) The new Ralph Lauren Polo advert, *The Guardian*, 27 September. http://www.theguardian.com/tv-and-radio/2014/sep/27/ralph-lauren-polo-advert-hard-sell (accessed 10 June 2015).

Telegraph Sport (2012) Manchester United survey reveals they have doubled their global fan base to 659 million over five years, *The Telegraph*, 29 May 2012. http://www.telegraph.co.uk/sport/football/teams/manchester-united/9298384/Manchester-United-survey-reveals-they-have-doubled-their-global-fan-base-to-659-million-over-five-years.html (accessed October 2018)

The UK Sponsorship Database (2015) Casillero del Diablo announces Sky Movies partnership, March. http://www.uksponsorship.com/ukjan15-Casillero-del-Diablo-announces-Sky-Movies-partnership.htm#.VX3mxPlVhBc (accessed October 2018)

Tomkins, R. (2003) The Hidden Message: Life's a Pitch, and Then You Die, *Financial Times*, 24 October, 14.

Tylee, J. (2018) Has Sir Martin Sorrell been a positive force for the ad industry? *Campaign* 18 April, https://www.campaignlive.co.uk/article/sir-martin-sorrell-positive-force-ad-industry/1462404 (accessed October 2018)

Ungoed-Thomas, J. and Neal, W. (2018) Kiddy vapes are trick not treat, *The Sunday Times*, 14 October, 4.

Vize, R., Coughlan, J., Kennedy, A. and Ellis-Chadwick, F. (2011) B2B Relationship Quality: Conceptualisation of Relationship Quality in online B2B Retail services, *18th Recent Advances in Retailing and Services Science Conference*, The European Institute of Retailing and Services Science, San Diego USA, 12–18 July.

Vaughn, R. (1980) How advertising works: A planning model. *Journal of Advertising Research*, October, 27–33.

Warc (2018) *Warc AA Expenditure report*, http://www.warc.com/content/article/warc-datapoints/uk_advertsining_expenditure_by_medium/112791 (accessed Nov 2018).

Ward, A. and Grant, J. (2005) PepsiCo Admits Curbing Adverts to Children, *Financial Times*, 28 February, 23.

West, R. and Turner, L. (2010) *Uses and Gratifications Theory, Introducing Communication Theory: Analysis and Application*, Boston, USA: McGraw-Hill.

White, J. (1991) *How to Understand and Manage Public Relations*, London: Business Books.

Wikipedia (2012) Product placement, http://en.wikipedia.org/wiki/Product_placement (accessed October 2018)

Wikipedia (2018) FCB (advertising agency). https://en.wikipedia.org/wiki/FCB_(advertising_agency) (accessed October 2018)

Willan, B. (2017) Why Unilever's sustainable living brands are driving growth, *Campaign*, 25 May. https://www.campaignlive.co.uk/article/why-unilevers-sustainable-living-brands-driving-growth/1434506 (accessed October 2018)

Williams, A. (2011) TV product placement is here, *The Marketer*, April, 17.

Wilson, B. (2015) Fifa scandal 'a disaster' for sponsors, *BBC News*, 28 May. http://www.bbc.co.uk/news/business-32912445

Wilson, R. (2005) Brands Need Not Pay the Price, *Marketing Week*, 7 July, 39–41.

Wood, O. (2010) An Emotional model of advertising, *Marketing Week*, 18 March, https://www.marketingweek.com/2010/03/18/an-emotional-model-of-advertising (accessed October 2018)

Wright, L.T. and Crimp, M. (2003) *The Marketing Research Process*, London: Prentice-Hall, 180.

CASE 27

Volvo: Buying a Car by Simply Using an App

While the Swedish car company Volvo (part of the Holding Group AB Volvo) was established way back in 1927, its recent history has been somewhat turbulent. Acquired by Ford, the quintessentially American company, in 1999, Volvo was sold to the Chinese company Zhejiang Geely Holding Group in 2010. Since then, Geely's love affair with the Volvo brand has only grown stronger, with Geely having acquired an 8.2 per cent stake in AB Volvo (the former parent company of the Volvo car division), a major manufacturer of trucks, in December 2017 for $3.2 billion. This move made Geely AB Volvo's largest shareholder and, by the same token, a strategic decision-maker in terms of future market moves.

Volvo benefits from its reputation of Scandinavian values of safety, environmental concern and classic understated design, while at the same time it tries to appeal to affluent Chinese buyers who demand more luxury and performance from their cars. The latter will certainly appreciate the fact that the Volvo XC40 was awarded the 'Car of the Year' trophy at the 88th International Motor Show held in Geneva, Switzerland, in March 2018. Chen Lizhe, sales chief at Volvo Car Greater China, announced in July 2018 that the company would launch an imported all-new XC40 compact sports utility vehicle (SUV) in the Chinese market before the end of the year and start local production of the model in China at the start of 2019. In addition to the highly praised XC40, Volvo China also plans to offer Chinese customers a locally made S60 mid-sized sedan, an imported V60 crossover wagon and an imported XC90 SUV, all in 2019 as well. The goal of all of these strategic moves being pursued by Volvo is to grow its market share in the largest automotive market in the world and to eventually sell 200,000 units by 2020 (6,000 units more than were sold in 2017), which will represent more than a quarter of Volvo's global annual sales.

In addition to its attempts to blend Scandinavian sensibilities with Chinese demands for luxury, while at the same time trying to move upmarket, Volvo recently announced its intention that fully electric cars will make up half of its sales by 2025. In 2017, Volvo announced an industry first by stating that all new models released from 2019 will be mild hybrid, plug-in or battery electric vehicles. The move to electrify

50 per cent of its cars by 2025 is part of a plan to position Volvo as a powerful player in China, which has become the world's leading market for electrified cars. Håkan Samuelsson, Chief Executive of Volvo Cars, said in 2017 that, 'The past 90 years have been exciting, but the 10 years left until the 100-year anniversary may come to be more exciting, as industry focus shifts to autonomous driving, electrification and connectivity.'

In its efforts to appeal to the Chinese upscale market, Volvo also announced that it would be cutting back drastically on corporate sponsorship activities in Europe and in the USA, while increasing them in Asia, especially through the organizing of the high-profile golf tournaments that Volvo sponsors, such as the Volvo Golf Masters event in China, Malaysia and in Thailand. The brand also hosts global golf's most popular customer tournament, the Volvo World Golf Challenge, in which more than 40,000 clients participate, mostly from Asia. Perhaps counterintuitively, Volvo has stopped its participation in car racing, as it is no longer considered to be in line with the brand. Still, the company continues to sponsor the Volvo Ocean Race, a triennial event in which boats race across four oceans and around six continents, covering 30,000 miles over nine months. The next race is planned for 2021 and, as Kina Wileke, Executive Vice President of Volvo Group Communication, puts it, 'The Volvo Ocean Race has been a great vehicle for building customer relationships, strengthening the Volvo brand and presenting our company and our products to a global audience.' Volvo also now focuses on just one auto show in each major region once a year: Detroit in the USA, Geneva in Europe, and Shanghai/Beijing in China. This reduced number of events will then be complemented and supported by additional mass communication and branding activities in other important markets. The strategy behind limiting the number of corporate events but focusing more intensely on the ones that remain is to differentiate Volvo from other car companies and allow it to get its message out more clearly.

Since 2014, Volvo has also made an effort to improve its digital platform in an effort to better communicate with, engage and serve its customers. The company upgraded its online platform in order to better integrate the online brand experience with the in-showroom brand experience. Customers who go online are given a standard-choice model which they then can personalize and upgrade, designing the eventual car they would like to buy. They receive a short video showing what the car will look like when finally delivered. Volvo does not see online purchasing as a replacement for car dealerships, but rather as a complement, since cars bought online will still have to 'pass through the dealer network', said Alain Visser, a Volvo sales executive. These efforts were put on display by Volvo with the launch of its XC40 model in November 2017 at the L.A. Auto Show. The company presented an app called 'Care by Volvo' with the following pitch: 'The official Care by Volvo app lets you customize and subscribe to your new Volvo right from your phone. Just download, subscribe, and drive. Your subscription includes personalized options, insurance, maintenance, wear and tear, and roadside assistance. You can also upgrade to a new car in as little as 12 months. Your new Volvo is also compatible with our fully integrated on-demand app, Volvo On Call, which gives you complete control of your vehicle right from your phone.' 'It is a revolutionary way to look at car ownership,' said Kristina Vasandani, Volvo's Manager of Campaigns and Digital Marketing, who added that the Care by Volvo set-up 'includes everything from maintenance to insurance [with] no negotiations and no down-payment. It's as simple as acquiring a new phone.' The plan for Volvo is, so to speak, to kill two marketing birds with one stone: introduce a new model while also helping to make life less complicated for its customers.

Questions

1. **What factors are pushing Volvo to change its marketing communication strategy?**
2. **Identify and evaluate the different elements of Volvo's marketing communication strategy. How can Volvo differentiate itself from other car makers and give the company a competitive edge?**
3. **How does Volvo plan to use digital marketing in its communication strategy and improve its relationship with customers?**

This case study was written by Tom McNamara and Irena Descubes from Rennes School of Business, Rennes—France.

References

Based on: Groves, E. (2011) 3 ways to create unique customer experiences, American Express, 27 April, https://www.americanexpress.com/us/small-business/openforum/articles/3-ways-to-create-unique-customer-experiences; Taylor III, A. (2000) Ford's Mr. Continental WOLFGANG REITZLE, once BMW's enfant terrible, wants to make Ford a luxury-car superpower. Can he love a Lincoln?, *Fortune Magazine*, 16 October, http://archive.fortune.com/magazines/fortune/fortune_archive/2000/10/16/289641/index.htm; Hudson, N. (2014) Volvo boss says motorsport 'does not conform with our brand', *Touring Car Times*, 15 December, http://www.touringcartimes.com/2014/12/15/volvo-boss-says-motorsport-does-not-conform-with-our-brand; Volvo (2014) Volvo Cars announces new global marketing strategy Volvo Press release, 15 December, https://www.media.volvocars.com/global/en-gb/media/pressreleases/155208/volvo-cars-announces-new-global-marketing-strategy; Bruell, A. (2014) Volvo Consolidates Global Media with Mindshare, *Ad Age*, 24 February, http://adage.com/article/agency-news/volvo-consolidates-global-media-mindshare/291822; Scrutton, A. (2014) Volvo's Make Or Break Moment For $11 Billion In China Plan Happens, 26 August, edited by Will Waterman, *Reuters*, 18 August, http://www.businessinsider.com/r-with-cigars-and-crystal-volvo-makes-eyes-at-chinese-rich-2014-18#ixzz3MN7tufZV; Edelstein, S. (2014) Volvo may swap auto shows for online sales and more digital marketing, *Digital Trends*, 17 December, http://www.digitaltrends.com/cars/volvo-may-swap-auto-shows-online-sales-digital-marketing/#ixzz3MORNGQBe; Sui-Lee Wee (2017) Geely Buys Stake in Volvo Trucks, Despite China Restrictions, *The New York Times*, 27 December, https://www.nytimes.com/2017/12/27/business/dealbook/china-volvo-geely.html; Gong Zhengzheng and Li Fusheng (2018) Volvo pins hopes on China market expansion with more models, *China Daily*, 23 July, http://www.chinadaily.com.cn/a/201807/23/WS5b554878a3107 96df4df8136.html; Fleet News (2018) Volvo eyes Chinese market with 50% EV sales move, *Manufacturer News*, 25 April, https://www.fleetnews.co.uk/news/manufacturer-news/2018/04/25/volvo-strengthens-position-in-chinese-market-with-50-ev-sales-move; Patrick Coffee (2018) Volvo's New Campaign and App Promote a Radical Concept: Subscribing to a Car-Owning a vehicle is something you 'used to' do, 18 April, *AdWeek*, https://www.adweek.com/brand-marketing/volvos-new-campaign-and-app-promote-a-radical-concept-subscribing-to-a-car

CASE 28
Toyota and Buddy

Steve Campbell was about to retire. As he went through his paperwork, he thought about all the previous experiences and challenges he had faced as the marketing communication director of Toyota Motors South Africa (TMSA). He had many memories. Some were good (such as healthy sales figures), while others were not so good. And then there was Buddy, his favourite character in Toyota advertising. He thought about the events of that time and was drawn back into those events.

Steve had received the newspaper report from his American colleagues. 'Toyota recall: reports of runaway cars' was the headline provided by ABC News. Others were more dramatic. "'There's no brakes . . . hold on and pray": Last words of man before he and his family died in Toyota Lexus crash'. He imagined how his colleagues would be feeling, or even the families of those affected by the situation. He thought of how it would feel if this were *his* family that had been involved. As marketing communication director at Toyota, he knew he had to do something. Steve was worried about how the news reports would affect Toyota owners and the general public. Toyota was such a reliable and trustworthy name in South Africa (as it was in many other parts of the world). As he travelled home, he decided. A marketing communication campaign was needed. But what type of campaign? What should the message be at a time like this? What did he want to achieve with the marketing campaign? What would be the best way to compile such a programme?

Background Information

Based in Japan, Toyota is an international manufacturer of passenger and commercial vehicles. Manufacturing takes places via 51 manufacturing companies in 28 countries. Toyota vehicles are sold in more than 170 countries.

One country where Toyota has a manufacturing company is South Africa, where the motor vehicle industry is important to the local economy. Currently, the industry accounts for 7.2 per cent of the country's GDP, and the total industry (including associated industries) creates approximately 30,000 direct jobs. It is estimated that 900,000 people are dependent on the automotive industry in both direct and indirect employment (either their own or a family member's), which includes the component industry and other informal activities. Toyota South Africa has a reputation in South Africa of producing and selling reliable, good quality motor vehicles. Toyota has consistently been the top-selling motor vehicle manufacturer in South Africa, despite strong competition from Volkswagen South Africa.

In the midst of this positive situation for Toyota, technical problems were identified in November 2009 with the accelerator of various models. Initially the problem was identified in the USA, but by January 2010 the necessity for a recall of Toyota vehicles in South Africa was identified. This situation had the potential to affect trust in the brand, as well as the perceptions of quality associated with the brand, if not managed well.

The Objectives of the Campaign

Steve knew that building trust in a brand is part of the task of any marketing manager, and that once it has been built, it is important to keep the trust. This was important with existing customers, but also with people who may be customers in the future. This would have to be one of the goals of the campaign. It was important to find a way to connect to the core brand values—namely, quality, durability and reliability—that built trust in the brand and the company (as a whole). Not only was it a question of maintaining trust, it was also about creating an emotional connection with the viewer (both existing and potential Toyota owners). That gave him another idea.

Why a Dog? Why Buddy?

Underpinning the campaign that was developed to rebuild the brand and prevent brand erosion was the use of a dog ('Buddy') in an integrated marketing communication campaign. The purpose of using the dog was to 'break through the advertising clutter' that was identified in the mass media. Further, Buddy (like all dogs) showed 'reliability, honesty, loyalty and warm-heartedness', and he was the symbol selected to appeal to people from various ages and races. Selecting the type of dog was important, as each breed is associated with certain characteristics. It is suggested that boxers are 'a combination of all dogs' while still being 'careful and cautious'. Buddy is a boxer in all ways, except in his lips, which are 'human'; thus use is made of anthropomorphism. The breed of dog selected was required to have a flat snout so that the creative team could incorporate human lips. The campaign used both print and broadcast media and advertised all Toyota brands (Corolla, Hilux, as well as the used-vehicle division). The campaign commenced on 23 September 2009 and consisted of different versions that reflected different components of the Toyota business and brands (such as the used vehicles).

Components of the Campaign

Use of social media When the problems with the cars were identified, Toyota published an open letter to the public which indicated the impact of the recall on customers and, in so doing, attempted to address customer concerns and apologize for the situation. This letter was placed in the mass media as well as on the website. The Toyota website was also used so that customers could determine whether they were affected by the recall and the actions necessary in this situation. Toyota owners could access the official website and supply their vehicle's details. This would enable the owner to check whether their specific vehicle was affected by the recall, and Toyota could advise the owner on the appropriate steps. Blogs managed by Toyota SA were also used to discuss the situation and advise customers. An address from the managing director of Toyota South Africa was also placed on YouTube. Buddy had his own Facebook page and Twitter account.

Use of mass media Use was made of a print and television campaign in the national media. Magazines selected included those that focused on the motor enthusiast, as well as other popular magazines. The advertising was positively perceived, and in the case of the television campaign, *Buddy and the Corolla* were number 2 on the most-liked advertising list for 2010, while *Buddy and the Hilux* were at number 10.

What Effect did Buddy have on the Toyota Brand?

Research was conducted among both Toyota and non-Toyota owners. These people were shown the storyboard for the advertisement and asked several questions, including:

- *How did the advertisement make you feel about Toyota?*
  Among Toyota owners, 85 per cent found Toyota much more appealing (in contrast with 51 per cent of owners of other vehicles). By contrast, 31 per cent of owners of other vehicles felt that the advertisement made Toyota a little more appealing, while a further 18 per cent indicated that it didn't change their feelings about Toyota. Toyota owners were exceedingly positive towards Toyota after having seen the storyboard. Non-Toyota owners were also positive towards the brand, but not as positive as Toyota owners. The advertisement was positively perceived by all those who viewed the advertisement, affecting the perception of the brand.
- *Has the advertisement improved your perceptions of the brand?*
  Among Toyota owners, 93 per cent agreed strongly that the advertisement had improved their perceptions of the brand, compared with 62 per cent of owners of other vehicles. In the case of 'agree slightly', 25 per cent of owners of other cars responded in this way compared with 5 per cent of Toyota owners. This increase shows the effect of the advertisement on changes in brand perception. The effect was more pronounced among Toyota owners.
- *Thinking about this advertisement, if you were to change/replace your current vehicle, how would this advertisement affect your consideration of Toyota?*
  Among Toyota owners, 89 per cent indicated it would make them much more likely to consider Toyota, while 42 per cent of owners of other vehicles were much more likely to consider Toyota. A further 36 per cent of owners of other vehicles indicated that the advertisement would make them a little more likely to consider Toyota. This indicates the ability of the advertisement to change not only perceptions, but also the actions of customers.
- *Thinking about the recalling of Toyota vehicles, if you were to change/replace your current vehicle, how would this recall issue affect your consideration of Toyota?*
  This question was relevant, as the campaign was part of the attempt to limit any potential damage associated with the recall of Toyota motor vehicles. Among Toyota owners, 49 per cent indicated that it would make them much more likely to consider Toyota, while in the case of owners of other vehicles,

»

21 per cent indicated it would make them much more likely to consider Toyota. Among both groups, 12 per cent indicated that they would be a little more likely to consider Toyota. For 37 per cent of Toyota owners and 57 per cent of non-owners, the recall issue made no difference to their considering buying a Toyota.

Exploiting the Buddy Effect

The campaign was a great success. It built connection and trust, and opinions of consumers were reflected in the research and the statistics. It was just what was needed. The campaign had started out with just Buddy, then his son was introduced, and then a friend (ChiChi), to introduce novelty into the campaign. A short-term campaign using a guinea pig exploited this animal connection for the launch of one of the Aygo models, attracting the younger target market buying their first car.

What is next?

Steve recalled Buddy and the other animals fondly. Toyota owed much to animals. They had all worked together to build not only the Corolla and the Aygo, but also the Toyota brand—but it was time for a change. How could the positive connections, specifically Buddy, be leveraged and carried on in the new ranges such as the Etios being launched to replace the Corolla? The time for animals was over—or was it? If something totally different should be developed, what could be done?

Questions

1. **Comment on the use of the various components of the integrated marketing communication strategy that Toyota South Africa used in its Buddy campaign.**
2. **How do you think Buddy was able to connect with Toyota owners and the general public?**
3. **How does a dog (like Buddy) reflect the brand? How does this benefit the brand?**
4. **Comment on the negative situation facing Toyota South Africa. What role does a marketing communication campaign play in this situation?**
5. **What suggestions do you have for Steve concerning a follow-up campaign for future ranges and models?**

This case study was written by Adele Berndt, Associate Professor, Jonkoping International Business School.

References

Based on: Kruger, C. (2010) Personal interview with the author; Kruger, C. (2010) Presentation at Southern African Institute of Management Scientists Conference 2010 Mpekweni Sun, 12–15 September; Toyota http://www.toyota-global.com/company/profile/facilities/worldwide_operations.html (accessed 2 April 2015); Connor, M. (2010) Toyota Recall: Five Critical Lessons http://business-ethics.com/2010/01/31/2123-toyota-recall-five-critical-lessons/ (accessed 14 April 2015); ABC News (2010) Toyota recall: Reports of runaway cars http://abcnews.go.com/Blotter/RunawayToyotas/runaway-toyotas-problem-persists-recall/story?id=9618735&page=2 (accessed 14 April 2015); *Mail Online* (2010) 'There's no brakes . . . hold on and pray': Last words of man before he and his family died in Toyota Lexus crash, http://www.dailymail.co.uk/news/article-1248177/Toyota-recall-Last-words-father-family-died-Lexus-crash.html#ixzz1YaJKrtWw (accessed 21 September 2011); SouthAfrica.info (2012) South Africa's automotive industry; http://www.southafrica.info/business/economy/sectors/automotive-overview.htm#.VTUYhiGeDGc (accessed 2 April 2015). https://city-press.news24.com/Business/r2567-billion-the-vehicle-industrys-massive-gdp-contribution-20170310 (accessed 27 August 2018)

CHAPTER 15
Direct Marketing Communications

> *Understand the power of asking.*
> **DRAYTON BIRD**

LEARNING OBJECTIVES

After reading this chapter, you should be able to:

1. discuss the key direct communication tools: direct marketing, personal selling and exhibitions
2. explain the concept of direct marketing and how to manage campaigns
3. describe the reasons for the growth in direct marketing communication activity
4. discuss the importance of database marketing and how database marketing creates a foundation for customer relationship management
5. describe the media used in direct marketing
6. discuss the ethical issues in direct communications
7. discuss the characteristics of personal selling and the stages in the selling process
8. consider the key issues involved in sales management
9. explain key account management in business-to-business (B2B) markets
10. discuss exhibitions and trade shows in a business-to-business context

The world of communications is changing rapidly. Digital and mobile communication platforms are blurring the boundaries between communication tools and media. Websites (potentially) carry text, audio and video messages as well as acting as information sources, means of data collection and sales channels (Chaffey and Ellis-Chadwick, 2019). In this chapter, we explore elements of the promotional mix that are direct forms of communication and generally do not require media to carry the communications messages, but which do offer a level of personalization not afforded by the mass communication tools discussed in Chapter 14. The chapter provides insight into how each of the direct communication tools might contribute to an integrated marketing communications (IMC) campaign strategy. The chapter begins by exploring direct marketing, then examines personal selling and sales management, and finally looks at exhibitions and trade fairs.

Principles of Direct Marketing Communications

Direct marketing is an effective means of communicating with consumer and B2B target audiences, using methods that attempt to acquire, retain and convert customers. Campaigns are usually designed to stimulate an immediate response from the recipient. A key advantage of direct marketing is that campaigns are easier to measure than for mass-communication tools, and therefore it is easier to determine the effectiveness of campaigns.

Direct marketing campaigns are not necessarily short-term, response-driven activities. Increasingly, companies are using direct marketing methods to develop ongoing direct personal relationships with customers (Key and Czaplewski, 2017). Some marketers believe that the cost of attracting a new customer is five times that of retaining existing customers. Direct marketing techniques can be used effectively as part of an IMC campaign and create further opportunities for retaining customers and selling more products using cross-selling (encouraging the purchase of a wider range of products) and up-selling (encouraging the purchase of higher value products). Direct marketing covers a wide array of techniques, and each technique offers a marketing manager a set of potential benefits and limitations that need to be considered when planning to incorporate these techniques into an IMC campaign. Direct marketing is a major component of the promotional mix and uses various media and technologies to target consumers precisely and request an immediate direct response. Originally, this communication method mainly involved **direct mail** and mail-order catalogues, but today's direct marketers use a wide range of media, including telemarketing, **direct response advertising**, the web, social media and mobile channels.

Figure 15.1 shows the main techniques used for direct marketing; each is discussed below.

Direct mail

Direct mailings are addressed to the target consumer (or business) and may include promotions, invitations, discounts, coupons, catalogues and other informative content. Spend on this form of communication is increasing in the UK by nearly 6 per cent annually, making it the third-largest method of communication after online and television. Direct mail can be used to meet different marketing communication objectives, from creating brand awareness to eliciting action. Direct mail is widely used, and campaigns often involve sending highly creative mailshots to capture the recipient's attention. A significant change in direct marketing is the move from mass marketing to mass customization; technology and effective database management are enabling marketers to achieve much greater accuracy with their direct mailing campaigns. This new level of knowledge facilitates more effective and efficient campaigns.

Many different types of brands are now increasingly using this form of communication. For example, Thames Water ran a successful direct mail campaign designed to inform customers about a complex behavioural change. They wanted to get the message over to 'Bin it—not block it' to stop water pipes becoming blocked with fat and grease poured down drains (Hemsley, 2018).

Direct response advertising

Direct response advertising is designed to elicit an immediate response, encouraging consumers to take action, and can appear in print, on television and online. This method is increasingly used online, where

FIGURE 15.1
Direct marketing communications techniques

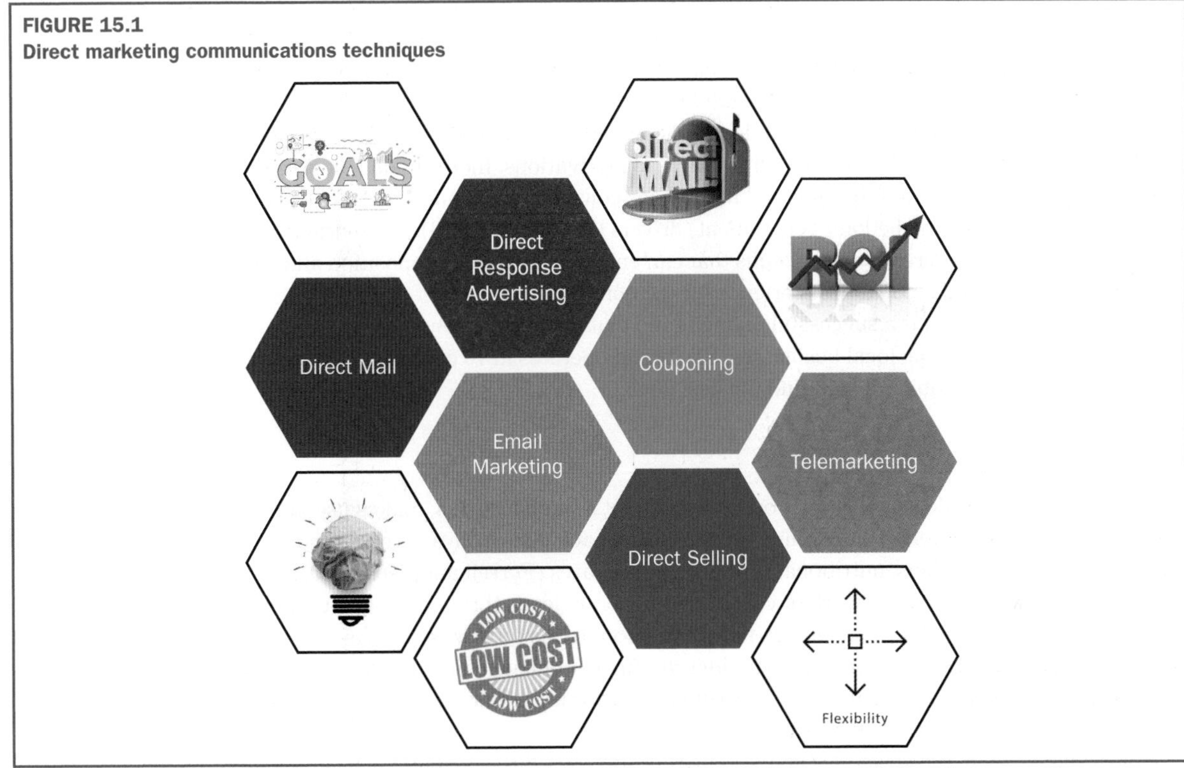

campaigns capture attention and then lead customers to a web page where they can take the desired action. Direct response advertising is a highly measurable form of communication. Also, because the advert requires action, it enables the advertiser to gather information about the customer. This forms a direct connection with the customer which can then be made again, enabling the sending of highly personalized messages and helping to build longer term relationships. 'Buy this' and 'shop now' are examples of triggers that can appear on web and mobile sites to encourage instant action. But objectives can also be to encourage customers to read a post on an online platform or sign up to a newsletter. These are also forms of direct response advertising.

Email marketing

Email marketing is important for building and maintaining close customer relationships, and this mode of direct marketing has been widely adopted as a means of distributing promotional messages and offers. Once established, this is a low-cost method for distributing discounts, coupons, sales promotions and vouchers. Care should be taken to gain the end customer's permission to send email marketing messages by inviting them to opt in to receive messages and promotions. Unsolicited emails (spam) are largely illegal. One of the major challenges for email marketing campaigns is to get the intended recipient to open the mailing rather than just delete the message. Ellis-Chadwick and Doherty (2012) found executional tactics that could enhance the likelihood of success. A recipient's attention depends on whether the subject line of the email is attention-grabbing and relevant. Also important is the sender; if a recipient perceives that the email is from an unknown or unwanted source, they will delete it rather than open it. To develop sustained attention, the message should be personally relevant to the recipient and have interactive content to engage further interest. Personalized messages can enhance performance but the recipients have passed through the opt-in permission stage first. PayPal regularly uses email campaigns to send personalized and targeted messages. Using financial, timed incentives increases customer engagement.

Coupons

Coupons are a marketing tool used to acquire customers and encourage trial of new products and services. Price promotions form an important tactic and the main motivation for customers to redeem coupons. Typically, coupons were printed, but now the use of electronic and mobile versions is widespread (Leva et al., 2018). Greater use of electronic formats has also changed the tactical motivations. Increasingly, 'deal of the day' offers are used to engage customers. Research has found that younger consumers will purchase the deal of the day motivated by both rational (price) and hedonic (enjoyment) drivers (Leva et al., 2018). For marketers, this opens up opportunities to develop creative campaigns that can enhance the value proposition and make the redemption of coupons an exciting and enjoyable experience for the consumer.

For example, Groupon is a successful online brand that connects consumers with coupons, sales give-aways and promotional codes from local businesses. The brand operates in 15 countries and has nearly 50 million users who visit the web and mobile sites to find the best deals.

Direct selling

Direct selling offers a sales channel that operates without a fixed location, makes use of personal contact and is big business. Billions of dollars of revenue are generated each year from a diverse range of product and services: cosmetics, cleaning products, nutritional products, homewares (Ferrell and Ferrell, 2012). This method of direct marketing relies on a seller's network of contacts to generate leads through which products can be promoted (Ponder, 2011). Social media have added a new dimension to this form of selling, as it extends the reach and diversity of personal networks. The opportunities are further enhanced by the use of smartphones. Digital technology and social media networks are creating opportunities to not only find new customers but also to recruit new advocates (Ferrell and Ferrell, 2012).

For example, Avon, the cosmetics and jewellery brand, uses direct selling via a catalogue (printed and online). Avon representatives sell products door to door through their networks. To stay relevant, the brand is finding ways to use digital advertising channels and social media to expand (Trefis Team, 2018).

Telemarketing

Telemarketing makes use of the phone to sell goods and services to target customers. There are two types: 1) inbound, where the customer contacts the firm, and the customer may consider this type of telemarketing to be part of the service offer; and 2) outbound, where the firm contacts the customer, which is often perceived as a nuisance—customers can become aggressive when they receive calls they are not expecting. There is also a downside for employees making the outbound calls, as they experience the negative attitudes of customers. Absenteeism and low morale are high in outbound telemarketing call centres (Maulana and Nurulfirdausi, 2015).

Despite the issues associated with managing a campaign, telemarketing is a versatile approach and can be used to support other forms of direct marketing, for example to follow up on sales leads generated from online campaigns, establish contact with customers, and provide customer sales support. Telemarketing is a relatively low-cost and effective means of interacting with target customers.

Regal Fish, for example, is a company using telemarketing very effectively to deliver freshly caught seafood directly to homes across the UK from its base in Barton-upon-Humber. By using customer referrals and telemarketing, the company has built a customer base of 80,000 to whom they regularly deliver by making 1,000 delivery rounds each year.

Care should be taken to ensure that calls are not perceived as aggressive, and the frequency of calls should be managed. If a customer feels that they are being hounded by telemarketing calls, this can create negative brand associations (Ritsema and Piest, 1990).

Direct Marketing

Direct marketing is no longer synonymous with junk mail, as it is a suite of communication techniques that are an integral part of the relationship marketing concept, where companies attempt to establish ongoing direct and profitable relationships with customers. As with all marketing communications, direct marketing campaigns

MARKETING IN ACTION 15.1

Has Direct Marketing been Given a One-way Ticket to Extinction?

Marketing is in flux as the use of digital technology intrudes into every aspect of marketing activity and every nook and cranny of human activity. Digital thinking has been heralded as an essential part of marketing strategy development and central to the mindset of marketers. Indeed, Ashley Friedlein, founder of Econsultancy, reported that '*If you don't "get digital" then you cannot be a modern marketer.*' Consequently, direct marketers are constantly wrestling with decisions about which media and which technology should be used to deliver which style of message to ensure the best *reach* and generate the highest level of returns. Marketers also must contend with increasingly detailed information about the transient whims of the customers in their target markets, who are increasingly willing to publicly parade the most intimate details of their daily lives online. So the database that was at the heart of marketers' campaigns is now overloaded with data, and the internet holds a further vast store: anecdotally, there is more than a terabyte of information on the millennials alone.

There is no strong lead from industry bodies, either, to help beleaguered direct marketers choose between the old and the new approaches. For several years, the Direct Marketing Association (DMA) and the Institute of Direct and Digital Marketing (IDM) have been discussing whether to merge to form Europe's largest trade body in marketing. And while they have finally taken the plunge and merged, they will still serve the industry using their separate identities.

Confusion appears to reign, but before direct marketers abandon everything physical and move over completely to the digital world, they should consider their capacity for being creative. Analysis of digital behaviour can be insular and inward facing; arguably selfies, pictures of food and pet videos reveal more about consumers than can currently be captured by machine code. For some, their meal cannot begin until a photograph is taken and shared on social media. Savvy restaurateurs have latched on to this trend and adapted their menus to make their food 'Instagrammable'. Giles Hedger (CSO, Leo Burnett) argues that: '*Marketing, however efficiently it runs, will never be about reductive computation . . . it will continue to be a test of the imagination, and there is no algorithm or app for that.*' MetaEyes is an image recognition analytics tool that can detect faces, sentiment and locations and even identify celebrities, suggesting that there may be challenges ahead.

Based on: Friedlein (2013); Milington (2015); Hedger (2015); Lee (2017); Metaeyes.com (2018)

should be integrated both within themselves and with other communication tools such as advertising, publicity and personal selling. Uncoordinated communication leads to blurring of brand positioning and customer confusion. See Marketing in Action 15.1 for further discussion of the challenges of the distinction between direct and digital marketing.

Direct Marketing Campaigns

Direct marketing is growing in popularity as a communication tool in both consumer and industrial markets.

Drivers of direct marketing:

- *Market and media fragmentation* has meant that the effectiveness of mass-marketing techniques (e.g. using television and other broadcast media) has declined as the requirement to reach target segments with

highly individualized needs has increased. Consequently, the importance of direct marketing media that can not only target specialized niche markets but also distribute highly personalized appeals has grown. Direct response advertising is more effective, since market niches can be tightly targeted, and this is used extensively online.
- *Technological advances* have led to the increasing sophistication of software, allowing the generation of personalized letters and telephone scripts and enabling direct marketers to develop highly targeted and sophisticated campaigns. Databases and data warehouses hold detailed information on individuals and businesses and, once analysed, this enhances targeting. Customer relationship management software has enabled companies to manage one-to-one relationships with huge numbers of consumers. Automated telephone systems make it possible to handle dozens of calls simultaneously, reducing the risk of losing potential customers. Furthermore, developments in technology in telephone, cable and satellite television and the internet have triggered the rise in home-based electronic shopping.
- *Emerging analytical techniques* mean that by using geodemographic analysis, households can be classified into a neighbourhood type, for example 'modern private housing, young families' or 'private flats, single people'. These, in turn, can be cross-referenced with product usage, media usage and lifestyle statements to create market segments that can be targeted by direct mail (see Chapter 7 for more detailed discussion).

Marketing databases

The **marketing database** is central to direct marketing, as activities depend on customer information. A marketing database holds customer data—for example, names, addresses, telephone numbers, and lifestyle and transactional data. Information such as the types of purchase, frequency of purchase, purchase value and responsiveness to promotional offers may be held. By using the marketing database, companies can take an interactive approach towards developing highly targeted direct communication campaigns using individually addressable marketing media and channels (such as mail, telephone and the salesforce) to provide information to a target audience.

Some key characteristics of marketing databases are that, first, they allow direct communication with customers through a variety of media, including direct mail, telemarketing, direct response advertising and digital media channels. Second, it usually requires the customer to respond in a way that allows the company to act (such as through contact by telephone, sending out literature or arranging sales visits). Third, this type of marketing communication is traceable and measurable.

Sophisticated databases provide the capability of storing and analysing large quantities of data from diverse sources and presenting information in a convenient, accessible and useful format. The creation of a database relies on the systematic collection and storage of information. Table 15.1 shows examples of basic sources and types of data.

Typical information stored in a database

Perhaps the most important thing to acknowledge about a marketing database is that it is a systematic way of gathering data that can be collated and analysed to provide information that has implications for marketing campaigns. Figure 15.2 shows typical information that is recorded in a database. This is described in more detail below (Stone, Davies and Bond, 1995).

Customer and prospect information

This provides the basic data required to access customers and prospects (e.g. name, home and email addresses, telephone number) and contains their general behavioural characteristics (e.g. psychographic and behavioural data). For organizational markets, information on key decision-makers and influencers and the choice criteria they use would also be stored.

Transactional information

Past transactions are a key indicator of likely future transactions. Transactional data must be sufficiently detailed to allow FRAC (frequency, recency, amount and category) information to be extracted for each customer.
- *Frequency* refers to how often a customer buys. Both the average frequency and the trend (is the customer tending to buy frequently?) is of use to the direct marketer.

TABLE 15.1 Basic Sources and types of data

Data source	Examples of data type
Company records	Purchase behaviour, name, address, telephone number
Warranty and guarantee cards	Product types
Enquiries	Clarifications of data held; e.g. an account holder at an HSBC bank might enquire about a new loan, at which point credit and personal finance data will be updated
Exchanging data with other companies	Loyalty cards like Nectar gather data and share information between companies in the group (e.g. American Express, Sainsbury's, BP, Ford Hertz, Viking Direct)
Salesforce records	Account details, customer leads, past sales data
Application forms	Personal or business data
Complaints	Reasons for returns, outcomes
Responses to direct marketing activities	Sales promotions, direct marketing: e.g. timing, frequency, purchase activity
Organized events	At corporate events/conferences business cards are often collected
Website engagement	Personal data, email addresses, personal preferences, usage data
Emails	Requirements, requests, qualitative data
Social media	Personal data, email addresses, connections, personal likes and dislikes, social media usage

FIGURE 15.2
A marketing database

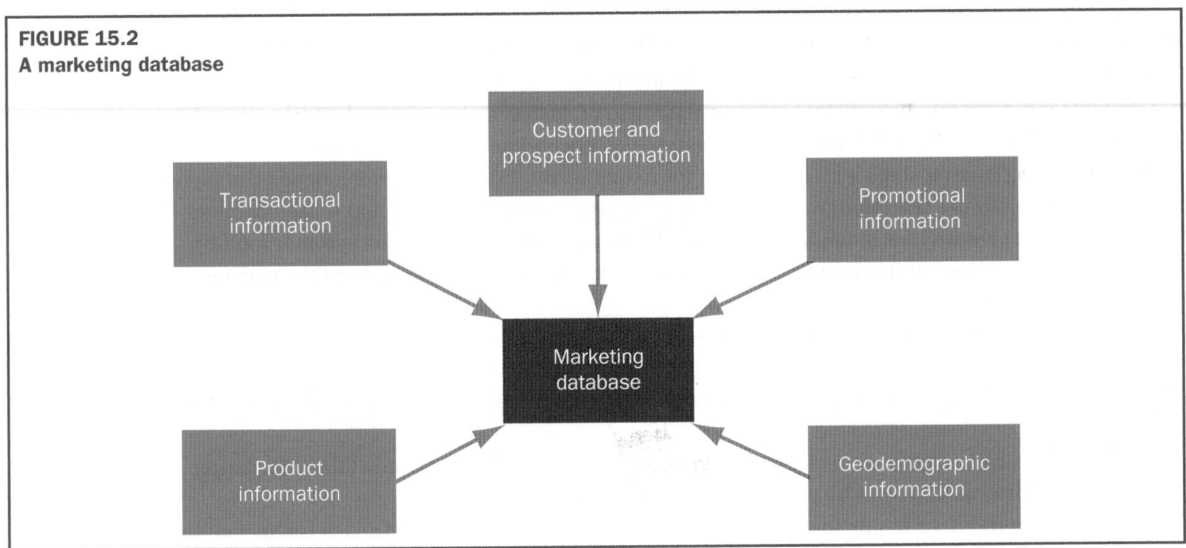

- *Recency* measures when the customer last bought. If customers are waiting longer before they rebuy (i.e. recency is increasing), the reasons for this (e.g. less attractive offers or service problems) need to be explored.
- *Amount* measures how much a customer has bought and is usually recorded in value terms. Analysis of this data may reveal that 20 per cent of customers are accounting for 80 per cent of the value of transactions.
- Finally, *category* defines the type of product being bought. Cross-analysing category data with type of customer (e.g. geodemographics or lifestyle data) can reveal the customer profile most likely to buy a product. Also, promotions can be targeted at those individuals known to be interested in buying from a product category.

Promotional information

This covers information on what promotional campaigns have been run, who has responded to them and what the overall results were in terms of contacts, sales and profits. The database will contain information on which customers were targeted and the media and contact strategy employed.

Product information

This information would include which products have been promoted, who responded, when, and from where.

EXHIBIT 15.1
Ryman's stationers gathers detailed information when opening business accounts

Geodemographic information

Information about the geographic areas of customers and prospects, and the social, lifestyle or business category they belong to is stored. By including postcodes in the addresses of customers and employing the services of an agency such as Acorn, that conducts a geodemographic analysis a customer profile can be built up. Direct mail could then be targeted at people with similar geodemographic profiles.

The main application of marketing databases

Marketing databases have the following uses.

- Developing targeted direct marketing campaigns: for example, a special offer on garden tools from a mail-order company could be targeted at those people who have purchased gardening products in the past. Another example is a car dealer which, by holding a database of customers' names and addresses and dates of car purchase, could use direct mail to promote service offers and new model launches.
- Strengthening relationships with customers: for example, direct marketing techniques can be used strategically to improve customer retention, with long-term programmes established to maximize customer lifetime value. Mini Case 15.1 shows how a database could be used by a retailer to develop customer loyalty.
- Developing an information resource for use in direct marketing campaigns. For this, various techniques are employed:
  - *Direct mail*: a database can be used to select customers for mailings.
  - *Telemarketing*: a database can store telephone numbers so that customers and prospects can be contacted. Also, when customers contact the company by telephone, relevant information can be stored, including when the next contact should be made.
  - *Distributor management systems*: a database can be the foundation on which information is provided to distributors and their can be performance monitored.
  - *Loyalty marketing*: highly loyal customers can be selected from the database for special treatment as a reward for their loyalty.
  - *Target marketing*: other groups of individuals or businesses can be targeted as a result of analysing the database. For example, buyer behaviour information stored by supermarkets can be used to target special promotions to those individuals likely to be receptive to them. For example, a consumer promotion for organic baby foods could be sent exclusively to mothers with young babies.
  - *Campaign planning*: the database can be used as a foundation for sending consistent and coordinated campaigns and messages to individuals and market segments.
  - *Marketing evaluation*: by recording responses to marketing mix inputs (e.g. price promotions, advertising messages and product offers), it is possible to assess how effective different approaches are to various individuals and market segments.

The marketing database is at the heart of customer relationship management systems.

MINI CASE 15.1
Using a Marketing Database in Retailing

Marketing databases offer great potential for planning and developing integrated marketing communications campaigns. Suppose a retailer wanted to increase sales and profits using a database. How might this happen? First, the retailer analyses its database to find distinct groups of customers for whom the retailer has the potential to offer superior value. The identification of these target market segments allows tailored products, services and communications to be aimed at them.

The purchasing patterns of individuals are established by means of a loyalty card programme which enables companies to use the data generated to work out patterns of shopper behaviour at a detailed level. Retailers might argue that the aim of their loyalty scheme is to improve customer retention by rewarding various shopping behaviours, but the reality is that such schemes allow customers to be tracked by frequency of visit, expenditure per visit and expenditure per product category. Loyalty schemes are less about garnering customer allegiance to a particular brand and more about creating an opportunity for companies to capture data that can be used for future marketing initiatives. Retailers can gain an understanding of the types of products that are purchased together. For example, Boots, the UK retailer, uses its Advantage card loyalty scheme (which has 15 million active members) to conduct these kinds of analysis. Analysis of Advantage card data revealed a link between the purchase of digital photo frames and new-baby products, for example. Because its products are organized along category lines, it never occurred to the retailer to create a special offer linked to picture frames for the baby products buyer, yet these are the kinds of products that new parents are likely to want.

If a retailer's customers are classified into market segments based on their potential, their degree of loyalty, and whether they are predominantly price- or promotion-sensitive, analysis of loyalty data means that it is possible to tailor the marketing strategy at a very personal level. For example, to trade up high-potential, promotion-sensitive, low-loyalty shoppers who do their main shopping elsewhere, high-value manufacturers' coupons for main shopping products might be mailed every two months until the consumer is traded up to a different group. Also, high-loyalty customers can be targeted for special treatment such as receiving a customer magazine.

The Tesco Clubcard gathers a rich stream of information from 16 million Clubcard members across the UK, which is then used, for example, to: define segments—for example, discount-driven 'price sensitives', 'foodies', 'heavy category users' and 'brand loyalists'; test consumer response to promotions; test the effects of different prices and the use of different media; and communicate more effectively with consumers. Product assortments in stores can also be fine-tuned according to the buying habits of customers.

Both the Boots Advantage and Tesco Clubcard schemes have worked hard to tailor the rewards offered to consumers. For example, Boots launched a Health Club and a Parenting Club to offer card holders rewards relevant to their lifestyles and interests. Tesco Clubcard enabled its users to collect green Clubcard points when they used their own shopping bags. Tesco is also using its Clubcard data to influence the choices its customers make, encouraging healthier choices. Insights from the loyalty card data enable profiling of customers using a health score for every basket of food sold to a Clubcard member. Customers are then sent targeted mailings and offers. This data is also used to inform the content of the supermarket's free monthly magazine with healthy recipes and tips on making better choices.

The success of the Boots Advantage card and the Tesco Clubcard continues to prompt other retailers to launch loyalty cards: for example Waitrose, the high-quality UK supermarket, has invested in developing a loyalty card as part of its strategy to reward customers, and Morrisons has its Match & More card. Rewarding customers has been found to be a highly successful strategy for improving return on investment. Staples, the office and business stationery supplier, has introduced a reward card targeting small businesses and uses the data on purchasing patterns to drive online promotional offers. Nectar is Britain's biggest loyalty card, with over 18 million subscribers. It started as a joint initiative launched by its founders (Sainsbury's, BP, Barclaycard and Debenhams) and is constantly expanding its company membership in order to extend the rewards it can

»

offer to signed-up shoppers. For example, Nectar points can be collected from Sainsbury's, eBay, Amazon, Sky and other Nectar member companies and then be used to buy goods.

In the early days when the technology needed to set up loyalty schemes was expensive, only the largest retailers offered loyalty cards, but implementation costs have fallen dramatically, which has meant that more companies in different industries are developing such schemes. For example, Tata Group, which is India's biggest family conglomerate, has set up a loyalty scheme modelled on Nectar.

Questions:

1 Why do companies launch loyalty cards?
2 Explain the type of data you might need to gather if you wanted to improve customer retention.

Based on: Mitchell (2002); James (2003); Barnes (2005); McCawley (2006); Murphy (2008); Finch (2009); Charles (2011); Clews (2011); The Economist (2011); Hammett (2018)

Managing a Direct Marketing Campaign

Direct marketing can be very effective when integrated with other elements of the promotional mix and used to support a coherent *marketing strategy*. In Chapter 13, on integrated marketing communications, it was stressed that all of the communication tools should send a consistent message and reinforce other elements of the marketing mix (product, place and price). Following this logic, messages sent out using various direct marketing media should also form a coherent whole. For example, information disseminated through advertising should be consistent with that sent out via a direct mail campaign. In the past, there was sometimes a tendency for direct marketing campaigns not to use multiple contacts or multiple media. However, increased use of digital channels gives direct marketers the opportunity to use a combination of media in sequence to achieve their objectives. For example, a business-to-business company marketing a new adhesive might place a direct response advertisement in trade magazines to stimulate trial and orders. A response coupon, freephone telephone number and email address would be provided, and prospects invited to choose their most convenient method of contact. An inbound telemarketing team would be trained to receive calls and take either orders or requests for samples for trial. Another team would deal with mail and email correspondence. An outbound telemarketing team would follow up prospects judged to be of small and medium potential and the salesforce would target large potential customers and prospects.

FIGURE 15.3
Managing a direct marketing campaign

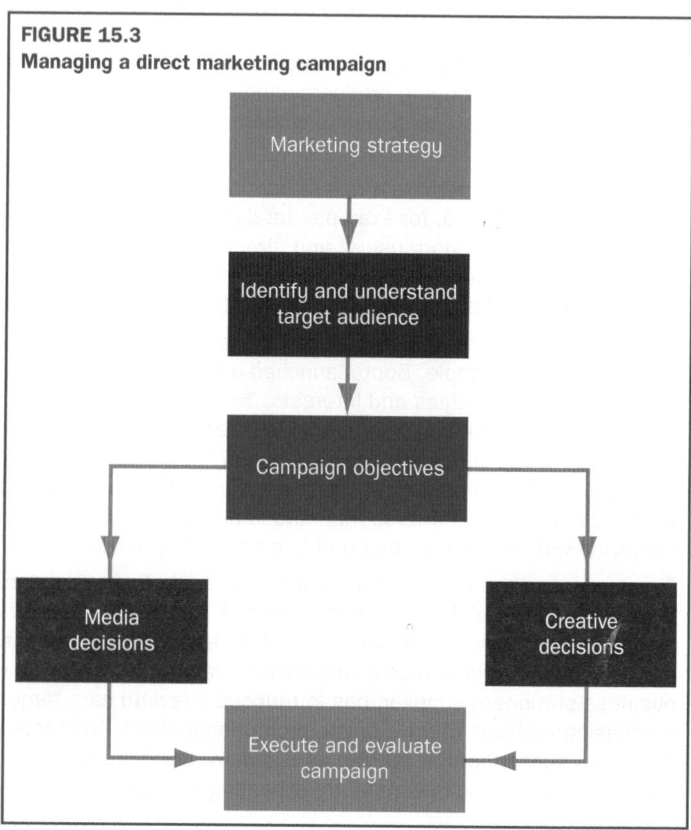

Accordingly, direct marketers need to understand how a product is positioned and its target market, as it is crucial that messages sent out as part of a direct marketing campaign do not conflict with those communicated by other channels such as advertising or the salesforce. The integrating mechanism is a clear definition of marketing strategy. Figure 15.3 shows the steps in the management of a direct marketing campaign.

In essence, the key stages in a direct marketing campaign are similar to those in a mass communication plan (as discussed in Chapter 14). However, there are certain differences at each of the stages.

Identifying and understanding the target audience

The target audiences are the groups of people at whom the direct marketing campaign is aimed (targeting strategies are described in Chapter 7). Lifestyle is often targeted, but a particularly useful method of segmentation for direct marketing purposes involves considering the following groups.

- *Competitors' customers*: all people who buy the types of product that the company produces but from its competitors.
- *Prospects*: people who have not bought from the company before but who qualify as potential purchasers (e.g. if the customers are large companies, other large companies should be targeted).
- *Enquirers*: people who have contacted the organization and shown interest in one or more products but, as yet, have not bought.
- *Lapsed customers*: people who have purchased in the past but appear to have ceased buying.
- *Referrals*: people who have been recommended to the organization as potential customers.
- *Existing customers*: people who are continuing to buy.

Read Marketing in Action 15.2 to appreciate the usefulness of target audience identification to Butchers & Bicycles.

MARKETING IN ACTION 15.2
Society Profits from Cyclists, but Who is Doing the Driving?

Morten Wagener, Morten Mogensen and Jakob Munk are Danish designers and innovators who founded the cargo and personal transportation bicycle company Butchers & Bicycles. They identified a business opportunity to improve the future of urban transport. The idea was that most of the trikes (three-wheeled bikes) on the market lacked good design, manoeuvrability and styling. With their backgrounds in engineering, the partners set out to design a new trike that would meet the needs of the target market, which their research identified as well-educated individuals who were very interested in aesthetics. The team was convinced that trikes were one of the answers to future urban transportation problems, so they decided to develop the best trike they could in terms of quality, style, design, manoeuvrability, safety and a great riding experience. Each trike is hand-made, and there is a waiting time of up to two months between order and delivery.

From a marketing perspective, one of the differentiating factors of the Butchers & Bicycles product is the quality of the ride (compared with that of competing products). The team coined the slogan 'built to tilt', because even though the vehicle is a trike, it feels like a two-wheeled bicycle to ride. The challenge was how to go to market with a marketing budget close to zero.

The target group had been clear from the beginning: consumers who were lifestyle orientated, such as readers of *Monocle* and *Wallpaper* magazines—first movers who appreciate quality and are willing to pay for it. Many of these customers were young urban families that might buy a Butchers & Bicycles trike as an alternative to a second car. Also, Copenhagen (Denmark's capital city) is number one in investment in cycling infrastructure, which makes it easier for families to adopt this form of transport.

How to reach the target market was initially a challenge, but the team at Butchers & Bicycles invested in the design of the website and in a professional promotional video that has reached hundreds of thousands people since its launch. It also has Facebook and Instagram pages, which are used to build and develop customer relationships. This approach is rather organic insofar as the company has built a reputation through word of mouth and social media, but it has proved highly effective.

Based On: Butchers & Bicycles (n.d.); Colville-Andersen (2015)

Once a target group is identified, the marketing manager has to consider how to access the group. This may be done through existing internet information from the customer relationship management system and marketing database, which will provide a list of existing contacts, or it may come from an external list broker. Experian is a global provider of individual and company information for direct marketing initiatives. Understanding current trends and changes in buying behaviour is important. For example, consumers have become increasingly in favour of opening direct mail letters if they perceive that the offer is relevant to them. In fact, consumers seem to have become less cynical about this form of communication and are often prompted to open the mailing to see whether there are any reward vouchers or coupons (Handley, 2011).

Campaign objectives

Campaign objectives vary and may focus on: financial goals—sales, profits and return on investment; marketing goals—acquire or retain customers or generate enquiries; and communication goals—create awareness or change beliefs. However, one of the benefits of direct marketing is its capacity to deliver against short-term objectives, which are easily measured and evaluated.

Acquisition

Acquisition objectives can be costly, as it is more expensive to attract new customers than develop and keep existing ones. So a consideration when setting this type of campaign objective is the concept of *lifetime value*. This measures the profits that can be expected from customers over their expected life with a company. Banks know, for example, that gaining student accounts has very high lifetime value, since switching between banks is unusual. This means that the allowable marketing cost per acquisition (or how much a company can afford to spend to acquire a new customer) can be quite high. If the calculation was based on potential profits while a student, the figure would be much lower. The establishment of a marketing database can, over time, provide valuable information on buying patterns, which aids the calculation of lifetime value.

Retention

Retention objectives focus on keeping customers and can have a direct impact on profitability. Customer loyalty programmes have blossomed as a result, with direct marketing playing a key role. Retention programmes are aimed at maximizing a customer's lifetime value to the company. Maintaining a long-term relationship with a customer provides the opportunity to up-sell, cross-sell and renew business. Up-selling involves the promotion of higher-value products, for example a more expensive car. Cross-selling entails the switching of customers to other product categories, as when a music club promotes a book collection. Renewal involves timing communications to existing customers for when they are about to repurchase. For example, car dealers often send direct mail promotional material two years after the purchase of a car, since many people change cars after that period.

Creative decisions

Most direct marketing campaigns have different objectives from those of advertising. Whereas advertising usually attempts to create awareness and position the image of a brand in the prospects' minds, the aim of most direct marketing is to make a sale. It is more orientated to immediate action than advertising is. Recipients of direct marketing messages (particularly through direct mail) need to see a clear benefit in responding.

Costa Coffee Club offers its members (in return for signing up via the website and providing personal data) five points per pound on purchases. The Costa Coffee Club has worked very well and has a positive impact on customers' frequency of consumption (Baker, 2012).

Marmite, the savoury spread, developed an IMC campaign based on a scientific study, and called it the gene project. A humorous television advert suggested that people are genetically predisposed to love or hate Marmite and invited them to get a test kit to find out online by sharing images and videos. Subsequently, a gene test kit was sent through direct mail. Sales of the brand increased by 14 per cent (D&DAD, 2018).

Creative decisions will be captured using a creative brief, which is a document that usually contains details of specific communications objectives, product benefits, target market analysis, details of the offer being made, the message that is to be communicated and the action plan (i.e. how the campaign will be run).

Executing and evaluating the campaign

Execution of the campaign may be in-house or through the use of a specialist agency. Direct marketing activity usually has clearly defined short-term objectives against which performance can be measured. Some of the most frequently used measurements are:

- response rate (the proportion of contacts responding)
- total sales (volume and value)
- number of contacts purchasing
- sales rate (percentage of contacts purchasing)
- number of enquiries
- enquiry rate
- cost per contact
- cost per enquiry
- cost per sale
- conversion rate from enquiry to sale
- average order value
- renewal rate
- repeat purchase rate.

Direct marketers should bear in mind the longer-term effects of their activities. A campaign may seemingly be unprofitable in the short term, but when renewals and repeat purchases are considered, the long-term value of the campaign may be highly positive.

Selling and Sales Management

Building and exploiting relationships for mutual benefit is at the heart of personal selling and traditionally involves face-to-face contact with a customer. But, increasingly, e-commerce is expanding selling opportunities, and more consumer and B2B transactions take place online (Palmatier et al., 2013). Personal selling is important in consumer marketing, as it is a communication technique widely used in the B2B market, especially when a high value contract is at stake. Unlike advertising, promotion, sponsorship and other forms of non-personal communication, personal selling permits a direct interaction between buyer and seller (in physical face-to-face situations). This two-way communication means that the seller can identify the specific needs and problems of the buyer and tailor the sales presentation in the light of this knowledge. The concerns of the buyer can also be dealt with on a one-to-one basis.

This flexibility comes only at a cost. The cost of time to be involved in the selling process, and the costs of travel and sales office overheads can mean that the field salesperson is a relatively costly asset. In B2B marketing, large proportions of the communications budget can be spent on the salesforce. US firms spend more than $140 billion on advertising and $800 billion on personal selling (Lee, Sridhar and Palmatier, 2017). This cost is often because of the technical nature of the products being sold and the need to maintain close personal relationships between the selling and buying organizations. By removing barriers, sales teams can reassure customers about products and services.

However, the nature of the personal selling function is changing. Organizations are reducing the size of their salesforces in the face of greater buyer concentration, moves towards centralized buying, and recognition of the high costs of maintaining a field sales team. Innovative digital solutions exist which are also helping to make sales teams more effective and their responses to customers more responsive and efficient. For example, Salesforce.com developed an innovative digital platform in the cloud that enables its users to manage collaborations, within- and across sales channels, customer relationships, employee workload and performance, plus a range of other functions (Salesforce.com, 2018). It has been estimated that, by 2020, 85 per cent of customer transactions will not require the involvement of a salesperson, and, ultimately, this will reduce the need for sales teams (Baumgartner, Hatami and Valdivieso, 2016). Artificial intelligence applications are being developed to handle sales leads, contact and follow-up, and to respond to customer queries.

This trend towards automation of the sales process is likely to lead to further concentration of buying power into fewer hands and to heighten the importance of customer relationship management and of key account selling, which involves the use of dedicated sales teams that service the accounts of major buyers.

The changing marketing environment is affecting selling and sales management, and many companies are looking for ways to optimize the performance of their sales teams. The next section explores the characteristics of selling that are required to cope with the changing and challenging marketing environment.

Characteristics of Selling

In today's competitive environment, a salesforce must have a wide range of skills to compete successfully. Gone are the days when salespeople required simple presentational and closing skills to be successful. The characteristics of selling require a wide array of skills, and without such an understanding salespeople will be ill-equipped to tackle the following activities successfully.

Customer retention and deletion

Many companies find that 80 per cent of their sales come from 20 per cent of their customers. This means that it is vital to devote considerable resources to retaining existing high-volume, high-potential and highly profitable customers. **Key account management** (see later in this chapter) has become an important form of sales organization, as it means that a salesperson or sales team can focus their efforts on fewer major customers.

At the other end of the spectrum, companies are finding that some small customers cost the organization money. This is because servicing and distribution of products to these customers may push costs beyond the revenue generated; but technology-driven solutions, for example customer relationship management, **telemarketing** and **e-commerce** systems, are providing ways to service accounts and control costs using digital solutions.

Customer relationship management

Growing emphasis on customer retention as part of strategic customer management has led to an increasing use of **customer relationship management** systems (see Chapter 10). The challenge is to reposition sales as a core element of a company's competitiveness, where the sales organization is closely integrated into marketing strategy and planning (Stephens, 2003). This process places the customer at the centre of the company's focus, with the sales organization charged with taking a strategic view of designing and implementing superior customer relationships (Lane and Piercy, 2004). This requires sales management to work towards the total integration of how customer relationships are designed, established, managed and sustained. For example, Cisco Systems has developed sales strategies and selling tools to support the personal selling process: Webex Teams is transforming how IBM Norway manages its teams. See Exhibit 15.2.

Knowledge management

Knowing your customers and how they want to interact with a firm is becoming increasingly important. Equally important is understanding how the salesforce interacts with and responds to customers. Technological advances such as email, mobile phones, web conferencing and sales support systems have transformed the way in which knowledge is transferred, which is becoming increasingly automated. The cloud and mobile computing devices mean that salespeople can store customer and competitor information, make presentations and communicate with head office electronically. Furthermore, all the information needed to make a sale, such as price lists, product availability and delivery times, can be held electronically so that it is readily available anywhere.

EXHIBIT 15.2
IBM Norway works with Cisco Webex Teams to improve meetings, interactions and collaboration

Source: https://www.cisco.com/c/en/us/solutions/collaboration/ibm-norway.html

Salesforce.com is leading the way in salesforce automation. Its digital platforms are designed to speed up the closing of sales deals, automatically generate leads and help to make decisions. In addition, they provide account and contact management.

Problem-solving and system selling

Personal selling, particularly in B2B situations, is based upon the salesperson acting as an expert/consultant who works with the customer to identify problems, determine needs, and propose and implement effective solutions (Rackham and DeVincentis, 1999). This approach is fundamentally different from the traditional view of the salesperson as a smooth fast-talker who breezes in to see a customer, persuades them to buy and walks away with an order. Selling often involves multiple interactions, online and by phone calls, the use of a team-selling approach and considerable analytical skills. Furthermore, customers are increasingly looking for a systems solution rather than buying an individual product. This means, for example, that to sell door handles to a firm like Ford Motor Company, a supplier must be able to sell a door *system* that includes door handles, locking and opening devices, as well as having a thorough knowledge of door technology and the ability to suggest to Ford solutions to problems that may arise.

Satisfying needs and adding value

A salesperson must have the ability to identify and satisfy customer needs. Some customers do not recognize that they have a need. It is the salesperson's job in such situations to stimulate need recognition. For example, a customer may not realize that a machine in the production process has low productivity compared with newer, more technologically advanced machines. The salesperson's job will be to make the customer aware of the problem to convince him/her that they have a need to modernize the production process. In so doing, the salesperson will have added value to the customer's business by reducing costs, and created a win/win situation for both the company and the customer.

Personal Selling and Sales Management

Success in selling comes from implementing the marketing concept when face to face with customers; increasingly this involves building long-term relationships with more emphasis on customer needs and wants and less on short-term sales transactions. Salespeople have an opportunity to implement unique presentations tailored to individual customers and to rapidly adjust messages in response to customer reactions. Indeed, research has shown that such customer-orientated selling is associated with higher levels of salesforce performance (Román, Ruiz and Munuera, 2002). Research has shown that making the customer central to the selling activity can deliver greater success than high-pressure selling tactics. But there are also many challenges to overcome if a sales team is to be successful.

Understanding buyer behaviour

Thought should also be given to understanding *buyer behaviour* (see Chapters 3 and 4). Questions should be asked, such as who are the likely key people to talk to, what are their probable choice criteria, are there any gatekeepers preventing access to some people, who need to be circumvented, and what are the likely opportunities and threats that may arise in the selling situation. All of the answers to these questions need to be verified when in the actual selling situation, but prior consideration can help salespeople to be clear in their own minds about the important issues.

The internet can provide a wealth of information about the buying organization. The buyer's website, online product catalogues and blogs are useful sources of information. Customer relationship management systems allow salespeople to access customer information held by their company, via the internet. But herein lies a potential problem: as customers expect more, sales teams need to be more informed and more able to search vast stores of information to find out about their customers' needs. See Marketing in Action 15.3 to find out more about how technology is changing the rules of the selling game.

MARKETING IN ACTION 15.3
Technology Rules, Online and on the Road

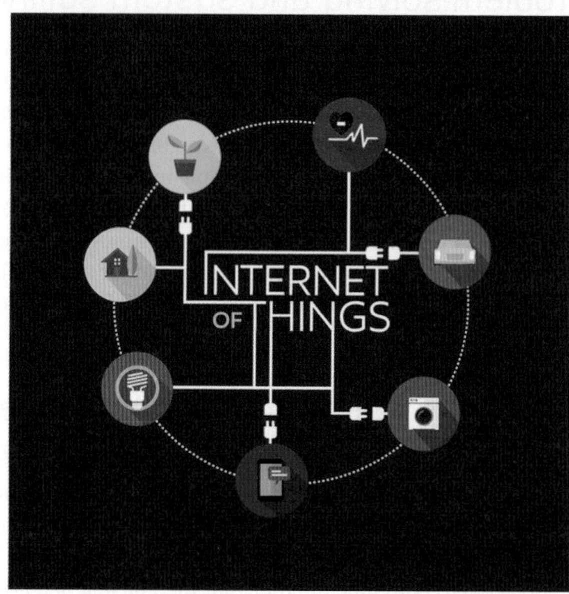

Technology is enabling sales teams to be more informed about their customers' behaviour and is providing better and more responsive sales experiences. Mobile apps, analytics, cloud computing and mobile peripherals mean that sales representatives can have a wealth of information at their fingertips. From the software industry through to the financial sector and pharmaceuticals to the toy industry, companies are increasingly using sophisticated technology to enhance the selling process. For example, sales representatives who work for French toy manufacturer Juratoys use iPads and mobile phones to take orders, check stock availability and show their customers new lines and back-catalogue items.

These are the key technology trends that marketers in direct selling should be aware of.

- The Internet of Things (IoT) is enabling communications between people, between people and things, and between things and other things. This concept is not new, but it has become significant in recent years because there are now more interactions and communications between an ever-growing number of people and things. And when these interactions occur, data is created that can be collected and analysed. So, the challenge is for companies to be able to set up systems that ensure that their sales teams have access to such information.

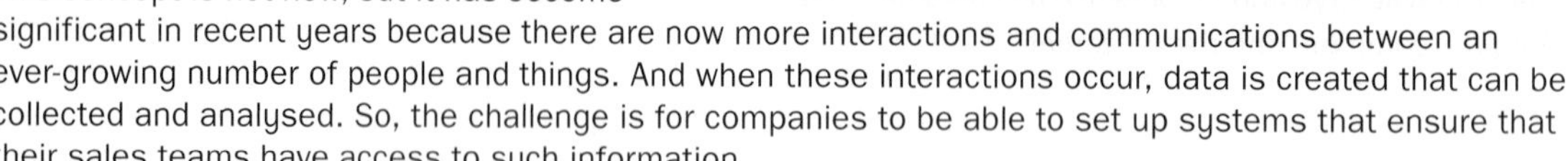

- Data analytics are providing greater insight into opportunities and customer behaviour. By linking customer relationship management systems to other forms of data capture devices linked to the IoT, salespeople can provide decisions and sales solutions. But companies must ensure that all their information systems are connected if they are to gain the most benefit.
- Cloud computing is creating opportunities to link up all the way through the sales process. This is improving the *richness* of available information and improving flexibility. For example, iPads are widely used in pharmaceutical sales; in this setting, technology is providing both sales representatives and doctors with access to extensive information and other collaborative sales tools such as web conferencing.

The impact of these trends is that buyers and sellers can collaborate in real time, negotiations can be handled and supported anywhere in the world, and the speed of selling is increasing.

Based on: Vongsingthong and Smanchat (2014); Zoltners, Sinha and Lorimer (2015); Movahhed (2014)

Identifying customer needs

People buy products because they have problems that give rise to needs. For example, a machine's unreliability (problem) causes the need to replace it with a new one (purchase). Therefore the first task is to identify the needs and problems of each customer. Only by doing so can the salesperson connect with each customer's situation. Having done so, the salesperson can select the product that best fits the customer's need and sell the appropriate benefits. It is benefits that link customer needs to product features, as in:

$$\text{customer need} \rightarrow \text{benefit} \leftarrow \text{product feature}$$

In the previous example, it would be essential to convince the customer that the salesperson's machine possessed features that guaranteed machine reliability. Knowledge of competitors' products would allow salespeople to show how their machine possessed features that gave added reliability. In this way, salespeople are in an ideal situation to convince customers of a product's differential advantage. Whenever possible, factual evidence of product superiority should be shown to customers. This is much more convincing than mere claims by the salesperson.

Effective needs and problem identification requires the development of questioning and listening skills. The problem is that people are more used to making statements than asking questions. Therefore the art of asking sensible questions that produce a clear understanding of the customer's situation requires training and considerable experience. The hallmark of inexperienced salespeople is that they do all the talking; successful salespeople know how to get the customer to do most of the talking. In this way, they gain the information necessary to make a sale. For example, Best Buy is a consumer electronics company that has struggled in recent years due to aggressive competition, especially from online retailers like Amazon. However, the business has been turned around by finding out about its end consumers and sharing this information with its suppliers. Best Buy began listening to its customers through the web and looking at online reviews, and has been able to tailor its product offer to better suit customer needs (Reid, 2015).

Dealing with cultural nuances

Salespeople operating in overseas markets need to be aware of the cultural nuances that shape business relationships. For example, in the west, a deadline is acceptable, whereas in many Middle Eastern cultures it would be taken as an insult. In China, salespeople need to acknowledge the importance of personalized and close business relationships, known as *guanxi*. *Guanxi* is a set of personal relationships/connections on which a person can draw to secure resources or advantage when doing business. *Guanxi* can lead to preferential treatment in the form of easy access to limited resources, increased accessibility to information and preferential credit terms. For foreigners, this means having as part of their *guanxi* network an influential person in an organization or government position. Another key issue in Chinese culture is the avoidance of 'loss of face'. Visiting salespeople should avoid creating a situation where a Chinese person might 'lose face' by finding themselves in an embarrassing situation (e.g. by displaying lack of knowledge or understanding).

Many salespeople make the mistake of using self-reference criteria when selling abroad. They assume that the values and behavioural norms that apply in their own country are equally applicable abroad. To avoid this failing, they need training in the special skills required to sell to people of different cultures.

Sales Management

In many respects, the functions of the sales manager are like those of other managers. Sales managers, like their production, marketing and finance counterparts, need to recruit, train, motivate and evaluate their staff. However, there are several peculiarities of the job that make effective sales management difficult and the job considerably demanding.

Problems of sales management

Geographic separation

The geographic separation between sales managers and their field salesforce creates problems of motivation, communication and control.

Repeated rejections

Salespeople may suffer repeated rejections when trying to close sales. This may cause attrition of their enthusiasm, attitudes and skills. A major role for sales managers is to provide support and renew motivation in such adverse circumstances.

The salesperson's personality versus the realities of the job

Most people who go into sales are outgoing and gregarious. These are desirable characteristics for people who are selling to customers. However, the reality of the job is that, typically, only 30 per cent of a salesperson's time is spent face to face with customers, with travelling (50 per cent) and administration (20 per cent) making up the rest (McDonald, 2002). This means that over half of the salesperson's time is spent alone, which can cause frustration in people who enjoy the company of others.

Oversimplification of the task

Some sales managers cope with the difficulties of management by oversimplifying the task. They take the attitude that they are interested only in results. It is their job to reward those who meet sales targets and severely punish those who fail. Such an attitude ignores the contribution that sales management can make to the successful achievement of objectives. Figure 15.4 shows the functions of a sales manager and the relationship between marketing strategy and the personal selling function.

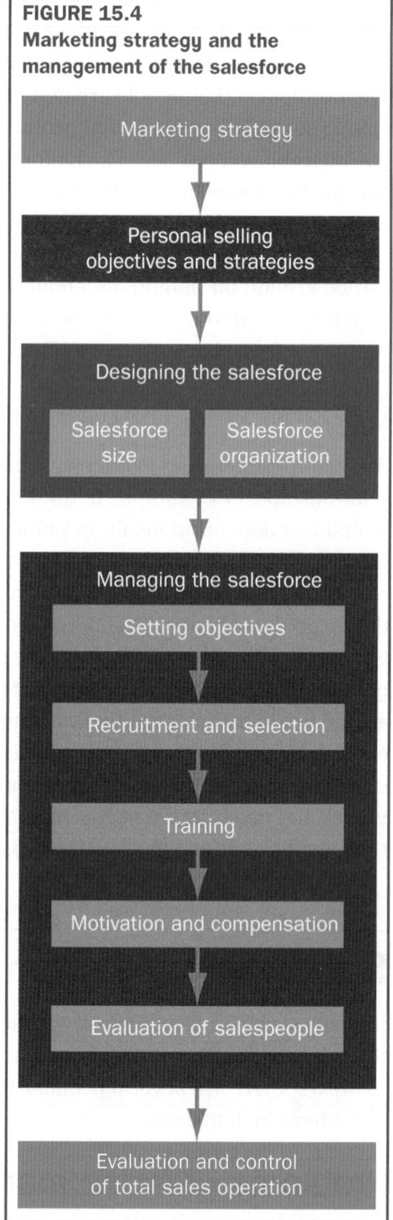

FIGURE 15.4
Marketing strategy and the management of the salesforce

Marketing strategy

As with all parts of the marketing mix, the personal selling function is not a standalone element, but one that must be considered in the light of the overall marketing strategy. At the product level, two major marketing considerations are:

1 choice of target market
2 the creation of a differential advantage.

Both of these decisions affect personal selling.

The definition of the target market has clear implications for sales management because of its relationship to **target accounts**. Once the target market has been defined (e.g. organizations in a particular industry over a certain size), sales management can translate that specification into individual accounts to target. Salesforce resources can, therefore, be deployed to maximum effect.

The creation of a differential advantage is the starting point of a successful marketing strategy, but this needs to be communicated to the salesforce and embedded in a sales plan which ensures that the salesforce is able to articulate it convincingly to customers. There are two common dangers. The first danger is that the salesforce undermines the differential advantage by repeatedly giving in to customer demands for price concessions. The second danger is that the features that underlie the differential advantage are communicated but the customer benefits are neglected. Customer benefits need to be communicated in terms that are meaningful to customers. This means, for example, that advantages such as higher productivity may require translation into cash savings or higher revenue for financially minded customers.

Four strategic objectives

Marketing strategy also affects the personal selling function through strategic objectives. Each objective—build, hold, harvest and divest—has implications for *sales objectives* and strategy; these are outlined in Table 15.2. Linking business or product area strategic objectives with functional area strategies is essential for the efficient allocation of resources and effective implementation in the marketplace (Strahle and Spiro, 1986).

Personal selling objectives and strategies

As we have seen, selling objectives and strategies are derived from marketing strategy decisions and should be consistent with other elements of the marketing mix. Indeed, marketing strategy will determine whether there is a need for a salesforce at all or whether the selling role can be accomplished better by using some other medium such as **direct mail**. Objectives define what the selling function is expected to achieve. Objectives are typically defined in terms of:

- sales volume (e.g. 5 per cent growth in sales volume)
- market share (e.g. 1 per cent increase in market share)
- profitability (e.g. maintenance of gross profit margin)

TABLE 15.2 Marketing strategy and sales management

Strategic marketing objective	Sales objective	Sales strategy
Build	Build sales volume Increase distribution Provide high service levels	High call rates on existing accounts High focus during call Call on new accounts (prospecting)
Hold	Maintain sales volume Maintain distribution Maintain service levels	Continue present call rates on current accounts Medium focus during call Call on new outlets when they appear
Harvest	Reduce selling costs Target profitable accounts Reduce service costs and inventories	Call only on profitable accounts Consider telemarketing or dropping the rest No prospecting
Divest	Clear inventory quickly	Quantity discounts to targeted accounts

Source: adapted from Strahle and Spiro (1986).

- service levels (e.g. 20 per cent increase in number of customers regarding salesperson assistance as 'good or better' in annual customer survey)
- salesforce costs (e.g. 5 per cent reduction in expenses).

Salesforce strategy defines how those objectives will be achieved. The following may be considered:

- call rates
- percentage of calls on existing versus potential accounts
- discount policy (the extent to which reductions from list prices are allowed)
- percentage of resources
  - targeted at new versus existing products
  - targeted at selling versus providing after-sales service
  - targeted at field selling vs telemarketing
  - targeted at different types of customers (e.g. high versus low potential)
- improving customer and market feedback from the salesforce
- improving customer relationships.

Once sales managers have a clear idea of what they hope to achieve and how best to set about accomplishing these objectives, they can make sensible decisions regarding salesforce design.

Designing the salesforce

Two critical design decisions are those of determining salesforce size and salesforce organization.

Salesforce size

The most practical method for deciding the number of salespeople is called the *workload approach*. It is based on the calculation of the total annual calls required per year divided by the average calls per year that can be expected from one salesperson (Talley, 1961). The procedure follows seven steps, as outlined below.

1 Customers are grouped into categories according to the value of goods bought, their potential for the future, and the need for prospecting.
2 The call frequency (number of calls per year to an account) is assessed for each category of customer.
3 The total required workload per year is calculated by multiplying the call frequency by the number of customers in each category and then summing for all categories.
4 The average number of calls that can be expected per salesperson per week is estimated.
5 The number of working weeks per year is calculated.
6 The average number of calls a salesperson can make per year is calculated by multiplying items 4 and 5.
7 The number of salespeople required is determined by dividing the total number of annual calls required by the average number of calls one salesperson can make per year.

Salesforce organization

There are three basic forms of *salesforce organization*: geographic, product and customer-based structures. The strengths and weakness of each are as follows.

1. *Geographic*: the sales area is broken down into territories based on workload and potential, and a salesperson is assigned to each one to sell all of the product range. This provides a simple, unambiguous definition of each salesperson's sales territory, and proximity to customers encourages the development of personal relationships. It is also a more cost-efficient method of organization than product- or customer-based systems. However, when products are technically different and sell in a number of diverse markets, it may be unreasonable to expect a salesperson to be knowledgeable about all products and their applications. Under such circumstances, a company is likely to move to a product- or customer-based structure.
2. *Product*: product specialization is effective where a company has a diverse product range selling to different customers (or at least different people within a given organization). However, if the products sell, essentially, to the same customers, problems of route duplication (and, consequently, higher travel costs) and multiple calls on the same customer can arise. When applicable, product specialization allows each salesperson to be well informed about a product line, its applications and customer benefits. Hewlett-Packard uses a product-based system because of its wide product range. The salespeople are assigned to one of its three divisions: PCs, laptops and handheld devices; printers and printing; or IT solutions for large enterprises.
3. *Customer-based*: the problem of the same customer being served by product divisions of the same supplier, the complexity of buyer behaviour that requires input not only from the sales function but from other functional groups (such as engineering, finance, logistics and marketing), centralization of purchasing, and the immense value of some customers have led many suppliers to rethink how they organize their salesforces. Companies are increasingly organizing around customers and shifting resources from product or regional divisions to customer-focused business units (Homburg, Workman and Jensen, 2000). Salesforces can be organized along market segment, account size or new versus existing account lines. Computer firms have traditionally organized their salesforce on the basis of industry served (e.g. banking, retailing, manufacturing), in recognition of their varying needs, problems and potential applications. Specialization by these *market segments* allows salespeople to gain in-depth knowledge of customers and be able to monitor trends in the industry that may affect demand for their products. In some industries, the applications knowledge of market-based salespeople has led them to be known as *fraternity brothers* by their customers (Magrath, 1989). An increasing trend in many industries is towards key account management, which reflects the increasing concentration of buying power into fewer but larger customers. These customers are serviced by a key account salesforce comprising senior salespeople who develop close personal relationships with customers, can handle sophisticated sales arguments and are skilled in the art of negotiation. For more detailed discussion of key account management, see later in this chapter. Table 15.3 illustrates some important distinctions between traditional (transactional selling) and key account management.

TABLE 15.3 Distinctions between transactional selling and key account management

	Transactional selling	Key account management
Overall objective	Sales	Preferred supplier status
Sales skills	Asking questions Handling objections Closing	Building trust Negotiation Providing excellent service
Nature of relationship	Short, intermittent	Long, more intensive interaction
Salesperson goal	Closed sale	Relationship management
Nature of salesforce	One or two salespeople per customer	Many salespeople, often involving multifunctional teams

Managing the salesforce

Besides deciding personal selling objectives and strategies and designing the salesforce, the company has to manage the salesforce. This requires setting specific salesperson objectives, recruitment and selection, training, motivation and compensation, and evaluation of salespeople. These activities have been shown to improve salesperson performance, indicating the key role that sales managers play as facilitators in helping salespeople to perform better (Piercy, Cravens and Morgan, 1998).

Setting objectives

To achieve aggregate sales objectives, individual salespeople need to have their own sales targets to achieve. Usually, targets are set in sales terms (sales quotas) but, increasingly, profit targets are being used, reflecting the need to guard against sales being bought cheaply by excessive discounting. To gain commitment to targets, consultation with individual salespeople is recommended, but, in the final analysis, it is the sales manager's responsibility to set targets. Payment may be linked to the achievement of the targets. Sales management may also wish to set input objectives, such as the proportion of time spent developing new accounts and the time spent introducing new products. They may also specify the number of calls expected per day and the precise customers who should be called.

Recruitment and selection

The importance of recruiting high-calibre salespeople cannot be overestimated. Clearly, the quality of the salespeople that sales managers recruit has a substantial effect on performance.

The recruitment and selection process follows five stages:

1. preparation of the job description and personnel specification
2. identification of sources of recruitment and methods of communication
3. design of the application form and preparation of a shortlist
4. the interview
5. use of supplementary selection aids.

Training

Sometimes, more traditional sales managers believe that their salespeople can best train themselves by doing the job. This approach ignores the value of a training programme that provides a frame of reference in which learning can take place, and the potential benefits such as enhanced skill levels, improved motivation, and greater confidence in the ability to perform well at selling, a factor that has been shown to be related to improved sales performance (Krishnan, Netemeyer and Boles, 2002).

B2B customers expect a seamless experience whether they are buying face to face or online (Arli et al., 2018), so a training programme should include knowledge about the company (its objectives, strategies and organization), its products (features and benefits), its competitors and their products, selling procedures and techniques, work organization (including report preparation), and relationship management. Salespeople need to be trained in the management of long-term customer relationships as well as in context-specific selling skills (Wilson, 1993) and should also be aware of the significance of the shift in power towards the customer.

Motivation and compensation

Effective motivation is based on a deep understanding of salespeople as individuals, their personalities and value systems. In one sense, sales managers do not motivate salespeople—they provide the enabling conditions in which salespeople motivate themselves. Motivation can be understood through the relationship between needs, drives and goals. Luthans stated that, 'the basic process involves needs (deprivations) which set drives in motion (deprivations with direction) to accomplish goals (anything which alleviates a need and reduces a drive) (Luthans, 1997). For example, the need for more money may result in a drive to work harder to receive increased pay. Improving motivation is important to sales success; research has shown that high levels of motivation lead to (see Pullins, 2001; Holmes and Srivastava, 2002):

- increased creativity
- working smarter and a more adaptive selling approach

- working harder
- increased use of win/win negotiation tactics
- higher self-esteem
- a more relaxed attitude and a less negative emotional tone
- enhancement of relationships.

It is important to note that motivation needs to encourage the types of behaviour that contribute to a company's marketing strategy and success. Therefore any reward schemes should benefit those who exhibit the correct behaviour.

Stimulating appropriate behaviour in the current sales environment means understanding how to foster trust, commitment and shared values, as these form the basis of strong customer relationships (Morgan and Hunt, 1994).

Evaluation of salespeople

Salesforce evaluation provides the information necessary to check whether targets are being achieved, and it provides the raw information to guide training and motivation. By identifying the strengths and weaknesses of individual salespeople, training can be focused on the areas in need of development, and incentives can be aimed at weak spots such as poor prospecting performance.

Often performance will be compared using standards of performance such as sales or profit quotas, although other comparisons such as salesperson to salesperson or current to past sales are also used. Two types of performance measures are used, based on quantitative and qualitative criteria.

Quantitative measures of performance may include sales revenue, profits generated, gross profit margin, sales per active account, and number of new accounts opened. Input criteria include number of calls and number of prospects visited.

These quantitative measures can be compared against target figures to identify strengths and weaknesses. Many of the measures are diagnostic, pointing to reasons why a target is not being reached. For example, a poor call rate might be a cause of low sales achievement. Measuring call rate is important, as call frequency has been found to have a positive effect on sales volume and customer satisfaction. Some results will merit further investigation. For example, a low prospecting success ratio should prompt an examination of why new accounts are not being opened despite the high number of prospects visited. A survey of evaluation metrics has shown that there is an increasing tendency to use profit-orientated criteria.

Qualitative measures of performance rely on soft data. They are intrinsically more subjective and include assessment of:

- sales skills, for example questioning and making presentations
- customer relationships, for example how much confidence do customers have in the salesperson, and is rapport good
- product knowledge, for example, how well informed the salesperson is regarding the company's and competitors' products
- self-management, for example how well are calls prepared and routes organized
- cooperation and attitudes, for example to what extent does the salesperson show initiative or follow instructions.

An increasing number of companies are measuring their salespeople based on the achievement of customer satisfaction. The use of quantitative and qualitative measures is interrelated. For example, a poor sales per call ratio will mean a close qualitative assessment of sales skills, customer relationships and product knowledge.

Evaluation and control of the total sales operation

Evaluation of the total personal selling function is necessary to assess its overall contribution to marketing strategy. The results of this assessment may lead to a more cost-efficient means of servicing accounts being introduced (e.g. direct mail or telemarketing), the realization that the selling function is underresourced, or the conclusion that the traditional form of sales organization is in need of reform. One company that suspected that its salesforce had become complacent moved every salesperson to a different territory. Despite having to forge new customer relationships, sales increased by a quarter in the following year.

Evaluation of the personal selling function should also include assessing the quality of the function's relationship with marketing and other organizational units. Salespeople who manage the external relationship with distributors (e.g. retailers) must collaborate internally with their colleagues in marketing to agree joint business objectives and to develop marketing programmes (e.g. new products and promotions) that meet the needs of distributors as well as consumers, so that they are readily adopted by them. This means that close collaboration and good working relationships are essential (Dewsnap and Jobber, 2002).

Business-to-Business Relationship Development Strategies

Customer relationships are becoming increasingly important in both business-to-consumer (B2C) and business-to-business (B2B) markets. A key tool for implementing relationship marketing is **key account management (KAM)**. In many industries, there is a trend towards the use of KAM, which reflects the increasing concentration of buying power into fewer but larger customers. Developing relationships with key accounts is often crucial to the survival of a business. Key accounts are serviced by a key account salesforce comprising senior salespeople who develop close personal relationships with customers, can handle sophisticated sales arguments and are skilled at negotiation.

Several advantages may be derived from adopting a key-account-structured approach towards relationship development; see Figure 15.5.

FIGURE 15.5
Potential advantages of KAM

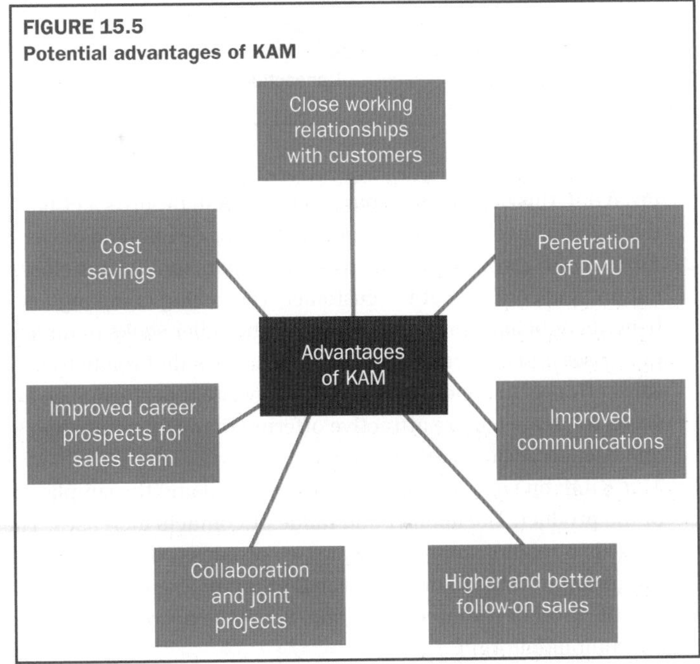

A potential advantage of the KAM approach is that it can lead to the development of close connective relationships. For example, the salesperson can get to know who the decision-makers are in a company and who influences the buying decision. This creates opportunities to gain greater penetration of the decision-making unit and cultivate relationships within the key account. Salespeople can *pull* the buying decision through the organization from the users, deciders and influencers to the buyer, rather than the more difficult task of pushing it through the buyer into the organization, as is done with more traditional sales approaches. Closer relationships can foster better communication, as the buyer becomes familiar with a dedicated salesperson or sales team and knows who to contact for information or if a problem occurs. The selling company can devote extra resources to the key account, which can result in higher sales and better follow-up and after-sales service. Effective KAM can also benefit the selling team. As the KAM relationship develops, the sales team may have the opportunity for career development: a tiered salesforce system with key (or national) account selling at the top provides promotional opportunities for salespeople who wish to advance within the salesforce rather than enter a traditional sales-management position. Lower costs can be achieved through joint agreement of optimum production and delivery schedules, and by demand forecasting. And finally, there may be cooperation on research and development for new products and joint promotions (e.g. within the fast-moving consumer goods/retail sector).

The development and management of a key account can be understood as a process that takes place over time between buyers and sellers. The KAM relational development model plots the typical progression of a buyer–seller relationship based on the nature of the customer relationship (transactional–collaborative) and the level of involvement with customers (simple–complex) (Wilson et al., 2000). Figure 15.6 shows the five stages: pre KAM, early KAM, mid KAM, partnership KAM and synergistic KAM. A sixth stage (uncoupling KAM) represents the breakdown of the relationship, which can happen at any point during the process.

FIGURE 15.6
Key account relational development model

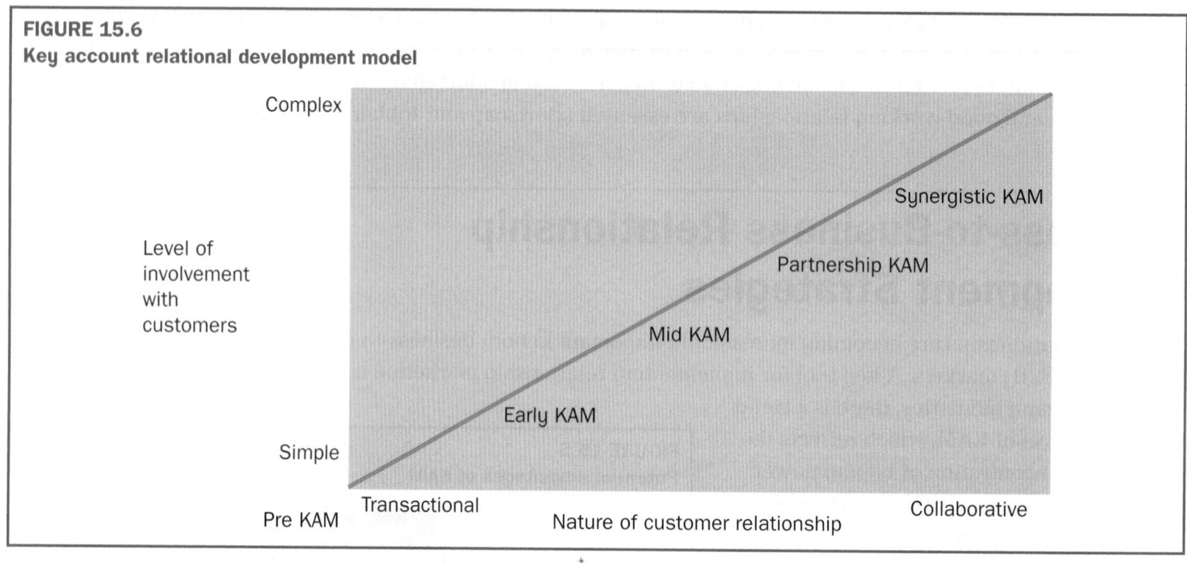

1 *Pre KAM*: this describes preparation for KAM, or 'prospecting'. The task is to identify accounts with potential that can be developed, and opportunities for developing closer relationships.
2 *Early KAM*: involves the exploration of opportunities for closer collaboration by identifying the motives, culture and concerns of the customer. The selling company needs to convince the buying company of the benefits of being a preferred supplier. The seller seeks to understand the buyer's decision-making unit and processes and the problems and opportunities that relate to the value-adding activities. An objective of the sales effort is to build trust based on consistent performance and open communications. The account manager seeks to create a more attractive offering than any competing supplier and attempts to establish credibility and deepen personal relationships.
3 *Mid KAM*: by now, trust has been established and the supplier is one of a small number of preferred sources of the product. The number and range of contacts increases. These may include social events, which help to deepen relationships across the two organizations. The account-review process carried out at the selling organization tends to move upwards to involve senior management, because of the importance of the customer and the level of resource allocation. Since the account is not yet exclusive, the activities of competitors require constant monitoring.
4 *Partnership KAM*: at this stage, the buying organization regards the supplier as an important strategic resource. The level of trust is sufficient for both parties to be willing to share sensitive information. The focus of activities moves to joint problem solving, collaborative product development and mutual training of the other company's staff. The buying company is now channelling nearly all of its business in the relevant product group(s) to the one supplier. The arrangement is formalized in a partnership agreement, which has a timeframe that can ensure stability. Performance is monitored and contacts between departments of the two organizations are extensive. The buying organization expects guaranteed continuity of supply, excellent service and top-quality products. A key task of the account manager is to reinforce the high levels of trust to form a barrier against potential competitors.
5 *Synergistic KAM*: this is the ultimate stage of the relational development model. Buyer and seller see one another not as two separate organizations but as part of a larger entity. Top management commitment manifests itself in joint board meetings. Joint business planning, research and development, and marketing research take place. Costing systems become transparent, unnecessary costs are removed, and process improvements are mutually achieved. For example, a logistics company together with one of its retail key accounts may have six cross-boundary teams working on process improvements at any one time (Wilson and Millman, 2003).
6 *Uncoupling KAM*: this is when transactions and interaction cease. The causes of uncoupling need to be understood so that uncoupling can be avoided.

Breakdowns are more often attributable to changes in key personnel and relationship problems than price conflicts. The danger of uncoupling is particularly acute in early KAM, when the single point of contact prevails. If, for example, the key account manager leaves to be replaced by someone who, in the buyer's eyes, is less skilled, or there is a personality clash, the relationship may end.

A second cause of uncoupling is breach of trust: for example, the breaking of a promise over a delivery deadline, product improvement or equipment repair can weaken or kill a business relationship. The key to handling such problems is to reduce the impact of surprise. The supplier should let the buying organization know immediately when a problem becomes apparent. It should also show humility when discussing the problem with a customer.

Companies also uncouple through neglect. Long-term relationships can foster complacency, and customers can perceive themselves as being taken for granted. Cultural mismatches can occur—for example, when the customer stresses price, whereas the supplier focuses on lifecycle costs. Difficulties can also occur between bureaucratic and entrepreneurial styles of management. Product or service quality problems can provoke uncoupling. Any kind of performance problem, or the perception that rivals now offer superior performance, can trigger a breakdown in relations. 'In' suppliers must build entry barriers by ensuring that product quality is constantly improved and any problems dealt with speedily and professionally.

Not all uncoupling is instigated by the buying company. A key account may be de-rated or terminated because of loss of market share or the onset of financial problems that impair the attractiveness of the account.

The importance of KAM on a worldwide scale is reflected in the employment of global account managers by many multinational organizations. **Global account management (GAM)** is the process of coordinating and developing mutually beneficial long-term relationships with a select group of strategically important customers (accounts) operating in globalized industries (Montgomery and Yip, 1999). Global account managers perform two key roles: 1) managing the internal interface between global and national account management, which is often embedded in a headquarters/subsidiary relationship; and 2) managing the external interface between the supplier and the dispersed activities of its global accounts (Wilson and Millman, 2003). Multinational customers are increasingly buying on a centralized or coordinated basis and seek suppliers who are able to provide consistent and seamless service across countries (Montgomery and Yip, 1999). Consequently, suppliers are developing and implementing GAM and are creating global account managers to manage the interface between seller and buyer on a global basis.

Personal selling enables individuals to interact and form bonds which can develop into long-term relationships that are beneficial for all parties concerned.

Exhibitions and Trade Shows

Another element of the promotional mix which comes under the banner of direct communications is trade fairs and exhibitions, which are a platform for personal selling as well as other communication tools. **Trade shows** and **exhibitions** offer marketing managers a unique opportunity to engage with buyers, sellers and the competitors under one roof. These types of event are used in both industrial and consumer markets, but are highly effective in the industrial buying process, second only to personal selling and ahead of direct mail and print advertising (Parasuraman, 1981). Indeed, exhibitions have been shown to increase the effectiveness of personal selling activities directly after the event (Smith, Gopalakrishna and Smith, 2004). A key role of trade fairs and exhibitions is to enable manufacturers, buyers, distributors, agents, present and future customers and media representatives to meet at a live event, which often has restricted access for the trade. This type of event has a long heritage and can be traced back over 4000 years. Trade shows and exhibitions play an important part in B2B trade and global economic growth (Sarmento and Simoes, 2018).

Why choose exhibitions and trade fairs as part of the communication mix?

Good relationships are essential in industrial trade situations, and these types of event have been found to be very useful for developing strong buyer–seller relationships (Geigenmüller, 2010).

Trade fairs and exhibitions generally bring together all the major players in an industry, and in doing so provide an opportunity for buyers and sellers to engage across an industrial sector. There are many potential advantages: for example, buyers may spot new products and companies can interact with other companies working in the same industry, discuss issues and save money, as all companies are exhibiting in one place. Other potential benefits are gathering market intelligence (Shipley and Wong, 1993) about competitors and industry trends (Hansen, 2004), and exchanging information and news about products, innovations, promotions and new marketing strategies. Exhibitions and trade shows are an ideal arena in which to demonstrate a company's new products, and despite the high cost associated with exhibiting, this is a widely used approach.

Events vary in style depending on the industry: for example, in the clothing industry a week-long series of events is held in leading fashion capitals around the world, such as New York, Paris, Milan and London. These events act as a showcase for designers, highlight new trends and present new product ranges. Buyers from around the world join the designers and media representatives in visiting runway shows. These events reveal cutting-edge designs that will shape what's in and what's out for the coming season. For many designers, a key aim is to be outstanding to maximize press coverage.

Trade fair and exhibition objectives

Trade fairs are a means of extending a firm's personal selling activities. There are various objectives that this element of the promotional mix can achieve and in doing so contribute to an IMC strategy. Research suggests that it is important to consider whether objectives are selling or non-selling oriented and whether they are aimed at new or existing customers (Bonoma, 1985; Sarmento and Simoes, 2018). Selling objectives include:

- generating leads/enquiries and a contact list
- gaining access to key decision-makers
- reaching an audience with a distinct interest in the market and the products on display
- creating awareness and developing relationships with new prospects
- providing product and service demonstrations
- launching new products and services
- recruiting dealers or distributors
- responding to customer account problems and strengthening existing customer relationships
- selling products and services

Non-selling objectives include:

- enhancing the firm's image
- evaluating reactions to new products
- gathering market intelligence from competitors who are exhibiting
- evaluating new products.

When developing objectives for an event, it is important to consider visitor (buyer) objectives. The exhibition stand should be both functional and attract attention. For example, regarding the simple logistics of the stand where the buyer and seller interact: is there appropriate seating, and are there refreshments? To be effective, the stand should be attractive, facilitate contact between buyer and seller, and create an environment that enhances sales conversions (Sarmento and Simoes, 2018).

Planning an exhibition

Success at an exhibition involves considerable pre-event planning. Clear objectives should be set, selection criteria for evaluating exhibition attendance determined, and design and promotional strategies decided. Pre-show promotions to attract visitors to the stand include a website, social media, direct mail and telemarketing; a personal sales call before the event or an advertisement in the trade or technical press can be highly effective.

Because exhibitions and trade fairs bring together both customer and competitor, a high degree of professionalism is required by the staff who attend the exhibition stand. Typically, such events should:

- introduce innovative products and new ranges
- exhibit a wider range of products, particularly large items that cannot be demonstrated on a sales call
- provide product and service expertise; event staff should be well-informed
- provide access to informative literature and links to follow-up resources online
- be a great customer experience, as this is an opportunity to showcase the company.

Trade shows and exhibitions tend to be located where there are large conference facilities with the necessary prestige to attract industry leaders. For example, leading international auto shows are held in major cities such as Beijing, Chicago and Berlin. Events can also be located close to the centre of economic activity: for example,

Slush is a fair that aims to bring together technology entrepreneurs, start-ups and technology innovators from across the world. It is held annually in Helsinki, Finland, because the Nordic region is known for being a hotbed of technology innovation and many innovative products have emerged from this region, for example Rovio, Supercell and MySQL (Slush, 2015).

For an event to be successful, organizers have to ensure that the location will be suitable and sufficiently attractive to potential attendees. For example, the organizers of the Spielwarenmesse international toy fair (Spielwarenmesse, n.d.) in Nüremberg, Germany, invest heavily to ensure that, at the end of January each year, over 2,800 exhibitors and 76,000 trade visitors from 120 nations visit 12 exhibition halls at the fair (each dedicated to a different type of toy-related product, such as dolls, hobbies, action toys, games, educational) to see over a million different products. Each company exhibiting at the fair has to put together its own event plan, set objectives and decide how to allocate the budget to get best value. But there are many benefits, according to Pascal Bernard, CEO of Juratoys, France: '*Nuremberg is the place to be, since everyone is here. It is the only trade fair where you meet everyone from everywhere. Our company is represented with sales representatives from 50 countries here.*'

Trade fairs and exhibitions also need to be at a time in the calendar when buyers are considering new products and suppliers can attend. So the Nüremberg toy fair and others in this industry tend to be in the winter and spring after the busy end-of-year trading period around the festive season.

Evaluating an exhibition

Post-show evaluation will examine performance against objectives. This is a learning exercise that will help to judge whether the objectives were realistic, how valuable the exhibition appears to have been and how well the company was represented.

Quantitative measures include:

- the number of visitors to the stand
- the number of key influencers/decision-makers who visited the stand
- how many leads/enquiries were generated
- the cost per lead/enquiry
- the number and value of orders
- the cost per order
- the number of new distributorships opened/likely to be opened.

Other, more subjective, qualitative criteria include:

- the worth of competitive intelligence
- interest generated in the new products
- the cultivation of new/existing relationships
- the value of customer query and complaint handling
- the promotion of brand values.

Sales and marketing departments may not always agree on the key evaluation criteria to use. For example, sales may judge the exhibition on the number of leads, while marketing may prefer to judge the show on the longer-term issue of the promotion of brand values. The most important consideration is to measure variables that enable assessment against marketing objectives. Therefore, since a major objective of many exhibitors is to stimulate leads and enquiries, mechanisms must be in place to ensure that these are followed up promptly.

Ethical Issues in Direct Communications

Personal selling and direct marketing methods are increasingly subject to scrutiny by industry bodies, consumer groups, governments and, ultimately, the national and international legal systems. Under the heading of personal selling deception, the hard sell, bribery and reciprocal buying are issues which marketing managers should plan to avoid. The implications of each of these issues are as follows.

- *Deception.* A dilemma that, sooner or later, faces most salespeople is the choice of telling the customer the whole truth and risk losing the sale, or misleading the customer to clinch it. The deception may take the form of exaggeration, lying or withholding important information that significantly reduces the appeal of the product. Such actions should be avoided by influencing salespersons' behaviour by training, by sales management encouraging ethical behaviour by their own actions and words, and by establishing codes of conduct for their salespeople. Nevertheless, sometimes evidence of malpractice in selling is discovered and action taken to recompense the injured party: for example, UK banks Barclays, HSBC, Lloyds and Royal Bank of Scotland have set aside billions of pounds to compensate customers for mis-selling loan insurance (Gard, 2015).

- *The hard sell.* Personal selling is criticized for employing high-pressure sales tactics to close a sale. Car dealerships and the timeshare industry have been deemed unethical in using hard-sell tactics to pressurize customers into making a quick decision on a complicated purchase that may involve expensive credit facilities.
- *Bribery.* This is the act of giving payment, gifts or other inducements to secure a sale. Bribes are considered unethical, as they violate the principle of fairness in commercial negotiations. A major problem is that, in some countries, bribes are an accepted part of business life: to compete, bribes are necessary. So, organizations in such a situation face an ethical dilemma. On the one hand, they will be castigated in their home country if they use bribes and this becomes public knowledge. On the other hand, without the bribe, the organization could be operating at a commercial disadvantage. Taking an ethical stance may cause difficulties in the short term but in the long run the positive publicity that can follow is likely to be of greater benefit.

Direct marketing methods also face different types of ethical issues associated with consumer concerns:

- *Poorly targeted direct mail.* Although designed to foster closer relationships in targeting of consumers, some direct mail is of little relevance to the recipient and can be a clear source of irritation and distress. As more attention is paid to the natural environment, the waste of natural resources caused by poorly directed mailshots is a questionable practice (Reed, 2008).
- *Intrusive nature of telemarketing calls.* Consumers complain about the annoyance caused by unsolicited telephone calls pressuring them to buy products at inconvenient times. Technological developments have the capacity to take this to a new level—for example, with robo calls (via computerized auto-diallers)—and while some countries legislate against this style of communication, there are still some types of call that manage to circumvent these controls.
- *Invasion of privacy.* Many consumers fear that every time they subscribe to a website, club, society or magazine, apply for a credit card, or buy anything by telephone or direct mail, their names, addresses and other information will be entered in to a database that will guarantee a flood of mail from the supplier.

The direct marketing industry and governments are responding to the public concerns noted above.

Review

1 The key direct marketing communication tools: personal selling, exhibitions, direct marketing

- Direct communications enable a direct dialogue between buyers and sellers; moreover, they do not involve the purchase of media space.
- Personal selling allows buyers and the seller to communicate in a face-to-face manner, which facilitates relationship development, but from a marketing management perspective this is relatively costly.
- Exhibitions are an opportunity to bring together all of the buyers and sellers in a particular market under one roof and create an environment for furthering customer relationships, enhancing corporate ideas and gathering competitive information.
- Direct marketing is a means of creating a dialogue between buyers and sellers using various techniques such as direct mail, digital marketing, telemarketing and catalogue marketing.

2 The meaning of direct marketing

- Direct marketing is the distribution of products, information and promotional benefits to target customers through interactive communication in a way that allows response to be measured.
- It includes such methods as direct mail, telemarketing, direct response advertising, catalogue marketing and digital media.

3 The reasons for the growth of direct marketing activity

- Direct marketing activity has grown because of market and media fragmentation, developments in technology, the expansion of lists of potential clients, sophisticated analytical techniques, and coordinated marketing systems.

4 The importance of database marketing

- Database marketing is an approach to marketing communications that targets individuals using various media channels.
- Databases are central to all forms of direct marketing activity as they store customer contact and behavioural data which helps marketing strategy and planning, for example when planning promotional campaigns designed to target very loyal customers who are to receive special treatment. Databases are useful for planning campaigns, as they hold details of past customer behaviour, such as responses to price promotions.

5 How to manage a direct marketing campaign

- A direct marketing campaign should not be designed in isolation but be based on a clear understanding of marketing strategy in particular positioning. Then the steps are as follows.
- Identify and understand the target audience; never sell to a stranger. Who is to be reached, their motives and choice criteria need to be understood.
- Campaign objectives: these can be expressed in financial (e.g. sales), in marketing (e.g. acquire or retain customers) or communication (e.g. change beliefs) terms.
- Media decisions: major media options are direct mail, telemarketing, mobile marketing, direct response advertising, catalogue marketing and the internet.
- Creative decisions: a creative brief will include a statement of communication objectives, product benefits (and weaknesses), target market analysis, development of the offer, communication of the message, and an action plan.
- Execute and evaluate the campaign: execution of the campaign may be in-house or through the use of a specialist agency. Evaluation should be taken against defined objectives such as total sales, number of enquiries, cost per sale and repeat purchase rate.

6 Ethical issues in direct communications

- Using direct communication tools can mean that marketing managers face difficult choices. Personal selling has been criticized for using deception, bribery and the hard sell in order to secure sales orders. Direct marketing tools can be seen by customers as poorly targeted, a waste of natural resources and an intrusion of privacy.

7 Characteristics of personal selling

- The characteristics are customer acquisition, retention and deletion, customer relationship management, adding value and satisfying customer needs.

8 The stages in the selling process

- Salespeople should prepare for selling by gaining knowledge of their own and competitors' products, planning sales presentations, setting up call objectives and seeking to understand buyer behaviour.

9 The key tasks of sales management

- The tasks of a sales manager are to: understand marketing strategy; set personal selling objectives and strategies; design the salesforce; manage the salesforce by setting objectives, organize recruitment and training, set reward structures and performance measures for salespeople; and evaluate and control the total sales operation.

10 The objectives, conduct and evaluation of exhibitions

- Objectives of exhibitions can be classified as selling objectives in the context of current customers (e.g. stimulate extra sales), selling objectives for potential customers (e.g. determine needs and transmit benefits), non-selling objectives for current customers (e.g. maintain image and gather competitive intelligence) and non-selling objectives for potential customers (e.g. foster image building and gather competitive intelligence).
- Staff conduct at an exhibition should ensure that there is always someone in attendance to talk to visitors. Staff should be well informed and provide informative literature, and a seating area/office and refreshments should be provided.
- Evaluation of an exhibition includes number of visitors/key influencers/decision-makers who visit the stand, number of leads/enquiries/orders/new dealerships generated and cost per lead/enquiry/order. Qualitative evaluation includes the worth of competitive intelligence, and interest generated in new products.

Key Terms

buying signals statements by a buyer that indicate an interest in buying

campaign objectives goals set by an organization in terms of, for example, sales, profits, customers won or retained, or awareness creation

customer benefits those things that a customer values in a product; customer benefits derive from product features

customer relationship management the methodologies, technologies and e-commerce capabilities used by companies to manage customer relationships

direct mail material sent through the postal service to the recipient's house or business address promoting a product and/or maintaining an ongoing relationship

direct response advertising the use of the prime advertising media such as television, newspapers and magazines to elicit an order, enquiry or request for a visit

e-commerce all electronically mediated transactions between an organization and any third party it deals with, including exchange of information

exhibition an event that brings buyers and sellers together in a commercial setting

key account management an approach to selling that focuses resources on major customers and uses a team selling approach

marketing database an interactive approach to marketing that uses individually addressable marketing media and channels to provide information to a target audience, stimulate demand and stay close to customers

product features the characteristics of a product that may or may not convey a customer benefit

salesforce evaluation the measurement of each salesperson's performance so that strengths and weaknesses can be identified

target accounts organizations or individuals whose custom the company wishes to obtain

telemarketing a marketing communications system whereby trained specialists use telecommunications and information technologies to conduct marketing and sales activities

trade show similar to an exhibition, as it brings together buyers, sellers and competitors under one roof, but it is not open to the public

Study Questions

1. **Discuss the challenges that a direct marketer might face when selecting direct marketing methods.**
2. **Define direct marketing. Identify the different forms of direct marketing. Give an example of how at least three methods can be integrated into a marketing communications campaign.**
3. **Discuss why databases are important for marketing communication campaigns. Explain the types of information that are recorded in a database.**
4. **What are the stages of managing a direct marketing campaign? Why is the concept of lifetime value of a customer important when designing a campaign?**
5. **Select a car with which you are familiar. Identify its features and translate them into customer benefits.**
6. **Imagine you are face to face with a customer for that car. Write down five objections to purchase and prepare convincing responses to them.**
7. **You are the new sales manager of a company selling natural ingredients to the pharmaceutical industry. Discuss how you would motivate and manage your salesforce.**
8. **From your own personal experience, do you consider salespeople to be unethical? Can you remember any sales encounters when you have been subject to unethical behaviour?**
9. **Explain the benefits of using exhibitions for buyers and sellers.**
10. **Discuss the importance of setting clear marketing objectives for trade fairs and exhibitions.**

Recommended Reading

Communicating directly with many customers simultaneously means getting the message right. Read about how email marketing is empowering consumers, the revolutions taking place in sales and the future possibilities of trade fairs.

Mari Hartemo (2016) Email marketing in the era of the empowered consumer, *Journal of Research in Interactive Marketing* 10(3), 212–30.

Marshall, G., Moncrief, W., Rudd, J. and Lee, N. (2012), Revolution in Sales: The Impact of Social Media and Related Technology on the Selling Environment, *Journal of Personal Selling & Sales Management* 32(3), 349–63.

Anja Geigenmüller (2010) The role of virtual trade fairs in relationship value creation, *Journal of Business & Industrial Marketing* 25(4), 284–92.

References

Arli, D., Bauer, C. and Palmatier, R. (2018) Relational selling: past present and future, *Industrial Marketing Management* 69(2), 169–84.

Baker, R. (2012) Costa eyes loyalty scheme for vending business, *Marketing Week*, 10 January.

Barnes, R. (2005) Nectar Readies B2B Loyalty Card Launch, *Marketing*, 19 January, 14.

Baumgartner, T., Hatami, H. and Valdivieso M. (2016) Why salespeople need to develop 'machine intelligence', *Harvard Business Review*,10 June. https://hbr.org/2016/06/why-salespeople-need-to-develop-machine-intelligence (accessed October 2018)

Bonoma, T.V. (1985) Get more out of your trade show, in Gumpert, D.E. (ed.) *The Marketing Renaissance*, New York: Wiley.

Butchers & Bicycles (n.d.) About, http://www.butchersandbicycles.com (accessed October 2018)

Chaffey, D. and Ellis-Chadwick, F. (2019) Digital Marketing: Strategy, Implementation and Practice, 7th edn, Harlow, UK: Pearson.

Charles, G. (2011) Waitrose unveils loyalty-card programme in strategic shift, *Marketing*, 26 October, 1.

Clews, M.-L. (2011) The evolution of loyalty, *Marketing Week*, August, 42–3.

Colville-Andersen, M. (2015) The Most Bike-Friendly Cities on the planet, *Wired*, 6 February.

D&AD Awards (2019) https://www.dandad.org/en/d-ad-awards (accessed October 2018)

Dewsnap, B. and Jobber, D. (2002) A Social Psychological Model of Relations Between Marketing and Sales, *European Journal of Marketing* 36(7/8), 874–94.

Ellis-Chadwick, F.E. and Doherty, N.F. (2012) Web advertising: the role of e-mail marketing, *Journal of Business Research* 65(6), 843–48.

Ferrell, L. and Ferrell, O.C. (2012) Redirecting direct selling: High-touch embraces high-tech, *Business Horizons* 55(3), 273–81.

Finch, J. (2009) Tesco Sales Top £1 billion a Week, *The Guardian*, 22 April, 22.

Friedlein, A. (2013) Our Modern Marketing Manifesto: will you sign? Econsultancy, 8 May. https://econsultancy.com/blog/62668-our-modern-marketing-manifesto-will-you-sign (accessed October 2018)

Gard, S. (2015) New Mis-Selling Scandal set to Rock Barclays, HSbC Holdings plc, Lloyds Banking group & Royal Bank of Scotland Plc, The Motley Fool, 2 February. http://www.fool.co.uk/investing/2015/02/02/new-mis-selling-scandal-set-to-rock-barclays-plc-hsbc-holdings-plc-lloyds-banking-group-plc-royal-bank-of-scotland-group-plc (accessed October 2018)

Geigenmüller, A. (2010) The role of virtual trade fairs in relationship value creation, *Journal of Business and Industrial Marketing* 25(4), 282–92.

Hammett, E. (2018) Tesco uses Clubcard data to help people eat more healthily, 15 October https://www.marketingweek.com/2018/10/15/tesco-clubcard-data-to-help-people-eat-healthier/ (accessed October 2018)

Handley, L. (2011) Do you want to know an open secret? *Marketing Week*, 20 October, 25.

Hansen, K. (2004) Measuring Performance at Trade Shows: Scale Development and Validation, *Journal of Business Research* 54, 1–13.

Hedger, G. (2015) The fallacy of our time, *Brand Republic*, 23 April. http://www.brandrepublic.com/article/1343640/fallacy-time (accessed October 2018)

Hemsley, S. (2018) Innovations in direct mail help brands shout louder in the digital era, *Marketing Week*, 19 February. https://www.marketingweek.com/2018/02/19/innovations-direct-mail/ (accessed October 2018)

Holmes, T.L. and Srivastava, R. (2002) Effects of Job Perceptions on Job Behaviours: Implications for Sales Performance, *Industrial Marketing Management* 31, 421–8.

Homburg, C., Workman, J.P., Jr, and Jensen, O. (2000) Fundamental Changes in Marketing Organization: the Movement Toward a Customer-Focused Organizational Structure, *Journal of the Academy of Marketing Science* 28, 459–78.

James, M. (2003) The Quest for Fidelity, *Marketing Business*, January, 20–2.

Key, T.M. and Czaplewski, A.J. (2017) Upstream social marketing strategy: An integrated marketing communications approach, *Business Horizons* 60(3), 325–33.

Krishnan, B.C., Netemeyer, R.G. and Boles, J.S. (2002) Self-efficacy, Competitiveness, and Effort as Antecedents of Salesperson Performances, *Journal of Personal Selling and Sales Management* 20(4), 285–95.

Lane, N. and Piercy, N. (2004) Strategic Customer Management: Designing a Profitable Future for Your Sales Organization, *European Management Journal* 22(6), 659–68.

Lee, J.-Y., Sridhar, S. and Palmatier, R.W. (2017) The effect of firms' structural designs on advertising and personal selling returns, *International Journal of Research in Marketing* 34(1), 173–93.

Leva, M., Canio, F., Ziliani, C. (2018) Daily deal shoppers: What drive social couponing? *Journal of Retailing and Consumer Services* 40(1), 299–303.

Luthans, F. (1997) *Organizational Behaviour*, New York: McGraw-Hill.

Magrath, A.J. (1989) To Specialise or Not to Specialise?, *Sales and Marketing Management* 14(7), 62–8.

McCawley, I. (2006) Nectar Loyalty Card Set for Global Roll-out, *Marketing Week*, 19 January, 3.

McDonald, M.H.B. (2002) *Marketing Plans*, London: Heinemann.

Maulana, A.E. and Nurulfirdausi, K. (2015) Permissive, Aggressive or Apathetic? Indonesian Telemarketing Customer, *Procedia Social and Behavioral Sciences* 169, 69–74.

Metaeyes.com (2018) Features, www.metaeyes.com (accessed December 2018).

Milington, A. (2015) DMA merger with IDM will create all-inclusive direct marketing organisation, *Marketing Week*, 22 May. http://www.marketingweek.com/2015/05/22/dma-merger-with-idm-will-create-all-inclusive-direct-marketing-organisation (accessed October 2018)

Mitchell, A. (2002) Consumer Power Is on the Cards in Tesco Plan, *Marketing Week*, 2 May, 30–1.

Morgan, R.M. and Hunt, S.D. (1994) The Commitment—Trust Theory of Relationship Marketing, *Journal of Marketing* 58, 20–38.

Movahhed, M. (2014) Tales for a Road Warrior, Handshake, 12 September. https://www.handshake.com/blog/wholesale-selling-strategies-toys (accessed 10 May 2015).

Murphy, C. (2008) No Such Thing as a Freebie, *The Marketer*, May, 28–31.

Palmatier, R., Houston, M.B., Dant, R.P. and Grewal, D. (2013) Relationship velocity: Toward a theory of relationship dynamics, *Journal of Marketing* 77(1), 13–30.

Parasuraman, A. (1981) The Relative Importance of Industrial Promotional Tools, *Industrial Marketing Management* 10, 277–81.

Piercy, N., Cravens, D.W. and Morgan, N.A. (1998) Salesforce Performance and Behaviour Based Management Processes in Business-to-Business Sales Organisations, *European Journal of Marketing* 32(1/2), 79–100.

Ponder, K. (2011). The ultimate social business model, *Direct Selling News* (supplement to *The Wall Street Journal*), 4–6.

Pullins, E.B. (2001) An Exploratory Investigation of the Relationship of Sales Force Compensation and Intrinsic Motivation, *Industrial Marketing Management* 30, 403–13.

Rackham, N. and DeVincentis, J. (1999) *Rethinking the Sales Force: Redefining Selling to Create and Capture Customer Value*, New York: McGraw-Hill.

Reed, D. (2008) Making a Visible Difference, *Marketing Week*, 14 August, 27.

Reid, A. (2015) 3 BRANDS THAT PROVE LISTENING TO CUSTOMERS IS KEY TO COMPANY COMEBACKS, www.fastcompany.com, 2 September. http://www.fastcompany.com/3035054/hit-the-ground-running/3-brands-that-prove-listening-to-customers-is-key-to-company-comeback (accessed 14 May 2015).

Ritsema, H. and Piest, B. (1990) Telemarketing: the case for self regulation *European Management Journal* 8(1) 63–6.

Salesforce.com (2018). About, www.salesforce.com (accessed December 2018)

Román, S., Ruiz, S. and Munuera, J.L. (2002) The Effects of Sales Training on Salesforce Activity, *European Journal of Marketing* 36(11/12), 1344–66.

Sarmento, M. and Simões, C. (2018) The evolving role of trade fairs in business: A systematic literature review and a research agenda, *Industrial Marketing Management* 73, 154–70.

Shipley, D. and Wong, K.S. (1993) Exhibiting, strategy and implementation, *International Journal of Advertising* 12(2), 117–30.

Slush (2015) About, Slush. http://www.slush.org/about/media (accessed 10 May 2015).

Smith, T.M., Gopalakrishna, S. and Smith, P.M. (2004) The Complementary Effect of Trade Shows on Personal Selling, *International Journal of Research in Marketing* 21(1), 61–76 (accessed October 2018).

Spielwarenmesse (n.d.) Fair Profile. http://www.spielwarenmesse.de/about-the-fair/fair-profile/?L=1 (accessed 10 May 2015).

Stephens, H. (2003) 'CEO', American Marketing Association Summer Educators' Conference, The H. R. Challey Group, August, Chicago.

Stone, M., Davies, D. and Bond, A. (1995) *Direct Hit: Direct Marketing with a Winning Edge*, London: Pitman.

Strahle, W. and Spiro, R.L. (1986) Linking Market Share Strategies to Salesforce Objectives, Activities and Compensation Policies, *Journal of Personal Selling and Sales Management*, August, 11–18.

Talley, W.J. (1961) How to Design Sales Territories, *Journal of Marketing* 25(3), 16–28.

The Economist (2011) Spies in your wallet, 5 November.

Trefis Team (2018) Will Avon be able to rise from its slump in 2018? Nasdaq, https://www.nasdaq.com/article/will-avon-be-able-to-rise-from-its-slump-in-2018-cm908711 (accessed October 2018)

Vongsingthong, S. and Smanchat, S. (2014) Internet of Things: A Review of Applications & Technologies, *Journal of Science and Technology* 21(4), 359–74.

Wilson, K. (1993) Managing the Industrial Salesforce in the 1990s, *Journal of Marketing Management* 9(2), 123–40.

Wilson, K., Croom, S., Millman, T. and Weilbaker, D. (2000) The SRTSAMA Global Account Management Study, *Journal of Selling and Major Account Management* 2(3), 63–84.

Wilson, K. and Millman, T. (2003) The Global Account Manager as Political Entrepreneur, Industrial Marketing Management 32, 151–8.

Zoltners, A., Sinha, P. and Lorimer, S. (2015) The Technology Trends That Matter to Sales Teams, *Harvard Business Review*, 7 May. https://hbr.org/2015/05/the-technology-trends-that-matter-to-sales-teams (accessed 10 May 2015).

CASE 29
Airbnb: Don't Go There, Live There!

Introduction

Airbnb was founded in San Francisco by Brian Chesky and Joe Gebbia. It is a community marketplace that allows property owners and travellers to connect with each other, via website or mobile applications,for renting properties.The company began in late 2007 when its founders, struggling to pay for their shared apartment in San Francisco, decided to rent out airbeds to conference attendees. Cleverly, they provided breakfast cereals which were custom branded to suit the convention their guests were attending—such as 'Obama Os' for the Obama convention. They quickly recruited other accommodation providers and started a basic website. Their entrepreneurial spirit captured a lot of attention and resulted in their securing significant investment from venture capitalists such as movie star Ashton Kutcher and music manager Guy Oseary. This investment enabled the company to process customer rental payments, and by 2012 the website had processed more than 10 million bookings.

Today, Airbnb provides a flexible and cost-effective form of accommodation for millions of leisure and business travellers around the world. Airbnb's business model is simple: it earns revenue by charging service fees to both guests and hosts.The cost to the renter of Airbnb lodgings is determined by the property owner. By not directly owning physical locations, Airbnb has been able to quickly scale its business to accommodate growing demand. In 2018, the company offered more than 3 million listings in over 65,000 cities and nearly 200 countries. Airbnb surpassed competitors such as Booking.com, Hotels.com and Marriott International in web traffic and was valued at $32 billion worldwide—a similar amount to the Marriott hotel group, even though it does not own any of its properties.

By 2020, Airbnb's revenue is projected to be as much as $8.5 billion. The rise of Airbnb can be attributed in part to its innovative direct marketing communications, with the 'Live There' campaign being a significant success.

Target Audience

Airbnb has always defined its core audience, 'head-first explorers' (younger millennials), as a psychographic consumer segment that drives its business. Millennials account for approximately 60 per cent of all guests. This market segment consists of travellers looking for a spacious and comfortable place to stay that is also affordable and functional. In Europe and the USA, Airbnb is typically 8–17 per cent cheaper than a regional hotel's average daily rate. The fastest-growing Airbnb host demographic is seniors, with over 200,000 senior hosts (senior women are also consistently rated as the best hosts on Airbnb).

Although Airbnb traditionally has mostly leisure travellers, which account for 90 per cent of its bookings, the company is now anxious to breach that ceiling and acquire more business travellers. Additionally, the company wants to expand its market reach to connect with groups outside its usual millennial demographic, such as young families and LGBT couples.

The 'Live There' Campaign

According to Airbnb, 86 per cent of its customers choose the platform because they want to experience the world like locals when travelling. That insight of living rather than visiting inspired the company's 2016 marketing campaign, 'Live there'. The campaign aimed to capture the idea that people shouldn't simply go to a new place—they should live there, even if only for one night. The campaign also aimed to inspire a reimagining of travel through a single global message that would resonate with a variety of travellers. In 2017, reflecting on the campaign, Brian Chesky (CEO) highlighted that Airbnb's hosts offer more than just generic hospitality—'they welcome travellers from around the world into their communities'.

Airbnb used a multi-faceted direct marketing communications approach to raise awareness of the 'Live there' campaign and to increase direct dialogue between buyers and sellers. Four media channels were used to target individuals: the Airbnb website, its app, email marketing and social media.

The Airbnb Website

The Airbnb website, while primarily an accommodation search and reservation site, has evolved significantly over the years, providing a suite of useful features

»

»

for travellers. The Airbnb guidebooks are both curated by Airbnb staff and populated with local information from Airbnb hosts. Guidebook content is significantly user-generated, meaning that hosts can provide very personal representations of a particular location, and this, in turn, feeds into the whole 'Live there' ethos. Airbnb's underlying technology parses through these guidebooks and compiles top-ten lists per location, based on provided content and traveller reviews. The Airbnb guidebooks allow visitors to get a taste of what day-to-day life is like for people who actually live in the location. Following on from the community-focused trend for engagement, Airbnb also provides stories which are simple but effective overviews of various hosts. These are in place to allow users to get detailed host information and feedback if they need further convincing to make a booking. Another element is the Airbnb neighbourhood guides—these are created by Airbnb staff and focus only on the 23 largest conurbations where Airbnb hosts are in abundance. Local photographers are utilized to lend authenticity to the content presented in these guides, which again feeds into the 'Live there' concept. To further enhance direct communication with users, Airbnb launched 'Trips' to allow travellers to book individual experiences (salsa dancing, yoga, etc.) in the locations to which they are travelling. These customized trips are promoted to the client on the Airbnb website, in Facebook live feeds, by the app, by email and by mini movies akin to trailers.

To increase engagement among the host community, Airbnb provides a 'Learn about Airbnb' section on the website. This enables potential hosts to quickly understand how the Airbnb systems work and how they can benefit from joining the service.

Mobile App

Airbnb redesigned its mobile app as part of the 'Live there' campaign launch. The new design presents users with a simple interface that is personalized to user preferences, history and context (e.g. directions from their current location to their selected accommodation). The app provides trip-planning information, and its goal is to become the de-facto travel planning tool for users. Leveraging Airbnb's strong social community, with the help of celebrity endorsements, was critical when launching the app. Celebrities such as Beyoncé, Gwyneth Paltrow, Kendall Jenner and Aston Kutcher supported this process. For example, Gwyneth Paltrow took to Instagram to enthuse about her accommodation, stating 'Airbnb who knew?? Such a beautiful trip. Adios Vallarta. Hasta la proxima!' (which translates to 'Goodbye. See you next time').The company continuously listens to its users and provides updates to its mobile service to meet users' requirements. Airbnb ensures that every new app release is accompanied by a detailed blog post which explains any updates, always keeping the customer informed.

Email Marketing

Airbnb used email marketing to help facilitate the conversation between hosts and guests during the 'Live there' campaign. A personalised email was sent to both hosts and guests to welcome them to Airbnb and to alert them when they had new messages. A simple community invitation email garnered a 70+ per cent opening rate and a 30+ per cent click-through rate. This, in turn, had the effect of bringing users back to the Airbnb platform. The company included attention-grabbing subject lines, such as 'Imagine yourself here', with an accompanying image featuring a unique and interesting destination. Care was taken to send emails during the week rather than over the weekend, which was the popular time with other travel companies. The company also ensured that emails were sent at strategic times during the day. For example, it discovered that email traffic to Spain was more effective later in the evening.

Social Media

Airbnb won the Twitter #creativity award for its #LiveInTheMovies initiative as part of its 'Live there' campaign. Through an analysis of social media conversations during the 2015 Oscars, the company discovered that the chat on Twitter spiked during commercial breaks. Airbnb created a short animated movie, released a week before the 2016 Oscars, which asked consumers to imagine what movie they would like to live in. As Twitter users tweeted about their favourite movie locations, Airbnb's social media team responded to each directly with a property listing to match the movie location or theme. For example, for *Jurassic Park* fans, a remote island off Costa Rica was highlighted. This early targeting enabled Airbnb to capture an audience prior to the event. As the Oscars progressed, Airbnb live-tweeted the event and, using social listening tools, matched tweets and winning films to locations in real time. The result of this innovative drive was the creation of 63 million Twitter impressions (the total number of times a tweet was seen by individual users on the Twitter platform), 1.3 million video views, 6.5 times the number of new Twitter followers versus daily average, and the placement of Airbnb as number two in visibility on Twitter compared with Oscar sponsors and paid advertisers. Additionally, #LiveInTheMovies resulted in more user-generated content than for any other brand during the Oscars.

Campaign Outcome

The 'Live there' campaign was a huge success for Airbnb and generated a significant increase in consumer awareness. Overall, the company raised global awareness by 20 per cent and almost completely closed the gap to competition. The 'Live there' YouTube movie, for example, gained 5.5 million views, with 12 million Facebook video views and 17,000 Instagram #livethere posts. The campaign also increased travellers' understanding of the Airbnb 'Live there' experience, particularly among young families. The company's latest campaign, #WeAccept, focuses on diversity, rehousing minorities, and acceptance, and is gaining similar traction since its launch in 2017.

Questions

1. **Discuss the potential benefits and limitations of direct marketing communications for Airbnb.**
2. **Discuss direct marketing techniques, other than the ones presented in this case study, that Airbnb could use as part of its future campaigns.**
3. **Select a major event where there could be significant demand for accommodation, for example the Oscar Awards in the USA or the Football World Cup. Discuss how you would manage a direct mail campaign for Airbnb for your chosen event.**

This case study was written by Dr Ethel Claffey, Waterford Institute of Technology, Republic of Ireland.

References

Based on: Amazon Web Services (2018) Airbnb Case Study, https://aws.amazon.com/solutions/case-studies/airbnb/ (accessed 17 August 2018); McGee, T. (2017) Airbnb: It's good to be a revolution, https://www.targetmarketingmag.com/post/airbnb-its-good-to-be-a-revolution (accessed 17 August 2018); iPropertyManagement (2018) Airbnb Statistics for Demographics and Growth, https://ipropertymanagement.com/airbnb-statistics (accessed 12 August 2018); Powell, S. (2017) Is Airbnb able to target more business travelers with new marketing & search tool? https://loyaltylobby.com/2017/05/06/is-air-bnb-able-to-target-more-business-travelers-with-new-marketing-search-tool (accessed 18 August 2018); Richards, K. (2016) Put Away the Selfie Stick and Live Like a Local, Urges Airbnb's New Campaign, https://www.adweek.com/brand-marketing/put-away-selfie-stick-and-live-local-urges-airbnbs-new-campaign-170920 (accessed 20 August 2018); Diaz, A. (2016) Airbnb Asks, 'Why Vacation Somewhere When You Can Live There?', http://creativity-online.com/work/airbnb-dont-go-there-live-there/46533 (accessed 20 August 2018); Rankin, S. (2016) How Celebrities Became Obsessed with Airbnb—and How to Vacation Just Like Them, https://www.eonline.com/news/783934/how-celebrities-became-obsessed-with-airbnb-and-how-to-vacation-just-like-them (accessed 12 August 2018) van Rijn, J. (2013) Email marketing at Airbnb: An eye for conversion and community, https://www.tnooz.com/article/email-marketing-airbnb-eye-conversion-community (accessed 12 August 2018); Twitter (2017) The #Creativity award: celebrating the right-brainers among us, https://marketing.twitter.com/na/en/success-stories/the-creativity-award-celebrating-the-right-brainers-among-us.html (accessed 22 August 2018); Airbnb Twitter Feed (2016) What movie would you live in?

Available at: https://tinyurl.com/airbnbLiveInTheMovies (accessed 22 August 2018); Chen, J. (2018) What Are Twitter Impressions & Why Are They So Important to Twitter?

https://sproutsocial.com/insights/twitter-impressions/ (accessed 12 August 2018); Mobile Marketing Association (2017) Airbnb: #LiveInTheMovies, http://www.mmaglobal.com/case-study-hub/case_studies/view/41911 (accessed 18 August 2018); Jay Chiat Awards (2017) Don't go there. Live there. https://tinyurl.com/JayChiatAwards (accessed 12 August 2018).

CASE 30
The Taste of Success: Nestlé's Direct Marketing Communications

Introduction

Nestlé was founded in 1867 by Henry Nestlé. The company has grown significantly since then, expanding its offerings beyond its early condensed milk and infant formula products. Today, Nestlé is the world's largest packaged food company, with its company headquarters in Vevey, Switzerland. Nestlé offers over 2,000 brands, including global icons such as Nespresso, Nescafé, Kit Kat, Smarties and Nesquik, in 191 countries around the world. In 2018, Nestlé reported sales of €80 billion with net profits of €51 billion, an increase of 19 per cent from the previous year. Nestlé has credited its focus on innovation and marketing for its success over the years. In 2017, CEO Ulf Mark Schneider noted the importance of Nestlé establishing a direct channel of communication with its consumers so that it can continue to offer improved service and communicate with its target audiences. Nestlé also uses direct marketing communications to increase its online sales, which at the end of 2017 accounted for 5 per cent of its total sales. This case study will examine some of the most innovative approaches to direct marketing that have been deployed by Nestlé in recent years.

Nestlé Nespresso

Nestlé's premium coffee brand Nespresso has a large brand community, the 'Nespresso Club', which was developed initially to give members who had purchased Nespresso machines 24-hour customer service. In 2005, using club member recommendations, George Clooney was enlisted as the brand ambassador for Nespresso. Since then, the company has launched several direct marketing campaigns to improve customer service and to increase overall sales and brand awareness of Nespresso. The company uses club members' data for direct mail and emails which typically feature a personalized message and the value of the recipient's club points. Club members receive regular offers based on their potential and degree of loyalty, which influences their accumulated points.

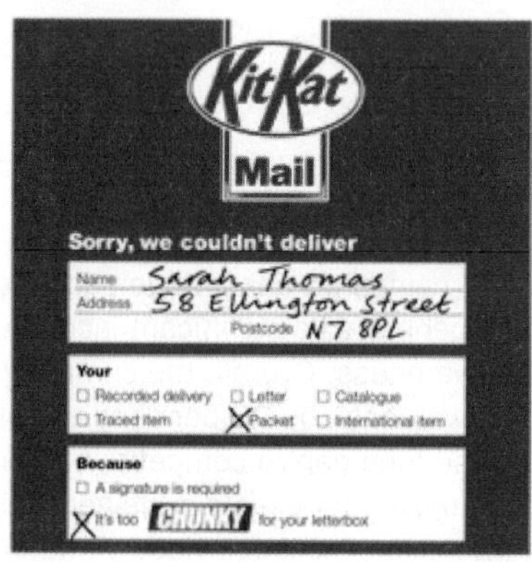

These include free delivery of coffee capsules, 10 per cent off accessories such as capsule dispensers or designer cups, and money-off vouchers to spend on coffee.

In 2017, Nespresso introduced a subscription service which allows members to purchase a coffee machine for €1 if they purchase a year's supply of coffee. Coffee pods are delivered monthly and no delivery charge applies. Additionally, high-loyalty customers are emailed a product catalogue on a monthly basis and posted high-quality fold-out leaflets to present the latest limited-edition coffee variants. All promotional materials are produced to an exceptionally high standard, thereby reinforcing the feeling of exclusiveness associated with Nespresso products.

Kit Kat Chunky Mail

In 2012, the company created a direct mail campaign 'Chunky mail' with a humorous twist on everyday mailing in order to drive the trial of its new Kit Kat Chunky in the UK. The campaign carefully targeted new and existing customers who were familiar with a standard Kit Kat but not the Chunky variant. This involved sending its target audience a note that mimicked the typical note used by postal carrier services when a package is too big to be delivered through the standard postbox. The note card stated that Kit Kat tried to deliver the new Chunky bar to the customer (with a graphic to illustrate its chunkiness), but it was 'too chunky to fit through the letterbox'. This was accompanied by a voucher to get the new Kit Kat Chunky free in a shop locally. The eye-catching flyer was a simple idea which promoted the chocolate bar's unique chunkiness. A reported 87 per cent of recipients went to their local newsagent to collect their Kit Kat Chunky. Overall, the direct mail campaign increased company awareness and gave Nestlé the opportunity to treat its target audience individually.

The following year, Nestlé launched its 'Choose a Chunky champion' campaign in the UK and Ireland, which invited fans to vote for the next permanent addition to its Kit Kat Chunky range from four limited edition flavours: mint, coconut, hazelnut and choc fudge. The company used social media to specifically target 18- to 30-year-old men who spend more than 30 minutes a day on Facebook. These recipients were encouraged to vote for their favourite flavour by visiting a dedicated Facebook page or using the augmented reality app Blippar. The campaign successfully increased engagement among this target market, resulting in over 600,000 votes cast on Facebook and 11 million bars sold.

In another, slightly tangential, move Nestlé teamed up with Google on its Android mobile operating system by revealing it would be called Android KitKat. This was the first time Android had been given a licensed name (previous versions of Android were called 'Jellybean' or 'Cupcake', for example). To mark the release of Android KitKat, more than 50 million specially branded Kit Kat bars were available in 19 markets, including Australia, Brazil, Germany, India, Japan, Middle East, Russia, the UK and USA. The packs led consumers to the website android.com/kitkat where they had the opportunity of winning prizes including Google Nexus 7 tablets and credits to spend in Google Play, Google's online store for apps, games, music, movies and books. The campaign enabled the company to store valuable customer contact and behavioural data which helped them to plan future direct marketing initiatives while also creating an environment for furthering customer relationships.

Additionally, Kit Kat has become a popular good-luck charm for exam-sitting students in Japan, because it sounds similar to the Japanese phrase kitto katsu: 'you will surely win'. In 2016, Nestlé used this opportunity to create a special holographic campaign targeting students through direct response advertising and direct mail, where good luck messages could be shared. The bars included a plastic pyramid that, when placed over a mobile phone, projected a hologram of the popular boy band 'DISH//' singing a good-luck song.

Nestlé's 'Maison Cailler'

In 2012, Nestlé created a new brand, 'Maison Cailler', as the launching pad for a new form of direct marketing. The campaign was rolled out in Switzerland via social media in order to bypass conventional retailers, so that Nestlé could test different chocolate flavours such as milk, caramel, nut, fruit, vanilla and cocoa. This was accompanied by a website which allowed consumers to 'discover their chocolate personality' and, within 48 hours, be sent a personalized box of chocolates that matched their individual preferences. The campaign was a huge success, allowing Nestlé to create a new database which contained a rich stream of information on customers. This enabled the company to tailor products and communications for future campaigns.

Nestlé is currently experimenting with location and mapping services to deliver fresh chocolate directly to consumers. This service determines the route to a customer's premises and calculates the required levels of refrigeration to counterbalance the environmental temperature in the location, so that the company can provide chocolates in mint condition.

Nestlé's MILO

In 2017, Nestlé's MILO brand (a chocolate and malt energy drink) ran a direct marketing campaign in Malaysia to create awareness about the importance of nutrition among children. The company used direct response advertising on the web, television and print media to urge mothers to enroll in its back-to-school programme. The programme encouraged these mothers to go to school with their children for one day and follow the same schedule as their child. Nestlé wanted mothers to gain an appreciation of the importance of a healthy diet for their children. The entire experience was filmed and edited into a series of four web films. In total, 60,000 Malaysians across seven locations in the country participated in the event. The campaign allowed Nestlé to communicate and engage with its key audience.

Nestlé Continues to Innovate

Nestlé's recent innovation drives include reducing sugar, salt and saturated fat content and increasing positive nutrients to improve the nutritional profile of its products. Nestlé continues to use innovative direct marketing approaches to target its customers. The 'Nestlé cocoa plan' direct marketing campaign promotes the fact that Nestlé is the first major confectionery company to source 100 per cent certified sustainable cocoa. The campaign is driven in conjunction with Tesco, Asda and Morrisons and

»

includes a direct mail campaign to loyalty customers. The company also recently launched its chocolate bar Milkybar Wowsomes, which uses Nestlé's new structured sugar to reduce sugar by 30 per cent by using only natural ingredients and no sweeteners. Primarily, direct-response advertising through the web and mobile communications is used to reach Nestlé's health-conscious target audience.

Questions

1. **Discuss the factors that have influenced the growth of direct marketing in recent years.**
2. **Why do you think that the Kit Kat Chunky mail campaign was so successful for Nestlé?**
3. **Explain the type of data Nestlé's might need if it wants to improve customer retention.**
4. **Discuss why marketing sustainability is important for businesses like Nestlé. Support your answer with examples.**

This case study was written by Dr Ethel Claffey, Waterford Institute of Technology, Republic of Ireland.

References

Based on: Koltrowitz, S. (2018) Nestlé counts on better second half to keep third point at bay, https://www.reuters.com/article/us-Nestlé-results/Nestlé-counts-on-better-second-half-to-keep-third-point-at-bay-idUSKBN1KG0GM (accessed 10 August 2018); Askew, K. (2018) 'Innovation leadership is key': Nestlé reorganises its R&D operations, https://www.foodnavigator.com/Article/2018/05/24/Nestlé-takes-innovation-to-new-level-with-R-D-reorganisation (accessed 12 August 2018); Vizard, S. (2017) Nestlé focuses on going direct-to-consumers as ecommerce sales hit 5 per cent, https://www.marketingweek.com/2017/02/17/Nestlé-focuses-going-direct-consumers-ecommerce-sales-hit-5 (accessed 10 August 2018); Nestlé-Nespresso.com (2018) Creating Long-lasting Consumer Relationships, https://www.nestle-nespresso.com/about-us/strategy/creating-long-lasting-consumer-relationships (accessed 10 August 2018); CampaignDrive (2018) 6 Great Examples of Print Marketing (And Why They Worked), https://www.campaigndrive.com/blog/6-great-examples-print-marketing-worked (accessed 20 August 2018); Royal Mail Market Research (2017) KitKat Grabbed Attention by Spoofing an Everyday Mailing, http://www.getmemedia.com/ideas/kit-kat-grabbed-attention-by-spoofing-an-everyday-mailing/royal-mail-marketreach.html (accessed 20 August 2018); Washington Direct Mail (2017) 10 Creative Examples of Direct Mail Marketing, https://www.wdmonline.co.uk/10-creative-examples-direct-mail-marketing/ (accessed 20 August 2018); Joseph, S. (2013) Kit Kat Chunky revives crowdsourcing push, https://www.marketingweek.com/2013/01/03/kit-kat-chunky-revives-crowdsourcing-push (accessed 20 August 2018); Nestlé Press Release (2013) Google and Nestlé announce Android Kitkat, https://www.corporate.nestle.ca/en/media/pressreleases/google-and-Nestlé-announce-android-kitkat (accessed 10 August 2018; Wyers, R. (2016) Nestlé Technology Innovator: 'We want to be the FMCG leader in leveraging digital and social media', http://www.foodingredientsfirst.com/news/Nestlé-Technology-Innovator-We-Want-to-be-the-FMCG-Leader-in-Leveraging-Digital-Social-Media.html (accessed 20 August 2018); SAS.com (2017) How to keep fresh products on the shelves, https://www.sas.com/en_us/customers/forecasting-supply-chain-nestle.html (accessed 17 August 2018); Wikipedia (2018) Milo definition, https://en.wikipedia.org/wiki/Milo (accessed 17 August 2018); Hew, V. (2017) Nestlé MILO's latest campaign brings mothers back to school, https://www.marketing-interactive.com/Nestlé-milos-latest-campaign-brings-mothers-back-to-school (accessed 17 August 2018); Utz.com (2018) The secrets behind Nestlé's successful consumer sustainability campaign, https://utz.org/better-business-hub/marketing-sustainable-products/secrets-behind-Nestlés-successful-consumer-sustainability-campaign/ (accessed 17 August 2018); Gebhart, A. (2017) What is Alexa? https://www.cnet.com/news/what-is-alexa/ (accessed 10 August 2018); Amazom.com (2018) GoodNes, https://www.amazon.com/Nestlé-GoodNes/dp/B06XX4T2MQ (accessed 20 August 2018).

CHAPTER 16
Digital Marketing and Media

> *Digital marketing has transformed how business and other organizations communicate with their target audiences.*
>
> **CHAFFEY AND ELLIS-CHADWICK (2019)**

LEARNING OBJECTIVES

After reading this chapter, you should be able to:

1 explain the concepts of digital marketing and digital media
2 explain each of the forms of digital media
3 identify the dimension of the digital marketing environment
4 discuss digital marketing campaign planning
5 discuss digital marketing implementation
6 discuss the dark side of digital marketing

Digital technologies are becoming increasingly important in all sectors of economic activity; these technologies and related innovations are disrupting traditional methods of marketing, communications and business models. Due to its high level of interconnectivity, the internet has been likened to the wheel and the airplane in terms of its ability to affect the future development of business, the economy and society. Consequently, companies are rethinking the role of technology and revising business models and processes to future-proof their businesses and seize new opportunities. But while firms concentrate on the adoption of the ever-expanding range of digital solutions, platforms (e.g. mobile phones, wireless and digital television) and technologies, the speed of innovation and change is constantly intensifying. For example, the global system for mobile communications (GMS) has become the fastest-growing communications technology of all time. And artificial intelligence (AI) and augmented reality (AR) applications are on the horizon and already changing how we trade, interact and live our daily lives. Consequently, adoption of digital technologies must be a part of every firm's business strategy, as these technologies have profound implications for marketing planning and implementation. In this chapter, we explore digital marketing by concentrating on communication channels and platforms. In previous chapters, we examined big data and the Internet of Things (Chapter 6), targeting and segmentation (Chapter 7), and data management and evaluation (Chapter 15)—areas that are also important to the application of digital marketing.

We begin by defining key terms—digital marketing and digital media— and then we explore the key dimensions of the digital communications environment. This is followed by a section exploring how to plan digital media campaigns and then a section on implementation, evaluation and control of digital marketing. Finally, we consider the dark side of digital marketing: ethical and societal issues.

What are Digital Marketing and Digital Media?

Digital marketing can be defined as 'achieving marketing objectives through applying digital media, data and technology' (Chaffey and Ellis-Chadwick, 2019). Even though *digital platforms* offer a fundamentally different environment for marketing activities insofar as the technology has unique properties that facilitate many-to-many interactive communications, the goals of the digital communication activities remain like those guiding the application of more traditional communication tools, for example raising awareness, encouraging action and increasing engagement.

But it is important to understand the way in which digital technologies are increasingly used to interact with target audiences. Digital technologies can emulate almost every aspect of marketing communications and traditional media channels and, in doing so, span the marketing mix. This means that the boundaries are less than clear, because digital technology is not only a means of communication but also a method of distribution. The flexibility afforded by the technology means that it is highly complex. Marketers are faced with learning how to use and understand emerging technologies, determining how to make strategic decisions that enable them to make the best use of the technology and implementing digital marketing plans that benefit their businesses. See Marketing in Action 16.1 to find out more about the meaning of digital marketing at Gucci, the luxury fashion brand. Furthermore, the widening application of digital technologies suggests that marketers should extend their thinking beyond the internet to encompass all the platforms—for example, mobile, web—that permit a company to communicate and do business electronically.

Digital media are the channels used to communicate and interact with a target audience online; see Figure 16.1. According to Chaffey and Ellis-Chadwick (2019), it is important to recognise that there are not only various digital media, but they also take different forms: paid-for media, owned media and earned media. Each form is now discussed.

Social media networks

Social media and social networking are shaping the way some sectors of society communicate. Social media cut across two forms of media: owned and earned. A company will 'own' its social media presence on Facebook, Instagram and Pinterest, but will also 'earn' engagement through social media market campaigns, i.e. by earning 'likes' and followers.

The growth of social media networks has been rapid since the mid 2000s, kick-started by digital natives (Prensky, 2001)—keyboard warriors and serial bloggers who live out their lives online, in communities created at

MARKETING IN ACTION 16.1
Gucci goes Digital in Style

Gucci is seen as being the embodiment of Italian luxury (despite being owned by a French company). Less well known is how the company has been able to combine old-world tradition with a deep understanding of modern technology and marketing techniques. Research named Gucci a 'fashion genius' due to its online capabilities regarding the use of e-commerce, social media, digital marketing and the integration of smartphone apps.

Unlike other luxury retailers, Gucci believes in providing a broad selection of products both in its boutiques and on its website. The reason for this is to ensure that customers have the same Gucci 'experience' in both the real world and the virtual one. In the early days of the web, many luxury brands struggled to move online, but Gucci led the way by having a well-defined and well-branded digital presence. The brand was an early adopter of Flipboard, a social network and social news aggregator that combines 'the beauty and ease of print with the power of social media'. Gucci also invested in an e-commerce infrastructure, so the company was well positioned to take advantage of the anticipated growth in online luxury markets.

Gucci's digital marketing strategy involves a multi-faceted approach using a variety of social media platforms. The company uses elaborate store-window displays in conjunction with superbly designed online video ads. Gucci has also cleverly tied promotional campaigns to the anniversaries of some of its iconic products, one example being the 60th anniversary of its famous Horsebit loafers when famous fashion bloggers were asked to show off the celebrated shoes. The brand has successfully created an immersive digital experience, which resonates with millennials. Gucci involves its customers through interactive features and displays. Gucci also invited fans to get involved, and simultaneously generated even more interest by asking them to post their favourite pictures on Instagram. The success of these efforts can be seen in the size of Gucci's online community, with the company having almost 19 million followers on Instagram and well over 17.5 million fans on Facebook in 2018.

Another example of Gucci's digital skills is its recent 'Made to Measure' campaign. Here, the company tied the promotion of a new cologne to an existing line of men's suits using Hollywood actor James Franco. The company ingeniously used Facebook, hashtags and social media postings in a coordinated effort to arouse interest in its new fragrance. In previous promotional campaigns, Gucci has used Facebook pages that included videos and apps for locating stores that carry a particular product.

Based on: Prepared from various published sources including Gucci (2018a, b)

virtual meeting places like Facebook, Biip, Habbo, Pinterest or Weibo. Social networking is proving to be the most pervasive digital innovation so far, and so online activity in this space is of great interest to marketers who see social networks as a communication and e-commerce channel. To put the adoption of social media into context, it took radio nearly 40 years to reach 50 million listeners and television 13 years to reach the same number, but in just four years 50 million users had internet access, and in less than one year over 100 million people had a Facebook account (Tuten and Solomon, 2013). Table 16.1 shows examples of social media sites, their country of origin and key community users. There are many online communities, focusing on various interests from art to education, but by far the most compelling driver of community growth is the ability to socialize and share information, pictures, music and video.

Social networks are nothing new and certainly were not invented by Tom Anderson (Myspace), Mark Zuckerberg (Facebook) or Joseph Chen (Renren). Social networks have existed almost since the beginning of humankind. They consist of people who are connected by relationships, friendships or interests. In 1975, Burke and Weir (1975) found that individuals prefer to turn to friends and family in times of need, and that being part of a social community gives individuals a sense of purpose (Argyle and Henderson, 1985). Sociologists suggested that a great deal of our daily lives involves relationships between *helpers* and *recipients* (of help) (Amato and Saunders, 1990), and the nature of these relationships is at the heart of the creation of social networks.

Online social media networks have spread throughout global societies, and research provides insight into this rapid diffusion (Katona, Zubcsek and Sarvary, 2010). It has been found that potential adopters of a social network who are connected to many adopters (already members of a social network) are predisposed towards becoming adopters themselves. In other words, if you know many people who are, say, connected to Facebook, you are more likely to become a member than if very few of your friends, family and work colleagues are members. You are also more likely to join a network that already has many members than one that is new with few members. The purpose of a social network is to enable an online community to use the functionality and tools of the site (e.g. Pinterest, enable the sharing of pictures and images; YouTube, the sharing of video) to share messages, ideas and content with an online community of *friends* (term used by Facebook).

FIGURE 16.1
Digital media channels

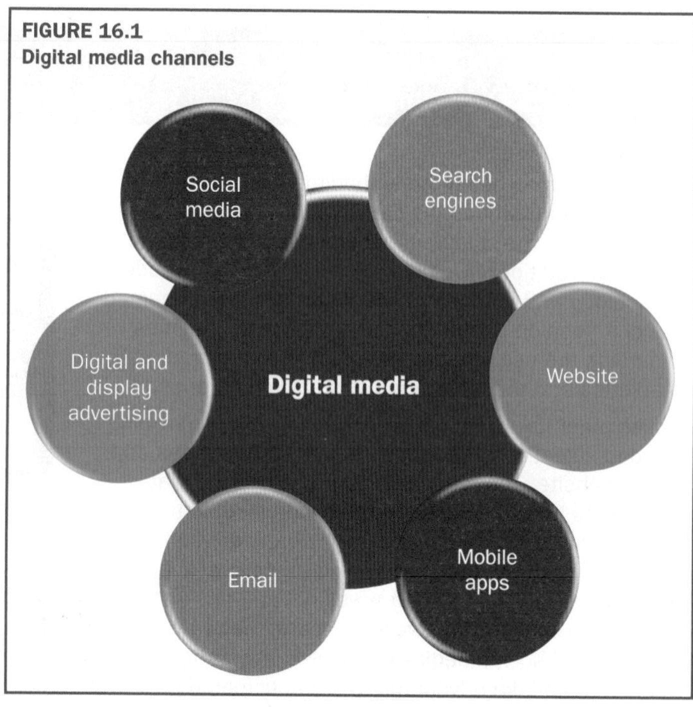

Social networks are a well-established part of the digital marketing world, and even though user communities differ in terms of the value proposition to members and the demographic profile, it is important for marketers to understand the nature and reach of the platforms they might use as part of their digital campaigns. For example, PepsiCo developed a 'meaningful social media following' in conjunction with strong retail promotional marketing as the main part of its campaign to launch and promote its Bubly water. The brand aimed to position its new sparkling water brand as fun and playful, and this was reflected in the launch campaign, the product features and flavour names. The use of social media is attributed with helping the brand to grow by 63 per cent in its launch year (Schultz, 2018).

TABLE 16.1 Social media sites, their country of origin and users

Social network	Country of origin	User community	Number of members	Geographical scope
Facebook	USA	Youth 13+	2.2 billion	Global
WeChat	China	Youth 13+	1 billion	China, Asia
QQ	China	Business and professionals	803 million	China, Asia
LinkedIn	USA	Businesspeople and professionals, mainly aged 30–50	467 million	Europe, Asia, South Africa
Badoo	Europe	Dating focused social network	252 million	Russia, Europe and Latin America
Instagram	USA	Under-35s	1 billion	USA
Pinterest	USA	Tablet users, young adults, mainly female	73 million	USA, Europe
Twitter	USA	Mainly under-40s	675 million	Global

Source: http://en.wikipedia.org/wiki/List_of_social_networking_websites (accessed June 2018)

According to Tuten and Solomon (2013: 33–41), 'social media is the way digital natives live a social life . . . it is all about a culture of participations; a belief in democracy, the ability to freely interact with other people, companies and organizations; open access to platforms allows users to share content from simple comments to reviews, ratings, photos, stories and more.' Being part of a social media network means that individuals and companies share ideas, interact with one another, work together, learn, enjoy group entertainment and even buy and sell.

Here are examples of some social media:

- *social community media* like Facebook and LinkedIn, which enable sharing of ideas and interests, socializing and having conversations
- *social publishing media* like YouTube, Pinterest and Flickr, which enable signed-up members to publish and distribute editorial content, movies, audio, photos
- *social commerce media* like TripAdvisor, Groupon and Facebook, which enable buying and selling, trading and building relationships
- *social entertainment media* like *Candy Crush*, *Clash of the Clans*, *Pet Rescue Saga*, which enable game playing and entertainment across communities

It is important to consider the network element of social media, as it is that which makes everything possible, including the interconnections, and informs the types of marketing message, content and interaction that might be used. For example, if you are a member of the Facebook social community, the network elements are the message boards, forums and wikis that facilitate communication and conversation. In a social publishing environment, a **blog** (online diary) often forms the underlying technology. In the commerce arena, the technology can be deal sites, deal aggregators and social e-commerce shopping markets.

The greater the number of members of the social media community, and the greater the number of interactions between them, the more interesting the network becomes to all involved. In other words, social (life), media (environment) and network (interconnections—technology and human) are the three elements that have come together to create social media networks—currently the fastest-growing online phenomenon, which has relevance for marketing. Leveraging the opportunities afforded by social media networks for marketing purposes has led to different tactical marketing applications: viral and buzz marketing.

Viral marketing is defined as the passing of information about products and services by verbal or electronic means in an informal person-to-person manner. It is also about identifying triggers that will prompt new conversations among target audiences. For example, Red Bull wanted to drive awareness for its Stratos mission, which aimed to test the limits of human capabilities and to contribute to scientific understanding. So, Red Bull set up a team of medical and aerospace experts and, using a helium-filled balloon, took Felix Baumgartner to the edge of the stratosphere, where he jumped back to Earth. To engage a global audience for this event, Red Bull created a destination website and a social media site and created a game with a prize of £12,000 for the person who guessed most accurately (on an interactive map) where Felix would land. The viral part of the campaign attracted over 250,000 followers on Twitter after one day. This turned out to be one of the biggest events on the internet: 9 million people watched the jump online, 8 million streamed the video on YouTube, there were 26 million unique visits to the website, and on the day of the event there were 29,000 shares on Facebook of Felix on the ground, in just 40 minutes (Ryan, 2014).

The spread of messages through viral marketing is usually driven by personal interests, which will determine which messages are successfully shared through social networks and messaging services. However, this can lead to unpredictable trends emerging. For example, Shabani, a gorilla at the Hiashiyama Zoo, captured the imagination (and hearts) of Japanese women, who referred to him with similar words they would use for actors like George Clooney and Hugh Jackman: 'dark and brooding', 'hunky', 'heart throb'. Shabani went viral as pictures and comments were widely shared on social media. This has also sent visitors flocking to the zoo to get a closer look at this primate (Murphy, 2015).

Buzz marketing is like viral marketing and more traditional word-of-mouth marketing, long recognized as one of the most powerful forms of marketing, but it has enjoyed a renaissance due to advances in technology such as email, websites and mobile phones. The first step in a buzz marketing campaign involves identifying and targeting 'alphas'—that is, the trendsetters who adopt new ideas and technologies early on—and the 'bees', who are the early adopters. Brand awareness then passes from these customers to others, who seek to emulate the trendsetters. In many instances, the alphas are celebrities who either directly or indirectly push certain brands. Once the target audience has been identified, the next key decisions, like those for all forms of promotion, are the message and the medium. The message may take many forms, such as a funny video clip or email attachment, a blog or story, an event such as a one-off concert, and so on. But, as with all aspects of buzz marketing, the only limitation is the imagination. For example, many individuals have used parts of their bodies or their private cars to carry commercial messages.

Given its novelty, evaluating the effectiveness of buzz marketing is difficult. Numbers are available regarding how many times a video clip is viewed, but marketers will not be able to determine by whom. For example, when a nearly naked image of model and reality television star Kim Kardashian appeared on the cover of *Paper* magazine, it created an instantaneous buzz and went viral on a global scale. Jean-Paul Goude aimed to #BreakTheInternet with his controversial image of Kim. And in just two hours, the image had been re-tweeted over 70,000 times, and, within a day, nearly 1 per cent of the US browsing traffic had seen the story (Hershkovits, 2014).

Search engines

Search engine marketing involves optimization of search listings and keyword searching. For instance, if searching Google using keywords such as 'jewellery shop', the search engine will provide a list of companies offering such services. Search engines like Google, Yahoo! and Bing generate revenue by charging each time an individual clicks on a sponsored link. The higher up the listing, the higher the price for click-through. Google sells a product called Google Ads and claims that it can enable users to attract more customers, help messages reach the *right* target audience, and be used on a local and global scale (Google Ads, 2018). From this perspective, search is a type of paid-for digital media. Google Ads connects companies with new customers at the precise moment they are looking for the company's products or services. With Google Ads, companies create their own adverts, choose keywords to help Google match their adverts to their audience, and pay only when someone clicks on them.

It has been argued that it is very important for advertisers to appear in the optimum position on the computer screen if they are to attract the greatest number of visitors to their online offering. By paying for a sponsored link, an advertiser gains a prominent position on the search engine's listings. The amount a company pays depends on how much it bids for keywords that internet users seeking a product are likely to enter: the higher the keyword bid compared with those of rivals, the higher the listing. While the average cost per click is 10–20p, in some competitive industries such as financial services it can be as high as £3. To make effective use of this mode of connecting with customers, companies should ensure that they choose the *right* keyword search terms, understand the analytical data and are measuring audience responses appropriately (Miles, 2018).

A second method of traffic building to a website is known as *search engine optimization* (SEO). This involves the achievement of the highest position in the natural listings on the search engine results pages after a keyword or phrase has been entered. The position depends on a calculation made by a search engine (e.g. Google) that matches the relevant site page content with the keyword (phrase) that is typed in. Unlike sponsored search (pay per click), SEO does not involve payment to a search engine to achieve high rankings. What a digital marketer needs is an understanding of how to achieve high natural rankings. Search engines use 'spiders' to identify the titles, links and headings that are employed to assess relevance to keywords and phrases. It is therefore important to ensure that the website includes the keywords (phrases) that a potential visitor might use to search for a company. For example, Ragdale Hall Spa's website includes terms such as 'weekend spa break', 'spa resort' and 'health spa', because they are key phrases used by consumers when searching for that type of hotel. This has achieved high ranking for the hotel on search engine listings (Chaffey, 2008).

However, SEO has become more of an exercise in behavioural segmentation than a technical website-development exercise, and so driving the *right* type of person to a site might be more important than where the website ranks for a key phrase. Google suggests that 200 separate variables can influence where and how a website finds itself in a search result. Google has set in place changes that might see website owners 'penalized' for overzealous SEO activity. There are clearly some organizations that play the SEO game with consummate success. A search for almost any consumer product will often find Amazon and eBay returned within the first few results, by virtue of their size, their authority as sites, their high-level linking, their involvement in advertising programmes and sophisticated automation of the SEO process. Within the hotel sector, many specialists admire Laterooms.com for its ability to perform highly against hotel brands and other booking services. Firms within highly competitive industries such as the insurance business expend huge resources to compete with other firms on Google. However, some brand names, such as GoCompare, prefer to spend that resource in pay-per-click campaigns than on SEO activity—perhaps an indication that brand awareness and a large pay-per-click budget might be more important than SEO for certain types of firms. SEO is not a type of paid-for digital media but is a strategic option for improving performance.

Digital and display advertising

Digital advertising is considered as a type of paid-for media. Online, advertisers make an investment to reach a target audience in much the same way as they would pay for space and time in print and broadcast media (Chaffey and Ellis-Chadwick, 2019). Online is a complex media environment. There are various forms of this type of media: digital display advertising, online video, internet television, and affiliate marketing.

Digital display advertising

This aims to get a target customer to act immediately by clicking on the advert or watching a video. Display adverts include banner adverts, skyscrapers (vertical tall and narrow banner ads that often appear at the right-hand side of the page) and pop-ups. There are many different forms of this type of advertising; see Figure 16.2. This is a popular and effective form of advertising; it can be used to elicit various responses and meet a range of communications objectives—for example, to raise awareness, increase action, change opinions and increase recall. It is measurable, relatively low cost—as payment is typically by each click-through—and easy to create. Digital display ads are flexible, come in different forms and can be sites on websites, social media platforms and on mobile devices, the latter having created opportunities for more creative forms of display advertising. Despite the advantages, some forms have been criticized: banner ads, are said to be distracting and interfere with the content of web pages, or are not noticed, and ad-blocking programs can be used to stop them from appearing to users. Nevertheless, better and more careful targeting has led to a renaissance for display advertising. Recently, Google, Facebook and Twitter have seen a significant increase in the spend on this form of advertising.

Online video advertising

Media-sharing sites have become increasingly popular and provide organizations and individuals with a platform on which to share visual, video and audio content. Popular platforms like YouTube, Flickr and Vimeo enable sharing of such content in an online environment. There are different types of content being produced depending on whether it is for an individual or a business.

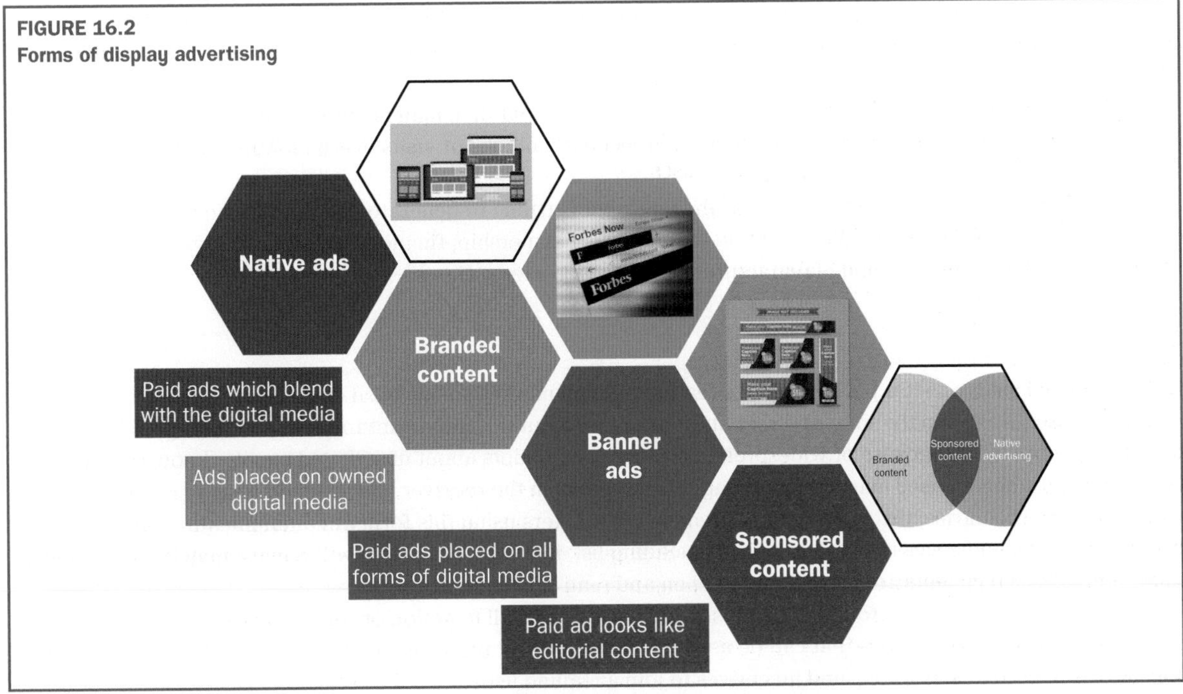

FIGURE 16.2
Forms of display advertising

Interactive television (iTV) advertising

The growth of digital television has given rise to an increase in this form of advertising, where viewers are invited to 'press the red button' on their remote control handset to see more information about an advertised product. This form of advertising has several advantages from being highly measurable, which means that advertisers can track the success of adverts displayed on different channels and at different times of the day. It also allows the targeting of niche audiences through specialist digital channels that focus on leisure activities such as sport, music and motoring and the provision of more in-depth information than a single television or press advertisement. For the user, it is a convenient means of buying a product without having to use a telephone or computer.

Affiliate marketing

This was a popular form of digital advertising. One business rewards another for placing advertising on its website. Each time a potential customer clicks on the link through to the originator of the advert website, the third party earns revenue. However, while sophisticated SEO techniques are increasingly being favoured for brand building over this technique, it should not be completely dismissed as an option (Olenski, 2014).

Websites

Websites are an important part of an organization's communication strategy and are classed as owned media (Chaffey and Ellis-Chadwick, 2019). The web offers a high degree of flexibility in terms of what can be created on a website, along with supporting digital technologies, which have revolutionized how organizations communicate.

Some organizations have developed highly sophisticated websites that target various global audiences with an extensive range of products. However, others have been far more timid, developing small-scale experimental applications; for example, there is a stark contrast between the reach and sophistication of Tesco.com compared with Morrison.co.uk (Doherty and Ellis-Chadwick, 2009). Websites are potentially much more than a form of advertising, as they can be used as an online store, an information repository, a portal or a gateway for many different services. Two examples of website types are the following.

1 *Intermediaries' websites*, which act as a portal or gateway to a variety of content. Examples are:
   - *Mainstream news media sites or portals*. These include traditional sites, for example *FT.com*, *The Times*, *The Guardian*, Pureplay and Google News.
   - *Social networks*, for example, Facebook, Twitter, LinkedIn, Renren and Google+.
   - *Price comparison sites* (also known as aggregators), for example Moneysupermarket, Kelkoo, Shopping.com, confused.com, mysupermarket.com.
   - *Super-affiliates*. Affiliates gain revenue from a merchant they refer traffic to, by being paid commission based on a proportion of the sale or a fixed amount. They are important in e-retail markets, accounting for significant sales.
   - *Niche affiliates or bloggers*. These are often individuals, but they may be important; for example, in the UK, Martin Lewis of Moneysavingexpert.com receives millions of visits every month. Smaller affiliates and bloggers can be important collectively.

2 *Destination sites*. These are the sites that the marketer is trying to generate visitors for and which may be transactional sites. For example, retailers—John Lewis Partnership; financial services—Aviva.com; travel companies—ryanair.com; and manufacturers' brands—Procter & Gamble.

Email

Email is owned media, as it is part of website features. Email marketing has been discussed in Chapter 15, as it is now an essential tool in the suite of direct marketing tools. But it is important to remember that permission-based emails are in use because of widespread consumer complaints about unsolicited emails (known as 'spam'). Generally, permission-based marketing messages are sent when the receiver has given consent to receive direct emails (in some countries, this is a legal requirement). Marketers using this form of communication find ways to encourage target audiences to opt in to a firm's emailing list; in return, recipients will receive materials that match their interests, as recipients are more likely to open and read such messages.

Email marketing has been found to be most widely used as a call to action or for sales promotion offers. There are many techniques and tactics that can be used to ensure the best performance for email marketing campaigns, such as sales discounts, rewards, and incentives to join a mailing list.

Mobile apps and messaging

Mobile marketing refers to the creation and delivery of marketing communications messages through mobile devices (phones, smartphones or tablet computers). Like websites and email, mobile is a type of media that is owned. Early examples of mobile marketing involved sending text messages containing advertising to willing recipients. *Messaging* can be a powerful marketing tool. WhatsApp, Facebook Messenger, Viber and WeChat are examples of messaging applications. These apps have an advantage over email, as the users do not have to share email addresses or sign up to receive content. For example, the *Washington Post* used a chat bot in its marketing strategy, which allowed users to find news articles and tailor the news feed they wanted to receive. The chat bot worked in the Facebook Messenger environment to enable sharing and exchange of information with users' personal networks. The Facebook Messenger platform has more than 1.3 billion monthly users and provides instantaneous interactions (Jenblat, 2018).

However, widespread adoption of smartphones and wireless tablet computers has increased capacity for visual content as well as text-based content. Mobile marketing is becoming increasingly popular, but not all consumers are keen to receive marketing messages via their phones. Research found that 75 per cent of consumers in the UK were happy to get offers via their handsets compared with 72 per cent in the USA, 50 per cent in France and 46 per cent in Germany (Akhtar, 2012). Nevertheless, one of the most rapidly growing forms of mobile marketing is smartphone applications (apps). See Marketing in Action 16. 2, which discusses how Shazam is partnering with Office Depot to create a whole new retail experience.

MARKETING IN ACTION 16.2
Shazam Joins with Retailers and Expands the Future of Mobile Marketing

Shazam has over 300 million users every month, who enjoy being able to identify songs and audio messages. The value proposition for Shazam's customers is that it connects users to the world around them through music, adverts, cinema, television and radio. Shazam has now extended the offer to retail. Shazam In-Store is a location-based mobile marketing app that allows users to create a personalized mobile shopping experience by linking together loyalty programmes, social media and the latest deals and offers. Retailers are able to target shoppers using in-store music, and once the shopper's smartphone recognizes the signal, that person can receive a Shazam song along with a tailored offer from the retailer. For example, Shazam and Office Depot have joined forces to create an innovative shopping experience using the app's music-based digital signature and iBeacons. An iBeacon is a digital innovation that is very flexible and can be used to communicate with any smartphone. Designed by Apple, iBeacons work on a localized basis, and many retailers, bars, restaurants and transport companies have adopted this technology to give customers information on the latest deals and offers. Arguably, iBeacons are bridging the gap between the digital and physical world by seamlessly linking together communication devices, creating opportunities for peer-to-peer sharing of coupons and vouchers, and creating Retail 2.0, whereby companies can push content to their customers depending on where they are in a store.

In 2017, Apple bought Shazam and incorporated it with its virtual assistant Siri, allowing the app's users to verbally ask for information about the songs being played. By combining with Shazam, Apple is aiming to be able to compete more strongly with rival its Swedish rival Spotify, which has the edge over Apple as it provides better targeted music selections. Shazam gives Apple access to a very large database, so it can offer a strong 'music discovery service'.

Based on: Vanhemert (2014); Shazam (2018); Bold (2014); Kelion (2017)

Mobile marketing has several advantages. It is:

- *cost-effective*. The cost per message is between 15p and 25p, compared with 50p to 75p per direct mail shot, including print production and postage.
- *targeted and personalized*. For example, operators like Vodafone, Virgin Mobile and Blyk offer free texts and voice calls to customers if they sign up to receive some advertising. In signing up, customers have to fill out questionnaires on their hobbies and interests.
- *interactive*. The receiver can respond to the text message, setting up the opportunity for two-way communication.
- *personal*. It enables dialogue and relationship development. Retailers like Dixons Carphone are developing ongoing 'conversations' with their customers across a range of mobile and digital media.
- *time-flexible*. Text messages can be sent at any time, giving greater flexibility when trying to reach the recipient.
- able to *engage the audience*. This is becoming known as *proximity marketing*. Messages can be sent to mobile users in nightclubs and shopping centres and at festivals and universities—indeed, wherever recipients are at any time of the day or night.
- *immediately available*. For example, the US consumer electronics retailer Best Buy sends special offers and deals to customers' smartphones using a technology that pinpoints when they are entering a Best Buy store.
- *immediate and measurable*. It can assist in database development.
- the *gateway to other channels*. For example, while most marketers spend less than 5 per cent of their marketing budgets on mobile marketing, smartphones are increasingly replacing other devices as the means by which users download music, films and other multimedia content, access the web, answer their emails and navigate (e.g. satnav apps).
- **Snap codes** and **Spotify codes** are other applications that may increasingly be linked to an app store, where coupons can be downloaded for instant use. Snapchat, Spotify, Messenger, WeChat and others are using **QR code** technology to instantly connect users to online content and destinations by scanning codes using a mobile phone camera. Snapchat launched snap codes in 2015 as an easy way to find a friend and a shortcut to marketing offers, games and other online content. WeChat in China is experimenting with how its codes can be used as a way to receive vouchers and pay for a meal when the user walks into a restaurant (Pierce, 2017).

The Digital Communication Environment

Since 1982, *digitization* has taken place and there has been a steady increase in the use of digital technologies. Products such as televisions, telephones, watches, cameras and music have changed to digital formats. As digitization spreads, the level of *connectivity* across devices, people and locations increases. For example, photographs can be shown on computer screens, shared on social networks and stored remotely in the computing cloud. The internet connects billions of people and organizations around the world, allowing fast transfer of information. Intranets connect people within a company, facilitating communications, and extranets connect a company with its trading partners, such as suppliers and distributors. In a similar vein to the marketing environment discussed in Chapter 2, the digital communication environment is shaped by four key dimensions, with implications for marketing: 1) technology, 2) marketing, 3) applications, and 4) audiences (see Figure 16.3).

Technology

The *internet* is at the heart of the digital age; it has facilitated the creation of a global network of computer networks, which creates the infrastructure for all online activity. Wireless networks and cloud computing are a growing part of the internet and are enabling users to access the internet remotely. *Mobile and satellite technologies* are revolutionizing the communication industry. They are widely used in logistics, from the transportation industry and air traffic control to the individual shopper at home. Tesco, for example, uses mobile and satellite technology throughout the supply chain; at the shopper end, there is a Tesco app that lets you add your shopping list to a smartphone and then it will create a map to show you the shortest route to your product selection. In store, one of Tesco's best-selling items is bananas, and there are technology systems in place to make sure the fruit is readily available on the shelves to meet customer demand (tesco.com, 2018). On the road there is a satellite grid system that updates managers on the distance from the store of the next bunch of bananas (Fenwick, 2010).

FIGURE 16.3
Key dimensions of the digital age

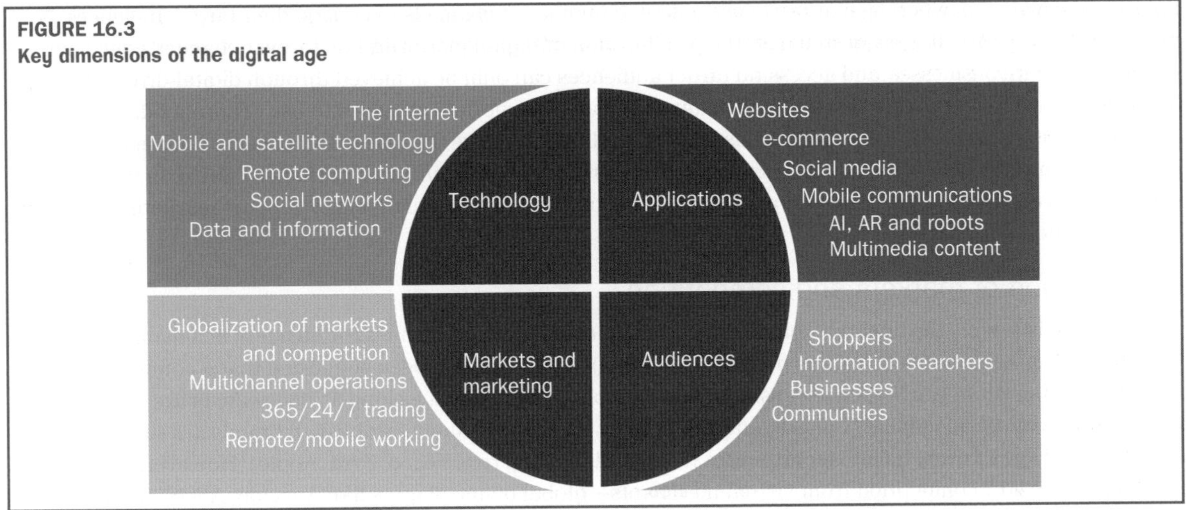

One of the main factors driving the use of digital technology is convergence, the bringing together into one device of the functions that were previously performed by several. For example, smartphones perform the functions of telephones, cameras, computers, audio systems and televisions. Convergence brings the convenience of being able to carry out several tasks using just one device. Platforms are switching from analogue to digital (e.g. television) and from fixed to wireless (e.g. telephones and computers); services are offered over multiple platforms (e.g. online television—BBC iPlayer; television over broadband—iTV by Apple; instant streaming of video content—Netflix and Amazon Prime Video). Convergence is creating many opportunities for developing new ways to provide access to multimedia content and a range of additional services.

Convergence has also prompted the development of *remote computing* and given rise to the concept of cloud computing. We probably all have many documents, spreadsheets, business and personal files and photographs which we are saving on an increasing array of storage devices. But the problem can be finding a document in its latest version. Cloud computing offers a solution to this problem, as all documents can be stored in a single secure remote location. Google and Apple offer different ways to access cloud computing, but both are aiming to make these services more accessible. Steve Jobs said 'keeping these devices in sync is driving us crazy' when he launched Apple's iCloud service (Nuttall, 2011).

Web 2.0 is a second generation of internet technology and applications to enable the sharing of content. Discussion boards, wikis, blogs and *social networks* are the underlying technologies that facilitate community developments and the sharing of information.

Data and information: data are the building blocks on which many of the applications are built; information is the 'intelligence' that can be gleaned from the data. We covered these topics in Chapter 6.

Intelligent technology: artificial intelligence (AI), augmented reality (AR) and other immersive technologies are likely to shape the next generation of applications, products and services that have relevance for marketers. Google Home and Amazon's Echo, Dot and Tap are voice-activated devices driven by AI. These devices enable users to use natural speech to ask for information, order goods, set alarms, manage energy in the home and a range of other tasks. The devices are learning from how they are used so that they can increase the range of services. Already, over 30 million smart speakers have been sold globally; this is providing a great deal of user data to learn from (Marr, 2018). AR enables digital data to be interwoven into a real experience. You don't need a headset to experience AR, as this technology is being incorporated into apps. Timberland has an AR virtual fitting room where shoppers can try on clothes, select different styles and colours, and see them on an AR image of themselves (Hall, 2017).

Markets and marketing

The development of digital technologies and their subsequent widespread adoption has significant implications for the reach and nature of markets and marketing. The rapid pace of innovation and change in the digital environment means there are many challenges for marketers to manage. There is also a growing debate about how *digital* is affecting the concept of marketing. On one side, it is suggested that the *marketing funnel* approach to planning, whereby marketers use a limited number of channels to engage their target audiences, is no longer appropriate. It is suggested that 'the proliferation of digital platforms has forever changed consumer engagement with businesses' and accessing target audiences can only be achieved through digital-driven data analysis of customer conversion rates to determine the most appropriate channels to use (Thorogood, 2015). But on the other side of the debate, the focus is more traditional, where the marketing concept remains central, and it is business as usual in what has been referred to as the '*post-digital world*' (Friedlein, 2015). In this world, *digital* is merely a new set of tools and platforms that should be applied creatively to support marketing and communication objectives.

Globalization of markets and competition

According to research, the internet's 'global connectivity opens up new avenues for business in a manner that traditional commerce conduits cannot match' (Pyle, 1996), and it has also been suggested that a company based anywhere in the world can launch a website to compete on a global basis, as long as its products are easily transportable or downloadable (Doherty and Ellis-Chadwick, 2010a). Many established brands are successfully taking advantage of these online opportunities to expand globally (e.g. Tesco, Zara, Apple). However, they inevitably face stiff competition from virtual merchants—global online players like Amazon, ASOS, Netflix and 'disintermediators' that have cannibalized the supply chain by going straight from manufacturer to the end consumer (e.g. Dell.com, and the Alibaba Chinese e-commerce platform, which serves all markets via its websites). Retailers and consumer brands are likely to face growing pressure from a variety of new businesses that are keen to get their share of the electronic market.

One thing that has become very clear during the last years of online trading is that there is always the opportunity for an innovative and dynamic company that has read the market well, and which has an effective business model, to make a strong impact, and, in so doing, to grow very big and powerful, very quickly, as in the case of Google, Facebook and eBay. The experiences of these organizations demonstrate that the internet can be a very fertile environment for global expansion if organizations have good ideas supported by an appropriate set of core competences and capabilities (Doherty and Ellis-Chadwick, 2010a). These discussions link to the later chapters on competition (Chapter 19) and global strategy (Chapter 21).

Multichannel operations

Multichannel operations are becoming the de-facto approach to managing online and offline operations. Most businesses have harnessed the internet's capacity to provide information, facilitate two-way communication with customers, collect market research data, promote goods and services and, ultimately, support the online ordering of merchandise as an extremely rich and flexible new channel (Basu and Muylle, 2003). The internet has given retailers a mechanism for broadening target markets, improving customer communications, extending product lines, improving cost efficiency, enhancing customer relationships and delivering customized offers (Srinivasan, Anderson and Kishore, 2002) through their cross-operations (Doherty and Ellis-Chadwick, 2010a).

Dixon's Carphone Warehouse is an example of a European retailer that is using the web and mobile technology to provide multichannel assistance and drive customers to its stores. To begin with, Carphone Warehouse developed a multichannel service by building a mobile-optimized website incorporating a 'click to call' feature that allowed users to contact the call centre and make a purchase. Carphone Warehouse then also promoted the service through mobile and web channels and included a link on its main website's store-finder page. This enabled customers in the high street who were thinking about buying a new mobile phone to be instantly directed to the nearest store (Jones, 2011).

Many retailers are finding that they are achieving a much higher return on investment if they use their websites and mobile apps as an integral part of their businesses (Barnett, 2011). A multichannel strategy brings together the different routes a company uses to access its market. Arguably, the aim is to create a customer journey that seamlessly links together every point where the customer touches a business, to create what appears to be a single-channel approach, even though many different channels are involved (**omnichannel**). This includes traditional and digital communications and distribution channels operating together. These discussions link to further issues associated with channel development and management in Chapter 17.

Continuous trading

The internet never closes; 365, 24/7 trading is a reality, and companies are being pressurized to manage their interface with customers on an 'open all hours' basis. Many companies provide self-help information on their websites, which customers can access around the clock. But they also provide call centres, customer services and returns departments, which provide real-time support, via the phone or online.

Remote and mobile working

Many more people are now working remotely than in the past. In the UK, 13.6 per cent of the working population are working on a remote basis. A surprisingly large proportion do so from their home premises (37.5 per cent). However, the biggest group of 62.5 per cent work remotely away from home (e.g. transport drivers, sales representatives) (Frary, 2012). New technology is facilitating this process and making more things possible. For home workers, there are many advantages and disadvantages to consider. On the plus side, travel costs are reduced, and workers have more control over how they plan their working day. On the negative side, there can be an increase in family conflict, lack of understanding from family members about the tasks the worker must complete, and pressure on the space needed to successfully carry out a job at home. There is also the loss of interaction with other members of the workforce, and managerial support is only available on a remote basis.

However, research has found that if there is increased social support from the workplace for remote workers, many of the negatives of working at home are reduced (Wylie et al., 2010). Social media have been found to offer support and boost employee satisfaction, trust and productivity (Snoad, 2011). Aviva World (available to over 36,000 staff worldwide) is very popular and regularly receives over 7 million hits a month. Aviva encourages its staff to get involved with the business at various levels through social media, and in doing so it is enabling remote workers to feel more involved in the business. These are not isolated examples; companies including Coca-Cola, the BBC, Unilever and Sainsbury's are using social media networks and intranets to communicate, interact and, ultimately, improve job satisfaction and productivity.

Applications

In the early days, the internet was viewed primarily as a means to facilitate two-way communications between companies and their customers. However, very quickly the underlying technology and widespread adoption of websites became far more sophisticated and enabled more applications and uses to be introduced. (See Chapter 13 for further detailed discussion of the use of digital communication in integrated marketing communications (IMC) strategies, and Chapter 15 for discussion of direct marketing.) Given the internet's potential to radically reconfigure underlying business processes, and because of the highly dynamic and innovative nature of the online marketplace, it is not surprising that there has been a rapid expansion in the application of these relatively new technologies. Furthermore, it should be remembered that commercial exploitation of the internet has far-reaching implications—technical, logistical, strategic, behavioural, social and legal. Companies wishing to take advantage of the opportunities created by the internet need to make sure that these opportunities are integrated into their wider strategic goals if they are to garner the best advantage from digital applications (Doherty and Ellis-Chadwick, 2010b). (See Chapter 18 for further discussion of marketing strategy and planning.)

Websites and e-commerce

The internet enabled the creation of websites that could be used to purchase and pay for merchandise, sell and promote goods and services, collect market research data, and track orders (Basu and Muylle, 2003; Doherty and Ellis-Chadwick, 2009). Currently, the internet provides businesses with a highly effective mechanism for broadening target markets, improving customer communications, extending product lines, improving cost-efficiency, enhancing customer relationships and delivering customized offers (Srinivasan, Anderson and Kishore, 2002). Indeed, target audiences have taken to the new technology, and whether companies are trading in business-to-business or business-to-consumer markets, an increasing range of applications are being used—e-commerce, information repositories, social media, interactive communications and multimedia content delivery.

Social media

These networks created an arena for multi-faceted applications and social communication. Facebook, Twitter, Instagram, Snapchat and WeChat are just some of the social media platforms where vast numbers of people spend hours each day online engaging with businesses and each other. Facebook and Facebook Messenger remain the most popular (Chaffey 2018). The emergence of successful social networking sites such as Facebook, LinkedIn and Google+ and **microblogging** sites like Twitter and Tumblr have had a significant impact on global society. Social networking has become pervasive throughout the world, even in China, where Facebook was censored in

2009 and remains inaccessible. Digital and social media have given a voice to masses of individuals, businesses and communities around the world, and adoption rates have been rapid. For example, at the turn of the century there were approximately 1.5 million internet users in China (Chaffey et al., 2000); now there are over 772 million (Internet World Stats, 2018), and reportedly 91 per cent of users have accounts with social media platforms like Renren (the Chinese equivalent of Facebook), Weibo (microblogging site) and Twitter.

Mobile communications

Mobile communications network technology has undergone significant change, switching from analogue to digital circuits, and mobile phone networks and handsets have become increasingly sophisticated. When Apple launched the iPhone in 2007, it kick-started a revolution in mobile applications (see earlier discussion) and a rapid increase in the number of users. Mobile phones have increased facilities for receiving multimedia content, and online television has become widely available. Mobile has significantly increased the potential for digital marketing and extended reach through digital media.

AI, AR and robots

New intelligent computing applications are reshaping how we interact with devices, applications and digital content.

- AI applications are set to transform marketing as big data is used to power customer analysis and predict behavioural responses.
- AR applications are creating immersive applications that enable users to use their mobile phones to link together the physical and the digital worlds. For example, Home Depot (US retailer) added 3D AR to its app to enable customers to visualize how products might look in their own homes.
- Robotics applications that can be used in the digital marketing and media space are also emerging.
- Chatbots are computer programs that can respond to customer queries and messages automatically.

Audiences

For its users, the internet and digital media have not only provided the means to find, buy and sell products, but they have also created an environment for building communities, where like-minded people can network, socialize and be entertained. Figure 16.4 shows levels of internet penetration in various countries around the world.

The trend for exponential growth in internet users started in the USA, where the internet's commercialization began early in the 1990s, and spread throughout Europe to Oceania, Asia, the Middle East and Africa. As use of the

FIGURE 16.4
Levels of internet penetration in selected countries across the world

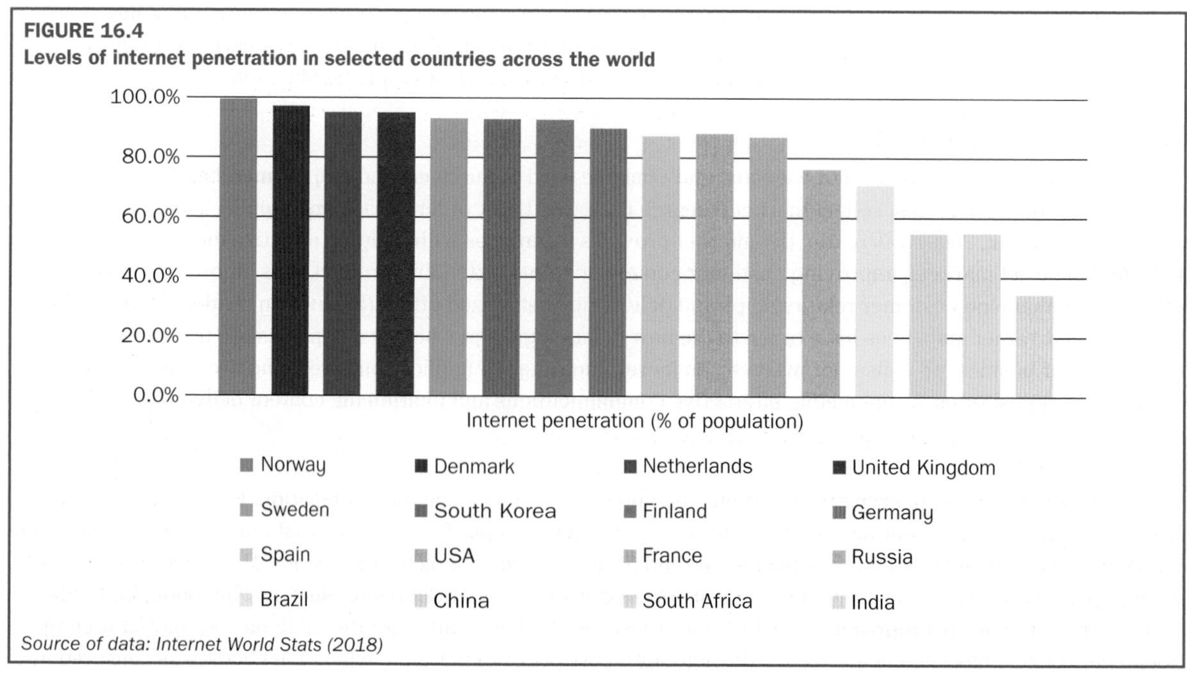

Source of data: Internet World Stats (2018)

internet and digital media grows, a major challenge for marketers is how to make best use of what digital media offer. Across the world, there are different types of audience; *shoppers, information searchers, businesses* and *communities' members* are now happy to use internet technology as part of their daily lives. Target audiences are discussed further in the section on digital marketing and digital media campaign planning. The dimensions of the digital age have far-reaching implications for marketers. Technology is driving the development of new routes and channels to market. Digital markets are growing and extending reach and opportunities to trade, and challenging the definition of marketing. Existing and new companies are continually in competition for market share. Myriad new applications are used to entice growing audiences to live part of their lives online and are changing how we interact with technology. To succeed, online companies should plan carefully how they are using digital technology.

Digital Marketing and Digital Media Campaign Planning

This section explores digital marketing planning. Deciding how to plan, resource, integrate, implement and monitor digital marketing activities can be guided by applying established marketing management principles and planning activities (as discussed in detail in Chapters 2 and 18). Digital media can be used to meet a range of different business objectives: achieve sales, communicate, or focus on the development and maintenance of mutually satisfying long-term relationships with customers by using digital technologies. Therefore, the types of activities will determine the strategic significance of the plan and give focus to the operational context.

Elements of digital marketing planning

The formulation of the digital marketing plan is likely to be informed by four significant and interdependent elements (Doherty and Ellis-Chadwick, 2004). See Figure 16.5.

1 *Strategic alignment* of digital marketing activities with corporate marketing and marketing communication strategies is important, as it should ensure development of a potentially successful digital marketing plan. This process should also help to define the purpose of the digital marketing activities.

2 *Integration* of digital marketing and social media with traditional tools and techniques is essential. This means that planning is required to consider all the touchpoints in a customer's journey and ensure that customers receive a consistent message. But integration also requires a cross-company approach, bringing together cross-company teams to achieve unified strategic-level corporate and marketing goals as well as tactical communication goals (Chaffey and Ellis-Chadwick, 2019).

3 The *value proposition* should emphasize the unique advantages created using digital technologies, for example *choice* (amazon.com offers the world's widest and deepest range of books at very low prices), *convenience* (tesco.com offers round-the-clock shopping), *community* (Facebook brings people together around the world). The value proposition created through the relative advantage afforded by digital technologies should reinforce core brand values and be clearly articulated to target audiences. It will also determine the extent to which organizational change is required.

4 *Implementation and organizational change* is likely if the digital marketing plan is to be delivered successfully. A good example to consider is how retailers like Tesco and Sainsbury's have developed unique logistical solutions to support online ordering. E-commerce initiatives can involve applying a wide range of digital technologies: internet, EDI (an electronic data format that allows companies to complete transactions online), email, electronic payment systems, advanced telephone systems, mobile and handheld digital appliances, interactive television, self-service kiosks and smart cards. Consequently, the integration of such technologies may require significant changes to operations and working practices in order to ensure that the right skill sets (capabilities) and resources are available when required. *Implementation* of the plan should be executed in a timely manner. Additionally, the success of the digital marketing plan is likely to be affected by senior management

FIGURE 16.5
Elements of digital marketing planning

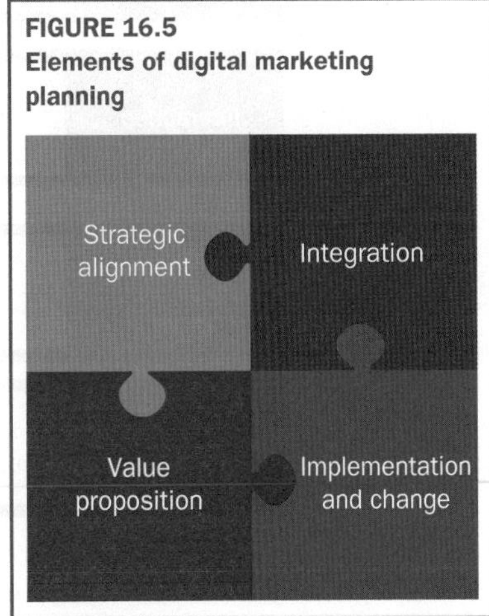

commitment, availability of appropriate resources and the appropriateness of the strategic vision that is guiding the implementation. The significance of the digital marketing plan for a company's overall strategy will also largely be dependent upon levels of technology adoption, investment and integration.

In addition, analysis of the marketing environment (as discussed in Chapter 2) should take place in order to determine the likely relevance of digital marketing and opportunities that might be pursued.

Objectives and analytics

Developing a plan for using digital marketing and media is much the same as any other marketing planning exercise insofar as there is a requirement to understand the situation in which they are going to be used, and the needs of the target audience and their behaviour. Once environmental analysis is complete and the broad focus of the campaign established, the next step is to determine its direction and purpose and to set objectives. This is perhaps where the planning process becomes more complicated. In order to state objectives, a company must be clear about the types of objectives that can be achieved. According to Chaffey and Ellis-Chadwick (2019), the RACE planning framework (Reach, Act, Convert, Engage) is important for managing key planning activities and aids clarity when evaluating objectives. See Figure 16.6.

- *Reach*: this relates to objectives of increasing awareness and driving visitor numbers in different forms of digital media: web mobile and social networks. A campaign aiming to capture the attention of new digital audiences or introduce existing audiences to new products and services will need to consider which digital media are the most appropriate for the desired target audience. This may include paid, owned and earned media to raise the number of unique visitors. Measurement analytics may include website bounce rates, time on site and comparison with rates achieved by competing brands online and number of brand searches.
- *Act*: this relates to objectives of increasing interactions and generating new prospects. Measurement analytics may include percentage of conversions in relation to the number of leads generated, goal value per visit, and page views per visit. For these types of objective, it is important to consider where the customer is in their brand journey and use data profiling to gain greater understanding of their behaviour. Also, it is important to link these objectives closely to content management strategy.
- *Convert*: this relates to sales and profits objectives. By this stage, companies will have a very clear understanding of the target audience, which should enable high levels of personalization, tailoring of customer experiences and multichannel selling opportunities. Analytics may measure the percentage of conversions, sales values and the average order value.
- *Engage*: these objectives relate to encouragement of customer loyalty and increasing advocacy. Objectives will focus on the percentage of active customers, and measurement may include percentage of customers

FIGURE 16.6
RACE framework: digital marketing objectives and analytics

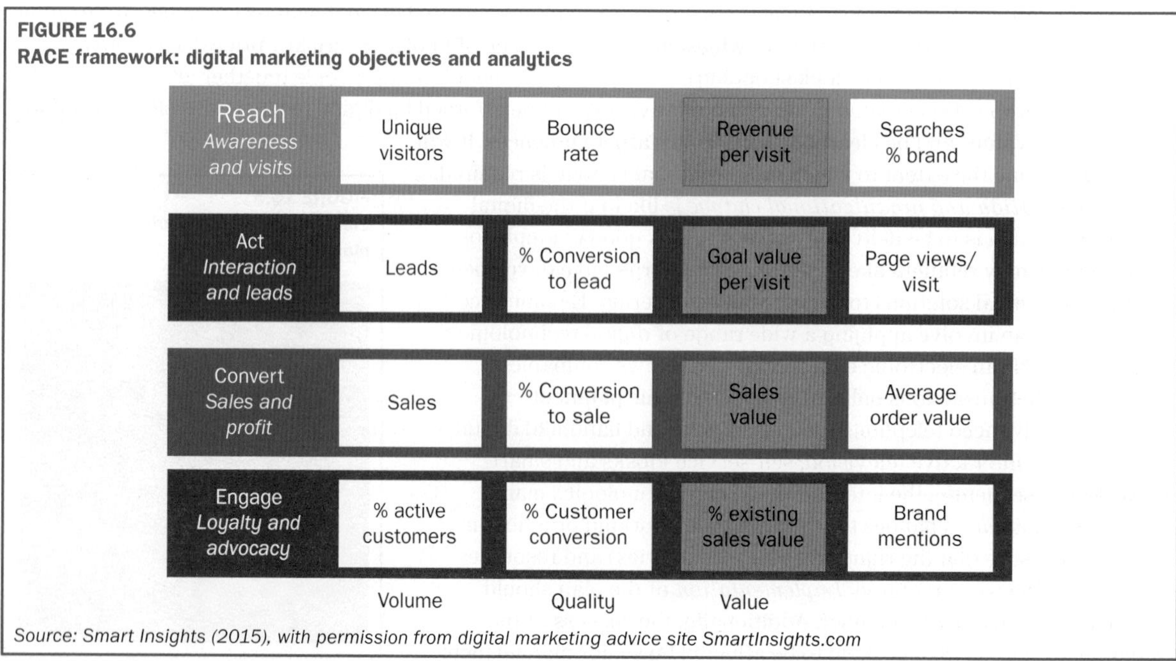

Source: Smart Insights (2015), with permission from digital marketing advice site SmartInsights.com

converted from inactive to active, percentage of existing sales, and brand mentions in social media networks. To achieve these objectives, companies can consider ways of attracting and signing up customers, ensuring a great customer experience and high levels of customer service. Social media play an important role in achieving these objectives. (Discussion based on Chaffey and Ellis-Chadwick, 2019.)

Digital media competency

It is worthwhile considering that companies are not all at the same level of competency when using digital media. According to Tuten and Solomon (2015), companies using social media can be at different stages, which can have implications for the types of objectives they are likely to pursue.

Trial phase—at this level, a company has just begun using social media and is testing what it can deliver. There is a tendency to 'play' and experiment. At this stage, there is little consideration of longer-term strategic objectives, as the focus is on making use of social media platforms like Facebook, Twitter and YouTube. The types of objectives typically pursued at the level are increasing website traffic and improving public relations.

Transition phase—this occurs when companies are making more significant use of social media. This can be considered as a mature phase. Beall's, a US department store, began using internet advertising in the early days to drive traffic to its website and promote sales and so on. Currently, the company makes extensive use of social media in order to engage its target audiences in conversation. The company's Facebook pages are updated several times a day, and commercial fan coupons are released so they can be shared among the community. At this phase, the use of social media becomes more sophisticated and more integrated with the IMC and marketing strategy. At this level, examples of objectives are improving public relations and increasing product awareness.

Strategic phase—this occurs when an organization enters the final level. At this point, the use of social media will be fully integrated across the business activities and incorporated into all levels of planning. At this level, most adopters are pursuing objectives such as increasing brand awareness, improving brand reputation and increasing website traffic.

Across all the phases, limited attention is given to objectives associated with increasing sales or reducing costs. Exhibit 16.1 shows World Animal Protection's sophisticated levels of competency when using digital media.

Evaluation and control

Evaluation and control systems need to be created that permit management to rapidly identify variance in actual performance versus forecast for all aspects of the digital marketing mix. Management also requires mechanisms that generate diagnostic guidance on the cause of any variance. To achieve this aim, control systems should focus on the measurement of key variables within the plan, such as targeted market share, customer attitudes, awareness objectives for digital marketing and distribution targets. Typically, in traditional marketing planning, measurement and control are not considered until later in the planning process. In digital campaigns, evaluation and control are an integral part of the objectives; while, in reality, the action of setting up these measures will not take place until the implementation stage, it is vitally important for marketers to know how they are going to measure the achievement of objectives, and this is why this aspect is included at this stage in our discussions.

Digital analytics is a catch-all term for the methods used to evaluate the success of digital marketing programmes. Such techniques allow the checking of whether objectives have been achieved, by recording traffic volume, website visitor numbers, the most popular pages and products, how long visitors spend on site, which pages they visit (clickstreams), referrals, sales, and

EXHIBIT 16.1
World Animal Protection crosses the boundary between the digital and physical world to raise awareness of the plight of elephants used in the tourism industry

the individual sites or search terms used by visitors to find digital content (Chaffey and Ellis-Chadwick, 2019). For example, Google Analytics is an excellent analytical tool which offers some basic-level analysis for free.

Analytics tools and techniques offer various solutions for measuring the performance of different online digital channels. Determining which to use will be dependent on the goals set for a campaign. Refer to Figures 16.5 and 16.6 and the description of the RACE framework above for examples of how objectives might be measured using digital analytics.

Research has shown that marketing managers often measure digital effectiveness using criteria such as brand awareness, word of mouth, customer satisfaction, and popular measures such as page views, cost per thousand impressions and click-throughs. However, Chaffey (2015) suggests that it is important to use appropriate key performance indicators in a planned manner to consider more than just the volume of traffic. Chaffey recommends that, for the best results, it is important to determine the quality of the traffic and the value. For example, if a company is seeking to build a new customer base, it should be determining the value of unique visitors. It should then be considering how extensively visitors navigate around the site (the bounce rate), which helps to determine the quality of the online customers. To determine the value, the revenue per visit needs to be monitored. Finally, the company should evaluate the number of searches the brand is attracting.

Evaluation of digital marketing activities is also important, and so a planner should decide which tactics might be the most effective and then optimize (focus on) the use of specific tools and techniques. For example, a fashion retailer like Net-a-Porter might be pursuing engagement objectives (for its Net Set app). If this were the case, according to Chaffey (2018) it would need to optimize its content management strategy, contact strategy, customer service and support, mobile market campaigns and social customer relationship management (CRM). However, if a company were following a customer acquisition strategy, it would need to optimize its SEO, pay-per-click advertising, affiliate and partner marketing, online public relations, and social media marketing (Chaffey, 2018).

As the complexity of the digital world increases, so do the number of tools and techniques that can be used to monitor and evaluate digital performance. This has become a growing subject, which goes beyond the remit of this chapter. Analytics have been discussed in Chapter 6, and recommended further reading on this topic is provided at the end of the chapter.

Once objectives have been set, the next stage in planning social media initiatives is to gather insight into target audiences by finding out which segments to target and which type of digital media is the most appropriate. It is especially important to find out about customer media habits, interests and online behaviour.

Selecting the target segment

For marketing managers, it is increasingly important to understand target audiences from a digital perspective, as significant changes are taking place resulting from more and more interactions between organizations and their audiences via digital technology. (For a more detailed discussion of target audiences and related segmentation strategies, see Chapter 7.) Arguably, every dimension of real-world relationships is replicated in a digital form.

When assessing a target audience, the following information will be useful (Chaffey and Ellis-Chadwick, 2019).

1 *Customer connectivity*: the proportion of the target markets that have access to relevant technologies.
2 *Customer channel usage*: how often target market participants use online channels and how they use the digital channel/platform (e.g. purchase or research?). For instance, for each customer segment and digital channel (e.g. web, digital television, social media or mobile), a company should know the proportion of the target market that:
   - *makes use* of and has access to a channel
   - *browses* and, as a result, is influenced by using the channel for pre-purchase research and evaluation
   - *buys* through the channel.
3 *Digital media consumption*: how many hours each week are spent using the web, social media and mobile in comparison with traditional media such as watching television, reading newspapers or magazines, or listening to the radio?

In addition, marketers should also consider the competition and be able to answer the following questions.

- What specific strategic resources, capabilities and competences are required for successful digital marketing?
- How well are the expectations of consumers being fulfilled by the company's digital marketing activities? For example, is the website easy to use? Are the email or mobile campaigns well received or regarded as intrusive?

- What is the number of visitors to the website per month? How many viewers watch the interactive television (iTV) commercials?
- What is the average length of time visitors spend on the website?
- What are the most popular pages and products? What are the least popular?
- Which product categories generate most sales?
- Conversion rates: what is the proportion of visitors who place an order? What is the proportion of recipients of email or mobile campaigns or proportion of iTV viewers who place an order?
- Click-through rates: how many visitors arrive at the website from banner advertisements or web links from other sites?

Findings of the internal and external analysis should feed into marketing objectives, the creation of competitive advantage and communication plans.

Other important considerations are the following.

Digital engagement: perhaps one of the most compelling reasons for consumers to go online is that there is a wealth of information that can improve the efficiency of their shopping behaviour and reduce their risk. Information in the digital world is enhanced by user participation. Product descriptions and price comparisons and reviews, generated by sellers and buyers, abound and provide a rich tapestry of information. Ranking systems exist to help reduce the guesswork: for example, Feefo, the global feedback engine (http://www.feefo.com/web/en), produces product ratings for buyers and customer experience insight for sellers. Marketers have become interested *not* in whether customers are using digital sources as part of their decision-making, but in what types of information customers are signing up to. Research has shown that digital and social media platforms have become increasingly important in the purchasing decision-making process.

For instance, in the consumer services sector, there is an increasingly intense struggle for power between the consumer and the service provider. Sites like Tripadvisor and Trivago freely allow visitors to find hotels, restaurants and other places of entertainment and to air their views of the service they received. However, while service providers need to take heed and be aware of what their customers are saying online, they too make use of highly sophisticated customer databases to track and trace their customers so that they can implement highly targeted 'one-to-one' marketing campaigns (Arora et al., 2008) and other initiatives that build strong customer relationships and deliver even more value (Kim, Zhao and Yang, 2008). On one hand, consumer audiences have access to tools that can help them disseminate their levels of satisfaction and dissatisfaction far and wide. On the other hand, consumer service providers have a wealth of consumer-oriented data that could enable them better to predict their customers' needs and requirements, and in doing so create more effective IMC campaigns. For example, Britvic set out to create a 'light touch' communication strategy that would engage the interest of parents of 10-year-olds. The soft drinks company monitored online behaviour when it launched its Fruit Shoot website. Once the site was established, Britvic launched its 'Parents for playgrounds' campaign and monitored what people were responding to, then tailored the content to suit their interests. This is a very different approach to planning an eight-week advertising campaign with fixed content and messages (Nutley, 2011).

Behavioural targeting: digital marketing and media allows advertisements to be targeted on an individual basis. *Behavioural targeting* (or personalized digital advertising) is a method of directing advertisements at consumers based on their previous online behaviour. At its most basic, it is the Amazon 'you've bought this, so you might like to buy this' approach. However, more sophisticated behavioural techniques log where internet users have been surfing online, using cookies. Once this is known, advertisements on other sites appear based on that information. For example, an online user could be browsing cinema listings when a banner advertisement for bargain breaks in Rome appears—something the user had been researching a few days previously.

Digital buyer behaviour: a huge amount of research has been conducted to try to understand typical online buyer behaviour. In Chapter 3, we learnt how pre-family man uses online technology depending on lifecycle stages, cultural differences and personal priorities. Other influences identified from a body of academic research carried out during the past 20 years (Doherty and Ellis-Chadwick, 2010a) are as follows.

a) *Demographic variables*: personal attributes that tend to remain static throughout an individual's lifetime, such as gender and race, or that evolve slowly over time, such as age, are demographic variables. Key elements of a customer's demographic profile that have been found to influence their online behaviour include such variables as income, education, race, age, gender and lifestyle (Hoffman and Novak, 1997).

b) *Psychographic and behavioural variables*: any aspect of a person's perceptions, beliefs and attitudes that might influence their online behaviour and their intention to shop. Indeed, behavioural characteristics—such as knowledge, attitude, innovativeness and risk aversion—can also affect a person's intention to shop. For example, it has been found that consumers who are primarily motivated by convenience were more likely to make purchases online, while those who value social interactions were found to be less interested (Swaminathan, Lepkowska-White and Rao, 1999).

c) *Personal profiles*: age, gender, education, salary. Indeed, it is important to note that online shoppers are no longer likely to be greatly different from their offline counterparts (Jayawardhena, Wright and Dennis, 2007). However, it is perhaps useful to differentiate between the most enthusiastic and profitable internet shoppers. For example, it has been found that the internet is a favourite channel for the compulsive shopper, as consumers are able to 'buy unobserved', 'without contact with other shoppers', and in so doing, 'experience strong positive feelings during the purchase episode' (Kukar-Kinney, Ridgway and Monroe, 2009). This study, which looked at the behaviour of internet shoppers from six countries, including both developing and developed countries, found a surprisingly high degree of homogeneity in their characteristics and habits (Brashear et al., 2009). Online shoppers were found to share their desire for convenience, were more impulsive, have more favourable attitudes towards direct marketing and advertising, were wealthier and were heavier users of both email and the internet.

Logistics of buyer behaviour: where consumers are making their purchases is changing, but online is not always the first choice. According to a recent survey by Gallup, the number of online shoppers is increasing: for example, in the USA in 2014 approximately a third of the population shopped online, and this number has grown year on year. But a study also found that some shoppers are increasingly going to physical stores, attracted by the service offer from their favourite retailers. Indeed, if the online experience does match up to customers' expectations, they are likely to become disengaged with the digital offer. Furthermore, the digital experience, if repeated frequently, can lead to customers becoming *agnostic* towards a brand if they become frustrated with the technology associated with websites and mobile apps (Borges and Veríssimo, 2014; Deneen and Yu, 2015).

When consumers shop is changing too. Research suggests that shopping online and via mobile apps can occur when consumers are at work, watching television or even in bed. Shop Direct, the UK's leading digital retailer, discovered that laptops and PCs are still the principal shopping devices, but more people are going mobile. This flexibility in purchasing methods means that the times we buy are changing Shop Direct (2014). For example, on Black Friday, Cyber Monday and other peak online shopping days, we buy throughout the day and night, and eBay sellers in the UK know that Sunday evening is a peak buying time. Nevertheless, if you go to Oxford Street a few days before Christmas, the streets will still be crammed with people and the tills ringing at a cumulative rate of nearly a £1 million a minute.

Who are social media consumers?

Social media deserve further consideration.

In 2018, over 4 billion people had internet access, 3 billion people accessed social networking sites, and over 5 billion mobile phone handsets were in operation. Globally, mobile penetration represented 85 per cent in terms of unique users against total population (We Are Social, 2018). Social media users are most likely to be aged between 16 and 55, as almost three-quarters of all adults in these age bands say they use one or more social networking sites. They are most likely to have some form of post-16 education and are slightly more likely to be female than male.

Age has been a key differentiator of the users of social networks since the networks' inception. Although the number of users over the age of 65 is increasing, those under 30 are more likely than any other age group to use a social networking site. Social media are increasingly being added to campaigns targeting younger audiences and for commercial and non-commercial marketing campaigns. For example, a partnership between World Animal Protection and Netherlands advertising agency FVV BBDO used a 3D printer and social media to raise awareness of the harm done by tourists riding elephants when they go on holiday. Each time someone in the Netherlands (or a visitor to Schiphol airport) made a pledge online, another section of the elephant was printed (Oakes, 2015). See Exhibit 16.2.

A word of warning: GDPR, discussed in Chapter 2, has introduced new legislation to control the use of data. For digital marketers this means rethinking how they use cookies (text files that recognize users). In the past, cookies have been used as digital mechanisms that remember login details and store individual preferences. However, the EU sees cookies as a means of tracking online behaviour that potentially represents an intrusion of privacy. As a result, new legislation has been implemented to ensure that website visitors explicitly agree to the use of cookies when browsing websites.

Creative Implementation

A successful digital marketing campaign often comes down to a company's capabilities for monitoring performance and implementing continual improvements. The quality of web analysis and management processes will signal the extent to which a company can expect improvement in a digital campaign and media performance (Chaffey and Ellis-Chadwick, 2018: 470–1). As well as ensuring that all the metrics and analytics associated with campaign objects are implemented, marketers should also consider competitive advantage and creative executions.

Creating competitive advantage

Marketers have long accepted that success demands identification of some form of *competitive advantage* capable of distinguishing an organization from other firms operating in the same market sector. The unique properties of digital technologies offer opportunities to establish new forms of competitive advantage. These include highly tailored communication campaigns that can be designed to meet very specific communication objectives. The secret of the success of most digital operations is that they have exploited digital market advantages and new technologies in order to deliver a value proposition superior to that of their competitors. See how Amazon, and other leading brands have used creative ad IMC campaigns to capture seasonal market share. See Marketing in Action 16.3.

MARKETING IN ACTION 16.3
Deck the Halls with Boughs of Holly—Retailers Aim to Go Viral with their Festive IMC Campaigns

Implementing a successful digital campaign is important, gaining the attention of required visitors and engaging their interest sufficiently for them to take action. During the festive season, retailers have traditionally launched their advertising via broadcast and print media, but now they rely heavily on digital media. In 2018, UK retailers deployed different creative executions to grab the limelight and create excitement ahead of the campaign launch.

John Lewis Partnership opted for superstar celebrity Elton John as the star of their Christmas ad. Elton's hit 'Your song' played throughout, while *moments of truth* (in his life) were revealed to the viewing audience, taking us back to when the young Reginald Dwight received a piano for Christmas. The television premier of the ad was during a primetime show, *Dark Heart*, on ITV, but a teaser campaign had leaked the news and by the time the ad was shown there had been over 1.8 million views on YouTube. Interestingly, not one product was displayed and the strapline—'some gifts are more than just a gift'—did not appear until the last frame.

In 2018, Marks & Spencer (M&S) opted for a feelgood approach, with festive must-haves appearing in a Bridget Jones style production with Holly Willoughby and David Gandy. M&S aimed to reach its core target audience of females aged 50+. Like the John Lewis ad, the ad could be previewed online before its launch date.

Amazon's campaign used smiling animated boxes and music to grab viewers' attention. Unlike those of other retailers, this campaign was run across nine countries. The smiling boxes' rendition of the Jacksons' 'Can you feel it' aimed to be reach high levels of memorability following on from Amazon's success with its 2017 campaign. The timing of the ad was planned to coincide with Amazon's announcement of the Black Friday shopping extravaganza.

»

»

Iceland frozen foods also chose animation, which was a change of direction for the brand as it has tended to use celebrities, which fitted its target audience in the past. But for this Christmas, Iceland chose to use technology—special effects—to create a highly controversial campaign that told a story of a young person and an orang-utan. The tale was far from creating the warm feeling and jollity of the ads of other retailers. This was a somewhat harrowing story about the effects of deforestation and the destruction of the rainforest and the use of palm oil in foodstuffs. The advert was launched online and on television and was accompanied by a life-size animatronic orang-utan, which appeared in strategic locations around the UK. But shortly after its launch, the advert was banned due to breaching political rules of advertising. Banning the advert prompted a public outcry; politicians, celebrities and other well-known faces from James Cordon to Anna Friel supported a campaign to reinstate the advert, which had over 12 million people views on Facebook and YouTube, outstripping the views achieved by other adverts (at the time). There was also an online petition, which had over three-quarters of a million supporters within a few days of the ban.

Retailers in the UK have taken different routes to getting their ads to go viral in the festive season, but it appears that getting an ad banned might just be the most effective tactic.

Based on: Heritage, 2018; Heath, 2018; Sweeney, 2018

Creative content marketing

According to Chaffey and Ellis-Chadwick (2016), this form of marketing is central to digital campaigns. The reason for this is that content drives engagement with target audiences through searches and social media. Ultimately, having the *right* content will affect customer conversion rates, help a brand to increase its visibility on the web, mobile and social media platforms, aid customer motivation and engagement, and eventually help develop sales.

Effective content can vary depending on the goals of a digital campaign. Campaigns that seek to raise awareness and foster engagement and customer retention are more likely to succeed with a content marketing approach than those that seek to stimulate action through sales promotions. In the latter case, the customer is likely to engage in a swift purchase rather than interact with content. While content should be engaging for the audience, it should also be designed to meet communication campaign objectives. To be effective, the content that conveys a brand's stories must be interesting, communicate brand values and reflect customer needs. This is a challenge, and content marketing efforts can have a negative effect if they are too *editorial* in tone and fall into the trap of becoming 'the creation of vague and generic brand visions' (Ritson, 2015). However, Hertz Europe has found a way to inspire customer engagement using thousands of pieces of local content at each of its car hire locations, and its 'Hertz in 60 seconds' video provides lots of local information, including how to find a parking space in central London (Hemsley, 2015) (see Exhibit 16.2).

Another example of a company that knows how to use and manage content is Net-a-Porter, the fashion retailer. It values content highly and has taken the use of content to a new level with its Net Set social shopping offer. Natalie Massenet, founder of Net-a-Porter, got the inspiration for this shopping innovation when she saw an increase in mobile sales to 40 per cent of sales. The Net Set app brings together the online retailer's e-commerce capabilities and knowledge of social media, and in doing so creates a value-added offer for millennials, who form the majority of its target audience (O'Connor, 2015). Members of the Net Set can buy with confidence using shared recommendations from friends and '*shoppable live feeds of items trending on Net-a-Porter worldwide*' and follow guidance from the in-house 'Style Council'.

Given the current importance placed on content marketing, many companies develop a content marketing strategy as part of their digital marketing planning. As with all strategies, this will involve review of the current approach, setting specific objectives and developing strategies to create and share content (Chaffey and Ellis-Chadwick, 2016).

Online newsletters, magazines and user-generated content (UGC). This form of digital marketing tends to focus on a specific set of issues or interests. The items can be sent at different frequencies and serve different communication objectives. Online newsletters and magazines form an important element of content marketing strategies, and often include user-generated content, depending on whether a company is telling its customers about a brand or conversing with them. For example, Notcutts Garden Centres often include real customer reviews in its magazine contributions. Cineworld invited users of its app to post photos and comments on its Facebook page to promote the launch of the superhero movie *Marvel's Avengers Assemble*.

EXHIBIT 16.2
Hertz Europe engages its digital audiences using value-added content marketing

UGC can be highly effective, as it creates a tone of authenticity that cannot be achieved by even the most creative marketers. Ikea found when it launched Ikeafamilylive.com, enabling its customer to upload pictures and stories of their homes, that it was an excellent source of indirect marketing material, as 'Alongside Ikea's own roomsets, you can now browse shelving arrangements created by Monika in Poland or Eline in Belgium on a Pinterest-style mood board.' The value of this approach is that if used appropriately, UGC can create loyalty and customer engagement (Handley, 2013).

See Mini Case 16.1 to discover how crowdsourcing can be used to develop advertising campaigns.

MINI CASE 16.1
Crowdsourcing of Advertising

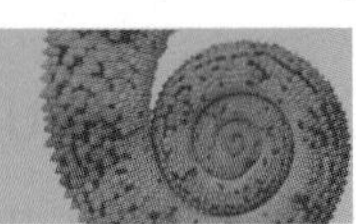

Marketing is increasingly using the internet in more innovative ways. One of these is crowdsourcing as a means of exploiting user-generated content (UGC) as part of an advertising campaign. The internet has helped crowdsourcing to spread and campaigns often involve many people who come together to support a particular event.

One great example of crowdsourcing is the 'Crash the Super Bowl' campaign from Doritos. This annual competition is run to unearth a television advert that Doritos will air live on one of its prestigious and hugely expensive television slots during the NFL Super Bowl in the USA. Since its launch in 2006, thousands of adverts have been submitted. The winner not only gets to see the advert shown live during one of the world's largest sports events, but also wins $1 million and a job at Universal Pictures. Perhaps one of the most interesting aspects of this competition is that the public decides who the winner is from a shortlist of eight finalists whose 30-second videos are uploaded to YouTube a month before the Super Bowl is played. This innovative and hugely engaging campaign puts crowdsourcing at the centre of not only the production but also the decision-making behind which advert will be shown.

The impact of this competition is that it generates great public relations and uncovers a talented mix of video producers who can be used by the company for more standard promotional work. The real positive for Doritos is that it can create a narrative that runs alongside the sporting event. The public are engaged in

»

the process, and the impact and brand awareness of the company grows as interest in the potential winner increases. The narrative is also enhanced by the fact that official odds are given as to the likely winner and people can place bets not only on the winner of the Super Bowl but also on who will win the Doritos advert competition. This type of organized crowdsourcing, although appearing to give control to the general public, can legitimately be included as part of a conventional media execution.

Crowdsourcing is still in its infancy and has the potential to grow using other platforms. One that has attracted a large amount of interest is the crowdsourcing content of the 'Our Stories' feature on Snapchat. When at an event, anyone using the app with the location setting turned on and posting their pictures to 'Our Stories' may have their post collated into an 'official' collection of snaps for that event. These are uploaded by Snapchat in near real time (after a moderating process) and appear as part of the timeline of the event. The timeline can be viewed by anybody. Snapchat often utilizes the 'Our Stories' feature for NCAA College Football matches, and the timeline regularly features snaps taken from not only the fans but also players, giving a unique view not offered anywhere else. These 'Our Stories' include pre-event, in-event and post-event content, with the added interest of the sportsmen/musicians and so on also snapping behind-the-scenes action. The rise of this type of activity is particularly powerful in the area of event marketing, where new perspectives can be generated that would not be possible using conventional media.

Questions:

1. A big factor in crowdsourcing is that it enables the public to influence a marketing communication. What are the pros and cons of this type of influence?
2. To what extent do you think that crowdsourcing and conventional marketing approaches are compatible?
3. Organizational structures have adapted to the rapid rise of the web. To what extent do you expect crowdsourced marketing campaigns, such as the Doritos 'Crash the Super Bowl' campaign, to continue to be popular, and what are the consequences of this to a marketing organization?

Based on: Schultz, E (2016), Velasco, H. (2017).

The Dark Side of Digital Marketing

Increased adoption of digital technologies within marketing has had many beneficial effects, such as increasing customer choice and convenience and enabling smaller companies to compete in global markets across a range of digital platforms. However, there are some key ethical issues emerging as a result of increased usage of digital technologies.

Cyber security

Malicious cyberattacks are largely beyond the remit of this text, but data security is fundamental to future success for digital brands and online marketing campaigns. According to Shattuck (2018), there is a great temptation to deploy ruthless tactics to increase revenues, visitor numbers and engagement online. But Shattuck cautions companies to seek a balance between achieving hard sales objectives and maintaining softer—and often more valuable in the longer term—objectives like brand reputation, brand experience and protecting consumer perceptions. Facebook's failure to protect the privacy of its users has enabled data to be used for political advertising and unethical campaigning. It is claimed that 87 million users had their data harvested in this political scandal. To redress the balance and restore confidence, Facebook had to contact its 2.2 billion users and explain how they would protect their privacy in the future (Badshah, 2018).

The digital divide and social exclusion

The historical timeline of the development of internet technologies reveals that, in the early days, the internet served highly specialized purposes and was used by expert technologists. Expansion and changes in the development of the web have made internet technology more accessible to a greater number of people, but there remains a virtual divide between the technology's 'haves' and 'have nots'. Hoffman and Novak (1999) examined the extent to which the internet has become indispensable, and found significant differences in usage based on race and educational attainment. They concluded that educational attainment is crucial if the digital divide is to be closed, and that efforts should be made to improve access for Hispanic and black populations in North America (Hoffman, Novak and Venkatesh, 2004).

Public and private organizations around the globe need to find creative solutions to improve internet access for all citizens, regardless of their demographic background, as they should not be deprived of internet access due to financial restrictions, a poor education and/or a lack of computer skills. From a commercial perspective, it is also important to acknowledge that while the networks forming the internet reach around the globe, access is far from equal and equitable.

However, mobile phones have been more widely adopted and reach into the community. For example, mobile phone ownership is currently nearing 85 per cent of the adult population in Europe (GSMA, 2018) The digital divide in computing might has also been bridged, with initiative such as the £7 laptop being launched in India (Ramesh, 2009).

Recent research suggests that there is a new form of digital divide forming (Office of Communications, 2005). As digital technologies become more widespread, it is specific aspects of the technologies that form divisions. For example, Londoners prefer to talk rather than text, whereas in Northern Ireland more texts are sent per week than anywhere else in the UK; rural internet users are stuck with slow connections in comparison with their urban neighbours, and three hours more television is watched per week in Scotland than anywhere else in the UK.

There is a risk of technological exclusion of the poorest members of society who cannot afford a computer, broadband connection, interactive television, digital radio or 4G network connection and smartphone and therefore cannot benefit from the vast array of products and services available or access to information sources.

However, there is also evidence of technology delivering advantages to socially deprived sectors of society. Mobile phones have aided homeless people by allowing them to avoid the embarrassment of not having a permanent address by giving a mobile number on job applications (Office of the Deputy Prime Minister, 2005). GSMA (2018) The Mobile Economy, Europe 2018 https://www.gsma.com/mobileeconomy/europe/ accessed dec 2018

Human obsolescence?

Claims that technology is replacing the human workforce have occurred throughout human history. I remember as a child being told by my teacher how advances in technology would mean my working week would be only a few hours and that my days would be spent pursuing leisure activities. His prophecies were made over 40 years ago, but there is now evidence, at least in part, of machines replacing humans.

AI has facilitated a growing number of automated decision-making systems. These systems can make real-time decisions based on analysis of vast quantities of data. For example, Amazon's Alexa is the personification of its AI applications. With 200 million adopters of these devices since its launch in 2016, every second, hour and day, vast quantities of data are being generated, analysed and used to improve Alexa's capacity to serve its human owners. But as well as enhancing human existence, sophisticated AI systems are also replacing human decision-makers due to their capacity to collect and curate data, analyse sentiments and then generate sophisticated analysis.

Salesforce.com has an application called Einstein, which is integrated into its customer relationship management systems. Einstein helps businesses to identify new sales opportunities, create customer predictive journeys and personalize customer experiences with an accuracy which outperforms human capabilities (salesforce.com, 2018a). Einstein is enabling analysis of the causes of customer satisfaction—an important KPI—but in a study by Salesforce.com of over 2,900 sales professionals, it found out that over 50 per cent of customers and businesses agree that technology has changed how they interact with sales teams.

Face-to-face sales interactions have been reduced and AI is automating the sales process and at the same time improving customer experiences. Data insights from analysis of rich data are improving AI's knowledge of customers and their likes and dislikes. The research concludes that virtual selling is becoming the norm (salesforce.com, 2018b).

Review

1 The concept of digital marketing and digital media

- Digital marketing can be defined as achieving marketing objectives through applying digital media, data and technology.
- Digital media are the channels we use to communicate and interact with target audiences online. The application of digital technologies forms digital media channels to market and includes, social media; search engines, digital and display advertising websites, emails and mobile apps.

2 Social media networks

These are online social communities that facilitate the sharing of ideas and information, publishing documents and video content. The concept is increasingly being used by marketing managers as part of their digital marketing campaigns. Social networking is shaping the way some sectors of society communicate. Social media cut across two forms of media: owned and earned. A company will 'own' its social media presence on Facebook, Instagram and Pinterest, but will also 'earn' engagement through social media market campaigns, i.e. earning 'likes' and followers.

3 Dimensions of the digital communication environment

- There are four key dimensions to consider: technology (the internet, mobile and satellite technology, remote computing, social networks, data and information intelligent technology), applications (websites, e-commerce, social media, mobile communications, artificial intelligence (AI), augmented reality (AR) and robots), marketing (globalization of markets and competition, multichannel operations, continuous trading, remote and mobile working) and audiences (shoppers, information searchers, businesses and community' members).

4 Digital marketing and digital media planning

- Deciding how to plan, resource, integrate, implement and monitor digital marketing activities can be guided by applying established marketing management principles and planning activities (as discussed in detail in Chapters 2 and 3). Elements of digital marketing planning include strategic alignment, integration, value proposition, implementation and change. Objectives and analytics are a fundamental part of digital marketing planning, and the RACE framework provides marketing managers with a guiding template for achieving reach (R), interactions (act; A), sales conversions (C) and engagement (E). New technologies can be used to meet a range of different business objectives: sales, communications, or to focus on the development and maintenance of mutually satisfying long-term relationships with customers by using digital technologies.
- Digital marketing planning can be affected by a company's digital media competency.
- Evaluation and control is a key consideration when setting campaign objectives.

5 Selecting a target segment digital marketing

For marketing managers, it is increasingly important to understand their target audiences from a digital perspective, as significant changes are taking place resulting from more and more interactions between organizations and their audiences via digital technology. Assessing a target segment involves considering customer connectivity, channel usage, media consumption, digital engagement, behavioural targeting and digital buyer behaviour.

6 Creative implementation

Implementing a successful digital marketing campaign often comes down to a company's capabilities for monitoring performance and implementing continual improvements. And the quality of web analysis and management processes will signal the extent to which a company can expect an improvement in digital campaign and media performance. Creating competitive advantage and managing creative content are key to campaign success.

7 The dark side of digital marketing

Increased adoption of digital technologies within marketing has had many beneficial effects, such as increasing customer choice and convenience and enabling smaller companies to compete in global markets across a range of digital platforms. Key ethical issues emerging as a result of increased usage of digital technologies include cyber security, the digital and social divide and human obsolescence.

Key Terms

blog short for weblog—a personal diary/journal on the web; information can easily be uploaded on to a website and is then available for general consumption by web users

buzz marketing the passing between individuals of information about products and services that is sufficiently interesting to act as a trigger for the individuals to share the information with others

digital marketing the application of digital technologies that form channels to market (the internet, mobile communications, interactive television and wireless) to achieve corporate goals through meeting and exceeding customer needs better than the competition

digital media the channels used to communicate and interact with a target audience online

microblogging involves the posting of short messages on social media sites like Twitter and Reddit

mobile marketing the sending of text messages to mobile phones to promote products and build relationships with consumers

multichannel involves an organization that is using different channels—physical retailer stores, the web and mobile, to enable its customers to buy, communicate, gain access to information or pay for goods and services. The organization in return provides consistent levels of service and marketing mix across all of the channels

omnichannel the bringing together of all of the customer touchpoints into a seamless shopping journey, which means that every time the customer 'touches' or interacts with a company their experiences are the same, whichever channel they use, for example by store, by phone, by the web, or by mobile.

QR codes a form of barcode which, once scanned, can link the user directly to web content, digital adverts and other available content. They are easy to use, and smartphones can read the codes

snap code a button in snapchat which links friends in the Snapchat environment; similar to 'following' a friend in Facebook

social media online community websites with individuals who can become members, share ideas and interests, for example Facebook; publish and distribute articles and video and other multimedia content, for example YouTube; carry out social commerce activities like writing reviews, buying and selling, for example TripAdvisor; or play games across communities, for example Zynga

Spotify code like a scannable QR code, a code that gives a quick link to a specific music download in Spotify environment

Study Questions

1. **Explain the meaning of the terms digital marketing and digital media.**
2. **Identify the key dimensions of the digital communication environment.**
3. **Identify and explain the different types of digital media.**
4. **Discuss the differences, advantages and limitations of social media and a communication tool.**
5. **Suggest how a business-to-consumer organization might use a multichannel approach. Give examples of companies using a multichannel approach.**
6. **Discuss the key considerations when developing a digital and social media campaign.**
7. **Explain what additional considerations a marketer should make (going beyond segmentation, targeting and positioning discussed in Chapter 7) when planning the targeting digital campaign.**
8. **Explain social media and suggest how this growing phenomenon might be used by marketing managers.**
9. **Debate the extent to which brands should consider the dark side of digital marketing when planning campaigns.**
10. **Discuss how digital marketing is challenging traditional marketing.**

Recommended Reading

The connected world places new demands on marketers. Read about the 10 trends affecting marketing, find out how small and medium sized businesses are adopting digital media and discover the dark side of social media

Baccarella, Christian V., Wagner, Timm F., Kietzmann, Jan H. and McCarthy, Ian P. (2018) Social Media? It's serious! Understanding the dark side of social media, *European Journal of Management* 36(4): 413–38.

References

Akhtar, T. (2012) Brands search for higher level of reception, *Marketing Week*, 5 January, 18–20.

Amato, R. and Saunders, J. (1990) Personality and social network involvement as predictors of helping behaviour in everyday life, *Social Psychology Quarterly* 53(1), 31–43.

Argyle, M. and Henderson, M. (1985) *The Anatomy of Relationships and the Rules and Skills Needed to Manage Them Successfully*, London: Heinemann.

Arora, N., Dreze, X., Ghose, A., Hess, J.D., Iyengar, R., Jing, B., Joshi, Y., Kumar, V., Lurie, N., Neslin, S., Sajeesh, S., Su, M., Syam, N., Thomas J. and Zhang, Z.J. (2008) Putting One-to-One Marketing to Work: Personalization, Customization, and Choice, *Marketing Letters* 19, 305–21.

Badshah, N. (2018) Facebook to contact 87 million users affected by data breach, *The Guardian* https://www.theguardian.com/technology/2018/apr/08/facebook-to-contact-the-87-million-users-affected-by-data-breach (accessed November 2018)

Barnett, M. (2011) Why websites generate much more than sales, *Marketing Week*, 16 June, 22–3.

Basu, A. and Muylle, S. (2003) Online support for commerce processes by web retailers, *Decision Support Systems* 34(4), 379–95.

Bold, B. (2014) Greggs gives lesson in Twitter crisis management after fake logo debacle, *Marketing Week*, 20 August, Greggs' Twitter campaign (accessed 20 June 2015).

Borges, T.M.T.P.M. and Veríssimo, J.M.C. (2014) Digital marketing and social media: Why bother? *Business Horizons* 57(6), 703–8.

Brashear, T.G., Kashyap, V., Musante, M.D. and Donthu, N. (2009) A profile of the Internet shopper: evidence from six countries, *Journal of Marketing Theory and Practice* 17(3), 267–281.

Burke, R.J. and Weir, T. (1975) Receiving and giving help with work and non-work related problems, *Journal of Business Administration* 6, 59–78.

Chaffey, D. (2008) Rise Through the Ranks, *The Marketer*, November, 51–3.

Chaffey, D. (2015) Introducing RACE: a practical framework to improve your digital marketing, Smart Insights, 24 June. http://www.smartinsights.com/digital-marketing-strategy/race-a-practical-framework-to-improve-your-digital-marketing (accessed November 2018)

Chaffey, D. (2018) Global Social media research summery 2018, Smart Insights, https://www.smartinsights.com/social-media-marketing/social-media-strategy/new-global-social-media-research/ (accessed November 2018)

Chaffey, D. and Ellis-Chadwick, F. (2016) *Digital Marketing: Strategy, Implementation and Practice*, 6th edn, Harlow, UK: Pearson.

Chaffey, D., Johnston, K., Mayer, R. and Ellis-Chadwick, F. (eds) (2000) *Internet Marketing: strategy, implementation and practice*, Harlow: Prentice Hall/Financial Times, 411.

Deneen, K. and Yu, D. (2015) Online Shopping Is Making Many Customers Antagonistic, *Gallup.com/Business Journal*, 17 March. http://www.gallup.com/businessjournal/182006/online-shopping-making-customers-antagonistic.aspx (accessed November 2018)

Doherty, N. and Ellis-Chadwick, F. (2004) Strategic Thinking in the Internet Era, *British Rail Consortium [BRC] Consortium Solutions* 3, 59–63.

Doherty, N.F. and Ellis-Chadwick, F. (2009) Exploring the drivers, scope and perceived success of e-commerce strategies in the UK retail sector, *European Journal of Marketing* 43(9/10), 1246–62.

Doherty, N.F. and Ellis-Chadwick, F. (2010a) Internet retailing: the past, the present and the future, *International Journal of Retail & Distribution Management* 38(11/12), 943–65.

Doherty, N.F. and Ellis-Chadwick, F. (2010b) Evaluating the role of electronic commerce in transforming the retail sector, *The International Review of Retail, Distribution and Consumer Research* 20(4), 375–78.

Fenwick, T. (2010) *Bar Code Technology, Retail Management and Marketing*, The Open University, iTunes.

Frary, M. (2012) Staff may be remote but they're not out of touch, *The Times*, 1 May.

Friedlein, A. (2015) Are we witnessing a reverse takeover of marketing by digital? *Marketing Week*, 18 May. http://www.marketingweek.com/2015/05/18/our-modern-marketing-manifesto-revisited (accessed 28 May 2015).

Google Ads (2018) Get your ad on Google today. https://ads.google.com (accessed November 2018)

Gucci (2018a) Gucci (Facebook page). https://www.facebook.com/GUCCI/ (accessed November 2018)

Gucci (2018b) Stories. https://www.gucci.com/us/en/st/stories/advertising-campaign (accessed November 2018)

Hall, J. (2017) How Augmented Reality Is Changing The World Of Consumer Marketing *Forbes*, 8 November, https://www.forbes.com/sites/forbesagencycouncil/2017/11/08/how-augmented-reality-is-changing-the-world-of-consumer-marketing/#161b061854cf (accessed November 2018)

Handley, L. (2013) For the best user-generated content, look to the newsstand, *Marketing Week*, 20 March. http://www.marketingweek.com/2013/03/20/for-the-best-user-generated-content-look-to-the-newsstand (accessed 20 June 2015).

Heath, O. (2018) The singing boxes return for Amazon's Christmas advert, *House Beautiful*, 5 November. https://www.housebeautiful.com/uk/lifestyle/a24634544/amazon-christmas-advert/ (accessed November 2018)

Hemsley, S. (2015) How to create content relevant to your business, *Marketing Week*, 12 June. http://www.marketingweek.com/2015/06/12/how-to-create-content-relevant-to-your-business (accessed November 2018)

Heritage, S. (2018) Elton John's John Lewis Christmas ad: it could have been so different, *The Guardian*, 15 November https://www.theguardian.com/tv-and-radio/2018/nov/15/elton-johns-john-lewis-christmas-ad-it-could-have-been-so-different (accessed November 2018)

Hershkovits, D. (2014) How Kim Kardashian broke the internet with her butt, *The Guardian*, 17 December. http://www.theguardian.com/lifeandstyle/2014/dec/17/kim-kardashian-butt-break-the-internet-paper-magazine (accessed 25 June 2015).

Hoffman, D.L. and Novak T.P. (1997) A New Marketing Paradigm for Electronic commerce, *The Information Society* 13, 43–54.

Hoffman, D. and Novak T. (1999) *The Growing Digital Divide: Implications for an Open Research Agenda*, eLab Owen Graduate School of Management Vanderbilt University (http://ecommerce.vanderbilt.edu/) (accessed November 2018).

Hoffman, D.L., Novak, T.P. and Venkatesh, A. (2004) Has the Internet Become Indispensable? *Communications of the ACM* 47(7), 37–42.

Internet World Stats (2015) Internet Stats and Facebook Usage in Europe, Internet World Stats, 21 June. http://www.internetworldstats.com/stats4.htm (accessed November 2018)

Internet World Stats (2018) https://www.internetworldstats.com (accessed November 2018)

Jayawardhena, C., Wright, L.T. and Dennis, C. (2007) Consumers online: intentions, orientations and segmentation, *International Journal of Retail and Distribution Management* 35(6), 512–26.

Jenblat, O. (2018) Messenger Marketing: The new way to do business, *Forbes*, 29 August. https://www.forbes.com/sites/forbesagencycouncil/2018/08/29/messenger-marketing-the-new-way-to-do-business/#23a558b252d0 (accessed Nov 2018).

Jones, G. (2011) The Carphone Warehouse harnesses the power of the mobile medium to facilitate multi-channel assistance and drive sales, *Marketing Week*, May, 43.

Katona, Z., Zubcsek, P.P. and Sarvary, M. (2010) Network effects and personal influence: the diffusion of an online social network, *Journal of Marketing Research* 48(3), 425–43.

Kelion (2017) Apple Shazam: Why is the US company buying the music app? BBC News https://www.bbc.co.uk/news/technology-42309311 (accessed November 2018)

Kim, C.S., Zhao, W.H. and Yang, K.H. (2008) An Empirical Study on the Integrated Framework of e-CRM in Online Shopping: Evaluating the Relationships Among Perceived Value, Satisfaction, and Trust Based on Customers' Perspectives, *Journal of Electronic Commerce in Organisations* 6(3), 1–19.

Kiss, J. (2011) Facebook began as a geeks hobby now it's more popular than google, *The Guardian*, 4 January, 23.

Kukar-Kinney, M., Ridgway, N.M. and Monroe, K.B. (2009) The relationship between consumers' tendencies to buy compulsively and their motivations to shop and buy on the Internet, *Journal of Retailing* 85(3), 298.

Marr, B. (2018) Machine Learning in Practice: How Does Amazon's Alexa Really Work? 5 October https://www.forbes.com/sites/bernardmarr/2018/10/05/how-does-amazons-alexa-really-work/#27d44ecd1937 (accessed November 2018)

Miles, D. (2018) 10 costly Googles Ads mistakes, https://www.smartinsights.com/guides/10-common-adwords-mistakes/ (accessed Nov 2018).

Murphy, F. (2015) Japanese women go ape over 'handsome' gorilla named Shabani, *The Telegraph*, 26 June. http://www.telegraph.co.uk/news/worldnews/asia/japan/11700427/Japanese-women-go-ape-over-handsome-gorilla-named-Shabani.html (accessed November 2018)

Nutley, M. (2011) Constant communication takes marketers down a beta channel, *Marketing Week*, 1 September.

Nuttall, C. (2011) Our future is up in the clouds, *Financial Times*, 17 June, 14.

Oakes, O. (2015) Can data really be creative? *Campaign*, 19 June, http://www.campaignlive.co.uk/news/1352173 (accessed November 2018)

O'Connor, C. (2015) Net-a-Porter's New Social Shopping App Might Be Fashion's Smartest Data Play, *Forbes*, 13 May. http://www.forbes.com/sites/clareoconnor/2015/05/13/net-a-porters-new-social-shopping-app-might-be-fashions-smartest-data-play (accessed 10 June 2015).

Ofcom (2005) Digital Television UK Household Penetration, www.ofcom.org.uk/media/news/2005/09/nr_20050915#content (accessed November 2018).

Office of Communications (2005) http://www.ofcom.org.uk. (accessed November 2018)

Office of the Deputy Prime Minister (2005) Digital Solutions to Social Exclusion, at http://egovmonitor.com/node/3362 (accessed November 2018).

Olenski, S. (2014) 4 Myths About Affiliate Marketing You Need To Know, *Forbes*, 8 July. http://www.forbes.com/sites/steveolenski/2014/07/08/4-myths-about-affiliate-marketing-you-need-to-know (accessed November 2018)

Pierce, D. (2017) The curious comeback of the dreaded QR code, *Wired*, 18 July, https://www.wired.com/story/the-curious-comeback-of-the-dreaded-qr-code/ (accessed Nov 2018)

Prensky, M. (2001) Digital natives digital immigrants, *On the Horizon* 9(5), 1–6.

Pyle, R. (1996) Electronic Commerce and the Internet, *Communications of the ACM* 39(6), 22–4.

Ramesh, R. (2009) After the World's Cheapest Car, India Launches £7 Laptop, *The Guardian*, 3 February, 19.

Ritson, M. (2015) Brands' inane 'visions' have lost touch with what consumers really use them for, *Marketing Week*, 20 May. https://www.marketingweek.com/2015/05/20/mark-ritson-brands-inane-visions-have-lost-touch-with-what-consumers-really-use-them-for (accessed November 2018)

Ryan, D. (2014) *The Best Digital Marketing Campaigns in the World*, London: Kogan Page.

salesforce.com (2018a) Einstein helps everyone blaze new trails with artificial intelligence, https://www.salesforce.com/uk/products/einstein/faq/ (accessed November 2018)

salesforce.com (2018b) State of Sales, 3rd Edition, https://www.salesforce.com/form/pdf/state-of-sales-3rd-edition (accessed November 2018)

Schultz, E (2016) How crash the super bowl changed advertising, AdAge, 4th January https://adage.com/article/special-report-super-bowl/crash-super-bowl-changed-advertising/301966/ (accessed Feb 2016)

Schultz, E.J. (2018) PepsiCo debuts 'Bubly' brand at Oscars in chase for more water sales, AdAge, August, https://adage.com/article/cmo-strategy/pepsico-chases-sparkling-water-growth-bubly-brand/312308/ (accessed November 2018)

Shattuck, M. (2018) Confronting the dark side of strategy *Smart Insights*, 2 October, https://www.smartinsights.com/digital-marketing-strategy/confronting-the-dark-side-of-strategy/ (accessed November 2018)

Shazam (2018) About Us, http://www.shazam.com/company (accessed November 2018)

Shop Direct (2014) Shop Direct Celebrates 20 years of online Shopping, Shop Direct, 1 August. https://www.shopdirect.com/shop-direct-celebrates-20-years-online-shopping (accessed November 2018)

Smart Insights (2017) http://www.smartinsights.com/digital-marketing-strategy/race-a-practical-framework-to-improve-your-digital-marketing (accessed November 2018)

Snoad, L. (2011) The vital connection between staff and the bottom line, *Marketing Week*, 10 November, 14–18.

Srinivasan, S., Anderson, R. and Kishore, P. (2002) Customer Loyalty in e-commerce: an Exploration of its Antecedents and Consequences, *Journal of Retailing* 78(1), 41–50.

Swaminathan, V., Lepkowska-White, E. and Rao, B.P. (1999) Browsers or buyers in cyberspace? An investigation of factors influencing electronic exchange, *Journal of Computer-Mediated Communication* 5(2), 1–19.

Sweeney, M. (2018) Iceland to let loose animatronic orang-utan after Christmas ad ban *the Guardian*, 14 November. https://www.theguardian.com/business/2018/nov/14/iceland-let-loose-animatronic-orangutan-after-christmas-advert-ban-palm-oil tesco.com (2018) Addressing the sustainability challenges in our top 20 products and ingredients, https://www.tescoplc.com/little-helps-plan/products-sourcing/top-20-products/ (accessed Nov 2018)

Throrogood, P. (2015) Let's split the funnel, American Marketing Association, 10 June. http://ama-academics.communityzero.com (accessed Aug 2015).

Tuten, T.L. and Solomon, M.R. (2013) *Social Media Marketing*, Upper Saddle River, NJ: Pearson, 3.

Tuten, T. and Solomon, M. (2015) *Social Media Marketing*, London: Sage Publications Ltd.

Vanhemert, K. (2014) 4 reasons why Apple's Ibeacon is about to disrupt interaction design, *Wired*, 11 November. http://www.wired.com/2013/12/4-use-cases-for-ibeacon-the-most-exciting-tech-you-havent-heard-of (accessed 20 June 2015).

Velasco, H. (2017) Brands capitalize on live video on Snapcahat, Instagram fro Superbowl LI The Drum, https://www.thedrum.com/news/2017/02/05/brands-capitalize-live-video-snapchat-instagram-super-bowl-li (accessed Jan 2018)

WeAreSocial (2018) Digital in 2018: World's Internet users pass the 4 billion mark, https://wearesocial.com/blog/2018/01/global-digital-report-2018 (accessed November 2018)

Wylie, E., Moore, S., Grunberg, L., Greenberg, E. and Sikora, P. (2010) What Influences Work-Family Conflict? The Function of Work Support and Working from Home, *Current Psychology* 29, 104–120.

CASE 31
Digital Disrupters Competing for Our Attention

Google, Apple, Facebook, Amazon and Microsoft (GAFAM)

Google, Apple, Facebook, Amazon and Microsoft (GAFAM) vie for pole position in the world's most valuable brand listings. They are all big US-based tech firms that have risen in value significantly since 2000. Their business models have evolved in the digital environment created by the internet (and associated technologies) into sophisticated and streamlined plans that create value. This case looks at how these five brands have created competitive advantage and become global brands which are shaping our lives. See Table C31.1.

Microsoft and Apple Microsoft and Apple both have portfolios of products and services which make up their revenue streams. Both make hardware, software and deliver other services.

Microsoft's products and services include Surface computers, Azure, cloud service, Microsoft Office suite of software solutions, and gaming consoles. Over 60 per cent of its revenue comes from software solutions and applications: Windows, Azure and Office. The Xbox and Surface account for less than 20 per cent of revenue.

Apple generates over 80 per cent of its revenue selling the iPhone, iPad and Mac computers. iTunes, the App Store, Apple Music, Apple Pay and AppleCare are complementary products and services which support and extend the brand's offer.

Microsoft has relied for some time on the popularity of the Windows operating system, which is used by around 1.4 billion users globally, for its competitive advantage. Apple, however, has built an ecosystem around the iPhone, which has enabled it to create strong competitive advantage, bypassing Microsoft's strengths in the computer operating system market and attacking by using the mobile operating system. Microsoft (Windows) and Apple (iOS), along with Google (Android), provide computing platforms for around 5.4 billion personal users. Arguably, these brands are

TABLE C31.1 GAFAM timelines, founders and vision

Company	Founded (when)	Founded (by whom)	Business activity sector	Vision
Microsoft	April 1975	Bill Gates and Paul Allen	Hardware and software applications	To allow every person and every organization on the planet to achieve more
Apple	April 1976	Steve Jobs and Steve Wozniak	Hardware manufacturer, software applications	Apple designs Macs, the best personal computers in the world, along with OS X, iLife, iWork and professional software. Apple leads the digital music revolution with its iPods and iTunes online store.
Amazon	July 1995	Jeff Bezos (and family)	Retail, B2B digital services	Amazon's vision is to be the Earth's most customer-centric company
Google	September 1998	Larry Page and Sergey Brin	Advertising, search	To organize the world's information and make it universally accessible and useful
Facebook	February 2004	Mark Zuckerberg and Eduardo Saverin	Advertising, social	Give people the power to build a community and bring the world closer together

reshaping how we work, by providing the tools and services that we need to communicate.

Amazon Amazon began as a retailer, setting up an e-commerce system that not only enabled it to become the world's largest book seller but, as it has expanded its ranges, to edge ever closer to Walmart, which is currently the biggest retailer globally. Amazon earns 70 per cent of its revenue from retailing and the rest from its Amazon Web Services (on-demand cloud computing and database services), Amazon Prime and other related services. Amazon has been growing at a rate of 20 per cent for the last few years and does not appear to be slowing. The company's success can be attributed to:

- sustainable competitive advantage, which comes from three areas:
  1. delivering high standards of customer service, great prices, fast and reliable delivery
  2. winning and retaining customers—Amazon offers a vast range of products and has the network structure to fulfil orders faster than its competitors
  3. sustaining competitive superiority, for example: world's largest book store; invented the Kindle e-reader, which created a new market for electronic books; Amazon's prices, delivery and media services; Echo, the artificial-intelligence-driven speaker
- visionary leadership from founder Jeff Bezos, who believes in the importance and power of the customer and has great insights into market opportunities.
- successfully exploiting market opportunities; for example, Amazon Web Services (AWS) (the systems that originally ran the company's e-commerce operations) are a fast-growing revenue stream in business-to-business (B2B) markets.

Amazon is reshaping how we shop and are entertained and is creating innovative devices which are market creators.

Google Google's rapid rise to become 'the world's biggest and best-loved search engine' can, in part, be attributed to the smart algorithms (mathematical instructions that computers can understand) devised by Larry Page and Sergey Brin. But equally important is the value proposition (the benefits to the user) that the search engine provides. Google enables its users to find relevant information quickly and easily, and delivers search results in an uncluttered format, which improves usability and increases user enjoyment online. However, in return, users of the search engine provide valuable information about their interests, lifestyles and behaviour. Indeed, Google gathers information every step of the way from when we search and browse the web, to sending and receiving Gmail communications, to using maps to find directions. By gathering this data from its users, Google can sell highly targeted advertising space, which enables advertisers to reach the customers they need.

Google can pool data about signed-up users across over 60 different services including Google search, YouTube, Gmail, Google Maps, web browsing and Blogger. The debate about access to, uses of and management of personal data continues; meanwhile, Google carries on (within legal parameters) using its unique access to data sources to provide highly targeted advertising services through services like Google Ads. Data is only part of the story; the technology infrastructure is also key to Google's leadership in the search engine marketplace. Google has developed sophisticated information technology resources that offer distinctively better functionality and services than those of its competitors.

By making creative use of information technology resources to enhance the capabilities of its search engine, Google created a search service that was quickly perceived by its users as superior to the competition. The Google brand differentiated itself from the competition by introducing the customer benefit of 'relevance' to online searching. The business continued to grow as consumers and business users increasingly turned to the internet as a primary source of information (searching is the second most common function of the web).

In addition to its effective and efficient use of technology resources and capabilities, Google's strong market position was supported by its financial success, generated by the application of an e-business model that provides free-to-user search services and highly targeted and yet discreet advertising, and by licensing the search technology to third parties (Google currently provides search services for several other search services). Advertisers pay per click for referrals to their web pages via the Google interface using Google Ads: search terms chosen by the advertisers are paid for at a rate determined by the popularity of the term. The cost per click varies according to the level of competition from advertisers for a keyword.

Since it was established, Google has used technology resources creatively and, in so doing, has developed superior technology-based capabilities that have enabled the company to become financially successful and stay ahead of the competition. In terms of the search market advertising revenues, Google's share of searches worldwide is 92.7 per cent, with Yahoo! accounting for just 2.3 per cent, Bing 2.2 per cent and Baidu 0.8 per cent.

The shift in focus towards mobiles created an opportunity for Google, with its Android mobile

»

operating system, which is currently the most widespread, with over 2.7 billion users, many of whom are in the southern hemisphere.

Google is a dynamic technology company which has created markets and been a market challenger. The company has not always anticipated changes in the marketplace but seems to find an effective response when its markets are threatened. One of the advantages that Google can always rely on is access to unique market information from users of its products and services. The cross-platform analytics give valuable insights into market behaviour, and this is a real strength of the business. To google is a verb in the *Oxford English Dictionary*. This demonstrates the power this brand has over the way we search and find information.

Facebook Facebook has reshaped how many people find friends, organize events and socialize. Facebook is the world's largest social media platform, with over 2.1 billion users.

Facebook utilizes its vast stores of users' data to sell highly targeted advertising space. The company generates close to 100 per cent of its revenue by selling advertising. Facebook charges advertisers by how many people see an ad; this specialized approach to targeting gives the social media network an advantage, as it means advertisers can provide interesting, relevant and attention-grabbing content, which can then be freely shared.

Facebook operates on a global scale and is the largest social network, giving advertisers global reach. The profile of the reach of Facebook's adverting in terms of gender is 43 per cent female and 57 per cent male. In terms of age, 64 per cent are under 34 and 13 per cent are older than 50. Over half of the users speak English, with Spanish the next most popular language.

Who Will be Next?

These five brands have become pervasive. But according to David Roth of WWP (global communications services), '*We're at the threshold of a new normal and a changing consumer*' and technology is a key feature in the leading brands' markets. GAFAM have been reshaping how we find the things we want, the types of devices we use to communicate, how we find our friends and how we shop for over a decade. While these brands are likely to be enduring for years to come, the next generation of disrupters have already begun changing more aspects of our lives. Netflix, Tesla, AirBnB and Uber (NTAU) are changing how we consume media and entertainment, the vehicles we drive, the type of places where we stay and how we get around. There are also significant brands developing in Asia—Alibaba, Tencent and WeChat—which share the capabilities of bringing world-beating technology solutions to market.

Questions

1. **Explain how each of the GAFAM brands create competitive advantage.**
2. **Suggest why they have become so successful.**
3. **Think about a typical day in your life. Map how you interact with the GAFAM brands, and also note how much of your day is spent in touch with each. Then estimate how much of your attention is given over to each brand in a typical day.**
4. **Imagine you are about to deliver a talk to a group of digital marketing trainees. Your challenge is to explain in your session how the GAFAM brands are valued by their users.**

This case study was written by Fiona Ellis-Chadwick, Senior Lecturer in Marketing and Retailing, Loughborough University.

References

Based on: Barney, J.B. (1991) From Resources and Sustained Competitive Advantage, *Journal of Management* 17(1), 99–120; Brit, B. (2005) Google Moves Beyond Search, *Marketing*, September, 19; Gallup, S. (2015) It's closing in on a billion users, http://fortune.com/2015/05/29/gmail-users (accessed July 2015); Griffin, A. (2015), Google Play Music goes free, days before launch of Apple's streaming service, *The Independent*, 24 June (accessed July 2015); Kiss, J. (2015) Dear Google: open letter from 80 academics on 'right to be forgotten, *The Guardian*, 14 May (accessed July 2015); Reisinger, D. (2015) For Google and search ad revenue, it's a glass half full, CNET, 31 March, http://www.cnet.com/uk/news/all-google-all-the-time-in-search-ad-biz-new-data-shows (accessed July 2015); Rose, F. (2006) Are you ready for Googlevision? *Wired* 14(5), www.wired.com/wired/archive/14.05/google_pr.html (accessed July 2015); Palmer, M. and Campbell, C. (2018) Top 100 Global brands, 2018, *Financial Times*, 9 July, https://ig.ft.com/top-100-global-brands/2018/; Carlson, N. (2010) At Last—The Full Story Of How Facebook Was Founded, *Business Insider*, 5 March, https://www.businessinsider.com/how-facebook-was-founded-2010-3?r=US&IR=T (accessed Nov 2018); Dunn, J. (2017) The tech industry is dominated by 5 big companies — here's how each makes its money, *Business Insider*, 26 May, http://uk.businessinsider.com/how-google-apple-facebook-amazon-microsoft-make-money-chart-2017-5 (accessed Nov 2018); Facebook (2018) About, https://www.facebook.com/pg/facebook/about/ (accessed Nov 2018); Google (2018) About, https://www.google.co.uk/about/ (accessed Nov 2018); Lotz, A. (2018) 'Big Tech' isn't one big monopoly—it's 5 companies all in different businesses, *The Conversation*, 23 March, http://theconversation.com/big-tech-isnt-one-big-monopoly-its-5-companies-all-in-different-businesses-92791 (accessed Nov 2018); Microsoft (2018) About Microsoft, https://www.microsoft.com/en-gb/about/ (accessed Nov 2018); Wong, J. (2018) Amazon posts record $2.5bn profit fueled by ad and cloud businesses, *The Guardian*, 26 July, https://www.theguardian.com/technology/2018/jul/26/amazon-profit-second-quarter-2018-advertising-cloud; Cohan, P. (2018) 3 reasons Amazon is the World's best business, *Forbes*, 2 Feb, https://www.forbes.com/sites/petercohan/2018/02/02/3-reasons-amazon-is-the-worlds-best-business/#50a473df6356 (accessed Nov 2018); *Strategist* (2018) Apple vs Microsoft, https://www.thestrategist.media/Apple-vs-Microsoft-Investor-s-choice_a2511.html (accessed Nov 2018); We Are Social (2018) The state of the internet in Q4 2018, https://wearesocial.com/uk/blog/2018/10/the-state-of-the-internet-in-q4-2018 (accessed Nov 2018).

»

CASE 32
Online Media—Brand Marketing in Real Time

Over the past decade, social media have exploded onto the marketing scene, with brands' budgets and organizational structures attempting to respond to the opportunities that this form of communication offers. With Facebook passing 2.23 billion active monthly users and Twitter having 335 million active monthly members, companies are fighting to gain a dominant presence in the social media space. With such a large audience and widespread connectivity, social media platforms are now seen to rival conventional broadcast news channels in the speed at which a message can be posted or news communicated. This has led to the rise of real-time content becoming part of an organization's marketing activity.

Real-time Marketing Real-time marketing is a reactive piece of content posted during a live event. It relies on the 'second screen experience', where a person is online on another device or has opened up a split screen while watching something else. Sporting events tend to attract this two-screen approach, as the viewer is often a fan who is emotionally engaged with the event and is seeking additional information as the match or game progresses. Real-time marketing has become increasingly prevalent at big sporting events when a brand attempts to 'own' a key moment in the sporting encounter. By placing the brand message at a key moment in the event, the aim is for the consumer to recall both the incident and the brand.

The 'Oreo—You Can Still Dunk In The Dark' moment is widely regarded as the first successful piece of real-time marketing content. It came in 2013 when there was a power outage during the NFL Super Bowl XLVII between the Baltimore Ravens and the San Francisco 49ers. With a Super Bowl commercial costing millions of dollars, social media gave the opportunity to own a moment of the match online, with the only cost being staff time. When the power cut happened, the Oreo social media team produced a post in a matter of minutes. Due to the second-screen nature of the sports event, spectators all over the globe saw this clear call to action by Oreo, and it gained 10,000+ retweets and 18,000+ likes on Facebook in just one hour, earning 525 million impressions worldwide for a grand total of zero media dollars being spent. Since then, real-time marketing via social media has continued to develop.

The 2018 Football World Cup saw brands with no organic connection to the sport capitalize on the online conversation. An example of this is Scotland-based soft drink company Irn-Bru publishing this tongue-in-cheek message on Twitter ahead of the event for which Scotland did not qualify.

However, real-time marketing does not have to be specifically around the event itself but can be used as a tool to humanize or showcase the personality of the brand.

ASOS, the global e-commerce platform in the fashion vertical, is targeted towards 20-somethings. In 2017, the brand printed a typo on its packaging and its customers were quick to publicize the mistake all over social media. The company, instead of hiding from the issue or publishing a formal press release (which would

be unlikely to be read by its customer base), directly owned up to its mistake. The @Asos Twitter account, once the mistake had been acknowledged, published this quick-witted response, which was received with great humour by its customers but also avoided having to reprint the 17,000 bags.

Similarly, when fast food chain KFC ran out of chicken in 2018, it published a tweet with a humorous apology which also doubled up as a print advert.

Spontaneous marketing Part of the attraction of this type of activity is the ad hoc, 'on the fly', type of feel to both the content as well as the timing. It gives the impression of spontaneity and that the company or brand is sharing the experience with you—it is part of the event. There has, however, been a radical change in the way real-time marketing happens. Brand teams are now setting up reactive social media centres. These centres often have an array of copywriters, a design team and a community manager to manage the social media aspect of the job. It takes months to organize, and many brainstorms take place to maximize the efficiency of the copy being inserted onto the relevant imagery that will be posted—ideally in seconds, but more likely within a couple of minutes of an incident taking place.

Real-time marketing also offers the opportunity for brands to combine user-generated content on their social media platforms. An example of this is EA Sports, the producer of the widely popular console game NFL Madden. Madden launched in a unique manner during the 2015/16 season. EA created an online platform called the #MaddenGiferator that ingested real match footage as it happened from throughout the National Football League (NFL). Everything from player celebrations to highlight plays were ingested onto the online platform, which then converted the action to appear like it happened in the Madden game. This allowed users to access the footage, insert their own messages and directly publish it on their social media channels. The # MaddenGiferator became an online sensation and thousands of people every hour created highly relevant miniature promotions of the game and published it across their social media channels.

Social media, and specifically real-time content, has opened up many opportunities for brands, especially in the area of ambush marketing. Owing to the lack of legislation around sponsorship rights on social media, the social media platform sees innovative and often humorous ambush marketers make a connection to an event that would not have been previously possible. Therefore, this arguably devalues the paid rights of an official sponsor.

Social media opens doors Social media have swung open a new door for marketers to maximize their brand reach. However, since the Oreo moment, this space has become saturated with brands trying to catch the eye of the consumer with real-time content. This has created pressure to recruit high-quality staff in a new type of industry that did not exist 15 years ago. Also, social media platforms have realized the potential for income through paid promotions, therefore this previously inexpensive marketing tool now requires more budget if it is to be well staffed, along with media spend to maximize the impact of a real-time intervention. The challenge will be to integrate real-time marketing into the overall marketing strategy of an organization.

Questions

1. **What are the pros and cons of using real-time marketing?**
2. **Who do you feel will be the audience for two-screen viewing? What implications will this have for its use?**
3. **A lot of discussion is taking place regarding the integration of social media and other forms of marketing activity. To what extent does real-time marketing lead to the possible fragmentation of marketing activity?**

This case study was written by James Saker, senior digital manager at a leading Premier League Football Club, in conjunction with the School of Business and Economics at Loughborough University.

References

Facebook passing 2.23 billion active monthly users https://www.statista.com/statistics/264810/number-of-monthly-active-facebook-users-worldwide/ (accessed April 2019)

Twitter having 335 million active monthly https://www.statista.com/statistics/282087/number-of-monthly-active-twitter-users/ (accessed April 2019)

Oreo social media post during Superbowl XLVII https://leonardom.com/case-studies/oreo-super-bowl-blackout-tweet/ (accessed April 2019)

Ecommerce retailer, Asos 2017 packaging typo https://www.huffingtonpost.co.uk/entry/asos-spelling-mistake-onilne_uk_5ab235f3e4b0decad0459250 (accessed April 2019)

NFL #MaddenGiferator https://www.thinkwithgoogle.com/marketing-resources/experience-design/ea-sports-madden-giferator/ (accessed April 2019)

CHAPTER 17
Distribution and Channel Management

> *Retail businesses that have ignored or failed to understand how consumers make use of digital channels are at best playing catch-up or at worst have gone out of business.*
>
> **FIONA ELLIS-CHADWICK (2018)**

LEARNING OBJECTIVES

After reading this chapter, you should be able to:

1 describe the functions and types of channels of distribution
2 explain how to determine channel strategy
3 discuss the three components of channel strategy: channel selection, intensity and integration
4 discuss the five key channel management issues: member selection, motivation, training, evaluation and conflict management
5 explain retailing, physical and digital channels to market distribution
6 explain how to improve customer service standards in physical distribution
7 discuss retailing and retail marketing
8 explain online social and mobile commerce
9 discuss ethical issues in distribution

Distribution, along with location of services, makes up the place element of the marketing mix. Products need to be available in adequate quantities, in convenient locations and at times when customers want to buy them. In this chapter, we examine the functions and types of distribution channels, the key decisions that determine channel strategy, and how to manage channels. We also explore the relevance of place in terms of where goods are purchased, by looking at the retail industry and the importance of physical and digital on distribution in this sector.

Producers should consider not only the needs of their ultimate customer but also the requirements of **channel intermediaries** (the organizations that facilitate the distribution of products to customers). For example, success for Müller yoghurt in the UK was dependent on convincing a powerful retail group (Tesco) to stock the brand. The high margins the brand supported were a key influence in Tesco's decision. Without retailer support, Müller would have found it uneconomical to supply consumers with its brand. Clearly, establishing a supply chain that is efficient and meets customers' needs is vital to marketing success. The supply chain is often referred to as a **channel of distribution** and is the means by which products are moved from producer to final customer. Logistics is a related term, which is used to refer to the movement of goods through the supply chain; this function has become increasingly complex as retailers offer their customers multiple collection points. Management of the supply chain is also important, as it is often the criterion considered by decision-making units when choosing suppliers. (See Chapter 4 for further discussion of influences on buying decisions.) To be successful, manufacturers and suppliers need access to their end customers and need to gain distribution outlets. Advertising to channel intermediaries is sometimes used to explain the benefits of the brand to encourage channel members to stock products. For example, Chupa Chups encourages retailers to stock its sugar-free products using promotional discounts to drive sales.

Choosing the most effective channel of distribution is an important aspect of marketing strategy. Supermarkets effectively shortened the distribution channel between producer and consumer by eliminating the wholesaler. Prior to the introduction of supermarkets, the typical distribution channel for products like food, drink, tobacco and toiletries was producer to wholesaler to retailer. The wholesaler would buy in bulk from the producer and sell smaller quantities to the retailer (typically a small grocery shop). By building up buying power, supermarkets could shorten this chain by buying directly from producers. This meant lower costs to the supermarket chain and lower prices for the consumer. The competitive effect was to drastically reduce the numbers of small grocers and wholesalers in this market. By being more efficient and meeting customers' needs better, supermarkets had created a competitive advantage for themselves.

Digital technologies are making further changes to distribution channels. In some cases, the change is from physical to virtual, for example the distribution of music and video (downloads), airline bookings (electronic ticketing) and hotel reservations (electronic booking). In other cases, the shift is from store to home and office purchasing, for example groceries (home shopping). Mobile networks permit the distribution of such products as music, video and ringtones (Bunwell, 2005). Increasingly, retailers are adopting a multichannel approach, which means they supply products and communicate with their customers in store, online, via mobile and through social media. In business-to-business markets, customers can place orders, receive quotes and track deliveries over the internet.

Next, we explore the functions of channel intermediaries and then examine the different types of channels that manufacturers can use to supply their products to customers.

Functions of Channel Intermediaries

The most basic question to ask when deciding channel strategy is whether to sell directly to the ultimate customer or to use channel intermediaries such as retailers and/or wholesalers. To answer this question, we need to understand the functions of channel intermediaries, that is, what benefits producers and consumers might derive from their use. Channel intermediaries add value by providing useful functions for producers and consumers. These functions are to reconcile the needs of producers and customers, improve efficiency by reducing the number of transactions or creating bulk, improve accessibility by lowering location and time gaps between producers and consumers, and provide specialist services to customers. Each of these functions is now examined in more detail.

Reconciling the needs of producers and consumers

Manufacturers typically produce a large quantity of a limited range of goods, whereas consumers and businesses usually want only a limited quantity of a wide range of goods (Coughlan et al., 2005). The role of channel intermediaries is to reconcile these conflicting situations. For example, a manufacturer of tables sells to retailers, each of which buys from a range of manufacturers of furniture. The manufacturer can gain economies of scale by producing large quantities of a product and then selling to many companies further along the supply chain, for example retailers like DFS, Harvey's, and Furniture Village. Each retailer can then offer its customers a wide assortment of products, offering its customers considerable choice under one roof. It is important to remember that the key function of channel intermediaries is *breaking bulk*. A wholesaler may buy large quantities from a manufacturer (perhaps a container load) and then sell smaller quantities (such as by the case) to retailers. Alternatively, large retailers such as supermarkets buy large quantities from producers and break bulk by splitting the order between outlets. In this way, producers make large quantities while consumers are offered limited quantities at the point of purchase. But there are also other combinations of using channels. David Grundy Limited is a specialist furniture manufacturer which sells both to retailers and directly to individual consumers online.

Improving efficiency

Channel intermediaries can improve distribution efficiency by *reducing the number of transactions* and *creating bulk for transportation*. Figure 17.1 shows how the number of transactions between three producers and three customers is reduced by using one intermediary. Direct distribution to customers results in nine transactions, whereas the use of an intermediary cuts the number of transactions to six. Distribution (and selling) costs and effort, therefore, are reduced.

Small producers can benefit by selling to intermediaries, which then combine many small purchases into bulk for transportation. Without the intermediary, it may prove too costly for each small producer to meet transportation costs to the consumer. Agricultural products such as fruit and vegetables—for example, green beans from Kenya, pineapples and bananas from Central America—are grown by small producers, who sometimes benefit from this arrangement.

Improving accessibility

Two major divides that need to be bridged between producers and consumers are the location gap and the time gap. The *location gap* derives from the geographic separation of producers from the customers they serve. Many of the cars produced in the UK by Nissan and Toyota are exported to Europe. Car dealers in Europe provide customer access to these cars in the form of display and test-drive facilities and the opportunity to purchase locally rather than deal directly with the producer thousands of miles away. The internet is reducing the location gap, allowing buyers to purchase without the need to visit a producer or distributor. Producers can play their part in improving accessibility by making consumers aware of the location of their distributors.

The *time gap* results from discrepancies between when a manufacturer wants to produce goods and when consumers wish to buy. For example, manufacturers of spare parts for cars may wish to run their manufacturing processes from Monday to Friday, but shoppers may wish to purchase goods every day of the week. By opening at the weekend, car accessory outlets bridge the time gap between production and consumption. The internet has facilitated 365/24/7 buying, which is streamlining communications throughout global supply chains. This is also very popular in consumer markets.

Providing specialist services

Channel intermediaries can perform specialist customer services that manufacturers may feel ill-equipped to provide themselves. Distributors may have long-standing expertise in such areas as selling, servicing and installation to customers. Producers may feel that these functions are better handled by channel intermediaries so that they can specialize in other aspects of manufacturing and marketing activity.

FIGURE 17.1
How a channel intermediary increases distribution efficiency

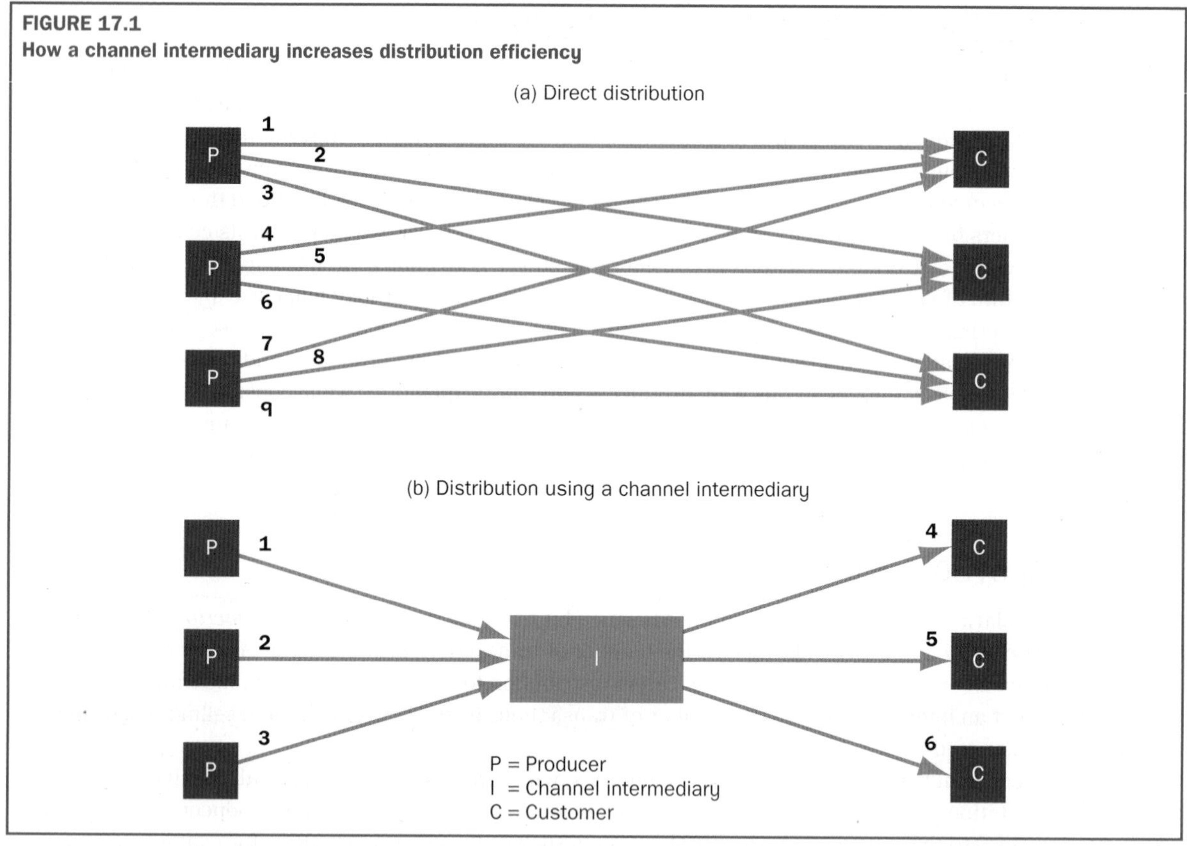

Types of Distribution Channel

Everything we buy, whether consumer goods or business-to-business goods or services, requires a channel of distribution. Business channels tend to be shorter than consumer channels because of the small number of ultimate customers, the greater geographic concentration of customers, and the greater complexity of the products that require close producer–customer liaison. Service channels also tend to be short, because of the intangibility of services and the need for personal contact between the service provider and consumer.

Consumer channels

Figure 17.2 shows four alternative consumer channels. Each one is described briefly below.

Producer direct to consumer

Cutting out distributor profit margin may make this option attractive to producers, as they can sell directly to consumers. Many companies, from men's outfitters such as Charles Tyrwhitt, to iTunes and Dell Computers, have adopted this approach. The internet has provided the technology infrastructure to supply consumers directly rather than through retailers. Manufacturers of digital products such as music, films and software have benefited from these types of distribution channel as their products are readily downloadable via a customer's computer.

Eliminating a layer of intermediaries from a distribution channel is called **disintermediation** (Mills and Camek, 2004). This is a term coined in the banking industry with the advent of retail banking. The basic idea is that the 'middleman' is removed and manufacturers sell directly to consumers. But this is also occurring at

FIGURE 17.2
Distribution channels for consumer goods

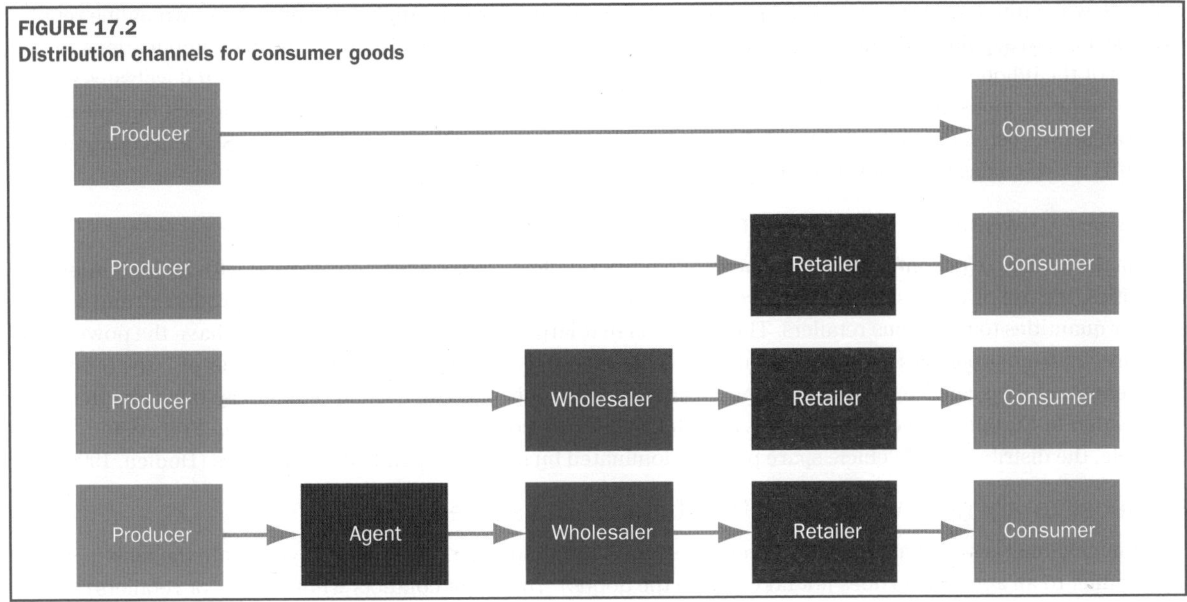

other stages in the supply chain; Amazon, eBay and ASOS refine their business models and streamline supply chains by eliminating intermediaries between themselves and the end consumer. This trend, adopted by many online retailers, has gone a step further by reducing the need for physical stores and is leading to the closure of many traditional high street retail brands (Bhaiya, 2017, Ellis-Chadwick, 2018). Examples in other industries include airlines such as easyJet and Ryanair, who have moved towards internet bookings, eliminating the need to go through a travel agent. Dell Computers has largely eliminated retailers from the traditional PC distribution channel. A broader definition of disintermediation includes the displacement of traditional channel intermediaries with new forms of distribution. For example, iTunes music stores are replacing specialist record shops in the distribution of music. Disintermediation occurs when a new type of channel intermediary or structure serves customers better than the old channels. Spotify and Last.fm provide access to almost limitless musical choice through streaming technology for a small monthly fee. YouTube provides a distribution platform for new recording artists.

At the opposite end of the spectrum is **reintermediation**. In this case, retailers use the internet for different purposes ranging from a simple poster website advertising the company to a fully integrated online business operation that facilitates online sales, builds customer relationships, and acts as a portal for new business opportunities. Research has found that, in general, retailers tend to lack the skills and technical resources required to develop their online presence. A solution is to use web service providers that act as 'cyber intermediaries' for designing, developing, hosting and managing their websites. Adding this extra level in the supply chain enables retailers to exploit the potential of the internet by using third-party web service providers who have the technical expertise and knowledge necessary for all the retailer's online business requirements. Many retailers are taking this action to protect their investment in increasingly competitive and challenging online trading environments. They also try to build strong collaborative relationships with their web service providers (Doherty and Ellis-Chadwick, 2010; Vize et al., 2010).

Producer to retailer to consumer

The growth in retailer size has meant that it has become economical for producers to supply retailers directly rather than through wholesalers. Consumers then have the convenience of viewing and/or testing the product at the retail outlet. Supermarket chains such as Sainsbury's exercise considerable power over manufacturers because of their enormous buying capabilities. However, technology has created new channels to consumers. Internet retailers such as Amazon (books and consumer goods), ASOS (fashion) and Expedia (travel and hotel bookings) compete with store-based retailers supplying directly from their websites. Apple has created its own online retail store, iTunes, to supply music downloads for the iPod, and the App Store to distribute software applications to owners of the iPhone. Store-based retailers have responded by developing their own sophisticated websites selling a wide range of goods. Increasingly, these types of retailer are developing a multichannel approach that means they can serve customer needs in store, online and on the move via mobile communications. See Marketing in Action 17.1, which describes how Costco shortens its distribution channel to keep costs low.

Producer to wholesaler to retailer to consumer

For small retailers (e.g. confectionery, tobacco and news retailers, and convenience stores) with limited order quantities, the use of wholesalers makes economic sense. Wholesalers can buy in bulk from producers and sell smaller quantities to numerous retailers. The danger is that large retailers in the same market have the power to buy directly from producers and thus cut out the wholesaler. In certain cases, the buying power of large retailers has meant that they can sell products to their customers more cheaply than a small retailer can buy from the wholesaler. In Europe, long channels involving wholesalers are common in France and Italy. In France, for example, the distribution of vehicle spare parts is dominated by small independent wholesalers (Dudley, 1990).

Producer to agent to wholesaler to retailer to consumer

This long channel is sometimes used by companies entering foreign markets. They may delegate the task of selling the product to an agent (who does not take title to the goods). The agent contacts wholesalers (or retailers) and receives commission on sales. Overseas sales of books are sometimes generated in this way.

Some companies use multiple channels to distribute their products. Grocery products, for example, use both producer to wholesaler to retailer (small grocers), and producer to retailer (supermarkets). The internet has also encouraged the use of multiple channels. For example, in the tourist industry, package holidays can be booked through travel agencies or via the internet, and hotels and flights can be booked over the phone or by using the internet. Such multichannel strategies allow companies to differentiate their services to take advantage of the inherent strengths of each channel (Wikström, 2005). Multiple channels also provide wide market coverage. For example, Sony achieves wide distribution coverage by using multiple channels such as its own Sony Centres, electrical goods chain stores such as Currys/PC World, catalogue shops such as Argos, and online retailers such as Amazon. In Japan, distribution channels to consumers tend to be long and complex, with close relationships between channel members, a fact that has acted as a barrier to entry for foreign companies.

MARKETING IN ACTION 17.1
Fingerprinting the Supply Chain Leads to Success for Costco

Costco is the fourth-largest retailer in the world after Walmart, the Kroger Company and Amazon. It is the largest US membership warehouse club and is rapidly expanding its global store portfolio. The firm has 761 warehouses worldwide, including 28 in the UK, two in Spain and one in France. There are ambitious plans for more international expansion. Costco sales are approaching $100 billion per year; the company has 195,000 employees, and has warehouses in important strategic locations around the world. The operational structure is organized to support the movement of goods, and Costco's global supply chain is important to the firm's success. Costco spans the boundary between business and consumer by operating a membership model that encourages both business buyers and individual shoppers to use its warehouses. All buyers become members of Costco, and this allows them to enjoy different levels of discounts. The prices and benefits of membership programmes vary depending on the type of customer, their spending patterns and whether they are businesses or individuals. The club membership fee, paid annually in advance, is another important factor in the company's success. The level of loyalty among Costco's members is very high, which supports its global purchasing strategy. Costco is a low-cost operator and its spend on servicing the supply chain, administration costs and costs associated with generating sales is lower than that of other global retailers, for example Walmart and Amazon. How Costco achieves this low-cost position, even when its buyers are constantly looking for new products to tempt its customers, is by reducing the 'fingerprints' on its products. In other words, it reduces the number of times products are *touched* as they move through the distribution chain, because each touchpoint generates a handling cost that must be attributed to the products. The firm also has a limited range of products (10,000 compared with around 40,000 in a large Walmart supermarket). Following the traditional distribution model, goods would pass from the manufacturers to distributors, and then to retailers. Costco buys most of its products from manufacturers, and this approach to distribution reduces the number of handling points using cross-dock distribution depots, which is where manufactured goods are sorted, gathered together and allocated to individual stores. The result is that Costco can maximize the efficiency of its distribution chain. Ultimately, this approach shortens the distribution channel for both business and consumers.

This business model enables Costco to reward both employees and customers: employees with wages that are higher than industry average, and customers with lower prices and cost savings. Customers who enjoy the cost-savings often make impulse purchases of high-ticket items like 3D televisions. Arguably, everyone benefits from this somewhat counterintuitive retail strategy.

Based on: Wulfratt (2014); Costco (2015); National Retail Federation (2018); Faran (2018)

Business-to-business channels

Common business-to-business distribution channels are illustrated in Figure 17.3. Usually a maximum of one channel intermediary is used.

Producer to business customer

Supplying business customers directly is common for expensive industrial products such as gas turbines, diesel locomotives and aero engines. There needs to be close liaison between supplier and customer to solve technical problems, and the size of the order makes direct selling and distribution economical.

Producer to agent to business customer

Instead of selling to business customers using their own salesforce, a business-to-business goods company could employ the services of an agent, who may sell a range of goods from several suppliers (on a commission basis), which spreads selling costs and may be attractive to companies without the reserves to set up their own sales operation. The disadvantage is that there is little control over the agent, who is unlikely to devote the same amount of time selling on products as a dedicated sales team would.

FIGURE 17.3
Distribution channels for business-to-business goods

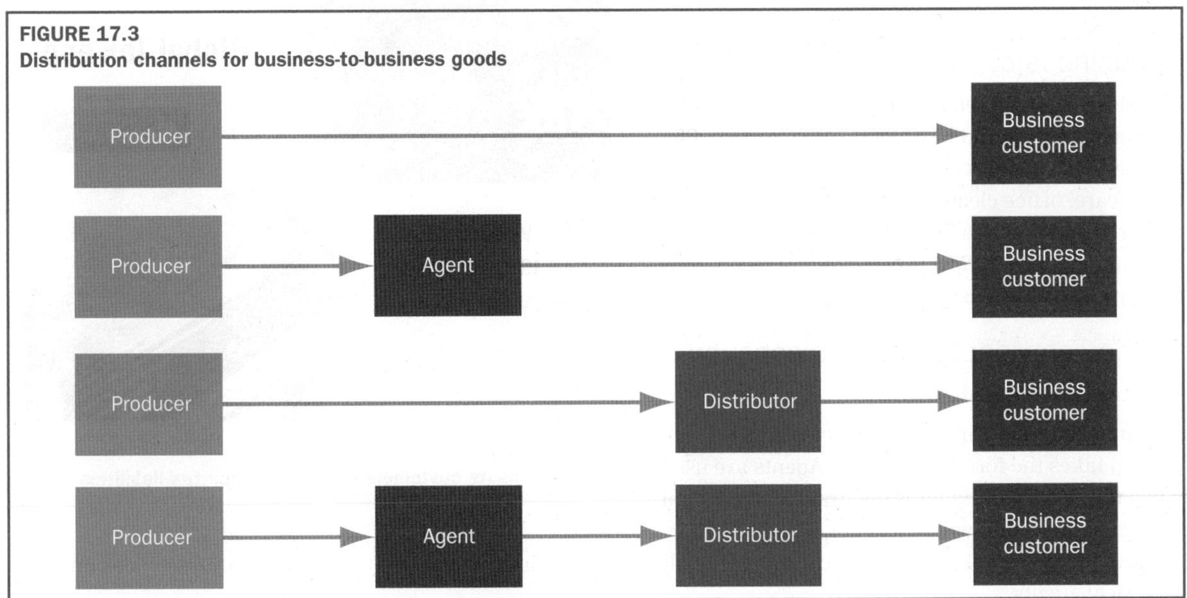

FIGURE 17.4
Distribution channels for services

Service provider
Consumer or business customer
Service provider
Agent
Consumer or business customer

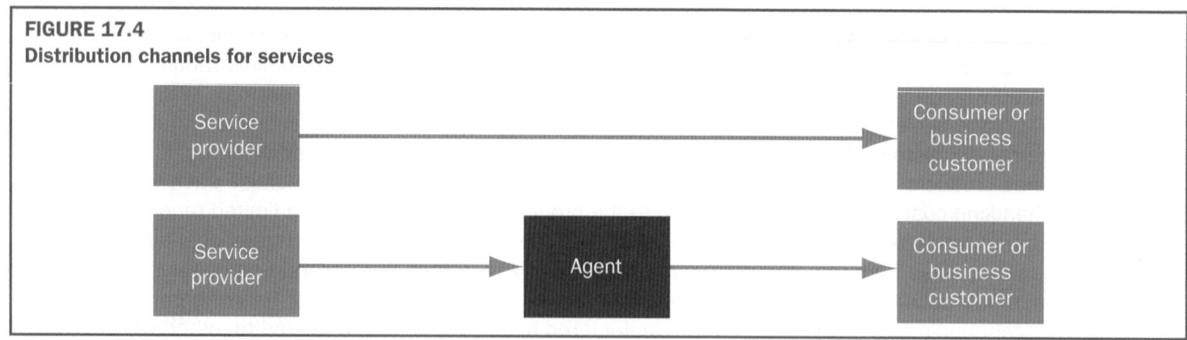

Producer to distributor to business customer

For less expensive, more frequently bought business-to-business products, distributors are used. These may have both internal and field sales staff (Narus and Anderson, 1986). Internal staff deal with customer-generated enquiries and order placing, order follow-up (often using the internet) and checking inventory levels. For many goods that are routinely purchased, fully automated digital systems are used. Outside sales staff are more proactive: their practical responsibilities are to find new customers, get products specified, distribute catalogues and gather market information. The advantage to customers of using distributors is that they can buy small quantities locally.

Producer to agent to distributor to business customer

Where business customers prefer to call upon distributors, the agent's job will require selling into these intermediaries. The reason why a producer may employ an agent rather than a dedicated salesforce is usually cost based (as previously discussed).

Services channels

Distribution channels for services are usually short—either direct or using an agent. While, in many situations, stocks are not held, the role of the wholesaler, retailer or industrial distributor is different in service supply chains. For example, in the fast food industry and beauty industries, products are purchased to use in the 'production' of service deliverables such as a Big Mac burger or a manicure and painted nails. Figure 17.4 shows the two alternatives, whether they be to consumer or business customers. Service organizations look for innovative ways to reach customers, as Marketing in Action 17.2 describes.

Service provider to consumer or business customer

The close personal relationships between service providers and customers often mean that service supply is direct. Examples include healthcare, office cleaning, accountancy, marketing research and law. See Exhibit 17.1 for how global accountancy firm KPMG is using digital technology to stay close to its customers.

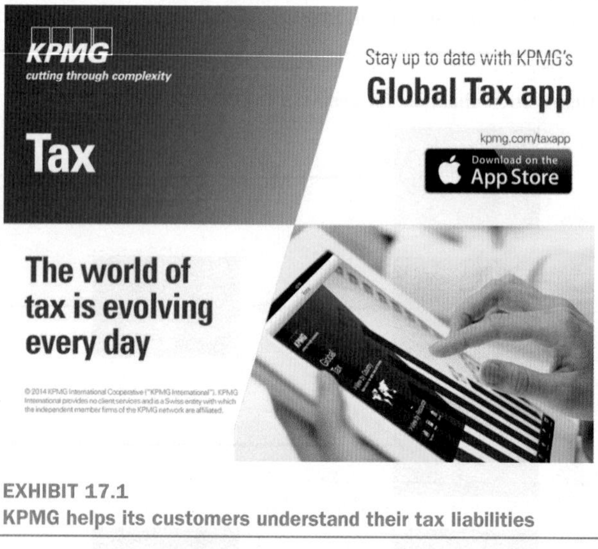

KPMG
cutting through complexity
Tax
Stay up to date with KPMG's
Global Tax app
kpmg.com/taxapp
Download on the App Store
The world of tax is evolving every day

EXHIBIT 17.1
KPMG helps its customers understand their tax liabilities

Service provider to agent to consumer or business customer

A channel intermediary for a service company usually takes the form of an agent. Agents are used when the service provider is geographically distant from customers and where it is not economical for the provider to establish its own local sales team. Examples include insurance, travel, secretarial services and theatrical agents.

Channel Strategy

Channel strategy decisions involve the selection of the most effective distribution channels, the most appropriate level of distribution intensity and the degree of channel integration (see Figure 17.5). Each of these decisions will now be discussed.

FIGURE 17.5
Channel strategy

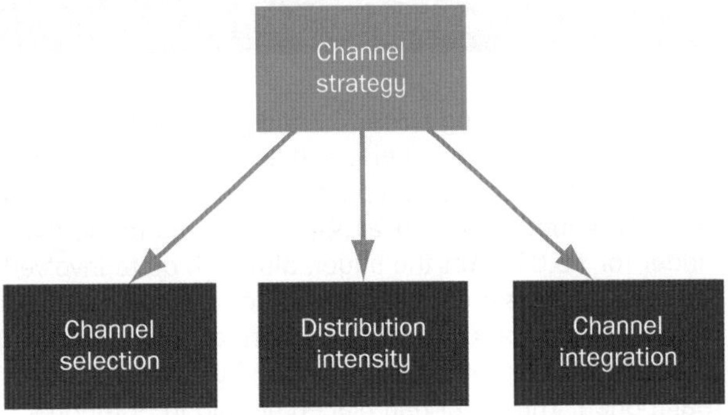

Channel selection

Why does Procter & Gamble sell its brands through supermarkets rather than selling direct? Why does General Electric sell its locomotives direct to train-operating companies rather than use a distributor? The answers are to be found by examining the following factors that influence *channel selection*. These influences can be grouped under market, producer, product and competitive factors.

Market factors

An important market factor is buyer behaviour: buyer expectations may dictate that the product be sold in a certain way. Buyers may prefer to buy locally in a shop. Failure to match these expectations can have serious consequences.

Buyer needs regarding product information, installation and technical assistance also have to be considered. A judgement needs to be made about whether the producer or channel intermediary can best meet these needs in terms of expertise, commitment and cost. For example, products that require facilities for local servicing, such as cars, often use intermediaries to carry out the task. Where the service requirement does not involve large capital investment, the producer may carry out the service. For example, supplier of pest control Rentokil trains its staff to conduct annual inspections and servicing as well as fulfilling their sales roles. But the firm also works to raise awareness of wider pest control issues. Working with Brunel University students on a 'Green Week' project, Rentokil's specialist teams together started Pestaurants, where sweet chilli pigeon burgers and savoury edible insects are supplied for free and experts are available to discuss which insects are edible and how to avoid pest problems. Pestaurants have been popping up since 2013 and continue to be an important part of the firm's fundraising efforts for Malaria Charities (Rentokil Initial plc, 2018). See Exhibit 17.2 for how Rentokil invites people from around the world to try alternative foods in its Pestaurants.

The willingness of channel intermediaries to market a product is also a market-based factor that influences channel decisions. Direct distribution may be the only option if distributors refuse to handle the product. For industrial products, this may mean the recruitment of salespeople, and for consumer products direct mail may be employed to communicate to and supply customers. The profit margins demanded by wholesalers and retailers and the commission rates expected by sales agents also affect the attractiveness of channel intermediaries. These costs need to be assessed in comparison with those of a salesforce.

The location and geographical concentration of customers also affects channel selection. The more local and clustered the customer base, the more likely direct distribution is to be feasible. Direct distribution is also more prevalent when buyers are few and buy large quantities. For products with many small customers, using channel intermediaries may be the only economical way of reaching them (hence supermarkets).

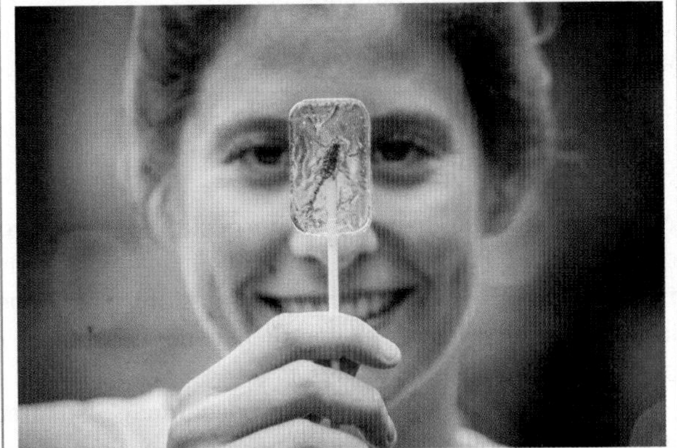

EXHIBIT 17.2
Rentokil invites people from around the world to try alternative foods in its Pestaurants

MARKETING IN ACTION 17.2
Sotheby's—Bidding on a New Distribution Channel

'Going once . . . going twice . . . and gone! Sold to . . .' is sometimes a relief to buyers, and at other times a bigger relief to sellers of auction lots. A print by the American photographer Berenice Abbott, *New York at Night*, was sold to the highest bidder for $6,000. Yet the buyer, although quite involved with the process, was not present to bid for the item at the Sotheby's New York salesroom. The sale was, in fact, conducted by a click of a mouse (or a tap with a quick finger) by a 'virtual bidder', yet with real money. The buyer had placed her bid in Sotheby's first 'live' auction on eBay on 1 April 2015.

The collaboration between Sotheby's and eBay represents the coupling of two seemingly different worlds. Sotheby's, established in 1744 by London bookseller Samuel Baker, is the world's oldest fine art auctioneers. Traditional auction houses such as Sotheby's and Christie's are often seen as intimidating places that are the exclusive domain of the wealthy elite. eBay, on the other hand, is a mass online marketplace founded in Pierre Omidyar's living room in Silicon Valley in 1995. The online auction and shopping website, which has won over 155 million customers in 190 countries, sells basically anything from toys to screwdrivers to cars.

It has never been easier for art aficionados or casual collectors to purchase art, whether a print, painting or sculpture. However, the new live auction platform of eBay.com and Sotheby's is like being there in person. Live video of the auctioneer and images of the item being sold appear on the screen, attempting to replicate the real-time saleroom bidding experience. It even provides a 'museum view' that simulates the experience of walking through a museum or gallery. Registered users (upon registration for each sale, users receive a unique paddle number associated with their eBay account) can place a bid with a click of the blue 'bid' button. This real-time bidding is sensitive to the millisecond. Following the bids can be quite dramatic, and the sound of the auctioneer's gavel has a lasting impact. However, buying at auction is not for the faint-hearted. Some works can be bought at below $5,000, but several valuations are more than $500,000. All bidders are notified that, 'By bidding, you agree to buy this item if you win.'

Sotheby's new online strategy has seized on a fresh growth opportunity. According to the TEFAF Art Market Report 2015, global sales of art and antiques reached their highest ever recorded level in 2014: a total of just over 51 billion euros worldwide. Online sales were estimated to account for only 6 per cent of global sales, but are expected to grow at least 25 per cent annually. Sotheby's online sales are low at around 1 per cent, but collaboration with eBay will allow Sotheby's to expand beyond the showroom to eBay's 155 million buyers worldwide. It will also bring the 'auction house appeal' to a younger generation that are not only technologically savvy, but also have an increasing interest in art, antiques and collectibles. These consumers are likely to be the biggest winners, assuming their good taste translates into bids that prove to be wise investments.

Source: Prepared from various published sources

Producer factors

A constraint on the channel decision occurs when the producer lacks adequate resources to perform the functions of the channel. Producers may lack the financial and managerial resources to take on channel operations. Lack of financial resources may mean that a salesforce cannot be recruited, and sales agents and/or distributors are used instead. Producers may feel that they do not possess the customer-based skills to distribute their products and prefer to rely on intermediaries.

The product mix offered by a producer may also affect channel strategy. A wide mix of products may make direct distribution (and selling) cost-effective. Narrow or single-product companies, on the other hand, may find the cost of direct distribution prohibitive unless the product is extremely expensive.

The final product influence is the desired degree of control of channel operations. The use of independent channel intermediaries reduces producer control. For example, by distributing their products through supermarkets, manufacturers lose total control of the price charged to consumers. Furthermore, there is no guarantee that new products will be stocked. Direct distribution gives producers control over such issues.

Product factors

Large, complex products are often supplied directly to customers. The need for close personal contact between producer and customer, and the high prices charged, mean that direct distribution and selling is both necessary and feasible. Perishable products such as frozen food, meat and bread require relatively short channels to supply the customer with fresh stock. Finally, bulky or difficult to handle products may require direct distribution, because distributors may refuse to carry them if storage or display problems arise (Rosenbloom, 1987). The increase in online shopping in Europe has encouraged retailers to explore increasingly innovative ways to get goods to their customers and add collection points to the end of the distribution chain. See Marketing in Action 17.3 to find out more.

MARKETING IN ACTION 17.3
Online Order Delivery

The delivery side of online shopping presents many challenges for retailers as they aim to create seamless shopping experiences for their customers when they buy online. As well as traditional delivery services by post, an array of different collection solutions by courier have been developed.

Click and collect: this is a simple concept: customers buy online and then choose where they would like to collect the goods—for example, at petrol stations, local corner shops and Royal Mail post offices. The concept has proved so popular for retailers like John Lewis that it is predicted that soon over three-quarters of online purchases will be delivered through click-and-collect schemes. eBay has even set up a collection scheme by partnering with Argos so that its sellers can offer this delivery option.

Remote click-and-collect locker: this delivery solution enables shoppers to pick up their goods from secure lockers. Amazon first used this method so that London commuters could get their orders from tube stations. The service has been extended to supermarkets, universities and libraries across the UK.

Temperature-controlled lockers: grocery retailers such as Asda and Waitrose have developed collection lockers that are sited in convenient locations for customers who do not want to visit the retailer's store. The locations of the lockers are carefully chosen to give consumers maximum convenience—for example, in car parks and near rail stations.

Additionally, there are multiple options for the timing and level of service of the delivery—for example, one-hour delivery, same day, next day, nominated days, weekend delivery. Each service has a different pricing structure. Amazon used delivery as part of its customer acquisition strategy and introduced Amazon Prime, providing members who sign up for a yearly fee an all-inclusive delivery service. There are over 100 million members and counting, and the firm introduced Amazon Prime Day, which has become one of the biggest annual online shopping events in the world.

In the future, Amazon, Domino's Pizza and others are experimenting with innovative delivery solutions.

Drones: Prime Air is Amazon's drone delivery service. This method is in its infancy, but sunscreen has been successfully delivered to people at a conference in Palm Springs. Domino's pizza, Mercedes and the Ukrainian post office are also experimenting with drone services.

Driverless cars: Domino's is trialing this technology for driverless home delivery services; Uber (in partnership with Toyota) is experimenting with the same technology.

Delivery innovations are changing the distribution and logistics industry, and automated or remotely operated vehicles are set to revolutionize the industry even more.

Based on: Felsted (2013); Planet Retail (2014); Dodds (2014); Vincent (2014); Vanian, (2018); O'Brien (2017)

Competitive factors

If the competition controls traditional channels of distribution—for example, through franchise or exclusive dealing arrangements—an innovative approach to distribution may be required. Two alternatives are to recruit a salesforce to sell direct or to set up a producer-owned distribution network (see the section on vertical marketing systems, under 'Conventional marketing channels', below). Producers should not accept that the channels of distribution used by competitors are the only ways to reach target customers. Direct marketing provides opportunities to supply products in new ways. Traditional channels of distribution for personal computers through high-street retailers are being circumvented by direct marketers who use direct response advertising to reach buyers. The emergence of the more computer-aware and experienced buyer, and the higher reliability of these products as the market reaches maturity, have meant that a local source of supply (and advice) is less important. Digitization of product not only changes the mode but also changes timings, access and availability.

Technology factors

Widespread use of the internet has encouraged greater use of e-commerce solutions, and many manufacturers have adopted web-based and mobile solutions as new channels to market, two major benefits being lower distribution cost and access to new markets (Palmatier et al., 2016). But digital channels can create problems relating to territories and lead to less control over access to customers. This friction can mean intensified competition between distributors and wholesalers using digital channels (Lee et al., 2003; Cunningham, 2013). Technology has also improved transparency: every transaction can be monitored, bringing greater transparency into channel relationships.

Distribution intensity

The second channel strategy decision is the choice of *distribution intensity*. The three broad options are intensive, selective and exclusive distribution.

Intensive distribution

Intensive distribution aims to achieve saturation coverage of the market by using all available outlets. With many mass-market products, such as soft drinks, foods, toiletries, alcohol and newspapers, sales are a direct function of the number of outlets penetrated. This is because consumers have a range of acceptable brands from which they can choose. If a brand is not available in an outlet, an alternative is bought. The convenience aspect of purchase is paramount. New outlets may be sought that hitherto had not stocked the products, such as petrol stations to sell confectionery and grocery items. In the UK, this trend has also encouraged supermarkets to locate convenience stores with a wide range of products at motorway service stations, for example Marks & Spencer's Simply Food stores in Moto service stations, and Waitrose as the latest food brand in Welcome Break's service stations (see Exhibit 17.3) (Motorway Services Online, 2015).

Selective distribution

Market coverage may also be achieved through **selective distribution**, in which a producer uses a limited number of outlets in a geographical area to sell its products. The advantages to the producer are the opportunity to select only the best outlets on which to focus its efforts to build close working relationships, to train distributor staff on fewer outlets than with intensive distribution, and, if selling and distribution is direct, to reduce costs. Upmarket aspirational brands are often sold in carefully selected outlets. Retail outlets and industrial distributors like this arrangement, since it reduces competition. Selective distribution is more likely to be used when buyers are willing to shop around when choosing products. This means that it is not necessary for a company to have its products available in all outlets—for example,

EXHIBIT 17.3
Supermarket convenience stores are now found in motorway service stations

Jaguar Land Rover (vehicles), Louis Vuitton and Chanel (luxury apparel), Moët Hennessy (fine champagne and cognac)—and brands can restrict where their products can be sold.

Problems can arise when a retailer demands distribution rights but is refused by producers, as in the case of Jaguar Land Rover refusing to allow Auto 24, an authorized car dealership, to sell Land Rover vehicles in Perigueux, France (Court of Justice of the European Union, 2012).

Exclusive distribution

This is an extreme form of selective distribution in which only one wholesaler, retailer or industrial distributor is used in a geographic area. Cars are often sold on this basis with only one dealer operating in each town or city. This reduces a purchaser's power to negotiate prices for the same model between dealers, since to buy in a neighbouring town may be inconvenient when servicing or repairs are required. It also allows very close co-operation between producer and retailer over servicing, pricing and promotion. Initially, Apple's iPhone was subject to exclusive distribution in the UK through the mobile phone operator O_2 and retailer Carphone Warehouse (Ritson, 2008), but this was soon extended to include other retailers. The right to **exclusive distribution** may be demanded by distributors as a condition for stocking a manufacturer's product line. Many luxury brands use this approach. Similarly, producers may wish for exclusive dealing where the distributor agrees not to stock competing lines. Adidas even refused to supply Sports Direct with replica football shirts, because of the retailer's 'pile em high, sell em cheap' approach to merchandizing (Joseph, 2013). The selection of an exclusive set of distributors can provide the basis for excellent customer service. For example, Caterpillar, the tractor manufacturer, is renowned for the quality of its exclusive dealer network. Dealers undergo rigorous selection procedures but, once accepted, are treated royally to make them feel part of the Caterpillar family. This is because Caterpillar recognizes the importance of dealer service in backing up its reputation for highly reliable machines (Nagle and Hogan, 2006).

Exclusive dealing can reduce competition in ways that may be considered contrary to consumers' interests. The European Court rejected an appeal by the French Leclerc supermarket group over the issue of the selective distribution system used by Yves St Laurent perfumes. The judges found that the use of selective distribution for luxury cosmetic products increased competition and that it was in the consumer's and manufacturer's interest to preserve the image of such luxury products.

Channel integration

Channel integration can range from conventional marketing channels comprising an independent producer and channel intermediaries, through a franchise operation, to channel ownership by a producer. Producers need to consider the strengths and weaknesses of each system when setting channel strategies.

Conventional marketing channels

The independence of channel intermediaries means that the producer has little or no control over these intermediaries. Arrangements such as exclusive dealing may provide a degree of control, but separation of ownership means that each party will look after its own interests. Conventional marketing channels are characterized by hard bargaining and, occasionally, conflict. For example, a retailer may believe that cutting the price of a brand is necessary to move stock, even though the producer objects because of brand image considerations.

However, separation of ownership means that each party can specialize in the function in which it has strengths: manufacturers produce, intermediaries distribute. Care needs to be taken by manufacturers to stay in touch with customers and not abdicate this responsibility to retailers.

A manufacturer that dominates a market through its size and strong brands may exercise considerable power over intermediaries, even though they are independent. This power may result in an **administered vertical marketing system** where the manufacturer can command considerable co-operation from wholesalers and retailers. Major brand builders such as Procter & Gamble and Unilever traditionally held great leverage over distribution but, more recently, power has moved towards the large dominant supermarket chains through their purchasing and market power. Marks & Spencer is a clear example of a retailer controlling an administered vertical marketing system. Through its dominant market position, it is capable of exerting considerable authority over its suppliers.

Franchising

A **franchise** is a legal contract in which a producer and channel intermediaries agree each member's rights and obligations. Usually, the intermediary receives marketing, managerial, technical and financial services in return for a fee. Franchise organizations such as McDonald's, Benetton, Hertz, the Body Shop and Anytime Fitness combine the strengths of a large sophisticated marketing-orientated organization with the energy and motivation of a locally owned outlet. Franchising is also commonplace in the car industry, where dealers agree exclusive deals with manufacturers in return for marketing and financial backing. Although a franchise operation gives a degree of producer control, there are still areas of potential conflict. For example, the producer may be dissatisfied with the standard of service provided by the outlet, or the franchisee may believe that the franchising organization provides inadequate promotional support. Goal conflict can also arise. Also, compared with ownership, the franchise organization lacks total control over franchisees. For example, Marriott, which franchises many of its hotels, had to rely on persuasion rather than control when it asked its franchisees to spend more than $1 billion worldwide on its new bedding design (Lambert, 2005).

A franchise agreement provides a **contractual vertical marketing system** through the formal co-ordination and integration of marketing and distribution activities. Some franchise organizations exert a considerable degree of control over financial and marketing operations. For example, to become a KFC franchisee, there is a licence fee of $45,000, a monthly royalty of 6 per cent, a 5 per cent contribution to advertising, plus the cost of buying and fitting out the restaurant, which can be more than $100,000. Additional funding is required for purchasing stock, paying for training, wages, utility bills and insurance premiums (KFC, 2018).

Despite the cost of setting up and running a franchise, there are compelling reasons why a producer might choose franchising as a means of distribution. Franchising allows the producer to overcome internal resource constraints by providing access to the franchisee's resources, as can be seen in the KFC example. The franchisee not only pays a set-up fee but also makes an ongoing contribution through regular royalty payments. Using this method, companies can gain access to geographically dispersed areas. KFC dominates the fast food franchise market in China, beating McDonald's to highly sought-after locations in major Chinese cities. Read Marketing in Action 17.4 to find out more about franchising Yum! and its successful franchise operations.

MARKETING IN ACTION 17.4
Alone We're Delicious, Together We're Yum!

Yum! Brands Inc. (http://www.yum.com) is based in Louisville, Kentucky, USA, and has four highly successful brands in its portfolio: KFC, Pizza Hut, Taco Bell and Wingstreet, which makes it one of the world's largest restaurant companies, with over 41,000 outlets in over 125 countries. Yum! operates 3,700 fast-food restaurants in China, of which KFC is currently the most profitable. Initially, Yum! took care to recruit managers who understood the local area and was also careful to select the right joint-venture partners: Beijing Corporation of Animal Production, Processing, Industry and Commerce, and Beijing Travel and Tourism Corporation. The reasons for not using the franchise model to expand in the early days were because of stringent Chinese rules and legislation. Changing economic conditions favour franchising, and there is plenty of demand from the 600-million-strong middle class.

Yum! aims to expand the number of outlets in this area to 20,000. The franchise approach has enabled the company to become the most successful foreign company operating in China. The business has been so successful because it has used local foods and management teams to build partnerships and drive expansion. If you visit a KFC in China, you can not only buy a bucket of fried chicken, you can also have a bowl of rice porridge with pork, pickles, mushrooms and preserved egg.

Yum! has also moved into Africa with its highly successful franchise approach. There is a Pizza Hut in Johannesburg, South Africa.

Based on: Mellor (2011); Hernandez (2011) Yum! (2018)

Regarding franchises, producers may value the notion of the owner-manager who has a vested interest in the success of the business. Although some control may still be necessary, the franchisee benefits directly from increases in sales and profits and so has a financial incentive to manage the business well. Finally, franchising may be a way for a producer to access the local knowledge of the franchisee. Franchising may therefore be attractive when a producer is expanding into new markets and where potential franchisees have access to information that is important in penetrating such markets.

The three most common levels where franchising is used in the distribution chain are:

1 *Manufacturer and retailer*: the car industry is dominated by this arrangement. The manufacturer gains retail outlets for its cars and repair facilities without the capital outlay required by ownership.
2 *Manufacturer and wholesaler*: this is commonly used in the soft drinks industry. Manufacturers such as Schweppes, Coca-Cola and Pepsi grant wholesalers the right to make up and bottle their concentrate in line with their instructions, and to distribute the products within a defined geographic area.
3 *Retailer and retailer*: a frequently used method that often has its roots in a successful retailing operation seeking to expand geographically by means of a franchise operation, often with great success. Examples include McDonald's, Benetton, Pizza Hut and KFC. See Table 17.1 for examples of some of the top franchises.

TABLE 17.1 Examples of top franchises in Europe

Rank	Franchise name	Number of units in Europe	Industry	Origin
1.	7-Eleven	60,000	Food convenience stores	USA
2.	Subway	44,819	Food sandwich bars	USA
3.	McDonald's	36,500	Food restaurants	USA
4.	Kumon Institution of Education	25,840	Education	Japan
5.	KFC (Yum! restaurants)	19,955	Food restaurants	USA
6.	Pizza Hut (Yum! restaurants)	15,605	Food restaurants	USA
7.	Burger King	15,000	Food restaurants	France
8.	Domino's Pizza	13,200	Food restaurants	USA
9.	Spar	12,176	Food convenience stores	Netherlands
10.	Dunkin' Donuts	12,000	Food restaurants	Netherlands

Source: Franchise Europe (2018) https://www.franchisedirect.co.uk/top500/

Channel ownership

Total control over distributor activities comes with channel ownership. This establishes a **corporate vertical marketing system**. By purchasing retail outlets, producers control their purchasing, production and marketing activities. Control over purchasing means a captive outlet for the manufacturer's products. For example, channel ownership is common in the clothing industry, with companies such as Zara and H&M owning their own chains of retail outlets.

The advantages of control must be weighed against the high price of acquisition and the danger that the move into retailing will spread managerial activities too widely. Nevertheless, corporate vertical marketing systems have operated successfully for many years in the oil industry, where companies such as Shell and BP own not only considerable numbers of petrol stations but also the means of production.

Channel Management

Once the key channel strategy decisions have been made, effective implementation is required. Specifically, several channel management issues must be addressed (see Figure 17.6). These are the selection, motivation, training and evaluation of channel members, and managing conflict between producers and channel members.

FIGURE 17.6
Channel management

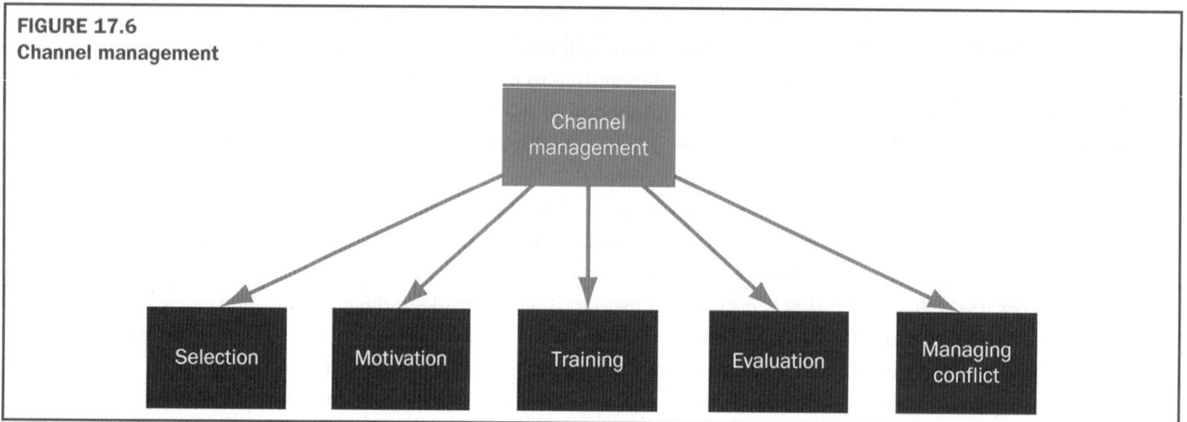

Selection

For some producers, the distribution problem is not so much channel selection as channel acceptance. The selection decision can vary depending on the size of the producer; for example, very small companies face difficulties when trying to persuade large retailers to stock their products. Selection then involves identifying candidates and developing *selection criteria*.

Identifying sources

Sources for identifying candidates include trade sources, reseller enquiries, customers of distributors and the field salesforce. *Trade sources* include trade associations, exhibitions and trade publications. Talking to trade associations can lead to the supply of names of prospective distributors. Exhibitions provide a useful means of meeting and talking to possible distributors. Sometimes channel members may be proactive in contacting a producer to express an interest in handling their products. Such *reseller enquiries* show that the distributor is enthusiastic about the possibility of a link. *Customers of distributors* are a useful source, since they can comment on distributors' merits and limitations. Finally, if a producer already has a *field salesforce* calling on intermediaries, salespeople are in a good position to seek out possible new distributors in their own territory.

Developing selection criteria

Common selection criteria include market, product and customer knowledge, market coverage, quality and size of the salesforce (if applicable), reputation among customers, financial standing, the extent to which competitive and complementary products are carried, managerial competence, and the degree of enthusiasm for handling the producer's lines. In practice, selection may be complex because large, well-established distributors may carry many competing lines and lack enthusiasm for more, whereas smaller distributors may be more enthusiastic and hungrier for success. The top selection criteria of overseas distributors are market knowledge, enthusiasm for the contract, hunger for success, customer knowledge, and the fact that the distributor does not carry competitors' products.

Motivation

Once selected, channel members need to be motivated to agree to act as a distributor and allocate adequate commitment and resources to the producer's lines. The key to effective motivation is to understand the needs and problems of distributors, as they are linked. For example, a distributor that values financial incentives may respond more readily to high commission than one that is more concerned with having an exclusive territory. Possible motivators include financial rewards, territorial exclusivity, providing resource support (e.g. sales training, field sales assistance, provision of marketing research information, advertising and promotion support, financial assistance and management training) and developing *strong work relationships* (e.g. joint planning, assurance of long-term commitment, appreciation of effort and success, frequent interchange of views and arranging distributor conferences).

Producers should seek to develop strong long-term relationships with their distributors, based on a recognition of their performance and integrated planning and operations. Jointly determined sales targets can motivate salespeople, who might receive a bonus on achievement. Targets are also useful for monitoring performance.

At the outset, establishing a long-term commitment is important, especially with international partners, as this can foster trust. Mutual commitment between channel members is central to successful relationship marketing. Two types of commitment are *affective commitment*, which expresses the extent to which channel members like to maintain their relationship with their partners, and *calculative commitment*, where channel members need to maintain a relationship. Commitment is highly dependent on interdependence and trust between the parties (Kumar, Scheer and Steenkamp, 1995).

Training

The need to train channel members obviously depends on their internal competences. Large-market supermarket chains, for example, may regard an invitation by a manufacturer to provide marketing training as an insult. However, many smaller distributors have been found to be weak on sales management, marketing, financial management, stock control and personnel management, and may welcome producer initiatives on training (see Webster, 1976; Shipley and Prinja, 1988). From the producer's perspective, training can provide the necessary technical knowledge about a supplier company and its products and help to build a spirit of partnership and commitment.

When training is provided, it usually takes the form of product and company knowledge, relationship management, service standards and a range of other key knowledge points. Sharing this knowledge can help to build strong personal relationships and give distributors the confidence to sell those products.

Evaluation

The evaluation of channel members has an important bearing on distributor retention, training and motivation decisions. Evaluation provides the information necessary to decide which channel members to retain and which to drop. Shortfalls in distributor skills and competences may be identified through evaluation, and appropriate training programmes organized by producers. Where a lack of motivation is recognized as a problem, producers can implement plans designed to deal with the root causes of demotivation (e.g. financial incentives and/or fostering a partnership approach to business) (see Pegram, 1965; Shipley, Cook and Barnett, 1989).

However, the scope and frequency of evaluation may be limited where power lies with the channel member. If producers have relatively little power because they are more dependent on channel members for distribution than channel members are on individual producers for supply, in-depth evaluation and remedial action will be restricted. Channel members may be reluctant to spend time providing the producers with comprehensive information on which to base evaluation. Remedial action may be limited to tentative suggestions when producers suspect there is room for improvement.

Where manufacturer power is high, through having strong brands and many distributors from which to choose, evaluation may be more frequent and wider in scope. Channel members are more likely to comply with the manufacturer's demands for performance information and agree for their sales and marketing efforts to be monitored by the manufacturer.

Evaluation criteria include sales volume and value, profitability, level of stocks, quality and position of display, new accounts opened, selling and marketing capabilities, quality of service provided to customers, market information feedback, ability and willingness to meet commitments, attitudes and personal capability.

Although the evaluation of overseas distributors and agents is more difficult than that of their domestic counterparts, research has shown that over 90 per cent of producers carry out evaluation, usually at least once a year (Philpot, 1975; Shipley, Cook and Barnett, 1989).

Managing conflict

Conflict has been defined as *the tension between two or more social entities (large organizations, individuals or groups)* (Sharma and Parida, 2018) when they have different expectations, for example of financial, behavioural, social outcomes. The intensity of conflict can range from occasional minor disagreements that are quickly forgotten to major disputes that fuel continuous bitter relationships. Channel conflicts can cause significant financial losses. Kodak and Walgreen's were at odds over the sale of photos printed on Kodak paper; the channel conflict cost around $500 million a year in sales (Bell et al., 2002). Channel 4 lost £20 million a month in revenue—caused by the absence of advertising on the television channel by major brands such as EE, Barclays Bank, Kuoni and BSkyB—when it entered into a conflict with Group M over the cost of advertising (O'Reilly, 2013). It is important to be aware of various sources of conflict.

Sources of channel conflict

The major sources of *channel conflict* are differences in goals, multiple distribution channels, and inadequacies in performance.

- *Differences in goals*: most resellers attempt to maximize their own profit. This can be accomplished by improving profit margin, reducing inventory levels, increasing sales, lowering expenses and receiving greater allowances from suppliers. In contrast, producers might benefit from lower margins, greater channel inventories, higher promotional expenses and fewer allowances given to channel members. These inherent conflicts of interest mean that there are many potential areas of disagreement between producers and their channel members.
- *Multiple distribution channels*: in trying to achieve market coverage, a producer may use multiple distribution channels. For example, a producer may decide to sell directly to key accounts, because their size warrants a key account salesforce, and use channel intermediaries to give wide market coverage. Conflict can arise when a channel member is denied access to a lucrative order from a key account because it is being serviced directly by the producer. Disagreements can also occur when the producer owns retail outlets that compete with independent retailers that also sell the producer's brands.
- *Inadequacies in performance*: an obvious source of conflict is when parties in the supply chain do not perform to expectations. For example, a channel member may underperform in terms of sales, level of inventory carried, customer service, standards of display and salesperson effectiveness. Producers may give poor delivery, inadequate promotional support, low profit margins, poor-quality goods and incomplete shipments. Retailer Monsoon Accessorize is potentially intensifying the number of opportunities for areas of conflict. CEO, Paul Allen, says about a new delivery service, 'Ship from store is a transformational project for our business, an important milestone on the road to becoming a fully integrated omnichannel retailer' Rigby (2018). To ensure success, the retailer will need to have ways to resolve all potential areas of conflicts, as it must deal with channel members across the supply chain and the end-consumer when seeking to fulfil strategic aims based on channel performance.

Sharma and Parida (2018) suggest that conflict is almost inevitable in marketing channels and is largely due to interdependencies between channel members which are mediated by the balance of power, levels of trust, and extent of loyalty and commitment, which if positive can moderate causes of conflict and if negative can intensify them. Marketing managers constantly try to avoid or resolve conflict.

Avoiding and resolving conflict

How can producers and channel members avoid and resolve conflict? There are several ways of managing conflict.

- *Developing a partnership approach*: this calls for frequent interaction between producer and resellers to develop a spirit of mutual understanding and co-operation. Producers can help channel members with training, financial help and promotional support. Distributors, in turn, may settle mutually agreed sales targets and provide extra sales resources. The objective is to build confidence in the manufacturer's products and relationships, based on trust. When conflicts arise, there is more chance they will be resolved in a spirit of co-operation. Organizing staff exchange programmes can be useful in allowing each party to understand the problems and tensions of the other, to avoid giving rise to animosity.
- *Training in conflict handling*: staff who handle disputes need to be trained in negotiation and communication skills. They need to be able to handle high-pressure conflict situations without resorting to emotion and *blaming behaviour*. Instead, they should be able to handle such situations calmly and be able to handle concession analysis, the identification of *win–win situations*. These are situations where both the producer and reseller benefit from an agreement.
- *Market partitioning*: to reduce or eliminate conflict from multiple distribution channels, producers can try to partition markets on some logical basis, such as customer size or type. This can work if channel members accept the basis for the partitioning. Alternatively, different channels can be supplied with different product lines.
- *Improving performance*: many conflicts occur for genuine reasons. For example, poor delivery by manufacturers or inadequate sales effort by distributors can provoke frustration and anger. Rather than attempt to placate the aggrieved partner, the most effective solution is to improve performance so that the source of conflict disappears. This is the most effective way of dealing with such problems.

- *Channel ownership*: an effective but expensive way of resolving conflicting goals is to buy the other party. Since producer and channel member are under common ownership, the common objective is to maximize joint profits. Conflicts can still occur, but the dominant partner is in a position to resolve them quickly. Some producers in Europe have integrated with channel intermediaries successfully.
- *Coercion*: In some situations, conflict resolution may be dependent on coercion, where one party induces compliance using force. For example, producers can threaten to withdraw supply, deliver late or withdraw financial support; channel members, on the other hand, can threaten to delist the manufacturer's products, promote competitive products and develop own-label brands.

Retailing: Physical and Digital Channels to Market

In the first part of this chapter, we examined channel strategy, focusing on the key areas of channel management decisions. In this section, we examine physical, digital and multichannel distribution decisions and the implications for channel management and for retailing.

Physical distribution

Physical distribution is defined as a set of activities concerned with the physical flows of materials, components and finished goods from producer to channel intermediaries and consumers. The combination of channels used by retailers is becoming increasingly diverse as they try to provide customers with non-stop access to goods and services. For retailers, the aim is to provide customers with the right products, in the right quantities, in the right locations, at the right time. Physical distribution activities have been the subject of managerial attention for some time, because of the potential for cost savings and improving customer service levels. Cost savings can be achieved by reducing inventory levels, using cheaper forms of transport and shipping in bulk rather than small quantities. Customer service levels can be improved by: fast and reliable delivery, including just-in-time delivery; holding high inventory levels, so that customers have a wide choice and the chances of stockouts are reduced; fast order processing; and ensuring products arrive in the right quantities and quality. But now channel selection has become a means of adding customer value. Zara uses the distribution channel as a source of competitive advantage (see Exhibit 17.4).

In the clothing industry, fast-changing fashion demands mean that companies such as H&M and Zara use extremely short lead times to create a competitive advantage over their slower, more cumbersome, rivals. Such methods used are discussed in Mini Case 17.1.

Physical distribution management concerns the balance between cost reduction and meeting customer service requirements. Trade-offs are often necessary. For example, low inventory and slow, cheaper transportation methods reduce costs but lower customer service levels and satisfaction. Determining this balance is a key marketing decision, as physical distribution can be a source of competitive advantage. A useful approach is to analyse the market in terms of customer service needs and price sensitivity. The result may be the discovery of two segments:

1 low service needs, high price sensitivity
2 high service needs, low price sensitivity.

Unipart was first to exploit segment 2 in the do-it-yourself car repair and servicing market. It gave excellent customer service but charged a high price. Unipart's analysis, therefore, defined the market segment to target and the appropriate marketing mix. Alternatively, both segments could be targeted with different marketing mixes. In business-to-business markets, large companies may possess their own service facilities, while smaller firms require producer or distributor service as part of the product offering and are willing to pay a higher price.

EXHIBIT 17.4
Zara uses the distribution channel as a source of competitive advantage

MINI CASE 17.1
Managing the Supply Chain the Zara Way

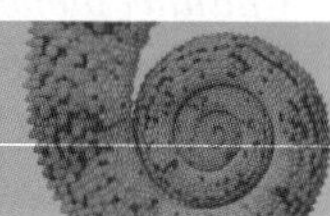

Zara, the Spanish clothing company owned by Inditex, has revolutionized the fashion industry by becoming the first global retailer to sell fashion lines designed especially for seasons in the southern as well as the northern hemisphere. Zara has a successful business model that has enabled the retail chain to expand to over 5,000 outlets and stores in Europe, South America, Oceania and Africa, so developing ranges to suit the seasons is an important part of the expansion strategy. Its key competitive advantage lies in its ability to match fashion trends that change quickly. This, in turn, relies on an extremely fast and responsive supply chain. While other retailers moved production to the Far East to save money, Zara knew that it could make its best-selling clothes faster in Spain (see Exhibit 17.4).

Zara uses its stores to find out what consumers want, what styles are selling, what colours are in demand, and which items are hot sellers and which are failures. The data are fed back to Zara headquarters through a sophisticated marketing information system. At the end of each day, Zara sales assistants report to the store manager using wireless headsets to communicate inventory levels. The store managers then inform the Zara design and distribution departments at headquarters about what consumers are buying, asking for and avoiding. Top-selling items are requested and low-selling items are withdrawn from shops within a week. There is a big incentive for the store managers to get it right, as up to 70 per cent of their salary is based on commission.

Garments are made in small production runs to avoid overexposure, and no item stays in the shops for more than four weeks, which encourages Zara shoppers to make repeat visits. Whereas the average high-street store in Spain expects shoppers to visit on average three times a year, Zara shoppers visit up to 17 times.

The company's designers use the feedback from the stores when preparing new designs. The fabrics are cut and dyed at Zara's own highly automated manufacturing facilities, which gives it control over this part of the supply chain. Seamstresses in 350 independently owned workshops in Spain and Portugal stitch about half of the pre-cut pieces into garments; the other half are stitched in-house. Only basic items such as T-shirts are bought from low-cost regions such as eastern Europe, Africa and Asia. Although wages are higher in Spain, Zara saves time and money on shipping.

The finished garments are sent back to Zara's headquarters with its state-of-the-art logistics centre, where they are electronically tagged, quality checked and sorted into distribution lots for shipping to their destinations. Although Zara supplies every market from warehouses in Spain, it manages to get new merchandise to European stores within 24 hours and, by flying goods via commercial airlines, to stores in the Americas and Asia in 48 hours or less.

So efficient are Zara's production and distribution systems that the average turnaround time from design to delivery is 10–15 days, with around 12,000 garments being marketed each year. In this way, Zara stays on top of fashion trends rather than being outpaced by the market. And, by producing smaller batches of clothing, it adds an air of exclusivity that encourages customers to shop often. As a result, the chain does not have to slash prices by 50 per cent, as rivals often do, to move mass quantities of out-of-season stock. Since Zara is more in tune with current looks, it can also charge slightly more than, for example, Gap, which it has now overtaken to become the world's largest clothing retailer.

Questions:

1 Discuss the implications of shorter product life-cycles for a clothing manufacturer like Zara and H&M.

2 Suggest why Zara doesn't just use the garment ranges developed in the winter for the northern hemisphere and then sell them on in the southern hemisphere.

3 At the opposite end of the spectrum from fast fashion is the 'slow fashion' movement, which advocates buying fewer clothes of better quality that will last longer and help to save the environment. Do you think this growing trend will affect the demand for fast fashion, and do fast fashion brands only appeal to the young?

Based on: The Economist (2002); Roux (2002); BBC (2003); Mitchell (2003); Fahy and Jobber (2015); Capell (2008); Johnson and Falstead (2011)

Not only are there trade-offs between physical distribution costs and customer service levels, but there are also possible conflicts between elements of the physical distribution system itself. For example, an inventory manager may favour low stocks to reduce costs, but if this leads to stock-outs this may raise costs elsewhere—the freight manager may have to accept higher costs resulting from fast freight deliveries to guarantee the safety of the products. A key role the physical distribution manager would perform would be to reconcile the conflicts inherent in the system, so that total costs are minimized subject to required customer service levels.

Virtual distribution and the impact of the e-commerce

E-commerce systems facilitate transactions, the flow of products, cash and information, and revertse product logistics (returns) and can be used to meet the customers' demands in terms of timing, location and speed of delivery. But these demands place additional pressures on channel partners. The bringing together of physical and digital channels to achieve shared goals raises extra challenges for all channel members. Marketing managers need to plan and prepare guidelines and training to avoid conflict. Those involved must also ensure that all efforts are pointing in the same direction. But there is an additional layer of complexity, as e-commerce systems can be both marketplace and sales and inventory management systems. Trust plays an important role and can either be confirmed or lost based on the performance of these integrated channels (Sharma and Parida, 2018).

Multichannel distribution

Digital channels have increased the number of touchpoints where a customer can engage with a business (see Chapter 10, Figures 10.2 and 10.3 for details). The desire to provide seamless customer service across all these touchpoints is at the heart of the multichannel distribution system. So, whether it is the point of purchase, the payment system, a customer service encounter, delivery or reverse logistics (returning/recycling goods)—in fact, wherever a customer touches the brand—the experience, i. e. the product offer, customer service and marketing message, should be the same (Sharma and Parida, 2018).

Managing logistics in multichannel relationships

The supply chain has been transformed in the retail industry by digital technology. The movement of goods and the flow of information between retailers and their suppliers are critical to operational success, and whereas retailers used to be 'passive recipients of products, allocated to stores by manufacturers in anticipation of demand', now they are in control and manage supplies in response to customer demand (Fernie et al., 2010). ASOS sells over 20,000 branded and own-label products through its online e-commerce operation. Digital systems and barcode technologies are enabling ASOS to offer 'a much wider product range than its high-street competitors'. Lean and agile supply chains that support large retail operations manage the purchasing, processing and movement of vast quantities of products, so that individual items are in the right place at the right time to satisfy customer needs.

Online shopping is on the increase, but it creates operational and logistical challenges, especially for grocery retailers Ellis-Chadwick (2011). A typical online grocery order consists of 60–80 items, across three temperature regimes picking from a total range of 10,000–25,000 products within 12–24 hours for delivery to customers within one to two-hour time slots. Supermarket retailers have made significant investment in technology to manage the complexities associated with receiving products from thousands of suppliers, and picking and then delivering millions of consumer orders. Ocado (2018), the online-only grocery retailer, makes extensive use of digital technology to enable its business to operate. To manage its complex online operations, Ocado has developed in-house software and uses state-of-the-art gaming software to visualize and identify problems, with the aim of streamlining operations in its automated warehouse and national supply chain. Ocado's IT team is pushing the boundaries in every aspect of the business by developing online and mobile apps for all the latest platforms, for example Android and iPad.

Retailing: In-store, Online and Mobile

Traditionally, retailing was considered a rather passive activity, with goods passing from the manufacturer to the wholesaler then to the retailer and, finally, to individual customers. Retailers would display available products and attempt to sell them to their customers with limited regard for what the customers wanted. However, eventually, retailers discovered that understanding what was important to the customer meant they could stock the right products, sell at the right price and ultimately *increase profits*, rather than having to *push* the products they had in stock, often at reduced prices. The era of 'stack them high and sell them cheap' ended. Retailers had discovered the importance of *understanding and satisfying customer needs*, and this represented an important landmark in the development and definition of modern retailing (Ellis-Chadwick, 2011). The implication of this shift towards a customer-centric operation is at the heart of many of the channel management decisions we have discussed so far in this chapter. In the remaining part of the chapter, we consider retail marketing decisions and the retail mix, and online and mobile retailing.

Retail marketing decisions

Like any modern business, retailers must understand the environment in which they trade and anticipate and adapt to changing environmental circumstances. We shall now explore some of the key retailing decisions necessary to prosper in today's competitive climate. These decisions are retail positioning, store location, product assortment and services, price and store atmosphere. These call for decisions to be taken against a background of rapid change in information technology.

Retailers are no strangers to information technology developments, with electronic point of sale (EPOS) systems allowing the counting of products sold and money taken, and faster service at checkouts. Barcodes, Universal Product Codes (UPCs; used for tracking items in stores and across the supply chain), scanners and associated technology have revolutionized retail supply chains, stock management and retail operations. A further technological innovation is using the internet to shop. Online shopping is growing as more people become accustomed to electronic payment, have broadband access to the internet and are prepared to shop via a mobile phone. See Exhibit 17.5 to find out how virtual retailer Yihaodian became the number one retailer in China.

Retail positioning

As with all marketing decisions, **retail positioning** involves the choice of target market and differential advantage. Targeting allows retailers to tailor their marketing mix—which includes product assortment, service levels, store location, prices and promotion—to the needs of their chosen customer segment. Differentiation provides a reason to shop at one store rather than another. For some retailers, the low-cost strategic option remains viable—Aldi, Costco, Asda Walmart, Amazon—and for others, the high-quality differentiated route—for example Waitrose, John Lewis Partnership, Harrods. But many retailers find themselves stuck in the middle, falling between low cost and high quality (Berman, 2010). Often this occurs when retailers attempt to be all things to all people. The outcome can be that the retailer needs to respond rapidly if it is to survive. For example, in 2015, leading UK supermarket retailer Tesco was facing falling profits and market share, and, in response, cut its prices to compete with limited range discounters Aldi and Lidl.

Many of the changes occurring in retail are as a result of the effect of the internet on traditional models. Retailers are left facing challenging decisions about which market positions to inhabit, which locations to utilize, how to communicate with their customers, and the extent to which their products can be augmented by additional services. Consequently, the way in which retailers are using the marketing mix to differentiate their brands has changed (Verhoef, Kannan and Inman, 2015). The rest of this section explores how retailers seek to differentiate their offer.

EXHIBIT 17.5
Yihaodian, number 1 retailer in China

Place: in-store location

Multichannel retailing, whereby retailers add new channels to their existing offer, is becoming increasingly important. For example, traditional store-based retailers have introduced online and mobile digital stores, for example Dixons Carphone and John Lewis Partnership. Alternatively, online-only retailers have moved onto the physical high street, for example eBay and Amazon.

But the discussion of the channels that retailers might choose to serve their customers does not end here. As the journey that customers take to purchase becomes more complex, crossing over from the physical to the virtual, they may encounter many touchpoints. For example, a shopper who likes a product in a magazine may then go to the web to find out about the product, visit a store to see what the product looks like, make a purchase online and finally go to a social media site to review the product. The decision for the retailer ceases to be which channels, but how to create a seamless journey for the customer.

The solution is to adopt a multichannel approach whereby, regardless of where shoppers interact with the retailer, their experience is the same. This means that a retailer should ensure that products, prices, customer service and communication messages are consistent. The increasing use of digital, mobile and social media channels, giving rise to new types of customer journey—for example: reserve online, collect from store; order in store, delivered to home; buy online, return unwanted goods to store—should be addressed alongside sales performance and marketing strategy.

As channel decisions become more complex, it is increasingly important to understand the target customers. However, convenience remains an important issue for many shoppers, and so store location can still have a major bearing on sales performance. Also, given that approximately 90 per cent of retail sales take place in physical stores, retailers must decide on regional coverage, the towns and cities to target within regions, and the precise location within a given town or city. Location for Ted Baker, the clothes and home furnishings fashion retailer, is key, as the company does not advertise. Ted Baker is on the high street as well as having in-store concessions and standalone stores, for example at Gatwick and Heathrow airports, Bluewater and Glasgow, and also in Miami, Paris and New York's Bloomingdale's. One of its London stores sits opposite Paul Smith, the designer clothes store, in one of the city's trendiest enclaves (Ryle, 2002). Many retailers begin life as regional suppliers and grow by expanding geographically. In the UK, for example, the Asda supermarket chain expanded from the north of England, while the original base for Sainsbury's was in the south of England.

The location of stores can be greatly aided by geographic information systems (GISs), which profile geographical areas according to such variables as disposable income, family size, age and birth rates. We saw in Chapter 7, on market segmentation and positioning, how such systems can be used to segment markets. GISs allow marketers to understand the profiles of people living in specific geographic areas. Asda, the UK supermarket chain, uses GIS data as a method of finding new store locations. By understanding the number and profile of consumers living in different geographical areas, it can plan its stores (and product assortment) to be in the right areas to serve its target market (Hayward, 2002).

Product assortment and customer services

Retailers must decide upon the breadth of their product assortment and its depth. A supermarket, for example, may decide to widen its product assortment from food, drink and toiletries to include clothes, electrical goods and toys; this is called *scrambled merchandising*. Within each product line it can choose to stock a deep or shallow product range. Some retailers specialize their product ranges, like Rymans the stationery retailer. Department stores like Debenhams and House of Fraser offer a much broader range of products, including toys, cosmetics, jewellery, clothes, electrical goods and household accessories. Some retailers begin with one product line and gradually broaden their product assortment to maximize revenue per customer. For example, petrol stations broadened their product range to include motor accessories, confectionery, drinks, flowers and newspapers. A by-product of this may be to reduce customers' price sensitivity, since selection of petrol station may be based on the ability to buy other products rather than the lowest price. The choice of product assortment will be dependent on the positioning strategy of the retailer, customer expectations and, ultimately, on the profitability of each product line.

Another product decision concerns own-label branding. Large retailers may decide to sell a range of own-label products to complement national brands. Often the purchasing power of large retail chains means that prices can be lower and yet profit margins higher than for competing national brands. This makes the activity an attractive proposition for many retailers. Consumers also find own-label brands attractive, with many of them in the grocery field being regarded as at least equal to, if not better than, established manufacturer brands (Burt, 2000).

Finally, retailers need to consider the nature and degree of *customer service*. Discount stores traditionally provided little service but, as price differentials have narrowed, some have sought differentiation through service. For example, many electrical goods retailers provide a comprehensive after-sales service package for their customers. Superior customer service may make customers more tolerant of higher prices. Also, even where the product is standardized (as in fast-food restaurants), training employees to give individual attention to each customer can increase loyalty to the outlet (Bloemer et al., 1999).

Price

For some market segments, price is a key factor in store choice. Consequently, some retailers use price as their differential advantage. This requires vigilant cost control and significant buying power. Where price is a key choice criterion, retailers that lose price competitiveness can suffer. For example, Carrefour, the world's second-largest retailer after Walmart, lost its reputation for low prices in France because of its focus on profit margins rather than volume. Market share plummeted in the face of intense competition from its domestic rivals Leclerc and Auchan and discounters such as Germany's Aldi and Lidl (*The Economist*, 2005). The popular trend is towards the *everyday low prices* favoured by retailers, rather than higher prices supplemented by promotions, supported by manufacturers. Retailers such as Aldi, Lidl and Asda maintain that customers prefer predictable low prices rather than occasional money-off deals, three-for-the-price-of two offers and free gifts. Supermarket chains are also pressurizing suppliers to provide consistently low prices rather than temporary promotions. This action is consistent with the desire to position themselves on a low-price platform.

Store atmosphere

This is created by the design, colour and layout of a store. Both exterior and interior design affect atmosphere.

External factors include architectural design, signs, window display and use of colour, which together create an identity for a retailer and attract customers. Retailers aim to create a welcoming rather than an intimidating mood. The image that is projected should be consonant with the ethos of the shop. The Body Shop, for example, projects its environmentally caring image through the green exterior of its shops and through window displays that feature environmental issues.

Interior design also has a major impact on atmosphere. Store lighting, fixtures and fittings, and layout are important considerations. Supermarkets that have narrow aisles, which contributes to congestion, can project a negative image, and poorly lit showrooms can feel intimidating. Colour, sound and smell can affect mood. Sometimes red-toned lighting is used in areas of impulse purchasing. For example, one stationer uses red tones at the front of its stores for impulse buys such as pens and stationery. Supermarkets often use music to create a relaxed atmosphere, whereas some boutiques use contemporary music to attract their target customers. Department stores often place perfume counters near the entrance, and supermarkets may use the smell of baking bread to attract their customers.

Online and mobile retailing

Selling online is not new. In business-to-business markets, dedicated e-commerce systems have facilitated trading between channel members across the supply chain for nearly half a century. However, selling to consumers using e-commerce systems is relatively new. While the first consumer sales online took place in 1994, it was not until 2005 that online shopping really took hold and became a significant retail marketplace (Ellis-Chadwick, 2018). European shoppers are spending significant amounts online, which represent approximately 10 per cent of retail sales; however, while overall sales continue to increase, the rate of growth is slowing. Forecasts suggest that by 2020 global online sales will increase to $4.058 trillion, accounting for 14.6 per cent of total retail sales (Chaffey, 2018).

Buying and selling online is more complex than physical retailing where the goods and services are offered by the retailer to the consumer. Online there are many new possibilities to trade, interact and engage with online markets (Chaffey and Ellis-Chadwick, 2019). Consumers can trade with consumers through online gateways like eBay (peer-to-peer auction site) and Etsy (e-commerce site selling handmade and vintage items).

Social commerce is possible via social media networks like Facebook, Pinterest and Instagram. Social commerce is creating opportunities for brands. Pinterest has 60 million purchasable pins, which can be bought with one click. Facebook's marketplace is approaching 600 million users. Many young consumers prefer to buy in social spaces. The expansion of this form of purchasing raises new challenges for retailers, who must determine where their consumers spend most of their time online (Brown, 2018). See Exhibit 17.6 Buyable pins from Pinterest.

EXHIBIT 17.6
Buyable pins from Pinterest

Mobile commerce enables communication and purchasing online via wireless telecoms networks using mobile phones and other mobile devices. Apple launched the iPhone in 2007, which arguably started the mobile shopping revolution (Ellis-Chadwick, 2013). Increased functionality of the smartphone, longer battery life, improved Wi-Fi networks and greater broadband capacity also contributed to driving more shoppers to search, compare and buy while on the move. To succeed in this channel, retailers must be prepared to adapt their websites so they translate accurately to the screen of a mobile phone and offer the shopping efficiency, price benefits and the transaction security that shoppers expect (Chi, 2018). In response to this opportunity to reach and sell to consumers almost everywhere, many retailers have developed apps—specially designed applications for a mobile device—enabling shopping on the go. Shoppers are increasingly making use of apps, and savvy retailers and service providers have developed solutions that are easy to use. The UK is leading the way in the uptake of retail apps, with many national high street retailers offering this service, for example Argos, Boots the chemist, John Lewis and Tesco. Retailers are extending their services and enabling shoppers to order products, arrange deliveries and track orders through apps. Service, leisure and travel and tourism sector brands have also launched apps so consumers can, for example, book an eye test appointment (Specsavers), order and pay for a meal from their table (JD Wetherspoons), or buy a train ticket (East Midlands Trains).

Ethical Issues in Distribution

The final section in this chapter discusses ethical issues associated with distribution. Ethical issues in distribution include the use of slotting allowances, exclusive dealing, restrictions on supply, grey markets and fair trading. Ethical issues associated with online shopping, social media and mobile commerce are discussed in Chapter 16.

Slotting allowances, exclusive dealing and restrictions to supply

Food is big business, and most products find their way to supermarket shelves rather than the local corner shop. The retail grocery business, therefore, tends to be dominated by mega brands, for example Walmart, Carrefour and Tesco. The power shift from manufacturers to retailers in this industry has meant that slotting allowances are often demanded by large retailers. A *slotting allowance* is a fee paid in exchange for an agreement to place a product in a preferential space on the retailer's shelves. Retailers say they are simply charging rent for a valuable, scarce commodity: shelf space (Stanton and Herbst, 2006). Tesco got into a row over slotting allowances, and the dispute was blamed for destabilizing the power it exerted over suppliers (Meville, 2014). Critics argue that these charges represent an abuse of power and work against small manufacturers who cannot afford to pay the fee. Research in the grocery sector found that nearly 40 per cent of manufacturers complained of being asked to pay fees for the retailer to stock their produce (Butler, 2015).

Another concern of small suppliers is that the power of large manufacturers and retailers will mean that they are squeezed out of the supply chain. In the UK, farmers and small grocery suppliers have joined forces to demand better treatment from large supermarket chains, which are forging exclusive deals with major manufacturers. They claim that the problem is made worse by the growth of category management, where retailers appoint 'category captains' from their suppliers, who act to improve the standing of the whole product category, such as breakfast cereals or confectionery. The small suppliers believe this forces them out of the category altogether, as category captains look after their own interests. They would like to see a system similar to that in France, where about 10 per cent of shelf space is by law given to small suppliers (McCawley, 2000).

Grey markets

These occur when a product is sold through an unauthorized distribution channel. When this occurs in international marketing, the practice is called parallel importing. Usually, a distributor buys goods in one country (where prices are low) and sells them in another (where prices are high) at below the going market price. This causes anger among members of the authorized distribution channel, who see their prices being undercut. Furthermore, the products may well be sold in downmarket outlets that discredit the image of the product, or be sold cheaply online. Quality fashion brands such as Burberry, Armani and Abercrombie & Fitch have experienced the 'grey market effect' on their brands. Nevertheless, supporters of grey markets argue that they encourage price competition, increase consumer choice and promote the lowering of price differentials between countries.

Fair trading

One problem of free market forces is that when small commodity producers are faced with large powerful buyers, the result can be very low prices. This can bring severe economic hardship to the producers, who may be situated in countries of the developing world. In the face of a collapse in world coffee prices, a fair-trading brand, Cafédirect, was launched. Fair trade business models provide benefits to small producers by helping them to achieve higher prices and retain access to important markets, and by providing training and improvements to working practices. But there are drawbacks; for example, prices may be fixed at a commodity level rather than at a country level, and certified Fairtrade coffee producers can be made to pay the cost of marketing of the Fairtrade brand, through licensing fees as a proportion of their sales (Macatonia, 2013).

Review

1 The functions and types of channels of distribution

- The functions are to reconcile the needs of producers and consumers, improve efficiency, improve accessibility and provide specialist services.
- Four types of consumer channel are: producer direct to consumer; producer to retailer to consumer; producer to wholesaler to retailer to consumer; and producer to agent to wholesaler to retailer to consumer.
- Four types of industrial channels are: producer to industrial customer; producer to agent to industrial customer; producer to distributor to industrial customer; and producer to agent to distributor to industrial customer.
- Two types of service channel are: service provider to consumer or industrial customer; and service provider to agent to consumer or industrial customer.

2 How to determine channel strategy

- Channel strategy should be determined by making decisions concerning the selection of the most effective distribution channel, the most appropriate level of distribution intensity and the correct degree of channel integration.

3 The three components of channel strategy: channel selection, intensity and integration

- Channel selection is influenced by market factors (buyer behaviour, ability to meet buyer needs, the willingness of channel intermediaries to market a product, the profit margins required by distributors and agents compared with the costs of direct distribution, and the location and geographic concentration of customers), producer factors (lack of resources, the width and depth of the product mix offered by a producer, and the desired level of control of channel operations), product factors (complexity, perishability, extent of bulkiness and difficulty of handling), and competitive factors (need to choose innovative channels because traditional channels are controlled by the competition or because a competitive advantage is likely to result).
- Channel intensity options are intensive distribution to achieve saturated coverage of the market by using all available outlets, selective distribution, where a limited number of outlets in a geographical area are used, and exclusive distribution, which is an extreme form of selective distribution where only one wholesaler, retailer or industrial distributor is used in a geographic area.
- Channel integration can range from conventional marketing channels (where there is separation of ownership between producer and distributor, although the manufacturer power of channel intermediaries may result in an administered vertical marketing system), franchising and channel ownership.

4 The five key channel management issues: member selection, motivation, training, evaluation and conflict management

- Selection of members involves identifying sources and establishing selection criteria.
- Motivation of distributors involves understanding the needs and problems of distributors, and methods include financial rewards, territorial exclusivity, providing resource support, and the development of strong work relationships.
- Training may be provided where appropriate. It can provide the necessary technical knowledge about a supplier company and its products and help to build a spirit of partnership and commitment.
- Evaluation criteria include sales volume and value, profitability, level of stocks, quality and position of display, new accounts opened, selling and marketing capabilities, quality of service, market information feedback, willingness and ability to meet commitments, attitudes and personal capability. Evaluation should be based on mutually agreed objectives.
- Conflict management sources are differences in goals, differences in desired product lines, the use of multiple distribution channels by producers, and inadequacies in performance. Conflict-handling approaches are developing a partnership approach, training in conflict handling, market partitioning, improving performance, channel ownership and coercion.

5 Retailing: physical and digital channels to market

- Physical distribution management concerns the balance between cost reduction and meeting customer service requirements. An example of a trade-off is incompatibility between low inventory and slow, cheaper transportation methods that reduce costs, and the lower customer service levels and satisfaction that result.
- Virtual channels facilitate the flow of products, cash and information, but increase the complexity of channel management.
- Digital channels have encouraged businesses to adopt a multichannel approach to distribution in pursuit of providing a seamless customer journey. The supply chain has been transformed by digital technology, enabling increasingly sophisticated marketing initiatives.

6 How to improve customer service standards in physical distribution

- Customer service standards can be raised by improving product availability (e.g. by increasing inventory levels), improving order cycle time (e.g. faster order processing), raising information levels (e.g. information on order status) and raising flexibility (e.g. fast reaction time to problems).

7 Retailing and retail marketing

- Retailing fulfils an essential role in the supply chain by breaking bulk and enabling goods manufactured in very large quantities to be supplied to consumers in very small quantities. This process has many implications for channel management. Furthermore, marketing mix decisions, positioning and other marketing concepts have particular meaning when applied to retailing.

- Retail positioning involves the choice of target marketing and use of the marketing mix to develop differential advantage.
- Store location decisions are made using a number of variables, from convenience to disposable income of a particular catchment area.
- Product assortment decisions focus on the breadth and depth of range, which enables retailers to tailor their product mix to suit particular audiences.
- Pricing is important in retailing, and retailers need to ensure that they manage cost control and levels of pricing effectively.
- Store atmosphere—the internal and external design, colour and store layout can all have an impact on consumer buying behaviour.

8 Online, social and mobile commerce

- Selling online has become popular and accounts for around 10 per cent of retail sales. Buying and selling online is more complex than physical retailing, and retailers have to work out where best to engage with their customers: social medial networks, the web or mobile apps.

9 Ethical issues in distribution

- There are potential problems relating to slotting allowances, exclusive dealing, restrictions on supply, grey markets and fair trading.

Key Terms

administered vertical marketing system a channel situation where a manufacturer that dominates a market through its size and strong brands may exercise considerable power over intermediaries even though they are independent

channel integration the way in which the players in the channel are linked

channel intermediaries organizations that facilitate the distribution of products to customers

channel of distribution the means by which products are moved from the producer to the ultimate consumer

channel strategy the selection of the most effective distribution channel, the most appropriate level of distribution intensity and the degree of channel integration

contractual vertical marketing system a franchise arrangement (e.g. a franchise) that ties together producers and resellers

corporate vertical marketing system a channel situation where an organization gains control of distribution through ownership

disintermediation the removal of channel partners by bypassing intermediaries and going directly from manufacturer to consumer via the internet

exclusive distribution an extreme form of selective distribution where only one wholesaler, retailer or industrial distributor is used in a geographical area to sell the products of a supplier

franchise a legal contract in which a producer and channel intermediaries agree each other's rights and obligations; usually the intermediary receives marketing, managerial, technical and financial services in return for a fee

intensive distribution the aim of this is to provide saturation coverage of the market by using all available outlets

reintermediation the introduction of new forms of channel intermediary that provide services which link members of the supply chain, for example web service providers and retailers

retail positioning the choice of target market and differential advantage for a retail outlet

selective distribution the use of a limited number of outlets in a geographical area to sell the products of a supplier

Study Questions

1. **The best way of distributing an industrial product is directly from manufacturer to customer. Discuss.**
2. **Why is channel selection an important decision? What factors influence choice?**
3. **What is meant by the partnership approach to managing distributors? What can manufacturers do to help build partnerships?**
4. **Describe situations that can lead to conflict between channel members. What can be done to avoid and resolve conflict?**
5. **What can be done to improve customer service standards in physical distribution?**
6. **What are the considerations a retailer might make when planning its channel strategy?**

Recommended Reading

Getting goods the last few miles to the consumer involves moving goods through distribution channels using complex logistics systems. Read about the evolution of retail logistics, the history of online retail, the growth of the internet as a retail channel and how to deploy multichannel strategies in retailing.

Doherty, N.F. and Ellis-Chadwick, F. (2010) Internet retailing: the past, the present and the future, *International Journal of Retail & Distribution Management* 38(11/12), 943–65.

Saghiri, S. Wilding, R. Mena, C. and Bourlakis, M. (2017) Towards a three-dimensional framework for omni-channel *Journal of Business Research*, 77 (August), 53–77.

References

BBC (2003) Store Wars: Fast Fashion, *The Money Programme*, 19 February.

Bell, D.R., Iyer, G. and Padmanabhan, V. (2002) Price competition under stockpiling and flexible consumption, *Journal of Marketing Research* 39(3), 292–303.

Berman, B. (2010) *Competing in Tough Times*, London: FT Press.

Bhaiya, A. (2017) The New Disintermediation, *Huffington Post*, 14 February, *https://www.huffingtonpost.com/amit-bhaiya/the-new-disintermediation_b_14681752.html?guccounter=1* (accessed October 2018)

Bloemer, S., de Ruyter, K. and Wetzels, M. (1999) Linking Perceived Service Quality and Service Loyalty: A Multi-Dimensional Perspective, *European Journal of Marketing* 33(11/12), 1082–106.

Brown, E. (2018) Will social commerce ever replace e-commerce? *Zdnet*, 20 August, https://www.zdnet.com/article/will-social-commerce-ever-replace-e-commerce/ (accessed November 2018)

Bunwell, S. (2005) One channel, many paths, *The Mobile Channel*, supplement to *Marketing Week*, 7 June, 5.

Burt, S. (2000) The strategic role of retail brands in british grocery retailing, *European Journal of Marketing* 34(8), 875–90.

Butler, S. (2015) Suppliers scared to blow the whistle on big retailers, *The Observer*, 8 February, 41.

Capell, K. (2008) Zara Thrives By Breaking All the Rules, *Business Week*, 20 October, 66.

Chaffey, D. (2018) Forecast growth in percentage of online retail/ecommerce sales, *Smart Insights*, 7 May

Chaffey, D. and Ellis-Chadwick, F (2019) *Digital Marketing: Strategy, Implementation and Practice*, Harlow, UK: Pearson Education Limited.

Chi, T. (2018) Understanding Chinese consumer adoption of apparel mobile commerce: An extended TAM approach, *Journal of Retailing and Consumer Services* 44, 274–84.

Costco (2015) *Investor Relations*, www.costco.com, 2 May. http://phx.corporate-ir.net/phoenix.zhtml?c=83830&p=irol-news&nyo=0 (accessed November 2018)

Cunningham, M.K. (2013) Reducing channel conflict, *Journal of Marketing Development and Competitiveness* 7(1), 78.

Coughlan, A., Anderson, E., Stern, L.W. and El-Ansany, A.I. (2005) *Marketing Channels*, Englewood Cliffs, NJ: Prentice-Hall, 6.

Court of Justice of the European Union (2012) press release No 80/12 Luxembourg, 14 June, Judgment in Case C-158/11 Auto 24 SARL v Jaguar Land Rover France SAS. http://curia.europa.eu/jcms/upload/docs/application/pdf/2012-06/cp120080en.pdf (accessed May 2015).

Dodds, L. (2014) eBay and Argos' click-and-collect deal goes nationwide, *The Telegraph*, 20 July. http://www.telegraph.co.uk/finance/newsbysector/retailandconsumer/10943206/eBay-and-Argos-click-and-collect-deal-goes-nationwide.html (accessed 20 April 2015).

Doherty, N. and Ellis-Chadwick, F. (2010) Internet retailing: the past, the present and the future, *International Journal of Retail & Distribution Management* 38(11/12), 943–65.

Dudley, J.W. (1990) *1992 Strategies for the Single Market*, London: Kogan Page, 327.

Ellis-Chadwick, F. (2011) An introduction to retail management and marketing, *The Open University*, block 1, 8–9.

Ellis-Chadwick F E (2013) History of online retailing, 14 October, http://www.open.edu/openlearn/money-management/management/business-studies/history-online-retail# (accessed October 2018)

Ellis-Chadwick (2018) The Future of Retailing: From Physical to Digital, in *The Routledge Companion of the History of Retailing*, Stobart, J. and Howard, V. (eds), 67–79.

Fahy, J. and Jobber, D. (2015) *Foundations of Marketing*, Maidenhead: McGraw-Hill.

Faran, B. (2018) Costco's retail innovation craze, *The Balance: Small Businesses*, https://www.thebalancesmb.com/costco-international-expansion-and-retail-innovation-2891768 (accessed October 2018)

Felsted, A. (2013) Waitrose to open remote click-and-collect food lockers, *The Financial Times*, 11 July. http://www.ft.com/cms/s/0/b1f3598a-ea43-11e2-b2f4-00144feabdc0.html#axzz3Z06RP4x2 (accessed 2 May 2015).

Fernie J., Sparks, L. and McKinnon, A.C. (2010) Retail logistics in the UK: past, present and future, *International Journal of Retail & Distribution Management* 38(11/12), 894–914.

Hayward, C. (2002) Who, Where, Win, *Marketing Week*, 12 September, 43.

Hernandez, H. (2011) Franchising in China, http://www. businessforum-china.com/article_detail.html?articleid 333, December (accessed October 2018).

Johnson, M. and Falstead, A. (2011) Inditex breaks new ground for season in the south, *Financial Times*, May, 17.

Joseph, S. (2013) Addias clamp down on discount retailers in about protecting brand legacy, *Marketing Week*, https://www.marketingweek.com/2013/12/04/adidas-clamp-down-on-discount-retailers-is-about-protecting-brand-legacy/ (accessed October 2018)

KFC (2018) Want to open a KFC? http://www.kfc.co.uk/our-restaurants/franchise (accessed October 2018).

Kumar, N., Scheer, L.K. and Steenkamp, J.-B.E.M. (1995) The effects of perceived interdependence on dealer attitudes, *Journal of Marketing Research* 32 (August), 248–56.

Lambert, K. (2005) Marriott Hip? Well, It's Trying, *Business Week*, 26 September, 79.

Lee, Y., Lee, Z. and Larsen, K.R. (2003) Coping with internet channel conflict, *Communications of the ACM* 46(7),137–42.

Macatonia, S. (2013) Going beyond fair trade: the benefits and challenges of direct trade, *The Guardian*, 13 March, 42.

McCawley, I. (2000) Small suppliers seek broader shelf access, *Marketing Week*, 17 February, 20.

Mellor, W. (2011) McDonald's no match for KFC in China as Colonel rules fast food, http://www.bloomberg.com/news/2011-01-26/mcdonald-s-no-match-for-kfc-in-china-where-colonel-sanders-rulesfast-food.html, 26 January (accessed October 2018).

Meville, S. (2014) Tesco share price: what analysts are saying, *The Independent*, 10 December. http://www.independent.co.uk/news/business/news/tesco-share-price-what-analysts-are-saying-9916346.html (accessed May 2015).

Mills, J.F. and Camek, V. (2004) The risks, threats and opportunities of disintermediation: a distributor's view, *International Journal of Physical Distribution and Logistics Management* 34(9), 714–27.

Mitchell, A. (2003) When push comes to shove, it's all about pull, *Marketing Week*, 9 January, 26–7.

Motorway Services Online (2015) Waitrose. http://motorwayservicesonline.co.uk/Waitrose (accessed October 2018).

Nagle, T.T. and Hogan, J.E. (2006) *The Strategy and Tactics of Pricing*, Upper Saddle River, NJ: Pearson.

Narus, J.A. and Anderson, J.C. (1986) Industrial distributor selling: the roles of outside and inside sales, *Industrial Marketing Management* 15, 55–62.

National Retail Federation (2018) Top 100 retailers, https://stores.org/2018/06/28/2018-top-100-retailers/ (accessed October 2018)

O'Brien, B (2017) 3 Innovative new delivery methods that are changing shipping, http://www.tradeready.ca/2017/topics/supply-chain-management/3-innovative-new-delivery-methods-changing-shipping-knowepidemi as we know it (accessed October 2018).

Ocado (2018) Ocado technology, http://www.ocadotechnology.com (accessed October 2018)

O'Reilly, L. (2013) Channel 4 contract marketers over WPP row, *Marketing Week*, 1 January, https://www.marketingweek.com/2013/01/01/channel-4-contacts-marketers-over-wpp-row/ (accessed October 2018)

Palmatier, R., Stern, L., El-Ansary, A. and Anderson, E. (2016) *Marketing Channel Strategy*, New York: Routledge.

Pegram, R. (1965) *Selecting and Evaluating Distributors*, New York: National Industrial Conference Board, 109–25.

Philpot, N. (1975) Managing the Export Function: Policies and Practice in Small and Medium Companies, *Management Survey Report No. 16*, British Institute of Management.

Planet Retail (2014) 76% of online shoppers to use click & collect by 2017. http://www1.planetretail.net/news-and-events/press-release/76-online-shoppers-use-click-collect-2017 (accessed 2 April 2015).

Rentokil Initial plc (2018) Pestaurant History, https://www.rentokil.co.uk/pestaurant-history/ (accessed October 2018)

Rigby, C. (2018) Monsoon make an extra £1.4 million in the first month of its ship-from-store project, 25 September, https://internetretailing.net/location/location/monsoon-makes-an-extra-14m-in-the-first-month-of-its-ship-from-store-project-18415 (accessed October 2018)

Ritson, M. (2008) iPhone strategy: no longer a grey area, *Marketing*, 11 June, 21.

Rosenbloom, B. (1987) *Marketing Channels: A Management View*, Hinsdale, IL: Dryden, 160.

Roux, C. (2002) The Reign of Spain, *The Guardian*, 28 October, 6–7.

Ryle, S. (2002) How to get ahead in advertising at no cost, *Observer*, 1 December, 8.

Sharma, D. and Parida, B. (2018) Determinants of conflict in channel relationships: a meta-analytic review, *Journal of Business and Industrial Marketing* 33(7), 911–30, https://doi.org/10.1108/JBIM-08-2016-0195

Shipley, D.D. and Prinja, S. (1988) The services and supplier choice influences of industrial distributors, *Service Industries Journal* 8(2), 176–87.

Shipley, D.D., Cook, D. and Barnett, E. (1989) Recruitment, motivation, training and evaluation of overseas distributors, *European Journal of Marketing* 23(2), 79–93.

Stanton, J. and Herbst, K. (2006) Slotting allowances: short-term gains and long-term negative effects on retailers and consumers, *International Journal of Retail & Distribution Management* 34(3), 187–97.

The Economist (2002) Chain Reaction, 2 February, 1–3.

The Economist (2005) Carrefour at the Crossroads, 22 October, 79.

Vanian, J. (2018) Amazon has over 100 million Prime members, *Fortune*,19 April, http://fortune.com/2018/04/18/amazon-prime-members-millions/ (accessed October 2018)

Verhoef, P., Kannan, P. and Inman, J. (2015) From multi-channel retailing to omni-channel retailing, *Journal of Retailing*, 8. http://ac.els-cdn.com/S0022435915000214/1-s2.0-S0022435915000214-main.pdf?_ tid=a237e420-f19e-11e4-b844-00000aab0f27&acdnat=1430662615_9950500b09ba86261ca27172443b4bf5 (accessed October 2018)

Vincent, J. (2014) Shop during your commute and pick it up at the station—Amazon Lockers arrive on the Tube. *The Independent*, 25 June. http://www.independent.co.uk/life-style/gadgets-and-tech/shop-during-your-commute-and-pick-it-up-at-the-station--amazon-lockers-arrive-on-the-tube-9562079.html (accessed 2 May 2015).

Vize, R., Coughlan, J., Kennedy, A. and Ellis-Chadwick, F. (2010) B2B relationship quality: do trust and commitment lead to loyalty? Exploring the factors that influence retailers' loyalty with web solution providers, 17th Recent Advances in Services Science Conference, European Institute of Retailing and Services Science, 2–5 July.

Webster, F.E. (1976) The role of the industrial distributor in marketing strategy, *Journal of Marketing* 40, 10–16.

Wikström, S. (2005) From e-channel to channel mix and channel integration, *Journal of Marketing Management* 21, 725–53.

Wulfratt, M. (2014) The secret to Costco's success lies in supply chain efficiency, *Canadian Grocer*, 13 May. http://www.canadiangrocer.com/blog/the-secret-to-costcos-success-lies-in-supply-chain-efficiency-40691 (accessed 2 May 2015).

Yum! (2018) *Building and defining global company that feeds the world.* Yum! 28 April. http://www.yum.com/company (accessed October 2018)

CASE 33
ASOS

Setting the Pace in Online Fashion

ASOS is the UK's largest online-only fashion retailer. The company has experienced phenomenal growth based on showing young shoppers how to emulate the designer looks of such celebrity magazine favourites as Kate Moss, Alexa Chung and Sienna Miller at a fraction of the cost.

ASOS was founded in 2000 by Nick Robertson. In 1996, he set up a business called Entertainment Marketing to place products in films and television programmes. By 2000, Robertson was running a website called AsSeenOnScreen, showing and selling brands that were used in films and on TV—from a pair of Oakley sunglasses worn by Tom Cruise in *Mission Impossible* to a pestle and mortar used by Jamie Oliver the *TV Chef*. But it was fashion that proved the biggest success, and Robertson decided to focus on that. ASOS was born. In 2015 Robertson was succeeded by the group's chief operating officer, Nick Beighton.

The company offers 85,000 branded and own-label product lines including womenswear, menswear, footwear, accessories, jewellery and beauty—a much wider range than that offered by other online rivals such as Topshop and New Look. Its key target market is women aged 18—34, with half of the online retailer's customers aged under 25. They demand new items to choose from, and ASOS provides this. Stock turnover (the speed at which items are replaced) is nine weeks, ensuring that visitors to the site are rewarded with new items on offer.

The company has its own design team and prefers to use suppliers based in Europe rather than the Far East. Between 60 and 70 per cent of its stock is made in Europe. This means that from spotting a celebrity wearing a new style of dress ASOS designers and buyers are in a position to have similar ones made and ready to sell in four weeks.

The ASOS Website

A major factor in the success of ASOS is its website. Visitors to the site can click on their favourite celebrity or pop star and view clothes they have been seen in. Perhaps a shopper prefers the style of Kate Moss. The cheapest way is not to visit ASOS's bricks-and-mortar competitor Topshop, but to choose a £6 ASOS Lurex vest 'in the style of' the London supermodel. At any one time on the website there are over 400 styles of dresses plus mountains of tops, trousers, shoes, bags, lingerie, swimwear and jewellery and an entire men's section, all of which is modelled by people walking on a catwalk. At the ASOS headquarters in North London, there are four studios where a pool of 30 models attempt to bring the clothes to life and transmit the excitement of the catwalk to the consumer.

The range of brands has expanded from own-label celebrity-lookalike items to include its own luxury brand, together with well-established labels such as Nike, Levi's, Calvin Klein and Tommy Hilfiger. The website attracts 100 million visitors a month and 12 million active customers (those who have bought within the past six 6 months), who place orders worth, on average, £60. Women's fashion items make up the vast majority of sales. Menswear accounts for 20 per cent of sales with beauty and cosmetics a further 3 per cent.

One problem with buying online rather than in a traditional retail outlet is that returns are higher. An average catalogue company experiences about 40 per cent returns, but ASOS achieves the much lower figure of 22 per cent. A key feature of ASOS's marketing tactics is to offer free delivery anywhere in the world and free returns in the UK. In 2016, the offer of free returns was expanded to customers in all European countries where it operates. It also offers

customers the opportunity to try on their products before buying them. This means that they do not have to claim a refund for items they return to ASOS.

Customer Service

ASOS aims for fast speed of delivery, and, when a delay is foreseeable, every effort is made to contact the customer. For example, when snow was forecast, emails were sent warning customers of probable delays. When it did snow, an apology email was sent offering a delivery refund and 10 per cent off next orders. The customer care team is available 24 hours a day. They are required to reply to customer enquiries within an hour and are assessed by the speed and quality of their reply. For a small charge, next day delivery is offered to UK customers.

Promotion

ASOS's success has provided many opportunities for public relations activity in newspapers, including quarterly reports on record profits and sales, and features on the reasons for its success. ASOS prefers digital to traditional media, although the latter is sometimes used, including poster advertising. Digital channels such as Instagram and Snapchat are used to connect with customers; ASOS has a total of 20 million social media followers. Search engine optimization and pay-per-click advertising on women's magazine sites such as *Look* and *Grazia* help to generate traffic to ASOS's site. Social networking also plays a part in raising awareness. ASOS has the second-largest UK fan group for any fashion retailer on Facebook (behind H&M). In 2011, ASOS launched a Facebook application that allows customers to make purchases from the store without leaving the social networking site. In the UK, half of sales come from mobile devices, and ASOS has launched a mobile app that allows customers to upload photos snapped from pages of magazines or social media to search for a similar outfit from their website.

ASOS's largest marketing expenditure is on a print magazine which is carefully targeted to reach 450,000 active customers. It showcases well-known brands as well as its own brands, and photos are blended with editorial content to rival the standards of newsstand glossies. It is also available online. This is supplemented by 24-page supplements in magazines such as *Glamour* and *Cosmopolitan* and sponsorship of the Sky Living show *America's Next Top Model*. ASOS achieves 60 per cent awareness among its target market. All this activity is supported by an in-house content team that produces video and editorial content for its print magazine, website and social media.

New Ventures

A major source of sales and profit growth has been overseas expansion with new websites being established in the USA, Germany, France, Spain, Denmark, Russia, Italy and Australia. Two European hubs have been built in Germany, and in 2019 in the USA a dedicated £30 million warehouse in Atlanta will be operational to supplement the one in Ohio. However, a setback to ASOS's overseas expansion plans occurred in 2016: ASOS closed its local operations in China when faced with problems from the Chinese postal service and fierce competition from Alibaba, which dominates online fashion in China. The company supplies goods to an additional 230 countries. Around 60 per cent of revenue is now generated from international sales.

ASOS has also launched a number of extensions from the core brand including:

- ASOS Marketplace: this allows customers to sell their own clothes and accessories on the ASOS site—whether they are recycling their clothes for cash or opening a boutique to sell their own designs. ASOS receives commission on sales.
- Little ASOS: this site caters for babies and children aged two to six years. As well as stocking ranges from high-fashion brands such as Diesel and Tommy Hilfiger, Little ASOS offers a number of boutique and independent labels such as Cath Kidston and No Added Sugar.
- ASOS Outlet: this is the discount arm of ASOS, offering end-of-line and previous season products at discounts of up to 75 per cent.
- ASOS Fashion Finder: showcases fashion trends and allows customers to research outfit building and creation. Visitors to the site are redirected to rival retailers if the product the shopper wants is not available at ASOS.

ASOS is not alone in selling online fashion worldwide. For example, boohoo.com dispatches to 100 countries and is differentiated from ASOS, as all its clothes are own brand and sell at lower price points. Its target market is 16- to 24-year-olds who are looking for inexpensive fashion items.

Questions

1. **Discuss the advantages and disadvantages of marketing fashion items online rather than through traditional retail stores.**
2. **To what extent does ASOS operate an integrated distribution channel system?**

3. **Perform a strengths, weaknesses, opportunities and threats (SWOT) analysis on ASOS.**
4. **On the basis of the SWOT analysis, what are your recommendations for ASOS?**

This case study was prepared by David Jobber, Emeritus Professor of Marketing, University of Bradford.

References

Based on: Finch, J. (2008) Nick Robertson: Wannabe Celebs Provide The Silver On Screen, *The Guardian*, 18 April, 31; Kollewe, J. (2008) Asos Defies Shopping Gloom by Reaching Height of Online Fashion, *The Guardian*, 18 November, 32; Barda, T. (2009) Winning Looks, *Marketer*, April, 24–7; Armstrong, L. (2009) Asos.com: As Seen On The Screens of The Fashion Savvy, *The Times*, 21 January, 26; Asos.com http://en. wikipedia.org/w/index; Costa, M. (2011) Fashion Leader Maps Out an International Future, *Marketing Week*, 16 June, 17–20; Treanor, J. (2012) Asos Managers Share £66m Bonus Pot, *The Guardian*, 25 May, 33; Butler, S. and S. Farrell (2014) Soaring Asos Is Latest Online Success Story, *The Guardian*, 15 January, 20;Butler, S. (2016) Asos to Reinvest China Savings in Euro Operations, *The Guardian*, 13 April, 19; Wood, Z. (2017) Asos App Allows Shoppers to Snap Up Fashion, www.theguardian.com/business, 15 July; Farrell, S. (2017) Asos Marches On, *The Observer*, 15 November, 39; Asos Annual Report 2017 www.annualreports.co.uk/Company/asos-plc; Wood, Z. (2018) Asos's 'Try Before You Buy' Pitch to Young Shoppers Pushes Up Sales, *The Guardian*, 26 January, 37; Fletcher, N. (2018) Fashion Forward—Asos Has Ambitions for Big Expansion, *The Observer*, 8 April, 58.

CASE 34
Walmart and Asda

Battling for Retail Success

Enter any Walmart store in the USA and you are struck by the sheer scale of the operation. These are stores of over 200,000 square feet in which seven UK superstores could be accommodated. Next come the 'greeters', who welcome customers into the stores, give them their card in case they need help and put a smiley sticker on them. Then come the prices where, for example, a cotton T-shirt that would sell for the equivalent of around $15 (£11/€13) in a UK department store sells for $1 (£0.80/€0.90) in Walmart. The choice of products is wide ranging, from clothes via groceries and pharmaceuticals to electrical goods. Stores are well organized with the right goods always available, are kept neat and clean in appearance and have goods helpfully displayed.

At the heart of the Walmart operation are its systems and information technology: 1,000 information technologists run a massive database; its information collection, which comprises over 65 million transactions (by item, time, price and store), drives most aspects of its business. Within 90 minutes of an item being sold, Walmart's distribution centres are organizing its replacement. Distribution is facilitated by state-of-the-art delivery tracking systems. So effective is the system that when a flu epidemic hit the USA, Walmart followed its spread by monitoring flu remedy sales in its stores. It then predicted its movement from east to west so that Walmart stores were adequately stocked in time for the rise in demand.

Walmart also uses real-time information systems to let consumers decide what appears in its stores. The internet is used to inform suppliers of what was sold the day before. In this way, it only buys what sells.

Its relationship with its suppliers is unusual in that they are only paid when an item is sold in its stores. Not only does this help cash flow, it also ensures that the interests of manufacturer and Walmart coincide. Instead of the traditional system where once the retailer had purchased stock it was essentially the retailer's problem to sell it, if the product does not sell it hurts the manufacturer's cash flow more than Walmart's. Consequently, at a stroke, the supplier's and retailer's interests are focused on the same measures and rewards. There is no incentive for the supplier to try to sell Walmart under-performing brands, since they will suffer in the same way as the retailer if they fail to sell in the store.

Walmart staff are called 'associates' and are encouraged to tell top management what they believe is wrong with their stores. They are offered share options and encouraged to put the customer first.

Walmart has enjoyed phenomenal success in the USA, but faced a tough challenge by its rival, Target, which has built its business by selling similar basic consumable goods like soap at low prices, but also higher-margin, design-based items such as clothing and furnishings. The problem Walmart faced was that consumers were buying groceries and toiletries at its stores but not its clothing, furnishing or electronics ranges. Target was stealing customers by positioning itself as an upmarket discounter using designers such as Isaac Mizraki and stylish lifestyle advertising to attract consumers to its clothing and furnishings. Walmart, by contrast, was using mundane in-store advertising focusing on low prices.

Walmart's response was to commission, for the first time, a marketing research survey. Hitherto it had believed that marketing research was the province of its suppliers. The survey of its customers revealed that Walmart's clothing was considered dull. This led to the launch in 2005 of a more upmarket fashion brand, Metro 7, targeted at the group Walmart called 'selective shoppers'—those who buy groceries and toiletries but who previously would not have bought clothing. The new clothing range was backed by a change in advertising, including a spread in *Vogue* magazine and a move to lifestyle advertising, designed to appeal to what the retailer termed 'fashion-savvy' female customers with an urban lifestyle. However, Metro 7 failed, as the line was not 'hip' enough to attract fashion buyers or cheap enough to appeal to traditional Walmart customers.

Walmart also redesigned its electronics and furnishings departments and improved the product ranges to appeal to wealthier customers. In consumer electrics, for example, it added high-end products from Sony LCD televisions, to Toshiba laptops and Apple iPods, and backed the new ranges with aggressive advertising campaigns. Departments were redesigned with wider aisles and lower shelves. Walmart revamped all its stores to make them appear less dull and appeal to middle-income shoppers trading down in the recession.

The retailer also employed what it termed its 'win, play or show' strategy. 'Win' product categories are those where Walmart can outmanoeuvre rivals with low prices on high-demand products such as flat-screen TVs, including higher-end models. This has increased Walmart's share of TVs while increasing margins. 'Play' applies to areas like clothing where Walmart can be a player but is unlikely to dominate. Here, product lines are pruned to top sellers like $20 Levi jeans while cutting back on higher-end items. 'Show' are the one-stop-shopping essentials such as hardware, which are necessary to compete in the USA with rivals like Home Depot. Here, product lines like hammers and tape measures are restricted to one or two brands.

However, Walmart has been criticized for being slow to fully embrace the opportunities provided by online shopping. In response, the company embarked on a major investment programme to rectify this weakness.

Walmart's Overseas Operations

Since 1992, Walmart has moved into 28 countries, and this strategy has been the engine for most of its sales and profit growth in recent years. In Canada and Mexico it is already market leader in discount retailing. In Canada, it bought Woolco in 1994, quickly added outlets, and by 1997 became market leader with 45 per cent of the discount store market—a remarkable achievement. In countries such as China and Argentina it has been surprisingly successful and international sales have grown to over 25 per cent of total revenue.

In 1998, it entered Europe with the buying of Germany's Wertkauf warehouse chain, quickly followed by the acquisition of 74 Interspar hypermarkets. It immediately closed stores and then reopened them with price cuts on 1,100 items, making the items 10 per cent below competitors' prices. Walmart's German operation was not a success, however, because of the presence of more aggressive discounters such as Aldi. In 2006, it admitted failure by selling its 85 stores to a local rival, Metro, at a loss of £530 million (€600 million).

Walmart's entry into the UK was the next step in its move into the European market. Asda was a natural target since it shared Walmart's 'everyday low prices' culture. It was mainly a grocery supermarket, but also sold clothing. Its information technology systems lagged badly behind those of its UK supermarket competitors, but it has acted as 'consumer champion' by selling cosmetics and over-the-counter pharmaceuticals for cheaper prices than those charged by traditional outlets. Walmart decided to keep the Asda store name rather than rebranding it as Walmart. Most of Asda's stores are located in the north of the UK.

The early signs were that the acquisition was a success with sales and profits rising. A major move was to create a speciality division that operates pharmacy, optical, jewellery, photography and shoe departments. The aim was to make store space work harder (i.e. improve sales revenue and profits per square metre). Asda has also benefited from the introduction of thousands of non-food items across a wide range of home and leisure categories. Space has been made for these extra products in existing food-dominated supermarkets by decreasing the amount of shelf space devoted to food and reducing pack sizes.

The George line of clothing was a huge success and was expanded to include a lower-priced version of the brand called Essentially George. So impressed were Walmart management with the success of George clothing that they introduced the range in their own stores. Asda took the George brand to the high street by launching standalone 10,000-square-foot clothing stores branded George. The stores carried the complete line of George-brand men's, women's and children's clothing at prices which were the same as those offered in the George departments in Asda supermarkets. However, in the face of competition from Primark and New Look, they were only moderately successful.

Besides expanding its product lines, Asda has also focused on cutting prices, aided by its inclusion in the Walmart stable, which brings it enormous buying power. For example, since the takeover, it has made 60 per cent savings on fabrics and 15 per cent on buttons. This has meant price reductions on such clothing items as jeans, ladies' tailored trousers, skirts, silk ties and baby pyjamas. In four years, the price of George jeans fell from £15 (€17) to £6 (€6.80).

»

»

Change of Fortune

Asda's initial success was reflected in its overtaking of Sainsbury's to become the UK's number two supermarket chain behind Tesco in 2004. Shortly afterwards, however, Asda's fortunes changed. Faced with a rampant Tesco and a resurgent Sainsbury's, the company lost market share. When Walmart bought Asda, the intention was to build huge, US-style hypermarkets. Unfortunately, shortly after the acquisition, UK planning rules tightened to prevent out-of-town shopping developments. Tesco, and to a lesser extent Sainsbury's, entered the smaller store market, opening outlets in town and city centres and petrol stations where planning restrictions were much less severe. Asda kept its focus on large supermarkets.

In 2005, Andy Bond was promoted internally to replace Tony de Nunzio, who left to join Dutch non-food retailer Vendex. Faced with a dominant Tesco with over 30 per cent market share, and a more aggressive Sainsbury's under the leadership of Justin King, Bond faced an enormous challenge. Helped by Asda's positioning as a cut-price, full-range supermarket, Bond met with early success. Some of his key actions were as follows.

- Removed 1,400 managers: 200 jobs at Asda's head office and 1,200 junior managerial positions in stores were cut. Part of the savings were invested in front-line customer service staff in stores.
- Opened 17 more Asda Living stores to bring the total to 22 and developed the Living range online: these are non-food stores offering such products as homeware, electrical goods, George clothing, music and video, health and beauty, and toys and baby products. It was planned that by 2015, 150 Asda Living stores would have been opened. However, by 2017 only 33 were operating.
- Slowed the growth of George fashion store openings and in 2010 closed all of them, citing high rental costs.
- Trialled two Asda Essentials stores: these were small-format stores to challenge Tesco Express and Sainsbury's Local convenience stores. They stocked a limited range of products, including fresh food, and were based on the French Leader Price chain, which sells fresh fruit, vegetables, meat, grocery products and cosmetics. The stores sold almost entirely Asda own-label products. After less than a year one of these trial stores was closed and Asda announced it had no plans to open any more.
- Improved the product line: healthier food sourced from local producers, and sold new products online such as contact lenses and airline tickets.
- Urged the Office of Fair Trading to open an inquiry into Tesco's land bank of 185 development sites with a view to preventing it buying land and opening stores close to existing outlets without reference to the OFT. And if an existing store was sold by one supermarket chain to another, the deal had to be scrutinized by the competition authority.
- Responded to the recession by selling hundreds of products for £1, offering 50p bargains including 400 g of mince, 2 pints of milk, a white loaf, six eggs and 2 kg of carrots, and launching a TV campaign (supported by evidence from the price comparison website moneysupermarket.com) showing how Asda was cheaper than Tesco.
- Adopted the 'less is more' strategy, which includes dropping secondary brands to concentrate on the biggest brand names.

Changes at the Top

In 2010, Bond resigned from his post as chief executive to take up the role of part-time chairman. He was replaced by Andy Clarke, formerly Asda's chief operating officer. One of Clarke's first moves was to buy the 193 UK stores off Danish discount retailer Netto. Netto stores averaged only 750 square metres compared with Asda's average superstore of 4,300 square metres.

Clarke soon faced an onslaught from the discount chains Aldi and Lidl, which competed by offering lower prices than Asda and smaller local stores. He responded by slashing prices, revamping Asda's 170 medium stores, giving more space to fresh food, hot food, and health and beauty products, while taking out a fifth of the space devoted to goods now bought mainly online, such as televisions, DVDs and CDs. Asda has also grown its online grocery business, including expanding click-and-collect locations from 250 in 2013 to 650 by 2018. Further, unlike Tesco, which retrenched, Asda opened more stores, particularly small and medium-sized supermarkets and outlets at petrol outlets. However, Clarke decided to avoid expansion into the convenience store sector, which is dominated by Tesco and Sainsbury's. 'Online and click and collect is our convenience solution,' he said.

In 2016, Andy Clarke stood down to make way for Sean Clarke, who was chief executive officer at Walmart China, in the face of declining sales and consumer perceptions of the brand. Sean Clarke, too, was replaced—by his deputy Roger Burnley—after just 18 months. Burnley returned to Asda after working for Sainsbury's as retail and operations director.

In 2018, it was announced that Sainsbury's and Asda had agreed a merger in a £10 (€11) billion deal that would see Walmart retain 42 per cent of the new company. The deal between the UK's second and third biggest supermarkets, if approved by the Competition and Markets Authority, would give the combined company 31 per cent of the supermarket sector just ahead of the current leader Tesco. Sainsbury's is no stranger to takeovers, having bought Argos, the catalogue store, in 2016 and loyalty scheme Nectar in 2018.

Questions

1. **Did Walmart's acquisition of Asda make competitive sense?**
2. **Why did Asda's fortunes worsen around 2004?**
3. **Assess the actions taken by Andy Bond and Andy Clarke to revive Asda.**
4. **What advantages does a Sainsbury's and Asda merger provide for the combined company, and what are the risks?**

This case was written by David Jobber, Emeritus Professor of Marketing, University of Bradford.

References

Based on: Merrilees, B. and D. Miller (1999) Defensive Segmentation Against a Market Spoiler Rival, *Proceedings of the Academy of Marketing Conference*, Stirling, July, 1–10; Teather, D. (2003) Asda's £360m Plan Will Create 3,900 Jobs, *The Guardian*, 19 February, 23; Troy, M. (2003) 'Buy' George! Wal-Mart's Asda Takes Fashion to UK's High Street, *DSN Retailing Today*, 23 June, 1; Finch, J. (2005) Asda to Open Hundreds of Discount Shops, *The Guardian*, 10 December, 22; Finch, J. (2005) Asda Cuts 1400 Managers in Fight to Stay No 2 Grocer, *The Guardian*, 6 July, 16; Birchall, J. (2005) What Wal-Mart Women Really Want, *Financial Times*, 10 October, 11; Birchall, J. (2005) Supermarket Sweep, *The Financial Times*, 10 November, 17; Anonymous (2006) Wal-Mart Admits Defeat in Germany and Sells Stores, *The Guardian*, 24 July, 32; Palmeri, C. (2008) Wal-Mart Is Up For This Downturn, *Businessweek*, 30 October, 42; Finch, J. and A. Clark (2008) 70,000 Extra Customers a Week Head For Asda, *The Guardian*, 10 July, 27; Finch, J. (2009) Asda Sales Continue To Soar As 'Intelligent Offers' Pull in Record 18m Shoppers a Week, *The Guardian*, 14 August, 23; Wood, Z. and G. Wearden (2010) Asda Boss Andy Bond Stuns City by Quitting, *The Guardian*, 13 April, 24; Finch, J. and Z. Wood (2010) Asda Buys Netto for £778m in Attempt to Close Gap on Tesco, *The Guardian* 28 May, 33; Boyle, M. and D. MacMillan (2011) Wal-Mart's Rocky Path From Bricks to Clicks, *Bloomberg Business Week*, 25–31 July, 31–3; Felsted, A. (2012) Asda Goes for Growth but Tesco Pulls Back, *The Financial Times*, 24 January, 18; Butler, s. Asda Launches Tube Station Grocery Collections, Guardian, 20 November, 31; Butler, S. (2015) Tesco Is Having Heart Surgery, Says Asda Boss, *The Guardian*, 6 February, 28; Butler, S. (2015) Asda Reveals Plans to Open More Stores As Sales Slip, Guardian, 20 February, 27; Butler S. (2015) Asda Sales Slump Worst of the Big Four, *The Guardian*, 20 May, 19; Vizard, S. (2016) Asda's New Boss Will Need to Turn Around the Brand, Not Just Its Sales, www.marketingweek.com, 13 June; Vizard, S. and R. Parsons (2018) Sainsbury's and Asda in 'Advanced Talks Over Shock Merger, www.marketing week.com 28 April; Hammett, E. (2018) Sainsbury's and Asda to Operate 'Dual-Brand Strategy' in Merger That Creates New Supermarket, www.marketingweek.com 30 April.

PART 4 MARKETING PLANNING AND STRATEGY

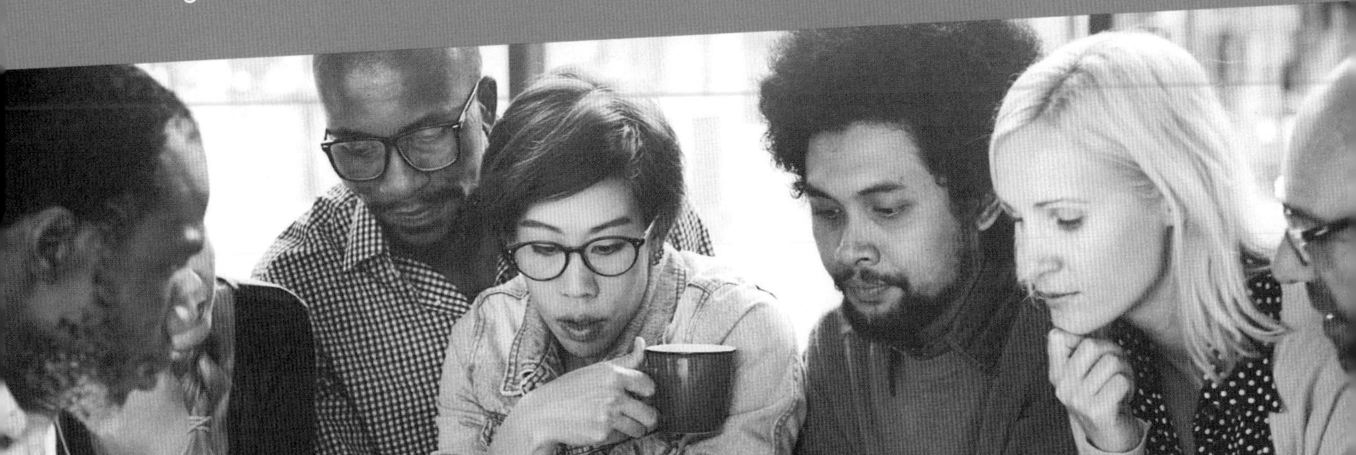

A number of videos featuring CEOs, CMOs, brand and PR managers related to the Chapters in this Part are available to lecturers for presentation and class discussion.

CHAPTER 18
Marketing Planning: An Overview of Strategic Analysis and Decision-making

> *Fact is, inventing an innovative business model is often mostly a matter of serendipity.*
>
> **GARY HAMEL (VAN VLIET, 2011)**

LEARNING OBJECTIVES

After reading this chapter, you should be able to:

1. describe the role of marketing planning within businesses
2. identify the key planning questions
3. discuss the process of marketing planning
4. describe the concept of the business mission
5. explain the marketing audit and SWOT analysis
6. discuss the nature of marketing objectives
7. identify the components of core strategy and how to test its effectiveness
8. explain marketing mix decisions in relation to the planning process
9. discuss implementation and control in the marketing planning process
10. describe the rewards and problems associated with marketing planning
11. discuss recommendations to overcome marketing planning problems

Part 1 explores the fundamentals of marketing, which inform the development of a marketing plan; Part 2 considers how core elements of marketing can be used to create value for customers; Part 3 studies how to communicate and deliver customer value. In Part 4, our attention turns to how to bring all these elements of marketing theory and practice together in a cohesive and coherent manner. The focus is on managing, planning and applying strategic thinking within the framework of marketing.

This chapter explores the marketing planning framework and discusses ways to develop a manageable approach towards implementing the marketing concept (as discussed in Chapter 1). Chapter 19 focuses on specific strategic notions—competitor analysis—and in doing so presents ways of creating competitive advantage. Chapter 20 examines product strategy and looks at ways in which products can be used for growth. Chapter 21 investigates what is involved in developing global marketing strategies. Chapter 22 discusses implementation and many issues at the heart of the application of the principles and practice of marketing.

Marketing planning and strategy comprises a complex and resource-intensive set of processes that can deliver great rewards if fully embraced. However, the marketing environment is in flux: digital technologies are disrupting and reshaping the marketing landscape and speeding up the rate of change. No longer does it take years to bring a new product to market; Twitter emerged within less than 18 months from concept to global adoption as a marketing tool. Arguably, this situation makes Gary Hamel's notion of serendipitous business planning (in the quotation above) seem quite compelling. But for marketing to function effectively across an organization, it should act as a guiding business philosophy for improving performance. Therefore, to gain the potential advantages that marketing might bring, managers must make and communicate many marketing planning decisions, for example which customer groups to serve, how to create value-added products and services, which technology to use and which marketing strategies are most likely to deliver competitive advantages. Managers must also consider the impact of the environment and determine how to get the best strategic fit between their organization's capabilities and resources and the market opportunities.

This chapter presents the **marketing planning** framework, which addresses many of the key questions and decisions a manager might encounter and provides a straightforward structured framework for handling all the complexities that marketers must accommodate. We begin the chapter by considering the marketing planning context. Then we delve into the key functions of marketing planning, before exploring the stages in the marketing planning process. The chapter concludes by looking at the rewards and problems of marketing planning.

Marketing Planning Context

Marketing planning is part of a broader concept of *corporate strategic planning* which involves all business functions: marketing, operations, finance, human resources, information management, distribution and the trading environment. The aim of corporate strategic planning is to provide direction, so that a firm can direct its activities to meet high-level corporate objectives, for example being market leader or improving profitability. Marketing links to this high level of strategic planning by managing the interface between a company and its environment; for example, a corporate objective to be market leader will take account of the economic forces and their impact on a market. So, the marketing planning team carrying out a marketing audit, for example, should produce enough knowledge to enable the corporate management team to make long-term strategic decisions, thereby creating a link between strategy and marketing planning.

The role of marketing planning in strategy development is complex and can vary considerably in terms of what is involved. At the simplest level, a company may market only one product in one market. In this case, the role of marketing planning is to ensure that the marketing plan for the product matches its customers' needs. Also, the company can use all available resources to achieve its marketing objectives—for example, to sell more products. This should also enable the marketing plan to feed into the corporate objective of becoming market leader. However, this is rarely the case, as companies tend to offer many products and/or services to many different target markets. In this situation, decisions should be made about the allocation of resources to each product and/or service. This is far from a straightforward process, as resource allocation is dependent on the attractiveness of the market for each product and the capabilities and resources of the company.

EXHIBIT 18.1
Virgin is a disruptive and innovative brand that aims to stand out; see how StartJG's graphic captures the essence of the Virgin brand

To add to the complexity, a company may comprise several discrete but connected divisions (or totally separate companies) each of which serves distinct groups of customers and has a distinct set of competitors (Day, 1984). For example: the Virgin Group operates many companies in different activity sectors, such as media (Virgin Media); music (Virgin Megastore); travel (Virgin Atlantic Airways). Each business may be strategically autonomous and thus form a **strategic business unit** (SBU). For example, the Virgin Group is made up of a *community* of independently operating companies (see Exhibit 18.1). A major component of a strategic plan—at the corporate level—is allocation of resources to each SBU. Strategic decisions at the corporate level are normally concerned with acquisition, divestment and diversification (Weitz and Wensley, 1988). In the Virgin Group example, each company contributes to the overarching aims of the group—that is, Virgin Media was created through mergers with NTL, Telewest and Virgin Mobile. The decisions to add or release a business are taken at the corporate and strategic planning level. Richard Branson, the founder of the Virgin empire, expanded the business's reach by entering diverse markets: finance and insurance—Virgin Money (Australia, South Africa, UK); health clubs—Virgin Active (UK, Italy, South Africa, Thailand); gaming—Virgin Casino (USA, UK). Marketing feeds into such corporate decision-making by identifying opportunities and threats in the environment. So, the opportunity to develop the travel arm of the Virgin Group by adding Virgin Hotels is likely to have emerged from marketing planning actions.

In summary, marketing planning is part of the overarching corporate strategic planning process and provides a range of insights from the trading environment to identify target markets and customer needs. There are two other aspects of marketing planning to consider: the core functions and key planning processes of marketing planning.

The Functions of Marketing Planning

Arguably, the core function of a marketing plan is to answer the following questions:

1 Where are we now?
2 Where would we like to be?

3 How do we get there?
4 Are we on course?

For the marketing planning team at Virgin, answering these questions means considering:

- Where are we now? Looking at the current position of the business in terms of its past performance, considering the effectiveness of previous marketing plans and questioning what might happen if there were no changes in current practice. In its annual financial statement, Virgin Atlantic reported strong performance against its objectives, managing its resources effectively through continuing tough economic conditions and against strong competition in the airline industry (Virgin Atlantic, 2018).
- Where would we like to be? The future direction of the business is defined by its marketing objectives. Virgin's corporate objective is to 'offer *the best business product* in the air', so the implications for the marketing planning team are setting suitable objectives which ensure improved customer service of its *business* products.
- How do we get there? This can be answered in the case of Virgin Atlantic by looking at the needs of business travellers and considering their expectations and experiences. Virgin has won industry awards for its Upper Class Suite, which is designed to be a first-class product for a business-class fare. The marketing planning team looked at this key target audience (business travellers) and devised a marketing mix strategy that it could implement to achieve its marketing objectives.
- Are we on course? This question is answered by looking at performance measures. Like many companies, Virgin measures sales and profitability but it uses other measures such as increase in fuel efficiency and reduction in carbon emissions, targeting the use of sustainable products and renewable resources.

The core functions of marketing planning addressed by these questions link into specific stages in the marketing planning process (see Table 18.1). 'Where are we now?' is forecast by reference to the marketing audit and SWOT (strengths, weaknesses, opportunities and threats) analysis. 'Where would we like to be?' is determined by the setting of marketing objectives. 'How do we get there?' refers to core strategy, marketing mix decisions, organization and implementation. Finally, 'Are we on course?' is answered by the establishment of a control system.

TABLE 18.1 Key questions and the process of marketing planning

Key questions	Stages in marketing planning
Where are we now?	Business mission, marketing audit, SWOT analysis
Where would we like to be?	Marketing objectives
How do we get there?	Core strategy, marketing mix decisions, organization, implementation
Are we on course?	Control

The next section discusses the process of marketing planning in detail.

The Process of Marketing Planning

Planning is rarely straightforward. Different people are involved at various stages of the planning process. The key marketing planning process can broadly be divided into two distinct areas:

1 the business unit level—e.g. Virgin Atlantic
2 the product level—e.g. Virgin flights to America.

The process of marketing planning is outlined in Figure 18.1. This overview of the framework provides a systematic way for understanding the analysis and the decision-making processes involved in marketing planning. Additionally, the framework shows how key elements of marketing—discussed in subsequent chapters—relate to each other and fit into the planning process.

FIGURE 18.1
The marketing planning process

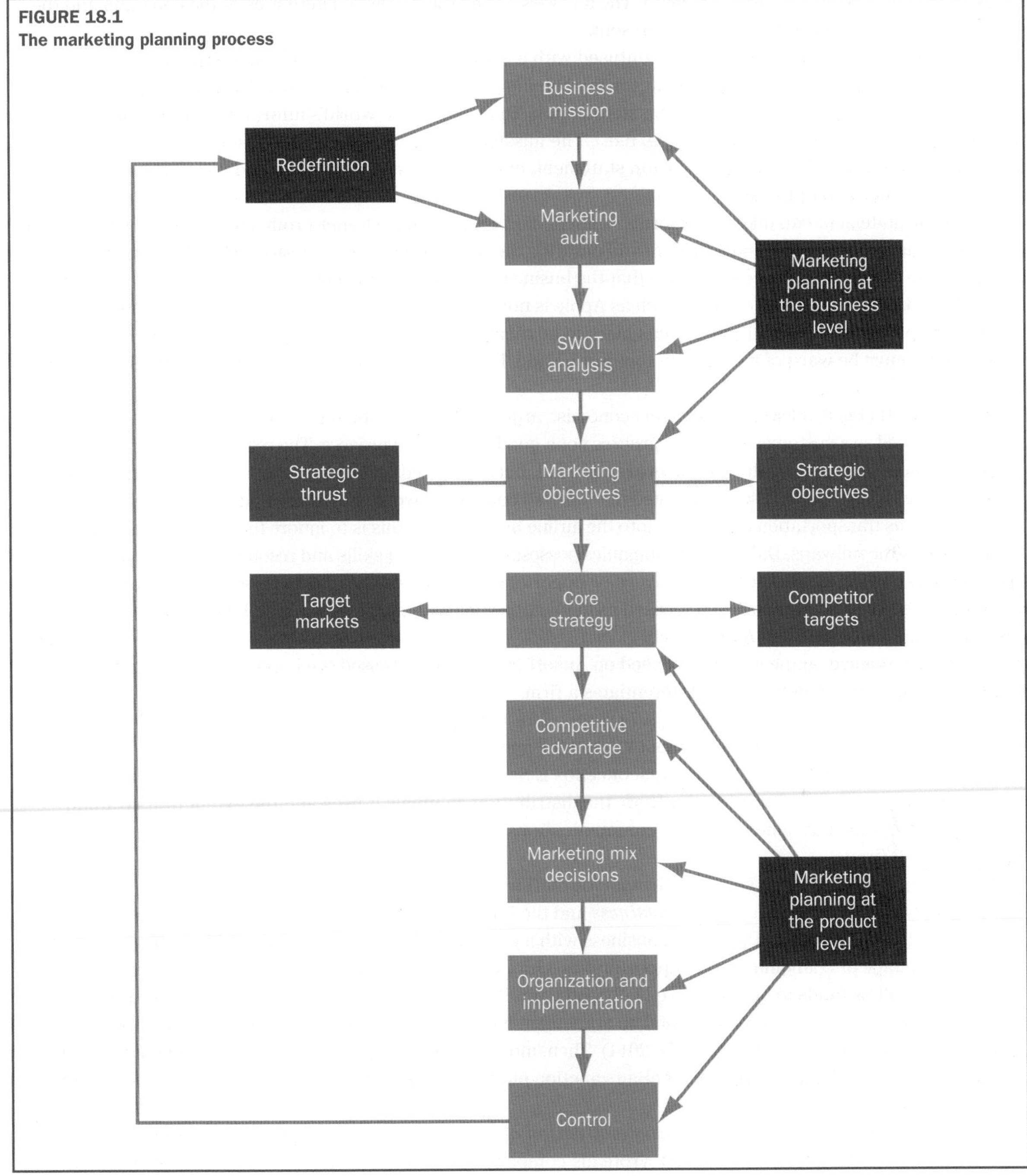

Business mission: how to define a business

Simply answer this question: 'What does a business do to make a living?' (Vasconcellos E Sa, 2014). But the answer is not always straightforward. According to Russell Ackoff, an American organizational theorist, a **business mission** is: 'A broadly defined, enduring statement of purpose that distinguishes a business from others of its type' (Ackoff, 1987). This definition captures essential ingredients of mission statements: they are enduring and specific to the individual organization (Hooley, Cox and Adams, 1992) and set out 'What business are we in?' and 'What business we want to be in?' (Drucker, 2007). The answers define the scope and activities of the company and the reason for its existence, and focus on the present.

The mission statement should not be confused with a vision statement, which looks to the future; for example, Samsung's 2020 vision statement for the coming decade is 'Inspire the world, create the future' (Samsung, n.d.), whereas Google's mission statement is 'to organize the world's information and make it universally accessible and useful' (Google, n.d.). The mission statement defines the business and is the foundation on which to build a future vision statement, and both mission statement and vision statement can inspire confidence and optimism.

A mission statement can take many forms, but it should reflect the customer groups being served (the market), refer to the customer needs being satisfied, and describe the process by which a customer need can be satisfied. The inclusion of market and needs ensures that the business definition is market focused rather than product based. Thus, the purpose of a company such as Apple is not to manufacture computers but to solve customers' information problems. While this advice has merit in advocating the avoidance of a narrow business definition, management must be wary of a definition that is too wide. Four key influences on shaping a business mission are described below.

Firstly, Levitt (1960), a leading American economist, argued a mission should focus on *needs* and that a business should be viewed as a customer-satisfying process not a goods-producing process. The reason for ensuring a business definition is market focused is that products are transient, but basic needs such as transportation, entertainment and eating are lasting. Levitt (1960) suggested that railway companies would have survived had they defined their business as transportation and moved into the airline business. But this is to ignore the limits of the business competence of the railways. Did railway companies possess the necessary skills and resources to run an airline? However, by adopting a customer perspective, new opportunities are more likely to be revealed. For example, Apple has streamlined its product ranges and focused its innovations on customers' needs for mobile computing, through the MacBook, iPhone, iPad and Apple Watch.

A second influence on the mission is based on Ansoff (1987), who stressed the importance of the *product* (or service) offer, which defines and differentiates a firm.

A third influence proposed by Hanan (1974) argued for the importance of the *client*, and suggested that a business should focus the mission statement around the importance of the customer.

A forth influence is global *location* (Vasconcellos E Sa, 2014). The location of a firm's target markets can define the products and services it offers, the distribution channels it uses and the extent of its trading operation. Free trade agreements, global communications and transportation systems have widened horizons for all firms.

Ultimately, a firm's mission should reflect all four influences and also:

- *provide a solid understanding of the business* and the forces acting on its operations, which might change in the future. For example, PayPal is a business with a clear mission, which it has been able to adapt to take advantage of changing market opportunities. Originally, Confinity Inc. created PayPal as a service that would allow funds to be transferred between Palm Pilots (handheld personal digital devices). But it was not long before the company signed an agreement with eBay to enable instantaneous payments for the millions of auction transactions (Davis, 2014). Then, mobile commerce proved to be another tipping point for PayPal as it extended its offer beyond eBay's auction platform to offer a truly one-touch financial payment solution (Hazan, 2014).
- *encapsulate the personal conviction and motivation of the leader*, who can make his or her ideas become contagious. For example, Walt Disney wrote his company's mission statement, 'To make people happy', which is both contagious and motivating for staff (Sanghera, 2005). Jeff Bezos's vision and mission for Amazon is 'to be the Earth's most customer-centric company, to build a place where people can come to find and discover anything they might want to buy online' (Gapper and Jopson, 2011). His passion and commitment have led the company through challenging times to become the world's leading consumer e-commerce company. See Marketing in Action 18.1 to find out more about the passion that drives Jeff Bezos's leadership style.
- *create strategic intent of winning throughout the organization*. This helps to build a sense of common purpose and stresses the need to create competitive advantages rather than settle for imitative moves.
- *enable success*. Managers must believe they have the latitude to make decisions about strategy without being second-guessed by top management.

MARKETING IN ACTION 18.1
Jeff Bezos and the Two-pizza Rule

Jeff Bezos is passionate about customers, and he wants his employees to share his level of commitment in everything they do. His leadership style is said to be full of quirks, and he has exacting standards. Standards at Amazon include a set of leadership principles which demand that all employees share Jeff's obsession with customers, are frugal and don't spend company resources on things that are not customer centric, and are vocally self-critical and always seeking ways to innovate and simplify the way the company operates. For example, Amazon was one of the first e-commerce websites to allow negative customer reviews. But this initiative gave the company an opportunity to identify the things it needed to get right to improve customer service.

When it comes to innovation, Jeff has an unusual rule for building teams: the two-pizza rule. This rule means that a team can have no more members than can be fed by two pizzas (approximately five to seven people). There is a logic behind this rule, which is that active teams are small and can all communicate with one another in a meaningful way. Jeff's leadership style relies on empowering his teams to act fast and innovate, so the pizza rule reduces complexity within a group *and* increases in-group communication and overall productivity. And he will never be seen at a meeting if this rule cannot be applied.

Based on: Sanghani (2013); Amazon (2015); Connley (2018)

In summary, the mission statement provides the framework within which managers decide which opportunities and threats to address and which to disregard. A well-defined mission statement is a key element in the marketing planning process, as it defines boundaries within which new opportunities are sought and motivates staff to succeed in the implementation of marketing strategy.

Marketing Audit

According to Brownlie (1993), the **marketing audit** is a systematic examination of a business's marketing environment, objectives, strategies and activities, with a view to identifying key strategic issues, problem areas and opportunities. The marketing audit provides the basis for developing a plan of action to improve marketing performance, should be done regularly and provide answers to the questions: 'Where are we now?', 'How did we get here?' and 'Where are we heading?'

Answers to these questions depend upon an analysis of the internal and external environment of a business. This analysis benefits from a clear mission statement, since the latter defines the boundaries of the environmental scan and helps decisions regarding which strategic issues and opportunities are important.

The internal audit focuses on those areas that are under the control of marketing management, whereas the external audit is concerned with those forces over which management has no control. The results of the marketing audit are a key determinant of the future direction of the business and may give rise to a redefined business mission statement. Alongside the marketing audit, a business may conduct audits of other functional areas such as production, finance and personnel. The coordination and integration of these audits produces a composite business plan in which marketing issues play a central role, since they concern decisions about which products to manufacture for which markets. These decisions clearly have production, financial and personnel implications, and successful implementation depends upon each functional area acting in concert.

A checklist of issues is a useful and common approach to carrying a marketing audit (Wilson, 1982). See Table 18.2 (for external marketing) and Table 18.3 (for internal marketing). External analysis covers the **macroenvironment** and the microenvironment. The macroenvironment consists of broad environmental issues that may affect business performance: political/legal, economic, ecological/physical, social/cultural and technological forces. Auditing these issues is known by the acronym PEEST analysis. Originally, Francis J. Aguilar alerted managers to the importance of scanning the business environment, and he is credited with inventing the PEST acronym, a structured method of analysis that assisted an organization's future planning (Aguilar, 1967). (PEST analysis does not include the influence of changes in the physical environment.) Since then, various acronyms have been used in management literature, for example STEP, STEEP and PESTLE (Gillespie, 2007). The key point to remember is that scanning the business environment in a systematic manner is crucially important for all organizations, as changes in the environment can have dramatic effects on long-term success.

TABLE 18.2 External marketing audit checklist

Forces	Key topics / Trends
Macroenvironment	
Political/legal	EU and national laws; codes of practice; political instability
Economic	Economic growth; unemployment; interest and exchange rates; global economic trends (e.g. the growth of the BRICS economies—Brazil, Russia, India, China and South Africa)
Ecological/physical environmental	Global warming; pollution; energy and other scarce resources; environmentally friendly ingredients and components; recycling and non-wasteful packaging
Social/cultural	Changes in world population, age distribution and household structure; attitude and lifestyle changes; subcultures within and across national boundaries; consumerism
Technological	Innovations; communications; technology infrastructures; bio-technology, smart technologies
Microenvironment	
Market	Size; growth rates
Customers	Who they are, their choice criteria, how, when and where they buy; how they rate the competition on product, promotion, price and distribution; how customers group (market segmentation), and what benefits each group seeks
Competitors	Who the major competitors (actual and potential) are; their objectives and strategies; strengths and weaknesses; size, market share and profitability; entry barriers to new competitors
Distributors	Channel attractiveness; distributor decision-making unit, decision-making process and choice criteria; strengths and weaknesses; power changes; physical distribution methods
Suppliers	Who they are and location; strengths and weaknesses; power changes

Table 18.2 lists the forces and key topics for each area. Chapter 2 explores the marketing environment in depth.

The **microenvironment** consists of the actors in the firm's immediate environment that affect its capabilities to operate effectively in its chosen markets. The key actors are customers, distributors, suppliers and competitors and microenvironmental analysis will consist of an analysis of issues relating to these actors and an overall analysis of market size, growth rates and trends (see Table 18.2).

More specifically, microenvironmental analysis consists of:

- **market analysis**, which involves the statistical analysis of market size, growth rates and trends
- **customer analysis** of buyer behaviour—how customers rate competitive offerings, and how they segment

- **competitor analysis**, which examines the nature of actual and potential competitors, and their objectives and strategies. It also seeks to identify their strengths and weaknesses, size, market share and profitability. Finally, entry barrier analysis identifies the key financial and non-financial barriers that protect the industry from competitor attack
- **distribution analysis**, which covers an examination of the attractiveness of different distribution channels, distributors, buyer behaviour, the strengths and weaknesses of different distribution channels, movements in power bases, and alternative methods of physical distribution
- **supplier analysis** examines who and where suppliers are located, their strengths and weaknesses, power changes and trends in the supply chain.

The internal audit allows the performance and activities of the business to be assessed in the light of environmental developments. Operating results form a basis of assessment, through analysis of sales, market share, profit margins and costs. **Strategic issues analysis** examines the suitability of marketing objectives and segmentation bases in the light of changes in the marketplace. Competitive advantages and the core competences on which they are based would be reassessed and the positioning of products in the market critically reviewed. Core competences are the principal distinctive capabilities possessed by a company, which define what it really is good at.

TABLE 18.3 Internal marketing audit checklist

Operating results (by product, customer, geographic region)	Marketing mix effectiveness
Sales	Product
Market share	Price
Profit margins	Promotion
Costs	Distribution
Strategic issues analysis	**Marketing structures**
Marketing objectives	Marketing organization
Market segmentation	Marketing training
Competitive advantage	Intra- and interdepartmental communication
Core competences	**Marketing systems**
Positioning	Marketing information systems
Portfolio analysis	Marketing planning system
Performance measurement	Marketing control system

An example of a company that has invested in its core competences is Eddie Stobart Ltd (see Exhibit 18.2). When Eddie set about transforming his dad's haulage business, he knew that customers 'hated slovenly drivers and old dirty lorries', and so focusing on dress code and cleanliness helped him to transform not only his own company but the whole of the haulage industry in the UK. Other core competencies included just-in-time stock management and highly effective logistics solutions (Madden, 2011). Zara is another example of a company that has utilized its supply-side competencies to build a global fashion brand.

EXHIBIT 18.2
Eddie Stobart transformed the image of his dad's haulage company by focusing on presenting the company as smart and clean

One danger that companies face is moving away from their core competences into areas where their skills and capabilities do not provide a competitive advantage. Management can become distracted, leading to poor performance. For example, IBM suffered as demand for its computing hardware and IT solutions declined and competition from Hewlett Packard and other more agile competitors increased. For several years, IBM seemed to be searching for markets where the business could leverage its expertize. Eventually, the focus of the business has shifted from selling hardware to software, business analytics and cloud computing.

Finally, **product portfolios** should be analysed to determine future strategic objectives.

Each element of the marketing mix is reviewed in the light of changing customer requirements and competitor activity. The **marketing structures** on which marketing activities are based should be analysed. Marketing structure consists of the marketing organization, training, and intra- and interdepartmental communication that takes place within an organization. Marketing organization is reviewed to determine fit with strategy and the market, and marketing training requirements are examined. Finally, communications and the relationship within the marketing department and between marketing and other functions (e.g. R&D, engineering, production) need to be appraised.

Marketing systems are audited for effectiveness. These marketing systems consist of the marketing information, planning and control systems that support marketing activities. Shortfalls in information provision are analysed, the marketing planning system is critically appraised for cost-effectiveness, and the marketing control system is assessed in the light of accuracy, timeliness (does it provide evaluations when managers require them?) and coverage (does the system evaluate the key variables affecting company performance?).

Marketing systems can be vital assets. For example, marketing information systems at British Airways, Qantas and Singapore Airlines provide knowledge regarding repeat passengers' preferred seats, newspapers, food and drinks, allowing customization of their offerings.

This checklist provides the basis for deciding on the topics to be included in the marketing audit. However, to give the same amount of attention and detailed analysis to every item would grind the audit to a halt under a mass of data and issues. In practice, the audit is critical in deciding the key items to focus upon. Those factors that are considered of crucial importance to the company's performance will merit most attention. For small businesses, setting priorities and carrying out the audit can have added challenges, as owners/managers can be overstretched, time poor, and find it difficult to critique their own strengths and weaknesses. One by-product of the marketing audit may be a realization that information about key environmental issues is lacking.

All assumptions should be made explicit as an ongoing part of the marketing audit: for example, key assumptions might be:

- Inflation will average 3 per cent during the planning period.
- VAT levels will not be changed.
- Worldwide overcapacity will remain at 150 per cent.
- No new entrants into the market will emerge.

The marketing audit should be an ongoing activity, not a desperate attempt to turn around an ailing business. Some companies conduct an annual audit as part of their annual planning system; others operating in less turbulent environments may consider two or three years to be an adequate period between audits. Others might consider the use of an outside consultant to coordinate activities and provide an objective outside view to be beneficial, while some may believe that their own managers are best equipped to conduct the analyses. Clearly, there is no set formula for deciding when and by whom the audit is conducted. The decision ultimately rests on the preferences and situation facing the management team.

SWOT analysis

A **SWOT analysis** is a structured approach to evaluating the strategic position of a business by identifying its strengths, weaknesses, opportunities and threats. It provides a simple method of synthesizing the results of the marketing audit (Piercy and Giles, 1989). Internal strengths and weaknesses are summarized as they relate to external opportunities and threats (see Figure 18.2), and strategies can be based on a good fit. But the results of SWOT should also fit into the business context set out by the mission statement, link to the marketing environment and fit with organizational resources (Agarwal, Grassi and Pahl, 2012).

FIGURE 18.2
SWOT analysis

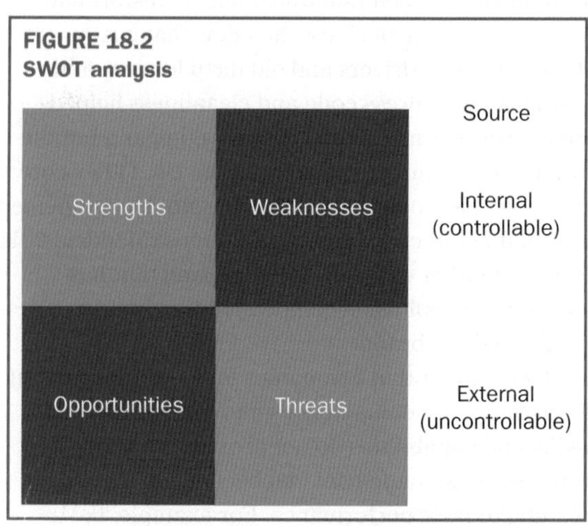

When evaluating strengths and weaknesses, only those resources or capabilities that would be valued by the customer should be included (Piercy, 2008). Strengths such as 'We are an old established firm', 'We are a large supplier' and 'We are technologically advanced' should be questioned for their impact on customer satisfaction. It is conceivable that such bland generalizations confer as many weaknesses as strengths. Also, opportunities and threats should be listed as anticipated events or trends *outside* the business that have implications for performance. Once a simple SWOT analysis has been completed, thought can be given to how to turn weaknesses into strengths, and threats into opportunities. For example, a perceived weakness in customer care might suggest the need for staff training to create a new strength. A threat posed by a new entrant might call for a strategic alliance to combine the strengths of both parties to exploit a new opportunity. Because these activities are designed to convert weaknesses into strengths and threats into opportunities, they are called *conversion strategies* (see Figure 18.3). Another way to use a SWOT analysis is to match strengths with opportunities. An example of a company that successfully matched strengths with opportunities is Charles Tyrwhitt, the men's clothing retailer, whose founder Nick Wheeler saw an opportunity in the growing demand for online sales. One of the company's strengths was the fact that it had run its own catalogue business for more than a decade to service its existing home-shopping operation. The result is that Charles Tyrwhitt has created a highly profitable online business, outselling its rivals Thomas Pink and TM Lewin in terms of online sales.

FIGURE 18.3
SWOT analysis and strategy development

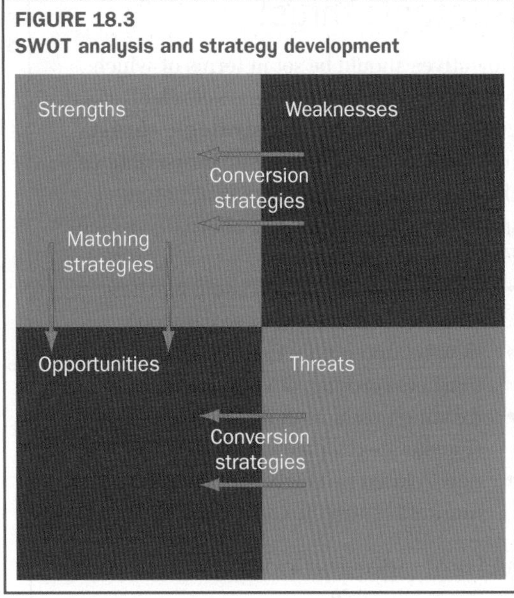

SWOT analysis is a strategic management tool generally applied when a firm is looking to improve or develop a part of its business. But the simplicity of the matrix belies the complexity involved in making the output of the SWOT analysis useful. According to Pandya (2017), 'Most SWOT exercises end up being laundry lists of bullet points put together under each of the four headings.' Pandya suggests that to gain value out of a SWOT analysis, firms should take a fresh look and use additional lenses to determine the outcomes of their analysis, by finding ways to:

- create a fit between strengths and opportunities to leverage advantages and seize opportunities
- reduce vulnerability by improving weaknesses and ensuring acute and current awareness of threats.

Remember, SWOT is a means of developing structured guidelines for managerial actions; it does not provide strategic direction (Pandya, 2017).

Marketing Objectives

The results of the marketing audit and SWOT analysis lead to the definition of **marketing objectives**. These objectives also link through the business mission to corporate objectives. Imagine you are responsible for managing Danone's yoghurt portfolio, which includes the Activia, Shape and Actimel product ranges. The corporate objective is to become number one in the yoghurt markets, overtaking Muller, the existing market leader. You will need to develop a marketing plan that contributes to this corporate objective. How you do this involves deciding on which markets to target with which products and then setting specific objectives for individual products. There are two levels of objective used in marketing planning:

1 *Strategic thrust objectives*, which shape the direction of the plan and involve deciding on which markets to target and which products/service to sell. So, in the Danone case, you might decide to target new customers (Muller yoghurt eaters) with existing products (Activia fruit yoghurts).
2 *Strategic objectives*, which set specific objectives for individual products. So, to implement your plan, you will need to build market share (of Activia fruit yoghurts).

Each type of objectives is now discussed in more detail.

Strategic thrust

Objectives should be set in terms of which products to sell in which markets (McDonald, 2007). This describes the **strategic thrust** of the business. The strategic thrust defines the future direction and areas of potential growth for a business. The alternatives (see Figure 18.4) comprise:

- existing products in existing markets (market penetration or expansion)
- new/related products for existing markets (product development)
- existing products in new/related markets (market development)
- new/related products for new/related markets (entry into new markets).

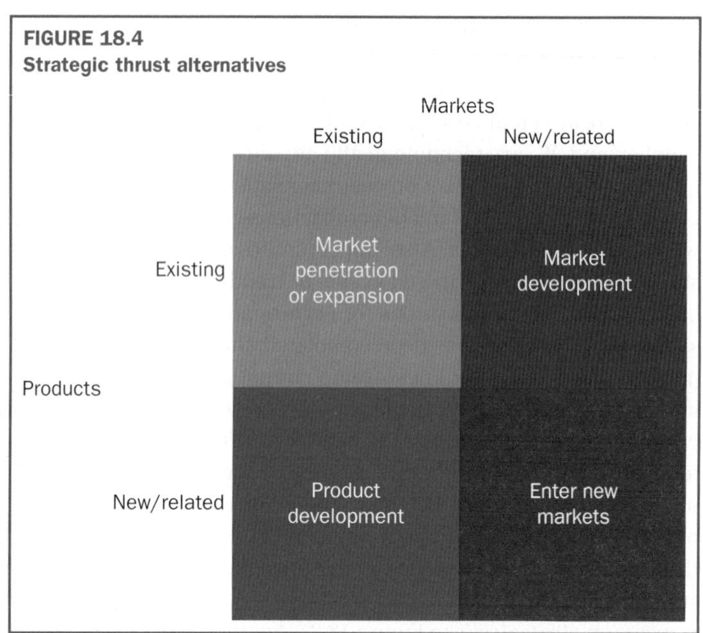

FIGURE 18.4
Strategic thrust alternatives

Market penetration

This strategy is to take the existing product in the existing market and to attempt increased penetration. Existing customers may become more brand loyal (brand-switch less often) and/or new customers in the same market may begin to buy the brand. Other tactics to increase penetration include getting existing customers to use the brand more often (e.g. wash their hair more frequently) and to use a greater quantity when they use it (e.g. two spoonfuls of tea instead of one). The latter tactic would also have the effect of expanding the market; for example, Glasses Direct, the online reseller of spectacles and sunglasses, launched a two-for-one offer encouraging existing customers to buy several pairs of glasses at a time (Glasses Direct, n.d.). Glasses Direct also uses incentives to encourage existing customers to introduce their friends and seek and encourage new customers in the same market to switch to their brand. See Exhibit 18.3.

EXHIBIT 18.3
Glasses Direct 'share with a friend'

Product development

This strategy involves increasing sales by improving present products or developing new products for current markets. New product replacements that fail to provide additional benefits are unlikely to succeed. Google Glass, smart glasses that linked to the internet and allowed wearers to take photos and videos, were withdrawn as usability, privacy and safety issues created problems for the product's early adopters (Cellan-Jones, 2015). Product development may take the form of brand extensions (Cadbury's Dairy Milk Caramel bars and Caramel Nibbles, Cadbury's Crunchie bars and Crunchie Rocks) that provide slightly modified features for target customers. See Mini Case 18.1 to find out more about how jewellery maker Pandora used its products to develop markets.

Market development

This strategy is used when current products are sold in new markets. This may involve moving into new geographical markets. Many consumer durable brands, such as cars, consumer electronics and household appliance brands, are sold in overseas markets with no or only very minor modifications to those sold at home. An alternative market development strategy is to move into new market segments. For example, BSkyB has expanded its market share through the acquisition of Virgin Media's TV channel. This has enabled BSkyB to gain access to Virgin's customers by providing Sky's existing content. Santander, one of the world's largest banking groups, has also developed markets for its existing financial products in both Latin America and the UK (*The Economist*, 2010).

Entry into new markets

Developing new products for new markets is the riskiest strategy, but may be necessary when a company's current products and markets offer few prospects for future growth. When there is synergy between the existing and new products, this strategy is more likely to work. For example, Apple's experience and competences in

MINI CASE 18.1
Pandora: Wherever Life Takes You, Take it With You

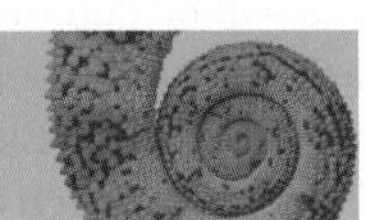

Pandora developed its markets from a single store in Copenhagen, Denmark, into an international jewellery brand. Having established a manufacturing base in Thailand, Per and Winne Enevoldsen—who founded the company—concentrated on building their business through wholesale jewellery markets. On the supply side, they focused on manufacturing products and introduced the Pandora charm bracelet into Denmark, where it was a great success, and then moved on to Germany, Austria and the USA. The innovativeness of the product, positioned at affordable prices, enabled Pandora to develop these markets quickly. More factories were opened in Thailand, and a vertically integrated system—in-house designers, the company's own factories and retail stores and franchises—used to service the increased demand. The manufacturing resources and capabilities facilitate agile manufacturing, so enabling rapid response to changes in market demands and capacity to capitalize on new opportunities. On the demand side, much attention has been given to the customer journey and ensuring this is a seamless experience across multiple channels (in-store, online and mobile) and communication platforms (broadcast, print, web, social media).

The company continued to use its products to reinforce the brand's market position. Its 'Wherever life takes you, take it with you' campaign aimed to encourage loyalty from existing customers, who were targeted to build up their collection of Pandora products as keepsakes of the special moments in their lives.

The company's mission is 'to inspire every woman to feel creative in her self-expression', which ties in to the future vision, which is to be the branded manufacturer that delivers the most personal jewellery experience.

The strategic marketing plan involves continuing to position the brand as affordable, innovative jewellery. New products are continually added in the form of charms, bracelets and necklaces, but Pandora aims to develop the product portfolio beyond the bracelets and charms into rings, earrings and necklaces by adding culturally relevant and seasonal ranges.

Questions:

1. Draw up a SWOT analysis for Pandora.
2. Suggest what Pandora should do in order to create a fit between strengths and opportunities and reduce any vulnerabilities (their weaknesses and threats).
3. Propose marketing objectives for product and markets which might enable Pandora to achieve its strategic aim of delivering the most personal jewellery experience.

Based on: Pandora Group (2015); West (2014); Pandora Group (2018) computer electronics provided the platform for designing a new product, the iPod, targeting a different market: young people who want downloadable music on a portable music player (Helmore, 2005). This, in turn, has been followed by the launch of the iPhone, which has placed Apple in a strong position in the market for smartphones (Allison, 2008), and the development of the iPad. Intel also believes it has the core competence required to move into smartphones, netbooks and tablet computing. Companies in technology markets are constantly investing in new developments and looking for markets for their offers.

Strategic objectives

Alongside objectives for product/market direction, **strategic objectives** for each product need to be agreed. Simply, this begins the process of planning at the product level. There are four basic options:

1 build
2 hold
3 harvest
4 divest.

For new products, the strategic objective will inevitably be to build sales and market share. For existing products, the appropriate strategic objective will depend on the particular situation associated with the product. This will be determined in the marketing audit, SWOT analysis and evaluation of the strategic options outlined earlier. Product portfolio planning tools are tools such as the Boston Consulting Group Growth–Share Matrix and the General Electric Market Attractiveness–Competitive Position Model. These will be discussed in detail in Chapter 20, which deals with managing products.

The important point to remember at this stage is that *building* sales and market share is not the only sensible strategic objective for a product. As we shall see, *holding* sales and market share may make commercial sense under certain conditions; *harvesting*, where sales and market share can fall but profit margins are maximized, may also be preferable to building; and finally, *divestment*, where the product is dropped or sold, can be the logical outcome of the situation analysis.

Together, strategic thrust and strategic objectives define where the business and its products intend to go in the future.

Core Marketing Strategy

Once objectives have been set, the next stage in the plan involves deciding how to meet the objectives and answer the question: how do we get there? The **core marketing strategy** focuses on how objectives can be accomplished. There are three key elements to consider: target markets, competitor targets and establishing a competitive advantage. Each element is interlinked, and together the elements form the key aspects of **competitive positioning** (Hooley, Piercy and Nicoulaud, 2012). We will consider each of the three elements in turn.

Target markets

A central plank of core strategy is the choice of **target market(s)**. Marketing is not about chasing any customer at any price. Decisions should be taken about which groups of customers (segments) are most attractive to the business and best fit with its capabilities. *The Economist* targets business professionals who wish to be regarded as well informed about business matters. This periodical can 'offer authoritative insight and opinion on international news, politics, business, finance, science and technology'. It can achieve high standards of journalism across a wide range of subjects, as it attracts many writers who wish to work together to produce thought-provoking articles. This is an example of a company that has a clear target market, and it can use its capabilities and resources to produce a product that satisfies the needs of its customers.

The choice of target market can emerge from the SWOT analysis and the setting of marketing objectives (strategic thrust). For existing products, marketing management should consider its current target markets and their changing needs. Consequently, a company should focus on customers' needs across its established product

MARKETING IN ACTION 18.2
Birds Eye Looks Closely at its Target Marketing Strategy

American frozen food manufacturer Birds Eye invests heavily in getting its products to the right markets. A new marketing strategy aiming to double its market share in Europe by 2020 cost £16 million; a rebranding campaign cost a further £8 million. Arguably, the reasoning driving these investments was to reduce missed opportunities, because when the brand assessed its marketing situation it found (in the UK market) that while over 80 per cent of households were aware of and used the brand, only 2 per cent used it at all meal times. In fact, its analysis revealed that many customers perceived Birds Eye as just a 'teatime fish fingers and peas brand'. This was also a cause for concern, as adults represented 65 per cent of customers, but fish fingers were perceived as food for 'kids'.

The marketing strategy across European used a marketing communications campaign designed to reposition the brand in the minds of its customers. The aim was to get existing customers to consider the brand as a 'food' rather than a frozen alternative. The aim was to penetrate the large market of customers who trust the brand in both the UK and the rest of Europe, by encouraging them to change the way they use Birds Eye products.

Even Captain Birds Eye had a makeover, returning to a more rugged look to bring a more authentic appearance to the brand icon. The frozen food manufacturer relaunched 57 of its products with a new slogan, 'the Birds Eye difference'. The company tied up sponsorship deals with mainstream TV channels to get access to its core target markets: i.e. families with children, when they are eating their evening meals. The deal involved scheduling the advertising campaign during the popular TV show *The Simpsons*.

Based on: Tesseras (2014), Hobbs (2016); Challouma (2018)

ranges. For example, smart televisions are constantly evolving in response to technology innovations and changing customer needs, and to retain its market share Samsung should make changes to the marketing mix to adapt to new requirements. In other cases, current target markets may have decreased in attractiveness, so products will need to be repositioned to target different market segments. The process of market segmentation and targeting is examined in depth in Chapter 7. See Marketing in Action 18.2 for discussion of how Birds Eye, leading European frozen brand, adapted its target marketing strategy.

Competitor targets

Competitor targets are the organizations against which a company chooses to compete directly. Samsung competes directly with Apple in the tablet computer market. Weak competitors may be viewed as easy prey, and resources channelled to attack them. The importance of understanding competitors and strategies for attacking and defending against competitors are discussed in Chapter 19, which examines in detail the areas of competitor analysis and competitive strategy.

Competitive advantage

The link between target markets and competitor targets is the establishment of a competitive advantage. A competitive advantage is the achievement of superior performance through differentiation to provide superior customer value, or by managing to achieve lowest delivered cost. For major success, businesses need to achieve a clear performance differential over the competition on factors that are important to target customers. The most successful methods are built upon some combination of three advantages (Day, 1984).

1. *Being better*—providing superior quality or service (e.g. Mercedes-Benz, Dulux paints, Singapore Airlines).
2. *Being faster*—anticipating or responding to customer needs faster than the competition does (e.g. Zara).
3. *Being closer*—establishing close long-term relationships with customers (e.g. Amazon).

Another route to competitive advantage is achieving the lowest relative cost position of all competitors (Porter, 1980). Lowest cost can be translated into a competitive advantage through low prices or by producing standard items at price parity when comparative success may be achieved through higher profit margins than those of competitors. Achieving a highly differentiated product is not incompatible with a low-cost position, however (Phillips, Chang and Buzzell, 1983). Since high-quality products suffer lower rejection rates through quality control and lower repair costs through their warranty period, they may incur lower total costs than their inferior rivals. Methods of achieving competitive advantages and their sources are analysed in Chapter 19.

Tests of an effective core strategy

Figure 18.5 shows six key considerations that can be used to test a core strategy. The six considerations are that the strategy should:

1 be based upon a *clear definition of target customers and their needs*
2 show understanding of competitors and be able to create *competitive advantage*
3 *incur acceptable risk*; challenging a strong competitor with a weak competitive advantage and a low resource base would not incur acceptable risk
4 be *resourced and managerially supportable*; the strategy should match the resources, capabilities and managerial competences of the business
5 be derived from the *product and marketing objectives* established as part of the planning process; extensive use of promotions that makes commercial logic when following a build objective may make no sense when following a harvesting objective
6 be *internally consistent*; each of the elements of the core strategy should be consistent with the rest of the marketing plan.

Marketing mix decisions

At this stage in the planning process, managers consider the marketing mix. The tools they use and the choices they make will be informed by the core strategy. Decisions about use of each of the elements of the mix will vary depending on whether the focus is on a product or service. Nevertheless, decisions will consist of judgements about how to select and blend each of the relevant elements of the mix. Such decisions will not be taken in isolation, as marketing managers will also consider how their close competitors use the mix. For example, major supermarkets Asda, Sainsbury's, Morrisons and Tesco constantly vie for market share. As there is limited growth in the overall size of the grocery market, so each of these major players grows its share of the market by attracting its competitors' customers. This is achieved through the marketing mix, and each of these supermarket brands uses the mix differently. At a basic level, Asda creates its competitive advantage by focusing on keeping

FIGURE 18.5
Testing core strategy

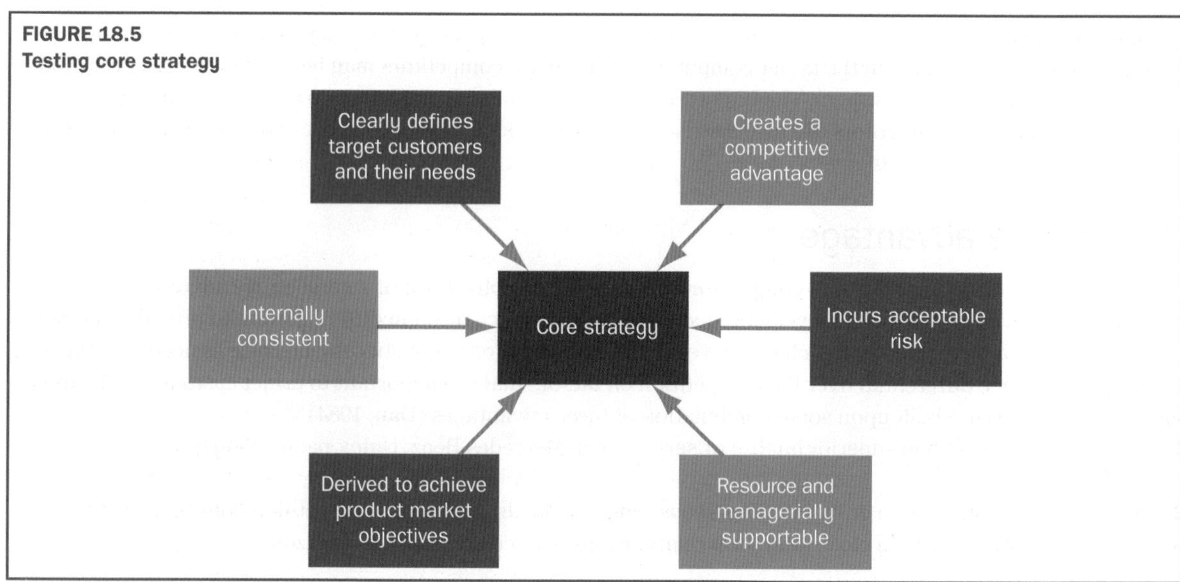

prices very low. Sainsbury's creates competitive advantage through the quality of its products. Morrisons differentiates itself through the freshness of its products and its store destinations, and Tesco positions its brand on offering the greatest value across the widest product range.

As with all other stages of the marketing plan, there are many complex choices involved in selecting an effective marketing mix. Part 3 of the book devotes several chapters to exploring each of elements of the mix in detail: product (Chapters 8, 11 and 20), services (Chapter 9), price (Chapter 12), promotion (Chapters 13, 14, 15, 16) and place (Chapter 17).

Organization and implementation

No marketing plan will succeed unless it 'degenerates into work' (Drucker, 1993). Consequently, the business must design an organization that has the capability of implementing the plan. Indeed, organizational weaknesses discovered as part of the SWOT analysis may restrict the feasible range of strategic options. Reorganization could mean the establishment of a new marketing organization or department in the business. In the past, many manufacturing organizations did not have a marketing department (Piercy, 1986). In some cases, marketing was done by the chief executive, or the sales department dealt with customer enquiries—so there was no further need for other marketing input. In other situations, environmental change caused strategy change and subsequent reorganization of marketing and sales business functions. More recently, the growth of large corporate customers with enormous buying power has resulted in businesses focusing their resources more firmly on meeting their needs (strategy change), which, in turn, has led to dedicated marketing and sales teams being organized to service these accounts (reorganization). Implementation and organizational issues are explored in Chapter 22.

Because strategy changes and reorganization affect the balance of power in businesses and the daily life and workloads of people, resistance may occur. Consequently, marketing personnel need to understand the barriers to change, the process of change management and the techniques of persuasion that can be used to effect the implementation of the marketing plan. These issues are dealt with in Chapter 22.

Control

The final stage in the marketing planning process is **control**. The aim of control systems is to evaluate the results of the marketing plan so that corrective action can be taken if performance does not match objectives. Short-term control systems can plot results against objectives on a weekly, monthly, quarterly and/or annual basis. Measures include sales, profits, costs and cash flow. There is a growing need for marketing managers to assess the payoff from their investments and justify them. This has resulted in the use of marketing metrics, which are quantitative measures of the outcomes of marketing activities and expenditures. There is extensive coverage of marketing metrics in Chapter 22. Strategic control systems are more long term. Managers need to stand back from week-by-week and month-by-month results to reassess critically whether their plans are in line with their capabilities and the environment.

Lack of this long-term control perspective may result in the pursuit of plans that have lost strategic credibility. New competition, changes in technology and moving customer requirements may have rendered old plans obsolete. This, of course, returns the planning process to the beginning, since this kind of fundamental review is conducted in the marketing audit. It is the activity of assessing internal capabilities and external opportunities and threats that results in a SWOT analysis. This outcome may be a redefinition of the business mission and, as we have seen, changes in marketing objectives and strategies to realign the business with its environment.

So how do the stages of marketing planning relate to the fundamental planning questions stated earlier in this chapter? Table 18.1 illustrates this relationship. The question 'Where are we now?' is answered by the business mission definition, the marketing audit and SWOT analysis.

Rewards of Marketing Planning

Many authors have suggested that there is a positive relationship between market-orientated business and performance (Jaworski and Kohli, 1993; Kumar, Subramaniam and Yauger, 1998; Narver and Slater, 1998), and companies with a highly developed market orientation tend to derive greater benefits from marketing planning

(Pulendran, Speed and Widing, 2003). Moreover, various authors have attributed the following benefits to marketing planning (Greenley, 1986; Leppard and McDonald, 1991; Terpstra and Sarathy, 1991).

1. *Consistency*: the plan provides a focal point for decisions and actions. By reference to a common plan, management decisions should be more consistent and actions better coordinated.
2. *Encourages the monitoring of change*: the planning process forces managers to step away from day-to-day problems and review the impact of change on the business from a strategic perspective.
3. *Encourages organizational adaptation*: the underlying premise of planning is that the organization should adapt to match its environment. Marketing planning, therefore, promotes the necessity to accept the inevitability of change. This is important as the capability to adapt has been linked to superior performance (Oktemgil and Greenley, 1997).
4. *Stimulates achievement*: the planning process focuses on objectives, strategies and results. It encourages people to ask 'What can we achieve given our capabilities?' As such, it motivates people to set new horizons for objectives when they otherwise might be content to accept much lower standards of performance.
5. *Resource allocation*: the planning process asks fundamental questions about resource allocation, for example which products should receive high investment (build), which should be maintained (hold), which should have resources withdrawn slowly (harvest) and which should have resources withdrawn immediately (divest).
6. *Competitive advantage*: planning promotes the search for sources of competitive advantage.

However, it is important to realize that this logical planning process (sometimes called *synoptic planning*) may conflict with the culture of the business, which may plan effectively using an *incremental approach* (Raimond and Eden, 1990). The style of planning should match business culture (Driver, 1990). Saker and Speed (1992) argue that the considerable demands on managers in terms of time and effort implied by the synoptic marketing planning process may mean that alternative planning schemes are more appropriate, particularly for small companies. (For information on marketing and planning in small and medium-sized firms, see Carson, 1990; Fuller, 1994.)

Incremental planning is more problem-focused in that the process begins with the realization of a problem (for example, a fall-off in orders) and continues with an attempt to identify a solution. As solutions to problems form, so strategy emerges. However, little attempt is made to integrate consciously the individual decisions that could possibly affect one another. Strategy is viewed as a loosely linked group of decisions that are handled individually. Nevertheless, the effect of incremental planning may be to attune the business to its environment, through its problem-solving nature. The drawback of incremental planning is the lack of a broad situation analysis and strategy option generation, which renders the incremental approach less comprehensive. For some companies, however, its inherent practicality may support its use rather than its rationality (O'Shaughnessy, 1995).

Problems in Making Planning Work

Empirical work into the marketing planning practices has found that most commercial companies did not practise the kinds of systematic planning procedures described in this chapter and, of those that did, many did not enjoy the rewards described in the previous section (Greenley, 1987). However, others have shown that there is a relationship between planning and commercial success; see, for example, Armstrong (1982) and McDonald (1984). A more recent study (Pulendran, Speed and Wildin, 2003) also confirmed that marketing planning is linked to commercial success. The problem is that the *contextual difficulties* associated with the process of marketing planning are substantial and need to be understood. In as much as forewarned is forearmed, the following is a checklist of potential problems that have to be faced by those charged with making marketing planning work.

Political

Marketing planning is a resource allocation process. The outcome of the process is an allocation of more funds to some products and departments, and the same or less to others. Since power bases, career opportunities and salaries are often tied to whether an area is fast or slow growing, it is not surprising that managers view planning as a highly political activity. An example is a European bank, whose planning process resulted in the decision to insist that its retail branch managers divert certain types of loan application to the industrial/merchant banking arm of the group, where the return was greater. This was required because the plan was designed to optimize the return to the group. However, the consequence was considerable friction between the divisions concerned, because the decision lowered the performance of the retail branch.

In another European bank, the introduction of a series of market-based products was blocked by managers of existing product-orientated offerings who feared the launch would mean, for them, losing their jobs. Both of these examples demonstrate how political factors can be a barrier to marketing planning initiatives. See Marketing in Action 18.3 to find out how Uber is encountering and overcoming political resistance as it moves into European markets.

MARKETING IN ACTION 18.3
Uber and the Ride-sharing Economy in Sweden

Uber is a market-maker. The taxi service is equivalent to the services offered by fast-food companies. I need a ride, I need it now—call digitally and hail Uber. Drivers typically respond in a few minutes. The Uber app links customers and drivers through a unique digital platform. This innovative peer-to-peer service has disrupted establish markets and created new levels of service. But as with other market makers, Uber is facing many challenges from established taxi firms, both public and private hire services. London's black-cab drivers are seeking to sue Uber for loss of earnings; Uber has been banned in Denmark, but the European Commission has asked member states to consider such bans only as a last resort, as they have a responsibility to create an environment that encourages new and disruptive businesses to prosper. Nevertheless, European taxi drivers came out in force against Uber, as shown in the photo above.

Marketing planning can hit problems. Great ideas that fulfil customer needs do not necessarily succeed, as unforeseen barriers and resistance can arise. Therefore, it is essential to understand *contextual difficulties* that might get in the way of a marketing strategy. Uber's ride-sharing concept is popular and is based on customer needs, but the company has come up against strong political resistance when moving into European markets.

Politically, drink-driving is a big issue; globally, around a third of road deaths are alcohol related. In many countries, it is illegal to have even one drink and then drive, but often a night out, lunch with friends or even a business meeting can involve more than one drink and going over legal limits. This behaviour creates a problem: how to get home when the party is over. Public transport services may have stopped running—especially late in the evening—and taxi services are often limited to urban boundaries, can be expensive and, on a busy Saturday night, difficult to find. Uber offers a solution to the problem and has started making a difference to the drink-driving statistics in the USA by making it easier to 'get a ride home'.

The idea was born out of a very simple need: two guys looking for a taxi in Paris after attending a business conference. These two people were Travis Kalanick and Garrett Camp, who were already successful technology entrepreneurs, so developing the Uber mobile app got off to a good start. Launched in San Francisco, the UberCab idea is based on carpooling. Uber is a mini-cab service that is accessed via mobile phone. Drivers and riders sign up through the Uber app and are then connected together based on the riders' needs and the drivers' availability. The idea proved to be very popular in California and soon spread to other parts of the USA. Market expansion to Europe was the next step.

Globally, there are over 160,000 active Uber drivers, but the launch of Uber in Europe has been far from straightforward. A German court banned Uber from offering its ride-sharing services countrywide. The German taxi association claimed that Uber was involved in illegal practices by providing unlicensed drivers; similar problems in the Netherlands, Spain and France have been tarnishing Uber's image and halting expansion into European markets.

However, in Sweden the Uber roll-out has been successful but challenged politically. Uber has turned threats into opportunities in this market. Consequently, initial resistance has been overcome, as the benefits of Uber have been conveyed to the Swedish Government and the people. Issues and questions include suggestions of tax avoidance by Uber, but this has created an opportunity for the company to show how its digital systems

»

are superior to those of many other transport companies. The Uber principle has been embraced as an innovative approach to transportation that delivers benefits to Uber riders and has the potential to improve the industry. Taxi Stockholm has already responded to competition from Uber by improving and extending its services. And Taxi Stockholm's head of marketing is quoted as saying, 'Uber is good for the market by pushing the industry to use a different technique, a new platform.'

Uber is learning how to manage contextual difficulties, and Sweden's innovative and forward-thinking culture is providing ideas about how Uber's marketing team might counter resistance in other parts of Europe.

Based on: Ewing (2015); Alert Driving (2010); Benson Strategy Group (2015); Frizell (2015); CBS Money Watch (2015); Topham (2018);

Opportunity cost

Some busy managers view marketing planning as a time-wasting ritual that conflicts with the need to deal with day-to-day problems. They view the opportunity cost of spending two or three days away at a hotel thrashing out long-term plans as too high. This difficulty may be compounded by the fact that people who are attracted to the hectic pace of managerial life may be the type who prefer to live that way (Mintzberg, 1975). Hence, they may be ill at ease with the thought of a long period of sedate contemplation.

Reward systems

The reward systems of many businesses are geared to the short term. Incentives and bonuses may be linked to quarterly or annual results. Managers may thus overweigh short-term issues and underweigh medium- and long-term concerns if there is a conflict of time. Thus, marketing planning may be viewed as of secondary importance.

Information

To function effectively, a systematic marketing planning system needs informational inputs. Market share, size and growth rates are basic inputs into the marketing audit but may be unavailable. More perversely, information may be wilfully withheld by vested interests who, recognizing that knowledge is power, distort the true situation to protect their position in the planning process.

Culture

The establishment of a systematic marketing planning process may be at variance with the culture of the organization. As has already been stated, businesses may 'plan' by making incremental decisions. Hence, the strategic planning system may challenge the status quo and be a threat. In other cases, the values and beliefs of some managers may be hostile to a planning system altogether.

Personalities

Marketing planning usually involves a discussion between managers about the strategic choices facing the business and the likely outcomes. This can be a highly charged affair where personality clashes and pent-up antagonisms can surface. The result can be that the process degenerates into abusive argument and sets up deep chasms within the management team.

Lack of knowledge and skills

Another problem that can arise when setting up a marketing planning system is that the management team do not have the knowledge and skills to perform the tasks adequately (McDonald, 1989). Basic marketing knowledge about market segmentation, competitive advantage and the nature of strategic objectives may be lacking. Similarly, skills in analysing competitive situations and defining core strategies may be inadequate.

How to Handle Marketing Planning Problems

Some of the problems revealed during the market planning process may be deep-seated managerial inadequacies rather than being intrinsic to the planning process itself. As such, the attempt to establish the planning system may be seen as a benefit to the business by revealing the nature of these problems. However, various authors have proposed recommendations for minimizing the impact of such problems (Abell and Hammond, 1979; McDonald, 1984).

- *Senior management support*: top management must be committed to planning and be seen by middle management to give it total support. This should be ongoing support, not a short-term fad.
- *Match the planning system to the culture of the business*: how the marketing planning process is managed should be consistent with the culture of the organization. For example, in some organizations, the top-down/bottom-up balance will move towards top-down; in other less directive cultures, the balance will move towards a more bottom-up planning style.
- *The reward system*: this should reward the achievement of longer-term objectives rather than focus exclusively on short-term results.
- *Depoliticize outcomes*: less emphasis should be placed on rewarding managers associated with build (growth) strategies. Recognition of the skills involved in defending share and harvesting products should be made. At General Electric, managers are classified as 'growers', 'caretakers' and 'undertakers' and matched to products that are being built, defended or harvested in recognition of the fact that the skills involved differ according to the strategic objective. No stigma is attached to caretaking or undertaking; each is acknowledged as contributing to the success of the organization.
- *Clear communication*: plans should be communicated to those charged with implementation.
- *Training*: marketing personnel should be trained in the necessary marketing knowledge and skills to perform the planning job. Ideally, all members of the management team should attend the same training course, so that they each share a common understanding of the concepts and tools involved and can communicate using the same terminology.

Review

1 The role of marketing planning within business

- Marketing planning is part of a broader concept known as strategic planning.
- For one-product companies, the role of marketing planning is to ensure that the product continues to meet customers' needs as well as seeking new opportunities.
- For companies marketing a range of products in a number of markets, marketing planning's role is as above plus the allocation of resources to each product.
- For companies comprising a number of businesses (strategic business units, SBUs), marketing planning's role is as above plus a contribution to the allocation of resources to each business.

2 The key planning questions

- These are: 'Where are we now?', 'How did we get there?', 'Where are we heading?', 'Where would we like to be?', 'How do we get there?' and 'Are we on course?'

3 The process of marketing planning

- The steps in the process are: deciding the business mission, conducting a marketing audit, producing a SWOT analysis, setting marketing objectives (strategic thrust and strategic objectives), deciding core strategy (target markets, competitive advantage and competitor targets), making marketing mix decisions, organizing and implementing, and control.

4 The concept of the business mission

- A business mission is a broadly defined, enduring statement of purpose that distinguishes a business from others of its type.
- A business mission should answer two questions: 'What business are we in?' and 'What business do we want to be in?'

5 The nature of the marketing audit and SWOT analysis

- The marketing audit is a systematic examination of a business's marketing environment, objectives, strategies and activities, with a view to identifying key strategic issues, problem areas and opportunities.
- The marketing audit consists of an examination of a company's external and internal environments. The external environment is made up of the macroenvironment, the market and competition. The internal environmental

audit consists of operating results, strategic issues analysis, marketing mix effectiveness, marketing structures and systems.

- A SWOT analysis provides a simple method of summarizing the results of the marketing audit. Internal issues are summarized under strengths and weaknesses, and external issues are summarized under opportunities and threats.

6 The nature of marketing objectives

- There are two types of marketing objective: i) strategic thrust, which defines the future direction of the business in terms of which products to sell in which markets; and ii) strategic objectives, which are product-level objectives relating to the decision to build, hold, harvest or divest products.

7 The components of core strategy and the criteria for testing its effectiveness

- The components of core strategy are target markets, competitor targets and competitive advantage.
- The criteria for testing its effectiveness are that core strategy clearly defines target customers and their needs, creates a competitive advantage, incurs acceptable risk, is resource and managerially supportable, is derived to achieve product–market objectives and is internally consistent. All elements are interlinked, and together they form the core aspects of competitive positioning.

8 Where marketing mix decisions are placed within the marketing planning process

- Marketing mix decisions follow those of core strategy, as they are based on an understanding of target customers' needs and the competition so that a competitive advantage can be created.

9 The importance of organization, implementation and control within the marketing planning process

- Organization is needed to support the strategies decided upon. Strategies are unlikely to be effective without attention to implementation issues. For example, techniques to overcome resistance to change and the training of staff who are required to implement strategic decisions are likely to be required.
- Control systems are important, so that the results of the marketing plan can be evaluated and corrective action taken if performance does not match objectives.

10 The rewards and problems associated with marketing planning

- The rewards are consistency of decision-making, encouragement of the monitoring of change, encouragement of organizational adaptation, stimulation of achievement, aiding resource allocation and promotion of the creation of a competitive advantage.
- The potential problems with marketing planning revolve around the context in which it takes place and are political, high opportunity cost, lack of reward systems tied to longer-term results, lack of relevant information, cultural and personality clashes, and lack of managerial knowledge and skills.

11 Recommendations for overcoming marketing planning problems

- Recommendations for minimizing the impact of marketing planning problems are attaining senior management support, matching the planning system to the culture of the business, creating a reward system that is focused on longer-term performance, depoliticizing outcomes, communicating clearly to those responsible for implementation, and training in the necessary marketing knowledge and skills to conduct marketing planning.

Key Terms

business mission the organization's purpose, usually setting out its competitive domain, which distinguishes the business from others of its type

competitive positioning consists of three key elements: target markets, competitor targets and establishing a competitive advantage

competitor analysis an examination of the nature of actual and potential competitors, and their objectives and strategies

competitor targets the organizations against which a company chooses to compete directly

control the stage in the marketing planning process or cycle when the performance against plan is monitored so that corrective action, if necessary, can be taken

core marketing strategy the means of achieving marketing objectives, including target markets, competitor targets and competitive advantage

customer analysis a survey of who the customers are, what choice criteria they use, how they rate competitive offerings and on what variables they can be segmented

distribution analysis an examination of movements in power bases, channel attractiveness, physical distribution and distribution behaviour

macroenvironment a number of broader forces that affect not only the company but the other actors in the environment, for example social, political, technological and economic

market analysis the statistical analysis of market size, growth rates and trends

marketing audit a systematic examination of a business's marketing environment, objectives, strategies and activities with a view to identifying key strategic issues, problem areas and opportunities

marketing objectives there are two types of marketing objective: strategic thrust, which dictates which products should be sold in which markets, and strategic objectives—that is, product-level objectives such as build, hold, harvest and divest

marketing planning the process by which businesses analyse the environment and their capabilities, decide upon courses of marketing action and implement those decisions

marketing structures the marketing frameworks (organization, training and internal communications) upon which marketing activities are based

marketing systems sets of connected parts (information, planning and control) that support the marketing function

microenvironment the actors in the firm's immediate environment that affect its capability to operate effectively in its chosen markets—namely, suppliers, distributors, customers and competitors

product portfolio the total range of products offered by the company

strategic business unit a business or company division serving a distinct group of customers and with a distinct set of competitors, usually strategically autonomous

strategic issues analysis an examination of the suitability of marketing objectives and segmentation bases in the light of changes in the marketplace

strategic objectives product-level objectives relating to the decision to build, hold, harvest or divest products

strategic thrust the decision concerning which products to sell in which markets

supplier analysis an examination of who and where suppliers are located, their competences and shortcomings, the trends affecting them and the future outlook for them

SWOT analysis a structured approach to evaluating the strategic position of a business by identifying its strengths, weaknesses, opportunities and threats

target market a market segment that has been selected as a focus for the company's offering or communications

Study Questions

1. **Discuss how to carry out a situation analysis and explain why it is an important part of marketing planning.**

2. **Discuss how macro and micro level influences might affect marketing planning decisions.**

3. **Explain why SWOT analysis has been quoted as mostly just producing a 'laundry list'. Suggest how to remedy this and ensure that this tool is used effectively as part of strategic marketing planning.**

4. **Explain how each stage of the marketing planning process links with the fundamental planning questions identified in Table 18.1.**

5. **The quote at the beginning of the chapter by business guru Gary Hamel suggests that marketing planning is somewhat irrelevant. Discuss the extent to which you agree with this comment.**

6. **Evaluate the extent to which the marketing planning process is a true reflection of how businesses plan their marketing strategies.**

7. **Explain the extent to which a clear business mission statement is a help to marketing planners?**
8. **What is meant by core marketing strategy? What role does it play in the process of marketing planning?**
9. **Discuss the key decisions that marketing planners should make when setting marketing objectives.**
10. **Discuss the importance of digital technology in the marketing planning process.**

Recommended Reading

Without a plan, it is difficult to know where you are going or measure when you have arrived. Read how to make SWOT analysis work with the help of LISA; about the calculated risks Apple is taking with its i-phone X marketing strategy and about how marketing improved business performance.

Heracleous, L. (2017) Apple makes a $999 gamble on its aspirational brand, *The conversation*, https://theconversation.com/apple-makes-a-999-gamble-on-its-aspirational-brand-83996 (accessed October 2018)

Morgan, N. A. (2012), Marketing and business performance, *Journal of the Academy of Marketing Science* 40(1), 102–19.

Pandya, S. (2017), 'Improving the learning and developmental potential of SWOT analysis: introducing the LISA framework', Strategic Direction, 33(3), pp.12–14,

References

Abell, D.F. and Hammond, J.S. (1979) *Strategic Market Planning*, Englewood Cliffs, NJ: Prentice-Hall.

Ackoff, R.I. (1987) Mission Statements, *Planning Review* 15(4), 30–2.

Aguilar, F.J. (1967) *Scanning the Business Environment*, New York, NY: Macmillan.

Agarwal, R., Grassi, W. and Pahl, J. (2012) Meta-SWOT: introducing a new strategic planning tool, *Journal of Business Strategy* 33(2), 12–21.

Alert Driving (2010) DRUNK DRIVING INCREASING CONCERN WORLDWIDE. Retrieved from Alertdriving.com: http://www.alertdriving.com/home/fleet-alert-magazine/international/drunk-driving-increasing-concern-worldwide (accessed 2 June 2015).

Allison, K. (2008) Apple Unveils iPhone Grand Plan, *Financial Times*, 10 March, 23.

Amazon (2015) Leadership Principles, Amazon, April. http://www.amazon.com/Values-Careers-Homepage/b?tag=skim0x680-20&ie=UTF8&node=239365011 (accessed October 2018)

Armstrong, J.S. (1982) The Value of Formal Planning for Strategic Decisions: Review of Empirical Research, *Strategic Management Journal* 3(3), 197–213.

Benson Strategy Group (2015) More Options, Shifting Mindsets, Driving Better Choices, Uber and MADD. https://newsroom.uber.com/wp-content/uploads/2015/01/UberMADD-Report.pdf (accessed 2 June 2015).

Brownlie, D. (1993) The marketing Audit: A Metrology and Explanation, *Marketing Intelligence and Planning* 11(1), 4–12.

Carson, D. (1990) Some Exploratory Models for Assessing Small Firms' Marketing Performance: A Qualitative Approach, *European Journal of Marketing* 24(11), 8–51.

CBS Money Watch (2015) Uber faces another setback in Europe, CBS Money Watch, 18 March. http://www.cbsnews.com/news/uber-faces-another-setback-in-europe (accessed October 2018)

Cellan-Jones, R. (2015) Google Glass sales halted but firm says kit is not dead, *BBC*, 15 January. http://www.bbc.co.uk/news/technology-30831128 (accessed October 2018)

Challouma, S. (2018) *Campaign*, 2 July, https://www.campaignlive.co.uk/article/birds-eye-marketing-director-why-gave-captain-rugged-new-look-2018/1486490 (accessed October 2018)

Connley, C. (2018) Jeff Bezos' 'two pizza rule' can help you hold more productive meetins, *CNBC* 30th April https://www.cnbc.com/2018/04/30/jeff-bezos-2-pizza-rule-can-help-you-hold-more-productive-meetings.html (accessed October 2018)

Davis, M. (2014) Six Companies That Changed Direction And Found Success, The richest.com, 10 February. http://www.therichest.com/business/companies-business/six-companies-that-changed-direction-and-found-success (accessed 28 March 2015).

Day, G. S. (1984) *Strategic Marketing Planning: The Pursuit of Competitive Advantage*, St Paul, MN: West, 41.

Driver, J.C. (1990) Marketing Planning in Style, *Quarterly Review of Marketing* 15(4), 16–21.

Drucker, P.F. (1993) *Management Tasks, Responsibilities, Practices*, New York: Harper and Row, 128

Drucker, P. (2007) *Management: Tasks, Responsibilities, and Practices*, New York: Truman Talley Books/E.P. Dutton, 285.

Ewing, A. (2015), 'Uber draws Teslas, Therapy Out of Taxi Rivals in Sweden. http://www.bloomberg.com/news/articles/2015-01-26/uber-draws-teslas-therapy-out-of-swedish-rivals-unfazed-by-apps (accessed October 2018)

Frizell, S. (2015) Uber Just Answered Everything You Want to Know About Your Driver, *Time*, 22 January. http://time.com/3678507/uber-driver-questions (accessed 2 June 2015).

Fuller, P.B. (1994) Assessing Marketing in Small and Medium-Sized Enterprises, *European Journal of Marketing* 28(12), 34–9.

Gapper, J. and Jopson, B. (2011) An inventor with fire in his belly and Jobs in his sights, *Financial Times*, 30 September.

Gillespie, A. (2007) Foundation of Economics, *Oxford University Press*, 12: http://www.oup.com/uk/orc/bin/9780199296378/01student/additional/page_12.htm (accessed October 2018).

Glasses Direct (n.d.) http://www.glassesdirect.co.uk/about/story/#os2006 (accessed 15 January 2012).

Google (n.d.) http://www.google.com/about/corporate/company (accessed 15 January 2012).

Greenley, G. (1987) An Exposition into Empirical Research into Marketing Planning, *Journal of Marketing Management* 3(1), 83–102.

Greenley, G.E. (1986) *The Strategic and Operational Planning of Marketing*, Maidenhead: McGraw-Hill, 185–7.

Hanan, M. (1974) Reorganize your company around its markets, *Harvard Business Review*, November–December, 63–74.

Hazan, E. (2014) Paypal's vision for a global market place, McKinsey & Company, August. http://www.mckinsey.com/insights/high_tech_telecoms_internet/paypals_vision_for_a_global_marketplace (accessed 4 April 2015).

Helmore, E. (2005) Big Apple, *Observer*, 16 January, 3.

Hobbs, T. (2016) Birds Eye Launches expansive rebrand as Captain Birds Eye Returns, *Marketing Week*, 19 March, https://www.marketingweek.com/2016/03/19/birds-eye-launches-expansive-rebrand-as-captain-birdseye-returns-yes-again/ (accessed October 2018)

Hooley, G.J., Cox, A.J. and Adams, A. (1992) Our Five Year Mission: To Boldly Go Where No Man Has Been Before . . . , *Journal of* Marketing *Management* 8(1), 35–48.

Hooley, G., Piercy, N.F. and Nicoulaud, B. (2012) *Marketing Strategy & Competitive Positioning*, Harlow: FT Prentice Hall, 32.

Jaworski, B.J. and Kohli, A.K. (1993) Market orientation: antecedents and consequences, *Journal of Marketing* 57, 53–70.

Kumar, K., Subramaniam, R. and Yauger, C. (1998) Examining the market orientation performance relationship: a context-specific study, *Journal of Management* 24(2), 201–33.

Leppard, J.W. and McDonald, M.H.B. (1991) Marketing Planning and Corporate Culture: A Conceptual Framework which Examines Management Attitudes in the Context of Marketing Planning, *Journal of Marketing Management* 7(3), 213–36.

Levitt, T. (1960) Marketing Myopia, *Harvard Business Review*, July–August, 45–6.

Madden, R. (2011) The best form of innovation is simply doing things better, *Marketing Week*, 5 May, 12.

McDonald, M.H.B. (1984) The Theory and Practice of Marketing Planning for Industrial Goods in International Markets, Cranfield Institute of Technology, PhD thesis.

McDonald, M.H.B. (1989) The Barriers to Marketing Planning, *Journal of Marketing Management* 5(1), 1–18.

McDonald, M.H.B. (2007) *Marketing Plans*, London: Butterworth-Heinemann, 2nd edn.

Mintzberg, H. (1975) The Manager's Job: Folklore and Fact, *Harvard Business Review*, July–August, 49–61.

Narver, J.C. and Slater, S.F. (1998) Additional thoughts on the measurement of market orientation: a comment on Deshpande and Farley, *Journal of Market-Focused Management* 2(1), 233–6.

O'Shaughnessy, J. (1995) *Competitive Marketing*, Boston, Mass: Allen & Unwin.

Oktemgil, M. and Greenley, G. (1997) Consequences of High and Low Adaptive Capability in UK Companies, *European Journal of Marketing* 31(7), 445–66.

Pandora Group (2015) *Business Strategy*, Pandora Group, 2 April. http://pandoragroup.com/About-Pandora/Business-Strategy (accessed October 2018)

Pandora Group (2018) *Business Strategy* https://pandoragroup.com/About-Pandora/Business-Strategy (accessed October 2018)

Pandya, S. (2017) Improving the learning and developmental potential of SWOT analysis: introducing the LISA framework, *Strategic Direction* 33(3), 12–14.

Phillips, L.W., Chang, D.R. and Buzzell, R.D. (1983) Product Quality, Cost Position and Business Performance: A Test of Some Key Hypotheses, *Journal of Marketing* 47(Spring), 26–43.

Piercy, N. (1986) The Role and Function of the Chief Marketing Executive and the Marketing Department, *Journal of Marketing Management* 1(3), 265–90.

Piercy, N. (2008) *Market-led Strategic Change: Transforming the Process of Going to Market*, Oxford: Butterworth-Heinemann, 259.

Piercy, N. and Giles, W. (1989) Making SWOT Analysis Work, *Marketing Intelligence and Planning* 7(5/6), 5–7.

Porter, M.E. (1980) *Competitive Strategy: Techniques for Analysing Industries and Competitors*, New York: Free Press, Ch. 2.

Pulendran, S., Speed, R. and Widing, R. (2003) Marketing planning, market orientation and business performance, *European Journal of Marketing* 37(3/4), 476–97.

Raimond, P. and Eden, C. (1990) Making Strategy Work, *Long Range Planning* 23(5), 97–105.

Saker, J. and Speed, R. (1992) Corporate Culture: Is it Really a Barrier to Marketing Planning? *Journal of Marketing Management* 8(2), 177–82.

Samsung (n.d.) http://www.samsung.com/uk/aboutsamsung/corporateprofile/vision.html (accessed 15 January 2012).

Sanghani, R. (2013) How Jeff Bezos rules his Amazonian empire, *The Telegraph*, 15 October. http://www.telegraph.co.uk/technology/amazon/10379912/How-Jeff-Bezos-rules-his-Amazonian-empire.html (accessed 28 March 2015).

Sanghera, S. (2005) Why So Many Mission Statements are Mission Impossible, *Financial Times*, 22 July, 13.

Terpstra, V. and Sarathy, R. (1991) *International Marketing*, Orlando, FL: Dryden, Ch. 17.

Tesseras, L. (2014) Birds Eye readies £16m marketing campaign to reveal new brand positioning, *Marketing Week*, 28 February. https://www.marketingweek.com/2014/02/28/birds-eye-readies-16m-marketing-campaign-to-reveal-new-brand-positioning (accessed 28 February 2015).

The Economist (2010) Breaking and entering: Why it is hard to copy Santander, 13 May: http://www.economist.com/node/16078452 (accessed January 2012).

Vasconcellos, E. Sa, J. (2014) From Levett to the global age: one more time, how do we define our business? *Management Decision* 49(1), 9–115.

Van Vliet, V. (2011) *Gary Hamel*, ToolsHero. http://www.toolshero.com/gary-hamel

Virgin Atlantic (2018) Virgin Atlantic 2018 financial results, *Virgin Atlantic*, 10 March. http://www.virgin-atlantic.com/gb/en/footer/media-centre/press-releases/financial-results-2018.html (accessed October 2018)

Weitz, B.A. and Wensley, R. (1988) *Readings in Strategic Marketing*, New York: Dryden, 4.

West, G. (2014) Pandora put life's unforgettable moments centre stage in 'Wherever life takes you, take it with you' campaign, *The Drum*, 14 November. http://www.thedrum.com/news/2014/11/14/pandora-put-lifes-unforgettable-moments-centre-stage-wherever-life-takes-you-take-it (accessed 2 April 2015).

Wilson, A. (1982) *Aubrey Wilson's Marketing Audit Checklists: A Guide to Effective Marketing Resource Realization*, 1st edn, Maidenhead, UK: McGraw-Hill.

CASE 35
Marks & Spencer: Challenging Times Ahead

Introduction

Marks & Spencer (M&S) was founded in 1884 when Michael Marks, a Polish refugee, opened a market stall in Leeds. In 1894, Marks went into partnership with Thomas Spencer, a former cashier from wholesale company Dewhirst, and in 1904 Marks & Spencer opened its first shop, selling a range of general goods. Over more than 100 years, the M&S name has grown and evolved, with M&S becoming a public company in 1936. M&S is often viewed as a quintessentially British brand. As one the UK's leading retailers, M&S sells homeware, food and clothing to the masses. One of the elements that makes the retailer so unique is that it has remained consistent with its corporate image while, at the same time, continuously evolving. The retailer has always had a clear vision for the brand that concentrated on bringing quality to British consumers.

Over the years, the retailer has had to deal with many changes in its internal and external environment which have impacted on its business operations. The M&S customer has evolved, but M&S hasn't always kept up with its customers' changing needs. Some would argue that the retailer has lost its competitive edge and has failed to respond adequately to new entrants into the marketplace. Throughout troubled times for the UK high street, the M&S brand has maintained its premium price, even when its competitors have slashed theirs. The retailer has also survived recessions and has had to adapt to growing environmental concerns, social and cultural changes and technological advances. M&S has responded to these growing environmental and social concerns by launching Plan A, which is its way of helping to build a sustainable future by being a business that enables its customers to have a positive impact on well-being, communities and the planet through everything it does. In terms of economic factors, the UK's decision to leave the EU is also likely to have an impact on the retailer's business going forward, and this has left people wondering whether M&S will continue to be a formidable presence on the high street in future years.

Challenging Times

M&S's fortunes have changed over the years. Its profits peaked in the financial year 1997/98, when it became the first British retailer to make a pre-tax profit of over £1 billion. However, it subsequently went into a sudden slump, which took the company and its shareholders, who included hundreds of thousands of small investors, by surprise. Even though the retailer recovered somewhat from this slump, in recent years it has been experiencing financial decline. M&S reported headline pre-tax profits of £613.8 million in 2017, but in 2018 this declined further to £573 million. Shares in the retailer have also almost halved in value since peaking at 59p in 2015. While M&S has dominated the UK clothing market for decades, its position as the clothes retailer with the largest market share is now 'perilously close to being lost to Primark', according to Maureen Hinston of data firm Global Data. Faced with these financial difficulties, in early 2016, Steve Rowe took over the reins as the new CEO of the retail chain. Tasked with turning the retailer's fortunes around, Rowe unveiled a new five-year turnaround plan to overcome some of the challenges facing the retailer and to revive the brand and make M&S special again.

Changing the M&S Business Model

A three-stage turnaround plan, launched in November 2017, focuses first on restoring the M&S basics, then shaping the retailer's future, before finally making

M&S special. M&S is implementing the plan over the next few years while flexing and adapting the plan as it goes, at pace. Rowe's turnaround plan has made 'recovering and growing' M&S clothing and home as one of the top priorities, while at the same time not losing the retailer's focus on food. When it comes to the food side of their business, M&S has always done an excellent job of positioning its food as a premium treat to aspire to, through attractive communication and clever activation. At present, food sales are positive, with M&S's food business accounting for around half of its revenue. Maintaining this momentum will be key to the retailer's success, but this will be no easy task for the retailer given the fact that its food is viewed as too expensive by some, and as the discounters such as Aldi and Lidl have caught up. M&S believes that it must broaden its appeal, getting its pricing and product ranges right, so that it can retain its core customers and attract busy families who want great-tasting quality food at outstanding value. In April 2017, M&S announced its plan to further expand the food area of the business, opening many new Simply Food outlets. Every M&S Simply Food store offers a handy range of high quality foods, including ready meals, fresh produce and staple groceries, plus wine, beer and flowers. These stores tend to have a smaller footprint than their clothing stores, and the hope is that this will help drive the ratio of turnover to shelf space.

M&S is a divided business. While its food offering is seen as premium, British, high quality and aspirational, its clothing and other merchandise have failed to gain traction. Its clothing division has been a perennial headache for M&S, with years of falling sales. Customers have been steadily losing interest in this side of the retailer's business, and the retailer has been trying to rework this. Rowe's predecessor, Boland, attempted a number of times to revamp M&S's clothes without much joy. The solution isn't necessarily getting rid of the clothing side of M&S's business, as general merchandise still accounts for £4 billion of sales for the retailer. Rowe has recently announced the retailer's intentions to slash prices, make it clearer who its clothing product lines are for, and simply be more in tune with who the M&S customer is, in an attempt to re-establish its price position in the market. According to Rowe, 'Our ambition is to be the UK's essential clothing retailer—famous for quality products that offer contemporary wearable style at great prices.'

M&S's turnaround plan includes attempting to transform the retailer's UK store estate. Critics argue that the retailer simply has too many shops and that its store portfolio needs to be reduced. Big shops used to be the route to bigger revenues, but, in the age of e-commerce, that is no longer the case. Some of its small outlets need investment and some of its bigger stores have become too difficult to navigate. Bringing in coffee shops and other services has helped improve matters somewhat. In May 2018, the retailer announced the radical decision to close more than 100 of its stores by 2022, with these closures affecting its clothing and home stores, which have underperformed for several years. Through store closures, the retailer hopes to better deal with the company's deteriorating financial performance. M&S says that, to date, the closure programme is producing good results, with significant sales transfer to nearby more profitable sites.

M&S's turnaround plan focuses on the retailer's desire to become a digital-first retailer. The retailer has suffered in recent times due to its slow-moving and unimpressive approach to e-commerce. The retail market is highly competitive, and about a quarter of fashion and footwear in the UK is now bought online. M&S has struggled to adapt to this changing retail environment, and its slow response to develop the online side of its business has left it playing catch-up with savvier retailers like ASOS and Zara. The retailer is taking steps to change this and plans to become a digital-first organisation and the UK's 'essential clothing retailer', building on strengths in lingerie, schoolwear, denim and suits to sharpen its ranges and provide 'better choices with fewer options' and 'contemporary wearable style'. It aims to make a third of its clothing and home sales online while rationalising in-store space by closing stores, reducing space and making relocations. M&S's ambition is to become a truly digital business, not only competitive online but adept at using artificial intelligence to better interact with customers to develop a more personalized relationship.

Conclusion

M&S is an organization that is undergoing substantial change, and the overall outlook for the retailer is uncertain. There is an accepted view that the retailer has not done enough to capture the public's attention over the last few years. M&S has been described as complacent, too inward-looking and too corporate. Its business has been drifting for over a decade, and M&S is going through a crucial period of transition—growing its online business and revitalizing its business model and market positioning. Implementation of its five-year plan is in its first phase. According to Rowe, 'M&S needs to change and change fast. We are now in the first phase of our transformation, restoring the basics so that we can deliver sustainable, profitable growth to investors, colleagues and the communities in which we operate.' Although the turnaround is underway, it is obvious that M&S still has a lot of work to do in the coming years as the 134-year-old retailer battles to revive its fortunes.

»

Questions

1. **Conduct a marketing audit of M&S. Which aspects of the marketing environment do you think have the greatest impact on M&S's business?**
2. **The development of Plan A is M&S's response to changing social and environmental concerns. Visit the retailer's website and learn more about its Plan A 2025 commitments. Comment on how Plan A differs from the retailer's five-year turnaround plan.**
3. **Identify the main challenges that M&S is facing. Comment on how the retailer's five-year turnaround plan is addressing these challenges.**
4. **Perform a SWOT analysis of M&S. On the basis of your SWOT analysis, outline recommendations you would make to the retailer.**

This case was written by Marie O' Dwyer, Waterford Institute of Technology, Republic of Ireland.

References

Based on: A Short History of Marks & Spencer, https://marksintime.marksandspencer.com/download?id=996; Hodgson, S. (2017) Quintessentially British brands: It's not just branding, it's Marks & Spencer branding, *Fabric*, 30 November, http://fabrikbrands.com/marks-and-spencer-branding; *The Telegraph* (2008) Marks & Spencer: A recent history, 2 July, https://www.telegraph.co.uk/finance/newsbysector/retailandconsumer/2792584/Marks-and-Spencer-A-recent-history.html; *Craft*, Marks & Spencer profile, https://craft.co/marks-spencer; *Business World* (2018) Profits dive 62pc at M&S, 21 November, *Independent*, https://www.independent.ie/business/world/profits-dive-62pc-at-ms-36937362.html; Halliday, S. (2018) Primark to gain top UK clothing retailer title from M&S say analysts, *Fashion Network*, 22 May, http://uk.fashionnetwork.com/news/Primark-to-gain-top-UK-clothing-retailer-title-from-M-S-say-analysts,979889.html; Press Association (2018) Marks & Spencer profits plunge as transformation costs weigh, *Daily Mail*, 23 May, http://www.dailymail.co.uk/wires/pa/article-5760907/Marks—Spencer-profits-plunge-transformation-costs-weigh.html; Tan, L. (2016) How Marks & Spencer could fashion a desirable new brand image, *The Drum*, 11 January, http://www.thedrum.com/opinion/2016/01/11/how-marks-spencer-could-fashion-desirable-new-brand-image; McMillan Woods (2017) M&S to close stores at home and abroad as profits fall, 11 September, http://www.mcmillanwoods.com/2017/09/11/ms-to-close-stores-at-home-and-abroad-as-profits-fall; Wood, Z. (2017) New M&S chair promises new radical shake-up to fix 'drifting' business, *The Guardian*, 8 November, https://www.theguardian.com/business/2017/nov/08/marks-and-spencer-speeds-up-shut-down-of-clothing-scales-back-simply-food; Shapland, M. (2017) Profits plummet at Marks & Spencer but boss Steve Rowe wins backers with food-only store openings, *This is Money*, 24 May, http://www.thisismoney.co.uk/money/markets/article-4536734/Clothes-sales-fall-Marks-Spencer.html; Wood, Z. (2016) M&S to close 30 UK stores and cut back on clothing, *The Guardian*, 8 November, https://www.theguardian.com/business/2016/nov/08/m-and-s-marks-spencer-close-80-stores-major-overhaul; Smith, R. (2016) The five big challenges facing M&S boss Steve Rowe, *Management Today*, 25 May, https://www.managementtoday.co.uk/five-big-challenges-facing-m-s-boss-steve-rowe/article/1389807; *Financial Times* (2018) Marks and Spencer confirms expanded store closure programme, 22 May, https://www.ft.com/content/e2de940a-5d9e-11e8-ad91-e01af256df68; Wood, S. and Butler, S. (2018) Seven reasons why Marks & Spencer is in trouble, *Internet Retailing*, 23 May, *The Guardian*, https://www.theguardian.com/business/2018/may/23/seven-reasons-why-marks-spencer-is-in-trouble; Rigby, C. (2017) M&S closes stores and targets online growth in a digital-first future, *Internet Retailing*, 8 November, https://internetretailing.net/themes/themes/mamps-closes-stores-and-targets-online-growth-in-a-digital-first-future-15532; Ritson, M. (2017) Mark Ritson: This is not just a decline, this is an M&S decline, *Marketing Week*, https://www.marketingweek.com/2017/07/12/mark-ritson-ms-decline

CASE 36

From Value Added in Africa (VAA) to Proudly Made in Africa (PMIA)—A Strategic change

> "Delivering beautiful, ethical goods from Africa to the world, reliably."
>
> **(VAA FOUNDER, CONALL O'CAOIMH, 2014)**

The idea of finding a way to provide African producers with access to markets where they could export ready-to-retail products came to the founder of VAA when he was on a trip to Mozambique in 1996. Conall O'Caoimh saw large 50 kilogram bags of cashew nuts being exported and thought that there must be a way to allow producers to trade in value-added goods, by supporting them to export products in ready-to-export packaging. However, it would be over a decade before that idea came to fruition in the form of Value Added in Africa (VAA).

With the 'cashew nut' idea always in mind, VAA was set up in 2008 under the original name Value Added Africa with a mandate to support African producers in overcoming cultural and institutional barriers to penetrating markets with value-added goods. Table C36.1 gives an overview of VAA.

At the start-up stage, the founders were working from a charitable model; they believed that retail businesses would support them because of the 'good work' they were doing, but they soon realized that businesses need to make profits and would only engage with VAA if what it was offering made business sense. Creating social value alone was not enough. They moved to a social enterprise model, enabling better engagement with businesses, offering services that businesses would want to take on and moving towards becoming self-financing. VAA acted as 'sales reps for producers' and spent time trying to engage buyers. However, VAA did not achieve significant sales; it was waiting for 'better products' to offer retailers. VAA knew the benefits of the manufactured African-made retail-ready products, but also recognized the outstanding challenges it had to overcome in order to advance its mission (see Table C36.2).

Addressing the Challenges

Understanding these challenges, VAA continued to work with African producers, building their capacity

TABLE C36.1 Overview of VAA

Category	Non-profit social enterprise
Established	In 2008, as VAA, by Co-founders Conall O'Caoimh, Michelle Hardiman and Professor Matt Murphy
Mission	To open channels for African businesses to market their processed goods in international markets
Purpose/role	Formed to act as a 'trade facilitator' between African producers with retail-ready products and European businesses
Objectives	• To enable African communities to lift themselves out of poverty through the development of sustainable livelihoods, decent work and economic growth • To make it 'normal' for international retailers and brands to source responsibly made finished goods from Africa • To make it 'normal' for African countries to add value to their natural resources before they export them

Source: www.proudlymadeinafrica.org

»

TABLE C36.2 The benefits and challenges for manufactured goods from Africa

Benefits	Challenges
• Security of supply	• Understanding of the marketplace
• New and different products	• Product consistency and volume
• Cost advantages	• Infrastructural and institutional barriers
• Preferential tariff rates	• Finding appropriate products
• Traceability and transparency	• Capacity and skills
• A good story	• Distance from the marketplace
• Less waste	
• Income and community development	
• Creation of jobs and a boost to the regional economies	
Source: Brouder and Tulej (2015)	

and organizing meetings throughout Europe, but in a more focused way than before, through the packaging design programme, which involved top-level Irish and British design companies, who worked with African producers to redesign their brand identities for the European market, as well as the networking programme, the aim of which was to create a forum for African business leaders to network and exchange business ideas. However, one of the main challenges faced by VAA was in addressing the retail buyers' poor comprehension of African produce and a negative bias against trade with Africa. VAA decided to focus on its marketing communications strategy in an attempt to educate and inform buyers and consumers alike of the quality of African produce and the consistency of this produce for the marketplace. As a result, VAA embarked on a process, facilitated by Brand Led Growth (www.brandledgrowth.com), through which it revisited its core values and vision and rethought the VAA strategy.

A number of stakeholders (producers, advertisers, buyers, customers, VAA board, and creatives) were invited to participate in that process, in which they identified the core values of the brand (see figure).

Once the core values were established, a second outcome of the Brand Led Growth project was an assessment of the organization's name. Market research showed that the name Value Added Africa was too esoteric a name to have traction in the marketplace and with commercial traders outside the development sector, and that there was potential to develop a more commercially focused sub-brand to better reflect the values of both the organization and the producers it worked with.

'Our concern at the time was that there was potentially a lot of African brands whose reputation we would need to build with consumers, and this would be a challenge, given limited marketing resources . . . a big impetus for us was to build a strong reputation for a single brand entity' (Donogh Lane, CEO, Brand Led Growth).

Quality: *The producer has the required systems and checks in place for export to the US and EU:*

- *Has robust quality management systems in place*
- *Independent QC checks for fashion lines and HACCP training for food lines. For bigger organisations, has international certifications such as ISO standards*

Origin: *African-made:*

- *Has minimum 65% inputs sourced in Africa, before packaging*

Ready to retail: *No raw materials, fresh or unprocessed goods*

- *Value added at source as much as possible*

Positive social impact: *Transparent supply chains and good control on lower supply chain tiers:*

- *Accredited or following an international standard of labour rights, independently assessed workplace standards or robust management systems in place to monitor social responsibility*
- *Fair trade or open negotiation price setting with sub-producers*
- *Workers are supported and provided with every opportunity to upskill and develop in their roles*

VAA brand values

Source: www.proudlymadeinafrica.org

Proudly Made in Africa Brand was Born

The new concept was tested with stakeholders and revised a number of times. Up to this point, there was no visual identity. Once the concept was agreed, a company called Dynamo was engaged to help build

Proudly Made in Africa (PMIA) brand 2012

Proudly Made in Africa (PMIA) brand 2017

the brand identity, the look and feel, and to create the visual that is the Proudly Made in Africa (PMIA) brand (see figure). After thorough testing and research, VAA launched the PMIA brand in 2012 as a mechanism by which buyers and consumers could recognize authentic African products. PMIA is a standard that African producers can aim to achieve through stringent procedures, as the brand ensures that the finished products are quality assured, responsibly sourced, manufactured from locally grown materials and socially beneficial.

After the 2012 launch of the PMIA brand, the VAA strategy was revised in 2013 and it was decided that a new, more commercially experienced team was needed to focus efforts on the trade facilitation work. In addition, the tagline of the PMIA logo, 'Products that build communities', was felt to be too development-focused and not reflective of a brand or award that would inspire producers to want to carry it on their products. The tagline was amended to 'Promoting excellence in African industry'.

In 2016, the founders stepped down and Vikki Brennan was hired as the new CEO, shortly followed by programme and sourcing manager, Feena Kirrkamm. Both Vikki and Feena began their careers in commercial procurement, so have a deep understanding of brand development, product supply chains and sourcing finished goods from developing countries. Prior to joining PMIA, Vikki spent her career creating responsible supply chain standards for international brands and global tripartite initiatives, so was seen as a logical successor to continue the good work started at VAA on building responsible African supply chains. On the board, new trade-focused members were brought in to replace the outgoing founders. The new commercial team decided to rebrand the entire organization as PMIA to ensure that the VAA and PMIA brands were not competing against each other.

African businesses engaging with PMIA wanted to ensure that they met the criteria for the desirable PMIA award as a way of guaranteeing to consumers their own high standards (see Table C36.3).

Brett Beach, CEO and founder of Mia Chocolate, was keen to get the PMIA award on his company's products

TABLE C36.3 Sample of Businesses working with PMIA

Company	Product offering	Relationship with PMIA
Meru Herbs, Kenya	Produces a range of organic herbal teas, gourmet fruit jams and tomato based sauces	• 90% of its produce is exported to Europe and Japan, and 10% is sold to the local market • Helped connect with potential new international buyers, formulation of a marketing strategy and product packaging • Facilitated in gaining new wholesale customers in England and Scotland
Eswatini Kitchens, Swaziland	Produces a range of chilli sauces	• Supported in fulfilling EU compliance standards in the labelling of its products • Facilitated in gaining a new wholesale customer in the UK
MIA, Madagascar	Gourmet chocolate made from bean to bar in Madagascar	• PMIA verified the Mia value chain and granted Mia the PMIA award of excellence • Available in gourmet food stores and markets in the UK, Belgium and Ireland
Soul of Africa, Ethiopia	Shoe manufacturer	• Supported to gain market entry to the UK high street. Currently selling in Clarks and Vivo Barefoot stores

Source: Vikki Brennan, CEO of Proudly Made in Africa. Interview date 1 August 2018.

»

»

to reinforce the quality of the product offering: 'PMIA embodies what we stand for, which is adding value in Madagascar, as a way to create jobs there . . . it's not only a way to improve prosperity, it's also about the quality of the product. We want to demonstrate to the market that the continent that produces the best ingredients can also introduce the best products.'

PMIA verified the Mia value chain and, in 2017, granted Mia an award to use the PMIA brand on its packaging. Mia, with the PMIA certification, launched in February 2018 and is currently available in selected gourmet stores across the UK, Belgium and Ireland.

The Future for PMIA

PMIA emerged as a result of the passion of a small group of people who believed that change can be made. It is a relatively young organization that has achieved much with limited resources in a competitive market environment and has stayed true to its mission. It had to adapt its business model and review organizational strategies on an ongoing basis, learning as it developed and continuing to learn from each opportunity and risk it took. The PMIA brand and standard has contributed to the development of the business, providing recognition and an integral identity between African produce and quality. It is hoped that, over time, this brand will be as recognizable as other brands such as Fairtrade.

Questions

1. **Based on your own experience and awareness, what are your perceptions of African-produced goods on your supermarket shelf?**
2. **What do you consider were the top three challenges originally faced by Value Added in Africa in bringing African products to the marketplace?**
3. **Based on your understanding of this case, what do you perceive is the significance of the Proudly Made in Africa (PMIA) brand image from a consumer's and a retailer's perspective?**
4. **Discuss the six considerations that can be used to test the core strategy of PMIA.**

This case study was written by Dr Christina O'Connor, Lecturer in Marketing, Maynooth University, Vikki Brennan, CEO of PMIA and Grace Carson, Queens University Belfast

References

Based on: Brouder, A.-M. and S. Tulej (2015) Africa: Making it#- A UK Business Perspective, http://www.proudlymadeinafrica.org/images/uploads/docs/VAA-FFF_Africa_Making_It_-_A_UK_Business_Perspective_report.pdf, 22–4; www.proudlymadeinafrica.org; www.brandledgrowth.com; www.africacashewalliance.com; www.madecasse.com

CHAPTER 19
Analysing Competitors and Creating a Competitive Advantage

> *If you don't have a competitive advantage, don't compete.*
>
> **JACK WELCH, FORMER CHIEF EXECUTIVE OF GENERAL ELECTRIC**

LEARNING OBJECTIVES

After reading this chapter, you should be able to:

1. describe the determinants of industry attractiveness
2. explain how to analyse competitors
3. distinguish between differentiation and cost leader strategies
4. discuss the sources of competitive advantage
5. discuss the value chain
6. explain how to create and maintain a differential advantage
7. explain how to create and maintain a cost leadership position
8. discuss the nature of competitive behaviour
9. explain the key elements of a competitive marketing strategy

Satisfying customers is central to the marketing concept, but it is not enough to guarantee success. The real question is whether a company can satisfy customers better than the competition. For example, many car manufacturers market cars that give customer satisfaction in terms of appearance, reliability and performance. They meet the basic requirements necessary to compete. Customer choice, however, will depend on creating more value than the competition. Extra value is brought about by establishing a competitive advantage—a topic that will be examined later in this chapter.

Since corporate performance depends on both customer satisfaction and creating greater value than the competition, companies need to understand their competitors as well as their customers. By understanding its competitors, a firm can better predict their reactions to any marketing initiative that the firm might make and exploit any weaknesses. Competitor analysis is thus crucial to the successful implementation of marketing strategy. Our discussion of competitors in this chapter begins by examining competitive industry structure, explains how to create competitive and differential advantage, and then explains cost leadership. Finally, we explore the key elements associated with developing a competitive marketing strategy.

Analysing Competitive Industry Structure

An **industry** is a group of companies that market products that are close substitutes for each other. There is more to understanding an industry and how it works than the core product or service being sold. Commonly, we refer to the oil, computer or retail industry. Some industries are more profitable than others. In the past, the car, steel, coal and textile industries have been highly profitable; in more recent years, however, they have had poor profitability records, whereas the creative industries, (e.g. television, publishing, web development), pharmaceuticals and soft drinks industries have recently enjoyed high profits. Not all this difference can be explained by the fact that one industry provides better customer satisfaction than another. Other determinants of industry attractiveness and long-run profitability shape the rules of competition. These are the threat of entry of new competitors, the threat of substitutes, the bargaining power of buyers and of suppliers, and the rivalry between the existing competitors (Porter, 1980). The intensity of these forces shapes an industry and its levels of performance. Their influence is shown diagrammatically in Figure 19.1, which shows what is known as the Porter model of competitive industry structure. Each of the five forces, in turn, comprises a number of elements that, together, combine to determine the strength of each force and its effect on the degree of competition. Each force is discussed below.

The threat of new entrants

New entrants can raise the level of competition in an industry, which may ultimately reduce its attractiveness. For example, Starbucks entered the coffee capsules market to take on market leaders Nespresso. Nestlé owns the Nespresso brand and has made significant investment in building the market for this product in Europe using an extensive advertising campaign fronted by Hollywood actor George Clooney, which led to a 20 per cent rise in sales. Nespresso's high levels of profitability have attracted many new entrants, including Green Mountain, Côte D'Or and Kenco (see Exhibit 19.1) (Simonian and Lucas, 2012). The threat of new entrants depends on the barriers to entry. High entry barriers exist in some industries (e.g. pharmaceuticals), whereas other industries are much easier to enter (e.g. restaurants). Key **entry barriers** include:

- economies of scale
- capital requirements
- switching costs
- access to distribution
- expected retaliation.

For present competitors, industry attractiveness can be increased by raising entry barriers. High promotional and research and development (R&D) expenditures are some methods of raising barriers, as in the situation with the Nespresso coffee pods. Nestlé continues to make a significant investment in these areas and, to further protect its market, Nestlé has struck a deal worth billions of dollars with its competitor Starbucks. Both brands benefit from wider distribution networks and greater access to new markets (BBC, 2018). Other ways of raising barriers are by taking out patents and developing strong relationships/partnerships with suppliers and/or distributors.

FIGURE 19.1
The Porter model of competitive industry structure

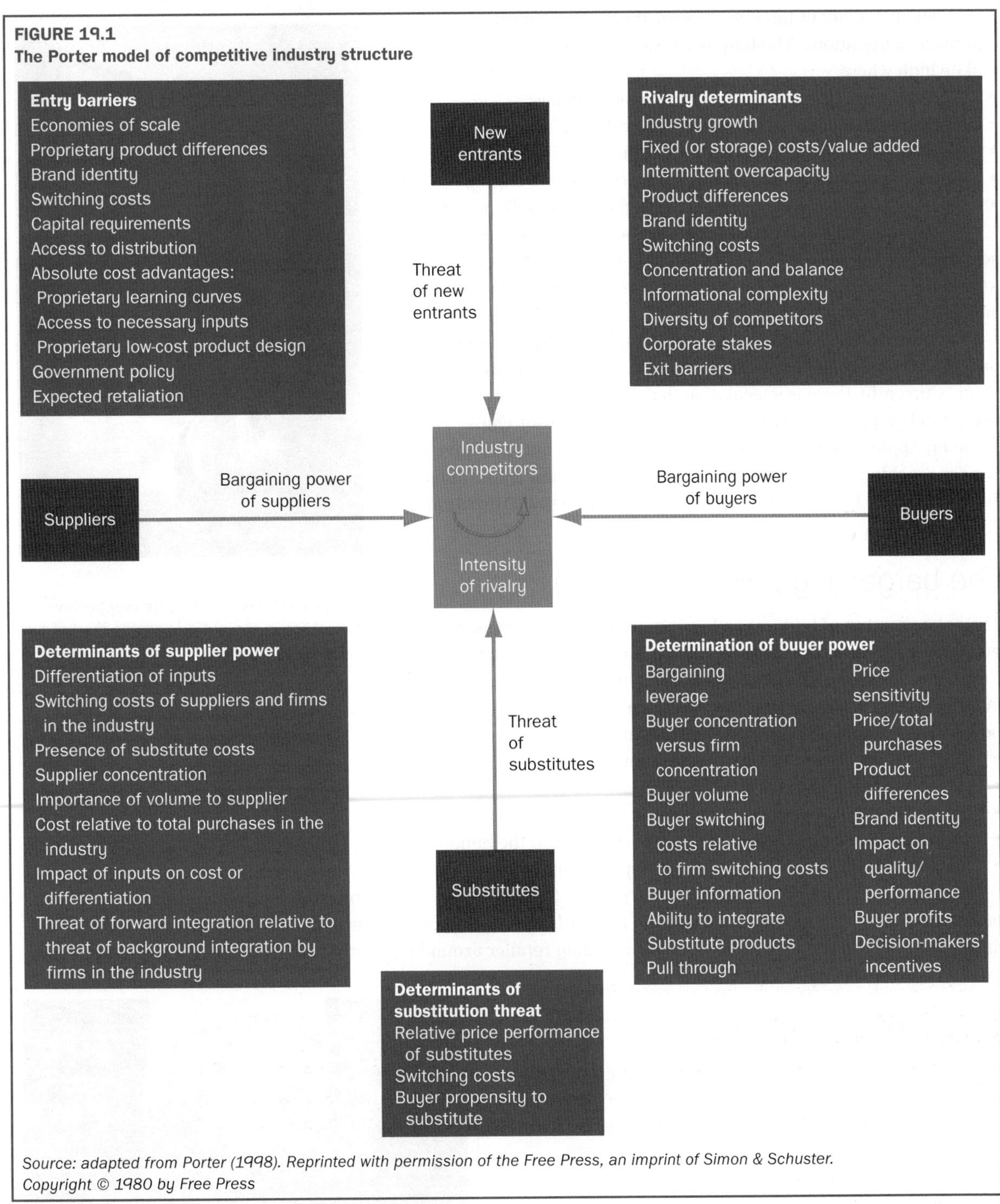

Source: adapted from Porter (1998). Reprinted with permission of the Free Press, an imprint of Simon & Schuster. Copyright © 1980 by Free Press

Some managerial actions can unwittingly lower barriers. For example, new product designs that dramatically lower manufacturing costs can ease entry for newcomers.

The bargaining power of suppliers

The cost of raw materials, components and intellectual skills can have a major bearing on a company's profitability. The higher the bargaining power of suppliers, the higher the cost of the goods. For example, when

Apple decided to adopt Intel processors, there were lengthy extensive negotiations. The bargaining power of suppliers will be high when:

- there are many buyers and few dominant suppliers
- there are differentiated highly valued products
- suppliers threaten to integrate forward into the industry
- buyers do not threaten to integrate backwards into supply
- the industry is not a key customer group to the suppliers.

A company can reduce the bargaining power of suppliers by seeking new sources of supply, threatening to integrate backwards into supply, and designing standardized components so that many suppliers can produce them.

Backwards integration means that a buyer (like Apple Inc.) purchases the supplier and a form of vertical integration takes place. Currently, there is speculation that Apple might switch from using Intel chips and replace them with ARM (processor chips made by Apple, through an acquisition of PA Semi), but this move has far-reaching implications that would mean popular Apple apps such as iTunes, TextEdit and Logic Pro would need to be rewritten (Barrett, 2018).

EXHIBIT 19.1
Nespresso aims to retain its competitive advantage in the coffee capsule market by using celebrity endorsement of the brand

The bargaining power of buyers

The concentration of buyers can lower manufacturers' bargaining power. For example, the large retailers in Europe (e.g. Dixons Carphone, Carrefour and Bauhaus GMbH) buy from many suppliers in large volumes, and this has increased the bargaining power. The bargaining power of buyers is greater when:

- there are few dominant buyers and many sellers
- products are standardized
- buyers threaten to integrate backwards into the industry
- suppliers do not threaten to integrate forwards into the buyer's industry
- the industry is not a key supplying group for buyers.

Manufacturing companies in the industry can attempt to lower buyer power by increasing the number of buyers they sell to, threatening to integrate forwards into the buyer's industry, and producing highly valued, differentiated products. Apple has become a leading retailer around the world with its dedicated high-tech Apple product stores; see Exhibit 19.2.

Threat of substitutes

The presence of substitute products can lower industry attractiveness and profitability, because these put a constraint on price levels. For example, tea and coffee are close substitutes in many European countries. Raising the price of coffee, therefore, would make tea more attractive. The threat of substitute products depends on:

- buyers' willingness to substitute
- the relative price and performance of substitutes
- the costs of switching to substitutes.

The threat of substitute products can be lowered by building up switching costs or, for example, by creating a strong, distinctive brand and maintaining

EXHIBIT 19.2
The design of Apple's Store in Shanghai reflects the innovativeness of its products

a price differential in line with perceived customer values. If these tactics fail to deter a rival from launching a substitute product, the incumbent is faced with the following options: copy the substitute and build in a differential advantage (Discount retailer Aldi sells Norpak butter, which is strikingly similar to (but cheaper than) the Danish brand Lurpak); form a strategic alliance with the rival (Nestlé and Starbucks coffee); buy the rival (LVMH got control of Christian Dior in a €12 billion deal); or move to a new market (Amazon is always on the lookout for new market opportunities, so its move into digital advertising to challenge Google and Facebook comes as no surprise).

Industry competitors

The intensity of rivalry between competitors in an industry will depend on the following factors.

- *Structure of the competition*: there is more intense rivalry when there are many small competitors or a few equally balanced competitors, and less rivalry when a clear market leader exists with a large cost advantage. Software markets are intense, highly dynamic and competitive, especially in analysis software; Microsoft, Oracle, IBM and SAP vie for market share at the top of the market, but there are hundreds of companies around the world in this market.
- *Structure of costs*: high fixed costs encourage price-cutting to fill capacity. Unilever, Anglo-Dutch manufacturer of Dove soap and Magnum ice cream, has seen sales fall, especially in US markets. Its response has been to lower its prices to maintain demand for production outputs (Chaudhuri, 2018).
- *Degree of differentiation*: basic commodity products encourage rivalry, while highly differentiated products that are hard to copy are associated with less intense rivalry. T-Mobile stands out in mobile phone markets with its one unlimited price plan. T-Mobile is positioned as an innovator in the industry—a company that is transparent and customer friendly (Trefis Team, 2017).
- *Switching costs*: rivalry is reduced when switching costs are high because the product is specialized, the customer has invested a lot of resources in learning how to use the product, and there are strong relational ties. In Europe, co-operative banks have a large market share in retail and corporate banking sectors; however, research indicates that co-operative banks like Credit Agricole (France), Dz Bank (Germany) and Banche Populari (Italy) have lower switching costs than commercial banks, suggesting that high switching costs are not necessarily robust protection from rivals (Egarius and Weill, 2016).
- *Strategic objectives*: when competitors are pursuing build strategies, competition is likely to be more intense than when following **hold objectives** or **harvesting objectives**.
- *Exit barriers*: when barriers to leaving an industry are high due to such factors as lack of opportunities elsewhere, high vertical integration, emotional barriers or the high cost of closing down plant, rivalry will be more intense than when exit barriers are low.

Companies need to balance their own position against the well-being of the industry so as not to spoil a situation of competitive stability. For example, an intense price or promotional war may gain a company a few percentage points in market share but lead to an overall fall in long-run industry profitability as competitors respond to these moves. It is sometimes better to protect industry structure than follow short-term self-interest. Revenue in investment banking is in decline, and a price war could intensify and increase competition, leading to lost revenue and profits for all the major players such as Credit Suisse, Deutsche Bank, Goldman Sachs and Morgan Stanley (Noonan, 2018).

A major threat to favourable industry structure is the use of a no-frills low-price strategy by a minor player seeking positional advantage. For example, the launch of generic products in the pharmaceutical and airline industries has lowered overall profitability. But low-cost operators face many challenges to maintain their position once established. Ryanair staff showed their dissatisfaction by going on strike, and many thousands of travellers were left stranded. The low-cost airline operator is faced with aggrieved flight crews because of poor pay and working conditions. This leaves the airline facing challenges, as increases to pay and conditions would hurt profits and create opportunities for competitors (Davies, 2018).

An intensive competitive environment means that the value created by companies in satisfying customer needs is given away to buyers through lower prices, dissipated through costly marketing battles (e.g. advertising wars) or passed on to powerful suppliers through higher prices for raw materials and components.

See Marketing in Action 19.1 to find out more about one of the world's most competitive industries.

MARKETING IN ACTION 19.1
Rovio and Supercell Battle for Market Share in the Intensely Competitive Apps Market

There are more mobile devices in the world than there are people, according to the US Census Bureau. So, it is perhaps no surprise that the competitive pressure for mobile app developers is intense. What also makes this such a highly competitive industry are the low entry barriers, the large number of competitors with similar capabilities, low switching costs for the customers, and many competitors trying to build market share. As a result, there are apps for almost every aspect of modern life, for example games, photo editors, magic pianos, healthy living and stargazing.

The app industry is reliant on downloads and revenues, but the increase in the quality of freely downloadable games has succeeded in getting customers to switch to new products. The industry has been affected by this change in pricing structure, and free downloads have come to dominate. So, companies competing in this market must find different ways to ensure a strong revenue stream and create competitive advantage. Some examples follow.

Rovio, the Finnish developer of *Angry Birds*, a highly successful mobile game app, regularly tops the charts in the app market. In 2014, *Angry Birds* was downloaded by 600 million mobile gamers. Despite the popularity of this game, the company has seen its profits fall. Part of the reason for this was a reduction in sales from associated merchandise, for example soft toys, clothing and gifts. So the company had to find other ways to extend the franchise around this game title, for example with the *Angry Birds Movie*, which produced strong revenues. *Angry Birds 2*, a second-generation game, has also started to perform, and Rovio is also developing new apps for the live games market. But licensing deals from the movies and the game in the longer term are in decline, so Rovio is looking to diversify into cloud-based gaming and streaming services.

Supercell is also a Finnish developer and one of the fastest growing technology companies in Europe. The company is known for producing successful game apps, for example *Clash of the Clans*, *Hay Day* and *Boom Beach*. Supercell has managed to take market share from market-leading app developers like Electronic Arts. The key to its success has been its ability to enter Asian markets, something that other developers have failed to achieve. This market capability did not go unnoticed by Tencent, a Chinese tech company, which bought out Supercell and created Europe's first $10 billion technology company.

These are just two examples of successful app companies. Finnish app developers seem to have been able to garner competitive advantage from several sources to ensure their success in this highly competitive industry—for example with distinctive graphics that have global appeal, successful targeting of Apple's iPad and smartphone platforms with high-quality apps that have been through extensive product testing prior to launch, and by developing creative pricing strategies.

Based on: Boren (2014); Sinclair (2015); Rovio (2018); Kuittinen (2013, 2014); Reisinger (2015); Cellan-Jones (2015); Hern, (2016)

Competitor Analysis

The analysis of how industry structure affects long-run profitability has shown the need to understand and monitor competitors. The actions of competitors can spoil an otherwise attractive industry, their weaknesses can be a target for exploitation, and their response to a firm's marketing initiatives can have a major impact on that firm's success. Indeed, companies that focus on competitors' actions have been found to achieve better business performance than those who pay less attention to their competitors (Noble, Sinha and Kumar, 2002). Competitive information can be obtained from marketing research surveys, secondary sources (e.g. the web, trade magazines, newspaper articles), analysing competitors' products and gathering competitors' sales literature.

Competitor analysis seeks to answer five key questions.

1 Who are our competitors?
2 What are their strengths and weaknesses?
3 What are their strategic objectives and thrust?
4 What are their strategies?
5 What are their response patterns?

These issues are summarized in Figure 19.2.

FIGURE 19.2
Competitor analysis

Identifying competitors
• Product form • Product substitutes • Generics • New entrants

↓

Audit competitor capabilities
• Financial • Technical • Managerial • Marketing assets • Strengths and weaknesses

↓

Infer competitor objectives and strategic thrust
• Build • Hold • Harvest • Growth directions

↓

Deduce competitor strategies
• Target segments • Differential advantages • Competitive scope • Cost leadership

↓

Estimate competitor response patterns
• Retaliator • Complacent • Hemmed-in • Selective • Unpredictable

Who are our competitors?

We need to take a wide view of potential competition. If only those companies producing technically similar products are the competition (e.g. paint companies), it is possible to miss other sources of competition, for example by ignoring companies that produce substitute products performing a similar function (e.g. polyurethane varnish companies) and those that solve a problem or eliminate it in a dissimilar way (e.g. PVC double-glazing companies). The actions of all types of competitors can affect the performance of a company and should be monitored and their responses also need to be assessed, as they will determine the outcome of any competitive move that the competing companies may wish to make. All competing companies face loss of market share or being made irrelevant if they do not understand the competitive landscape. Making the competition irrelevant is a strategic option discussed later in this chapter.

The marketing environment needs to be scanned for potential entrants into the industry. Entrants can take two forms: entrants with technically similar products, and those invading the market with substitute products. Companies with similar core competences to the present incumbents' may pose the threat of entering with technically similar products. For example, Apple's skills in computer electronics provided the springboard for it to become market leader in several key technology markets, for example the portable music player market with its iPod brand, tablet computers with its iPad, and mobile phone with its iPhone. The source of companies entering with substitute products may be more difficult to locate, however. A technological breakthrough may transform an industry by rendering the old product obsolete, for example voice-activated speakers such as Amazon Echo replacing radios and alarm clocks. In such instances, it is difficult to locate the source of the substitute product well in advance. Figure 19.3 illustrates this competitive arena.

What are competitors' strengths and weaknesses?

Having identified our competitors, the next stage is to complete a **competitor audit** to assess their relative strengths and weaknesses. Understanding competitor strengths and weaknesses is an important prerequisite for developing a competitor strategy and identifying a competitor's vulnerabilities.

The process of assessing competitors' strengths and weaknesses may take place as part of a marketing audit (see Chapter 18). As much internal, market and customer information should be gathered as is needed. For example, the following may be relevant: financial data concerning profitability, profit margins, sales and investment levels; market data relating to price levels, market share and distribution channels used; and customer data concerning awareness of brand names, perceptions of brand and company image, product and service quality and selling ability.

Not all information will be easily accessible. Management needs to decide the extent to which each element of information is worth pursuing. For example, a decision is required regarding how much expenditure is to be allocated to measuring customer awareness and perceptions through marketing research.

This process of data gathering needs to be managed so that information is available to compare the company with its competitors on the *key factors for success* in the industry. A three-stage process can then be used.

1 Identify key factors for success in the industry.

Key factors should be restricted to about six to eight factors, otherwise the analysis becomes too diffuse (Macdonald and Wilson, 2011). Which factors to use is a matter of managerial judgement. Factors may be functional (such as financial strength or flexible production) or generic (for example, the ability to respond quickly to customer needs, innovativeness, or the capability to provide other sales services). Since these factors are critical for success, they should be used to compare the company with its competitors.

2 Rate the company and competitors on each key success factor, using a rating scale.

Each company is given a score on each success factor, using a rating device such as a scale ranging from 1 (very poor) to 5 (very good). The ratings result in a set of company capability profiles. An example is given in Figure 19.4. In this example, the company is rated alongside two competitors on six key success factors. Compared with the company, competitor 1 is relatively strong regarding technical assistance to customers and access to international distribution channels, but relatively weak on product quality. Competitor 2 is relatively strong on international distribution channels but relatively weak on innovativeness, financial strength and having a well-qualified workforce.

3 Consider the implications for competitive strategy.

The competitive profile analysis helps to identify possible competitive strategies. The analysis in the example above suggests that the company should consider taking steps to improve technical assistance to customers to match or exceed competitor 1's capability on this factor. Now the company enjoys a differential advantage over competitor 1 on product quality. The company's strength in innovativeness should be used to maintain this differential advantage, and competitor 1's moves to improve product quality should be monitored carefully.

FIGURE 19.3
Competitor identification

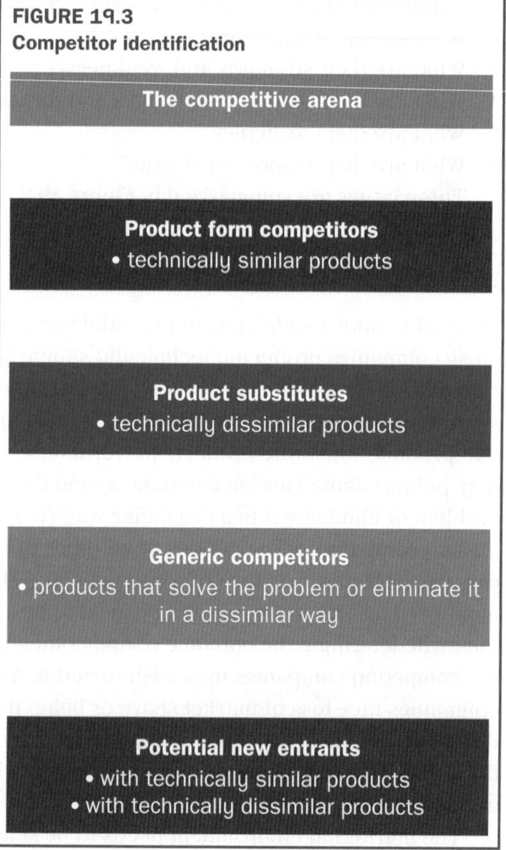

FIGURE 19.4
Company capability profiles

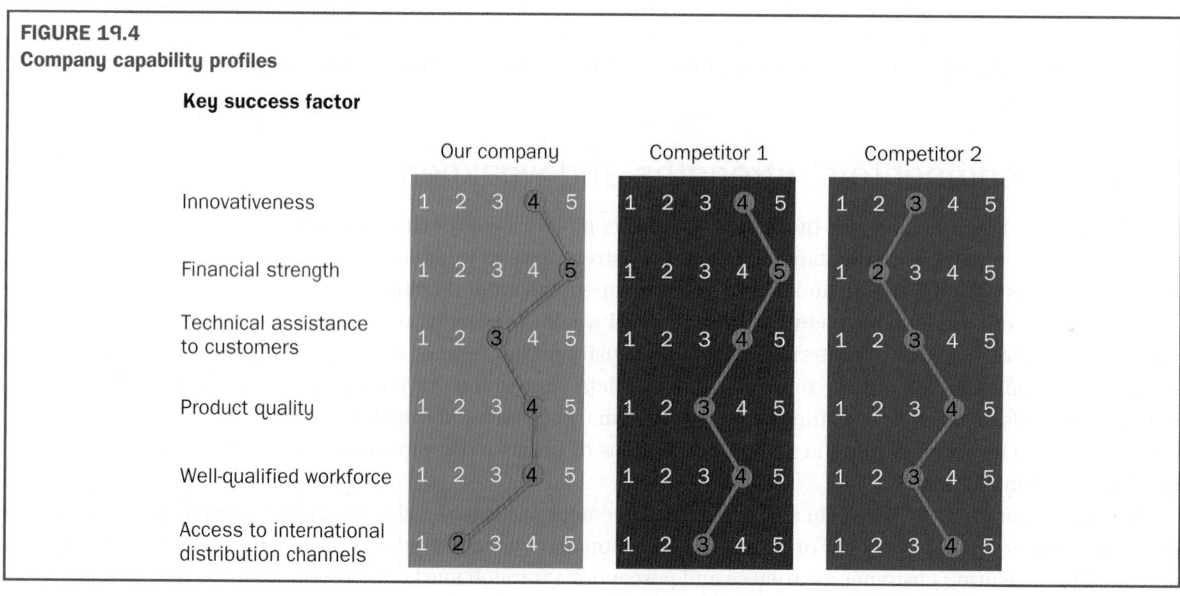

What are competitors' strategic objectives and thrust?

The third part of competitor analysis is to infer competitors' *strategic objectives*. In Chapter 18, we discussed how companies might determine their broader strategic aims by deciding which products they need to sell into particular markets. Likewise, knowing the strategic thrust of competitors can help with strategic marketing planning decision-making and also set the overall direction which defines the target market (Varadarajan, 2010). Equally, it is useful to know which strategic objectives are being pursued by competitors, because competitors' response patterns and marketing strategies may depend upon their objectives. Knowing whether a competitor is planning to build, hold, harvest or **divest** products and/or strategic business units is also important for planning.

Determining a competitor's objectives can be difficult, as information of a strategic nature can be hard to come by. However, by studying market conditions, it is possible to garner insight into what objectives a competitor might be seeking to achieve, and then infer the possible implementation actions it might pursue to succeed. Table 19.1 summarizes the market conditions and implementation actions that might occur when a competitor starts to pursue a strategic marketing objective.

TABLE 19.1 Market conditions and implementation actions related to different marketing objectives

Strategic objectives	Market conditions	Implementation actions
Build	Growth markets Exploitable competitor weaknesses Firm has exploitable strengths, capabilities and resources	**Market expansion**, e.g. attract new customers; finding ways to develop new uses for the goods; increasing the frequency of use **Win marketing share** through innovative application of the marketing mix, e.g. exploit new channels to market; new products **Mergers and acquisition** **Form strategic alliances**
Hold	Firm is market leader in a mature or declining state Costs exceed the possible benefits of building market share	**Continually monitor the competition**, e.g. in a market characterized by competitive stability where no one is willing to destabilize the industry structure. Monitoring is necessary to check that there are no significant changes in competitor behaviour **Confront the competition**, e.g. where rivalry is intense and strategic action may be required to defend market share from aggressive challenges
Harvest	Market in decline Core of loyal customers exist Firm has future new products	**Eliminate R&D expenditure**, e.g. reduce investment in the products **Reformulate product**, e.g. reduce costs **Rationalize product lines**, e.g. cut product variants, keeping best-sellers **Reduce marketing spend**, e.g. cut promotional budgets and spend on advertising **Increase prices**, as loyal customers will continue to buy
Divest	Low market share in declining markets Too expensive to revive products Removal will not impact on other products	**Exit the market**, e.g. get out quickly to minimize costs and potential future losses
Niche	Niche market opportunities Small budget available Opportunities to create competitive advantage	**Market segmentation**, e.g. survey the market, apply segmentation strategies to identify underserved market opportunities. **Focused R&D**, e.g. focus on developing sustainable differential advantage **Differential advantage**, e.g. understand the needs of the customer group and satisfy their needs better than the competition **Thinking small**, e.g. place emphasis on high margins not high volume

What are their strategies?

At the product and/or service level, competitor analysis will attempt to deduce positioning strategy. This involves assessing a competitor's target market and the differential advantage of its product and/or service. The marketing mix strategies (e.g. price levels, media used for promotion, and distribution channels) may indicate target market, and marketing research into customer perceptions can be used to assess relative differential advantages.

Companies and competitors should be monitored continuously for changes in positioning strategy. For example, Volvo's traditional positioning strategy, based on safety, has been modified to give more emphasis to performance and style, enabling the company to compete with other high-performance cars.

Strategies can also be defined in terms of competitive scope. For example, are competitors attempting to service the whole market or a few segments of a **niche?** If a competitor is a niche player, is it likely that it will be content to stay in that segment or will it use the niche as a beachhead to move into other segments in the future? Japanese companies are renowned for their use of small niche markets as springboards for market segment expansion (e.g. the small car segments in the USA and Europe).

Competitors may use cost leadership, focusing on cost-reducing measures rather than expensive product development and promotional strategies. (Cost leadership will be discussed in more detail later in this chapter.) If competitors are following this strategy, it is more likely that they will be focusing R&D expenditure on process rather than product development in a bid to reduce manufacturing costs.

What are their response patterns?

A key consideration in making a strategic or tactical move is the likely response of competitors. Indeed, it is a major objective of competitor analysis to be able to predict competitor response to market and competitive changes. A competitor's past behaviour is also a guide to what they might do in the future. Market leaders often try to control competitor response by retaliatory action. These are called *retaliatory* competitors, because they can be relied on to respond aggressively to competitive challenges. For example, Amazon acquired LoveFilm, a video-streaming and DVD disc rental service, in a competitive move against US rival Netflix. LoveFilm was eventually sidelined as the demand for discs declined and the competitive intensity in streaming video markets increased. Amazon Prime now offers live video streaming and video on demand services.

By punishing competitor moves, market leaders can condition competitors to behave in predicted ways— for example, by not taking advantage of a price rise by the leader. It is not only market leaders that retaliate aggressively. Where management is known to be assertive and a move is likely to have a major impact on their performance, a strong response is usual.

The history, traditions and managerial personalities of competitors also have an influence on competitive response. Some markets are characterized by years of competitive stability with little serious strategic challenge to any of the incumbents. This can breed complacency, with predictably slow reaction times to new challenges. For example, innovation that offers superior customer value may be dismissed as a fad and unworthy of serious attention.

Another situation where competitors are unlikely to respond is where their previous strategies have restricted their scope for retaliation. An example of such a *hemmed-in competitor* was a major manufacturer of car number plates that were sold to car dealerships. A new company was started by an ex-employee, who focused on one geographical area, supplying the same quality product but with extra discount. The national supplier could not respond, since to give a discount in that region would have meant granting the discount nationwide.

A fourth type of competitor may respond *selectively*. Because of tradition or beliefs about the relative effectiveness of marketing instruments, a competitor may respond to some competitive moves but not others. For example, extra sales promotion expenditures may be matched but advertising increases to, say, build brand awareness may be ignored. Another reason for selective response is the varying degree of visibility of marketing actions. For example, giving extra price discounts may be highly visible, but providing distributors with extra support (e.g. training, sales literature, loans) may be less discernible.

A final type of competitor is totally *unpredictable* in its response pattern. Sometimes there is a response and, at other times, there is no response. Some moves are countered aggressively; with others, reaction is weak. No factors explain these differences adequately; they appear to be at the whim of management.

Interestingly, research has shown that managers tend to overreact more frequently than they underreact to competitors' marketing activities (Leeflang and Wittink, 1996).

Competitive Advantage

The key to superior performance is to gain and hold a *competitive advantage*. Companies can gain a competitive advantage through *differentiation* of their product offering to provide superior customer value, or by managing for *lowest delivered cost*. Increasingly, how companies are using digital technologies and social media is fundamental to remaining competitive. See Marketing in Action 19.2 to find out more.

Competitive strategies

These two means of competitive advantage, when combined with the **competitive scope** of activities (broad versus narrow), result in four generic strategies: differentiation, cost leadership, differentiation focus, and cost focus. The differentiation and cost leadership strategies seek competitive advantage in a broad range of market or industry segments, whereas differentiation focus and cost focus strategies are confined to a narrow segment (Porter, 1980).

Differentiation

Differentiation strategy involves the selection of one or more choice criteria that are used by many buyers in an industry. The firm then uniquely positions itself to meet these criteria. Differentiation strategies are usually associated with a premium price and higher than average costs for the industry, as the extra value to customers (e.g. higher performance) often raises costs. The aim is to differentiate in a way that leads to a price premium in excess of the cost of differentiating. Differentiation gives customers a reason to prefer one product over another, and thus is central to strategic marketing thinking. Here are some examples of brands that have achieved success using a differentiation strategy.

- Nissan produced the Leaf, a battery electric car, which met the needs of customers looking for a *greener* solution. The innovations incorporated into the car enabled it to become the best-selling electronic vehicle in Europe.
- Toyota has built its success and reputation by targeting a broad market with highly reliable, high build quality, stylish and environmentally friendly cars, which differentiate the brand from its competitors, such as GM, Ford and Fiat.
- Dyson differentiated its vacuum cleaners by inventing a bagless version that outperformed its rivals by providing greater suction and convenience, and that eliminated the need to buy and install dust bags. Its vacuum cleaners are also differentiated from other brands by their distinctive design.
- Google created a differential advantage over its search engine rivals by enabling the most relevant websites to be ranked at the top of listings.

Cost leadership

This strategy involves the achievement of the lowest cost position in an industry. Many segments in the industry are served, and great importance is attached to minimizing costs throughout the business. As long as the price achievable for its products is around the industry average, cost leadership should result in superior performance. Thus, cost leaders often market standard products that are believed to be acceptable to customers. Heinz and United Biscuits are believed to be cost leaders in their industries. They market acceptable products at reasonable prices, which means that their low costs result in above-average profits. Walmart is also a cost leader, which allows the company the option of charging lower prices than its rivals to achieve higher sales and yet achieve comparable profit margins, or to match competitors' prices and attain higher profit margins. Zara, owned by Inditex, has an extremely efficient supply chain that not only enables the brand to produce very low-cost fashion garments, but also to get products to market faster than its competitors.

Differentiation focus

With this strategy, a firm aims to differentiate within one or a small number of target market segments. The special needs of the segment mean that there is an opportunity to differentiate the product offering from that of the competition, which may be targeting a broader group of customers. For example, some small speciality chemical companies thrive on taking orders that are too small or specialized to be of interest to their larger competitors. Differentiation focusers must be clear that the needs of their target group differ from those of the broader market (otherwise there will be no basis for differentiation) and that existing competitors are underperforming.

MARKETING IN ACTION 19.2
Creating a Digital Advantage

Adidas is the most shared brand logo on social networks, even outperforming Google.

A brand extension, Adidas Originals, used social media to extend the brand's reach online. The strategy involved using celebrity endorsement, in particular connecting closely with Kanye West, Pharrell Williams, Stella McCartney and other celebrities, with the aim of bringing an added dimension of authenticity to capture the attention of users of Twitter, Facebook and social media platforms.

Andy Murray and Derrick Rose took part in the 'The return of Stan Smith' campaign. The Stan Smith brand first launched in the 1970s is making a comeback. In return for a tweet at #stansmith, brand followers get the opportunity to win a personalized pair of the iconic shoes.

But this is just the beginning when it comes to creating digital advantage. Brands like Adidas, Nike and Vans are becoming highly skilled at using social media to create a buzz around their products and build a loyal customer base. Brands need to adapt and learn how to create competitive advantage in the digital as well as the physical world. Standing out online is a challenge. Successful brands should ensure that they are true to their brand values and promises as well as being visually and aesthetically pleasing. In the digital landscape, there are opportunities to connect to a tribe of followers who extend beyond a traditional target segment and to foster long-term customer loyalty. Successful digital brands build loyal customers through building emotional ties and optimizing their customers' lifetime value. Digital communications can increase visibility of a brand but also make more strategically important connections. For example, Adidas's Stan Smith 'Put your face here' campaign engaged customers through Twitter.

In the future, brands are likely to be competing for measurable digital KPIs (key performance indicators) such as the number of 'likes' and unique visitors per month, as well as revenue.

Based on: McCarthy (2018); Joseph, (2014); Interbrand (2018)

Examples of differentiation focusers are Burberry, Mercedes and Ferrari; each of these markets differentiated products to one or a small number of target market segments. Not all attempts to differentiate succeed, as Marketing in Action 19.2 explains.

Cost focus

With this strategy, a firm seeks a cost advantage with one or a small number of target market segments. By dedicating itself to the segment, the cost focuser can seek economies that may be ignored or missed by broadly targeted competitors. In some instances, the competition, by trying to achieve wide market acceptance, may be overperforming (for example, by providing unwanted services) to one segment of customers. By providing a basic product offering, a cost advantage will be gained that may exceed the price discount necessary to sell it. Examples of cost focusers are easyJet and Ryanair, who focus on short-haul flights with a basic product trimmed to reduce costs. Lidl is also a cost focuser, targeting price-sensitive consumers with a narrow product line (around 300 items in stock), but with large buying power. Ibis, the no-frills hotel brand in the Accor Hotels portfolio, is another example with its focus on one market segment: price-conscious consumers.

Choosing a competitive strategy

The essence of corporate success is to choose a generic strategy and pursue it with passion. Below-average performance is associated with the failure to achieve any of these generic strategies. The result is no competitive advantage: a *stuck-in-the-middle position* that results in lower performance than that of the cost leaders, differentiators or focusers in any market segment. An example of a company that made the mistake of moving to a stuck-in-the-middle position is Fiat. The Fiat 500 was sold in the USA through a stand-alone dealership network. Dealers were required to make a heavy investment in creating an Italian feel in their showrooms. This was in preference to launching the car through the 500-strong Chrysler dealers (Chrysler acquired a stake in Fiat in 2009). The advantages of the first option were an image of exclusivity, but heavy investment was required—for example, $3 million for the showroom makeover. In the second option, leveraging advantage from Chrysler could have meant making use of existing sales and service infrastructures (Wunker, 2012). One of the downsides was that the Fiat 500 had a higher ticket price than similar-performing cars like the Nissan Versa or Toyota Yaris, and being sold in the same location could have had a negative impact on sales. So, the Fiat 500 was, arguably, stuck in the middle, and its strategy did not lead to the coverage needed to establish the brand as rapidly as it would have liked. Sales in the USA have continued to be challenging, as the car has a relatively high price, less functionality and does not offer similar value to competing brands (McIntyre, 2018).

Companies need to understand the generic basis for their success and resist the temptation to blur strategy by making inconsistent moves. For example, a no-frills cost leader or focuser should beware the pitfalls of moving to a higher cost base (perhaps by adding expensive services). A focus strategy involves limiting sales volume. Once domination of the target segment has been achieved, there may be a temptation to move into other segments to achieve growth with the same competitive advantage. This can be a mistake if the new segments do not value the firm's competitive advantage in the same way.

In most situations, differentiation and cost leadership strategies are incompatible: differentiation is achieved through higher costs. However, there are circumstances when both can be achieved simultaneously. For example, a differentiation strategy may lead to market share domination, which lowers costs through economies of scale and learning effects; or a highly differentiated firm may pioneer a major process innovation that significantly reduces manufacturing costs, leading to a cost-leadership position. When differentiation and cost leadership coincide, performance is exceptional since a premium price can be charged for a low-cost product.

Sources of competitive advantage

To create a differentiated or lowest cost position, a firm needs to understand the nature and location of the potential *sources of competitive advantage*. The nature of these sources is the superior skills and resources of a firm. Management benefits by analysing the superior skills and resources that are contributing, or could contribute, to competitive advantage (i.e. differentiation or lowest cost position). Their location can be aided by value chain analysis. A **value chain** is the discrete activities a firm carries out to perform its business (Porter, 1985).

Superior skills

Superior skills are the distinctive capabilities that set key personnel apart from the personnel of competing companies (Day and Wensley, 1988). The benefit of superior skills is the resulting ability to perform functions more effectively than other companies. For example, Sergey Brin and Larry Page worked together to produce a search engine that outperformed its rivals. Their technical know-how enabled them to use their superior skills not only to create Google, but also to lead the company to become the world's most influential internet search tool and global digital brand.

Superior resources

Superior resources are the tangible requirements for advantage that enable a firm to exercise its skills. Examples of superior resources include:

- the number of salespeople in a market
- expenditure on advertising and sales promotion
- distribution infrastructure
- expenditure on R&D
- scale of and type of production facilities
- financial resources
- brand equity
- knowledge.

Core competences

A company's distinctive skills and resources make up its **core competences**. For example, Google can use its technical skills and vast resources to enable the company to operate a global search engine. Google's operation has grown in part due to responsiveness to change, innovative use of technology, its skills, and the deployment of data centres in the USA, Northern Europe and Asia.

Value chain

A useful method for locating superior skills and resources is the value chain (Porter, 1985). All companies consist of a set of activities that are conducted to design, manufacture, market, distribute and service its products. The value chain categorizes these activities into primary and support activities (see Figure 19.5). This categorization enables the sources of costs and differentiation to be understood and located.

Primary activities include inbound physical distribution (e.g. materials handling, warehousing, inventory control), operations (e.g. manufacturing, packaging, reselling), outbound physical distribution (e.g. delivery, order processing), marketing (e.g. advertising, selling) and service (e.g. installation, repair, customer training). A key skill of Walmart is its inbound logistics, which are based on real-time information systems and let customers decide what appears in its stores. The internet is used to inform suppliers of what was sold the day before. In this way, Zara buys only what sells. Zara's competitive advantage relies on its marketing skills which relate product design to fashion trends, and on operational and logistical skills that get new clothing designs in stores faster than competitors do.

Support activities are found within all these primary activities and consist of purchased inputs, technology, human resource management and the firm's infrastructure. Support activities are not defined within a given primary activity, because they can be found in all of them. Purchasing can take place within each primary activity, not just in the purchasing department. Technology is relevant to all primary activities, as is human resource management. The firm's infrastructure, which consists of general management, planning, finance, accounting and quality management, supports the entire value chain.

By examining each value-creating activity, management can look for the skills and resources that may form the basis for low-cost or differentiated positions.

To the extent that skills and resources exceed (or could be developed to exceed) those of the competition, they form the key sources of competitive advantage. Not only should the skills and resources within value-creating activities be examined, but the *linkages* between them should be examined too. For example, greater coordination between operations and inbound physical distribution may give rise to reduced costs through lower inventory levels.

Value chain analysis can extend to the value chains of suppliers and customers. For example, just-in-time supply could lower inventory costs; providing salesforce support to distributors could foster closer relations. Thus, by looking at the linkages between a firm's value chain and those of suppliers and customers, improvements in performance can result which can lower costs or contribute to the creation of a differentiated position.

Overall, the value chain provides a framework for understanding the nature and location of the skills and resources that are the basis for competitive advantage and it is a means of systematic analysis of costs. Assigning operating costs and assets to value activities is the starting point of cost analysis, so that improvement can be made and cost advantages defended. For example, if a firm discovers that its cost advantage is based on superior production facilities, it should be vigilant in upgrading those facilities to maintain its position against competitors. Similarly, by understanding the sources of differentiation, a company can build on these sources and defend against competitive attack. For example, if differentiation is based on skills in product design, then management

FIGURE 19.5
The value chain

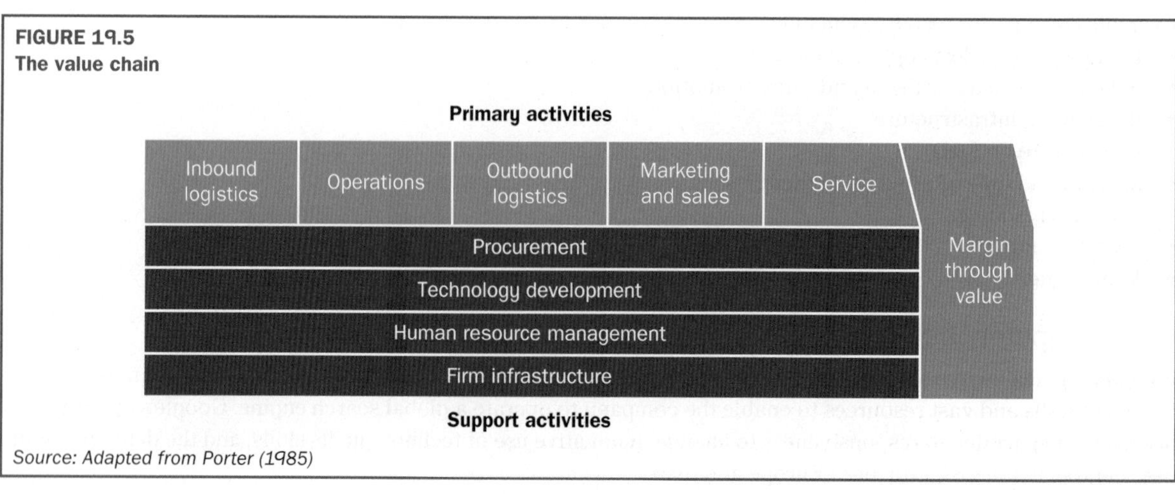

Source: Adapted from Porter (1985)

knows that sufficient investment in maintaining design superiority is required to maintain the firm's differentiated position. Also, the identification of specific sources of advantage can lead to their exploitation in new markets where customers place a similarly high value on the resultant outcome. For example, Marks & Spencer's skills developed in clothing retailing were successfully extended to provide differentiation in food retailing. Finally, analysis of the value chain can lead to its reconfiguration so as to fundamentally change the way a market is served. Figure 19.6 provides some examples.

FIGURE 19.6
Value chain reconfiguration

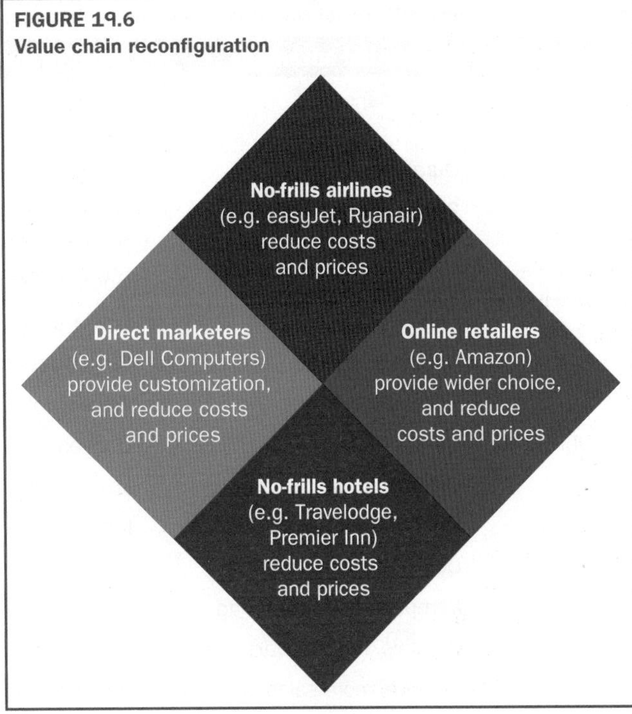

Creating a Differential Advantage

Although skills and resources are the sources of competitive advantage, they are translated into a **differential advantage** only when the customer perceives that the firm is providing value above that of the competition. (For methods of calculating value in organizational markets, see Anderson and Narus (1998).) The creation of a differential advantage comes from linking skills and resources with the key attributes (choice criteria) that customers are looking for in a product offering. However, it should be recognized that the distinguishing competing attributes in a market are not always the most important ones. For example, if customers were asked to rank safety, punctuality and onboard service in order of importance when flying, safety would undoubtedly be ranked at the top. Nevertheless, when choosing an airline, safety would rank low because most airlines are assumed to be safe. Therefore, airlines look to less important ways of differentiating their offerings (e.g. by giving superior onboard service).

A differential advantage can be created with any aspect of the marketing mix. Product, distribution, promotion and price are all capable of creating added customer value (see Figure 19.7).

The key to knowing whether improving an aspect of marketing is worthwhile is to know whether the potential benefit provides value to the customer. Table 19.2 lists ways of creating differential advantages and their potential impact on customer value.

Product

Product performance can be enhanced by, say, raising speed, comfort and safety levels, capacity and ease of use, or improving taste or smell. For example, improving comfort levels (e.g. of a car), taste (e.g. of food), or smell (e.g. of cosmetics) can give added pleasure to consumption. There are many ways to enhance performance. For example, Apple has enhanced the performance of its iPhone with the creation of its App Store, which allows users to access software applications from independent developers. This creates additional functions that the iPhone can carry out: for example, Foursquare allows users to find the location, price range and reviews of restaurants nearby. For further discussion of marketing apps, see Marketing in Action 19.1.

FIGURE 19.7
Creating a differential advantage

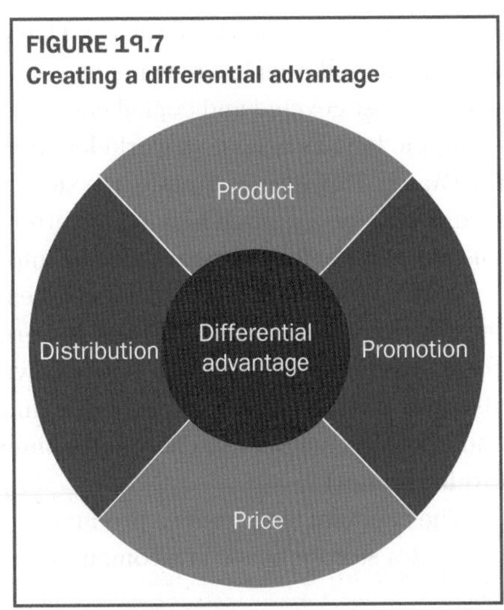

Exclusive designs and style are another way in which products can be used to differentiate a brand. Manufacturers Bang & Olufsen and Audi are two companies that have used style to compete in

TABLE 19.2 Creating a differential advantage using the marketing mix

Marketing mix	Differential advantage	Value to the customer
Product	Performance	Lower costs; higher revenue; safety; pleasure; status; service; added functions
	Durability	Longer life; lower costs
	Reliability	Lower maintenance and production costs; higher revenue; fewer problems
	Style	Good looks; status
	Upgradability	Lower costs; prestige
	Technical assistance	Better-quality products; closer supplier–buyer relationships
	Installation	Fewer problems
Distribution	Location	Convenience; lower costs
	Quick/reliable delivery	Lower costs; fewer problems
	Distributor support	More effective selling/marketing; close buyer–seller relationships
	Delivery guarantees	Peace of mind
	Computerized reordering	Less work; lower costs
Promotion	Creative/more advertising	Superior brand personality
	Creative/more sales promotion	Direct added value
	Cooperative promotions	Lower costs
	Well-trained salesforce	Superior problem-solving and building close relationships
	Dual selling	Sales assistance; higher sales
	Fast, accurate quotes	Lower costs; fewer problems
	Free demonstrations	Lower risk of purchase
	Free or low-cost trial	Lower risk of purchase
	Fast complaint handling	Fewer problems; lower costs
Price	Lower price	Lower cost of purchase
	Credit facilities	Lower costs; better cash flow
	Low-interest loans	Lower costs; better cash flow
	Higher price	Price–quality match

highly competitive markets. Bang & Olufsen has long been regarded as the style leader in audio and television equipment, and Audi has become one of the car industry's most successful luxury brands, producing some of the world's most coveted and copied cars.

Apple Inc has become a world-leading brand by continually introducing innovative products, the latest being the iWatch. However, currently, the small battery means that the watch has to be charged regularly; so, while the iWatch may be a desired high-status product, its performance might create an opportunity for competitors to enter this market. Performance can also be improved by added functions that create extra benefits for customers.

The *durability* of a product has a bearing on costs, since greater durability means a longer operating life. Improving product *reliability* (i.e. lowering malfunctions or defects) can lower maintenance and production costs, raise revenues through lower downtime and reduce the hassle of using the product. Product *styling* can also give customer value through the improved looks that good style brings. This can confer status to the buyer and allow the supplier to charge premium prices, for example Bridgestone (Japanese), Michelin (French) and Pirelli (Italian).

The capacity to *upgrade* a product (to take advantage of technological advances) or to meet changing needs (e.g. extra storage space in a computer) can lower costs and confer prestige by maintaining state-of-the-art features.

The Apple MacBook Pro and MacBook Air computers demonstrate how style can be used to create a differential advantage.

Products can be augmented by the provision of *guarantees* that give customers peace of mind and lower costs should the product need repair, as well as giving *technical assistance* to customers, so that they are provided with better-quality products. Both parties benefit from closer relationships and from the provision of product *installation*, which means that customers do not incur problems in properly installing a complex piece of equipment.

Distribution

Wide distribution coverage and/or careful selection of distributor *locations* can provide convenient purchasing for customers. *Quick and/or reliable delivery* can lower buyer costs by reducing production downtime and lowering inventory levels. Reliable delivery reduces the frustration of waiting for late delivery. Providing distributors with *support* in the form of training and financial help can bring about more effective selling and marketing and offers both parties the advantage of closer relationships. Working with organizational customers to introduce *digital replenishment* systems can lower their costs, reduce their workload and increase the cost for them of switching to other suppliers.

Third party logistics firm DHL made *a game-changing* adjustment to its logistical operations to help retailers get large appliances and items of heavy furniture to customers' homes. DHL introduced two-man delivery services, which not only helped streamline processes but also improved levels of service and customer satisfaction (Hartshorne, 2017).

Promotion

A differential advantage can be created by the *creative use of advertising*. For example, *spending more on advertising* can also aid differentiation by creating a stronger brand personality than that of competitive brands. For example, Amazon Prime, which provides preferential delivery and video streaming to paying members of the service, uses online and TV advertising to differentiate the brand. Linked to its annual promotional events like Amazon Prime Day, Digital Day and Black Friday, Prime also uses sales promotions, direct marketing and other forms of digital marketing communications techniques to drive sales and brand awareness.

Similarly, using *more creative sales promotional methods* or simply *spending more on sales incentives* can give direct added value to customers. By engaging in *cooperative promotions* with distributors, producers can lower their costs and build goodwill. The salesforce can also offer a means of creating a differential advantage. Particularly when products are similar, a *well-trained salesforce* can provide superior problem-solving skills for their customers.

Price

Using low price as a means of gaining differential advantage can fail unless the firm enjoys a cost advantage and has the resources to fight a price war. For example, budget airlines such as Ryanair and easyJet have challenged more traditional airlines by charging low prices based on low costs. Aldi and Lidl, discount retailers, have successfully used price to gain market share from leading supermarket brands. A less obvious means of lowering the effective price to the customer is to offer *credit facilities* or *low-interest loans*. Both serve to lower the cost of purchase and improve cash flow for customers.

Finally, a *high price* can be used as part of a premium positioning strategy to support brand image. Where a brand has distinct product, promotional or distributional advantages, a premium price provides consistency within the marketing mix. Louis Vuitton maintains high prices across its ranges to give a consistent message of the value and quality of its products and designs. The pricing policies of luxury brands seek to achieve a balance between accessibility and exclusivity. Bulgari and Hermès maintain high-level entry prices targeting customers with very high levels of disposable income. Chanel, Dior, Burberry, Tiffany and Vera Wang have a slightly different approach, having slightly lower entry price products to enable wider diffusion of the brand (Wealth-X, 2018).

This analysis of how the marketing mix can be used to develop a differential advantage has focused on how each action can be translated into value to the customer. Remember, however, that for a differential advantage to be realized, a firm needs to provide not only customer value but also value that is superior to that offered by the competition. If all companies provide distributor support in equal measure, for example, distributors may gain value, but no differential advantage will have been achieved.

Fast reaction times

In addition to using the marketing mix to create a differential advantage, many companies are recognizing the need to create *fast reaction times* to changes in marketing trends. For example, H&M and Zara have developed fast-reaction systems so that new designs can be delivered to stores within three weeks, top-selling items are requested and poor sellers are withdrawn from shops within a week. This is made possible by sophisticated marketing information systems that feed data from stores to headquarters every day.

Scale of operations

Companies can also create a differential advantage when the scale of their operations creates value for their customers. For example, eBay has built a sustainable differential advantage by building a large participant base. As the customer value of an auction site is directly related to the size of the participant base, once eBay gained a large user base advantage it became extremely difficult for any competitor to duplicate the value that it offers (Nagle and Hogan, 2006).

Sustaining a differential advantage

When searching for ways to achieve a differential advantage, management should pay close attention to factors that cannot easily be copied by the competition. The aim is to achieve a *sustainable differential advantage*. Competing on low price can often be copied by the competition, meaning that any advantage is short-lived. Other attempts at creating a differential advantage may also be copied by the competition. For example, when DHL challenged FedEx and UPS in the US postal delivery market, all its attempts at gaining a competitive edge were copied by its rivals. When DHL hired the US Postal Service to carry out its domestic deliveries, a move that was popular with customers, FedEx and UPS followed suit. The result was that DHL could not find a way of creating a differential advantage and was forced to exit the US market (*The Economist*, 2008). The key to achieving a long-term advantage is to focus on areas that the competition finds impossible or, at the very least, very difficult to copy, including:

- patent-protected products
- strong brand personality
- close relationships with customers
- high service levels achieved by well-trained personnel
- innovative product upgrading
- high entry barriers (e.g. R&D or promotional expenditures)
- strong and distinctive internal processes that deliver the above and are difficult to copy
- scale (where the scale of operations provides value to the customer, e.g. eBay) (De Chernatony, Harris and Dall'Olmo Riley, 2000).

Eroding a differential advantage

However, many advantages are contestable. For example, IBM's stronghold on personal computers was undermined by cheaper clones. Three mechanisms are at work that can erode a differential advantage (Day, 1999).

1. Technological and environment changes create opportunities for competitors by eroding the protective barriers (e.g. long-standing television companies challenged by satellite television and digital video streaming services).
2. Competitors learn how to imitate the sources of the differential advantage (e.g. competitors engage in a training programme to improve service capabilities).
3. Complacency leads to lack of protection of the differential advantage.

Read Marketing in Action 19.3 to discover how IBM invented an artificial intelligence computer and, in doing so, acquired a new source of competitive advantage.

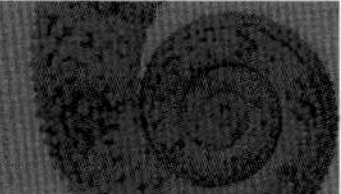

MARKETING IN ACTION 19.3

Want to Know How to Beat the Competition? Ask Watson

Watson is an artificial intelligence computer system that can answer *spoken* questions using natural language rather than computer code. The machine, devised by IBM, has won the television quiz show *Jeopardy* in the USA by outperforming human opponents in answering questions. Watson's advantage comes from its vast memory store and the speed at which information can be retrieved.

But IBM is not intending to use Watson for playing games; it is being used in various commercial settings in the health industry as a diagnostic tool for use with cancer patients. Watson has been fed information relating to oncology (lung, prostate and breast cancers), which has provided a knowledge base that the machine can interpret. This information includes more than 2 million pages of information from medical journals and 1.5 million patient records. Wellpoint's Samuel Nessbaum claims that Watson can interrogate the knowledge base and produce a diagnosis that is correct 90 per cent of the time, which once again outperforms humans; doctors are found to be correct only 50 per cent of the time.

IBM has now launched Watson Health, which is a cloud-computing-based supercomputer for analysing healthcare data on a global basis. The company has also entered into partnership with Apple and Johnson & Johnson (leading pharmaceutical product manufacturer) to develop consumer and medical devices. At Apple, Watson Health Cloud services will be linked to the Apple Health Kit, which will enable Apple iWatch wearers to take part in a huge health data study.

At Johnson & Johnson, the focus will be on creating intelligent healthcare coaching systems, including joint replacement and spinal surgery. Johnson & Johnson also intends to launch new apps for targeting chronic conditions such as diabetes and obesity.

Based on: IBM (2015); Steadman (2013); Mearian (2015)

Creating Cost Leadership

Creating a cost-leadership position requires an understanding of the factors that affect costs. Porter has identified 10 major *cost drivers* that determine the behaviour of costs in the value chain (see Figure 19.8) (Porter, 1985).

FIGURE 19.8
Cost drivers

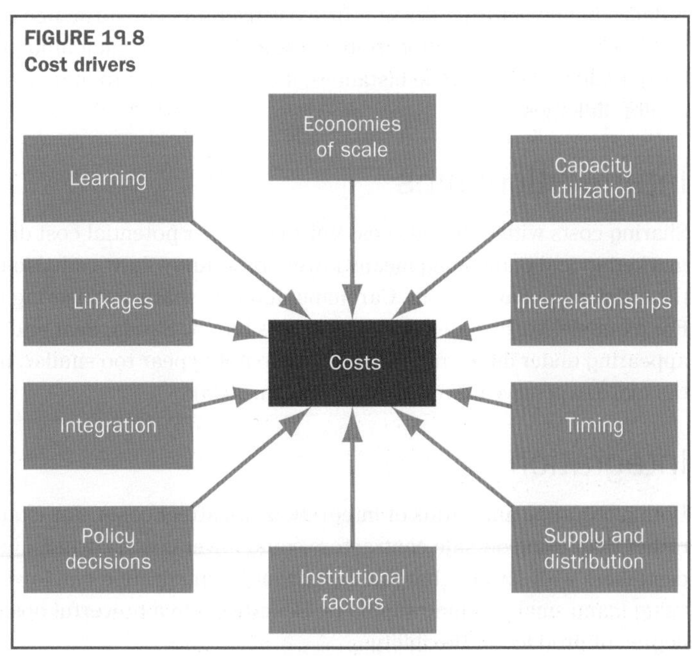

Economies of scale

Scale economies can arise from the use of more efficient methods of production at higher volumes. For example, United Biscuits benefits from more efficient machinery that can produce biscuits more cheaply than that used by Fox's Biscuits, which operates at much lower volume. Scale economies also arise from the less-than-proportional increase in overheads as production volume increases. For example, a factory with twice the floor area of another factory is less than twice the price to build. A third scale economy results from the capacity to spread the cost of R&D and promotion over a greater sales volume. Such scale economies mean that companies such as Coca-Cola, General Electric, Intel, Microsoft and Walmart have a huge advantage over their competitors. However, economies of scale do not proceed indefinitely. At some point, diseconomies of scale are likely to arise as size gives rise to overcomplexity and, possibly, personnel difficulties.

Learning

Costs can also fall because of the effects of learning. For example, people learn how to assemble more quickly, pack more efficiently, design products that are easier to manufacture, lay out warehouses more effectively, cut driving time and reduce inventories. The combined effect of economies of scale and learning as cumulative output increases has been termed the **experience curve**. The Boston Consulting Group has estimated that costs are reduced by approximately 15–20 per cent on average each time cumulative output doubles. This suggests that companies with greater market share will have a cost advantage through the experience curve effect, assuming that all companies are operating on the same curve. However, a move towards a new manufacturing technology can lower the experience curve for adopting companies, allowing them to leap-frog more traditional companies and thereby gain a cost advantage even though cumulative output may be lower.

Capacity utilization

Since fixed costs must be paid whether a plant is manufacturing at full or zero capacity, underutilization incurs costs. The effect is to push up the cost per unit for production. The impact of capacity utilization on profitability was established by the PIMS (profit impact of marketing strategy) studies, which have shown a positive association between utilization and return on investment (Buzzell and Gale, 1987). Changes in capacity utilization can also raise costs (e.g. through the extra costs of hiring and laying off workers). Careful production planning is required for seasonal products such as ice cream and fireworks, to smooth output.

Linkages

These describe how the costs of activities are affected by how other activities are performed. For example, improving quality-assurance activities can reduce after-sales service costs. In the car industry, the reduction in the number of faults on a new car reduces warranty costs. The activities of suppliers and distributors also link to affect the costs of a firm. For example, the introduction of a just-in-time delivery system by a supplier reduces the inventory costs of a firm. Distributors can influence a company's physical distribution costs through their warehouse location decision. To exploit such linkages, though, the firm may need considerable bargaining power. In some instances, it can pay a firm to increase distributor margins or pay a fee in order to exploit linkages.

Interrelationships

Sharing costs with other business units is another potential cost driver. Sharing the costs of R&D, transportation, marketing and purchasing means lower costs. Know-how can also be shared to reduce costs by improving the efficiency of an activity. Car manufacturers share engineering platforms and components to reduce costs. For example, Volkswagen does this across its VW, Skoda, Seat and Audi cars. Care must be taken that the cars appearing under different brand names do not appear too similar, however, or this may detract from the appeal of the more expensive marques (MacKintosh, 2005).

Integration

Both integration and forms of integration can affect costs. For example, owning the means of physical distribution rather than using outside contractors could lower costs. Ownership may allow a producer to avoid suppliers or customers with sizeable bargaining power. De-integration can lower costs and raise flexibility. For example, by using many small clothing suppliers, Benetton is in a powerful position to keep costs low while maintaining a high degree of production flexibility.

Timing

Both first movers and late entrants have potential opportunities for lowering costs. First movers in a market can gain cost advantages: it is usually cheaper to establish a brand name in the minds of customers if there is no competition. Also, they have prime access to cheap or high-quality raw materials and locations. However, late entrants to a market can buy the latest technology and avoid high market development costs.

Policy decisions

Companies have a wide range of discretionary policy decisions that affect costs. Product width, level of service, channel decisions (e.g. small number of large dealers versus large number of small dealers), salesforce decisions (e.g. in-company salesforce versus sales agents) and wage levels are some of the decision areas that have a direct impact on costs. Southwest Airlines, for example, cuts costs by refusing to waste time assigning seats and does not wait for late arrivals. The overriding concern is to get the aeroplane in and out of the gate quickly, so that it is in the air earning money. Southwest flies only one kind of aircraft, which also keeps costs down (McNulty, 2001).

Companies can also collaborate to reduce costs. For example, Vodafone has teamed up with O2 to share mobile network infrastructure (e.g. masts, equipment and power supply) in a billion-pound deal to speed up network rollout and to keep up with competitors British Telecom (Williams, 2018).

Ryanair accepts bookings via digital channels, eliminating the need for an inbound telemarketing team, and uses digital e-ticketing to further reduce costs. Other sectors, such as insurance, rail, banking, package holidays and hotels, encourage transactions over the internet to reduce costs. Care must be taken, however, not to reduce costs about activities that have a major bearing on customer value. For example, moving from a company-employed salesforce to sales agents may not only cut costs but at the same time also destroy supplier–customer relationships.

Supply and distribution

With global supply chain networks, the movement of goods around the world is much faster and is easily scalable. Fast time to market is very important in the digital age, and goods can be transported on an on-demand basis, but there are high costs to consider. It is important to ensure that manufacturing processes and resources are streamlined so that goods are available when required, which involves detailed forecasting of product demand. Galfeter supplies speciality paper and engineering products on a global basis, and it cut the time to market by 25 per cent by using digital decision-making systems. This, in turn, enabled the firm to get ahead of its competitors (Sopheon, 2018). Being close to the point of consumption can also bring benefits. Coca-Cola's bottled water brand, Dasani, is bottled in close proximity to consumer markets, giving cost advantages from its logistical operations. Locating near customers can lower outbound distributional costs, while locating near suppliers reduces inbound distributional costs.

Institutional factors

These include government regulations, tariffs and local content rules. For example, regulations regarding the maximum size of lorries affect distribution costs. Businesses based in the UK may be facing further tariff barriers on the movement of goods if the Brexit negotiations do not go in their favour.

Companies employing a cost leadership strategy will be vigilant in pruning costs. This analysis of cost drivers provides a framework for searching out new avenues for cost reduction.

Once a company has identified a strategic direction and has developed an understanding of the nature of the competition and how it might compete, it then must decide on developing a competitive marketing strategy.

Competitive Marketing Strategy

When developing a marketing strategy, companies need to be aware of their own strengths and weaknesses, customer needs, and the competition. This three-pronged approach to strategy development has been termed the 'strategic triangle' and is shown in Figure 19.9. This framework recognizes that to be successful it is no longer enough to be good at satisfying customers' needs; companies need to be better than the competition.

So far, we have considered creating and sustaining competitive advantage; now we explore the development of marketing strategies in the face of competitive activity and challenges, by looking at alternative modes of competitive behaviour and then examining when and how to achieve strategic marketing objectives.

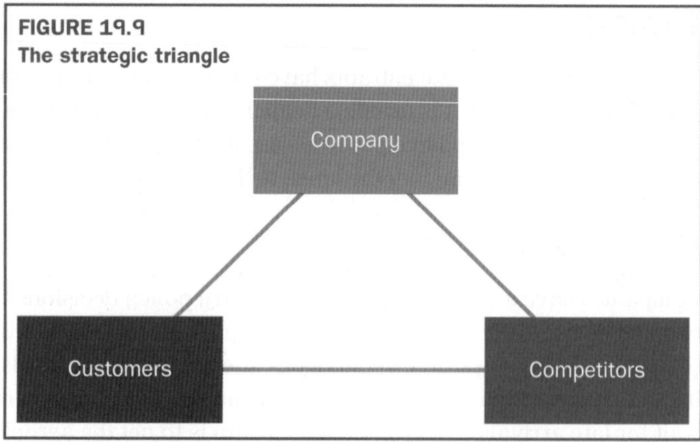

FIGURE 19.9
The strategic triangle

Competitive Behaviour

Rivalry between companies does not always lead to conflict and aggressive marketing battles. **Competitive behaviour** can take five forms: conflict, competition, co-existence, cooperation and collusion (Easton and Araujo, 1986).

Conflict

Conflict is characterized by aggressive competition, where the objective is to drive competitors out of the marketplace. The retail industry is highly competitive. Compounded by the global economic recession, many businesses have been forced to close because of competitive conflict or devise ways of strengthening their market position.

Dixons Retail changed the face of its business in the UK by merging with Carphone Warehouse. The move created a very large retailer with over 3,000 physical stores and additional product ranges, strengthened the company's buying power, and created opportunities for growth and costs savings on operational costs (Garside and Farrrell, 2014).

Competition

The objective of competition is not to eliminate competitors from the marketplace, but to perform better than them. This may take the form of trying to achieve faster sales and/or profit growth, larger size or higher market share. Competitor reaction will be an important consideration when setting strategy and should also consider the level of aggression with which the competitor will respond. Players will avoid spoiling the underlying industry structure, which is an important influence on overall profitability. For example, price wars will be avoided if competitors believe that their long-term effect will be to reduce industry profitability.

Co-existence

Three types of co-existence can occur. First, co-existence may arise because companies do not recognize their competitors, owing to difficulties in defining market boundaries. For example, Waterman and Mont Blanc, makers of fine-quality and luxury writing instruments, fountain pens and propelling pencils, may ignore competition from jewellery companies, since their definition may be product-based rather than market-centred (i.e. the gift market). Second, companies may not recognize other companies they believe are operating in a separate market segment. For example, Mont Blanc and Waterman are likely to ignore the actions of Mitsubishi Pencil Company, which manufactures Uniball rollerball pens, as the companies are operating in different market segments. Third, companies may choose to acknowledge the territories of their competitors (for example, geography, brand personality, market segment or product technology) to avoid harmful head-to-head competition.

Cooperation

This involves the pooling of the skills and resources of two or more companies to overcome problems and take advantage of new opportunities. A growing trend is towards **strategic alliances**, where companies join

MINI CASE 19.1
Growing Markets the Diageo Way

Diageo is a company that owns over a quarter of the world's leading brands of spirits, for example Smirnoff vodka, Johnnie Walker whisky and Guinness, which is a leading global beer brand. In addition, Diageo also owns local brands, which are used to broaden market penetration in parts of the world. For Diageo, growth opportunities are in new markets in Asia Pacific, Latin America and Africa, and the company is making acquisitions of strong local brands that appeal to its target customers.

Diageo's strategies for winning market share make use of the company's marketing knowledge and expertise. Elements of the marketing mix are used innovatively to differentiate its brands—for example, the global Johnnie Walker 'Keep walking' marketing communications campaign, which has increased sales and market share for over a decade. This creative idea has grown and been reinvented for a new generation of digital consumers. Products also undergo regular reinventions, and new flavours, packaging and formats are introduced to ensure the interest of new and existing customers, for example the 'From the bar' premixed drinks range using Gordon's, Pimm's and Smirnoff.

Collaboration with partners is another method used by Diageo to build market share. The company's 'Diageo way of selling' programme aims to help retailers and other trade partners achieve high levels of sales through education and sharing best practices, which creates value for all involved in the collaboration. Diageo has made a significant investment in facilitating partnerships. The European Customer Collaboration Centre provides a state-of-the-art facility for Diageo to bring together customers, retailers, trade partners and distributors to aid brand development, integrated planning and R&D for new products and services. This investment not only helps Diageo show support to its business partners and customers, but also to foster constant brand development and innovation, which ultimately increases sales and growth of market share.

Recently, Diagio acquired Belsazar—a German aperitif—through its Distill Ventures programme. This programme aims to accelerate business growth, support entrepreneurs and build global brands from the ground up. Diageo provides the funding and business support; the entrepreneurs do the rest.

Questions:

1 Explain the actions Diageo has used to build market share.
2 Discuss the difference between strategic thrust and strategic objectives, using examples from Diageo.
3 Discuss the importance of setting marketing objectives as part of the marketing planning process.

Based on: BBH (2015); Diageo (2018); Distill Ventures (2018)

through a joint venture, licensing agreement, long-term purchasing and supply arrangements, or joint R&D contract to build a long-term competitive advantage. For example, Shell International Petroleum, Rolls-Royce and Airbus have worked in collaboration to develop alternative fuels for the A380, which has led to the use of cleaner aviation fuels. In today's global marketplace, where size is a key source of advantage, cooperation is a major type of competitive behaviour (Airbus, 2012). See Mini Case 19.1 to find out more about the Diageo way of growing markets.

Collusion

The final form of competitive behaviour is collusion, whereby companies come to some arrangement that inhibits competition in a market. Collusion is more likely where there are a small number of suppliers in each national market, the price of the product is a small proportion of buyer costs, cross-national trade is restricted by tariff barriers or prohibitive transportation costs, and buyers can pass on high prices to their customers. For example, Apple joined forces with five major book publishers (Hachette Book Group, HarperCollins, Penguin, Simon & Schuster, and Macmillan) to raise the price of e-books. The US Justice Department and the European Commission decided that Apple's decision to side with the publishers was tantamount to collusion and an example of anti-competitive behaviour. The publishers settled, but Apple went to trial and was found guilty of price fixing and collusion (Hughes, 2014).

Developing Competitive Marketing Strategies

Researchers Ries and Trout (2005) and Kotler and Singh (1981) have drawn attention to the relationship between military and marketing 'warfare'. Their work has stressed the need to develop strategies that are more than customer based. They placed the emphasis on attacking and defending against the competition and used military analogies to guide strategic thinking. They saw competition as the enemy and thus recognized the relevance to business of the principles of military warfare as put forward by such writers as Sun Tzu (1963) and von Clausewitz (1908). As von Clausewitz wrote:

> 'Military warfare is a clash between major interests that is resolved by bloodshed—that is the only way in which it differs from other conflicts. Rather than comparing it to an art we could more accurately compare it to commerce, which is also a conflict of human interests and activities.'

Earlier in the chapter we discussed analysing competitors and their marketing objectives, which shape their direction in terms of products and markets and, more specifically, objectives for individual products and services. We now consider the marketing strategies that companies might apply when pursuing strategic marketing objectives.

Attack and defence strategies

Attack strategies

If a market cannot be expanded, a build strategy implies gaining marketing success at the expense of the competition. Winning market share is an important goal, as market share has been found to be related to profitability in many studies (see Chapter 11). There are several reasons why this should be. Market leaders are often high-price brands (e.g. Coca-Cola, Kellogg's, Heinz, Nestlé and Nike). They are also in a stronger position to resist distributor demands for trade discounts. Because of economies of scale and experience curve effects, market leaders' costs are likely to be lower than those of their smaller-volume rivals. Therefore, market leaders' profit margins should be greater than those of their competitors. Since they are market leaders, the unit sales volume is higher and consequently their overall profits (profit margin × sales volume) should be higher than those of their rivals. Therefore, companies such as GE, Unilever, Procter & Gamble and Heinz are willing to compete only in those markets where they can reach number one or two position.

Companies seek to win market share through product, distribution, promotional innovation and penetration pricing. Kotler and Singh (1981) have identified five competitor confrontation strategies designed to win sales and market share. See Table 19.3.

Table 19.4 shows examples of companies that are regularly in head-to-head competitive confrontation.

Defence strategies

In circumstances where there is rivalry among competitors, strategic action may be required to defend sales and market share from aggressive challenges. The principles of defensive warfare provide a framework for identifying strategic alternatives that can be used in this situation. Table 19.5 illustrates six methods of defence derived from military strategy.

Working together in competitive markets

When companies are trading in intensely competitive markets, there is a likelihood that they will interact through attacking and defending market territories. However, in increasingly turbulent and changing markets, collaboration and cooperation often occur. Marketing managers can find themselves considering whether to compete or cooperate with companies that operate in similar market territories. Collaborative networks of competing companies can develop based on shared interests, with the aim of solving common problems (Meng and Layton, 2011). For example, Nissan, BMW and Tesla are rivals in the electronic car market, but they have agreed to collaborate and share patents to speed up the development of electric cars. Growth in this relatively new industry has been slow, so by cooperating there is potential for all partners to benefit. Adidas has joined with Parley for the Oceans (a movement raising awareness of the plight of the oceans visit https://www.parley.tv/#fortheoceans for further details). This savvy partnership brings additional credibility for the sportswear manufacturer's new range of trainers made from reused plastic waste gathered from the sea. Amazon has partnered with Visa to launch the Amazon Prime rewards Visa Signature card. McDonald's is offering home delivery through its relationship with Uber Eats in the UK and USA (Hammett, 2018).

TABLE 19.3 Competitor confrontation strategies designed to win sales and market share

Frontal attack		Involves the market challenger taking on the defender head-on. The challenger should have a clear and sustainable competitive advantage. If the advantage is based on cost leadership, this will support a low-price strategy to fight the market leader. Success is more likely if there is some restriction on the leader's ability to retaliate, for example through patent protection, which can make it difficult for the market leader. However, the challenger needs adequate resources to withstand any battle that occurs should the leader decide to retaliate.
Flanking		Involves attacking unguarded or weakly guarded ground—in marketing terms, attacking geographical areas or market segments where the defender is poorly represented. The advantage of a flanking attack is that it does not provoke the same kind of response as head-on confrontation. Since the defender is not challenged in its main market segments, there is more chance that it will ignore the challenger's initial successes. If the defender dallies too long, the flank segment can be used as a beachhead from which to attack the defender in its major markets.
Encirclement		Involves attacking the defender from all sides. Every market segment is hit with every combination of product features to completely encircle the defender. An example is Seiko, which produces over 2,000 different watch designs for the worldwide market. These cover everything the customer might want in terms of fashion and features. A variant on the encirclement attack approach is to cut off supplies to the defender. This could be achieved by the acquisition of major supply firms.
Bypass		Circumvents the defender's position. This type of attack changes the rules of the game, usually through technological leap-frogging. A bypass attack can also be accomplished through diversification. An attacker can bypass a defender by seeking growth in new markets with new products.
Guerrilla		Hurts the defender with pin-pricks rather than blows. Unpredictable price discounts, sales promotions or heavy advertising in a few television regions are some of the tactics that attackers can use to cause problems for defenders. Guerrilla tactics may be the only feasible option for a small company facing a larger competitor. Such tactics allow the small company to make its presence felt without the dangers of a full-frontal attack. By being unpredictable, guerrilla activity is difficult to defend against. Nevertheless, the defender may choose to retaliate with a full-frontal attack if sufficiently provoked.

Based on source: Kotler and Singh (1981); Varadarajan, (2010)

TABLE 19.4 Major marketing head-on battles

Companies	Competitive area
Nike vs Adidas	Footwear
Coca-Cola vs Pepsi	Soft drinks
Unilever vs Procter & Gamble	Fast-moving consumer goods
Apple (iPhone) vs Samsung Galaxy	Smartphones
Intel vs Advanced Micro Devices	Microchips
Boeing vs Airbus	Aircraft
Google/Facebook	Digital advertising

TABLE 19.5 Defence strategies

Position		Involves building a fortification around a firm's existing territory. This reflects the philosophy that the company has good products, and all that is needed is to price them competitively and promote them effectively. This is more likely to work if the products have differential advantages that are not easily copied, for example through patent protection. Marketing assets like brand names and reputation may also provide a strong defence against aggressors, although it can be a dangerous strategy.
Flanking		Is characterized by the defence of a hitherto unprotected market segment. The danger is that if the segment is left unprotected, it will provide a beachhead for new entrants to gain experience in the market and attack the main market later. This means that if it helps to avoid or slow down competitive inroads, it can make sense to a defender to compete in a segment that, in short-term profitability terms, looks unattractive.
Mobile		When a firm's major market is under threat, a mobile defence may make strategic sense. The two options are diversification and market broadening. A classic example of a company using diversification as a form of mobile defence is Imperial Tobacco, which responded to the health threat to its cigarette business by diversifying into food and leisure markets.
Counter-offensive		A defender can choose from three options when considering a counter-offensive defence. It can embark on a head-on counter-attack, hit the attacker's cash cow or encircle the attacker. With a head-on counter-attack, a defender matches or exceeds what the attacker has done. This may involve heavy price cutting or promotion expenditure, for example. This can be a costly operation but may be justified to deter a persistent attacker. This strategy was employed by Meublein when its Smirnoff vodka brand was attacked by the cheaper Wolfschmidt brand in the USA.
Preemptive		Follows the philosophy that the best form of defence is to attack first. This may involve continuous innovation and new product development: for example, Apple Inc. invests heavily in design and innovation. Failure to maintain the ability to lead the market could result in loss of market share and eventual collapse of the brand.
Strategic withdrawal		Market exit strategy requires a company to define its strengths and weaknesses and then to hold on to its strengths while divesting its weaknesses. This results in the company concentrating on its core business. An example is Diageo, which withdrew from the fast-food business by selling Burger King, and from food by selling Pillsbury to concentrate on premium drinks.

Based on source: Kotler and Singh (1981); Varadarajan (2010)

Review

1 The determinants of industry attractiveness

- Industry attractiveness is determined by the degree of rivalry between competitors, the threat of new entrants, the bargaining power of suppliers and buyers, and the threat of substitute products.

2 How to analyse competitors

- Competitor analysis should identify competitors (product from competitors, product substitutes, generic competitors and potential new entrants); audit their capabilities; analyse their objectives, strategic thrust and strategies; and estimate competitor response patterns.

3 The difference between differentiation and cost leadership strategies

- Differentiation strategy involves the selection of one or more choice criteria used by buyers to select suppliers/brands and uniquely positioning the supplier/brand to meet those criteria better than the competition.
- Cost leadership involves the achievement of the lowest cost position in an industry.

4 The sources of competitive advantage

- Competitive advantage can be achieved by creating a differential advantage or achieving the lowest cost position.
- Its sources are superior skills, superior resources and core competences. A useful method of locating superior skills and resources is value chain analysis.

5 The value chain

- The value chain categorizes the value-creating activities of a company. The value chain divides these into primary and support activities. Primary activities are inbound physical distribution, operations, outbound physical distribution, marketing and service. Support activities are found within all of these primary activities and consist of purchased inputs, technology, human resource management and the company's infrastructure.
- By examining each value-creating activity, management can search for the skills and resources (and linkages) that may form the basis for low cost or differentiated positions.

6 How to create and maintain a differential advantage

- A differential advantage is created when the customer perceives that the company is providing value above that of the competition.
- A differential advantage can be created using any element in the marketing mix: superior product, more effective distribution, better promotion and better value for money by lower prices. A differential advantage can also be created by developing fast reaction times to changes in marketing trends.
- A differential advantage can be maintained (sustained) through the use of patent protection, strong brand personality, close relationships with customers, high service levels based on well-trained staff, innovative product upgrading, the creation of high entry barriers (e.g. R&D or promotional expenditures), and strong and distinctive internal processes that deliver the earlier points and are difficult to copy.

7 How to create and maintain a cost leadership position

- Cost leadership can be created and maintained by managing cost drivers. These cost drivers are economies of scale, learning effects, capacity utilization, linkages (e.g. improvements in quality assurance can reduce after-sales service costs), interrelationships (e.g. sharing costs), integration (e.g. owning the means of distribution), timing (both first movers and late entrants can have low costs), policy decisions (e.g. controlling labour costs), location, and institutional factors (e.g. government regulations).

8 The nature of competitive behaviour

- Competitive behaviour can take five forms: conflict, competition, co-existence, cooperation and collusion.

9 Competitive marketing strategy can appear as a military initiative

- Military analogies have been used in the past to guide strategic thinking, because of the need to attack and defend against competition. While the underlying thinking remains important, the language of war appears less in modern business-speak.
- Attack strategies are the frontal attack, the flanking attack, encirclement, the bypass attack and the guerrilla attack.
- Defence strategies are the position defence, the flanking defence, the preemptive defence, the counter-offensive defence, the mobile defence and strategic withdrawal.

Key Terms

competitive behaviour the activities of rival companies with respect to each other; this can take five forms—conflict, competition, co-existence, cooperation and collusion

competitive scope the breadth of a company's competitive challenge, for example broad or narrow

competitor audit a precise analysis of competitor strengths and weaknesses, objectives and strategies

core competences the principal distinctive capabilities possessed by a company—what it is really good at

counter-offensive defence a counter-attack that takes the form of a head-on counter-attack, an attack on the attacker's cash cow or an encirclement of the attacker

differential advantage a clear performance differential over the competition on factors that are important to target customers

differentiation strategy the selection of one or more customer choice criteria and positioning the offering accordingly to achieve superior customer value

divest to improve short-term cash yield by dropping or selling off a product

entry barriers act to prevent new companies from entering a market: for example, a high level of required investment

encirclement attack attacking the defender from all sides: i.e. every market segment is hit with every combination of product features

experience curve the combined effect of economies of scale and learning as cumulative output increases

flanking attack attacking geographical areas or market segments where the defender is poorly represented

flanking defence the defence of a hitherto unprotected market segment

frontal attack a competitive strategy where the challenger takes on the defender head on

guerrilla attack making life uncomfortable for stronger rivals through, for example, unpredictable price discounts, sales promotions or heavy advertising in a few selected regions

harvest objective the improvement of profit margins to improve cash flow even if the longer-term result is falling sales

hold objective a strategy of defending a product in order to maintain market share

industry a group of companies that market products that are close substitutes for each other

mobile defence involves diversification or broadening the market by redefining the business

niche a small market segment

position defence building a fortification around existing products, usually through keen pricing and improved promotion

preemptive defence usually involves continuous innovation and new product development, recognizing that attack is the best form of defence

strategic alliance collaboration between two or more organizations through, for example, joint ventures, licensing agreements, long-term purchasing and supply arrangements, or a joint R&D contract to build a competitive advantage

strategic withdrawal holding on to the company's strengths while getting rid of its weaknesses

value chain the set of a company's activities that are conducted to design, manufacture, market, distribute and service its products

Study Questions

1. **Using Porter's 'five forces' framework, suggest why there is intense rivalry between leading European supermarket brands.**

2. **For any product of your choice, identify the competition using the four-layer approach discussed in this chapter.**

3. **Why is competitor analysis essential in today's turbulent environment? How far is it possible to predict competitor response to marketing actions?**

4. **Distinguish between differentiation and cost-leadership strategies. Is it possible to achieve both positions simultaneously?**

5. **How might Google use differential advantage to stand out from its rivals?**

6. **How can value chain analysis lead to superior corporate performance?**
7. **What are cost drivers? Should marketing management be concerned with them, or is their significance solely the prerogative of the accountant?**
8. **Discuss the favourable conditions for pursuing build and hold marketing strategic objectives.**
9. **Explain the attack and defence strategies that a company might need to use if it is the market leader.**

Recommended Reading

Knowing who you are competing against, and competitors' strengths and weaknesses, enables you to create competitive advantage. Read about how smart products are transforming competition.

Porter, M. E. and Heppelmann, J.E. (2014) *How Smart, Connected Products Are Transforming Competition*, Harvard Business Review 92(11) 64–88.

References

Airbus (2012) Alternative Fuel Sources http://www.airbus.com/innovation/eco-efficiency/operations/alternative-fuels (accessed November 2018)

Anderson, J.C. and Narus, J.A. (1998) Business Marketing: Understand What Customers Value, *Harvard Business Review*, Nov–Dec, 53–65.

Barrett, B. (2018) For Apple Quitting Intel won't come easy. *Wired*, 4 March, https://www.wired.com/story/apple-quitting-intel-processors (accessed November 2018)

BBC (2018) Nestle pays Starbucks $7.1bn to sell its coffee, 7 May, https://www.bbc.co.uk/news/business-44027773 (accessed November 2018)

BBH (2015) Case Study: Johnnie Walker, *CreativeBrief.com*, April. http://www.creativebrief.com/agency/work/686/12/johnnie-walker-advertising-keep-walking-by-bartle-bogle-hegarty-bbh-london (accessed November 2018)

Boren, Z. (2014) There are officially more mobile devices than people in the world, *The Independent*, 7 October. http://www.independent.co.uk/life-style/gadgets-and-tech/news/there-are-officially-more-mobile-devices-than-people-in-the-world-9780518.html (accessed November 2018)

Buzzell, R.D. and Gale, B.T. (1987) *The PIMS Principles*, New York: Free Press.

Cellan-Jones, R. (2015) Supercell: Europe's supercharged games success, *BBC.co.uk*, 15 October. http://www.bbc.co.uk/news/technology-24541073 (accessed November 2018)

Chaudhuri, S. (2018) Price war eats into Unilever profits, *The Wall Street Journal*, 19 July, https://www.wsj.com/articles/price-war-eats-into-unilever-profit-1531991997 (accessed November 2018)

Davies, R. (2018) Ryanair strikes: their brand is built on being reliable bastards, *The Guardian*, 7 July, https://www.theguardian.com/business/2018/jul/07/ryanair-strikes-their-brand-is-built-on-being-reliable-bastards. (accessed November 2018)

Day, G.S. (1999) *Market Driven Strategy: Processes for Creating Value*, New York: Free Press.

Day, G.S. and Wensley, R. (1988) Assessing advantage: a framework for diagnosing competitive superiority, *Journal of Marketing* 52, April, 1–20.

De Chernatony, L., Harris, F. and Dall'Olmo Riley, F. (2000) Added value: its nature, roles and sustainability, *European Journal of Marketing* 34(1/2), 39–56.

Diageo (2018) Diageo acquires premium aperitif Belsazar, the first company to graduate from Distill Ventures, 15 March, https://www.diageo.com/en/news-and-media/features/diageo-acquires-premium-aperitif-belsazar-the-first-company-to-graduate-from-distill-ventures (accessed November 2018)

Distill Ventures (2018) About us, https://www.distillventures.com/about-us (accessed November 2018)

Easton, G. and Araujo, L. (1986) Networks, bonding and relationships in industrial markets, *Industrial Marketing and Purchasing* 1(1), 8–25.

Egarius, D. and Weill, L. (2016) Switching cost and market power in the banking industry: the case of cooperative banks, *Journal of International Financial Markets, Institutions and Money* 42(1), 155–65.

Garside, J. and Farrrell, S. (2014) Carphone Warehouse and Dixons agree £3.8bn merger, *The Guardian*, 15 May. http://www.theguardian.com/business/2014/may/15/carphone-warehouse-dixons-agree-merger (accessed 20 April 2015).

Hammett, E. (2018) Strategic partnerships are helping the world's most valuable brands accelerate growth, *Marketing Week*, 29 May, https://www.marketingweek.com/2018/05/29/brandz-partnerships-accelerate-growth (accessed November 2018)

Hartshorne, J. (2017) Why two-man delivery is a game changer, *Retail Week*, 29 September, https://www.retail-week.com/retail-voice/why-two-man-delivery-is-a-game-changer/7026208.article?authent=1 (accessed November 2018)

Hern, A. (2016) Clash of Clans maker Supercell becomes Europe's first 'decacorn', *The Guardian*, 23 June, https://www.theguardian.com/technology/2016/jun/23/clash-of-clans-maker-supercell-becomes-europes-first-decacorn (accessed November 2018)

Hughes, N. (2014) Apple agrees to pay $450 million to settle ebook price fixing lawsuit, *Appleinsider*, 16 July, http://appleinsider.com/articles/14/07/16/apple-settles-ebook-price-fixing-complaint-with-states-consumers-could-pay-450m (accessed November 2018)

IBM (2015) What is Watson? http://www.ibm.com/smarterplanet/us/en/ibmwatson/what-is-watson.html (accessed November 2018)

Interbrand (2018) Building breakthrough brands in the digital age. https://www.interbrand.com/best-brands/interbrand-breakthrough-brands/2016/articles/building-breakthrough-brands-in-the-digital-age/ (accessed November 2018)

Joseph, S. (2014) Adidas enlists Stan Smith and Andy Murray for star-studded brand revival. *Marketing Week*, 14 Jan https://twitter.com/adidasuk/status/423423732145598464 (accessed November 2018)

Kotler, P. and Singh, R. (1981) Marketing Warfare in the 1980s, *Journal of Business Strategy*, Winter, 30–41.

Kuittinen, T. (2013) 5 Reasons Why Finnish Apps Are Beating American Rivals On US iPad Market, *Forbes*, 22 November. http://www.forbes.com/sites/terokuittinen/2013/11/22/5-reasons-why-finnish-apps-are-beating-american-rivals-on-us-ipad-market/ (accessed 20 April 2015).

Kuittinen, T. (2014) Rovio's Revenue Crisis and the App Market Evolution, *Forbes*, 6 March. http://www.forbes.com/sites/terokuittinen/2013/03/06/rovios-revenue-crisis-and-the-app-market-evolution (accessed 20 April 2015).

Leeflang, P.H.S. and Wittink, D.R. (1996) Competitive reaction versus consumer response: do managers over-react? *International Journal of Research in Marketing* 13, 103–19.

Macdonald, M.H.B. and Wilson, H. (2011) *Marketing Plans*, Oxford: Butterworth Heinemann.

MacKintosh, J. (2005) Car Design in a Generalist Market, *Financial Times*, 6 December, 20.

McCarthy, J. (2018) Brandwatch: Adidas has the most shared brand logo on social media; *The Drum*, 3 May, https://www.thedrum.com/news/2018/05/03/brandwatch-adidas-has-the-most-shared-logo-any-brand-social-media (accessed November 2018)

McIntyre, D. (2018) For Fiat brand, a disastrous end to a difficult year, *USA Today*, 8 January, https://eu.usatoday.com/story/money/cars/2018/01/08/fiat-brand-disastrous-end-difficult-year/1013536001 (accessed November 2018)

McNulty, S. (2001) Short on Frills, Big on Morale, *Financial Times*, 31 October, 14.

Mearian, L. (2015) IBM launches Watson Health global analytics cloud, *Computerworld*, 14 April. http://www.computerworld.com/article/2909534/ibm-launches-watson-health-global-analytics-cloud.html (accessed 20 April 2015).

Meng, J. and Layton, R. (2011) Understanding managers' marketing strategy choice in a collaborative competition industry, *European Business Review* 23(5), 477–501.

Nagle, T.T. and Hogan, J.E. (2006) *The Strategy and Tactics of Pricing*, Upper Saddle River, NJ: Pearson.

Noble, C.H., Sinha, R.K. and Kumar, A. (2002) Market orientation and alternative strategic orientations: a longitudinal assessment of performance implications, *Journal of Marketing* 66(October), 25–39.

Noonan, L. (2018) Price war between banks could offset benefits of volatility, *The Financial Times*, 19 February, https://www.ft.com/content/56c65c20-122e-11e8-8cb6-b9ccc4c4dbbb (accessed November 2018)

Porter, M.E. (1980) *Competitive Strategy: Techniques for Analysing Industries and Competitors*, New York: Free Press.

Porter, M.E. (1985) *Competitive Advantage*, New York: Free Press.

Porter, M.E. (1998) *Competitive Strategy*, New York: Free Press, 4.

Reisinger, D. (2015) Angry Birds maker's earnings fall while games rise, Cnet, 19 March. http://www.cnet.com/uk/news/angry-birds-maker-rovio-revenue-earnings-fall-but-games-rise (accessed November 2018)

Ries, A. and Trout, J. (2005) *Marketing Warfare*, New York: McGraw-Hill.

Rovio (2018)Annual statement, http://assets-production.rovio.com/s3fs-public/rovio_q2-2018_interim_report.pdf?AQnMFQIkR8MJmvQUy11w.Jc8KCofIrKi&_ga=2.143486261.1640735939.1534687033-1941294554.1534687033 (accessed November 2018)

Simonian, H. and Lucas, L. (2012) Starbucks takes coffee wars to Nespresso, *Financial Times*, 5 March, http://www.ft.com/cms/s/0/d90109a4-66ec-11e1-9e53-00144feabdc0.html (accessed November 2018)

Sinclair, B. (2015) Apps are the most competitive market ever—Rovio exec, Gamesindustry.biz, 16 April. http://www.gamesindustry.biz/articles/2015-04-16-apps-are-the-most-competitive-market-ever-rovio-exec (accessed November 2018)

Sopheon (2018) How New Product Time To Market Impacts Revenue and Profitability, https://www.sopheon.com/new-product-time-to-market (accessed November 2018)

Steadman, I. (2013) IBM's Watson is better at diagnosing cancer than human doctors, *Wired*, 11 February. http://www.wired.co.uk/news/archive/2013-02/11/ibm-watson-medical-doctor (accessed 20 April 2015).

Sun Tzu (1963) *The Art of War*, London: Oxford University Press.

The Economist (2008) Failure to Deliver, 15 November, 80.

Trefis Team (2017) Why T-Mobile's All-in pricing strategy could pay off, *Forbes*, 12 January, https://www.forbes.com/sites/greatspeculations/2017/01/12/why-t-mobiles-all-in-pricing-strategy-could-pay-off/#76bf3f275302 (accessed November 2018)

Varadarajan, R. (2010) Strategic marketing and marketing strategy: domain, definition, fundamental issues and foundational premises, *Journal of Academy of Marketing Science* 38, 119–40.

von Clausewitz, C. (1908) *On War*, London: Routledge and Kegan Paul.

Wealth-X (2018) Luxury Brand Pricing strategy: Consistency is Key to Brand Success, https://www.wealthx.com/intelligence-centre/exclusive-content/wealth-x-institute/2018/luxury-brand-pricing-strategy-consistency-key-brand-success (accessed November 2018)

Williams, C. (2018) O2 and Vodaphone hope mast deal will help battle BT, *The Telegraph*, https://www.telegraph.co.uk/business/2017/01/15/o2-vodafone-hope-mast-deal-will-help-battle-bt (accessed November 2018)

Wunker, S. (2012) Fiat's Smart US launch strategy—really, *HBR Blog Network*, 1 February. http://blogs.hbr.org/cs/2012/02/fiats_smart_us_launch_strategy_really.html (accessed November 2018)

CASE 37

General Motors

Deciding on the Future Strategic Direction for US Car Giant

On 1 June 2009, General Motors (GM; www.gm.com) filed for bankruptcy protection, a historic landmark event. GM has been leading the automotive business for over a century. The company owns several internationally known automotive brands, which it markets around the world. It builds nearly 9.6 million vehicles a year, making it an industry colossus. For many, GM represents the heartbeat of the US manufacturing industry and is viewed as an exemplar in the effective management, strategic thinking and organization of a modern corporation. Yet it faced the perfect storm in 2009, as sales fell by a staggering 30 per cent. Most alarmingly, the company had over $176 billion in liabilities and lost a staggering $30 billion in 2008. Low-cost competition was eroding its market share. It had lost its mantle as the world's largest car manufacturer to Toyota in 2007. Now even the German VW group and Korean Hyundai had surpassed GM.

GM was once the iconoclast of US multinational corporations. The contribution of GM to US industry is gargantuan, with the corporation spending billions of dollars a year on parts and being one of the USA's largest employers. However, it had lost a colossal $88 billion since 2004—an untenable situation. At the height of the financial crisis, GM had to be bailed out by the US government due to bankruptcy. The US government invested over $862 billion into the motor vehicle industry. The company then offloaded several brands so that it could concentrate on core car models, and shed thousands of dealerships to make it leaner. The bankruptcy meant that original investors lost everything as the share price collapsed. Backed by the US and Canadian governments, the company had undergone radical change. The company's sheer size and impact on US economic life meant that it was too big to countenance failure.

GM slowly emerged from this traumatic period. In November 2010, it completed the world's largest initial public offering on the stock exchange, with the US government selling its stake in the business. Under its new leadership of CEO Mary T. Barra, the company expected to sell a colossal 1,000 new cars every hour

in 2015, globally. The company now employs 180,000 staff, based in 396 facilities, and produces around 9.6 million vehicles a year for over 125 countries. By 2017, the company had shaken off its shackles, earning net income of $300 million on revenue of $145.6 billion. Yet global markets experience peaks and troughs: for example, sales in Russia have been decimated due to political and economic uncertainty. GM sold its European Opel and Vauxhall car brands for €2.2 billion to Peugeot owner PSA. In addition, it exited from Indian and some African markets. GM sells more cars in China than in the USA and through its joint venture with Chinese manufacturer Baojun it sold over 4 million vehicles in China compared with 3 million in the USA in 2017.

GM had a huge product portfolio, selling cars in nearly every single market. Now the company has undergone radical transformation. GM has disposed of several leading automotive brands such as Opel/Vauxhall, Saturn, Hummer, Pontiac and Saab. The company has set up a number of manufacturing centres in low-cost countries such as Mexico, India, South Africa and China. The company had hoped to grow through a series of acquisitions and alliances, designed to strengthen the brand portfolio even further. In 2000, GM gained 100 per cent control of Swedish luxury carmaker Saab. However, the luxury car brand ceased manufacturing cars in 2011, due to the accumulation of huge losses. In 2002, GM took over troubled South Korean carmaker Daewoo. The firm produces low-cost cars under the Chevrolet brand in 10 different

»

>>

international markets, using low-cost manufacturing bases. GM dropped the Daewoo brand in 2004, using the Chevrolet brand, with the aim of turning Chevrolet into a global brand and moving it away from the firm's overreliance on the North American market. However, this strategy of a global automotive car brand has failed, with the firm pulling the Chevrolet brand out of Europe, citing difficult economic conditions. Its grand vision of a global car brand failed to materialize. The brand began sponsoring the UK football team Manchester United and in 2017 agreed a five-year deal worth £53 million.

GM is attempting to strengthen its international presence by focusing on growth areas such as China and developing countries. Growth there has been stellar, achieving 5.6 per cent quarterly sales growth. In China, it operates 10 joint ventures with local companies and employs over 58,000, selling international brands like Cadillac, Chevrolet and Buick, coupled with domestic Chinese automotive brands like Baojun, Wuling, and Jiefang. In 2002, GM formed a three-way strategic alliance with two domestic Chinese partners, SAIC and Liuzhou Wuling. To see a synopsis of GM's eight main automotive brands, see Table C37.1. The company uses these different brands to target different segments of the market and in different countries. In the USA, its uses four different car brands: Chevrolet, GMC, Buick and Cadillac. In Australia, it sells GM car marques under the Holden brand.

TABLE C37.1 GM's main automotive brands

Current GM brands			
Chevrolet	**Cadillac**	**Buick**	**GMC**
The Chevrolet brand is the third biggest car brand in the world and GM's most important brand. Has offering in nearly every sector of market. GM sells this brand in Asian markets, focusing on small/medium size cars that are value for money. Sold 4.1 million cars.	The luxury car brand in the GM stable. The quintessential luxury US car brand, with an emphasis on luxury, comfort, performance and technology. Aims to hold on to its premium brand. Sales up 14.8 per cent worldwide, selling 356,000 cars.	A mid-tier brand, with several luxury saloon cars and SUV offerings. Criticized for lacking distinction and rationalizing its current car model portfolio. Focuses on safety, quality and premium interiors at attainable prices. Brand has been successful in China. Selling 1.4 million cars.	It focuses on producing SUVs, pickup trucks and a range of commercial vehicles. Formerly known as GMC Truck. Sales up 20 per cent; strong demand for SUVs due to cheap petrol. Sales up 3.9 per cent.
GM brands sold or defunct			
Pontiac	**Saab**	**Hummer**	**Vauxhall/Opel**
Pontiac was a mid-level brand, aimed typically at a young market. Focused on projecting an image of performance, sport and youth. Was only available in North America. Sold roadsters, saloons and SUVs. Brand was phased out as part of restructuring.	Focused on premium market with sporty designs. Small niche brand. Sold to Swedish super luxury car market with support from the Swedish government. Now in receivership. Production stopped in 2011.	The former military vehicle jeep was transformed into a highly popular and ridiculously expensive 4 × 4 vehicle. Launched in 1999, earned a cache for cool. Sold for $100 million to Chinese manufacturer. Stopped production in 2010.	Struggling European division was sold for €2.2 billion. Produced a range of saloons, MPVs, and SUVs. Vauxhall brand used in the UK, and Opel for rest of Europe. Reasons cited for sale were Brexit, lack of mass-market opportunity in Europe, and greater opportunities in mobility technologies.
GM brands sold in China (SGMW)			
Wuling Motors		**Baojun Motors**	
Wuling's brand orientation is called 'Quality drives life'. The Chinese brand produces a range of mini-vans, MPVs and small pickup trucks. The focus is low cost yet high value. Sold 1.1 million cars in 2017.		Baojun Motors was launched in 2011. Sells a range of sedans and MPVs. Sold 996,000 cars in 2017.	

One of the biggest difficulties for the GM stable of car brands was the lack of distinction between the various car marques. Car buyers view many of the models launched by GM as very similar to other cars in its range. GM adopted a 'euthanasia' policy on several of its underperforming brands in an effort to quell costs and create a stronger brand proposition. It argues that the cars sold under the various brands confuse customers, and that better returns could be gained by a coordinated branding strategy that communicated the true brand essence of each of the brands. For example, you could have bought a similar saloon car under the Pontiac, Buick and Chevrolet brand names with few or no discernible differences. GM suffers from the curse of sameness. Other companies have developed stronger reputations with a smaller repertoire of vehicles. Originally, each of the GM brands had a strong distinctive image, with various brands focusing on different tiers of the market. For instance, Chevrolet focused on the value end, while Cadillac focused on the premium spectrum of the market. GM has culled its line-up in the past in an effort to rationalize its product portfolio; it scrapped the Oldsmobile brand in 2000. This famous US car brand suffered perennially from a decline in its revenue due to a poor product offering and the brand's lack of differentiation.

To put the malaise into perspective, in the USA the four different brands had four different slogans.

- GMC—'We are professional grade'
- Chevrolet—'Find new roads'
- Buick—'That's a Buick?'
- Cadillac—'The new standard of the world'

Coupled with this, these four brands produce over 41 different types of car: saloons, pickup trucks, SUVs and MPVs. One of the key challenges for its brand stable is the production of eco-friendly cars in response to oil prices and growing environmental concerns. GM launched the Chevrolet Volt in 2011, which is an electric hybrid car. However, this is not GM's first foray into green energy, as it launched the EV11 car, an innovative electric car, in 1999. This car was immortalized in a documentary called *Who Killed the Electric Car?*, which accused oil companies, car dealers and the car companies themselves of helping to accelerate the project's downfall. This green initiative failed to be capitalized upon by GM, whereas Toyota's Prius hybrid car became an instant hit. GM let this innovative technology languish, while driving ahead with its traditional product portfolio. Hybrid technology, ethanol or electricity were seen as viable technologies. Sales of new rival Tesla for its luxury range of electric cars have proved positive. The sales of the Volt, however, have failed to electrify industry pundits, despite receiving very positive reviews and awards. GM had high hopes for selling electric cars, projecting to sell 500,000 electric vehicles by 2017; however, only 180,000 were sold. Yet electric vehicles still are only a very tiny proportion of GM's total sales. Americans still have a love affair with their huge pickup jeeps, with Chevrolet Silverado being their best seller. Still, GM now has plans to launch over 20 all-electric models by 2023.

The Near End

The company has been prone to difficulties throughout its history. It managed to stave off bankruptcy by 40 minutes in 1992 during a credit crunch. During that turbulent period, it bounced back by slashing 21 plants and cutting 70,000 jobs, eliminating corporate bureaucracy and improving productivity and quality. GM is heavily reliant on the North America market, where most of its problems resided. Excess capacity, diminishing margins, a rigid sales channel structure, confusing brand propositions, falling market share, labour problems and exorbitant legacy costs have all made a serious impact. The majority of GM's revenue still comes from North America, making it very susceptible to market shocks within the US market. Sales in key Western European markets are still falling. It has the number one market share in the Americas, and the number two position in Asia, while it languished at number six in Europe. Now it has exited the European market altogether.

In recent years, the firm had focused on churning out gas-guzzling SUVs (sports utility vehicles) and pickup trucks, diverting its attention from normal saloon cars. These vehicles at the time were much sought-after by the market and yielded higher margins. The company lost sight of developing a solid car range, while foreign competitors developed strong reputations in the sector. In the wake of rising oil prices, demand for these expensive-to-run SUVs has slumped, and consumers have turned to more fuel-efficient cars. Much of GM's portfolio is solely focused on large cars. The price of oil has serious ramifications on GM's future success. The oil price stabilization has proved serendipitous for the firm, making Americans still love their gas guzzlers, despite climate change and environmental concerns such as VW's Dieselgate debacle.

GM's US market share is continuing to slide: where it garnered 41 per cent of the market in 1985, it now accounts for only 17.6 per cent. In an effort to stave off the decline, the company has deployed an aggressive price-discounting strategy, which has devalued many of GM's venerable brands. It offered its cars at 'employee discount for everyone'.

»

»

Sales drop when a promotion ends and consumers wait for the latest rebate or promotional offer. The company shifted away from price promotions and focused on building brands through lower advertised prices, more advertising expenditure and extra equipment as standard.

Key to the future survival is the efficiency and effectiveness of GM's manufacturing capabilities. GM factories have won several awards for quality processes; however, this is not reflected in the market, where consumers have poor-quality perceptions of GM brands. Continued improvement in its manufacturing capabilities is vital, focusing on quality, efficiency and costs. For instance, it takes 34 hours to build a typical GM car, while a Toyota takes 28 hours. The company has only recently focused on harmonizing production and sharing parts and car platforms. The new GM company has formed a partnership, with its powerful trade unions now owning 17.5 per cent of the new company and agreeing to profit-sharing incentives.

GM has been criticized for launching numerous new models under different brands and then subsequently ditching them if they did not prove a stellar success, which thus created huge levels of product churn. This is a substantial investment in terms of marketing expenditure, with GM constantly investing in brand recognition campaigns for these new brands. Other car-makers have several cornerstone car marques, which they frequently update with the latest technology and revamp with subtle stylistic changes. GM has increased the level of new product launches to unprecedented levels, placing the emphasis on getting newer models out to market very quickly. Also, GM had too many dealers. GM had five times more dealers than Toyota. Now it has cut nearly a half of its dealer network. Dealer margins have slipped to 1.6 per cent. The dealership structure has been consolidated to become more sustainable. Continued efforts to alter GM sales channels have been restricted due to franchised dealers' rights under US law. However, bankruptcy enabled the company to make radical changes that would normally be impossible. The only way to change a dealership contract is through expensive compensation to the franchise. Over 1,100 GM dealers were culled in 2009, with subsequent sizeable job losses. Fleet sales make up over 13.8 per cent of global car sales.

GM's Rebirth and Turnaround Strategy

Between 2009 and the end of 2010, GM had a total of four different CEOs. This highlights the extent of the calamity at the company. On 18 November 2010, GM emerged from bankruptcy a very different company, free from the shackles that potentially obliterated it. The group has launched several initiatives in order to reverse its declining fortunes, namely, reducing exorbitant fixed costs, maximizing manufacturing capacity and revitalizing a weak product offering through improved research and development (R&D). Manufacturing plants that are not operating at full capacity really hurt the business, especially in high-cost manufacturing countries. Previously, the company had allowed autonomous R&D within divisions, but now the firm is seeking to leverage engineering expertise across its global operations. This, it is hoped, will improve design, reduce costs and avoid fruitless duplication of activities. GM is spending nearly $8 billion on R&D every year, which equates to approximately 5 per cent of its revenue. GM also hopes to eliminate look-alike products from its portfolio, developing best-in-segment cars. It has culled a swath of middle managers in a bid to eliminate bureaucracy. The company wants to radically overhaul its cost base, rationalizing its engineering centre in Italy and trimming options and the sheer variety of models—all of which costs money. From a marketing perspective, GM has placed a renewed focus on customer satisfaction, earning customers for life. It has initiated programmes to improve the customer experience through all touchpoints, measuring customers' net promotor scores, in an effort to delight the customer.

GM is placing a huge emphasis on its new car-sharing endeavour, called Maven. With the emergence of the sharing economy and the success of companies such as Uber, Zipcar and Airbnb, GM has now entered the foray. Maven hopes to provide all-electric car fleets to Maven members, under a car sharing mobility solution. Now consumers do not necessarily need to own a car outright, but can use Maven to access the shared vehicle fleet. The solution has been launched in over 30 US cities, and members can access a car for a few hours, a day, a week or a month. The platform offers four key services: Maven City—where members access on-demand car rental; Maven Home—a car sharing service for people in a residential community or commercial entity, providing access at their address; Maven Gig—allowing members to earn money as drivers; Maven Reserve—allowing members to rent a car for a month with a dedicated parking space. This new business model responds to changing attitudes to vehicle ownership and driving patterns. The company is testing opportunities for allowing owners of GM cars to rent out their cars to the Maven platform. The platform now has nearly 150,000 members and attracts a core urban millennial demographic. Will car-sharing become more popular than ride-hailing?

GM is now attempting to amalgamate several brands into one sales channel. For instance, in the USA, it is creating dealerships where Buick and GMC are sold under the same dealership, creating strong sales propositions. Obviously, developing markets like China and Brazil are the big hope for the automotive trade. Yet with increased threats to globalization, such as potential trade tariffs, and possible future trade wars, this could represent a very difficult trading environment. The Chinese market is a key priority for the firm. Developing cars that Chinese consumers want is critical, and leveraging relationships with local partners will be important. GM is developing an array of crossover cars, supermini cars and fuel-efficient electric cars. In 2017, GM earned over $145 billion. The new GM vision is to design, build and sell the world's best vehicles. Furthermore, the technological promise of ride sharing and autonomous vehicles will have an impact on the future of GM. Can it maintain the positive momentum?

Questions

1. **Using Porter's 'five forces' framework, discuss the competitiveness of the global automobile market.**
2. **Identify and discuss the weaknesses associated with GM's marketing strategy. (Visit its affiliated sites: www.gm.com, www.cadiliac.com, www.chevrolet.com.)**
3. **What are GM's sources of competitive advantage? Discuss how GM could achieve a differential advantage over competitors.**

This case was written by Dr Conor Carroll, Lecturer in Marketing, University of Limerick.

References

The material in the case has been drawn from a variety of published sources and research reports.

»

CASE 38

Coca-Cola in India: An Unstoppable Powerhouse or a Stumbling Giant?

While Coca-Cola is often thought of as being as American as baseball and apple pie, it is, in reality, an international brand, immediately recognizable the world over. One of its most important markets is India, where Coca-Cola is the largest producer of beverages, with a reported 40 per cent market share in the branded beverage sector. The President of Coca-Cola India and South West Asia, T. Krishnakumar, says that the Indian market is vital to the future success of the company, and that his strategy is to eventually make the country one of the top three places where Coca-Cola does business (India is currently Coca-Cola's sixth-largest market, after the USA, Mexico, Japan, Brazil and China)—an impressive goal considering that India currently makes up less than 1 per cent of Coca-Cola's global sales and that the majority of India's 1.3 billion citizens have never tasted any product made by the company.

This doesn't deter Krishnakumar, an unconventional executive who avoids traditional business suits in favour of more comfortable short-sleeved shirts and khaki trousers, and who starts his morning with hour-long prayers and lives in a modest two-bedroom apartment. He emphatically believes that Coca-Cola can eventually provide a value proposition for every single Indian consumer.

Luckily for Krishnakumar, according to the PWC consultancy, the Indian market for non-alcoholic beverages is one of the fastest growing on the planet, with per capita consumption expected to double between 2017 and 2020. But India has a relatively short cola history compared with the USA's. And unlike in the USA, where soda is often seen as an alternative to water, carbonated drinks are considered to be somewhat of a luxury product, to be consumed only occasionally. But PWC believes that the opportunity exists for companies to build a strong brand image that consumers can identify with—that is, if they have the capacity to effectively compete in this highly competitive and culturally diverse marketplace.

Today, India is seen as an attractive emerging market with a high potential for success, but that was not always the case. In the 1970s the country had severe political upheaval, with a state of emergency existing from 1975 to 1977. Turmoil, and a disadvantageous legal environment for foreign multinationals, caused many large companies to leave India during this period, Coca-Cola being just one of them. The company would not have the courage to re-enter the Indian beverage market again until 1993, after a 17-year absence.

In terms of strategy, Coca-Cola manages its business around five categories of drinks: 1) carbonated, 2) energy, 3) plant/juice/dairy based, 4) water/sports and 5) pre-prepared coffees and teas. But the future market in India is expected to be juices, with a compounded annual growth rate of about 17 per cent expected between 2016 and 2021.

It is this last statistic, unfortunately, that appears to pose the biggest problem for Coca-Cola. Simply selling more fizzy drinks to thirsty Indian consumers doesn't seem to be a realistic option. Even more troubling, global tastes look as if they are changing as well, putting pressure on Coca-Cola's revenue. Since about 2002, carbonated drinks, as a percentage of revenue, have gone from 90 per cent to approximately 70 per cent, and it is believed that by 2030 soda could make up only 50 per cent of Coca-Cola's sales.

»

The company needs new products and new markets if it hopes to survive, let alone thrive.

Competition is another serious problem facing Coca-Cola in India. Not only does the company have to deal with its arch nemesis Pepsi, it is also being seriously challenged by a relatively new Indian startup called Hector Beverages. In an ironic twist of fate, Hector Beverages was founded in 2010 by a former Coca-Cola executive, Neeraj Kakkar.

An Indian David Takes on an Atlanta Giant

While its first product was an energy drink, Hector Beverages' flagship brand is its Paper Boat line of 'ethnic', or traditional, drinks. This segment, according to Wazir Advisors, a consultancy, is estimated to be worth as much as $250 million, and Paper Boat is already the market leader with a broad array of different flavours for people to choose from (by comparison, Coca-Cola and Pepsi have only one or two flavours each). Kakkar is passionate about the ethnic drinks market, saying that 'At Hector Beverages, we believe that if we don't do something now, these recipes will disappear in the next 20 to 30 years.'

Historically speaking, the ethnic beverage market in India was highly unorganized, primarily being the domain of street vendors; also people prepared such drinks at home. The genius of Hector Beverages was to come up with the prepackaged and ready-to-drink format for beloved traditional drinks. Furthermore, Hector Beverages has been able to readily penetrate urban markets and increase production as demand has increased.

The idea to sell ethnic beverages came to the founders of Hector Beverages in the summer of 2012, when one of them, James Nuttall, was trying to find the traditional Indian drink *aam panna* (made from raw mangos) for his parents, who were visiting him in India. Not satisfied with the selection (and hygiene) of those being offered by the traditional street vendors found throughout India, the founders of Hector Beverages 'realized that traditional Indian drinks could have a great market if produced and packaged hygienically. We didn't do any formal market research. We just followed our instincts,' says Kakkar.

Those instincts could prove to be killer. As V.T. Bharadwaj, an early investor in Hector Beverages, puts it, 'India has a rich history of traditional beverages, and it's a shame that no one has tried to present them in an attractive and aspirational manner.' Ethnic beverages have the 'potential to transform the beverages landscape in India. It is a category that is waiting to explode and has the potential to break the back of the cola market.'

Staring in 2013 with just two flavours, Paper Boat now offers consumers 13 different distinct, and uniquely Indian, flavours in convenient 250-millilitre Doy Pak packs (sealed plastic bags, originally designed to be used by astronauts in space), with selected products also offered in 500 millilitre Tetra Pak containers. Keeping with Indian tradition, Paper Boat uses no preservatives, carbonation or colour additives. It reportedly takes 18 months for the company to go from an idea to actually having a product on the shelf, and Paper Boat always tries to have several new flavours in the development pipeline. Kakkar says that the secret to Paper Boat's success is simple. 'We are extremely strong in product development. Whether it is identifying the right vendors, sourcing at the right time or establishing the right processing standards, we have developed a very strong knowledge base.'

Paper Boat's Strategy: Navigating the Ethnic Drinks Market

Right from the beginning, the brand strategy for Paper Boat was to create something 'that our mothers and grandmothers made, [but] that we don't have the time/recipes/ingredients to make today, but the taste of which have left a "limbic print" on our minds'. Unfortunately, the marketing challenge for Hector Beverages was to find the balance of bringing back fond childhood memories while at the same time not being seen as old fashioned. The company addressed this concern by way of the fun, bright modern design of its packaging, which also provides convenience as well as adequate shelf life, something that is important in the hot tropical zones of India. What differentiates Paper Boat from competing western firms is the 'emotional benefit' the company has, due to the fact that many Indians have pleasant memories of drinking ethnic beverages during the hot months of summer as children. Oddly, the name Paper Boat was deliberately chosen because it has nothing to do with beverages. It was believed that this would actually entice consumers by making them curious.

Hector Beverages definitely gets kudos from marketing experts. As one consultant says, 'The company has been innovative in terms of product, packaging and marketing to create the consumer wow factor. It can certainly take credit for that.' At first, Paper Boat had difficulty finding space on retailers' shelves due to the fact that is was perceived as being not upscale enough. But after a series of advertisements on the front pages of some of the country's top-selling newspapers, Paper Boat was able to make its way into stores.

»

Hector Beverages always had an active presence in online media, but has only recently turned to mainstream media as a way of regularly reaching customers. A positive element that is helping the company is the trend in India of going from an unbranded to a branded goods market. A key component of Paper Boat's brand, according to Kakkar, is showing consumers that its products are 'authentic' and 'alive'. To achieve this, Paper Boat focuses its marketing campaigns around such simple childhood memories as walking home from school and playing with paper boats and kites, as well as using well-known Indian melodies. Paper Boat also uses 'stories', which it promotes on various digital platforms. According to a marketing executive at the company, 'There are stories that we put up on Facebook, Instagram and Twitter every day, and we keep doing films that are hosted on YouTube. A lot of it is done in-house with some exclusive partners who help us create those ideas.'

Paper Boat's Potential to Spring a Leak?

Hector Beverages says that it travels all over India to find the right recipes for Paper Boat. By interacting with people in small town and villages, the company can get a feel for what flavours are popular in a particular region. For Hector Beverages, no part of the country is too remote to find a great idea for a new recipe. But herein lies a major criticism of the company.

The recipes that Hector Beverages uses to make Paper Boat have been taken from vendors located in such places as railway stations, as well as from temples and people's homes. They are not owned by Hector Beverages. This means that the company has almost no intellectual property (IP) to speak of (as opposed to Coca-Cola's world-famous secret formula). But executives at Hector Beverages disagree. 'Our IP is our brand and all the qualities associated with the product. Our IP is the processes we follow which make our drinks very different in their unique way. For example, all our mangoes are naturally processed. No other company is doing it,' the company says.

Paper Boat can mostly be found in large cities, with the ideal target consumer being someone between 25 and 40 years old. However, because Paper Boat is actually a niche market player, proper distribution is a never-ending concern. You can therefore also buy its products online (a link on Paper Boat's website sends you to Amazon.com). The challenge, as Kakkar sees it, is to penetrate the largely untouched rural Indian market, something that Hector Beverages seems well placed to do. But Indian consumers are very demanding, expecting value for their money, resulting in squeezed profit margins.

For his part, Kakkar doesn't seem to be too worried about competing with one of the largest soft drinks companies in the world. When speaking of his former employer, he has only nice things to say about upper management at Coca-Cola. Kakkar says, 'They have got in some of the best performers from Coca-Cola worldwide. This will result in faster decision making.' For Paper Boat's sake, let's hope that faster doesn't necessarily mean better.

Coca-Cola Fires Shots over the Bow of Paper Boat

But Coca-Cola hasn't remained in business for over 130 years by taking things lying down. Managers at the company realized that they had made a strategic blunder by not having the 'right product at the right price point' in India. Between 2017 and 2018, Coca-Cola went on a counter-attack, hoping to show Hector Beverages that it can beat the company at its own game, or at least show that it is willing to die trying. The company decided that it would go 'hyper local', introducing such flavours as orange, pomegranate, guava, litchi and a special variety of mango that is only grown in West Bengal—all of this in an effort to cater to the highly selective taste buds of the average Indian consumer.

This reinvigorated strategy for the juice sector builds on what were already seen as previously favourable results. Between 2012 and 2017, according to research firm Euromonitor, Coca-Cola's share of the fruit juice market went from about 28.5 per cent to a little over 31 per cent. Not spectacular, but positive nonetheless. The problem is that profit margins in the juice sector are fairly low. More worryingly is the fact that this growth might have come at the expense of the company's flagship (and more profitable) carbonated drinks sector. During the same period, Coca-Cola's share of the fizzy drinks market went from almost 61 per cent to a still impressive 56.3 per cent. But in another troubling sign that momentum might not be on Coca-Cola's side, its share of the bottled water market (again, during the same period) dropped from over 12.5 per cent to almost 10 per cent.

While still in an advantageous position in terms of brand image and financial resources, Coca-Cola is not prepared to sit idly by and watch its market share slowly erode. In a bold move, the company has gone 'blue ocean' in its strategy, trying to create a whole new market by mixing fruit juice with some of its carbonated drinks. The advantage here, in addition to quite possibly creating a new market segment, is that these drinks are taxed by the Indian government at a lower rate. In a bid to expand its product selection even further, the company has announced a new line of frozen desserts, again using local fruits.

Coca-Cola: As Indian as Cricket and *Kaju ki Barfi* (a Traditional Indian Dessert)?

In an effort to show the seriousness of its commitment to India, Coca-Cola has announced plans to spend almost US $2 billion building its own agricultural ecosystem in the country over the next several years. This will, in effect, create a supply chain that will provide Coca-Cola with all the ingredients and infrastructure that it needs to go from the 'grove to glass', while at the same time supporting the local Indian economy. By being more local, Coca-Cola should also be able to adapt itself better to changing market conditions. In 2017 alone, the company launched 17 new products, the majority of them local, with many more reportedly in development as well. As one Coca-Cola executive says, 'The India strategy replicates the global strategy of providing choice. In India, we will localize these choices.'

Previously, Coca-Cola had focused on big cities and the urban (and wealthy) market. However, analysts believe that if the company really wants to grow it needs to reach the almost 650,000 villages in India. That is where the real growth will come from. And this is not necessarily an impossible task. According to consultant Jagdeep Kapoor, thanks to mass media and advertising, there is a ready, and thirsty, market waiting for Coca-Cola products. The trouble, however, is that in the countryside, consumers prefer fresh juices not bottled ones.

In an effort to better adapt itself to Indian culture, in July of 2017, Coca-Cola redesigned its website, employing a story-telling format that they call 'Journey'. The goal is to better engage with its target consumers in a way that is more authentic, providing a two-way form of dialogue. In addition to hosting content created by Coca-Cola itself, the site also hosts content written by consumers. The goal is to better align the company's marketing strategy with India's gloried story-telling tradition.

Coca-Cola has also engaged in a 'mass-personalized' branding initiative by way of its 'Share a Coke' campaign. This involves the use of slogans that celebrated different family and social relationships (e.g. 'Daddy: My teacher. My friend', 'Mom: Above the rest. Simply the best') printed in 12 different Indian languages. An executive at Coca-Cola says the idea is to take 'a refreshing new look at relationships. This campaign aims to encourage Indian consumers to celebrate relationships that have evolved over the years and reignite them by creating a moment of happiness that comes from sharing a Coke.'

As another sign that it is fully implemented in Indian society, in June of 2018, Coca-Cola announced a recycling initiative to protect the local environment. 'We have pledged to recover and recycle one package for every single one that we put out in the market by 2030,' the company says. Furthermore, Coca-Cola has 'adopted' 1,000 schools in socially disadvantaged areas. The company also does everything it can to encourage diversity in its hiring and promotion decisions; women reportedly make up a majority of top positions in the areas of quality and innovation at Coca-Cola India.

But is all of this enough?

As one astute beverage executive puts it, 'For Coca-Cola to boost its growth it needs to recruit more consumers at the front-end and at a much faster pace than it is doing at present. It needs to bring them into the fold of packaged beverages and then work at moving them up the value chain. One answer to this is product innovation. You have to create new and exciting products which offer high value for money.' The executive who said this? None other than Kakkar, head of Hector Beverages.

But Kakkar should be wary. When you play with giants, there is always the danger that you might get crushed. As Saurabh Uboweja, head of the consultancy Brands of Desire, puts it, the solution is quite simple. He believes that, 'for Coke . . . , Paper Boat would be a logical target brand to buy out at some stage to strengthen its increasingly diversified product portfolio.'

For Coca-Cola, it looks like it just might be a case of 'if you can't beat them, buy them'.

Questions

1. **What are the main characteristics of Coca-Cola's brand-building strategy in India?**
2. **What are the features of Coca-Cola's 'blue-ocean' strategy in response to Paper Boat's position in the Indian Market?**
3. **How can Coca-Cola counter Paper Boat's aggressive competitive marketing strategy?**

This case study was written by Tom McNamara and Irena Descubes, The Rennes School of Business, France.

References

Based on: BW People (2018) A Quiet Revolution at Coca-Cola, 2 August 2, http://bwpeople.businessworld.in/article/A-Quiet-Revolution-at-Coca-Cola/02-08-2018-156570; Mitra, S. (2018) Amid a shift by Indian

consumers from carbonated beverages to fruit-based drinks, Coca-Cola is going local to ensure a product for every region, *Livemint*, 6 April, https://www.livemint.com/Companies/DxLDLNzSi9sHDEG03ul82H/Fruits-the-real-deal-for-CocaCola-in-India.html; Bansal, S. (2016) Paper Boat sails ahead on Indian drinks, *Livemint*, 13 December, https://www.livemint.com/Companies/FYypavmzDOI9kkmiG3TtxO/Paper-Boat-sails-ahead-on-Indian-drinks.html; *Knowledge@Wharton* (2017) Can an Ethnic Beverage Brand Challenge Coca-Cola in India? 11 January; The Indian Express (2018) Coca Cola, Infosys, others pledge to beat plastic pollution in India, 2 June, https://indianexpress.com/article/india/coca-cola-infosys-others-pledge-to-beat-plastic-pollution-in-india-5201438; Dsouza, S. (2018) Coca-Cola Turns Apple Grower In Push Beyond Sugary Sodas, *Bloomberg Quint*, 3 August, https://www.bloombergquint.com/business/2018/08/03/coca-cola-turns-apple-grower-in-push-beyond-sugary-sodas; *WARC* (2017), Ethnic beverages could pass colas, 16 January, https://www.warc.com/NewsAndOpinion/news/Ethnic_beverages_could_pass_colas/f53564e7-c52b-43eb-ab4b-4967286ae32f; Gangal, A. (2018) 'Designers must let go of the idea of being "boutique"': Ashwini Deshpande, Elephant Design, *Afaqs!* 12 July, http://www.afaqs.com/interviews/index.html?id=588_Meet-the-Design-Mahouts; Panchal, S. (2014) Economic Milestone: Exit of the MNCs (1977), *Forbes India*, 14 August, http://www.forbesindia.com/article/independence-day-special/economic-milestone-exit-of-the-mncs-(1977)/38431/1; Patar, P. (2017) Hector Beverages (Paper Boat)-India's answer to Coca Cola? *LinkedIn Pulse*, 21 July, https://puneet3210.wordpress.com/2017/07/21/hector-beverages-paper-boat; PWC India (2017) Retail and Consumer Quarterly Newsletter Q1 FY 2018, PWC India, September; Qureshi, W. (2018) HP brings Coca-Cola 'personal relationships' campaign to India, *Packaging News*, 11 July, https://www.packagingnews.co.uk/top-story/hp-brings-coca-cola-relationships-campaign-indian-market-11-07-2018; Singh, R. (2014) How Hector Beverages' Paper Boat is making waves in a cluttered soft drinks market, *The Economic Times*, 5 October, http://economictimes.indiatimes.com/articleshow/44333187.cms?utm_source=contentofinterest&utm_medium=text&utm_campaign=cppst; Venkatesh, S. (2016) Ethnic drinks: How Paper Boat plans to keep its lead, *Forbes India*, 7 September, http://www.forbesindia.com/article/work-in-progress/ethnic-drinks-how-paper-boat-plans-to-keep-its-lead/44219/1; Buzz in Content (2018) When Coca-Cola India reimagined company's website into a digital magazine 'Journey', 26 July, http://www.buzzincontent.com/story/when-coca-cola-india-reimagined-company–single–s-website-into-a-digital-magazine—journey–single/; *Knowledge@Wharton* (2017) Will Coca-Cola's New India Strategy Have Fizz or Go Flat? 17 November.

CHAPTER 20
Product Strategy: Lifecycle, Portfolio and Growth

> *Innovation distinguishes between a leader and a follower.*
>
> **STEVE JOBS, APPLE INC.**

LEARNING OBJECTIVES

After reading this chapter, you should be able to:

1. describe the concept of the product lifecycle
2. discuss the uses and limitations of the product lifecycle
3. describe the concept of product portfolio planning
4. explain the Boston Consulting Group Growth-Share Matrix
5. explain the General Electric Market Attractiveness–Competitive Position Model
6. discuss the contribution of product portfolio management
7. discuss product strategies for growth

This chapter examines the application of analytical tools used in strategic product planning, beginning with considering the implications for managing brands over time: the product lifecycle. The next key topic is managing brand and product line portfolios. Many companies handle numerous products and serve multiple market segments. Consequently, managers need to address the question of where to place investment for product growth and where and when to withdraw resources. Such questions are considered in the second part of the chapter. Finally, the topic of product strategies for growth is explored.

Managing Product Lines and Brands over Time: The Product Lifecycle

No matter how wide the product mix, both product lines and individual brands need to be managed over time. A useful starting point for conceptualizing the changes that occur during the lifetime of a product is the **product lifecycle (PLC)**. The PLC is a flexible model that can be applied to both brands and product lines (Polli and Cook, 1969). For simplicity, in the rest of this chapter, brands and product lines will be referred to as products. We shall now look at the product lifecycle before discussing its uses and limitations.

The classic product lifecycle has four stages (see Figure 20.1): introduction, growth, maturity and decline.

Introduction

When first introduced to the market, a product's sales growth is typically low and financial losses are incurred because of heavy development and promotional costs. Companies should monitor the speed of product adoption and, if this is disappointing, consider terminating the product at this stage.

Leading companies such as Samsung, IBM, Mercedes, Toyota and Apple invest heavily in new product development to create products that confer new features and benefits for consumers. Because of heavy investment, high promotional expenditures and low sales, losses are often suffered during product introduction. Nokian Tyres made long-term investment in product research and innovations, which improved the firm's knowledge and capabilities. The company's expertise in heavy-tyre manufacturing has enabled it to become a world-leading specialist manufacturer. Nokian Tyres also invests in communicating the benefits of its products in business-to-business markets to ensure continued growth (Nokian, 2015). Coca-Cola invested heavily in launching Fuze Tea, an iced tea drink, with the aim of enabling the brand to diversify and build market share in a growing market (Fleming, 2018).

Growth

This stage is characterized by a period of faster sales and profit growth. Sales growth is fuelled by rapid market acceptance and, for many products, repeat purchasing. Profits may begin to decline towards the latter stages

FIGURE 20.1
The product lifecycle

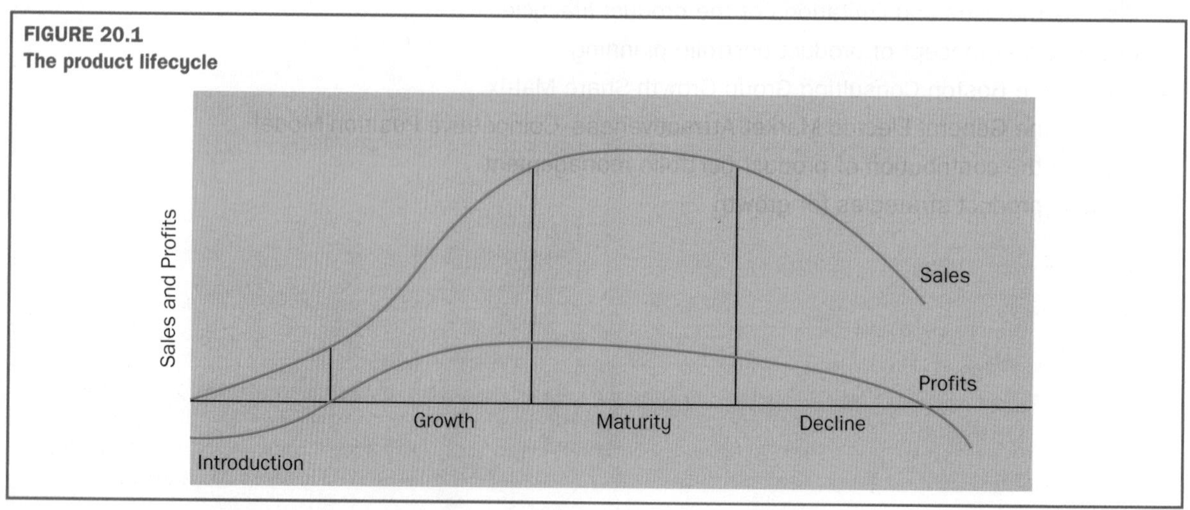

of the growth cycle as new rivals enter the market, attracted by fast sales growth and high profit potential. The tablet computer market is an example of this. Apple introduced the iPad in 2010, and the rapid sales growth was mirrored by an increase in competing products, for example Samsung Galaxy Tab and Hewlett-Packard TouchPad (see Exhibit 20.1). The smartphone market developed as technology innovation enabled mobile computing to be integrated into modern handsets; smartphones began to take market share from some brands of tablets. During the growth stage, many rival technology companies entered the market with operating systems for the new types of phones, including Apple iOS, Google Android and Microsoft Windows. The end of the growth period is often associated with *competitive shakeout*, when weaker suppliers cease production. Technology markets are particularly susceptible to rapidly escalating periods of growth followed by dramatic market collapse. Read Marketing in Action 20.1 to find out about the winners and losers in the dot-com bubble(s).

EXHIBIT 20.1
Samsung reminds its customer there are no limits

MARKETING IN ACTION 20.1
The Dot-com Bubble(s): Winners and Losers

The size of the internet economy started to grow rapidly from 1996. Between 1999 and 2001, there was a period of intense growth in the value of technology stocks. Forrester Research estimated that the total internet economy was worth US$15 billion, and, by 2000, revenues from online consumer spending in the USA alone were estimated at US$45 billion (Boston Consulting Group, 2001). Predictions about the growth of online markets and the rapidly rising share prices got everyone excited. This was a rapid growth market. But there were very few internet-savvy businesses offering stocks for sale. Investors scrambled to buy internet stocks. The high demand and low level of supply created a trading frenzy, which stimulated exponential market growth (see graph). Extreme examples of increases in valuations and personal gains for the entrepreneurs (dot-com millionaires) helped to drive growth even more. For example, Xcelera.com, developed by Norwegian Alexander Vik, saw its stock soar from a few cents to over $200 a share in less than a year, giving the company a market capitalization of $3.8 billion. Indeed, in 2000 there were 63 dot-com millionaires on the Sunday Times Rich List, but by 2001 this was down to just 26. The bubble burst and many innovative companies—which had rushed to move online—collapsed almost overnight. There were some notable winners and losers.

Winners:

- Google
- Amazon
- Lastminute.com
- eBay

Losers:

- Boo.com (spent $180 million in six months trying to create a global fashion store, but went bankrupt in 2000)
- Webvan (filed for bankruptcy in 2001)
- FreeInternet.com (filed for bankruptcy in October 2000)
- Pets.com (pet supplies retailer; filed for bankruptcy in 2000)

In 2015, after many years of relative stability, tech stocks began to rise in value to similar levels seen at the height of the 2000 dot-com boom-and-bust era (see graph). Likewise, there were signs that the underlying real value of the tech firms was not rising as fast as the price of their stocks and shares. In such a turbulent environment, demand for tech stocks is high and can lead to overvaluation of untested or new-to-market products. Uber ($60 billion), Airbnb ($30 billion), Deliveroo ($1 billion) and Dropbox ($10 billion) are examples of digital brands with such high valuations. But tech firms can fall out of favour: Snapchat (digital messaging service), which generates money through advertising revenue, alienated

»

millions of its users when it redesigned its app, and, consequently, there were fewer advertisers, which put a squeeze on revenues and profits, which is likely to affect its $18 billion valuation.

The timing of another period of bust is unpredictable, but what is much more certain is that tech products will come and go over time in much the same way as physical products do.

Based on: Boston Consulting Group (2001); Pavitt (1997); Wikipedia (n.d.); Virzi (2000); Hudson (2010); Roberts (2018); Lynn (2016); Cohan (2018)

Maturity

Eventually, sales peak and flatten as saturation occurs, hastening competitive shakeout. The survivors battle for market share by employing product improvements, advertising and sales promotional offers, dealer discounts and price cutting; the result is a strain on profit margins, particularly for follower brands. The need for effective brand building is acutely recognized during maturity, as brand leaders are in the strongest position to resist the pressure on profit margins (Doyle, 1989). Heinz has been advertising its brand of beans for over 50 years. The manufacturer differentiated the brand using the slogan 'Beanz Meanz Heinz'. Investment in this iconic advertising campaign enabled Heinz to fend off competitors and stimulate sales in a mature market. See Exhibit 20.2 to find out how Heinz celebrated the 50th anniversary of its baked beans with iconic product packaging.

EXHIBIT 20.2
Heinz created limited-edition labels with 50 different catchphrases

Decline

Sales and profits fall during the decline stage as new technology or changes in consumer tastes work to reduce demand for the product. For example, Sony lost out when the market for cathode-ray TVs went into decline following the development of flat-screen TVs. The technological advance resulted in Samsung and Panasonic overtaking Sony in sales of TVs (Gapper, 2006). Suppliers may decide to cease production completely or reduce product depth. Sony responded by developing the Bravia brand of flat-panel LCD televisions. When faced with declining sales, firms may also revise promotional and product development budgets by reducing the spend, and marginal distributors would be dropped as suppliers seek to maintain (or increase) profit margins. Alternatively, advertising may be used to defend against rivals and prevent the sales of a brand from falling into decline.

Uses of the Product Lifecycle

The product lifecycle (PLC) concept is useful for product management in several ways.

Product termination

First, the PLC emphasizes the fact that nothing lasts forever. There is a danger that management may fall in love with certain products. Maybe a company was founded on the success of a product; perhaps the product champion of a past success is now the chief executive. Under such circumstances there can be emotional ties with the product that can transcend normal commercial considerations. The PLC highlights the fact that products need to be terminated and new products developed to replace them. Without this sequence, a company may find itself with a group of products all in the decline stage of their PLC. Steve Jobs, Apple's co-founder, pioneered the market for selling computers into schools and educational markets in the USA, but recently the global brand's executives have produced the latest iPad, which appears to be out of touch with the needs of educational markets. Google's Chromebook, which is cheaper and better suited to the needs of school children has 60 per cent share of this market (Braithwaite, 2018). See Exhibit 20.3 to discover how the tech giants are seeking to lock in consumers from a very young age.

EXHIBIT 20.3
Apple, Google, and Sony are funding schools to capture the attention of consumers at a very young age

Growth projections

The second use of the PLC concept is to warn against the dangers of assuming that growth will continue. Swept along by growing order books, management can fall into the trap of believing that the heady days of rising sales and profits will continue forever. The PLC reminds managers that growth will end and suggests a need for caution when planning investment in new production facilities.

Marketing objectives and strategies over the PLC

The PLC emphasizes the need to review marketing objectives and strategies as products pass through the various stages. Changes in market and competitive conditions between the PLC stages suggest that marketing strategies should be adapted to meet them. Table 20.1 shows a set of stylized marketing responses to each stage. Note that these are broad generalizations and serve to emphasize the need to review marketing objectives and strategies in the light of environmental change.

The strategic marketing objective is to build sales by expanding the market for the product. The brand objective will be to create product (as well as brand) awareness so that customers will become familiar with generic product benefits.

The generic product is likely to be fairly basic, with an emphasis on reliability and functionality rather than special features to appeal to different customer groups. Once, desktop computers were the de facto machine for all our computing needs. Then the laptop arrived which was a mobile equivalent. Generally, these machines were expensive, heavy and suffered from poor battery life. There was therefore a gap in the market to meet the needs of target audiences who wanted lighter machines to last longer while on the move. The netbook was able to fill this gap. Fairly basic models were offered, providing mobile computing and internet access at affordable prices (e.g. Asus, Acer, Samsung). The functionality was basic, and the processor speed and memory fairly limited compared with that of their desktop and laptop counterparts. This lack of benefits eventually enabled other faster devices with a greater range of benefits to supersede the netbook—for

TABLE 20.1 Marketing objectives and strategies over the product lifecycle

	Introduction	Growth	Maturity	Decline
Strategic marketing objective	Build	Build	Hold	Harvest/manage for cash/divest
Strategic focus	Expand market	Penetration	Protect share/innovation	Productivity
Brand objective	Product awareness/trial	Brand preference	Brand loyalty	Brand exploitation
Products	Basic	Differentiated	Differentiated	Rationalized
Promotion	Creating awareness/trial	Creating awareness/trial/ repeat purchase	Maintaining awareness/ repeat purchase	Cut/eliminated
Price	High	Lower	Lowest	Rising
Distribution	Patchy	Wider	Intensive	Selective

example, tablet computers like the iPad and Microsoft Surface Pro, and smartphones like the Apple iPhone and Samsung Galaxy.

Promotion will support the brand objectives by gaining awareness for the brand and product type and stimulating trial. Advertising has been found to be more effective in the beginning of the life of a product than in later stages (Vakratsas and Ambler, 1999). Typically, price will be high because of the heavy development costs and the low level of competition. Distribution will be patchy, as some dealers are wary of stocking the new product until it has proved to be successful in the marketplace.

Growth

The strategic marketing objective during the growth phase is to build sales and market share. The strategic focus will be to penetrate the market by building brand preference. To accomplish this task, the product will be redesigned to create differentiation, and promotion will stress the functional and/or psychological benefits that accrue from the differentiation. Awareness and trial to acquire new customers are still important, but promotion will begin to focus on repeat purchases. As development costs are defrayed and competition increases, prices will fall. Rising consumer demand and increased salesforce effort will widen distribution.

Maturity

As sales peak and stabilize, the strategic marketing objective will be to hold on to profits and sales by protecting market share rather than embarking on costly competitive challenges. Since sales gains can only be at the expense of competition, strong challenges are likely to be resisted and lead to costly promotional or price wars. Brand objectives now focus on maintaining brand loyalty and customer retention, and promotion will defend the brand, stimulating repeat purchase by maintaining brand awareness and values. For all but the brand leader, competition may erode prices and profit margins, while distribution will peak in line with sales.

A key focus will be innovation to extend the maturity stage or, preferably, inject growth. This may take the form of innovative promotional campaigns, product improvements, and extensions and technological innovation. Unilever, Anglo Dutch manufacturer of consumer goods, introduced Persil Powergems to its laundry products—'a completely new format with triple power to clean'—a product that is more concentrated and more effective than previous product iterations. Unilever also redesigned the bottle as a way of communicating the product's revolutionary evolution (Unilever, 2017).

Decline

The conventional advice to companies managing products in the decline stage of the product lifecycle is to harvest or divest. A harvest strategy would result in the raising of prices while slashing marketing expenditures in an effort to boost profit margins. The strategic focus, therefore, is to improve marketing productivity rather than holding or building sales. The brand loyalty that has been built up over the years is, in effect, being exploited to create profits that can be used elsewhere in the company (e.g. new products). Product development will cease, the product line will be cut to the bare minimum of brands, and promotional expenditure will be cut, possibly to zero. Distribution costs will be analysed with a view to selecting only the most profitable outlets. The internet will be examined to explore its potential as a low-cost promotional and distribution vehicle.

Divestment may take the form of selling products to other companies or, if there are no willing buyers, product elimination. The strategy is to extract any residual value in the products, where possible, and to free up managerial time and resources to be redirected at more attractive products and opportunities. For example, Unilever sold its brands of margarine (Flora, Stork, Blue Band) due to falling consumer demand (Ruddick and Kollewe, 2017).

Two other strategies that can be applied at the decline stage are: 1) industry revitalization; and 2) pursuit of a profitable survivor strategy.

Industry revitalization: some products go into decline not because they are inherently unpopular, but because of lack of investment. For example, years of underinvestment in cinemas meant that the facilities were often dilapidated and the programming offered limited choice of films. However, one company saw this scenario as a marketing opportunity. Showcase Cinemas was launched, offering a choice of around 12 films in modern purpose-built premises near large conurbations. This completely changed the experience of going to the cinema, resulting in revitalization of the industry and growth in cinema attendances and profits. Thus, the classic PLC prescription of harvesting in the decline stage was rejected by a company that was willing to invest to reposition cinemas as an attractive means of offering evening entertainment.

Profitable survivor strategy: this is another alternative to harvesting or divestment (Aaker, 2007). It involves deciding to become the sole survivor in a declining market. This may involve being willing to incur losses while competitors drop out, or, if it is thought that this process is likely to be lengthy and slow, to accelerate it by:

- further reducing the attractiveness of the market by such actions as price cuts or increases in promotional expenditure
- buying competitors (which may be offered at a low price due to the unattractive markets they operate in) or their product lines that compete in the same market
- agreeing to take over competitors' contracts (e.g. supplying spare parts or service contracts) in exchange for their agreement to drop out of the market.

Once in the position of sole supplier, the survivor can reap the rewards of a monopoly by raising prices and resuming profitable operations.

Limitations of the Product Lifecycle

The product lifecycle is an aid to thinking about marketing decisions, but it needs to be handled with care. Management needs to be aware of the limitations of the PLC so that it is not misled by its prescriptions.

Fads and classics

Not all products follow the classic curve of the product lifecycle (Figure 20.1). The sales of some products 'rise like a rocket then fall like a stick'. This is normal for *fad* products such as hula hoops (popularized in the 1950s), 'pet rocks' (1970s), Pokemon cards (1990s), Zumba classes, superfoods such as quinoa (2010s) and vegan foods (2018). For example, when vegan foods became popular, leading ice cream brands Ben & Jerry's, Haagen-Daz and Halo Top released vegan flavours. Even vegan butchers selling plant-based 'meat products' appeared. See Marketing in Action 20.2.

Other products (and brands) appear to defy entering the decline stage. For example, classic confectionery products and brands such as Mars bars, Cadbury's Milk Tray and Toblerone have survived for decades in the mature stage of the PLC.

MARKETING IN ACTION 20.2
Japp Kortweg: The Vegetarian Butcher

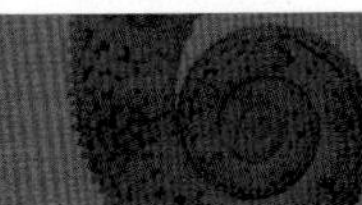

Jaap Kortweg grew up on a farm, and breeding cows goes back nine generations in his family. But Kortweg experienced the results of swine fever and bovine spongiform encephalopathy (mad cow disease) on the family's estate in the Netherlands. In 1998, at the height of the outbreak of the disease, he started thinking very seriously about how many animals were being killed to enable him to eat meat three times a day and also more philosophically about the fact that the reason for animals to exist is the product(s) they produce after they are killed.

It was several years before Kortweg became a full-time vegetarian. At first, he began by eating organic meat and even tried keeping his own animals for five years to give them a life before killing them. But this became like killing a family pet. So Kortweg gave up meat, but his hankering for eating sausages and chicken wings didn't abate. He took the radical step of creating vegetarian 'meat' products. It took him 10 years to find and develop a suitably tasty meat substitute with the right texture and bite. Kortweg worked with leading chefs to produce a range of meat-free products that would have wide market appeal. Kortweg's aim is to become the world's biggest 'butcher' with his sausages, meatballs and nuggets. He's made a strong start, as leading supermarkets in Europe are selling his products, and his restaurant in The Hague is growing in popularity.

Based on: Sandu (2018); The Vegetarian Butcher (2018)

Nevertheless, research has shown that the classic S-shaped curve does apply to a wide range of products, including grocery food products and pharmaceuticals (Polli and Cook, 1969).

EXHIBIT 20.4
Toblerone uses magic and fantasy to maintain its position as a classic chocolate brand

Marketing effects

The PLC is the *result* of marketing activities, not the cause. One school of thought argues that the PLC is not simply a fact of life—unlike living organisms—but is simply a pattern of sales that reflects marketing activity (Dhalia and Yuspeh, 1976). Clearly, sales of a product may flatten or fall simply because the product has not received enough marketing attention or has had insufficient product redesign or promotional support. Using the PLC, argue the critics, may lead to inappropriate action (e.g. harvesting or dropping the product), when the correct response should be increased marketing support (e.g. product replacement, positioning reinforcement or repositioning). Toblerone has used creative marketing solutions to maintain sales of its classic chocolate bars; see Exhibit 20.4.

Unpredictability

The duration of the PLC stages is unpredictable. The PLC outlines the four stages that a product passes through, without defining their duration. Clearly; this limits its use as a forecasting tool, since it is not possible to predict when maturity or decline will begin. The exception to this problem is when it is possible to identify a comparator product that serves as a template for predicting the length of each stage. Two sources of comparator products exist: 1) countries where the same product has already been on the market for some time; and 2) where similar products are in the mature or decline stages of their lifecycle but are thought to resemble the new product in terms of consumer acceptance. In practice, the use of comparator products is fraught with problems. For example, the economic and social conditions of countries may be so different that simplistic exploitation of the PLC from one country to another may be invalid; the use of similar products may offer inaccurate predictions in the face of ever-shortening product lifecycles.

Misleading objective and strategy prescriptions

The stylized marketing objectives and strategy prescriptions of the PLC may be misleading. Even if a product could accurately be classified as being in a PLC stage and sales are not simply a result of marketing activities, critics argue that the stylized marketing objectives and strategy prescriptions can be misleading. For example, there can be circumstances where the appropriate marketing objective in the growth stage is to harvest (e.g. in the face of intense competition), in the mature stage to build (e.g. when a distinct, defensive differential advantage can be developed), and in the decline stage to build (e.g. when there is an opportunity to dominate).

A Summary of the Usefulness of the Product Lifecycle Concept

Like many marketing tools, the product lifecycle should not be viewed as a panacea to marketing thinking and decision-making but as an aid to managerial judgement. By emphasizing the changes that are likely to occur as a product is marketed over time, the concept is a valuable stimulus to strategic thinking. Yet as a prescriptive tool it is blunt. Marketing management must monitor the real-life changes that are happening in the marketplace before setting precise objectives and strategies. Mini Case 20.1 explores how technology and the digital world are having an impact on the PLC.

MINI CASE 20.1
Disruptive Innovations

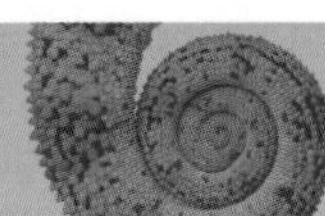

Disruptive Digital Technology: Permanent Beta and the Big Bang

Twenty-five years ago, few people were aware of the impact that the internet and associated digital technologies might have on our lives and the way we behave, communicate and trade.

The internet has affected many aspects of marketing, and product development is no exception. Two fundamental changes affect the PLC: 'permanent beta' and the big bang.

Permanent beta

Companies finding that the traditional product development lifecycle is taking too long before a product can reach the market have now adopted the 'permanent beta'. While some traditional products still require a formal development process, particularly where safety, warranty or legality is concerned (e.g. cars, aircraft, electrical goods), services and digital products can be released ahead of their final version.

There are potential advantages of early product release. One is that it *allows for errors*: in a freemium economy model (where products are provided free of charge, e.g. Google Search, Internet Explorer web browser), mistakes can be made, and customers are far more forgiving of a service that does not work as expected if they are not paying. Companies such as Dropbox do this regularly for new features in their cloud storage service to see how they work for a broad range of customers. Because many businesses regard their products as constantly evolving, it makes sense for them to be described as in a state of permanent beta. Arguably, permanent beta is *work in progress*, and this has implications for product management insofar as the whole concept of product development becomes highly fluid and constantly evolving. For the marketing manager, this means changing planning horizons between pre-launch activity, launch and eventual divestment.

The big bang

The date 11 August 1994 was a landmark date, as the first consumer e-commerce purchases were made. The product was a compact disk (CD): *Ten Summoner's Tales* by UK musician Sting. From that date forward, the internet developed as a new channel to market. Initially, CDs books, chocolates, wine and computers were sold to those individuals with access online. And it was this demand for consumer goods and access to the internet in consumer markets—rather than in business-to-business markets—that had a profound influence on the growth and development of the internet as a marketing channel. Why?

First, the market potential of the virtual world offered access to new markets, both locally and globally, and the internet enabled businesses to target new customers. This potential played a fundamental role in driving the growth of the online economy. The internet also offered the opportunity to trade continuously

>>

24 hours a day and allowed innovators to develop exciting ways to interact with the new target markets. For example, in 1995, Pierre Omidyar founded eBay, bringing online auctions and flexible pricing to a global audience. The global success of businesses like eBay and Amazon played a part in establishing the internet as a mainstream retail channel.

Second, the internet offered scope to satisfy customer needs. Communicating digitally, continuously, and in real-time—at first through email, then discussion boards and eventually social media networks—opened new ways to interact with customers and find out even more about their needs and wants.

Third, the internet facilitated diffusion of digital innovations: digital technology developed and spread rapidly. **Disruptive innovations** like Facebook, Twitter, Tumblr are digital innovations that have the capacity to infect the world in days. Many new digital apps have been developed at hackathons—late night sessions in Silicon Valley. The outcome is that disruptive innovations enter markets as a big bang rather than following the patterns of diffusions described by Everett Rogers (1983).

The impact of the internet on marketing has been profound. Digital technology innovations are great enablers of the principles of marketing: getting to know the customer better through digital analytics and behavioural information; satisfying their needs better than the competition does; providing greater opportunities for tailored and personalised offers across all aspects of product and service delivery; identifying innovative products and services, for example smart phones and wearable technology such as Fitbit, which show us new ways of doing things. Moreover, while digital technology continues to evolve at a rapid pace and have an increasing impact on the world we inhabit, marketing continues to be strongly related to the strategic aims of organizations. But changes are emerging: market-orientated firms that search proactively for market opportunities are discovering greater scope to develop their market offer through analysis of digital information.

Questions:

1. What are the implications of the big-bang disruption for a firm launching new technology products?
2. Discuss the extent to which the lifecycle of physical products is influenced by the big bang.
3. How might the digital technology landscape affect product development in the future?

Based on: Doherty, Ellis Chadwick and Hart (1999); Leckart (2012); Rogers (1983); Downes and Nunes (2013); Rowan (2012)

Managing Brand and Product Line Portfolios

So far, we have treated the management of products as distinct and independent entities. However, many companies are multi-product, serving multiple markets and segments. Some of these products will be strong, others weak. Some will require investment to finance growth; others will generate more cash than required. Somehow companies must decide how to distribute their limited resources among the competing needs of products so as to achieve the best performance for the company as a whole. Specifically, within a product line, management needs to decide which brands to invest in or hold, and which to withdraw support from. Similarly, within the product mix, decisions regarding which product lines to build or hold, or to withdraw support from, need to be taken. Canon, for example, took the strategic decision to focus on its profitable products—mainly copiers, printers and cameras—while divesting personal computers, typewriters and liquid crystal displays (LCDs) (Rowley and Tashiro, 2005). Managers who focus on individual products often miss the bigger picture that helps ensure the company's entire portfolio of products fits together coherently rather than being a loose confederation of offerings that has emerged out of a series of uncoordinated historical decisions (Shah, 2002). Philips found itself in this position, marketing a sprawling set of products, namely, semiconductors, consumer electronics, medical equipment, lighting and small electrical appliances (Marsh and Bickerton, 2005). To bring coherence to its product lines, Philips responded by selling its semiconductor business to focus on consumer lifestyle (consumer electronics and domestic appliances) and healthcare. Philips' exit from the incandescent lighting market is a result of a big bang technology disruption (as discussed in Marketing in Action 20.2). The technology innovation was light emitting diodes (LEDs), and Phillips' management recognized that this technology would lead to better, more energy-efficient and cheaper lighting technologies, which would eventually lead to the end of the firm's existing product ranges (Nunes and Downes, 2015). See Exhibit 20.5.

EXHIBIT 20.5
Phillips' innovations in LED lighting products

Clearly, portfolio-planning decisions are strategic decisions, since they shape where and with what brands/product lines a company competes and how its resources should be deployed. Furthermore, these decisions are complex, because many factors (e.g. current and future sales and profit potential, and cash flow) can affect the outcome. The process of managing groups of brands and product lines is called **portfolio planning**.

Key decisions regarding portfolio planning involve the choice of which brands/product lines to build, hold, harvest or divest. Marketing in Action 20.3 discusses several companies' approach to portfolio planning.

Two methods for managing products are widely discussed in management literature: 1) Boston Consulting Group Growth-Share Matrix; and 2) General Electric Market Attractiveness–Competitive Position portfolio-evaluation models. Like the PLC, these are flexible tools and can be used at both the brand and product line levels. Indeed, corporate planners can also use them when making resource allocation decisions at the strategic business unit level.

MARKETING IN ACTION 20.3
Portfolio Planning to the Core

The composition of a company's product portfolio is a vital strategic issue for marketers. Few companies have the luxury of starting with a clean sheet
and creating a well-balanced set of products.
An assessment of the strengths and weaknesses of the current portfolio is, therefore, necessary before taking the strategic decisions of which ones to build, hold, harvest or divest.

Major multinationals like Nestlé, Mondelez Foods, Procter & Gamble, GE and Unilever constantly review their product portfolios to achieve their strategic objectives. The trend has been to focus on core brands and product categories, and to divest minor peripheral brands.

»

»

Nestlé is the world's largest producer of packaged foods and constantly strives to manage its product portfolio. Nestlé sold Crosse & Blackwell and Davigel frozen and chilled foods to focus on key product categories and maintain market leadership. The focus is on the core categories of beverages, confectionery, chilled dairy, milks and nutrition. In line with this strategy, Nestlé has acquired the Ski and Munch Bunch dairy brands from Northern Foods, propelling it into the number two position behind Müller in the chilled dairy market.

Mondelez Foods has many globally recognized food brands in its product portfolio, for example Oreo, Nabisco, Trident and Tang. It has a mixed portfolio, with 49 per cent of its business in North America, 23 per cent in Europe and 28 per cent in developing markets. Of these businesses, the largest concentration are in the confectionery sector (28 per cent), followed by biscuits (22 per cent), beverages (18 per cent), cheese (14 per cent), convenience meals (10 per cent) and grocery (8 per cent). These holdings in its portfolio make Mondelez Foods the second-largest food company in the world; in order to maintain this position, Mondelez Foods constantly reviews the product portfolio, as 80 per cent of its revenues come from products that are market leaders in their categories. In 2008, Mondelez acquired LU, a global biscuit business, but got rid of Post, its cereal food operation. In 2010, Cadbury was added to the portfolio to help build its dominance in the confectionery sector in Europe, while DiGiono, its pizza business, was divested, as convenience foods account for only a small part of the portfolio.

This trend is not confined to the grocery business, however. For example, Adidas sold its ski and surf equipment firm Salomon to Amer Sports Corporation so that it could focus on its core strength in the athletic footwear and apparel market as well as the growing golf category. IBM sold its PC division to Lenovo to concentrate on software and services.

Philips rationalized its product portfolio, selling its semiconductor business to focus on consumer lifestyle, healthcare and lighting. Its mission is to focus on health and well-being, and it has invested in healthcare, moving away from its medical imaging business and into patient monitoring and home healthcare. One example is its acquisition of Respironics, a medical equipment maker specializing in sleep therapy. Phillips sees healthcare as a growth market as people live longer.

One advantage of this portfolio-planning strategy is to enable maximum firepower to be put behind core brands.

Based on: Costello (2015); Mondelez Foods (n.d.); Mason (2002); Tomlinson (2005); Milner (2006); Steen (2008)

The Boston Consulting Group Growth-Share Matrix

A leading management consultancy, the Boston Consulting Group (BCG), developed the well-known BCG Growth-Share Matrix (see Figure 20.2) (also known as the 'Boston box'). The matrix allows portfolios of products to be depicted in a 2 × 2 box, the axes of which are based on market growth rate and relative market share. The analysis is based upon cash flow (rather than profits), and its key assumptions are:

- market growth has an adverse effect on cash flow, because of the investment in such assets as manufacturing facilities, equipment and marketing needed to finance growth
- market share has a positive effect on cash flow, as profits are related to market share.

The following discussion will be based on an analysis at the product line level.

Market growth rate forms the vertical axis and indicates the annual growth rate of the market in which each product line operates. In Figure 20.2, it is shown as 0–15 per cent, although a different range could be used, depending on economic conditions. In this example, the dividing line between high and low growth rates is 7 per cent. Market growth rate is used as a proxy for market attractiveness.

FIGURE 20.2
The Boston Consulting Group Growth-Share Matrix

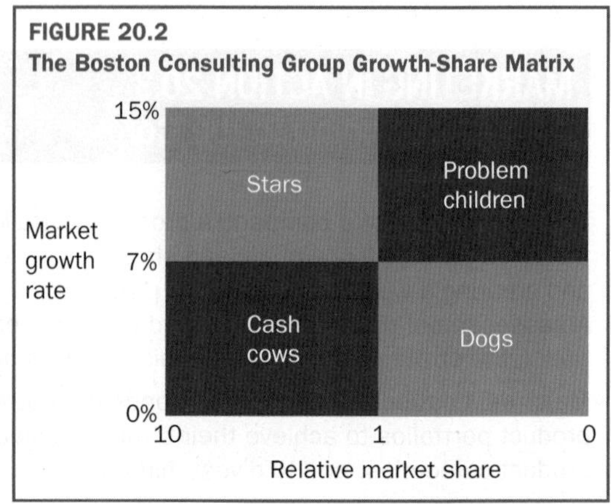

Relative market share is shown on the horizontal axis and refers to the market share of each product relative to its largest competitor. It acts as a proxy for competitive strength. The division between high and low market share is 1. Above this figure, a product line has a market share greater than its largest competitor. For example, if our product had a market share of 40 per cent and our largest competitor's share were 30 per cent, this would be indicated as 1.33 on the horizontal axis. Below 1, we have a share less than the largest competitor. For example, if our share were 20 per cent and the largest competitor had a share of 40 per cent, our score would be 0.5.

The BCG argued that cash flow is dependent on the box in which a product falls. Note that cash flow is not the same as profitability. Profits add to cash flow, but heavy investment in such assets as manufacturing facilities, equipment and marketing expenditure can mean that a company can make profits and yet have a negative cash flow.

Stars are likely to be profitable because they are market leaders, but they require substantial investment to finance growth (e.g. new production facilities) and to meet competitive challenges. Overall cash flow is therefore likely to be roughly in balance. *Problem children* are products in high-growth markets that cause a drain on cash flow. But these are low-share products; consequently, they are unlikely to be profitable. Overall, problem children are big cash users. *Cash cows* are market leaders in mature (low-growth) markets. High market share leads to high profitability, and low market growth means that investment in new production facilities is minimal. This leads to a large positive cash flow. *Dogs* also operate in low-growth markets but have low market share. Except for some products near the dividing line between cash cows and dogs (sometimes called *cash dogs*), most dogs produce low or negative cash flows. Relating to their position in the product lifecycle, they are the also-rans in mature or declining markets.

What are the strategic implications of the BCG analysis? It can be used for setting strategic objectives and for maintaining a balanced product portfolio.

Guidelines for setting strategic objectives

Having plotted the position of each product on the matrix, a company can begin to think about setting the appropriate strategic objective for each line. As you may recall from Chapter 18, there are four possible strategic objectives: build, hold, harvest and divest. Figure 20.3 shows how each relates to the star, problem child, cash cow and dog categories. However, it should be emphasized that the BCG Matrix provides guidelines for strategic thinking and should not be a replacement for managerial judgement.

- *Stars*: these are the market leaders in high-growth markets. They are already successful, and the prospects for further growth are good. As we have seen when discussing brand building, market leaders tend to have the highest profitability, so the appropriate strategic objective is to build sales and/or market share. Resources should be invested to maintain/increase the leadership position. Competitive challenges should be repelled. These are the cash cows of the future and need to be protected.
- *Problem children*: as we have seen, these are cash drains, because they have low profitability and need investment to keep up with market growth. They are called problem children because management must consider whether it is sensible to continue the required investment. The company faces a fundamental choice: to increase investment (*build*) to attempt to turn the problem child into a star, or to withdraw support by either *harvesting* (raising price while lowering marketing expenditure) or *divesting* (dropping or selling it). In a few cases, a third option may be viable: to find a small market segment (*niche*) where dominance can be achieved. Unilever, for example, identified its speciality chemicals business as a problem child. It realized that it had to invest heavily or exit. Its decision was to sell and invest the billions raised in predicted future winners such as personal care, dental products and fragrances (Brierley, 1997).
- *Cash cows*: the high profitability and low investment associated with high market share in low-growth markets means that cash cows should be defended. Consequently, the appropriate strategic objective is to *hold* sales and market share. The excess cash that is generated should be used to fund stars, problem children that are being built, and research and development for new products.

FIGURE 20.3
Strategic objectives and the 'Boston box'

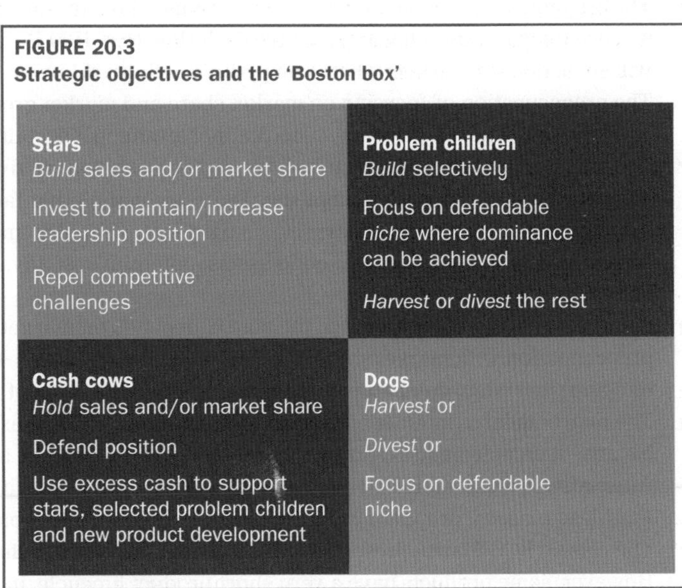

- *Dogs*: dogs are weak products that compete in low-growth markets. They are the also-rans that have failed to achieve market dominance during the growth phase and are floundering in maturity. For those products that achieve second or third position in the marketplace (*cash dogs*) a small positive cash flow may result, and for a few others it may be possible to reposition the product into a defendable *niche*. But for the bulk of dogs the appropriate strategic objective is to *harvest* to generate a positive cash flow for a time, or to *divest*, which allows resources and managerial time to be focused elsewhere.

FIGURE 20.4
The case of an unbalanced product portfolio

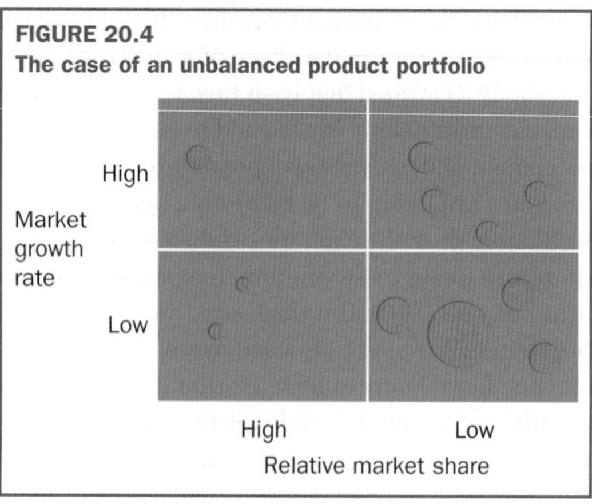

Maintaining a balanced product portfolio

Once all the company's products have been plotted, it is easy to see how many stars, problem children, cash cows and dogs are in the portfolio. Figure 20.4 shows a product portfolio that is unbalanced. The company possesses only one star, and the small circle indicates that sales revenue generated from the star is small. Similarly, the two cash cows are also low revenue earners. In contrast, the company owns four dogs and four problem children. The portfolio is unbalanced, because there are too many problem children and dogs and not enough stars and cash cows. What many companies in this situation do is to spread what little surplus cash is available equally between the products in the growth markets (Hedley, 1977). To do so would leave each with barely enough money to maintain market share, leading to a vicious circle of decline.

The BCG remedy would be to conduct a detailed competitive assessment of the four problem children and select one or two for investment. The rest should be harvested (and the cash channelled to those that are being built) or divested. The aim is to build the existing star (which will be the cash cow of the future) and to build the market share of the chosen problem children so that they attain star status.

The dogs also need to be analysed. One of them (the large circle) is a large revenue earner, which despite low profits may be making a substantial contribution to overheads. Another product (on the left) appears to be in the cash dog situation. But for the other two, the most sensible strategic objective may be to harvest or divest.

Criticisms of the BCG Growth-Share Matrix

The simplicity, ease of use and importance of the issues tackled by the BCG Matrix has led to its widespread adoption to help firms get a handle on the complexities of strategic resource allocation. But the tool has also attracted a litany of criticism (see, for example, Wensley, 1981; Haspslagh, 1982; Day and Wensley, 1983). The following list draws together many of the points raised by the BCG's critics.

- The assumption that cash flow will be determined by a product's position in the matrix is weak. For example, some stars will show a healthy positive cash flow (e.g. IBM PCs during the growth phase of the PC market), as will some dogs in markets where competitive activity is low.
- The preoccupation of focusing on market share and market growth rates distracts managerial attention from the fundamental principle in marketing: attaining a sustainable competitive advantage.
- Treating the market growth rate as a proxy for market attractiveness, and market share as an indicator of competitive strength is over-simplistic. There are many other factors that must be taken into account when measuring market attractiveness (e.g. market size, strengths and weaknesses of competitors) and competitive strengths (e.g. exploitable marketing assets, potential cost advantages), besides market growth rates and market share.
- Since the position of a product in the matrix depends on market share, this can lead to an unhealthy preoccupation with market share gain. In some circumstances, this objective makes sense (e.g. brand building), but when competitive retaliation is likely the costs of share building may outweigh the gains.
- The matrix ignores interdependencies between products. For example, a dog may need to be marketed because it complements a star or a cash cow—the dog may be a spare part for a star or a cash cow. Alternatively, customers and distributors may value dealing with a company that supplies a full product line. For these reasons, dropping products because they fall into a particular box may be naive.
- The classic BCG Matrix prescription is to build stars because they will become the cash cows of the future. However, some products have a very short product lifecycle, in which case the appropriate strategy should be to maximize profits and cash flow while in the star category (e.g. fashion goods).

- Marketing objectives and strategy are heavily dependent on an assessment of what competitors are likely to do. How will they react if prices are lowered or raised when implementing a build or harvest strategy, for example? This is not considered in the matrix.
- The matrix assumes that products are self-funding. For example, selected problem children are built using cash generated by cash cows. But this ignores capital markets, which may mean that a wider range of projects can be undertaken as long as they have positive net present values of their future cash flows.
- The matrix is vague regarding the definition of 'market'. Should we take the whole market (e.g. for confectionery) or just the market segment that we operate in (e.g. expensive boxed chocolates)? The matrix is also vague when defining the dividing line between high- and low-growth markets. A chemical company that tends to generate in lower-growth markets might use 3 per cent, whereas a leisure goods company whose markets on average experience much higher rates of growth might use 10 per cent. Also, over what period do we define market growth? These issues question the theoretical soundness of the underlying concepts and allow managers to manipulate the figures so that their products fall in the right boxes.
- The matrix was based on cash flow. but perhaps profitability (e.g. return on investment) is a better criterion for allocating resources.
- The matrix lacks precision in identifying which problem children to build, harvest or drop.
- 2×2 matrices, in general, are limited and act more as a screening tool to facilitate further analysis than to provide definite answers (Calandro and Lane, 2007).

General Electric Market Attractiveness–Competitive Position Model

As we have already noted, the BCG Matrix enjoyed tremendous success as management grappled with the complex issue of strategic resource allocation. Stimulated by this success and some of the weaknesses of the model (particularly the criticism of its over-simplicity), McKinsey & Co developed a more wide-ranging market attractiveness–competitive position (MA–CP) model in conjunction with General Electric (GE) in the USA.

Market attractiveness criteria

Instead of market growth alone, a range of market attractiveness criteria were used, such as:

- market size
- market growth rate
- beatable rivals
- market entry barriers
- social, political and legal factors.

Competitive strength criteria

Similarly, instead of using only market share as a measure of competitive strength, a number of factors were used, such as:

- market share
- reputation
- distribution capability
- market knowledge
- service quality
- innovation capability
- cost advantages.

Assessing market attractiveness and competitive strength

Management is allowed to decide which criteria are applicable for their products. This gives the MA–CP Model flexibility. Having decided on the criteria, management's next task is to agree upon a weighting system for each set of criteria, with those factors that are more important having a higher weighting. Table 20.2 shows a set of weights for market attractiveness. Management has decided that the key factors that should be used to assess market attractiveness are market size, market growth rate, beatable rivals and market entry barriers. Ten points are then shared between these four factors depending on their relative importance in assessing market attractiveness. Market size (weighting = 4.0) is considered the most important factor, and market entry barriers (1.5) is the least important of the four factors.

Next, management assesses the market for the product under examination on each of the four factors on a scale of 1 to 10. The market is rated very highly on size (rating = 9.0), it possesses beatable rivals (8.0), its growth

TABLE 20.2 An example of market attractiveness assessment

Market factors	Relative importance weightings (10 points shared)	Factor ratings (scale 1–10)	Factor scores (weightings × ratings)
Market size	4.0	9.0	36
Market growth rate	2.0	7.0	14
Beatable rivals	2.5	8.0	20
Market entry barriers	1.5	6.0	9
			79%

TABLE 20.3 An example of competitive strength assessment

Strengths needed for success	Relative importance weightings (10 points shared)	Factor ratings (scale 1–10)	Factor scores (weightings × ratings)
Market share	2.5	8.0	20
Distribution capability	1.0	7.0	7
Service quality	2.0	5.0	10
Innovation capability	3.0	9.0	27
Cost advantages	1.5	8.0	12
			76%

rate is also rated highly (7.0), and there are some market barriers, although they are not particularly high (6.0). By multiplying each weighting by its corresponding rating and then summing, a total score indicating the overall attractiveness of the market for the product under examination is obtained. In this case, the market attractiveness for the product achieves an overall score of 79 per cent.

Competitive strength assessment begins by selecting the strengths that are needed to compete in the market. Table 20.3 shows that market share, distribution capability, service quality, innovation capability and cost advantages were the factors considered to be needed for success. Management then assigns a weight by sharing 10 points between each of these strengths according to their relative importance in achieving success. Innovation capability (weighting = 3.0) is regarded as the most important strength required to compete effectively. Distribution capability (1.0) is considered the least important of the five factors. The company's capabilities on each of the required strengths are rated on a scale from 1 to 10. Company capabilities are rated very highly on innovation capability (rating = 9.0), market share (8.0) and cost advantages (8.0), and highly on distribution capability (7.0), but service quality (5.0) is mediocre. By multiplying each weighting by its corresponding rating and then summing, a total score indicating the overall competitive strength of the company is obtained. In this example, the competitive strength of the company achieves an overall score of 76 per cent.

The market attractiveness and competitive strength scores for the product under appraisal can now be plotted on the MA–CP matrix (see Figure 20.5). The process is repeated for each product under investigation, so that the products' relative positions on the MA–CP matrix can be established. Each product position is given by a circle, the size of which is in proportion to its sales.

Setting strategic objectives

The model is shown in Figure 20.5. Like the BCG Matrix, the recommendations for setting strategic objectives are dependent on the product's position on the grid. Five zones are shown in Figure 20.6. The strategic objectives associated with each zone are as follows (Hofer and Schendel, 1978).

- *Zone 1*: build—manage for sales and market share growth, as the market is attractive and competitive strengths are high (equivalent to star products).

- *Zone 2*: hold—manage for profits consistent with maintaining market share, as the market is not particularly attractive but competitive strengths are high (equivalent to cash cows).
- *Zone 3*: build/hold/harvest—this is the question-mark zone. Where competitors are weak or passive, a build strategy will be used. In the face of strong competitors, a hold strategy may be appropriate—or harvesting, where commitment to the product/market is lower (similar to problem children).
- *Zone 4*: harvest—manage for cash, as both market attractiveness and competitive strengths are fairly low.
- *Zone 5*: divest—improve short-term cash yield by dropping or selling the product (equivalent to dog products).

In the example shown in Figure 20.5, the circle labelled A indicates the position of the product, which falls within Zone 1 as it operates in an attractive market and its competitive strengths are high. This would suggest a build strategy that probably involves investing in raising service quality levels, which were found to be relatively weak.

FIGURE 20.5
The General Electric Market Attractiveness–Competitive Position Matrix

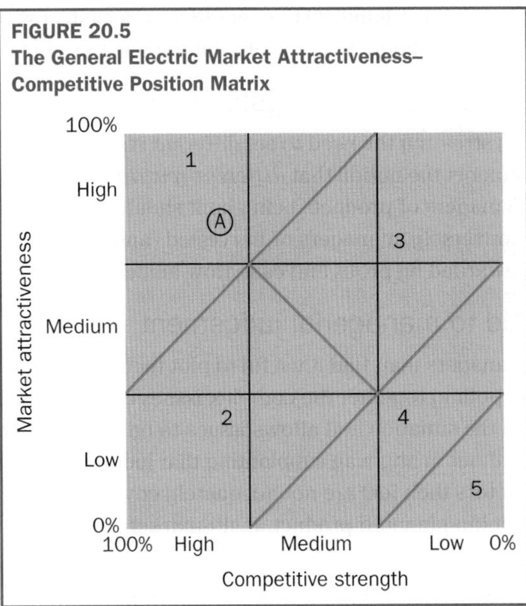

Criticisms of the GE MA–CP Model

The proponents of the GE MA–CP portfolio model argue that the analysis is much richer than BCG analysis—thanks to more factors being considered—and more flexible. These are substantial advantages and the model is widely used, with companies such as BP, IBM, Honda, Nissan, Philips, Centrica, Mitsubishi and GE employing it to aid their strategic thinking. Critics argue, however, that it is harder to use than the BCG Matrix, since it requires managerial agreement on which factors to use, their weightings and scoring. Furthermore, its flexibility provides a lot of opportunity for managerial bias to enter the analysis, whereby product managers argue for factors and weightings that show their products in a good light (Zone 1). This last point suggests that the analysis should be conducted at a managerial level higher than that being assessed. For example, decisions on which product lines to be built, held, and so on, should be taken at the strategic business unit level, and allocations of resources to brands should be decided at the group product manager level.

The contribution of product portfolio planning

Despite the limitations of the BCG and the GE MA–CP portfolio evaluation models, both have contributed to the practice of portfolio planning. We shall now discuss this contribution and suggest how the models can usefully be incorporated into product strategy.

Different products and different roles

The models emphasize the important strategic point that *different products should have different roles* in the product portfolio. Hedley points out that some companies believe that all product lines and brands should be treated equally—that is, set the same profit requirements (Hedley, 1977). The portfolio planning models stress that this should not necessarily be the case and may be harmful in many situations. For example, to ask for a 20 per cent return on investment (ROI) for a star may result in underinvestment to meet the profit requirement.

FIGURE 20.6
Implications of portfolio planning

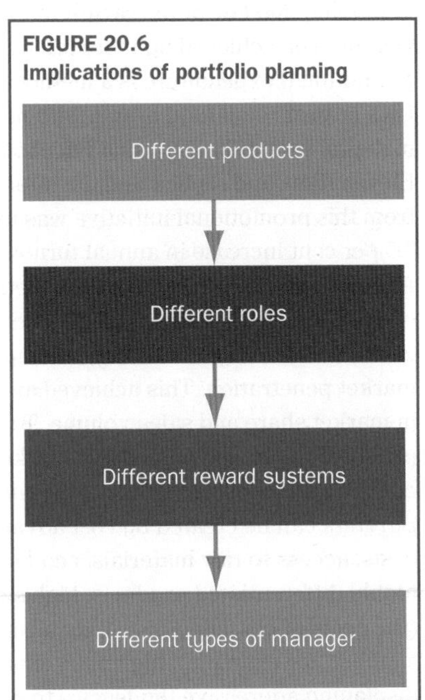

On the other hand, 20 per cent ROI for a cash cow or a harvested product may be too low. The implication is that products should be set profitability objectives in line with the strategic objective decisions.

Different reward systems and types of manager

By stressing the need to set different strategic objectives for different products, the models, by implication, support the notion that *different reward systems and types of manager* should be linked to them. For example, managers of products being built should be marketing led and rewarded for improving sales and market share. Conversely, managers of harvested (and to some extent cash cow) products should be more cost orientated and rewarded by profit and cash flow achievement (see Figure 20.6).

Aid to managerial judgement

Managers may find it useful to plot their products on both the BCG and GE MA–CP portfolio grids as an initial step in pulling together the complex issues involved in product portfolio planning. This can help them to get a handle on the situation and allows issues to be resolved. The models can then act as an *aid to managerial judgement* without in any way supplanting that judgement. Managers should feel free to bring into the discussion any other factors they feel are not adequately covered by the models. The models can therefore be an aid to strategic thinking in multi-product, multi-market companies.

Product Strategies for Growth

The emphasis in product portfolio analysis is on managing an *existing* set of products in such a way as to maximize their strengths, but companies also need to look to new products and markets for future growth. Sir James Dyson, inventor and entrepreneur, announced that the brand was to take the radical step of ending the development of corded vacuum cleaners in favour of cordless models, the Cyclone V10 being the most advanced version to date. Dyson is also developing an electric car, which it expects to launch in 2020. Both product strategies aim to ensure the future of the brand (Field, 2018).

A useful way of looking at growth opportunities is the Ansoff Matrix, as shown in Figure 20.7 (Ansoff, 1957). By combining present and new products and present and new markets into a 2 × 2 matrix, four product strategies for growth are revealed. Although the Ansoff Matrix does not prescribe when each strategy should be employed, it is a useful framework for thinking about the ways in which growth can be achieved through product strategy.

Figure 20.8 shows how the Ansoff Matrix can be used to implement a growth strategy. The most basic method of gaining **market penetration** in existing markets with current products is by *winning competitors' customers*. This may be achieved by more effective use of promotion or distribution or by cutting prices. Increasing promotional expenditure is a method of winning competitors' customers and market penetration. Greggs, the UK's largest retail food brand, with more shops than McDonald's and Subway, made a significant investment in digital promotion by using Facebook to find out what its 20,000 customers thought about the brand. Eleven thousand replied and the information gathered from this promotional initiative was used to deliver a 7.5 per cent increase in annual turnover (Handley, 2012). Another way of gaining market penetration is to *buy competitors*. An example is the Morrisons supermarket chain, which bought Safeway, a competitor, to gain market penetration. This achieved an immediate increase in market share and sales volume. To protect the penetration already gained in a market, a business may consider methods of *discouraging competitive entry*. *Barriers* can be created by cost advantages (lower labour costs, access to raw materials, economies of scale), highly differentiated products, high switching costs (the costs of changing from existing supplier to a new supplier, for example), high marketing expenditures and displaying aggressive tendencies to retaliate.

FIGURE 20.7
Product growth strategies: the Ansoff Matrix

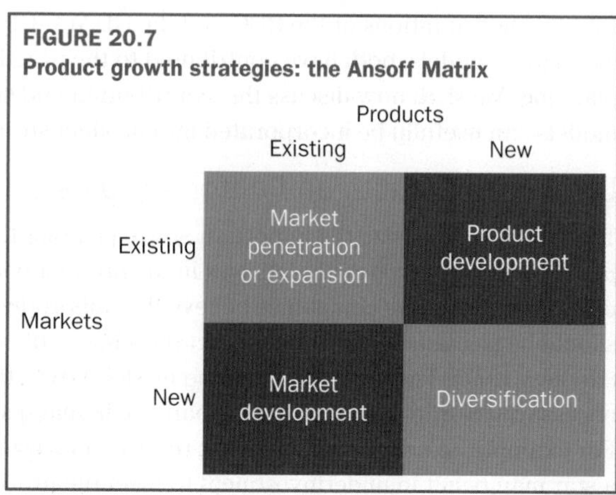

FIGURE 20.8
Strategic options for increasing sales volume

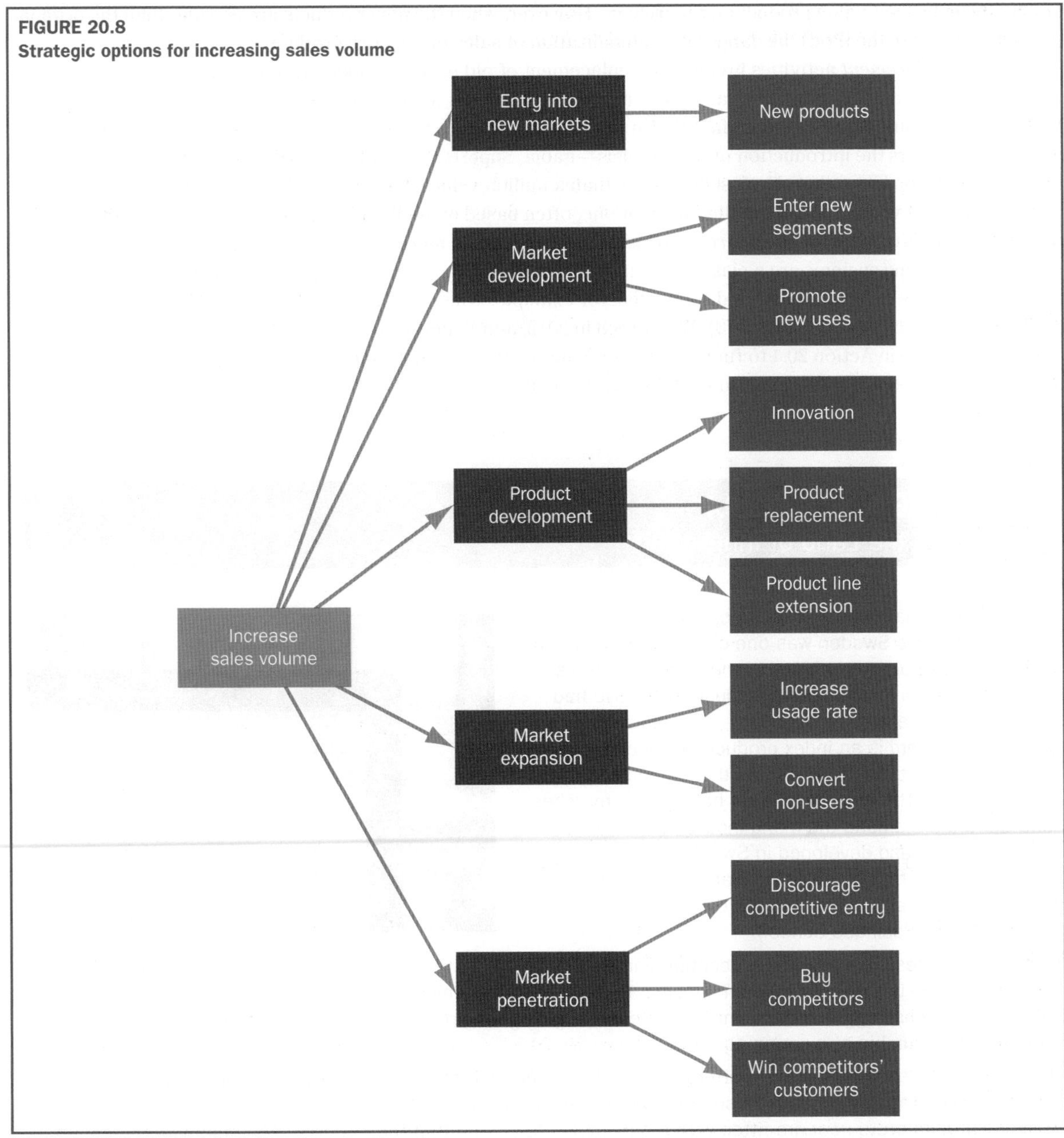

A company may attempt **market expansion** in a market that it already serves by converting *non-users to users* of its product. This can be an attractive option in new markets when non-users form a sizeable segment and may be willing to try the product given suitable inducements. Lapsed users can also be targeted. Kellogg's has targeted lapsed breakfast cereal users (specifically fathers) who rediscover the pleasure of eating cornflakes when feeding their children. Market expansion can also be achieved by *increasing usage rate*. Kellogg's has also tried to increase the usage (eating) rate of its cornflakes by promoting eating in the evening as well as at breakfast. Affordability and improving sustainability market expansion have also been found to aid market expansion (Banga and Joshib, 2010). The **product development** option involves the development of new products for existing markets (Ansoff, 1957). One variant is to *extend existing product lines* to give current customers greater choice. For example, the original iPod has been followed by the launches of the iPod nano, shuffle and touch, giving its target market of young music lovers greater choice in terms of size, capacity and price. When new features are added (with an accompanying price rise), trading up may occur, with customers buying the enhanced-value product on repurchase. However, when the new products are cheaper than the original (as is the case with the iPod) the danger is cannibalization of sales of the core product.

Product replacement activities involve the replacement of old brands/models with new ones. This is common in the car market and often involves an upgrading of the old model with a new (more expensive) replacement. For Skoda, the third oldest car manufacturer in the world, product replacement has been essential to its survival, and in recent years the introduction of new models—Fabia, Superb, Citigo and Rapid—has enabled the brand to retain and develop its market share, selling more than a million vehicles a year. A final option is the replacement of an old product with a fundamentally different one, often based on technology change. The business thus replaces an old product with an *innovation* (although both may be marketed side by side for a time). Microsoft operating systems are a classic example of replacement products being introduced, but the older products continue to be marketed and supported; for example, Windows Vista (released in 2006) was superseded by Windows 7 in 2009 (Microsoft, 2013), Windows 8 in 2012, and Windows 10 in 2015.

See Marketing in Action 20.4 to find out about the innovative products and technology applications that have helped Sweden become Europe's third most innovative nation.

MARKETING IN ACTION 20.4
Sweden is the Land of Innovation

Sweden is a small country with a population of 9.5 million. Once Sweden was one of the poorest nations in Europe, but today it is home to many of the world's most successful innovations—products that have had an impact on the lives of individuals. The Innovation Union Scoreboard is an index produced by the European commission that ranks Sweden as the leading country for innovation. The three-point seat belt, safety matches and Spotify are among the many innovations to have been designed and developed in Sweden. The country also ranks very highly on the Innovative Capacity Index (Harvard Business School) and the Global Innovation Index (INSEAD Business School).

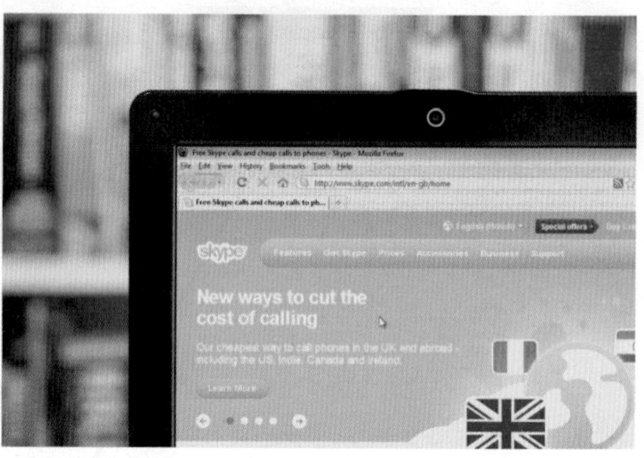

Sweden's success is attributed to: continual investment in research and design; its focus on specific areas in which to achieve excellence, for example medicine, bioscience, technology and the climate; and encouraging young people to become interested in technology and entrepreneurship at a young age.

In the field of medicine, the first battery-run heart pacemaker that was small enough to be implanted under a patient's skin was developed by a surgeon at the Karolinska University Hospital in Stockholm. Over half a million patients every year are fitted with a pacemaker to ensure that their hearts keep beating regularly and they subsequently benefit from normalized heart rhythms.

The Tetrapak is a revolution in paper-based packaging that allows billions of shoppers to take home their milk and other liquids in a carton instead of a glass bottle. Erik Wallenberg came up with the idea, and it was then produced by Ruben Raising, who was instrumental in setting up the first specialized packaging company in Sweden. Since then, the company has grown, and it now supplies more than 8.5 billion packs a year, which can be recycled. The company has won many awards for being an environmentally responsible manufacturer.

Skype is another globally recognized application to emerge from Scandinavia. Niklas Zennstrom (from Sweden) worked with Janus Friis (from Denmark) with Estonian developers to produce this innovative software application that enables internet users to make free voice calls via the web.

The Swedish government has a strategy that aims to continue to foster the right conditions for the development of many more innovations. The strategic focus for investment in innovations are medicine and bioscience, technology and climate. The strategy aims to meet global societal challenges by placing emphasis on sustainability, increasing competitiveness and creating jobs in the knowledge economy, and increasing the efficiency of public services. The Swedish government is aiming to create the best possible conditions for innovation by enabling people to be innovative, investing in research and higher education, and creating an infrastructure that provides solid foundations for the future. The strategy extends beyond business and to the heart of innovation in schools. Finn Upp is a programme that brings together Sweden's successful entrepreneurs and innovators and young people in schools. Ung Företagsamhet is another school-based programme aimed at developing young entrepreneurship. Snilleblixtarna (flashes of genius) is aimed at younger children and seeks to stimulate curiosity.

Based on: Swedish Institute (2018); Tetrapak (2015); Swedish Ministry of Enterprise, Energy and Communications (2015)

Market development entails the promotion of *new uses of existing products to new customers* or the marketing of *existing products (and their current uses) to new market segments.* The promotion of new uses accounted for the growth in sales of nylon, which was first marketed as a replacement for silk in parachutes but expanded into being used in shirts, carpets, tyres, etc. Tesco, the UK supermarket chain, practised market development by marketing existing grocery products, which were sold in large out-of-town supermarkets and superstores, to a new market segment—convenience shoppers—by opening smaller grocery shops in town centres and next to petrol stations. Market development through entering new segments could involve the search for overseas opportunities. Andy Thornton Ltd, an interior design business, successfully increased sales by entering Scandinavia and Germany, two geographic segments that provided new expansion opportunities for the business's services. The growth of overseas markets in China, India, Russia and eastern Europe is providing major market development opportunities for companies such as BP, Vodafone, Walmart and Carrefour (*The Economist*, 2008). When Wagner, the German manufacturer of spray guns for painting, expanded to the USA in search of market development, it found that it had to refocus on an entirely different market segment. In Europe it sells its products to professional painters, but in the USA its products are bought by people who use spray guns in their own homes to paint interiors and outside surfaces such as fences (Bolfo, 2005).

The **entry into new markets (diversification)** option concerns the development of *new products for new markets*. This is the most risky option, especially when the entry strategy is not based on the *core competences* of the business. However, it can also be the most rewarding, as exemplified by Honda's move from motorcycles to cars (based on its core competences in engines), and Apple Computer's launch of the iPod mobile music player, which can download music via a computer (based on its core competences in computer electronics). This was followed by its highly successful diversification into smartphones (the iPhone), based on its new-found competences in mobile communication, and tablet computers with the iPad. It is the lure of such rewards that has tempted the internet networking equipment maker Cisco to venture into consumer electronics, and Intel, which manufactures microprocessors that power personal computers, to diversify into platforms combining silicon and software, which has led to new devices and technologies in consumer electronics, wireless communications and healthcare (see Edwards, 2006; Palmer, 2006).

Ethical Issues and Products

The final section in this chapter considers the three major ethical issues relating to products.

1 *Product safety* is a major concern, particularly in relation to consumables. Genetically modified (GM) products have attracted the attention of pressure groups such as Greenpeace, who have spoken out about the dangers of genetic modification. People are sharply divided as to whether GM products are safe. Although plant breeders have, for thousands of years, been tampering with the genes of plants through traditional cross-pollination of plants of the same species, genetic modification goes one step further as it allows scientists to cross the species barrier.

   Concerns about product safety also relate to tobacco (lung cancer), the levels of fat, sugar and salt in foods (obesity and heart problems), and sugar in soft drinks (obesity and tooth decay). Such issues have led to bans on tobacco advertising, the setting up of independent bodies to protect consumers' interests in the food and drinks industries, and reductions in the levels of fat, sugar and salt in many food and drink brands; particularly the level of sugar in food and soft drinks consumed by children. For example, Nestlé has reduced the level of sugar in its cereals targeted at children and reformulated its Rowntree range of children's sweets to make them free from artificial flavours and colours. The UK government introduced a sugar tax on soft drinks, which has encouraged many more leading brands to cut the sugar content of their soft drinks. Coca-Cola has developed many new products to target the low-sugar markets: vitaminwater, Fuze, Gold Peak Tea.

2 *Planned obsolescence.* Many products are not designed to last a long time. From the producer's point of view this is sensible, as it creates a repeat purchase situation. Hence consumer electronics break and are superseded by newer models, clothes wear out, and fashion items are replaced by the latest styles. Consumers accept that nothing lasts forever, but the issue concerns what is an acceptable length of time before replacement is necessary. For physical goods, issues of environmental sustainability and impact on the planet are changing how manufacturers view obsolescence. But technology firms regularly introduce changes that render existing products obsolete, for example upgrades and new releases of software. Smartphones are a prime example: new features, are regularly introduced and battery life and memory capacity extended, rendering older phones near to obsolete

3 *Deceptive packaging.* This can occur when a product appears in an oversized package to create the impression that the consumer is buying more than is the case. This is known as 'slack' packaging and has the potential to deceive when the packaging is opaque. Products such as soap powder and breakfast cereals have the potential to suffer from 'slack' packaging. A second area where packaging may be deceptive is through misleading labelling, for example the failure of a package to state that the product contains genetically modified soya beans. This relates to the consumer's 'right to be informed', which can include stating ingredients (including flavouring and colourants), nutritional contents and country of origin on labels. Nevertheless, labelling can be misleading. For example, in the UK, 'country of origin' is only the last country where the product was 'significantly changed'. So oil pressed from Greek olives in France can be labelled 'French', and foreign imports that are packed in the UK can be labelled 'produce of the UK'. Consumers should be wary of loose terminology. For example, smoked bacon may well have received its 'smoked' flavour from a synthetic liquid solution, 'farm fresh eggs' are likely to be un-date-marked eggs of indeterminate age laid by battery hens, and 'farmhouse cheese' may not come from farmhouses but from industrial factories.

The use of loose language and meaningless terms in the UK food and drink industry has been criticized by the Food Standards Agency (FSA). A list of offending words has been drawn up, which includes 'fresh', 'natural', 'pure', 'traditional' and 'original'. Recommendations regarding when it is reasonable to use certain words have been drawn up. For example, 'authentic' should only be used to emphasize the geographic origin of a product, and 'homemade' should be restricted to the preparation of the recipe on the premises and must involve 'some degree of fundamental culinary preparation'. The FSA has also expressed concern about the use of meaningless phrases such as 'natural goodness' and 'country style' and recommended that they should not be used.

Review

1 The concept of the product lifecycle

- A four-stage cycle in the life of a product, illustrated as sales and profit curves, the four stages being introduction, growth, maturity and decline. It is quite flexible and can be applied to both brands and product lines.

2 The uses and limitations of the product lifecycle

- Its uses are that it emphasizes the need to terminate old and develop new products, warns against the danger of assuming growth will last forever, stresses the need to review marketing objectives and strategies as products pass through the four stages, emphasizes the need to maintain a balanced set of products across the four stages, and warns against the damages of overpowering (setting too high prices early in the cycle when competition is low).
- The limitations are that it is wrong to assume that all products follow the classic S-shaped curve, and it is misleading to believe that the product lifecycle sales curve is a fact of life: it depends on marketing activity.

The duration of the stages is unpredictable, limiting its use as a forecasting tool, and the stylized marketing objectives and strategy prescriptions associated with each stage may be misleading in particular cases.
- Overall, it is a valuable stimulus to strategic thinking, but as a prescriptive tool it is blunt.

3 The concept of product portfolio planning
- This is the process of managing products as groups (portfolios) rather than separate, distinct and independent entities.
- The emphasis is on deciding which products to build, hold, harvest and divest (i.e. resource allocation).

4 The Boston Consulting Group Growth–Share Matrix ('Boston box'), its uses and associated criticisms
- The matrix allows portfolios of products to be depicted in a 2 × 2 box, the axes of which are based on market growth rate (proxy for market attractiveness) and relative market share (proxy for competitive strength).
- Cash flow from a product is assumed to depend on the box in which a product falls.
- Stars are likely to have cash flow balance, problem children cause a drain on cash flow, cash cows generate large positive cash flow, and dogs usually produce low or negative cash flow.
- The matrix provides guidelines for setting strategic objectives (e.g.: stars should be built; problem children should be built selectively, harvested or divested; cash cows should be held; and dogs should be harvested or divested) and emphasizes the need to maintain a balanced product portfolio. The matrix is criticized for: distracting management from focusing on sustainable competitive advantage; treating market growth rate and market share as proxies for market attractiveness and competitive strength; being over-simplistic, as making the assumption that products are self-funding ignores capital markets; the theoretical soundness of some of the underlying concepts (e.g. market definition), which is questionable; cash flow possibly not being the best criterion for allocating resources; and the matrix lacking precision in identifying which problem children to build, harvest or divest.

5 The General Electric Market Attractiveness–Competitive Position Model, its uses and associated criticisms
- The model is based on market attractiveness (e.g. market size, market growth rate, strength of competition) and competitive strength (e.g. market share, potential to develop a differential advantage, cost advantages). By weighting the criteria and scoring products, these can be positioned on a matrix.
- Its advantages over the 'Boston box' are that more criteria than just market growth rate and market share are used to determine the position of products in the matrix, and the model is more flexible.
- Its uses are that the matrix provides guidelines for setting strategic objectives based upon a product's position in the matrix, and that the analysis is much richer than that of the Boston box, because more factors are being taken into account, leading to better resource allocation decisions.
- The criticisms are that it is harder to use than the Boston box, and its flexibility can provide an opportunity for managerial bias.

6 The contribution of portfolio planning
- The models emphasize the important strategic point that different products should have different roles in a product portfolio, and different reward systems and managers should be linked to them.
- The models can be useful as an aid to managerial judgement and strategic thinking, but should not supplant that judgement and thinking.

7 Product strategies for growth
- A useful way of looking at growth opportunities is offered by the Ansoff Matrix, as it is a practical framework for thinking about how growth can be achieved through product strategy.
- It comprises four general approaches to sales growth: market penetration/expansion, product development, market development and diversification.
- Market penetration and expansion are strategies relating to growing existing products in existing markets. Market penetration depends on winning competitors' customers or buying competitors (thereby increasing market share). Defence of increased penetration may be through discouraging competitive entry. Market expansion may be through converting non-users to users or increasing usage rate. Although market share may not increase, sales growth is achieved through increasing market size.

- Product development is a strategy for developing new products for existing markets. It has three variants: 1) extending existing product lines (brand extensions) to give current customers greater choice; 2) product replacement (updates of old products); and 3) innovation (developing fundamentally different products).
- Market development is a strategy for taking existing products and marketing them in new markets. This may be through the promotion of new uses of existing products to new customers, or the marketing of existing products to new market segments (e.g. overseas markets).
- Diversification (entry into new markets) is a strategy for developing new products for new markets. It is the most risky of the four growth strategies, but also potentially the most rewarding.

8 **Ethical issues**

- Ethical issues associated with products fall into three main categories: 1) product safety; 2) planned obsolescence; and 3) deceptive packaging.

Key Terms

disruptive innovations innovations that can disrupt existing market and make changes to the value expectations, thereby creating new markets

entry into new markets (diversification) the entry into new markets by new products

market development to take current products and market them in new markets

market expansion the attempt to increase the size of a market by converting non-users to users of the product and by increasing usage rates

market penetration to continue to grow sales by marketing an existing product in an existing market

portfolio planning managing groups of brands and product lines

product development increasing sales by improving present products or developing new products for current markets

product lifecycle a four-stage cycle in the life of a product illustrated as sales and profit curves, the four stages being introduction, growth, maturity and decline

Study Questions

1. **To what extent can the product lifecycle help to inform marketing management decision-making? Discuss.**
2. **Discuss the extent to which digital technology is disrupting the PLC?**
3. **Identify one of the latest fads, for example vegan products, and then evaluate its market potential.**
4. **Explain why it is important for firms to manage their product portfolio.**
5. **Evaluate the usefulness of the BCG Matrix. Do you believe that it has a role to play in portfolio planning?**
6. **What is the difference between product and market development in the Ansoff Matrix? Give examples of each form of product growth strategy.**
7. **How does the GE Matrix differ from the BCG Matrix? What are the strengths and weaknesses of the GE Matrix?**
8. **Evaluate the contribution of product portfolio planning models to product strategy.**
9. **Suggest how product portfolio planning might be affected by changing forces in the marketing environment.**
10. **Discuss the ethical issues relating to product development and suggest how these issues are changing in response to environmental and technological issues. (Refer to Chapter 2 for more detailed insights into these two areas.)**

Recommended Reading

Extending the reach and life of a brand can involve launching new products. Read about how technology is disrupting the product lifecycle with a big bang; also find out what happens in a hackathon and about the origins of diffusion of innovations.

Downes, L. and Nunes, P. (2013) *Big-Bang Disruption*, Harvard Business Review, March, https://hbr.org/2013/03/big-bang-disruption

Leckart, S. (2012) The Hackathon is on: pitching programming the next killer app, *Wired* 18(12). https://www.wired.com/2012/02/ff_hackathons/all/1/

Rogers, E.M. (1983) *Diffusions of Innovations*, New York: The Free Press.

References

Ansoff, I. (1957) Strategies for Diversification, *Harvard Business Review*, Sept.–Oct., 113–24.

Banga, V.V. and Joshib, S.L. (2010) Market expansion strategy—performance relationship, *Journal of Strategic Marketing* 18(1), 57–75.

Bolfo, B. (2005) The Art of Selling One Product to Two Markets, *Financial Times*, 10 August, 11.

Boston Consulting Group (2001) On-line Retail Market in North America to reach $65 billion in 2001, http://www.beg.com (accessed October 2018).

Braithwaite, P. (2018) As Apple and Google fight for edtech dominance, the industry is still failing kids and teachers, *Wired*, 10 April, https://www.wired.co.uk/article/apple-ipad-pencil-school-education-google-chromebook (accessed October 2018)

Brierley, D. (1997) Spring-Cleaning a Statistical Wonderland, *European*, 20–6 February, 28.

Calandro, J. and Lane, S. (2007) A new competitive analysis tool: the relative profitability and growth matrix, *Strategy & Leadership*, 35(2), 30–8.

Cohan, P. (2018) Snap will keep falling unless Apple of Google buys it, says Wharton Professor, *Forbes*, 14 June. https://www.forbes.com/sites/petercohan/2018/06/14/wharton-prof-snap-will-keep-falling-unless-apple-or-google-buy-it/#5032175e70cd (accessed October 2018)

Costello, M. (2015) Nestlé to shed frozen and chilled goods brand Davigel, *The Times*, 16 April. http://www.thetimes.co.uk/tto/business/industries/consumer/article4412839.ece (accessed October 2018)

Day, G.S. and Wensley, R. (1983) Marketing theory with a strategic orientation, *Journal of Marketing*, Fall, 79–89.

Dhalia, N.K. and Yuspeh, S. (1976) Forget the product life cycle concept, *Harvard Business Review*, Jan–Feb, 102–12.

Doherty, N.F. Ellis Chadwick, F. and Hart, C.A. (1999) Cyber retailing in the UK: the potential of the Internet as a retail channel, *International Journal of Retail & Distribution Management* 27(1), 22–36.

Downes, L. and Nunes, P. (2013) Big-bang disruption, *Harvard Business Review*, March, https://hbr.org/2013/03/big-bang-disruption (accessed October 2018)

Doyle, P. (1989) Building successful brands: the strategic options, *Journal of Marketing Management* 5(1), 77–95.

Edwards, C. (2006) Inside Intel, *Business Week*, 9 January, 43.

Field, M. (2018) Dyson to stop developing corded vacuum cleaners after 25 years. 6 March, https://www.telegraph.co.uk/technology/2018/03/06/dyson-stop-developing-corded-vacuum-cleaners-25-years/ (accessed October 2018)

Fleming, M. (2018) Coca-Cola's Fuze tea launches first UK TV campaign. *Marketing Week*, 5 October, https://www.marketingweek.com/2018/10/05/coca-colas-fuze-tea-first-uk-tv-campaign/ (accessed October 2018)

Gapper, J. (2006) Sony is Scoring Low at its Close Game, *Financial Times*, 6 November, 17.

Handley, L. (2012) Greggs finds ingredient for growth on Facebook, *Marketing Week*, 1 March, 15–18.

Haspslagh, P. (1982) Portfolio planning: uses and limits, *Harvard Business Review*, Jan–Feb, 58–73.

Hedley, B. (1977) Boston Consulting Group approach to the business portfolio, *Long Range Planning*, February, 9–15.

Hofer, C. and D. Schendel, (1978) *Strategy Formulation: Analytical Concepts*, St Paul, MN: West.

Hudson, A. (2010) Whatever happened to the dotcom millionaires? http://news.bbc.co.uk/1/hi/technology/8505260.stm (accessed October 2018).

Leckart, S. (2012) The Hackathon is on: pitching programming the next killer App, *Wired* 18(12). https://www.wired.com/2012/02/ff_hackathons/all/1/ (accessed October 2018)

Lynn, M. (2016) There's already another dotcom bubble–we just haven't noticed, *The Telegraph*, 11 August https://www.telegraph.co.uk/business/2016/08/11/theres-already-another-dotcom-bubble–we-just-havent-noticed/ (accessed October 2018)

Marsh, P. and Bickerton, I. (2005) Stewardship of a Sprawling Empire, *Financial Times*, 18 November, 13.

Mason, T. (2002) Nestlé Sells Big Brands in Core Strategy Focus, *Marketing*, 7 February, 5.

Microsoft (2013) A history of Windows, http://windows.microsoft.com/en-US/windows/history (accessed October 2018)

Milner, M. (2006) £1.2bn Sale of Schweppes' European Drinks Business Agreed, *The Guardian*, 22 November, 26.

Mondelez Foods (n.d.) About Us. http://www.Mondelezfoodscompany.com (accessed October 2018)

Nokian (2018) Innovation. https://www.nokianheavytyres.com/innovation/tailored-special-expertise/ (accessed October 2018)

Nunes, P. and Downes, L. (2015) How Phillips Thrived in Lighting's 'big crunch', *Forbes*, https://www.forbes.com/sites/bigbangdisruption/2015/03/31/how-philips-thrived-in-lightings-big-crunch/#4702ed943818 (accessed October 2018)

Palmer, M. (2006) Cisco Lays Plans to Expand into Home Electronics, *Financial Times*, 16 January, 21.

Pavitt, D. (1997) Retailing and the super highway: the future of the electronic home shopping industry, *International Journal of Retail & Distribution Management*, 25(1), 38–43.

Polli, R. and Cook, V. (1969) Validity of the Product Life Cycle, *Journal of Business*, October, 385–400.

Roberts, L. (2018) Are tech stocks entering dotcom bubble territory again? *EFT Daily News*, 13 March, https://etfdailynews.com/2018/03/13/are-tech-stocks-entering-dotcom-bubble-territory-again-qqq (accessed October 2018)

Rogers, E.M. (1983) *Diffusions of Innovations*, The Free Press. New York.

Rowan, D. (2012) Reid Hoffman: The network philosopher, *Wired*, April. http://www.wired.co.uk/magazine/archive/2012/04/features/reid-hoffman-network-philosopher (accessed 20 April 2015).

Rowley, I. and Tashiro, H. (2005) Can Canon Keep Printing Money? *Business Week*, 5/12 September, 18–20.

Ruddick, G. and Kollewe, J. (2017) Unilever to ditch Flora and Stork as consumers turn to butter, *The Guardian*, 6 April, https://www.theguardian.com/business/2017/apr/06/unilever-flora-stork-kraft-heinz-bid (accessed October 2018)

Sandu, S. (2018) People are hooked on meat–they don't like to think about animals'–farmer who couldn't bear to eat meat created a vegetarian version, News The Essential Daily Briefing, 13 September, https://inews.co.uk/news/long-reads/vegetarian-butcher-fake-meat/ (accessed October 2018)

Shah, R. (2002) Managing a Portfolio to Unlock Real Potential, *Financial Times*, 21 August, 13.

Steen, M. (2008) Reinventing the Philips Brand, *Financial Times*, 27 March, 18.

Swedish Institute (2018) Innovation in Sweden, Sweden.Se, https://sweden.se/business/innovation-in-sweden (accessed 20 November 2018).

Swedish Ministry of Enterprise, Energy and Communications (2018) The Swedish Innovation Strategy, https://sweden.se/business/innovation-in-sweden (accessed: September 2018).

Tetrapak (2015) About Tetrapak, Tetrapak. http://www.tetrapak.com/uk/about-tetra-pak/the-company/history/ourfounder (accessed 20 April 2015).

The Economist (2008) Face Value, 31 May, 86.

The Vegetarian Butcher (2018) Our Story, https://www.thevegetarianbutcher.com/about-us/the-vegetarian-butcher (accessed October 2018)

Tomlinson, H. (2005) Adidas Sells Ski and Surf Group for £329m, *The Guardian*, 3 May, 5.

Unilever plc (2017) Unilever unveils world-first innovation in laundry with Persil Powergems, https://www.unilever.com/news/news-and-features/Feature-article/2017/unilever-unveils-world-first-innovation-in-laundry-with-persil-powergems.html (accessed October 2018)

Vakratsas, D. and Ambler, T. (1999) How advertising works: what do we really know? *Journal of Marketing* 63, January, 26–43.

Virzi, A.M. (2000) Billionaire builds wealth at Internet speed, *Forbes*, http://www.forbes.com/2000/06/30/feat.html (accessed October 2018).

Wensley, R. (1981) Strategic marketing: betas, boxes and basics, *Journal of Marketing*, Summer, 173–83.

Wikipedia (n.d.) Dot-com bubble. http://en.wikipedia.org/wiki/Dot-com_bubble (accessed October 2018)

CASE 39
Growth Strategies at Unilever

In February 2000, when Niall FitzGerald, chairman of Unilever, rose in front of his shareholders to reveal his plans for the most comprehensive restructuring and strategy review to hit the company in over a hundred years, there was a sharp intake of breath. His four-year 'Path to growth' strategy was to see 1,200 of its 1,600 consumer brands axed to concentrate marketing muscle behind 400 high-growth brands. All brands that were not among the top two sellers in their market segment would be dropped either immediately or over a period of time.

Buyers would be sought for those that were to be divested immediately; the rest would be harvested (milked) and the cash generated ploughed into support for the 400 big brands. This would mean £450 million (€510 million) of extra marketing expenditure put behind such global brands as Magnum ice cream, Dove soap, Knorr soup and Lipton's tea. Local successes such as Persil washing powder and Colman's mustard in the UK would also be supported heavily.
The promise was to increase profit margins from 11 to 16 per cent and to achieve target annual growth rates of between 4.5 and 5 per cent from Unilever's 400 top brands. Brands scheduled to be harvested or divested included Timotei shampoo, Brut deodorant, Radion washing powder, Harmony hairspray, Pear's soap and Jif lemon.

The analysis that Unilever had done revealed that only a quarter of Unilever's brands provided 90 per cent of its turnover and that disposing of the other three-quarters would lead to a more efficient supply chain and reduced costs of £1 billion (€1.13 billion) over three years. As FitzGerald explained, 'We were doing too many things. We had too many brands in too many places. Many were just not big enough to move the needle so we had to focus and simplify. That simplification would allow us to take cost out of the business.'

Not everyone was convinced. There were £3.5 billion (€4 billion) of restructuring costs (bigger than most companies' market capitalizations) and the prospect of 25,000 jobs going. The exercise would require a highly effective internal communications programme to obtain buy-in from Unilever staff.

By the end of 2002, FitzGerald could claim considerable achievements. Cost savings of over £450 million (€510 million) had already been banked and margins had moved from 11 to 15 per cent.
The top 400 leading brands accounted for 88 per cent of sales and achieved an average growth rate of 4.5 per cent. Three businesses had also been bought. Bestfoods, the US foods giant, brought the Hellmann's mayonnaise, Knorr soups and Skippy peanut butter brands into the Unilever portfolio; the acquisition of Ben & Jerry's gave the company one of two major brands in the premium ice cream sector, and Slimfast provided major penetration of the diet food market.

Unilever was also busy dropping or selling off Elizabeth Arden, Batchelor's soups, Oxo, Knight's Castille soap, Frish toilet cleaner and Stergene handwashing liquid. Some of Unilever's unwanted brands were bought by small companies. For example, Buck UK bought Unilever's Sqezy—the washing-up liquid formerly marketed as 'easy, peasy, lemon Sqezy'.
Also, Unilever sold its Harmony hairspray and Stergene fabric conditioner brands to Lornamead. Others such as Oxo and Batchelors were sold to larger companies—in this case Campbell Grocery Products.

A number of brand extensions were also planned in 2002, most notably in the Bertolli olive oil, Dove soap, Knorr soup, Lynx (Axe) male grooming and Slimfast diet food brands. The Lynx (Axe) men's deodorant was launched in the USA, and three new flavours of Hellmann's mayonnaise and an Asian side-dishes range were introduced.

The result of all this activity was that Unilever posted a 16 per cent increase in 2002 profits—that is,

>>

£1.5 billion compared with £1.3 billion (€1.7 billion compared with €1.5 billion) in 2001. Sales of its top 400 brands grew by 5.4 per cent, above the company's target of 4.5 and 5 per cent. The company invested £5.1 billion (€5.8 billion) in advertising and promotion, up 8.5 per cent on the 2001 level.

During 2003, Unilever earmarked an additional 20 per cent of marketing investment in its global ice cream portfolio over the next three years. The ice cream group has a remarkable global brand portfolio. For example, in the UK, Unilever owns Walls, in France it bought Miko, in Portugal it owns Ola, and in Sweden it owns GB Glace. Over Europe as a whole, Unilever owns and operates more than 12 different ice cream brands, each with its own strong heritage and relationships with customers. Unilever has retained the names of its national brands while replacing original brand symbols with a single heart-shaped logo.

Unfortunately, the successes of the early years were followed by two years of performance below expectations, leading to the departure of FitzGerald in May 2004. Poor sales and profit performance was blamed on poor organizational structure, lack of innovation and poor advertising. Poor structure stemmed from Unilever's Anglo-Dutch heritage, which resulted in joint chairmen—one for the Dutch arm and one for the UK—and no chief executive. The company was run by two boards and separate headquarters in London and Rotterdam. Consequently, decision-making was cumbersome and slow with the ever-present threat of conflict between the two groups compounding the problems. The group was also divided into divisions: health and personal products, food, and frozen foods. These were regarded as fiefdoms under which different management teams managed their products separately in each country.

Following FitzGerald's departure, Unilever carried out a strategic review under its joint chairmen, Patrick Cescau in the UK and Antony Burgmans in the Netherlands. Cescau, the driving force behind the review, became Unilever's chief executive, with Burgmans becoming non-executive chairman. The board was unified and headquarters were centralized in London. These changes gave Cescau the autonomy to push through the reform needed to get Unilever back on track. Under the slogan 'One Unilever' he dismantled the fiefdoms which were merged to form one executive team covering all divisions and nationalities, resulting in the loss of almost a fifth of senior management. A cull of about 30,000 jobs took place, and some loss-making factories were closed to cut costs.

Cescau also changed focus from 'Path to growth's fixation on profit margins to boosting market share. This meant price reductions and the introduction of cheaper product ranges to complement the premium priced brands. The Magnum ice cream brand was complemented in this way, for example.

Cescau also sold Unilever's cosmetics and fragrances arm Unilever Cosmetics International to Coty International for £438 million (€494 million) in a move that allowed Unilever to focus on its core categories of food, cleaning and personal care brands, such as Ben & Jerry's ice cream, Knorr soups, Flora margarine, Cif cleaning products, Persil detergents, Dove personal care products, Sunsilk shampoos and Lynx (Axe) men's deodorants. This was quickly followed by the sale of its frozen-food division (Birds Eye) to Permira, a venture capitalist, for £1.2 billion (€1.4 billion). At the time of the sale, Birds Eye was the number one food brand in the UK with a turnover of £500 million (€565 million) a year and profits of around £50 million (€57 million). It was also the UK's second-biggest supermarket brand after Walker's crisps. Unilever also sold its North American detergents business in 2008 to a private equity firm.

A greater emphasis was placed on emerging markets such as China, India, Brazil, Russia, Africa, and central and eastern Europe. Advertising budgets in western Europe were tightened to fund extra investment in these growth markets. In line with this strategy, Inmarko, Russia's largest ice cream brand, was acquired in 2008. By 2009, emerging markets accounted for around 50 per cent of Unilever's sales revenue.

Another change in strategy was to adopt a more standardized approach to global marketing. The company moved from autonomous localized initiatives to the roll-out of innovation and marketing programmes on a global basis. Power was taken away from country managers and given to global marketing teams to oversee the development and marketing of new products. Brand marketing was split into two divisions: the brand development team and brand building. The brand development team devise a global strategy for each brand including innovation. A package of recommendations is then created, usually in conjunction with two key countries. This is then sent to brand building teams in each country and they 'make it happen' within local markets.

Cescau also invested in 'healthy living' brands to capitalize on the trend towards health and well-being. For example, a number of 'healthy' sauces and soups under the Knorr brand were launched with no artificial flavours or colourings, reflecting Unilever's 'vitality' positioning.

In 2008, Cescau stepped down as chief executive after achieving what most commentators regard as a fairly successful period at the helm, transforming the company from a lumbering, regionally driven bureaucracy into a more streamlined, globally managed business. However, Unilever's performance did not match that of Reckitt Benckiser, maker of Cillit Bang cleaner, whose strategy was to launch brands such as stain removers targeting niche markets that avoided direct head-to-head competition with Procter & Gamble and Unilever.

Cescau's successor was Paul Polman, a former Procter & Gamble and Nestlé man, breaking with an 80-year-old tradition of appointing insiders. Faced with a recession, Polman embarked on a cost-cutting programme, including a freeze on management salaries and travel budget cuts of 30 per cent (replacing travel with teleconferencing), designed to achieve £45 million (€50 million) savings. A job-cutting and factory closure programme that began in 2007 was accelerated, and a global procurement officer was recruited to seek savings by using the company's vast scale to obtain better prices. Acquisitions were also made, including the purchase of Toni & Guy and Alberto Culver (both haircare), and Sara Lee's personal care business. The Russian personal care group Kalina was also bought in 2011. By 2012, emerging markets accounted for over half of Unilever's sales revenue. The impact of Unilever's brand portfolio strategy is reflected in the fact that 75 per cent of sales are now made from its top 25 brands.

Polman has continued his quest for cost efficiencies and constantly reviews his product portfolio. For example, in 2014 he sold the troubled Slimfast brand, which was hit by the Atkins diet craze in the USA. Unilever also sold its Peperami, Ragu and Bifi brands as it focuses on its health and beauty businesses. In 2017 the company's margarine brands, Flora, Becel and I Can't Believe It's Not Butter, were sold as consumers turned away from margarine spreads.

Polman's third focus is on product 'premiumization'. By developing premium brands, such as Regenerate toothpaste, priced at £10 (€11) and Maille mustard with wine and truffles, costing £29 (€33), together with a constant drive towards lower costs, Unilever has improved profits margins from 12.8 per cent in 2010 to 16.5 per cent in 2017.

In 2017, Polman successfully repelled a hostile takeover by the US food group Kraft Heinz. Following this, he undertook a review of Unilever's structures, which resulted in a move from its traditional dual headquarters to a single headquarters. Unilever is in the process of relocating their headquarters, but the final decision on location had not been made at the time of going to press. The business was also restructured into three divisions with more autonomy and financial responsibilities. Two—beauty and personal care, and home care—have headquarters in London, while the third—food and refreshments—is based in Rotterdam.

Questions

1. **What were the advantages to Unilever of reducing the size of its brand portfolio? What were the risks?**
2. **To what extent does it appear that Unilever followed (i) the BCG Growth–Share Matrix, and (ii) the General Electric Market Attractiveness–Competitive Position Model approaches to portfolio planning during the FitzGerald era?**
3. **What are the attractions to small companies of buying marginal Unilever brands? What are the dangers of doing so?**
4. **Comment on Unilever's approach to the global marketing of its brands.**
5. **Why did the sale of Birds Eye and Unilever's North American detergent business make strategic sense for Unilever?**

This case study was prepared by David Jobber, Emeritus Professor of Marketing, University of Bradford.

References

Based on: Farrell, S. (2014) Unilever to Revamp Products to Lure Back cash-Strapped Customers, theguardian.com/business, 23 October; Jack, L. (2009) The Soaps, the Glory and the Universal Truths in Marketing, *Marketing Week*, 23 April, 20–4; Kilby, N. (2005) Coty Scents Growth Potential in Unilever Cosmetics, *Marketing Week*, 26 May, 11; Kilby, N. (2006) Permira Aims to Make Birds Eye Cooler than Chilled, *Marketing Week*, 7 September, 10; Kollewe, J. (2014) Unilever Puts Slimfast and US Pasta Sauce Range up for Sale, the guardian.com/business, 24 April; Lucas, L. (2011) Unilever 'On Front Foot' but Full-Year Margins Disappoint, *Financial Times*, 4 November, 22; Mortished, C. (2009) Unilever Chief Paul Polman Ditches Pay Rises and Targets, *The Times*, 6 February, 18; Pratley, N. (2015) Unilever's Weak Results Show It's a Low Growth, Low Inflation World, theguardian.com/business, 21 January; Ritson, M. (2003) Unilever Goes with its 'Heart' to Make Global Brand of Local Ices, *Marketing*, 1 May, 18; Ritson, M. (2012) Bereft of Stars, Premier's Plan Will Flop, *Marketing Week*, 26 January, 58; Vizard, S. (2014) Unilever Eyes More 'Agile' Marketing for Spreads Brands as Bisiness Splits into Standalone Unit, theguardian.com/business, 4 December; Wiggins, J. (2008) Unilever Hangs on to European Laundry List, *Financial Times*, 29 July, 18; Wiggins, J. (2008) Unilever Buys Russia's Inmarko Ice Cream, *Financial Times*, 5 February, 21; Wiggins, J. (2009) Unilever Looks to the Silver Lining, *Financial Times*, 6 February, 19; Treanor, J. (2017) Unilever Sells Household Name Spreads to KKR for £6bn, www.theguardian.com/business, 15 December; Pratley, N. (2018) Unilever's Shy Rabbits, *The Guardian*, 2 February, 37; Kollewe, J. (2018) Unilever Says Brexit Not a Factor in Opting for Rotterdam HQ, *The Guardian*, 16 March, 31.

CASE 40

Fever-Tree: Capitalizing on Market Trends

Capitalizing on market trends is not easy, especially when you are going head to head with one of the world's biggest brands, Coca-Cola (Schweppes), plus supermarket own-brand labels, which account for a significant share of the soft drinks market. But Charles Rolls and his business partner, Tim Warrillow, are entrepreneurs who were not daunted by the challenge. Rolls built his reputation and business skills in the Plymouth gin industry. Warrillow had ambitions to start his own gin distillery. At the time, the craze for craft gin was in its infancy, but Rolls was looking at a different market: he saw an opportunity to develop a mixer to complement the slowly growing number of speciality gins.

Tonic generally makes up three-quarters of a gin and tonic. Rolls had discovered that many tonics were filled with artificial sweeteners and cheap aromatics, and felt there was something special to be done by creating a new tonic that was differentiated from the market-leading giants. Rolls persuaded Warrillow to join him in his quest to produce the finest-quality mixers on the planet to complement the newly created craft gins. Their 18-month journey involved extensive travel (the Democratic Republic of Congo, India, Sicily and Spain), being held at gunpoint, and much tasting to source the finest ingredients. But the journey resulted in the formation of the company Fever-Tree, named after the colloquial term for the Congolese cinchona tree, which produces quinine, the main ingredient in tonic water.

Competing against giants may be frightening, but Rolls and Warrillow knew they had developed something so special that it could take on the big brands and win. Since the outset, Fever-Tree has maintained its decision to use only the highest quality ingredients in its products and uses this as a clear differentiator from the competition and a key driver of the brand's authenticity and credibility.

Insurgent Brand

Fever-Tree is a plucky insurgent brand with bags of character. It is a small, fast-growing brand that is out-manoeuvring the big brand leaders. Research highlighted that smaller brands tend to be more agile, operating with simpler structures, which allows faster response to emerging trends. Often, small brands use social media at launch, although many later move

into traditional media to get reach. Fever-Tree followed this route, and its move into sponsoring the Queen's Club tennis tournament represents a move into more tradition marketing communication methods.

But even though smaller brands are flexible and dynamic, they must also have clear goals. From the outset, Fever-Tree knew the direction it wanted to take, and Rolls and Warrillow set about defining their business with a clear mission statement. Charles Rolls stated, 'Our mission—to combine the highest quality naturally sourced ingredients with expert manufacturing techniques to produce an unrivalled drinks experience'. His fellow co-founder, Tim Warrillow, added the vision, 'Our vision—to be the world's leading supplier of premium carbonated mixers'.
These statements give the company direction, focus and structure for a future strategy of growth. It is possibly this sense of purpose, clarity and passion that enabled this insurgent brand to become market leader in the UK by 2017, just 13 years after its inception.

Fever-Tree Brand Growth Timeline

2003: Charles Rolls and Tim Warrillow have an idea, experiment and create a new brand made from natural ingredients.

2005: Fever-Tree launches following 18 months of testing and travelling the world to source the best quinine, a vital ingredient for creating a high-quality tonic water. The bark from the cinchona tree—the 'Fever-Tree'—which is used in the production of quinine was found in the Democratic Republic of Congo. Very soon after this discovery, production began, and it was only a few short weeks before the supermarket Waitrose began selling Fever-Tree tonic.

2007: Fever-Tree launches in the USA and Spain, two of the largest gin-drinking markets in the world.

2010: Direct-to-consumer marketing campaign and adverts in selected specialist magazines, *The Week, The Spectator and Private Eye*, help Fever-Tree double its turnover to £8 million and see its profits continue to soar up 90 per cent.

2013: Fever-Tree's marketing efforts see it appearing in more locations, from agricultural fairs to cocktail festivals, and the company increases its following on social media networks.

2014: Highly successful initial public offering on the London Stock Exchange.

2017: As the market for special craft gins continues to grow rapidly, Fever-Tree is able to capitalize on the increased demand for premium tonic and overtake Schweppes—the established market leader in the UK—to become the biggest-selling mixer brand.

2018: Fever-Tree replaces Aegon as the Queen's Tennis Club sponsor, boosting is profile and reinforcing its market positioning in the minds of some of its core target customers. Tim Warrillow has his eye on other key sports sponsorships, but to become lead sponsor for the prestigious tennis tournament is a defining moment for the brand.

Fever-Tree Mixers
@FeverTreeMixers

@imbibeuk Live stand starting to take shape! See you all tomorrow for a G&T!

First Mover to the Future

As the first mover in the premium mixer market and new market leader, Fever-Tree faces the challenge of maintaining that position. Fever-Tree's growth has been built on tonic water and coincided perfectly with the gin revival in western Europe, particularly in the UK, Spain, Belgium and the Netherlands. This success has allowed it to create a portfolio of 12 varieties that are available in 60 countries. These varieties include: Sicilian lemonade, elderflower tonic, ginger ale and Madagascan vanilla cola. Since Fever-Tree's launch, Tim Warrillow estimates that rivals have created 85 'me-too' brands, but they claim only a combined 3 per cent market share. New entrants like 1724 (named because quinine was discovered at 1724 metres above sea level on the Inca Trail) and Schweppes 1783, a premium tonic launched to take on Fever-Tree, have not halted Fever-Tree's growth. As Tim says, 'By their own admission, they've thrown the kitchen sink at it, but recent statistics show clearly who consumers are supporting.'

Drinkers, however, can be fickle and tend to quickly latch on to new trends. But this is not a threat to Fever-Tree. In 2017, sales rose by 39 per cent in the USA, and ginger beer is a new best-seller as a mixer with Moscow Mule, a vodka and lime creation. Created in 1941, this cocktail is reportedly taking the planet by storm—a great new opportunity for Fever-Tree to develop a market with Vodka drinkers.

And to the future. Fever-Tree is a successful exporter, as 75 per cent of its business comes from outside the UK, and trade in the home market is ahead of market expectations. Sales rose by 66 per cent to £170 million after an increase of 58 per cent. These levels of performance are funding the company's growth ambitions. Fever-Tree has entered into a strategic partnership with Patron to create the first tonic specifically designed to be mixed with tequila.

Again, the principles of the founding directors guided the development of Fever-Tree citrus tonic water.

Members of the product development team travelled to Mexico—home to tequila, the fiery spirit made from the blue agave plant, grown in the hills surrounding the city of the same name—to source ingredients that would enable the production of a tonic suitable to complement Patron tequila and balance the spirit's sweet, peppery taste.

This is not the only innovation the company has in development. Currently, Warrillow has his eye on developing drinks for new market sectors and on greater expansion in international markets, especially in North America. Tim Warrillow is quoted as saying, 'There remains a significant opportunity in front of us, across all our regions, as Fever-Tree continues to drive the evolution of the mixer category.'

This multiple-award-winning brand has been voted the best-selling and top trending tonic, confirming the brand's position as the world's leading premium mixer brand.

Questions

1. **Discuss Fever-Tree, using the product lifecycle (PLC) model. Suggest the extent to which this brand is following the classic S curve.**
2. **The market for craft gin may yet prove to be a fad. How is Fever-Tree planning to protect the brand and develop markets in the future?**
3. **Do some desk research to identify all of Fever-Tree's products and then classify each of the products according to the Boston box matrix.**
4. **Suggest two different options for product growth strategies for Fever-Tree.**
5. **Explain what is meant by an insurgent brand and suggest how Fever-Tree can maintain the qualities of an insurgent brand now that it is market leader in the UK.**

This case study was written by Brian Searle, Programme Director MSc Marketing, Loughborough University.

References

Based on: Brownsell, A. (2018) Fever-tree replaces Aegon as Queen's club Tennis title sponsor, *Campaign*, 20 March, https://www.campaignlive.co.uk/article/fever-tree-replaces-aegon-queens-club-tennis-title-sponsor/1459837; Brandgym (2018) Drinks International's 2018 Annual Brand Report; Fever-Tree (2018) How it all began, https://fever-tree.com/en_GB/our-approach; Rear, J. (2018) Fever-Tree is smashing the tonic water markets: here's why, Verdict, 13 March, https://www.verdict.co.uk/fevertree-shares-smashing-tonic-water-market-heres/; Davies, R. (2018) Fever-Tree's value fizzes to £4.5bn on back of strong gin sales, *The Guardian*, 24 July; Taylor, D. (2018) Are big brands really doomed? How big brands can adapt to the threat from small insurgents, *WARC* Best Practice, October; Hall, E. (2015) You give me Fever-Tree: Upstart British mixer becomes a global brand, *AdAge*, December; Walsh, D. (2018) Fevertree fizzes past Schweppes, *The Times*, 16 July

CHAPTER 21
Global Marketing Strategy

I want to be a good Frenchman in France and a good Italian in Italy. My strategy is to go global when I can and stay local when I must.

ERIC JOHANNSON, FORMER PRESIDENT OF ELECTROLUX

LEARNING OBJECTIVES

After reading this chapter, you should be able to:

1 explain why companies seek foreign markets
2 discuss the factors that influence which foreign market to enter
3 identify and discuss the range of foreign market entry strategies
4 identify the factors influencing foreign market entry strategies
5 discuss the influences on the degree of standardization or adaptation
6 discuss the special considerations involved in designing a marketing mix for foreign markets
7 explain how to organize for global marketing operations

From a marketing perspective, the world is becoming more accessible; as a result, global brands like Apple, Nike, Coca-Cola, Google and Samsung are widely recognized. But not all brands have such reach, and trading overseas raises many challenges for companies wishing to export their goods. While new technologies are making it easier to communicate with a global audience, many internal and external factors need to be considered if new market entry is to be successful. Consequently, managers need the *right* marketing skills to be able to compete in this increasingly global marketplace. Companies require the capabilities to identify and seize opportunities that arise across the world. Failure to do so could bring stagnation and decline, not only to individual companies but also to whole regions.

Global expansion and exports are important to all nations and all sectors, but the contribution to the economy varies by sector: for example, in China exporting electrical goods and apparel is important, whereas in the European Union (EU) key sectors are machinery and motor vehicles and, in the UK, manufactured goods, fuels and chemicals (CIA, 2015).

The importance of international trade is reflected in the support given by governmental bodies set up to encourage and aid export activities. For example, the UK Department for International Trade (DIT) is a government body that works with UK-based businesses to help them succeed in overseas markets. Whether businesses are trying to establish a new business or exporting to a new country, DIT offers various services, including: expert advice on international trade and export; taking part in trade fairs and outward trade missions; providing market intelligence; identifying international business opportunities; helping to develop international business relationships; and trading with integrity (DIT, 2018).

This chapter explores the challenges of global marketing. It is organized around the key issues associated with developing global marketing strategies: 1) whether to go global or stay domestic; 2) the factors that have an impact on the selection of countries in which to market; 3) foreign market-entry strategies; and 4) the options available for companies developing global marketing strategies. It also builds on earlier chapters and considers how the principles of marketing might be applied in a global marketplace.

Deciding Whether to Go Global or Stay Local

Some companies do not look to compete internationally. They know their domestic markets well, and if they chose to go global they would have to come to terms with the customs, language, tariff regulations and transport systems of other countries and with trading in foreign currencies. Furthermore, their products might require significant modifications to meet foreign regulations and different customer preferences. So, why do companies choose to market abroad? There are seven triggers for global expansion (see Figure 21.1).

Saturated domestic markets

The pressure to raise sales and profits, coupled with few opportunities to expand in current domestic markets, provides one condition for international expansion. This was a major driving force behind Tesco's expansion into Europe and Asia. In 1997, less than 2 per cent of the group's profits were generated by international trade; by 2014, the figure had risen to over 30 per cent (Tesco plc, 2014). Made.com, the online retailer seeking to disrupt the furniture industry, attributes part of its growing success to market expansion into France, Netherlands, Germany and Belgium (Cassidy, 2017). Many of the foreign expansion plans of European supermarket chains are fuelled by the desire to take a proven retailing formula out of their saturated domestic market into new overseas markets. Currently, many retailers, including Carrefour, Walmart and Tesco, are focusing on emerging markets in India and Asia and looking at expansion opportunities with existing formats or new offerings.

FIGURE 21.1
Triggers for expansion to global markets

Small domestic markets

In some industries, survival means broadening scope beyond small national markets to the international arena. For example, Philips and Electrolux (electrical goods) could not compete against the strength of global competitors by servicing their small domestic market alone. For them, internationalization was not an option; it was a fundamental condition for survival.

Low-growth domestic markets

Often recession at home provides the spur to seek new marketing opportunities in more buoyant overseas economies. Luxury car manufacturers Mercedes, Audi and BMW exploited the demand for luxury cars in China while home markets in Europe were experiencing slow growth. BMW has enjoyed high sales growth in China, as sales rose by 76 per cent compared with 13 per cent in Europe, although, more recently, this rate has begun to slow due to challenges in the supply chain and uncertainty over changes to import tariffs (Bryant, 2015; Sachgau, 2018). VW has reported very strong growth and profit increases in China. The car manufacturer delivered over 3.1 million cars into the Chinese market in 2017—through its own brand and two joint ventures—which is approaching 12.8 per cent of the total number of cars sold in 2017. Indeed, growth in Chinese markets continues to drive VW's aspirations to become the world's largest car manufacturer, with market opportunities in the SUV and electric car segments (Attwood, 2018).

Customer drivers

Customer-driven factors may also affect the decision to go global. In some industries, customers may expect their suppliers to have an international presence. This is increasingly common in advertising, with clients requiring their agencies to coordinate worldwide campaigns. A second customer-orientated factor is the need to internationalize operations in response to customers expanding abroad.

Competitive forces

There is a substantial body of research which suggests that when several companies in an industry trade internationally, others feel obliged to follow suit to maintain their relative size and growth rate (see Aharoni, 1966; Knickerbocker, 1973; Agarwal and Ramaswami, 1992). This is particularly true in oligopolistic industries, which are dominated by a small number of large brands. We can see evidence of this from the earlier example of luxury car manufacturers entering China, for example Audi, Mercedes and BMW. A second competitive factor may be the desire to attack, in their own home market, an overseas competitor that has entered their domestic market. This may make strategic sense if the competitor is funding its overseas expansion from a relatively attractive home base. Chinese car manufacturer Geely invested in Volvo cars and trucks, enabling the Swedish brand to become a significant global brand. Geely invests in technology and innovation, which is key to its growth strategy, and benefits in its home markets from tax incentives, especially in the new-energy vehicle sector. It also owns part of Proton, the Malaysian car business and London (black cab) taxi business (Tovey, 2017)

Cost factors

High national labour costs, shortages of skilled workers, and rising energy charges can raise domestic costs to uneconomical levels. These factors may stimulate moves towards foreign direct investment in lower-cost areas such as China, Taiwan, South Korea, and central and eastern Europe. Expanding into foreign markets can also reduce costs by gaining economies of scale through an enlarged customer base.

Portfolio balance

Marketing in a variety of regions provides the opportunity to achieve portfolio balance, as each region may be experiencing different growth rates. At any one time, China, USA, Japan and individual European and Far Eastern countries will be enjoying varying growth rates. By marketing in a selection of countries, the problems of recession in some countries can be balanced by the opportunities for growth in others.

Deciding Which Markets to Enter

Having made the commitment to enter international territories, marketing managers require the analytical skills necessary to pick those countries and regions that are most attractive for overseas operations. There are various factors that govern this decision to enter a foreign market. These are shown in Figure 21.2.

FIGURE 21.2
Selecting foreign markets

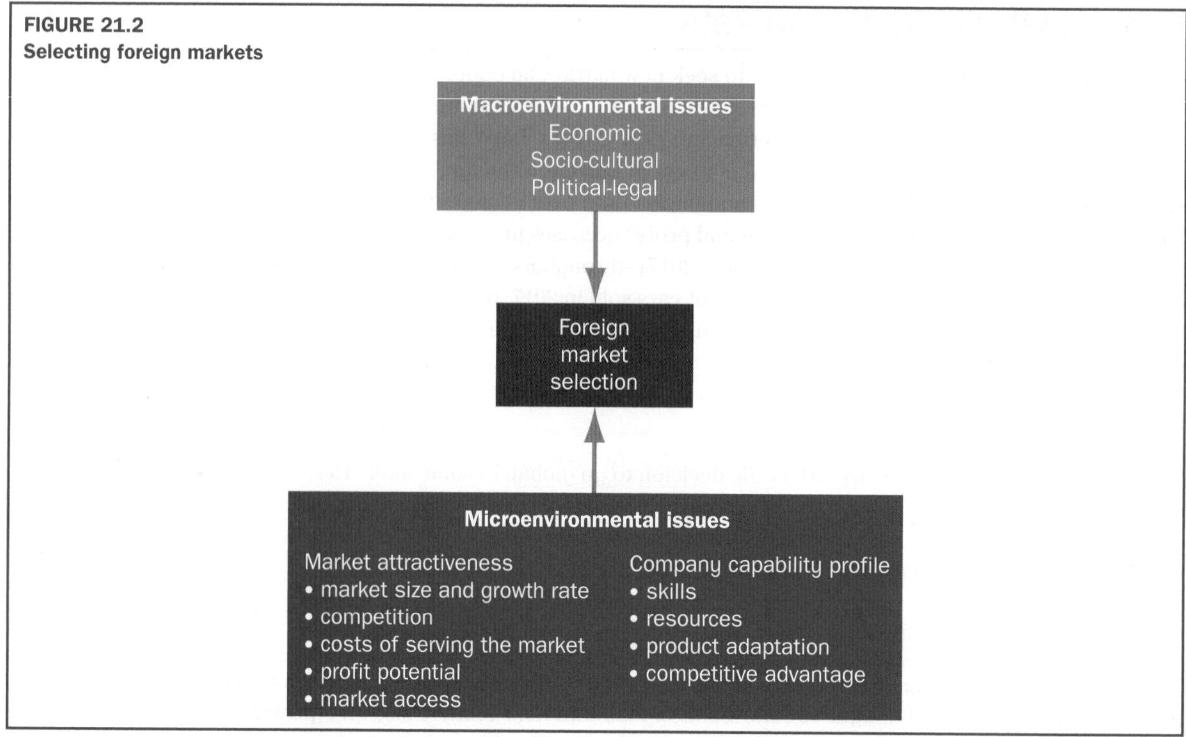

Macroenvironmental issues

These consist of *economic, socio-cultural* and *political-legal technological influences* on market choice.

Economic influences

A country's size, per capita income, stage of economic development, infrastructure, and exchange rate stability and conversion affect its attractiveness for international business expansion. Small markets may not justify setting up a distribution and marketing system to supply goods and services. Low per capita income will affect the type of product that may sell in that country. The market may be very unattractive for car manufacturers, but feasible for bicycle producers. Less developed countries in the early stages of economic development may demand inexpensive agricultural tools but not computers. Research into the decision to enter a new foreign market found that the extent to which a country had a developed economy was an important influencing factor (Whitelock and Jobber, 2004). Research also found intensity of competition, controls on quality, and international competitiveness to be important (Isa, Saman and Rashidah, 2014).

The economic changes that have taken place globally have had varying effects on each country's attractiveness. For example, China has become the world's second-largest economy; it has shifted from being a centrally planned to a market-based economy, and this has aided both economic and social development. Direct foreign investment is on the increase, as cumbersome administrative procedures have been relaxed and financial controls liberalized.

Another economic consideration is a nation's infrastructure. This comprises the transportation structures (roads, railways, airports), information technology and communication systems (broadband, mobile, telephone, television, the press, radio) and energy supplies (electricity, gas, nuclear). A poor infrastructure may limit the ability to manufacture, advertise and distribute goods and to provide adequate service back-up. Some central and eastern European countries suffer because of this. In other areas of Europe, infrastructure improvements are enhancing movement of goods—for example, the Eurotunnel linking the UK with mainland Europe, and the Øresund Bridge and Drogden Tunnel that connect Sweden and Denmark.

Finally, exchange rate stability and conversion may affect market choice. A country that has an unstable exchange rate or one where it is difficult to convert to hard currencies such as the dollar or euro may be considered too risky to enter. Equally important are exchange rates, as countries can find that their goods become too expensive in export markets if their currency rates are high. See Marketing in Action 21.1.

Socio-cultural influences

Differences in socio-cultural factors between countries are often termed *psychic distance*. These are the barriers created by cultural disparities between the home country and the host country, and the problems of communication resulting from differences in social perspectives, attitudes and language (Litvak and Banting, 1968). This psychic distance can have an important effect on selection. International marketers sometimes choose countries that are psychically similar to begin their overseas operations. This has a rationale in that barriers of language, customs and values are lower. It also means that less time and effort is required to develop successful business relationships (Conway and Swiff, 2000). Research looking at Swedish manufacturing companies showed that they often begin by entering new markets that are psychically close—that is, both culturally and geographically—and gain experience in these countries before expanding operations abroad into more distant markets (Johanson and Vahlne, 1977). This has also been found to be the case for service companies that move from culturally similar foreign markets into less familiar markets as their experience grows (Erramilli, 1991).

Language, in particular, has caused many well-documented problems for marketing communications in foreign markets. Classic communication faux pas resulting from translation errors in brand names include the following. General Motors called a car Nova, which means 'doesn't go' in Spanish; Mitsubishi had to change the name Pajero in Spanish-speaking countries, because it is a slang word meaning masturbator; Toyota's MR2 is pronounced 'merde' in French, which translates to excrement; Nissan's Moco means mucus in Spanish.

In addition, history, religion and culture have also been found to influence the attractiveness of a global market and competitive positioning (Prasad, 2011). Greater knowledge of the history of a country and the resulting culture and economic performance can assist marketing managers in developing a better understanding of the social fabric of a new market. For example, Indian supermarkets do not display as many varieties of

MARKETING IN ACTION 21.1
Brexit and the Pound

In June 2016, after the UK Brexit referendum, which resulted in a vote signalling that the country should leave the EU, sterling (the UK pound) fell in value against the euro and 15 other currencies used in the world's biggest economies. Volatility in the currency markets continued as political announcements reflected uncertainty about the UK government's plans for the final terms of the Brexit deal, to be concluded by 29 March 2019. But currency fluctuations tend not to be uniform, and sterling did not fall everywhere during the Bexit negotiations: in Turkey and Egypt, where political unrest has had a destabilising effect, the pound rose 8 per cent in 2018.

However, the UK economy performed better than expected in this turbulent period: for example, in the tourism sector, the weak pound turned the UK into a visitor attraction, with international bargain hunters from Europe, the USA and China spending over £2.8 billion on visiting the UK in peak summer months. Hotels, historical sights and designer brands all benefited from this boom.

So, marketers seeking to invest in the international market must take note of the potential impact of currency fluctuations and factor this into their planning.

Based on: Butler (2017); Gottilieb and Connington (2017)

individual products such as bread as western supermarkets do. Careful analysis of the history of a nation and its cultural heritage can offer an insight into its business behaviour. See Marketing in Action 21.2.

MARKETING IN ACTION 21.2
Cultural Differences and Leadership Styles in the Global Marketplace

As more companies operate on a global scale, there is a greater need for cross-cultural understanding. Leadership styles need to recognize that leading a global team requires the ability to operate with eastern and western cultures to achieve the best outcomes, as successful leadership in developed economies is very different from the approaches used in emerging economies. According to research, US and Chinese approaches often appear incompatible: for example, Americans tend to view Chinese negotiators as inefficient and indirect, while the Chinese see American negotiators as aggressive and impersonal. Therefore, it is important to develop ways that enable both sides to move forwards. So, when negotiations take place between US and Chinese companies, they should seek to find ways to cooperate—for example, build relationships, shape attitudes towards each other that foster win–win situations, strike a balance of emotions and set mutually acceptable timeframes.

Research also examined business culture and management styles in Europe using two dimensions: type of leadership and organization. Figure 21.3 shows the position of each of the 13 nations according to these

FIGURE 21.3
Positions of European countries by type of leadership and organization

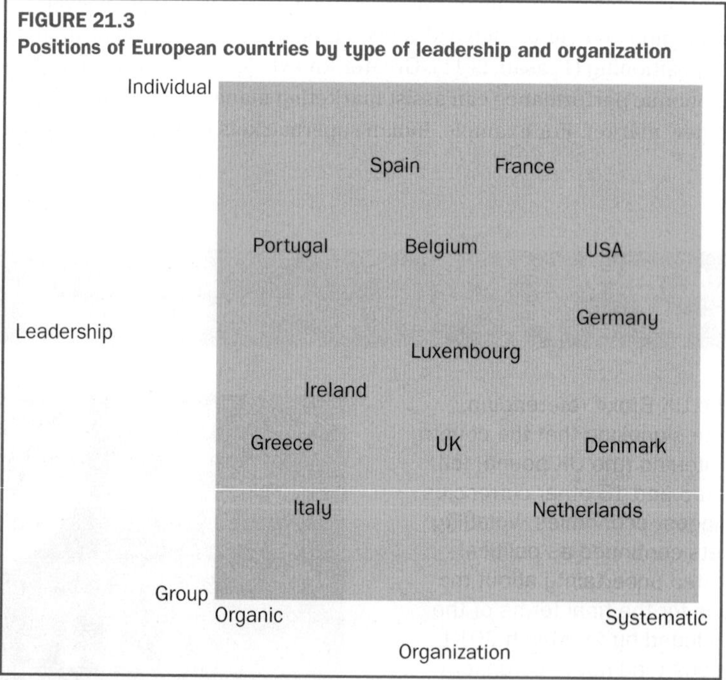

two characteristics. Individual leadership (autocratic, directive) is found in Spain and France, whereas an organic leadership style (democratic, equalitarian) tends to be found in Italy and the Netherlands. Systematic organization (formal, mechanistic) is found in Germany, Denmark and the Netherlands, while organic companies (informal, social) are more likely to exist in Spain, Italy, Portugal and Greece.

Studies have also shown that business life in Italy, Spain and the Netherlands is very different. Italian organizations tend to be informal, with democratic leadership. Decisions are taken informally, usually after considerable personal contact and discussion. Italian managers are flexible improvisers who have a temperamental aversion to forecasting and planning. Interpersonal contact with deciders and influencers in the decision-making unit (DMU) is crucial for suppliers. Finding the correct person to talk to is not easy, since DMUs tend to be complex, with authority vested in trusted individuals outside the apparent organizational structure. Suppliers must demonstrate commitment to a common purpose with their Italian customers.

In Spain, business is typified by the family firm, where the leadership style is autocratic and the organizational system informal. Communications tend to be vertical with little real teamwork. Important purchasing decisions are likely to be passed to top management for final approval, but good personal relationships are vital to prevent middle management blocking approaches.

Leadership in the Netherlands is more democratic, although the organizational style tends to be systematic, with rigorous management systems designed to involve multilevel consensus decision-making. Buying is, therefore, characterized by large DMUs and long decision-making processes as members attempt to reach agreement without conflict or one-sided outcomes.

Ultimately, it is important to understand how management and leadership styles vary and then to develop market strategies that can facilitate collaborative relationships. In India and China, this means focusing on developing strong skillsets and effective implementation. In Benelux and Nordic countries, leaders focus on planning and communications. In the USA and UK, there tend to be *hybrid leadership models*, with leaders adopting a *push-orientation towards change*.

Based on: Mole (1990); Wolfe (1991); Salacuse (2004); Bersin (2012)

Political–legal influences

Political factors that have implications for global marketing are: the general attitudes of foreign governments to imports and foreign direct investment; political stability; governmental policies; and trade barriers. Negative attitudes towards foreign companies may also discourage imports and investment, because of the threat of protectionism and expropriation of assets (the taking by the state of private property for public purposes, normally without compensation). Positive governmental attitudes can be reflected in the willingness to grant subsidies to overseas companies to invest in a country and a willingness to cut through bureaucratic procedures to assist foreign companies and their imports. The willingness of the UK government to grant investment incentives to Japanese companies was a factor in Nissan, Honda and Toyota setting up production facilities in the UK. However, speculation over Brexit and the threat of new trade barriers having an impact on profits, as well as the loss of *frictionless* access to EU markets, has caused concern for these and other firms that have manufacturing facilities in the UK (Pitas, 2018).

Countries with a history of political instability may be avoided because of the inevitable uncertainty regarding their future. Countries such as Iraq and Lebanon have undoubtedly suffered because of their respective political situations.

Government policies can also influence market entry. For example, the Chinese government still operates censorship of information, which can act as a barrier to entry, especially for media and information-based web companies. YouTube, Twitter and Facebook are blocked from accessing Chinese consumers, although foreign visitors can access these platforms in some of the southern islands, which are also a free trade zone (Chan, 2018).

Finally, a major consideration when deciding which countries to enter will be the level of tariff barriers. Undoubtedly, the threat of tariff barriers to imports to the countries of the EU has encouraged US and Japanese foreign direct investment into Europe. Within the single market, the removal of trade barriers is making international trade in Europe more attractive, as not only do tariffs fall but, in addition, the need to modify products to cater for national regulations and restrictions is reduced. See Mini Case 21.1 to find out more about how Amazon helps sellers reach customers in the worldwide marketplace.

Technological influences

The internet has had a profound influence on global market expansion, and we have discussed many examples throughout the book of how companies have used the internet and associated technologies to grow market share both nationally and internationally. However, when considering the influence of technology on market entry, it is important to understand the information and communication technology (ICT) infrastructure of a nation, as it is essential—particularly in emerging economies—to understand the quality of infrastructure that is in place. The costs of direct entry to such an economy can be high, not only due to the need for upgrades to the infrastructure but also due to the high training cost to overcome any knowledge and skills gap that may exist (Chen, 2018). ICT is particularly important for the coordination of the movement of goods, transportation, global production and for cross-border investment (Ngwenyama and Morawczynski, 2009). See Mini Case 21.1 to find out how Amazon helps support global business expansion.

MINI CASE 21.1

Amazon Helps Companies Grow their Businesses around the Globe

Online companies like eBay and Amazon pioneered the development of global markets. Together they have hundreds of millions of active accounts for buyers and sellers, which generates billions of dollars of revenue. These marketplaces have also enabled more companies (and even individuals) to trade in foreign markets than ever before and have fostered the development of other trading platforms, for example La Redoute (France), Rakuten (Japan) and Alibaba (China).

Amazon actively trades in 13 global marketplaces in the USA, Europe, India and Asia and takes a proactive role in encouraging and helping its sellers to trade around the world. While developing its global digital marketplace, it has accumulated knowledge about how to succeed in distance selling, especially when crossing national boundaries. Amazon now shares this information to help its own customers trade in foreign markets.

The Amazon marketplaces provide companies with advice for sellers—large and small—about what is required when trading in different parts of the world. Amazon has a four-step plan that guides sellers through the international selling process. This plan involves:

1. *Deciding what and where to sell*. Amazon operates country-specific marketplaces in three broad regions: North America, Europe and Asia. Each region has country-specific domains, for example Amazon.ca (Canada), Amazon.de (Germany), Amazon.co.jp (Japan). A seller simply chooses a region in which to sell, and registers with the particular marketplace; the seller then has access to customers in that region. Consideration should be given to the type of products that are to be sold to ensure they comply with country-specific laws and standards. Amazon even provides its sellers with help with languages and coaching in how to maximize selling opportunities.
2. *Setting up and registering an account*. Once steps 1 and 2 are complete, a seller is then ready to prepare for step 3 and can begin trading in foreign markets. The seller sets up a *seller central* account, establishes payment methods and begins listing products for sale. The Amazon marketplace then acts as a gateway to the global market, making it easier for sellers that are new to international trade to access these markets.
3. *Shipping and fulfilment of global orders*. No matter where in the world buyers live, they will want to receive the goods they purchase in a timely and secure fashion. Amazon marketplace sellers can arrange their own methods of delivery or use Amazon's fulfilment service. With Amazon's fulfilment service, Amazon helps sellers with the complexities of exporting and importing around the globe.
4. *Managing global business and providing customer support and returns*. Amazon is a highly customer-centric company and so insists that sellers provide high-quality aftersales support and returns policies and procedures.

Amazon also provides some country-specific guidance on tax laws, duties and selling restrictions, but advises that sellers must ensure they are fully aware of legal and industry requirements.

Arguably, Amazon and similar international digital marketplaces are lowering the entry barriers for international trade by providing access to global markets. But political and legal barriers remain and must be recognized by all companies wishing to trade in global markets.

Questions:

1. Visit Amazon services at http://services.amazon.com/global-selling and then, using the information provided, select a region—a country-specific domain—and suggest a range of products you might sell to a new market in this region.
2. Suggest what difficulties you might encounter when deciding which marketplace to enter.
3. Based on your answers to questions 1 and 2, devise your own set of priorities that companies should consider when selecting and entering foreign markets.

Based on: Amazon.com Inc. (2018); Raconteur (2013)

Microenvironmental issues

While the macroenvironmental analysis provides indications of how attractive each country is to an international marketer, microenvironmental analysis focuses on the attractiveness of the particular market being considered and the company capability profile.

Market attractiveness

Market attractiveness can be assessed by determining market size and growth rate, competition, costs of serving the market, profit potential and market access.

- *Market size and growth rate*: large, growing markets (other things being equal) provide attractive conditions for market entry. Research supports the notion that market growth is a more important consideration than market size (Knickerbocker, 1973). It is expectations about future demand rather than existing demand that are important, particularly for foreign direct investment. It is China's enormous market size and growth rate that is attracting many European companies, for example Tesco, Carrefour, Louis Vuitton, Metro and Tengelmann (Birchall and Parkers, 2006). Russia's technology boom, subsidies and tax cuts for foreign investors have stimulated growth, but recent political unrest has also been a limiting factor (Henni, 2012).
- *Competition*: markets that are already served by strong, well-entrenched competitors may dampen enthusiasm for foreign market entry. However, when a competitive weakness is identified, a decision to enter may be taken. For example, in China there is growing demand for *clean* energy, and while local producers of solar energy dominate this market, there are opportunities for foreign exporters that can supply specialized niche services, for example engineering and environmental consultancy. Volatility of competition also appears to reduce the attractiveness of overseas markets. Highly volatile markets, with many competitors entering and leaving the market and where market concentration is high, are particularly unattractive (Whitelock and Jobber, 1994). Dixons Carphone sold off its Electro World operations in central Europe and Turkey to enable it to focus on its core business. The firm has also created competitive advantage around the service side of its business, through its in-store Know How clinics and computer and mobile phone repairs to differentiate the brand from online retailers like ao.com and Amazon (Armstrong, 2017).
- *Costs of serving the market*: two major costs of servicing foreign markets are distribution and control. As geographic distance increases, so these two costs rise. Many countries' major export markets are in neighbouring countries—such as the USA, whose largest market is Canada. Costs are also dependent on the form of market entry. Obviously, foreign direct investment is initially more expensive than using distributors. Some countries may not possess suitable low-cost entry options, making entry less attractive and more risky. Long internal distribution channels (e.g. as in Japan) can also raise costs, as middlemen demand their profit margins. If direct investment is being contemplated, labour costs and the supply of skilled labour will also be a consideration. Finally, some markets may prove unattractive because of the high marketing expenditures necessary to compete in them.
- *Profit potential*: some markets may be unattractive because industry structure leaves them with poor profit potential. For example, the existence of powerful buying groups may reduce profit potential through their ability to negotiate low prices. Also, technology firms like Netflix face high costs when entering some international markets, due to low bandwidth and poor digital infrastructure, which can also limit international growth.
- *Market access*: some foreign markets may prove difficult to penetrate because of informal ties between existing suppliers and distributors. Without the capability of setting up a new distribution chain, this would mean that market access would effectively be barred. Links between suppliers and customers in organizational markets would also form a barrier. In some countries and markets, national suppliers are given preferential treatment. China is said to be moving away from using foreign technology companies for its banks, military and key government agencies, in favour of Chinese suppliers (Yang, 2014).

Company capability profile

Company capability to serve a foreign market also needs to be assessed: this depends on skills, resources, product adaptation and competitive advantage.

- *Skills*: does the company have the necessary skills to market abroad? If not, can sales agents or distributors compensate for any shortfalls? Does the company have the necessary skills to understand the requirements of each market? For example, when VW established Volkswagen Financial Services in the UK, one of the biggest concerns about locating this operation in this country was the availability of a workforce with the right skills. The operation is now based in Milton Keynes and employs 400 people, who serve 250,000 customers.

- *Resources*: different countries may have varying market servicing costs. Does the company have the necessary financial resources to compete effectively in different countries? Human resources also need to be considered, as some markets may demand domestically supplied personnel.
- *Product adaptation*: for some foreign markets, local preferences and regulations may require the product to be modified. Does the company have the motivation and capability to redesign the product?
- *Competitive advantage*: a key consideration in any market is the ability to create a competitive advantage. Each foreign market needs to be studied in the light of the company's current and future ability to create and sustain a competitive advantage.

Deciding How to Enter a Foreign Market

Once a firm has decided to enter a foreign market, it must choose a mode of entry—that is, select an institutional arrangement for organizing and conducting marketing activities.

The choice of foreign market entry strategy is likely to have a major impact on a company's performance overseas (Young et al., 1989). Each mode of entry has its own associated levels of commitment, risks, control and profit potential. The major options are indirect exporting, direct exporting, licensing, joint ventures, and direct investment, either in new facilities or through acquisition (see Figure 21.4).

Indirect exporting

Indirect exporting involves the use of independent organizations within the exporter's domestic market; these include the following.

- *Domestic-based export merchants* who take title to the products and sell them abroad.
- *Domestic-based export agents* who sell on behalf of the exporter but do not take title to the products; agents are usually paid by commission.
- *Piggy-backing*, whereby the exporter uses the overseas distribution facilities of another producer.
- *Cooperative organizations*, which act on behalf of a number of producers and are partly controlled by them; many producers of primary products, such as fruit and nuts, export through cooperative organizations.

Indirect exporting has three advantages. First, the exporting organization is domestically based, making communication easier than using foreign intermediaries. Second, investment and risk are lower for the exporter than setting up its own sales and marketing facility. Third, use can be made of the exporting organization's knowledge of selling abroad.

FIGURE 21.4
Foreign market entry strategies

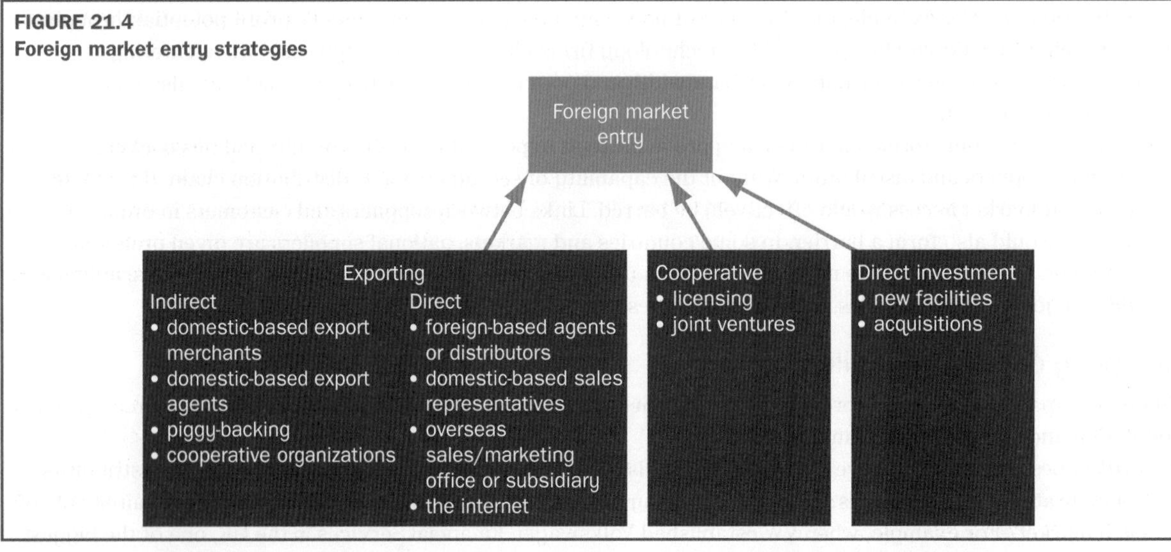

Direct exporting

As exporters grow more confident, they may decide to undertake their own exporting task. This will involve building up overseas contracts, undertaking marketing research, handling documentation and transportation, and designing marketing-mix strategies. **Direct exporting** modes include export through foreign-based agents or distributors (independent middlemen), a domestic-based salesforce, an overseas sales/marketing office or subsidiary, or via the internet.

Foreign-based agents or distributors

Most companies use specialist agents or distributors in some or all their exporting abroad. Over 60 per cent of US companies use them for some or all their export activity, and for European companies the figure rises to over 70 per cent (West, 1987). Agents may be: *exclusive*, where the agreement is between the exporter and the agent alone; *semi-exclusive*, where the agent handles the exporter's goods along with other non-competing goods from other companies; or *non-exclusive*, where the agent handles a variety of goods, including some that may compete with the exporter's products.

Distributors, unlike agents, take title to the goods and are paid according to the difference between the buying and selling prices rather than commission. Distributors are often appointed when after-sales service is required, as they are more likely than agents to possess the necessary resources.

The advantages of both agents and distributors are that they are familiar with the local market, customs and conventions, have existing business contracts and employ foreign nationals. They have a direct incentive to sell, through either commission or profit margin, but, since their remuneration is tied to sales, they may be reluctant to devote much time and effort to developing a market for a new product. Also, the amount of market feedback may be limited, as agents or distributors may see themselves as being purchasing agents for their customers rather than as selling agents for the exporter.

Overall, exporting through independent middlemen is a low-investment method of market entry, although significant expenditure in marketing may be necessary. Also, it can be difficult and costly to terminate an agreement with an independent agent or distributor, which suggests that this option should be viewed with care and not seen as an easy method of market entry.

Domestic-based sales representatives

As the sales representative is a company employee, greater control of activities compared with that when using independent middlemen can be expected. A company has no control over the attention an agent or distributor gives to its products or the amount of market feedback provided, whereas it can insist that various activities be performed by its sales representatives.

Also, the use of company employees shows a commitment to the customer that the use of agents or distributors may lack. Consequently, sales representatives are often used in industrial markets, where there are only a few large customers who require close contact with suppliers, and where the size of orders justifies the expense of foreign travel. This method of market servicing is also found when selling to government buyers and retail chains, for similar reasons.

Overseas sales/marketing office or subsidiary

This option displays even greater customer commitment than using domestic-based sales representatives, although the establishment of a local office requires a greater investment. However, the exporter may be perceived as an indigenous supplier, improving the chances of market success. In some markets, where access to distribution channels is limited, selling directly through an overseas sales office may be the only feasible way of breaking into a new market. The sales office or subsidiary acts as a centre for foreign-based sales representatives, handles sales distribution and promotion, and can act as a customer service centre.

The internet

The global reach of the internet means that companies can now engage in exporting activities directly to customers. (See Mini Case 21.1 to learn how Amazon and other digital companies are helping.) By creating a website, the company can make overseas customers aware of its products and ordering can be direct. Products can be supplied straight to the customer without the need for an intermediary. The internet is not only a channel to market but also a useful research tool.

Licensing

Licensing refers to contracts in which a foreign licensor provides a local licensee with access to one or a set of technologies or know-how in exchange for financial compensation (Young et al., 1989). The licensee will normally have exclusive rights to produce and market the product within an agreed area for a specific period in return for a *royalty* based on sales volume. A licence may relate to the use of a patent for a product or process, copyright, trademarks and trade secrets (e.g. designs and software) or know-how (e.g. product and process specifications).

Licensing agreements allow the exporter to enter markets that otherwise may be closed for exports or other forms of market entry, without the need to make substantial capital investments in the host country. However, control of production is lost, and the reputation of the licensor is dependent on the performance of the licensee. A grave danger of licensing is the loss of product and process know-how to third parties, which may become competitors once the agreement is at an end.

The need to exploit new technology simultaneously in many markets has stimulated the growth in licensing by small high-tech companies that lack the resources to set up their own sales and marketing offices, engage in joint ventures or conduct direct investment abroad. Licensing is also popular in research and development intensive industries such as pharmaceuticals, chemicals and synthetic fibres, where rising research and development costs have encouraged licensing as a form of reciprocal technology exchange.

Sometimes the licensed product has to be adapted to suit local culture. For example, packaging that uses red and yellow, the colours of the Spanish flag, is seen as an offence to Spanish patriotism; in Greece, purple should be avoided as it has funereal associations; and the licensing of a movie, TV show or book whose star is a cute little pig will have no prospect of success in Muslim countries, where the pig is considered an unclean animal (Bloomgarden, 2000).

In Europe, licensing is encouraged by the EU, which sees the mechanism as a way of offering access to new technologies to companies lacking the resources to innovate; licensing provides a means of technology sharing on a pan-European scale. Licensing activities have been given exemption in EU competition law (which means that companies engaged in licensing cannot be accused of anti-competitive practices), and *tied purchase* agreements, whereby licensees must buy components from the licensor, have not been ruled anti-competitive, since they allow the innovating firm protection from loss of know-how to other component suppliers.

Franchising

Franchising is a form of licensing where a package of services is offered by the franchisor to the franchisee in return for payment. The two types of franchising are, *product and trade name franchising*, the classic case of which is Coca-Cola selling its syrup together with the right to use its trademark and name to independent bottlers, and *business format franchising*, where marketing approaches, operating procedures and quality control are included in the franchise package as well as the product and trade name. Business-format franchising is mainly used in service industries such as restaurants, hotels and retailing, where the franchisor exerts a high level of control in the overseas market since quality-control procedures can be established as part of the agreement. For example, McDonald's specifies precisely who should supply the ingredients for its fast-food products wherever they are sold, to ensure consistency of quality in its franchise outlets.

The benefits to the franchisor are that franchising may be a way of overcoming resource constraints, an efficient system to overcome producer–distributor management problems, and a way of gaining knowledge of new markets (Hopkinson and Hogarth-Scott, 1999). Franchising provides access to the franchisee's resources. For example, if the franchisor has limited financial resources, access to additional finance may be supplied by the franchisee. Franchising may overcome producer—distributor management problems in managing geographically dispersed operations, through the advantages of having owner-managers who have vested interests in the success of the business. Gaining knowledge of new markets by tapping into the franchisee's local knowledge is especially important in international markets, where local culture may differ considerably between regions.

There are risks, however. Although the franchisor will attempt to gain some control of operations, the existence of multiple geographically dispersed owner-managers makes control difficult. Service delivery may be inconsistent because of this. Conflicts can arise through dissatisfaction with the standard of service, lack of promotional support and the opening of new franchises close to existing ones, for example. This can lead to a breakdown of relationships and deteriorating performance. Also, initial financial outlays can be considerable because of expenditures on training, development, promotional and support activities.

The franchisee benefits by gaining access to the resources of the franchisor, its expertise (sometimes global) and buying power. The risks are that it may face conflicts (as discussed above) that render the relationship unviable.

Franchising is also exempt from EU competition law, as it is seen as a means of achieving increased competition and efficient distribution without the need for major investment. It promotes standardization, which reaps scale economies with the possibility of some adaptation to local tastes. For example, in India, McDonald's uses goat and lamb rather than pork or beef in its burgers, and Benetton allows a degree of freedom to its franchisees to stock products suitable to their customers (Welford and Prescott, 2000).

Joint ventures

Two types of joint venture are *contractual* and *equity* joint ventures. In **contractual joint ventures**, no joint enterprise with a separate personality is formed. Two or more companies form a partnership to share the cost of an investment, the risks and long-term profits. The partnership may be to complete a project or for a longer-term cooperative effort (Wright, 1981). Contractual joint ventures are found in the oil exploration, aerospace and car industries, and in co-publishing agreements (Young et al., 1989). An **equity joint venture** involves the creation of a new company in which foreign and local investors share ownership and control.

Joint ventures are sometimes set up in response to government conditions for market entry or because the foreign firm lacks the resources to set up production facilities alone. Also, the danger of expropriation is less when a company has a national partner than when the foreign firm is the sole owner (Terpstra and Sarathy, 1999). Finding a national partner may be the only way to invest in some markets that are too competitive and saturated to leave room for a completely new operation. Many of the Japanese/US joint ventures in the USA were set up for this reason. The foreign investor benefits from the local management talent and knowledge of local markets and regulations. Also, joint ventures allow partners to specialize in their areas of technological expertise in a given project. They may also be the only means of entering a country, because of national laws. For example, in India overseas supermarket chains are not allowed to operate as retailers unless they can find a local partner to own and operate the store (Rigby and Leaky, 2008). For this reason, Marks & Spencer's stores are operated by Indian retailer Reliance Retail, and the firm aims to make India its largest overseas market (Ram, 2018). Finally, the host firm benefits by acquiring resources from its foreign partners. Now read Marketing in Action 21.3.

MARKETING IN ACTION 21.3
Harnessing the Power of the *Guanxi*

China's economy has been growing at an average of a 7 per cent year-on-year increase since 2000. The country possesses considerable strengths in mass manufacturing and is currently building large electronics and heavy industrial factories and is also investing heavily in education and training, especially in the development of engineers and scientists. China poses new opportunities and threats to western companies. China has a population of over 1.38 billion people and they are spending their growing incomes on consumer durables such as cars, mobile phones computers and other digital technologies. Western companies such as Microsoft, Procter & Gamble, Coca-Cola, BP and Siemens have already seen the Chinese market as an opportunity with the aid of local joint-venture partners.

Although the Chinese economy undoubtedly possesses many strengths, it also has several weaknesses. First, it lacks major global brands. When business people around the world were asked to rank Chinese brands, Haier, a white goods and home appliance manufacturer was ranked first, and Lenovo,

»

»

a computer company, famous for buying IBM's personal computer division, was second. Neither company is a major global player in their respective markets. Second, China suffers from the risk of social unrest, resulting from the widening gap between rich and poor, as well as from corruption. Third, the country has paid a heavy ecological price for rapid industrial and population growth, with thousands of deaths attributed to air and water pollution. Fourth, while still a low labour cost economy, wage levels are rising fast, particularly in skilled areas, reducing China's competitive advantage in this area. Finally, bureaucracy can make doing business in China difficult.

Although western companies have made successful entries into the Chinese market, some such as Whirlpool, a US white goods manufacturer, and Kraft, the food multinational, have made heavy losses. Overseas companies hoping to sell successfully in China need to understand several realities of the market there. First, the country is very diverse: 1.38 billion people speak 100 dialects and, covering such a large geographic area, the climate is very different across regions. For example, parts of the south are humid, while the north is more temperate. Also, income levels vary considerably between less affluent rural districts and richer cities.

Many western companies enter China by means of a joint venture, but they need to be aware of the different business conditions in the country. In China, there is no effective rule of law governing business. Bureaucracy and governmental interference can also bring difficulties. For example, Thames Water pulled out of a 20-year water treatment project in Shanghai after the government ruled that the guaranteed rate of return to investors was illegal.

A key element in Chinese business dealings is the existence of *guanxi* networks. *Guanxi* is a set of personal connections on which a person can draw to obtain resources or an advantage when doing business. *Guan* means a gate or a hurdle, and *xi* refers to a tie, relationship or connection. Therefore, *guanxi* literally means 'pass the gate and get connected'. The existence of *guanxi* or personal relationships is global, but *guanxi*'s ubiquitous nature makes it unique and distinctive to China. Intermediaries may be useful in establishing *guanxi*. For example, if person A wants to make a request of person C, with whom A has no *guanxi*, A may seek out a member of C's *guanxi* network, person B. If B provides A with an introduction to C, a *guanxi* relationship may begin between A and C. Developing such a network may involve performing favours or giving gifts. For example, a business person may participate in a public ceremonial function, or a professor could send books to a Chinese university. Favours are 'banked' and there is a reciprocal obligation to return a favour. Three important elements of *guanxi* are *ganqing* (feelings or affection), *renquing* (reciprocation and favour) and *xinren* (trust). All three elements are important in fostering good buyer–seller relationships.

An important aspect of Chinese culture is the avoidance of loss of face. This can occur when a Chinese person finds him/herself embarrassed by, for example, displaying lack of knowledge or understanding. Chinese people like to gather as much information as possible before revealing their thoughts to avoid losing face and displaying ignorance. They value modesty and reasoning. They also regard the signing of a contract to be only the beginning of a business relationship.

Source: prepared by David Jobber, Emeritus Professor of Marketing, University of Bradford

There are potential problems with joint ventures, however. The national partner's interests relate to the local operation, while the foreign firm's concerns relate to the totality of its international operations. Areas of conflict can be the use made of profits (pay out versus plough back), product line and market coverage of the joint venture, and transfer pricing.

Equity joint ventures are common between companies from western European and eastern European countries. Western European companies gain from low-cost production and raw materials, while former Eastern bloc companies acquire western technology and know-how. Eastern European governments are keen to promote joint ventures rather than wholly owned foreign direct investment in an attempt to prevent the exploitation of low-cost labour by western companies. A joint research project between French car makers and British designers led to the Renault Clio winning European Car of the Year Award.

Direct investment

This method of market entry involves investment in foreign-based assembly or manufacturing facilities. It carries the greatest commitment of capital and managerial effort. Wholly owned **direct investment** can be through the acquisition of a foreign producer (or by buying out a joint venture partner) or by building *new facilities*. Acquisition offers a quicker way into the market and usually means gaining access to a qualified labour force, national management, local knowledge, and contacts with the local market and government.

Acquisition also is a means of getting ownership of global brands. But such investments do not always deliver immediate profits: for example, when Tata Motors bought Jaguar and Land Rover, it took several years before significant profits were declared. This was a risky investment, as it took Tata Motors into the luxury car market and away from its trucks and small cars, which were the mainstay of its business at the time of the investment (Gribeben, 2013). In saturated markets, acquisition may be the only feasible way of establishing a production presence in the host country (*The Economist*, 2008). However, coordination between the foreign investor and the local management team, and different styles of management, may cause problems. Whirlpool, the US white goods (washing machines, fridges, etc.) manufacturer, is an example of a company that has successfully entered new international markets using acquisition. The company has successfully entered European markets through its acquisition of Philips' white goods business and its ability to develop new products that serve cross-national Euro-segments. European companies have also gained access to North American markets through acquisition.

Central and eastern Europe have been the recipients of high levels of direct investment as companies have sought to take advantage of low labour costs. Car companies have opened production facilities there, notably VW in the Czech Republic and Slovakia, Renault in Romania, Slovakia and Turkey, and Fiat in Poland.

Wholly owned direct investment offers a greater degree of control than licensing or joint ventures and maintains the internalization of proprietary information for manufacturers. It accomplishes the circumvention of tariff and non-tariff barriers and lowers distribution costs compared with domestic production. A local presence means that sensitivity to customers' tastes and preferences is enhanced, and links with distributors and the host nation's government can be forged. Foreign direct investments can act as a powerful catalyst for economic change in the transition from a centrally planned economy. Foreign companies bring technology, management know-how and access to foreign markets (Ghauri and Holstius, 1996). Direct investment is an expensive option, though, and the consequent risks are greater. If the venture fails, more money is lost, and there is always the risk of expropriation. Furthermore, closure of plant may mean substantial redundancy payments.

The selection of international market entry mode is dependent on the trade-offs between the levels of control, resources and risk of losing proprietary information and technology. Figure 21.5 summarizes the levels associated with exporting using middlemen, exporting using company staff, licensing, joint ventures and direct investment.

Considerable research has gone into trying to understand the factors that have been shown to have an impact on selection of market entry method. Both external (country environment and buyer behaviour) and internal (company issues) factors have been shown to influence choice. A summary of these research findings is given in Table 21.1.

FIGURE 21.5
Selecting a foreign market entry mode: control, resources and risk

Level	Factor: Risk of losing proprietary information	Resources	Control
High		Direct investment	Direct investment Exporting (own staff)
Medium	Licensing Joint venture	Joint venture Exporting (own staff)	Joint venture Licensing
Low	Exporting (own staff) Exporting (middlemen) Direct investment	Licensing Exporting (middlemen)	Exporting (middlemen)

Developing Global Marketing Strategy

Standardization or adaptation

A fundamental decision that managers have to make regarding their global marketing strategy is the degree to which they standardize or adapt their marketing mix around the world. (These options are referred to, respectively, as the **adapted marketing mix** and the **standardized marketing mix**.) Many writers on the

TABLE 21.1 Factors affecting choice of market-entry method

External variables
Country environment
• Large market size and market growth encourage direct investment (Sungwook, Namwoon and Ge, 2017)
• Barriers to imports encourage direct investment (Buckley, Mirza and Sparkes, 1987)
• The riskiness of the host country, resource commitments and host government restrictions (Taylor, Zou and Osland, 2000)
• Geocultural distance encourages independent modes, for example agents, distributors (Anderson and Coughlan, 1987)
• Psychical distance does not favour integrated modes, for example own salesforce, overseas sales/marketing offices (Klein and Roth, 1990)
• Low market potential does not necessarily preclude direct investment for larger companies (see Agarwal and Ramaswami, 1992)
Buyer behaviour
• Project and protectionist buying encourages cooperative entry, for example licensing and joint ventures (Sharma, 1988)
Internal variables
Company issues
• Lack of market information, uncertainty and perception of high investment risk lead to the use of agents and distributors (Johanson and Vahlne, 1977; Lu, 2002)
• Companies pay more attention to the behaviour firms in the home market than foreign competition (Chan and Makino, 2007; Mas-Ruiz, Ruiz-Cone and Calderon-Martinez, 2018)
• Perception of high investment risk encourages joint ventures (Buckley, Mirza and Sparkes, 1987)
• Small firm size or resources encourages reactive exporting (Sharma, 1988)
• Limited experience favours integrated entry modes (Klein and Roth, 1990)
• Service companies that expand abroad by following their clients' expansion plans tend to favour integrated modes (Erramilli, 1991)
• When investment rather than exporting is preferred, lack of market information leads to a preference for cooperative rather than integrated modes (Buckley, Mirza and Sparkes, 1987)
Adapted from Whitelock and Jobber (1994)

subject discuss standardization and adaptation as two distinct options, but the literature on the subject is full of contradictions (Hise and Choi, 2010). Pure standardization means that a company keeps the same marketing mix in all countries to which it markets. Such an approach is in line with Levitt's view that world markets are being driven 'towards a converging commonality' (Levitt, 1983). However, the world has moved on since Levitt made this comment. There are compelling arguments for and against standardization. The commercial reality is that few marketing mixes are totally standardized.

EXHIBIT 21.1
McDonald's: a truly global brand

Some of the brands that are most often quoted as being standardized are Coca-Cola, McDonald's and Levi Strauss. It is true that many elements of these brands' marketing mixes are identical in a wide range of countries, but even here adaptation is found (Exhibit 21.1). First, in Coca-Cola, the sweetness and carbonization vary between countries. For example, sweetness is lowered in Greece and carbonization lowered in eastern Europe. Diet Coke's artificial sweetener and packaging differ between countries (Quelch and Hoff, 1986). Second, Levi Strauss uses different domestic and international advertising strategies (Banerjee, 1994). As Dan Chow Len, Levi's US advertising manager, commented (Mayer, 1991):

> 'The markets are different. In the US, Levi's is both highly functional and fashionable. But in the UK, its strength is as a fashion garment. We've tested UK ads in American markets. Our primary target market at home is 16–20-year-olds, and they hate these ads, won't tolerate them, they're too sexy. Believe it or not, American 16–20-year-olds don't want to be sexy. . . . When you ask people about Levi's here, it's quality, comfort, style, affordability. In Japan, it's the romance of America.'

Third, in McDonald's, menus are changed to account for different customer preferences. For example, in France, McDonald's offers 'Croque McDo', its version of the French favourite the *croque monsieur*. McDonald's also works with French companies to offer local products such as yoghurts from Danone and coffee from Carte Noire, and buys 80 per cent of its products from French farmers. The proportion of meat in the hamburgers also varies between countries.

Most global brands adapt to meet local requirements. Even high-tech electronic products have to conform to national technical standards and may be positioned differently in various countries.

How do marketers tackle the standardization–adaptation issue? A useful rule of thumb was cited at the start of this chapter: go global (standardize) when you can; stay local (adapt) when you must.

Figure 21.6 provides a grid for thinking about the areas where standardization may be possible and where adaptation may be necessary. The example shows a highly standardized approach to the product and service elements and brand name, some adaptation of advertising, packaging, selling and sales promotion, and an adapted approach towards pricing, finance and distribution.

There are many variations in which elements are standardized and which are adapted. For example, IKEA's product offering and stores are largely standardized, but its advertising is varied between countries. SEAT's car models are standardized, but its positioning alters: for example, it is positioned as a more upmarket brand in Spain than in the UK. Also, the Kronenbourg product is standardized, but it is positioned as more of a premium beer in the UK than in Germany. Occasionally, the brand name changes for the same product. For example, Unilever's male toiletries brand is marketed as Lynx in the UK and Ireland, because of trademark problems, and as Axe across the rest of the world (Lewis, 2006) (see Exhibit 21.2).

FIGURE 21.6
An example of a grid to aid thinking about standardization and adaptation of the marketing mix

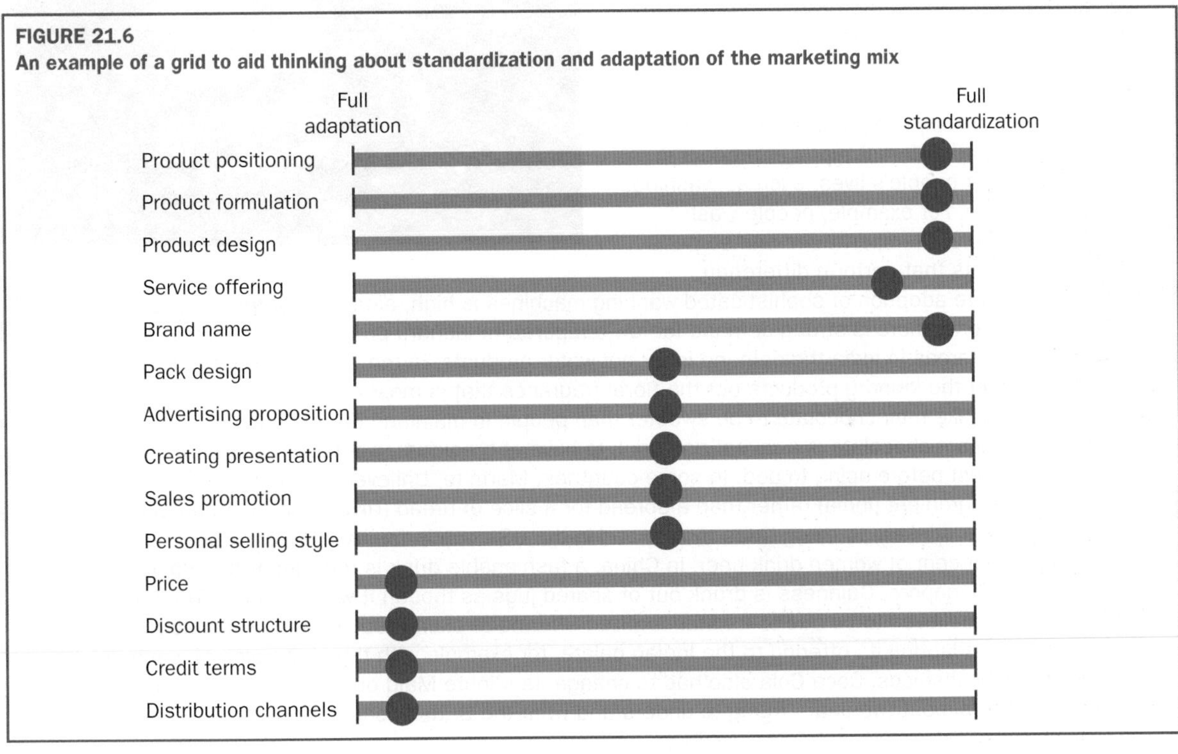

Standardization is an attractive option because it can create massive economies of scale. For example, lower manufacturing, advertising and packaging costs can be realized. Also, the logistical benefit of being able to move stock from one country to another to meet low-stock situations should not be underestimated. This has led to the call to focus on similarities rather than differences between consumers across Europe and the rest of the world. Procter & Gamble, for example, standardizes most of its products across Europe, so Pampers nappies and Pringles crisps are the same in all western European countries, although Procter & Gamble's detergent Daz does differ (Mazur, 2002). However, there are a number of barriers to developing standardized global brands. These are discussed in Marketing in Action 21.4

EXHIBIT 21.2
Unilever's male toiletry brand is marketed as Axe across the rest of the world

MARKETING IN ACTION 21.4
Barriers to Developing Standardized Global Brands

The cost of the logistical advantages of developing standardized global marketing approaches has meant that many companies have looked carefully at standardizing their approach to the European market. Mars, for example, changed the name of its chocolate bar Marathon in the UK to conform to its European brand name Snickers. Full standardization of the marketing mix is difficult, however, because of five problems.

1 *Culture and consumption patterns*: different cultures demand different types of product in every aspect of people's lives, such as washing, eating, drinking. For example, people wash clothes at different temperatures and so need laundry products that perform differently.
   In Europe, where adoption of sophisticated washing machines is high, along with interest in reducing carbon emissions, there is strong demand for low-temperature laundry products, for example Ariel gel with Actilift, whereas in India the demand is for hot-water products. In the USA, it is not the temperature/performance of the laundry products but the floral fragrance that is most important.
   UK consumers like their chocolate to be sweeter than people in mainland Europe do. Also, in South America hot chocolate is a revitalizing drink to have at breakfast, whereas in the UK it is a comfort drink to have just before going to bed. In some countries, Marmite, Unilever's savoury spread, is promoted as a cooking ingredient (India) rather than a spread for a slice of bread (UK). In South America there are two female beer drinkers to every three males, and in the USA one in four women drink beer—yet in the UK, only 10 per cent of women drink beer. In China, a fashionable drink is red wine with a dash of Coca-Cola, and, in Singapore, Guinness is drunk out of shared jugs as though it were Sangria. The failure of KFC in India is believed to be due to its standardized offering of plain fried chicken, while McDonald's succeeded by adapting its offering to the Indian palate, for example with the Maharajah Mac made from chicken and local spices. Coca-Cola also had to change its Minute Maid orange juice for the UK market. After spending almost two years trying to understand what the British consumer wanted, Coca-Cola

changed its US formulation of concentrate and water to fresh orange juice without concentrate. Consumer electrical products are less affected, though.

2 *Language*: brand names and advertising may have to change because of language differences. For example, PSCHITT is a soft drink developed by Perrier in the mid-1950s. If it were to be launched in the UK, the name might have to be adapted because of the English pronunciation.
3 *Regulations*: while national regulations are being harmonized in the single market, differences still exist—for example, with colourings and added vitamins in food.
4 *Media availability and promotional preferences*: varying media practices also affect standardization. For example, wine cannot be advertised on television in Denmark, but in the Netherlands this is allowed. Beer cannot be advertised on television in France, but this is allowed in most other European countries. In Italy, levels of nudity in advertising that would be banned in some other countries are accepted.
5 *Organizational structure and culture*: the changes necessary for a standardized approach may be difficult to implement where subsidiaries have, historically, enjoyed considerable power. Also, where growth had been achieved through acquisition, strong cultural differences may lead to differing views about pan-European brand strategy.

As discussed, standardization is rarely possible. Even brands that are regarded as global, such as Sony, Nike, Visa, IBM, Disney, Heineken, McDonald's and Pringles, are not as globally identical as they may first appear. For example, Visa uses different logos in some countries, Heineken is positioned as a mainstream beer in some countries but as a premium beer in others, Pringles uses different flavours and advertising executions in different countries and, although McDonald's core food items are consistent across countries, some products are customized to local tastes. Setting the objective as being to develop a standardized global brand should not be the priority; instead, global brand leadership—strong brands in all markets backed by effective global brand management—should be the goal.

Based on: De Chernatony (1993); Kirby (2000); Aaker and Joachimsthaler (2002); Luce (2002); Benady (2003); Charles (2008); Lovell (2008); Neff (2010)

Developing global and regional brands requires commitment from management to a coherent marketing programme. The sensitivities of national managers need to be accounted for, as managers may perceive a loss of status associated with greater centralized control. One approach is to have mechanisms that ensure the involvement of national managers in planning and that encourage them to make recommendations. The key is to balance this local involvement with the need to look for similarities rather than differences across markets. It is the essential differences in consumer preferences and buyer behaviour that need to be recognized in marketing mix adaptation, rather than the minor nuances. Managers must also be prepared to invest heavily and over a long time period to achieve brand penetration. Success in international markets does not come cheaply or quickly. Market research should be used to identify the required positioning in each global market segment (De Chernatony, 1993).

This discussion has outlined the difficulties in achieving a totally standardized marketing mix package. Rather, the tried-and-tested approach of market segmentation based on understanding consumer behaviour and identifying international target markets, which allows the benefits of standardization to be combined with the advantages of customization, is recommended. The two contrasting approaches are summarized in Figure 21.7.

International marketing mix decisions

When developing an international market entry strategy and when trading in global markets, consideration should be given to the marketing mix; marketers need to avoid falling into the trap of applying national stereotypes to country targets. As with domestic markets, overseas countries contain market segments that need to be understood to design a tailored marketing mix.

Before entering an overseas market, a firm should develop an understanding of its target customers, as there are many challenges to expanding overseas. The reason for understanding target consumers is to avoid the danger of using self-reference criteria, where there is an assumption that the choice criteria, motivations and behaviour that are important to overseas customers are the same as those used by domestic customers.

For example, although Audi adopts a standardized approach to product design, it still researches overseas customers. Audi sent members of its design team to California and China for eight weeks each, to live with families and better understand how they live and drive. Its research in the USA persuaded Audi to put cup and bottle holders on its car doors. Also, Chinese drivers' liking of tea led to the installation of a cup holder in the Audi A8

FIGURE 21.7
Two approaches to developing international marketing strategies

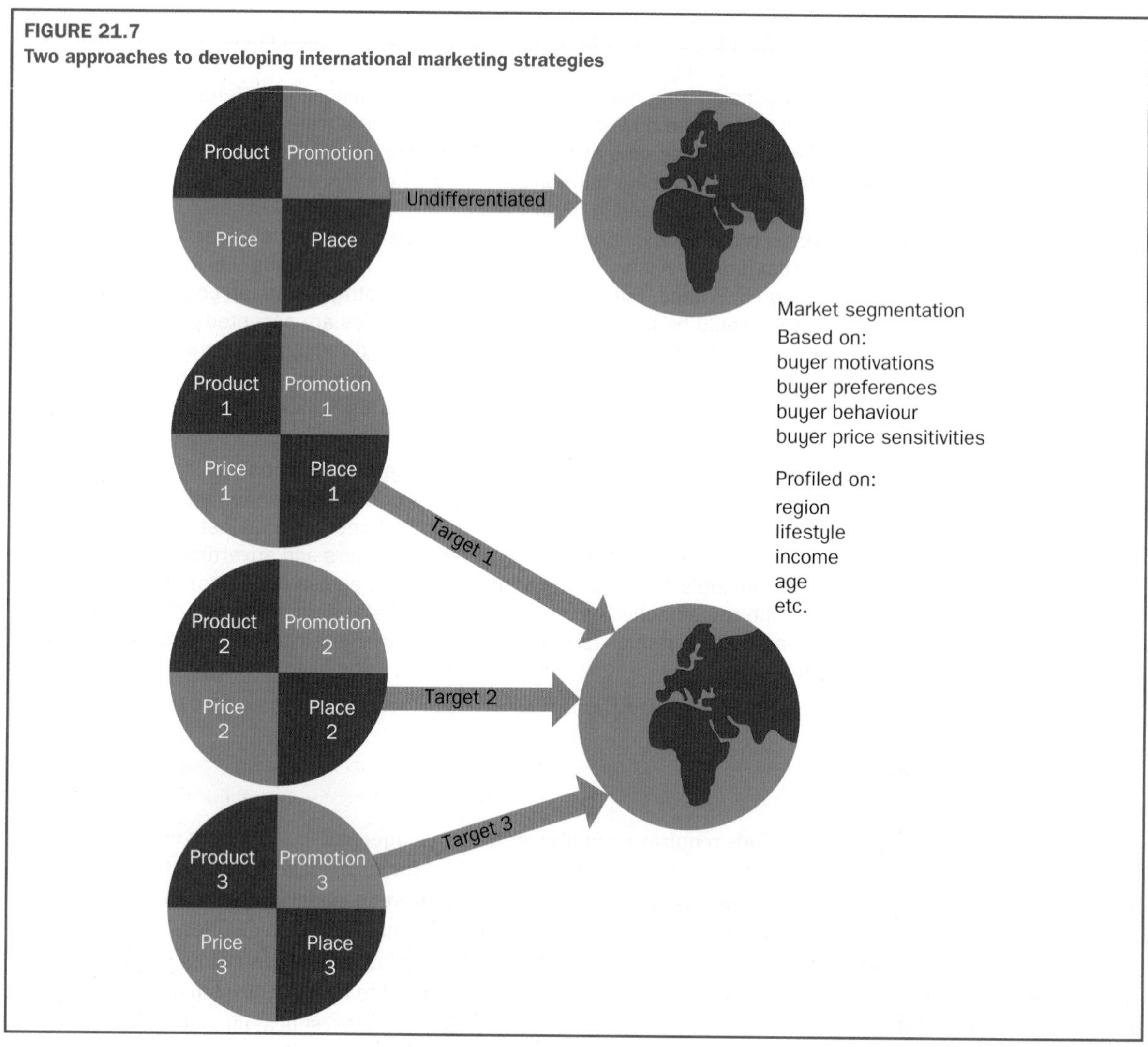

that can be heated or cooled. Rather than incur the expense of changing designs for specific countries, Audi has made these features standard globally. The cup holder used by Chinese drivers for green tea is promoted for use as a baby bottle holder elsewhere.

Once a thorough understanding of the target market has been achieved, marketing managers can then tailor a marketing mix to fit those requirements. We will now explore some of the special considerations associated with developing an effective *marketing mix* for global markets.

Product

Some companies rely on global markets to provide the potential necessary to justify their huge research and development costs. For example, in the pharmaceutical industry, GlaxoSmithKline's Zantac and Zovirax could not have been developed (R&D costs exceeded £30 million in both cases) without a worldwide market. Once the product is developed, the company can offer a standardized product to generate huge positive cash flow, as the benefits that these products provide span national boundaries. Many car companies also standardize as much of each car model as possible, particularly those parts that are not visible to drivers, such as the air-conditioning system, suspension and steering column.

A second situation that supports a standardized product is where the brand concept is based on *authentic national heritage* across the globe: Scotch whisky, Belgian chocolate and French wine are relevant examples. Clearly, there are sound marketing reasons for a standard product.

A third basis for standardization is where a global market segment of like-minded people can be exploited. This is the basis for the success of such products as Swatch and Rolex watches, Gucci fashion accessories and Chanel perfume. Where brands make statements about people, the *worldwide properties* of the brand add significantly to its appeal; this is particularly relevant for luxury brands.

In other cases, products need to be modified. Product adaptations come in two forms: permanent and temporary (Dudley, 1989). A company may make a fairly standard product worldwide, but make adaptations for particular markets. For example, Mattel's Barbie doll is a standardized product for most countries, but for some international markets , the doll was redesigned to suit cultural features and these were an example of *permanent adaptation*.

Sometimes, a change is only a *temporary adaptation* to see if the local consumer needs time to adjust gradually to a new product. This often occurs with food products. For example, when McDonald's entered Japan it had to alter the red meat content of its hamburgers, because Japanese consumers prefer fat to be mixed with beef. Over time, the red meat content has been increased, making it almost as high as in the USA. Also, the movement of large multinational companies to seek global brand winners can provide opportunities for smaller companies to exploit emerging market segments. For example, in the Netherlands, a small company took the initiative to sell environmentally friendly products and captured a quarter of the household cleaning market (Mitchell, 1993).

Brand names may require modification because of linguistic idiosyncrasies. Many companies are alive to this type of problem now. Mars, for example, changed the name of its Magnum ice cream in Greece to Magic. However, in France, McVitie's had problems trying to convince consumers that the word 'digestive' has nothing to do with stomach disorders. Brand name changes also occur in the UK, with Brooke Bond PG Tips being called Scottish Blend in Scotland and coming in distinctive Scottish packaging (Harris and McDonald, 1994).

Promotion

Standardized promotional campaigns can realize cost economies and a cohesive positioning statement in a world of increasing worldwide travel. Standardization allows the multinational corporation to maintain a consistent image identity throughout the world and minimizes confusion among consumers who travel frequently (Papavassiliou and Stathakopoulos, 1997). As with all standardization–adaptation debates, the real issue is one of degree. Rarely can a campaign be transferred from one country to another without any modifications because of language difference. The clever use of pop music (arguably a universal language) in Levi's advertising was one exception. Coca-Cola is also close to the full standardization position with its one-sound, one-sight, one-appeal philosophy. Audi successfully used the strapline '*Vorsprung durch Technik*' globally. Other examples of the same copy being used globally are McDonald's ('I'm lovin' it'), Johnnie Walker ('Keep walking') and HSBC ('The world's local bank'). Yet research has found that full standardization of advertising is rare (Harris and Attour, 2003).

Other companies find it necessary to adopt different positions in various countries, resulting in the need for advertising adaptation. In Mexico, Nestlé managed to position the drinking of instant coffee as an upmarket activity: it is smarter to offer guests a cup of instant coffee than ground coffee. This affects the content of Nestlé's advertising. When brands are used differently in various countries, the advertising may need to be changed accordingly. For example, Marmite is used as a savoury spread and often eaten at breakfast in the UK, but in India it is preferred as a cooking ingredient (Rampton, 2010). An analysis of the extent of advertising adaptation that is necessary can be assisted by separating the advertising proposition from the creative presentation of that proposition. The advertising platform is the aspect of the seller's product that is most persuasive and relevant to the potential customer—it is the fundamental proposition that is being communicated. The *creative presentation* is the way in which that proposition is translated into visual and verbal statements (Killough, 1978). Advertising platforms, being broad statements of appeal, are more likely to be transferable than creative presentations. If this is the case, the solution is to keep the platform across markets but change the creative presentation to suit local demands. In other cases, both platform and presentation can be used globally, as is the case with the McDonald's 'I'm lovin' it' campaign.

Advertising can be used to position brands using one of three strategies, as outlined below (Alden, Steenkamp and Batra, 1998).

1 **Global consumer culture positioning**: this strategy defines the brand as a symbol of a given global culture. For example, Benetton, whose slogan ('The United Colours of Benetton') emphasizes the unity of humankind and promotes the idea that people all over the world consume the brand. Fresh Intelligence developed a

measure of global brands to identify the closeness between brand and country values; this 'Glocalization' score has been found to be important to the success of brand development in foreign markets (Sandler and Churkina, 2011).

2 **Foreign consumer culture positioning**: with this strategy, the brand is associated with a specific foreign culture. The brand becomes symbolic of that culture so that the brand's personality, use occasion and/or user group are associated with a foreign culture. For example, Gucci in the USA is positioned as a prestigious and fashionable Italian product; Singapore Airlines' use of the 'Singapore girl' in its global advertising campaign, and the positioning of Louis Vuitton as representing French style and gracious living are two further examples (Wachman, 2004).

3 **Local consumer culture positioning**: this involves the association of the brand with local consumer culture. The brand is associated with local cultural meanings, reflects the local culture's norms and identities, is portrayed as consumed by local people in the national culture, and/or is depicted as locally produced for local people. For example, Dr Pepper soft drink is positioned in the USA as part of the 'American' way of life. Irn-Bru also has a strong brand personality influenced by its powerful Scottish heritage. This soft drink is manufactured under licence in Russia, Canada, Australia and Norway and is exported to Spain, Netherlands, Germany and other parts of Europe, as well as Africa and Asia.

The unwritten rules of doing business are often at variance, too. In the west, business may be discussed over lunch or at dinner in the business-person's home. In India, this would violate hospitality rules. Western business relies on the law of contract for sales agreements, but in Muslim culture a person's word is just as binding. In fact, a written contract may be a challenge to a person's honour (Jobber and Lancaster, 2015). Salespeople need to adapt their behaviour to accommodate the expectations of customers abroad. For example, in Japan, sales presentations should be low key with the use of a moderate, deliberate style, reflecting Japanese people's preferred manner of doing business. Salespeople should not push for a close of sale; instead they should plan to cultivate relationships through sales calls, courtesy visits, the occasional lunch and other social events.

Digital marketing is creating opportunities for companies to advertise globally by setting up a website. Using electronic media as a promotional tool may be hampered by the need to set price lists, however. Where prices are currently very different across national borders, some companies may decide that the risks of establishing a global internet presence outweigh the advantages.

Country images may have a role to play in the selection of goods in overseas markets. For example, a negative image of a country may influence a consumer's attitude towards products originating from that country. Country of origin is sometimes used to promote products abroad when associations are believed to be favourable and the national image is considered suitable for the specific type of product being marketed. For example, the product categories most often promoted by means of the Danish image are foodstuffs and dairy produce, design goods and products related to agriculture (Niss, 1996). Germany is highly regarded for its engineering excellence, which is a major asset for companies such as Audi, BMW and Volkswagen. So strong is this image that Citroën ran an advertising campaign for its C5 claiming German engineering excellence, even though the car is made in France (Whitehead, 2008).

A trend in organizing global advertising campaigns is for consolidation. Advertisers are either using an agency network where the agency has a global presence, or a holding group that contains many agencies spread worldwide; both routes provide the opportunity for greater coordination than employing different agencies in different countries. This also provides the client with the likelihood of negotiating a reduction in fees because of the large budgets involved.

Price

Price setting is a key marketing decision, because price is the revenue-generating element of the marketing mix. Poor pricing decisions can undermine previous cost-saving strategies.

In the face of more intense global competition, marketers need to consider six issues when considering cross-national pricing decisions.

1 Calculating extra costs and making price quotations
2 Understanding the competition and customers
3 Using pricing tactics to undermine competitor actions
4 Parallel importing

5 Transfer pricing
6 Counter-trade.

Each of these special considerations will now be explored.

Calculating extra costs and making price quotations: the extra costs of doing business in a foreign market must be taken into account if a profit is to be made. *Middlemen and transportation costs* need to be estimated. Distributors may demand different mark-ups, and agents may require varying commission levels in different countries. The length of the distribution channel also needs to be understood, as do the margins required at each level before a price to the consumer can be set. These can sometimes almost double the price in an overseas market compared with at home. Overseas transportation may incur the additional costs of insurance, packaging and shipping. *Taxes and tariffs* also vary from country to country. A tariff is a fee charged when goods are brought into a country from another country. Although tariff barriers have fallen among the member states of Europe, they can still be formidable between other countries. Companies active in non-domestic business need to protect themselves against the costs of *exchange rate fluctuations*. Nestlé, for example, lost $1 million in six months due to adverse exchange rate moves (Cateora, Graham and Ghauri, 2006). Companies are increasingly asking that transactions be written in terms of the vendor company's national currency, and *forward hedging* (which effectively allows future payments to be settled at around the exchange rate in question when the deal was made) is commonly practised.

Care should be taken when *quoting a price* to an overseas customer. The contract may include such items as credit terms, currency of exchange, quality standards, quantities, responsibilities for the goods in transit and who pays insurance and transportation charges, and it may specify the currency. The price quoted can vary considerably, depending on these factors.

Understanding the competition and customers: as with any pricing decision, these factors play a major role. The difference is that information is often more difficult to acquire for exporters, because of the distances involved. When making pricing moves, companies need to be aware of the present *competitors' strategic degrees of freedom*, how much room they have to react, and the possibility of the price being used as a weapon by companies entering the market from a different industry. Where prices are high and barriers to entry are low, incumbent companies are especially vulnerable.

Companies also need to be wary of using **self-reference criteria** when evaluating overseas customers' perceptions. This occurs when an exporter assumes that the choice criteria, motivations and behaviour that are important to overseas customers are the same as those used by domestic customers. The viewpoints of domestic and foreign consumers to the same product can be very different. For example, a small Renault car is viewed as a luxury model in Spain but utilitarian in Germany. This can affect the price position vis-à-vis competitors in overseas markets.

Marketers entering products into foreign markets need to *understand how to use appropriate pricing tactics* in the face of increasingly fierce global competition.

Parallel importing: a major consideration in foreign markets is the threat of parallel imports. These occur when importers buy products from distributors in one country and sell them in another to distributors who are not part of the manufacturer's normal distribution system. The motivation for this practice occurs when there are large price differences between countries and the free movement of goods between member states means that it is likely to grow. Companies protect themselves by:

- lowering price differentials
- offering non-transferable service/product packages
- changing the packaging—for example, a beer producer, by offering differently shaped bottles in various countries, ensured that the required recyclability of the product was guaranteed only in the intended country of sale (Leszinski, 1992).

Another means of parallel importing (or 'grey market' trading, as it is sometimes called) is by supermarkets buying products from abroad to sell in their stores at reduced prices. A landmark legal battle was won by Levi Strauss to prevent Tesco, the UK supermarket chain, from selling Levi's jeans imported cheaply from outside Europe.

Transfer pricing: this is the price charged between profit centres (e.g. manufacturing company to foreign subsidiary) of a single company. Transfer prices are sometimes set to take advantage of lower taxation in some countries than others. For example, a low price is charged to a subsidiary in a low-tax country and a high price in one where taxes are high. Similarly, low transfer prices may be set for high-tariff countries. Transfer prices should not be based solely on taxation and tariff considerations, however. For example, transfer pricing rules can cause subsidiaries to sell products at higher prices than the competition even though their true costs of manufacture are no different.

Counter-trade: not all transactions are concluded in cash; goods may be included as part of the asking price. Four major forms of counter-trade are as follows.

1 *Barter*: payment for goods with other goods, with no direct use of money; the vendor then has the problem of selling the goods that have been exchanged.
2 *Compensation deals*: payment using goods and cash. For example, General Motors sold $12 million worth of locomotives and diesel engines to former Yugoslavia and received $8 million in cash plus $4 million worth of cutting tools (Cateora, Graham and Ghauri, 2006).
3 *Counter-purchase*: the seller agrees to sell a product to a buyer and receives cash. The deal is dependent on the original seller buying goods from the original buyer for all or part of the original amount.
4 *Buy-backs*: these occur when the initial sale involves production plant, equipment or technology. Part or all of the initial sale is financed by selling back some of the final product. For example, Levi Strauss set up a jeans factory in Hungary that was financed by the supply of jeans back to the company.

A key issue in setting the counter-trade 'price' is valuing the products received in exchange for the original goods and estimating the cost of selling on the bartered goods. However, according to Shipley and Neale, this forms 20–30 per cent of world trade, with yearly value exceeding $100 billion (Shipley and Neale, 1988).

Place

A key market decision when trading abroad is whether to use importers/distributors or the company's own personnel to distribute a product in a foreign market. Initial costs are often lower with the former method, so it is often used as an early method of market entry. For example, Sony and Panasonic originally entered the US market by using importers. As sales increased, Sony and Panasonic entered into exclusive agreements with distributors, before handling their own distribution arrangements by selling directly to retailers (Darlin, 1989).

Marketers must not assume that overseas distribution systems should resemble their own. As we have mentioned, Japan is renowned for its long, complex distribution channels; in Africa, the physical landscape and the underdeveloped transport infrastructure create many challenges. Nonetheless, Kenyan growers have established distribution networks that enable beans, mangoes and other fresh produce to be picked, processed, packed and transported to markets in northern Europe and the USA within a few short days. An important consideration when evaluating a distribution channel is the power of its members. Selling directly to large powerful distributors such as supermarkets may seem attractive logistically, but the distributors' ability to negotiate low prices needs to be considered.

Customer expectations are another factor that has a bearing on the channel decision. For many years, in Spain, yoghurt was sold through pharmacies (as a health product). As customers expected to buy yoghurt in pharmacies, suppliers had to use pharmacies as an outlet. Regulations also affect the choice of distribution channel. For example, over-the-counter pharmaceuticals are sold only in pharmacies in Belgium, France, Spain and Italy, whereas in Denmark, the UK and Germany, other channels (notably grocery outlets) also sell them.

Nevertheless, there can be opportunities to standardize at least part of the distribution system. For example, BMW standardizes its dealerships so that customers have the same experience when they enter their showrooms around the world (*Campaign*, 2005). Fiat adopted a similar approach when launching the Fiat 500 in the USA. The Italian car manufacturer insisted that all dealerships invested heavily to convert showrooms to create an 'Italian' feel to the customer experience.

As with domestic marketing, the marketing mix in a foreign market needs to be blended into a consistent package that provides a clear position for the product in the marketplace. Furthermore, managers need to display high levels of commitment to their overseas activities, as this has been shown to be a strong determinant of performance (Chadee and Mattsson, 1998).

Review

1 **The reasons why companies seek foreign markets**

- The reasons are: to find opportunities beyond saturated domestic markets; to seek expansion beyond small, low-growth domestic markets; to meet customer expectations; to respond to competitive forces (e.g. the desire to attack an overseas competitor); to act on cost factors (e.g. to gain economies of scale); and to achieve a portfolio balance where problems of economic recession in some countries can be balanced by growth in others.

2 **The factors that influence which foreign markets to enter**

- The factors are macroenvironmental issues (economic, socio-cultural and political–legal) and microenvironmental issues (market attractiveness, which can be assessed by analysing market size and growth rate, degree of competition, the costs of serving the market, profit potential and market accessibility) and company capability profile (skills, resources, product adaptability and the ability to create a competitive advantage).

3 **The range of foreign market entry strategies**

- Foreign market entry strategies are indirect exporting (using, for example, domestic-based export agents), direct exporting (using, for example, foreign-based distributors); licensing (using, for example, a local licensee with access to a set of technologies or know-how); joint venture (where, for example, two or more companies form a partnership to share the risks, costs and profits) and direct investment (where, for example, a foreign producer is bought or new facilities built).

4 **The factors influencing foreign market entry strategies**

- The factors are the risk of losing proprietary information (for example, direct investment may be used to avoid this risk), resources (for example, when resources are low, exporting using agents or distributors may be favoured) and the desired level of control (for example, when high control is desired, direct investment or exporting using the company's staff may be preferred).

5 **The influences on the degree of standardization or adaptation**

- A useful rule of thumb is to go global (standardize) when you can and stay local (adapt) when you must.
- The key influences are: cost; the need to meet local regulations, language and needs; the sensitivities of local managers, who may perceive a loss of status associated with greater centralized control; media availability and promotional preferences; and organizational structure and culture (for example, where subsidiaries hold considerable power).

6 **The special considerations involved in designing a marketing mix for global markets**

- The special considerations are where there are huge research and development costs, where a brand concept is based on an authentic national heritage that transcends global boundaries, where a global segment of like-minded people can be exploited, and where a cohesive positioning statement makes sense because of increasing global travel. All of these considerations favour a standardized marketing mix. Where there are strong local differences, an adapted marketing mix is required.

7 **How to organize for global marketing operations**

- Many companies begin with an export department, but this may be replaced later by more complex structures.
- Four types of structure for managing a worldwide business enterprise are: international (where overseas operations are appendages to a central domestic operation), global (where overseas operations are delivery pipelines to a unified global market), multinational (where overseas operations are managed as a portfolio of independent businesses) and transnational organizations (which are characterized by a complex process of coordination and cooperation in an environment of shared decision-making).

Key Terms

adapted marketing mix an international marketing strategy for changing the marketing mix for each foreign target market

contractual joint venture two or more companies form a partnership but no joint enterprise with a separate identity is formed

counter-trade a method of exchange where not all transactions are concluded in cash; goods may be included as part of the asking price

direct exporting the handling of exporting activities by the exporting organization rather than by a domestically based independent organization

direct investment market entry that involves investment in foreign-based assembly or manufacturing facilities

equity joint venture where two or more companies form a partnership that involves the creation of a new company

foreign consumer culture positioning positioning a brand as associated with a specific foreign culture (e.g. Italian fashion)

franchising a form of licensing where a package of services is offered by the franchisor to the franchisee in return for payment

global consumer culture positioning positioning a brand as a symbol of a given global culture (e.g. young cosmopolitan men)

indirect exporting the use of independent organizations within the exporter's domestic market to facilitate export

licensing a contractual arrangement in which a licensor provides a licensee with certain rights, for example to technology access or production rights

local consumer culture positioning positioning a brand as associated with a local culture (e.g. local production and consumption of a good)

self-reference criteria the use of one's own perceptions and choice criteria to judge what is important to consumers. In global marketing the perceptions and choice criteria of domestic consumers may be used to judge what is important to foreign consumers

standardized marketing mix a marketing strategy for using essentially the same product, promotion, distribution, and pricing in all the company's global markets

transfer pricing the price charged between the profit centres of the same company, sometimes used to take advantage of lower taxes in another country

Study Questions

1. **What are the factors that drive companies to enter global markets?**
2. **Discuss possible entry methods for markets in Europe.**
3. **For a company of your choice, research its reasons for expanding into new foreign markets and describe the moves that have been made.**
4. **Using information in this chapter and from Chapter 17 on distribution, describe how you would go about selecting and motivating overseas distributors.**
5. **Why are so many companies trying to standardize their global marketing mixes? With examples, show the limitations to this approach.**
6. **What are the factors that influence the choice of market entry strategy?**
7. **Select a familiar advertising campaign in your country and examine the extent to which it is likely to need adaptation for another country of your choice.**
8. **Describe the problems of pricing in overseas markets and the skills required to price effectively in the global marketplace.**

9. **Explain the importance of Guanxi when seeking to enter Chinese markets.**

10. **Suggest how technology is affecting the expansion of digital brands.**

Recommended Reading

Acting local and thinking global is becoming easier -in principle- read about developing international marketing strategies; entering new markets and the influence of strategic groups on foreign market entry.

Cadogan, J. (2012) International marketing, strategic orientations and business success: Reflections on the path ahead, *International Marketing Review* 29(4), 340–8.

Chen, H.-C. (2018) Entry mode, technology transfer and management delegation of FDI, *International Review of Economics & Finances* 54 (March), pp 232–243.

Mas-Ruiz, F. Ruiz-Conde, E. and Calderon-Martinez, A. (2018) Strategic group influence on entry mode choices in foreign markets, *International Business Review* 27, pp 1259–1269

References

Aaker, D.A. and Joachimsthaler, E. (2002) *Brand Leadership*, New York: Free Press, 303–9.

Agarwal, S. and Ramaswami, S.N. (1992) choice of foreign market entry mode: impact of ownership, location and internalisation factors, *Journal of International Business Studies*, Spring, 1–27.

Aharoni, S. (1966) *The Foreign Investment Decision Process*, Boston, MA: Harvard University Press.

Alden, D.L., Steenkamp, J.-B.E.M. and Batra, R. (1998) Brand positioning through advertising in asia, north america, and europe: the role of global consumer culture, *Journal of Marketing*, 63, January, 75–87.

Amazon.com Inc. (2018) *Amazon Services Europe*, amazon.co.uk, 10 May. http://services.amazon.co.uk/services/global-selling/overview.html (accessed October 2018)

Anderson, E. and Coughlan, A.T. (1987) international market entry and expansion via independent or integrated channels of distribution, *Journal of Marketing* 51, January, 71–82.

Armstrong, A. (2017) Dixons Carphone posts record full-year profits, *The Telegraph*28th June https://www.telegraph.co.uk/business/2017/06/28/dixons-carphone-posts-record-full-year-profits/ (accessed October 2018)

Attwood, J. (2018) Analysis: How Volkswagen is Conquering China, *AutoCar*, 7 June https://www.autocar.co.uk/car-news/industry/analysis-how-volkswagen-conquering-china (accessed August 2018).

Banerjee, A. (1994) Transnational advertising development and management: an account planning approach and a process framework, *International Journal of Advertising* 13, 95–124.

Benady, D. (2003) Uncontrolled immigration, *Marketing Week*, 20 February, 24–7.

Bersin, J. (2012) How Does Leadership Vary Across the Globe? *Forbes*, 31 October. http://www.forbes.com/sites/joshbersin/2012/10/31/are-expat-programs-dead (accessed 10 May 2015).

Birchall, J. and Parkers, C. (2006) Assault on West Coast market, *Financial Times*, 10 February, 21.

Bloomgarden, K. (2000) Branching out, *Marketing Business*, April, 12–13.

Bryant, C. (2015) BMW warns earnings growth will slow as China car market cools, *The Financial Times*, 18 March. http://www.ft.com/cms/s/0/3446253c-cd66-11e4-9144-00144feab7de.html#axzz3abkp6PRp (accessed October 2018)

Buckley, P.J., Mirza, H. and Sparkes, J.R. (1987) Foreign direct investment in japan as a means of market entry: the case of European companies, *Journal of Marketing Management* 2(3), 241–58.

Butler, S. (2017) Weak pound brings record number of tourists to UK in August, *The Guardian*, 17 November, https://www.theguardian.com/business/2017/nov/17/weak-pound-record-number-tourists-uk-august (accessed October 2018)

Campaign (2005) When the World is your Market, 27 May, 46–7.

Cassidy, A. (2017) Made.com founder: 'We want to be the new IKEA', *The Guardian*, 18 September. https://www.theguardian.com/small-business-network/2017/sep/18/madecom-founder-we-want-to-be-the-new-ikea (accessed October 2018).

Cateora, P.R., Graham, J.L. and Ghauri, P.J. (2006) *International Marketing*, London: McGraw-Hill, 376.

Chadee, D.D. and Mattsson, J. (1998) Do service and merchandise exporters behave and perform differently? *European Journal of Marketing* 32(9/10), 830–42.

Chan, T.F. (2018) China will lift part of its @Great fire wall@ to give foreigners access to Facebook, YouTube and Twitter, on a tropical island dubbed 'Hawaii of the east. *Business Insider*, 25 June, http://uk.businessinsider.com/china-great-firewall-hainan-censorship-2018-6 (accessed October 2018)

Chan, C. and Makino, S. (2007) Legitimacy and multi-level institutional environments: Implications for foreign subsidiary ownership structure, *Journal of International Business Studies* 38(4), 621–38.

Charles, C. (2008) Coors Seeks Feminine Touch, *Marketing*, 27 August, 16.

Chen, H.-C., (2018) Entry mode, technology transfer and management delegation of FDI, *International Review of Economics & Finances* 54 (March), 232–43.

CIA (2015) The World Factbook, https://www.cia.gov/library/publications/the-world-factbook/rankorder/2078rank.html (accessed October 2018)

Conway, T. and Swiff, J.S. (2000) International relationship marketing, *European Journal of Marketing* 34(1/2), 1391–413.

Darlin, D. (1989) Myth and marketing in Japan, *Wall Street Journal*, 6 April, B1.

De Chernatony, L. (1993) Ten hints for EC-wide brands, *Marketing*, 11 February, 16.

DIT (2018) About DIT, https://www.gov.uk/government/organisations/department-for-international-trade/about-our-services (accessed October 2018) (Accessed August 2018).

Dudley, J.W. (1989) *1992: Strategies for the Single Market*, London: Kogan Page.

Erramilli, M.K. (1991) Entry mode choice in service industries, *International Marketing Review* 7(5), 50–62.

Ghauri, P.N. and Holstius, K. (1996) The role of matching in the foreign market entry process in the Baltic states, *European Journal of Marketing* 30(2), 75–88.

Gottilieb, J. and Connington, J. (2017) Mapped: how the pound has fared against currencies around the world since Brexit, *The Telegraph*, 18 August, https://www.telegraph.co.uk/money/consumer-affairs/mapped-pound-has-fared-against-currencies-around-world-since/ (accessed October 2018)

Gribeben, R. (2013) Jaguar Land Rover: £1.3bn Tata gamble pays off as big cat purrs at last, *The Telegraph*, 15 September. http://www.telegraph.co.uk/finance/newsbysector/transport/10310725/Jaguar-Land-Rover-1.3bn-Tata-gamble-pays-off-as-big-cat-purrs-at-last.html (accessed 10 May 2015).

Harris, G. and Attour, S. (2003) The international advertising practices of multinational companies: a content analysis study, *European Journal of Marketing* 37(1/2), 154–68.

Harris, P. and McDonald, F. (1994) *European Business and Marketing: Strategic Issues*, London: Chapman.

Henni, A. (2012) Russia's technology boom attracts foreign investment, *The Telegraph*, 3 April. http://www.telegraph.co.uk/sponsored/rbth/technology/9183881/Russia-technology-foreign-investors.html (accessed 2 May 2015).

Hise, R. and Choi, Y.-T. (2010) Are US companies employing standardization or adaptation strategies in their international markets? *Journal of Business and Cultural Studies* 4, 1–29.

Hopkinson, G.C. and Hogarth-Scott, S. (1999) Franchise relationship quality: microeconomic explanations, *European Journal of Marketing* 33(9/10), 827–43.

Jobber, D. and Lancaster, G. (2015) *Selling and Sales Management*, London: Pitman.

Johanson, J. and Vahlne, J.-E. (1977) The internationalisation process of the firm: a model of knowledge development and increasing foreign market commitments, *Journal of International Business Studies* 8(1), 23–32.

Isa, C. Saman, H. and Rashidah, S. (2014) Specific-factors Influencing Market Selection Decision by Malaysian Construction Firms into International Market, *Procedia Social and behavioural Sciences* 129, 4–10.

Killough, J. (1978) Improved pay-offs from transnational advertising, *Harvard Business Review*, July–Aug., 58–70.

Kirby, K. (2000) Globally led, locally driven, *Marketing Business*, May, 26–7.

Klein, S. and Roth, J.R. (1990) Determinants of export channel structure: the effects of experience and psychic distance reconsidered, *International Marketing Review* 7(5), 27–38.

Knickerbocker, F.T. (1973) *Oligopolistic Reaction and Multinational Enterprise*, Boston, Mass: Harvard University Press.

Leszinski, R. (1992) Pricing for a single market, *McKinsey Quarterly* 3, 86–94.

Levitt, T. (1983) The globalization of markets, *Harvard Business Review*, May/June, 92–102.

Lewis, E. (2006) Going global, *The Marketer*, June (Issue 25), 7–9.

Litvak, I.A. and Banting, P.M. (1968) A Conceptual Framework for International Business Arrangements, in King, R. L. (ed.) *Marketing and the New Science of Planning*, Chicago: American Marketing Association, 460–7.

Lovell, C. (2008) Universal truths cross booze borders, *Campaign*, 15 August, 8.

Lu, J. (2002) Intra- and inter-organisational imitative behavior: Institutional influences on Japanese firms' entry mode choice, *Journal of International Business Studies* 33(1), 19–37.

Luce, E. (2002) Hard sell to a billion consumers, *Financial Times*, 15 April, 14.

Mas-Ruiz, F. Ruiz-Conde, E. and Calderon-Martinez, A. (2018) Strategic group influence on entry mode choices in foreign markets, *International Business Review* 27, 1259–69.

Mayer, M. (1991) *Whatever Happened to Madison Avenue? Advertising in the '90s*, Boston, MA: Little, Brown, 186–7.

Mazur, L. (2002) No Pain, No Gain, *Marketing Business*, September, 10–13.

Mitchell, A. (1993) Can branding take on global proportions? *Marketing*, 29 April, 20–1.

Mole, J. (1990) *Mind Your Manners*, London: Industrial Society.

Neff, J. (2010) The dirt on laundry trends around the world: Unilever, P&G, Henkel adjust products to suit cultural preferences—and washing temperatures, *Advertising Age*, 14 June. http://adage.com/article/global-news/global-marketing-dirt-laundry-trends-world/144398 (accessed October 2018)

Ngwenyama, O. and Morawczynski, O. (2009) Factors affecting ICT expansion in emerging economies: an analysis of ICT infrastructure expansion in five Latin American countries, *Information Technology for Development* 15(4), 237–58.

Niss, N. (1996) Country of origin marketing over the product life cycle: a Danish case study, *European Journal of Marketing* 30(3), 6–22.

Papavassiliou, N. and Stathakopoulos, V. (1997) Standardisation versus adaptation of international advertising strategies: towards a framework, *European Journal of Marketing* 31(7), 504–27.

Pitas, C. (2018) Nissan Honda, Toyota warn about Brexit high stakes, *Reuters*, 9 February, http://europe.autonews.com/article/20180209/ANE/180209764/nissan-honda-toyota-warn-about-brexit-high-stakes (accessed October 2018)

Prasad, A. (2011) The impact of non-market forces on competitive positioning understanding global industry attractiveness through the eyes of M. E. Porter, *Journal of Management Research*, 11(3), 131–7.

Quelch, J.A. and Hoff, E.J. (1986) Customizing global marketing, *Harvard Business Review*, May–June, 59–68.

Raconteur (2013) Marketplaces: underpinning the growth in e-commerce, Raconteur.net, 24 September. http://raconteur.net/business/marketplaces-underpinning-the-growth-in-e-commerce (accessed October 2018)

Ram, A. (2018) Foreign retailers seek to overcome barriers to Indian expansion, *The Telegraph*, 16 February, https://www.ft.com/content/299457fa-ef7c-11e6-930f-061b01e23655 (accessed October 2018)

Rampton, J (2010) Trying to sell Marmite to Indians? *The Telegraph*, 6 May, https://www.telegraph.co.uk/culture/tvandradio/7685963/Trying-to-sell-Marmite-to-Indians-We-must-be-mad-Theo-Paphitis-on-his-latest-business-idea.html (accessed October 2018)

Rigby, E. and Leaky, J. (2008) Tesco finds its passage to India, *The Guardian*, 13 August, 17.

Sachgau, O. (2018) BMW Trails Mercedes, Audi in China with sales drop in May, *Bloomberg* https://www.bloomberg.com/news/articles/2018-06-12/bmw-trails-mercedes-audi-in-china-with-sales-drop-in-may (accessed August 2018).

Salacuse, J.W. (2004) Negotiating: The Top Ten Ways That Culture Can Affect Your Negotiation, *Ivey Business Journal*.

Sandler, C. and Churkina, O. (2011) *Glocalization—a measure of global brands*. ESOMAR.

Sharma, D.D. (1988) Overseas market entry strategy: the technical consultancy companies, *Journal of Global Marketing* 2(2), 89–110.

Shipley, D. and Neale, B. (1988) Countertrade: reactive or proactive, *Journal of Business Research*, June, 327–35.

Sungwook, M. Namwoon, K. and Ge, Z. (2017) The impact of market size on new market entry: contingency approach, *European Journal of Marketing* 51(1), 2–22.

Taylor, C., Zou, S. and Osland, G. (2000) Foreign market entry strategies of Japanese MNCs, *International Marketing Review* 17(2), 146–63.

Terpstra, V. and Sarathy, R. (1999) *International Marketing*, Fort Worth, TX: Dryden.

Tesco plc (2014) Annual Report and Financial Statement 2014. http://www.tescoplc.com/files/pdf/reports/ar14/download_strategic_report.pdf (accessed 2 May 2015).

The Economist (2008) The Challengers, 12 January, 61–3.

Tovey, A. (2017) China's Geely adds to Swedish Assets with AB Volvo stake, *The Telegraph*, 27 December https://www.telegraph.co.uk/business/2017/12/27/chinas-geely-adds-swedish-assets-taking-major-stake-truck-maker/ (accessed August 2018).

Wachman, R. (2004) Papa of the branded bags, *Observer*, 25 July, 16.

Welford, R. and Prescott, K. (2000) *European Business*, London: Pitman.

West, A. (1987) *Marketing Overseas*, London: Pitman.

Whitehead, J. (2008) More to Citroën campaign than stereotypes, *The Guardian*, 22 September, 7.

Whitelock, J. and Jobber, D. (1994) The Impact of Competitor Environment on Initial Market Entry in a New, Global market, *Proceedings of the Marketing Education Group Conference*, Coleraine, July, 1008–17.

Whitelock, J. and Jobber, D. (2004) An evaluation of external factors in the decision of UK industrial companies to enter a new nondomestic market: an exploratory study, *European Journal of Marketing* 38(1/2), 1437–56.

Wolfe, A. (1991) The 'Eurobuyer', How European businesses buy, *Market Intelligence and Planning* 9(5), 9–15.

Wright, R.W. (1981) Evolving International Business Arrangements, in Dhawan, K. C., H. Etemad and R. W. Wright (eds) *International Business: A Canadian Perspective*, Reading, MA: Addison Wesley.

Yang, S. (2014) China Said to Plan Sweeping Shift From Foreign Technology to Own, *Bloomberg Business*, 17 December. http://www.bloomberg.com/news/articles/2014-12-17/china-said-to-plan-sweeping-shift-from-foreign-technology-to-own (accessed 2 May 2015).

Young, S., Hamill, J., Wheeler, C. and Davies, J.R. (1989) *International Market Entry and Development*, Englewood Cliffs, NJ: Prentice-Hall.

CASE 41
IKEA

Building a Cult Global Brand

IKEA is a global colossus built on contemporary design, low prices and an enthusiasm that few organizations can equal. Perhaps more than any other company in the world, IKEA has become a curator of people's lifestyles, if not their lives. At a time when consumers face so many choices for everything they buy, IKEA provides a one-stop sanctuary for coolness. It is a trusted safe zone that people can enter and where they can immediately be part of a like-minded cost/design/environmentally sensitive global tribe.

The IKEA concept has plenty of room to run: the retailer accounts for just 5–10 per cent of the furniture market in most of the countries in which it operates. It is, however, a global phenomenon. This is because IKEA is far more than a furniture merchant. It sells a lifestyle that consumers around the world embrace as a signal that they've arrived, have good taste and recognize value. 'If it wasn't for IKEA,' wrote British design magazine *Icon*, 'most people would have no access to affordable contemporary design.' The magazine even voted IKEA founder, Ingvar Kamprad, the most influential taste master in the world.

As long as consumers from Moscow to Beijing and beyond keep striving to enter the middle class, there will be a need for IKEA. No mass-market retailer has had more success globally—not Walmart, which, despite vast strengths, has stumbled in Brazil, Germany and Japan, nor France's Carrefour, which has never made it in the USA. IKEA has had its slip-ups, too. But right now its 313 stores, mainly in Europe, Asia, Australia and the USA, are thriving, hosting over 500 million shoppers a year.

Why the Uproar?

IKEA is the quintessential global cult brand. Just take its stunts. Before an Atlanta opening, IKEA managers invited locals to apply for the post of ambassador of *kul* (Swedish for fun). The five winners wrote an essay on why they deserved $2,000 in vouchers. There was one catch. They would have to live in the store for three days before the opening, take part in contests and sleep in the bedding department. 'I got about

eight hours of sleep total because of all the drilling and banging going on,' says winner Jordan Leopold, a manager at Costco Wholesale.

Leopold got his bedroom set. And IKEA got to craft another story about itself—a story picked up in the press that drew even more shoppers. More shoppers, more traffic. More traffic, more sales. More sales, more buzz. Such buzz has kept IKEA's sales growing at a healthy rate: in 2017, sales revenues were a colossal $39.9 billion, with profits of $2.9 billion. IKEA maintains these profits even while it cuts prices steadily. IKEA's operating margins of approximately 10 per cent are among the best in home furnishing.

To keep growing at that pace, IKEA has continued its new store openings around the world, with up to 20 per year (although that number has reduced in recent years). IKEA has boosted its profile in three of its fastest-growing markets: the USA, Russia (where IKEA is already a huge hit—today's Russian yuppies are called 'the IKEA generation') and China (now worth over $1 billion in sales). In the USA, the number of stores has grown from 25 in 2005 to 45 in 2017. IKEA is also investing in emerging markets such as the Czech Republic and India. In the UK, IKEA has built smaller multi-level city stores in Coventry and Southampton in response to restrictions on building out-of-town retail establishments.

The key to these roll-outs is to preserve the strong enthusiasm IKEA evokes—an enthusiasm that has inspired endless shopper comment on the internet. Examples: 'IKEA makes me free to become what I

TABLE C41.1 IKEA at a glance

Privately owned home products retailer that markets flat-pack furniture, accessories, and bathroom and kitchen items globally.
Ikea is the world's largest furniture manufacturer.
Sales of $39.9 billion (2017).
Estimated profits of $2.9 billion (2017).
Number of stores in 2017: 301 in 313 countries, mainly in Europe, USA, Canada, Asia and Australia. The largest number of stores are in Germany (53) and USA (45). Ikea owns 276 stores, and 37 are franchises.

want to be' (from Romania). Or this: 'Half my house is from IKEA—and the nearest store is six hours away' (the USA). Or this: 'Every time, it's trendy for less money' (Germany).

The Shopping Experience

What enthrals shoppers and scholars alike is the store visit, a similar experience the world over. The blue-and-yellow buildings average 28,000 square metres in size, about equal to five football fields. The sheer number of items—7,000, from kitchen cabinets to candlesticks—is a decisive advantage. 'Others offer affordable furniture,' says Bryan Roberts, research manager at Planet Retail, a consultancy in London, 'But there's no one else who offers the whole concept in the big shed.'

The global middle class, which IKEA targets, share buying habits. The $50 Billy bookcase, $13 Lack side table and $190 Ivar storage system are best-sellers worldwide. Even spending per customer is similar. According to IKEA, the figure in Russia is $85 per store visit—exactly the same as in affluent Sweden.

Wherever they are, customers tend to think of the store visit as more of an outing than a chore. That's intentional. IKEA practises a form of 'gentle coercion' to keep you for as long as possible. Right at the entrance, for example, you can drop off your kids at the playroom, an amenity that encourages more leisurely shopping.

Then, clutching your dog-eared catalogue (the print run is over 160 million—more than the Bible, IKEA claims), you proceed along a marked path through the warren of showrooms. 'Because the store is designed as a circle, I can see everything as long as I keep walking in one direction,' says Krystyna Gavora, an architect who frequents IKEA in Schaumburg, Illinois, USA. Wide aisles let you inspect merchandise without holding up traffic. The furniture itself is arranged in fully accessorized displays, down to the picture frames on the nightstand, to inspire customers and get them to spend more. The settings are so lifelike that one writer staged a play at IKEA in Renton, Washington, USA.

Along the way, one touch after another seduces the shopper, from the paper measuring tapes and pencils to strategically placed bins with items like pink plastic watering cans, scented candles and picture frames. These are things you never knew you needed, but at less than $2 each you load up on them anyway. You set out to buy a $40 coffee table but end up spending $500 on everything from storage units to glassware. 'They have this way of making you believe nothing is expensive,' says Bertille Faroult, a shopper at IKEA on the outskirts of Paris. The bins and shelves constantly surprise. IKEA replaces a third of its product line every year.

Then, there's the stop at the restaurant, usually placed at the centre of the store, to give shoppers a breather and encourage them to keep going. You proceed to the warehouse, where the full genius of founder Kamprad is on display. Nearly all the big items are flat-packed, which not only saves IKEA millions in shipping costs from suppliers, but also enables shoppers to haul their own stuff home—another saving. Finally, you have the fun, or agony, of assembling at home, equipped with nothing but an Allen key and those cryptic instructions.

A vocal minority rails at IKEA for its long queues, crowded car parks, exasperating assembly experiences and furniture that's hardly built to last. The running joke is that IKEA is Swedish for particle board. But the converts outnumber the critics. And for every fan who shops at IKEA, there seems to be one working at the store itself.

The fanaticism stems from founder Ingvar Kamprad, who died in 2018, a figure as important to global retailing as Wal-mart's Sam Walton. Kamprad started the company in 1943 at the age of 17, selling pens, Christmas cards and seeds from a shed on his family's farm in southern Sweden. In 1951, the first catalogue appeared. Kamprad penned all the text himself until 1963. His credo of creating 'a better life for many' is enshrined in his almost evangelical 1976 tract, *A Furniture Dealer's Testament*. Peppered with folksy titbits—'divide your life into 10-minute units and sacrifice as few as possible in meaningless activity', 'wasting resources is a mortal sin' (that's for sure: employees are the catalogue models) or the more revealing 'it is our duty to expand'—the pamphlet is given to all employees the day they start.

»

Employees at IKEA will never get rich, but they do get to enjoy autonomy, very little hierarchy and a family-friendly culture. In return, they buy in to the culture of frugality and style that drives the whole company.

Kamprad initiated the practices that define IKEA culture. One is egalitarianism. IKEA regularly stages anti-bureaucracy weeks, during which executives work on the shop floor or tend the checkouts.

Prices and Costs

A feature of IKEA is its steely competitiveness. You get a sense of this at one of IKEA's main offices, in Helsingborg, Sweden. At the doorway, a massive bulletin board tracks weekly sales growth, names the best-performing country markets and identifies the best-selling furniture. The other message that comes across loud and clear: cut prices. IKEA designers found a way to pack the Ektorp three-seater sofa more compactly, doubling the amount of sofa they could get into a given space. The cost saving meant that $135 could be shaved from its price.

The montage vividly illustrates IKEA's relentless cost-cutting. The retailer aims to lower prices across its entire offering by an average of 2 per cent to 3 per cent each year. It goes deeper when it wants to hit rivals in certain segments. 'We look at the competition, take their price and then slash it in half,' says Mark McCaslin, manager of IKEA Long Island, in Hicksville, New York.

It helps that frugality is as deeply ingrained in the corporate DNA as the obsession with design. Managers, even the top brass, fly economy. Steen Kanter, who left IKEA in 1994 and now heads his own retail consultancy in Philadelphia, USA—Kanter International—recalls that while flying with founder Ingvar Kamprad once, the boss handed him a coupon for a car rental he had ripped out from an in-flight magazine.

This cost obsession fuses with the design culture. 'Designing beautiful-but-expensive products is easy,' says Josephine Rydberg-Dumont, president of IKEA of Sweden. 'Designing beautiful products that are inexpensive and functional is a huge challenge.'

No design—no matter how inspired—finds its way into the showroom if it cannot be made affordable. To achieve that goal, the company's 12 full-time designers at Almhult, Sweden, along with 80 freelances, work hand in hand with in-house production teams to identify the appropriate materials and least costly suppliers, a trial-and-error process that can take as long as three years. Example: for the PS Ellan, a $39.99 dining chair that can rock back on its hind legs without tipping over, designer Chris Martin worked with production staff for a year and a half to adapt a wood-fibre composite, an inexpensive blend of wood chips and plastic resin used in highway noise barriers, for use in furnishings. Martin also had to design the chair to break down into six pieces, so it could be flat-packed and snapped together without screws.

With a network of 2,000 suppliers in over 50 countries, IKEA works overtime to find the right manufacturer for the right product. It once contracted with ski makers—experts in bent wood—to manufacture its Poang armchairs, and it has tapped makers of supermarket carts to turn out durable sofas. Simplicity, a tenet of Swedish design, helps keep costs down. The 50-cent Trofé mug came only in blue and white, the least expensive pigments. IKEA's conservation drive extends naturally from this cost-cutting. For its PS line, it challenged 28 designers to find innovative uses for discarded and unusual materials. The results: a table fashioned from reddish-brown birch heartwood (furniture makers prefer the pale exterior wood) and a storage system made from recycled milk cartons.

Adaptation to Local Tastes

Adding to the challenge, the suppliers and designers have to customize some IKEA products to make them sell better in local markets. In China, the 250,000 plastic placemats IKEA produced to commemorate the year of the rooster sold out in just three weeks. Julie Desrosiers, the bedroom line manager at IKEA of Sweden, visited people's houses in the USA and Europe to peek into their closets, learning that 'Americans prefer to store most of their clothes folded, and Italians like to hang.' The result was a wardrobe that features deeper drawers for US customers.

The US market poses special challenges for IKEA, because of the huge differences inside the USA. 'It's so easy to forget the reality of how people live,' says IKEA's US interior design director, Mats Nilsson. For example, IKEA realized it might not be reaching California's Hispanics, so its designers visited the homes of Hispanic staff. They soon realized they had set up the store's displays all wrong. Large Hispanic families need dining tables and sofas that fit more than two people, the Swedish norm. They prefer bold colours to the more subdued Scandinavian palette and display tons of pictures in elaborate frames. Nilsson warmed up the showrooms' colours, adding more seating and throwing in numerous picture frames.

IKEA is particularly concerned about the USA, since it is key to expansion—and since IKEA came close to blowing it. 'We got our clocks cleaned in the early 1990s because we really didn't listen to the consumer,' says Kanter. Stores weren't big enough to offer the full IKEA experience, and many were in poor locations. Prices were too high. Beds were measured in centimetres, not king, queen and twin. Sofas weren't deep enough, curtains were too short, and kitchens didn't fit US-size appliances. 'American customers were buying vases to drink from, because the glasses were too small,' recalls Goran Carstedt, the former head of IKEA North America, who helped engineer a turnaround. Parts of the product line were adapted (no more metric measurements), new and bigger store locations chosen, prices slashed and service improved. Now US managers are paying close attention to the tiniest details. 'Americans want more comfortable sofas, higher-quality textiles, bigger glasses, more spacious entertainment units,' says Pernille Spiers-Lopez, head of IKEA North America.

In 2018, IKEA opened its first store in India, where 1,000 families were researched to understand their aspirations, their frustrations and what they wanted. IKEA also took into account their customs, tastes and disposable incomes. Consequently, alongside the normal IKEA furniture like Billy bookshelves, the store sells locally relevant products like masala boxes, Indian frying pans called tawas, rice cake makers and mattresses with coconut-fibre centres. Over 1,000 products are priced at less than 200 rupees ($2.5), and the research revealed that Indians were averse to assembling furniture, with small, family-owned businesses usually providing the service. In response, IKEA has teamed up with UrbanClap, an online platform that connects consumers looking for an assembly service with tradespeople.

The Future

Can the cult keep thriving? IKEA has stumbled badly before. A foray into Japan 30 years ago was a disaster (the Japanese wanted high quality and great materials, not low price and particle board). The company returned to Japan in 2006. IKEA is also seeing more competition than ever. In the USA, Target recruited top designer Thomas O'Brien to develop a range of low-priced furnishings. An IKEA-like chain called Fly is popular in France. In Japan, Nitori is the major player in low-cost furniture. ILVA is successfully selling upmarket furniture in Denmark and Sweden, although its foray into the UK market was unsuccessful.

Perhaps the bigger issue is what happens inside IKEA. 'The great challenge of any organization as it becomes larger and more diverse is how to keep the core founding values alive,' says Harvard Business School professor Christopher A. Bartlett. IKEA is still run by managers who were trained and groomed by Kamprad himself—and who are personally devoted to the founder. As the direct links with Kamprad disappear, the culture may start to fade.

For now, the fans keep clamouring for more. At least once a year, Jen Segrest, a 36-year-old freelance web designer, and her husband make a 10-hour round-trip from their home in Middletown, Ohio, USA, to IKEA in Schaumburg, Illinois, near Chicago. 'Every piece of furniture in my living room is IKEA—except for an end table, which I hate. And next time I go to IKEA I'll replace it,' says Segrest. To lure the retailer to Ohio, Segrest has even started a blog called OH! IKEA. The banner on the home page reads 'IKEA in Ohio—because man cannot live on Target alone.'

Questions

1. **IKEA has chosen to enter new markets mainly by direct investment. What advantages does this form of entry give it? Why doesn't IKEA use franchising like McDonald's and Benetton do as its main method of entering new markets?**
2. **How would you categorize IKEA's approach to developing an international marketing strategy in terms of standardization and adaptation?**
3. **What are the factors that have helped IKEA to build a successful global brand?**

This case study was written by David Jobber, Emeritus Professor of Marketing, University of Bradford.

References

Based on: Sains, A., C. Lindblad, A. T. Palmer, J. Bush, D. Roberts and K. Hall (2005) IKEA: How The Swedish Retailer Became a Golbal Cult Brand, *Business Week*, 14 November, 45–54; Wearden, G. (2009) IKEA to Cut More Jobs, *The Guardian*, 8 July, 22; Clark, N. (2008) ILVA, Marketing, 30 January, 20; Boyle, C. (2009) IKEA to Cut More Staff as Demand Falls Falls, www.business.timesonline.co.uk/tol/business; Anonymous (2011) The Secret of Ikea's Success, *Economist*, 26 February, 634; BBC News (2012) Ikea Profits Rise Ten Per Cent as Emerging Markets Boost Sales, www. bbc.co.uk/news/business; Anonymous (2015) Ikea Repeats Flat Profits Despite Rising Sales, www.bbc.co.uk/news/business, 28 January; Anonymous (2018) About Ikea, www.ikea.com/ms/jp_GB/about ikea/factsand figures; France-Presse, A. (2018) Masala Boxes and Swedish Meatballs—IKEA Opens Its First Store in India, *The Guardian*, 10 August, 29.

CASE 42

Subway Germany: Getting Steadily Underway

The world loves fast food. And Germany is no exception. Burgers? Pizza? Kebabs? Sushi? Currywurst? There has never been a wider choice of fast-food offerings. According to Euromonitor, the German fast-food market recorded a value of €13.3 billion in 2017 and is expected to reach sales of €14 billion by 2022.

So, what is driving fast-food consumption in Europe's largest economy? First, the increase in the number of fast-food outlets. There are about 42,200 outlets in Germany, which means that a quick bite is within easy reach. Moreover, Germans are more willing to experiment with more exotic cuisines such as Asian or Mexican. Second, aggressive pricing strategies; for example, a cheeseburger at McDonald's costs just €1.30 and has created new 'snacking' opportunities. Third, consumers are attracted to the convenience of fast food. The rise of the gig economy and flexible working times has created a need for fast food available at all times of the day or night. Hectic lifestyles mean that time has become a scarce commodity. Fast food saves all the time and hassle of cooking at home—particularly in single households. Next, fast-food outlets have become a social space to spend time with family and friends. The 'Starbucks experience' has been extended to other settings—such as McCafé, where consumers are trading up to enjoy a latté with a muffin. Finally, the fast food-industry has responded to consumer health concerns with the introduction of perceived healthier options. For example, a choice of salads and wraps are now omnipresent at McDonald's.

Subway: Global Success

This should all seem like good news for the restaurant chain Subway, which has long been positioned as the 'healthier' fast-food alternative. It is claimed that the sandwich was invented by John Montagu, the fourth Earl of Sandwich in 1762. Fast-forward more than 300 years to 1965 when Fred DeLuca and Peter Buck opened the first Subway store in the US state of Connecticut: consumers rediscovered a new way to appreciate what had become boring old sandwiches. The submarine sandwich (known as a 'sub') was born and named for its resemblance to naval vessels of that shape. The number of Subway outlets in the USA is currently 25,166. The long-standing advertising slogan 'Eat fresh' has been replaced by 'Make it what you want', which explains how every sandwich is made to order using a variety of baked breads, fillings, toppings and sauces. With 2 million different combinations available, there is something for everyone—as long as they have an appetite!

The Subway sub may not be a major product innovation breakthrough, but it has, just the same, become an exponential success in the global market. Subway opened its first international restaurant in Bahrain in 1984. This was the start of an aggressive global expansion plan. The franchise format ensured Subway's expansion, not only rapidly, but with limited capital investment required by the franchisee and the franchisor.

Subway now has more restaurants in the world than any other restaurant chain does: 43,202 outlets in over 100 countries, with outlets from Afghanistan to the Virgin Islands. Subway claims on its website that 'We've become the leading choice for people seeking quick, nutritious meals that the whole family can enjoy.'

Subway Germany: Sink or Swim?

The expansion of Subway's network accelerated across the globe with a curious exception—Germany. The first German Subway restaurant opened in Berlin in 1999, and Subway was able to expand, as in other international markets, with its franchise model that emphasizes small, low-cost outlets. Franchisees at Subway pay a fee of 12.5 per cent of their sales turnover to the franchiser, from which 4.5 per cent is put aside for advertising support. The franchisee is also able to benefit from Subway's franchise support system, which includes employee training, product development and advertising, as well as a purchasing cooperative and field support.

By 2009, the German Subway chain had grown to 798 outlets. However, while Subway was able to sustain growth in the fast-food market in other European markets, in Germany consumers were turning up their noses and turning their backs on the chain.

TABLE C42.1 Selected fast-food companies in Germany, 2017

	McDonald's	Nordsee	KFC	Starbucks
Number of outlets	1,480	310	161	154
Turnover (million euro)	3,255*	285,2	243,7	125**

** Estimated*

***2016*

Source: Bundesverband der Systemgastronie (BdS)

TABLE C42.2 Sub of the day (U-Bahn des Tages)

Monday	Italian B.M.T.
Tuesday	Salami
Wednesday	Turkey
Thursday	Chicken fajita
Friday	Tuna
Saturday	Turkey and ham
Sunday	Chicken breast

The result was the closure of Subway restaurants up and down the country, with only 619 Subway restaurants remaining in 2016.

This anomaly of Subway Germany's market performance was more pronounced given that bread is deeply rooted in German culinary culture (a mouth-watering 58.9 kg of bread was consumer per household in 2017) and that Germans are collectively striving to follow healthier lifestyles. Subway's highly customized offering even includes ultra-healthy options, such as subs with 6° g or less of fat.

So why was Subway leaving a sour taste in the mouths of German consumers? If Subway were to turn around the business, it was critical to understand why Germans were jumping overboard.

Competitive Overpressure

McDonald's is undoubtedly the giant of the German fast-food market. However, the fast-food market in Germany remains fairly fragmented and diverse, giving the consumer greater choice. It is estimated that there are about 16,000 independent doner kebab outlets, generating an annual turnover of €2.5–3 billion. Moreover, Subway is not the only quick-service restaurant chain to offer so-called 'better-for-you' meals. The increasingly popular burger chains (e.g. Five Guys) and sushi restaurant chains (e.g. Sushi Circle) are offering premium fast-food alternatives.

Significantly, Subway in Germany is subject to direct competition from approximately 11,347 master bakeries: 46,000 sales outlets can be found on the high streets. For instance, the bakery chain Wiener Feinbäcker has over 250 outlets in Germany. These bakeries sell bread rolls (*Brötchen*) that are freshly prepared with conventional fillings such as ham and cheese with a slice of pickle, using traditional German bread. Lunchtime queues are not uncommon as consumers seek the convenience of consistent home-style quality closer to their workplace.

However, the recent success of low-cost discount bakery chains that also sell filled rolls has created new competitive price pressures. Backwerk, for example, has over 300 outlets in Germany, Austria and Switzerland, and offers a wide selection of traditional filled rolls at competitive low prices.

In this competitive environment, many Subway franchise holders looked towards the franchiser for an action plan to revive their business fortunes—a recipe for success.

Local Taste Buds

Germans' passion for bread may have actually been turning them off the Subway sandwich. There are more than 3,000 different varieties of bread in Germany, and it may be that Germans do not wish to accept 'imposed quality and taste'. Product localization, which has been the forefront of McDonald's global strategy, is now subtly being adopted by Subway to adapt the chain to the culinary expectations of the German market.

The introduction of locally inspired breads such as wholemeal bread, familiar to the average German, is one example. Similarly, fillings such as barbecue ribs and meat balls, considered too strange and foreign for the German palate, have since been dropped from the menu. However, this doesn't mean that Germans are not open to new flavours. Chicken teriyaki is, according to Subway's managing director, the favourite sub in Germany!

The Product Proposition

As in other global markets, Subway has attempted to boost sales through expanding its customer base and increasing restaurant frequency. The 'sub of the day' ('U-Bahn des Tages') initiative allows customers to enjoy a different sandwich each day for a set price of €2.90. This price point might well be a critical factor, as Germans are regarded as being particularly value-conscious consumers. Subway has also introduced a breakfast menu for early morning commuters in selected outlets and a kids' menu (Kids' Pack), including collectable toys such as 'Beyblades', to build a stronger relationship with younger customers.

»

New Communication Routes

Fast-food brands appeal to the emotions and behaviours of the fast-food consumer to win over their hearts and minds, and wallets and purses. Although it remains difficult for Subway to compete against the huge media budgets of its international competitors, it has returned to television brand advertising. Its latest campaign brings to life the core message, '*Von Hand. Für Dich*', which translates to 'Hand crafted. For you.' (The campaign can be viewed at https://www.youtube.com/watch?v=I0Ef81GyUVY.)

Subway, however, continues to invest in social media to connect with its younger and technologically savvy customer base. Subway Germany has over 900,000 likes on Facebook, and it launched a digital storytelling campaign that showcases behind-the-scenes stories of Subway employees. (The Storytelling campaign can be viewed at http://alles-fuer-dein-sub.subway-sandwiches.de)

Moreover, Subway was the first fast-food player in Germany to launch an electronic loyalty card. The SUBCARD, which is also available as an app, encourages customers to take advantage of special promotions and collect points for purchases made at Subway, which can be redeemed for Subway products.

The Right Direction?

The German market has been traditionally difficult for many foreign retailers. Dunkin Donuts is the latest casualty to close down outlets in Germany.

Latest data suggest that Subway Germany may indeed have weathered the storm and may be heading in the right direction. According to internal data, 2017 was a record year for Subway Germany, with a sales turnover increase of 4.5 per cent. Subway has returned to expansion with the opening of 41 new outlets in 2017.

Has Subway passed dangerous waters? There are future potential routes to be followed, including plans to expand its collaboration with Shell petrol stations and develop its home delivery service in collaboration with Delivery Hero. Further, Subway has embarked on revamping its store design to be consistent with its new 'Fresh Forward' concept.

However, Subway cannot assume that further storms do not lie ahead. The fast-food industry remains fiercely competitive as battles still wage to win over the fast-food customer with new and innovative marketing initiatives. For example, McDonald's has launched made-to-order burgers and has even introduced table service in some restaurant outlets.

Can Subway Germany do better than just stay afloat?

'Fresh Forward' Subway, Hauptbahnhof Frankfurt Oder

Source: the Subway Media Site: https://www.subway-franchise.de/presse/

Questions

1. **Conduct a strengths, weaknesses, opportunities and threats (SWOT) analysis of Subway Germany. Prioritize your key findings and discuss options for Subway Germany to deal with them.**
2. **Discuss the advantages and disadvantages of Subway using franchising in order to enter new international markets.**
3. **Discuss Subway Germany's approach to developing an international marketing strategy in terms of standardization and adaptation. Maybe also visit the Subway Germany website and make comparisons with the Subway UK or US local site for specific examples.**

This case was prepared by Glyn Atwal, Burgundy School of Business, France, and Douglas Bryson, Rennes School of Business, France.

References

Based on: Deutsches Brotinstitut e. V. (2017), Zahlen und Fakten zu Brot https://www.brotinstitut.de/brotinstitut/zahlen-und-fakten-zu-brot/; Subway Germany (2018), Pressebereich Subway® Deutschland!, https://www.subway-franchise.de/presse/; Wachter, D.S. (2017), Herr Fux, sind Ihre Sandwiches wirklich so gesund, wie Sie behaupten?, https://www.stern.de/genuss/essen/subway-chef-deutschland—sind-ihre-sandwiches-wirklich-so-gesund—7890282.html; Zentralverband des Deutschen Bäckerhandwerks e. V. (2017), Wirtschaftsfaktor Bäckerhandwerk, https://www.baeckerhandwerk.de/baeckerhandwerk/zahlen-fakten/

CHAPTER 22
Managing Marketing Implementation, Organization and Control

> *There is nothing more difficult than to take the lead in the introduction of a new order of things.*
>
> **MACHIAVELLI**

LEARNING OBJECTIVES

After reading this chapter, you should be able to:

1. describe the relationship between marketing strategy, implementation and performance
2. identify the stages that people pass through when they experience disruptive change
3. describe the objectives of marketing implementation and change
4. discuss value-based approaches to delivering the marketing concept
5. discuss the forms of resistance to marketing implementation and change
6. explain how to develop effective implementation strategies
7. describe the elements of an internal marketing programme
8. discuss the skills and tactics that can be used to overcome resistance to the implementation of the marketing concept and plan
9. discuss marketing organizational structures
10. explain the nature of a marketing control system

Designing marketing strategies and positioning plans that meet today's and tomorrow's market requirements is a necessary but not a sufficient condition for corporate success—they need to be translated into action through effective implementation. Throughout this book, we explore the theoretical principles and business practices that are key to understanding this dynamic and complex subject. In this chapter, we focus on: the importance of implementation for business outcomes; the relationship between strategy, implementation and performance; how people react to change; and the objectives of implementation. We also explore resistance to change that might result from implementing the marketing strategy, and the skills and tactics that marketing managers can use to bring about marketing implementation and change. Finally, we examine how companies organize their marketing activities and establish control procedures to check that objectives have been achieved.

Marketing Strategy, Implementation and Performance

Marketing strategy concerns the issues of *what* should happen and *why* it should happen. Implementation focuses on actions: *who* is responsible for various activities, *how* the strategy should be carried out, *where* things will happen and *when* action will take place. Managers devise marketing strategies to meet new opportunities, counter environmental threats and match core competences. The framework for strategy development was discussed in Chapter 18 as part of the marketing planning process. Although implementation is a consequence of strategy, it also affects planning and is an integral part of the strategy development process. The proposition is straightforward: without a well-organized implementation, even the best strategy is likely to fail. Implementation capability is an integral part of strategy formulation, and the link between the two is shown in Figure 22.1. Implementation affects marketing strategy choice. For example, a company that traditionally has been a low-cost, low-price operator may have a culture that finds it difficult to implement a value-added, high-price strategy. Strategy also determines implementation requirements: for example, a value-added, high-price strategy may require the salesforce to refrain from price discounting.

Combining strategies and implementation

Bonoma has argued that combinations of appropriate/inappropriate strategy and good/poor implementation will lead to various business outcomes (Bonoma, 1985). Figure 22.2 shows the four-cell matrix, with predicted performances.

Appropriate strategy–good implementation

This is the combination most likely to lead to success. No guarantee of success can be made, however, because of the vagaries of the marketplace, including competitor actions and reactions, new technological breakthroughs and plain bad luck; but with strong implementation backing sound strategy, marketing management has done all it can to build success.

Appropriate strategy–bad implementation

This combination is likely to lead to trouble if substandard performance is attributed to poor strategy. Management's tendency to look for strategy change in response to poor results will result in a less appropriate strategy being grafted onto an already wayward implementation system.

Inappropriate strategy–good implementation

Two effects of this combination can be predicted. First, the effective implementation of a poor strategy can hasten failure. For example, very effectively

FIGURE 22.1
Marketing strategy and implementation

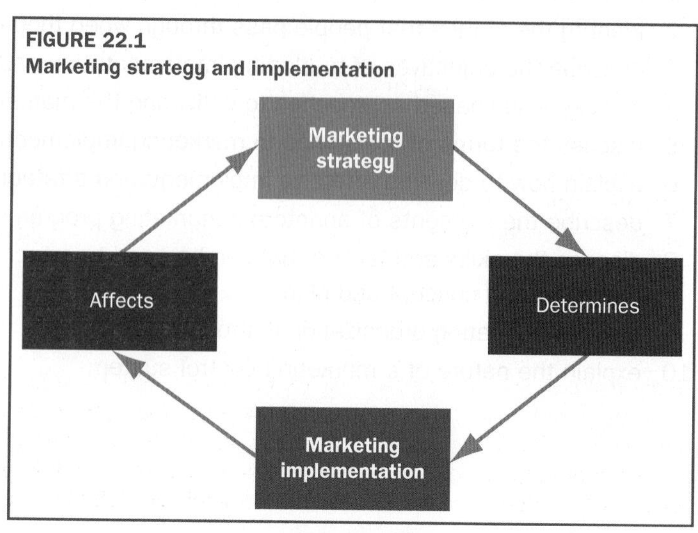

communicating a price rise (which is part of an inappropriate repositioning strategy) to customers may accelerate a fall in sales. Second, if good implementation takes the form of correcting a fault in strategy, then the outcome will be favourable. For example, if strategy implies an increase in sales effort to push a low margin *dog* product to the detriment of a new *star* product in a growing market (perhaps for political reasons), modification at the implementation level may correct the bias. The reality of marketing life is that managers spend many hours supplementing, subverting, overcoming or otherwise correcting shortcomings in strategic plans.

FIGURE 22.2
Marketing strategy, implementation and performance

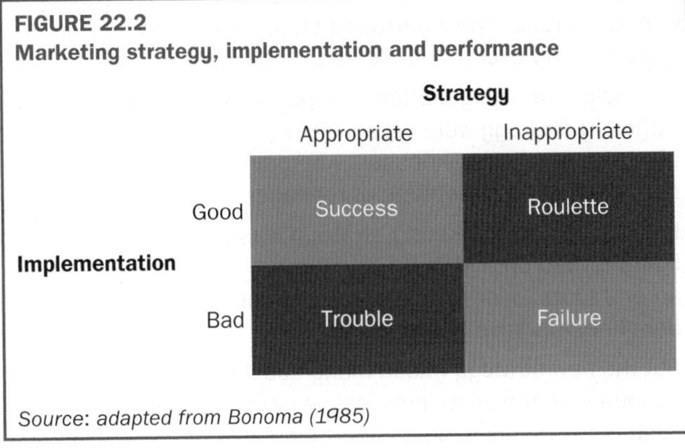

Source: adapted from Bonoma (1985)

Inappropriate strategy–bad implementation

This obviously leads to failure, which is difficult to correct because so much is wrong. An example might be a situation where a product holds a premium price position without a competitive advantage to support the price differential. The situation is made worse by an advertising campaign that is unbelievable and a salesforce that makes misleading claims leading to customer annoyance and confusion.

Implications

So, what should managers do when faced with poor performance? First, strategic issues should be separated from implementation activities and the problem should be diagnosed. Second, when in doubt about whether the problem is rooted in strategy or implementation, implementation problems should be addressed first so that strategic adequacy can be assessed more easily. Read Mini Case 22.1 to find out how Abercrombie & Fitch is struggling to find an appropriate strategy to revive the brand.

MINI CASE 22.1
Is Abercrombie & Fitch playing roulette?

Abercrombie & Fitch has been said to be *the best-run fashion brand on the planet*, but declining sales and falling share prices in recent years have led to doubts about whether this iconic fashion brand can survive in the digital age.

Mike Jeffries became CEO of Abercrombie & Fitch in 1992. He had a vision for developing the brand that would turn it into an '*exclusive club for teenagers*'. His implementation of the vision was striking: he alienated and offended the parents of his target audience—teenagers—but this approach appealed to the young people. In his first two years in control the turnover doubled, and within five years the brand had reached $1 billion in sales.

However, the dimly lit stores—which were designed to have the look and feel of an exclusive nightclub, with loud music and perfumed air, and to give the target audience (*cool kids . . .* with *attitude and a lot of friends*) a feeling of belonging to an exclusive, high-status echelon of youth society—began to alienate the more mainstream customers. Ordinary teenagers who dared to venture into a store, passing by the slender assistants with highly toned bodies and polished looks, were disappointed if they were looking for a size XL or larger. The brand's policy of only selling smaller sizes was part of its controversial positioning of only selling to *beautiful people*. Other alienated groups were potential gift buyers—parents, relatives and older friends of the target teenagers—who found Abercrombie & Fitch stores unpleasant to visit and highly over-priced.

»

Feminist groups were outraged by its provocative slogans on T-shirts; Hispanic, black and Asian groups sued the company over its employment policies.

Arguably, the highly proficient implementation of Mike Jeffries' vision, brand positioning and exceedingly focused targeting strategy were responsible for the brand's success and failure. The factors that made the brand strong also exposed its weaknesses. Abercrombie & Fitch's positioning became out of kilter with the expectations of the newly emerging generation of teenagers, and the brand was also losing touch with its ageing core market.

In 2015, a new marketing strategy was implemented to revive the brand. Larger sizes were introduced, the lights turned up and the music turned down. The new leadership stopped hiring the 'beautiful' people and put an end to its 'overtly sexualized marketing with the iconic images of half-naked teenagers'. Finally, the athletic door-keepers have been retired.

But the new strategy raised many questions. What does this implementation mean for the brand? What has happened to the edgy, provocative heritage of the brand, and what are today's anarchic teenagers expected to latch onto? Perhaps most importantly, has the new strategy turned around the failing brand? Apparently not. Abercombie & Fitch has seen revenue fall by almost 70 per cent and has begun closing stores. Store closures have boosted profitability, but the reach of the brand has arguably been reduced on the high streets of the world.

So in 2017, Fran Horowitz, the latest CEO, is to take on the challenge of Abercombie & Fitch. She is quoted as saying that the brand is a 'quintessential part of American pop culture', with a 125-year history. Applying her optimistic and collaborative approach towards management, she has plans to reinvigorate the brand and make much greater use of online channels to reach target markets and put the customer first.

Questions:

1 How have the key strategic issues facing Abercrombie & Fitch changed since Fran Horowitz took over?

2 Fran aims to reinvigorate the brand. Suggest ways of using digital channels to put the customer first.

3 Imagine you had replaced Mike Jeffries. Suggest where you would have taken the brand and how you would implement your new strategy.

Based on: Ritson (2015); Saner (2012); Trefis Team (2014), Bergstein, (2017); Total Retail (2018)

Implementation and the Management of Change

A key factor in implementing a change programme is top management support. Without management's clear, visible and consistent backing, a major change programme is likely to falter under the inertia created by vested interests (Johannessen, Olaisen and Havan, 1993). It is important for companies to monitor change and ensure that systems are in place to gather and disseminate information throughout the organization. For example, Cisco invites key clients to discussions, workshops and collaboration meetings, using a combination of face-to-face and technology-driven approaches such as video and WebEx cloud conferencing to enhance customer relationships. The objectives are to analyse how the company can develop to better serve the customers. Cisco's partnership approaches not only enable it to gain first-hand knowledge of customer preferences, but also to ensure that the entire organization is immediately aware of customers' experiences and demands, which helps to build stronger and closer customer relationships (Cisco, 2015).

The implementation of a new strategy may have profound effects on people in organizations. Brand managers who discover that their product is to receive fewer resources (be harvested) may feel bitter and demoralized; a salesperson who loses because of a change in the payment system may feel equally aggrieved. The implementation of a strategy move is usually associated with the need for people to adapt to *change*. The cultivation of change, therefore, is an essential ingredient in effective implementation.

It is helpful to understand the emotional stages that people pass through when confronted with an adverse change. These stages are known as the **transition curve** and are shown in Figure 22.3 (Wilson, 1993).

Numbness

The first reaction is usually shock. The enormity of the consequences leads to feelings of being overwhelmed, despair and numbness. The outward symptoms include silence and lack of overt response. The news that a field salesforce is to be replaced by a telemarketing team is likely to provoke numbness in the field salespeople. More people are likely

FIGURE 22.3
The transition curve

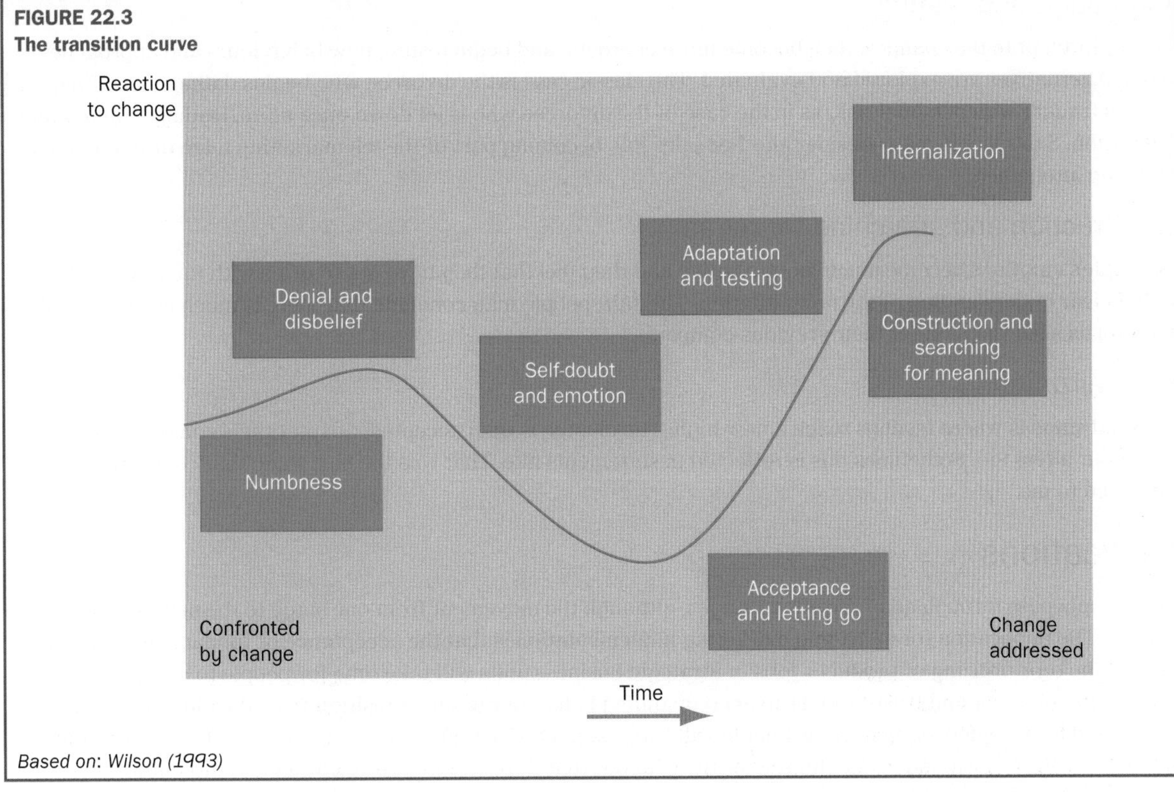

Based on: Wilson (1993)

to experience being replaced as rapid advances in technology such as artificial intelligence, robotics and self-service systems enable machines to do the work of humans. This means that managers must be more aware of how to manage change and must reassess the changing skills needed. See Exhibit 22.1.

EXHIBIT 22.1
Automation and the world of work

Denial and disbelief

Denial and disbelief may follow numbness, leading to trivializing the news, denying it or joking about it. The aim is to minimize the psychological impact of the change. News of the abandonment of the field salesforce may be met by utter disbelief and sentiments such as 'They would never do that to us.'

Self-doubt and emotion

As the certainty of the change dawns, so personal feelings of uncertainty may arise. The feeling is one of powerlessness, of being out of control—the situation has taken over the individual. The likely reaction is one of anger: both as individuals and as a group, salesforce staff are likely to vent their anger and frustration on management.

Acceptance and letting go

Acceptance is characterized by tolerating the new reality and letting go of the past. This is likely to occur at an emotional low point but is the beginning of an upward surge as comfortable attitudes and behaviours are severed and the need to cope with the change is accepted. In the salesforce example, salespeople would become accustomed to the fact that they will no longer be calling upon certain customers and receiving a particular salary.

Adaptation and testing

As people adapt to the changes, they become more energetic and begin testing new behaviours and approaches to life. Alternatives are explored and evaluated. The classic case is the divorcee who begins dating again. This stage is fraught with personal risk, as in the case of the divorcee who is let down once more, leading to anger and frustration. Salespeople may consider another sales job, becoming part of the telemarketing team or moving out of selling altogether.

Construction and searching for meaning

As people's emotions become much more positive and they feel that they have got to grips with the change, they seek a clear understanding of the new situation. The salespeople may conclude that there is much more to life than working as a salesperson for their previous company.

Internalization

The final stage is where feelings reach a new high. The change is fully accepted, adaptation is complete, and behaviour alters too. Sometimes this is reflected in statements like 'That was the best thing that could have happened to me.'

Implications

Most people pass through all of the above stages, although the movement from one stage to the next is rarely smooth. The implication for managing marketing implementation is that the acceptance of fundamental change such as the reprioritizing of products, jobs or strategic business units will take time for people to accept.
The venting of anger and frustration is an accompanying behaviour to this transition from the old to the new and should be accepted as such. Some people will leave as part of the fifth stage—the testing of new behaviours—but others will see meaning in and internalize the changes that have resulted from strategic redirection.
See Marketing in Action 22.1 to find out how large companies adapt to change.

MARKETING IN ACTION 22.1
The New Nokia: Leader in Smart Cities and the Internet Of Things

Remember Nokia, the failed mobile handset producer? Meet the new Nokia, leader in smart cities and Internet of Things (IoT) solutions.

A senior management team should provide leadership and ensure that a company provides goods and services in accordance with market demand. As the pace of change increases and competition intensifies, companies must become more agile and the senior management teams more responsive. So why do market leaders fail? For example, Nokia dominated the mobile phone market but lost out to its competitors, Apple and Samsung, in the handset market.

Entrenched management processes. Budgeting, planning performance reviews and succession planning—the processes that drive a business—are often not adapted in line with new trading environments and conditions. Sometimes, these processes are so deeply engrained in the company that they are rarely challenged. So companies should regularly review their processes and be prepared to change any that no longer add value.

Failure to monitor the competition. As markets change and develop, the key success factors on which companies compete can change rapidly, too, particularly for those companies operating in high-tech markets. For example, Nokia was not benchmarking carefully enough against competitors like Apple. Nokia's problems were not due to lack of technological invention, as it had a smartphone prototype, or because it hadn't recognized the changing market. The problem for Nokia was that it failed to successfully implement changes and did not make decisive, timely decisions—which ultimately meant it was not able to compete effectively in the emerging smartphone market.

Lack of management diversity. Senior management teams that have been successful over time tend to become homogeneous, that is, made up of people with similar world views. Consequently, there is a propensity for events, opportunities and marketplace changes to be missed. This was an issue for Nokia, as the top executives were all very similar in outlook, age and culture. In contrast, successful technology company Infosys proactively sought to avoid this situation by implementing a programme—the Voice of Youth programme—that gave the under-30s an opportunity to influence senior management decisions.

Intolerance of failure. Large companies can become risk-averse, as they perceive that there is more to lose if they make mistakes. Therefore, it is important to ensure that there is an innovative culture that tolerates failure if a company is to remain vital. Google, Amazon and Netflix all actively encourage an entrepreneurial and innovative culture.

In the mobile phone handset market, Nokia has paid a heavy price, as the brand largely disappeared when it became Microsoft Mobile in April 2015. Microsoft also took over Nokia's social media presence, as the new owner did not want any confusion over the positioning of the new brand. So, will those who remain on Nokia's team—satellite telecoms networks—have to watch the gradual disappearance of what was once an innovative market leader and iconic brand?

The answer is no. Nokia has been transformed; the company now focuses on creating the infrastructure and networks that are the foundation of the connected world. For example, Nokia's enterprise cloud and integrated solutions for IoT and smart cities are bringing innovations into the urban landscape.

Based on: Burke et al. (2007); Birkinshaw (2013); Chang (2012); Gokey (2015); Nokia (2018)

Objectives of Marketing Implementation and Change

The overriding objective of marketing implementation and change from a strategic standpoint is the successful execution of the marketing plan. This may include:

- gaining the support of key decision-makers in the company for the proposed plan (and overcoming the opposition of others)
- gaining the required resources (e.g. people and money) to be able to implement the plan
- gaining the commitment of individuals and departments in the company who are involved in frontline implementation (e.g. marketing, sales, service and distribution staff)
- gaining the cooperation of other departments needed to implement the plan (e.g. production and research and development).

For some people, the objectives and execution of the plan are consistent with their objectives, interests and viewpoints; gaining support from them is easy. But there are likely to be others who are involved with implementation who are less willing to support the planned change. They are the losers and neutrals. Loss may be in the form of lower status, a harder life or a reduction in salary. Neutrals may be left untouched overall with gains being balanced by losses. For some losers, support will never be forthcoming; for others they may be responsive to persuasion, whereas neutrals may be more willing to support change. Read Marketing in Action 22.2 to see how SAS gained support for its new marketing strategy.

FIGURE 22.4
The ladder of support

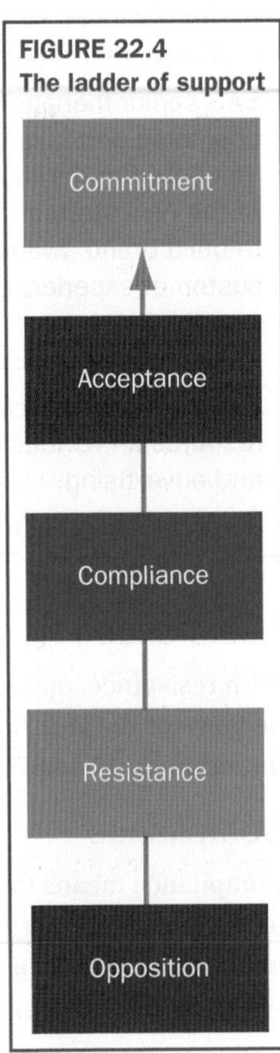

The ladder of support

What does support mean? Figure 22.4 illustrates the degree of support that may be achieved; this can range from outright opposition to full commitment.

Opposition

The stance of direct opposition is taken by those with much to lose from the implementation of the marketing strategy and who believe they have the political strength to stop the proposed change. Opposition is overt, direct and forceful.

MARKETING IN ACTION 22.2
SAS and Marketing Strategy: Success is in the Details

Scandinavian Airlines (SAS) is one of Scandinavia's most popular carriers, transporting over 28 million passengers a year with services to cities in 193 countries around the world. The company's business model is to efficiently serve its core customer group—frequent fliers in Scandinavia who want ease and convenience when they travel.

Compared with the rest of Europe, the Nordic market for air travel is fairly large, with Scandinavians usually preferring short-haul flights. These are the types of trips that SAS is well placed to provide and which are at the centre of its business strategy. But, like many other airlines, SAS is facing the challenge of continued economic weakness in Europe. This has caused the company to re-emphasize improving operating efficiencies as well as refocus its marketing strategy to better control its brand and communication efforts (especially digital ones). This last part is not surprising given that SAS has an estimated 700,000 fans on Facebook and 50,000 followers on Twitter, along with 100 million hits to its website every year.

The new marketing strategy is called 'We are travelers', and a key component is an innovative editorial concept called Scandinavian Traveler. The platform will incorporate and integrate 'a new onboard magazine, website, web TV, social media content, and newsletters' to better serve passengers and fans. SAS believes its marketing strategy will promote 'the idea of travel as part of our way of life' while celebrating 'the joy and anticipation we feel before a flight.' While the strategy might sound a bit idealistic, the company says that it arose from a clear analysis and deep understanding of its customers and the markets that it serves (the initial target audience is Sweden, Norway and Denmark). This provided senior management with some indication that implementation capabilities were already in place at SAS.

SAS senior management were sure to make the objectives of the new marketing strategy clear from the very beginning and take efforts to communicate them effectively throughout the organization in order to ensure 'buy in' from the over 13,000 people who work for the airline. These actions were critical if the implementation of the new strategy was to have any chance of success. The focus of the 'We are Travelers' campaign aimed to build brand awareness, and changes to the marketing implementation were aimed at improving the overall customer experience. Additionally, it was important to create a sense of community for the 80,000 people who fly SAS every day. The performance of the campaign was carefully tracked through detailed recording and measurement of data, another key element about successful marketing strategy implementation.

Along with the new strategy came a change in the way SAS allocated its marketing and communication resources. Previously, the company spent over 90 per cent of its budget on traditional paid media and advertising.

Based on: SAS (2019a), SAS (2019b).

Resistance

With resistance, opposition is less overt and may take a more passive form such as delaying tactics. Perhaps because of the lack of a strong power base, people are not willing to display open hostility but, nevertheless, their intention is to hamper the implementation process.

Compliance

Compliance means that people act in accordance with the plan but without much enthusiasm or zest. They yield to the need to conform but lack conviction that the plan is the best way to proceed. These reservations limit the lengths to which they are prepared to go to achieve the successful implementation of the plan. Staff feel valued when included in key organizational practices/activities.

Acceptance

A higher level of support is achieved when people accept the worth of the plan and actively seek to realize its goals. Their minds may be won, but their hearts are not set on fire, limiting the extent of their motivation.

Commitment

Commitment is the goal of an effective implementation programme. People not only accept the worth of the plan but also pledge themselves to secure its success. Both hearts and minds are won, leading to strong conviction, enthusiasm and zeal. This can be encouraged by making people feel valued. From Toyota to B&Q, a market-leading DIY chain in the UK, companies are using members of staff in their advertising campaigns. Pizza Hut used YouTube for an open casting call to find eight employees to feature in its ad campaigns. In this way, it was able to involve many hundreds of employees. The chief marketing officer said, 'There is no better way to express the emotional side of the brand than through the employees that actually deliver the brand experience every day' (Bruno, 2010). The trend for using employees in commercials has grown and is used by many brands. See Exhibit 22.2.

Value-based Approaches to deliver the Marketing Concept

Increasingly, marketing managers need to be adept at managing the internal environment of the company as well as the external. Furthermore, making a transition from a basic product offer to a value-based offer—which is increasingly the norm—raises many challenges (Matthyssens and Vandenbempt, 2008). We examine barriers to the implementation of the marketing concept (discussed in Chapter 1) from a value-based perspective.

EXHIBIT 22.2
Autoglass features its staff in TV adverts and online

Making the shift and implementing value-based approaches requires firms to make a significant transition. The marketing concept states that business success will result from creating greater customer satisfaction than the competition does. In today's markets, co-value creation is fundamental to businesses that want to move forwards from just offering a basic core product towards achieving a superior market position with a highly differentiated offer. Figure 22.5 shows the drivers and effects of moving from commoditized product offers to superior value-based solutions. Each element is now explained in relation to implementation.

FIGURE 22.5
Model of superior value creation

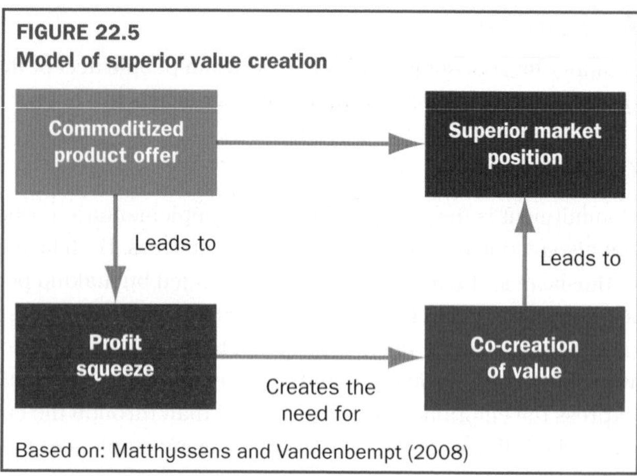

Based on: Matthyssens and Vandenbempt (2008)

Commoditization

Maximizing returns for a firm's stakeholders is a necessary but no longer a sufficient condition for creating superior economic performance (Barney, 2002). Marketing managers are increasingly put under pressure by the commoditization of their products and services due to intense global rivalry, shortening product lifecycles and increased transparency of pricing and products. **Commoditization** occurs when differentiated products lose their uniqueness and no longer stand out in the marketplace. For marketers, this is a significant issue and highlights the need for customized solutions that add value and ensure sustainable competitive advantage.

Profit squeeze

Commoditization can put pressure on firms wanting to provide highly differentiated offers and can lead to a squeeze on profits. Gillette introduced the Mach3 multi-blade razor, which enabled it to stand out—but the razor was quickly followed by Gillette's single-blade competitors. Sales growth and profits were squeezed due to price drops needed to maintain market share. The value of being in a commoditized market falls away and only the lowest-cost operators in the market survive as the emphasis is placed on efficiencies rather than effectiveness. For survival and growth, it becomes crucial for firms to understand how customer value is changing in each market (Boudier et al., 2015). Marketing managers should watch for signs of commoditization—for example increasing price sensitivity from customers, competitors frequently cutting prices, and/or consolidation occurring across the industry—as companies look to maintain competitive advantage through increased scale, expanded reach and improved capability. In the supermarket sector, Sainsury's and ASDA are planning a merger, expanding the range of products and services to give both brands protection from disruptive discounters Aldi and Lidl (Leyland and Quinn, 2018).

Co-creation of value

To deal with commoditization and falling profits, market-orientated firms should find ways to restore differentiation by increasing the value proposition. But be aware that customers may see price reductions as a desirable benefit, and therefore enjoy the effects of increased commoditization. However, firms are unlikely to survive in the longer term under such conditions—and if they fail, everyone potentially loses. So, customers need to understand the benefits of a value-based solution. Implementation of a value creation strategy should seek to inform and engage stakeholders across the value chain. Matthyssens and Vandenbempt (2008) suggest that this can be achieved by designing transition paths that guide a firm towards superior value creation. This involves overcoming barriers such as antagonistic relationships, based on resisting change, and personal ambitions, which can hinder the progress of marketing in an organization. Another force blocking implementation can be the gap between what senior managers say and what they do. Webster suggests that senior management must give clear signals and establish clear values and beliefs about serving the customer (Webster, 1988). However, Argyris (1966) found that senior executives' behaviour often conflicted with what they said—for example, they might say 'Be customer orientated' and then cut back on marketing research funds. This resulted in staff not really believing that management was serious about achieving a customer focus. Matthyssens and Vandenbempt (2008) argue for carefully planned, incremental steps towards co-creation of value that enable internal and external stakeholders to contribute to the implementation.

Superior Value

Value-adding strategies will, to a certain extent, be dependent on the industry and its critical success factors. Strategies might include: augmenting services to provide increased customization which delivers stronger ties with customers; innovations in products, process and or services which seek to make the competition irrelevant; identifying specialist niches and following a market focus strategy; and innovations in service delivery. Implementing one or a combination of these generic value-adding strategies can lead to the creation of superior value (Matthyssens and Vandenbempt, 2008). See Figure 22.5.

Forms of Resistance to Marketing Implementation and Change

Opposition to the acceptance of marketing and the implementation of marketing plans is direct, open and conflict driven. Often, arguments such as the lack of tangible benefits and the extra expense of marketing proposals will be used to cast doubt on their worth. Equally likely, however, is the more passive type of *resistance*. Kanter (1997) and Piercy (2008) suggest 10 forms of resistance.

1. Criticism of specific details of the plan
2. Foot-dragging
3. Flow response to requests
4. Unavailability
5. Suggestions that, despite the merits of the plan, resources should be channelled elsewhere
6. Arguments that the proposals are too ambitious
7. Hassle and aggravation created to wear the proposer down
8. Attempts to delay the decision, hoping that the proposer will lose interest
9. Attacks on the credibility of the proposer with rumour and innuendo
10. Deflation of any excitement surrounding the plan by pointing out the risks.

Market research reports supporting marketing action can also be attacked. Johnson (1987) describes the reaction of senior managers to the first marketing research report commissioned by a new marketing director.

> 'As a diagnostic statement the research was full, powerful, prescriptive. The immediate result of this analysis was that the report was rubbished by senior management and directors. The analysis may have been perceived by its initiator as diagnostic but it was received by its audience as a politically threatening statement.'

Ansoff and McDonnell (1990) argue that the level of resistance will depend on how much the proposed change is likely to disrupt the culture and power structure of the organization and the speed at which the change is introduced. The latter point is in line with the previous discussion about how people adapt to adverse change, requiring time to come to terms with disruptions. The greatest level of opposition and resistance will come when the proposed change is implemented quickly and is a threat to the culture and politics of the organization; the least opposition and resistance will be found when the change is consonant with the existing culture and political structure and is introduced over a period of time. Further, Pettigrew states that resistance is likely to be low when a company is faced with a crisis, arguing that a common perception among people that the organization is threatened with extinction also acts to overcome inertia against change (Pettigrew, 1985).

Developing Implementation Strategies

Faced with the likelihood of resistance from vested interests, a **change master** should develop an implementation strategy that can deliver the required change (Kanter, 1997). For example, when Anne Mulcahy was CEO at Xerox, the company was in trouble and she had to act as a change master. She began by talking to customers and employees to gain an understanding of what was wrong. She ran meetings differently, forcing people to face the tough decisions that were necessary, and used the severity of the crisis at Xerox to gain acceptance for the

FIGURE 22.6
Managing implementation

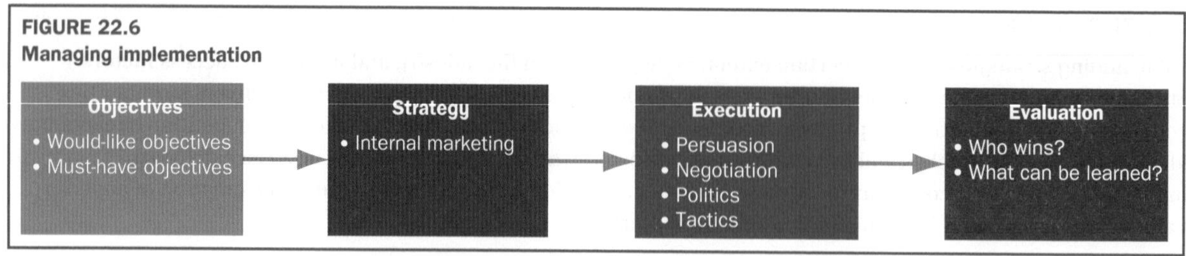

required changes, which included cutting $1 billion of overheads and closing unprofitable businesses (London and Hill, 2002). The workforce was cut by almost 40 per cent, while gaps in Xerox's product portfolio were filled with lower-priced products. This gave the company its largest product portfolio and has made it more competitive. Mulcahy was succeeded in 2009 by Ursula Burns, who was instrumental in pulling Xerox back from the brink of bankruptcy (Forbes Media, 2018). See Exhibit 22.3 to see what drives Ursula Burns to succeed.

A change master is a person who is responsible for driving through change within an organization. This necessitates a structure for thinking about the problems to be tackled and the way to deal with them. Figure 22.6 illustrates such a framework. The process starts with a definition of objectives.

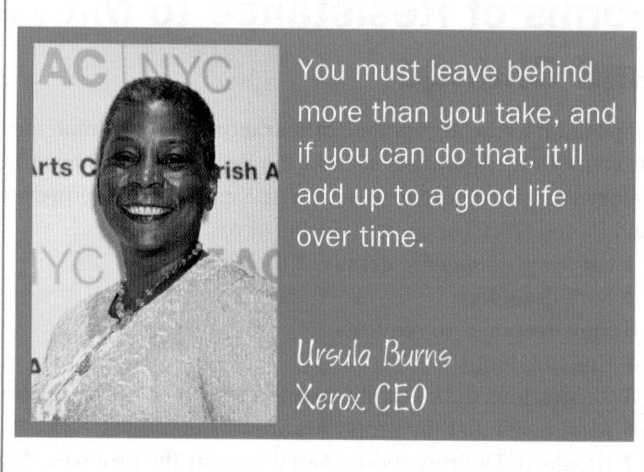

EXHIBIT 22.3
Ursula Burns believes in the power of people to help themselves through education

Implementation objectives

These are formulated at two levels: what we would like to achieve (*would-like objectives*) and what we must achieve (*must-have objectives*). Framing objectives in this way recognizes that we may not be able to achieve all that we desire. Would-like objectives are our preferred solution; they define the maximum that the implementer can reasonably expect (Kennedy, Benson and MacMillan, 1987). Must-have objectives define our minimum requirements; if we cannot achieve these, then we have lost, and the plan or strategy will not succeed. Between the two points there is an area for negotiation, but beyond our must-have objective there is no room for compromise.

By clearly defining objectives at the start, we know what we would like, the scope for bargaining, and the point where we have to be firm and resist further concessions. For example, suppose our marketing plan calls for a move from a salary-only payment system for salespeople to salary plus commission. This is predicted to lead to strong resistance from salespeople and some sales managers who favour the security element of fixed salary. Our would-like objective might be a 60:40 split between salary and commission. This would define our starting point in attempting to get this change implemented. But to give room for allowances, our must-have objective would be somewhat lower, perhaps an 80:20 ratio between salary and commission. Beyond this point we refuse to bargain: we either win or lose on the issue. In some situations, however, would-like and must-have objectives coincide: here there is no room for negotiation, and persuasive and political skills are needed to drive through the issue.

Internal marketing strategy

All worthwhile plans and strategies necessitate substantial human and organizational change inside companies (Piercy, 1990). Marketing managers, therefore, need a practical mechanism for thinking through strategies to drive change. One such framework is known as internal marketing and is widely seen as an important element of value creation (Boukis and Gournairs, 2014; Shyh-Rong et al., 2014;).

FIGURE 22.7
Internal marketing

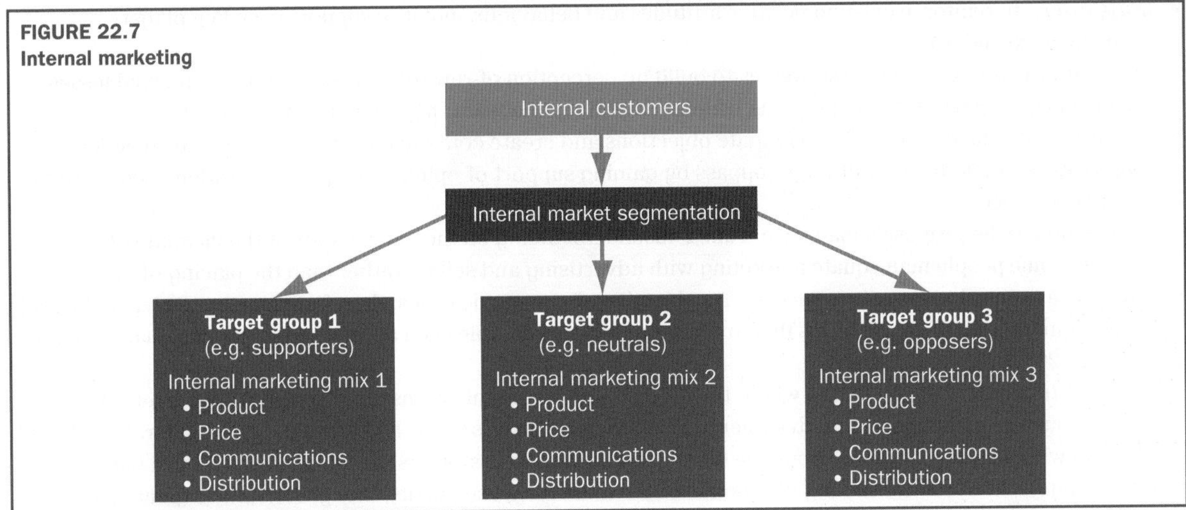

Originally the idea of internal marketing was developed within services marketing and it applied to the development, training, motivation and retention of employees, in retailing, catering and financial services (see Grönroos, 1985; Gummesson, 1987; Mudie, 1987). However, the concept can be expanded to include marketing to all employees with the aim of achieving successful marketing implementation. The framework is appealing as it draws an analogy with external marketing structures such as market segmentation, target marketing and the marketing mix. The people inside the organization to whom the plan must be marketed are considered *internal customers*. We need to gain the support, commitment and participation of a sufficient number of these to achieve acceptance and implementation of the plan. For those people where we fail to do this, we need to minimize the effectiveness of their resistance. They become, in effect, our competitors in the internal marketplace.

Internal market segmentation

As with external marketing, analysis of customers begins with market segmentation. One obvious method of grouping internal customers is into three categories.

1 *Supporters*: those who are likely to gain from the change or are committed to it.
2 *Neutrals*: those whose gains and losses are in approximate balance.
3 *Opposers*: those who are likely to lose from the change or are traditional opponents.

These three market segments form distinct *target groups* for which specific *marketing mix* programmes can be developed (see Figure 22.7).

Internal marketing mix programmes

Product is the marketing plan and strategies that are being proposed, together with the values, attitudes and actions that are needed to make the plan successful. Features of the product may include increased marketing budgets, extra staff, different ways of handling customers, different pricing, distribution and advertising, and new product development strategies. The product will reflect our would-like objectives; however, it may have to be modified slightly to gain acceptance from our opponents. Hence the need for must-have objectives.

The *price* element of the marketing mix is what we are asking our internal customers to pay because of accepting the marketing plan. The price they pay may be lost resources, lower status, fear of the unknown, harder work and rejection of their pet projects because of lack of funds. Clearly, price sensitivity is a key segmentation variable that differentiates supporters, neutrals and opposers.

Communications is a major element of the internal marketing mix and covers the communication media and messages used to influence the attitudes of key players. A combination of personal (presentations, discussion groups) and non-personal (the full report, executive summaries) can be used to inform and persuade. Communication should be two-way: we should listen as well as inform. We should also be prepared to adapt the product (the plan) if necessary in response to our internal customers' demands. It may be necessary to fine-tune the language of marketing (e.g. eliminating jargon) to fit the corporate culture and background of the key players. Communication objectives will differ according to the target group, as follows.

- *Supporters*: to reinforce existing positive attitudes and behaviour, mobilize support from key players (e.g. chief executive).
- *Neutrals*: the use of influence strategies to build up perception of rewards and downgrade perceived losses; display key supporters and explain the benefits of joining 'the team'; negotiate to gain commitment.
- *Opposers*: disarm and discredit; anticipate objections and create convincing counter-arguments; position opposers as 'stuck in their old ways'; bypass by gaining support of opinion and political leaders; negotiate to lower resistance.

Opposition to the proposals may stem from a misunderstanding on the part of staff of the meaning of marketing. Some people may equate marketing with advertising and selling rather than the placing of customer satisfaction as central to corporate success. An objective of communications, therefore, may be to clarify the real meaning of marketing or to use terms that are more readily acceptable such as 'improving service quality' (Laing and McKee, 2001).

Distribution describes the places where the product and communications are delivered to the internal customers, such as meetings, committees, seminars, informal conversations and away days. Consideration should be given to whether presentations should be direct (proponents to customers) or indirect (using third parties such as consultants). Given the conflicting viewpoints of the three target segments, thought should be given to the advisability of using different distribution channels for each group. For example, a meeting may be arranged with only supporters and neutrals present. If opponents tend to be found in a department, judicious selection of which departments to invite may accomplish this aim.

Execution

To execute an implementation strategy successfully, certain skills are required and particular tactics need to be employed. Internal marketing has provided a framework to structure thinking about implementation strategies. Within that framework, the main skills are persuasion, negotiation and politics.

Persuasion

The starting point of persuasion is to try to understand the situation from the internal customer's standpoint. The new plan may have high profit potential, the chance of real sales growth and be popular among external customers, but if it is perceived to cause grief to individuals and/or internal departments, resistance is likely to occur. As with personal selling, the proponents of the plan must understand the needs, motivations and problems of their customers before they can hope to develop effective messages. For example, appealing to a production manager's sense of customer welfare will fail if that person is interested only in smooth production runs. In such a situation, the proponent of the plan needs to show how smooth production will not be affected by the new proposals, or how disruption will be marginal or temporary.

The implementer also needs to understand how the features of the plan (e.g. new payment structure) confer customer benefits (e.g. the opportunity to earn more money). Whenever possible, evidence should be provided to support claims. Objectives should be anticipated and convincing counter-arguments produced. Care should be taken not to bruise egos unnecessarily.

Negotiation

Implementers have to recognize that they may not get all they want during this process. By setting would-like and must-have objectives (see earlier in this chapter), negotiators are clear about what they want and have given themselves negotiating room wherever possible. Two key aspects of negotiation will be considered next: concession analysis and proposal analysis.

The key to **concession analysis** is to value the concessions the implementer might be prepared to make from the viewpoint of the opponent. By doing this, it may be possible to identify concessions that cost the implementer very little and yet are highly valued by the opponent. For example, if the must-have objective is to move from a fixed salary to a salary plus commission, a salesperson's compensation plan that concedes that the proportions should be 80:20 rather than 70:30 may be trivial to the implementer (an incentive to sell is still there) and yet highly valued by the salesperson, as they will gain more income security and value the psychological bonus of winning a concession from management. By trading concessions that are highly valued by the opponent and yet cost the implementer little, painless agreement can be reached.

Proposal analysis: another sensible activity is to try to predict the proposals and demands that opponents are likely to make during the process of implementation. This provides time to prepare a response rather than relying on quick decisions during the heat of negotiation. By anticipating the kinds of proposals opponents are likely to make, implementers can plan the types of counter-proposal they are prepared to make.

Politics

Success in managing implementation and change also depends on the understanding and execution of political skills. Understanding the sources of power is the starting point from which an assessment of where power lies and who holds the balance can be made. The five sources of power are: reward, expert, referent, legitimate and coercive power (French and Raven, 1959).

Reward power derives from the implementer's ability to provide benefits to members in the organization. The recommendations of the plan may confer natural benefits in the form of increased status or salary for some people. In other cases, the implementer may create rewards for support—for example, promises of reciprocal support when required, or backing for promotion. The implementer needs to assess what each target individual values and whether the natural rewards match those values, or whether created rewards are necessary. A limit on the use of reward power is the danger that people may come to expect rewards in return for support. Created rewards, therefore, should be used sparingly.

Expert power is based on the belief that implementers have special knowledge and expertise that renders their proposals more credible. For example, a plan outlining major change is more likely to be accepted if produced by someone who has a history of success rather than by a novice. Implementers should not be reluctant to display their credentials as part of the change process.

Referent power occurs when people identify with and respect the architect of change. That is why charismatic leadership is often thought to be an advantage to those who wish to see change implemented.

Legitimate power is wielded when the implementer insists on an action from a subordinate as a result of their hierarchical relationship and contract. For example, a sales manager may demand compliance with a request for a salesperson to go on a training course, or a board of directors may exercise its legitimate right to cut costs.

The strength of **coercive power** lies with the implementer's ability to punish those who resist or oppose the implementation of the plan. Major organizational change is often accompanied by staff losses. This may be a required cost-cutting exercise, but it also sends messages to those not directly affected that they may be next if further change is resisted. The problem with using coercive power is that, at best, it results in compliance rather than commitment.

The balance of power will depend on who holds the sources of power and how well they are applied. Implementers should pause to consider any sources of power they hold and the sources and degree of power held by supporters, neutrals and opposers. Power held by supporters should be mobilized, those neutrals who wield power should be cultivated, and tactics should be developed to minimize the influence of powerful opposers. The tactics that can be deployed will be discussed shortly, but two applications of power will be discussed first: overt and covert power plays.

Overt power plays are the visible, open kind of power plays that can be used by implementers to push through their proposals. Unconcealed use of the five sources of power is used to influence key players. The use of overt power by localized interests who battle to secure their own interests in the process of change has been well documented (see Hickson et al., 1971; Hinings et al., 1974).

Covert power plays are a more disguised form of influence. Their use is more subtle and devious than that of overt power plays. Their application can take many forms, including agenda setting, limiting participation in decisions to a few select individuals/departments, and defining what is and what is not open to decision for others in the organization (Wilson, 1992).

Tactics

The discussion of overt and covert power plays has introduced some of the means by which implementers and change agents can gain acceptance of their proposals and overcome opposition. Now we examine in more detail the tactics and skills needed to win implementation battles and how they can be applied in the face of some hostile reaction within the organization. These can be grouped into tactics of persuasion, politics, time and negotiation (see Figure 22.8), and are based on the work of a number of authorities (see Kanter, 1983; Ansoff and McDonnell, 1990; Kanter, Stein and Jick, 1992; Piercy, 2008). The tactics provide a wide-ranging checklist of approaches to mobilizing support and overcoming resistance.

FIGURE 22.8
Tactics for implementing marketing plans

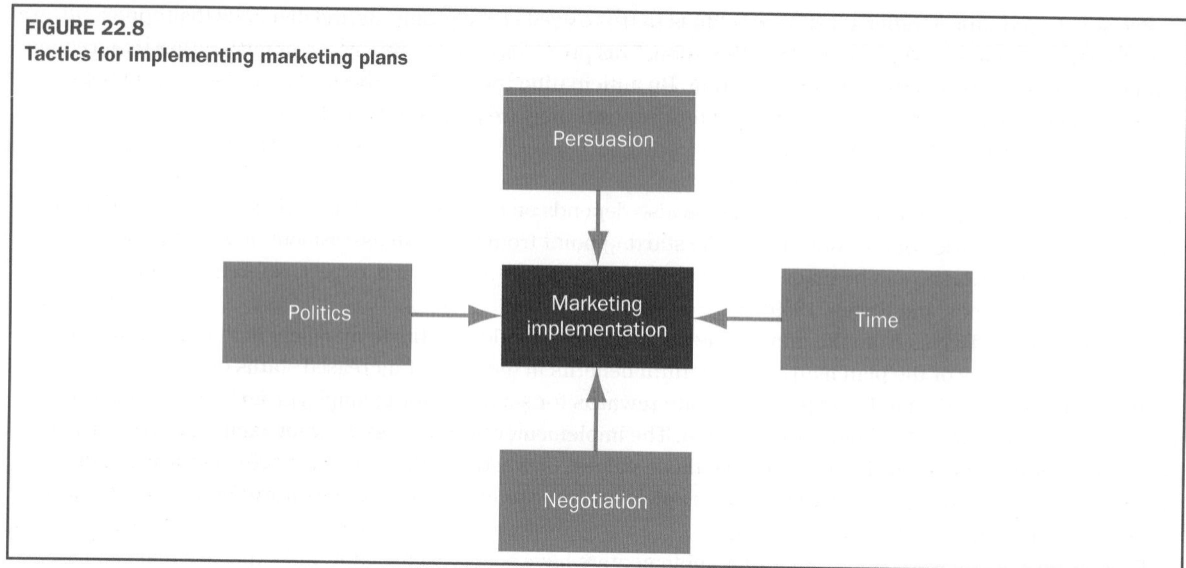

Persuasion

- *Articulate a shared vision*: the vision of where the organization is heading and the desired results of the change need to be clearly stated to key players in the organization. For example, if the marketing plan calls for a reduction in staffing levels, the vision that this is required to reposition the company for greater competitiveness needs to be articulated. Without an understanding of the wider picture, people may regard the exercise as 'just another cost drive' (Kanter, Stein and Jick, 1992). Since most change involves risk and discomfort, a clear vision of its purpose and consequences can make the risk acceptable and the discomfort endurable.
- *Communicate and train*: implementation of the marketing concept or a fundamentally different marketing plan means that many individuals re-orientate and engage in new activities. To achieve this requires a major commitment to communicating the nature and purpose of the change, as well as to training staff in the new skills to be mastered. Major changes require face-to-face communication at discussion sessions and management education seminars. Formal training programmes are needed to upgrade skills and introduce new procedures.
- *Eliminate misconceptions*: a major part of the communication programme will be designed to eliminate misconceptions about the consequences of the change. Unfounded fears and anxieties should be allayed. Certain individuals will exaggerate the negative consequences of the proposed changes, and their concerns need to be addressed.
- *Sell the benefits*: the needs of key players must be identified and the benefits of the change sold to them on that basis. The benefits may be economic (e.g. increased salary) or psychological (e.g. increased status, enhanced power). Whereas shared vision provides evidence of a wider general benefit (e.g. increased competitiveness), personal benefits should also be sold. This recognizes the fact that individuals seek to achieve not only organizational goals but also personal ambitions.
- *Gain acceptance by association*: position the plan against some well-accepted organizational doctrine such as *customer service or quality management*. Because the doctrine is heavily backed, the chances of the plan being accepted and implemented are enhanced. Another positioning strategy is to associate the plan with a powerful individual (e.g. the chief executive). The objective is to create the viewpoint that if the boss wants the plan, there is no point in opposing it.
- *Leave room for local control over details*: leaving some local options or local control over details of the plan creates a sense of ownership on the part of those responsible for implementation and encourages adaptation to different situations. Thought should be given to the extent of uniformity in execution and the areas where local adoption is both practical and advisable.

- *Support words with action*: when implementation involves establishing a more marketing-orientated culture, it is vital to support words with corresponding action. As we saw when discussing resistance to the marketing concept, it is easy for managers to contradict their words with inappropriate actions (e.g. stressing the need to understand customers and then cutting the marketing research budget). An illustrative case of how management actions supported the culture that management were trying to create is the story of a regional manager of US company United Parcel Service (UPS), who used his initiative to untangle a misdirected shipment of Christmas presents by hiring an entire train and diverting two UPS-owned 727s from their flight plans (Bonoma, 1984). Despite the enormous cost (which far exceeded the value of the business), when senior management learned what he had done they praised and rewarded him—their actions supported and reinforced the culture they wanted to foster. As this story became folklore at UPS, its staff knew that senior management meant business when they said that the customer had to come first.
- *Establish two-way communication*: it is important that the people who are responsible for implementation feel that they can put their viewpoints to senior management, otherwise the feeling of top-down control will spread, and resistance will build up through the belief that 'no one ever listens to us'. It is usually well worth listening to people lower down the management hierarchy and especially those who come face to face with customers. One way of implementing this approach is through staff suggestion schemes, but these need to be managed so that staff believe it is worth bothering to take part.

Asda, the UK supermarket chain acquired by Walmart, is well known for its policy of tapping into the collective wisdom of its 85,000 staff. It encourages them to put forward suggestions for improved customer service, and the best ideas are presented at an annual meeting called the National Circle. It also invites staff to write directly to its chief executive officer, with the most promising ideas being rewarded with 'star points' that staff can redeem against a catalogue of offers including clothes and holidays.

See Marketing in Action 22.3 to find out more about how Unilever is chatting with its employees on a global scale.

MARKETING IN ACTION 22.3
Unilever Creates Virtual Jams while Chatting with its Employees

Unilever has over 400 brands, 170,000 employees and is number one in fast-moving consumer goods markets in 26 countries, so managing internal communications creates many challenges. However, to ensure that it can maintain its record of excellent customer service and high product quality, the company is always looking at innovative ways to interact with its customers and employees around the globe. More specifically, in 2013 it looked for ways to bring internal teams together more effectively, improve morale and inspire and motivate personal and professional development.

Unilever's global brands

The solution was a 'virtual jam lobby'—a virtual conference that enabled employees working across the globe to communicate and take part in a scheduled event using a digital communications hub. The event created an opportunity to share live content, cut the costs of employees having to travel to a single location, enabled multiple collaborations and delivered very effective internal communications.

Unilever constantly finds ways to involve its large workforce in the running of its many businesses. Using innovative technology platforms to enable the sharing of ideas, solutions to problems and personal opinions produces rich feedback from employees.

Based on: McDonagh (2014); Unilever (2018)

Politics

- *Build coalitions*: the process of creating allies for the proposed measures is a crucial step in the implementation process. Two groups have special significance: power sources that control the resources needed for implementation—such as information (expertise or data) and finance and support (legitimacy, opinion leadership and political backing)—and stakeholders, who are those people likely to gain or lose from the change (Kanter, Stein and Jick, 1992). Discussion with potential losers may reveal ways of sharing some rewards with them ('invite the opposition in'). At the very least, talking to them will reveal their grievances and so allow thought to be given as to how these may be handled. Another product of these discussions with both potential allies and foes is that the original proposals may be improved by accepting some of their suggestions.
- *Display support*: having recruited powerful allies, these should be asked for a visible demonstration of support. This will confirm any statements that implementers have made about the strength of allies' backing ('gain acceptance by association'). Allies should be invited to meetings, presentations and seminars so that stakeholders can see the forces behind the change.
- *Invite the opposition in*: thought should be given to creating ways of sharing the rewards of the change with the opposition. This may mean modifying the plan and how it is to be implemented to take account of the needs of key players. As long as the main objectives of the plan remain intact, this may be a necessary step towards removing some opposition.
- *Warn the opposition*: critics of the plan should be left in no doubt as to the adverse consequences of opposition. This has been called *selling the negatives*. However, the tactic should be used with care, because statements that are perceived as threats may stiffen rather than dilute resistance, particularly when the source does not have a strong power base.
- *Use of language*: in the political arena, the potency of language in endorsing a preferred action and discrediting the opposition has long been apparent. Language can be used effectively in the implementation battle. For example, critics of the new plan may be being labelled 'outdated', 'backward looking' and 'set in their ways'. In meetings, implementers need to avoid the temptation to *overpower* in their use of language. For people without a strong power base (such as young newcomers to a company), using phrases like 'We must take this action' or 'This is the way we have to move' to people in a more senior position (e.g. a board of directors) will provoke psychological resistance, even to praiseworthy plans. Phrases like 'I suggest' or 'I have a proposal for you to consider' recognize the inevitable desire on the part of more senior management to feel involved in the decision-making rather than being treated like a rubber stamp.
- *Decision control*: this may be achieved by agenda setting (i.e. controlling what is and is not discussed in meetings), limiting participation in decision-making to a small number of allies, controlling which decisions are open for debate in the organization, and timing important meetings when it is known that a key critic is absent (e.g. on holiday or abroad on business).
- *The either/or alternative*: finally, when an implementation proposal is floundering, a powerful proponent may decide to use the either/or tactic in which the key decision-maker is required to choose between two documents placed on the desk: one asks for approval of the implementation plan, the other tenders the implementer's resignation.

Time

- *Incremental steps*: people need time to adjust to change; therefore consideration should be given to how quickly change is introduced. Where resistance to the full implementation package is likely to be strong, one option is to submit the strategy in incremental steps. A small, less controversial strategy is implemented first. Its success provides the impetus for the next implementation proposal, and so on.
- *Persistence*: this tactic requires the resubmission of the strategy until it is accepted. Modifications to the strategy may be necessary on the way, but the objective is to wear down the opposition by resolute and persistent force. Implementation can be a battle of wills and requires the capability of the implementer to accept rejection without loss of motivation.
- *Leave insufficient time for alternatives*: a different way of using time is to present plans at the last possible minute so that there is insufficient time for anyone to present or implement an alternative. The proposition is basically, 'We must move with this plan as there is no alternative.'

- *Wait for the opposition to leave*: for those prepared to play a waiting game, withdrawing proposals until a key opposition member leaves the company or loses power may be feasible. Implementers should be alert to changes in the power structure in these ways as they may present a window of opportunity to resubmit hitherto rejected proposals.

Negotiation

- *Make the opening stance high*: when the implementer suspects that a proposal in the plan is likely to require negotiation, the correct opening stance is to start high but be realistic. There are two strong reasons for this. First, the opponent may accept the proposal without modification; second, it provides room for negotiation. When deciding how high to go, the limiting factor is the need to avoid unnecessary conflict. For example, asking for a move from a fixed salary to a commission-only system with a view to compromising with salary plus commission is likely to be unrealistic and to provoke unnecessary antagonism among the salesforce.
- *Trade concessions*: sometimes it may be possible to grant a concession simply to secure agreement to the basics of the plan. Indeed, if the implementer has created negotiating room, this may be perfectly acceptable. In other circumstances, however, the implementer may be able to trade concession for concession with the opponent. For example, a demand from the salesforce to reduce list price may be met by a counter-proposal to reduce discount levels. A useful way of trading concessions is by means of the *if . . . then* technique: '*If* you are prepared to reduce your discount levels from 10 to 5 per cent, I am then prepared to reduce list price by 5 per cent' (Kennedy, Benson and MacMillan, 1980). This is a valuable tool in negotiation, because it promotes movement towards agreement and yet ensures that concessions given to the opponent are matched by concessions in return. Whenever possible, an attempt to create win–win situations should be made in which concessions that cost the giver very little are highly valued by the receiver.

Evaluation

Finally, during and after the implementation process, evaluation should be made to consider what has been achieved and what has been learned. Evaluation may be in terms of the degree of support gained from key players, how well the plan and strategy have been implemented in the marketplace (e.g. using customer surveys), the residual goodwill between opposing factions, and any changes in the balance of power between the implementers and other key parties in the company.

Marketing Organization

The marketing organization provides the context in which marketing implementation takes place: companies may have no marketing departments; those that do may have functional, product-based, market-centred or matrix organizational structures.

No marketing department

As we have seen, it is common to have no marketing department, for example in small companies that cannot afford the luxury of managerial specialism, or in production- or financially driven organizations that do not see the value of a marketing department. In small companies, the owner-manager may carry out some of the functions of marketing, such as developing customer relationships and product development. In larger companies, which may use the traditional production, finance, personnel and sales function division, the same task may be undertaken by those departments, especially sales (e.g. customer feedback, sales forecasting).

It should be noted that not all companies that do not have a marketing department are poor at marketing; nor does the existence of a marketing department guarantee marketing orientation. Nevertheless, marketing should be a company-wide phenomenon, not something that should be delegated exclusively to the marketing department.

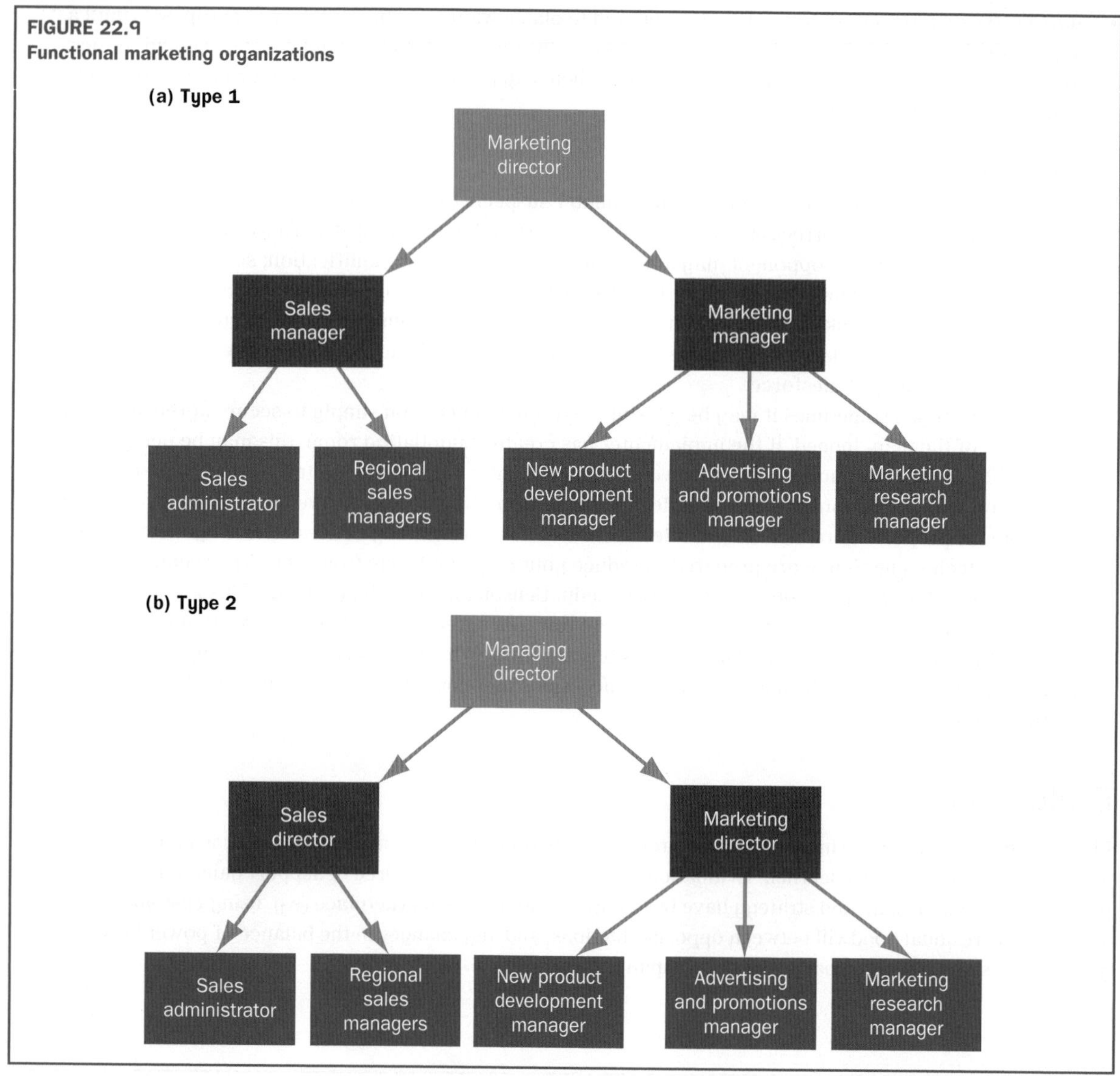

FIGURE 22.9
Functional marketing organizations

Functional organization

As small companies grow, a formal marketing structure might emerge as a section within the sales department. As the importance of marketing is realized and the company grows, a marketing manager could be appointed with equivalent status to the sales manager, who reports to a marketing director (see Figure 22.9). If the marketing director title is held by the previous sales director, little may change in terms of company philosophy: marketing may subsume a sales support role. This is the case in many companies where a more appropriate name for the person given the title 'marketing manager' would be 'communications manager'. An alternative route is to set up a *functional structure* under a sales director and a marketing director (see Figure 22.9(b), Figure 22.10 and Table 22.1).

There are two sources of friction between sales and marketing.

1 Economic—wrangles over budget allocations. For example, the salesforce tends to blame marketers for the way they spend money on promotions, and the marketers look to the salesforce to achieve the highest possible prices; friction is rife between the two groups.
2 Cultural—the two job roles attract different types of individual: marketers tend to be analytical and project focused, whereas salespeople are skilled relationship builders and have an acute insight into which products will sell (Kotler, Rackham and Krishnaswamy, 2006).

FIGURE 22.10
Product-based organization

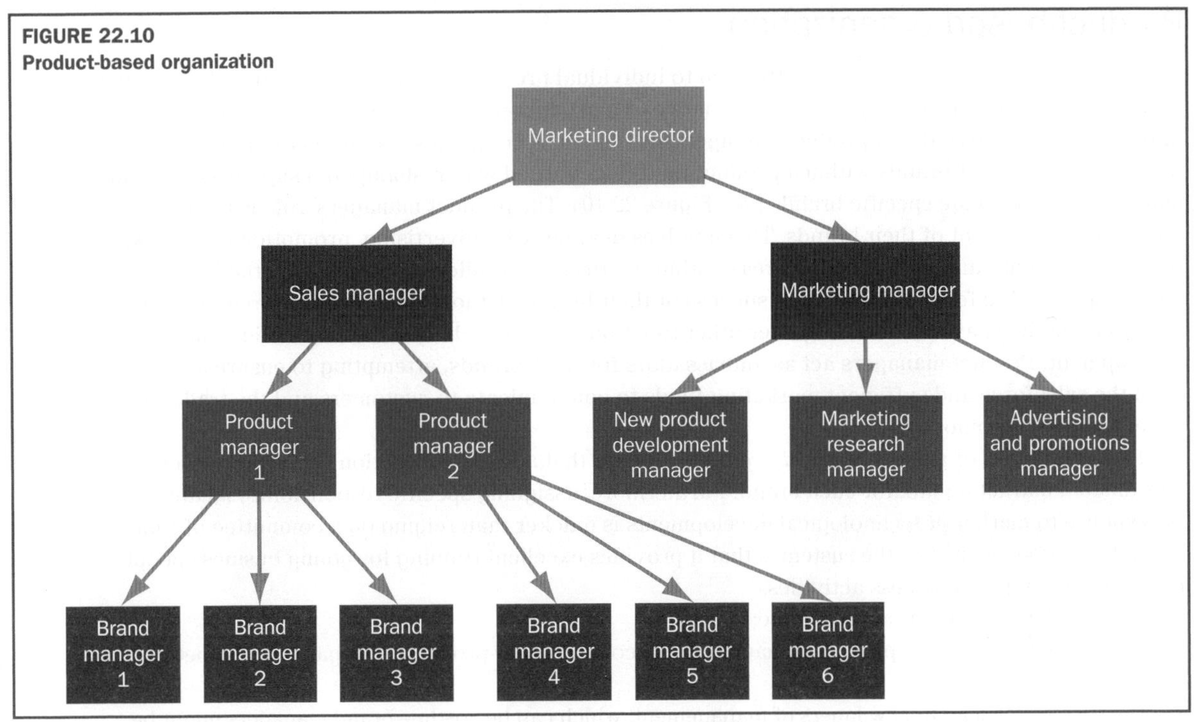

TABLE 22.1 Potential areas of conflict between marketing and sales

Area	Sales	Marketing
Objectives	Short-term sales	Long-term brand/market building
Focus	Distributors/retail trade	Consumers
Marketing research	Personal experience with customers/trade	Market research reports
Pricing	Low prices to maximize sales volume. Discount structure in the hands of the salesforce	Price set consistent with positioning strategy. Discount structure built in to the marketing implementation plan
Marketing expenditure	Maximize resources channelled to the salesforce	Develop a balanced marketing mix using a variety of communication tools
Promotion	Sales literature, free customer give-aways, samples, business entertainment, sales promotions	Design a well-blended promotional mix including advertising, promotion and public relations

Table 22.1 adds to this discussion, identifying more sources of conflict. Therefore, it is important to appoint a marketing director who understands the relationship between sales and marketing and has the power to implement marketing strategies that recognize sales as a key element of the marketing mix.

Functionalisms bring the benefit of specialization of task and a clear definition for responsibilities of a marketing organization (Workman, Homburg and Gruner, 1998). However, as the product range widens and the number of markets served increases, the structure may become unwieldy with insufficient attention being paid to specific products and markets, since no one has full responsibility for a product or market.

Marketing organization and implementation are inevitably intertwined, as the former affects the day-to-day activities of marketing managers. It is important that we understand the organizational world as marketing managers have come to understand it; in particular, the activities that constitute their job (Brownlie and Saren, 1997).

Product-based organization

The need to give sufficient care and attention to individual products has led many companies (particularly in the fast-moving consumer goods field) to move to a product-based structure. For example, Nestlé has moved from a functional to a product management system. A common structure is for a product manager to oversee a group of brands within a product field (e.g. bottled water, shampoos) supported by brand managers who manage specific brands (see Figure 22.10). The product managers' role is to coordinate the business management of their brands. This involves dealing with advertising, promotion and marketing research agencies, and with function areas within the firm. Their dilemma stems from the fact that they have responsibility for the commercial success of their brands without the power to force through their decisions, as they have no authority over other functional areas such as sales, production and research and development. Product managers act as ambassadors for their brands, attempting to ensure adequate support from the salesforce and sufficient marketing funds to communicate to customers and the trade through advertising and promotion.

The advantages of a *product-based organization* are that adequate attention is given to developing a coordinated marketing mix for each brand. Furthermore, assigning specific responsibility means that speed of response to market or technological developments is quicker than relying on a committee of functional specialists. A by-product of the system is that it provides excellent training for young business people, as they meet a wide range of business activities.

The drawbacks with this approach are:

- Healthy rivalry between product managers can become counter-productive, negatively competitive and cause conflict.
- The system can lead to new layers of management, which can be costly—brand managers might be supplemented by assistants—as brands increase and additional brand managers are recruited. Companies like Procter & Gamble and Unilever are eliminating layers of management in the face of increasing demands from supermarkets to trim prices (and thus increase efficiency).
- Brand managers can be criticized for spending too much time coordinating in-company activities and too little time talking to customers. **Category management** can be an effective solution; it involves management of brands in a group, or *category*, with specific emphasis on the retail trade's requirements. Suppliers such as Unilever, Heinz and L'Oréal have moved to category management to provide greater clarity in strategy across brands in an age where retailers themselves are managing brands as categories. (For further insights into category management, see: Aaker, 2009; Ambler, 2001.)

Market-centred organization

Where companies sell their products to diverse markets, *market-centred organizations* should be considered. Instead of managers focusing on brands, *market managers* concentrate their energies on understanding and satisfying the needs of markets. The salesforce, too, may be similarly focused. For example, Figure 22.11 shows a market-centred organization for a hypothetical computer manufacturer. The specialist needs and computer applications in manufacturing, education and financial services justify a sales and marketing organization based on these market segments.

Occasionally, hybrid product/market-centred organizations based on distribution channels are appropriate. For example, at Philips, old organizational structures based on brands or products have been downgraded and replaced with a new focus on distribution channels. Product managers who ensure that product designs fit market requirements still exist. However, under a new combined sales and marketing director, the emphasis has moved to markets. Previously, different salespeople would visit retailers selling different products from the Philips range. This has been replaced by dedicated sales teams concentrating on channels such as the multiples, the independents and mail order.

The enormous influence of the trade in many consumer markets has forced other companies besides Philips to rethink their marketing organization. This has led to the establishment of **trade marketing** teams which serve the needs of large retailers.

The advantage of the market-centred approach is the focus it provides on the specific customer requirements of new opportunities and on developing new products that meet customer's needs. By organizing around

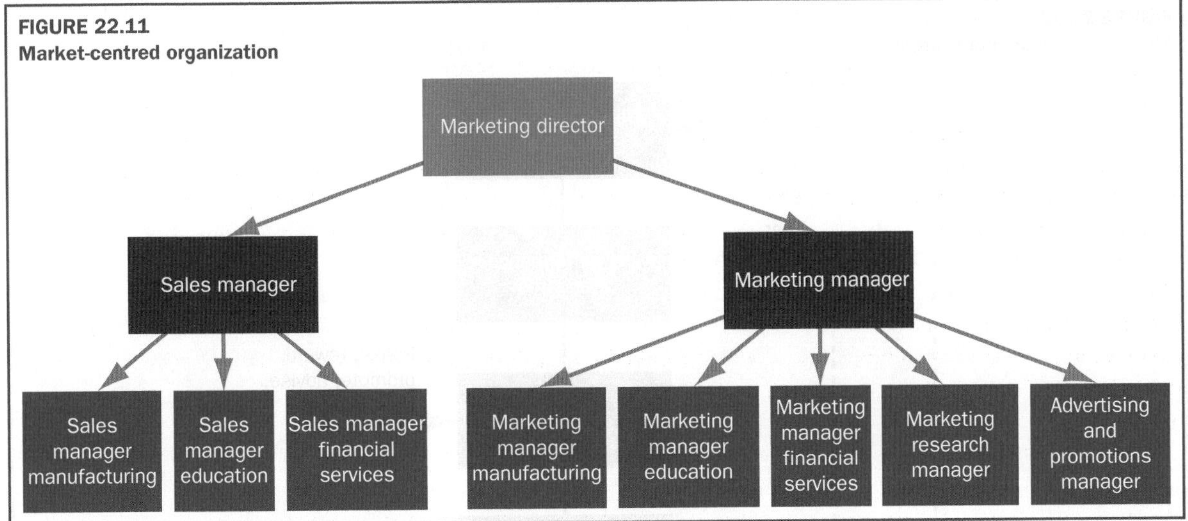

FIGURE 22.11
Market-centred organization

customers, this approach embodies the essence of the marketing concept. However, for companies competing in many sectors it can be resource-hungry.

Matrix organization

For companies with a wide product range selling in diverse markets, a *matrix structure* may be necessary. Both product and market managers are employed to give due attention to both facets of marketing activity. The organizational structure resembles a grid; an example is shown in Figure 22.12, again using a hypothetical computer company. Product managers are responsible for sales and profit performance for their group of products and they monitor technological developments that impact on their products. Market managers focus on the needs of customers in each market segment.

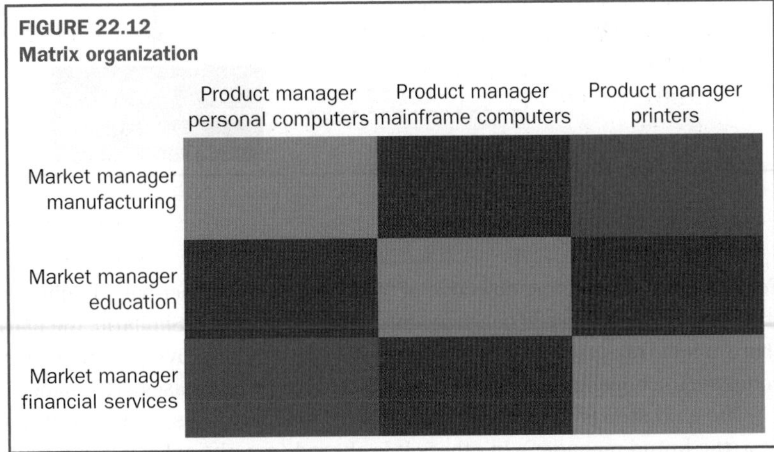

FIGURE 22.12
Matrix organization

For the system to work effectively, clear lines of decision-making authority need to be drawn up because of the possible areas of conflict. For example, who decides the price of the product? If a market manager requires an addition to the product line to meet the special needs of some customers, who has the authority to decide whether the extra costs are justified? How should the salesforce be organized: along product or market lines? Also, it is a resource-hungry method of organization. Nevertheless, the dual specialism does promote the careful analysis of both product and markets so that customer needs are met.

Marketing Control

Marketing control is an essential element of the marketing planning process, because it provides a review of how well marketing objectives have been achieved. A framework for controlling marketing activities is given in Figure 22.13. The process begins by deciding marketing objectives, leading to the setting of performance standards.

FIGURE 22.13
The marketing control system

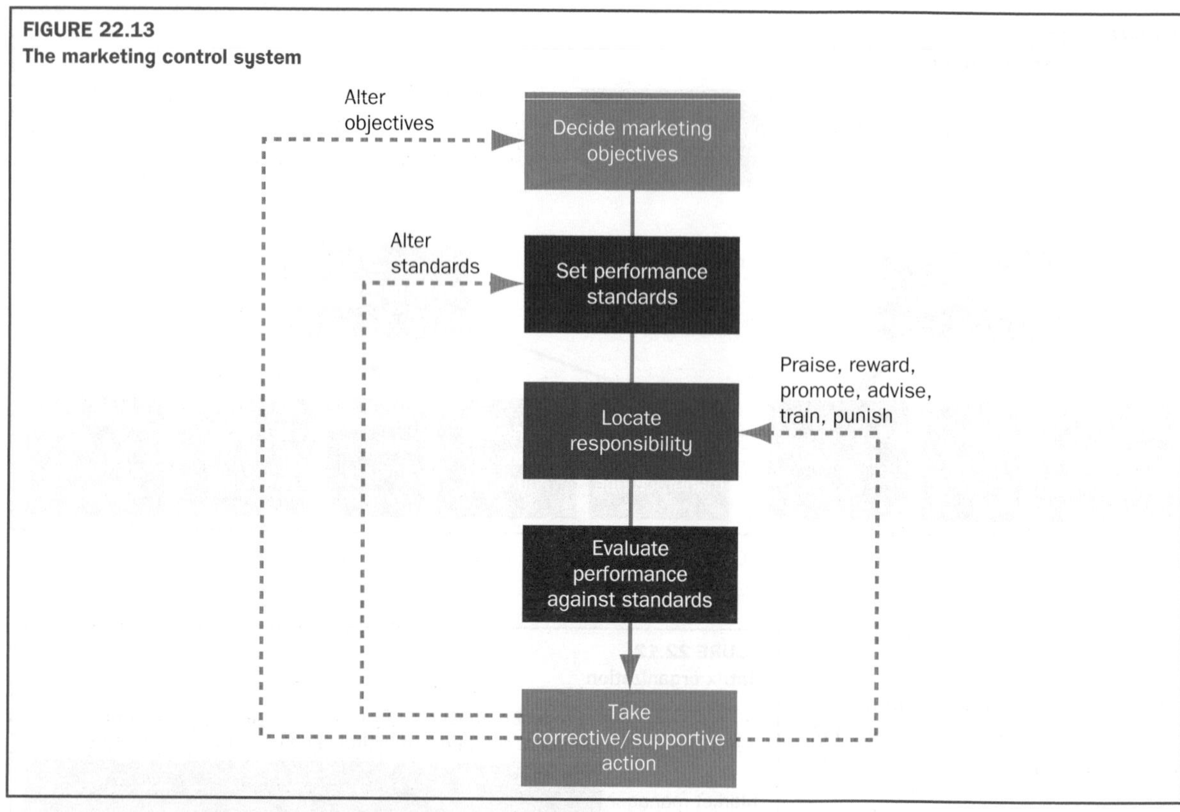

For example, a marketing objective of 'widening the customer base' might lead to the setting of the performance standard of 'generating 20 new accounts within 12 months'. Similarly, the marketing objective of 'improving market share' might translate into a performance standard of 'improving market share from 20 per cent to 25 per cent'. Some companies set quantitative marketing objectives, in which case performance standards are automatically derived.

The next step is to locate responsibility. In some cases, responsibility ultimately falls on one person (e.g. the brand manager); in others it is shared (e.g. the sales manager and salesforce). It is important to consider this issue, since corrective or supportive action may need to focus on those responsible for the success of marketing activity.

Performance is then evaluated against standards, which relies on an efficient information system, and a judgement has to be made about the degree of success and/or failure achieved, and what corrective or supportive action is to be taken. This can take various forms.

- Failure that is attributed to poor performance of individuals may result in the giving of advice regarding future attitudes and actions, training and/or punishment (e.g. criticism, lower pay, demotion, termination of employment). Success, on the other hand, should be rewarded through praise, promotion and/or higher pay.
- Failure that is attributed to unrealistic marketing objectives and performance standards may cause them to be lowered for the subsequent period. Success that is thought to reflect unambitious objectives and standards may cause them to be raised next period.
- The attainment of marketing objectives and standards may also mean modification for the next period. For example, if the marketing objective and performance standard of opening 20 new accounts is achieved, this may mean that the focus for the next period may change. The next objective may focus on customer retention, for instance.
- The failure of one achieved objective to bring about another may also require corrective action. For example, if a marketing objective of increasing calls to new accounts does not result in extra sales, the original objective may be dropped in favour of another (e.g. improving product awareness through advertising).

Strategic Control

Two types of control system may be used. The first concerns major strategic issues and answers the question 'Are we doing the right thing?' It focuses on company strengths, weaknesses, opportunities and threats, and the process of control is through a marketing audit. This is discussed in depth in Chapter 18 under the heading 'The process of marketing planning'.

Operational Control and the Use of Marketing Metrics

The second control system concerns tactical ongoing marketing activities and is called operational control. An array of measures (often referred to as **marketing metrics**) are available to marketing managers who wish to measure the effectiveness of their activities (Faris et al., 2006). However, it is often difficult to determine the exact contribution of marketing efforts, because outcomes are usually dependent on several factors. For example, higher sales may be caused by increased (or better) advertising, a more motivated salesforce, weaker competition, more favourable economic conditions, and so on. This makes it difficult to justify, for example, increased advertising expenditure, because it is hard to quantify the past effects of advertising. This contrasts with the situation in production, where the effects of the introduction of a new machine can be calculated by measuring output, or in finance, where a cost-cutting programme's effect on costs is easily calculated.

Despite these problems, there are now demands on marketing to become accountable for its activities. In order to be accountable, marketing managers are using *marketing metrics*, which are quantitative measures of the outcomes of marketing activities and expenditures. No longer can marketing executives attend budget meetings expecting to spend more money on advertising, promotion, direct marketing and other marketing activities without quantitative justification of these expenditures. The new mantra is **marketing accountability**—the requirement to justify marketing investment by using marketing metrics. Without such justification, it is hardly surprising that marketing budgets are often the first to be cut in an economic downturn.

A research study has identified the kinds of marketing metrics being employed by companies; the 10 most used metrics are shown in Table 22.2, together with an importance measure (Ambler, Kokkinaki and Puntoni, 2004). Although discussed under operational issues, the information can also usefully be fed into the marketing audit for strategic purposes.

TABLE 22.2 The use of marketing metrics in UK companies

Rank	Metric	% using measure	% rating it as important
1	Profit/profitability	92	80
2	Sales: value and/or volume	91	71
3	Gross margin	81	66
4	Awareness	78	28
5	Market share (value/volume)	78	37
6	Number of new products	73	18
7	Relative price	70	36
8	Customer dissatisfaction	69	45
9	Customer satisfaction	68	48
10	Distribution/availability	66	18

Source: Ambler, Kokkinaki and Puntoni (2004)

Each of these metrics—as shown in Figure 22.14—will now be assessed, and specific measures identified, together with their calculation.

FIGURE 22.14
Key marketing metrics

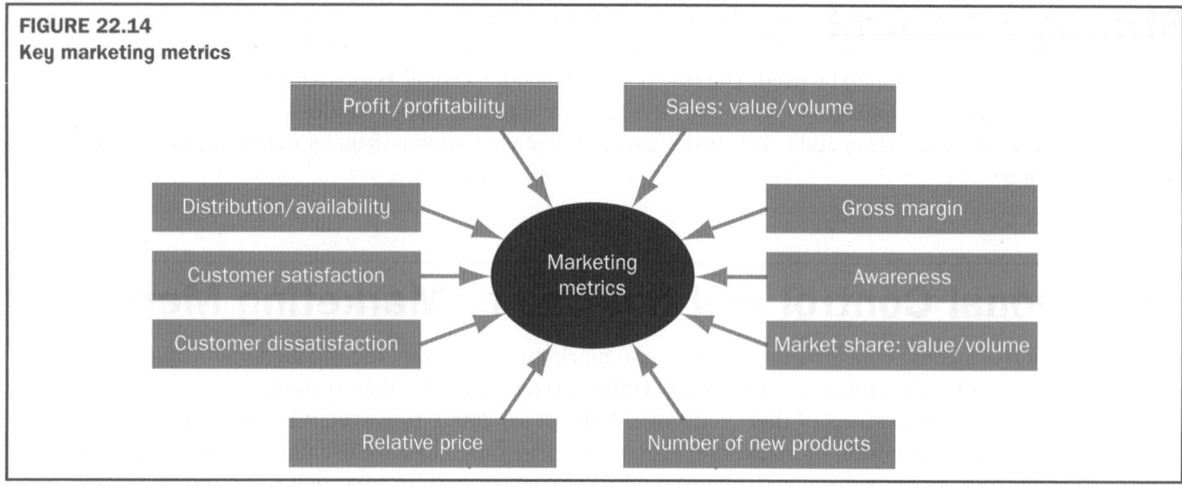

Profit/profitability

Table 22.3 shows some typical profit metrics.

TABLE 22.3 Some typical profit metrics

Typical metrics	Calculation
Profit	Profit = total revenue − total costs
Return on investment (ROI)	$\text{ROI} = \dfrac{\text{net profit}}{\text{investment}}$

Profit is the financial objective of most organizations, so it is the most used metric. Similarly, profitability, which measures the profit return on investments such as products or advertising campaigns, is a popular metric since it relates to the financial objectives of companies. It is usually measured as return on investment (ROI) and, increasingly, marketers are attempting to measure return on marketing investment, although, as discussed earlier, accounting for marketing contribution to a sales (and hence profit) increase is sometimes difficult. What is required is a baseline figure (i.e. what would have happened without the marketing expenditure). Apart from direct marketing, where experiments can be conducted to test effects, such baseline figures can be difficult to establish. Also, ROI is usually measured over a short time period (e.g. a year), and so such calculations can underestimate the full effects of marketing investments, which, through brand building, often have positive long-term effects (Ambler and Roberts, 2008).

For operational control, **profitability analysis** can provide useful information on the profit performance of key aspects of marketing, such as products, customers or distribution channels. The example given focuses on products. The hypothetical company sells three types of product: paper products, printers and copiers. The first step is to measure marketing inputs to each of these products; these are shown in Table 22.4. Allocation of sales calls to products is facilitated by separate sales teams for each group.

TABLE 22.4 Allocating functional costs to products

Products	Salesforce (number of sales calls per year)	Advertising (number of one-page ads placed)	Order processing (number of orders placed)
Paper products	500	20	1,000
Printers	400	20	800
Copiers	250	10	200
Total	1,150	50	2,000
Total cost	£190,000	£130,000	£80,000
Functional cost per unit	£165 per call	£2,600 per ad	£40 per order

If the sales teams were organized on purely geographic lines, an estimate of how much time was devoted to each product, on average, at each call would need to be made. Table 22.4 shows how the costs of an average sales call, advertising insertion and order are calculated. This provides vital information to calculate profitability for each product.

Table 22.5 shows how the net profit before tax is calculated. The results show how copiers are losing money. Before deciding to drop this line, the company would have to take into account the extent to which customers expect copiers to be sold alongside paper products and printers, the effect on paper sales of dropping copiers, the possible annoyance caused to customers who already own one of its copiers, the extent to which copiers cover overheads that otherwise would need to be paid for from paper products and printer sales, the scope for pruning costs and increasing sales, and the degree to which the arbitrary nature of some of the cost allocations has unfairly treated copier products.

TABLE 22.5 Profitability statement for products (£)

	Paper products	Printers	Copiers
Sales	1,000,000	700,000	300,000
Cost of goods sold	500,000	250,000	250,000
Gross margin	500,000	450,000	50,000
Marketing costs			
Salesforce (at £165 per call)	82,500	66,000	41,250
Advertising (at £2,600 per advertisement)	52,000	52,000	26,000
Order processing (at £40 per order)	40,000	32,000	8,000
Total cost	174,500	150,000	72,250
Net profit (or loss) before tax	325,500	300,000	(25,250)

Sales

Table 22.6 shows some typical sales metrics.

TABLE 22.6 Some typical sales metrics

Typical metrics	Calculation
Sales revenue	Sales revenue = unit sales × price
Sales volume	Sales volume = unit sales
Sales revenue against target	Variance = sales revenue – target sales revenue

Processing sales revenue and sales volume is easy, and the metrics are important determinants of marketing investments. Sales increases are normally sought to justify higher marketing expenditures—but without corresponding profit, metrics can be misleading. This is because sales can be bought with excessive discounting, leading to higher sales but lower profit. For this reason, rewarding salesforces for higher sales without also measuring profits can be harmful.

Despite these dangers, **sales analysis** of actual against target sales revenue can be useful for operational control. Negative variance may be due to lower sales volume or lower prices. Product, customer and regional analysis will be carried out to discover where the shortfall arose. A change in the product mix could account for a sales fall, with more lower-priced products being sold. The loss of a major customer may also account for a sales decline. Regional analysis may identify a poorly performing area sales manager or salesperson. These findings would identify the direction of further investigations to uncover the reasons for such outcomes.

Gross margin

Table 22.7 shows some typical gross margin metrics.

TABLE 22.7 Some typical gross margin metrics

Typical metrics	Calculation
Gross margin per unit (GMU)	GMU = price − cost of goods sold (material plus labour)
Gross margin percentage (GMP)	$\text{GMP} = \frac{\text{GMU} \times 100}{\text{price}}$

The third most popular metric is gross margin. Different industries can achieve widely varying gross margins. For example, high-volume, low-price supermarkets achieve low single-digit margins, while traditional jewellers typically require and achieve 50 per cent or more gross margins because their business is lower volume. Calculated as a percentage, gross margin is an indication of the percentage of the selling price that is a contribution to profit. It is not necessarily actual profit, as other expenses such as sales, marketing, distribution and administrative costs have not been deducted. A problem with using gross margin as a marketing metric is that it can be misleading if these other expenses are high. The answer is to calculate unit margin, where all costs are included.

Awareness

Table 22.8 shows some typical awareness metrics.

TABLE 22.8 Some typical awareness metrics

Typical metrics	Calculation
Recall	Survey respondents are asked to name all the brands in a product category that they can think of
Recognition	Survey respondents are shown a list of brands and asked to name those that they have heard of

Awareness is an important metric because it measures whether a marketing communications campaign is entering target consumers' minds. Awareness measures before and after a campaign are particularly useful. However, awareness does not necessarily raise purchase levels if the brand is not liked. It is therefore best used alongside other communications-orientated metrics such as measures of beliefs, liking, willingness to recommend, and purchase intention.

Market share

Table 22.9 shows some typical market share metrics.

TABLE 22.9 Some typical market share metrics

Typical metrics	Calculation
Market share (value)	$\text{Market share (value)} = \frac{\text{sales revenue}}{\text{total market revenue}}$
Market share (unit)	$\text{Market share (unit)} = \frac{\text{unit sales}}{\text{total market unit sales}}$
Relative market share	$\text{Relative market share} = \frac{\text{brand's market share}}{\text{largest competitor's share}}$

Market share analysis evaluates a company's performance in comparison with that of its competitors. Sales analysis may show a healthy increase in revenues, but this may be due to market growth rather than an improved performance over competitors. An accompanying decline in market share would sound warning bells regarding relative performance. This would stimulate further investigation to root out the causes.

It should be recognized that a market share decline is not always a symptom of poor performance. This is why outcomes should always be compared with marketing objectives and performance standards. If the marketing objective was to harvest a product, leading to a performance standard of a 5 per cent increase in profits, its achievement may be accompanied by a market share decline (through the effect of a price rise). This would be a perfectly satisfactory outcome, given the desired objective. Conversely, a market share gain may not signal improved performance if it was brought about by price reductions that reduced profits.

The relative market share metric (percentage) was used when calculating a brand's position on the Boston Consulting Group Matrix (see Chapter 20). When a brand is a market leader, relative market share has a value greater than 1.

Number of new products

Table 22.10 shows some typical new product metrics.

TABLE 22.10 Some typical new product metrics

Typical metrics	Calculation
Number of new products	Number of new products launched per year
Number of successful new products	Number of new products achieving objectives
Proportion of sales attributable to new products (PSANP)	$\text{PSANP} = \dfrac{\text{sales revenue of product on the market for more than } n \text{ years}}{\text{total sales revenue}}$

Innovation is the lifeblood of success, and, as a consequence, it is not surprising that an important marketing metric is the number of new products. However, simply counting the number of new products launched per year does not take into account their success rate. Two other metrics can be used to measure success: 1) the number (and proportion) of successful launches, where success is recognized when objectives are achieved, and 2) the proportion of sales revenue (and profits) attributable to new products (within a given time period). For example, 3M measures the proportion of sales attributable to new products launched within six years as a check on their innovative capability.

Care needs to be taken when defining what is a new product. As we saw in Chapter 11, there are many categories of new product, stretching from brand extensions to radical innovation (new-to-the-world products). Therefore, it can be sensible to categorize each of the metrics according to type of new product.

Relative price

Table 22.11 shows some typical relative price metrics.

TABLE 22.11 Some typical relative price metrics

Typical metrics	Calculation
Ratio of brand A's price to the average price charged in the product category (RPAP)	$\text{RPAP} = \dfrac{\text{brand A's price}}{\text{average price in the product category}}$
Ratio of brand A's price to the price of its main competitor (RPPM)	$\text{RPPM} = \dfrac{\text{brand A's price}}{\text{price of its main competitor}}$

The relative price metric indicates the extent to which a brand is operating at a price premium or discount in a product category. A benchmark is required, which is usually the average price charged or the price of the brand's main competitor or the market leader. If brand A was priced at £4 and the average price charged was £3, the ratio of brand A's price to the average price charged in the product category (RPAP) would be 1.33, demonstrating that the brand was charging a price premium (over the market average) of 33 per cent. If this metric was supported by market leadership (indicated by using a market share metric), this would suggest a strong differential advantage for the brand: not only does the brand outsell its rivals but it does so with a higher price. Therefore, when used with other metrics, relative price measures can be indicative of the strength of a brand (brand equity).

Customer dissatisfaction

Table 22.12 shows some typical customer dissatisfaction metrics.

TABLE 22.12 Some typical customer dissatisfaction metrics

Typical metrics	Calculation
Number of customer complaints	Number of complaints per period
Number of lost customers	Number of lost customers per period
Proportion of lost customers (PLC)	$\text{PLC} = \dfrac{\text{number of lost customers per period}}{\text{total number of customers at the start of the period}}$

Companies measure customer dissatisfaction because it is associated with losing customers. Companies monitor customer complaints to assess weaknesses in the product offering, including service levels. The outcomes of customer complaints should also be measured, as research has shown that the successful resolution of a complaint can cause customers to feel more positive about the company than before the service failure (Maxham and Netemeyer, 2002). The number and proportion of lost customers are also useful metrics. These can be measured for consumer packaged goods by consumer panels and for business-to-business accounts directly from sales data.

Customer satisfaction

Table 22.13 shows some typical customer satisfaction metrics.

TABLE 22.13 Some typical customer satisfaction metrics

Typical metrics	Calculation
Satisfaction rating scales	Responses to 'Very dissatisfied' and to 'Very satisfied' rating scales
Satisfaction compared to expectations	Responses to 'Worse than expected' and to 'Better than expected' rating scales
Willingness to recommend	Responses to 'Would you recommend brand X to a friend or colleague?' question

An increasingly common barometer of marketing success is **customer satisfaction measurement**, which is encouraging as customer satisfaction is at the heart of the marketing concept. Although this measure does not appear directly on a company's profit and loss account, it is a fundamental condition for corporate success. The process involves setting customer satisfaction criteria, designing a questionnaire to measure satisfaction on those criteria, choosing which customers to interview, and analysing and interpreting results. The use of a market research agency is advised, to take advantage of its skills and unbiased viewpoint. A potential problem measuring customer satisfaction can lead to harmful behaviour on the part of the employees whose performance is being measured. For example, in one company, salespeople gave price concessions to customers simply to build up goodwill that they hoped would improve their scores on a customer satisfaction questionnaire (Piercy and Morgan, 1995).

One business-to-business marketing research agency advocates interviewing three customer groups to give a valid picture of customer satisfaction and marketing effectiveness:

1. ten current customers
2. ten lapsed customers (who bought from the company in the past but do not now)
3. ten non-customers (who are in the market for the product but hitherto have not bought from the company).

Invaluable information can be gained concerning customer satisfaction, how effective the salesforce is, why customers have switched to other suppliers, and why some potential customers have never done business with the company.

A powerful question to ask customers is 'Would you recommend brand X to a friend or colleague?' It provides insight into the strength of customer relationships and, therefore, likely future performance. Research by Reichheld into 14 companies in six industries in the USA showed that the answers to this question provided the best or second-best predictor of future customer behaviour in 11 out of 14 tests (Reichheld, 2006). Responses are given on a scale of 1–10, with 9s and 10s being defined as promoters, and 6s and below as detractors. The difference between the two gives the Net Promoter Score (NPS). A major benefit of this score is its simplicity, but NPS has been criticized because a given score can arise from very different sets of responses. For example, an NPS of 40 may arise from 70 per cent promoters and 30 per cent detractors, or one of 40 per cent promoters and zero detractors. Also, the method does not allow measurement of satisfaction of particular aspects of the product offering such as product performance, service quality and salesperson satisfaction. In practice, the question is normally followed by the open-ended 'why' question, to tease out these elements. It also tends to be used alongside the normal customer satisfaction rating scales rather than as a replacement for them (Mitchell, 2008).

Distribution/availability

Table 22.14 shows some typical distribution/availability metrics.

TABLE 22.14 Some typical distribution/availability metrics

Typical metrics	Calculation
Availability ratio (AR)	$AR = \frac{\text{number of outlets stocking brand A}}{\text{total number of outlets}}$
Out of stock ratio (OSR)	$OCR = \frac{\text{number of outlets where brand A is listed but unavailable}}{\text{total number of outlets where brand A is listed}}$

The availability of a brand in distribution outlets is an important marketing metric because, if a brand in an outlet is out of stock, a consumer may be unwilling to visit another shop, preferring the convenience of buying a rival brand instead. Two important metrics are the availability ratio, which measures the proportion of outlets stocking the brand, and the out-of-stock ratio, which measures the proportion of outlets that normally stock the brand but are out of stock at a particular time. Poor scores on these ratios mean that the causes need to be identified and remedial action taken.

In practice, marketing managers need to decide on the set of metrics that are relevant to their business and seek ways of gathering them, which may mean employing a marketing research agency.

Review

1 The relationship between marketing strategy, implementation and performance

- Appropriate strategy with good implementation will have the best chance of successful outcomes; appropriate strategy with bad implementation will lead to trouble, especially if the substandard implementation leads to strategy change; inappropriate strategy with good implementation may hasten failure or may lead to actions that correct strategy and therefore produce favourable outcomes; and inappropriate strategy with bad implementation will lead to failure.

2 The stages that people pass through when they experience disruptive change

- The stages are numbness, denial and disbelief, self-doubt and emotion, acceptance and letting go, adaptation and testing, construction and meaning, and internalization.

3 The objectives of marketing implementation and change

- The overall objective is the successful execution of the marketing plan.
- This may require gaining the support of key decision-makers, gaining the required resources and gaining the commitment of relevant individuals and departments.

4 Value-based approaches to deliver the marketing concept

- Increased commoditization of products and services is leading to squeezed profits
- Co-creation of value is a way to refocus marketing efforts and approaches towards creating sustainable superior value

5 The forms of resistance to marketing implementation and change

- The 10 forms of resistance are: criticisms of specific details of the plan; foot-dragging; slow response to requests; unavailability; suggestions that, despite the merits of the plan, resources should be channelled elsewhere; arguments that the proposals are too ambitious; hassle and aggravation created to wear the proposers down; attempts to delay the decision; attacks on the credibility of the proposer; and pointing out the risks of the plan.

6 How to develop effective implementation strategies

- A change master is needed to drive through change.
- Managing the implementation process requires the setting of objectives ('would like' and 'must have'), strategy (internal marketing), execution (persuasion, negotiation, politics and tactics) and evaluation (who wins, and what can be learned).

7 The elements of an internal marketing programme

- An internal marketing programme mirrors the structures used to market externally, such as market segmentation, targeting and the marketing mix.
- The individuals within the organization are known as internal customers. These can be segmented into three groups: supporters, neutrals and opposers. These form distinct target markets that require different internal marketing mixes to be designed to optimize the chances of successful adoption of the plan.

8 The skills and tactics that can be used to overcome resistance to the implementation of the marketing concept and plan

- The skills are persuasion (the needs, motivations and problems of internal customers need to be understood before appealing messages can be developed), negotiation and political skills (the understanding of the sources of power, and the use of overt and covert power plays).
- The tactics are persuasion, politics, timing and negotiation.

9 Marketing organizational structures

- The options are: no marketing department, and functional, product-based, market-centred or matrix organizational structures.

10 The nature of a marketing control system

- There are two types of marketing control: strategic and operational control systems.
- Strategic control systems answer the question 'Are we doing the right things?' and are based on a marketing audit.
- Operational control systems concern tactical ongoing marketing activities. Marketing metrics are used for this purpose and to justify marketing investments. The most commonly used metrics are profit/profitability, sales (value and/or volume), gross margin, awareness, market share, number of new products, relative price, customer dissatisfaction, customer satisfaction, and distribution/availability.

Key Terms

category management the management of brands in a group, portfolio or category, with specific emphasis on the retail trade's requirements

change master a person who develops an implementation strategy to drive through organizational change

coercive power power inherent in the ability to punish

concession analysis the evaluation of things that can be offered to someone in negotiation, valued from the viewpoint of the receiver

commoditization is when differentiated products lose their uniqueness and no longer stand out in the marketplace.

covert power play the use of disguised forms of power tactics

customer satisfaction measurement a process through which customer satisfaction criteria are set, customers are surveyed and the results interpreted in order to establish the level of customer satisfaction with the organization's product

expert power power that derives from an individual's expertise

legitimate power power based on legitimate authority, such as line management

market share analysis a comparison of company sales with total sales of the product, including sales of competitors

marketing accountability the requirement to justify marketing investment by using marketing metrics

marketing control the stage in the marketing planning process or cycle when performance against plan is monitored so that corrective action, if necessary, can be taken

marketing metrics quantitative measures of the outcomes of marketing activities and expenditures

overt power play the use of visible, open kinds of power tactics

profitability analysis the calculation of sales revenues and costs for the purpose of calculating the profit performance of products, customers and/or distribution channels

proposal analysis the prediction and evaluation of proposals and demands likely to be made by someone with whom one is negotiating

referent power power derived by the reference source, for example when people identify with and respect the architect of change

reward power power derived from the ability to provide benefits

sales analysis a comparison of actual with target sales

trade marketing marketing to the retail trade

transition curve the emotional stages that people pass through when confronted with an adverse change

Study Questions

1. **Think of a situation when you experienced a dramatic change in your life. Using Figure 22.3 for guidance, recall your feelings over time. How closely did your experiences match the stages in the figure? How did your feelings at each stage (e.g. denial and disbelief) manifest themselves?**
2. **Can good implementation substitute for an inappropriate strategy? Give an example of how good implementation might make the situation worse, and an example of how it might improve the situation.**
3. **Discuss commoditization and its potential effects on firm survival.**
4. **Suggest strategies for the implementation of co-value creation that can lead to superior value and differentiation.**
5. **Describe the ways in which people may resist the change that is implied in the implementation of a new marketing plan. Why should they wish to do this?**
6. **What is internal marketing? Does the marketing concept apply when planning internal marketing initiatives?**
7. **What tactics of persuasion are at the implementer's disposal? What are the advantages and limitations of each one?**

8. Discuss the options available for organizing a marketing department. How well is each form likely to serve customers?

9. Discuss the problems involved in setting up and implementing a marketing control system.

Recommended Reading

Implementation can determine the success or failure of a marketing strategy. Read about how to implement change, the importance of management rewards systems and managing people in marketing organizations.

Armstrong, M. (2015) *Armstrong's Handbook of Reward Management Practice*, London: Kogan Page.

Olson, E., Slater, S., Hult, T., Olson, K. (2017) The application of human resource management policies within the marketing organization: The impact on business and marketing strategy implementation, *Industrial Marketing Management* 69(Feb), https://www.sciencedirect.com/science/article/pii/S0019850118300440

Sarin, S., Challagalla, G. and Kohli, A.K. (2012) Implementing changes in marketing strategy: the role of perceived outcome- and process-oriented supervisory actions, *Journal of Marketing Research* 49(4), August 2012, 564–80.

References

Aaker, D. (2009) *Brand Leadership*, New York: Free Press

Ambler, T. (2001) Category Management is Best Deployed for Brand Positioning, *Marketing*, 29 November, 18.

Ambler, T. and J. H. Roberts (2008) Assessing Marketing Performance: Don't Settle For a Silver Metric, *Journal of Marketing Management* 24, 733–50.

Ambler, T., F. Kokkinaki and S. Puntoni (2004) Assessing Marketing Performance: Reasons for Metrics Selection, *Journal of Marketing Management* 20, 475–98.

Ansoff, I. and E. McDonnell (1990) *Implanting Strategic Management*, Englewood Cliffs, NJ: Prentice-Hall.

Argyris, C. (1966) Interpersonal Barriers to Decision Making, *Harvard Business Review* 44 (March–April), 84–97.

Barney, J.B. (2002) *Gaining and Sustaining Competitive Advantage*, Reading MA: Addison Wesley.

Bergstein, R. (2017) How Abercombie & Fitch went from aspirational to out-of-touch, *Forbes*, 10 May, https://www.forbes.com/sites/rachellebergstein/2017/05/10/how-abercrombie-fitch-went-from-aspirational-to-out-of-touch/#3b1996d01fa0 (accessed October 2018)

Birkinshaw, J. (2013) Why corporate giants fail to change, *Fortune*, 8 May. http://fortune.com/2013/05/08/why-corporate-giants-fail-to-change (accessed 2 May 2015).

Bonoma, T. V. (1984) Making your Marketing Strategy Work, *Harvard Business Review* 62 (March–April), 68–76.

Bonoma, T.V. (1985) *The Marketing Edge: Making Strategies Work*, New York: Free Press.

Boudier, E., Reeves, M., Porsborg-Smith, A. and Venjara, A. (2015) Escaping the doghouse: winning in commiditized markets, https://www.bcg.com/en-gb/publications/2015/business-unit-strategy-escaping-dog-house-winning-commoditized-markets.aspx (accessed October 2018)

Brownlie, D. and Saren, M. (1997) Beyond the One-Dimensional Marketing Manager: The Discourse of Theory, Practice and Relevance, *International Journal of Research in Marketing* 14, 147–61.

Bruno, K. (2010) Marketers turn employees into Ad stars, http://www.forbes.com/sites/marketshare/2010/09/23/marketers-advertising-employees-yum-pizza-hut-bp-cathay-pacific (accessed October 2018)

Burke, D., Hajim, C., Elliot, J., Mero, J. and Tkaczy, C. (2007) Top 10 Companies for Leaders, *Fortune*, October 1, 109-116.

Boukis, A. and Gounaris, S. (2014) Linking IMO with employees' fit with their environment and reciprocal behaviours towards the firm, *Journal of Services Marketing*, 28(1), 10–21.

Chang, A. (2012) Headline: 5 reasons why Nokia lost its handset sales lead and got downgraded to 'Junk', *Wired*, 27 April. http://www.wired.com/2012/04/5-reasons-why-nokia-lost-its-handset-sales-lead-and-got-downgraded-to-junk (accessed 2 May 2015).

Cisco (2015) Cisco Collaboration Meeting Rooms, 3 May. http://www.cisco.com/c/en/us/solutions/collaboration/index.html (accessed October 2018)

Faris, P.W., Bendle, N.T., Pfeifer, P.E. and Reibstein, D.J. (2006) *Key Marketing Metrics*, Harlow: Pearson.

Forbes Media (2018) https://www.forbes.com/profile/ursula-burns/#3a5674c940a0 (accessed October 2018)

French, J.R.P. and Raven, B. (1959) The Bases of Social Power, in Cartwright, D. (ed.) *Studies in Social Power*, Ann Arbor: University of Michigan Press, 150–67.

Gokey, M. (2015) It's official: Nokia to become Microsoft Mobile April 25—What happens next? *Tech Times*, 22 April. http://www.techtimes.com/articles/5872/20140422/its-official-nokia-to-become-microsoft-mobile-april-25-what-happens-next.htm (accessed 2 May 2015).

Grönroos, C. (1985) Internal Marketing: Theory and Practice, in Bloch, T. M., Upah, G.D. and Zeithaml, V.A. (eds) *Services Marketing in a Changing Environment*, Chicago: American Marketing Association.

Gummesson, E. (1987) Using Internal Marketing to Develop a New Culture: The Case of Ericsson Quality, *Journal of Business and Industrial Marketing* 2(3), 23–8.

Hickson, D. J., Hinings, C.R., Lee, C.A., Schneck, R.E. and Pennings, J.M. (1971) A strategic contingencies theory of intraorganisational power, *Administrative Science Quarterly* 16(2), 216–29.

Hinings, C.R., Hickson, D.J., Pennings, J.M. and Schneck, R.E. (1974) Structural conditions of intraorganisational power, *Administrative Science Quarterly* 19(1), 22–44.

Johannessen, J.-A., Olaisen, J. and Havan, A. (1993) The challenge of innovation in a Norwegian shipyard facing the Russian market, *European Journal of Marketing* 27(3), 23–38.

Johnson, G. (1987) *Strategic Change and the Management Process*, Oxford: Basil Blackwell.

Kanter, R. M. (1983) *The Change Masters*, London: Allen and Unwin.

Kanter, R. M. (1997) *The Change Masters*, London: Allen & Unwin.

Kanter, R.M., Stein, B.A. and Jick, T.D. (1992) *The Challenge of Organisational Change*, New York: Free Press.

Kennedy, G., Benson, J. and MacMillan, J. (1987) *Managing Negotiations*, London: Business Books.

Kotler, P., Rackham, N. and Krishnaswamy, S. (2006) Ending the War Between Sales and Marketing, *Harvard Business Review*, July–August. https://hbr.org/2006/07/ending-the-war-between-sales-and-marketing (accessed October 2018)

Laing, A. and L. McKee (2001) Willing volunteers or unwilling conscripts? professionals and marketing in service organisations, *Journal of Marketing Management* 17(5/6), 559–76.

Leyland, A. and Quinn, I. (2018) Sainsbury's Asda £51bn combination play: what we know and what it means, *The Grocer*, 4 May, https://www.thegrocer.co.uk/home/topics/sainsburys-asda-merger/sainsburys-and-asda-mega-merger-what-we-know-and-what-it-means/566476.article (accessed October 2018)

London, S. and Hill, A. (2002) A recovery strategy worth copying, *Financial Times*, 16 October, 12.

Marketing Business (2005) 100 Days, June, 15–17.

Matthyssens, P. and Vandenbempt, K. (2008) Moving from basic offerings to value-added solutions: Strategies, barriers and alignment, *Industrial Marketing Management* 37(8), 316–28.

Maxham, J.G. and Netemeyer, R.G. (2002) A longitudinal study of complaining customers' evaluations of multiple service failures and recovery efforts, *Journal of Marketing* 66(October), 57–71.

McDonagh, M. (2014) Top 3 Takeaways from Unilever's Virtual Event, WorkCast, 13 October. http://www.workcast.com/uk/blog/showcasing-unilevers-virtual-event (accessed October 2018)

Mitchell, A. (1994) Dark night of marketing or a new dawn? *Marketing*, 17 February, 22–3.

Mitchell, A. (2008) The only number you need to know does not add up to much, *Marketing Week*, 6 March, 15–16.

Mudie, P. (1987) Internal marketing: cause of concern, *Quarterly Review of Marketing*, Spring–Summer, 21–4.

Nokia (2018) Networks, https://networks.nokia.com

Pettigrew, A. M. (1985) *The Awakening Giant: Continuity and Change in ICI*, Oxford: Basil Blackwell.

Piercy, N. (1990) Making marketing strategies happen in the real world, *Marketing Business*, February, 20–1.

Piercy, N. (2008) *Marketing-Led Strategic Change*, Oxford: Butterworth-Heinemann.

Piercy, N. and Morgan, N.A. (1995) Customer satisfaction measurement and management: a processual analysis, *Journal of Marketing Management* 11, 817–34.

Reichheld, F. (2006) *The Ultimate Question*, Boston: Harvard Business School Press.

Ritson, M. (2015) Abercrombie's new direction hasn't revitalised the brand but eradicated it, *Marketing Week*, 29 April. http://www.marketingweek.com/2015/04/29/abercrombies-new-direction-hasnt-revitalised-the-brand-but-eradicated-it (accessed 30 April 2015).

Saner, E. (2012) Abercrombie & Fitch: for beautiful people only, *The Guardian*, 28 April. http://www.theguardian.com/fashion/2012/apr/28/abercrombie-fitch-savile-row (accessed 2 May 2015).

SAS (2019a) Corporate webpages https://www.sasgroup.net/en/ (accessed March 2019)

SAS (2019b) Scandinavian airlines pays tribute to travelers – travelers are the future https://www.sasgroup.net/en/scandinavian-airlines-pays-tribute-to-travelers-travelers-are-the-future/ (accessed March 2019)

Shyh-Rong, F., Enchi, C., Chang, C.-C. and C, C.-H. (2014) Internal market orientation, market capabilities and learning orientation, *European Journal of Marketing* 48(1/2), 170–92.

Total Retail (2018) Top Women in Retail 2018: Fran Horowitz, CEO, Abercombie & Fitch, https://www.mytotalretail.com/article/top-women-in-retail-2018-fran-horowitz-abercrombie-fitch-co/ (accessed October 2018)

Trefis Team (2014) Abercrombie and Fitch's CEO Mike Jeffries To Step Down Immediately, *Forbes*, 10 December. http://www.forbes.com/sites/greatspeculations/2014/12/10/abercrombie-and-fitchs-ceo-mike-jeffries-to-step-down-immediately (accessed 2 May 2015).

Unilever (2018) About us, www.unilever.com (accessed June 2015).

Webster, F. E. Jr. (1988) Rediscovering the Marketing Concept, *Business Horizons* 31 (May–June), 29–39.

Wilson, D. C. (1992) *A Strategy of Change: Concepts and Controversies in the Management of Change*, London: Routledge.

Wilson, G. (1993) *Making Change Happen*, London: Pitman.

Workman J.P. Jr, Homburg, C. and Gruner, K. (1998) Marketing organisation: an integrative framework of dimensions and determinants, *Journal of Marketing* 62 July, 21–41.

CASE 43

Marimekko—a Story of Design, Determination and Leadership

This is a historic case that demonstrates the importance of enduring company values, strong leadership and powerful and innovative leadership.

Marimekko is a distinctive Finnish brand which imbues the country's heritage and culture. Its iconic fashion design principles were established by founders Armi and Viljo Ratia in 1951, and since then the company has become well known for its folk-based approach to design and creativity. Armi Ratia employed young artists just starting out on their careers and encouraged them to create striking designs for fabrics. In 1953, Vuokko Eskolim-Nurmesniemi joined the company and made radical changes to the garment designs, which are still evident today; she wanted to see clothes that allowed the wearer to move freely. Her radical loose-fitting dress designs and the unisex Jokapoika shirt launched the brand onto the world's stage. Marimekko's designs were bold and chic and worn by celebrities around the world, including Jackie Kennedy, who wore Marimekko dresses during her husband's presidential campaign in the USA in 1959. This became a showcase for the brand and earned it media coverage in over 300 glossy magazines, which, at the time, were influential in persuading women which brands to wear.

An Unorthodox Sense of Tradition

Originally, this was a brand made by women for women to wear, and in the 1960s the brand was positioned as strident and liberating and was 'a component in women's liberation' through its clothes and accessories. Armi Ratia's values were seen in everything the brand did; Ratia didn't use professional models in the advertising, but instead people who would wear the brand in their daily lives. The bright-coloured prints and wearables became the 'uniform of the intelligentsia'. The *folk dress* became one of the iconic designs, which buyers were encouraged to wear so that they could relax and be themselves. Marimekko continued to produce unisex designs and started to grow internationally in the 1970s, expanding through licensing agreements into Sweden, Japan and the USA.

Marimekko designs are infused with a strong sense of national culture, and this is through the very heart of the brand from its design stage to the stores. The company uses quality fabrics to bring *colour and joy for everyday life*. Every year, 1 million metres of fabric are still produced in the company's printing factory in Helsinki. Unikko, the rebel flower, was designed by Maija Isola for the 1960s flower-power era—a movement in opposition to the Vietnam war. This design was counter to the wishes of Armi Ratia, who had declared that they would never 'do florals'. But Maija was a free thinker and her poppy design (see image) captured the DNA of the company and has lived on in hundreds of different styles, homeware products, and even shoes.

The energy and passion which launched this brand onto the global stage faded in 1979 when Armi Ratia died. Marimekko was left without strong leadership and soon lost its direction. The company fell into a period of decline.

Management Revival

Even iconic brands can hit a low spot. Following a period of lacklustre management in the 1980s, Kirsti Paakkanen, a successful Finnish entrepreneur, bought the company in 1991 from the Amer Group, a Finnish conglomerate. In the €6 million deal, she took over the responsibility for Marimekko's €20 million debt. She was determined to save the Marimekko design, and had a clear vision of where she wanted to take the business and how she would revive its fortunes. Her two key objectives were:

1 to provide strong visionary leadership by utilising her skills, reputation and capabilities to re-image the brand and enable it to develop into a prestige brand

2 to create an international chain of high-quality retail stores which would act as flagships for the brand. The stores would be a showcase of Finnish design and culture.

Turning around this failing brand required courage, determination and vision.

Following the Amer Group ownership, Marimekko had gone through a period of harsh rationalization, and 360 workers had been laid off. While this left the company in a weak position, Paakkanen was able to ensure that the remaining staff understood the ethical and economic values of the company. She sent memos to employees to constantly remind them that '*You have to trust in yourself. Only selves succeed. World needs strong individuals. How many statues have been erected to committees? None!*' Everyone was required to work by these principles and at the same time cut costs wherever viable and work to increase revenues. She also took what might seem an unconventional step to ground these values in the minds of the workforce; she invited post-modernist academics, philosophers and psychiatrists to give inspiring lectures on personal development and creativity to the staff.

Paakkanen followed traditional values and launched an advertising campaign, 'Get the masses on the move', with over 70 major design events. These events used ordinary people to showcase the designs backed by music celebrities and performers. The Marimekko *road show* popped up in parks, on high streets and in the Opera House in Helsinki. Everyone freely attended the events, giving the *masses* access to the fashion. Mass-media advertising was deemed to be too expensive, so public relations events, exhibitions, shows and local poster campaigns were the mainstay of the company's communication campaigns.

Paakkanen's vison extended to the stores, which she visited to gain better knowledge of the customers and the staff. By understanding every aspect of the business, she was able to be better informed and had a great sense of the market demand. She regularly shared this knowledge throughout the company via computer printouts.

By 1998, she had opened her envisioned flagship stores in Stockholm and Cologne and then in New York and London. Paakkanen introduced new styles and gave the brand a more elegant and empowering look.

Design Culture for Living

As tastes and fashions evolve over time, Marimekko continues to use artists who can capture the mood with simple clean colourful ideas, which Armi Ratia had originally felt was at the heart of keeping loyal customers. Inspired by resonating the cultural values of the Finnish people, the freedom and creativity has enabled to brand to grow. In 2018, Satu Maaranen became head designer and carries on the tradition of making iconic ready-to-wear fashion and bags.

Currently, products are sold in over 40 countries, from 160 stores, annual sales exceed €193 million and the online store is reaching new customers in 30 other countries. Marimekko's design culture reaches beyond its own stores: its fabrics and ready-made garments can be found in stores such as Crate and Barrel, H&M, Converse and Banana Republic.

Founder Armi Ratia wanted the designs to live on and is quoted saying 'Marimekko is not about trendy fashion, with a few minor exceptions. We make lasting and timeless products. Timelessness may, however, occasionally come into fashion by chance, like now.' The fabric designs are inspired by life and nature and are created into products which people can enjoy every day. And so Armi Ratia's vision lives on as creative women have carried the baton and inspired the next generation to wear Marimekko.

Questions

1. **Discuss the importance of the Armi Ratia's vision and describe how this has shaped the cultural values of the Marimekko brand.**
2. **Discuss the steps Kirsti Paakkanen took to relaunch the brand.**
3. **Explain whether the marketing strategy of Marimekko can be considered as good implementation. Give examples to support your answer.**
4. **Imagine you are given the responsibility for implementing a new marketing campaign for Marimekko. Explain how you would go about this task.**

This case study was written by Fiona Ellis-Chadwick, who would like to thank Professor Heli Marjanen for her support in writing the case study, and the team in the Marimekko store on 3 Centralgatan, Helskini, Finland, who inspired this case.

References

Based on: Marimekko (2018) The brand story, https://www.marimekko.com/eu_en/the-brand/marimekko-story (accessed Nov 2018); Chatarji, S. (2001) Memories of a Lost War: American

»

Poetic Responses to the Vietnam War, Oxford University Press, 2001, 42; Barrot, L., Lecordier, S., Bichet, L. and Meunier, S. (1996) Description and analysis of the marketing strategy of and export product: Marimekko's clothes line in Europe, Helsinki, Finland: Marimekko, 6 November; Marimekko (2018) Joy of everyday life, https://www.marimekko.com/eu_en/the-brand/design/design-philosophy (accessed Nov 2018); Marimekko (2017) Financial Statement 2017, Marimekko Corporation; Ruokonen, H.-M., Simon, G. and Cho, D.-S. (1995) Marimekko (Case Study), Helsinki: Helsinki School of Economics & Business Administration; Clarke, I., Moore, C. and Marjanen, H. (1999) Retail Internationalisation by Design? The cultural context of the fashion brand, Academy of Marketing Conference, 'New Marketing, New Relevance: Evolution & Innovation for the Next Generation', University of Stirling, Scotland, 7–9 July; Koncuis, J. (2014) Marimekko's Unikko: 50 years of flower power, *Home & Garden*, 28 May, https://www.washingtonpost.com/lifestyle/home/marimekkos-unikko-50-years-of-flower-power/2014/05/27/65eff10a-db98-11e3-bda1-9b46b2066796_story.html?noredirect=on&utm_term=.92741c90d347

CASE 44

Managing a Changing Musical Portfolio: HMV

HMV is a British retailer that opened its first shop in 1921, becoming recognized through its famous 'dog and gramophone' trademark. At the end of 2012, it was the UK and Ireland's leading music retailer, with over 200 stores offering a specialist selection of entertainment content and technology products, an online store at hmv.com and a download service at hmvdigital.com. The company had, prior to this, experimented with a number of related areas, including cinemas, juice bars and ticketing, although success was limited. None of these services are currently offered as part of HMV's product portfolio. More successful in recent years has been the sale of technology products such as headphones, speakers and turntables to play vinyl records.

HMV has struggled to make headway since the early 2010s, as the advent of the internet led to demand for its traditional products falling away. Annual sales dropped nearly 20 per cent to £923.2 million during the year 2011; as HMV faced increasing competition from websites such as Amazon and the supermarkets, this led to it shutting stores. The markets for HMV's main products—computer games, digital video discs (DVDs) and compact discs (CDs)—shrunk by between 10 and 20 per cent during this period. Financial problems culminated in the company entering administration on 14 January 2013. The assets were bought by Hilco Capital, a company that specializes in investing in and restructuring companies, for an estimated £50 million on 5 April 2013. Hilco Capital had previously purchased HMV's Canadian assets, including the retail stores, in 2011, although all the shops in Canada had ceased trading by May 2017.

Consolidating and Restructuring

After the restructuring, business in the UK has improved, although a number of stores have been closed and others relocated to smaller premises, as budgets have been reduced. The company is still a major player in the CD and DVD market, but it only deals in physical entertainment. Since 2013, HMV has not operated in the digital download music market, unlike Amazon and Apple. Nor has it ever been in the streaming market like Spotify, Apple Music and Deezer. Demand for new products such as headphones and speakers appears, to some extent, to be offsetting falling sales of CDs, DVDs and computer games, although, of course, these are not purchased as frequently. The retailer has tried to position itself as an entertainment chain, with new departments dedicated to the latest gadgets and accessories such as headphones, speakers and vinyl turntables. It has yet to enter the voice-controlled smart speaker market and follow in the footsteps of Amazon, which launched the Echo in 2014, and of Google, which followed with its Home version in 2016.

The current product/service range can be divided into:

- books and magazines
- computer games
- DVDs, including Blu-ray discs
- fashion (such as T-shirts and casual clothing) and merchandise
- music CDs and vinyl
- technology (speakers, headphones and vinyl turntables).

Building Relationships

In recent years, the company has rebuilt its relationship with record companies and film studios, which are keen to see it survive. For all parties in the entertainment industry, working together allows for the promotion of artists through special events at shops. This is something Amazon finds difficult to do.

»

»

TABLE C44.1 UK digital, CD, digital downloads, vinyl, DVD and streaming sales 2010–2017 (millions of units unless stated)

	Annual sales							
	2010	2011	2012	2013	2014	2015	2016	2017
CDs (millions of units)	98.6	86.2	69.6	60.6	55.9	53.6	47.4	41.8
Digital (millions of units)	21.0	27.0	30.5	32.6	29.7	25.7	18.1	13.8
Vinyl (millions of units)	0.2	0.3	0.4	0.8	1.3	2.2	3.2	4.1
DVDs (millions of units)	223	207	179	162	143	120	101	N/A
Streaming (billions of audio streams)				7.5	14.8	26.8	44.9	68.1

Notes:

Sales of vinyl albums were over 3 million in the 1970s, falling to a low of 205,000 in 2007. They have risen every year since then.

Figures for streaming exclude YouTube.

DVD sales peaked at 257 million in 2008.

Sources: British Phonographic Industry (2018); British Film Institute (2018); Music Business Worldwide (2018); Toesland (2017)

Each year, HMV stages over 200 events, such as book and album signings, in stores to attract visitors, and this helps to increase sales on these days. It tries to give each event a local feel and uses social media as a form of word-of-mouth promotion.

In 2016, HMV's sales of physical music in the UK overtook those of Amazon for the first time since September 2013, meaning that it became the UKs largest physical music retailer. Fiona Keenan, Strategic Insight Director at the market research company Kantar Worldpanel, says that the company has been successful in attracting shoppers in store, particularly those who want to browse through its extensive range of products before deciding what to buy, which historically was an area of strength for the high street specialist.

Table C44.1, however, shows that a number of HMV's markets are in decline. The CD and DVD markets have struggled as they face increased competition from digital alternatives such as iTunes and Netflix and, more recently, through the increased use of streaming—a market in which the company does not operate and that has grown rapidly in recent years as companies like Spotify have taken advantages of developments in technology. The games market has seen many users also switch from tangible products to online digital alternatives.

Uncertain Future for the HMV brand

Declining sales have, to some extent been offset by sales in other product categories and by the customers of these products tending to purchase more frequently. The revival of vinyl has also helped: annual sales passed 3 million in 2016 for the first time since 1991; see Table C44.1. HMV has also seen growth in the sales of turntables on which to play vinyl records. HMV's head of marketing, Patrizia Leighton, in a 2017 interview with Hobbs argues:

> 'There is still an audience out there for physical media, irrespective of what the media believes. Young people like to own a physical product as it makes them feel closer to the artist and have something tangible to hold in their hand. We are seeing a trend [towards this way of thinking] particularly among young women.' (Hobbs, 2017).

HMV has continued to invest in its digital media strategy with a redesigned e-commerce website (see http://store.hmv.com). When originally launched in 2013, the website was only used as part of the brand's communication strategy, as it only had news of HMV'S product range and did not allow users to place orders. The new site operates a multichannel click-and-collect service from over 120 stores. Orders via this channel have grown rapidly, with average order size increasing. The website is also used for cross-selling and up-selling and customer retention; by using the browsing history of visitors to the site, recommendations can be made as to music and film purchases. HMV also operates a loyalty scheme branded as 'pure hmv'; the scheme rewards cardholders with points for orders, which can be redeemed on several items. Challenging economic conditions in retailing in the UK have continued to test the implementation of HMV's strategy in the longer term. In 2019, the brand went into administration but was bought out by a Canadian music entrprenuer Doug Putman, who plans to retain the HMV stores and the develop the brand's high street presence in the UK.

Questions

1. **HMV implemented a strategy in 2010 based on marketing via retail shops; this could be described as inappropriate. Discuss this statement. Many retailers in the UK have not coped well as consumers changed from buying in shops to buying online. Explain the difficulties HMV faces in adapting to this changing market.**
2. **Explain what is meant by internal marketing and why it is such an important issue in this case. How can the company 'build a coalition' between staff based at head office and those who work in the shops?**
3. **Describe what is meant by category management. How can HMV implement this system in its marketing department? Assess the usefulness of this form of staff organization in the addition of new product lines.**
4. **Explain what is meant by marketing metrics. What measures can be used to measure the performance of HMV's shops?**

This case study was written by Adrian Pritchard, Coventry University

References

Based on: British Film Institute (2018); *BFI statistical yearbook 2017*, https://www.bfi.org.uk/sites/bfi.org.uk/files/downloads/bfi-statistical-yearbook-2017.pdf; British Phonographic Industry (2018). *All about the music 2018*, https://www.bpi.co.uk/shop/; Hobbs, T. (2017) HMVs marketing boss on bringing the brand back from the brink, *Marketing Week*, 3 April, https://www.marketingweek.com/2017/04/03/hmv-rebuilding-brand-ashes-keeping-faith-physical-media/; Kantar World Panel (2016) HMV becomes UK's largest physical music retailer, Published 1 November, https://www.kantarworldpanel.com/global/News/HMV-becomes-UKs-largest-physical-music-retailer-once; Music Business Worldwide (2018) UK albums sales have been cut in half since 2010, https://www.musicbusinessworldwide.com/uk-album-sales-have-been-cut-in-half-since-2010/; Toesland, F. (2017) Vinyl gets to play it again in UK revival, https://www.raconteur.net/culture/retro-revival-the-resurgence-of-vinyl

Glossary

A

adapted marketing mix an international marketing strategy for changing the marketing mix for each foreign target market

administered vertical marketing system a channel situation where a manufacturer that dominates a market through its size and strong brands may exercise considerable power over intermediaries even though they are independent

advertising any paid form of non-personal communication of ideas or products in the prime media: i.e. television, the press, posters, cinema and radio, the Internet and direct marketing

advertising agency an organization that specializes in providing services such as media selection, creative work, production and campaign planning to clients

advertising message the use of words, symbols and illustrations to communicate to a target audience using prime media

agency an organization that specializes in providing services such as media selection, creative work, production and campaign planning to clients

attitude the degree to which a customer or prospect likes or dislikes a brand

augmented product the core product plus extra functional and/or emotional values combined in a unique way to form a brand

awareness set the set of brands of which the consumer is aware may provide a solution to the problem

B

beliefs descriptive thoughts that a person holds about something

benefit segmentation the grouping of people based on the different benefits they seek from a product

blog short for weblog – a personal diary/journal on the web; information can easily be uploaded on to a website and is then available for general consumption by web users

bonus pack giving a customer extra quantity at no additional cost

brand a distinctive product offering created by the use of a name, symbol, design, packaging, or some combination of these, intended to differentiate it from its competitors

brand assets the distinctive features of a brand

brand domain the brand's target market

brand equity a measure of the strength of a brand in the marketplace by adding tangible value to a company through the resulting sales and profits

brand extension the use of an established brand name on a new brand within the same broad market or product category

brand heritage the background to the brand and its culture

brand performance metrics **brand performance metrics** how customers respond to a brand. Measures include market share, sales, sales growth, market size, share-of-wallet

brand personality the character of a brand described in terms of other entities such as people, animals and objects

brand reflection the relationship of the brand to self-identity

brand stretching the use of an established brand name for brands in unrelated markets or product categories

brand valuation the process of estimating the financial value of an individual or corporate brand

brand values the core values and characteristics of a brand

broadcast sponsorship a form of sponsorship where a television or radio programme is the focus

business analysis a review of the projected sales, costs and profits for a new product to establish whether these factors satisfy company objectives

business ethics the moral principles and values that guide a firm's behaviour

business mission the organization's purpose, usually setting out its competitive domain, which distinguishes the business from others of its type

buying centre a group that is involved in the buying decision (also known as a *decision-making unit*)

buzz marketing the passing between individuals of information about products and services that is sufficiently interesting to act as a trigger for the individuals to share the information with others

C

campaign objectives goals set by an organization in terms of, for example, sales, profits, customers won or retained, or awareness creation

category management the management of brands in a group, portfolio or category, with specific emphasis on the retail trade's requirements

change master a person that develops an implementation strategy to drive through organizational change

channel integration the way in which the players in the channel are linked

channel intermediaries organizations that facilitate the distribution of products to customers

channel of distribution the means by which products are moved from the producer to the ultimate consumer

channel strategy the selection of the most effective distribution channel, the most appropriate level of distribution intensity and the degree of channel integration

choice criteria the various attributes (and benefits) people use when evaluating products and services

classical conditioning the process of using an established relationship between a stimulus and a response to cause the learning of the same response to a different stimulus

coercive power power inherent in the ability to punish

cognitive dissonance post-purchase concerns of a consumer arising from uncertainty as to whether a decision to purchase was the correct one

cognitive learning the learning of knowledge and development of beliefs and attitudes without direct reinforcement

combination brand name a combination of family and individual brand names

commitment a process whereby individuals (and companies) establish a bond to reduce negative aspects of a relationship

Commoditization is when differentiated products lose their uniqueness and no longer stand out in the marketplace.

Commodity businesses those firms which sell goods and materials that are freely traded, e.g.agricultural products – rice, coffee, grain; raw materials, metals

commodity market one where commodities – a primary good, e.g. cocoa, wheat, precious metals, oil – is traded

communications-based co-branding the linking of two or more existing brands from different companies or business units for the purposes of joint communication

competitive advantage the achievement of superior performance through differentiation to provide superior customer value or by managing to achieve lowest delivered cost

competitive behaviour the activities of rival companies with respect to each other; this can take five forms—conflict, competition, co-existence, cooperation and collusion

competitive bidding drawing up detailed specifications for a product and putting the contract out to tender

competitive positioning consists of three key elements: target markets, competitor targets and establishing a competitive advantage

competitive scope the breadth of a company's competitive challenge, for example broad or narrow

competitor analysis an examination of the nature of actual and potential competitors, and their objectives and strategies

competitor audit a precise analysis of competitor strengths and weaknesses, objectives and strategies

competitor targets the organizations against which a company chooses to compete directly

concept testing testing new product ideas with potential customers

concession analysis the evaluation of things that can be offered to someone in negotiation valued from the viewpoint of the receiver

consumer a person who buys goods and services for personal use

consumer decision-making process the stages a consumer goes through when buying something—namely, problem awareness, information search, evaluation of alternatives, purchase and post-purchase evaluation

consumer movement an organized collection of groups with the objective of protecting consumer rights

consumer panel household consumers who provide information on their purchases over time

consumer pull the targeting of consumers with communications (e.g. promotions) designed to create demand that will pull the product into the distribution chain

consumerism organized action against business practices that are not in the interests of consumers

contractual joint venture two or more companies form a partnership but no joint enterprise with a separate identity is formed

contractual vertical marketing system a franchise arrangement (e.g. a franchise) that ties together producers and resellers

control the stage in the marketing planning process or cycle when the performance against plan is monitored so that corrective action, if necessary, can be taken

core competences the principal distinctive capabilities possessed by a company—what it is really good at

core marketing strategy the means of achieving marketing objectives, including target markets, competitor targets and competitive advantage

core product anything that provides the central benefits required by customers

corporate social responsibility the ethical principle that an organization should be accountable for how its behaviour might affect society and the environment

corporate vertical marketing system a channel situation where an organization gains control of distribution through ownership

counter-offensive defence a counter-attack that takes the form of a head-on counter-attack, an attack on the attacker's cash cow or an encirclement of the attacker

counter-trade a method of exchange where not all transactions are concluded in cash; goods may be included as part of the asking price

covert power play the use of disguised forms of power tactics

cultural norms the systems of societal (or group) beliefs and values, which are accepted by the members of the society or group

cultural values culture is a system of meaning, which is ingrained into society and groups. The values are shaped by individuals that are connected to the society or group

culture the combination of traditions, taboos, values and attitudes of the society in which an individual lives

customer analysis a survey of who the customers are, what choice criteria they use, how they rate competitive offerings and on what variables they can be segmented

customer relationship management (CRM) a term for the methodologies, technologies and e-commerce capabilities used by companies to manage customer relationships

customer satisfaction the fulfilment of customers' requirements or needs

customer satisfaction measurement a process through which customer satisfaction criteria are set, customers are surveyed and the results interpreted in order to establish the level of customer satisfaction with the organization's product

customer value perceived benefits minus perceived sacrifice

customer-based brand equity the differential effect that brand knowledge has on consumer response to the marketing of that brand

customized marketing the market coverage strategy where a company decides to target individual customers and develops separate marketing mixes for each

D

decision-making process the stages that organizations and people pass through when purchasing a physical product or service

decision-making unit (DMU) a group of people within an organization who are involved in the buying decision (also known as the buying centre)

demography changes in the population in terms of its size and characteristics

descriptive research research undertaken to describe customers' beliefs, attitudes, preferences and behaviour

differential advantage a clear performance differential over the competition on factors that are important to target customers

differential marketing strategies market coverage strategies where a company decides to target several market segments and develops separate marketing mixes for each

differentiated marketing a market coverage strategy where a company decides to target several market segments and develops separate marketing mixes for each

differentiation strategy the selection of one or more customer choice criteria and positioning the offering accordingly to achieve superior customer value

diffusion of innovation process the process by which a new product spreads throughout a market over time

digital marketing the application of digital technologies that form channels to market (the Internet, mobile communications, interactive television and wireless) to achieve corporate goals through meeting and exceeding customer needs better than the competition

Digital media the channels used to communicate and interact with a target audience online

digital promotion the promotion of products to consumers and businesses through electronic media

digital surveys various methods of gathering qualitative (and in some cases quantitative) data using email or web-based surveys

direct exporting the handling of exporting activities by the exporting organization rather than by a domestically based independent organization

direct investment market entry that involves investment in foreign-based assembly or manufacturing facilities

direct mail material sent through the postal service to the recipient's house or business address promoting a product and/or maintaining an ongoing relationship

direct marketing (1) acquiring and retaining customers without the use of an intermediary; (2) the distribution of products, information and promotional benefits to target consumers through interactive communication in a way that allows response to be measured

direct response advertising the use of the prime advertising media such as television, newspapers and magazines to elicit an order, enquiry or request for a visit

direct-cost pricing the calculation of only those costs that are likely to rise as output increases

disintermediation the removal of channel partners by bypassing intermediaries and going directly from manufacturer to consumer via the Internet

disruptive innovations innovations that can disrupt existing market and make changes to the value expectations, thereby creating new markets

distribution analysis an examination of movements in power bases, channel attractiveness, physical distribution and distribution behaviour

distribution push the targeting of channel intermediaries with communications (e.g. promotions) to push the product into the distribution chain

divest to improve short-term cash yield by dropping or selling off a product

E

e-commerce all electronically mediated transactions between an organization and any third party it deals with, including exchange of information

e-procurement digital systems that facilitate the management of the procurement process; often integrates with e-commerce systems

economic value to the customer (EVC) the amount a customer would have to pay to make the total lifecycle costs of a new and a reference product the same

effectiveness doing the right thing, making the correct strategic choice

efficiency a way of managing business processes to a high standard, usually concerned with cost reduction; also called 'doing things right'

encirclement attack attacking the defender from all sides; i.e. every market segment is hit with every combination of product features

entry barriers that act to prevent new companies from entering a market, for example the high level of investment required

entry into new markets (diversification) the entry into new markets by new products

environmental scanning the process of monitoring and analysing the marketing environment of a company

environmentalism the organized movement of groups and organizations to protect and improve the physical environment; their concerns are production and consumption of products that lead to global warming, pollution, the destruction of natural resources such as oil and forests, and non-biodegradable waste

equity joint venture where two or more companies form a partnership that involves the creation of a new company

ethical consumption when individual consumers, when making purchase decisions, consider not only personal interests but also the interests of society and the environment

ethics the moral principles and values that govern the actions and decisions of an individual or group

ethnography a form of qualitative research which involves detailed and prolonged observation of consumers in the situations which inform their buying behaviour

event sponsorship sponsorship of a sporting or other event

evoked set the set of brands that the consumer seriously evaluates before making a purchase

exaggerated promises barrier a barrier to the matching of expected and perceived service levels caused by the unwarranted building up of expectations by exaggerated promises

exchange the act or process of receiving something from someone by giving something in return

Exclusive distribution channels manufacturers make agreements with specific retailers to sell the goods; the retailer is given exclusive rights, which cover a specified geographic region

exclusive distribution an extreme form of selective distribution where only one wholesaler, retailer or industrial distributor is used in a geographical area to sell the products of a supplier

exhibition an event that brings buyers and sellers together in a commercial setting

experience curve the combined effect of economies of scale and learning as cumulative output increases

experimental research research undertaken in order to establish cause and effect

expert power power that derives from an individual's expertise

F

fairtrade marketing a movement that aims to help producers in developing countries to produce goods ethically and enhance the wellbeing and wealth of the workers in these countries; the movement also promotes sustainability

family brand name a brand name used for all products in a range

fighter brands low-cost manufacturers' brands introduced to combat own-label brands

flanking attack attacking geographical areas or market segments where the defender is poorly represented

flanking defence the defence of a hitherto unprotected market segment

focus group a group normally of six to twelve consumers brought together for a discussion focusing on an aspect of a company's marketing

focused marketing a market coverage strategy where a company decides to target one market segment with a single marketing mix

foreign consumer culture positioning positioning a brand as associated with a specific foreign culture (e.g. Italian fashion)

franchise a legal contract in which a producer and channel intermediaries agree each other's rights and obligations; usually the intermediary receives marketing, managerial, technical and financial services in return for a fee

franchising a form of licensing where a package of services is offered by the franchisor to the franchisee in return for payment

frontal attack a competitive strategy where the challenger takes on the defender head on

full-cost pricing pricing so as to include all costs and based on certain sales volume assumptions

G

geodemographics the process of grouping households into geographic clusters based on information such as type of accommodation, occupation, number and age of children, and ethnic background

global account management (GAM) the process of coordinating and developing mutually beneficial long-term relationships with a select group of strategically important customers (accounts) operating in globalized industries

global branding achievement of brand penetration worldwide

global consumer culture positioning positioning a brand as a symbol of a given global culture (e.g. young cosmopolitan men)

going-rate pricing pricing at the rate generally applicable in the market, focusing on competitors' offerings rather than on company costs

guerrilla attack making life uncomfortable for stronger rivals through, for example, unpredictable price discounts, sales promotions or heavy advertising in a few selected regions

H

halo customers customers that are not directly targeted but may find the product attractive

harvest objective the improvement of profit margins to improve cash flow even if the longer-term result is falling sales

hold objective a strategy of defending a product in order to maintain market share

I

in-depth interviews the interviewing of consumers individually for perhaps one or two hours, with the aim of understanding their attitudes, values, behaviour and/or beliefs

inadequate delivery barrier a barrier to the matching of expected and perceived service levels caused by the failure of the service provider to select, train and reward staff adequately, resulting in poor or inconsistent delivery of service

inadequate resources barrier a barrier to the matching of expected and perceived service levels caused by the unwillingness of service providers to provide the necessary resources

indirect exporting the use of independent organizations within the exporter's domestic market to facilitate export

individual brand name a brand name that does not identify a brand with a particular company

industry a group of companies that market products that are close substitutes for each other

information framing the way in which information is presented to people

information processing the process by which a stimulus is received, interpreted, stored in memory and later retrieved

information search the identification of alternative ways of problem-solving

ingredient co-branding the explicit positioning of a supplier's brand as an ingredient of a product

innovation the realization of an invention by bringing it to market

inseparability a characteristic of services, namely that their production cannot be separated from their consumption

intangibility a characteristic of services, namely that they cannot be touched, seen, tasted or smelled

integrated marketing communications (IMC) the concept that companies coordinate their marketing communications tools to deliver a clear, consistent, credible and competitive message about the organization and its products

intensive distribution the aim of this is to provide saturation coverage of the market by using all available outlets

internal marketing training, motivating and communicating with staff to cause them towork effectively in providing customer satisfaction; more recently the term has been expanded to include marketing to all staff, with the aim of achieving the acceptance of marketing ideas and plans

invention the discovery of new methods and ideas

J

just-in-time (JIT) this concept aims to minimize stocks by organizing a supply system that provides materials and components as they are required

K

key account management (KAM) an approach to selling that focuses resources on major customers and uses a team selling approach

L

latent markets markets not yet served by existing products and service offers. These markets present opportunities for market orientated companies

learning any change in the content or organization of long-term memory as the result of information processing

legitimate power power based on legitimate authority, such as line management

licensing a contractual arrangement in which a licensor provides a licensee with certain rights, for example to technology access or production rights

lifecycle costs all the components of costs associated with buying, owning and using a physical product or service

lifestyle the pattern of living as expressed in a person's activities, interests and opinions

lifestyle segmentation the grouping of people according to their pattern of living as expressed in their activities, interests and opinions

local consumer culture positioning positioning a brand as associated with a local culture (e.g. local production and consumption of a good)

loyalty a term used to explain repeated purchasing behaviour

M

macroenvironment a number of broader forces that affect not only the company but also the other actors in the microenvironment

manufacturer brands brands that are created by producers and bear their chosen brand name

market analysis the statistical analysis of market size, growth rates and trends

market development to take current products and market them in new markets

market expansion the attempt to increase the size of a market by converting non-users to users of the product and by increasing usage rates

market orientation companies with a market orientation focus on customer needs as the primary drivers of organizational performance

market penetration to continue to grow sales by marketing an existing product in an existing market

market segmentation the process of identifying individuals or organizations with similar characteristics that have significant implications for the determination of marketing strategy

market share analysis a comparison of company sales with total sales of the product, including sales of competitors

market testing the limited launch of a new product to test sales potential

market-orientated pricing an approach to pricing that takes a range of marketing factors into account when setting prices

marketing accountability the requirement to justify marketing investment by using marketing metrics

marketing audit a systematic examination of a business's marketing environment, objectives, strategies and activities with a view to identifying key strategic issues, problem areas and opportunities

marketing concept the achievement of corporate goals through meeting and exceeding customer needs better than the competition

marketing control the stage in the marketing planning process or cycle when performance against plan is monitored so that corrective action, if necessary, can be taken

marketing database an interactive approach to marketing that uses individually addressable marketing media and channels to provide information to a target audience, stimulate demand and stay close to customers

marketing environment the actors and forces that affect a company's capability to operate effectively in providing products and services to its customers

marketing ethics the moral principles and values that guide behaviour within the field of marketing

marketing information system a system in which marketing information is formally gathered, stored, analyzed and distributed to managers in accordance with their informational needs on a regular, planned basis

marketing metrics quantitative measures of the outcomes of marketing activities and expenditures

marketing mix a framework for the tactical management of the customer relationship, including product, place, price, promotion (the Four-Ps); in the case of services, three other elements to be taken into account are process, people and physical evidence

marketing objectives there are two types of marketing objective: strategic thrust, which dictates which products should be sold in which markets, and strategic objectives—that is, product-level objectives such as build, hold, harvest and divest

marketing planning the process by which businesses analyse the environment and their capabilities, decide upon courses of marketing action and implement those decisions

marketing structures the marketing frameworks (organization, training and internal communications) upon which marketing activities are based

marketing systems sets of connected parts (information, planning and control) that support the marketing function

media channel the means used to transmit a message, including spoken words, print, radio, television or the Internet. Also called the *medium*

media class the press, cinema, television, posters, radio, or some combination of these

media planning an advertising strategy most commonly employed to target consumers using a variety of informational outlets. Media planning is generally conducted by a professional media planning or advertising agency and typically finds the most appropriate media outlets to reach the target market

media relations the communication of a product or business by placing information about it in the media without paying for time or space directly

media type (also referred to as a *content type*) is a general category of data content, such as: application (executable program), audio content, an image, a text message, a video stream, and so forth

media vehicle the choice of the particular newspaper, magazine, television spot, poster site, etc.

media vehicle decision the choice of the particular newspaper, magazine, television spot, poster site, etc.

message the use of words, symbols and illustrations to communicate to a target audience using prime media

microblogging involves the posting of short messages on social media sites like Twitter and Reddit

microenvironment the actors in the firm's marketing environment: customers, suppliers, distributors and competitors

misconception barrier a failure by marketers to understand what customers really value about their service

mobile defence involves diversification or broadening the market by redefining the business

mobile marketing the sending of text messages to mobile phones to promote products and build relationships with consumers

modified rebuy where a regular requirement for the type of product exists and the buying alternatives are known but sufficient change (e.g. a delivery problem) has occurred to require some alteration to the normal supply procedure

money-off promotions sales promotions that discount the normal price

multichannel involves an organization that is using different channels – physical retailer stores, the web and mobile, to enable its customers to buy, communicate, gain access to information or pay for goods and services. The organization in return provides consistent levels of service and marketing mix across all of the channels

N

new task refers to the first-time purchase of a product or input by an organization

niche a small market segment

non-commodity those which are involved in facilitating processes and exchanges, but are not in themselves commodities. For example, when you buy electricity, a large proportion of the cost is attributed to the network of cables used to deliver the supply. In the UK, the National Grid owns the electricity transmission system

not-for-profit marketing involves the use of marketing frameworks, concepts and ideas used by an organization that operates on a not-for-profit basis; this type of organization often employs a volunteer workforce and relies on donations and external funding

O

omnichannel the bringing together of all of the customer touchpoints into a seamless shopping journey, which means that every time the customer 'touches' or interacts with a company, for example by store, by phone, by the web by mobile

operant conditioning the use of rewards to generate reinforcement of response

overt power play the use of visible, open kinds of power tactics

own-label brands brands created and owned by distributors or retailers

P

parallel co-branding the joining of two ormore independent brands to produce a combined brand

Parallel importing the movement of goods from one country to another without the permission of the owner/designer. These types of imports are sometimes referred to as 'grey' imports

PEEST analysis the analysis of the political/legal, economic, ecological/physical, social/cultural and technological environments

perception the process by which people select, organize and interpret sensory stimulation into a meaningful picture of the world

perishability a characteristic of services, namely that the capacity of a service business, such as a hotel room, cannot be stored—if it is not occupied, this is lost income that cannot be recovered

personal selling oral communication with prospective purchasers with the intention of making a sale

personality the inner psychological characteristics of individuals that lead to consistent responses to their environment

place the distribution channels to be used, outlet locations, methods of transportation

portfolio planning managing groups of brands and product lines

position defence building a fortification around existing products, usually through keen pricing and improved promotion

positioning the choice of target market (where the company wishes to compete) and differential advantage (how the company wishes to compete)

positioning strategy the choice of target market (*where* the company wishes to compete) and differential advantage (*how* the company wishes to compete)

pre-emptive defence usually involves continuous innovation and new product development, recognizing that attack is the best form of defence

premiums any merchandise offered free or at low cost as an incentive to purchase

price (1) the amount of money paid for a product; (2) the agreed value placed on the exchange by buyer and seller

price unbundling pricing each element in the offering so that the price of the total product package is raised

price waterfall the difference between list price and realized or transaction price

product a good or service offered or performed by an organization or individual, which is capable of satisfying customer needs

product churning a continuous and rapid spiral of new product introductions

product development increasing sales by improving present products or developing new products for current markets

product lifecycle a four-stage cycle in the life of a product illustrated as sales and profit curves, the four stages being introduction, growth, maturity and decline

product line a group of brands that are closely related in terms of the functions and benefits they provide

product mix the total set of products marketed by a company

product placement the deliberate placing of products and/or their logos in movies and television, usually in return for money

product portfolio the total range of products offered by the company

product-based co-branding the linking of two or more existing brands from different companies or business units to form a product in which the brand names are visible to consumers

profile segmentation the grouping of people in terms of profile variables, such as age and socio-economic group, so that marketers can communicate to them

profitability analysis the calculation of sales revenues and costs for the purpose of calculating the profit performance of products, customers and/or distribution channels

project teams the bringing together of staff from such areas as R&D, engineering, manufacturing, finance and marketing to work on a project such as new product development

proposal analysis the prediction and evaluation of proposals and demands likely to be made by someone with whom one is negotiating

proprietary-based brand equity is derived from company attributes that deliver value to the brand

psychographic segmentation the grouping of people according to their lifestyle and personality characteristics

public relations (PR) the management of communications and relationships to establish goodwill and mutual understanding between an organization and its public

Q

QR codes a form of barcode which, once scanned, can link the user directly to web content, digital adverts and other available content. They are easy to use and smartphones can read the codes

qualitative research exploratory research that aims to understand consumers' attitudes, values, behaviour and beliefs

quantitative research a structured study of small or large samples using a predetermined list of questions or criteria

R

reasoning a more complex form of cognitive learning where conclusions are reached by connected thought

rebranding the changing of a brand or corporate name

reference group a group of people that influences an individual's attitude or behaviour

referent power power derived by the reference source, for example when people identify with and respect the architect of change

reintermediation the introduction of new forms of channel intermediary that provide services which link members of the supply chain, for example web service providers and retailers

relationship marketing the process of creating, maintaining and enhancing strong relationships with customers and other stakeholders

repositioning changing the target market or differential advantage, or both

retail positioning the choice of target market and differential advantage for a retail outlet

reward power power derived from the ability to provide benefits

rote learning the learning of two or more concepts without conditioning

S

sales analysis a comparison of actual with target sales

sales promotion incentives to customers or the trade that are designed to stimulate purchase

salesforce evaluation the measurement of each salesperson's performance so that strengths and weaknesses can be identified

sampling process a term used in research to denote the selection of a sub-set of the total population in order to interview them

satisfaction an indicator of the extent to which customer expectations have been met. As a concept it is important to long-term relationship building

selective attention the process by which people screen out those stimuli that are neither meaningful to them nor consistent with their experiences and beliefs

selective distortion the distortion of information received by people according to their existing beliefs and attitudes

selective distribution the use of a limited number of outlets in a geographical area to sell the products of a supplier

selective retention the process by which people only retain a selection of messages in memory

self-reference criteria the use of one's own perceptions and choice criteria to judge what is important to consumers. In global marketing the perceptions and choice criteria of domestic consumers may be used to judge what is important to foreign consumers

service any deed, performance or effort carried out for the customer

service mix an extended framework of tactical management processes specifically focusing on service delivery

service quality involves the experience a customer has of a company's offer. Services vary in complexity and the investment and risk a customer makes in the purchase

services marketing mix product, place, price, promotion, people, process and physical evidence (the 'Seven-Ps')

Snap codes a button in snapchat which links friends in the Snapchat environment, similar to 'following' a friend in Facebook

social marketing seeks to change behaviour for the benefit of the individual and society and its applications come in many different guises.

social media online community websites with individuals who can become members, share ideas and interests, for example Facebook; publish and distribute articles and video and other multimedia content, for example YouTube; carry out social commerce activities like writing reviews, buying and selling, for example TripAdvisor; or play games across communities, for example Zynga

sponsorship a business relationship between a provider of funds, resources or services and an individual, event or organization that offers in return some rights and association that may be used for commercial advantage

Spotify codes like a scannable QR code, a code that gives a quick link to a specific music download in Spotify environment

stakeholder an individual or group that either (i) is harmed by or benefits from the company, or (ii) whose rights can be violated or have to be respected by the company

stakeholder theory this contends that companies are not managed purely in the interests of their shareholders alone but a broader group including communities associated with the company, employees, customers and suppliers

standardized marketing mix a marketing strategy for using essentially the same product, promotion, distribution, and pricing in all the company's global markets

straight rebuy refers to a purchase by an organization from a previously approved supplier of a previously purchased item

strategic alliance collaboration between two or more organizations through, for example, joint ventures, licensing agreements, long-term purchasing and supply arrangement, or a joint R&D contract to build a competitive advantage

strategic business unit a business or company division serving a distinct group of customers and with a distinct set of competitors, usually strategically autonomous

strategic issues analysis an examination of the suitability of marketing objectives and segmentation bases in the light of changes in the marketplace

strategic objectives product-level objectives relating to the decision to build, hold, harvest or divest products

strategic thrust the decision concerning which products to sell in which markets

strategic withdrawal holding onto the company's strengths while getting rid of its weaknesses

strong theory of advertising the notion that advertising can change people's attitudes sufficiently to persuade people who have not previously bought a brand to buy it; desire and conviction precede purchase

supplier analysis an examination of who and where suppliers are located, their competences and shortcomings, the trends affecting them and the future outlook for them

sustainable marketing focuses on reducing environmental damage by creating, producing and delivering sustainable solutions while continuing to satisfy customers and other stakeholders

SWOT analysis a structured approach to evaluating the strategic position of a business by identifying its strengths, weaknesses, opportunities and threats

T

target accounts organizations or individuals whose custom the company wishes to obtain

target audience the group of people at which an advertisement or message is aimed

target market a market segment that has been selected as a focus for the company's offering or communications

team sponsorship sponsorship of a team – for example, a football, cricket or motor racing team

telemarketing a marketing communications system whereby trained specialists use telecommunications and information technologies to conduct marketing and sales activities

test marketing the launch of a new product in one or a few geographic areas chosen to be representative of the intended market

touch points contact points where customers interact with a firm. Contact can occur in physical and digital situations

touchpoints points at which a customer interacts with a company across a customer journey and where data can be collected

trade marketing marketing to the retail trade

trade show similar to an exhibition, as it brings together buyers, sellers and competitors under one roof, but it is not open to the public

trade-off analysis a measure of the trade-off customers make between price and other product features so that their effects on product preference can be established

transfer pricing the price charged between the profit centres of the same company, sometimes used to take advantage of lower taxes in another country

transition curve the emotional stages that people pass through when confronted with an adverse change

trust a customer's level of confidence in a company's ability to supply the required goods, its reliability and integrity

U

undifferentiated marketing a market coverage strategy where a company decides to ignore market segment differences and develops a single marketing mix for the whole market

V

value analysis a method of cost reduction in which components are examined to see if they can be made more cheaply

value chain the set of a company's activities that are conducted to design, manufacture, market, distribute and service its products

variability a characteristic of services, namely that, being delivered by people, the standard of their performance is open to variation

vicarious learning learning from others without direct experience or reward

W

weak theory of advertising the notion that advertising can first arouse awareness and interest, nudge some consumers towards a doubting first trial purchase and then provide some reassurance and reinforcement; desire and conviction do not precede purchase

Companies and Brands Index

L

M

N

Subjects and Authors Index

C

D

E

F

J

K

S

T